What Happened When

A Chronology of Life and Events in America

Gorton Carruth

Abridged edition of
The Encyclopedia of American Facts & Dates

A SIGNET BOOK

SIGNET
Published by the Penguin Group
Penguin Books USA Inc., 375 Hudson Street,
New York, New York 10014, U.S.A.
Penguin Books Ltd, 27 Wrights Lane,
London W8 5TZ, England
Penguin Books Australia Ltd, Ringwood,
Victoria, Australia
Penguin Books Canada Ltd, 2801 John Street,
Markham, Ontario, Canada L3R 1B4
Penguin Books (N.Z.) Ltd, 182–190 Wairau Road,
Auckland 10, New Zealand

Penguin Books Ltd, Registered Offices:
Harmondsworth, Middlesex, England

Published by Signet, an imprint of New American Library, a division
of Penguin Books USA Inc. This is an authorized reprint of a
hardcover edition published by Harper & Row, Publishers.

First Signet Printing, February, 1991
10 9 8 7 6 5 4 3 2 1

This work is an abridged edition of the *The Encyclopedia of American
Facts & Dates*, eighth edition, published by Harper & Row, Publishers.

REGISTERED TRADEMARK—MARCA REGISTRADA

Printed in the United States of America

To Gisèle Carruth

STAFF

Executive Editor	Raymond V. Hand, Jr.
Contributing Editors	Fon W. Boardman, Jr.
	David H. Scott
Copy Editor	Felice Levy
Indexer	Cynthia Crippen
Computer Keyboarder	Antje Munroe
Researchers	Sally Bunch
	Ellen Sackelman
Proofreaders	Barbara Bergeron
	Bernie Borok
	Rina Cascone
	Bitite Vinklers
	Brenda Woodward

Preface

What Happened When is a chronologically arranged encyclopedia of the most important events in American history, from 986 A.D., when Europeans first sighted North America, to the presidential elections of 1988. It contains the essential information students and general readers need in order to understand our country's past. And its unique arrangement makes it an indispensable desk reference book.

Its coverage of subjects is exceptionally broad. A partial listing would include:

Architecture
Art
Books and publishing
Business
Crime
Disasters
Discovery, exploration, settlement
Economics
Education
Fashions
Foreign affairs
Inventions
Politics and government
Religion
Science
Sports
Suffrage
Technology

Television
Theater
Treaties
Vital statistics
Wars and battles
Women

The entries are arranged in convenient time periods, for example, one-year or five-year periods, making it easy to find the entries for contemporaneous events. Within each of these time periods the entries are placed under four broadly conceived topic heads:

I. Civil Rights
   Exploration and Settlement
   Government
   Statistics
   Wars

II. Architecture
   Arts and Music
   Popular Entertainment
   Publishing
   Theater

III. Business and Industry
   Education
   Philosophy and Religion
   Science

IV. Fashion
   Folkways
   Holidays
   Social Issues and Crime
   Sports

Entries concerning civil rights, say, or sports are thus placed together, which speeds the location of events of the same kind.

A brief but detailed introduction under each topic head provides an overview of what was then happening in the country in that subject area, for example, a political campaign or in sports.

With the addition of an exceptionally complete index *What Happened When* becomes the most accessible and comprehensive of inexpensive desk encyclopedias on American life and events.

The parent volume for *What Happened When* is *The Encyclopedia of American Facts and Dates,* now in its eighth edition and a standard reference in its field. In the preface to *American Facts and Dates* are acknowledgments that should be repeated here:

Acknowledgment should be made to those single-volume American date and reference books that have been especially valuable: *The Reader's Encyclopedia* edited by William Rose Benét (Harper & Row); *Documents of American History* by Henry Steele Commager (Prentice-Hall); *The Columbia Encyclopedia* (Columbia University Press); *Information Please Almanac* (Houghton Mifflin); *Famous First Facts* by Joseph Nathan Kane (H. W. Wilson); *A Short Chronology of American History, 1492–1950* by Irving S. and Nell M. Kull (Greenwood); *The Encyclopedia of Sports* by Frank Menke (A. S. Barnes); *Encyclopedia of American History* edited by Richard B. Morris (Harper & Row); *The World Almanac* (Newspaper Enterprise Association). Acknowledgment should especially go to *The New York Times* for much of the recent detail. Thanks should go to the many readers who have made corrections and suggestions for improvement. Warm thanks must be extended to librarians across the country who have adopted *American Facts and Dates* as a standard reference, but the staff of the Mount Pleasant Public Library in Pleasantville, N.Y., must be singled out for special thanks for their cheerful assistance given in every stage of our research.

In addition, I am especially grateful for the contributions made by Fon W. Boardman, Jr., who has written extensively in American history and who has helped immeasurably to make *What Happened When* a more accurate, useful book.

Gorton Carruth
1989

986–1599

I. Civil Rights
   Exploration and Settlement
   Government
   Statistics
   Wars

The first Europeans to see the North American continent were Norsemen, led by the navigator Bjarni Herjulfson, who, in 986, while seeking Eric the Red's settlement on the coast of Greenland, was blown off course and sighted an unidentified land mass. In 1000 Leif Ericson, a son of Eric the Red, explored the coast of North America and established a settlement he called Vinland. In the 1960s evidence of such a settlement was unearthed at L'Anse aux Meadows, Newfoundland. Between 1004 and 1008 Leif's brothers, Thorvald and Thorstein, carried out further exploration of the North American coast and may well have seen what is now New England. Thorfinn Karlsefni, a trader from Iceland, visited the coast of North America between 1010 and 1013. The last Norse voyage to the New World took place in 1014–1015 when, according to the Greenland Saga, Eric's daughter, Freydis, sailed with Thorfinn Karlsefni.

1492 Oct 12: The expedition of **Christopher Columbus** sighted what was probably present-day Watling Island, in the Bahamas. That day they went ashore and claimed the island for the king and queen of Spain. Columbus explored the northeastern coast of Cuba and northern coast of Hispaniola, then set sail for

Spain on Jan. 16, 1493. On his second expedition (1493–1496) he discovered Jamaica, and on his third (1498–1500) he made further discoveries, including the island of Trinidad. During his fourth and final expedition (1502–1504) Columbus discovered Martinique and explored the coasts of present-day Honduras, Nicaragua, Costa Rica, and Panama.

1513 Apr 2: Juan Ponce de León discovered Florida, claiming it for the king of Spain.

1526 Summer: The **first European settlement** in what is now the U.S., San Miguel de Guadalupe, was established by Lucas Vazquez de Ayllón, who led some 500 or 600 settlers from Hispaniola to the coast of South Carolina. The site of the settlement was thought to have been just north of the mouth of the Peedee R. Many of the settlers died of fever. After Ayllón succumbed on Oct. 18, the approximately 150 surviving settlers returned to Hispaniola.

1539 May 30: Fernando de Soto landed in Florida and began the consolidation of Spain's dominion over the peninsula.

1541 May 8: The **first Europeans to reach the Mississippi R.** were members of the de Soto expedition. De Soto died the next year and was buried in the river.

1542: The **first Europeans to reach the Pacific coast** of what is now the U.S. were members of the expedition of Juan Rodriquez Cabrillo, who was sent on an exploratory voyage by Spanish administrators in Mexico. Cabrillo landed near what is now Ballast Point, San Diego, Calif., then continued his explorations and discovered Santa Catalina Island, San Pedro Bay, the Santa Barbara Channel, and other West Coast landmarks.

1562 Apr 30: The **first French colonizers** in what was to become the U.S., Huguenots led by Jean Ribaut, established Port Royal on Parris Island, off the coast of present-day South Carolina. In early 1564, when supplies failed to arrive from France, the colony was abandoned.

1565 Sep 8: The **first permanent white colony** in what is now the U.S. was founded at St. Augustine, Fla., by the Spanish under Pedro Menéndez de Avilés, a naval officer.

1565 Sep 20: Fort Caroline was destroyed by the Spanish under Menéndez, who massacred most of its inhabitants. He renamed it San Mateo and in the next two years built a string of forts to Tampa Bay while looking for a water passage across Florida.

1579 June 17: The expedition of **Sir Francis Drake** anchored in a harbor just north of present-day San Francisco Bay in California, during Drake's celebrated circumnavigation of the globe. Drake named the land Nova Albion and claimed it for England. The members of the expedition spent a month repairing their ship. Then on July 26 Drake sailed from California, continuing north and then west across the Pacific Ocean.

1585 Aug: The **Roanoke Island colony,** sponsored by Sir Walter Raleigh, was established on Roanoke Island, off the northeast coast of what is now North Carolina, under the leadership of Sir Richard Grenville and Sir Ralph Lane. The settlers fared badly and returned to England in June of 1586. In 1587 Raleigh sent out another group, under John White, consisting of 117 men, women, and children. White returned to England for supplies but was unable to get back to Roanoke until Aug. 17, 1590. He found all the colonists gone; the only clue to their fate was the word *CROATOAN* carved on a tree. The meaning of this remains unexplained and no trace was ever found of the settlers.

II. Architecture
Arts and Music
Popular Entertainment
Publishing
Theater

Almost as soon as the early explorers of America returned to Europe, they wrote accounts of their adventures. These accounts expressed great enthusiasm and, like later accounts, might be classed as promotional material. The first eyewitness report in English of what today is part of the U.S. was written in 1588 by Thomas Hariot, who took part in the Roanoke Island adventure sponsored by Sir Walter Raleigh.

Hariot's account was entitled *A Brief and True Report of the New Found Land of Virginia.* It depicted America as a paradise where a little work would yield great prosperity. In the following year appeared *The Principal Navigations, Voyages, Traffics, and Discoveries of the English Nation* by Richard Hakluyt. Not an explorer himself but a collector of the reports of others, Hakluyt later enlarged his book and included the adventures of Sir Francis Drake, Sir Humphrey Gilbert, Sir Martin Frobisher, and others. In the early seventeenth century, further works were written by such explorers as John Smith and Samuel de Champlain. Mapmakers also went to work almost as soon as the New World was found, although their maps were very inexact by today's standards and reflected the prevailing belief or hope that America was but a minor obstacle in the way of ships seeking the riches of the Far East. One such map was prepared by Sebastian Cabot in 1544 and another by Gerardus Mercator in 1569.

1507: The term *America* was first used for the New World in Martin Waldseemüller's short geography book *Cosmographiae Introductio.* Wrote Waldseemüller, "But now that these parts have been more extensively examined, and another fourth part has been discovered by Americus Vespuccius . . . I do not see why anyone should by right object to name it America . . . after its discoverer, Americus, a man of sagacious mind, since both Europe and Asia took their names from women." Waldseemüller mistakenly attributed discovery of the New World to Amerigo Vespucci.

1584: Richard Hakluyt wrote *A Discourse Concerning Western Planting,* at the request of Sir Walter Raleigh, for Queen Elizabeth I of England. This work urged that the queen promote English settlement in America and offered a complete plan for such a program. Hakluyt said such settlement would help promote religion, supply goods for England, employ men who would otherwise be idle, increase revenues, provide overseas bases for use in the event of war with Spain, and be useful in the search for a Northwest Passage to the Orient. Hakluyt wrote enthusiastically that "this Realm shall have by that meane Shippes of great burden and of great strengthe" for defense. Further, he wrote, colonial trade would "breed more skilfull, connynge and stowte pilotts and maryners than any other belonging to this land: For it is the long voyaiges . . . that harden seamen and open unto them the secrets of navigation." The queen apparently read the *Discourse* but did not act on it. It was not published until almost three centuries later, when it was issued by the Maine Historical Society. As for Hakluyt, an ordained clergyman of the Church of England, he never saw America. Although he had intended to go to Jamestown, Va., in 1607 as rector, he was not physically able to make the trip. He died and was buried in Westminster Abbey in 1616.

1598 Apr 30: The **first theatrical performance** given in North America was acted on the Rio Grande near present-day El Paso, Tex. The play was a Spanish *comedia* dealing with an expedition of soldiers. On July 10 the same group produced *Moros y los Cristianos* (Moors and Christians), an anonymous play.

III. Business and Industry
Education
Philosophy and Religion
Science

When John Cabot discovered Newfoundland in 1497, he also discovered one of the world's great fishing areas. He enjoyed the codfish his crew found and he saw nets on shore, but not their Indian owners. England, however, was slow to develop this economic and trade resource. The French and Portuguese were the first to exploit it. They took fish home for trading purposes and also traded fish, which they cured on shore, with the Indians for furs. By 1577, according to Richard Hakluyt, there were 150 French fishing craft, 100 Spanish, and 50 Portuguese, but only 15 English vessels fishing in Newfoundland. English fishing, however, became dominant in the next century. Despite the competition of the European nations in other areas, this fertile fishing ground provided a peaceful international exchange.

1112: The **first bishop of America** was appointed. He was Eric Gnupsson, named by Pope Paschal II. His see included Greenland and Vinland.

1540: The **first recorded baptism** in what is now the U.S. was performed by priests accompanying the Fernando de Soto expedition. They baptized an Indian guide, Peter, in the waters of the Acmulgee R., near present-day Macon, Ga.

1550-1600: Discovery of **new agricultural products** during the Spanish explorations of the New World proved a great benefit to European economic development. Spanish expeditions brought back to the Old World such things as potatoes, tomatoes, quinine extracted from the bark of the cinchona tree, cocoa, tapioca from the cassava root, and tobacco. In return settlers brought to the Americas such things as barley, oats, rye, sugar cane, cattle, pigs, poultry, rabbits, and horses, which later found a natural home on the plains.

1565 Sep 8: The **first Catholic parish** in what is now the U.S., the parish of St. Augustine, Fla., was founded by Fr. Don Martin Francisco Lopez de Mendozo Grajales, chaplain of the Spanish expeditionary forces.

1566: The **first Jesuit missionaries** in what was to become the U.S., three Jesuits sponsored by Pedro Menéndez de Avilés, arrived in Spanish Florida, followed by a second group two years later. The first missions were established at Guale, in present-day Georgia, and Orista and Santa Elena, in present-day South Carolina. The Jesuits were forced out of Florida by the Indians within a few years.

1579: The **first Protestant service** in the New World, and the first religious service in English held there, was conducted in California. Participants were members of the crew of Adm. Francis Drake's expedition. Having sailed around South America, the expedition put into a bay at the 38th parallel where, according

to the ship's log, "the admiral ordered divine service
to be performed at his tent."

1587: The **first Indian convert** to Protestant Christianity was Manteo, who was baptized into the Church of
England by members of Sir Walter Raleigh's expedition to Roanoke. Manteo was later named Lord of
Roanoke by Raleigh.

IV. Fashion
Folkways
Holidays
Social Issues and Crime
Sports

At the beginning of European colonization, there
were some 600 tribes of North American Indians,
speaking some 500 different dialects. They were
chiefly hunters and gatherers, but some tribes had
developed agriculture, and bartered or used wam-
pum to exchange goods. There was a good deal of
warfare between tribes and most Indians prided
themselves on their courage in battle. But the Indians' chief weapon, the bow and arrow, was no match
for European firearms, and against Old World diseases such as smallpox they had no defense. As soon
as European settlement began in the early sixteenth
century, the fragile structure of North American Indian society began to crumble.

1007: The **first white child** born in North America was
Snorro, the son of Thorfinn and Gudrid Karlsefni,
members of Leif Ericson's expedition to Vinland.
Later Snorro became an important member of the
Norse community in Iceland.

1540: The **horse was first introduced** on a large scale
into what is now the U.S. by Francisco Coronado, the
Spanish explorer, who traveled through Kansas with
260 horses, most escaping to the Midwest, Mexico,
and Canada. These animals eventually mingled with
large French Norman horses brought to Canada by
French settlers, producing the wild horses later
found in North America.

1565: Smoking of tobacco was introduced to England by John Hawkins. Hawkins was primarily a slave trader, carrying Africans to the West Indies. Most of his dealings were with the Spanish in the West Indies, but during his second trip to the region (1564–1566) he visited the small French colony in Florida and learned to smoke tobacco from the colonists, who had learned from the Indians. Hawkins returned to England with a shipload of tobacco. He described the Indian use of the plant this way: "The Floridians when they travell have a kinde of herbe dried, who with a cane and an earthen cap in the end, with fire, and dried herbs put together, doe sucke thorow the cane the smoke thereof, which smoke satisfieth their hunger, and therwith they live foure or five days without meat or drinke, and this all the Frenchmen used for this purpose."

1585: The first eyewitness picture of **American Indians at play,** a drawing by John White, showed Indians participating in lacrosse, archery, and foot racing, and pitching balls at a target on top of a high tree.

1587 Aug 18: The **first English child** born in North America was Virginia Dare. Her parents were Ananias and Ellinor Dare, members of Sir Walter Raleigh's colony at Roanoke Island, in present-day North Carolina. Ellinor Dare was the daughter of Gov. John White, who had led a company of 150 householders to establish a colony on the island.

1600–1609

I. Civil Rights
   Exploration and Settlement
   Government
   Statistics
   Wars

From the beginning a chief purpose of voyages to the New World was to find a trade route to the Far East. When it became clear that there was a large land mass between Europe and the East, the search for a found the route, and in 1610 when he discovered Hudson Bay he was on a similar mission. In 1616 William Baffin discovered Baffin Bay, which many years later was to provide a key to the actual route, long after the Northwest Passage had lost any commercial appeal.

1602 May 15: The **first Englishman** to land in what is now New England was Capt. Bartholomew Gosnold, who anchored at what is now New Bedford, Mass. He had sailed on Mar. 26 from Falmouth, England, on the *Concord*, touched at the Maine coast, and explored the New England coastline. He named Cape Cod, Martha's Vineyard, and other landmarks.

1604: The **first northern French colony** was established by Pierre du Guast, Sieur de Monts, at Neutral Island in the St. Croix R. in southeastern Maine. His patent had been granted by the French king.

1606: Colonial charters were granted to the Virginia Company of London and the Virginia Company of Plymouth by the English Crown. The grants extended from Cape Fear, N.C., to the St. Croix R. on the border between what are now Maine and New Brunswick, Canada. The London Company was permitted to establish settlements in a tract between 34 and 41 degrees north latitude. The Plymouth Company was granted an equal tract between 38 and 45 degrees north latitude. The overlapping area was a neutral zone where both companies could establish settlements.

1607 May 13: The **first permanent English colony** in North America, Jamestown, Va., was founded by more than 100 colonists on the left bank of the "River of Powhatan" (James R.). Dispatched by the London Company, the colonists had sailed aboard the *Sarah Constant, Goodspeed,* and *Discovery*.

1607 Dec: Capt. **John Smith** and two companions were captured by Indians while in search of provisions.

His companions were killed, but he was spared, Smith reported, by the intercession of Pocahontas, Chief Powhatan's daughter.

1607 Dec: Probably the **first act of rebellion** in the American colonies, a conspiracy against the Council of Jamestown, was uncovered in Virginia. George Kendall, its leader, was shot for mutiny.

II. Architecture
Arts and Music
Popular Entertainment
Publishing
Theater

The key factor determining the design of the first colonial structures was the availability of building materials. In New England, the settlers tried to copy the architecture of their homelands, using wood, which was in abundance. In the South, brick soon displaced wood as the favorite building material. In the Southwest, the Spaniards adapted Indian materials and methods for their buildings. Such a structure, the oldest surviving non-Indian building in the U.S., was the governor's palace in Santa Fe, N. Mex., built in 1609 by Don Pedro de Peralta. The building of forts, usually of logs, for defense against Indian attacks, became a necessity. The Jamestown colonists began such work less than a month after they landed in 1607. In August of that year, a Plymouth Company expedition to Maine erected a fort that encompassed other structures.

1606 Nov 14: One of the **earliest theatrical performances** in North America, the French masque *Le Théâtre de Neptune en la Nouvelle-France* (Neptune's Theater in New France), took place at Port Royal, Acadia (Nova Scotia).

1608: What is considered the **first American book,** *A True Relation of Such Occurrences and Accidents of Noate as Hath Hapned in Virginia Since the First Planting of that Collony* by Capt. John Smith, was printed in London. The book strangely omitted the

famous tale of Pocahontas. It was not until 1624, with
the publication of his book *The Generall Historie of
Virginia, New-England, and the Summer Isles,* that
Smith included a reference to the famous romance.

1609: The last work of **Richard Hakluyt,** *Virginia
Richly Valued,* was published. It was based upon a
Portuguese work, *Relacam,* which was written by a
voyager who claimed to have been with Fernando de
Soto on the expedition through Florida, Georgia, Alabama, Arkansas, and Louisiana. One of three extant
histories of this voyage, *Virginia Richly Valued* has
been attributed to the original authorship of de
Soto.

III. Business and Industry
Education
Philosophy and Religion
Science

In the early days of the English colonies, trade was
a one-way street. The colonists badly needed supplies
from the homeland. The colony at Jamestown, Va.,
for example, was not self-sufficient for many years.
On June 22, 1607, Capt. Christopher Newport left
Jamestown with a cargo for England. Unfortunately,
the cargo was fool's gold, but it was an indication of
the economic motives of those who sponsored outposts in the New World. In Dec. 1608 Newport sailed
with a more practical cargo: pitch, tar, soap, ashes,
and glass. There is evidence that sassafras was
shipped from Cape Cod earlier, but this Jamestown
cargo was the first instance of American manufactures being exported.

1603: A **monopoly of the fur trade,** granted for a ten-
year period to Pierre du Guast, Sieur de Monts, by the
king of France, reflected the importance the French
placed on the trade. The English and Dutch were far
behind in developing a fur trade with the Indians.
Monts was associated with Pierre Chauvin, Sieur de
Tonnetuit, a naval officer and trader; and with Samuel de Champlain, who in 1608 founded Quebec and

the following year discovered the lake that now bears his name, in what is now New York State. They established trading posts in eastern Canada, working their way south to the Penobscot R. in what is now Maine. Monts' monopoly of the fur trade was rescinded in 1607, then restored for a year in 1608. He withdrew from the trade about 1612. Even with a monopoly, it was difficult to prevent others from engaging in fur trading. Eventually the English and Dutch became strong competitors in the fur trade.

IV. Fashion
   Folkways
   Holidays
   Social Issues and Crime
   Sports

Settlers as well as explorers were beginning to come to the English territories on the Atlantic coast. Unfortunately, some of the earliest pioneers, as at Jamestown, Va., were adventurers interested more in making a quick fortune from the alleged riches of the New World than in engaging in agriculture or forestry. In later years, though, a greater diversity of settlers arrived and brought with them a variety of skills. They ranged from wealthy Englishmen, who wanted to carve out large estates, to servants. Merchants saw the opportunity for trade as populations grew. Groups seeking religious freedom were also prominent, bringing with them a tradition of hard work and a willingness to start life anew.

1600: The **Indian population** of what was to become the U.S. was about 1,000,000 when European exploration began. Because the pattern of settlement here differed from that of the Spanish penetration of Central and South America, the change in customs of the Indians was, at first, comparatively slow. Pioneer groups of European colonists were small. They entered regions with sparser populations and more fluid cultures than the larger and more stable Indian communities of Central America, the Andes, and the

Caribbean islands. Contact was sometimes mutually beneficial, but there was no fusion of European and Indian cultures as occurred in South America. In retrospect, the first decade of the seventeenth century was the twilight of aboriginal Indian life.

1608: John Smith had two Indians teach him how to raise **Indian corn.** Faced with starvation the colonists accepted this new grain, although opposition to it existed everywhere. In French Louisiana, the women, accustomed to fancier European fare, staged a petticoat rebellion against daily consumption of corn. The governor reported that the women " . . . inveigh bitterly against His Grace, the Bishop of Quebec, who, they say has enticed them away from home under the pretext of sending them to enjoy the milk and honey of the land of promise."

1609: In what was probably the **first marriage** in the American colonies, Anne Burrows and John Laydon were wed in Virginia.

1610–1619

I. Civil Rights
Exploration and Settlement
Government
Statistics
Wars

The colonies, as soon as they were established, had to have leadership and a system of government. The proprietors of the companies that were granted colonizing rights appointed their own colonial governors. The Virginia Company, on Feb. 28, 1610, named Thomas West De La Warr, Lord Delaware, the first lord governor and captain general of the Virginia colony. On May 23, 1611, he was succeeded by Sir

Thomas Dale, whose new law code amounted almost to martial law. Within a few years, however, the colonists had more voice in government, and the New England colonies, although theocratic, were not under comparably absolute rule.

The estimated European **population** in the colonies was 210.

1612: The **foundation of New York City** was laid when the Dutch sent two ships, *Tiger* and *Fortune*, to trade with the Indians on the Hudson R. Huts were built on Manhattan Island (approximately where 45 Broadway now stands) to house trade goods. One year later, a permanent trading post was established. The next year a fort was erected on the tip of the island.

1614: The **first important Dutch settlement** in the New World, preceding New Amsterdam, was Fort Nassau, a stockaded post at Castle Island, near present-day Albany, N.Y. Established by Dutch fur traders, it was abandoned in 1617 and a new fort was built on the shore of the Hudson R. Fort Orange, near Albany, was established in 1624 by the Walloons. The region was later dominated by the patroonship of Rensselaerswyck.

1619 July 30: The **first legislative assembly** in America, the House of Burgesses, convened at Old Church, Jamestown, Va. All legislation needed the approval of the London Company.

1619 Aug: The **first slaves** arrived in Virginia when a Dutch ship carried 20 blacks to Jamestown, Va., for sale.

II. Architecture
   Arts and Music
   Popular Entertainment
   Publishing
   Theater

An important figure in early colonial literature was John Smith, the explorer and adventurer who wrote seven books about the New World. Among these were

A Map of Virginia (1612), probably his best-known work; *A Description of New England* (1616); and *New England's Trials* (1620). These works contributed to further exploration and settlement and offer excellent views of early colonization. Smith's autobiography, *The True Travels, Adventures, and Observations of Captain John Smith,* was published in 1630, the year before his death.

1610: An **early report of Virginia** was contained in *A True Reportory of the Wrack and Redemption of Sir Thomas Gates, Knight, upon and from the Islands of the Bermudas, his coming to Virginia and the Estate of that Colony then and after the Government of the Lord La Ware,* a firsthand account of New World settlement by William Strachey. First published in 1625, the manuscript has been offered as one of the sources that might have suggested *The Tempest* to William Shakespeare.

1612: An early **detailed study of Virginia** was provided in *A Map of Virginia* by Capt. John Smith. The book, describing Virginia's land, its commodities, people, government, and religion, was published in Oxford, England.

III. Business and Industry
    Education
    Philosophy and Religion
    Science

Early explorers were astonished to see Indians smoking tobacco, a plant unknown in Europe. Tobacco leaves were soon taken to Europe, where smoking became a rage. For a time it was believed that the fumes had miraculous curative powers. As a result of its popularity, tobacco became an economic asset in America, especially in Virginia, where a young planter, John Rolfe, planted the first successful crop in 1612. By 1619 tobacco was the leading export of Virginia, and it was later used as a basis for currency. Unfortunately, tobacco production came to require a large number of slaves, and the crop quickly depleted the soil.

1611: The **first Presbyterian congregation** in America was established at Jamestown, Va., by the Rev. Alexander Whitaker, a volunteer from the Puritan community at Cambridge, England. He is best known as the clergyman who instructed Pocahontas in Christianity and baptized her.

1613: Pocahontas, daughter of Powhatan, head of a confederacy of Algonquian tribes in Virginia, was baptized, perhaps the first Indian convert in the colony. Taken hostage to compel the release of colonists held by her father's tribe, she came into contact with the Rev. Alexander Whitaker, was converted, baptized, and given the Christian name of Rebecca. On Apr. 14, 1614, she married the young planter John Rolfe. On a trip to England, her old friend, Capt. John Smith, introduced her to the royal court.

1616: A **smallpox epidemic** among Indians relieved future New England colonies of the threat of major hostilities with the Indians. The tribes from the Penobscot R. in Maine to Narragansett Bay in Rhode Island were virtually destroyed.

IV. Fashion
   Folkways
   Holidays
   Social Issues and Crime
   Sports

Colonists from Europe brought with them their customs with regard to recreation. As early as May of 1611, the men of Jamestown, Va., played a game of bowls in the street, the first such event on record. At Christmas in 1625, a Virginian recorded that "the extreame winde, rayne, froste and snow caused us to keepe Christmas among the savages where we were never more merry, nor fed on more plenty of good Oysters, Fish, Flesh, Wilde fowl and good bread, nor never had better fires in England." In 1619, however, Virginia prohibited gaming at dice or cards. A few years later the Pilgrim and Puritan fathers of New England frowned on almost all frivolity.

1617: Women started to arrive in Virginia. Unlike the Puritans in the North, Virginia settlers came over "not as men, but more as soldiers sent out to occupy an enemy's country." The arrival of women insured the growth and development of permanent communities.

1618: In a move to **compel church attendance,** Gov. Samuel Argall of Virginia decreed that all who failed to attend church service would be imprisoned in the guardhouse, "lying neck and heels in the Corps of Gard ye night following and be a slave ye week following." Sunday dancing, fiddling, card playing, hunting, and fishing were also forbidden.

1620–1629

I. Civil Rights
Exploration and Settlement
Government
Statistics
Wars

In 1629 the Dutch West India Company introduced the patroon system to New Netherland. To encourage emigration, the company on June 7 proclaimed a Charter of Freedoms and Exemptions, by which large tracts of land were granted to those who could establish settlements of 50 persons within four years. In return, the landholder, or patroon, received what amounted to feudal rights and authority. By 1630 five such patroonships had been established, but only three were ever colonized: Pavonia, which included what is now Staten Island, N.Y.; Swaanendael on Delaware Bay; and Rensselaerswyck on the upper Hudson R. Of these, only Rensselaerswyck was successful.

The estimated colonial **population** was 2499.

1620 Nov 21: The **Mayflower Compact,** the first social contract for a New England colony, was drafted and signed by 41 adult males in Provincetown Harbor, Mass. The Pilgrims did not settle there, but went on after a time to Plymouth.

1620 Dec 26: The **Pilgrims reached Plymouth,** Mass., aboard the *Mayflower* after setting out from England on Sept. 16. The company consisted of 41 men and their families.

1621: A **peace treaty and defensive alliance** between the Wampanoag Indians and the Pilgrims was concluded at Strawberry Hill, Plymouth, Mass. Arranged by Squanto, an English-speaking Indian, it was one of the earliest recorded treaties between Europeans and Indians in North America. Squanto had been kidnaped and sold as a slave in Spain. He escaped to England, where he learned English, and lived in Newfoundland for a time before returning to Massachusetts in 1619.

1622 Mar 22: The **first Indian massacre,** led by Powhatan's brother, almost wiped out the settlements outside Jamestown, Va., which was itself heavily fortified.

1622 Aug 10: The province of **Maine** was granted to John Mason and Ferdinando Gorges. It included the land between the Merrimack and Kennebec rivers.

1624 May: The Dutch colony of **New Netherland,** which at this time consisted of the Hudson River Valley north to Fort Orange, was established when Cornelis J. Mey reached what is now New York Bay with 30 families. Mey was the first governor of New Netherland.

1624 Dec 21: The **first Swedish colony** in America was authorized by a charter granted to the South Company of Sweden. No colony was established until 1638, after organization of the New Sweden Company (1637).

1625 Spring: The Dutch settlement of **New Amsterdam** was constructed at the tip of Manhattan, or Manhattes, Island. The settlement was under the direction of Willem Verhulst, who succeeded Cornelis

Mey as governor of New Netherland. On May 4, 1626,
Peter Minuit arrived with a new group of settlers and
succeeded Verhulst, with the title director general of
New Netherland.

1626: Manhattan Island was sold by the Indians for
goods valued at 60 guilders, later calculated as the
legendary sum of $24. The purchase was made by
Peter Minuit.

1629 June 27: The first settlers of **Massachusetts Bay
Colony** entered Salem Harbor. Led by John Winthrop, they were 900 strong, and arrived in five ships.

II. Architecture
Arts and Music
Popular Entertainment
Publishing
Theater

One of the great stories of American literature concerns Myles Standish, military leader of Plymouth
colony. According to tradition, in 1621 Standish,
whose wife Rose had just died, asked John Alden, a
young Pilgrim rising in importance, to court Priscilla
Mullens on his behalf. When Alden did so, the
maiden said to Alden, "Prithee, John, why do you not
speak for yourself?" John did so, they were married,
and Standish forgave Alden. This tale, although his-
torically unfounded, was enshrined in American tradition by Henry Wadsworth Longfellow's poem "The
Courtship of Miles Standish" (1858).

1620: The **first public library** in the English colonies
was established at a college planned for Henrico, Virginia. The library received bequests of books from
English estates; but the college was never developed,
and the collection of books was soon broken up.

1622: The journal of William Bradford and Edward
Winslow, long known as *Mourt's Relation* and containing the first detailed and accurate account of the
landing of the Pilgrims at Plymouth, was published.
Printed anonymously in England as *A Relation or
Journall of the Beginning and Proceedings of the English Plantation Setled at Plimoth in New England*, it

included a preface bearing the signature G. Mourt, possibly that of George Morton, who served as an agent for the colony.

1624: *The Generall Historie of Virginia, New England, and the Summer Isles* by John Smith was published in England. The book consisted of accounts of his observations in the New World. Besides helping to found Virginia, he had mapped the coastal area of New England around Cape Cod in 1614. This exciting report, which included the first complete account of Smith's rescue by Pocahontas, was in part promotional literature designed to encourage immigration.

III. Business and Industry
Education
Philosophy and Religion
Science

A major factor in the establishment of the English colonies was the search for religious freedom. Much of the seventeenth century was a period of religious dissent in the British Isles against the established Church of England. The best known of the dissenters were the Pilgrims, who were Separatists, and the more numerous Puritans, who established the Massachusetts Bay Colony. Their church, the Congregational Church, became established in New England and was supported by taxes. Maryland was founded as a Roman Catholic sanctuary, and later the persecuted Quakers found a haven in Pennsylvania. Baptists, Presbyterians, and, later, Methodists added to the denominational mix of English colonists in America. Virginia was settled largely by Anglicans.

1620: A **Congregational Church** was founded in Plymouth, Mass., by 102 Pilgrim Separatists under William Brewster, William Bradford, and Edward Winslow, all of whom were part of the Scrooby-Leiden congregation in Holland. In England, Congregationalists were known as Independents. Ralph Smith, the first successful pastor of the church, arrived later.

1624 Mar: The **first cattle** brought to New England were three heifers and one bull imported from Devon, England, by Edward Winslow, later governor of Plymouth colony.

1628: The **Reformed Protestant Dutch Church** was established in New Amsterdam under the leadership of the Rev. Jonas Michaelius. Before this date Dutch settlers had held informal meetings of worship. The Rev. Michaelius also established the first school in New Netherland. The Reformed Church was the established church of the colony until the English conquest in 1664. Four churches in New York City—Fort Washington Collegiate Church, Middle Collegiate Church, Marble Collegiate Church, and West End Collegiate Church—now collectively known as the Collegiate Reformed Dutch Church, grew out of this early church.

1629 July 10: The **first non-Separatist Congregational Church** in America was established in Salem, Mass. The church was founded by Francis Higginson and Samuel Skelton, two ministers newly arrived from England.

IV. Fashion
   Folkways
   Holidays
   Social Issues and Crime
   Sports

An important albeit lowly position in the colonial social structure, between free men and slaves, was that of the indentured servant. Indentured servants, in return for passage to America, agreed to work for a period of time, usually five years, in return for little more than their keep. Many came of their own free will, but the English government also sent over hundreds of hardened criminals on such terms. Often, after the servants' terms of service had expired, they were granted plots of land. Others became tenant farmers, as in Virginia, where by 1619 their farms extended for 20 miles along the James R.

1621 Dec: The **earliest American harvest festival** was celebrated by the Pilgrims at Plymouth, Mass.

1621 Dec 25: Game playing on Christmas Day by newcomers to Plymouth colony was halted by Gov. William Bradford. The governor, scandalized at the settlers' playing of such games as "pitching the barr" and "stoole-ball," confiscated the equipment needed to play the games.

1623: Seafood was the main source of nutrition for women and children arriving in New England this year to join their Pilgrim husbands and fathers. The settlers were feasted with "a lobster or a piece of fish without bread or anything else but a cup of spring water." Many lobsters weighed 25 lbs. and were so abundant that the smallest child could catch them.

1625: The **first child** born in New Amsterdam was in the family of Jan Joris Rapaelje, marking the beginning of family life in the Dutch settlement.

1627: 1500 kidnaped children arrived in Virginia. They came from Europe and some became great successes. A six-year-old, kidnaped by a sailor and sold in America, married his master's daughter, inherited his fortune, and bought the sailor, by then a prisoner.

1628 May 1: The celebration of **May Day** at Mare Mount, Thomas Morton's settlement at what is now Quincy, Mass., was colorfully although bitterly described by Gov. Bradford: "They allso set up a May-Pole, drinking and dancing aboute it many days together, inviting the Indean women, for their consorts, dancing and frisking together, (like so many faries or furies rather) and worse practices. As they had anew revived and celebrated the feasts of the Roman Goddes Flora, or the beastly practieses of the Madd Bacchinalians."

1630–1639

I. Civil Rights
Exploration and Settlement
Government
Statistics
Wars

The first of the many wars between whites and Indians was fought in 1637 between the Pequots and New England settlers. The Pequots were a warlike tribe centered along the Thames R. in southeastern Connecticut. By 1630, under their chief, Sassacus, they had pushed west to the Connecticut R. There they had numerous quarrels with colonists, culminating in the murder by the Pequots of a trader, John Oldham, on July 20, 1636. On Aug. 24 Gov. John Endicott of Massachusetts Bay Colony organized a military force to punish the Indians, and on May 26, 1637, the first battle of the Pequot War took place when the New Englanders, under John Mason and John Underhill, attacked the Pequot stronghold near present-day New Haven, Conn. The Indian forts were burned and about 500 men, women, and children were killed. The survivors fled in small groups. One group, led by Sassacus, was caught near present-day Fairfield, Conn., on July 28, and nearly all were killed or captured. The captives were made slaves by the colonists or were sold in the West Indies. Sassacus and the few who escaped with him were put to death by Mohawk Indians. The few remaining Pequots were scattered among other southern New England tribes.

The estimated colonial **population** was 5700.

1630: Rensselaerswyck, the only successful Dutch patroonship, was founded by Kiliaen Van Rensselaer, a director of the Dutch West India Company. The patroonship, comprising present-day Albany and Rensselaer counties, extended 24 miles on both sides of the Hudson R., and its inhabitants numbered several thousand tenants. It was never seen by Van Rensselaer, who managed the entire enterprise from his home in Old Amsterdam.

1630: A settlement at Trimountain, also known as Shawmut, an Indian name meaning living fountain, was established by John Winthrop. The settlement was an extension of the colony at Salem, Mass., which was under the governorship of John Endicott. On Sept. 17 the settlement was named Boston.

1630 Sep 30: The **first criminal executed** in the American colonies, John Billington, was hanged for murder. A member of the original Pilgrim band, he had waylaid and shot a man with whom he had quarreled.

1632 June 20: A charter for the settlement of **Maryland** was granted to Cecilius Calvert, second Lord Baltimore. Under his proprietorship, the Roman Catholic settlement of St. Marys was established. Leonard Calvert, his brother, was the first governor of Maryland.

1636 June: Rhode Island was founded by Roger Williams, who established Providence with a small group of colonists from Massachusetts Bay. It was the first English colony in America to grant complete religious tolerance.

1638 Mar: The **first Swedish settlers** in America landed at Fort Christiana, Del., after crossing in Dutch ships under Peter Minuit. They established the first Lutheran congregation in America, led by Rev. Reorus Rorkillus. In 1643 Swedish colonists from Delaware, under John Printz, settled at Upland, now Chester, Pa.

1639 Jan 14: The **first constitution** in the colonies, the Fundamental Orders, composed by Roger Ludlow, was adopted by representatives from Hartford, Windsor, and Wethersfield in Connecticut. The resulting instrument, with some changes, remained in force until 1818.

II. Architecture
Arts and Music
Popular Entertainment
Publishing
Theater

The history of American publishing dates from 1638, when the first printing press in the colonies arrived in Cambridge, Mass. It was the property of the Rev. Jose Glover, who died on the voyage from England. He had brought it with him under contract with Stephen Daye. In Cambridge, Glover's widow and Matthew Daye, Stephen's son, helped set up the press. In 1639 the press produced the first English document printed in America, "Oath of a Free-Man." This broadsheet read in part: "I doe solmenly bind myself in the sight of God, that when I shal be called to give my voyce touching any such matter of this State, in which Freemen are to deal, I will give my vote and suffrage as I shal judge in mine own conscience may best conduce and tend to the publike weal of the body, without respect of persons, or favour of any man." An almanac soon followed this broadsheet and in the course of the next decade more than 20 items were printed.

1630: *History of Plimmoth Plantation* by William Bradford, the first account of the settlement of Plymouth colony, was begun. Bradford was the second governor of Plymouth colony. His book took more than 20 years to complete and was first published in full in 1856. Devout, sincere, and learned, Bradford wrote feelingly of the *Mayflower* crossing and of the pioneer life of the early settlers. His authenticity earned him the title "father of American history."

1630 May 29: *The History of New England*, a chronicle of events from 1630 to 1649, was begun by John Winthrop, first governor of Massachusetts Bay Colony. The journal was the inspiration for many of Henry Wadsworth Longfellow's *New England Tragedies*. It was published in a two-volume edition in

1790. When an additional manuscript was found some time later, the whole work finally appeared as *The History of New England,* published in 1825–1826. Winthrop touched upon all major aspects of life. His work is a vast compendium of what the early colonists felt and thought and traces the evolution of their ideas and ideals. It remains an unparalleled primary source for the history of the period.

1634: The **first Roman Catholic** church built by English colonists was raised at St. Marys City, Md. Excavations have revealed its foundation, but nothing else is known about its appearance.

1636: The **oldest extant house** of the English-speaking colonies, the Adam Thoroughgood House, was built near Norfolk, Va. Its design typified that of the small, southern colonial brick farmhouse of the seventeenth century.

1637: The *New English Canaan,* a book by Thomas Morton describing New England life and satirizing the Plymouth Pilgrims, was published in Amsterdam. Morton founded the colony at Mare Mount, where Maypole dances and other so-called debauched customs stirred the wrath of Puritan leaders. Morton was the square peg in the round hole of New England Puritanism. He spent his life traveling back and forth across the Atlantic, spending enough time in various colonies to outrage the local authorities and be shipped back to England and prison. Before he published his book, he was engaged by the English as an informer against the Massachusetts Bay Colony. The book served partly as revenge for the treatment he had received from the Puritans and partly as justification for his own activities. Nathaniel Hawthorne wrote about Morton in "The Maypole of Merry-Mount."

1638: Construction of **Old College** was begun at Harvard College in Cambridge, Mass. The most ambitious building of its time in the U.S., it housed the entire student body, library, lecture halls, etc.

1638: The **American log cabin,** originally a Finnish building, was introduced to the New World by the

Swedish settlers of Delaware. Unlike other colonists, they brought over their own timber. The colonists also introduced the steam bath.

1638: The **first almanac** in the English colonies, *An Almanak for the Year of Our Lord, 1639, Calculated for New England* by William Pierce, was published at Cambridge, Mass., by Stephen Daye. Pierce, a shipmaster, used the almanac as a broadside to attract new settlers for the colonies and passengers for his ship.

1639: Hezekiah Usher, who became the **first American bookseller and publisher,** settled in Cambridge, Mass. He later (1657) imported presses and type from England to print John Eliot's *Indian Bible* (1661–1663).

III. Business and Industry
Education
Philosophy and Religion
Science

Education was an early concern of the colonists, in large part because it was believed necessary, especially in New England, that everyone be able to read the Bible. Also, many of the early settlers had some education—there were, in fact, about 130 university alumni in New England by 1640. The first schoolmaster was a Dutchman, Adam Roelantsen, who arrived in New Amsterdam in 1633 and set up the first school in America. It was an adjunct of the Dutch Reformed Church. That same year the first secondary school in America, the Boston Latin School, was established with a classical curriculum derived from English schools. By 1720 five public schools were maintained in Boston and were so well regarded that they enrolled students from as far away as the West Indies. Boston Latin School, the oldest public school in the U.S., is still in existence.

1630 Summer: Boston's first church was founded. It had been formed under a covenant adopted by John

Winthrop, Thomas Dudley, Isaac Johnson, and the pastor, John Wilson, in Charlestown before these men and their followers crossed the Charles R. and founded the settlement that became Boston. It was a Puritan but non-Separatist Congregational church.

1631 Feb 5: Roger Williams, the great early American dissenter and the founder of the American Baptist Church, arrived at Boston from England. He became pastor of the Separatist church at Plymouth in 1632.

1631 Nov 3: The Rev. **John Eliot,** who became the first Protestant minister in America to dedicate himself to the religious conversion of Indians, arrived at Boston from England. Settling as a teacher at Roxbury, now part of Boston, he began preaching to the Indians in 1646 and came to be called the apostle of the Indians.

1634 Mar 25: The **Roman Catholic Church** gained a permanent foothold in America when the *Dove* and the *Ark* arrived in Maryland with colonists carefully selected by Cecilius Calvert, second Lord Baltimore, proprietor of Maryland and a Roman Catholic. The colony was led by Leonard Calvert, Lord Baltimore's brother.

1636 Oct 28: Harvard College was founded by an act of the General Court of Massachusetts that allowed £400 for the establishment of a school. Its entrance requirements were: "When any scholar is able to understand Tully or such like classical author extempore, and make and speak true Latin in verse and prose . . . and decline perfectly the paradigms of nouns and verbs in the Greek tongue, let him then and not before, be capable of admission into the college." The Rev. Henry Dunster was Harvard's first president.

1637 Nov 7: Anne Hutchinson was banished from Massachusetts Bay Colony. Charged with heresy for preaching that faith alone was sufficient for salvation, a belief that contradicted Puritan orthodoxy, she was condemned by an ecclesiastical synod at Newtown, Mass., and fled to Rhode Island.

1638: The **first Baptist church** in America was established at Providence by Roger Williams, who became
its first pastor but remained in the church for only a
few months.

1639 May 20: The **first school maintained by community taxes** was established by the Council of Dorchester, Mass. Only certain property owners were taxed,
and no general tax rates were established.

IV. Fashion
Folkways
Holidays
Social Issues and Crime
Sports

The tavern, a favorite European institution, began to
thrive in America about this time. Drinking was
looked on with tolerance in some circles, deplored
and opposed in others. The first tavern in Boston was
opened by Samuel Cole on Mar. 4, 1634. Taverns became important social institutions and at the time of
the American Revolution were meeting places for
patriotic groups. Nevertheless, they were frowned on
by the authorities. In 1637 Gov. Willem Kieft of New
Amsterdam lamented that one-quarter of all the
buildings there were occupied by "grog-shops or
houses where nothing is to be got but tobacco and
beer." On Sept. 4, 1639, the General Court of Massachusetts enacted a law against drinking toasts, saying
that, "The common custom of drinking to one another is a mere useless ceremony, and draweth on the
abominable practice of drinking healths." It proved
impossible to suppress such a time-honored custom,
and the law was repealed in 1645.

1631 Feb 22: The **first public thanksgiving,** a fast day,
was celebrated in Massachusetts Bay Colony, though
many private celebrations had been recorded before
this.

1634: A **sumptuary law** was passed by the Massachusetts General Court prohibiting the purchase of
woolen, linen, or silk clothes with silver, gold, silk, or

thread lace on them. Slashed clothing was limited to one slash in each sleeve and in the back.

1638: Dutch justice was prompt and harsh during the early days of Manhattan. Guysbert Van Regerslard was sentenced to throw himself from the sail-yard of a yacht three times and receive three lashes from each sailor for "drawing his knife upon a person."

1639: New England laws governing the **clothing of men** reflected the gay attire of the day: men were censured for wearing "immoderate great breeches," broad shoulder-bands, capes, and double ruffles. Silk roses were worn as adornment on shoes.

1639: A woman of Plymouth convicted of **adultery** was sentenced to "be whipt at a cart tayle" and to "weare a badge upon her left sleeue during her aboad" in the community. If found in public without the badge, she was to be "burned in the face with a hott iron." Generally the letters AD made up the badge.

1640–1649

I. Civil Rights
Exploration and Settlement
Government
Statistics
Wars

The first federation of American colonies was formed on May 19, 1643, when representatives of Connecticut, Massachusetts Bay, New Haven, and Plymouth colonies met in Boston and organized the United Colonies of New England. The federation was to provide a "firm and perpetual league of friendship and amity, for offense and defense, mutual advice and succor upon all just occasions." John Winthrop of

Massachusetts Bay Colony was the first president. Two commissioners from each colony administered the federation, which could not interfere in internal affairs but could resolve boundary disputes among themselves and with the Dutch, who were attempting to encroach on territory claimed by New Englanders. The federation was also intended to provide support against the Indians when necessary. Provision was made for the return of runaway indentured servants, and a fund for the conversion of Indians to Christianity was administered. In 1653 Massachusetts Bay Colony, with the largest population and therefore liable for more soldiers and money than the others, refused to join a proposed war against the Dutch. The federation gradually declined but revived in 1675 on the occasion of King Philip's War. It was dissolved in 1684.

The estimated colonial **population** was 27,947.

c1640: The **first woman barrister** in America was Margaret Brent, colonial attorney for Cecilius Calvert, Lord Proprietor of Maryland.

1641 Dec: The **Body of Liberties,** a legal code framed by the General Court of Massachusetts, contained strong hints of the growing spirit of colonial independence. Five years later, in 1646, the court had occasion to reply to criticism of its provisions: "Our allegiance binds us not to the laws of England any longer than while we live in England."

1643: Development of the coastal towns of **Boston, Salem, Dorchester, and Charleston** in Massachusetts Bay colony dwarfed the Plymouth settlement. There were an estimated 20,000 inhabitants in the London Company's Bay Colony.

1643 Mar: **Roger Williams** left Providence for England to obtain a formal charter. In this way Rhode Island secured a legal position from which to fight against pressure from hostile New England colonies.

1647 May 29-31: The **Rhode Island General Assembly** convened at Portsmouth, drawing from the towns of Providence, Portsmouth, Newport, and Warwick. This body drafted a remarkably liberal constitution which, among other things, called for separation between church and state.

II. Architecture
Arts and Music
Popular Entertainment
Publishing
Theater

As mid-century approached, houses and commercial buildings in the colonies became larger, more imposing, and more like those of Europe than, for example, the first homes of Boston, which had been one-story structures covered with thatch and put up at random. By 1636 the Dutch West India Company had built in New Amsterdam five large stone structures for use as shops, although most houses there were built of wood. William Coddington, who founded Newport, R.I., in 1639, two years later built a large townhouse of the type that had a central chimney and two or four rooms on a floor, rather than the older pioneer style house of one room with the fireplace at one end. The City Tavern, the first inn built in New Amsterdam, in 1641, was a four-story stone house, an excellent example of the Dutch colonial style. In 1654 it became the Stadthuys, or Town-House. The first of the great Virginia mansions was erected in 1642 by Gov. William Berkeley about three miles north of Jamestown. Called Greenspring, it was L-shaped, with a brick main wing nearly 100 feet long.

1640: The **first book printed** in America, *The Whole Booke of Psalmes Faithfully Translated into English Metre,* was published in Cambridge, Mass. More commonly called the *Bay Psalm Book,* it contained new versions of all the psalms. Early editions had no music, but included explicit instructions on which tunes should be used for each psalm. Translations and tunes were crude, jog-trot ballads, easier to sing but much less interesting than older versions in Henry Ainsworth's or Thomas Sternhold and John Hopkins' psalters.

1643: The **first American word book,** *A Key into the Language of America, or an help to the language of the natives of that part of America called New England,* by Roger Williams, founder of Providence, R.I., was published in London. Williams compiled his Indian language dictionary aboard ship during a journey to Southampton, England.

1647: The **earliest painting** of New York, by an unknown artist, also provided the first representation of a striped flag. The flag's four stripes symbolized the confederacy of four colonies: Plymouth, New Haven, Connecticut, and Massachusetts.

III. Business and Industry
Education
Philosophy and Religion
Science

It was many years before manufacturing was of much importance in the colonies compared with agriculture, forestry, and fishing, but by this period stirrings of the entrepreneurial spirit could be seen. In 1642 Joseph Jencks, a skilled English ironmaker, was induced to come to America to help develop the iron and brass works at Lynn, Mass. Jencks obtained a Massachusetts patent for a scythe-grinding machine in 1646, the first American patent for machinery. In 1643, what was probably the first American textile factory, a small woolen and fulling mill, was established at Rowley, Mass. The next year the first successful ironworks in what is now the U.S. was founded on the Saugus R. near Lynn, Mass. Its founders were called the Company of Undertakers of Ironworks. They were headed by John Winthrop, a colonial governor who in 1663 became the first resident of the American colonies to become a member of the Royal Society.

1641 Oct: The **first patent** in the colonies was awarded to Samuel Winslow of Massachusetts for a process of manufacturing salt, the term of the patent to extend ten years.

1646 Nov 4: A severe **heresy law** enacted in Massachusetts made death the punishment for any person who persisted in denying that the Holy Scriptures were the word of God "or not to be attended to by illuminated Christians."

1647: The **first important public education law** in America was passed in Massachusetts, providing that every community of 50 homeowners maintain free elementary education and that communities of more than 100 households provide secondary school education as well.

1647 May 26: Roman Catholic priests were forbidden to enter territory under Puritan jurisdiction, according to a law passed in Massachusetts. Any person suspected who could not clear himself was to be banished. For a second offense death was the penalty.

1647 Nov 11: The **first American compulsory school law** was passed in Massachusetts. It provided for the appointment of a teacher in every community of more than 50 families and for the establishment of a grammar school in every community of more than 100 families.

1648: The **first person executed for witchcraft** in America was Margaret Jones of Charlestown, Mass. Gov. John Winthrop wrote "that she was found to have such a malignant touch, as many persons, (men, women and children), whom she stroked or touched with any affection or displeasure, etc., were taken with deafness . . . or other violent pains or sickness . . . Her behaviour at the trial was very intemperate, lying notoriously, and railing upon the jury and witnesses, etc., and in the like distemper she died."

1648 Oct18: The **first labor organization** in America was authorized by the Massachusetts Bay Colony. "The shoomakers of Boston" were permitted to meet whenever they wanted to choose officers and clerks.

1649 Apr 21: The **Toleration Act** was pushed through the Maryland Assembly by Lord Baltimore, Roman Catholic Proprietor of Maryland. Though the colony was a haven for Roman Catholics, Lord Baltimore had from the beginning encouraged Protestant immigration. As Protestant groups became more numerous, religious disturbances became frequent and bitter. The rise of Oliver Cromwell in England in 1642 intensified anti-Catholic feeling among the Puritans in Maryland and other colonies. Increased pressure from England for the suppression of Catholicism in the colonies led Baltimore to sponsor the Act of Toleration as a means of averting a serious test of authority.

IV. Fashion
   Folkways
   Holidays
   Social Issues and Crime
   Sports

As towns grew and more houses were crowded together, the danger of fire led to development of the volunteer firefighting system. In Massachusetts, laws of 1638 and 1646 forbade smoking "out of dores." This move was inspired not so much by Puritan mores as because "fires have beene often occasioned by taking tobacco." Boston in 1649 required that between nine in the evening and half past four in the morning all fires be covered or put out. In 1648 in New Amsterdam, Gov. Peter Stuyvesant forbade construction of chimneys of "wood or plaister in any house," since defective chimneys caused most fires. He appointed four firemasters to inspect chimneys and to collect three guilders for any chimney found "neglected and foul." The fines were to be used to buy hooks, ladders, and leather buckets for a firefighting organization called The Prowlers, a group of eight men who patrolled the streets at night.

1640: The **high-backed settle** appeared in American households. Designed to rest in front of fireplaces, it was fitted with a high back and arms to ward off drafts, with seats extremely narrow and left unupholstered.

1644: The **first Thanksgiving Day** celebrated in New Amsterdam commemorated the safe return of Dutch soldiers from the battle with Connecticut Indians near Stamford.

1647: An unusual blue law forbidding **social smoking** was enacted in Connecticut. Tobacco could be used once a day, at meals or elsewhere, "and then not in company with any other." Tobacco could only be used in one's own house. Behind this law lay the belief that smoking in a group paved the way to dissipation.

1647: Marriages by agreement were declared illegal in Rhode Island. Cases of common law marriage were frequent in the colonies, especially among the Quakers. In one case a New England woman, after living with her "husband" for 20 years, petitioned for separation and her property. The court stigmatized her as a fornicator, fined both £20, and ordered them "not to lead soe scandalose life."

1650–1659

I. Civil Rights
Exploration and Settlement
Government
Statistics
Wars

Of all the Indians the English colonists encountered in the colonies, none were more powerful or better organized than the Iroquois. The five tribes—Mohawk, Oneida, Onondaga, Cayuga, and Seneca—were concentrated in New York in that order between the Hudson R. and the Genesee R. to the west. Their league, possibly organized as early as 1570, numbered no more than 25,000 persons by about 1650 but it dominated others in all directions. Their particular enemies were the Hurons to the north, who with their French allies dominated the fur trade. In 1649 the Iroquois won a resounding victory over the Hurons; in 1651 they nearly wiped out the Neutral Nation along the northern shore of Lake Erie; and in 1656 they defeated and dispersed the Eries. They continued to increase their power and became allies of the English after the Dutch lost New Netherland. As a result, the Iroquois were a serious problem for the patriot forces during the American Revolution.

The estimated colonial **population** was 51,700.

1652: Exportation of **African slaves** to New Netherland was approved by the Dutch government. In the colony strict laws prevented mistreatment of slaves. Whipping was forbidden unless the owner received permission from the authorities.

1652: New Amsterdam was granted self-government by the Dutch authorities in the Netherlands. Peter Stuyvesant, since his arrival in the town in 1647 as governor of New Netherland, had ruled as an autocrat. A board of advisers he appointed was dismissed by him in 1651 when they complained of his rule to the homeland. By Feb. 2, 1653, Stuyvesant had no choice but to proclaim New Amsterdam a self-governing municipality, but he reserved the right to enact laws and ordinances.

1652 May 31: Maine was part of the Massachusetts Bay colony, according to a ruling by the Massachusetts General Court. Despite an appeal to the English Parliament, Maine was unable to resist and so was annexed.

1652 June 10: The **first mint** in America was established in Boston in defiance of English colonial law, with John Hull as its first master. It issued the famous Pine Tree Shilling, designed by Hull, a silversmith.

1653: Settlement of **North Carolina** by Virginia colonists began. They migrated through the Nansemond Valley and settled north of Albemarle Sound between the Chowan R. and the sea. The move was endorsed by the Virginia Assembly, which wanted a buffer settlement as protection for Virginia's southern frontier.

1655: New Netherland took **control of New Sweden,** the Swedish colony on the Delaware R., after years of pressure on the colony by Peter Stuyvesant. Much later, in 1683, the Swedes and Finns along the Delaware R. gladly became English citizens when William Penn founded Pennsylvania.

1656 Sep 22: The **first all-woman jury** in the colonies was empaneled by the General Provincial Court in session at Patuxent, Md., to hear evidence against Judith Catchpole. The defendant, accused of murdering her child, claimed she had never even been pregnant. After hearing her evidence, the jury acquitted her.

II. Architecture
Arts and Music
Popular Entertainment
Publishing
Theater

The Puritan settlers of New England were quick to defend their actions and their beliefs, and many felt that the substantial criticism of them being voiced in England during this time required answering. One of the stalwart defenders was Edward Johnson, who first emigrated to Boston in 1630. In 1653 he published in London *The Wonder-Working Providence of Sions Saviour in New England,* a history of Puritan settlement from 1628 to 1652. Johnson pictured the Puritan settlers as soldiers of Christ waging war against the wilderness and unbelievers.

1650: Anne Bradstreet became New England's first published poet when a volume of her verse, *The Tenth Muse Lately Sprung Up in America,* was published in London. Bradstreet was the wife of Simon Bradstreet, who later served as governor of Massachusetts colony from 1679 to 1686 and again from 1689 to 1692. The manuscript for her book had been taken to London by a brother-in-law who so admired her work that he arranged to have it published without her knowledge. Her poetry showed the influence of Edmund Spenser, Francis Quarles, Sir Philip Sydney, and others. The longer poems dealt with a variety of subjects, such as the four seasons and the four ages of man. Her shorter poems dealt with her New England experiences. Among the latter were "The Flesh and the Spirit," "On the Burning of Her House," "On My Son's Returning Out of England," and "The Author to Her Book." Cotton Mather and other eminent New England figures praised her poetry. A second edition of her poetry, *Several Poems*, was published posthumously in Boston in 1678.

1653: The **first Indian book** was a *Catechism* translated into a dialect of the Algonquian language by John Eliot, missionary to the Indians. Eliot later translated the complete Bible into Algonquian, the first Bible printed (1661, 1663) in the colonies.

III. Business and Industry
     Education
     Philosophy and Religion
     Science

Although many of the early settlers came to America to secure religious freedom, they were not always willing to extend this freedom to others. When the first Quakers, Mary Fisher and Ann Austin, arrived in Boston from Barbados on July 1, 1656, they were imprisoned and mistreated, then expelled by Massachusetts authorities. On Oct. 2 Connecticut enacted a law to fine and banish Quakers. Massachusetts legislation enacted on Oct. 14 decreed that 40-shilling fines be levied against anyone sheltering Quakers and prescribed various physical mutilations for those who returned to the colony after having been banished. The commissioners of the United Colonies of New England expressed their support for such legislation. The first five Quakers to land in New Amsterdam, on June 1, 1657, were imprisoned for eight days before they were allowed to leave for Rhode Island. On May 29, 1658, the Massachusetts General Court passed a law forbidding the holding of Quaker meetings. The first two Quakers hanged on Boston Common, on Oct. 27, 1659, for violating the law against returning to Massachusetts after they had been banished, were William Robinson and Marmaduke Stevenson. Except in Rhode Island, Quakers were persecuted in all the colonies in this period. It was not until the founding of Pennsylvania in 1682 that the Quakers had a haven in the New World.

1654: Production of wool became an important New England industry, partly because many early settlers had been in the wool business in England.

1654: A commission for the **first fire engine** in America was awarded by the Boston selectmen to Joseph Jencks, an ironmonger from Lynn, Mass. The machine, set on wheels, spurted water from a cistern filled by a bucket brigade.

1654: Probably the **first toll bridge** in what became the U.S. was authorized by the General Court of Massachusetts, which licensed Richard Thurley to build and maintain a toll bridge over the Newbury R. at Rowley. The court fixed the toll at two shillings for horses, cows, and oxen; one-half shilling for hogs, sheep, and goats. Humans crossed free.

1654 July 8: The **first Jew** to settle in North America, Jacob Barsimson, arrived on Manhattan Island, first of 24 Jewish immigrants that year. In September three Jews fleeing the Spanish Inquisition in Brazil arrived in New Amsterdam, and more followed. Their right to stay was upheld by the Dutch West India Company against the wishes of Gov. Peter Stuyvesant. They founded Congregation Shearith Israel, with Saul Brown as first rabbi.

1655: Illiteracy among women was about 50%, as shown by an examination of legal documents that required signatures of women in Massachusetts. More than half were obliged to sign with a cross. In New Netherland the rate was 60% and in Virginia 75%.

1656: The **Copernican system,** the conception of the solar system that has the sun rather than Earth at its center, was formally accepted by Harvard College only 23 years after Galileo Galilei had been forced by the Roman Catholic Inquisition to repudiate it.

1658: Perhaps the **first hospital** in what is now the U.S. was set up in New Amsterdam by a Dr. Varravanger, surgeon of the Dutch West India Company. It consisted of a clean house with plenty of firewood and a fire, and was supervised by a matron.

IV. Fashion
Folkways
Holidays
Social Issues and Crime
Sports

Furniture manufacture in the colonies began about this time. Production was hampered for some time by a shortage of carpenters and cabinetmakers. Since the early houses were small, there was not a great deal of space for furniture, and a cramped effect was not unusual. Chests and cupboards provided storage space. An alcove bed was common. Sometimes the parlor, the best room in the house, also seved as the parents' bedroom. The so-called Turkish carpet was placed on table tops, not on the floor. The first known American cabinetmaker, an example of whose work is still extant, worked during this period. He was Nicholas Disbrowe, active in the Connecticut Valley. This area, then the frontier, became the site of a flourishing furniture industry.

1653: An interesting example of **New England snobbery** was demonstrated by the arrest of two women in Newbury, Mass., for adorning themselves with silk hoods and scarves. They were released when they presented proof that both their husbands had net worths of £200.

1656: A Capt. **Kemble** of Boston was made to sit for two hours in the stocks for his "lewd and unseemly behavior" in kissing his wife "publicquely" on Sunday. He had just returned from a three-year sea voyage.

1656: To ensure that **Sunday** would be a day of rest, the burgomasters of New Netherland passed a law forbidding drinking, sowing, mowing, building, sawing, smithing, bleaching, hunting, fishing, dancing, card-playing, tick-tacking, bowling, jaunting in a boat or carriage, etc.

1657: The first reference to **golf** in America was a complaint issued by the sheriff of Fort Orange, now Albany, N.Y., against three men for playing kolven on Sunday. Kolven is believed to have been an early form of golf.

1658: A colonial writer took note of the **fortunes of women** in America: "They no sooner arrive than they are besieged with offers of matrimony, husbands being ready soon for those whom nature had apparently marked out and predestined for lives of single blessedness." Many servants, innocent country girls kidnaped in England and sent penniless to America, married well and attained distinction.

1659 Sep 30: The first mention of **tennis** in America appeared in a proclamation issued by Gov. Peter Stuyvesant of New Netherland forbidding tennis playing, among other things, on certain days.

1660–1669

I. Civil Rights
Exploration and Settlement
Government
Statistics
Wars

Some seeds of the American Revolution were sown at this time by the Navigation Acts of the English Parliament, aimed at the rising power of the Dutch merchant fleet. A law passed in 1651 required that most products be shipped to England in English-owned vessels. The First Navigation Act, of 1660, listed colonial articles that could be supplied only to England. Other Navigation Acts followed in 1662, 1663, 1670, and 1673. The 1663 law required that all foreign goods be shipped to the colonies through English ports. Colonists benefited from the laws to the extent that they were given a monopoly on the shipment of some products to England and preferential tariff treatment in some instances. Colonial businessmen nevertheless resented the restrictions imposed upon them.

The estimated colonial **population** was 84,800.

1660 Dec 1: The **First Navigation Act,** passed by the English Parliament to govern colonial trade, stated that all goods carried to and from England must be transported by British ships manned chiefly by British sailors. It further provided that certain articles, which included sugar, tobacco, cotton, wool, ginger, and dyestuffs, were to be exported to England only.

1662 May 3: A **legal charter for Connecticut** was secured through the efforts of Gov. John Winthrop, Jr. The charter united the colonies of New Haven and Connecticut, neither of which was protected by royal charter. New Haven, however, opposed merger with Connecticut.

1664: A **slavery act** in Maryland provided for lifelong servitude for black slaves. The law was designed to prevent slaves who had converted to Christianity from claiming freedom on the basis of English court decisions holding that infidel slaves must be freed once they had been baptized as Christians and had taken legal residence in the country. Similar acts were passed in Virginia, North Carolina, New York, South Carolina, and New Jersey. Such action was not taken in Georgia, Pennsylvania, or Delaware.

1664 June 24: Proprietorship of **New Jersey,** land between the Hudson and Delaware rivers, was granted by James, Duke of York, to Lord John Berkeley and Sir George Carteret. The new grant was named New Jersey for Carteret, who had been governor of the Isle of Jersey.

1664 Sep 7: Gov. **Peter Stuyvesant surrendered New Netherland** to an English naval force led by Col. Richard Nicolls. Not a shot was fired. Thus ended Dutch power in the New World. Dutch holdings were reorganized into the English colonies of New York and New Jersey. New Amsterdam was renamed New York, and Fort Orange was renamed Albany.

1665 Feb 28: The **Duke's Laws,** sponsored by the English proprietor of New York, James, Duke of York, provided for official recognition of all Protestant sects within the colony. Specific mention was made of the Reformed Protestant Dutch Church, the only church recognized by name. This unusual toleration of the Dutch Church by English authorities contrasted sharply with the restrictive policies of the Dutch West India Company before its loss of the colony to the British in 1664. Up to 1664 the Reformed Protestant Dutch Church was the only legal church in the colony. Despite this restriction, a great many unauthorized religious groups established footholds in the Dutch colony. This religious diversity inherited by the English proprietor in 1664 made the policy of toleration a practical necessity.

1667 July 21: New Netherland was ceded to England by the Dutch by the Peace of Breda, which ended the Second Anglo-Dutch War (1664–1667).

II. Architecture
Arts and Music
Popular Entertainment
Publishing
Theater

Puritans resorted to poetry as well as prose to defend and extend their beliefs. The poetry was always stronger on the theological side than on the poetic. Most famous of such seventeenth-century poet-preachers was Michael Wigglesworth, a clergyman in Malden, Mass. In 1662 his volume *The Day of Doom,* accurately labeled in its subtitle *A Poetical Description of the Great and Last Judgement,* was published. Eighteen hundred copies were sold the first year. It was estimated that one of every twenty persons in New England and one in every forty-five in all the colonies bought a copy. Wigglesworth continued his poetic efforts with *Meat Out of the Eater* (1670), a long poem presenting the Christian view of suffering and the benefits to be derived from it.

1661: The **first Bible printed in America,** the New Testament translated by John Eliot into the Algonquian language and financed by the Corporation for Propagating the Gospel in New England, was published. Of this remarkable work, Cotton Mather wrote: "Behold, ye Americans, the greatest honor that ever you were partakers of! This is the only Bible that ever was printed in all America from the very foundation of the world." Eliot's translation into Algonquian of the Old Testament was published in 1663.

1665 Aug 27: The **first play performed in the North American colonies,** *Ye Bare and Ye Cubb* by Philip Alexander Bruce, was presented at Acomac, Va. Three local residents were fined for acting in this play. Most colonies had laws forbidding public performances. What is strange is that this incident occurred in Virginia, where no such legislation existed.

1669: The first comprehensive **history of New England** was published in Boston, Mass.: *New England's Memoriall, or a Brief Relation of the Most Memorable and Remarkable Passages of the Providence of God, Manifested to the Planters of New England in America; With Special Reference to the First Colony Therefore, Called New Plymouth* by Nathaniel Morton, secretary of Plymouth colony.

III. Business and Industry
Education
Philosophy and Religion
Science

An early political document stressing religious toleration in America was *Fundamental Constitutions,* drawn up for the governance of the Carolinas in 1669. It was the work of the English philosopher John Locke, who prepared it for his friend Anthony Ashley Cooper, later first earl of Shaftesbury, one of the proprietors of Carolina. The document combined liberal principles and an aristocratic social system while stressing religious tolerance. Although it never became law, it exercised a profound influence on colonial religion, particularly in the Carolinas. *Funda-*

mental Constitutions provided that "Noe person whatever shall disturbe, molest or persecute another for his speculative opinions in Religion or his way of worship." Official recognition and support could be granted only to the Church of England, but it was specified that any seven adherents of a religious faith could establish a church under any name they desired, with the provisos that they accept the existence of God and declare that the parishioners of the church would worship Him.

1660: The **first Indian church** in New England was founded by John Eliot at Natick, Mass., on the Charles R. He had established Natick as a native village for "praying Indians" in 1657.

1661: The **first annual meeting of American Quakers** was held in Rhode Island.

1661 Mar 24: The **last Quaker executed** in Boston was William Leddra, who suffered the death penalty for returning from banishment.

1661 Sep: Persecution of Quakers in Massachusetts was halted by Gov. John Endicott on orders from Charles II, a personal friend of William Penn.

1662 Mar: Adoption of the **Half-Way Covenant** by a general synod of Massachusetts churches led to a schism in New England Congregationalism. The covenant permitted parents who had been baptized in the church, but who no longer professed their faith, to have their children baptized. The Half-Way Covenant was symptomatic of the decline of power of the New England founders and the emergence of a more liberal second generation.

1669: The **first Sunday school** of record was established at Plymouth, Mass.

IV. Fashion
Folkways
Holidays
Social Issues and Crime
Sports

Seventeenth-century colonists enjoyed a variety of sports and games. Since horses were a part of everyday life, it was not surprising that, in 1664, horse racing became the first organized sport in the colonies. Before then the governor of Virginia and his friends had raced their horses on a short stretch of road after church services, thereby developing the fast "quarter horse." The Dutch in New Amsterdam enjoyed the cruel sport of "riding the goose" until it was banned in 1658. In Boston, in spite of the Puritan atmosphere, football was played on the streets. Gambling and card playing also were popular there until laws were passed to forbid them. At Newport, R.I., from 1640 to 1690, men amused themselves by bowling on the green.

1660: The **first divorce case** in Delaware involved a Finnish couple. It was said that the "wife receives daily a severe drubbing and is expelled from the house like a dog." The husband was an adulterer, and the divorce was granted. New England at this time showed the most liberality in granting divorces. New Netherland and the rest of the Middle Atlantic colonies made divorce almost impossible except in cases of proved or confessed adultery.

1660: To promote **stable marriages,** a Connecticut law ordered all married men to live with their wives. Any man who was separated from his wife for more than three years was ordered out of the colony.

1660: A **sumptuary law** passed in Virginia forbade settlers from importing "silke stuffe in garments or in peeces except for whoods and scarfs, nor silver or gold lace, nor bone lace of silk or threads, nor ribbands wrought with gold or silver in them." But with the Restoration in England in 1660, periwigs came into fashion on both sides of the Atlantic. Authorities in New England made repeated efforts to prevent their use.

1660 May: The celebration of **Christmas** was forbidden by a law of Massachusetts, with a fine of five shillings levied on violators.

1664: Marriage by a justice of the peace instead of a clergyman was made lawful in New York by the Duke's Laws, actually a continuation of a Dutch law of 1590. The law has never been altered.

1664: The **first organized sport** in America, horse racing, began when New York's first governor, Richard Nicolls, established the Newmarket Course at Hempstead Plains, Long Island, instituted rules of racing, and offered prizes to winners. His purpose was to improve the breed of horses in the colonies.

1670–1679

I. Civil Rights
Exploration and Settlement
Government
Statistics
Wars

While the English colonists were settling along the Atlantic coast and river valleys, the French, from their bases in Canada, were using the St. Lawrence R. and the Great Lakes to explore and claim western North America. At Sault Sainte Marie in 1671, Daumont de St. Lusson claimed the entire interior for France. In 1673 the explorer Louis Joliet and the missionary Jacques Marquette reached the upper Mississippi R. and traveled down it as far as Arkansas. Marquette established a mission at what is now Chicago on Dec. 4, 1674. Another expedition began in late 1678 under the leadership of Robert Cavelier, Sieur de La Salle, and Father Louis Hennepin. They passed Niagara Falls, and later Hennepin was the first European to write a description of it. The party explored the upper Mississippi River Valley. On Apr. 9, 1682, La Salle reached the mouth of the Mississippi, where he claimed control of the whole valley for France and named it Louisiana after King Louis XIV of France.

The estimated colonial **population** was 114,500.

1670 Apr: Charleston, S.C., was founded. English colonists under Joseph West settled at Port Royal Sound, then moved northward to the Ashley R. at

Albemarle Sound for fear of Spaniards. There they established Charles Town, later known as Old Charles Town. In 1680, this settlement was moved once again to the juncture of the Ashley and Cooper rivers, the present site of the city.

1671: The first of the great **Hudson Valley manors** was established at Fordham by the English colony of New York. Others followed: Fox Hall (Kingston), 1672; Rensselaerswyck, 1685; Livingston, 1686; Pelham, 1687; Philipsborough, 1693; Morrisania, 1697; Cortlandt, 1697; and Scarsdale, 1701.

1671: A new **slavery act** in Maryland extended the scope of the slavery law passed in 1664 by declaring that conversion or baptism of slaves before or after their importation did not entitle them to freedom. The act was passed on behalf of slave owners who hesitated to import slaves for fear of losing their investments through prior or subsequent conversion and, also, to encourage slave owners to convert their slaves to Christianity.

1673: The **first native-born governor** of an American colony, Josiah Winslow of Plymouth, was elected governor of Plymouth colony. His term extended until his death in 1680. Winslow also succeeded Myles Standish as commander in chief of the Plymouth military defense.

1673 Aug 8: The **surrender of New York** was demanded by a Dutch force of 23 ships and 1600 men anchored near Sandy Hook. They held possession of the colony until Feb. 9, 1674, when the English regained control.

1674 Dec 4: The **first dwelling** in what is now Chicago was built by Father Jacques Marquette as a mission.

1675-1676: Pressures on the **Indian population** of New England resulted in King Philip's War. The tribes most affected by early colonial expansion were the Wampanoags, originally from the Atlantic coast, now forced back to east of Narragansett Bay; the Narragansetts, whose territory between Narragansett Bay and the Thames R. was menaced by a land company that claimed it held a mortgage to the areas; the Mohegans, between the Connecticut and Thames rivers; the Podunks, directly to the north; and the Nipmucks, who ranged over the northern parts of the Thames and Pawtucket rivers. A coalition of these tribes, known as the Five Nations, was headed by King Philip, Indian name Metacomet, chief of the Wampanoags.

1675 June 24: King Philip's War (1675–1676) began with a massacre of colonists at Swansee, Plymouth, by a band of Indians. The war was started by King Philip after three of his people were executed by the English for murdering an Indian in English employ.

1676 Feb 10: Lancaster, Mass., was attacked by Indians led by King Philip. The settlement was destroyed by fire after all the men were killed and the women and children taken prisoners.

1676 Aug 12: King Philip's War (1675–1676) ended when the Wampanoag leader was surprised and shot by an Indian in the service of Capt. Benjamin Church. The conflict had grown to include the Wampanoag, Nipmuck, Narragansett, Mohegan, and Podunk tribes and ended with their virtual destruction, opening southern New England to unimpeded colonial expansion.

1676 Sep 19: Jamestown, Va., was burned in **Bacon's Rebellion,** an uprising led by Nathaniel Bacon. The rebellion was prompted by Virginia Gov. William Berkeley's repeated refusal to organize necessary defensive measures against marauding Indians. Among the buildings destroyed was the Episcopal Church in Jamestown, the first Protestant church in America. The ruins of the church tower are still standing on the site of the community.

1678: The **first vessel** to penetrate Lake Ontario, the *Griffin,* carried a French expedition led by Robert Cavelier, Sieur de La Salle, from Fort Frontenac (later Kingston) to the present site of Fort Niagara.

1679: A **Boston fire,** the worst in the colonies in the seventeenth century, destroyed 150 houses in Boston. Thereafter, frame houses were abandoned by city ordinance, and all houses were constructed of "stone or bricke, & covered with slate or tyle."

II. Architecture
Arts and Music
Popular Entertainment
Publishing
Theater

A colonial tradition in architecture was that a house should be designed and built to last, and to grow as the family that owned it grew. This was reflected in the history of the House of the Seven Gables in Salem, Mass. Originally known as the Turner House, its first two rooms were built in 1670. Successive additions greatly expanded the structure, and it eventually came to have eight gables. Nathaniel Hawthorne was thought to have modeled the house in his novel *The House of the Seven Gables* (1851) after this structure, which he had visited in his youth.

1676: An example of **early American satire** was the ballad *A Looking-Glass for the Times; or, The former spirit of New England revived in this generation* by Peter Folger, grandfather of Benjamin Franklin. In strong, manly doggerel, he lashed into the Christians of New England for their behavior toward Quakers, Baptists, and others.

1677: A **classic historical book**, *Narrative of the Trouble with the Indians in New England* by William Hubbard, was published. The book reflected the colonials' hostility to red men, who were described as "treacherous villians," "children of the Devil," "the dross of mankind," and "dregs and lees of the earth."

1679: A colonial **best seller**, *A Guide to Heaven* by Samuel Hardy, was published in Boston. A book of Puritan rules and practices of piety, it was less fiery than Bishop Lewis Bayly's *The Practice of Piety*.

III. Business and Industry
Education
Philosophy and Religion
Science

By 1675 more than 600 ships and 4000 New England men were engaged in fishing. From early times, fishing had been important to the colonies not just for food for the settlers but for commerce. When the Pilgrims sailed for America in 1620, they intended their colony to be in part a fishing settlement. In the 1630s the Puritans entered the field. The Rev. Hugh Peter organized fisheries at Marblehead, Mass., and discovered a market for dried codfish. Fishing for cod became so important in the Massachusetts Bay Colony that a wooden image of a cod was installed in the capitol in Boston. Salted fish was in demand in Catholic Europe and in the West Indies. New England fishermen divided their catch into three classes. The largest and fattest, the most difficult to cure, were consumed at home. Somewhat smaller fish were cured and exported to Europe. The smallest fish were sold, usually traded for molasses, in the West Indies as food for slaves.

1673 Jan 1: The first regular **mounted mail service** was inaugurated between New York and Boston. A postman rode without a change of horse from New York to Hartford, through woods and over streams, keeping a lookout for runaway servants and soldiers. The road was little more than a trail but it would soon become the Boston Post Road, the first important highway in the colonies. A post road was so called because men or horses were posted at intervals along the route. They would take packages or messages and carry them to the next post. In this way goods and information were relayed with relative speed. Nonetheless, it still took three weeks to get the mail from Boston to New York City.

1674: Increase Mather was appointed a fellow at Harvard College, beginning a distinguished career in education. Although he once refused the presidency of Harvard, Mather was named acting president in 1685. The following year he took charge, with the title of rector, and held that post until 1701. Mather promoted the study of scientific subjects while maintaining the college's Congregationalist ties. In 1675 his eldest son, Cotton Mather, was admitted to Harvard at the age of 12. He was the youngest person ever admitted to the school. Cotton Mather, the son and grandson of Puritan clergymen, even at this early age believed himself destined to follow in their footsteps and become the preeminent religious and political leader of Massachusetts. Perhaps it was young Mather's sense of destiny that led his fellow students to consider him something of a prig.

1677: The first charter guaranteeing **separation of church and state** in the American colonies was framed by William Penn at the Quaker colony of West Jersey.

IV. Fashion
Folkways
Holidays
Social Issues and Crime
Sports

From the beginning, dress styles had varied from colony to colony, in large part because of national origin, class, or religion. New Englanders tended to be plain of dress, although not as austere as they were later depicted, while many Virginians copied the fashions of upper-class English men and women. By the later seventeenth century, colonial life had improved to where fashion became substantially more elegant and luxurious. This gave rise, particularly in New England, to sumptuary laws intended by colonial authorities to control excesses in dress, hairstyle, and the like.

1670: The **coffee house** appeared in America when a license was given by Boston authorities to a woman to sell coffee and chocolate.

1674: A rule against **horse racing** on public thoroughfares in Plymouth colony stated that "whatsoever person ran a race with any horse in any street or common road should forfeit five shillings or sit in the stocks for one hour."

1675: New York City, which had always had a mixed population, began to take on a really cosmopolitan air. The combination of religious toleration and commercial activity encouraged an influx of Englishmen,

Jews, Africans, Indians, Madagascan pirates, and French Huguenots.

1675: Laws upbraiding **current fashions** were enacted by the Massachusetts General Court. Indian attacks were blamed on the sins of the people, among which was "the manifest pride openly appearing amongst us in that long hair, like women's hair, is worn by some men, either their own or others' hair made into periwigs."

1675: In a case involving **sumptuary laws** in Connecticut, 38 women were brought before a magistrate for wearing clothes not befitting their social position. One young girl was accused of "wearing silk in a flaunting manner, in an offensive way and garb not only before but when she stood presented." This year 30 young men were arrested for wearing silk and sporting long hair.

1678: **Tobacco** consumption of the Dutch inhabitants of New York was substantial. An English chaplain reported that "the Dutch are obstinate and incessant smokers, whose diet . . . being sallets and brawn and very often picked buttermilk, require the use of that herb to keep their phlegm from coagulating and curdling."

1680–1689

I. Civil Rights
 Exploration and Settlement
 Government
 Statistics
 Wars

The flight of King James II of England to France, and his succession on the English throne by William of Orange and his wife Mary on Feb. 13, 1689, marked the climax of the Glorious Revolution, by which the

English Parliament asserted its authority over the king and ensured the succession of a Protestant to the throne. The abdication of James II, a Catholic and an autocratic ruler, had almost immediate repercussions in the colonies. In 1689 the unpopular governor of Virginia, Lord Howard, was removed; Gov. Edmund Andros surrendered in Boston; the counties of New York, Queens, and Westchester in New York ousted the royal government and set up their own rule; Rhode Island and Connecticut reestablished governments under their old charters; and a Protestant Association overthrew the old government in Maryland.

The estimated colonial **population** was 155,600.

1680 Sep: New Hampshire was separated from Massachusetts by royal commission.

1681 Mar 4: What is now roughly the state of **Pennsylvania was granted to William Penn,** a member of the Society of Friends (Quakers) by King Charles II of England. The grant was apparently made to offset a debt of £16,000 the king owed to Penn's father, Sir William Penn.

1682: A site for the city of **Philadelphia** was laid out by Thomas Holme, one of four commissioners who had been sent to Pennsylvania by William Penn to prepare settlers for the new government. Penn, who was in the colony at the time, helped in planning the city.

1682: The **first European settlement in Texas** was made by Spaniards at Yselta, on the site of present-day El Paso. The settlers were refugees from New Mexico who had been driven out after the Pueblo revolt of 1680. Several missions were established in this area but they did not flourish because the Comanche, Apache, and other Indian tribes were unfriendly.

1682 May 5: William Penn's *Frame of Government* was put into effect. An unusually liberal document, it provided for a governor, council, and assembly to be elected by freeholders. The council had legislative, judicial, and administrative powers. At first, the assembly could not initiate legislation, but this was altered in 1696.

1682 Aug 24: Delaware was awarded to William Penn by James, Duke of York, who had no legal title to the land. This made Penn's control over Delaware tenuous, particularly since it conflicted with other claims. The issue was finally resolved by the Charter of 1701, which gave Delaware autonomy.

1683 Oct 6: The first German settlers in America, Mennonites from Krefeld, Germany, arrived at Philadelphia. They settled Germantown, near Philadelphia, at the bidding of William Penn. Their leader, Francis Daniel Pastorius, was considered by many the most learned man in America at the time.

1684 June 21: The Massachusetts Bay Colony charter was revoked by King Charles II of England, acting through the Court of Chancery. Massachusetts had violated its charter by discriminating against the Church of England, setting religious rather than property qualifications for suffrage, and establishing an illegal mint. The revocation had been prompted by Edward Randolph, who had been appointed surveyor of customs and collector in 1678. He sent two unfavorable reports to England in 1682, then returned to England the next year to help prosecute Massachusetts for its charter violations. Revocation of the charter led to dissolution of the New England Confederation.

1687: The Charter Oak incident occurred as the result of the high-handed actions of Sir Edmund Andros, the English colonial governor. In 1685 King James II of England decided to consolidate the New England colonies into the Dominion of New England and named Andros governor. The dominion came to include New York and East and West Jersey. Andros dissolved colonial assemblies and infringed on other rights and customs. He also demanded that the colonial charters be turned over to him. According to legend, when he met with Connecticut officials in Hartford to demand their charter, the candles in the room were suddenly blown out and the royal charter, which had been granted Connecticut in 1662, disappeared. It was then hidden by Capt. Joseph Wadsworth in a hollow in a white oak tree, which became known as the Charter Oak. The tree was said to be 1000 years old and it stood until 1856.

II. Architecture
Arts and Music
Popular Entertainment
Publishing
Theater

A leading figure in colonial literature during this time was William Penn, one of the more unusual personalities among those who founded English colonies in America. The son of an English admiral, he became a Quaker in 1666, when he was 22. Two years later he was imprisoned for writing a religious tract. While in the Tower of London he composed another. Although a liberal in government and deeply religious, he was also politically adept at the royal court. During this period he founded Pennsylvania and wrote both in praise of the colony and in defense of his Quaker beliefs.

1681: An **early description of Pennsylvania** was provided in *Some Account of the Province of Pennsylvania* by William Penn. Like numerous other accounts of the colonies, this was intended to induce emigration from England by indicating ways in which one could earn a living in the New World.

1681: The **Old Ship Meeting House** was erected at Hingham, Mass., by the Puritans, who never referred to a house of worship as a church. This meeting house has been in continuous service since its completion, and it is the last remaining example of the four-square meeting house, a native American contribution to church construction. The meeting house was intentionally denied a cross or spire. Instead a functional tower held a bell and supported a practical weather vane.

1682: A famous **account of Indian life,** *The Sovereignty & Goodness of God, Together With the Faithfulness of His Promises Displayed; Being a Narrative of the Cap-*

tivity and Restoration of Mrs. Mary Rowlandson by Mary Rowlandson, was published. It was the first example of an American literary genre, the Indian captivity narrative. It reflected the hostile attitude of colonists to the American Indian. The book went through more than 30 editions.

1682: The **Newport Parish Church,** the most complete and authentic of extant seventeenth- century Virginia churches, was built at Smithfield, Isle of Wight County. Also called the Old Brick Church, it is a remarkable example of Tudor Gothic (late medieval) architecture transferred to America.

III. Business and Industry
Education
Philosophy and Religion
Science

By the late seventeenth century, the African slave trade was a large-scale business enterprise. Largely in the hands of the Dutch until the 1660s, it was continued by the English, with New Englanders especially active after the Royal Africa Trade Company lost its monopoly in 1696. In the trade, a ship sailed from New England with rum and other goods for the Slave Coast. The slaves were then carried, under the most miserable conditions, to the West Indies or to the colonial South, where they were exchanged for sugar, molasses, and tobacco for the North. During this period Virginia planters relied more on white indentured servants from Europe than on slaves from Africa. There were 6000 indentured servants in Virginia in 1681, compared with 2000 slaves. Some indentured servants came voluntarily, signing papers for five or more years, at the end of which time they would receive some clothing and perhaps a parcel of land. They often then became tenant farmers. Criminals, vagrants, and debtors were sent involuntarily to the New World, usually for a term of service of seven years; they were known as "His Majesty's Seven Year Passengers." Others, children and adults, were victims of kidnaping. They were sold to shipmasters who in turn sold them into servitude in America. Many servants caused trouble in the colonies. As a result, the end of the seventeenth century saw a steady growth in the slave trade.

1680: A major **scientific achievement** of colonial America was the calculation of the orbit of a comet of 1680 by Thomas Brattle, an early Boston mathematician. He sent word of his discovery to the royal astronomer at Greenwich, England, who checked Brattle's observation. Brattle's calculation supported Isaac Newton's theory of cometary orbits, and Newton acknowledged Brattle's work. Nonetheless, a curious mix-up by the Royal Society left Brattle's contribution to science unrewarded. In 1714, a year after he died, the society elected his brother, William, to membership. William Brattle declined the honor.

1686: The **importance of water transportation** to early colonial commerce was remarked on by a Frenchman traveling in Virginia, who noted: "None of the plantation houses, even the most remote, is more than 100 or 150 feet from a 'crik' and the people are thus enabled not only to pay visits in their canoes, but to do all their freight carrying by the same means." Until the coming of the railroads in the nineteenth century, most American commerce, particularly transportation of heavy goods, was conducted by water transportation.

1689: The **first public school** in America with such practical subjects as science and inventions, the William Penn Charter School, was founded in Philadelphia. The school charged tuition only for students who could afford it.

IV. Fashion
   Folkways
   Holidays
   Social Issues and Crime
   Sports

A new element was added to colonial society when in France the Edict of Nantes was revoked in 1685 by King Louis XIV. The edict had protected the Huguenots, French Protestants, from persecution, and its revocation led to a wave of Huguenot emigration to the New World. Thrifty and industrious middle-class merchants and artisans, they settled in New York, Massachusetts, Rhode Island, Virginia, and South Carolina, and established such illustrious family names as Jay, Revere, DeLancey, Faneuil, Bowdoin, and Maury. In New York they founded and named New Rochelle in 1688. The Huguenots were especially important in South Carolina, where 500 of them took up 50,000 acres along the Santee R. They were prominent in Charleston life, and in their cultivation of rice in the lowlands they did much to increase the use of slaves in the colony.

1681: The appearance of the **first dancing master** in Boston provoked an outburst from the authorities. He was cited as "a person of very insolent & ill fame that Raues & scoffes at Religion." He soon was driven out. Dancing was a constant source of complaint among the ministers. Shortly after ouster of the first dancing master, Increase Mather thundered forth his condemnation in the tract *An Arrow against Profane and Promiscuous Dancing, Drawn out of the Quiver of the Scriptures.*

1682: The **first Freemason** to settle in America, John Skene, arrived in Burlington, N.J. He belonged to the lodge in Aberdeen, Scotland, and came to the colonies through arrangements made by the Earl of Perth, chief proprietor of New Jersey and an outstanding Freemason.

1685: For **performing marriages in Boston,** a Huguenot minister was haled before a New England court. A growing tendency to make marriage an ecclesiastical function was strongly suppressed. Marriage was regarded as a civil contract and the courts were determined to enforce this.

1687 June 28: William Phipps, the **first knighted native American,** was dubbed by King James II of England in ceremonies at Windsor Castle. He was so honored for having found a treasure ship off the coast of Hispaniola. Later he returned to Massachusetts and became governor of the colony.

1690-1699

I. Civil Rights
Exploration and Settlement
Government
Statistics
Wars

King William's War (1689–1697) was the first of what came to be known in America as the French and Indian Wars. In fact, the French and Indian Wars were a series of colonial wars between Great Britain and France that lasted three-quarters of a century. Hostilities in King William's War began in 1690, when in the course of a few months Schenectady, N.Y., was burned by the French and Indians, and colonial English forces launched attacks on Port Royal (now Annapolis Royal), Nova Scotia, and on Quebec. Despite further raids by the French and Indians, the war ended in a stalemate. The Treaty of Ryswick, by which were ended the war and its European counterpart, the War of the Grand Alliance, restored all colonial possessions to their prewar status.

The estimated colonial **population** was 213,500.

1690 Feb 3: The **first paper money** was issued. It was used by Massachusetts to pay soldiers who had served the campaign in Quebec.

1690 Feb 8: In **King William's War** (1689–1697) French and Indian forces from Montreal attacked and burned Schenectady, N.Y.

1690 May 11: Port Royal (now Annapolis Royal), Nova Scotia, was captured by the English under Sir William Phips. French forces recaptured it in 1691.

1690 Oct 7: The city of **Quebec was attacked** by English forces in the first major military operation of King William's War. They were repulsed by the French under Louis de Buade, comte de Palluau et de Frontenac.

1691: A **charter** uniting the colonies of Plymouth and

Massachusetts Bay provided "liberty of conscience to all Christians, except Papists."

1691: Albemarle was renamed **North Carolina** and put under the governorship of a deputy answerable to the Crown.

1692 Apr: A patent to found a **post office** in the English colonies was issued to the Englishman Thomas Neale. It was first put into effect in Virginia. Andrew Hamilton, Neale's colonial deputy, later did much to organize widespread postal service.

1696: The **importation of slaves** by Quakers was forbidden at the yearly meeting of American Quakers, with expulsion from membership the penalty for violators.

1697: An epidemic of **smallpox** ravaged Charleston, S.C. After running its course for over a year, it diminished, only to be followed in Aug. 1699 by yellow fever, which killed 150 people in six days. Infections were generally brought from the West Indies.

1697 Sep 3: King William's War (1689–1697) was ended by the Treaty of Ryswick. From the standpoint of the American colonies, the war was completely pointless. Both French and English forces won a number of engagements and managed to occupy part of each other's territory. However, the treaty restored all possessions to their prewar status.

II. Architecture
   ## Arts and Music
   ## Popular Entertainment
   ## Publishing
   ## Theater

Printing and publishing, although hampered by government restrictions, had become more or less common in the larger cities by the end of the seventeenth century. John Foster had established Boston's first press in 1674, and by 1700 presses in Boston were producing more print than those in any English city except London. The first press in Philadelphia had been set up in 1685 by William Bradford, who that year issued an almanac, *Kalendarium Pennsil-*

vaniense or America's Messenger. Bradford, however, had trouble with the city council in 1693 and moved to New York City. In Philadelphia, Regnier Jansen established another press in 1698. In New York, Bradford began issuing almanacs in 1694, and in 1696 he published *Le Trésor des Consolations Divine et Humaine* [Treasury of Comforts Divine and Human]. Almanacs became popular in the eighteenth century. The most famous, *Poor Richard's Almanack*, was first issued by Benjamin Franklin in 1732.

1690: The famous **Wayside Inn** of Henry Wadsworth Longfellow's *Tales of a Wayside Inn* (1886) was built in Sudbury, Mass. It was called the Red Horse Tavern, and was characterized by a raftered ceiling and a bar in the form of a cage. It was damaged by fire in 1955 but was restored.

1690: The *New England Primer*, a standard colonial elementary textbook, made its first appearance. It combined the teaching of the alphabet and Puritan theology in moral couplets, as "In Adam's fall-We sinned all."

1690 Sep 25: The **first newspaper** in the colonies appeared in Boston. It was Benjamin Harris's *Publick Occurrences.* It expired four days later because Harris had presumed to publish without official permission.

1695: The cornerstone was laid for the first building at the **College of William and Mary in Virginia,** based on plans said to have been drawn in London by Christopher Wren. The building, an excellent example of early Georgian style in its purest, Virginian form, was completed in 1702.

1698: The **Old Swedes Church** in Wilmington, Del., said to be the oldest Protestant church in continuous use in America, was erected by Swedish Lutherans. It is now a Protestant Episcopal church.

III. Business and Industry
Education
Philosophy and Religion
Science

The history of New England's great religious leaders was magnified and epitomized in the prolific yet contradictory career of Cotton Mather, last and greatest of the Puritan divines. Pictured as a central figure in the Salem witch hunts because he helped bring on the witchcraft trials there in 1692, he later had second thoughts on witchcraft. He was smug and stern but was also a leader in the revolt against the autocratic rule of Gov. Edmund Andros in Massachusetts. Mather did much to promote education and was deeply interested in science. He wrote more than 440 works and collected a library of 4000 books. He was a man of his time in whom all traits good and bad were greatly magnified.

1690: The **first paper mill** in America was set up by German settlers in Pennsylvania. The paper was handmade from linen rags pounded into pulp. The first American watermark was the word "company" formed in paper made by William Rittenhouse.

1690: The American **whaling industry** first began large-scale operations out of Nantucket, Mass.

1692: The **first divinity degree** conferred in the American colonies was given to Increase Mather, sixth president of Harvard College. Mather received a Doctor of Divinity degree from Harvard under a new charter just granted by William and Mary, the English sovereigns.

1692 Mar: The **Salem witch hunt** was unleashed when some children, called upon to explain their odd behavior, claimed that three old women had bewitched them. The women were tried, convicted, and condemned on the testimony of the children. Although Gov. William Phips halted the trials in Oct. 1692, by Jan. 1693 twenty persons condemned for witchcraft had been executed and two had died in prison.

1693 Feb 8: A charter founding the **College of William and Mary in Virginia** was signed. A grant was given to James Blair to "furnish Virginia with a seminary of ministers, to educate the youth in piety, letters and good manners and to propagate Christianity among the Indians."

1697: Official repentance for the **Salem witch trials** was highlighted by a day of prayer for forgiveness by the Massachusetts Court. Samuel Sewall, one of the Salem judges, publicly confessed his feeling of guilt from his pew in the South Church.

1697 Oct: A severe enactment against **blasphemers and atheists** was passed in Massachusetts. Anyone denying the divine nature of the Bible could be imprisoned for six months, confined to the pillory, whipped, bored through the tongue with a hot iron, or forced to sit on the gallows with a rope around his neck.

IV. Fashion
    Folkways
    Holidays
    Social Issues and Crime
    Sports

As towns and cities grew, the problem of street cleaning arose. Throwing rubbish of all kinds into the street was an old English custom. The tidy Dutch in New Amsterdam were the first to do something about the problem when they forbade in 1657 the throwing of "any rubbish, filth, oyster shells, dead animal or anything like it" into the street. Boston first took action in 1662 when Thomas Willsheer was hired as a scavenger to get rid of "all Carrion & matters of Offenciue natuer." Beginning in 1684 four scavengers were at work. Street cleaning was introduced in New York in 1695 when a Mr. Vanderspiegle was hired at £30 a year. By 1710 the city was employing public cartmen to remove trash placed before houses.

1691: The **ducking stool,** a form of punishment for scolds, was ordered built on the wharf in front of City Hall, New York. Although this form of punishment by plunging into water was not used frequently in New York City, it was common in the South.

1693: The **Huguenots** of South Carolina, considered foreigners, were threatened with the loss of their estates upon death. Discrimination against the French was marked throughout the century in South Carolina, probably because of envy of their refinement, education, and superior economic ability.

1699 Spring: Capt. **William Kidd,** the notorious pirate, paid a visit to an old friend in Narrangansett, R.I., and left some treasure. Thus began the myth of Capt. Kidd's buried treasure, which has sent thousands digging up beaches for trinkets and pieces of eight. Legend says that Kidd murdered a helper and buried him with the treasure chest as a means or warding off searchers.

1699 June: A **card game** was suppressed by Judge Samuel Sewall of Boston. A few days later he found a pack of cards strewn over his lawn, as if to mock his efforts. Gambling was rampant in all the colonies despite numerous laws against it. Even lotteries came under ban in New England by an order promulgated in 1719.

1700–1704

I. Civil Rights
Exploration and Settlement
Government
Statistics
Wars

Queen Anne's War (1702–1713), the second of the French and Indian Wars, began May 4, 1702. In Europe it was known as the War of the Spanish Succession. The Grand Alliance (England, the League of Augsburg, Denmark, Portugal, and the Netherlands) declared war on France and Spain to prevent union of the French and Spanish thrones following the death of King Charles II of Spain. In North America British and French colonial forces, with their Indian allies, raided and attempted to capture a number of border settlements. New England colonists successfully attacked the French settlements of Minas and Beaubassin in Nova Scotia in July 1704, while the French destroyed Deerfield, Mass., in February and took the English colony of Bonavista on Newfoundland in August. The most notable colonial success was the British capture of Port Royal, Nova Scotia, on Oct. 16, 1710, following unsuccessful assaults in 1704 and 1707; however, a British naval attack on Quebec in 1711 failed. In the South, Carolina forces captured the town of St. Augustine, Fla., in Sept. 1702, although the fort there held out. Another force wiped out all but one of fourteen missions in northwestern Florida in 1704.

c1700: The **population** of the colonies was sparsely scattered over the large area. Below the Delaware R. an isolated farm was the usual settlement, save for Charleston, which had about 250 families. Philadelphia had approximately 700 houses, New York about 5000 inhabitants, Newport less than 2000, and Boston, the largest city, about 7000. There were approximately 275,000 inhabitants in the colonies.

1701: The capture of Capt. **William Kidd** marked the passing of the pirate era from colonial trade. William Kidd, at one time a wealthy New York landowner who had served as a privateer for the Crown against the French, was tried and hanged in London on May 23. He left many legends of buried treasure in his wake.

1701 July 24: A settlement at **Detroit** was established by Antoine de la Mothe Cadillac. The area of Michigan was early known to trappers, priests, and traders from French Canada. The Jesuits, led by Isaac Jogues, founded a mission at Sault Ste. Marie in 1641. There, in 1668, Jacques Marquette established the first permanent settlement in Michigan. When the French government lost interest in outposts in the West, Cadillac went to France with a proposal that would save the fur trade from the English. He was granted the land by the narrows of the river connecting Lake Huron with Lake Erie. There he set up a large colony he called Fort Pontchartrain. The name Detroit comes from the French words for the narrows (*détroit*), where the fort was located.

II. Architecture
Arts and Music
Popular Entertainment
Publishing
Theater

Journalism was one of the trades that followed the colonists to America. The first successful newspaper in the English colonies appeared on Apr. 24, 1704. This was the Boston *News-Letter*, founded by John Campbell, the Boston postmaster. It published until 1776. Although its early circulation was only about 300, the paper was passed from person to person and was available in coffee houses and taverns. It carried advertising, including notices placed by dancing and music teachers. Other early newspapers were the Boston *Gazette* (1719), Philadelphia *American Mercury* (1719), *New England Courant* (Boston, 1721), New York *Gazette* (1725), Maryland *Gazette* (Annapolis, 1727), and *Pennsylvania Gazette* (Philadelphia, 1728).

1700: Perhaps the **first denunciation of slavery** in the colonies was *The Selling of Joseph* by Samuel Sewall, which put forth antislavery arguments. Typical of his time, Sewall relied mainly on biblical citations.

1702: *Magnalis Christi Americana; or the Ecclesiastical History of New England,* the *magnum opus* of Cotton Mather, was published. Mather wanted to bring people back to the early spirit of Puritanism at a time when feeling against the clergy ran high because of witch burnings.

1704: The earliest known example of a **Dutch gambrel roof** in America was built on the Ackerman house in Hackensack, N.J. This roof type became common throughout New York and northern New Jersey in the eighteenth century.

1704 Oct: A **classic travel book**, *Private Journal*, was begun by Sarah Kemble Knight; she made entries until Mar. 1705. A schoolmistress (young Benjamin Franklin attended her school in Boston), she took a trip alone to New York and reported on her experiences. She also commented on the character and mores of the Yankee inhabitants she encountered. Her book was not published until 1825.

III. Business and Industry
Education
Philosophy and Religion
Science

The Church of England made great efforts in the eighteenth century to propagate its cause in the English colonies. The Society for the Propagation of the Gospel in Foreign Parts was granted a charter in 1701 by King William III of England. This charter was granted at the instigation of the Rev. Thomas Bray of London, who had been chosen in 1696 to establish the Anglican Church in Maryland. Bray recruited missionaries and sent out more than 30 parish libraries. Between 1702 and 1783 the society maintained 54 missionaries in South Carolina, 33 in North Carolina, 84 in New England, 47 in Pennsylvania, 58 in New York, 44 in New Jersey, 13 in Georgia, 5 in Maryland, and 2 in Virginia. In all, 202 central missions were maintained and the society spent £227,454 in this period. Although the Anglican Church made some gains as a result of this effort, the various other Protestant sects and denominations—Presbyterian, Congregationalist, Quaker, and Baptist—held their ground, as did the small Roman Catholic community. American Anglicans fought the establishment of an episcopate because the selection would be imposed from England. Southern laymen especially insisted on the right to choose their own clergymen. During the American Revolution the Patriot leadership was dominated by such southern Anglicans as George Washington and such northern Congregationalists as John Adams. The Loyalists for the most part were Anglicans.

1700 June 17: Massachusetts enacted a law requiring **Roman Catholic priests** to leave the colony within three months. If any priest remained, he was to be considered an "incendiary and disturber of the public peace and safety and an enemy to the true Christian religion." If found guilty, he could be imprisoned for life or executed.

1701 Oct 16: Yale was founded as Collegiate School in Killingworth, Conn., by Congregationalists dissatisfied with the growing liberalism at Harvard. The school was named after Elihu Yale, son of one of the founders of New Haven, who had gained great riches in India as governor for the East India Company. The school was moved in 1745 to New Haven, Conn., where it became Yale College. Yale became a university in 1887. Its first degrees were awarded in 1716.

IV. **Fashion**
Folkways
Holidays
Social Issues and Crime
Sports

The Bowery, about three miles north of New York City, was a popular recreation center. The well-known traveler Sarah Kemble Knight visited the Bowery in 1704 and found that visitors did not "spare for any diversion the place offered, and sociable to a degree." John Clap, a tavern keeper there, offered "any Gentlemen Travellers that are strangers to the City . . . good Entertainment, for themselves and Horses." Knight reached the Bowery by sleigh and on one occasion noted that she met "50 or 60 sleys."

c1700: The American **slat-back chair** made its first appearance simultaneously in New England, Pennsylvania, and New York. In the nineteenth century Shakers produced quantities of this type of chair, popular for general home use. An early type used a rope seat. This design should not be confused with the splat-back chair, which showed the influence of Dutch craftsmanship and design and was a product of this period.

1704: New York **women's fashions** were described by a contemporary traveler and diarist: "The English go very fasheonable in their dress. The Dutch, especially the middling sort, differ from our women, in their habitt go loose, were French muches which are like a Capp and a head band in one, leaving their ears bare, which are sett out with Jewells of a large size and many in number. And their fingers hoop't with Rings, some with large stones in them of many Coullers as were their pendants in their ears, which You should see very old women wear as well as Young."

1704 Sep 28: Separation of couples by a minister was legalized by a statute passed in Maryland. A minister could separate a man and woman if he disapproved of the woman. If the man did not obey, he was haled into court and, if convicted, fined or whipped until blood began to flow.

1705–1709

I. Civil Rights
Exploration and Settlement
Government
Statistics
Wars

In the early nineteenth century the prevailing political and economic theory held that colonies existed for the benefit of the mother country and that the colonies should produce only raw materials, accepting in return manufactured goods from the homeland. An English law of 1705, for example, expanded the list of goods that the American colonies could export to English ports only. Among these were rice, molasses, and naval stores—pitch, rosin, tar, hemp, masts, yards, and bowsprits. At this time there was little organized political opposition to the rule of Crown and Parliament. As long as home nation and colonies prospered, the political situation remained manageable.

1705: A Virginia **slavery act** decreed that all imported servants were to remain in lifelong servitude. Excepted were those who had been Christians in their native country or who had been free in a Christian country. This law limited slavery to blacks and confined almost all imported blacks to slavery. An interesting exception was inserted for "Turks and Moors in amity with her majesty."

1706: An important American **customhouse** was built at Yorktown, Va. Yorktown had been appointed the port of entry for New York, Philadelphia, and other northern cities, though many merchants disregarded the law. Yorktown was the site of Virginia's "tea party" in 1774, when Richard Ambler, collector of revenue, led a boarding party to the *Virginia* and tossed its tea cargo overboard. The customhouse was restored in 1928.

1709 Sep 3: The first major influx of **Swiss and German immigrants** came to the Carolinas. They had been encouraged by a grant of 13,500 acres by the proprietors to two sponsors representing German refugees from the Palatinate and Swiss emigrants from Berne.

II. Architecture
   Arts and Music
   Popular Entertainment
   Publishing
   Theater

Accounts of persons who had been held captive by Indians provided popular reading matter in colonial times. One of the best examples of the genre, and a best seller in the early eighteenth century, was *The Redeemed Captive, Returning to Zion* (1707) by John Williams, Congregational minister of Deerfield, Mass. Williams and his family were captured by the Indians in 1704 during the raid on Deerfield in Queen Anne's War. His book, written at the urging of Cotton Mather, recounted the cruelties he witnessed and suffered during two years of captivity; it also detailed attempts by Jesuits to convert him to Catholicism. William's narrative and an earlier account, *The Sovereignty of God, Together with the Faithfulness of His Promises Displayed; Being a Narrative of the Captivity and Restauration of Mrs. Mary Rowlandson* (1682) by Mary Rowlandson, were models for a number of books about Indian captivity published during the eighteenth and early nineteenth century.

1706: Work was begun on the **Governor's Palace** at Williamsburg, Va., the finest residence of its time in the colonies. It was not formally completed until 1720. The Governor's Palace was occupied by royal governors until the Revolutionary War, and thereafter by the state governors, Patrick Henry and Thomas Jefferson, until the capital was moved to Richmond in 1780.

1708: A **popular satirical poem** by one Ebenezer Cook was *The Sot-Weed Factor; or, A Voyage to Maryland,—a satire in which is described the laws, government, courts, and constitution of the country, and also the buildings, feasts, frolics, entertainments, and drunken humors of the inhabitants in that part of America.* Little is known about the author.

**III. Business and Industry
    Education
    Philosophy and Religion
    Science**

The various Protestant denominations were active in establishing themselves in the English colonies in the early eighteenth century. The first Anglican parish in Connecticut was established in 1706 at Stratford through the efforts of Caleb Heathcote. He was a wealthy merchant and public official who in 1701 had been granted the manor of Scarsdale in Westchester County, N.Y., the last manor to be granted in the colonies. In Mar. 1706 the first presbytery was established in Philadelphia, Pa., through the efforts of the Rev. Francis Makemie. Born in Ireland, Makemie first came to America in 1683 and began organizing

Presbyterian churches. In 1707 he was arrested in New York, charged with preaching without a license. Although he was acquitted, he incurred heavy costs. About this time the Baptists in Philadelphia organized their first church, which had quarters in a brew house. In 1707 the first meeting of a Baptist association was held in Philadelphia, with five churches represented. Connecticut Congregational churches, meeting at Saybrook, Conn., adopted the Saybrook Platform in 1708, which moved toward a church system like that of the Presbyterians rather than the more democratic Massachusetts Congregationalists. In Charleston, S.C., both the Baptists and the Quakers organized churches as early as 1699, but the largest religious groups there were the Huguenots and the Anglicans.

1706: What was perhaps the **first lithotomy** (surgical removal of stones from the bladder) in New England gave prominence to Zabdiel Boylston, the Boston surgeon who performed it. Following this, he performed many successful operations; in 1718 he removed a cancerous breast from a woman.

1709: The **first private home for mental illness** in America was established by the Quakers of Philadelphia, Pa. In 1751 it became a part of Pennsylvania Hospital.

IV. Fashion
   Folkways
   Holidays
   Social Issues and Crime
   Sports

With the introduction of paper money in the colonies, counterfeiting was not long in appearing. In 1705 Thomas Odell of Boston counterfeited the £4 notes of Massachusetts and tried to pass them in Pennsylvania. He was arrested and sentenced in Boston to a fine of £300 and a year in prison. James Mar, a New York engraver, applied his skill to counterfeit bills. He was sentenced to be hanged, but was granted clemency by the governor, who could not refuse a tearful petition from "Most of the Gentlewomen of the City." In Philadelphia in 1720 Edward and Martha Hunt were implicated in counterfeiting and sentenced to death and life imprisonment respectively.

1705: Intermarriage between a white person and a black was declared illegal in Massachusetts. Any minister performing such a marriage was fined £50. This prohibition remained in force until 1843, when the law was repealed.

1706: A closed season on deer hunting was established on Long Island, where continual hunting had almost eliminated this popular game.

1708: A closed season, Apr. 1 to July 31, was established on turkeys, heath hens, partridges, and quail in Kings, Queens, and Suffolk counties in New York.

1710–1714

I. Civil Rights
Exploration and Settlement
Government
Statistics
Wars

Settlers from European lands other than the British Isles began to come to the English colonies in large numbers. On Sept. 3, 1700, the proprietors of Carolina granted a tract of 13,500 acres to agents representing Swiss and German Palatinate emigrants. Besides wanting to better themselves economically, many of the emigrants sought religious freedom. New Bern, the second town in North Carolina, was settled in 1710 by some 650 Swiss and German colonists under the leadership of Baron Christopher de Graffenried and John Dawson. The same year 3000 Germans from the Palatinate settled near Livingston Manor, N.Y., intending to produce naval stores. They were brought to America by Robert Hunter, commissioned governor of New York and the Jerseys in 1709. The settlement was not successful and in 1713, under the leadership of Conrad Weiser, the settlers moved first to the Schoharie Valley and then to the Mohawk Valley. Eventually many of them moved to Berks and Bucks counties in Pennsylvania.

The estimated colonial **population** was 357,500.

1711 Sep 22: The **Tuscarora Indian War** (1711–1713) began with a massacre of settlers on the Chowan and Roanoke rivers in northeastern North Carolina. The settlement at New Bern was abandoned. White encroachment, which included the enslaving of Indian children, led to the war.

1712 May 9: The **Territory of the Carolinas** was provided with two governors, one for the north and one for the south. Though theoretically a single province, the settlements were far apart, and so each section was accorded its own governor. From 1691 to 1712 a single governor usually resided in Charleston.

1713 Mar 23: The **Tuscarora War** ended with the capture of the Indian stronghold at Fort Nohucke, S.C. The Indians fled northward and were admitted into the League of the Iroquois as a sixth nation.

1713 Apr 11: **Queen Anne's War** (1702–1713) was ended by the Treaty of Utrecht, which brought the War of the Spanish Succession to a close in Europe. By the treaty France ceded the Hudson Bay territory, Newfoundland, and Nova Scotia to Great Britain. France also agreed to a British protectorate over the Iroquois Indians. France kept Cape Breton Island and the islands of the St. Lawrence.

II. Architecture
   Arts and Music
   Popular Entertainment
   Publishing
   Theater

Bookselling in the colonies began before the turn of the century and so was flourishing by this time. Around 1698 Regnier Jansen, a printer in Philadel-

phia, was selling books. By 1714 Andrew Bradford's
Philadelphia store, the Bible and Crown, was filling
orders from as far away as Barbados. In 1718 John
Copson sold books along with other merchandise, a
common practice. William Bradford, who set up in
New York as a printer in 1694, also ran a bookshop,
as did Thomas Adams, a stationer, after 1698. Boston,
however, led the way in the book business, with
about 30 stores there by 1711. In 1724 the Boston
booksellers formed an association to fix prices and
otherwise regulate the trade. Boston supplied books
to all the other colonies, but its trade was especially
brisk in New England.

1713: King's Chapel, the Anglican church in Boston,
acquired an organ in a bequest from Thomas Brattle.
Few organs were to be found in colonial churches,
since Puritan practice prohibited instrumental music
in religious services and most congregations of other
denominations could not afford to import instruments from England.

III. Business and Industry
Education
Philosophy and Religion
Science

Deism, a rationalistic theology holding that the
course of the universe demonstrates the existence of
God, so no formal exercise of religion is necessary,
made considerable headway in the colonies. Published in 1711, *Characteristicks of Men, Manners,
Opinions, Times* by Anthony Ashley Cooper, third
earl of Shaftesbury, had much influence in America.
Shaftesbury postulated an innate moral sense that
did not require religious incentives to reveal itself.
Many of his admirers in America seized upon this
idea as the basis of deistic thought. Deism was strongest in the large towns, especially in Philadelphia,
where men such as Benjamin Franklin became believers. In New England even Cotton Mather, of the
leading family of Puritan divines, flirted with the idea
of "Nature and Nature's God" by 1715. The painter

Robert Feke led a group in Newport, R.I., that read and discussed deistic works. Later in the century men as prominent as Thomas Jefferson were deists.

1710: **Trinity School** was established in New York City under the auspices of the Society for the Propagation of the Gospel. The founding of Trinity School represented a victory of private and parochial school adherents over supporters of free public schools.

1712: The **first sperm whale** captured by an American was taken by Christopher Hussey, of Nantucket, Mass. The event radically changed the character of the Nantucket whaling business. Whalers previously had plied close to shore, seeking right whales. Thereafter they hunted in deep waters on longer voyages. In 1715 Nantucket had a fleet of six sloops engaged in sperm whaling.

1713: The **first American schooner** was built by Capt. Andrew Robinson in Gloucester, Mass.

1714: Support for **scientific observation** over dogma was demonstrated by the famous Puritan theologian Cotton Mather, who accepted the Copernican theory of the universe as against the Ptolemaic. His sermon of acceptance was unfavorably received by the eminent Puritan moralist Judge Samuel Sewall, who considered the subject too controversial.

IV. Fashion
    Folkways
    Holidays
    Social Issues and Crime
    Sports

By 1710 the favorite nonalcoholic beverage of the colonists was probably chocolate. This drink resulted from the discovery of the cacao tree and its seed by Spanish explorers in Mexico. They took it to Europe, where it spread to England and then back to the North American colonies. Coffee was introduced into North America about 1668, and the first coffee house was opened in October 1676 in Boston by John Sparry. It soon became the place where businessmen gathered to exchange news. Tea was first brought to Europe by the Dutch East India Company in the early seventeenth century. It was carried by settlers to America almost as soon as colonization began. Coffee did not take first place over tea and chocolate until the time of the Boston Tea Party (1773), when it became a patriotic duty not to drink English tea because of the tax on it and the monopoly on its trade. However, the popularity of tea actually increased in the first half of the eighteenth century because of widespread smuggling, which provided a plentiful and inexpensive supply. Among alcoholic beverages, rum was a favorite in New England and beer in the middle colonies. Madeira took first place in wines followed by canary, claret, burgundy, port, brandy, and champagne.

c1710: In contrast to the sober dress of the Quakers, **colonial fashions** were often extravagant. High heels, stiff stays, and large curled wigs were worn by both men and women. Men's coat skirts were stiffened with buckram, and sleeve cuffs often reached the elbows. The invention of the hoop in England in 1711 governed dress styles in America for many years. Originally these hoops were flat, projecting only at the sides. Over them were worn layers of skirts, and a sacque, or overdress, was hung on top. Women's hairstyles were characterized by the "tower," or "commode." From the top of this tower "lappets," or lace pendants, hung down alongside the face.

1712: The **first fines for speeding** were levied against reckless carters in Philadelphia.

1715–1719

I. **Civil Rights**
Exploration and Settlement
Government
Statistics
Wars

Another of the many conflicts between whites and Indians that were to go on until the late nineteenth century occurred at this time. The Yamassee Indians, encouraged by the Spanish, massacred several hundred Carolina settlers in Apr. 1715. In Jan. 1716 the South Carolina settlers, aided by Cherokee Indians, defeated the Yamassee northwest of Port Royal, at the southern tip of what is now South Carolina. The conflict was a result of the desire of Carolina settlers moving into Yamassee territory to take up large areas of coastal land for raising cattle. This southward movement also brought the English colonists into areas claimed by the Spanish.

1718: New Orleans was founded by French settlers from Canada and France. The Canadians generally brought their wives and families with them. French officers, however, usually younger sons of nobility, refused to marry below their rank, inspiring the plea of one of the early governors to France: "Send me wives for my Canadians; they are running in the woods after Indian girls."

II. Architecture
Arts and Music
Popular Entertainment
Publishing
Theater

When the colonists left England for new homes in America, they brought their music with them and in the eighteenth century were practicing and enjoying music in a variety of ways. In 1715 appeared the *Introduction to the Singing of Psalm-Tunes* by Rev. John Tufts. This was the first American instruction manual, and no copy of it is known to exist. In New York in 1720 gentlemen might gather at someone's home "to hear some good Musick, and to take a Tiff of fresh Lime Punch." The first public "Concert of Musick on Sundry Instruments" took place on Feb. 18, 1729, in Boston. The first piece of music criticism in America was perhaps an *article in the Philadelphia Mercury* in 1729. And in 1732 a school of "Vocal Musick" was opened at Newport, R.I., by a Mr. Beal, who had previously taught singing at Yale.

1716: The **first theater** in the colonies was built in Williamsburg, Va., by William Levingston.

1719: ***Divine and Moral Songs for the Use of Children,*** a juvenile best seller by Isaac Watts, was published. The book was popular for at least 150 years, with more than 240 editions being published in England and America.

1719: Fraunces Tavern, the earliest residential building remaining in Manhattan, was built at Pearl and Broad streets in New York. Originally built as a residence for Stephen De Lancey, it was purchased for a tavern by Samuel Fraunces in 1762. It became famous for its Long Room, where George Washington delivered his Farewell Address to his officers in 1783.

III. Business and Industry
Education
Philosophy and Religion
Science

The growth of shipping and commercial trade was encouraged in 1717 when colonial merchants were allowed to send ships to the French West Indies. The chief item of this lucrative trade was molasses, from which New England distilleries produced rum, a profitable staple of colonial trade. The Treaty of Utrecht (1713) provided for trading concessions with the Spanish colonies. Commercial fishing was also booming and shipbuilding began to be important in the economy. An early shipbuilder was Capt. Andrew Robinson of Gloucester, Mass., who in 1713 built a schooner of his own design. From Charleston, S.C., much trade was carried on, not only with the West Indies but also with Dutch settlements in South America. In 1718 £150,000 worth of goods, mostly woolens from England, came into Charleston. New York, Newport, and Philadelphia were also growing as shipping and trading centers, but Boston was the leading commercial center of the colonies in the early eighteenth century.

1716: Probably the **first lighthouse** in the colonies was put up by Massachusetts Colony on Little Brewster Island to guard Boston Harbor.

1719: **Potato cultivation** in the colonies began with the settlement of Londonderry, N.H., by Scottish-Irish immigrants.

IV. **Fashion**
  Folkways
  Holidays
  Social Issues and Crime
  Sports

Piracy, although declining, still existed on a fairly large scale and was not entirely frowned upon. This reflected the narrow difference between privateering, a wartime act in which a shipowner could legitimately attempt to capture merchant ships owned by his country's enemy, and piracy, which was much the same act in time of peace. Nevertheless, steps were taken to end piracy. The English Parliament in 1700 had ordered establishment of special courts in the colonies to try those accused of piracy. In 1718 Gov. Alexander Spotswood of Virginia offered a reward for capture of Blackbeard, the most notorious pirate of the time, whose real name was Edward Teach. He had been both a privateer and a pirate. Even though protected by the governor of North Carolina, who shared some of his booty, Blackbeard was caught and hanged. Also in 1718 another pirate, Stede Bonnet, was captured by an expedition from Carolina, and he too was hanged.

1719: Perhaps the **first street light** in America, a single lantern, was presented to the town of Boston by Eliakim Hutchinson. Boston's selectmen ordered that the town be "well fixed with Lights on all or Stormy Nights."

1719 Mar: New Jersey enacted its most important **marriage statute.** It provided that no person under 21 years of age could be married without the consent of a parent or guardian. It was the result of many instances of young people being enticed into clandestine marriages.

1720–1724

I. Civil Rights
   Exploration and Settlement
   Government
   Statistics
   Wars

In the eighteenth century northern New England was claimed both by the English and the French, and both established forts and settlements in the disputed area. The English in 1724 built Fort Dummer, named for William Dummer, lieutenant governor and acting governor of Massachusetts. It was near the site of present-day Brattleboro, Vt., named for William Brattle, who with Dummer had purchased the tract of land on which the fort stood. Brattleboro was the first permanent European settlement in Vermont. A French stronghold at this time was the Abnaki Indian village of Norridgewock on the Kennebec R. in Maine. The leader there was a French Jesuit missionary, Father Sébastien Rasle. Father Rasle escaped a British raid in 1721, leaving behind a dictionary of the Abnaki language he had been preparing. The raiders took it away, and it was not published until 1833. In 1724 the British again raided Norridgewock, captured it, and killed Father Rasle, gun in hand. These and similar events of the period became known as Dummer's or Lovewell's War (1721–1725). The Lovewell in question was John Lovewell, a Massachusetts Indian fighter who was killed in a skirmish with Pigwacket Indians at Fryeburg, Maine, on May 8, 1725.
c1720: A period of **French expansion and entrenchment** in the Mississippi Valley began. The French

erected forts in 1720 and 1726 at the mouths of the Kaskaskia and Illinois rivers, and made peace with the Indians in the South. Fort Toulouse was erected among the Creeks on the Alabama R. In the North powerful Fort Louisbourg on Cape Breton Island, constructed in 1720, guarded the entrance to the St. Lawrence R. Farther south the French established fortifications at Crown Point on Lake Champlain in 1731. Fort Miami, constructed in 1704, protected the northern approach to the Mississippi Valley. Fort Ouiataon on the Wabash R. was built about 1719, and Fort Vincennes on the lower Wabash R. about 1724.

1720: The estimated colonial **population** was 474,388. City populations were: Boston, 12,000; Philadelphia, 10,000; New York, 7000; Charleston, 3500; and Newport, 3800. All urban dwellers at this time were only 8% of the total population.

1722: The **League of Six Nations,** an Iroquois confederation that included the Tuscarora tribe, concluded in Albany, N.Y., a treaty with Gov. Alexander Spotswood of Virginia. The Indians agreed not to cross the Potomac R. or Blue Ridge Mts. The Iroquois league always remained friendly to the English and hostile to the French, mainly because the latter often aided Indian tribes who were enemies of the Iroquois. Thus the League of Six Nations was an effective and necessary guard for the English colonies' western borders during this period of French expansion in the Mississippi R. Valley.

II. Architecture
Arts and Music
Popular Entertainment
Publishing
Theater

Georgian architecture came into fashion in England and the English colonies at about this time. The style, named in honor of the three kings of England who reigned during the period, marked a return to classical forms. It was greatly influenced by the designs of the sixteenth-century Italian architect Andrea Palladio and the seventeenth-century English architect Inigo Jones. In Apr. 1723 the cornerstone was laid for Christ Church, known as Old North Church, in Boston. Designed by William Price, who had studied Christopher Wren's London churches, it was the first Georgian church in New England. Today it is the oldest church in Boston. From its steeple in 1775 were hung lanterns that started Paul Revere on his ride by horseback to Lexington and Concord to warn of the approach of British troops. In Philadelphia James Porteus designed a new Christ Church, completed in 1731 and the most ornate example of the Georgian style in America. A new state house for the Pennsylvania Assembly, completed in 1735, was the largest and most elaborately formal structure in the colonies. Perhaps the most distinguished private residence of the type was Westover, built about 1734 for William Byrd, II, on the James R. in Virginia. Another practitioner of the Georgian style was the Newport, R.I., architect Peter Harrison, sometimes called the first American architect. Among his works were Newport's Touro Synagogue and the Redwood Library.

1722: The Alamo, to become famous as the site of a great battle of the war for Texan independence in 1836, was constructed at about this time as a Franciscan mission.

1723: Perhaps the **first house with running water** in America was John Headly's in Newport, R.I. It was equipped in this year with a pipe "underground from the Spring."

III. Business and Industry
Education
Philosophy and Religion
Science

A major step forward in preventive medicine was introduced to the colonies. The first smallpox inoculations in America were given on June 26, 1721, in Boston by Dr. Zabdiel Boylston. He had been urged to do so by Cotton Mather, the influential Puritan clergyman. Even though an epidemic was raging in Boston at the time, many persons objected fiercely on religious grounds. The homes of both Mather and Boylston were stoned by mobs. Dr. Boylston first inoculated his son, Thomas, and two black slaves. In all he inoculated 240 persons, of whom all but six survived. During the epidemic there were 5889 cases of smallpox in Boston, and 844 persons died. It is said that Dr. Boylston's slave, Onesimus, had previously told him of similar inoculations administered in Africa. Smallpox epidemics were a constant menace in colonial times. In Charleston, S.C., in 1698 an epidemic raged unchecked for about ten months. During another Boston epidemic, in 1702, it was ordered that bodies be buried without elaborate funerals so as to prevent the spread of infection. There were serious outbreaks in New York and Philadelphia in 1731–1732. In New York it was estimated that 6% of the population died of smallpox at the time.

1721: A **Jesuit college,** founded at Kaskaskia, in what is now Illinois, was one of the first institutions of higher learning in the Middle West. It had an especially distinguished library containing many volumes of eighteenth-century French philosophers.

1723: The **first permanent school for Indians** in the colonies was established at Bafferton Hall, built at the College of William and Mary in Williamsburg, Va. The school was maintained by funds left for the purpose by Robert Boyle, the English scientist.

1723: The **first recorded commercial corporation** in America, a Connecticut trading company, was organized. Up to this time, land companies, universities, and philanthropic enterprises were the only forms of corporate enterprise. Colonial restrictions on the distribution of currency and restrictions from England on local trade and industry served to inhibit the formation of corporations in the modern sense.

IV. Fashion
   Folkways
   Holidays
   Social Issues and Crime
   Sports

An increase in crime was noted in the colonies. The cause was attributed to the growth of cities, increasing wealth, and the changes brought on by the colonial wars, the first of which began in 1689. From then on, Boston, New York, Philadelphia, and Charleston, S.C., had night watches most of the time. By 1709, for example, Charleston had an armed watch of ten men who patrolled the town nightly. In New York in 1711 one John Riemer reported the theft of 25 gallons of cider, beer, and Madeira from his house. There was a great deal of theft in Boston in 1720, and it was blamed on the fact that there was much wealth there. Also at that time some people felt that Bostonians were "inclined to Riots and Tumults." Death was the usual penalty for theft, and in Philadelphia in Mar. 1720 William Smith and Hannah Travis, the latter known as Dancing Hannah, were convicted of theft and received death sentences. By 1723 the Boston police force consisted of 12 men who were instructed "to walke Silently and Slowly, now and then to Stand Still and Listen in order to make discovery. And no smoking to be on their walking rounds."

1721 May: After a succession of **blue laws** limiting travel on Sunday, Connecticut passed a law providing that people could not go from their homes unless to attend worship or perform some indispensable

1722 Apr 30: The game of **billiards** was mentioned in the *New England Courant*, which reported that a public house in Charlestown, Mass., had set up tables for customers who wished "to Recreate themselves with a Game of Billiards."

1725–1729

I. Civil Rights
Exploration and Settlement
Government
Statistics
Wars

The French and English began to compete for control of the area west of the Allegheny Mts., especially in the Ohio R. Valley. The French, who claimed the region and had done the most to explore it, were alarmed by the number of English colonists beginning to cross the mountains. In 1729 they sent Chaussegros de Léry to fortify the river down to the Miami R. in Ohio. Earlier, in 1724, the French had built Fort Vincennes on the lower Wabash R. The British government had done little to oppose the French, even though the English colonies claimed their land grants extended westward to include the Ohio Valley. King George I had been petitioned by the Lords of Trade in 1721 to "fortify the passes in the back of Virginia" to interrupt French communications, but nothing was done. Meanwhile, the French built another fort in 1726 on the Mississippi R. at the mouth of the Illinois R., and, to protect their routes to the Ohio country from Quebec, had that same year erected Fort Niagara on the Niagara R. at its junction with Lake Ontario.

1725: The **slave population** in the American colonies reached 75,000.

1725 Feb 20: The first known instance of **scalping by Europeans** occurred in a fight between Indians and a party led by Capt. John Lovewell at Wakefield, N.H. Ten Indian scalps were taken. A bounty of £100 per scalp was paid to the victors in Boston.

1726: A **riot in Philadelphia** by the city's poorer residents broke out in the heart of town. The rioters tore down the pillory and stocks and set them on fire before the governor of Pennsylvania put down the uprising. Similar outbursts continued to crop up in the city: in 1729 crowds broke into the mayor's gardens and destroyed his plants; in 1738 a riot ensued when the administration limited fishing on the Schuylkill R.

1729 June: The **Carolina grant was purchased** by the English Crown from its proprietors for £17,500. Carolina was divided into two royal provinces, North Carolina and South Carolina, in 1730. Even after independence there were disputes as to the exact boundary between the two states. These were not resolved until 1815.

II. Architecture
Arts and Music
Popular Entertainment
Publishing
Theater

Printing and publishing in the colonies began to thrive during this period, and one of the leading figures in the field was William Bradford. Born in England, he became in 1685 the first printer in Philadelphia. In 1690 he was one of the founders of the first paper mill in the colonies. In 1693 he moved to New York, where, in the course of 50 years, he issued some 400 items, including the first American *Book of Common Prayer* (1710); the first printed American play, *Androboros* (1714) by Gov. Robert Hunter of New York; and many almanacs and pamphlets. In 1725 he established the first newspaper in the colony, the *New York Gazette* (1725–1744). The paper was royalist in its politics, as Bradford was the official government printer. Andrew Bradford, William Bradford, and other Bradford descendants also became printers.

1725: The *Astronomical Diary and Almanack* by Nathaniel Ames, a Massachusetts physician, was published. Extremely popular, it may have been used by Benjamin Franklin in preparing his own almanac. Typical of its entries were:

> Dec 7–10 Ladies take heed,
> Lay down your fans,
> And handle well
> Your warming pans.
>
> Dec 15–18 This cold, uncomfortable weather
> Makes Jack and Gill lie close
> together.

1725: The **Union Oyster House,** a famed Boston restaurant, was built as a private residence. It became a public eating place in 1826.

1729: The **Old South Meeting House** was built in Boston by Joshua Blanchard, a master mason who later built Faneuil Hall in Boston. The meeting house has been a museum since 1876.

1729 Oct: The *Pennsylvania Gazette* was bought by Benjamin Franklin. Under the title *Universal Instructor in All Arts and Sciences and Pennsylvania Gazette,* it was founded by Samuel Keimer in 1728. At that time it had a subscription list of 90. Under Franklin it became in time the leading newspaper between New York and Charleston. He managed the *Gazette* until 1766, and it was continued until 1815 by David Hall, Franklin's partner from 1748, and by Hall's descendants. The claim of the popular magazine *The Saturday Evening Post* that it was a continuation of the Gazette *is a* myth. The *Post* was founded in 1821, six years after the *Gazette* had expired, by men with no connection with the *Gazette.*

III. Business and Industry
Education
Philosophy and Religion
Science

Although few in number, Jewish immigrants were strong contributors to the religious life of America. The first permanent Hebrew congregation in the colonies was formed in 1729 in New York City; the next year the members constructed a synagogue on Mill St. that was described as a "solid, neat, stone Temple." The congregation later added the first school for Jewish children. Around this time Jewish communities were also developing in Charleston, S.C., Newport, R.I., and Philadelphia, Pa., and by the time of the American Revolution, there were between 2000 and 3000 Jews in the colonies, mostly merchants and traders. An act of Parliament in 1740 allowed Jews to be naturalized, and in the colonies they found more political and religious freedom than anywhere else in the world.

1725: The **U.S. Reformed Church** was established by John Philip Boehm at Falkner Swamp, Pa.

1729: The **third Anglican parish** in Boston was established in Trinity Church. The new parish reflected the rapid expansion of Anglicanism in New England.

1729 Mar 15: The **first Catholic nun** to be professed in the colonies was Sister St. Stanislaus Hachard, who celebrated the Ceremony of Profession at the Ursuline Convent in New Orleans, La.

IV. Fashion
Folkways
Holidays
Social Issues and Crime
Sports

Voluntary associations formed for a variety of purposes became a feature of colonial life. One of the prime movers was Benjamin Franklin of Philadelphia, who in 1727 organized a group of artisans and tradesmen into the Leather Apron Club, later called the Junto. The club held meetings in taverns to discuss morals, politics, literature, and science, and to exchange books. The idea for a subscription library grew out of this last function, and on July 1, 1731, the Library Company was formed with 24 members. It imported its first books from England the next year. The club registered formal opposition to slavery and what it considered other inhumane practices. Out of the Junto grew the American Philosophical Society, founded in 1743.

1725: Queen Anne–style furniture, characterized by double curves, broken pediments, and curved legs in furniture of walnut, became fashionable in the colonies five years after its greatest popularity passed in England and some 11 years after the death of Queen Anne of England. This period marked the first appearance of the cabriole, or curved, style for table and chair legs; and the first appearance of the American Windsor chair, in Philadelphia. Windsor chairs were generally painted green, brown, or red, but rarely white.

1728: Boston Common was enclosed in order to preserve its grass from carts and horses. Soon it became the custom after tea for gentlemen and ladies to stroll about the green before going to their homes.

1728: The arrival in Louisiana of **casket girls,** so called because they received a dress in a casket as a gift for their immigration, introduced a new element into Louisiana society. Since these girls were not inmates of penal institutions, as were many of their predecessors, it became and has remained an honor to be descended from a casket girl.

1728: Importation of rum in the colonies for this year amounted to 2,124,500 gal., or £25,000 of liquor. Drinking was extremely heavy. This printed doggerel gave one reason why people did not drink:

> There's but one Reason I can Think
> Why People ever cease to drink,
> Sobriety the Cause is not,
> Nor Fear of being deam'd a Sot,
> But if Liquor can't be got.

1730–1734

I. **Civil Rights**
   Exploration and Settlement
   Government
   Statistics
   Wars

Georgia, the last of the 13 original colonies to be founded, came into being under somewhat different circumstances than the others. On June 9, 1732, a royal charter was granted by King George II of England to James Edward Oglethorpe, an English general and philanthropist. Originally this region had been part of the grant of the Carolinas; it also was claimed by Spain. One of the purposes of founding Georgia, therefore, was to protect the other southern colonies from Spanish intrusion. Oglethorpe saw the colony as a refuge for English debtors. The first colonists, led by Oglethorpe, arrived on Feb. 12, 1733, and founded Savannah, the first settlement in Georgia. Forts were built and the friendship of the Creek Indians was secured. Slavery was originally prohibited, but members of Georgia's ruling class felt this would hinder them economically. In 1752 the colony was turned over to the Crown and thereafter became profitable, but by then it had already achieved its major objective, the blocking of Spanish northern expansion.

The estimated colonial **population** was 654,950.

1730: The **most populous area** of colonial America was New England, with 275,000 Europeans. By 1760 this number rose to 425,000, and at the close of the Revolution to 800,000.

1733: An **epidemic of influenza,** the first outbreak in North America, swept New York City and Philadelphia.

1733 May 17: The **Molasses Act** was passed, placing high duties on rum and molasses imported from the French and Spanish West Indies. Admission of American merchants into the rum trade of the French West Indies (1713) caused a boom in sugar on those islands. Planters on the English islands lost out as New England ships put into French and Dutch ports to load up with cheap sugar. The English planters petitioned Parliament and forced passage of the Molasses Act, which levied prohibitive duties on sugar and molasses brought to the colonies from other than British possessions.

II. Architecture
Arts and Music
Popular Entertainment
Publishing
Theater

Growth of American music was stimulated in colonial times by immigrant European musicians, many of whom were talented and creative composers as well as accomplished performers. Often the musicians were obliged to travel from place to place seeking work as church organists, teachers, or the like. Such a musician was Carl Theodorus Pachelbel, an organist and composer and son of Johann Pachelbel, who had been a noted influence on his younger contemporary Johann Sebastian Bach. Carl Theodorus Pachelbel emigrated from Germany to Boston in 1733. There he taught children to play the harpsichord and the spinet. He soon moved on to Newport, R.I., where he became organist at Trinity Church. In Jan. 1736 he gave a concert of vocal and instrumental music at Todd's Tavern in New York City, "the Harpsichord Part Perform'd by himself. The Songs, Violins, and German Flute by private hands." Enough people paid four shillings apiece to attend to allow another performance to be given in March. Later Pachelbel moved to Charleston, S.C., where he died on Sept. 14, 1750.

1730: The **Old State House** in Philadelphia, known as Independence Hall, was designed by Andrew Hamilton. Completed in 1753 and rebuilt in 1828, it is an excellent example of Georgian public architectural style.

1732 May: The *Philadelphische Zeitung* [Philadelphia Newspaper], the first foreign-language newspaper in the English colonies, was founded by Benjamin Franklin in Philadelphia, Pa.

1732 Dec 19: *Poor Richard's Almanack* was first published by Benjamin Franklin at Philadelphia, Pa. In continuous publication for 25 years, Franklin's *Almanack* sold on average more than 10,000 copies yearly and thus was one of the most popular writings of colonial America.

1734 Oct: In a landmark case involving **freedom of the press,** John Peter Zenger, founder and publisher of the New York *Weekly Journal,* was arrested for libel. Zenger had founded the *Weekly Journal* on Nov. 5, 1733, and had used its pages to oppose the administration and policies of Gov. William Cosby of New York. In 1735 he was acquitted after a defense by Andrew Hamilton that was later cited in many cases involving freedom of the press. The Sons of Liberty, an organization founded to aid Zenger's defense, later became the Tammany Society of New York. The *Weekly Journal* was published until 1751.

III. Business and Industry
Education
Philosophy and Religion
Science

The prominent part religion played in the settlement and development of the English colonies was emphasized by the revival movement known as the Great Awakening, which began in New England in 1734, triggered by the preaching at a revival in Northampton, Mass., of Jonathan Edwards, the theologian and philosopher. Edwards emphasized man's sinful nature and the torments of eternal damnation. His fame spread widely and he received many invitations to preach. His influence was strong among young people. Many converts were made, amid public scenes of great emotion. In the middle colonies, William Tennent, a Presbyterian clergyman, led the movement. The Great Awakening reached all the colonies with the 1739–1741 visit to America of George Whitefield, the Methodist evangelist who preached from New England to Georgia. In the South Samuel Davies carried the message to the Presbyterians of Virginia. The movement reached the Baptists of North Carolina in the 1760s, but by that time it had already died out in New England. The Great Awakening resulted in bitter doctrinal disputes in New England between two groups known as the New Lights and the Old Lights. The latter opposed revivalism as extravagant and impermanent. The Old Lights were led by Charles Chauncy, a Boston clergyman who became the leader of the theological liberals. His beliefs developed into Universalism, or Unitarianism. The theology of the New Lights was more conservative and developed into a somewhat modified Calvinism.

1731: The **Library Company of Philadelphia,** the first circulating library in the New World, was founded by Benjamin Franklin. The extent to which libraries were to grow and flourish in the U.S. is indicated by the fact that by 1984 there were 8796 public libraries, with an additional 6260 branches, in the U.S.

1732: The **first stage coach line** was established between Burlington and Amboy, N.J. Connections could be made from Amboy to New York City and from Burlington to Philadelphia by boat.

1732 Feb 26: The **only Roman Catholic Church** built and maintained in the colonies until the Revolutionary War held its first mass in Philadelphia.

c1733: **Pennsylvania Dutch kilns** produced perhaps the finest pottery in America. The earliest specimen dates from this period—a barber basin inscribed "Putz und Balwir mich heibsh und fein das ich gefal der liebste mein [Clean and shave me nicely and fine so that I'll please my loved one]." Later Pennsylvania

Dutch sgraffito, pottery in which a design is etched through the surface coating to show the layer beneath, and slipware bore short verses like the following:

> In the dish on the table
> Merry he who yet is single
> Sad is he who is engaged.

> If loving were unhealthy
> Surely the doctor would avoid it
> And if it would hurt the wives
> Surely they would not allow it.

IV. Fashion
   Folkways
   Holidays
   Social Issues and Crime
   Sports

By 1730 summer resorts were being patronized by the well-to-do. A Dr. Thomas Bond encouraged his patients to picnic and take the waters at Spring Garden on the outskirts of Philadelphia. Near Bristol, Pa., was the so-called Bath spring, which also became a popular summer resort. The most popular and fashionable resort was Newport, R.I., whose climate attracted patrons from the Carolinas and the West Indies who came ostensibly for reasons of health. Newport's offerings included excursions to New Shoreham and Prudence Island. There were races on the beach by Narragansett pacers, and the winners were awarded silver tankards. Tea parties, dances, and lavish dinners added to the atmosphere of pleasure and sophistication. Newport's popularity contributed to its growth as a cultural and trade center as well. In 1730 a Philosophical Society was established, out of which the Redwood Library was formed 20 years later. Within a few years Newport became an important port in the "triangular trade," whereby rum was traded for slaves in Africa and the slaves were exchanged for sugar and molasses in the West Indies.

c1730: A great craze for **white stockings** for men and women set in, replacing varicolored hose of the seventeenth century. The stockings were made of thread, silk, cotton, or worsted, and were supported by ornate garters. Often the name of the wearer was woven into the garter with a "posy." White hose were worn until the end of the century.

1732: The **oldest sporting organization** and first fishing club in North America was formed as the Schuylkill Fishing Company in Philadelphia. It is now known as the Fish House Club, its membership limited to 30, its function limited to annual meetings at the Andalusia, Pa., headquarters.

1735–1739

I. Civil Rights
Exploration and Settlement
Government
Statistics
Wars

The War of Jenkins' Ear (1739–1742), which began in Europe on Oct. 19, 1739, and a year later merged into the War of the Austrian Succession, had its repercussions in the southern colonies. England went to war with Spain over the mistreatment of English seamen whom the Spaniards accused of smuggling. The war took its name from Robert Jenkins, captain of the ship *Rebecca*, who claimed Spanish coast guards had cut off his ear in 1731. He exhibited the ear in the House of Commons and so aroused public opinion that the government of the British Prime Minister Robert Walpole reluctantly declared war on Oct. 23, 1739. Basically, the war was one of commercial rivalry between England and Spain. By the Treaty of Utrecht (1713), which ended Queen Anne's War, Britain was to be allowed to participate in slave traffic with the Spanish colonies. A special Spanish fleet, however, interfered with this activity and the Spanish also objected to the English logwooders operating on the coast of Honduras. The other cause of the war was the continued dispute over the boundary of Spanish Florida in relation to Georgia. As soon as war was declared, Gov. James Edward Oglethorpe called on the citizens of Georgia and South Carolina to join in an invasion of Florida. The Spanish retaliated by attempting to invade those colonies by sea.

1738: **Lewis Morris** was named the first governor of New Jersey colony. Since 1702 New York and New Jersey had shared the same governor, although New Jersey had become autonomous for all practical purposes. Morris, who had been born in New York to a wealthy and prominent family, served as governor of New Jersey until his death in 1746.

1739: Three **slave uprisings** broke out in South Carolina this year. The incidents have been attributed to the preaching of the Spanish missionaries who allegedly created in the slaves a false expectation of deliverance. On Sept. 9 a band of slaves from Charleston set out for St. Augustine, Fla., and freedom, slaying all Europeans they met on the way. They were themselves surrounded and massacred. Twenty-one Europeans and 44 blacks perished. At Stone River a slave named Cato led another insurrection. The third uprising was in St. John's Parish in Berkeley County.

II. Architecture
Arts and Music
Popular Entertainment
Publishing
Theater

Many colonists were deeply concerned with religion, and hymn singing was of major importance. This led to the publication of hymnals. When John Wesley, the founder of Methodism, visited America in 1737 he had published at Charleston, S.C., *A Collection of Psalms and Hymns.* Some of the selections were adaptations from the German Moravian *Gesangbuch*. Wesley had met Gov. James Edward Oglethorpe of Georgia in 1735, when Oglethorpe was in England. Oglethorpe invited Wesley and his brother Charles, then students at Oxford and members of an Oxford group known variously as the Holy Club, Bible Moths, and Methodists, to come to Georgia. They arrived in Georgia Feb. 5, 1736. Notwithstanding Oglethorpe's invitation, the visit was marked by difficulties. In Savannah John was charged with inserting into the Anglican church service unauthorized psalms and hymns. Charles Wesley is said to have produced about 5000 hymns in his lifetime, many of which became popular in America, including "Hark! The Herald Angels Sing." Another prolific and popular hymn writer was Isaac Watts, an English clergyman. The first American edition of his *Hymns and Spiritual Songs*, which appeared in England in 1707, was published in America in 1739, although his hymns had been sung there before that. Watts wrote "O God, Our Help in Ages Past," among several hundred hymns that reflected a stern Calvinism with touches of sympathy and tenderness.

1735 Feb 8: The **first opera** produced in the colonies was performed at the Courtroom, in Charleston, S.C. It was *Flora; or The Hob in the Well* by Colley Cibber.

c1737: The **oldest extant house** in the U.S. Midwest was built by an unknown French colonist at Cahokia, Ill. The house later became the Cahokia County Courthouse. The structure was of poteaux-sur-sole style construction, characterized by upright posts driven into the earth and chinked with clay, with a double-pitched, hipped roof, and a surrounding balcony.

III. Business and Industry
   Education
   Philosophy and Religion
   Science

Science and scientists were flourishing in the colonies. The first chair in mathematics and natural philosophy was endowed at Harvard in 1727, and its first incumbent was Isaac Greenwood, who gave a course in fluxions (calculus). He retired in 1737, his lectures having done much to stimulate interest in science. Greenwood was succeeded by John Winthrop, IV, who is sometimes called the father of seismology because of his studies of earthquakes. In 1746 he gave the first laboratory demonstration of magnetism and electricity. In 1766 Winthrop was elected a fellow of the Royal Society and in 1773 Harvard conferred on him an L.L.D. degree, the first ever awarded in America. The Rev. Jared Eliot of Connecticut, the first American experimenter in physiological botany, was interested in making agriculture more scientific and worked on the fructification of maize before 1739. He also developed a process for smelting iron from black magnetic sand. Ezra Stiles, a theologian as well as a scientist, calculated the true position of the sun and moon, using the work of Sir Isaac Newton. As president of Yale from 1778 to 1795, he liberalized the curriculum, bringing in the thought of the enlightenment of the eighteenth century.

1736 Feb 5: The history of **Methodism** in America began with the arrival in Georgia of John Wesley, at the invitation of Gov. James Edward Oglethorpe. When Wesley came to America his career had not yet reached the spectacular proportions later brought on by his achievements as a public preacher. Six years earlier the name Methodists had been applied to his group of religious ascetics, but Methodism as a religious movement was still in the future. His stay in America was notable for his romance with Sophia Hopkey, who wooed but did not win him. When Sophia married another, Wesley barred her from his congregation and her new husband retaliated with the threat of a lawsuit. Wesley then decided to return to England.

1737: The **first copper coinage** minted in the colonies was produced by John Higley at his furnace on Hop-meadow Brook, Simsbury, Conn. Known to numismatists today as "Higley pennies," the coins were stamped "I am good copper" and "Value me as you will."

1739: Caspar Wistar, the glass designer and manufacturer, set up his glassworks at Allowaystown, N.J., on tracts of land ideal for production of window and bottle glass. The factory went into operation July 30, 1740, and was staffed by Belgian glassblowers specially drafted from Europe. Wistar's enterprise was responsible for the most distinctive type of early American glass, South Jersey glass, known for its wide, bulbous forms, often with superimposed winding thicknesses on the bottom. Wistar's glassworks was one of the first successful co-ops in America.

IV. Fashion
   Folkways
   Holidays
   Social Issues and Crime
   Sports

Because of the religious atmosphere and growing colonial affluence, funerals became more elaborate and expensive. It was customary to give away mourning rings or gloves at funerals. At the funeral of Gov. Jonathan Belcher of Massachusetts in 1741, his widow gave away 1000 pairs of gloves. Clergymen and doctors accumulated hundreds of such items over their careers. In 1721 the General Court of Massachusetts passed laws against "extraordinary expenditures for funerals" to protect those who could not afford "gloves, scarfs and scutcheons," but when Andrew Faneuil was buried in 1738 more than 1100 persons accompanied his funeral cortege, which was described as "generous and expensive." Newport, R.I., also witnessed elaborate funerals, that of Rosewell Lavine in 1716 costing £55. One livery stable in Boston kept black horses for hire for funerals, while a "Mr. C.H." offered to supply engraved sets of ready-to-use obituaries, "With Void Spaces for the Name,

Age, Distinction, and Profession, or such Particular
and Eminent Qualities as do not properly fall under
the Notice of General Description."

c1735: The **status of women** changed with the increase
of wealth in the colonies. More women left their husbands when they found living together incompatible;
newspaper items told of runaway wives and elope-
ments.

1735 Jan: The often tense **relations between Europeans and blacks** in New York was demonstrated
when John van Zandt, a Dutch burgher of New York,
horsewhipped his slave to death for having been
picked up at night by a watch. The coroner's jury
judged the "Correction given by the Master was not
the Cause of his Death, but it was by the Visitation of
God." One reason for such tension was that the slave
population was about one-fifth that of the entire colony. Blacks were lynched and burned for theft, rape,
etc.

1737 Mar 17: The first celebration of **St. Patrick's Day**
outside the confines of the Roman Catholic Church
was held in Boston by the Charitable Irish Society,
which had been founded that year. The Friendly Sons
of St. Patrick in New York City followed suit in 1784.
An oddity of the New York society was its joint sponsorship by Irish Roman Catholics and Presbyterians,
with the first president of the organization being a
Presbyterian.

1738: A Masonic warrant for the **first Masonic lodge**
was issued by the Grand Lodge of Massachusetts to
Abraham Savage. A similar authority was granted to
Richard Gridley in 1756 for a military expedition
against Crown Point, N.Y., during the French and
Indian War (1754–1763).

1740–1744

I. Civil Rights
   Exploration and Settlement
   Government
   Statistics
   Wars

King George's War (1744–1748), the third of the French and Indian wars, was known as the War of the Austrian Succession in Europe, where it began in 1740. The war included most of the European nations in a complicated series of alliances. It began after the death of Charles VI, the Holy Roman Emperor and ruler of the Hapsburg lands. The Archduchess Maria Theresa succeeded her father but there were counterclaimants. Fighting began when King Frederick II of Prussia invaded Austrian-held Silesia. In America and elsewhere in the world, France and England fought for colonial power and possessions. The French unsuccessfully attacked Port Royal, Nova Scotia, in 1744, the year in which fighting broke out in America.

The estimated colonial **population** was 889,000.

1740 Jan: The **War of Jenkins' Ear** (1739–1742) continued with an invasion of Florida led by Gov. Oglethorpe of Georgia. He was protected on the west from the French by friendly Indians. He captured forts San Francisco de Pupo and Picolata on the San Juan R. From May to July he besieged St. Augustine, but broke off the attack when his rear guard was threatened by the Spanish.

1741: A group of **German Moravians** moved from Georgia, where their colony had been unsuccessful, to Pennsylvania. They joined others of their faith in the establishment of Bethlehem on the Lehigh R. Count Nikolaus Ludwig Zinzendorf, their leader, arrived from Europe this year, bringing with him a band of new immigrants. Zinzendorf returned to Europe in 1743.

1742 June 9: In the **Battle of Bloody Marsh** on St. Simons Island, one of the Sea Islands off the southeast coast of Georgia, the Spanish attacked Fort Frederica, which had been constructed by Gov. Oglethorpe in 1736 to protect the colony. The Spanish were repulsed in a bloody battle that was a decisive engagement of the War of Jenkins' Ear.

1744: An **Indian treaty** signed with the Iroquois League at Lancaster, Pa., ceded to England the territory of the Ohio R. Valley north of the Ohio R.

II. Architecture
Arts and Music
Popular Entertainment
Publishing
Theater

Before the American Revolution, about 15 magazines began publication in the colonies, but they had an average life of only ten months. The first of these, published by Andrew Bradford, was the *American Magazine; or, A Monthly View of the Political State of the British Colonies.* Bradford's magazine began in Philadelphia in Jan. 1741 but published only three monthly issues. Bradford by three days had beaten Benjamin Franklin, who started his *General Magazine and Historical Chronicle* also in Philadelphia and also in January. Franklin's magazine lasted for six issues. In Boston in 1743, Gamaliel Rogers and John Fowle began the *Boston Weekly Museum,* which died that same year. More successful was the *American Magazine and Historical Chronicle,* which began publication in Boston in 1743. It was edited by Jeremy Gridley and published for more than three years. Gridley was a lawyer, and while the magazine was devoted largely to politics, he also wrote about literary and cultural subjects.

1741: The **first symphony orchestra** in America was organized by Moravian settlers in Bethlehem, Pa. By

1748 it had 14 pieces: two first violins, two second violins, two violas, one cello, one double bass, two flutes, two trumpets, and two French horns.

1742: The **Carpenters' Company** was established by the master carpenters of Philadelphia, who sought to establish an architectural library and teach themselves the elements of design and craftsmanship. In 1770 they built Carpenters' Hall, which became the meeting place of the first Continental Congress in 1775.

1742 Sep 24: Faneuil Hall in Boston was opened to the public. A Georgian structure designed by the painter John Smibert, it was enlarged in 1805 according to plans by Charles Bulfinch that retained the original Georgian style. The famous weather vane on its cupola is a giant grasshopper of beaten copper.

III. Business and Industry
   ### Education
   ### Philosophy and Religion
   ### Science

The first American scientific association, the American Philosophical Society, was founded in Philadelphia in 1743 as an outgrowth of the Junto, a club Benjamin Franklin and a group of friends had begun in 1727. The society was formed "for the promotion of useful knowledge among the British planters in America." Its first president was a lawyer named Thomas Hopkinson, and Franklin was the first secretary. In 1769 it merged with the American Society for Promoting Useful Knowledge, and Franklin was elected the first president of the combined organization. He held the post until his death in 1790. He was succeeded by David Rittenhouse, an astronomer and instrument maker, who was succeeded by Thomas Jefferson. In 1769 the society began publication of its *Transactions*. The original inspiration for the society was the Royal Society of England. The society continues to exist with a membership of distinguished persons in intellectual and scientific fields. It has a large library especially rich in materials dealing with the American Revolution and the history of science in America.

1741: The **Great Awakening,** a religious revival movement in New England, reached an oratorical peak with the famous sermon delivered by Jonathan Edwards at Endfield, Mass. Entitled "Sinners in the Hands of an Angry God," Edwards's sermon proclaimed man's "abominable" sinfulness in the eyes of God.

1741: The **first true porcelain** manufactured in the colonies was produced by Andrew Duché, a craftsman of Huguenot descent who had founded a pottery in Savannah, Ga., in 1730. Lack of financial backing hampered pottery manufacture, but Duché prospered by exporting his clay to England. In 1764 the *Bristol Journal* acknowledged that the first porcelain made in an English-speaking country came from North America.

1742: The **Moravian Seminary for Women** was founded at Bethlehem, Pa. Men were first admitted in 1746, and in 1807 a full college curriculum was adopted. The institution is now known as Moravian College.

1742: The so-called **Franklin stove,** a variation on an open firebox of German design, was invented by Benjamin Franklin.

IV. Fashion
Folkways
Holidays
Social Issues and Crime
Sports

The growing problem of crime and racism in the increasingly populous cities, and a decline in social and economic stability, was reflected in the so-called Negro Conspiracy of 1741 in New York City. A number of robberies in February were attributed to the customers of John Hughson's dram shop, which was frequented by blacks. Hughson had a bad reputation and it was suspected that he was a fence for stolen goods. In March Fort George burned and the fire was thought to have some connection with the robberies. Many people panicked for fear of crimes by blacks, and their fears were fed by sensational tales of a conspiracy, described by one Mary Burton, a European servant. Hundreds of people fled to the Bowery and Harlem, and then outside the city proper, for fear of a black uprising. The militia was called out and many blacks were jailed and given summary judicial treatment. Two slaves, Quack and Cuffee, were burned at the stake, and Hughson and his wife were hanged. Before the frenzy subsided, 13 blacks had been burned alive, eight hanged, and 71 transported out of the colony. The claim of a conspiracy had no basis. Even Daniel Horsemanden, the prosecutor, admitted later that there had been no plot.

1741: The prevalence of **alcohol abuse** in the colonies was demonstrated in the death of a child about five years old after consuming a great quantity of rum. Drunkenness was the most prevalent vice of colonial settlers. Each colony had stringent laws meant to suppress excess drinking. Boston even went so far as to post the names of drunkards. A contemporary quatrain sounded this note:

> This town would quickly be reclaimed,
> If drams no more had vent,
> And all the sorts that could be named,
> To *Strombolo* were sent.

1745–1749

I. Civil Rights
Exploration and Settlement
Government
Statistics
Wars

The Treaty of Aix-la-Chapelle was signed on Oct. 18, 1748, ending the War of the Austrian Succession, known in America as King George's War (1744–1748). For the most part it restored the status quo in the New World, returning Fort Louisbourg, on Cape Breton Island in Canada, to France. The New Englanders, whose forces had fought brilliantly to capture heavily defended Louisbourg, were outraged. As a result, the English Crown agreed to bear the cost of the expedition. Great Britain's privilege of transporting slaves to Spanish America was renewed, but the treaty turned out to be merely a truce before the last and greatest of the French and Indian Wars.

1745: In **King George's War** (1744–1748), French and Indian forces began the year with raids on English fortifications in Maine.

1745 June 16: Fort Louisbourg, a powerful French stronghold on Cape Breton Island in Nova Scotia, was captured by New Englanders under William Pepperell and an English fleet under Sir Peter Warren.

1745 Nov 28-29: Saratoga, N.Y., was attacked and burned by French and Indian forces after the English had succeeded in persuading the Iroquois league to enter the war against the French.

**II. Architecture
Arts and Music
Popular Entertainment
Publishing
Theater**

In the mid-eighteenth century portrait painting flourished. The best colonial painter of this period was Robert Feke. He probably studied in Europe at one time, but he developed a personal style of painting. Feke practiced in New York City, Philadelphia, Newport, and Boston, painting excellent portraits of leading citizens. Perhaps his best, in terms of characterization, was a portrait of the Rev. Thomas Hiscox done in 1745. Feke's portraits were noted for their charm and for the elegance of the costumes worn by his subjects. Examples of his work include a portrait of Mrs. Barlow Trecothick done in Boston; and *Unknown Lady*, now in the Brooklyn Museum, noted for its almost cubist depiction of the subject's bell-shaped skirt and funnel-shaped torso. Feke's work was influenced by John Smibert, the first painter of skill in New England. Feke disappeared at sea in 1750.

1745: Selections from the writings of Charles de Secondat, Baron de la Brède et de **Montesquieu,** were first published in American periodicals. The selections were from *Lettres Persanes* (*Persian Letters*, 1721). These were followed several years later by excerpts from *L'Esprit des Lois* (*Spirit of the Laws*, 1748) in the Boston *Gazette*. This book had a profound effect on the evolution of American political theory and the formulation, some 40 years later, of the U.S. Constitution.

1749 Aug 22: Colonial **opposition to acting** was demonstrated when an early troupe of English actors, Murray and Kean's, performed Joseph Addison's *Cato* (1713) in a Philadelphia warehouse. Protests by the city council forced them to leave for New York.

III. Business and Industry
Education
Philosophy and Religion
Science

Seven colleges—Harvard, the College of William and Mary, Yale, Princeton, Columbia, Brown, and Rutgers—were established before the Revolution. Typical of them was Princeton, chartered Oct. 22, 1746, as the College of New Jersey and opened in 1747 in Elizabethtown, N.J. Its first president was Jonathan Dickinson, who taught the first classes in his home. He was a leading preacher of the Great Awakening and founded the college to train leaders for the revival movement. Its first degrees were conferred in 1748. In 1756 the college moved to Princeton, N.J., where its name was changed. In the years following its founding, Princeton became a stronghold of conservative doctrine in the bitter theological conflicts within the Presbyterian Church. Princeton's second president was Aaron Burr, whose son, also named Aaron Burr, was to kill Alexander Hamilton in a duel. During the Revolution both sides occupied the school buildings, which were heavily damaged. As time passed, the original purpose of training clergymen disappeared and the university devoted itself to higher education.

1745: The growth of **literacy** in early America was spurred by the founding of 22 newspapers between

1747: The **New York Bar Association,** the first legal society in America, was organized by lawyers of New York City to defend themselves against attacks by Lt. Gov. Cadwallader Colden. In 1765 the group spearheaded colonial resistance to the Stamp Act.

IV. Fashion
    Folkways
    Holidays
    Social Issues and Crime
    Sports

Coffee houses began to gain popularity about this time, as the populations of cities grew. New York had two coffee houses in 1744. A coffee house was opened in Charleston, S.C., by William Monat in 1743, but lost business to Charles Shepheard, whose British Coffee House grew in popularity after its owner became deputy postmaster. Three coffee houses were available to Philadelphians before 1750, two of them named the Widow Robert's and the Widow Jones's. The former was the most popular, providing newspapers and magazines, tea, coffee, and chocolate, and the "constant Attendance" of the proprietor until the Widow Roberts died in 1754. Boston had the Crown and the North End. Jacob Hassey, described as "a comicall old whimsical fellow," kept a coffee house at Newport, R.I. Prior to the opening of coffee houses, taverns fulfilled some of the same purposes, but many taverns became notorious for their patrons' heavy drinking and lawlessness. As a result, coffee houses became centers where businessmen met and where notices of ship sailings, sales, and other matters were posted.

c1745: Whist became very popular in the colonies, having been brought over from England, where it was the rage. The game afforded men the opportunity to keep company with women. Ladies often played for money, as evidenced in accounts of Thomas Jefferson and George Washington concerning their wives' expenses.

1749: The **consumption of cider** in New York rivaled that of beer. A Swedish visitor to the colonies noted the abundance of apple orchards and number of cider presses in New York. In winter cider was used extensively; in summer it was mixed with water, sweetened, and spiced with nutmeg.

1749: The **eating habits** of the Dutch in New York were carefully recorded by a foreign traveler: "Their Breakfast is tea, commonly without milk. . . . They never put sugar into the cup but put a small bit of it into their mouths while they drink. Along with tea they eat bread and butter with slices of hung beef. . . . They breakfast generally about seven. Their dinner is buttermilk and bread. . . . They sometimes make use of buttermilk instead of fresh milk to boil a thin kind of porridge with, which tastes very sour but not disagreeable in hot weather. To each dinner they have a great salad prepared with abundance of vinegar and little or no oil [probably koolslaa—modern coleslaw]. Their supper is generally bread and butter, or milk and bread."

1750–1754

I. Civil Rights
Exploration and Settlement
Government
Statistics
Wars

The first attempt to unite the English colonies was made at the Albany Congress, which was called in Albany, N.Y., in 1754 to negotiate a treaty with the Iroquois Indians in the event of further war with the French. Represented at the Albany Congress were the four New England colonies and New York, Pennsylvania, and Maryland. Benjamin Franklin took the occasion to present his "Plan of the Union" of the colonies, which the delegates approved on July 19, 1754. The plan included amendments proposed by Thomas Hutchinson of Massachusetts and would have united all the American English colonies, except Georgia and Nova Scotia, under a president general who would be named by the British government and paid by it. The various colonial assemblies would elect a grand council that would have legislative power, subject to the president general and the English Crown. However, the plan was rejected by the colonies and by the Crown. England proposed a looser union with a commander in chief and a commissioner for Indian affairs, but nothing came of the idea.

The estimated colonial **population** was 1,207,000.
1753 Oct 31: George Washington was sent by Gov. Robert Dinwiddie of Virginia to demand French withdrawal from the Ohio territory. Dinwiddie had been impressed by Washington's achievement as surveyor and fieldsman, and picked him for the commission although he was only 21. As adjutant general of the Northern Division, Washington set out from Williamsburg, Va. With Christopher Gist as his guide, he

made observations of French fortifications and estimations about needed English fortifications. During the expedition he kept a journal, which Dinwiddie later obtained and had printed. It indicted French intentions for the territory and attributed to a French officer the indiscreet admission that " . . . it was their absolute Design to take possession of the Ohio, and by G— they would do it."

1754 Apr 17: The **French continued to advance** on the Ohio River Valley with the occupation of the junction of the Allegheny and Monongahela rivers on the site of present-day Pittsburgh, Pa. There they built Fort Duquesne. The move anticipated similar intentions by an English force led by George Washington and dispatched by Gov. Dinwiddie.

1754 May 28: The **first skirmish of the French and Indian War** (1754–1763), the last and most significant of the French and Indian Wars, occurred when a small force under George Washington engaged and defeated a reconnaissance party of French and Indians near Fort Duquesne. Unable to proceed against the superior French forces in the fort, Washington erected Fort Necessity at nearby Great Meadows.

1754 July 4: George Washington surrendered **Fort Necessity** when attacked by a large French contingent from Fort Duquesne. This defeat left the French in possession of the Ohio River Valley.

II. Architecture
Arts and Music
Popular Entertainment
Publishing
Theater

The fortunes of American theater rose considerably when Lewis Hallam brought his theatrical troupe to America in 1752. The company's first performance was *The Merchant of Venice* in Williamsburg, Va. Moving to New York City in 1753, Hallam built a new theater on Nassau St. that was well patronized by upper-class New Yorkers. In April the company

moved on to Philadelphia, where it gave 30 performances at Plumstead's Theater, which had been renovated for them. The performance of *The Fair Penitent*
was received "with universal applause." After touring
the South, Hallam went to Jamaica in the West Indies, where he died in 1756. The company was said
to have had a repertoire of over 40 plays. Hallam's
widow married David Douglass. With him she
formed the American Company, which came to New
York in 1759. The opening bill at Cruger's Wharf was
Jane Shore, which played to "great applause, to a
most crowded audience." Hallam's son, Lewis, Jr.,
was a member of this troupe and a noted performer
of comedy. In 1767 he appeared in Thomas Godfrey's
Prince of Parthia, the first American drama to be produced professionally.

1750: Parlange, one of the finest plantation houses of
the bayou country in Louisiana and a classic example
of French colonial architecture, was built at New
Roads, Pointe Coupée Parish, La., by Marquis Vincent de Ternant, whose descendants still own it.

1752: The **Georg Muller House,** the best surviving example of Pennsylvania Dutch architecture, was built
at Milbach, Pa. Its layout was based on designs common in the Rhine Valley.

1754: What was perhaps the **first American political
cartoon** was published by Benjamin Franklin in his
Pennsylvania Gazette. The cartoon showed a snake
cut into eight parts, the head representing New England and the other seven parts representing the remaining colonies. The caption was "Join or Die." The
cartoon was prompted by rumors of an impending
war with the French.

III. Business and Industry
Education
Philosophy and Religion
Science

Medical care in the colonies was somewhat primitive
and unorganized in the early eighteenth century.

During this period both the quality and availability of medical treatment improved as medical education increased and general hospitals made their first appearance. In 1734 William Bull of South Carolina received a medical degree in Europe, the first of 40 or so colonial physicians to be educated abroad. Forerunners of hospitals were the pesthouses, such as those established in Boston (1717), Philadelphia (1742), Charleston, S.C. (before 1752), and New York City (1757). The first general hospital was organized in Philadelphia by Dr. Thomas Bond; it opened its doors Feb. 6, 1752, as the Pennsylvania Hospital. Admission was on a paying or charity basis for persons who were mentally or physically ill, except for incurables and those having infectious diseases.

1750: The **Great Awakening,** the New England religious revival sparked by Jonathan Edwards, came to an end when Edwards was compelled to resign from his pulpit at Northampton, Mass., by liberal members of his congregation. The liberals opposed his emphasis on the sinful nature of mankind.

1751: The **first sugar cane** grown in America was introduced into Louisiana by Catholic missionaries from San Domingo on the island of Hispaniola. It was used to make taffia, a kind of rum.

1752 Jan 31: The **first American-born nun** in the Roman Catholic Church was Sister St. Martha Turpin, who celebrated the Ceremony for the Profession at the Ursuline Convent, in New Orleans, La.

1752 June: Benjamin Franklin conducted his celebrated experiment with kite and key to prove lightning a manifestation of electricity. A kite with a projecting wire was flown during a thunderstorm, and an electrical charge was conducted to the key through light twine. The experiment was conducted in a pasture near what is now the corner of Fourth and Vine streets in Philadelphia, Pa.

1753: The **first steam engine** in the colonies was brought to North Arlington, N.J., by John Schuyler to pump water from his copper mine. The machine came from England and was assembled in America by Joshua Hornblower.

1754: The first clock made entirely in America was constructed by Benjamin Banneker, a 30-year-old black who had never seen a clock before. It continued to run accurately, striking all hours regularly, for 20 years.

IV. Fashion
Folkways
Holidays
Social Issues and Crime
Sports

By the mid-eighteenth century social customs and forms of entertainment were somewhat relaxed compared with earlier periods. At the same time, many forms of entertainment and recreation were those to be expected of small towns and farming areas—hunting, fishing, folk dancing, and corn husking bees, for example. One observer noted that at one of the husking bees the "neighboring Swains . . . cannot carry in the husks without a Rhum bottle." There was widespread observance of the custom that any young man who found a red ear of corn could kiss any girl he chose. It was recorded that one young woman, Sarah Tuttle, charged with having enjoyed the occasion too much, was brought before a magistrate who denounced her as a "Bould Virgin."

1752: The inscription for the **Liberty Bell,** the biblical sentence "Proclaim liberty throughout all the land unto all the inhabitants thereof," was chosen by the Pennsylvania Provincial Assembly. The bell was cast in England and delivered to the colony in this year. While being tested in Philadelphia, it suffered its first crack.

1754: Curious **Valentine customs** were recorded by a colonial girl: "Last Friday was St. Valentine's Day, and the night before I got five bay leaves and pinned four on the corners of my pillow and the fifth to the middle; and then if I dreamt of my sweetheart, Betty said we should be married before the year was out. But to make it more sure I boiled an egg hard and took out the yolk and filled it with salt; and when I went to bed ate it shell and all, without speaking or drinking after it. We also wrote our lovers' names on bits of paper, and rolled them up in clay and put them into water; and the first that rose up was to be our Valentine. Would you think it? Mr. Blossom was my man. I lay abed and shut my eyes all the morning, till he came to our house, for I would not have seen another man before him for all the world." It was about this time, in the middle of the century, that the history of American valentines began. A certain simplicity was apparent in the style of the sketches and verses of early valentines, though they often displayed some talent. So-called valentine writers, guides to the composition of valentines containing sample verses, were imported from England from 1723 on, and many senders were willing merely to copy their verses from these.

1755–1759

I. Civil Rights
Exploration and Settlement
Government
Statistics
Wars

The Seven Years' War (1756–1763), the European counterpart to the French and Indian War (1754–1763), began officially between France and England on May 15, 1756, when the latter made a formal declaration of war. Actually, fighting had been going on in America for two years. The war involved all the major European powers and was worldwide in scope, but to the colonists it was a struggle against the French for control of North America. The war did not go well for England until the elder William Pitt came to power in 1756. He concentrated on fighting the French and sent badly needed troop reinforcements to North America.

1755 July 9: In the **French and Indian War** (1754–1763), British Gen. Edward Braddock was mortally wounded when he and his force of British troops and colonial militia were caught in a French and Indian ambush. Braddock had just crossed the Monongahela R. on his way to attack Fort Duquesne, on the site of what is now Pittsburgh, Pa. Braddock died July 13, and George Washington assumed command of the retreating army.

1755 Nov 30: The **first refugees** from the French and Indian War, some 900 Acadian French deported by British authorities from Nova Scotia, arrived in Maryland. Years later Henry Wadsworth Longfellow used this exile as the background for his poem *Evangeline* (1847).

1756 Aug 14: Fort Oswego in north central New York was captured by the French under Gen. Joseph de Montcalm de Saint-Véran. Gen. Montcalm rendered the fort useless for military purposes and returned to Montreal.

1757 Aug 9: Fort William Henry, at the southern tip of Lake George in northeastern New York, capitulated to the French commanded by Gen. Montcalm. Many of the British soldiers in the garrison were killed by the Indian allies of the French on the next day.

1758 July 8: A British and colonial assault on **Ticonderoga,** at the northern end of Lake George in New York, was beaten back by the French under Gen. Montcalm. Nearly 2000 of the attacking force of 17,000 were killed or wounded.

1758 July 26: The French at the **fortress of Louisbourg,** Nova Scotia, surrendered to the British under Adm. Edward Boscawen and Gen. Jeffrey Amherst after a 48-day siege. Almost 6000 prisoners were captured and the fortress was razed.

1758 Nov 25: British forces drove the French from **Fort Duquesne,** which the British renamed Pittsburgh.

1759 July 26: Ticonderoga was abandoned by the

French as Gen. Amherst threatened a siege. The French commander, the Chevalier de Bourlamaque, withdrew to Crown Point, N.Y.

1759 Sep 13: The French were defeated on the **Plains of Abraham** at Quebec. Both Gen. Montcalm and the British commander Gen. James Wolfe were killed. The city of Quebec was surrendered to the British Sept. 18.

II. Architecture
Arts and Music
Popular Entertainment
Publishing
Theater

Colonial America was developing its own intellectual class, whose members were noted for their wide-ranging interests and varied talents. None of them was more versatile than Francis Hopkinson, a musician and poet, accomplished harpsichordist, and leader of musical pursuits in Philadelphia. In 1759 Hopkinson wrote what was probably the first secular song written by a native American, "My Days Have Been So Wonderous Free." The song, based on the poem by Thomas Parnell, was not published until the twentieth century. Hopkinson went on to become a signer of the Declaration of Independence, wrote the celebrated Revolutionary poem "The Battle of the Kegs" (1778), and, as a member of the Continental Navy Board (1776-1778), may have designed the American flag. His book *Seven songs, for the Harpsichord or Forte-Piano* (1788) was the first book of music published by an American composer.

1755: According to legend, the words of the song "Yankee Doodle" were written by Dr. Richard Shuckburg, a British army surgeon, as a satire on the ragged American troops. More likely the song was of folk origin among the British soldiers. Adopted as a favorite marching tune by American troops, "Yankee Doodle" quickly lost its satirical aspect. In 1781, during the American Revolution, the song was played at the British surrender at Yorktown, Va.

1757: Mount Vernon, a cottage of one and one-half stories acquired by George Washington, was remodeled for the first time. It was enlarged and remodeled at least three more times in the next 30 years, probably in accordance with Washington's own designs. The result was a structure not as well designed as other Virginia mansions but, aside from its historical associations, interesting for its record of architectural growth.

III. Business and Industry
Education
Philosophy and Religion
Science

The opening in 1756 of a through stage route linking Philadelphia and New York City marked another step forward in the development of colonial transportation. As the first colonial settlements grew into towns and then into cities, the need for roads and reliable means of transportation also grew. By 1717 there was a continuous road along the East Coast connecting all the colonies. Other roads went into the interior, but many were rough. The first stage line between Boston and Newport, R.I., began to operate in 1736. Beginning in 1744, part of the heavily traveled route between New York and Philadelphia was served by twice-weekly stages between New Brunswick and Trenton, N.J. Perhaps the most heavily traveled road was the Great Philadelphia Wagon Road, which ran west to Lancaster and then to York. The 1756 Philadelphia-New York stage used Jersey Wagons, wagons without spring suspensions, which operated in relays. Faster passenger service was offered in 1766 by the Flying Machine, a box wagon that ran from Camden, N.J., to what is now Jersey City, N.J. The 90-mile trip took two days and passengers had to use a ferry at each end.

1755 June 16: The **first nonsectarian college** in America, the University of Pennsylvania, was chartered as the College, Academy, and Charitable School in Philadelphia through the efforts of Benjamin Franklin. Its first degrees were awarded in 1757.

IV. Fashion
Folkways
Holidays
Social Issues and Crime
Sports

As soon as streets were laid out in colonial cities, citizens and city councils alike pointed to the necessity and desirability of paving them. Paving not only made streets drier and smoother, but also contributed to public health by providing drainage. After 1700, Boston, New York City, and Newport, R.I., began to pave streets. Later, between 1743 and 1760, paving became more common and colonial streets were probably in better shape than those in England. In 1757 over 16,000 yards of roadway on Boston Neck were paved at a cost of £3000. A lottery in Newport in 1752 provided funds for paving more streets. Philadelphia also used a lottery to pay the cost of paving.

1756 July 26: Bosom bottles were advertised in the *Boston Evening Post.* They were small, beribboned glasses worn on stiff dresses of the period, filled with water, and containing flowers that served much the same function as corsages do today.

1757: Street lights appeared in Philadelphia on a small scale. Whale oil lamps, specially designed by Benjamin Franklin, were installed on a few streets. The year before, Franklin had introduced a bill to the Pennsylvania Assembly for street illumination.

1760–1764

I. Civil Rights
Exploration and Settlement
Government
Statistics
Wars

The Treaty of Paris, signed by Great Britain, France, and Spain on Feb. 10, 1763, ended the Seven Years' War and its American counterpart, the French and Indian War (1754–1763). By terms of the treaty, France ceded Canada and all its territory east of the Mississippi R. to England, and Spain yielded Florida to England. France retained the islands of St. Pierre and Miquelon in the Gulf of St. Lawrence. Worldwide, France was humbled and the treaty marked the start of the colonial and maritime supremacy of Great Britain. Britain's success was costly, however, and Parliament's attempt to cover its debts, and to pay for a continuing military presence in America, by direct taxation of the colonists soon caused strained relations between mother country and colonies.

The estimated colonial **population** was 1,610,000.

1760 Aug 7: In the **French and Indian War** (1754–1763), Fort Loudon, Tenn., capitulated to the Cherokee Indians. Capt. Demere surrendered under condition that his troops be allowed to retreat unimpeded. On Aug. 10 the garrison was massacred by Indians while retreating to Fort Prince George in South Carolina.

1760 Sep 8: The **French surrendered Montreal** to Gen. Jeffrey Amherst. After the defeat of this last French stronghold, Canada was split into three parts: Quebec, Montreal, and Three Rivers.

1760 Nov 29: Detroit was surrendered to Maj. Robert Rogers by the French Commander Belêtre.

1763 May 7: Pontiac's Rebellion, named for the Ottawa Indian chief who led the uprising, began when Pontiac led an attack on the fort at Detroit. The raid failed and the Indians began a siege. News of the attack sparked similar raids throughout the region until all but three forts—Detroit, Pitt, and Niagara—had fallen. British forces rushed to their relief. With no French aid materializing, Pontiac in October secured a truce and withdrew to the west. A final peace agreement in 1766 marked the end of the rebellion.

II. Architecture
Arts and Music
Popular Entertainment
Publishing
Theater

The growth of the colonies brought with it a strong interest in cultural activities. In the mid-eighteenth century musical concerts were flourishing in the colonial centers, and musical societies, music dealers, and instrument makers all benefited. As in other matters, Boston, New York City, Philadelphia, and Charleston, S.C., led the way, with Charleston seeming to have a special affinity for music. The first music society in America, the St. Cecilia Society, was founded there in 1762. In Europe, Charleston was considered the chief cultural center of the colonies, and many artists, actors, and musicians chose to settle there when they emigrated to America. Other cities could boast of cultural achievements as well. In Boston a group of gentlemen sponsored a concert in Faneuil Hall as early as 1744, and in 1754 the first concert hall in Boston was opened by Gilbert Deblois. Philadelphia boasted four organ makers who produced spinets and virginals as well as organs.

1764: The *Connecticut Courant* began publishing as a weekly newspaper in Hartford, Conn. Renamed the

Hartford Daily Courant, it became a daily in 1837, changing to its present name, the *Hartford Courant,* in 1887. It became the oldest continuously published newspaper in the U.S. The *Courant* was a patriotic journal during the Revolution and after independence supported the Federalist Party.

III. Business and Industry
Education
Philosophy and Religion
Science

The most useful contribution to transportation produced in the colonies was the Conestoga Wagon. Although it existed in primitive form by about 1725, it came into its own after 1760, by which time craftsmen of Lancaster, Pa., living along the Conestoga Creek, had converted the wagon into an enormous conveyance using six horses and carrying up to eight tons of goods. The bottom was curved to help keep the load in place whether going uphill or down. The top was a huge white cover, first made of homespun hempen and later of canvas. It rose out and up at each end, giving a poke bonnet effect. The driver rode on the left wheelhorse or on a lazyboard that could be pulled out from the side of the wagon. By so doing, he could see oncoming traffic. This arrangement is thought to be the origin of the custom of driving on the right-hand side of the road. The Conestoga Wagon was vital to the settlement of the Allegheny region. Thousands of these wagons carried farm produce to the cities and hauled to the west the goods needed by pioneer settlers. The prairie schooner, which made up the wagon trains that later took settlers to Mississippi regions, was a light version of the Conestoga Wagon.

c1760: The **first bifocal lenses** were invented by Benjamin Franklin. Twenty years later Franklin wrote to a friend that he had become tired of carrying two pairs of spectacles and had ordered a pair made with two kinds of lenses cut in the same circle of glass.

1763: A pioneer attempt at **steam navigation** was made by Henry Williams. Inspired by the work of James Watt in England, Williams built the first steam-powered boat and tested it on the Conestoga Creek in Lancaster, Pa. Although the tests were a failure, they helped encourage Robert Fulton and his experiments.

IV. Fashion
Folkways
Holidays
Social Issues and Crime
Sports

Student life at colonial colleges was reflected in the experience of Thomas Jefferson, who entered the College of William and Mary at Williamsburg, Va., on Mar. 25, 1760, when not quite 17. About this time the students complained about the food. The faculty told the housekeeper, Isabella Cocke, that both salt and fresh meat must be served at dinner, puddings and pies provided on Sunday and two weekdays, and supper must be the same at all tables, even if made up of scraps. Jefferson described the buildings as "rude, mis-shapen piles, which, but that they have roofs, would be taken for brick-kilns." The College of William and Mary was the second oldest college in the colonies, opened in 1694, and its main building was already 60 years old.

1761 June 10: The influence of **Puritan morality** on colonial society was demonstrated in the production of a play presented at Newport, R.I., by the Douglass Company: *Moral Dialogues in 5 parts, Depicting the Evil Effects of Jealousy and other Bad Passions, and Proving that Happines can only Spring from the Pursuit of Virtue*. The play was actually Shakespeare's *Othello*. The advertisement for the performance read: " . . . Commencement at 7, conclusion at half past 10, in order that every spectator may go home at a sober hour and reflect upon what he has seen before he retires to rest." This description failed to disarm Puritan critics of theater. After a few performances by the company in Newport and Providence, the Rhode Island Assembly enacted legislation barring theatrical performances in the colony, with a penalty of £100 for each actor.

1765–1769

I. Civil Rights
Exploration and Settlement
Government
Statistics
Wars

The Stamp Act, passed by Parliament on Mar. 22, 1765, raised the subject that was to be a major cause of the American Revolution, taxation without representation. The act levied a tax on all newspapers, legal documents, pamphlets, almanacs, playing cards, and dice by requiring that they bear a stamp. The receipts from the tax were to be used to pay for defense of the colonies. The tax was to take effect on Nov. 1, but even before then American opposition was intense. Merchants refused to buy English goods, stamp agents were threatened with harm if they did not resign, and in some places the official stamps were destroyed. As a result the tax was repealed on Mar. 18, 1766, but not before delegates from nine of the thirteen colonies attended the Stamp Act Congress in Oct. 1765. The congress issued a series of resolutions stating the reasons for colonial opposition to the tax. The same day the tax was repealed, Parliament passed the Declaratory Act, asserting that the British government had the right to make any laws it wished concerning the American colonies.

1765 May 29: **Patrick Henry** attacked the Stamp Act in the Virginia House of Burgesses, declaring that only colonial legislatures could impose taxes on their respective colonies. Shouts of "Treason!" interrupted Henry's speech, to which he replied: "If this be treason, make the most of it."

1765 Oct 7-25: The **Stamp Act Congress** met at City Hall, New York City, in answer to a circular from the Massachusetts House of Representatives. Twenty-eight delegates from nine colonies attended to organize a united resistance to the Stamp Act. On Oct. 19 the congress adopted the Declaration of Rights and Grievances, a series of resolutions protesting taxes imposed by the act, and resolved not to import any goods that required payment of duty. This led to the Petition of London Merchants in 1766, which urged repeal of the act and stressed the injury to English trade caused by the colonial policy of nonimportation.

1766 Mar 17: The **Stamp Act was repealed** by Parliament. The repeal was approved the next day by King George III and became effective on May 1.

1767 June 29: The **Townshend Revenue Act** was passed by Parliament. It required that colonists pay an import duty on tea, glass, painter's colors, oil, lead, and paper. The £40,000 that the act was expected to yield was to pay salaries of royal governors and judges in the colonies. In Feb. 1768 the Massachusetts House of Representatives sent a letter to other colonial legislatures calling upon them to join with it in action against the duties. The British ordered the letter repudiated and threatened to dissolve any assembly in sympathy with Massachusetts. In Virginia the burgesses responded with a declaration that they had the exclusive right of taxation in the colony. While protesting loyalty to the king, they entered into an agreement not to import goods on which Parliament raised revenues and, after a certain date, to stop buying a long list of embargoed items.

**II. Architecture
Arts and Music
Popular Entertainment
Publishing
Theater**

The American school of painting, still in its infancy during this period, was diminished by the death in 1765 of Joseph Badger, whose use of realism in portraiture was a significant move away from traditional European techniques. Badger's works owed nothing to the more refined and technically superior British school of portraiture. Badger was a glazier and house painter who became Boston's favorite artist. His work had charm, but a stiff, archaic style. His best work portrayed children, such as Jeremiah Belknap. He also did portraits of Revolutionary era notables such as Jonathan Edwards and John Adams. Many thought his plain style was more suited to the young, raw, and vigorous colonials than to studied portraits of English nobles. His work reflected the general tendency in all the colonial arts during this period to establish independent styles and techniques.

1766 Oct: The **first permanent theater** in the colonies, the Southwark Theater, was erected on South St. in Philadelphia by David Douglass, owner and manager of the American Company of Comedians. Douglass also built New York City's first permanent theater, the John Street Theater, in 1767.

1767 Apr 24: Probably the **first professionally performed American play**, *The Prince of Parthia* by Thomas Godfrey, opened at the Southwark Theater

1768: A commemorative bowl molded in silver by **Paul Revere** was presented to each of 92 legislators in the Massachusetts House of Representatives who resisted royal authority by protesting to King George III about restrictive trade measures.

1769: Whitehall, an impressive late Georgian mansion, was built in Anne Arundel County, Md. It was equipped with the only known interior water closet in colonial America.

III. Business and Industry
Education
Philosophy and Religion
Science

The last of the large Protestant denominations to establish itself in America was the Methodist Church. In England it did not formally separate from the Church of England until late in the century. In 1766 Philip Embury, originally from Ireland, formed the John Street church in New York City and preached there. About the same time Robert Strawbridge started a congregation in Maryland, and in Virginia the Rev. Devereux Jarratt, an Anglican, acted as chaplain to the Methodists. Francis Asbury came from England in 1771 and made many converts to Methodism. The first annual Methodist conference in America was held in 1773. In 1784, with authority from John Wesley, the founder of Methodism, Thomas Coke formally organized the Methodist Episcopal Church in America.

1765: The **first chocolate** manufactured in North America was produced at Dorchester Lower Mills on the Neponset R. in Massachusetts by John Harmon. In 1780 the plant came into the possession of Dr. James Baker, who had sponsored Harmon. From Baker's business evolved the world-famous Walter Baker & Co., Ltd., chocolate manufacturers.

1765 May 3: The **first medical school** in the colonies, the medical department of the College of Philadelphia, was organized by Drs. John Morgan and William Shippen, Jr. The school later became the University of Pennsylvania School of Medicine.

1767: The **first planetarium** in America was built by David Rittenhouse of Philadelphia. Rittenhouse, a noted clockmaker, plotted the orbits of Venus and Mercury in 1769.

1768 Oct 30: The **first Methodist Church** in America was dedicated. It was the Wesley Chapel on John St. in New York City. The church was rebuilt in 1817 and again in 1840.

1769: A famous American **glassmaking plant** opened at Manheim, Pa., by Henry William Stiegel, whose name became identified with a type of American glassware that reflected a German tradition.

1769: Anthracite coal was used in a forge for the first time in Wilkes-Barre, Pa. It had been discovered as early as 1762 by Connecticut pioneers in Pennsylvania. It was little used until the beginning of the nineteenth century.

IV. Fashion
Folkways
Holidays
Social Issues and Crime
Sports

This period, following the last of the French and Indian Wars, saw the opening of vast new tracts for westward expansion and the rise of the western frontiersman as an American folk hero. The most celebrated folk hero was Daniel Boone who, after hunting and exploring his way through the Cumberland Gap, saw Kentucky for the first time on June 7, 1769. Boone spent two years exploring the region, then in 1773 made an unsuccessful attempt to settle Kentucky. In 1775, with a company of 30 men, he blazed the Wilderness Road and founded Boonesborough, Ky. The next year he joined the Patriot cause in the American Revolution as a captain in the Virginia militia. In 1778 he was captured by the Shawnee Indians but managed to escape and alert Boonesborough to an impending Indian raid. Boone's land titles in Kentucky were overturned in the courts on technicalities, and he eventually moved to Missouri, where he continued his pioneer existence until his death in 1820. Boone's adventures became widely known after publication in 1784 of *Discovery, Settlement, and Present State of Kentucky* by John Filson, which contained material purporting to be autobiographical.

1765: Education for women in colonial America emphasized practical learning, as illustrated by the advertisement of a Philadelphia teacher who promised to teach young ladies to spell and print with propriety. He advised them not to be discouraged in their pursuit of knowledge by their age or fear of not obtaining a husband, since he had given "the finishing stroke" to several New York ladies who married shortly afterward.

1766: Some **popular games** in New York City were suggested by James Rivington's advertisement that he imported "battledores, shuttlecocks, cricket balls, pellets, racquets for tennis and fives, and backgammon tables."

1770–1774

I. Civil Rights
Exploration and Settlement
Government
Statistics
Wars

The first clashes of the coming revolution occurred during this period, among them the Boston Massacre in 1770 and the Boston Tea Party in 1773. This period also saw the rise of organized political resistance to parliamentary and royal excesses in the form of the first Continental Congress, which met from Sept. 5 to Oct. 26, 1774, in Philadelphia. There were 55 delegates representing all the colonies except Georgia. Peyton Randolph of Virginia was elected president and Charles Thompson of Pennsylvania secretary. The most important action, taken on Oct. 20, was the formation of the Continental Association, which forbade the importation and use of English products and proposed that colonial exports be prohibited. The delegates also adopted a number of resolutions opposing the Intolerable Acts, the Quebec Act, the maintenance of British troops in towns in peacetime, and the dissolution of colonial assemblies. The rights of the colonists, including rights to "life, liberty, and property," were also expressed. The congress voted to assemble again on May 10, 1775.

The estimated colonial **population** was 2,205,000.

1770 Mar 5: In what came to be called the **Boston Massacre,** five colonists were killed when British troops fired on a mob of men and boys who had been taunting them and throwing stones. Capt. Thomas Preston, commander of the British contingent, and six of his men were charged with murder. They were defended in court by John Adams and Josiah Quincy. All were acquitted but two soldiers who were found guilty of manslaughter.

1770 Apr 12: The **Townshend Acts** were repealed through the efforts of Lord Frederick North. Realizing that the colonies were being pushed too far, Parliament was persuaded to withdraw all Townshend duties except that on tea. The colonies responded by lifting their embargo on goods shipped from England, thus improving relations between England and America. The tax on tea remained, as did the colonial embargo on tea.

1773 Apr 27: The **Tea Act** was passed by Parliament. The act was designed to save the East Indian Company from bankruptcy by remitting all British duties on tea while retaining the tax on tea exported to America. This enabled the company to cut its price and undersell colonial competition. The company's resulting monopoly all but destroyed American tea merchants.

1773 Dec 16: In the celebrated **Boston Tea Party,** a group of men dressed as Indians boarded three British ships in Boston harbor and threw their cargoes of tea, 342 chests worth £18,000, into the water. The action was the climax of growing colonial opposition to the Tea Act.

1774 Mar 31: The first of the **Intolerable Acts**, also known as the Coercive Acts, was passed by Parliament. The Coercive Acts were punitive measures against Massachusetts for the Boston Tea Party. This act closed the port of Boston until payment was made for the destroyed tea. The three subsequent acts were the Massachusetts Government Act (May 20), which forbade public meetings unless sanctioned by the governor; the Administration of Justice Act (May 20), under which any British officials accused of capital offenses were to be transferred from Massachusetts to England or to another colony for trial; and the Quartering Act (June 2), which required Massachusetts residents to house and feed British troops.

1774 June 22: The **Quebec Act** was passed by Parliament. It established a permanent government in Quebec and extended its boundaries south to the Ohio R. to include land contested by several American colonies. For this, it was considered by the colonists to be one of the Intolerable Acts.

1774 Dec 14: The **first military encounter of the American Revolution** occurred. On the report (the news was carried by Paul Revere) that the British intended to station a garrison at Portsmouth, N.H., Maj. John Sullivan led a band of militia to Fort William and Mary, broke into its arsenal, and carried off a store of arms and ammunition. Neither side suffered casualties.

II. Architecture
Arts and Music
Popular Entertainment
Publishing
Theater

The rising prestige of American artists in the world was reflected in the career of John Singleton Copley, who was at the peak of his powers at this time, and was soon to become one of America's earliest expatriate artists. A Bostonian and a successful portrait painter by the time he was 20, Copley moved to England about 1775 and remained there for the rest of his life. In England he enjoyed great popularity, and completed a number of his best historical paintings, such as *The Death of Lord Chatham* (c1780), which won him election to the Royal Academy, and the *Siege of Gibraltar* (1790). He also painted portraits of the royal family and the famous *Family Picture* of his wife and children. Nevertheless, Copley's reputation rests primarily on the portraits he painted in America, including those of many of the leading citizens of New England.

1770: The first house at **Monticello** was built by Thomas Jefferson from his own designs. Its plan showed his great interest in pure classicism and in the temple forms of Greek and Roman architecture, especially as evidenced by large porticoes. Monticello later was completely rebuilt and enlarged, but still in keeping with classical forms. Plans for Monticello absorbed Jefferson's attention from his early manhood. Its foundations were dug in 1769, the year of his first election to the House of Burgesses. Monticello stands to this day.

1774 Oct 20: American theater was suspended after an order of the Continental Congress that the colonies "discountenance and discourage all horse racing and all kinds of gaming, cock fighting, exhibitions of shows, plays and other expensive diversions and entertainments."

III. Business and Industry
Education
Philosophy and Religion
Science

The curious history of the American Shaker movement began during this period. The Shakers, officially the United Society of Believers in Christ's Second Coming, had been established in England for a number of years when Ann Lee, known as Mother Ann, arrived in New York State on Aug. 6, 1774, following a vision that told her to travel to America. In 1776 she and eight followers—six men and two women—settled at Watervliet, near Albany. Members of the movement became known as Shakers because of the trembling movements their bodies made when they were in a state of religious fervor. Mother Ann's tour of New England in 1781 aroused animosity because her followers claimed she embodied the second coming of Christ. The Shaker faith centered upon public confession of sins and preparation for the second coming, and Mother Ann added strictures against sexual intercourse and marriage (which ultimately doomed the sect), war, the bearing of arms, and oath-taking. After her death in 1785, her followers composed a life story that made much of the persecutions she encountered in England and America and the supposedly miraculous manner of her deliverance from them. By 1825, eighteen Shaker communities had been founded in eight states, as far west as Indiana, but by 1860 the movement had begun to decline. Today the movement is known especially for its furniture and handcrafts, which were famous for their simplicity and high quality of workmanship.

1770: The **first mental hospital** in the colonies, the Public Hospital for Persons of Insane and Disordered Minds, was opened at Williamsburg, Va. It later became the Eastern Lunatic Asylum, and still later the Eastern State Hospital.

1773 Jan 12: The **first museum** officially established in the American colonies was founded at Charleston, S.C. In 1915 it was incorporated as the Charleston Museum.

1773 July 14: The first annual **conference of American Methodists** convened at St. George's Church, Philadelphia, Pa.

IV. Fashion
    Folkways
    Holidays
    Social Issues and Crime
    Sports

The first large-scale street lighting projects began during this period, although street lighting had begun in the major colonial cities in the 1750s. Philadelphia had installed some 320 oil lamps by 1767, and in Charleston, S.C., in 1762 one Joseph Wilson contributed £300 for street lamps and three months of maintenance. The need for street lighting as an aid to citizens engaged in evening commerce or cultural activities and also as a deterrent to steadily rising urban crime, had been growing throughout the mid-eighteenth century. In 1770 Charleston began a program of street lighting at public expense, and in 1771 Philadelphia purchased a large number of new lamps. It also levied a £20 fine for breaking a lamp. Boston street lighting came comparatively late, but on Mar. 2, 1774, its streets were illuminated by 310 lamps, tended by one Edward Smith with the assistance of seven lamplighters. The lamps were kept lighted in the evenings from Oct. 1 to May 1.

1773: In a comment on **women's fashions,** a Virginia diarist sadly noted the arrival of a batch of women's stays (corsets): "[They] are produced upwards so high that we can have scarce any view at all of the Ladies' Snowy Bosoms; and on the contrary, they are extended downwards so low that whenever ladies who wear them, either young or old, have occasion to walk, the motion necessary for Walking, must, I think, cause a disagreeable Friction of some part of the body against the lower edge of the Stays which is hard and unyielding." Stays were worn by old and young alike. Even ten-year-old girls were forced to girdle their bodies.

1773 Mar: The rioting and wild festivities that marked **New Year's Day** in New York were somewhat curbed by the colonial legislature, which outlawed the discharge of firearms and explosives. New Year's Day had been the most important holiday in the colony during Dutch rule, when it was the traditional day to visit and exchange gifts. When the English took over the colony in 1664, they adopted Dutch customs completely and added a turkey shoot to the day's festivities.

1775–1779

I. **Civil Rights**
   Exploration and Settlement
   Government
   Statistics
   Wars

This period saw the beginning of the American Revolution (1775–1783). Of the numerous events that occurred, none was more momentous than the drafting and adoption of the Declaration of Independence at the Second Continental Congress, which convened in Philadelphia in May 1775. On June 6, 1776, Richard Henry Lee of Virginia introduced a resolution that "these united colonies are, and of right ought to be, free and independent states." On June 11 John Adams, Benjamin Franklin, Thomas Jefferson, Robert R. Livingston, and Roger Sherman were appointed to draft a declaration. Jefferson prepared the first draft; then improvements by Adams and Franklin were incorporated. Lee's resolution of independence was adopted on July 2 by a vote of 12 to 0, New York abstaining. The actual Declaration was approved July 4, after the congress made some further changes. It was not until Aug. 2, however, that a formal parchment copy was ready for signing. Eventually 61 patriots affixed their signatures. The importance of the document lay in its declaration that each person has certain unalienable rights, and that governments derive their powers from the consent of the governed. In an age of kings who were thought to rule by divine right, this was truly a revolutionary philosophy. The Declaration of Independence, combined with the ultimate success of the American Revolution, was destined to usher in a new political age.

1775 Mar 23: Patrick Henry, addressing the second Virginia convention in Richmond, Va., delivered his immortal speech against arbitrary British rule, closing with "Give me liberty or give me death."

1775 Apr 19: The opening volleys of the American Revolution were exchanged at the Battle of **Lexington** in Massachusetts. Capt. John Parker, commanding some 70 Minutemen, engaged a British column marching on Concord, Mass., to seize military stores there. The brief fight at Lexington left eight Minutemen dead and ten wounded. The British then marched to Concord, destroyed some colonial supplies, and fought another engagement before beginning a long and costly retreat under colonial fire back to Boston. By day's end, the British had suffered about 273 casualties, the Americans 93.

1775 May 10: Fort Ticonderoga, N.Y., was taken by American forces under the command of Col. Ethan Allen.

1775 June 15: The Second Continental Congress chose **George Washington** commander in chief of the Continental Army. He declined to accept pay for his services, but in 1783, after eight years of war, submitted records of his expenses totaling £24,700.

1775 June 17: The Battle of **Bunker Hill** was actually fought on Breed's Hill. British forces under Gen. Howe assaulted the Continental positions three times before the Americans, under Col. William Prescott, ran out of gunpowder and were forced to retreat. The British then occupied Bunker Hill after another skirmish.

1775 Sep 25: Col. **Ethan Allen** was captured while attacking Montreal. He was taken to England and held prisoner until the end of the war.

1775 Oct 13: A **naval force was established** by the Continental Congress when it authorized construction of two warships, increasing the number to four on Oct. 30. The Continental Navy was formally established on Nov. 28 and rules for its regulation approved.

1775 Nov 10: Two battalions of **Continental Marines** were organized by the Continental Congress as a component of its naval force. The U.S. Marine Corps was not formally established until July 11, 1789.

1775 Nov 29: In an important **naval victory,** the American cruiser *Lee* captured the British brig *Nancy,* which was laden with guns and ammunition destined for Quebec. *Nancy* was renamed *Congress* and played a key role in forcing the British evacuation of Boston in Mar. 1776.

1775 Dec 22: Esek Hopkins was appointed the **first commander in chief of the Continental Navy.** His rank was to correspond with Gen. Washington's. His first fleet consisted of the *Alfred, Columbus, Andrea Doria,* and *Cabot,* to which four more converted merchant ships were soon added. On Jan. 2, 1777, Hopkins was formally dismissed because he failed to follow orders from the Continental Congress.

1776 Mar 17: The **British evacuated Boston** after American forces seized and fortified Dorchester Heights on Mar. 4. Gen. Howe sailed for Halifax, Nova Scotia, to await reinforcements.

1776 Apr 12: North Carolina became the **first colony to propose independence** formally when the North Carolina Provincial Congress instructed its delegates to the Continental Congress to vote for independence.

1776 Aug 2: The **Declaration of Independence was signed** by the members of the Continental Congress. Though it had been approved on July 4, the draft document had been signed only by John Hancock and Charles Thomson, the president and secretary. The names of the signers were withheld from the public for more than six months because, if independence were not achieved, their treasonable act might result in their deaths.

1776 Aug 27: In the Battle of **Long Island,** N.Y., American forces commanded by Gen. Israel Putnam and Gen. John Sullivan were defeated by the British under Gen. Sir William Howe and Gen. Sir Henry Clinton. Howe took Gen. Sullivan prisoner. On Aug. 30 the Americans evacuated Long Island and crossed to Manhattan.

1776 Sep 6: The **first submarine attack,** by David Bushnell's submersible craft *Turtle,* was initiated unsuccessfully against Adm. Richard Howe's flagship *Eagle* in New York Bay off Manhattan Island. A second attempt to sink British shipping later in September also failed.

1776 Sep 15: The **Continental Army evacuated New**

York City, which was then occupied by the British under Howe.

1776 Sep 22: Capt. **Nathan Hale** of Connecticut was executed by the British in New York City for spying. Before he was hanged he said, "I only regret that I have but one life to lose for my country."

1776 Dec 19: The first number of *The Crisis* by Thomas Paine, a series of pamphlets written to bolster the morale of the Continental Army, was issued. It was immortalized by its famous first sentence, "These are the times that try men's souls."

1776 Dec 26: In the Battle of **Trenton,** N.J., Gen. Washington captured nearly 1000 mercenary Hessian troops in an early morning surprise raid.

1777 Jan 3: The Battle of **Princeton,** N.J., was fought and won by the Continental Army. Gen. Washington again attacked in the early morning, as he had at Trenton the previous week.

1777 July: The **Vermont state constitution,** drafted this month, made Vermont the first state to abolish slavery and adopt universal male suffrage without regard to property. It was followed to a lesser degree by other New England states, which with Vermont were destined to become strongholds of abolitionism in the 1850s. Vermont had declared itself an independent state on Jan. 16, 1777.

1777 Aug 16: Americans under Gen. John Stark defeated the British at **Bennington,** Vt., killing about 200 and capturing 600. The British detachment commanded by Lt. Col. Friedrich Baum had been sent by Gen. Burgoyne in search of provisions.

1777 Sep 11: In the Battle of **Brandywine,** Pa., the Continental Army under Gen. Washington was defeated by British forces under Gen. Howe, who continued to advance on Philadelphia.

1777 Sep 19: In the first Battle of **Bemis Heights,** also known as the Battle of Freeman's Farm, the British under Gen. Burgoyne gained some ground from the Americans under Gen. Horatio Gates but lost 500 men. Almost 300 Americans were killed.

1777 Sep 19: The **Continental Congress fled Philadelphia,** which was threatened by British forces.

1777 Sep 26: **Philadelphia was occupied** by British forces under Gen. Howe.

1777 Oct 4: At **Germantown,** near Philadelphia, Gen. Washington attacked the British but was repulsed by Gen. Howe. The Americans lost about 600 men in this battle.

1777 Oct 7: In the second Battle of **Bemis Heights,** near Saratoga, N.Y., the Americans routed a force of some 1500 British. Benedict Arnold was wounded while attempting to force an entrance into the Hessian camp, and British Gen. Simon Fraser was killed.

1777 Oct 17: At **Saratoga** Gen. Burgoyne, surrounded by a superior force, capitulated to Gen. Horatio Gates, surrendering 5642 British and German troops.

1777 Nov 15: The **Articles of Confederation** were adopted by the Continental Congress at York, Pa. They were ratified in 1781.

1777 Dec 17: Gen. Washington retired with his troops to **Valley Forge, Pa.,** for the winter.

1778 Feb 6: A **Treaty of Alliance with France** was signed. It was in part commercial and in part political and military. France recognized U.S. independence, which was for the Americans the goal of the treaty. It was the first and only treaty of alliance made by the U.S. until the North Atlantic Treaty Organization pact of 1949.

1778 June 18: The **British evacuated Philadelphia,** fearing blockade by French ships.

1778 June 28: In the Battle of **Monmouth,** N.J., American forces under Gen. Washington defeated the British under Gen. Clinton after initial reversals.

1779 July 15: The fort at **Stony Point,** N.Y., was seized by American forces under Gen. Anthony Wayne. More than 600 British were killed or taken prisoner.

1779 Sep 3-Oct 28: An unsuccessful **siege of Savannah,** Ga., which had been captured by the British in late 1778, was conducted by a French fleet under Adm. d'Estaing supported by American forces on land. On Oct. 9 Count Casimir Pulaski, a Polish officer in American service, was mortally wounded in a disastrous assault on the city.

1779 Sep 23: **John Paul Jones,** commanding the *Bon-*

homme Richard, defeated and captured the *Serapis,* a British man-of-war commanded by Capt. Richard Pearson. It was during this engagement that Jones, when asked if he had struck his colors (surrendered), replied "I have not yet begun to fight." After three hours of brutal fighting, Pearson surrendered to Jones. The Americans transferred to the *Serapis* from their own ship, which sank a day later.

II. Architecture
Arts and Music
Popular Entertainment
Publishing
Theater

The American Revolution provided fresh material for the new nation's poets. Philip Freneau, who was later to earn the title "poet of the American Revolution," wrote a number of satirical poems, among them "General Gage's Soliloquy" (1775) and "General Gage's Confession" (1775), before leaving America in 1776 for the Caribbean. Returning in 1778, he was captured by the British and released. He then turned his poetic talents to the revolutionary cause. Francis Hopkinson, in his ballad "The Battle of the Kegs" (1778), satirized the British reaction during an actual incident, a mine attack launched by David Bushnell on the British fleet in Philadelphia in Jan. 1778. The poem enraged the British and delighted the Patriots, and was the most popular poem of its day. Later poets found the American Revolution a rich source of material. Henry Wadsworth Longfellow immortalized Paul Revere's 1775 ride to alert the Minutemen at Lexington and Concord in his classic American poem "Paul Revere's Ride" (1861).

1776 Jan 10: *Common Sense* by Thomas Paine was published. The pamphlet, which contained the first demand for complete independence for the American colonies, sold 100,000 copies in less than three months. No other book in the U.S. has had such a quick or large sale relative to population. The pamphlet was highly influential in swinging the tide of popular opinion toward a clean break with the mother country.

1776 July 6: The **Declaration of Independence was published** for the first time in the *Pennsylvania Evening Post* under the title "A Declaration by the Representatives of the United States of America, in General Congress assembled." The *Post* was sold for "only two coppers" and was published every Tuesday, Thursday, and Saturday evening. A four-page paper, it devoted its entire front page and the first column of its second page to the Declaration.

1777: The first American edition of the **Bible** in English was published. It consisted of the New Testament alone. The first complete Bible in English published in America appeared in 1782.

III. Business and Industry
Education
Philosophy and Religion
Science

Despite the outbreak of war, new religious groups continued to find the colonies an excellent place in which to grow. Among them was the Universalist Church of America, founded by John Murray, a convert from Methodism who came to America from England in 1770. He traveled and preached for four years in New Jersey, New York, and New England before settling in Gloucester, Mass. In 1775 George Washington named him chaplain to the Rhode Island troops. In 1779 Murray became pastor of the Gloucester First Church, the first Universalist church in the U.S. The Universalist movement spread and in 1790 a convention was held in Philadelphia that drew up a profession of faith and a congregational organization. Murray's Universalism was basically Calvinistic. Later, under Hosea Ballou, pastor for may years of the Second Universalist Society in Boston, the Calvinist strains of Universalism began to diminish.

1775 Feb 22: The **first joint stock manufacturing company** in America, the American Manufactory of Woolens, Linens, and Cottons, was established to promote the production and distribution of textile products. Shares sold on a subscription basis at £10 apiece.

1775 Mar 10: Daniel Boone began blazing the **Wilderness Road,** from Fort Chiswell in the Shenandoah Valley of Virginia, southwest then west through the Cumberland Gap into Kentucky and to the Ohio R., where Boone established a fort and terminal station he named Boonesborough. Although the Wilderness Road was for many years the main route for western traffic, it was not improved for wagon traffic until 1795.

1776 Dec 5: The **Phi Beta Kappa** fraternity was founded at the College of William and Mary as a social fraternity of five students. It was the first social fraternity at an American college. In 1831 Phi Beta Kappa became an honorary fraternity for students of academic distinction.

IV. Fashion
   Folkways
   Holidays
   Social Issues and Crime
   Sports

The somewhat obscure and uncertain history of the American flag began during this period. In Oct. 1775, when Congress created the first naval force, it also set down rules for creation of a flag. The result, variously called Congress Colors, the Grand Union Flag, or the First Navy Ensign, was a flag of 13 alternating red and white stripes, with a field of blue bearing the crosses of St. George and St. Andrew. This flag is believed to be the one raised by Lt. John Paul Jones aboard Commodore Esek Hopkins's flagship *Alfred* on the Delaware R. at Philadelphia on Dec. 3, 1775. The first land raising of the Grand Union Flag occurred at Prospect Hill in Somerville, Mass., on Jan. 1, 1776, during the American siege of Boston. On June 14, 1777, Congress adopted what became known as the Stars and Stripes, a flag of 13 red and white stripes with a blue field bearing 13 stars, one for each state. The tradition that Betsy Ross designed the flag has been almost completely discredited. It has been suggested that Francis Hopkinson, a member of the Continental Navy Board from 1776 to 1778, was the father of the Stars and Stripes.

1775: James Adair wrote a description of a **lacrosse** game played by Cherokee Indians in Florida. They used a deerskin ball stuffed hard with deer's hair and bats two feet long with deerskin thongs. The game usually was played for high stakes between two large groups, equal in number, and the ball was kept in the air for long periods of time. The Indians were evidently very good at the game.

1775 June 17: The memorable words "**Don't fire until you see the whites of their eyes**" were uttered, according to tradition, by Col. William Prescott at the Battle of Bunker Hill. The injunction, by no means completely original, was also ascribed to Gen. Israel Putnam.

1775 Dec 3: Raising of the **first official American flag** took place aboard the *Alfred,* the flagship of Commodore Esek Hopkins, on the Delaware R. Because the Navy was governed by Congress the flag was called Congress Colors, and was later variously known as the Grand Union Flag and First Navy Ensign. This standard remained the colonial flag until superseded by the Stars and Stripes on June 14, 1777.

1777 June 14: Congress authorized the **Stars and Stripes,** a flag consisting of 13 stripes alternating red and white, and 13 white stars on a field of blue "representing the new constellation." June 14 has since been observed as Flag Day, although the resolution did not go into effect until Sept. 3, 1777.

1780–1784

I. Civil Rights
  Exploration and Settlement
  Government
  Statistics
  Wars

By 1780 the Continental Army had suffered its worst privations, its greatest defeats, and its darkest hours. It would continue to lose battles but, by this time turned into a well-trained fighting force by European officers and aided by allied French forces, it endured and marched to ultimate victory at Yorktown, Va., in Aug. 1781. The military phase of the conflict ended at Yorktown, but the diplomatic struggle continued. Preliminary articles of peace were secured on Nov. 30, 1782, after long and difficult negotiations. The Treaty of Paris, by which the war was officially ended and independence formally acknowledged by Great Britain, was not signed until Sept. 3, 1783.

1780: The estimated colonial **population** was 2,781,000.

1780 Mar 1: Pennsylvania became the **first state to abolish slavery** (Vermont had not yet joined the Union). The law provided that no child born after the date of its passage would be a slave.

1780 Aug 16: In the Battle of **Camden,** S.C., American forces uder Gen. Horatio Gates were defeated by the British under Gen. Charles Cornwallis. Baron Johann de Kalb, a Prussian officer who was commissioned a general in the Continental Army, was mortally wounded in the battle.

1780 Oct 2: Maj. **John André,** adjutant general to British Gen. Sir Henry Clinton, was hanged as a spy at Tappan, N.Y. André had been apprehended on Sept. 23 by three militiamen as he returned from a secret meeting with Gen. Benedict Arnold, who, as commander of West Point, had agreed to surrender the key American fort on the Hudson R. to the British. The plot uncovered, Arnold fled to safety in New York City.

1780 Oct 7: British and Tory forces were defeated at **King's Mountain,** S.C., by Americans under Col. William Campbell, Col. Isaac Shelby, and Col. Benjamin Cleveland. The British commander, Maj. Patrick Ferguson, and 150 others were killed. Nearly 800 prisoners were taken.

1781 Mar 1: The **Articles of Confederation** were ratified by Maryland, the last state to do so.

1781 Mar 15: In the Battle of **Guilford Court House,** N.C., Gen. Cornwallis defeated an American force led by Gen. Nathanael Greene, but heavy losses were suffered by both the British and Americans.

1781 Aug 1: Yorktown, Va., was occupied by the British under Gen. Cornwallis, who sought supplies and reinforcements from Gen. Clinton in New York City.

1781 Sep 9: At **Eutaw Springs,** S.C., the American forces under Gen. Nathanael Greene were forced to withdraw after an assault upon the British under Col. Alexander Stewart.

1781 Oct 19: Gen. **Cornwallis surrendered at Yorktown.** The capitulation, which yielded about 8000 British prisoners, virtually brought the war to an end.

1782: An **emancipation law** was enacted by the Virginia legislature under urging by Thomas Jefferson. The bill made it lawful for any man "by last will and testament or other instrument in writing sealed and witnessed, to emancipate and set free his slaves."

1782: The **Great Seal of the United States** was adopted. It was first used on Sept. 16, 1782, on a document granting Gen. Washington authority to consult with the British about prisoner exchanges. On Sept. 15, 1789, Congress declared that the Great Seal was to be the official seal of the U.S. and that it was to be kept in custody of the secretary of state. Since then six dies of the seal have been officially cut and used.

1783: Slavery was made illegal in Massachusetts by a judicial interpretation of the state constitution of 1780, in which text stating that all men were "born free and equal" was construed as legal nullification of slavery. This year also saw the slave trade outlawed in Maryland.

1783 Sep 3: The **Treaty of Paris** was signed by representatives of the U. S. and Great Britain, thus ending the American Revolution. American independence was recognized by the British and the boundaries of the new republic agreed upon: the Great Lakes and Florida to the north and south, and the Mississippi R. to the west. Benjamin Franklin, John Jay, and John Adams were the American agents during the peace negotiations in Paris.

1784: Slavery was abolished in Connecticut and Rhode Island.

II. Architecture
   Arts and Music
   Popular Entertainment
   Publishing
   Theater

During the American Revolution and the early uncertain days of independence, American intellectual life continued its steady development. The American Academy of Arts and Sciences, the second oldest learned society in the U.S., was founded in Boston on May 4, 1780. The academy, like others of the period, was largely local but kept in touch with other groups. It joined, for example, in an unsuccessful attempt to have the duty on foreign books repealed. The academy began publishing *Memoirs* in 1785 and *Proceedings* in 1846. The moving spirit in starting the academy was James Bowdoin, a leading political figure in Massachusetts who, like many other public figures of the time, was interested in arts and sciences. He was the academy's first president. Bowdoin College in Maine was named for him.

1782: *M'Fingal* by John Trumbull was published in its complete form. The first two of its four sections had been published in 1775. A lively debate on revolutionary matters, it was for a time considered one of the greatest of the American poems.

1782: *Letters from an American Farmer* by J. Hector St. John de Crèvecoeur, an extremely popular book on early American life around the time of the American Revolution, was published. The author, whose real name was Michel Guillaume Jean de Crèvecoeur, was a Frenchman who settled in New York, where he collected his famous impressions of the New World. The *Letters* reflected the "noble savage" views of the eighteenth century. The book was reprinted five times in English and appeared in three French editions and two German translations. Crèvecoeur traveled extensively in America, became a naturalized citizen, and was an experienced woodsman and farmer. *Letters from an American Farmer* contains 12 letters reflecting in warm and vivid detail his knowledge of farm life, animals, and the geography of the colonies. He believed in the simple life espoused by Jean Jacques Rousseau and popularized the idea of the Physiocrats that the goodness of man was traced from his connection with the soil. Crèvecoeur in his writings idealized the new man who was to come from the American experiment.

1783: *The American Speller* by Noah Webster was published. It was the first part of Webster's *A Grammatical Institute of the English Language*, which included a grammar (1784) and a reader (1785). As a separate work, Webster's *Speller* supplanted for a time the *New England Primer* as the principal text for the early grades of public school. It included stories, aphorisms, and maxims on ethical behavior.

1783 May 30: The **first daily newspaper** in the U.S., the *Pennsylvania Evening Post* published by Benjamin Towne, began publication in Philadelphia, Pa.

III. Business and Industry
Education
Philosophy and Religion
Science

By the late eighteenth century medical scientists in Europe and America were questioning older practices and theories. In the U.S. Benjamin Rush was the foremost medical scientist of his time, and he typified the new attitude. He was the author of the earliest important work on mental disorders, *Medical Inqui-*

ries and Observations upon the Diseases of the Mind
(1812). Another of Rush's studies, *An Inquiry into the
Effects of Spiritous Liquors on the Human Body and
Mind* (1784), provided scientific support for the temperance movement. Rush, a signer of the Declaration
of Independence, became the first professor of chemistry in America in 1769, at the College of Philadelphia and, at the University of Pennsylvania after 1792
he developed the best medical school in the U.S. Unfortunately, in spite of his pioneering investigations
of the relationship of bodily and mental illnesses,
Rush also remained a strong advocate of bloodletting
and purging and so delayed discontinuance of these
practices.

1781 Dec 31: The **Bank of North America** was established by Congress. Under the Articles of Confederation, Congress could not tax, so the Bank of North
America was founded with a capitalization of
$400,000 to supply the federal government with
money.

1783: The **first Protestant Episcopal bishop** in America, Dr. Samuel Seabury, was elected by ten of his
fellow ministers at Woodbury, Conn.

1784: A major **depression** crippled the U.S. economy,
prompting the states to institute separate measures to
aid recovery. The hardships suffered during this depression, which did not end until 1788, led to Shays'
Rebellion in 1787.

1784: A lucrative new **trade route** was opened to American merchantmen when the *Empress of China* sailed
from Sandy Hook, N.J., around Cape Horn with a
cargo of ginseng root for which the Chinese were
willing to pay enormous prices. The voyage lasted a
year and was very profitable. The trade route enabled
American commerce to recover from the crippling
British blockade during the American Revolution. By
1789, eighteen American merchantmen were plying
their way to the harbor of Canton. Salem, Mass., had
become the main American port for the China trade.

1784 Nov 18: Samuel Seabury, the first American Protestant Episcopal bishop, was consecrated by the Scottish bishops in Aberdeen and Moray in contravention
of the wishes of the Archbishop of Canterbury.

1784 Dec 24: The **Methodist Church** was organized in America at a conference in Baltimore, Md., even though in England the Methodists did not formally separate from the Church of England until 1791. John Wesley, the founder of Methodism, had sent the Rev. Thomas Coke to America this year as superintendent of the Methodist societies. Francis Asbury was to be associate superintendent. Asbury, however, dominated the conference, was elected superintendent, and then assumed the title of bishop. Although in ill health all his life, Asbury traveled on horseback more than 5000 miles a year to supervise and expand the Methodist Church.

IV. Fashion
   Folkways
   Holidays
   Social Issues and Crime
   Sports

American cabinetmakers and furniture designers were becoming the equal of any in artistic ability. Chief among them were William Savery, John Goddard, Jonathan Gostelow, and, beginning in the 1790s, Duncan Phyfe. Savery is believed to have lived in Philadelphia from about 1740 and was noted for his original interpretation of eighteenth-century English designs, especially the Queen Anne style. John Goddard was a member of a Newport, R.I., Quaker family of cabinetmakers. His pieces, especially his secretaries, were known for their stateliness. Goddard developed a characteristic block front design that divided the front of his pieces into three equal sections. Examples of Goddard's work are quite scarce. Gostelow worked in Philadelphia and showed originality at a time when many Americans were following English designs. His work had graceful but substantial lines rather than elaboration or ornamentation. In 1788 Gostelow was elected chairman of the Gentlemen Cabinet and Chair Makers of Philadelphia, and in 1789 he made and presented an elaborate font to Christ Church. Phyfe emigrated from

Scotland and about 1792 set up shop in New York. He was noted for his use of mahogany and held to high standards of workmanship. His early designs boasted excellent proportions and graceful curves. Later he adopted the Empire style. His final designs were heavily ornamented. He was so much copied that a Duncan Phyfe style came into being.

1783: The **pace of public transportation** in the U.S. was painfully slow. It took Thomas Jefferson five days to travel from Philadelphia to Baltimore.

1783: By this time some **100,000 Loyalists had fled the U.S.** Also known as Tories, they had suffered various penalties for their loyalty to the Crown, including confiscation of property, removal from public office, and punitive taxation. Probably no more than 10% of the colonials were Tories, who were generally well-to-do, engaged in commerce or the professions, or public officials. Many fled to Canada, some to England. Some returned after the war. Many, however, had remained behind. After the conflict many were able to recover at least some of their confiscated property.

1783 May 13: The **Society of Cincinnati** was founded by veteran officers of the American Revolution. Its membership was restricted to the eldest male descendants of Revolutionary soldiers. George Washington was its first president-general and Gen. Alexander Hamilton its second.

1785–1789

I. Civil Rights
Exploration and Settlement
Government
Statistics
Wars

In the nation's early years, it became clear that the Articles of Confederation, which had gone into effect in 1781, were inadequate for the effective government of the United States. On May 25, 1787, the Constitutional Convention convened in Philadelphia. Eventually, all the newly independent states except Rhode Island sent delegates to the session that at first was expected merely to amend the Articles of Confederation. As it turned out, the delegates wrote a new charter, the Constitution of the U.S. Many problems were solved after long debate, such as the question of fair representation for large and small states. This issue resulted in a compromise whereby in the Senate all states would be equally represented but in the House of Representatives representation would be based on population. George Washington was president of the convention and other leading delegates included Benjamin Franklin, James Madison, Gouverneur Morris, Roger Sherman, and Edmund Randolph. Final agreement was reached on Sept. 17 and the document was submitted to the states for ratification. This process reached a conclusion on June 21, 1788, by which time nine states had ratified, the number necessary to put the Constitution into effect. The debate had been long and aroused great passion along with much opposition. Eventually, the other four original states also ratified.

1785: Slavery was made illegal in New York.

1785 July 6: A new **coinage system,** based on the Spanish milled dollar, was proposed in Congress by Thomas Jefferson. He proposed a gold piece with a value of ten dollars, a dollar in silver, a tenth of a dollar in silver, and a hundredth of a dollar in copper. This proposal was adopted by Congress, and on Aug. 8, 1786, a full plan of coinage was enacted.

1786: Slavery was outlawed in New Jersey.

1787 Jan 25: Shays' Rebellion, a farmers' uprising named for its leader Daniel Shays, reached its climax when Shays led 1100 men in an attempt to seize the arsenal in Springfield, Mass. State militia commanded by Gen. William Shepherd routed the insurgents. The uprising had been caused by the harsh economic conditions faced by Massachusetts farmers, who sought reforms and the issuance of paper money.

1787 July 13: The **Northwest Ordinance,** enacted by Congress under the Articles of Confederation, established the Northwest Territory, the region bounded by the Great Lakes on the north, the Ohio R. on the south, and the Mississippi R. on the west. The ordinance established a government for the territory, provided that it could form no fewer than three nor more than five states, set up the procedure by which statehood was to be achieved, and barred slavery in the territory.

1787 Dec 7: Delaware became the first state to ratify the Constitution.

1787 Dec 12: Pennsylvania ratified the Constitution and became the second state of the Union.

1787 Dec 18: New Jersey ratified the Constitution and became the third state of the Union.

1788 Jan 2: Georgia ratified the Constitution and became the fourth state of the Union.

1788 Jan 9: Connecticut ratified the Constitution and became the fifth state of the Union.

1788 Feb 6: Massachusetts ratified the Constitution and became the sixth state of the Union.

1788 Apr 28: Maryland ratified the Constitution and became the seventh state of the Union.

1788 May 23: South Carolina ratified the Constitution and became the eighth state of the Union.

1788 June 21: New Hampshire ratified the Constitution and became the ninth state of the Union. With this ratification the Constitution became effective, though not declared in effect until Mar. 4, 1789.

1788 June 25: Virginia ratified the Constitution and became the tenth state of the Union.

1788 July 26: New York ratified the Constitution and became the 11th state of the Union. For a time North Carolina and Rhode Island refused to ratify, but the introduction of a bill of rights and the threat of economic sanctions eventually induced them to join.

1788 Sep 30-1790 Aug 31: In the **first congressional elections** under the Constitution the federalists gained a 17–9 Senate majority over the antifederalists. In the House the federalists took a 38–26 majority. Senators were chosen by state legislatures until 1913, when the Seventeenth Amendment provided for their popular election. Members of the House were elected by popular vote, but some states held statewide elections and others held elections by district. Also, some states held elections in odd-numbered years, a practice that faded out in the late nineteenth century.

1789: The **Federalist Party** was formed by those who had supported ratification of the Constitution. Considered pro-English, they enjoyed considerable success until 1800, when Thomas Jefferson, a Democratic-Republican, defeated John Adams for the presidency. Eventually the party lost its supporters and ceased to exist about 1820. Alexander Hamilton was one of the party's founders and foremost leaders.

1789 Mar 4: The **first session of the U.S. Congress** convened, but only 9 of 22 senators and 13 of 59 representatives appeared. The House had its first quorum on Apr. 1, the Senate on Apr. 5. On Apr. 6 the first Congress was formally organized.

1789 Apr 30: George Washington, Federalist of Virginia, was inaugurated president of the United States.

1789 July 27: The U.S. **State Department** was established by Congress. Thomas Jefferson became the first secretary of state in Feb. 1790.

1789 Aug 7: The U.S. **War Department** was established. Pres. Washington selected Henry Knox to be the first secretary of war. At this time the regular army numbered 840 men who supervised public lands and guarded the Indian frontier.

1789 Sep 2: The U.S. **Treasury Department** was established by Congress. Alexander Hamilton became the first secretary of the treasury.

1789 Sep 26: Congress confirmed John Jay's appointment as the **first chief justice of the U.S. Supreme Court.** He was appointed by Pres. Washington and served for six years.

1789 Sep 26: Samuel Osgood was appointed the **first postmaster general** of the U.S. by Pres. Washington. Osgood resigned in Aug. 1791 because of the government's removal from New York City to Philadelphia.

1789 Sep 26: Edmund J. Randolph was appointed **attorney general** of the U.S. by Pres. Washington. In 1794 he succeeded Thomas Jefferson as secretary of state.

1789 Nov 21: North Carolina ratified the Constitution and became the 12th state of the Union.

II. Architecture
Arts and Music
Popular Entertainment
Publishing
Theater

The leading publishing event of the period was the serial publication, beginning Oct. 27, 1787, of *The Federalist*, probably the greatest American work on political theory. This series of essays, an outgrowth of the debate over adoption of the Constitution, began with the intent of persuading New York State and others to ratify the new document. The last essay was published on Apr. 4, 1788. The series of 85 essays was initiated by Alexander Hamilton of New York, who wrote at least 51 of the papers. James Madison of Virginia wrote 14 and John Jay of New York wrote five. The authorship of the other 15 is debatable as between Hamilton and Madison. The essays were widely read as they appeared in newspapers, but actually had little effect on the debate over ratification. They did, however, make clear the basic problems of republican government and defended federalism as a means of creating a strong state while perserving individuals from tyranny. The essays appeared in book form in two volumes published between March and May of 1788.

1786: The **first extended theatrical engagements** in America were seen this year. Lewis Hallam, Jr.'s, American Company, performing in New York City, gave seven performances of Richard Brinsley Sheridan's *The School for Scandal* (1777) and 18 of John O'Keefe's *The Poor Soldier*. This year also saw the first U.S. performance of *Hamlet*, in New York City at the John Street Theater by Hallam's company with the Irish actor John Henry.

1787 Apr 16: *The Contrast* by Royall Tyler, the first American comedy to be performed on a regular stage by a company of professional actors, opened at the John Street Theater in New York City. It became an immediate success. The first stage Yankee in American history appeared as the hero in this pro-democratic play, which ridiculed aristocratic values while extolling the rustic virtues of the hero.

1788: A volume of *Miscellaneous Works* by Philip Freneau was published. This book, combined with Freneau's collected *Poems* (1786), marked Freneau's emergence as a major American poet. Some memorable poems appeared in these volumes, for example, "To the Hurricane" and "The Indian Burying Ground." "The Wild Honey Suckle" was considered Freneau's finest poem.

1789: What has been called the **first American novel,** *The Power of Sympathy; or The Triumph of Nature* by William Hill Brown, was published. The book was written "to expose the dangerous Consequences of Seduction and to set forth the advantages of female Education."

1789: The **Virginia Capitol** was built at Richmond from plans by Thomas Jefferson. It was generally considered the first building of the Classic Revival style in the U.S.

1789 Mar 2: A **law prohibiting theatrical performances** was repealed in Pennsylvania. A more permissive attitude toward theater was seen in all the states.

III. Business and Industry
Education
Philosophy and Religion
Science

Unitarianism took root in the U.S. during this period. Although the foundations of Unitarianism—the belief that God exists in only one being rather than in the trinity of Father, Son, and Holy Spirit—originated in the sixteenth century, it was 1785 before the doctrine came to the U.S. The Unitarian movement in America originated from a change in the Episcopalian liturgy at King's Chapel in Boston. The clergyman responsible was James Freeman, a Harvard graduate. In 1796 Joseph Priestley, the English scientist, established a Unitarian church in Philadelphia. Separate congregations gradually formed themselves into a denomination, adopting the name Unitarian about 1815. Unitarianism grew out of the liberal wing of Congregationalism and was strongest in New England.

1785: Regular stage routes linking New York City, Boston, Albany, and Philadelphia were initiated. The trip from Boston to New York took six days with coaches traveling from 3 A.M. until 10 P.M.

1785: The **first American turnpike,** known as the Little River Turnpike, was authorized by the state of Virginia.

1785: The charter of the **Bank of North America** was revoked by the Pennsylvania legislature. The bank's enemies charged it with causing the economic depression that had begun in 1784. When things did not get better, supporters of the bank claimed that trade was bad because the bank's charter had been lost. In 1787 Democratic-Republicans won control of the state legislature and rechartered the bank. It was the first bank owned and operated by and for merchants. It acquired capital and influence so quickly that it became a center of political rivalry and ambition.

1786: The **first steamboat in America,** built by John Fitch, sailed on the Delaware R. On Aug. 22, 1787, Fitch ran his second and improved boat on the Delaware R. It used a system of upright paddles at the sides of the boat and attained a speed of three mph.

1786: The first recorded **strike** in the U.S. was called by the printers of Philadelphia, Pa. They were successful in obtaining a wage of $6 a week.

1787: The **first cotton factory** in New England was established at Beverly, Mass., under the management of John Cabot and Joshua Fisher.

1787: In a move to promote **manufacturing**, the Pennsylvania Society for the Encouragement of Manufactures and Useful Acts was organized. It supported a protective tariff, inventions, and research. Its Committee on Manufactures, chosen by subscribers to a manufacturing fund, agreed to promote cotton manufacturing and ordered two English carding and spinning machines. By the end of 1788, its factory put out 10,000 yards of cotton and linen. New York City, Boston, and Baltimore established similar societies in the same year, and were soon followed by other cities.

1789 July 4: The **first tariff bill** enacted by Congress set up protective duties on more than 30 different commodities.

IV. Fashion
Folkways
Holidays
Social Issues and Crime
Sports

The widely practiced custom of bundling, prevalent in colonial days in New England and Pennsylvania especially, was dying out. The cold of northern winters, which had been a major contributor to the custom's popularity, was now alleviated by better heating and sturdier houses. To bundle, engaged or courting couples got into bed together, but with most or all of their clothes on. The couple was sometimes separated by a board and some girls tied their ankles together. Although bundling implied no improper relationship, it became the target of reformers and was abandoned by the early nineteenth century, although there were reports of bundling in the backwoods of western Pennsylvania in the 1840s.

c1785: The style of **men's clothing** during this period was reflected in a description by a printer of Boston: "He wore a pea-green coat, white vest, nankeen small clothes, white silk stockings, and pumps fastened with silver buckles which covered at least half the foot from instep to toe. His small clothes were tied at the knees with ribbon of the same colour in double bows, the ends reaching down to the ancles. His hair in front was loaded with pomatum, frizzled or craped and powdered. Behind, his natural hair was augmented by the addition of a large queue called vulgarly a false tail, which, enrolled in some yards of black ribbon, hung half-way down his back."

1788 May: A celebrated gray stallion, **Messenger,** believed to be the original sire of a fine breed of trotting horses, arrived from England. His line was so successful that upon his death he was buried with military honors on Jan. 8, 1808.

1789: The beginning of a **social courtesy** that was soon to spread elsewhere was seen in the following announcement at a performance in the Park Theater, New York City: "The offensive practice to Ladies, and dangerous to the House, of smoking segars during the performance, it is hoped, every gentlemen will consent to an absolute prohibition of."

1789 May 7: The **first inaugural ball,** to honor Pres. Washington, was held at the Assembly Rooms, New York City.

1789 May 12: The **Society of Tammany** held its first meeting in New York. Its name was derived from an ancient and wise chief of the Delaware Indians, Tammany, and the society was essentially anti-Federalist in character. Its chief founder and first grand sachem was William Mooney.

1789 Nov 26: Thanksgiving Day was celebrated for the first time as a national holiday. Pres. Washington, at the request of Congress, had proclaimed it a day of thanksgiving for the Constitution. Anti-Federalists protested that his proclamation violated states' rights.

1790–1794

I. Civil Rights
Exploration and Settlement
Government
Statistics
Wars

Probably the most important political event of this period was adoption of the Bill of Rights, the first ten amendments to the U.S. Constitution. Some had opposed adoption of the Constitution because of its lack of guarantees of such rights as freedom of worship, freedom of speech, freedom of the press, and freedom of assembly. Supporters of the Constitution had promised that if ratified, it would be amended in these respects. Accordingly, on Sept. 25, 1789, Congress voted to submit the amendments to the states. They became part of the Constitution on Dec. 15, 1791, when Virginia ratified them, thereby completing the required number of state ratifications for passage into law.

1790-1791: In **congressional elections** the Federalists took a 16–13 Senate majority over the Republicans. In the House the Federalists led 37–33.

1790 Mar 1: The **first U.S. Census** was authorized by Congress. It was completed on Aug. 1. The population was placed at 3,929,625 including 697,624 slaves and 59,557 free blacks. The most populous state was Virginia, with 747,610 people, and the largest city was Philadelphia, with a population of 42,444. The center of U.S. population was about equally divided between New England and the Middle Atlantic States, and the South. Massachusetts was the only state to report no slaves.

1790 Apr 10: The **first circumnavigation of the globe by an American vessel** was accomplished when Capt. Robert Gray docked the *Columbia* in Boston harbor. On a voyage for a group of Boston merchants, Gray had sailed from Boston in Sept. 1787 with a cargo of goods to be traded for furs with Indians of the Pacific Northwest. Gray then carried a valuable cargo of sea otter skins to Canton, China, and sailed on around the world, a voyage of almost 42,000 miles. His trip opened up trade between New England and the Pacific Northwest, which brought great wealth to New England merchants. The trip also helped establish U.S. claims to the Oregon Territory. On May 11, 1792, during a second voyage, Gray became the first white man to enter the Columbia R.

1790 Apr 17: Benjamin Franklin died in Philadelphia at 84. Lord Jeffrey, editor of the *Edinburgh Review*, wrote of him: "In one point of view the name of Franklin must be considered as standing higher than any of the others which illustrated the Eighteenth Century. Distinguished as a statesman he was equally great as a philosopher, thus united in himself a rare degree of excellence in both these pursuits, to excel in either of which is deemed the highest praise." Franklin's funeral and burial in Christ Church Yard drew 20,000 spectators, the largest gathering in the U.S. to that time.

1790 May 29: Rhode Island ratified the Constitution and became the 13th state of the Union.

1790 May 31: The first U.S. copyright act was signed by Pres. George Washington. The new law protected plays, maps, and books. The term of protection was for 14 years, with the right of renewal for another 14 years. The work's title page had to be deposited in the clerk's office of the local U.S. district court. Passage of the law was credited largely to the efforts of Noah Webster. Until the eighteenth century copyright had remained, on the whole, a matter of common law, and protection ebbed and flowed with the tides of political fortune. But in 1710 Parliament passed the Statute of Anne, which provided protection for up to 28 years. It became standard in the colonies as well as in England. After the American Revolution, however, the various states were lax about establishing copyright prerogatives. When Webster was ready to publish his *American Spelling Book,* he soon discovered that he would have no say in the disposition of his work. He began a tour of the states to campaign for new legislation. His campaign for a uniform copyright law coincided with the Federalists' desire for a strong central government, and the measure was passed.

1791 Mar 3: The **first internal revenue law** was passed by Congress. Fourteen revenue districts were created and a tax of 20 to 30 cents a gallon put on distilled spirits. The legislatures of North Carolina, Virginia, and Maryland passed resolutions of disapproval shortly thereafter.

1791 Mar 4: Vermont joined the Union, becoming the 14th state. It had ratified the Constitution in January.

1792–1793: In **congressional elections** the Federalists held a 17–13 Senate majority over the Republicans. In the House the Republicans took a 57–48 majority over the Federalists.

1792: The **Republican Party,** also known as the Democratic-Republican or Antifederalist Party, was formed. This party later became the Democratic Party. It was formed to oppose the Federalists, who were considered pro-English and against a republican form of government. Thomas Jefferson, who was sympathetic toward the French Revolution, became party leader. The Republicans enjoyed overwhelming popularity until 1820.

1792 Apr 2: Congress passed the **Coinage Act,** establishing the first U.S. Mint, to be constructed in Philadelphia, Pa. The act provided for a decimal system of coinage and a standard of bimetallism, with silver and gold as legal tender at a ratio of 15 to 1 by weight. David Rittenhouse, the astronomer and instrument maker who had succeeded Benjamin Franklin as president of the American Philosophical Society in 1791, was named first director of the mint.

1792 June 1: Kentucky became the 15th state. It previously had been part of Virginia territory.

1792 Dec 5: George Washington was reelected president of the United States. John Adams was elected vice president. The electoral vote was Washington, 132; Adams, Federalist of Massachusetts, 77; George Clinton, Antifederalist of New York, 50.

1794-1795: In **congressional elections** the Federalists gained two Senate seats for a 19–13 majority. In the House they gained six seats for a 54–52 majority.

1794 July-Nov: The **Whiskey Rebellion** broke out in western Pennsylvania among farmers opposed to a federal excise tax on liquor passed in 1791. On Aug. 7 Pres. Washington issued a proclamation ordering the insurgents to go home and calling out a militia force of several thousand from four states. He issued another proclamation on Sept. 24 and ordered the militia to suppress the uprising. For a time Washington led this force in person. By mid-November the trouble was over. Two men were convicted of treason but Washington pardoned them.

1794 Nov 19: The **Jay Treaty** was concluded between Great Britain and the U.S. It was widely denounced in America because it continued to allow the British the right to search U.S. ships and impress American seamen on the grounds that they were actually of British birth and citizenship.

II. Architecture
Arts and Music
Popular Entertainment
Publishing
Theater

Scientists traveled widely in the U.S. because there was much to study that was new and because there were unique flora and fauna. Invariably, such men wrote about their journeys. While these men wrote as scientists, their writings can also be categorized as travel books. The travelers gloried in the beauty and magnitude of American scenery and often were imbued with the spirit of the Romantic movement. Such a naturalist-author was William Bartram, son of John Bartram, who had earlier recorded his trips to Lake Ontario and Florida. William wrote *Travels Through North and South Carolina, Georgia, East and West Florida, the Cherokee Country, the Extensive Territories of the Muscogulges, or Creek Confederacy, and the Country of the Chactaws* (1791). In the book Bartram revealed a vision of "natural man." His enthusiastic descriptions of scenery influenced such writers as William Wordsworth and Samuel Taylor Coleridge, the latter terming the book one of "high merit."

1790: Printing began on ***Dobson's Encyclopaedia,*** a magnificent American edition in 18 volumes of the *Encyclopaedia Britannica.* Special types were prepared for the task, and a great number of engravings of fine workmanship were made on Pennsylvania paper. Printing required seven years, the cost of the venture being covered by subscription. When completed, the encyclopedia was hailed as the greatest achievement of the press in America up to that time.

1791 Mar: The first part of ***The Rights of Man*** by Thomas Paine was published in England. An incendiary document, it attacked monarchy, supported the French Revolution, and argued forcibly in favor of democracy, republican government, and personal freedom and rights. The British government considered the work seditious and charged Paine with treason. He fled to France in 1792, was tried in absentia, and was banished from Great Britain.

1792: The cornerstone of the **Capitol** was laid in Washington, D.C. The building was completed about 1830, though it was in use before then. It was designed by William Thornton following lines of English country mansions in the Palladian mode.

1792: Work on the **White House** in Washington, D.C., was begun, following plans by James Hoban. The building was a sumptuous example of post-colonial architecture, modeled after the palace of the Duke of Leinster in Ireland. Burned by the British in 1814, it was rebuilt in 1818 and restored in 1951.

1793: ***American Poems, Selected and Original,*** an anthology of poems selected by Elihu Hubbard Smith, was published at Litchfield, Conn. The anthology was devoted largely to the group of writers who became known as the Hartford Wits or Connecticut Wits, including John Trumbull, Joel Barlow, Timothy Dwight, and Lemuel Hopkins, all of whom were

1793: New York City's first daily newspaper and the second daily in the country, the *American Minerva,* was founded by Noah Webster. He edited the paper for ten years, during which time it was strongly Federalist and anti-French. In 1797 the name was changed to the *Commercial Advertiser.* In 1905 the *Advertiser* in turn was combined with the New York *Globe,* which in turn was absorbed by the New York *Sun* in 1923.

1794: The **Boston Theater** was opened under the management of Charles Stuart Powell after repeal of the law of 1750 prohibiting plays in Boston.

1794: The first part of *The Age of Reason* by Thomas Paine was published in Paris. This deistic work was written with frequently faulty logic but unmistakable fervor and conviction. The book had a profound effect and was especially popular with common people, who resented religious as well as political tyranny. On Dec. 27, 1793, after completing the first part of the book, Paine was thrown into prison for his opposition to the Reign of Terror then raging in revolutionary France. He completed the rest of his book under the shadow of the guillotine, and it was published on his release in 1795.

III. Business and Industry
Education
Philosophy and Religion
Science

Although the U.S. was primarily an agricultural nation, some manufacturing had begun. There were those who thought that with independence the new nation should encourage manufacturing as a way of avoiding dependence on other nations. Chief among these persons was Alexander Hamilton, first secretary of the treasury, who submitted his *Report on the Subject of Manufactures* in 1791. The report favored

tariffs and government bounties and said such policies would create employment, attract immigrants,
and stimulate investment. Hamilton, however, received little support. Merchant and shipping interests
had more to gain from free trade, and the expanding
cotton regions of the South did not want tariffs that
would increase their costs.

1790 July 31: The **U.S. Patent Office** was opened. It has
been said that a dozen men from Connecticut were
waiting at the door, a colorful way of noting that
traditionally more inventors from Connecticut have
registered patents than from any other state. However, the first U.S. patent was issued to Samuel Hopkins of Vermont for a new method of making pearl-
ash and potash.

1790 Aug 4: Interest-bearing **government bonds** were
authorized by Congress. The 6% bonds were sold to
pay off the federal debt.

1790 Aug 15: The **first Roman Catholic bishop** in the
U.S., Father John Carroll, was consecrated at Lul-
worth Castle, England. He was selected by Pope Pius
VI, who also chose Baltimore as the first episcopal
see in America. Bishop Carroll held his first synod on
Nov. 7, 1791.

1790 Dec 21: The **cotton mill** of Almy, Brown, and
Slater began operation in Pawtucket, R.I., using British industrial methods. Samuel Slater had come to
America with a thorough understanding of the new
machinery invented in Britain by Richard Ark-
wright, Samuel Crompton, and James Hargreaves.
His factory was manned by children between four
and ten years of age. Slater was the first American
industrialist to break down the production process
into simple parts, enabling child labor to outproduce
skilled artisans.

1791 Dec 12: The **Bank of the U.S.** opened its main
branch in Philadelphia and additional branches in
the main urban centers of America. The bank served
the federal government as its fiscal representative.

1792: The first important **wooden truss bridge,** invented to suit American needs, was completed by Col.

Ewel Hale at Bellows Falls, Vt. Wood was plentiful in the area but rafts and barges would have been impeded by a bridge built on piles or with rows of arches. Hale's bridge consisted of two spans of 175 ft. each resting on an island.

1792 May 17: The **New York Stock Exchange** was organized at the Merchants Coffee House, New York City.

1793 May 25: The **first Roman Catholic priest ordained** in the U.S., Father Stephen Theodore Badin, was ordained in Baltimore, Md. He was a refugee from the French Revolution. After his ordination he served in Kentucky where he dedicated the first Catholic chapel in Lexington in 1800.

1793 Oct 28: **Eli Whitney** of Mulberry Grove, Ga., filed an application for a patent on the cotton gin. The patent was granted on Mar. 14, 1794. Cotton production mounted spectacularly after Whitney's invention, rising from 138,000 lbs. exported in 1800. Whitney, however, received very little in return for his invention. His machine's operating principle was stolen or duplicated by others in spite of his patent, and powerful interests opposed his fight for royalties. In 1812 Congress refused to renew his patent.

1794: The first independent **Methodist Church for blacks** was established in Philadelphia by Richard Allen, a former slave. In 1816 Allen became the first bishop of the African Methodist Episcopal Church when 16 black congregations united to form the new denomination.

1794: The first major **turnpike** in America was completed between Philadelphia and Lancaster, Pa. The large profits that could be realized by sponsoring such a company led to the construction of many such roads throughout America, often in areas where they were not necessary. Lancaster Turnpike, 62 mi. long, was the first macadam road in the U.S.

1794: One of the earliest American **canals** was built to circumnavigate South Hadley's falls on the Connecticut R. in Massachusetts. Its lift operated by means of inclined planes and cables powered by the current. At

about the same time construction of the Middlesex
Canal from Boston to the Merrimack R. was begun.
Its first section opened in 1804. The Middlesex Canal
was 27 miles long, and it cost about $3.50 for a stan-
dard barge to go its length. The sizes of the barges
were fixed by regulations. The barges were pulled by
horses.

IV. Fashion
   Folkways
   Holidays
   Social Issues and Crime
   Sports

During and after the American Revolution patriotic
societies sprang up in several cities. Among them
were the Tammany societies founded in New York
City, Philadelphia, and other cities. The societies
were named for the Delaware Indian chief Tammany, who was said to have welcomed William Penn
to Pennsylvania. The Tammany Society, or Columbian Order of New York City, was formed in 1786 and
incorporated in 1789. The first Columbus Day was
celebrated on Oct. 12, 1792, under the auspices of this
society. The New York Tammany was the only such
society to have a long life, and it became the most
powerful political organization in the city in the nineteenth century. Its headquarters, Tammany Hall, became a symbol of graft, corruption, and machine politics in the 1860s and 1870s. The organization
maintained substantial political influence well into
the twentieth century.

1790: New York City, the state's capital, had a population of 30,000 and five markets. Gov. George Clinton
moved into Government House to save the $750 per
year rent he was paying for his own house.

1790: The phrase *not worth a continental* expressed
a common attitude toward the continental currency
issued by Congress at the end of the American Revolution. Paper money valued at $200,000,000 shrank
rapidly in purchasing power until it took $40 in paper
to buy one silver dollar.

1790: The **Pennsylvania system** of prison management, based on the concept of absolute solitary confinement, was introduced at the Walnut St. Prison in Philadelphia. It was supposed to promote moral regeneration by means of enforced meditation. The philosophy of the Pennsylvania system was opposed to that of the later Auburn system, which was initiated by the state penitentiary in Auburn, N.Y., in 1816, and which permitted congregation of prisoners during the day. At night, however, Auburn prisoners slept in separate cells. In general, the Auburn system came to prevail in the U.S.

1790 Dec 6: Philadelphia became the nation's capital when Congress opened its legislative session there. On July 10, 1790, the House of Representatives had approved, by a vote of 32 to 29, the move from New York City to Philadelphia as part of a deal to establish a permanent capital. Congress had authorized George Washington to select a site for a new capital on the Potomac R. Philadelphia remained the nation's capital until 1800, when Washington, D.C., became the permanent seat of government. In 1799 Philadelphia had ceased to be the capital of Pennsylvania when the state government moved to Lancaster.

1792: The first edition of *The Farmer's Almanac* was published. Edited by Robert Bailey Thomas, a native of Grafton, Mass., it contained much information about New England life and manners along with valuable data on weather and other practical matters. Its homespun flavor and its depiction of New England ways captivated readers and turned the almanac into an American institution. Thomas, until his death in 1746, edited *The Farmer's Almanac,* later retitled *The Old Farmer's Almanac* to differentiate it from its numerous imitators.

1792 June 1: Statehood Day in Kentucky was instituted to commemorate admission of the Blue Grass State to the Union on this date.

1792 Oct 12: The first celebration of **Columbus Day** in America was held in New York City under the auspices of the Society of St. Tammany. St. Tammany had been chosen as the patron saint in a spirit of ridicule since he had been an Indian savant. The ridicule was directed at such societies as those of St. George, St. Andrew, and St. David.

1794: Powdering of men's hair went out of fashion after more than 100 years. However, men's hair was still worn in a queue tied with a black ribbon.

1795–1799

I. Civil Rights
Exploration and Settlement
Government
Statistics
Wars

What came to be known as the XYZ Affair marked a new low in Franco-American relations at the end of the eighteenth century. A three-man commission, consisting of Elbridge Gerry, John Marshall, and Charles Cotesworth Pinckney, was sent to France in 1797 by Pres. John Adams to negotiate a treaty of commerce and amity. The French foreign minister, Charles Maurice de Talleyrand, refused to deal with them directly and instead on Oct. 18 sent three agents who later were designated X,Y, and Z in the reports of the American delegation. The French agents suggested that the U.S. make a loan to France and also offer a bribe of about $250,000 to Talleyrand. The Americans refused, with Pinckney replying, "No, no, not a sixpence." On Apr. 3, 1798, Pres. Adams submitted the XYZ correspondence to Congress, and the disclosure aroused great resentment in the U.S. against France.

1795 Jan 29: The **Naturalization Act** was passed. It required a residence period of five years and renunciation of allegiances and titles of nobility as prerequisites to citizenship.

1796-1797: In **congressional elections** the Federalists gained one Senate seat for a 20–12 majority over the Republicans. In the House the Federalists gained four seats for a 58–48 majority.

1796 June 1: Tennessee became the 16th state of the Union.

1796 Sep 17: What has come to be known as **Washington's Farewell Address** was delivered by Pres. Washington before Congress. One of the outstanding American political documents, the address warned against America's involvement in foreign disputes and thus paved the way for the isolationist policy of the nineteenth century.

1796 Dec: John Adams was elected president of the United States. Adams was the last Federalist candidate to gain the presidency. The electoral vote was Adams, 71; Thomas Jefferson, Democratic-Republican of Virginia, 68; Aaron Burr, Democratic-Republican of New York, 30; and Thomas Pinckney, Federalist of South Carolina, 59. Jefferson, the candidate with the second highest electoral vote, became vice president.

1798-1799: In **congressional elections** the Federalists lost one Senate seat but held a 19–13 majority over the Republicans. In the House they gained six seats for a 64–42 majority.

1798: The **first secretary of the Navy** was appointed by Pres. Adams. He was Benjamin Stoddert, and he found himself with a weak navy in a time of trouble with France. Within two years he acquired 50 ships and planned a marine corps, naval hospital, and dock yards.

1798 Jan 8: The **Eleventh Amendment** to the Constitution was adopted. It stipulated that federal courts shall not have jurisdiction over litigation between individuals from one state against individuals from another state.

1798 June 18: The first of four acts known collectively as the **Alien and Sedition Acts,** amending the Naturalization Act of 1795, was adopted. The act required of prospective citizens a residence period of 14 years and a declaration of intention for five years.

1798 June 25: The **Alien Act,** second of the Alien and Sedition Acts, was passed, granting the president power for two years to deport any alien he deemed dangerous to the country's safety.

1798 July 6: The **Alien Enemies Act,** third of the Alien and Sedition Acts, was passed. It provided for the apprehension and deportation of male aliens who were subjects or citizens of a hostile country.

1798 July 14: The **Sedition Act,** fourth and last of the Alien and Sedition Acts, was passed. It provided for arrest and imprisonment of any person who attempted to impede the lawful processes of government, foment insurrection, or write, publish, or utter any false or malicious statement about the president, Congress, or government of the U.S. The Alien and Sedition Acts reflected the panic of the Federalist Party in the face of the XYZ Affair, the general conflict with France, and the growing strength of the Democratic-Republican Party. Intended to curb domestic opposition, the acts caused confusion and injustice and brought the Federalist Party ultimately into contempt, political defeat, and dissolution.

II. Architecture
   Arts and Music
   Popular Entertainment
   Publishing
   Theater

After American independence was won, more and more periodicals began to be published, with over 70 appearing before 1800. Most of them did not last long. Among the periodicals were *Columbian Magazine* (1786–1792), *Massachusetts Magazine* (1786–1796), *New York Magazine* (1790–1797), and *Monthly Magazine and American Review.* The last one was established in New York in April of 1799 by Charles Brockden Brown, the nation's first professional novelist. In 1801 it became a quarterly under the title

American Review and Literary Journal; it published until the end of 1802. Brown also edited the *Literary Magazine and American Register* from its founding in Philadelphia in 1803 until 1807, when it too failed. Most magazines of the time carried a mix of educational, literary, and scientific material.

1796: Gilbert Stuart completed his portrait *George Washington,* probably the most famous portrait of the first president. It also came to be known as the Athenaeum head. Stuart made numerous tries before this successful result. Nothing but the head of Washington can be seen, his character being derived from his facial features alone. This likeness is the accepted one and has become familiar to millions. The portrait was placed in the Boston Athenaeum, and later on permanent loan to the Boston Museum of Fine Arts.

1799: The *Baltimore American,* the first newspaper outside Washington, D.C., to give verbatim reports of Congressional debates, began publication. The paper published for 130 years.

III. Business and Industry
Education
Philosophy and Religion
Science

Both in the U.S. and abroad, the day of the general scientists, who took many fields of inquiry as their province, was coming to an end. Professional, or at least more specialized, scientists were taking over. An outstanding example of the generalists who had contributed so much to eighteenth-century progress was Samuel Latham Mitchill. His accomplishments and interests revealed the scope of his life's work. Mitchill established the first medical journal, *Medical Repository,* in 1797; was professor of natural history at Columbia College from 1798 to 1801; published the first good description of the geology of eastern New York State in 1798; was professor of the College of

Physicians and Surgeons in New York City from 1807 to 1826; and served in the New York State Assembly and the House of Representatives and the U.S. Senate. In addition, he introduced into American science the chemical nomenclature of Antoine Lavoisier, founder of modern chemistry, and by 1814 was the foremost zoologist as a result of his work on the fish of New York.

1796: The first experiments with **gas illumination** were conducted in Philadelphia, Pa.

1796: The first important **suspension bridge** in the U.S. was built between Uniontown and Greensborough, Pa., over Jacob's Creek. The bridge, no longer standing, was based on a principle of suspension developed mainly by James Finley of Fayette County, Pa.

1797: The first U.S. **clock patent** was awarded to Eli Terry for his newly devised method of employing wooden works in his clocks. Terry's clocks were sold rather cheaply—$18 to $70—and sales were brisk. Terry became the first manufacturer to use water power to cut parts.

1797 June 26: The first U.S. **plow patent** was issued to Charles Newbold of New Jersey. After expending his entire fortune in developing a practical plow of cast iron, Newbold was unable to sell it to farmers because of their fear of harmful effects of iron on soil. Thomas Jefferson had made the first studies of plows in America and designed a moldboard plow according to the distinctive requirements of American soil, but he never applied for a patent.

1798: The revolutionary concept of manufacturing **interchangeable parts** was incorporated by Eli Whitney in production of firearms for the U.S. government.

1798 Dec 14: A patent for a **screw threading machine** was awarded to David Wilkinson of Rhode Island. In Aug. 1848, Congress awarded Wilkinson $10,000 for his invention.

IV. Fashion
   Folkways
   Holidays
   Social Issues and Crime
   Sports

Americans—at least those who could afford to—
dined well and heartily on holiday occasions, as the
menus of some presidential Christmas dinners indicated. A Christmas menu from Mount Vernon
showed that George and Martha Washington served
34 different dishes and wines on one holiday, beginning with onion soup and ending with port and
Madeira. Five different meat dishes were available.
In the White House John and Abigail Adams called
one of their holiday repasts "A Most Sinful Feast."
Among the 29 dishes was "Skillet Cranberries for a
Slack Oven."

1796: A social trend away from **capital punishment**
was reflected in reforms in the criminal code of Virginia, which reduced the number of crimes for which
capital punishment was decreed.

1796: Travel between the cities of America frequently
presented challenges and dangers to tradesmen and
vacationers. Harried travelers on the Philadelphia–
Baltimore roads complained of chasms six to ten feet
deep along the way. They were lucky when their vehicles did not overturn. It sometimes took a stagecoach
five days to make a trip.

1797: A new **water supply** for Philadelphia, Pa., drawing from the Schuylkill R., went into operation.
There were three underground tunnels for distributing water in the city, and these were supplied from a
tower in the center of the city. This was the first attempt in the U.S. to construct a centralized water
distribution system.

**1798 June 18: "Millions for defense, but not one cent
for tribute"** entered American political history at a
banquet at O'Eller's Tavern in Philadelphia, Pa., in
honor of John Marshall, one of the three presidential
envoys to French Foreign Minister Charles Maurice
de Talleyrand-Périgord. Honored by the Federalists

for refusing a bribe by one of Talleyrand's agents, Marshall listened to 16 toasts in honor of his part in the XYZ Affair. The 13th toast, proposed by Rep. Robert Goodloe Harper, Federalist of South Carolina, contained the well-known phrase. Although the statement was correctly attributed to Harper in Philadelphia's *American Daily Advertiser* on June 20, the expression came to be identified with Charles Cotesworth Pinckney, another of the American envoys to whom the bribe request had been directed. Pinckney, shortly before his death, denied ever having made the statement, but because the expression seemed more apt as a diplomatic reply than as a toast, the legend persisted that Pinckney had spoken these words to the French agent.

1799 Dec 26: "**First in war, first in peace, first in the hearts of his countrymen,**" forever associated with George Washington, was first said as part of Henry Lee's funeral oration before Congress, after Washington's death on Dec. 14. Lee, known as "Light Horse Harry" Lee, had served under Washington in the Revolution and become his close friend. He was the father of Robert E. Lee. On the same day as Lee's eulogy, the House of Representatives passed a resolution incorporating Lee's words almost verbatim: "First in war, first in peace, first in the hearts of his fellow citizens."

1800

I. Civil Rights
   Exploration and Settlement
   Government
   Statistics
   Wars

This year's contest for the presidency revealed a sharp political division between the Federalist Party and the Republican, or Democratic-Republican, Party (forerunner of the Democratic Party). The Federalists, advocates of a strong central government and representing the well-to-do business class, chose as their candidate Pres. John Adams. The Republicans, the party of limited government and the agricultural interests, selected Thomas Jefferson of Virginia. The Constitution provided for each elector in the electoral college to vote for two candidates. The candidate with the most votes would become president and the one with the second highest total, vice president. The Republican electors cast 73 votes for Jefferson and the same number for Aaron Burr, the Republican candidate for vice president. The Federalist electors cast 65 votes for Adams; 64 for Charles Cotesworth Pinckney, their candidate for the vice presidency; and one for John Jay. The tie between Burr and Jefferson for the presidency meant the election would have to be decided in early 1801 by the House of Representatives. The problems caused by this election contributed to the passage, and ratification in 1804, of the Twelfth Amendment to the Constitution.

The second U.S. **Census** recorded a population of 5,308,483, including 896,849 slaves. The total number represented a ten-year increase of 1,379,269; the number of slaves increased by 199,168. The center of U.S. population was 18 miles southwest of Baltimore, a westward shift from 1790 reflecting the expansion of the frontier.

1800-1801: In **congressional elections** the Republicans gained six Senate seats to take an 18–13 majority over the Federalists. In the House they gained 27 seats to take a 69–36 majority.

May 7: The **Northwest Territory was divided** by a law enacted by Congress into two territories, Ohio and Indiana, the latter out of the western portion, including Illinois, Wisconsin, Indiana, and parts of Michigan and Minnesota. The provisions of the Treaty of

Paris (1783), which ended the Revolutionary War, had defined the borders of the U.S. Among other concessions, Great Britain agreed to a line through the Great Lakes that placed in U.S. control the territory called the Old Northwest, between the Ohio and Mississippi rivers. States that had previously laid claim to parts of the region had ceded their territories in anticipation of the Northwest Ordinance of 1787.

June: The new city of **Washington** in the District of Columbia became the U.S. capital, succeeding Philadelphia. This occurred when government departments began to move into their new buildings on land ceded to the federal government by Maryland and Virginia. The radial design of the city was created by the French architect Pierre Charles L'Enfant. Construction began in 1791 but was delayed following L'Enfant's dismissal in 1792. The first Congress to sit in Washington convened on Nov. 17, 1800. The first president to live in the Executive Mansion, John Adams, moved in, also in November. The first president to be inaugurated there, Thomas Jefferson, was sworn into office March 4, 1801. The U.S. was probably the first modern nation to design a city exclusively as a capital.

Oct 1: The territory of **Louisiana,** the entire region of the Missouri-Mississippi river valleys, was ceded by Spain to France in the secret treaty of San Ildefonso, in effect giving back territory awarded Spain by France in the Treaty of Fontainebleau in 1762. This territory was acquired by the U.S. in 1803 through the Louisiana Purchase.

II. Architecture
Arts and Music
Popular Entertainment
Publishing
Theater

Almost as soon as George Washington died in 1799, writers began to depict him as a hero of almost myth-

ical proportions. Chief contributor to this legend was
Mason Locke Weems, an Episcopal clergyman usually referred to as Parson Weems, who is supposed to
have had Washington as a parishioner in Virginia. In
1800 the first edition of his best-known work appeared, *The Life and Memorable Actions of George
Washington*. There were nine editions of the book by
1809. It was in the fifth edition, issued in 1806, that
Weems first included the story of Washington and
the cherry tree. In all, the biography went through 86
printings between 1800 and 1927. Weems's practice
was to fictionalize biographies to increase their sales.
For more than 30 years he was primarily a book
peddler, selling his own books as well as those of
other authors. He worked for Mathew Carey, the
leading publisher and bookseller of Philadelphia.
Weems wrote biographies of Francis Marion, Benjamin Franklin, and William Penn. He also composed
moral tracts such as *The Drunkard's Looking Glass*
(1812) and *Hymen's Recruiting Sergeant* (c1799).

The number of **libraries** in the U.S. was about 50,
with holdings of some 80,000 volumes. Most of these
libraries required membership or payment of a fee
for access to their books. By 1825, however, the nation's four largest cities could claim a total of 50 libraries, including some 1,500,000 volumes. Between
1800 and 1830 about 50,000 pamphlets, books, and
magazine titles were issued in the U.S. Most of the
books sold no more than 1000 copies, a respectable
number considering the population of the country.

III. Business and Industry
Education
Philosophy and Religion
Science

The need to improve transportation facilities sparked
a boom in canal building in the early nineteenth century. In South Carolina the Santee Canal, the first
true canal in the U.S., was constructed between 1792
and 1800 to connect the Santee and Cooper rivers.

This canal was 22 miles long, with ten locks that raised and lowered boats 103 feet. Its construction was directed by Christian Senf, a Swedish engineer imported for the job. He employed 110 men and women, mostly black slaves, to do the hard work. The canal cost $1,000,000 but ultimately failed because of inadequate supply of water. In New York State the Western Inland Lock Navigation Company had started a canal at the same time. This was only one mile long, with five locks. It was constructed to make navigation possible around the rapids of the Little Falls Gorge, on the Mohawk R.

The **Library of Congress** was established by the federal government. Housed at first in the Capitol, it was moved in 1897 to its own building, the largest and most costly library building in the world.

The first shoemaker in America to make **shoes designed specifically for the right and left feet** was William Young of Philadelphia.

The **Church of the United Brethren in Christ** was organized. Philip William Otterbein and Martin Boehm were elected bishops. The movement to form the church had originated among Mennonites in Lancaster County, Pa., in 1766 and spread among the German settlers of Pennsylvania, Maryland, and Virginia through the evangelistic labors of Otterbein and Boehm.

Sep: Cayuga Bridge, an engineering marvel of its time, was completed. It crossed the northern end of Cayuga Lake and the Montezuma Swamp in west central New York. The bridge, one and one-eighth of a mile long, was built of wood and was wide enough for wagons to pass abreast. Stages of the Genesee Turnpike used it, as did American troops in the War of 1812 on their way to the Niagara frontier. The bridge cost $150,000. It was financed by a loan from the Manhattan Company of New York City, which was founded in 1799 by Aaron Burr. Ostensibly established as a water supply company, the Manhattan Company had a charter broad enough so that it could function as a bank.

IV. **Fashion**
   Folkways
   Holidays
   Social Issues and Crime
   Sports

The remarkable career of Johnny Appleseed began about 1800. Born John Chapman in Massachusetts about 1775, he moved to Pennsylvania, where he sold or gave away saplings and apple seeds to settlers moving west. Chapman then moved on to Ohio, sowing and giving away apple seeds en route. For more than 40 years he traveled throughout Ohio, Indiana, and western Pennsylvania. He pruned trees he had previously planted and helped pioneers care for the orchards grown from his seeds. His work bore fruit, literally, over an area of perhaps 100,000 sq. mi. Chapman was ragged in dress and eccentric in his ways. He was also an itinerant preacher, expounding his faith in the Church of the New Jerusalem, the religious organization that grew out of the teachings of Emanuel Swedenborg, the Swedish mystic whose teachings had been introduced to the U.S. in 1784 and whose empathy with the natural world apparently appealed to Chapman. During the War of 1812 Chapman traveled 30 miles to bring troops to Mansfield, Ohio, to forestall a raid by Indian allies of the British. Chapman also introduced and encouraged the raising of many useful medicinal herbs. He died near Fort Wayne, Ind., in 1847.

Four-tined forks came into common use in American homes at about this time. Two- and three-tined forks had been customary.

The **Sheraton and Directoire styles** in furniture, both reflecting a continued classical influence and a return to simpler design, appealed strongly to public taste. The New York City workshop of Duncan Phyfe turned out many superb examples.

1801

I. **Civil Rights**
   Exploration and Settlement
   Government
   Statistics
   Wars

As a result of the tie vote between Thomas Jefferson and Aaron Burr in the electoral college in the 1800 presidential election, the process of presidential selection went to the House of Representatives, where each state would have one vote. Burr publicly professed support for Jefferson, his fellow Republican, but did nothing to take himself out of the race, even though the Republicans intended that Burr become vice president. Many Federalists favored Burr for president, but Alexander Hamilton, the leading Federalist, detested Burr and worked behind the scenes on Jefferson's behalf, despite his disagreement with Jefferson's policies. Beginning Feb. 11, the House took 35 ballots without breaking the deadlock. On the 36th ballot, on Feb. 17, barely two weeks before a new president was to be inaugurated, Jefferson received a majority vote when certain Federalists gave up their support of Burr. Burr was elected vice president.

Jan 20: John Marshall was appointed chief justice of the U.S. Supreme Court. He became one of the greatest judges in U.S. history, establishing the Supreme Court as final authority in determining state and federal powers.

Mar 4: Thomas Jefferson, third president of the United States, became the first president to be inaugurated in Washington, D.C. He held the office for eight years, and was the first of the Republican (later Democratic) Party elected to the presidency.

II. Architecture
   Arts and Music
   Popular Entertainment
   Publishing
   Theater

With the new century and the establishment of political parties came newspapers and journals that strongly supported one side or another. Among the leading editors of such publications was Joseph Dennie, who first edited the *Farmer's Weekly Museum* in Walpole, N.H. The publication became influential because of the "Lay Preacher" essays Dennie wrote for it. Later, in Philadelphia, he edited *The Port Folio* from 1801 to 1809. An avid Federalist, Dennie made such strong verbal attacks on Thomas Jefferson that he was tried in 1805 for seditious libel but was acquitted. He did, however, publish literary articles of quality, including works of Thomas Moore, Leigh Hunt, and Thomas Campbell. Dennie was a founder of the Tuesday Club of Philadelphia, which supported both the magazine and the Federalist cause.

The **New York** *Evening Post,* a newspaper that enlisted some of the foremost editorial writers of the nineteenth century, was established. Under the editorship of William Cullen Bryant from 1826–1878, it was Free-soil and supported Abraham Lincoln. In the 1880s Carl Schurz and Edwin Lawrence Godkin steered the paper in its attack on local corruption. After passing through many hands, it became the New York *Post* in Mar. 1934.

III. Business and Industry
    Education
    Philosophy and Religion
    Science

A religious revival began to sweep the West in this period. It started with the preaching of James McGready, a Presbyterian minister who began preaching in Logan County, Ky., in 1797. Encampments at which he preached formed the beginnings

of the camp meeting, a gathering that for many typified evangelical Protestantism on the frontier. Such
meetings generally featured hell-fire sermons
preached at congregations gathered in open fields or
groves of trees.

Oct 19: The **first Philadelphia aqueduct** was opened,
providing a new supply of fresh water for the growing city.

IV. Fashion
   Folkways
   Holidays
   Social Issues and Crime
   Sports

Pioneer farmers in the backwoods had no opportunity to go to concerts or plays, but they created their
own recreation, geared to their circumstances and
their way of life. They met their neighbors at log-
rollings, barbecues, and religious camp meetings.
Some of them drank too much of the raw whiskey
produced on the frontier, or gambled on horses or at
cards. Since good marksmanship was a necessity,
competition arose out of men's pride in their skill.
There were competitive squirrel hunts and shooting
at targets for such prizes as a turkey or a barrel of
whiskey. Dances such as Virginia reels and country
jigs were popular; they gave the women some much-
needed social life.

Mar 4: The expression *entangling alliances* was
coined by Thomas Jefferson and used in his first inaugural address: "Peace, commerce, and honest friendship with all nations—entangling alliances with
none." These words have been commonly attributed
to George Washington; although Washington supported the idea expressed, there is no record of his
having used this phraseology.

1802

I. **Civil Rights**
   Exploration and Settlement
   Government
   Statistics
   Wars

In April the U.S. learned that Napoleon I of France in 1800 had secured through a secret agreement the return of the Louisiana territory from Spain. This was alarming news because the mouth of the Mississippi R. was now in the hands of an aggressive power, and Americans west of the Allegheny Mts. depended on free passage and use of the port of New Orleans to transfer their products to oceangoing ships. Pres. Thomas Jefferson ordered Robert R. Livingston, U.S. minister to France, to buy land on the lower Mississippi for use as a port, or to secure a guarantee of free navigation. In October Spanish officials, still in New Orleans, refused to allow Americans to use the port. This serious disruption of American commerce led Jefferson in the next year to begin negotiations for purchase of Louisiana.

1802-1803: In **congressional elections** the Republicans gained seven Senate seats for a 25–9 majority over the Federalists. In the House they gained 33 seats to the Federalists' gain of three, for a 102–39 majority.

Mar 16: The **U.S. Military Academy** at West Point, N.Y., was established by Congress. The academy opened officially on July 4.

Apr 30: Pres. Jefferson signed the **Enabling Act,** establishing procedures under which a territory organized by the provisions of the Ordinance of 1787 could become a state. The law authorized the people of Ohio Territory to hold a convention and frame a constitution. Subsequently, in 1803, Ohio became the 17th state of the Union and the first created out of the Northwest Territory. This precedent was later followed by other parts of the territory.

II. Architecture
Arts and Music
Popular Entertainment
Publishing
Theater

In the nineteenth century almost all American artists studied abroad and many of them became expatriates, chiefly in England and Italy. The first of these was Benjamin West, one of the best historical painters. West settled in London in 1763, becoming prominent as historical painter to King George III and president of the Royal Academy. He trained or advised a number of younger American painters. Among his paintings were *Saul and the Witch of Endor* and *The Death of Wolfe.* His paintings treating American subjects included *William Penn's Treaty with the Indians* (1772) and *Franklin Drawing Electricity from the Sky* (c1805). He completed an enormous canvas of *Christ Healing the Sick* in 1816, intended as a gift for the Pennsylvania Hospital in Philadelphia. It created such a sensation in London that he was offered 3000 guineas for it, so he painted a duplicate to send to America. The picture was so large that a special gallery had to be built to house it.

The **American Academy of Arts** was established in New York City. Shares of stock in the organization were sold as if the academy were a business corporation, reflecting the domination of the upper class in American culture.

III. Business and Industry
Education
Philosophy and Religion
Science

American scientists, often self-taught, showed a bent for practical matters rather than research in theoretical problems. A good example was Nathaniel Bowditch. After having learned algebra at age 14, Bowditch made five sea voyages between 1795 and 1803, during which he perfected his knowledge of mathe-

matics and navigation. As a result he corrected some
8000 errors in J. Hamilton Moore's *The Practical
Navigator,* a standard work. Bowditch devised a practical method of computing longitude with a sextant,
by measuring the angular distances between certain
fixed stars and the moon. A new edition of Moore's
work appeared under Bowditch's name in 1802 as
The New Practical American Navigator. Nine more
editions appeared in his lifetime, and in 1867 the
rights were acquired by the U.S. Hydrographic Office,
which has published it since. Bowditch also found
time to translate four volumes of Pierre Simon, Marquis de Laplace's *Mécanique Celeste,* and to be president of the Essex Fire and Marine Insurance Co.

The **first brass mill,** built by Abel Porter & Co. and
operated by horsepower, began operation in Water-
bury, Conn., which became the leading brass manufacturing center in America.

IV. Fashion
   Folkways
   Holidays
   Social Issues and Crime
   Sports

By the early nineteenth century the division between
North and South on the question of slavery was
becoming clear-cut. By 1802 all states north of the
Mason-Dixon line, except for New Jersey, had passed
antislavery laws or measures for gradual emancipation. In Congress a bill to make the Fugitive Slave
Law of 1793 more stringent was defeated by a narrow margin. In the South there was fear of slave
insurrections, which were reported in six North Carolina counties and nine Virginia counties in 1802.

The **first hotel** in the U.S., the Union Hotel in
Saratoga Springs, N.Y., was built by Gideon Putnam.
What distinguished the Union as a hotel was its emphasis on lodging and services rather than food and
drink.

1803

I. **Civil Rights**
   Exploration and Settlement
   Government
   Statistics
   Wars

A landmark decision was handed down by the Supreme Court this year in the case of *Marbury* v. *Madison*. In Mar. 1801, in the last hours of John Adams's presidency, William Marbury was awarded a commission as justice of the peace of the District of Columbia. The new president, Thomas Jefferson, instructed his secretary of state, James Madison, not to deliver the commission. Marbury and three other men in the same situation sued Madison. The Court's decision, written by Chief Justice John Marshall and issued on Feb. 24, held that the law under which the suit was brought was null and void because it contravened the Constitution. This was the first decision of the Supreme Court to declare an act of Congress unconstitutional, thereby establishing the doctrine of judicial review and expanding the power of the judiciary.

Feb 19: Ohio became the 17th state. Although slavery had been outlawed in the Northwest Territory by the Northwest Ordinance in 1787, Ohio was the first state in which slavery was forbidden by law from the beginning of statehood. Vermont had outlawed slavery with the adoption of its constitution in July 1777, some six months after its declaration of independence as a republic.

Apr 30: The **Louisiana Purchase,** the first territorial acquisition made by the U.S., added to the country some 828,000 sq. mi. of land between the Mississippi R. and the Rocky Mts. It was bought from France for 80,000,000 francs (about $15,000,000). The price included 20,000,000 francs for assumption by the U.S.

of claims against France by U.S. citizens. The Louisiana Purchase increased U.S. national territory about 140%. The territory later formed Missouri, Nebraska, Iowa, Arkansas, North and South Dakota, most of Louisiana, Kansas, Minnesota, Montana, Wyoming, and parts of Colorado and Oklahoma.

II. Architecture
Arts and Music
Popular Entertainment
Publishing
Theater

A versatile American of the early national period was William Wirt of Virginia. A lawyer, politician, and essayist, he served as U.S. attorney general for 12 years. His most popular literary work was *Letters of a British Spy*, purporting to be written by a member of the British Parliament during a visit to the southern U.S. Wirt's essays, attempting to mimic the style of Joseph Addison, first appeared anonymously in a Richmond, Va., newspaper. They followed the example of eighteenth-century commentators who posed as foreign observers of the customs of a strange society. Published in book form in 1803, the essays became very popular and went through 12 editions. The essays dealt with southern customs, education, politics, and history. In 1817 Wirt published *Life and Character of Patrick Henry*, the first book to appear under his own name. In it he recreated many of Henry's speeches.

Feb 4: William Dunlap, often called America's first professional playwright, adapted the French melodrama *La Voix de Nature* by L.C. Caigniez, and produced it in New York City. Melodrama, newly developed abroad, notably in France, involved virtuous and villainous stock characters, with the virtuous always triumphant. *The Voice of Nature* was the first melodrama to reach the American stage.

III. Business and Industry
Education
Philosophy and Religion
Science

Among the religious groups that attempted to fund utopias in the U.S. were the Rappites, so-called after their leader George Rapp, who emigrated from Germany in 1803. In 1805 he and his followers founded Harmony, Pa., where they developed a prosperous industrial and agricultural community. In 1814 and 1815 they moved to Indiana and founded another Harmony. There they also prospered but in 1825 sold their property to Robert Owen, the English manufacturer and social reformer. Moving back to Pennsylvania, the Rappites established Economy (now Ambridge), northwest of Pittsburgh. The Harmony Society was an austere group who practiced celibacy. The group weakened after Rapp's death and faded as its members grew old. It ceased to exist in 1906.

The **first tax-supported public library** was founded in Salisbury, Conn. It was launched by a gift from Caleb Bingham, a Boston publisher, and was continued by grants of town moneys.

IV. Fashion
Folkways
Holidays
Social Issues and Crime
Sports

The British Passenger Act of 1803 appeared to be a humanitarian measure, but its practical effect was to cut down dramatically on the number of immigrants coming to the U.S. Ships from Londonderry and Belfast, Ireland, had been carrying 400 to 500 emigrants on each voyage, but the new law required that 43 sq. ft. of space be allowed for each passenger, so they soon could transport only a few score. As a result, fares increased so after 1803 only about 1000 emigrants a year left Ireland for the U.S. Between 1810 and 1812 these ships were preyed upon by British naval vessels, which impressed hundreds of young men into service. The falling off of immigration to the U.S. during the early years of independence gave more time for earlier settlers to become assimilated before the next influx.

John Randolph of Roanoke, an aristocratic Virginia congressman, set tongues wagging in Philadelphia with an announcement that he had fathered an illegitimate child.

1804

I. Civil Rights
   Exploration and Settlement
   Government
   Statistics
   Wars

Pres. Thomas Jefferson's scientific curiosity, and his concern for the economic and political security of the western U.S., were reflected in his sponsorship of the Lewis and Clark Expedition of 1804–1806. The expedition was headed by Merriwether Lewis, Jefferson's private secretary, and William Clark, an Army officer. The expedition was to explore the Northwest from the Mississippi R. to the Pacific Ocean, find the best travel route, and establish U.S. claims to the Oregon Territory. The expedition, including about 30 persons, left St. Louis, Mo., on May 14, 1804, and traveled up the Missouri R., spending the winter in North Dakota. In July 1805, the group found the headwaters of the Missouri and learned there was no easy route to the Pacific. They were also the first Americans to cross the Continental Divide. Traveling down the Columbia R., the expedition reached the Pacific on Nov. 8, 1805, and wintered there. On Sept. 23, 1806, the expedition arrived back at St. Louis, bringing with it great quantities of information on vegetation, animals, Indians, and the geography of the region. As Theodore Roosevelt wrote later, the expedition "opened the door into the heart of the Far West."

1804-1805: In congressional elections the Republicans gained two Senate seats for a 27–7 majority over the Federalists. In the House they gained 14 seats for a 116–25 majority.

July 11: Alexander Hamilton was fatally wounded in a pistol duel with Aaron Burr. Hamilton had fought Burr's run for the presidency in 1800, and for the governorship of New York in 1804, when Hamilton and others suspected that Burr intended to attach New York to the disgruntled New England states in a plan to disunite from the Union and form a northern confederacy. Burr challenged Hamilton, who deliberately misfired before Burr fired with intent to kill.

Sep 25: The **Twelfth Amendment** to the U.S. Constitution was ratified, providing in part that voters shall "name in their ballots the person voted for as President and in distinct ballots the person voted for as vice president." In the election of this year, electors for the first time voted separately for president and vice president. Previously the candidate having the second largest number of votes in the electoral college became vice president.

Dec 5: Thomas Jefferson was reelected president of the United States. George Clinton, first governor of New York and like Jefferson a Democratic-Republican, was elected vice president. The electoral vote was Jefferson, 162; Charles C. Pinckney, Federalist of South Carolina, 14. This was the first election with separate ballots for president and vice president.

II. Architecture
    Arts and Music
    Popular Entertainment
    Publishing
    Theater

Like other American artists before and after them, Washington Allston and John Vanderlyn found

Europe more congenial for exercising their talents than the U.S. Beginning in 1801, Allston studied in England under Benjamin West, then spent four years in Rome. The period from 1810 to 1818, spent in England, was Allston's most productive. He was an early and important artist of the Romantic school, as exemplified in such works as *The Deluge* (1804) and *The Rising of a Thunderstorm at Sea* (1804). His work lost its vitality when he returned to the U.S. and was marked by such failures as *Belshazzar's Feast,* over which he labored for 26 years. John Vanderlyn was the first American painter to study in Paris instead of London or Rome. He spent the years from 1796 to 1815 in the French capital and in Rome. His early work featured nudes painted so realistically that they shocked viewers. Vanderlyn was primarily a historical painter, and such works as *Marius Amid the Ruins at Carthage* won him a high reputation but did not sell. He also did excellent portraits but worked so slowly that few people had the patience to pose for him.

The first volume of **Life of George Washington** by John Marshall was published. The fifth and final volume appeared in 1807. Although the work reflected Marshall's Federalist bias and lacked literary style, it was considered the most impressive and authoritative biography of the first president to appear in the 50 years following Washington's death. Shorter biographies of Washington were written by Aaron Bancroft (1807) and David Ramsay (1807).

III. Business and Industry
Education
Philosophy and Religion
Science

Even as late as the eighteenth century, religious and political persecution was spurring men of above ordinary talent to immigrate to the U.S. Such a man was Joseph Priestley, theologian and scientist. His greatest scientific achievement was the discovery of oxygen, although he did not realize the importance of his work. His strongly expressed Unitarian views and his support of the French Revolution made him many enemies. A mob wrecked his house and destroyed his scientific apparatus in 1791, prompting him to leave England for the U.S. in 1794. Among his friends and correspondents was Thomas Jefferson. Priestley settled at Northumberland, Pa., and spent the last years of his life writing and continuing his scientific studies. He died at Northumberland on Feb. 6, 1804.

What was perhaps the **first automobile** was built by Oliver Evans, an American inventor, who was commissioned by the Philadelphia Board of Health to build a steam engine for dredging the Schuylkill R. and cleaning the city docks. His five-hp engine propelled a scow 12 ft. wide and 30 ft. long. The scow weighed 15½ tons and was driven 1½ miles from its construction shed, down Center St., much to the amusement of Philadelphians. Evans offered to bet an onlooker $3000 that he could build a steam-driven vehicle that would go faster than any horse in the world. The scow's drive belt was shifted from its rollers to paddlewheels and it went steaming down the river against the wind, leaving all sailboats behind. Despite this demonstration, the public was not much impressed with the principle of steam locomotion.

IV. Fashion
   Folkways
   Holidays
   Social Issues and Crime
   Sports

One result of Napoleon's establishment of the French Empire in Europe in 1804 was the development of the Empire style in furniture and house furnishings. The style was not long in reaching the U.S. and dominated until after Napoleon's fall in 1815. By contrast with late eighteenth-century styles, which favored the classical manner of straight lines and minimal carving, Empire furniture was heavier and more massive. There were combinations of marble and brass, and ormolu and wood. Animal forms, such as claw feet and eagle heads, were used together with elaborate decorative carvings. Heavy textiles were used in upholstery. Larger and more imposing interiors were needed to set off the monumental furniture so couches were modeled after Roman beds and bookcases with facades like temples appeared. Although most American pieces were not as lush as the French originals, the furniture suggested wealth and power in the Napoleonic manner but did not provide a relaxed setting for social life.

The **Coonskin Library** was founded in Marietta, Ohio. This unique institution came into being when settlers along the Ohio R. bartered coonskins for books from Boston merchants.

1805

I. **Civil Rights**
   Exploration and Settlement
   Government
   Statistics
   Wars

U.S. merchant shipping, as it grew in volume, was increasingly preyed upon by pirates of the states of the Barbary Coast of North Africa, who had attacked the shipping of European nations for many years. These states were Tripolitania, Tunisia, Algeria, and Morocco. The Tripolitan War (1801–1805), the first of a number of conflicts, began when the American government refused to pay tribute to the rulers of these states in return for a guarantee of protection. After sporadic fighting, John Rodgers, a naval officer, negotiated a peace treaty, which was signed June 4, 1805. Tripoli renounced all rights to collect tribute or halt

U.S. shipping. The U.S. agreed to pay $60,000 to ransom the crew of the warship *Philadelphia,* which had been captured after having drifted aground. The treaty was the most favorable any nation had negotiated with the pirate states, but it did not put an end to piracy. Another decade was to pass before the threat was entirely ended.

Apr 27: In the **Tripolitan War,** the U.S. achieved its major victory when William Eaton, a special U.S. naval agent, led a small force of Marines and Arab mercenaries in capturing the Tripolitan port city of Derna. Eaton's force, a squad of U.S. Marines under Lt. Preston N. O'Bannon and about 100 Arab mercenaries, had marched 500 miles from Egypt to Derna and were assisted by a coordinated bombardment of Derna by U.S. naval vessels. Eaton's ultimate mission, approved by Pres. Thomas Jefferson, was to replace the ruling pasha of Tripoli with the rightful ruler. However, the coming of peace in early June aborted the plan. The phrase "to the shores of Tripoli" in the official song of the U.S. Marine Corps refers to the Derna campaign, which was the first engagement of U.S. land forces in North Africa. The campaign marked the first time that the U.S. flag was raised over an Old World fort.

II. Architecture
   Arts and Music
   Popular Entertainment
   Publishing
   Theater

In the early years of independence the U.S. was still dependent on Europe, especially England, for architects and architectural styles. Benjamin Henry Latrobe, who came to the U.S. from England in 1796, is considered the first professional architect in the U.S. Pres. Thomas Jefferson appointed him surveyor of public buildings in 1803. Latrobe introduced classical Greek designs and styles, which contributed

greatly to the Classical revival. His 1799 design for
the Bank of Pennsylvania in Philadelphia was modeled after a Greek Ionic temple. Latrobe also designed the Roman Catholic Cathedral in Baltimore.
Built between 1805 and 1815, it was the first cathedral in the U.S. and represented the best monumental
architecture of the period. In 1800 Latrobe designed
Sedgeley, a residence near Philadelphia, said to be
the first executed example of the Gothic revival in the
U.S. After the British burned the Capitol in Washington, D.C., in 1814, Latrobe took charge of its rebuilding.

The **Pennsylvania Academy of Fine Arts** was
founded by Charles Willson Peale. It is the oldest
extant art institution in the U.S. The New York Academy was founded in 1801 but survived only four
years.

III. Business and Industry
Education
Philosophy and Religion
Science

A book of theological thought published this year
marked a change in the course of belief within the
Universalist Church. The book was *A Treatise on the
Atonement* by Hosea Ballou, who for about 34 years
was pastor of the Second Universalist Society in Boston. After about 1796 Ballou was the most influential
voice in the denomination and turned it away from
its Calvinistic tendencies. Ballou emphasized
"Christ's subordination to the Father," giving Universalism a position much the same as that of Unitarianism. His basic viewpoint was that of anti-Trinitarian-
ism, with God the universal father and Jesus Christ,
His son, the spiritual authority and leader in uniting
man with God. Ballou affirmed the freedom of man's
will, with the sacrifice of Christ an example of the
perfection man can attain by turning away from sin.
The Winchester Profession, stating the doctrinal position of the church, had been adopted in 1803.

A **labor dispute** was taken into court for the first time by a struck employer. The result was conviction of leaders of the Philadelphia Society of Cordwainers, workers in cordovan leather, for criminal conspiracy for the purpose of increasing their wages. The conviction was secured under English common-law doctrine.

IV. Fashion
Folkways
Holidays
Social Issues and Crime
Sports

Not all commentators praised the morals and manners of the young U.S. Among those who emphasized the excesses of a raw democracy was Scottish-born Hugh Henry Brackenridge, author and jurist. The influence of satirists such as Miguel de Cervantes and Jonathan Swift was evident in his novel, *Modern Chivalry*, published between 1792 and 1815 in four volumes, a revision, and a final edition. In it he wrote: "In the American republic, we retain yet a great deal of the spirit of monarchy. . . . The first lesson I would give to a son of mine would be to have nothing to do with public business, but as a duty to his country. . . . beware of flatterers, whose object is not to serve them, but themselves. The demagogue in a democracy, and the courtier in a monarchy, are identical."

Sacajawea, a Shoshone Indian woman, gained a place in American folklore by her activities this year. The wife of the Lewis and Clark expedition's official interpreter, Toussaint Charbonneau, she joined the expedition in what is now South Dakota, and accompanied the party to the Pacific and part of the way back east. Her presence with the explorers helped convince the Indians they met en route that the newcomers were not members of a war party. Her knowledge of edible wild plants was a great help to the expedition. In February she gave birth to a baby boy. The midwife was Meriwether Lewis.

1806

I. Civil Rights
Exploration and Settlement
Government
Statistics
Wars

One of the most puzzling incidents of the early nineteenth century involved Aaron Burr, the brilliant but erratic political figure. Shortly after he fatally wounded Alexander Hamilton in a duel in 1804, Burr journeyed to New Orleans and entered into a conspiracy with U.S. Gen. James Wilkinson, although it is not clear what they conspired about. Wilkinson was actually in the pay of Spain at the time. Speculation was that Burr intended either to establish an independent nation in the Southwest or to seize territory for the same purpose in Spanish America. Burr secured financing from Harman Blennerhassett, of Blennerhassett Island in the Ohio R. near present-day Parkersburg, W. Va. He set out from there in the fall of 1806 with about 60 well-armed men and headed downstream. The expedition aroused suspicion and Wilkinson, seeking to save his own skin, turned against Burr. He spread stories of Burr's intentions and sent dispatches to the government in Washington accusing Burr of treason. Burr was arrested and charged with treason, but he was acquitted in 1807.

1806-1807: In **congressional elections** the Republicans gained one Senate seat for a 28–6 majority over the Federalists. In the House they gained two seats for a 118–24 majority.

July 15: Zebulon Pike began his exploration of what is now the southwestern U.S. He traveled up the Missouri R., through Kansas and southern Nebraska to New Mexico, through the Rio Grande Valley and on to Mexico City. On Nov. 15 Pike first saw the famous mountain named for him, Pike's Peak, in what is now Colorado.

II. Architecture
Arts and Music
Popular Entertainment
Publishing
Theater

More and larger book publishing firms began to emerge as the nation grew. The most important publisher before the turn of the century was Isaiah Thomas of Worcester, Mass., whose firm published everything from magazines to reference books to almanacs. Thomas wrote a valuable *History of Printing in America* (1810). Another publisher was Matthew Carey of Philadelphia, who also labored for a protective tariff system. His son, Henry Charles Carey, became the head of Carey, Lea, and Carey, whose authors included Washington Irving. Henry Carey, like his father, was deeply interested in economics and the protective tariff.

Noah Webster's *Compendious Dictionary of the English Language* represented a retreat from Webster's earlier attempts to Americanize the English language. Although many supporters of a purely American language continued to agitate for linguistic change, Webster's dictionary compromised with the British mother tongue, and its standards became the accepted practice in the U.S. The dictionary was the culmination of a series of works by Webster, beginning in 1783 with *The Grammatical Institute of the English Language* and including readers, spellers, and grammars with enormous circulation in America.

III. Business and Industry
Education
Philosophy and Religion
Science

Many trails long used by the Indians became roads for pioneer settlers. Such a trail was the Natchez

[203]   JEFFERSON • 1806

Trace, which ran from present-day Nashville, Tenn.,
southwest to Natchez, Miss. By 1806 it was much
used by traders, causing Congress to pass legislation
for construction of a better road over its route. In the
War of 1812 Andrew Jackson marched troops on the
Natchez Trace as he moved on New Orleans to oppose the British.

The **first industry-wide strike** in the U.S. resulted
when 200 journeymen shoemakers in New York City,
suspecting that struck employers were having their
work done in other establishments, obtained a nationwide strike order from the Journeyman Cordwainers' Society of Baltimore. Leaders of the strike
were indicted for criminal conspiracy in their attempt to secure higher wages.

**IV. Fashion
Folkways
Holidays
Social Issues and Crime
Sports**

Dueling was dying out but had not yet disappeared.
One of its most active practitioners was a future president of the U.S., Andrew Jackson. In 1803 he became
embroiled in a dispute with Gov. John Sevier of Tennessee who was said to have insulted Jackson's wife.
A duel was arranged, but the confrontation was
averted because of confusion at the scene. In 1806 a
duel resulted from a bet on a horse race and yet
another insult to Jackson's wife, this time by a lawyer, Charles Dickinson. When Jackson and Dickinson met on May 30, both men fired and Jackson suffered a broken rib. His shot felled Dickinson, who
bled to death.

The first picture of a soccer-type **football game** in
America showed president Timothy Dwight watching
Yale students kicking a ball. According to Yale tradition, the game of football had been played there for
45 years. The modern American game of football,
however, did not begin to develop until about 1869.

1807

I. **Civil Rights**
   Exploration and Settlement
   Government
   Statistics
   Wars

An early incident presaging the War of 1812 was the *Chesapeake-Leopard* affair of June 22, 1807. The U.S. warship *Chesapeake* was stopped by the British frigate *Leopard* off Norfolk, Va. The British commander insisted that the Chesapeake had four British deserters on board. When James Barron, commanding the *Chesapeake*, refused to surrender the men, the British ship opened fire, killing three Americans and wounding 18. The four alleged deserters were forcibly removed. In spite of Pres. Thomas Jefferson's protest, the British government on Oct. 17 announced it would continue its policy of impressing seamen on American ships who were thought to be British. As for Barron, he was court-martialed and suspended from active duty for five years, during which time he served in the French navy. In 1820 Barron killed Stephen Decatur in a duel sparked by Decatur's opposition to Barron's reinstatement.

Mar 2: The **African slave trade** was prohibited after Jan. 1, 1808, by an act of Congress, which outlawed importation of slaves into any place within the jurisdiction of the U.S.

Sep 1: Aaron Burr was acquitted of treason by a circuit court in Richmond, Va., on the grounds that he was not present when an overt act was committed. Pres. Thomas Jefferson, having been warned of Burr's activities with respect to annexation of Spanish territory, had issued a warning on Nov. 27, 1806, to all citizens forbidding any expedition against Spanish territory. Burr had been arrested in Alabama on Feb. 19 and indicted on June 24 on charges of treason.

II. Architecture
   Arts and Music
   Popular Entertainment
   Publishing
   Theater

The nation's new sense of political independence was reflected in the lives and works of its writers, who felt that American letters should also be independent of the Old World. Leaders in this movement were the Connecticut Wits, also known as the Hartford Wits because they were centered in that Connecticut city. This informal group began as one devoted to modernizing the Yale College curriculum. The members soon, however, entered the political arena. They shared the views of the conservative Federalists and collaborated on satirical verse attacking the liberal position. Among the group's members were Joel Barlow, John Trumbull, Timothy Dwight, Theodore Dwight, and Lemuel Hopkins. The group's political and literary importance was greatest in the late 1700s but continued to be an influence into the early 1800s.

Jan 24: The first number of *Salmagundi,* a series of whimsical, mildly satirical, and very popular essays written by William and Washington Irving and James Kirke Paulding, was published. Following the informal style of London essayists of the previous century, these pieces afforded delightful glimpses of New York's social, cultural, and political life in the early 1800s. They also marked the beginning of what came to be called the Knickerbocker movement in American literature. Many imitations followed at once. Paulding and the Irvings were men of affluent background and similar literary taste. At this point in their lives they were little concerned with the major issues of the day. *Salmagundi,* therefore, remains charming embroidery rather than basic fabric in the development of American literature. But the essays are a lasting memorial to the old days of New York City and its Hudson R. Valley suburbs, and they established the tradition of metropolitan wit that continues unbroken to our day.

III. Business and Industry
Education
Philosophy and Religion
Science

In the late eighteenth and early nineteenth centuries, American physicians and surgeons made significant contributions to medical science. Samuel Bard wrote a manual on midwifery and a forward-looking report on medical education. Nathan Smith helped found Yale's medical school and wrote a treatise on typhus fever. Philip Syng Physick performed many operations for cataracts and improved methods for treating fractures. Ephraim McDowell, who practiced in Kentucky, performed the first ovariotomy on record in 1808.

Aug 11: Robert Fulton's steamboat *Clermont* made its first run to Albany from New York in 32 hours, traveling at about 5 mph. The initial trial of the *Clermont* had taken place the previous spring when it crossed the Hudson R. from New York to New Jersey. Also in 1807 Pres. Jefferson corresponded with Fulton about the torpedoes Fulton was proposing as the chief defense of harbors. But Jefferson could not see gambling the safety of the nation on the success of a single weapon. Fulton had also proposed the development of submarines. Jefferson noted how effective torpedoes launched from submarines would be, and encouraged Fulton in his research and experiments.

IV. Fashion
Folkways
Holidays
Social Issues and Crime
Sports

Most Americans had plenty to eat, but few enjoyed a balanced diet. Farmers grew their own food and shot wild game. In the cities the lack of refrigeration and even of canning until about 1820 meant that much salt pork and other preserved items were staples. Fresh fruits and vegetables were not available for much of the year. Foreign visitors were impressed by the amount of greasy food consumed by Americans and the speed at which it was eaten. A visiting French count reported that he was nearly made ill by a breakfast that included fish, steak, ham, sausage, salt beef, and hot breads. "The whole day passes in heaping indigestions on one another," he complained.

Feb 27: Henry Wadsworth Longfellow, one of America's most popular and revered poets, was born in Portland, Me. His birthday came to be celebrated for many years in public schools throughout the nation. One of the earliest records of such a celebration appeared in the biennial report of the superintendent of schools in West Virginia in 1905. The Historical Society of Cambridge, Mass., celebrated the centenary of Longfellow's birth in 1907 with addresses by William Dean Howells, Charles W. Eliot, Charles Eliot Norton, and Thomas Wentworth Higginson.

1808

I. Civil Rights
   Exploration and Settlement
   Government
   Statistics
   Wars

The war between Great Britain and Napoleonic France in the early nineteenth century caused great damage to America's economy and led to government action to solve the problem. On Dec. 22, 1807, an Embargo Act became law. In effect the act banned all trade with foreign countries in an attempt to show England and France, who were trying to keep U.S. ships from reaching each other's ports, the importance of U.S. products and markets. Another Embargo Act was passed on Jan. 9, 1808, and still a third on Mar. 12. None of the acts had the desired effect. Trade to and from Canada was difficult to stop, and neither Britain nor France suffered. The chief result was damage to shipping and commercial interests of the North, especially New England.

1808-1809: In **congressional elections** the Republicans maintained their 28–6 Senate majority over the Federalists. In the House they lost 24 seats but kept a majority, 94–48.

Dec 7: James Madison was elected president of the United States. George Clinton, Republican of New York, was elected vice president. The electoral vote was Madison, Democratic-Republican of Virginia, 122; Charles Cotesworth Pinckney, Federalist of South Carolina, 47; George Clinton, 6. In the vice presidential race the electoral vote was Clinton, 113; Rufus King, Federalist of New York, 47.

II. Architecture
Arts and Music
Popular Entertainment
Publishing
Theater

Pocahontas (real name, Matoaka), daughter of the Indian chief Powhatan, became a favorite subject of American writers as a result of John Smith's tale of her intercession to save his life. The first book to treat Pocahontas as a literary figure was a novel, *The First Settlers of Virginia* (1805) by John Davis. The first play to use an American Indian as its subject was *The Indian Princess; or, La Belle Sauvage* by James N. Barker; it was first staged in Philadelphia on Apr. 6, 1808. The play was interspersed with songs and told the story of Pocahontas in a romantic vein. Another play, *Pocahontas* appeared in 1830; it was the work of George Washington Parke Custis, grandson of Martha Washington. Another drama with the same title, by Robert Dale Owen, the social reformer, appeared in 1837. Seba Smith, the humorist and journalist, wrote a verse romance, *Powhatan* (1841).

III. Business and Industry
Education
Philosophy and Religion
Science

One of America's first and most successful entrepreneurs was German-born John Jacob Astor, who came to the U.S. in 1784. On Apr. 6, 1808, he received a charter for the American Fur Company, planning to compete in the far Northwest with the long established Canadian firms. In 1811 a subsidiary company established Fort Astoria (now Astoria, Oreg.) on the Columbia R. estuary, the first permanent U.S. settlement on the Pacific coast. By the 1820s Astor held a virtual monopoly on fur trading in the U.S. West. Manuel Lisa, William Clark, Pierre Chouteau, and others operating out of St. Louis, Mo., formed the Missouri Fur Company on July 16, 1808, to compete but in 1821 Astor formed an alliance with them. Astor retired in 1834 and at his death on Mar. 29, 1848, was the wealthiest man in the U.S.

The first volume of *American Ornithology* by Alexander Wilson, a major contribution to American scientific scholarship, was published. Wilson's study ran to nine volumes and was completed in 1814. A pioneer work, it also appealed to laymen because of its attractive illustrations and frequent analogies to human nature.

IV. Fashion
Folkways
Holidays
Social Issues and Crime
Sports

Horses and horse racing continued to fascinate a large part of the population. The thoroughbred stallion Diomed was imported from England in 1798 and put out to stud. Diomed sired Sir Archie, sold to Gen. William R. Davie, a veteran of the American Revolution, for the unheard of sum of $5000. There was widespread mourning when Diomed died in 1808 in Virginia. The most important horse of the period was Justin Morgan, foaled in 1792 and the sire of the breed that became known by his name. The horse was named for its owner, a schoolteacher who brought him to Vermont, where there still is a Morgan horse farm near Middlebury. The Morgan horse is small, has great endurance, and can do almost anything but hunt or run well in long races.

Oct 30: Benjamin Ireson, skipper of the schooner *Betty*, brought his vessel into Marblehead, Mass., where he was accused unjustly of sailing away from another skipper's sinking ship because he feared losing his own vessel. The women of Marblehead tarred and feathered him and ran him out of town in a cart. This story was related years later by John Greenleaf Whittier in his ballad "Skipper Ireson's Ride" (1857).

1809

I. Civil Rights
Exploration and Settlement
Government
Statistics
Wars

Great Britain's attempts to restrict U.S. shipping during Britain's war with France continued to cause dissension in the U.S. The ineffective Embargo Act of 1807 was repealed on Mar. 1, 1809, largely through the efforts of Sen. Timothy Pickering of Massachusetts. Pickering was an ardent Federalist who typified the bitter opposition of New England to the law that had almost destroyed its shipping. The Non-Intercourse Act was passed the same day, permitting trade with all nations except England and France. Trade with the belligerents would be resumed when they agreed to respect the rights of the U.S. On Apr. 19 Pres. James Madison issued a proclamation allowing trade with England; the British minister to the U.S. had stated that British orders against U.S. shipping would be withdrawn on June 10. Unfortunately, the minister did not have the authority to make this promise, and on Aug. 9 Pres. Madison reinstated the Non-Intercourse Act.

Mar 1: The **Non-Intercourse Act** was signed by Pres. Thomas Jefferson in retaliation for English and French interference with American commerce. The act closed ports of the U.S. to France and England and outlawed their imports. It was repealed when the loss in customs revenue became excessive.

II. Architecture
Arts and Music
Popular Entertainment
Publishing
Theater

The Wyoming Valley Massacre of 1778, a relatively minor event in the course of the American Revolution, was remembered because of a later poem about it. On July 3, 1778, a force of Loyalists and Indians commanded by John Butler of Connecticut attacked a settlement in the Wyoming Valley of northeastern Pennsylvania. The Americans were promised safe conduct, but when they surrendered on July 4, the Indians killed the settlers and looted and burned their homes. In 1809 Thomas Campbell, a Scottish poet, wrote *Gertrude of Wyoming*, a long narrative poem that described horrible events that had never occurred. It also told the sad story of two fictional lovers whose future happiness was doomed by the massacre. The poem was one of the earliest works by a European writer based on an American historical incident.

A *History of New York* by Washington Irving, the first American humorous masterpiece, was published. It was also the first American work to impress European critics and readers. Written under the pseudonym Diedrich Knickerbocker, a comic scholar "a little queer in his ways," Irving's book was a tongue-in-cheek history of Dutch New Amsterdam. It became a best seller. Although it has been said that the descendants of the original Dutch settlers were put out by the treatment Irving gave their ancestors, the Dutch patroons were but one target among many. Irving had as good a time with Thomas Jefferson, Republicans, Yankees, Swedes, European literature, and historians who wrote the sort of books that did please the descendants of the Dutch. He also possessed the redeeming quality of being able to laugh at himself.

III. Business and Industry
Education
Philosophy and Religion
Science

Among those who contributed to the growing knowledge about the U.S. and to the achievements of American scientists was William Maclure, a well-to-do Scottish merchant who became a U.S. citizen in 1796. His *Observations on the Geology of the United States* (1809) included the first geological map of the U.S. In preparing a revised edition (1817), Maclure crossed the Allegheny Mts. dozens of times. He also introduced to the U.S. the educational theories of Johann Heinrich Pestalozzi, the Swiss educational reformer. Pestalozzi emphasized individual development and the study of nature.

The **Boston Crown Glass Company** was incorporated. The company had been in business since 1792, when it made the first successful window glass in the U.S. Its glass was said to be superior to any imported product. The charter of incorporation suspended company taxes and freed employees from military service.

IV. **Fashion**
   Folkways
   Holidays
   Social Issues and Crime
   Sports

One of the most impressive American Indian leaders was Tecumseh, chief of the Shawnees. Alarmed by the steady westward movement of settlers, Tecumseh on July 2, 1809, began a campaign to unite in a defensive confederacy the Indian tribes of the Old Northwest, the South, and the eastern Mississippi R. Valley. Americans had by treaty already acquired 30,000,000 acres of land in the region. Tecumseh was aided by his brother, Tenskwatawa, called the Shawnee Prophet. In spite of Tecumseh's efforts, on Sept. 30 William Henry Harrison, governor of the Indiana Territory, signed a treaty at Fort Wayne by which the Indian tribes ceded three more tracts of land along the Wabash R. Tecumseh's continuing efforts to halt further encroachment on Indian lands alarmed the settlers, who urged military action against him. The dream of an Indian confederacy died for good with the battle of Tippecanoe in Nov. 1811.

Oct 31: A **missing persons advertisement** was placed by one George Hicks of Brooklyn in the New York *Post.* Hicks offered a $25 reward for the return of a "Negro woman named Charity and her female child . . . 25 years of age, five feet high, of a yellowish complexion . . . has lost the use of one of her fingers, occasioned by a fellon . . . took with her several suits of clothes."

1810

I. Civil Rights
Exploration and Settlement
Government
Statistics
Wars

The western and northern boundaries of the area known as West Florida were long in dispute between the U.S. and Spain, England, or France—all three controlled it at various times. The U.S. claimed some of the area as part of the Louisiana Purchase of 1803. In dispute was the land between the Mississippi R. on the west and the Perdido R. on the east. In 1810 American settlers in the region rebelled against Spanish control. On Sept. 26 they captured the fort at Baton Rouge and proclaimed a republic. On Oct. 27 Pres. James Madison proclaimed U.S. annexation of West Florida and declared it part of Orleans Territory.

The third U.S. **Census** recorded a population of 7,239,881, an increase of 1,931,398 over 1800. Black population rose by 481,361 to 1,378,110. Of this total, 186,746 were free citizens, a group omitted in the 1800 census. The center of population moved to a point 40 mi. northwest of Washington, D.C.

1810-1811: In **congressional elections** the Republicans gained two Senate seats for a 30–6 majority over the Federalists. In the House they gained 14 seats for a 108–36 majority.

II. Architecture
Arts and Music
Popular Entertainment
Publishing
Theater

Interest and support for musical enterprises continued to grow. The first regular orchestra in the U.S.

was formed about this time in Boston by Gottlieb Graupner, a German-born musician who came to the U.S. in 1795. For nearly 25 years Graupner played a leading role in the musical life of Boston, especially as the founder of the Handel and Haydn Society. The semiprofessional Philharmonic Orchestra he founded played a significant role in the development of Boston's cultural life. The orchestra gave its last performance on Nov. 24, 1824, at the Pantheon, on Boylston Square.

A **theater season** was launched in Lexington, Ky., the first time west of the Appalachians. From then on, road companies mostly offering contemporary melodramas and farces brought stage presentations to the smaller cities of the U.S. until the high costs of production and travel in the mid-twentieth century made the business unprofitable.

III. Business and Industry
Education
Philosophy and Religion
Science

Because of the vast expanse of the U.S., the development of new means of transportation was inevitable. Cornelius Vanderbilt was one of the first of the new developers. He began his career in 1810, operating a small boat as a ferry between Staten Island and Manhattan, New York. By age 40 he was worth a small fortune as a result of his major share in shipping interests around New York harbor and on the Hudson R. During the gold rush of the mid-nineteenth century, he operated a shipping line to the West Coast by way of Nicaragua, where he put together a combined land and water route across Central America. Turning his attention to railroads after the Civil War, Vanderbilt built or secured control of the lines that became the New York Central Railroad between New York and Chicago. Some of his methods, like those of his competitors, were ethically questionable, but at his death in 1877 Vanderbilt was said to be worth $100,000,000.

The **Newburyport Bridge** over the Merrimack R. in Massachusetts, the most famous suspension bridge in nineteenth-century America, was erected by John Templeman, holder of several patents on suspension bridge improvements. The bridge had a span of 224 ft. In 1909 it was rebuilt, with its original structure carefully preserved.

Growth of higher education in the U.S. was reflected in the establishment of seven new colleges during the decade beginning in 1810. The new schools brought to 37 the number of institutions of higher learning in the nation.

July 12: The **Journeymen Cordwainers** trial began in New York City. Members of this trade union were accused of conspiring to raise their wages by calling a strike. They were found guilty and fined $1.00 each plus costs because "Even to do a thing which is lawful in itself, by conspiracy, is unlawful." This decision followed the precedent established in the 1806 trial of bootmakers in Philadelphia. In 1842 the Supreme Court of Massachusetts reversed the trend by stating that the legal definition of *conspiracy* excluded union actions.

IV. Fashion
  Folkways
  Holidays
  Social Issues and Crime
  Sports

Although cricket had a long headstart over baseball, it quickly lost out in popularity once baseball was introduced later in the century. A form of cricket was played in Virginia as early as 1709, and a match was played in New York City in 1751. Boston's first cricket club was organized in 1809, and the sport spread west with English settlers. There were reports of cricket being played in Kentucky in 1818 and in Illinois a year later. Chicago in 1840 had three teams. But Philadelphia was the center of cricket in the U.S., and its factory workers of English origin played weekly matches.

Dec 10: The first unofficial **heavyweight champion** of the U.S., Tom Molineaux, a freed slave from Virginia, was beaten in the 40th round by Tom Cribb, the English champion, in a boxing match at Copthall Common, London.

1811

I. Civil Rights
   Exploration and Settlement
   Government
   Statistics
   Wars

Two incidents involving warships were portents of the coming war between the U.S. and Great Britain. On May 1, off Sandy Hook, N.Y., the 38-gun British frigate *Guerrière* stopped the American brig *Spitfire* and seized an American-born seaman. On May 6 the 44-gun American frigate *President* was ordered to the area to protect U.S. shipping; en route it came upon a ship thought to be the *Guerrière*. Actually it was a British 20-gun corvette, *Little Belt*. The *President* attacked the *Little Belt* on May 16, disabling it, killing nine, and wounding 23 of the crew. The U.S. government told the British minister in Washington on Nov. 1 that it would reach an agreement about the incident if Great Britain would rescind orders that restricted American commercial shipping. The British refused to negotiate.

Feb 11: Trade with Britain was prohibited by Pres. Madison, the third time in four years that such action was taken. Madison hoped to effect repeal of the Orders in Council by which Britain placed restrictions on neutral commerce.

Apr 12: Colonists sent by **John Jacob Astor** on the *Tonquin* to operate a Pacific coast fur-trading center

of the newly formed Pacific Fur Company arrived at
the mouth of the Columbia R. via Cape Horn. Under
the leadership of a Capt. Thorn, they disembarked at
Cape Disappointment, Wash., but soon moved a few
miles upstream and founded Astoria in what is now
Oregon. This was the first permanent American colony in the Pacific Northwest.

II. Architecture
   Arts and Music
   Popular Entertainment
   Publishing
   Theater

An unusual case of plagiarism involved one of the
most popular American novels of the early nineteenth century. Isaac Mitchell, a newspaper editor,
serialized in 1811 in his Poughkeepsie, N.Y., *Political
Barometer*, a novel he had written, *The Asylum; or,
Alonzo and Melissa*. In the same year there appeared
Alonzo and Melissa; or, The Unfeeling Father, signed
by Daniel Jackson, a teacher at the Plattsburgh, N.Y.,
Academy. Mitchell died before he could sue for damages, but authorship later was restored to him. The
novel, a Gothic romance, featured ghosts, separated
lovers, haunted castles, and a happy ending for the
young couple. It sold well for some 40 years.

James Fenimore Cooper left the U.S. Navy to
marry Susan De Lancey and settle down in Mamaro-
neck, N.Y., as a gentleman farmer. Cooper did not
begin his career in letters for another nine years. In
1814 Cooper moved to Cooperstown, N.Y., then to
Scarsdale, N.Y., in 1817. There, it is said, he claimed
he could write a better book than the novel he was
then reading, and his wife challenged him to do so.
Thus began the career of one of the most popular
novelists in American literary history.

III. Business and Industry
    Education
    Philosophy and Religion
    Science

The first large-scale highway construction project of the federal government began this year. The project was the National Road, the first part of which was known as the Cumberland Road because it connected Cumberland, Md., already linked to Baltimore, with Wheeling, in present-day West Virginia. The Cumberland Road was completed in 1818. Originally the National Road was to run to the Mississippi R., but after it reached Vandalia, Ill., in 1830 construction stopped. Until it lost its importance, first to canals and then to railroads, the National Road was the main route west for settlers and a vital commercial artery for farm products moving to eastern cities.

The **first steamboat** to sail down the Mississippi R. was owned by a Mr. & Mrs. Roosevelt. After several interruptions, including an earthquake at New Madrid, Mo., and the birth of a baby to Mrs. Roosevelt, the boat reached New Orleans on Jan. 12, 1812, where it caused a sensation. The boat then commenced regular runs between New Orleans and Natchez, charging $18 for the downstream trip and $25 for the upstream trip.

IV. Fashion
   Folkways
   Holidays
   Social Issues and Crime
   Sports

Even as the nation grew in size, its social fabric was being enriched by the introduction of new national groups. In 1811 Russians were exploring and claiming areas of the Far West that eventually became U.S. territory. On Feb. 2 Russians landed at Bodega Bay, north of San Francisco, and established Fort Ross, a fur-trading post. Russians had been the first Europeans to reach Alaska, in 1741, under the leadership of Vitus Bering, a Dane in Russian employ. They established the first settlement in Alaska in 1784 on Kodiak Island, and further strengthened their claim to the region with the founding of the Russian-American Company in 1799.

Jan: A **slave insurrection** took place in Louisiana when some 400 slaves rose up, killed the son of a plantation owner, and marched on New Orleans. Armed soldiers and planters put down the uprising, and some 75 of the slaves were killed. The uprising was an indication of the frail foundation on which the southern economy and social fabric were based. Fear of further bloody uprisings was to play an important role in the nation's political and social history leading up to the Civil War.

1812

I. Civil Rights
Exploration and Settlement
Government
Statistics
Wars

The War of 1812 began on June 18, when Pres. James Madison officially proclaimed the U.S. to be at war with Great Britain. Congress had voted for war on June 4 and June 8. The war, which caused great harm to the U.S. economy, came after a long period of troubled relations between the two countries, caused mainly by Britain's conflict with Napoleonic France. The British seized American ships, impressed seamen from them, some of whom were U.S. citizens, and attempted to keep U.S. ships from reaching French ports. The war was also the result of the influence of the so-called War Hawks in Congress, Henry Clay and other westerners who wanted to acquire more land by conquering Canada. Ironically, on June 23 Great Britain, not yet aware of the declaration of war, suspended the orders that had hampered U.S. shipping.

1812-1813: In **congressional elections** the Republicans lost three Senate seats but still led the Federalists

27–9. In the House the Federalists gained 32 seats to the Republicans' four, but the latter maintained a majority, 112–68.

Apr 30: Louisiana was admitted to the Union, the 18th state. Formerly known as Orleans Territory, it was made up mainly of land from the Louisiana Purchase of 1803, but also included the part of West Florida annexed in 1810 west of the Pearl R.

May 14: Annexation by a congressional act added the **West Florida territory** to the territory of Mississippi and to the nation.

Aug 16: Brig. Gen. **William Hull surrendered Detroit** to British forces under Gen. Isaac Brock, making no attempt to defend the city though the attacking force was smaller than his own. Hull was court-martialed two years later for yielding without resistance.

Oct 13: Gen. **Stephen Van Rensselaer** was defeated in the battle of Queenstown Heights, Canada, on the Niagara frontier by the British and Indians. About 1000 U.S. troops were killed or wounded. British Gen. Isaac Brock, captor of Detroit, was killed during the engagement.

Dec 2: James Madison was reelected president of the United States, defeating De Witt Clinton of New York, who had been endorsed by the Federalists and by Democratic-Republicans opposed to the war. Elbridge Gerry, Democratic-Republican of Massachusetts, was elected vice president. The presidential electoral vote was Madison, 128; Clinton, 89. The vice presidential electoral vote was Gerry, 131; Charles Jared Ingersoll, Federalist of Pennsylvania, 86.

Dec 29: The U.S. frigate *Constitution* destroyed the British frigate *Java* in a fight off the coast of Brazil. *Old Ironsides* was under the command of Commodore William Bainbridge.

II. Architecture
   Arts and Music
   Popular Entertainment
   Publishing
   Theater

Thomas Sully was an Anglo-American who became the leading portrait painter of his day. Born in England, Sully came to the U.S. as a child and later lived and worked in both countries. He was influenced by Benjamin West and Sir Thomas Lawrence, and his portraits were in the Romantic style, urbane and elegant. They included likenesses of Queen Victoria, Fanny Kemble, Andrew Jackson, and Samuel Coates. The Coates portrait shows the subject standing by his desk, quill pen in hand, a cosmopolitan gentleman. Sully also did historical paintings, his best known being *Washington's Passage of the Delaware*. He produced some 2000 portraits in all as well as miniatures.

Apr 13: *Marmion* by James N. Barker, a highly successful dramatization of the poem by Sir Walter Scott, opened in New York City. With the U.S. at war with Great Britain, the anti-English sentiments expressed by Scott's characters held great appeal for New York audiences. Yet the producer listed the play as written by an Englishman, Thomas Morton, to cater to the esteem Americans placed on British culture.

III. Business and Industry
Education
Philosophy and Religion
Science

American religious groups, which in colonial days had been the object of missionary efforts from England and other countries, in the early nineteenth century began to proselytize abroad. The American Board of Commissioners for Foreign Missions was formed in 1810. The Baptists established a group to support missions in 1814, the Methodists in 1819, the Episcopalians in 1820, and the Presbyterians in 1837, although work by the Presbyterians had begun much earlier. Adoniram Judson, a leader of the missionary movement that had spawned the American Board, went to India in 1812. In 1813 he traveled to Burma, where he remained for 30 years and where he translated the Bible into Burmese. By 1848 there were 283 American missionaries in the Orient.

The **Academy of Natural Sciences of Philadelphia** was founded, dedicated to the advancement of the natural sciences. It was immediately popular and generously supported. Within two years the original membership of seven doubled, 33 correspondents were making contributions, and a program of lectures on plants and insects was scheduled. The public was admitted in 1828, two years after the museum had been expanded by the addition of another building. Among today's more than 140,000 volumes, those presented by the original donors maintain a place of honor.

IV. Fashion
Folkways
Holidays
Social Issues and Crime
Sports

The first use of *Uncle Sam* to personify the federal government occurred during the War of 1812. It seems to have been used derisively at first by those opposed to the war and stemmed probably from the "U.S." stamped on uniforms and government wagons. Some attribute the origin of the term to Samuel Wilson of Troy, N.Y. His nickname was Uncle Sam and he was an inspector of Army supplies. The "U.S." stamped on supplies was referred to by workmen as Uncle Sam. The first recorded use of the term in print was in the Troy *Post* of Sept. 3, 1813, and the first appearance in a book was in *Adventures of Uncle Sam* (1816) by an author who used the name Frederick Augustus Fidfaddy, Esq.

Gerrymandering entered the national vocabulary as a term indicating political abuse. The Massachusetts legislature had passed a bill that would facilitate the rigging of contests for senatorial offices by a systematic reapportionment of the electoral districts within the state. In 1812 the senatorial districts corresponded to the areas of the counties. When the Republicans gained control of the legislature, they cited a provision of the state constitution that invested the legislature with the power of determining electoral districts. Elbridge Gerry, the governor, signed the bill into a law. The districts followed no regular lines. One district resembled a salamander or, in the words of a Federalist, a *Gerrymander*.

1813

I. **Civil Rights**
   Exploration and Settlement
   Government
   Statistics
   Wars

An Indian uprising in the South brought on the Creek Indian War (1813–1814). Creeks who lived mainly in Alabama and Georgia were alarmed by encroachments on their lands and were convinced by Tecumseh, the Shawnee chief, to unite with many other tribes against the settlers. The leader of the Creeks was William Weatherford, also known as Red Eagle. On Aug. 30, 1813, he led an attack on Fort Mims, a temporary stockade near the confluence of the Tombigbee and Alabama rivers. Although Weatherford attempted to restrain his warriors, they massacred some 500 whites. The U.S. retaliated on Nov. 3 when Gen. John Coffee attacked and destroyed the Indian village Talladega, in Alabama, killing more than 500 warriors. In Jan. 1814, however, Tennessee militiamen were defeated in three minor engagements. The war did not end until the Battle of Horsehoe Bend in Mar. 1814.

Apr 27: British forces surrendered **York, Canada,** now Toronto, to Americans commanded by Brig. Gen. Zebulon M. Pike, who was killed in the battle.

June 1: Capt. **James Lawrence** cried "Don't give up the ship" to his crew as he lay mortally wounded aboard the *Chesapeake*, which was subsequently defeated and captured by the British frigate *Shannon* in an engagement off the Massachusetts coast.

Sep 10: The **Battle of Lake Erie** was a significant American naval victory. An improvised American fleet commanded by Oliver Hazard Perry decisively defeated the British after a bloody engagement. During the battle Perry's flagship *Lawrence* was crippled and he had to continue the fight from another ship. He returned to the *Lawrence* to accept the British surrender, then sent to Gen. William Henry Harrison, commander in the west, the victory dispatch containing the words "We have met the enemy, and they are ours." The Americans gained control of Lake Erie, and the British were obliged to withdraw from Detroit, further strengthening the U.S. position in the Great Lakes.

II. Architecture
Arts and Music
Popular Entertainment
Publishing
Theater

The most successful woman author of the late eighteenth and early nineteenth centuries was Susanna Rowson, who had come to America from England in 1793. In England she had published in 1791 the sentimental and didactic novel *Charlotte Temple: A Tale of Truth.* It was issued in America in 1794, described as "designed . . . for the perusal of the young and thoughtful of the fair sex." By 1933 it had gone through 161 editions in the U.S. Mrs. Rowson was also an actress and author of comedies and comic operas. Although she left the stage in 1797 and opened a girls' boarding school near Boston, Mrs. Rowson continued to write, her work including the novel *Sarah; or, The Exemplary Wife* (1813).

Sep 4: The **first religious weekly** in America, *Religious Remembrancer,* founded in Philadelphia by John W. Scott, began publication. Through successive mergers the magazine grew, and eventually became the *Christian Observer.*

III. Business and Industry
Education
Philosophy and Religion
Science

In 1813 Jethro Wood, a farmer in New York State, invented a cast-iron plow that he patented the following year. This was the 19th patent for a plow issued in the U.S. Charles Newbold had patented the first cast-iron plow in 1797. In 1819 Wood patented an improved plow that had replaceable iron parts and a curved plate, the moldboard. The modern moldboard derives from Wood's moldboard. Wood's design remains little changed today, but John Deere's substitution of steel for cast iron two decades later proved more effective in turning the heavy, sticky soil of the prairies.

Feb 26: **Robert R. Livingston,** one of the leading figures in the development of steam transportation, died. Livingston had financed Robert Fulton's first successful steamboat, the *Clermont,* which had sailed up the Hudson R. in 1807. As a result of Fulton's early support, Livingston had secured a monopoly on steamboat shipping in New York waters. Livingston was a man of many achievements. He had been a member of the committee that drafted the Declaration of Independence in 1776. As the first chancellor of the State of New York, he had administered the presidential oath of office to George Washington in 1789, and in 1801, as U.S. minister to France, conducted the negotiations that led to the Louisiana Purchase.

IV. Fashion
   Folkways
   Holidays
   Social Issues and Crime
   Sports

The gambling game of craps, derived from the English and French game of hazard, began to be played in the U.S. at about this time. At least as early as the sixteenth century, the throw of 1–1 with dice was called crabs, and the word *craps* stems from this term. According to one legend, blacks around New Orleans, La., began playing hazard about 1800, when the game was already sometimes called crabs or craps. Rules were so modified that craps became a separate game. Another explanation is that a rich playboy of New Orleans, Bernard Xavier Philippe de Marigny de Mandeville, introduced craps to America. He is said to have lost most of his money shooting craps. In any event, New Orleans seems to have been the starting point for the game of craps.

The celebrated "witch" **Moll Pitcher** died in Lynn, Mass. Her fame had spread throughout the region. Hundreds went to her for prophecy, love potions, and knowledge of lost things. She is reputed to have presided at conventions of witches at Lynn. Every time she visited a community, she entered its folklore. Years later she became the subject of the long poem *Moll Pitcher* (1832) by John Greenleaf Whittier.

1814

I. Civil Rights
   Exploration and Settlement
   Government
   Statistics
   Wars

The Treaty of Ghent, ending the War of 1812, was signed on Dec. 24 by representatives of the U.S. and Great Britain. The Senate ratified the treaty in Feb. 1815. The American negotiators were John Quincy Adams, James A. Bayard, Henry Clay, Jonathan Russell, and Albert Gallatin. By terms of the treaty, all conquered territory was to be returned by both sides, and a commission was to settle the boundary between the U.S. and Canada from the St. Croix R. west to Lake of the Woods. The British did not achieve their aim to set up an Indian buffer state in the Northwest. The emotional issues that helped cause the war—impressment of American seamen and the rights of neutral commerce—were not mentioned.

1814-1815: In **congressional elections** the Republicans lost two Senate seats but led the Federalists 25–11. In the House they gained five seats for a 117–65 majority.

Mar 29: The **Creek War** (1813–1814) ended as Gen. Andrew Jackson defeated the Creeks under Chief Weatherford at the decisive battle of Horseshoe Bend, Ala., where nearly 900 of 1000 Indians were killed. The Creeks had fought with British troops against the Americans in the War of 1812.

Aug 24: Washington, D.C., was captured by British troops under Gen. Robert Ross. The Capitol, White House, and other government buildings were set afire in retaliation for the earlier burning of Canadian government buildings in York, Toronto, by U.S.

Sep 11: At the **Battle of Lake Champlain** a newly built U.S. fleet under Master-Commandant Thomas Macdonough annihilated a British squadron. This forced British Gen. Sir George Prevost and his army to abandon their siege of the U.S. fort at Plattsburgh and to retreat to Canada on foot.

II. Architecture
Arts and Music
Popular Entertainment
Publishing
Theater

The words to "The Star Spangled Banner" were written during the War of 1812 by Francis Scott Key, a lawyer, on the night of Sept. 13–14, 1814, during the unsuccessful bombardment of an American fort by British warships. Key was on his way to the British fleet to try to secure release of an American citizen held by the British. He was detained by the British during their attempt to capture Fort McHenry, near Baltimore. Key was inspired by the sight of the American flag still flying and wrote the words that were set to the music of "Anacreon in Heaven," anthem of the Anacreontic Societies of England, which were clubs of amateur musicians. Key's song was first printed as a handbill; on Sept. 20 it appeared in the Baltimore *Patriot*. Although long considered the national anthem of the U.S., "The Star Spangled Banner" did not officially gain that status until 1931.

A report on the **Lewis and Clark Expedition** (1803–1806), based on the papers of Meriwether Lewis and made available by William Clark, was published by editors Nicholas Biddle and Paul Allen. The report, *History of the Expedition under the Command of Captains Lewis and Clark*, carried a preface by Thomas Jefferson in which the career of Lewis was related in succinct but memorable detail. In 1806 Jefferson himself had given advance notice of the findings of the expedition in his *Message from the President of the United States, Communicating Discoveries Made by Captains Lewis and Clark*. Lewis had intended to arrange publication of the material himself. But immediately after the expedition and retirement from the Army, Jefferson appointed Lewis governor of the Louisiana Territory. Lewis was so busy with the affairs of his office that he found no time to finish his revision before his mysterious death in an inn in Tennessee in 1809. Clark contributed to this edition of the journals, but final discretion was left to his editors. The complete papers remained unpublished until 1903.

III. Business and Industry
Education
Philosophy and Religion
Science

Important improvements in education in the early nineteenth century, especially education of women, were the result of the efforts of Emma Willard. In 1807, when only 20, she took charge of the Female Academy at Middlebury, Vt. She opened a school of her own in 1814. There she taught subjects not otherwise available to women. An appeal to the New York State legislature in 1818 to support her plan for improving the education of women induced Gov. De Witt Clinton to invite Mrs. Willard to move to New York. She accepted, and opened a school at Waterford in 1819. In 1821 she moved to Troy and established the Troy Female Academy. Mrs. Willard wrote textbooks and a volume of poems (1831), which included the popular "Rocked in the Cradle of the Deep."

Francis Cabot Lowell built the first U.S. plant designed to manufacture cloth from raw cotton by power machinery. A Boston importer, Lowell had observed power machinery in British textile plants and had violated British laws by smuggling secretly drawn sketches of that machinery out of the country. With the financial backing of his brother-in-law, Patrick Tracy Jackson, and the mechanical skill of machinist Paul Moody, Lowell secured a charter for the Boston Manufacturing Company, with a capitalization of $300,000. The machinery used in the Waltham factory and all subsequent equipment of the company came to be known as Lowell-Moody machinery and soon was quite different from the English models upon which they had been based. The city of Lowell, Mass., was named after Lowell.

IV. **Fashion**
   Folkways
   Holidays
   Social Issues and Crime
   Sports

A ubiquitous institution of the period was the country store. Most communities were too small to support a variety of retail stores, each specializing in a particular line of goods. The result was the country store, carrying virtually everything—food, clothing, farm equipment, housewares, and more. The Great Western Store, opened by Jedediah Barber at Homer, N.Y., in the central part of the state in 1813, was typical. Starting in one medium-sized room, Barber expanded his establishment to three stories, attic, and cellar. Like other storekeepers of the time, Barber did much of his business in barter, with customers exchanging products they had made or grown for store goods. Storekeepers often became leading citizens of their communities, sometimes adding real estate and banking to their business enterprises.

The **cost of education at Harvard** was about $300 a year. John Thornton Kirkland became president in 1810 and continued the innovations that had established the liberal bent of the college. He made it possible for poor students to meet fees by offering a number of jobs in which they could earn some money. He also supervised grants and scholarships, as well as an annual subsidy of $2500 that Massachusetts donated to encourage gifted but needy students. In Kirkland's time Harvard had the reputation of being a poor man's school, because he did so much to make it easy for indigent students to attend. Yet the tradition of gentility was already apparent, since the aim of the college was to create the same kind of gentlemen who were described in prospectuses of Cambridge and Oxford. Students attended classes five days a week from 6 A.M. to 4 P.M., with an hour free between the morning and afternoon sessions. Campus social life was encouraged by Kirkland. He contributed to the beginnings of some of the most famous clubs, including Hasty Pudding, Porcellian, Hermetic Society, and Speaking Club. There were extracurricular pleasures in parties and dances, and the college was just far enough from Boston to provide the attractions of both city and country life.

1815

I. Civil Rights
Exploration and Settlement
Government
Statistics
Wars

The greatest battle of the War of 1812 and its finest American victory came on Jan. 8, 1815, two weeks after the war had been ended officially by the Treaty of Ghent. The Battle of New Orleans was fought on the British side by 7500 veterans under the command of Gen. Sir Edward Pakenham. The U.S. force, under the command of Gen. Andrew Jackson, comprised about 4500 troops, many of them expert marksmen from Kentucky and Tennessee armed with exceedingly accurate long rifles. The U.S. troops were strongly entrenched when on the morning of Jan. 8 the British, in close ranks, made two assaults on their lines. In half an hour the British were driven back, Pakenham was killed, and 2036 of his men were killed or wounded. U.S. forces suffered 8 killed and 13 wounded. Although the battle had no bearing on the outcome of the war, it was a stimulus to U.S. pride, which had suffered from several embarrassing defeats during the conflict. The battle made a military hero of Gen. Jackson, whose political career was advanced.

Mar 3: War against Algeria was declared by Congress.

The dey of Algiers had molested U.S. ships and insisted on payment of tribute.

June 17: Commodore **Stephen Decatur** captured the Algerian frigate *Mashouda*. Hammida, the renowned Algerian admiral, was killed during this engagement.

June 19: Capt. **Decatur**'s squadron captured *Estido*, an Algerian brig, off Cape Palos in southeastern Spain.

June 30: The **war against Algeria** and the Barbary Coast pirates ended when a peace treaty was signed with the dey of Algiers. It was followed by similar treaties with Tunis on July 26 and Tripoli on Aug. 5. The treaties, exacted by Commodore Stephen Decatur, required the pirates to cease their hostile acts, free all American prisoners, and compensate the U.S. for vessels seized.

II. Architecture
Arts and Music
Popular Entertainment
Publishing
Theater

America's first professional journalist, Philip Freneau, was also the "poet of the American Revolution." In 1775, at the beginning of the war, he wrote eight satirical poems, such as "General Gage's Confession." During the war he was captured by the British on a voyage from the West Indies and in 1781 wrote of the brutal treatment he had received in "The British Prison Ship." Freneau's anti-British sentiments were also expressed during the War of 1812 in such poems as "On British Commercial Depredations." Freneau edited various newspapers, such as the *National Gazette* in Philadelphia from 1791 to 1793. As an editor he was a vigorous Jeffersonian, often involved in editorial quarrels. Beyond his political and patriotic activities, Freneau was the earliest American lyrical poet of importance, writing such poems as "The Wild Honeysuckle" and "Eutaw Springs." An edition of his *Collected Poems* was published in 1815.

The *North American Review,* for a century the most influential review in the U.S., was founded by William Tudor, Edward T. Channing, and Richard Henry Dana, Sr. It soon became a major influence among educated readers. The review published articles by leading American writers, who wrote in professional and scholarly fashion.

III. Business and Industry
Education
Philosophy and Religion
Science

One of the most important economic activities in the U.S. from the late eighteenth century to the middle of the nineteenth century was whaling. In 1791 American whalers for the first time rounded Cape Horn to hunt whales in the South Pacific. New Bedford, Mass., became the greatest whaling port in the world. Although set back by the War of 1812, whalers prospered more than ever after the virtual disappearance of British whaling ships. U.S. ships sailed throughout the Pacific Ocean, often on hunts of three years or more. Shortly before the Civil War, the whaling industry declined because the demand for sperm oil lessened with the coming of the petroleum industry. In addition, the number of whales had been reduced by overhunting.

The **Conestoga wagon** proved to be the most efficient mode of transportation for long treks from the East into the prairie regions. The "prairie schooner" was often bedecked with lively colors, its team of four-to-six horses festooned with bells. It carried a load of several tons and sometimes was built to a length of 60 ft.

IV. Fashion
Folkways
Holidays
Social Issues and Crime
Sports

With the end of the Napoleonic wars in Europe, immigration to the U.S. increased to new levels. Between 1815 and 1860, 5,000,000 persons came to the U.S. Over half of the immigrants came from the British Isles, mostly from Ireland. The next largest contingent arrived from Germany, 1,500,000, not counting German-speaking French citizens from Alsace and Lorraine. More than half the German immigrants settled in the upper Mississippi and Ohio river valleys.

Jean Lafitte, the pirate, became an American folk hero because of his actions at the Battle of New Orleans. Since 1810 Lafitte had been operating off the Baratarian coast, south of New Orleans, as a privateer, preying on Spanish commerce for several Latin American nations. In Sept. 1814, a few days after a U.S. naval force raided his base at Barataria, Lafitte was offered a commission by the Royal Navy. Instead of accepting, Lafitte offered to help Andrew Jackson in return for a U.S. pardon for his piratical offenses. Lafitte and his men acquitted themselves admirably in the Battle of New Orleans, but in 1817 he moved his crew to the site of present-day Galveston, Tex., where they resumed a life of piracy.

1816

I. Civil Rights
   Exploration and Settlement
   Government
   Statistics
   Wars

The presidential election of 1816 resulted in continuation of the so-called Virginia dynasty of presidents that had begun with Thomas Jefferson's election in 1800. The Democratic-Republican candidate was James Monroe of Virginia, who had been wounded in the American Revolution, and had served as diplomat, senator, and secretary of state. The Federalists by now scarcely existed as a national political party. They nominated Rufus King, who had been a delegate to the Constitutional Convention and one of New York's first senators. He carried only Massachusetts, Connecticut, and Delaware. The election was yet one more indication of the moribund condition of the Federalist Party. From this election on, it became ever weaker and ceased to exist in the 1820s.

1816-1817: In **congressional elections** the Republicans gained nine Senate seats for a 34–10 majority over the Federalists. In the House they gained 24 seats for

Dec 4: James Monroe was elected president of the United States. Daniel D. Tompkins was elected vice president. Monroe, secretary of state under Pres. James Madison, gained the presidency in a landslide victory over his Federalist opponent, Rufus King of New York. The presidential electoral vote was Madison, 183; King, 34; and four abstentions.

Dec 11: Indiana was admitted into the Union as the 19th state. Five years earlier, at the Tippecanoe R., it had been the scene of a decisive encounter between the confederated Indians under Tecumseh and U.S. forces under Gen. William Henry Harrison. After that encounter the Indians had made one last major raid, in 1812, then chose to sell out to the settlers and move beyond the Mississippi R. In June 1816 a constitution for the new state was drafted in the Indiana state capital at Corydon. In 1825 the state capital was moved to Indianapolis.

II. Architecture
   Arts and Music
   Popular Entertainment
   Publishing
   Theater

It was believed in some quarters and hoped in others
that one result of securing independence from England would be development of an American language. Differences in spelling and vocabulary increased, but the American language has never
achieved true independence from the mother tongue.

Aug: "The Culprit Fay," a poem of more than 600
lines, was written in three days by Joseph Rodman
Drake. Drake died of tuberculosis in 1820, and his
poem was not published until 1835, in the volume
The Culprit Fay and Other Poems. On his deathbed
Drake had ordered his wife to destroy the manuscripts of what he described as his "trifles in rhyme."
Fortunately, she did not do so. "The Culprit Fay," set
against the background of the Hudson R. Valley, is
considered an important milestone in the development of American literature.

III. Business and Industry
Education
Philosophy and Religion
Science

Black religious groups began to break away from
largely white Protestant denominations to form their
own churches. In 1796 black members of the Methodist Episcopal Church in New York City formed the
African Methodist Episcopal Zion Church, which in
1821 was organized as a national group. The African
Methodist Episcopal Church was founded in 1816 by
Richard Allen, a clergyman who had been born a
slave. He was pastor of a group that broke away from
the Methodist Church in Philadelphia. On Apr. 11 he
became the first bishop of the new denomination.

The **American Bible Society** was founded in New
York City. The purpose of the organization was to
increase circulation of the Bible. Through the society
translations of the Bible in over 1000 tongues have
been printed and distributed around the world. The
society emphasizes distribution of the Bible to the
poor. It was incorporated in 1841 and in cooperation

with the British and Foreign Bible Society has developed into an organization of worldwide influence with a large membership and many auxiliaries.

June: Baltimore, Md., became the first city in the U.S. to launch a **gas company.** The Gas Light Company of Baltimore was organized to provide coal gas for lighting the city's streets.

Dec 13: The **first savings bank** in the U.S. was organized in Boston as The Provident Institution for Savings.

IV. Fashion
Folkways
Holidays
Social Issues and Crime
Sports

Transportation of blacks from the U.S. to Africa was often proposed as a partial solution for the slavery question. The first important step along these lines was taken at a meeting in Washington, D.C., in Dec. 1816 and Jan. 1817, when the American Colonization Society was formed. The principal founder was Robert Finley, a clergyman. Freeing many black slaves created a new problem: freedmen did not enjoy equal status with whites. In 1821 land was secured in Africa that later became the independent nation of Liberia, but by 1860 only about 11,000 blacks had been transported there. Abolitionists opposed resettlement, claiming it merely made slavery stronger in the South by removing free blacks. At the same time, many blacks born in the U.S. showed little enthusiasm for resettlement in Africa.

"Our country, right or wrong" was included in a toast offered by Stephen Decatur at a Virginia dinner commemorating his success against the pirates of the Barbary Coast. Called on to propose a toast he said: "Our Country! In her intercourse with foreign governments may she always be in the right; but our country, right or wrong."

1817

I. Civil Rights
Exploration and Settlement
Government
Statistics
Wars

The first step in a process of mutual disarmament along the U.S.-Canadian border was taken this year in the Rush-Bagot Convention, signed on Apr. 28–29. The agreement was contained in an exchange of notes in Washington, D.C., between Richard Rush, acting secretary of state, and Charles Bagot, the British minister to the U.S. By its terms, each nation would have no more than four warships on the Great Lakes and Lake Champlain, and none would exceed 100 tons. The Senate unanimously approved the agreement on Apr. 16, 1818. The agreement set a precedent for solving Anglo-American disagreements by negotiation, although it was not until the Treaty of Washington of 1871 that complete mutual disarmament obtained along the U.S.-Canadian border.

Nov 20: The **First Seminole War** (1817–1818) began when settlers attacked Florida Indians and the Indians retaliated by raiding isolated Georgia homesteads. Americans believed Spain had incited the Seminoles against the white settlers.

Dec 10: Mississippi was admitted into the Union, the 20th state.

II. Architecture
Arts and Music
Popular Entertainment
Publishing
Theater

More than any other painter, John Trumbull provided future generations with a record of the Revolutionary era. After studying under Benjamin West in London, he began copying his teacher's grand style in historical paintings. An early and moving example was *The Death of General Montgomery at Quebec.* In 1816 Trumbull secured a commission from Congress to decorate the Capitol, and the best known result was *Signing of the Declaration of Independence* (1818). Others were *Surrender of Burgoyne at Saratoga, Surrender of Cornwallis at Yorktown,* and *Resignation of Washington.* In 1831 he founded Trumbull Gallery at Yale and placed much of his work in it.

Sep: The poem **"Thanatopsis"** by William Cullen Bryant won for American poetry its first attention and respect from British critics. Printed in the *North American Review,* the poem's appearance was "much as if a classic temple had been exorcised from the wilderness by the strains of a new Amphion." Its quiet reflections on death and nature created an entire school of American poets.

III. Business and Industry
Education
Philosophy and Religion
Science

The distribution by religious groups of Christian literature not only spread religion but also contributed significantly to education. The Connecticut Tract Society was formed in 1807. In 1814 it joined with half a dozen similar groups to form a national organization, the American Tract Society. After 1817 the society supplied much religious literature, which was distributed widely by circuit riders. In many homes these were the only books, and from them children learned to read and spell. Peter Cartwright, a Methodist circuit rider for nearly 50 years, wondered whether he "had done the most good by preaching or by distributing religious books." He felt "it was part and parcel of a Methodist preacher's most sacred duty to circulate good books." Cartwright sometimes handed out a thousand dollars worth of books a year, a large amount at that time.

July 4: Construction of the **Erie Canal** was begun under Gov. De Witt Clinton of New York, elected in spring of 1817. The canal was to affect the development of New York, both city and state, bringing Great Lakes trade to the Atlantic Ocean.

IV. Fashion
Folkways
Holidays
Social Issues and Crime
Sports

Fashions in clothing changed considerably in the early nineteenth century. Under the influence of the romantic movement and the French Revolution, women's fashions became simpler. Light dresses, low-cut and sleeveless, replaced the elaborate billowing gowns of the old aristocracy. Hair was cut shorter, not piled high. About 1815 fashion began moving back to the era of stiff corsets, leg-of-mutton sleeves, and full skirts that developed into the hoop skirt. Men's fashions also changed. Knee-length pantaloons, with buckles, silk stockings, and low-cut shoes, as well as the wig, were on their way out by 1800. Pres. James Monroe was the last chief executive to dress this way, and an 1823 painting of him and his cabinet shows Monroe the only person so clothed. Long trousers came in, reflecting the French Revolution, whose supporters came from the middle and lower classes and dressed this way to contrast with the nobility. The style seemed appropriate for democratic America.

Cup plates became the rage at about this time. They were miniature plates with a center cavity about the diameter of a cup bottom used as a dainty but practical perch for cups while a drinker sipped from his saucer. Cup plates were decorated with lavish attention to detail, came in a great variety of patterns, and fairly chronicled the taste of the period. They were introduced first as chinaware. The development of the glass industry, especially of the glass press, made them even more plentiful and, considering their use, necessary. Cup plates lasted as long as it was considered polite to drink from a saucer but went out of vogue before the Civil War.

1818

I. **Civil Rights**
   Exploration and Settlement
   Government
   Statistics
   Wars

The First Seminole War (1817–1818) began in earnest this year with a U.S. invasion of East Florida to punish hostile Seminole Indians, whose territory had become a refuge for runaway slaves. American troops on July 27, 1816, had destroyed the Seminole stronghold of Fort Apalachicola, on the river of that name. On Dec. 27, 1817, Gen. Andrew Jackson took command, with orders to pursue the Indians across the Florida boundary. Jackson marched his troops into Florida and captured St. Marks on Apr. 7, 1818, and Pensacola on May 24. In the course of his campaign, Jackson seized two British traders, Alexander Arbuthnot and Robert Ambrister. He accused them of aiding the enemy and had the former hanged and the latter shot. There was a great outcry in England and considerable criticism in Washington. Nevertheless, popular opinion approved the campaign, which brought East Florida under American control and resulted in its cession to the U.S. by Spain in 1819.

1818-1819: In **congressional elections** the Republicans gained one Senate seat for a 35–7 majority over the Federalists. In the House they gained 15 seats for a 156–27 majority.

Oct 20: A **diplomatic convention** signed between Britain and the U.S. gave fishing rights to American seamen off parts of Newfoundland and the coast of Labrador. The U.S. renounced such activity within three miles of any other British territory. The boundary between Canada and the U.S. between Lake of the Woods and the crest of the Rocky Mts. was fixed at the 49th parallel. No boundary was decided upon farther west, and Oregon was declared open territory for ten years.

Dec 3: **Illinois** was admitted into the Union, the 21st state.

II. Architecture
Arts and Music
Popular Entertainment
Publishing
Theater

An unusual example of an American playwright of the early years of independence who won acclaim, although not riches, on both sides of the Atlantic was John Howard Payne (1791–1852). Showing a precocious interest in the drama, he published the *Thespian Mirror* in New York City when he was only 14. It so impressed the literary and theater world that he was encouraged to write. He proceeded to write a melodrama, *Julia; or, The Wanderer* in 1806. His early fame waned, and it was not until 1818, in England, that he regained recognition. Success stemmed from the production by Edmund Kean, the noted British actor, of Payne's *Brutus; or, The Fall of Tarquin,* which opened on Dec. 3. This romantic tragedy, in blank verse, was equally successful in New York in 1819. It was performed for many years. By 1832, after other successes and writing the poem "Home, Sweet Home," which was put to music, Payne was honored but died in debt while working on further literary and dramatic works.

Jan 1: The **White House,** as the restored Executive Mansion in Washington, D.C., was now called because of its gleaming new coat of white paint, was opened for a general reception. Burned out by the British in 1814, the building was ready for occupancy in the fall of 1817, but lacked proper furnishings.

III. Business and Industry
Education
Philosophy and Religion
Science

Americans in the early nineteenth century continued to show interest in science. One of the foremost scientists was Benjamin Silliman, who in 1802 became the first professor of chemistry and natural history at Yale. In 1813 he began an illustrated lecture course in geology and mineralogy and in 1818 was one of the founders of the Yale Medical School. Also in 1818 he became one of the founders of the *American Journal of Science and Arts,* the first important scientific journal in the U.S., which he edited for nearly 28 years.

Jan: Transatlantic ship crossings on a regular monthly basis were initiated between U.S. and British ports when the *James Monroe* sailed from New York City and the *Courier* from Liverpool, England. Four ships formed the Black Ball Line.

IV. Fashion
Folkways
Holidays
Social Issues and Crime
Sports

Bowling had been introduced to America by the Dutch in the seventeenth century, when the game became a ten-pin rather than nine-pin game. There is an 1803 picture of ten-pin bowling in progress in Suffolk County, N.Y. By mid-nineteenth century there was a boom in the building of indoor alleys. Gambling began to invade the sport, and in 1841 bowling was banned in Connecticut for this reason. Still it remained a regular amusement at the fashionable Saratoga, N.Y., spa. In literature, the game of

ninepins plays an important part in Washington Irving's "Rip Van Winkle," probably his most popular
story, issued serially in *The Sketch Book* (1819–1820).

Apr 4: A **U.S. flag with 13 stripes** was settled on by
Congress. On admission of each new state to the
Union, another star would be added to the flag, the
number and pattern of stripes remaining the same.

1819

I. **Civil Rights**
   Exploration and Settlement
   Government
   Statistics
   Wars

The Supreme Court, under the leadership of Chief
Justice John Marshall, continued to set precedents
increasing the power of the judiciary and the national government. In the case of *McCulloch v. Maryland* in 1819, Marshall found an opportunity to assert
the power of the federal government over the states.
Maryland had levied a tax on a branch of the Bank
of the United States. Marshall argued that if the government had the right to coin money, which the Constitution gave it, it had the implied right to establish
a bank. Thus, the government was supreme in that
sphere and a state could not tax an instrument of the
central government. This argument is generally
agreed to be Marshall's most brilliant opinion on constitutional law, but it was not universally accepted at
the time.

Feb 22: The **Florida Purchase Treaty** was signed by
Spain and the U.S. In a triumph of diplomacy by Sec.
of State John Quincy Adams, Spain ceded the remainder of its old province of Florida at no cost beyond
that of U.S. assumption of up to $5,000,000 of the
claims of U.S. citizens against Spain. Adams also ob-

tained for the U.S. a transcontinental southern boundary that legitimized U.S. interests on the northern side of the line to the Pacific.

Dec 14: Alabama was admitted into the Union, the 22nd state.

II. Architecture
Arts and Music
Popular Entertainment
Publishing
Theater

One of the earliest satirical writers on public affairs in the U.S. was Joseph Rodman Drake, a poet of New York. A series of satirical poems called "The Croaker Papers" appeared anonymously in the New York *Evening Post* and *National Advertiser* this year. Of the 35 poems, Drake wrote 14 and collaborated on eight with his friend Fitz-Greene Halleck. Drake also wrote "The Culprit Fay," a serious poem, and "The American Flag," a patriotic poem that was declaimed on many occasions for years after. Drake died of consumption on Sept. 21, 1820, at 25. Halleck's poem "On the Death of Joseph Rodman Drake" is considered one of the finest elegies in American literature.

Washington Irving's *Sketch Book* became an immediate best seller and still ranks among the most popular American books of all time. With this book Irving established himself as a beloved literary genius.

III. Business and Industry
Education
Philosophy and Religion
Science

In the Dartmouth College case the Supreme Court, under Chief Justice John Marshall, continued to uphold the power of the federal government. In 1816 New Hampshire, without the consent of Dartmouth College, amended the college charter, which in legal terms was a contract. The college brought suit, with

Daniel Webster as counsel. Marshall wrote the court's opinion, holding that New Hampshire acted unconstitutionally, violating the Constitution's prohibition against any state passing laws "impairing the Obligation of Contracts." The decision became a major instrument for protection of property rights against state abridgment.

What was probably the **first food canning business** was begun in New York City when Ezra Daggett and Thomas Kensett started canning fish as a commercial enterprise. In 1825 Kensett obtained a patent, the first, for tin-plated cans. In Boston William Underwood opened a successful canning plant in 1820.

William Ellery Channing delivered his famous sermon, "Unitarian Christianity," in Baltimore. In it he outlined the Unitarian view and provided liberals with a platform. The sermon heightened tensions among Protestant factions and led to formation of the American Unitarian Association.

IV. Fashion
Folkways
Holidays
Social Issues and Crime
Sports

The eastern U.S. was slowly becoming urbanized, but the frontier, moving ever westward, was still the place for the vigorous outdoor activities associated with newly settled rural areas. Marksmanship was highly prized and involved such sports as squirrel shooting by four-man teams. On one occasion, a team shot 152 squirrels by nightfall and the other, 141. A brutal sport was the rough-and-tumble fight. There were no rules and the two contestants were free to bite off ears or gouge out eyes until a fighter gave up or was knocked unconscious.

Apr 26: The **Independent Order of Odd Fellows** made its first appearance in the U.S. with the organization of Washington Lodge No. 1 in Baltimore, Md., by Thomas Wildey, who had arrived from England in 1818. On Feb. 1, 1820, the new lodge was chartered by Duke of York Lodge, Preston, England.

1820

I. **Civil Rights**
   Exploration and Settlement
   Government
   Statistics
   Wars

The first serious clash between slavery and antislavery interests, in 1819 and 1820, strained relations between the North and the South and hinted at worse trouble to come. At the end of 1818 the Union consisted of 11 free and 11 slave states. The North, however, was rapidly outdistancing the South in population and held a growing numerical advantage in the House of Representatives. Southern leaders felt strongly, therefore, that the number of free and slave states should remain balanced so that the South would be equal to the North in the Senate. Ready for statehood were Maine, certain to be a free state, and Missouri, part of the Louisiana Purchase and likely to be a slave state. After much political maneuvering, Congress passed on Mar. 3, 1820, a bill that became known as the Missouri Compromise. By its terms Maine was to be admitted as a free state and Missouri as a slave state, but slavery was to be forever prohibited in the rest of the Louisiana Purchase north of the line of latitude 36°30′, which was the southern boundary of Missouri.

The fourth U.S. **Census** recorded a population of 9,638,453. The center of population was placed 16 miles east of Moorefield, W. Va.

1820-1821: In **congressional elections** the Republicans gained nine Senate seats for a 44–4 majority over the Federalists. In the House they gained two seats for a 158–25 majority.

Mar 15: Maine was admitted into the Union, the 23rd state.

Dec 6: James Monroe was reelected president of the United States. Daniel D. Tompkins was reelected vice president. The electoral vote was Monroe, 231; John Quincy Adams, a Federalist and Monroe's secretary of state, 1.

II. Architecture
Arts and Music
Popular Entertainment
Publishing
Theater

The Knickerbocker Group was a school of writers with similar literary tastes who were associated with New York City. The name was a tribute to Washington Irving's *Knickerbocker's History of New York* (1809); those who followed Irving tried to carry on his spirit and style. Among the Knickerbockers were William Cullen Bryant, James Kirke Paulding, Joseph Rodman Drake, Lydia Maria Child, and Fitz-Greene Halleck. In 1819 Halleck's long poem *Fanny* was published. In it, in imitation of the style of Lord Byron, he satirized in rollicking fashion life in New York—finance, society, women, etc. Halleck also found time to be personal secretary to the entrepreneur John Jacob Astor.

A great **literary theme** of the 1820s was the romantic treatment of the Indian. Works in this vein included *Frontier Maid, or the Fall of Wyoming* (1819); *Yamoyden* (1820) by Eastburn and Sands; *Logan, an Indian Tale* (1821) by Samuel Webber; *The Land of Powhatten* (1821) by a Virginian; and *Ontwa, Son of the Forest* (1822) by Henry Whiting.

III. Business and Industry
Education
Philosophy and Religion
Science

Americans were beginning to take an interest in the history and culture of the Indians. The foremost pioneer in this field was Henry Rowe Schoolcraft, a self-taught ethnologist and geologist. This year School-craft accompanied an expedition to the upper Mississippi R. and Lake Superior region, and two years later he was appointed Indian agent for the tribes in that area. This enabled Schoolcraft to carry on his research into Indian history and culture and resulted in voluminous writings. These included a six-volume history published between 1851 and 1857. Schoolcraft married the daughter of an Ojibwa woman and a fur trader. Henry Wadsworth Longfellow used Schoolcraft's writings as source material for his narrative poem *The Song of Hiawatha* (1855).

The **number of college graduates** in the U.S. was estimated by James Fenimore Cooper to be 8000, in a population of 10,000,000.

The evolution of **interchangeable machine parts** was stepped up by Thomas Blanchard's invention of a special lathe to finish off wooden stocks of firearms. Stocks could be cut out in rapid order and used with standardized metal parts of guns. Success with his lathe encouraged Blanchard to apply his invention to more general industrial uses.

IV. Fashion
   Folkways
   Holidays
   Social Issues and Crime
   Sports

The frontier attracted rugged types who liked to boast of their toughness, since the West was a region where physical strength was often a necessity. The phrase *half horse, half alligator,* first recorded in 1809 by Washington Irving, was an appellation such persons liked to use in referring to themselves. Mark Twain later wrote of a rough-and-tumble fighter who introduced himself in this way: "the original iron-jawed, brass-mounted, copper-bellied corpse-maker from the wilds of Arkansaw," concluding with "cast your eye on me, gentlemen, and lay low and hold your breath, for I'm 'bout to turn myself loose."

During this decade the **first soccerlike games** appeared in American colleges. A large round ball was kicked toward a goal. The game served as a form of hazing, especially at Yale and Harvard. Sophomores and freshmen were supposed to kick the ball, but sophomores generally kicked freshmen instead. The games were banned during the 1830s because of the large number of injuries sustained by students.

1821

I. Civil Rights
Exploration and Settlement
Government
Statistics
Wars

As part of the westward movement, American traders probed the Southwest, which put them in contact with Spanish regions. Traffic over what was to become the Santa Fe Trail began on Sept. 1, 1821, when William Becknell led a party from Independence, Mo., headed for Santa Fe, N. Mex. Spanish authorities had forbidden trading with Americans, but such trade was welcome after Mexico won its independence in Nov. 1821. The trip of about 780 miles was made yearly by caravans comprising as many as 100 wagons, the trip taking 40 to 60 days. The caravans carried textiles and hardware to Santa Fe, where the traders usually remained for four or five weeks before returning to Missouri.

Aug 10: Missouri was admitted into the Union, the 24th state.

Dec: The **first American settlement in Texas,** San Felipe de Austin, was established by Stephen Austin.

II. Architecture
   Arts and Music
   Popular Entertainment
   Publishing
   Theater

Music was made more available to amateurs and students by the publication of songbooks and by the introduction into schools of music education. A pioneer in this field was Lowell Mason, a banker and church organist in Savannah, Ga. In 1821 he helped compile the *Boston Handel and Haydn Society's Collection of Church Music.* Its success was one reason why Mason gave up banking and turned to music, becoming the musical director of three Boston churches. He was a founder of the Boston Academy of Music in 1832. Mason also found time to compose 1210 hymns, including "Nearer, My God, to Thee."

The Spy by James Fenimore Cooper, a romance of the American Revolution, was published and quickly went through three printings in its first year.

III. Business and Industry
    Education
    Philosophy and Religion
    Science

The need for more and better roads to transport people and goods also meant that more and better bridges were needed. Ithiel Town, an architect, contributed to the cause by patenting in 1820 a form of truss bridge with a diamond pattern of closely spaced diagonals. This was simple to construct and required no special materials. In 1821 he wrote an article that considered the problem of rigid iron bridges. It was to take 15 years before such structures were built in the U.S.

May 31: The **first Catholic cathedral** in the U.S., the Cathedral of the Assumption of the Blessed Virgin Mary, Baltimore, Md., was dedicated by Archbishop Maréchal. The cornerstone had been laid in 1806.

IV. **Fashion**
   Folkways
   Holidays
   Social Issues and Crime
   Sports

The most serious attempt to find a home outside the U.S. for freed black slaves was the establishment in 1821 of the colony of Liberia in western Africa. With government and private funds, the American Colonization Society purchased the area from local tribal chiefs. Settlement began in 1822, when the first of about 15,000 persons arrived in Liberia. The colony had many difficulties, and its survival in the early years was due mainly to the efforts of Jehudi Ashmun, who was sent there by the society and who built up the colony in spite of epidemics and native attacks. The colony was declared independent in 1847. Immigration of American blacks ended for the most part after the Civil War.

During the next decade and a half **coffee** came into general use in America. But temperance movements directed heavy campaigns against it, and in some quarters it was considered an aphrodisiac.

1822

I. **Civil Rights**
   Exploration and Settlement
   Government
   Statistics
   Wars

Fear of slave insurrections was common in the South in the early nineteenth century. While there were few actual instances of trouble, a serious uprising took place in Charleston, S.C., this year. It was led by a free black, Denmark Vesey, who had purchased his freedom in 1800. Over the years Vesey had organized a plot to seize control of Charleston, but word leaked out in June. Militia and federal troops were called out, many slaves were arrested, and Vesey and 34 others were executed. Some estimates put the number of slaves involved as high as 9000.

1822-1823: In **congressional elections** the Republicans kept their 44–4 Senate majority over the Federalists. In the House they gained 29 seats to the Federalists' gain of one, for a 187–26 majority.

II. Architecture
Arts and Music
Popular Entertainment
Publishing
Theater

Men with a variety of talents aided progress in literature, religion, and education in the first quarter of the nineteenth century. One of these was Timothy Dwight of New England, a leader of the Connecticut Wits, clergyman, and educator. His long poem *Greenfield Hill* (1794) was an attempt to convince Europeans that America provided suitable material for poetry. His *Travels in New England and New York* (four volumes, 1821–1822) is an indispensable source for the life of the period. An orthodox Congregational minister, Dwight was sometimes called the "Protestant pope of New England." He was president of Yale from 1795 to 1817 and did much to modernize its curriculum.

The Pilot by James Fenimore Cooper was published and became a best seller. Cooper's fourth novel, and the first with a maritime setting and theme, was a product of Cooper's determination to outdo Sir Walter Scott in the production of a sea novel. The unnamed hero, known only as the Pilot, represents John Paul Jones, the foremost U.S. naval figure of the time. The novel's action takes place during the American Revolution. Cooper's novel was long popular.

III. Business and Industry
Education
Philosophy and Religion
Science

Agitation by manufacturing interests for a protective tariff system, which had begun with Alexander Hamilton in the late eighteenth century, continued as industry grew. The chief proponent was Mathew Carey of Philadelphia. One of the most important publishers and booksellers of his day, Carey was also a self-taught economist who wrote and spoke in favor of what was beginning to be called the American system: tariffs and internal improvements at the federal government's expense. Carey's *Essays on Political Economy* was published in 1822. His frequent addresses before the Philadelphia Society for the Promotion of National Industry reflected the rise of protectionist sentiment.

The first patent for making **false teeth** was awarded to C.M. Graham.

IV. Fashion
Folkways
Holidays
Social Issues and Crime
Sports

Exploration of the western U.S. was aided by fur trappers and those who organized the fur trade. One such man was William Henry Ashley, whose 1822 expedition built a post at the confluence of the Yellowstone and Missouri rivers. Ashley's innovation in the fur trade was to initiate an annual rendezvous at which time the trappers gathered to sell their furs and purchase supplies. The trappers, who had had no taste of civilization for a year, sometimes spent on drinking and gambling everything they had earned for the year's work.

The primitive U.S. form of **football** was prohibited at Yale College by Pres. Timothy Dwight, who ordered any violations to be reported and violators to be penalized by a fine not to exceed half a dollar.

1823

I. Civil Rights
Exploration and Settlement
Government
Statistics
Wars

Many Americans, especially in the South, were beginning to cast eyes at Texas as an area for agricultural expansion. Long part of the Spanish Empire, Texas had become part of the independent nation of Mexico in 1821. Spain had made a grant of land and in 1820 given Moses Austin permission to bring in 300 settlers. The Mexican government having confirmed the grant, Moses's son Stephen took up the work of his late father and brought in settlers in Dec. 1821. Mexico further encouraged American settlement in 1823 with an offer of cheap land. More Americans came, and half a dozen settlements had been established within a decade.

Dec 2: What came to be called the **Monroe Doctrine** was enunciated by Pres. James Monroe. His annual message to Congress expounded a foreign policy based on two principles. First, any attempt by Europeans to colonize the Americas or interfere in the internal affairs of the Western Hemisphere would be viewed with displeasure by the U.S. Secondly, the U.S. would remain aloof from European quarrels. In essence, this was the foreign policy advocated by John Quincy Adams, Monroe's secretary of state.

II. Architecture
Arts and Music
Popular Entertainment
Publishing
Theater

The portrayal of blacks on the stage posed problems in a nation in which most blacks were slaves. The first acting group of blacks, the African Company, began giving performances in New York City in 1821. Both Shakespearean drama and lighter plays were produced. In 1823 Edwin Forrest, who was to become a national idol and one of the great tragedians of the century, appeared in blackface as Ruban in a farce by Sol Smith, *Tailor in Distress*. No white actress would black her face, so a black woman was engaged to play opposite Forrest.

May 8: "Home Sweet Home" by John Howard Payne, the most popular song yet written by an American, was sung for the first time at Covent Garden in London. It was an aria sung by the homesick heroine in a play by Payne with music composed by Sir Henry Bishop.

III. Business and Industry
   Education
   Philosophy and Religion
   Science

The banking system of the U.S. centered on the second Bank of the United States, chartered in 1816 by the federal government. Its headquarters was in Philadelphia and it had 25 branches around the land. It prospered under the presidency of Langdon Cheves, a legislator from South Carolina who assumed the post in 1819, and even more under Nicholas Biddle, who took over in 1823. Biddle was a financier, editor, and diplomat. State-chartered banks were growing in numbers. The leading private banker was Stephen Girard, a French-born financier who had helped the government finance the War of 1812.

Charles J. Ingersoll offered a major defense of American culture against the criticism of British intellectuals in an address before the American Philosophical Society. In his *Discourse Concerning the Influence of America on the Mind,* he accepted the challenge of British critics by comparing American culture with European, suggesting that the average intellect in America far surpassed the corresponding intellect in Europe. He suggested that America's great contribution to world civilization had been self-government.

IV. Fashion
Folkways
Holidays
Social Issues and Crime
Sports

In an era when entertainment in the home had to be supplied by family and guests, music with humorous or sentimental words that could be sung to well-known melodies, was popular. Among such songs were "Believe Me if All Those Endearing Young Charms" (1808); "'Tis the Last Rose of Summer" (1813); "The Minstrel's Return from the War" (1827); and "Zip Coon" (c1834), later known as "Turkey in the Straw."

May: The **first major horse race** in the U.S. was between American Eclipse from the North and the challenger Sir Henry from the South for a purse of $20,000. About 100,000 spectators jammed the Union Course on Long Island to see American Eclipse take two out of three heats, doing the four-miles in 7:49 and 8:24. Victory of the northern horse spread gloom in the South.

1824

I. Civil Rights
Exploration and Settlement
Government
Statistics
Wars

Russia and the U.S. settled a territorial dispute involving regions in the far Northwest. On Sept. 4, 1821, Czar Alexander I asserted a claim on all of the Pacific coast north of the 51st parallel, bisecting the Oregon Territory claimed jointly by the U.S. and Great Britain. On July 17, 1823, Secretary of State John Quincy Adams notified Russia that this claim was unacceptable under the principles set forth by Pres. James Monroe the following December. On Apr. 17, 1824, Russia and the U.S. signed a treaty by which Russia agreed to 54°40′ as the southern limit of its claim. The treaty also removed a ban Russia had tried to impose on commercial fishing off the coast of the land it claimed.

1824-1825: In **congressional elections** the traditional parties broke down. The Federalist party disappeared as a national force and the Republican party split into Administration supporters, who backed John Quincy Adams, and Jacksonians, who supported Andrew Jackson. In the Senate the Administration faction led the Jacksonians 26–20. In the House they took a 105–97 majority.

Aug: The **first nominating convention** was held at Utica, N.Y. For the first time, electors of nominees for office were chosen by popular vote. Nominations for president and for state offices had previously been made in caucus, but this method was replaced by the convention. The Utica convention nominated candidates for the offices of governor and lieutenant governor of New York.

Dec 1: In the **1824 presidential election** no candidate received an electoral majority. John Quincy Adams of Massachusetts received 84 votes; Andrew Jackson of Tennessee, 99; Secretary of State William H. Crawford, who had suffered a stroke and was effectively out of the running, 41; Henry Clay, 37. John C. Calhoun of South Carolina was elected vice president. On Feb. 9, 1825, John Quincy Adams was chosen as president by the House of Representatives.

II. **Architecture**
   Arts and Music
   Popular Entertainment
   Publishing
   Theater

Of the many accounts of Indian captivity, none was more popular than *A Narrative of the Life of Mrs. Mary Jemison* by James E. Seaver, published in 1824. Mary Jemison was captured by a French and Indian war party in western Pennsylvania in 1758, when she was 15. She was married twice, once to a Delaware and once to a Seneca, and had eight children. Becoming known as the "White Woman of the Genesee," Mrs. Jemison refused to leave the Senecas. In 1817 New York State confirmed her possession of a tract of land on the Genesee R. that had first been given to her in 1797.

The **Meeting House** at Deerfield, Mass., was built from plans by Isaac Damon, the most popular country architect of New England in the early nineteenth century. The building is considered a very good example of his somewhat monumental style.

III. **Business and Industry**
   Education
   Philosophy and Religion
   Science

A new institution with religious and secular functions was the Sunday school. Originating in England, Sunday schools were first established to educate children who worked in mines and factories. Under church sponsorship, the schools soon came to offer religious instruction. The Methodist leader, Francis Asbury, established the first Sunday school in the U.S. in 1786 in Hanover County, Va. On May 25, 1824, representatives of a number of denominations from several states founded the American Sunday School Union to coordinate activities of these schools. Publication of *Sunday School Magazine* began in 1824, and over the years an enormous amount of literature was issued to serve the widespread institution.

The first recorded **strike involving female employees** in the U.S. occurred in Pawtucket, R.I. Male and female weavers struck against a proposed decrease in wages and an increase in hours. Prior to this time, organized labor had met with little success in or out of court in improving working conditions. By 1820, however, textile mill workers had been organized into a union numbering some 100,000. This growth in union strength was one of the factors that contributed to the strike in Pawtucket.

IV. Fashion
   Folkways
   Holidays
   Social Issues and Crime
   Sports

Memories of the American Revolution were revived when the Marquis de Lafayette, who had come from France in 1777 to fight on the Patriot side, arrived in the U.S. on Aug. 14, 1824. He was 67 years old when he returned. In October of 1824, Gen. Lafayette met Pres. James Monroe, the last U.S. president to have fought in the Revolution. On his tour of the U.S., which lasted until Sept. 1825, Lafayette was welcomed with enthusiasm, his natural charm and easy self-confidence winning over men and women alike.

The **first written American Indian language,** Cherokee, was finished by Sequoyah, the son of a white trader and a Cherokee Indian woman. Sequoyah, who also used the name George Guess, devised a syllabary of 85 characters to represent the spoken sounds of the Cherokee language. He demonstrated the alphabet's utility in a dramatic way. He had his young daughter transcribe speeches at a tribal council in his absence. Then he entered the council chamber and read the speeches aloud from his daughter's transcription. In the years following, Sequoyah taught thousands of Cherokee Indians to read and

write. He also translated parts of the Bible into the
new language, and in 1828 began publication of a
weekly newspaper.

1825

I. Civil Rights
Exploration and Settlement
Government
Statistics
Wars

The first secular Utopian society in the U.S. was established on Jan. 3 by Robert Owen, a social reformer who had made a fortune as a cotton manufacturer in Great Britain. He took over Harmony, Ind.,
from the followers of George Rapp and set up New
Harmony, a community that was to have complete
equality of property and opportunity. About 1000 settlers were attracted to the 20,000 acres of New Harmony, including educators, scientists, and writers.
However, dissension arose and there was lack of direction among those who were supposed to cooperate. Owen left in 1827. In 1828 the community ceased
to exist as a Utopian enterprise.

Feb 9: John Quincy Adams was elected president of
the United States by the House of Representatives,
into which the election had been thrown by the failure of any of the four candidates to win a majority in
the electoral college. In the four-way race of Adams,
Andrew Jackson, Henry Clay, and William Crawford,
Jackson had received more electoral votes than
Adams, but no majority. Clay assisted the Adams
cause in the House.

Feb 12: The Creek Indian treaty was signed. Tribal
leaders agreed to turn over all their lands in Georgia

to the government and promised to migrate west by Sept. 1, 1826. The treaty was rejected by most Creeks.

II. Architecture
Arts and Music
Popular Entertainment
Publishing
Theater

Henry Wadsworth Longfellow, one of the first American poets destined to be read and honored in the U.S. and Europe, began to see his poems appear in print. His first poem to be published was "The Battle of Lovell's Pond," on Nov. 17, 1820, in the Portland, Maine, *Gazette*. In 1825, the year he was graduated from Bowdoin College, a number of Longfellow's early poems were published in the *United States Literary Gazette*. They included "Autumnal Nightfall," "Woods in Winter," "The Angler's Song," and "Hymn of the Moravian Nuns." Longfellow soon left for Europe to prepare for a teaching position at Bowdoin, to which he returned in 1829.

June 17: Word of the oratorical brilliance of **Daniel Webster** spread after his celebrated "Bunker Hill Oration" at the laying of the cornerstone for the Bunker Hill Monument in Boston. His other early speeches included "The Dartmouth College Case" (1818) and "The Landing of the Pilgrims" (1820), matched perhaps only by Webster's "Reply to Hayne" in the U.S. Senate in 1830.

III. Business and Industry
Education
Philosophy and Religion
Science

The era of canal building was gathering momentum. On Oct. 26, 1825, the most important and successful of all American canals, the Erie, was officially opened. The Erie Canal stretched for more than 350 miles between Lake Erie and the Hudson R. at Albany and thus connected the Great Lakes with the Atlantic Ocean at New York City by way of the Hudson R. The father of the Erie Canal was Gov. De Witt Clinton of New York, whose enthusiasm had gotten the project under way. Construction had begun on July 4, 1817, and on Oct. 22, 1819, the first boat to travel on the canal went from Rome to Utica. The canal cost $7,000,000, which was returned many times over by the traffic it attracted. The Erie Canal became the most important passenger and freight route from the East to the Midwest and made New York the Empire State.

Mechanical pressing of glass, the first technical innovation in glassmaking since ancient times, was introduced into American factories. The change enabled production of intricately designed glassware. Famous glassworks established this year by Deming Jarves at Sandwich, Mass., were noted for their large-scale production of pressed glass.

IV. Fashion
   Folkways
   Holidays
   Social Issues and Crime
   Sports

Controversy over women's place in society was stimulated by Frances Wright, who had moved from England to the U.S. in 1824. An earlier visit (1818–1820) had resulted in her volume *Views of Society and Manners in America* (1821), which praised the country enthusiastically. Now, however, she was lecturing from public platforms, addressing workmen's groups and openly discussing such forbidden subjects as equal rights, birth control, and abolition. One newspaper editor denounced her as a "bold blasphemer and voluptuous preacher of licentiousness."

"Devil tales," involving pacts with the Devil, were a popular form of short story. Washington Irving contributed to the vogue by his legendary tale "Tom and the Devil," in his *Tales of a Traveler,* published this year. Tom and his wife strike a bargain with Old

Nick when he promises them the treasure of Captain Kidd.

1826

I. Civil Rights
Exploration and Settlement
Government
Statistics
Wars

Trappers, explorers, adventurers, and scientists were beginning to unlock the secrets of the immense expanse of the American West, much of it still unknown to settlers. One of the most daring yet practical of these men was Jedediah Strong Smith. Already a veteran of various expeditions, Smith set out on Aug. 22, 1826, with a small band of men from Great Salt Lake, Utah. They crossed the Colorado R. and the Mojave Desert before arriving at the San Gabriel Mission on Nov. 27. On leaving California, Smith and two of his men became the first men other than Indians to cross the Sierra Nevada and the Great Salt Desert from west to east. In 1831, while traveling along the Santa Fe Trail, Smith was killed by Comanches. Smith's most important contributions were his mapping and establishment of trails in the areas he explored.

1826-1827: In **congressional elections** the Jacksonians gained eight Senate seats for a 28–20 majority over the Administration faction. In the House they gained 22 seats for a 119–94 majority.

Jan 24: The Creek Indians signed the **Treaty of Washington** with the federal government. It nullified a previous treaty and ceded less territory to the government. It also granted the Indians the right to stay on their lands until Jan. 1, 1827.

II. Architecture
Arts and Music
Popular Entertainment
Publishing
Theater

American actors were competing with their British counterparts, who long had dominated the stage. The most notable rivalry was between the American Edwin Forrest and William Charles Macready of Great Britain. Forrest became a great tragedian, first playing Othello in 1826. He was very popular but some thought he displayed his powerful voice too often. Macready made his first visit to the U.S. in 1826, making his debut Oct. 2 at the Park Theater in New York in the play *Virginius* by James Sheridan Knowles. He, too, was a great tragedian. Forrest played Macbeth in England in 1845 but met with hostility from those who preferred Macready. Their rivalry was to have fatal consequences in 1849.

James Fenimore Cooper's *The Last of the Mohicans* began its phenomenal publishing record. The most popular of Cooper's novels, selling over 2,000,000 copies, it was also a best seller across the Atlantic. The Leatherstocking Tales, of which *The Last of the Mohicans* is the second novel of five, are still popular in the U.S. and Europe, especially France.

III. Business and Industry
Education
Philosophy and Religion
Science

Legal scholarship flourished in the U.S. as the American legal system began to separate from British tradition and establish its own foundations and precedents. America's first great legal scholar was James Kent, who in 1794 became the first professor of law at Columbia and later became chief justice of New York State courts. Kent modified English chancery practice to conform to American institutions and vir-

tually created equity jurisdiction in the U.S. Out of
his opinions and lectures came his *Commentaries on
American Law* (4 volumes, 1826–1830). The section
on constitutional law was Federalist in approach.
The *Commentaries* were an immediate success. Kent
updated them five times since. Kent's influence on
the legal profession and the teaching of law in the
U.S. was second only to that of John Marshall. Kent's
classic work has been compared with that of William
Blackstone, the English jurist who wrote a similar
four-volume work (1765–1769).

IV. Fashion
Folkways
Holidays
Social Issues and Crime
Sports

Combining entertainment with education, the lyceum movement became a familiar part of American
life. A lyceum was an organization that provided a
platform for speakers on a great variety of subjects.
The first lyceum was organized in 1826 in Millbury,
Mass., by Josiah Holbrook, a teacher whose Agricultural Seminary had failed in 1825. Within two years
he helped establish more than 100 lyceums. The National American Lyceum was formed in 1831, and by
1834 some 3000 lyceums were in operation, offering
information on the arts, science, history, and public
affairs. Many so-called reformers took advantage of
this platform to promote their notions, but leading
figures of the day, such as Daniel Webster and Ralph
Waldo Emerson, also were happy to appear on lyceum platforms.

June 30: "**Independence now and Independence forever!**" was penned by John Adams in response to a
request for a toast to be offered in his name on July
Fourth. The entire toast by Adams read: "It is my
living sentiment, and by the blessing of God it shall
be my dying sentiment—Independence now and Independence forever!"

1827

I. Civil Rights
Exploration and Settlement
Government
Statistics
Wars

Oregon Country, the region north of the California border and extending to Alaska, was still claimed by both the U.S. and Great Britain. On Aug. 6, 1827, the two nations signed a treaty extending an 1818 agreement to continue joint occupation of the territory. American and British fur-trading companies were in competition in the region, with the English Hudson's Bay Company having the better of it. At the same time, Americans were exploring the area, and in 1829 Hall J. Kelley of Boston founded the American Society for Encouraging the Settlement of the Oregon Territory.

Nov 15: The **Creeks** ceded their remaining territory in the Southeast to the U.S. The area included all their lands in Georgia.

II. Architecture
Arts and Music
Popular Entertainment
Publishing
Theater

The birds of North America, abundant and colorful, attracted scientists and nature lovers alike. It remained for an artist and ornithologist, John James Audubon, to give them recognition by painting some 500 of the birds in all their splendor. Later paintings may be more scientific, but none has ever matched Audubon's in popular appeal. *The Birds of America* was published in elephant folio size in parts between 1827 and 1838 in London. An accompanying text, *Ornithological Biography*, was issued in five volumes between 1831 and 1839. In the text Audubon had the help of William MacGillivray, who supplied scientific information. Earlier, in the course of observing birds, Audubon had made the first American bird-banding experiments.

The first book of poems by **Edgar Allan Poe,** *Tamerlane and Other Poems*, was printed in Boston. Little attention was paid the slim volume. In 1829 a second volume, *Al Aaraaf, Tamerlane and Minor Poems*, also went unnoticed.

Feb 7: Ballet was introduced to the U.S. by Mme. Francisquy Hutin, famed French danseuse, with *The Deserter*, staged at the Bowery Theater, New York City. Mme. Hutin's light and scanty attire so shocked the public that every woman in the lower tier of boxes immediately left the theater.

III. Business and Industry
Education
Philosophy and Religion
Science

As the U.S. economy began to shift from agriculture to manufacturing, causing a relative decline in commerce and shipping, economists who favored manufacturing began finding arguments for protecting and encouraging it. Among these was a German-born economist, Friedrich List, who emigrated to the U.S. in 1820 and returned to Germany in 1832. List wrote *Outlines of American Political Economy* (1827), arguing that a nation's true wealth stemmed from its productive industrial forces rather than from commercial transactions. Such a view was especially popular in New England, where the shift to light and heavy manufacturing was most pronounced. Thus, New England favored high tariffs on imported goods to protect the young American industries.

Encyclopedia Americana was begun by the German refugee political philosopher, Francis Lieber. Organized along Germanic principles of research and scholarship, the 13-volume work began to appear in 1829. It made a significant contribution to American culture.

IV. Fashion
   Folkways
   Holidays
   Social Issues and Crime
   Sports

During the first half of the nineteenth century, the American diet and eating habits amazed English visitors. Frances Trollope noted: "They eat with the greatest possible rapidity and in total silence." Harriet Martineau reported a breakfast that consisted of "cornbread, buns, buckwheat cakes, broiled chicken, bacon, eggs, rich hominy, fish, fresh and pickled, and beef-steak." And Charles Dickens was repelled by "those dyspeptic ladies and gentlemen who eat unheard-of quantities of hot corn bread (almost as good for the digestion as a kneaded pincushion), for breakfast and supper."

July 23: The **first swimming school** in the U.S. opened in Boston, Mass. Swimming was taught by placing a belt "around the bodies, under the arms, attached to a rope and pole, by which the head and body are kept in the proper position in the water, while the pupil is learning the use of his limbs." The school was attended by many notables, including John James Audubon and John Quincy Adams. Adams is reputed to have done some diving from the 6-foot board when he was 61 years old.

1828

I. Civil Rights
Exploration and Settlement
Government
Statistics
Wars

Growing discord between North and South over the
tariff came to the fore this year when, on May 19,
Pres. John Quincy Adams signed into law what became known as the Tariff of Abominations. Political
maneuvering between supporters of Pres. Adams and
those of Andrew Jackson caused much bitterness.
The Jacksonians had hoped to discredit Adams by
making the bill so objectionable that it would be defeated. Southerners, led by Vice Pres. John C. Calhoun, felt the law discriminated against the agricultural South, which relied on imports from abroad,
and favored the North and West. With strong New
England support, the bill passed both houses of Congress.

The **Democratic Party** was formed. Essentially it
was an extension of the Democratic-Republican (Jeffersonian) Party (formed May 13, 1792), and was
backed by southern agrarians and northern urban
workers. It advocated Jeffersonian principles of personal liberty and attacked special privilege. Andrew
Jackson became the new party's first nominee for
president.

The **National Republican Party** was formed during Pres. John Quincy Adams's term of office (1824–
1828). Ill feeling between Adams and Jackson was
polarizing U.S. politics. The National Republican
Party of Adams advocated a nationalistic program
including a national bank, protective tariffs, federally sponsored internal improvements, and a conservative land-sale policy. This package, called the

American System, was put together by Henry Clay, an ally of Adams, to appeal to the North and West. After loss of the election to Jackson, the coalition of National Republicans, Whigs, and splinter groups fell apart, and the Whig Party emerged as the party of opposition to the Jacksonian Democrats.

1828-1829: In **congressional elections** the Democrats gained a 26–22 Senate majority over the National Republicans. In the House they took a 139–74 majority.

Dec 3: Andrew Jackson was elected seventh president of the United States. Jackson, a senator from Tennessee until his nomination, received 647,231 popular votes and 178 electoral votes against 509,097 popular votes and 83 electoral votes for John Quincy Adams, candidate of the National Republican Party. John C. Calhoun was reelected vice president, receiving 171 electoral votes. The election was swung by Martin Van Buren of New York on the understanding that he would continue to exercise power in the state through the spoils system.

II. Architecture
   Arts and Music
   Popular Entertainment
   Publishing
   Theater

Women were beginning to enter journalism, and the most prominent woman journalist was Sarah Josepha Hale. In 1828 in Boston she became editor of a new journal, *Ladies' Magazine.* She moved to Philadelphia in 1837, becoming editor of *Godey's Lady's Book* and holding that post for 40 years. In 1846 Mrs. Hale began using the pages of the magazine to agitate for a national Thanksgiving Day, and by 1858 all but six states celebrated thanksgiving on the last Thursday in November. Mrs. Hale had great influence on fashions and manners and regularly urged higher education for women. Her volume *Poems for Our Children* (1830) contained "Mary Had a Little Lamb."

The monumental *American Dictionary of the English Language* by Noah Webster was published, a labor of more than 20 years. Webster spent much time in England gathering material for his work and completed it while living in Cambridge, England.

III. Business and Industry
   Education
   Philosophy and Religion
   Science

For practical purposes, the age of the railroad in the U.S. began on July 4, 1828, when ground-breaking ceremonies for the Baltimore and Ohio Railroad, led by Charles Carroll, the last surviving signer of the Declaration of Independence, were held in Baltimore, Md. The first section of the B&O, as it came to be known, opened in May 1830 between Baltimore and Ellicott's Mills, Md. The first source of power was the horse, but on August 30 the line was converted to steampower. The B&O kept laying rails westward and reached St. Louis, Mo., in 1857.

A **strike of factory workers,** the first recorded, occurred in a textile plant in Paterson, N.J. The strike was doubly significant because it led to the first recorded summoning of the militia to end labor violence. The workers' agitation for a ten-hour day ended in failure.

IV. Fashion
   Folkways
   Holidays
   Social Issues and Crime
   Sports

Performances by white entertainers in blackface, destined to develop into the popular minstrel shows of the 1840s and 1850s, probably got their start in 1828. In that year Thomas Dartmouth Rice gave a solo performance in blackface, dancing and singing "Jim Crow." Rice is said to have taken the tune from an elderly black who worked near the Louisville Theater, in Louisville, Ky. When Rice went to England in 1836, "Jim Crow" became an international hit song and the term Jim Crow became a synonym for blacks. Rice became known as "the father of American minstrelsy."

America's **first archery club** was formed by a group of famous artists. The United Bowmen of Philadelphia was formally organized by Franklin Peale, Titian Ramsey Peale, Samuel P. Griffith, Jr., Thomas Sully, and others. The initiation fee was $5.00 and dues 50 cents a month. Members wore Lincoln green frock coats with gold trim and broad straw hats decorated with three black ostrich plumes. It held annual tournaments and awarded silver trophies until it disbanded in 1859. It was the forerunner of the National Archery Association, founded in 1879. The National Field Archery Association was founded in 1939.

1829

I. Civil Rights
   Exploration and Settlement
   Government
   Statistics
   Wars

Inauguration of Andrew Jackson as seventh president was a turning point in the history of the executive office. Jackson was a self-made man, in contrast with his six predecessors, four of them upper-class Virginians and two affluent New Englanders. Jackson was also the first president nominated by the Democratic Party, which had evolved from the old Jeffersonian Democratic-Republican Party. The events of his inauguration symbolized the new Jacksonian era. After the ceremony thousands of his followers accompanied him back to the White House where, uninvited, they took over the reception, stand-

ing on chairs and crowding so that people were trampled and china and glassware broken. Tubs of punch
were set out on the White House lawn to lure some
of the crowd before a disaster occurred. The new
president himself had to be eased out a rear door for
protection against his surging admirers. Jacksonians
felt that the true democracy of America had triumphed.

The **Workingmen's Party** began to appear in Philadelphia and New York and spread quickly into northern industrial cities. Really an association of like-
minded labor assemblies, the Workingmen's Party,
including in its ranks several liberal newspaper editors, called for universal suffrage, abolition of imprisonment for debts, a nonmonopolistic banking
system, and compulsory, tax-supported schools.
Jacksonians exploited the party for political purposes. Though the party did not last long, its members and platform found their way ultimately into the
Democratic Party.

II. Architecture
   Arts and Music
   Popular Entertainment
   Publishing
   Theater

Sculptors were never as numerous as painters in
nineteenth-century America, but the making of statues was becoming a profession. Horatio Greenough
was America's first professional sculptor. He is best
known for his colossal statue of George Washington,
but he did other notable work, such as *The Rescue*
(1846) for the Capitol in Washington, D.C., depicting
a settler saving his wife and children from attacking
Indians. He also created *The Chanting Cherubs*
(1829) for the novelist James Fenimore Cooper, but
the nude cherubs shocked public taste. Greenough is
remembered as well for his writings on architecture,
in which he advocated that form follow function.

Scrimshaw, the art of making pictures on or carving the teeth or jaw of a sperm whale, flourished

during this period. Busks for corsets, chessmen, vases, cutlery, etc. were carved as were historical scenes. The hobby filled long, lonely hours on whaling cruises.

III. Business and Industry
Education
Philosophy and Religion
Science

A landmark in American education and publishing was the work of a German-born political philosopher, Francis Lieber, who came to the U.S. in 1827. Between 1829 and 1833 he edited the 13-volume *Encyclopedia Americana*, the first such reference work published in the U.S. Important to the work was the fact that Lieber persuaded specialists in various fields to write for the general public. As a professor at the University of South Carolina (1835–1836), he wrote the first works in political science by an American scholar not in public life. Among his other activities was popularization of physical education, which he saw as contributing to the well-being of a cultivated mind. During the Civil War he wrote *Instructions for the Government of Armies of the United States in the Field* (1863).

Oct 17: The **Chesapeake and Delaware Canal** was formally opened. Linking the Delaware R. and Chesapeake Bay, the canal was 14 miles long and cost some $2,250,000, which was shared by the U.S. government, Delaware, Maryland, and Pennsylvania, and various private citizens.

IV. Fashion
Folkways
Holidays
Social Issues and Crime
Sports

Americans have always liked tales of men of outsized stature and achievement, and Mike Fink was an early favorite. Born at Fort Pitt, Pa., before the American

Revolution, Fink was an Indian scout but most of his fame came from his exploits as a keel-boatman on the Ohio and Mississippi rivers. The first account of his adventures appeared in print in 1829 in *The Western Souvenir,* in an article by Morgan Neville. The account told of Fink's marksmanship, physical prowess, and tall tales. There are about 11 versions of his death, but he probably was shot dead somewhere near the mouth of the Yellowstone R. while trapping and exploring up the Missouri R. in 1822. Bernard DeVoto described this legendary figure as one in which "Casanova, together with Paul Bunyan, merges with Thor."

Oct 16: The **Tremont Hotel** in Boston, the first luxurious hotel in the New World, opened with a dollar-a-plate dinner attended by such notables as Daniel Webster and Edward Everett. The 170-room hotel offered many first-time-ever luxuries and conveniences: private bedrooms with door locks, soap and a pitcher of water in each room, indoor toilets (eight water closets), menus in the dining room, room clerks, and bellboys, called rotunda men. Architects of luxury hotels in the next few decades generally used the Tremont as their model.

1830

I. Civil Rights
Exploration and Settlement
Government
Statistics
Wars

The constitutionality of internal improvements (roads and canals) carried out by the federal government continued to be debated and to cause political divisions. On May 27, 1830, Pres. Andrew Jackson vetoed the Maysville Road bill, which would have provided government financial support for a 60-mile road construction project entirely in Kentucky. On May 31 Jackson approved a bill to provide funds for the Cumberland Road because it involved more than one state. Jackson believed in internal improvements in principle but felt a constitutional amendment was necessary. His stand helped him politically. The South's belief in states' rights was supported by his veto, which was also aimed at Henry Clay and the

The U.S. **Census** recorded a population of 12,866,020. The center of population was placed 19 miles west-southwest of Moorefield, W. Va.

1830-1831: In **congressional elections** the Democrats and National Republicans each lost a Senate seat to minor parties, but the Democrats held a majority of 25–21. In the House they gained two seats for a 141–58 majority, with 14 seats going to minor parties.

Jan 19-27: The **Webster-Hayne debates** took place. They began when Sen. Samuel A. Foot of Connecticut offered a resolution to restrain sale of public lands in the West. Sen. Thomas Hart Benton of Missouri replied by declaring that eastern interests were trying to check the prosperity of the West. He was supported by Sen. Robert Y. Hayne of South Carolina, who defended states' rights. Hayne stated that "the very life of our system is the independence of the states, and that there is no evil more to be deprecated than the consolidation of this government." Sen. Daniel Webster of Massachusetts replied by criticizing the tendency of some senators "to habitually speak of the union in terms of indifference, or even of disparagement." The debate evolved into a discussion of the powers of the Constitution and the nature of the Union. In his speech of Jan. 26–27, Webster declared that the states were sovereign only in that area where their power is not qualified by the Constitution, and that the Constitution and the government were sovereign over the people.

Sep: The **Anti-Masonic Party,** the first major third party in the history of U.S. politics, held its first national convention in Philadelphia. Its candidate was

William Wirt of Maryland. It would draw votes from Henry Clay in the 1832 elections and win several House seats in New England.

II. Architecture
   Arts and Music
   Popular Entertainment
   Publishing
   Theater

Inspired by the Romantic movement while studying in Europe, a group of American painters, beginning about 1825 and lasting for half a century, formed what came to be called the Hudson River school. They took interest in the natural beauty of the U.S. and concentrated on painting the Hudson River Valley, Catskill Mts., White Mts., and Niagara Falls. Best known of the school were Thomas Doughty, Asher B. Durand, Thomas Cole, John Frederick Kensett, and George Innes.

Plays about Indians flooded the American stage in the decades before the Civil War. Among the more successful were the anonymous *Indian Wife* (1830), *Pontiac, or the Siege of Detroit* by General Alexander Macomb, and *Metamora, or The Last of the Wampanoags* by John A. Stone. Approximately 50 plays about Indians appeared between 1825 and 1860.

Sep 16: Oliver Wendell Holmes wrote the poem "Old Ironsides" for the Boston *Daily Advertiser*. Stirred by the notice that the frigate *Constitution* was to be dismantled, he composed his impassioned poem, which became so popular that the order for destruction of the ship was rescinded.

III. Business and Industry
    Education
    Philosophy and Religion
    Science

The Church of Jesus Christ of Latter-Day Saints, known as the Mormon Church, was founded on Apr. 6, 1830, by Joseph Smith at Fayette, N.Y., with 30 members. Smith in 1827 said he had unearthed golden tablets near Palmyra, N.Y., the writing on which he translated and published in 1829 as *Book of Mormon.* These writings of the prophet Mormon were an early history of America from about 600 B.C. to about A.D. 420, showing that colonization of America had been carried out by a lost tribe of Israel. Mormon also revealed God's special message for America. This made Mormonism a distinctly American religion at a time when nationalistic feeling was strong. Smith set up the headquarters of his church in Kirtland, Ohio, in 1831.

Canal mileage in America totaled 1277 as against 73 miles of railroads. By 1840 there were 3326 miles of canals and 2818 miles of railroads. By 1850 there were 3698 miles of canals and 9021 miles of railroads. In 1830 New York was first in canals, with 546 miles, while Pennsylvania had virtually all railroads, 70 out of 73 miles. In 1840 Pennsylvania seized first place with 954 miles of canals, keeping its lead in rail mileage with 576 miles. In 1850 Pennsylvania retained its lead in canal mileage with 954 miles, yielding rail leadership to New York with its 1361 miles.

Alexander Campbell and his followers, often called Campbellites, formed the Disciples of Christ. The denomination rejected all creeds and confessions and urged restoration of New Testament beliefs, practices, and polity. Undivided on the issue of slavery, the Disciples grew rapidly in number and influence throughout the last half of the nineteenth century.

IV. Fashion
   Folkways
   Holidays
   Social Issues and Crime
   Sports

Fads and reforms in diet attracted reformers and dieters alike. The most successful experimenter was Sylvester Graham, a clergyman and temperance lecturer of the period who believed proper diet would prevent alcoholism. He developed Graham bread, or Graham crackers, the name still linked to his product. Made of coarsely ground whole wheat flour, Graham's bread preserved vitamins, although nothing was known about vitamins at the time. His name also became attached to health clubs and boardinghouses. Graham advocated bathing at least three times a week, daily exercise, open bedroom windows in winter, and cheerful dispositions at meals. The well-known newspaper editor Horace Greeley at one time lived on a diet of beans, potatoes, boiled rice, milk, and Graham bread. In 1850 the American Vegetarian Society was founded.

Jan 27: **"Liberty and Union, now and forever, one and inseparable!"** was included in a speech delivered by Sen. Daniel Webster of Massachusetts in debate with Sen. Robert Y. Hayne of South Carolina. Webster held that the Union was stronger than the separate states, and that its acts could not be nullified by them.

Sep 18: A celebrated **race between horse and steam** was won by the horse over the Tom Thumb, the first locomotive built in America. During the race the locomotive pulled 40 passengers over a nine-mile course from Riley's Tavern to Baltimore, Md. Mechanical failure, ever the plague of railroads, caused Tom Thumb's poor showing. The engine sprang a leak in the boiler and failed to finish the course.

1831

I. Civil Rights
   Exploration and Settlement
   Government
   Statistics
   Wars

A bloody slave insurrection, long feared by many southerners, began on Aug. 21 in Southampton County, Va. It was led by Nat Turner, a black who believed he had been chosen to lead his people out of slavery. With about 70 followers, Turner first killed his master, Joseph Travis, and his family. Within 24 hours, 60 or 70 whites had been murdered. Militia and federal troops who were called out killed about 100 blacks. Turner was captured on Oct. 30 and, after confessing to the uprising, was hanged on Nov. 11. The shaken South retaliated by passing more stringent laws relating to slaves. Southerners blamed abolitionists for inciting the slaves.

Mar 4: John Quincy Adams returned to Congress, the first former president to do so. He represented the Plymouth, Mass., district in the House of Representatives for eight terms.

June 27: Black Hawk, leader of the Sauk Indians, and Gen. Edmund P. Gaines, commanding U.S. troops, reached an agreement under which the Sauks would move out of the Rock R. area of Illinois and across the Mississippi R. into Iowa. Once there, the Sauks nearly starved and in the spring of 1832 returned to their old corn fields in Illinois.

Dec 12: The **first nominating convention** of a major party was held by the National Republican Party. It nominated Henry Clay for President.

II. Architecture
Arts and Music
Popular Entertainment
Publishing
Theater

The early nineteenth century was a period of strong patriotic feeling on the part of Americans. Independence had been confirmed by the War of 1812, and the growing population was spreading over a vast

continent. One result of this fervor was the writing
of patriotic verse and song. The most notable song,
after "The Star Spangled Banner," was "America,"
which was first sung in public on July 4, 1831, at a
service in the Park Street Church, Boston. The
words had been written by the Rev. Samuel Francis
Smith, a Baptist clergyman, earlier in the year. The
words of this American hymn were sung to the tune
of "God Save the King," and it is said that Smith did
not know it was the British anthem.

Jan 1: The first issue of *The Liberator*, edited and
published by William Lloyd Garrison in Boston, was
issued. Probably the leading abolitionist journal, *The
Liberator* was published until 1865.

III. Business and Industry
Education
Philosophy and Religion
Science

American inventors, less hampered by tradition than
their European counterparts, and faced with a labor
shortage and an almost limitless expanse of arable
land, were early encouraged to invent labor-saving
devices for farmers. Chief among the inventors was
Cyrus H. McCormick, who demonstrated his reaper
in 1831 and patented it in 1834. A similar machine
was invented independently by Obed Hussey, who
first announced his invention in 1834. McCormick in
1847 built a factory in Chicago to produce his own
reaper and by 1850 had established a nationwide
business. In 1851 he introduced the reaper in England and later on the Continent. During the Civil
War McCormick's reaper helped make it possible to
feed Union armies.

Aug: The **Adventist movement** in American Protestantism was born when William Miller, a Baptist,
began public preaching. His theme was the immi-
nence of Christ's return to earth, based on his interpretation of passages from Daniel and Revelation.

Miller predicted that the "cleansing by fire" would begin at some point between March 21, 1843, and March 21, 1844.

IV. Fashion
Folkways
Holidays
Social Issues and Crime
Sports

In the first half of the nineteenth century the diet and health of Americans were improved by the introduction of canning and refrigeration. Canned foods began to be produced commercially in 1820 by William Underwood in Boston and Thomas Kensett in New York. Canning became more efficient after introduction of the tin can, first patented in the U.S. in 1825. By the 1840s canning was being done on a large scale. By this time, too, improvements in the cutting and storing of ice made ice cheaper, so refrigeration came into common use.

Aug 10: The term *Old Glory,* denoting the U.S. flag, was first used by William Driver, of Salem, Mass., captain of the *Charles Daggett.* Presented with a large American flag, Driver raised it to the masthead and proclaimed: "I name thee Old Glory." By the end of the 1850s, the term was in widespread use.

1832

I. Civil Rights
Exploration and Settlement
Government
Statistics
Wars

The issue of states' rights had come to the fore as a result of the tariff bill of 1828, known to its enemies in the South as the Tariff of Abominations. This year, for the first time, a state threatened both nullification and secession. On Nov. 24, 1832, a South Carolina convention passed an ordinance declaring null and void both the 1828 tariff and one enacted in 1832, reducing somewhat the tariff duties to which the South objected. The ordinance stated further that the state would secede if the federal government used force. Pres. Andrew Jackson reacted strongly to this declaration on Dec. 10 with a proclamation to South Carolina asserting supremacy of federal law and calling nullification an act of rebellion.

1832-1833: In **congressional elections** the Democrats and National Republicans fell into a 20–20 Senate tie, with eight seats held by minor parties. In the House the Democrats had a 147–53 majority over the Anti-Masonic Party, with 60 seats held by minor parties.

Apr 6: The **Black Hawk War** began soon after the Sauk Indians, led by Black Hawk, faring poorly in Iowa where the government had moved them, recrossed the Mississippi R. and moved back to their former corn fields to plant a new crop. As tensions mounted, panicky settlers killed two Indians seeking a parley and bearing a white flag. Black Hawk, enraged, began killing white settlers.

May 21: The **Democratic Party,** formerly known as "Republican Delegates from the Several States" and called both Republican and Democratic-Republican, formally adopted its present name at its convention in Baltimore, Md. The convention nominated Pres. Andrew Jackson for a second term and nominated Martin Van Buren of New York for vice president.

Aug 2: Sauk followers of **Black Hawk** were massacred at the mouth of the Bad Axe R. in Wisconsin by Illinois militia led by Gen. Henry Atkinson. Old men, women, and children were all killed without regard for pleas of mercy or white flags.

Aug 27: Black Hawk, deserted by his Winnebago allies, surrendered, thus ending the Black Hawk War.

Dec 5: Andrew Jackson was reelected president of the United States by 687,502 popular votes and 219 electoral votes, against 530,189 popular votes and 49 electoral votes for Henry Clay. Martin Van Buren was elected vice president.

II. Architecture
Arts and Music
Popular Entertainment
Publishing
Theater

As in the past, many of the most popular figures on the American stage during this period were English actors and actresses, some of whom remained in the U.S. and made careers there. The most popular of them all was Fanny Kemble, who made her debut with her father Charles at the Park Theater, New York City, in 1832. Two years later Miss Kemble married Pierce Butler, whose family owned a large plantation in Georgia. The marriage was a failure, largely because she could not stand life on a slave-operated estate. She wrote *Journal of a Residence on a Georgia Plantation in 1838–39*, which was published in 1863. She hoped it would turn British opinion against the South.

The collected *Poems* of **William Cullen Bryant** were published and hailed by the *North American Review* as "the best volume of American verse that has appeared." Among the 89 poems were such favorites as "O Fairest of the Rural Maids," "The Death of the Flowers," "June," "A Forest Hymn," "Hymn to Death," "A Meditation on Rhode Island," and "To a Fringed Gentian."

III. Business and Industry
Education
Philosophy and Religion
Science

The need for faster ships to connect the East and West coasts of the U.S. by way of Cape Horn, and to carry on the lucrative trade with China, resulted in the development of the clipper ship, the fastest merchant sailing vessel ever built. The clippers were characterized by great length in proportion to beam and an enormous area of sail. The first true clipper, the *Ann McKim,* was built in Baltimore in 1832. Donald McKay of Boston became the foremost builder, completing such famous clippers as *Flying Cloud* and *Lightning.* In 1854 *Flying Cloud* set a record for the Boston to San Francisco route of 89 days, 8 hours. The clipper as a type ruled the seas until the development of steam-powered vessels.

The **Ohio and Erie Canal** connected Cleveland to the Ohio R. at Portsmouth. Construction of the canal took seven years, with malaria and a shortage of funds crippling the year-round labor of some 2000 workers. The canal, opened in 1833, gave Ohio farmers an outlet to the Mississippi R. and to the markets of the South.

Nov 26: The **first streetcar in the world** was put into operation by the New York & Harlem Railroad in New York City. Built by John Stephenson, it was named *John Mason* and was a horse-drawn car that ran on lower Fourth Ave.

IV. Fashion
   Folkways
   Holidays
   Social Issues and Crime
   Sports

A unique link with the birth of the nation was broken this year when Charles Carroll, the last surviving signer of the Declaration of Independence, died on Nov. 14, at 95. He had inherited a large estate from his father near Frederick, Md., known as Carrollton Manor. Carroll was one of a delegation that tried unsuccessfully in 1776 to get support from Canada for the Revolutionary cause. Later he was a U.S. senator from Maryland (1789–1792). Said to be the wealthiest man in America in his time, Carroll was a pioneer in promoting transportation projects and was chairman in 1828, of the first board of directors of the Baltimore and Ohio Railroad.

Oranges and lemons entered the American diet with the arrival of the first large shipment, direct from Sicily. Previously they had been a delicacy for the rich. Oranges and lemons have both been traced to Asia. It was not until the conquests and migrations of the Arabs that the fruit became of major agricultural consequence. The Arabs planted lemon trees in Spain during their occupation. Christopher Columbus was credited with planting the first orange tree in the New World. Trees were distributed by the Spaniards throughout the regions they explored and settled. Neither the orange nor the lemon became of commercial importance in the U.S. until years later.

Apr 1: Robert the Hermit, of Massachusetts, one of the most colorful and famous hermits in American history, died in his hermitage at Seekonk, Mass. Robert was a bonded slave, born of an African mother and probably an Anglo-Saxon father, in Princeton, N.J. He obtained his freedom, was swindled out of it and shipped to a foreign slave market, escaped to America, was parted from his first wife by force, rejected by his second wife after a long voyage at sea, and otherwise buffeted about before withdrawing from the society of men.

1833

I. Civil Rights
Exploration and Settlement
Government
Statistics
Wars

That the abolition movement was gaining strength was demonstrated this year when the first national abolitionist organization, the American Anti-Slavery Society, was formed in Philadelphia on Dec. 4. Its first president was Arthur Tappan, who like his brother Lewis was a wealthy New York City business-man. Both were active in the antislavery cause for many years. Also prominent in the movement was William Lloyd Garrison, the fiery editor of *The Liberator*, who with his followers seized control of the society in 1840 because he did not think it was radical enough. The society saw slavery as a moral evil and called for immediate abolition. In 1835 it began a propaganda campaign that flooded the slave states with abolitionist literature.

Mar 2: In the continuing **controversy over nullification,** Pres. Andrew Jackson signed two bills. The first was Henry Clay's compromise Tariff of 1833, which was intended to ease the trouble between the federal government and South Carolina. The second was called the Force Act; it authorized the president to enforce collection of tariffs by use of the Army and Navy if necessary.

Mar 15: The South Carolina **Ordinance of Nullification** was revoked by a state convention. However, on Mar. 18 the convention passed an ordinance nullifying the Force Act.

II. Architecture
   Arts and Music
   Popular Entertainment
   Publishing
   Theater

The day of newspaper sensationalism dawned with the establishment of the New York *Sun* on Sept. 3. Founded by 23-year-old Benjamin H. Day, its first issue consisted of four pages, which Day wrote and set in type himself. The paper sold for one penny while all other New York papers sold for 6 cents. Day was the first publisher in the city to use newsboys and by 1835 he claimed that the 19,360 circulation of the *Sun* was the largest in the world.

Nathaniel Currier moved his lithography business from Philadelphia, Pa., to New York City, going into business with J.H. Bufford. In 1850 Currier went into business with James Merritt Ives, and by 1857 all of the prints issued by the company bore the Currier & Ives imprint. The lithographs, inexpensive and enormously popular, gave an eloquent pictorial account of sights and events of nineteenth-century America.

Jan 17: William Rush, the first native American sculptor, died at 76. Working in wood and clay, Rush in his work reflected the neoclassical influence. His work included busts of many notables, American and European; carved wooden female figureheads for ships; the personifications of Tragedy and Comedy seen at the Actor's Home outside Philadelphia; and also the *Spirit of the Schuylkill,* in Fairmount Park in Philadelphia.

III. Business and Industry
Education
Philosophy and Religion
Science

An invention that contributed as much to the history and folklore of the American West as it did to the firearms industry was the Colt revolver, invented by Samuel Colt in 1833 and patented on Feb. 25, 1836. Colt began producing the weapon at the Patent Arms Company in Paterson, N.J. As the first firearm that could be used effectively by a man on horseback, this six-shooter soon became associated with the frontier and the Great Plains. In time the name Colt became almost synonymous with the term revolver. Colt's business failed, but it was revived by an order from the government for 100 revolvers in 1847 for use in the Mexican War. Colt established a new company and plant in Hartford, Conn.

A **tax-supported public library** was established in Peterborough, N.H., under the leadership of the Rev.

Abiel Abbot. The library charged a small membership fee. It is considered the oldest public library in
the U.S. except for the Library of Congress, established in 1800 by an act of Congress.

IV. Fashion
   Folkways
   Holidays
   Social Issues and Crime
   Sports

The frontier and the westward movement produced
a number of semilegendary folk heroes. None of
these figures has ever surpassed Davy Crockett in
popularity or scope and number of alleged exploits.
Crockett began as a frontiersman and Indian fighter,
but by 1833 he was serving his third term as a congressman from Tennessee. As a legislator, he made
the most of his backwoods humor, style of dress, racy
language, and naive but often shrewd comments on
public affairs. More sophisticated politicians used
Crockett, who opposed Pres. Andrew Jackson's policies, to lure Democratic backwoodsmen to the Whig
Party. One of their ploys was to prepare books and
attribute them to Crockett, who may have had a hand
in some of them. *Sketches and Eccentricities of Col.
David Crockett* appeared in 1833. He died in 1836 as
one of the defenders of the Alamo in San Antonio,
Tex. That year there appeared posthumously *Col.
Crockett's Exploits and Adventures in Texas.*

The promotion of **fly-fishing** highlighted the angler's year. Jerome Van Crowninshield Smith's *Fishes
of Massachusetts* reported that the angler "enjoys the
sport and exults in its success, according as it re-
quires an exertion of his skill. . . . There are not only
individuals of whom we speak, but others who avail-
ing themselves of all the information to be acquired
from books and experience, are fully aware that fly-
fishing is the perfection of angling."

1834

I. **Civil Rights**
   Exploration and Settlement
   Government
   Statistics
   Wars

A new national political party coalèsced this year out of several groups whose common cause was opposition to Pres. Andrew Jackson and his policies. In 1834 this coalition formally adopted the name Whig, after the English political party that opposed excessive royal prerogatives. Its leaders were Henry Clay of Kentucky, John C. Calhoun of South Carolina, and Daniel Webster of Massachusetts. The party brought together those who favored the so-called American system of protective tariffs combined with internal improvements, states' rights groups, those opposed to Jackson's Bank of the United States policy, southern planters, and northern industrialists. In 1836 the party absorbed the remnants of the Anti-Masonic Party. Although in general it represented the conservative political view, the party lacked leadership and disappeared after it failed dismally in the 1852 presidential election.

1834-1835: In **congressional elections** the Democrats took a 27–25 Senate majority over the Whigs. In the House they lost two seats but held a majority of 145–98 over the Whigs.

June 24: Roger Brooke Taney, serving as secretary of the treasury on a recess appointment from Pres. Jackson, was rejected by the Senate when his name was sent up for confirmation. Again in 1835 Taney was rejected when nominated to be an associate justice of the Supreme Court, but in 1836 he was nominated and confirmed as chief justice.

II. **Architecture**
   Arts and Music
   Popular Entertainment
   Publishing
   Theater

American historians of the middle years of the nine-teenth century were not as objective in their treat-ment of the nation's history as most of those who came later. The last great subjective historian was George Bancroft, whose ten-volume *History of the United States* appeared between 1834 and 1874. Ban-croft was professionally trained as a historian, but he was nationalistic and rhetorical, using the story of the U.S. to express commonly held beliefs in democ-racy, manifest destiny, and the virtues of Anglo-American Protestantism. Bancroft also held public office and as secretary of the navy in 1845–1846 he established the U.S. Naval Academy at Annapolis, Md.

The song **"Zip Coon"** was performed in New York City by Bob Farrell. It would soon become known as "Turkey in the Straw" and gain popularity in minstrel shows. It originated as a folk song about 1815 in the frontier states of the Southwest.

III. **Business and Industry**
   Education
   Philosophy and Religion
   Science

Growing interest in science brought with it advocates and followers of pseudo-sciences. One was phrenol-ogy, which began in Germany and was now being popularized in the U.S. by Orson Fowler. Phrenology claimed that from the shape of the human skull one could determine character traits and mental abilities. Furthermore, phrenology taught that man could alter his personality and develop the brain by train-ing. The lectures and writings of Fowler, self-ap-pointed professor of phrenology, became very popular, and even so eminent a person as Horace Mann, the educator, said it helped him in his work.

A true prototype of the modern **electric motor** was constructed by Thomas Davenport, a Vermont blacksmith. Davenport recognized the versatility of Joseph Henry's electromagnet and saw that it could be adapted for use in an electric power machine. He connected four electromagnets to a battery and set them up on a wheel that rotated rapidly when current was turned on. This is the basic design of the standard electric motor of today. Davenport received a patent in 1837, but could not create a market for his device before his death in 1851.

Cyrus McCormick patented an early model of his famous reaper. Although 20 patents for reapers in the U.S. preceded his, McCormick's persistent experimentation and technical improvements soon made his product preeminent in its field. He did not put his reaper on the market until certain defects had been eliminated. He sold his first two reapers in 1841; produced 4000 in 1856; and 23,000 in 1857. McCormick's reapers revolutionized American agriculture.

IV. Fashion
Folkways
Holidays
Social Issues and Crime
Sports

From about 1825 to the outbreak of the Civil War in 1861, there was a strong atmosphere of reform in the U.S. Most noticeable was the antislavery movement, but it was only one of many causes for which people organized, labored, and contributed money. Dedicated people worked for women's rights, prison reform, educational reform, religious liberalism, social welfare, and other causes. One group called itself the Society to Improve the Condition of the Sailors. This urge to reform had several sources: the religious revival that began in the 1820s; the rational spirit of the Enlightenment with its idea of the possibility of progress, and the spirit of romanticism, which was related to the older notion that the New World was a second Eden where people could start over.

The legend of **Davy Crockett** was augmented by publication of his supposed autobiography, *A Narrative of the Life of David Crockett*. He was featured as a great bear hunter and congressman. Interspersed were tall tales. Anti-Jacksonians, of whom Crockett was one, expected to profit politically from promotion of Crockett's image. Political opponents meanwhile characterized him as "fresh from the backwoods, half-horse, half-alligator, a little touched with the snapping-turtle."

Americans began to eat **tomatoes** at about this time, but not until 1900 would they become popular. Despite the fact that tomatoes had been introduced into Europe from Mexico as ornamental plants c1550, and were soon afterward eaten in Italy, they were popularly regarded in the U.S. as poisonous and in France as an aphrodisiac.

1835

I. **Civil Rights**
   Exploration and Settlement
   Government
   Statistics
   Wars

The federal government was committed to a policy of removing all eastern Indians to reservations west of the Mississippi R. To that end a treaty had been signed in 1832 with the Seminole Indians of Florida. When the time came in 1835 to begin the move, many Seminoles refused to go. Resistance was led by the Indian chief Osceola, whose father was not an Indian. In November the Second Seminole War (1835–1842) erupted. Federal troops were sent to Florida but had little success against the Indians, whose raid-

ing parties struck quickly and then vanished. Osceola
was taken prisoner in 1837 while negotiating under
a flag of truce; he died in prison on Jan. 30, 1838. The
American forces did not overcome Seminole resistance until 1842. The cost to the U.S. was 1500 dead
and $20,000,000.

Jan: Daniel Webster of Massachusetts was nominated
for president by the Whigs of the Massachusetts legislature. With other Whig candidates in the field and
the Anti-Jacksonians divided, Webster won only his
home state.

Jan: Sen. Hugh L. White of Tennessee was nominated
for president by independent anti-Jacksonian Democrats in the legislatures of Tennessee and Alabama.
John Tyler was his running mate. White won the
electoral votes of Tennessee and Alabama in the 1836
election.

Jan 30: Pres. Andrew Jackson was attacked in the first
attempt on the life of a U.S. president. Richard Lawrence fired twice while Jackson was attending the
funeral of Rep. Warren Ransom Davis of South Carolina, but both shots misfired. Lawrence was later declared insane.

May 20: The **Democratic National Convention nominated Martin Van Buren** of New York for the presidency. Richard M. Johnson of Kentucky was nominated for the vice presidency.

Dec 16: The **Anti-Masonic Party nominated William
Henry Harrison** of Ohio for the presidency and Francis Granger of New York for the vice presidency.

II. Architecture
   Arts and Music
   Popular Entertainment
   Publishing
   Theater

Compared with that of Europe, the history of the U.S.
did not go back very far, but already it was being
recorded professionally. Scholars began to edit pa-

pers and documents of the first heroes of the nation.
Among these historians was Jared Sparks who, at
Harvard in 1839, became the first professor of American history in the U.S. Sparks did much to find and
publish previously unprinted manuscripts, but
he bowdlerized them to enhance the reputations of
his subjects. His largest work was *The Writings of
George Washington* (12 volumes, 1834–1837). The
initial volume was a biography of the first president.

The **New York** *Herald,* a penny daily, was begun
by James Gordon Bennett. It soon became pro-Tam-
many and proslavery. In 1869 it astounded everyone
by sending Stanley to Africa to find Livingstone. In
1924 it was merged with the New York *Tribune* to
form the *Herald Tribune.*

III. Business and Industry
Education
Philosophy and Religion
Science

Almost since its discovery, America had been popular
with European intellectuals, who visited here because of its novelty. Now the U.S. began to attract
visitors who wanted to study the world's preeminent
experiment in democracy. Perhaps the most thoughtful of these visitors was Alexis de Tocqueville, a
French liberal who visited the U.S. in 1831–1832. In
1835 his classic volume *De la Démocratie en Amé-
rique* was published in Belgium. It was issued in the
U.S. in an English-language edition, *Democracy in
America,* in 1838. Tocqueville had been favorably impressed with the U.S. and its attempt to have both
liberty and equality. His book, objective for the most
part, was the earliest important analysis of the American system of government.

A model **telegraph** was constructed by Samuel F.
B. Morse and demonstrated for a few friends.
Morse's model was severely limited and inefficient
because he was unfamiliar with advances made in

electromagnetism by his contemporaries. It had about the same applicability as a telephone with a range of 40 feet. In the next two years he applied the results of more recent research, improved his equipment, and extended the range of his system to ten miles. He received a patent in 1840.

Nov 23: A machine to manufacture **horseshoes** was patented by Henry Burden of Troy, N.Y., a Scottish immigrant. The machine could produce 60 horseshoes a minute. In the Civil War most of the shoes for Union cavalry came from Burden's plant in Troy.

IV. Fashion
   Folkways
   Holidays
   Social Issues and Crime
   Sports

Although the nation was still basically one of farms and small towns, a trend toward urbanization was becoming apparent. Between 1820 and 1850 the combined population of New York City, Philadelphia, Baltimore, and Boston nearly tripled. In 1830 farmers outnumbered city dwellers by about 10.5 to 1; by 1840 the ratio was only 5.5 to 1. The population of towns of 8000 or more nearly doubled between 1830 and 1850. Urbanization brought with it such problems as slums, poor sanitation, and crime. In 1835 *The People's Magazine* blamed the growth of cities for a new type of young man, characterized as unhealthy, badly postured, pale, and nervous.

A well publicized **ten-mile foot race** at Union Course, L.I., was watched by nearly 30,000 spectators. The offer of $1000 to any man who could run ten miles in less than an hour drew nine contestants. Henry Stannard of Killingsworth, Conn., won. He covered the first mile in 5:36, the last mile in 5:54, and the entire course in 59:44. At the conclusion of the race, amid great jubilation, Stannard leaped on a horse and triumphantly retraced his winning course.

1836

I. Civil Rights
Exploration and Settlement
Government
Statistics
Wars

The presidential election campaign of 1836 pitted Democratic Vice Pres. Martin Van Buren against a field of three Whig candidates. They were William Henry Harrison, who also ran on the Anti-Masonic ticket; Daniel Webster, representing the North; and Hugh L. White, whose support came from the South and Southwest. The Whig Party hoped the vote would be split enough to throw the election into the House of Representatives, where they had a chance of prevailing. Issues played little part in the campaign. Those who approved of Pres. Andrew Jackson's policies of the past eight years were for Van Buren; those who were anti-Jackson backed a Whig candidate.

1836-1837: In **congressional elections** the Democrats gained four Senate seats for a 30–18 majority over the Whigs, with four seats going to minor parties. In the House they lost 37 seats for a nominal majority of 108–107, with 24 seats going to minor parties.

Mar 2: Texas declared itself an independent republic. Two weeks later it wrote a constitution and organized a government. The new republic sent commissioners George Childress and Robert Hamilton to Washington, D.C., where their authority was not accepted because the U.S. was unwilling to recognize the Republic of Texas.

Mar 6: The Alamo, a fortified mission at San Antonio, Tex., where fewer than 200 Texans were garrisoned, was captured by the Mexican leader Gen. Antonio López de Santa Anna, who had led 3000 troops across the Rio Grande. Every Texan except a mother, a child, and a servant was killed.

Apr 21: At the **Battle of San Jacinto**, the Texas army under Gen. Sam Houston defeated the Mexican army under Santa Anna. This battle ended the war, and Texas earned its independence from Mexico.

June 15: Arkansas was admitted into the Union, the 25th state.

Oct 22: Sam Houston was sworn in as the first president of the Republic of Texas. He later became a U.S. senator from Texas.

Dec 7: Martin Van Buren was elected president of the United States. The electoral vote was Van Buren, 170; William Henry Harrison, Anti-Masonic candidate, 73; Sen. Hugh L. White of Tennessee, anti-Jacksonian Democrat, 26; Daniel Webster, Massachusetts Whig candidate, 14; and Willie P. Mangum of North Carolina, 11. The popular vote was Van Buren, 761,549; Harrison, 549,567; White, 145,396; Webster, 41,287. None of the four vice presidential candidates received a majority of the electoral votes. The Senate, for the first and only time, had to choose, naming Richard M. Johnson of Kentucky to the office.

II. Architecture
Arts and Music
Popular Entertainment
Publishing
Theater

This year proved a turning point in American intellectual life. Ralph Waldo Emerson's first book, *Nature*, in which he stated his fundamental philosophy, was published anonymously. Emerson had visited Europe in 1832 and 1833, where he met Thomas Carlyle, William Wordsworth, and Samuel Taylor Coleridge. Through them he was introduced to transcendental thought, derived from Immanuel Kant and German idealism. In *Nature* he set forth the principles of American Transcendentalism, which was to become the most influential school of philosophy of the nineteenth century. Transcendentalism also owed much to the Romantic movement. Emerson expressed a deeply felt love for the natural world in

Nature and went on to combine this with a belief in the spiritual nature of reality and the importance of self-reliance.

Building of the **Washington Monument** in Washington, D.C., was begun from plans by Robert Mills. The monument was outstanding for its freedom from ornamentation in a period when taste ran toward the decorative.

Maria Monk's scandalous narrative, *Awful Disclosures of Maria Monk, as Exhibited in a Narrative of Her Suffering During a Residence of Five Years as a Novice, and Two Years as a Black Nun, in the Hotel Dieu Nunnery at Montreal,* was published. The book, today known to be a hoax, quickly sold hundreds of thousands of copies. The period was one of considerable anti-Catholic feeling.

III. Business and Industry
Education
Philosophy and Religion
Science

Politics, religion, and education all shaped American thought and action. In the field of education, nothing was more influential than the *Eclectic Readers,* compiled by William Holmes McGuffey, a clergyman and teacher. His first and second readers appeared in 1836, the third and fourth in 1837, the fifth in 1844, and the sixth in 1857. They became almost universally used in the public schools of America and were often revised. After nearly two generations of use, they had sold 122,000,000 copies. The readers taught literary and moral lessons, and included selected writings of the best English-language authors.

The **Transcendental Club,** with Ralph Waldo Emerson, A. Bronson Alcott, George Ripley, Henry Hedges, Orestes Brownson, Theodore Parker, Margaret Fuller, William Ellery Channing, Nathaniel Hawthorne, Elizabeth Peabody, Henry David Thoreau, James Freeman Clark, and others as participants, began as a casual discussion group. The group convened frequently, but the note of informality was never lost. The club had no officers, office, or schedule, and membership waxed and waned. One outcome of the Transcendental Club was the beginning, in 1840, of the Transcendental organ, *The Dial.*

IV. Fashion
   Folkways
   Holidays
   Social Issues and Crime
   Sports

In the 1830s circuses developed into tent shows when acrobatic troupes merged with menageries and equestrian shows. By this time, 30 shows were traveling around the country and one, the Zoological Institute, boasted 47 carriages and wagons, over 100 horses, 14 musicians, and 60 performers. An integral part of the entertainment was a parade heralding the arrival of the circus in a town. Floating theaters in the form of showboats on the Mississippi and Ohio rivers in particular added to the entertainment. The first showboat was built in Pittsburgh, Pa., in 1831.

The political slogan *Tippecanoe and Tyler too* caught the public fancy during this year's presidential campaign. Troops under William Henry Harrison, the Whig candidate, had engaged the Indians at Tippecanoe and beaten them off with heavy losses. Harrison thus became identified with the place. John Tyler, a former Democratic senator from Virginia, was his running mate.

Remember the Alamo was the stirring battle cry of Texans at San Jacinto, where the army of Gen. Antonio López de Santa Anna was routed and revenge taken for the massacre of the previous year. The Alamo, a fort in San Antonio, had been besieged for ten days. After being taken, its defenders were slaughtered. Among the dead were Davy Crockett and James Bowie.

So-called **cold water societies** were introduced by the Rev. Thomas P. Hunt, who enlisted children, mainly through Sunday schools, in a temperance crusade. Each child was issued a pledge card and sent out to gather signatures of those who agreed to abstain from drink.

Nov 12: The telling phrase *the almighty dollar* was coined by Washington Irving in his story "The Creole Village," which appeared in *The Knickerbocker Magazine* on this date. The full phrase was "The Almighty Dollar, that great object of universal devotion throughout the land."

1837

I. Civil Rights
Exploration and Settlement
Government
Statistics
Wars

A severe financial panic struck the U.S. in 1837. It was triggered on May 10, when New York banks stopped making payments in specie, but the causes were more deep-seated. Pres. Andrew Jackson's administration had created too much credit. The result was inflation and speculation in western lands. The Specie Circular drained gold and silver to the West. During the year 618 banks failed. A depression followed, bringing widespread unemployment. The panic did not end until 1843.

Jan 26: **Michigan** was admitted into the Union as the 26th state.

Mar 3: The **Republic of Texas** was recognized by Pres. Andrew Jackson and approved by Congress.

Nov 7: Elijah P. Lovejoy was killed by proslavery rioters at Alton, Ill. His antislavery printing press had previously been smashed several times but was replaced by the Ohio Anti-Slavery Society. Lovejoy became known as the martyr abolitionist.

Dec 29: The *Caroline* Affair (1837–1842) began when, on the U.S. shore of the Niagara R. near Buffalo, Canadian authorities seized and burned the American vessel *Caroline.* The ship was leased to run supplies to Navy Island for support of Canadian revolutionaries led by William Lyon MacKenzie. In the fracas an American was killed by a Canadian militiaman. Ultimately the Canadian was acquitted.

II. Architecture
   Arts and Music
   Popular Entertainment
   Publishing
   Theater

While authors such as Nathaniel Hawthorne and Ralph Waldo Emerson were writing novels and essays that are still read and honored, other authors were publishing books of less than permanent quality. A good example of popular taste in historical fiction was a trilogy by William Ware, a Unitarian clergyman. The first part of the trilogy, *Zenobia,* appeared in 1837; the second, *Aurelian,* in 1838; and the final volume, *Julian,* in 1841. These epistolary novels dealt with the political and social struggles of Christians against the Roman Empire.

Twice-Told Tales by Nathaniel Hawthorne, the author's second book and first collection of tales, was published. Digging deep into chronicles and histories of colonial New England and adding symbolic overtones, Hawthorne achieved some of the finest moral allegory ever written.

Thomas Cole produced a masterpiece of the Hudson River school of landscape artists, *In the Catskills.* A resident of the region, Cole as usual romanticized the rural setting. In a clearing surrounded by trees, two figures rest by a winding stream that loses itself in the foliage of the background. In the rear the mountains rise gently.

Aug 31: **Ralph Waldo Emerson** delivered his celebrated *American Scholar* address before the Phi Beta

Kappa Society at Harvard. Oliver Wendell Holmes called it "our intellectual Declaration of Independence." Although many previous writers and speakers had dealt with the same theme, Emerson raised the subject to the level of philosophy.

III. Business and Industry
Education
Philosophy and Religion
Science

The U.S. was beginning to develop its own economists. These new economists approached their subject from the point of view of American optimism, in contrast to the pessimism of English economists. Chief among the Americans was Henry C. Carey of Philadelphia, who had gained substantial business experience by running efficiently the large bookstore he inherited from his father. In general, Carey believed in laissez-faire capitalism but favored a protective tariff for American industries. In his three-volume work *Principles of Political Economy* (1837–1840), his economic nationalism was apparent.

John Deere produced his first plow incorporating a steel blade at his blacksmith shop in Grand Detour, Ill. While visiting a sawmill he noticed a smooth-surfaced saw blade and thought that, shaped into a plow blade, it might easily cut furrows in the moist and sticky midwestern soil without clogging. His experiments proved successful and he soon moved to Moline, Ill., where he began to manufacture steel plows. Deere plows, known as singing plows, contributed greatly to the expansion of farming in the Midwest and West.

Sep: Samuel F.B. Morse filed for a patent on his telegraph. It was not granted until 1844.

Dec 29: A portable **combined thresher and fanning mill** earned a patent for the inventors, Hiram Avery and John Avery Pitts of Winthrop, Me. Eventually Hiram moved to Chicago where he manufactured

Chicago-Pitts brand threshers, which were widely used throughout the grain belt for more than half a century.

IV. Fashion
Folkways
Holidays
Social Issues and Crime
Sports

Americans liked showmanship, natural wonders, freaks, and all kinds of believe-it-or-not items. One man in the mid-nineteenth century gave them all this and more. He was Phineas T. Barnum, who began his career this year by exhibiting an old black woman, Joyce Heth. He claimed she was 161 years old and had been George Washington's nurse. She was actually about 80. A crowd of some 10,000 flocked to see her at Niblo's Garden in New York City. In 1842 Barnum opened his American Museum in New York City. There at various times he was to exhibit the original Siamese twins, Chang and Eng, and the Fiji Mermaid, half monkey and half fish. The most popular attraction, though, was Tom Thumb, a dwarf who stood only 40 inches tall. Exhibited in the U.S. and abroad, Thumb was seen by 20,000,000 people.

About this time **Amos Lawrence** became a well-known model of the virtuous merchant by his practicing of moral hygiene. Lawrence gave up tea and coffee in 1832, fish, meat, and gravies in 1835, and butter in 1836. Lawrence conducted regular family prayers, conscientiously observed the Sabbath, and contributed to many worthy charities. In the midst of his piety, Lawrence prospered as a landlord and businessman to such an extent that his example was cited as evidence of the rewards of good living. Lawrence died on Dec. 31, 1852. His sons collected his papers, published as *Extracts from the Diary and Correspondence of the Late Amos Lawrence* (1855).

1838

I. Civil Rights
Exploration and Settlement
Government
Statistics
Wars

The Underground Railroad was a loosely organized apparatus operated by northern abolitionists to bring slaves from the South and set them free. More than 3000 persons were involved in the effort. The name apparently was first used in 1831. The best known leaders were Levi Coffin, who is said to have assisted 3000 slaves, and Harriet Tubman, an escaped slave. Slaves were passed along from one safe station to another until they reached a free state. Some went on to Canada. By the time of the Civil War, the Underground Railroad may have assisted as many as 50,000 slaves to escape bondage, although after the passage of the Fugitive Slave Law of 1850 the number decreased to 500 to 1000 a year.

1838-1839: In **congressional elections** the Democrats lost two Senate seats but still led the Whigs 28–22. In the House the Democrats picked up 16 seats and the Whigs gained 11, for a Democratic majority of 124–118.

Jan 26: The **first prohibition law** in the U.S. was passed in Tennessee, making it a misdemeanor to sell alcoholic beverages in taverns and stores. Later in the year a political storm erupted in Massachusetts over a law prohibiting the sale of alcoholic beverages in amounts of less than 15 gallons, except for "medicinal or mechanical purposes."

May 18: Charles Wickes was placed by Congress in command of a naval exploring and surveying expedition of the South Seas. On Aug. 18 his fleet of six ships left Hampton Roads, Va., to explore hundreds of islands of the Pacific; a large sector of Antarctica, later named Wickes Land; and the American Northwest coastline. The expedition returned in July 1842. Wickes's five-volume report was published in 1844.

June 12: A new **Iowa Territory,** including the two Dakotas and much of Minnesota in addition to Iowa, was formed with its separation from Wisconsin Territory.

Dec: **Cherokee Indians** remaining in Georgia and southeastern Tennessee, 14,000 in all, were forcibly removed from their lands by 7000 U.S. soldiers and herded into Oklahoma. The phrase *Trail of Tears* refers to this final tragic act in the enforcement of the fraudulent treaty of New Echota in 1835. Four thousand Cherokees died en route; perhaps 1000 escaped. In the end 7,000,000 acres of Cherokee land had been seized by whites.

II. Architecture
   Arts and Music
   Popular Entertainment
   Publishing
   Theater

Although the North seemed to supply most of the nation's authors, the South was not without its contributors to the literary world. A worthy example was John Pendleton Kennedy, a lawyer and politician as well as author. His *Swallow Barn* (1832) was a series of sketches about Virginia, written in the manner of Washington Irving. Kennedy wrote two novels, *Horse-Shoe Robinson* (1832) and *Rob of the Bowl* (1838). Although its subject matter was melodramatic, the latter novel was a realistic tale of Maryland in 1681. It concerned an attempt by Protestants to overthrow Lord Baltimore, a Catholic.

   John Greenleaf Whittier joined the list of authors of books supporting abolition with the publication of his *Ballads and Anti-Slavery Poems.* Noteworthy among the pieces were "To William Lloyd Garrison,"

"The Hunters of Men," "The Slave Ships," "Stanzas for the Time," "Toussaint L'Ouverture," "Hymn," the extremely popular "Stanzas," and "The Moral Warfare."

III. Business and Industry
Education
Philosophy and Religion
Science

The Mormon Church was going through a difficult period. On Jan. 12, 1838, Joseph Smith, the founder, and his followers left Kirtland, Ohio, partly as a result of the panic of 1837. They moved to Independence, Mo., where they met with hostility, partly because of their beliefs and partly because of their communal economic organization and efficiency. Moving back east in 1839, the Mormons founded Nauvoo, Ill. By 1844 Nauvoo had a population of 15,000 and was the most prosperous city in Illinois. Again, however, the Mormons were distrusted for their religious beliefs and disliked for their economic competition.

Apr 23: The **first transatlantic steamship service** began with the arrival in New York harbor of the steamer *Great Western* after less than 16 days at sea. The previous day the *Sirius* had arrived from England. Both ships were British steam-sail packets. For the next generation Great Britain led the world in transatlantic steamer service. Scheduled service was not established until 1840.

IV. Fashion
Folkways
Holidays
Social Issues and Crime
Sports

Comparatively brief as American history was, Americans were exceedingly proud of it and were beginning to give a mythological flavor to the Revolutionary War period and its heroes. Foremost among these, of course, was George Washington. In 1832, on the 100th anniversary of Washington's birth, Daniel Webster had declaimed: "His age and his country are equally full of wonders; and of both he is the chief." An attempt in Congress at this time to have the remains of the first president removed from their Mount Vernon, Va., tomb and reburied in the capital city caused bitter debate. Southerners refused to have such a precious possession moved even a few miles north.

The term **_Trail of Tears_** referred to the route taken by the Cherokee Indians on their removal from Georgia to new lands in Oklahoma. The Indians were forced into prison camps by troops under Gen. Winfield Scott. The first migration began in October. Conservative estimates placed the Indian death toll at 10% of the population. The removal had been legalized by the Treaty of New Echota in 1835.

1839

I. Civil Rights
Exploration and Settlement
Government
Statistics
Wars

An unusual incident involving a mutiny on a slave ship added to the tension between North and South. A Spanish ship, the *Amistad,* sailed from Havana, Cuba, in June 1839 with 54 black slaves aboard. An uprising by the slaves on July 1, in which two men were killed, gave them control of the ship and they attempted to sail to Africa. However, the vessel was captured by a U.S. Navy ship off Long Island. Slave interests, led by Sec. of State John Forsyth, attempted to turn the slaves over to Spain. Abolitionists brought suit to prevent this, and the case reached the Supreme Court, which in Mar. 9, 1841, found that the slaves had been illegally kidnaped and set them free. Former Pres. John Quincy Adams defended the blacks.

Feb 12: The **Aroostock War** began with the seizure of Rufus McIntire, a U.S. land agent sent to the Aroostock region between New Brunswick, Canada, and Maine, to expel Canadian lumberjacks who had entered the disputed area. The boundary question had been an Anglo-American issue since 1783 and had never been satisfactorily settled. After McIntire's arrest, Maine and New Brunswick called out their militias, and the Nova Scotia legislature appropriated war funds. Congress authorized a conscription of 50,000 men and voted $10,000,000 toward the prosecution of this action. Calmer voices prevailed: Gen. Winfield Scott arranged a truce, and both parties agreed to refer the dispute to a boundary commission. The issue was settled in 1842 by the Webster-Ashburton Treaty.

Nov 13: The **Liberty Party,** an antislavery party, held its first national convention at Warsaw, N.Y. It nominated James G. Birney of New York for president. Birney, a former Kentuckian and slaveholder, wielded strong political influence in western New York and the Ohio R. Valley. Francis J. Lemoyne was nominated for vice president.

Dec 4-7: The **Whig National Convention nominated William Henry Harrison** for the presidency. John Tyler of Virginia was nominated for the vice presidency.

II. Architecture
Arts and Music
Popular Entertainment
Publishing
Theater

In architecture the Gothic Revival, beginning in the late 1830s, competed with the earlier Classic Revival.

Copying the tall towers and pointed arches of the Middle Ages, the Gothic style was used primarily for churches, schools, and libraries, but was adapted to country houses also. The first important architect of the Gothic Revival was Richard Upjohn, who in 1839 was given the task of rebuilding Trinity Church in New York City. His design was soon copied by other churches. James Renwick was also a leading architect of the style. He planned beautiful Grace Church in New York City (1843–1846), and was then chosen in 1853 to be the architect for St. Patrick's Cathedral, also in New York City. This was the most ambitious structure of the Gothic Revival. In the field of country houses and landscape gardening, Andrew Jackson Downing was the leading figure. His book, *Treatise on the Theory and Practice of Landscape Gardening Adapted to North America*, appeared in 1841. It at once became the standard work in its field, going through ten editions.

An Englishman, **Alexander Forbes**, wrote *California*, the first book in English about the territory. A businessman, Forbes stopped off at Yerba Buena (San Francisco) on a voyage to the Pacific and saw the possibilities of the new land. He urged the British government to take over the territory before Russian or American settlers pushed into it. To make the territory more accessible, he suggested cutting a canal across the Isthmus of Panama.

III. Business and Industry
Education
Philosophy and Religion
Science

Increased attention was now being paid to education: in requiring school attendance, in providing free public schools, and in teacher education. The leader in the field was Horace Mann of Massachusetts. It was through his efforts that in 1839 the first state-supported school to educate teachers was established in the U.S., in Massachusetts. As secretary of the state board of education there, Mann instituted longer school terms, insisted on better schoolhouses, and secured higher pay for teachers. His successful upgrading of education influenced states throughout the nation.

Vulcanized rubber was first made by Charles Goodyear, after many failed experiments. This was the first successful attempt to make rubber nonsticky and solid at high temperatures. Rubber had interested inventors for years but none had succeeded in creating a product that did not melt easily when subjected to heat. Goodyear made his first tests with rubber while in jail for debt in 1834. His ultimate success was the result of an accident—he dropped a mixture of sulfur and rubber on top of a hot stove, thereby discovering a process he called vulcanization. Goodyear secured patents for his process and made arrangements for royalties, but he became entangled in lawsuits. At the time of his death in 1860, he was $200,000 in debt.

The importance of **wheat** as a cash crop was increasing steadily. In 1839 production amounted to 84,823,000 bushels. Ten years later the number had climbed to 100,485,000 bushels. By the 1840s large areas of Iowa and Nebraska were being used to grow wheat. Canals and railroads were used to transport the bulky crop, and by 1840 there were 4354 grist mills in the U.S. to grind the wheat into flour. Large mills were located in Baltimore, Buffalo, and Rochester.

IV. Fashion
  Folkways
  Holidays
  Social Issues and Crime
  Sports

Even though a commission reported in 1908 that Gen. Abner Doubleday, veteran of the Mexican and Civil wars, had invented baseball in 1839 at Cooperstown, N.Y., hardly anyone credits this story any more. Too many other similar games, such as rounders, played mostly by children, antedated 1839. In addition, the game lacked many phases of its development until later in the century, when it became the American national sport. The first organized baseball team of which much is known was the Knickerbocker Base Ball Club in New York, organized in 1842. Three years later the club found a permanent home at the Elysian Fields in Hoboken, N.J., and adopted a set of rules.

The **first woman horse thief** of record in the U.S., Josephine Amelia Perkins achieved notoriety by a confession that was published with the following description of herself: "A young woman, who, in early life was deservedly esteemed for her exemplary behavior, yet for three years last past (friendless and unprotected) has been unhappily addicted to a criminal propensity, more singular and surprising in its nature (for one of her sex) than can be found on record; in the commission of which, she has been four times detected, twice pardoned on account of her sex, once for reasons of supposed insanity, and the fourth and last time, convicted and sentenced to two years imprisonment in Madison County jail, Kentucky. Annexed is a well-written Address to Parents and Children." Miss Perkins was born in Devonshire, England, in 1818. She stole her first horse from her father to make an elopement journey of 117 miles. Through a series of misadventures, she landed in America without any money and with only the clothes on her back. Her career in horse stealing soon began.

1840

I. Civil Rights
Exploration and Settlement
Government
Statistics
Wars

The presidential election campaign of 1840 was something new in American life, engaging as it did in the use of slogans, parades, campaign hats, and mud-slinging. The Democrats renominated Pres. Martin Van Buren, but could not agree on a vice presidential candidate. The Whigs nominated William Henry Harrison of Ohio and, for vice president, John Tyler of Virginia. The Democrats ran on a platform that emphasized strict construction of the Constitution. They opposed congressional interference with slavery, a national bank, and internal improvements paid for by the federal government. The Whigs, on the other hand, based their campaign on personalities. They pictured Van Buren as luxury-loving and aristocratic. Most of all, they made use of a remark of a Democratic newspaper, the Baltimore *Republican*, "that upon condition of his receiving a pension of $2000 and a barrel of cider, Gen. Harrison would no doubt consent to withdraw his pretensions, and spend his days in a log cabin on the banks of the Ohio." The Whigs used this statement to run a "Log Cabin and Hard Cider" campaign. They presented the hero of the Battle of Tippecanoe as a simple man of the people, although he came from an aristocratic Virginia family. The Whig campaign song was "Tippecanoe and Tyler Too," with a refrain, "Van, Van is a used up man." Their placards portrayed Harrison at the door of a log cabin, welcoming visitors to his humble home.

The U.S. **Census** recorded a population of 17,069,453. The center of population was placed 16 miles south of Clarksburg, W. Va.

1840-1841: In **congressional elections** the Whigs gained six Senate seats for a 28–22 majority over the Democrats, with two seats held by minor parties. In the House the Whigs gained 15 seats for a 133–102 majority, with six seats going to minor parties.

Jan 19: The **U.S. expedition** to the South Seas led by Capt. Charles Wilkes laid claim to a portion of the continent of Antarctica for the U.S.

May 5: The **Democratic National Convention nominated Pres. Martin Van Buren** for a second term. The convention was unable to agree on a vice presidential candidate.

Dec 2: **William Henry Harrison was elected president** of the United States. John Tyler of Virginia was elected vice president in a Whig landslide. The electoral vote was Harrison, 234; Martin Van Buren, incumbent Democrat, 60. The popular vote was Harrison, 1,275,017; Van Buren, 1,128,702; James G. Birney, Liberty Party candidate, 7059.

II. Architecture
   Arts and Music
   Popular Entertainment
   Publishing
   Theater

Magazines with high standards and espousing particular points of view were established in this period. The most notable was *The Dial,* first published in July 1840 and lasting only until April 1844. It was the voice of the transcendentalists and was edited by Margaret Fuller. It published articles by Ralph Waldo Emerson, Henry David Thoreau, Theodore Parker, and others. *The Living Age* was founded in 1844 by Eliakim Littel and edited by him until his death in 1870. It was a general magazine of fiction, poetry, and comment. *Brownson's Quarterly Review* was also first published in 1844, by Orestes Brownson; it reflected Brownson's conversion to Catholicism. *The Southern Literary Messenger* was founded in Richmond, Va., in 1834, while the year before James Hall had brought out the *Illinois Monthly Magazine,* the first literary magazine west of the Ohio R.

Two Years Before the Mast by Richard Henry Dana, Jr., an American classic dealing with the nineteenth-century maritime industry, was published. The book drew on the author's experience as a sailor to the West Coast and back (1834–1836). A sensitive man, Dana was revolted by the cruelty, especially the flogging, aboard ship, and later was instrumental in having the practice outlawed. His realistic approach to writing about life at sea set the standard for later writers.

Tales of the Grotesque and Arabesque, the first collection of short stories by Edgar Allan Poe, was published in Philadelphia in Dec. 1839 but bore the date 1840 on its title page. The two-volume collection included such classic tales of the macabre as "MS. Found in a Bottle," "The Fall of the House of Usher," and "William Wilson." Although Poe was gaining a substantial literary reputation, he failed to find a wide readership or any financial security from his writing. He spent his entire career in virtual penury.

III. Business and Industry
Education
Philosophy and Religion
Science

Dentistry was about to become a separate profession and the U.S. took the lead. The first dental school in the world, the Baltimore College of Dental Surgery, was founded this year in Baltimore, Md. It later became part of the University of Maryland. Chapin Aaron Harris, a pioneer in the field, was the founder. The previous year he had established the *American Journal of Dental Science* and in 1840 helped organize the American Society of Dental Surgeons.

Photography of the moon was accomplished for the first time by John William Draper, a physicist and astronomer at New York University. Draper's photograph of the moon was not impressive by later standards, but it foreshadowed America's pioneering role in astronomical photography. Draper also had the distinction of being the first photographer to capture an image showing a human subject with eyes open.

Mar 31: **A ten-hour workday** was established by executive order for all federal employees engaged on public works. It had long been a goal of U.S. labor.

IV. Fashion
Folkways
Holidays
Social Issues and Crime
Sports

An indication of the social issues confronting Americans during this period was the burgeoning of societies and associations formed to improve health, labor conditions, moral values, education, and other social conditions. The Washington Temperance Society, formed this year by a small group, held a series of meetings in which alcoholics discussed their problems with one another. Within three years the society claimed that 500,000 intemperate drinkers and 100,000 confirmed alcoholics had reformed under its auspices. As early as 1834 the North Carolina Temperance Society had 50 branches with 4700 members. A temperance novel, *My Mother's Gold Ring,* by Lucius Manlius Sargent, was published in 1833 and sold 113,000 copies. What had begun as a movement for temperance in drinking alcoholic beverages turned into a moral crusade for total abstinence, led primarily by Protestant clergymen. Many employers backed the drive on the grounds that nondrinking workers would be more efficient. Among laymen, Neal Dow of Maine was the foremost champion of temperance. He made his first temperance speech when he was 24 and in 1838 was instrumental in the founding of the Maine Temperance Union.

The expression *O.K.* came into popular use this year. The first recorded use of the term was in the Boston *Morning Post* of Mar. 23, 1839, as the initials of the jocularly misspelled phrase *oll korrect.* It came into use in Boston and New York City, then in the presidential election of 1840 was used also to mean *Old Kinderhook,* a reference to Martin Van Buren, whose birthplace and home were in Kinderhook, N.Y.

1841

I. Civil Rights
   Exploration and Settlement
   Government
   Statistics
   Wars

For the first time a vice president succeeded to the presidency because of the death of an incumbent. William Henry Harrison, 68, who caught cold at his inauguration on Mar. 4, died of pneumonia on Apr. 4. Harrison was succeeded by Vice Pres. John Tyler who, although he had run on the Whig ticket, was not a Whig at heart. He had previously supported the Democrat, Pres. Andrew Jackson, in 1828 and 1832, and had major political disagreements with the northern, conservative wing of the Whig Party. His administration was characterized by bickering and frustration, as Henry Clay and Daniel Webster tried to control Tyler and shape the Whig Party to their own interests.

Oct 27: What came to be called the *Creole* incident began when the U.S. brig *Creole* sailed from Hampton Roads, Va. At sea its cargo of slaves mutinied and took over the vessel, then made for the Bahamas, where the mutineers were arrested and the crew allowed to go free. Sec. of State Daniel Webster, arguing that the slaves were on an American vessel and therefore subject to U.S. law, led the attempt to recover the slaves. Rep. Joshua Giddings, Whig of Ohio, introduced a series of resolutions (Mar. 21–22, 1842) against federal sanction of slavery, and particularly against the coastal slave trade, and was censured (Mar. 23, 1842). He resigned from Congress but was returned the next month by his constituents in a special election.

II. Architecture
   Arts and Music
   Popular Entertainment
   Publishing
   Theater

A new literary genre, the detective story, was created in the U.S. this year. It was introduced by Edgar Allan Poe with "The Murders in the Rue Morgue." The story appeared in the April issue of *Graham's Lady's and Gentleman's Magazine,* of which Poe was editor. Poe followed this with "The Mystery of Marie Rogêt" in 1842–1843 and "The Purloined Letter" in 1845. The forerunner of the modern fictional detective appeared in these stories in the person of C. Auguste Dupin, an amateur who demonstrated his ability to find and analyze clues that baffled the police. Thus Poe introduced the puzzling crime, the eccentric detective, his loyal but unperceptive companion, the dull-witted policeman, the surprise solution, and the rational explanation. These works of Poe were popular, but it was later in the century that detective stories by foreign authors such as Wilkie Collins and Arthur Conan Doyle brought wide readership of the genre. Nevertheless, Poe brought this distinct form of fiction to a level matched by only a few later writers.

Essays (first series) by Ralph Waldo Emerson appeared. His second series of *Essays* was published in 1844. Initially both books had only a small sale, but with the advent of the "cheap libraries" of the 1870s and 1890s the *Essays* reached best-seller status. Transcendentalism found its best expression in these essays.

The Deerslayer by James Fenimore Cooper, the last of the frontier novels known as the Leather-Stocking Tales, was published. Leatherstocking, also called Natty Bumppo and Hawkeye, was shown in his youth, skillful in the hunt, resourceful, tough, and sinewy. Above all he was virtuous, sincere, and unspoiled by civilization. When asked about his church, he replied: "I am in church now; I eat in church, drink in church, sleep in church. The 'arth is the temple of the Lord. . . ."

Henry Wadsworth Longfellow gained wide readership with the publication of his *Ballads and Other Poems,* in which he displayed a spirited narrative technique. Poems such as "The Skeleton in Armor" and "The Wreck of the Hesperus" have become part of the American folk heritage. In seven years the Longfellow collection went through ten printings.

III. Business and Industry
   Education
   Philosophy and Religion
   Science

Nativism, chiefly an anti-Catholic movement, increased as the number of Catholic immigrants grew. By 1841 it began to involve education. At this time there were about 200 parochial schools in the country. In New York, on Oct. 29, Bishop John Joseph Hughes urged state support for such schools and encouraged Catholics to use their votes to achieve this purpose. His efforts led to the establishment of an independent Catholic school system, and aroused anger and fear among many American Protestants. Agitation over government support for parochial schools contributed to the founding of the Native American Party, which consisted of Protestants who saw a conspiracy on the part of the growing Catholic population and especially its clergy. Riots resulted, including an attack on Bishop Hughes's home in 1842.

The **Brook Farm Association** was created by members of the Transcendental Club to apply their theories in an experimental cooperative community on a farm nine miles from Boston. A stock company was formed, with George Ripley as its prime organizer and first manager. On April 1 he and his wife and some 20 others began seeking a life balanced between manual labor and intellectual pursuits. Emerson was a party to discussions but never committed himself. Hawthorne and two other transcendentalists lived at Brook Farm for a period. The experiment ended after a serious fire in 1847, with the problems of combining plain living and high ideals unresolved.

IV. Fashion
Folkways
Holidays
Social Issues and Crime
Sports

Foreign visitors continued to arrive in the U.S., look about them, return home, and publish their impressions. Perhaps the most indefatigable of all, both as to miles traveled and words written, was James Buckingham, a British lecturer and a member of Parliament. He made a four-year tour of the U.S., from 1837 to 1840. In 1841 appeared his *America: Historical, Statistical, and Descriptive*, in two volumes. In the following year he published four more volumes, two devoted to the eastern and western states and two to the slave states. His encyclopedic approach yielded a more or less impartial guide. In one observation he found upstate New York frugal and staid, but New York City speculative and extravagant.

The current vogue in **ladies' dresses**, *Godey's Lady's Book* commented, was for tight sleeves. Further, it predicted that the style would last and "again exhibit the beautiful contour of a lady's arm." Yet bare limbs were not proper. Ladies who attended summer resorts were warned against "brocade breakfast dresses" with sleeves and necklines so short that they caused brothers to blush "through the tediousness of three courses and dessert."

1842

I. Civil Rights
Exploration and Settlement
Government
Statistics
Wars

A turning point in U.S.-British relations came with the signing on Aug. 9, 1842, of the Webster-Ashburton Treaty, which settled several matters between the two nations. The treaty took its name from Sec. of State Daniel Webster and Lord Ashburton, the British envoy in Washington. It adjusted the Maine-New Brunswick boundary, which had been the cause of the Aroostock War of 1838–1839. The U.S. received most of the territory in dispute as well as navigational rights on the St. John R. The treaty also settled the question of the U.S.-Canada boundary between Lake Superior and Lake of the Woods. As a result, the U.S. gained territory that included the rich Mesabi iron deposits discovered later. The two nations also agreed to cooperate in suppressing the slave trade. In a separate action Ashburton apologized for the *Caroline* affair, which involved the seizure in 1837 of that American-owned small steamer on the Niagara R.

The **first expedition of John Frémont** began this year. Frémont was placed at the head of a party sent to explore the route to Oregon beyond the Mississippi R. as far as the South Pass of the Continental Divide in Wyoming. Frémont had previously traced the headwaters of the Des Moines R. in 1841.

1842-1843: In **congressional elections** the Democrats gained three Senate seats but the Whigs kept a majority, 28–25, with one seat going to a minor party. In the House the Democrats picked up 40 seats for a 142–79 lead, with one seat going to a minor party.

June 25: A **congressional reapportionment act** was passed. It provided that all congressmen were to be elected by districts equal in number to each state's quota of representatives.

II. Architecture
Arts and Music
Popular Entertainment
Publishing
Theater

Growing interest in classical music was indicated by the number of musical organizations founded in the mid-nineteenth century. Foremost among them was the New York Philharmonic Society, established on Apr. 2, 1842. The orchestra was led by a German-trained musician from Connecticut, Ureli Corelli Hill. It gave its first performance on Dec. 7. Only Hill and the librarian received salaries, while the 60-odd orchestra members, mostly Germans, shared in the modest ticket receipts. The Chicago Philharmonic Society was formed in 1850 but lasted only four years. The first important chamber music group was the Mendelssohn Quintette Club of Boston, founded in 1849.

Cheap publishing made its first appearance in the U.S. Because of low postal rates for newspapers and improvements in printing, novels were published in a newspaper format and sold for as little as 6 1/4 cents. This forced regular publishers to produce cheap paperbacks. The newspaper extras lasted only four or five years, having been killed off by the handier paperbacks.

III. Business and Industry
    Education
    Philosophy and Religion
    Science

Of the nineteenth-century advances in medical science, none was more welcome to patients than the development of anesthetics. The properties of chloroform had been discovered in 1831, but it was not used as an anesthetic until 1847 in Great Britain. In the meantime, on Mar. 30, 1842, Dr. Crawford W. Long of Jefferson, Ga., used ethyl ether while removing a tumor from the neck of a patient. For several years thereafter he continued to use ether. He even administered it to his wife during childbirth. Long, however, did not make his work public until 1849, after others had demonstrated the value of anesthetics. Dr. William T. G. Morton demonstrated the beneficial effects of ether in Boston on Oct. 16, 1846, before members of the medical profession.

The **legality of labor unions** was established by the Massachusetts Supreme Court in the case of *Commonwealth v. Hunt.* This included the right of workers to strike in order to obtain a closed shop, higher wages, shorter working hours, and better working conditions. It was held further that individual members of unions could not be indicted collectively for the illegal actions of other union members. This decision was significant in its reversal of traditional judicial hostility to labor organizations.

Mar 3: Child labor legislation was advanced when Gov. John Davis of Massachusetts signed a law to regulate the workday of children under 12 years of age. Such children were limited to a ten-hour day. But the law applied only to "manufacturing establishments" and was not easily enforceable. Similar laws were passed in other states, particularly in New England and the Middle Atlantic states, but it was not until after the Civil War that enforcement of minimum age and maximum hour provisions began to affect child employment practices.

IV. Fashion
Folkways
Holidays
Social Issues and Crime
Sports

At this time horse racing was the most popular spectator sport. It was also popular with those who liked to wager on sporting events. The Union Course, on Long Island, N.Y., held a series of intersectional races that drew large crowds. On May 20, 1842, the entry from the South, Fashion, and the entry from the North, Boston, raced for a purse of $20,000. Although Boston was the outstanding horse of the period, it lost to Fashion, which ran the four-mile course in a record 7:32. In 1845 Fashion raced Peytona, from Alabama, on the same course; the latter won. This time it was estimated that 50,000 people tried to reach the track, tying up traffic to the extent that some fans never arrived.

In **women's fashions,** the pelerine, a type of cape or mantle, was very popular, as were watered silk and velvet cardinals (short cloaks) and scarves. However, it was not considered good taste to wear a cardinal with a dress of the same color.

1843

I. Civil Rights
Exploration and Settlement
Government
Statistics
Wars

The U.S. was concerned over the interest shown in the Hawaiian Islands by France and Great Britain. In 1842 the U.S. recognized the islands' independence and Pres. John Tyler said the U.S. would be "dissatisfied" if any nation took possession of them. To affirm its interest, the U.S. signed a trade treaty with Hawaii in 1843 and sent a diplomatic agent, George Brown, to represent American interests. Earlier in the year the commander of a British frigate had made an abortive attempt to obtain cession to Great Britain from King Kamehameha III.

May 29: The second and most fruitful **Frémont expedition,** under John C. Frémont, left Kansas City. The journey yielded an accurate survey of the emigrant route to Oregon. The return journey allowed members of the expedition to correct many misconceptions about the geography of California. Frémont discovered the nature of the Great Basin, and probably first used that term to describe the independent system of lakes and rivers divided from the ocean by the mountains. Frémont made a great contribution to geographical knowledge. He arrived back in St. Louis on Aug. 7, 1844.

June: The **American Republican Party** was formed at New York City largely through the efforts of the Native American Association, an anti-Catholic, anti-immigrant organization. In 1845, this party evolved into the Native American Party, which called for sweeping changes in immigration laws. Having no position on the Mexican War, it failed. Revived in 1853, it collapsed again in division over the slavery issue.

Aug 31: The abolitionist **Liberty Party nominated James G. Birney** of Kentucky for the presidency and Thomas Morris of Ohio for the vice presidency.

II. Architecture
  Arts and Music
  Popular Entertainment
  Publishing
  Theater

American humor continued to favor the regional, folksy approach of the naive but shrewd storyteller. Two such storytellers were Seba Smith and William Tappan Thompson. The latter was the editor of the Savannah, Ga., *Morning News*. His humorous accounts of Georgia characters, which had first appeared in his paper, were collected in 1843 in *Major Jones's Courtship*. The sketches were written as letters to the editor, and the supposed author, Major Jones, appeared to be a semiliterate Georgia planter. The pieces were filled with descriptions of everyday events, weddings, military service, and the like, all in dialect. Thompson's book went through 20 printings. He published four more books in a similar vein. Seba Smith founded the Portland, Me., *Courier* and published in it letters from the fictional "Major Jack Downing," a Down East Yankee whose forte was political commentary. Smith, through his alter ego, was thus the first of a line of homespun political philosophers to delight American readers. Smith collected Downing's writings in book form first in 1833.

The Conquest of Mexico, an American historical and literary classic by William Hickling Prescott, was published. It was a monumental work for which he had to import a small reference library. Concerned always with style, Prescott had a passion for fact, making his work authoritative as well as compelling. In 1847 he added *The Conquest of Peru* to his history of Spanish America. Both books have sold hundreds of thousands of copies.

III. Business and Industry
Education
Philosophy and Religion
Science

The era of nineteenth-century Utopian communities came to a climax with the establishment this year of the North American Phalanx at Red Bank, N.J. Its founder was Albert Brisbane, a disciple of the social philosophy of Charles Fourier of France, who proposed organizing people into economic units called phalanxes. About 1200 formed the Red Bank group, which built a three-story phalanstery and a gristmill. The land was fertile and the group's members, mostly people of culture and refinement, developed a successful truck gardening operation. The members ate their meals together but each family had separate quarters. After the mill burned down in 1854, the association was dissolved, having enjoyed a longer life until then than any other community of its type.

The **Harvard Astronomical Observatory** acquired by private subscription the largest telescope available. In March a comet had appeared in daytime and aroused such interest that a subscription for fitting out the observatory with the latest astronomical equipment had been proposed. The purchase of the telescope indicated that lectures and public addresses by scientists were having the intended effect: establishing American astronomy. Harvard Observatory was begun through the initiative of William Cranch Bond, who had made observations for some years at his home and then moved to Dana House in 1839. A main branch of the Harvard Observatory is still maintained at Cambridge, Mass.

IV. Fashion
   Folkways
   Holidays
   Social Issues and Crime
   Sports

Rowing and sailing were popular sports. They were mainly enjoyed by the well-to-do and hence had high social status. Rowing was introduced at Harvard this year by a student, William Weeks, who bought and outfitted a shell. Yale took up the sport the next year. On Aug. 3, 1852, the Harvard crew defeated the Yale crew on Lake Winnepesaukee, N.H., in the first intercollegiate sports event of any kind. In the 1830s and 1840s in New York City, the Castle Garden Amateur Boat Club Association was restricted to "young men of the highest respectability, who were determined to combine with pleasure the utmost propriety of conduct."

July 12: Joseph Smith, leader of the Mormon Church,

announced that a divine revelation had sanctioned the practice of polygamy. This announcement caused bitter feeling both within Mormon ranks and between Mormons and non-Mormons around Nauvoo, Ill., where Smith's followers were settled at this time.

1844

I. Civil Rights
   Exploration and Settlement
   Government
   Statistics
   Wars

The presidential election campaign of 1844 saw some unusual happenings in American politics. Pres. John Tyler wanted a term in his own right, and a Democratic faction nominated him in 1844. It was clear, however, that he stood no chance, and he withdrew on Aug. 20, becoming the first president who did not stand for a second term. At the Democratic National Convention, former Pres. Martin Van Buren tried to secure the nomination but could not muster enough support, largely because of his opposition to the annexation of Texas. The Democrats nominated the first so-called dark horse in U.S. history, James K. Polk of Tennessee. The Whigs unanimously nominated Henry Clay of Kentucky for the presidency. There was a third party this year, the Liberty Party, which in 1843 had nominated James G. Birney of Kentucky on an antislavery platform. The Democratic platform was nationalistic, calling for annexation of Texas and control of the entire Oregon Territory, then shared with England. The Whig platform was more general, making no reference to Texas or to the question of a national bank.

1844-1845: In **congressional elections** the Democrats gained six seats for a 31–25 majority over the Whigs. In the House the Democrats gained one seat for a 143–77 majority, with six seats going to minor parties.

May 1: The **Whig National Convention nominated Henry Clay** of Kentucky for the presidency. Theodore Frelinghuysen of New Jersey was nominated for the vice presidency.

May 27-29: The **Democratic National Convention nominated James K. Polk** of Tennessee for the presidency on the ninth ballot. Polk won the nomination after all other candidates withdrew. Former Pres. Martin Van Buren was unable to secure the nomination largely because of his opposition to the annexation of Texas. George M. Dallas of Pennsylvania was nominated for the vice presidency. This was the first convention at which a dark horse candidate won, and also the first to be reported by telegraph.

June 8: The **Texas Annexation Treaty** failed to win the necessary two-thirds vote for passage in the Senate.

Dec 4: James K. Polk was elected president of the United States by a popular vote of 1,337,243 against 1,299,068 for Henry Clay, the Whig candidate, and 62,300 for James B. Birney, the Liberty candidate. Birney's strong showing in New York cost Clay the state's electoral votes and the election. The electoral vote was Polk, 170; Clay, 105.

II. Architecture
Arts and Music
Popular Entertainment
Publishing
Theater

Fictional tales of the violence, real or imagined, of the western frontier were popular. One of the most successful authors of such works was Charles W. Webber, who served in the Texas Rangers, studied at Princeton Divinity School, and died on an expedition to Nicaragua. Among his novels were *Jack Long; or,*

The Shot in the Eye (1844) and *Old Hicks* (1848). Emerson Bennett wrote 50 novels of adventure and intrigue, most of them with western settings. *Prairie Flower* and *Leni-Leoti*, both published in 1849, sold about 100,000 copies each.

The second series of *Essays* by Ralph Waldo Emerson was published. Among the essays included were "Experience," "Gifts," "New England Reformers," "The Poet," "Character," "Politics," "Nature," and "Manners." It proved more popular than Emerson's first series of *Essays* (1841), but it has not enjoyed equal literary reputation.

The Dial suspended publication. Founded in 1840, the publication was never popular and its 16 issues did not, from circulation reports, indicate that it ever would be. Yet it was of crucial importance in the history of New England transcendentalism and has had an influence on American life and letters that is belied by its short life. *The Dial* remains a primary source for an understanding of the views of the transcendentalists. As first editor, Margaret Fuller drew on an outstanding list of contributors, among them Ralph Waldo Emerson and Henry David Thoreau.

III. Business and Industry
Education
Philosophy and Religion
Science

American inventors tended to concentrate on the development of practical and marketable devices. Such a man was Charles Goodyear, who on June 15, 1844, received a patent for vulcanizing rubber. In 1839 Goodyear, while trying to find a way of making rubber useful at high temperatures, accidentally dropped some rubber that had been mixed with sulfur on a hot stove, and the vulcanization process was discovered. Poor and in debt, Goodyear sold his patent for far less than it was worth. He died in poverty.
May 24: The **first telegraph message**, "What hath God

wrought," was sent from the U.S. Supreme Court room in Washington, D.C., to Alfred Vail in Baltimore, Md., by Samuel F. B. Morse, the inventor of the telegraph. The federal government appropriated the money for the line.

June 27: The founder of Mormonism, **Joseph Smith,** and his brother, Hiram Smith, were murdered by a mob in Carthage, Ill.

Sep 19: The **Marquette iron range** in the Upper Peninsula of Michigan near Lake Superior was discovered accidentally by a group of government surveyors headed by William A. Burt. Burt observed that his compass was deviating 87 degrees from normal. Upon investigating the soil, he found evidence of large deposits of iron ore.

IV. Fashion
Folkways
Holidays
Social Issues and Crime
Sports

Foot racing was a popular sport, largely because it offered a fine opportunity for betting. The runners of the time were professionals and were called pedestrians. In 1835 in New York City a $1000 purse was offered to anyone who could run a ten-mile course in less than an hour. An enormous and unruly crowd turned out to see one of the nine starters finish in just under an hour. In 1844 at Hoboken, N.J., a similar race was run in which John Gildersleeve of New York triumphed out over several British entrants. Gildersleeve finished in 57:01.5 and won $1000. A crowd estimated at 25,000 watched the race and was again unruly.

The catchy phrase *Fifty-four Forty or Fight* was adopted as a campaign slogan by forces supporting James K. Polk, the expansionist Democrat, for the presidency. It applied to the Oregon controversy between Great Britain and the U.S. Many Americans felt that the country should press U.S. claims to the

54°40'th parallel. Settlement was finally made on the 49th parallel, with everything north becoming part of Canada and everything south part of the U.S. Northwest.

The **first private bath** in an American hotel was introduced at the New York Hotel. The first bridal suite in an American hotel was introduced at the Irving House in New York City.

The **first female mannequin** ever exhibited in America was employed by Paulina Wright in her public lectures on the physiology of women before female audiences.

June 26: Pres. **John Tyler was married** to Miss Julia Gardiner at the Church of the Ascension in New York City. Tyler was the first president to marry during his term of office.

July 29: The **New York Yacht Club** was founded on board the schooner *Gimcrack* docked off the Battery. John C. Stevens was elected its commodore. It is the oldest surviving yacht club in the U.S.

1845

I. Civil Rights
Exploration and Settlement
Government
Statistics
Wars

The annexation of Texas finally became a reality after long political bickering. Antislavery forces were opposed to annexation because Texas was certain to become a slave state. Others wanted to act lest Great Britain or France develop a relationship with the Republic of Texas, whose independence Mexico refused to recognize. In Apr. 1844 Pres. John Tyler submitted to the Senate a treaty of annexation, but the Senate rejected it in June. In December Tyler offered a joint resolution to cover annexation. This required only a majority vote by both houses of Congress instead of the two-thirds vote needed to ratify a treaty. Action on the resolution was completed on Feb. 28, 1845, when the House accepted it in revised form. On June 23 the congress of Texas accepted annexation.

Jan 23: A **uniform election day for presidential elections** was established by an act of Congress. States had previously set their own election days. The act named the first Tuesday after the first Monday in November as Election Day. The first national election fell on Nov. 4.

Mar 3: **Florida** was admitted to the Union, becoming the 27th state.

Spring: **John C. Frémont** left on his third expedition, this time directly to California, with 60 armed men. Ostensibly their mission was to survey the central Rockies and the Great Salt Lake region. However, war with Mexico was in the air. In 1846 Frémont supported and may have instigated the Bear Flag Revolt, in which American settlers in the San Francisco Bay area seized the town of Sonoma. The settlers raised a flag with the figure of a bear on it and proclaimed the Republic of California.

June 15: **U.S. protection of Texas** was assured if it agreed to annexation. Tangible evidence was given to the Texans when Gen. Zachary Taylor was ordered to defend a line "on or near the Rio Grande."

Dec 29: **Texas** was admitted to the Union, the 28th state.

II. Architecture
   ## Arts and Music
   ## Popular Entertainment
   ## Publishing
   ## Theater

Writings about the western frontier now included works by authors who saw the process of pioneering in realistic terms. One such author was Caroline

Kirkland, an early settler of Pinckney, Mich. Her first book was *A New Home—Who'll Follow?* (1839). In it she described many aspects of frontier life, from log houses to land booms, as well as social life, politics, and teaching methods, etc. Later Mrs. Kirkland wrote *Forest Life* (1842) and *Western Clearings* (1845), which were more sentimental and self-conscious than her first and more humorous book had been.

June: *Tales* by Edgar A. Poe was published in New York City by Wiley & Putnam, which also issued Poe's *The Raven and Other Poems* in October. The former contained 12 stories, including "The Gold-Bug," "The Fall of the House of Usher," "A Descent into the Maelstrom," and "The Murders in the Rue Morgue." The latter included all of Poe's best poems to date. Despite growing recognition and the publication of these volumes, his eighth and ninth books, Poe was in such dire need of money that his magazine, *Broadway Journal*, failed in December, ending a remarkably productive two years.

III. Business and Industry
Education
Philosophy and Religion
Science

There were as yet few leaders or writers who took up labor's cause, and those who did generally cloaked their efforts under the broad heading of social reform. There were also few attempts to form labor unions. Unusual for his time was George Henry Evans, who had retired in 1836. He emerged again in 1844, reestablishing his former paper, the *Workingman's Advocate*. In 1845 he formed the National Reform Association. At the heart of Evans's reform was his proposal to have the government give every workingman a free homestead of 160 acres. His strategy was to get candidates for public office to support this idea if they wanted the votes of labor.

Dr. **William Keil** founded the communal settle-

ment of Bethel in Shelby County, Mo. He led 500
German immigrants with Anabaptist backgrounds
and Utopian ideas into this haven. There he established his Church of the Living God, a successful enterprise. Keil held autocratic power. His subjects sel-
dom received any money for their efforts, but all
their needs were satisfied—food, clothing, shelter, education for their children, and other benefits.

Oct 10: The U.S. Naval Academy opened at Annapolis,
Md. It combined at one site a group of schools previously located in the port cities of New York, Boston,
Philadelphia, and Norfolk. Its first graduation exercises were held on June 10, 1854.

IV. Fashion
Folkways
Holidays
Social Issues and Crime
Sports

The exuberant, nationalistic, even jingoistic, spirit of
the times was perfectly exemplified in the phrase
manifest destiny, which first appeared this year in
connection with the annexation of Texas. In the July
issue of the *United States Magazine and Democratic
Review,* John L. O'Sullivan, its editor, wrote of "our
manifest destiny to overspread the continent allotted
by Providence for the free development of our yearly
multiplying millions." The phrase soon gained wide
usage in connection with the dispute over the Oregon
Territory, even by those who wanted to annex Cuba.

The popularity of **lectures** among American audiences was reflected in the career of John Bartholomew Gough, an English-born reformed alcoholic
who made a handsome living giving lectures on his
victory over drink. Every lecture ended with the taking of pledges of abstinence. At his peak Gough was
paid $175 per lecture, many times the fee of the aver-
age temperance speaker. Before his death Gough estimated he had given 9600 temperance lectures to

9,000,000 people. In 1843 he traveled 6840 miles to make 383 addresses.

Baseball took a giant step toward the modern game when Alexander J. Cartwright, a New York City fireman, drew up a set of rules and organized the first baseball club, The Knickerbockers. Other clubs were formed and adopted Cartwright's rules. Cartwright fixed four as the number of bases, not two, three, or five; set them 90 feet apart; stood the batter in a box at home plate, not at some distance from it; made the bases flat; and ruled out "plugging" a baserunner with a thrown ball to put him out.

1846

I. **Civil Rights**
Exploration and Settlement
Government
Statistics
Wars

With the annexation of Texas in early 1845, war with Mexico became all but inevitable. Pres. James K. Polk hoped to settle matters peacefully but was determined to have his way by war if necessary. In Nov. 1845 he sent John Slidell to Mexico with an offer of $5,000,000 for the purchase of New Mexico and $25,000,000 for California. The offer was refused. On May 9, 1846, word reached Washington, D.C., that American troops had been attacked by Mexican forces on Apr. 24. Polk asked Congress for, and was granted, a declaration of war. Congress authorized the president to call for 50,000 volunteers and appropriated $10,000,000. Congress and the nation, however, were far from united on the idea of waging war. Southerners favored war as likely to extend slave territory, while northerners opposed the war for the same reason.

1846-1847: In **congressional elections** the Democrats increased their Senate majority to 36–21, with one seat going to a minor party. In the House the Whigs gained 38 seats to take a 115–108 majority, with four seats going to minor parties.

Jan: Pres. **James K. Polk** ordered U.S. troops into the region in southern Texas disputed with Mexico, between the roughly parallel Nueces and Rio Grande rivers. The commanding general was Zachary Taylor.

Feb 10: The **Mormon migration** westward from Nauvoo, Ill., began. It was organized and led by Brigham Young after the murder of Joseph Smith, founder of Mormonism.

Apr 30-May 1: The **Mexican army** crossed the Rio Grande and on May 3 placed Fort Texas under siege.

May 4: Capital punishment was abolished for the first time in the U.S. by the Michigan legislature, effective Jan. 1, 1847. Treason against the state remained a capital crime.

May 8: The **Battle of Palo Alto,** the first important engagement of the Mexican War, was fought, with the Mexicans on the losing side.

May 9: In the **Battle of Resaca de la Palma,** U.S. forces under Gen. Taylor forced the Mexican army back across the Rio Grande.

May 13: A **declaration of war** against Mexico was passed several days after hostilities commenced. War measures were passed over Whig opposition, which increased as the war progressed.

May 18: U.S. forces crossed the Rio Grande, led by Gen. Zachary Taylor. The Americans occupied Matamoros.

June 14: The **Bear Flag Revolt** began with the proclamation by a group of California settlers of the Republic of California. The name came from their standard, which included the name of the republic, a grizzly bear, and a star on a field of white. On Aug. 17 Robert F. Stockton, a naval officer commanding

U.S. forces on the Pacific coast, issued a proclamation declaring the annexation of California by the U.S., and establishing himself as governor.

June 15: The **Oregon Treaty** with Great Britain was signed. It established the 49th parallel as the boundary between the U.S. and the British Northwest territory. Idaho, Oregon, Washington, and part of Montana became undisputed U.S. territory. This was a compromise from the campaign slogan of Polk in 1844: "Fifty-four Forty or Fight." Canada was granted navigation rights to part of the Columbia R. south of the 49th parallel.

Sep 25: **Monterrey, Mexico,** was captured by U.S. forces under Gen. Zachary Taylor after a four-day engagement that made "Old Rough and Ready" Taylor, a Whig, into a national hero. His relations with Pres. Polk, a Democrat, cooled subsequently.

Dec 28: Iowa was admitted into the Union, becoming the 29th state.

II. Architecture
Arts and Music
Popular Entertainment
Publishing
Theater

The talented author whose career becomes disjointed and whose works lapse into obscurity, only to be revived and hailed by a later generation, is not unique in literary history. No one fitted this situation better than Herman Melville, in 1846 deemed one of America's most promising new writers. In his lifetime Melville worked as a bank clerk, farmer, teacher, and sailor; he spent 19 of his later years working as customs inspector in New York City. His career seemed more than ensured when his first novel, *Typee*, was published in 1846. This romance of the South Seas, based on his own experiences, was followed by several more well received novels. His greatest work, *Moby-Dick* (1851), was misunderstood by readers and critics alike, and Melville began a long, heartbreaking slide into literary oblivion. His greatness was not fully appreciated until well into the twentieth century.

Margaret Fuller published her critical essays as *Papers on Literature and Art.* Up to and even past her time, Fuller was the most formidable American female intellectual. She was known in her own time for her support of the rights of women, her intellect, her knowledge of German, and her understanding of philosophy. From 1840–1842 she edited *The Dial,* and she was considered the best American critic up to 1850, but her writings had a limited and select audience. Hawthorne used her in conceiving his character Zenobia in *The Blithedale Romance.*

III. Business and Industry
Education
Philosophy and Religion
Science

One of the most important events in the scientific world at this time was the establishment by Congress this year of the Smithsonian Institution in Washington, D.C. In 1829 James Smithson, an illegitimate son of the Duke of Northumberland, left about $550,000 in his will to establish such an institution. Congress, however, did not resolve exactly how to use the money for 17 years, finally determining that it should be "for the increase and diffusion of knowledge among men." The Smithsonian over the years has grown into a complex of museums and other facilities serving professionals and nonprofessionals alike. It supports many scientific endeavors.

The **Eastern Exchange Hotel,** the first public building heated by steam, opened in Boston.

The **first rotary printing press** was devised and produced by Richard M. Hoe. It was capable of turning out 8000 newspapers an hour. The press was first installed in 1847 by Philadelphia's *Public Ledger.*

Sep 10: The **first sewing machine** in the U.S. with an eye-pointed needle was patented by Elias Howe, called the father of the modern sewing machine.

Oct 16: Anesthesia was given its first public demonstration before doctors by William T. G. Morton, a Boston dentist. Morton administered sulfuric ether during an operation performed by John Collins Warren at the Massachusetts General Hospital. A neck tumor was removed. Earlier, on Sept. 30, Morton had painlessly removed an ulcerated tooth from a patient anesthetized by ether.

IV. Fashion
Folkways
Holidays
Social Issues and Crime
Sports

The lecture circuit was popular with Americans, who found lyceum speakers entertaining and sometimes inspiring. The lecture hall became a center for promotion of social movements, including the rising agitation for prohibition laws. At this time there emerged a new voice for temperance, John Bartholomew Gough, an Englishman and reformed alcoholic. He lectured for 40 years, and thousands of people signed the teetotaler's pledge after hearing his story of the evils of drink. Gough advocated that a prohibition amendment be added to the Constitution.

The **exodus of the Mormons** from Nauvoo, Ill., after open hostilities with their Illinois neighbors came on the heels of a hard winter of preparation. The Mormons had turned their homes into workshops and equipped 12,000 wagons to carry their families and belongings. Beginning in February, small groups began to leave Nauvoo. They crossed the Mississippi R. by flatboat. Later in the month the river froze and some groups were able to cross on the ice. By the end of the month, 2000 men, women, and children were in Iowa and ready to move on. The sprawling caravan was broken into companies of 50 wagons. The leading parties advanced slowly, setting up resting spots along the route where tired people and cattle could recover from the ravages of ice, snow, and rain. By the middle of May 16,000 Mormons had crossed the Mississippi. The stragglers left Nauvoo by September. Through the fall and following winter, from fear of winter and Indians on the plain ahead, the main body of the wagon train was bogged down in the bottomlands of the Missouri R., near Council Bluffs, Iowa.

June 19: The **first recorded baseball game** in history resembling the modern sport was played at Elysian Field, Hoboken, N.J., between the New York Club and the Knickerbockers. The New York Club won 23–1. Davis, their pitcher, was fined six cents for swearing at the umpire. Alexander J. Cartwright, founder of the Knickerbockers, had written the rules under which the game was played.

1847

I. Civil Rights
Exploration and Settlement
Government
Statistics
Wars

One of the most horrifying incidents in the history of the westward movement occurred in early 1847 in the Sierra Nevada range of California. The previous December a pioneer group of 87 persons, headed by two brothers, Jacob and George Donner, had attempted to take a shortcut through the Wasatch Mountains, only to find themselves trapped by snow when they reached the Sierra Nevada. A party of eight men, five women, and two Indian guides set out for help. While they were gone, the rest of the party realized that no one would survive unless they practiced cannibalism on those who died. When relief

reached the stranded party on Feb. 19, there were
only 45 survivors.

Jan 16: The **Oregon Bill,** providing for territorial government of that area, passed the House. It excluded
slavery under the restrictions of the Northwest Ordinance. The bill was tabled in the Senate.

Feb 22-23: At the **Battle of Buena Vista,** U.S. forces
under Gen. Zachary Taylor defeated the Mexicans
under Gen. Antonio López de Santa Anna.

Mar 9: U.S. forces under Gen. Winfield Scott landed
near **Vera Cruz,** Mexico. Some 10,000 troops landed
just south of the city, site of the most powerful fortress in the Western Hemisphere, in what was the
first large-scale amphibious operation in U.S. history.
Scott began a siege of Vera Cruz on Mar. 22. The
fortress fell on Mar. 27 and was occupied two days
later. On Apr. 8 Scott moved toward Mexico City.

Sep 14: Gen. **Winfield Scott entered Mexico City.** A
battalion of U.S. Marines made its presence felt at the
"halls of Montezuma."

II. Architecture
   Arts and Music
   Popular Entertainment
   Publishing
   Theater

The death in New York City on Nov. 2 of Nathaniel
Bannister, a prolific southern playwright who ended
his days in poverty, was a reminder of the period's
love of historical and melodramatic plays. Bannister's work also reflected the vogue for foreign settings, as in *Gaulantus* (1837), *England's Iron Days*
(1837), and *Gentleman of Lyons* (1838). His most popular play, *Putnam,* however, which had been produced at the Bowery Theater in New York City in
1844, had a Revolutionary War setting.

   An idyllic tale in verse, *Evangeline* by Henry
Wadsworth Longfellow, was published. Based on an
account told to the poet by Nathaniel Hawthorne, the
narrative concerns the fate of two lovers in French

Acadie (Nova Scotia) who are separated when the French are expelled from Nova Scotia. It is a tale of virginal love that maintains itself through disappointments and frustrations.

Sep 11: "Susanna," by Stephen Foster, was performed for the first time at a concert in the Eagle Saloon, Pittsburgh, Pa. It became Foster's first widespread success, being taken up by minstrel troupes and carried to the West Coast by the forty-niners.

III. Business and Industry
Education
Philosophy and Religion
Science

Liberal Protestant clergymen were stirring controversy by their espousal of a less harsh view of humanity than that offered by Calvinism. The early intellectual leader of this group was Horace Bushnell, a Congregational clergyman who emphasized the divine in humanity and in nature. His views were expressed in *Christian Nurture* (1847) and *God in Christ* (1849). *Nature and the Supernatural* (1858) attacked transcendentalism. Bushnell was accused of heresy for his views on the Trinity but was never brought to trial.

May 1: The **Smithsonian Institution** was formally dedicated in Washington, D.C. Joseph Henry, a Princeton physicist, was named its first secretary.

July 1: The **first official U.S. postage stamps** were issued by the Post Office Department in five-cent and ten-cent denominations. This action had been authorized by Congress on Mar. 3. The new stamps were also the first adhesive postage stamps in the U.S.

July 24: **Brigham Young,** with a party of 143, reached the valley of Great Salt Lake. The flight of Joseph Smith from Missouri to Illinois had ended with a quarrel among the factions of the Mormon Church, the imprisonment of Smith by order of the Illinois governor, and his assassination by a mob that stormed the jail at Carthage and shot him and his brother to death. Brigham Young had been chosen to succeed Smith as leader of the Mormons. Hostility toward the Mormons continued and violence increased. Young was compelled to lead the Mormons' western trek, which was one of the great migrations of the American West. When Salt Lake City was established, Young returned to lead the rest of the eastern Mormons from Council Bluffs, Iowa, to their permanent home in Utah.

IV. Fashion
Folkways
Holidays
Social Issues and Crime
Sports

Light entertainment in the 1840s consisted of burlesque and *tableaux vivants*. Burlesque usually took the form of musical satire. Even William Shakespeare was burlesqued, as in *Much Ado about the Merchant of Venice*. Most daring were *tableaux vivants* in which scantily clad men and women posed in such classical scenes as "Venus Rising from the Sea" and "Psyche Going to the Bath."

The **legal status of women** was slightly improved in Vermont by passage of a state law that guaranteed to the wife full ownership of real estate held by her at the time of her marriage or gained by gift or bequest afterward. The husband's consent was still necessary, however, if the wife wished to transfer ownership of the property.

Flogging boys and girls as an educational practice was attacked by Lyman Cobb in *The Evil Tendencies of Corporal Punishment as a Means of Moral Discipline in Families and Schools*. Cobb listed some 60 arguments against the practice. An advanced educator, Cobb even announced that he did not want his pupils to suffer over tedious reading. His views were widely held by those opposing the old-fashioned "school of the rod."

Oct: Maria Mitchell, a Nantucket, Mass., librarian and astronomical observer, discovered a new comet. For this she received a gold medal from the astronomy-minded King of Denmark and election into the American Academy of Arts and Sciences, the first woman so honored. When Vassar College opened in 1865 she was named to the staff as the first woman professor of astronomy in the U.S.

1848

I. Civil Rights
Exploration and Settlement
Government
Statistics
Wars

The Treaty of Guadalupe Hidalgo, signed by the U.S. and Mexico on Feb. 2, 1848, formally ended the Mexican War (1846–1848). By its terms Mexico recognized Texas as part of the U.S. and ceded to the U.S. over 500,000 square miles of territory, including all of the future states of California, Nevada, and Utah, almost all of New Mexico and Arizona, and parts of Colorado and Wyoming. In return the U.S. agreed to pay Mexico $15,000,000 and to assume the claims of U.S. citizens against Mexico, amounting to $3,250,000. The U.S. became an enormous continental republic, but the acquisition of the new territory aggravated the dispute between slavery and antislavery forces. The war resulted in 1721 dead and 4102 wounded. In addition, some 11,155 Americans died of disease as a result of the war. The total cost of the war was estimated at $97,500,000.

1848-1849: In **congressional elections** the Democrats lost one Senate seat for a 35–25 majority over the Whigs, with one seat held by a minor party. In the

House they gained four seats for a 112–109 majority, with nine seats held by minor parties.

May 22-26: The **Democratic National Convention nominated Lewis Cass** of Michigan for the presidency and William O. Butler of Kentucky for the vice presidency.

May 29: Wisconsin was admitted to the Union, becoming the 30th state.

June 7-9: The **Whig National Convention nominated Gen. Zachary Taylor** of Louisiana for the presidency and Millard Fillmore of New York for the vice presi-

July 19-20: A **women's convention at Seneca Falls,** N.Y., called by Lucretia Mott and Elizabeth Cady Stanton, discussed women's rights. Susan B. Anthony joined the convention, where such subjects as voting, property rights, and divorce were debated. Similar conventions were held annually until the Civil War.

July 27: The **Clayton Compromise,** named for Sen. John M. Clayton, National Republican of Delaware, was passed by the Senate. It excluded slavery from Oregon, prohibited legislation regarding slavery by the new territories of California and New Mexico, and authorized the appeal of territorial slave cases to the Supreme Court. The House tabled the bill the next day.

Nov 7: Zachary Taylor was elected president of the United States. Millard Fillmore was elected vice president. The electoral vote was Taylor, 163, Lewis Cass, Democratic candidate, 127. The popular vote was Taylor, 1,360,101; Cass, 1,220,544; Martin Van Buren, Free-Soil and Barnburners candidate, 291,263.

II. Architecture
Arts and Music
Popular Entertainment
Publishing
Theater

New developments in cast-iron production combined during this period with innovative architectural con-

cepts to produce a new kind of structure, both as to
materials and design. Pioneer architect James Bogardus built in 1848 and 1849 the first cast-iron building,
a five-story structure located in New York City at
Centre and Duane streets. It consisted of cast iron
instead of masonry, except that the floor beams may
have been timber. The facade consisted of cast-iron
columns similar to the stone columns of the Classical
style, interspersed with windows. The style remained
popular for the rest of the century. Foundries such
as Badger's Iron Works in New York City began to
turn out prefabricated parts for columns and capitals.

   James Russell Lowell had a banner year with the
publication of three major poetic works. *The Biglow
Papers* (first series) consisted of nine poems that hu-
morously voiced opposition to the war with Mexico
and the annexation of Texas. The Yankee dialect of
Ezekiel and Hosea Biglow immediately caught popular fancy. *A Fable for Critics,* in the tradition of Pope's
Dunciad and Byron's *Vision of Judgment,* dealt with
contemporary writers and critics. Lowell also published *Poems: Second Series* and *The Vision of Sir
Launfal.*

III. Business and Industry
   ## Education
   ## Philosophy and Religion
   ## Science

The only successful industrial Utopian community
was established in 1848 in Oneida, N.Y. It was
founded by John Humphrey Noyes and his followers.
In 1839 Noyes had established a so-called Perfection-
ist community at Putney, Vt. His system of polyga-
mous marriage so outraged his neighbors that the
group was forced to flee. They moved to Oneida
where they established the Oneida Community.
There the group held all property in common and
children were raised in a communal nursery. The

community prospered, at first by manufacturing a trap for small animals and later by producing silverware. In 1879, however, opposition again arose to the community's style of living and Noyes went to Canada, where he remained for the rest of his life. In 1881 the group, having abandoned Noyes's theories, was reorganized as a business corporation.

The **Associated Press** (AP) was organized by a group of New York City journalists. The AP was a result of the impatience of Moses Beach, publisher of the New York *Sun,* with established news lines. He experimented with ways of getting the news faster, including use of carrier pigeons. Reports from the Mexican War came in so slowly that Beach finally set up his own express service. The arrangement was successful enough to convince other New York publishers to carry the expense of a private news-gathering service, which became the Associated Press.

June 27: Air conditioning for a theater was offered by the Broadway Theater in New York City, perhaps for the first time. The theater issued this notice in its bill: "The public is respectfully informed that an Extensive Apparatus for the Perfect Ventilation of the Entire Building is now in operation. The Steam Power by which it is impelled, being capable of conveying to the Audience part alone, 3000 Feet of Cool Air per minute, thus rendering the Establishment during the hottest and most crowded nights in all respects comfortable. The machinery patented by Mr. J. E. Coffee."

Sep: The **American Association for the Advancement of Science** was founded. The charter of the association expressed a determination to "advance science in the New World" in every possible way. The association developed as a joint endeavor of American and Canadian scientists.

Nov 1: The **first medical school for women** opened with an enrollment of twelve. It was founded and further developed by Samuel Gregory, a pioneer in medical education for women. Known as the Boston Female Medical School, it was merged in 1874 with the Boston University School of Medicine to form one of the first coed medical schools in the world.

IV. Fashion
Folkways
Holidays
Social Issues and Crime
Sports

The first significant sign that women were becoming an organized force in American society was seen in 1848. A group of women called a convention to be held in Seneca Falls, N.Y., on July 19. There they formulated a "Declaration of Sentiments," which cleverly paraphrased the Declaration of Independence, addressing "man" rather than King George III of England. The document called for women's "immediate admission to all the rights and privileges which belong to them as citizens of the United States." The organizers of the convention were Lucretia Mott and Elizabeth Cady Stanton; they led the movement for many years. Mrs. Mott was one of the earliest women lecturers for temperance, the rights of labor, and abolition. Mrs. Stanton was particularly interested in securing the right to vote. When she married Henry B. Stanton in 1840, she refused to have the word "obey" used in the ceremony.

New York State granted **property rights for women** equal to those of men. This was a significant improvement in women's legal status, but New York's example was not copied elsewhere. Similar women's property rights laws had been passed in Mississippi (1839) and Maine (1844).

John B. Curtis of Bangor, Maine, manufactured the first chewing gum commercially sold in the U.S. Curtis later traveled as a drummer throughout western territories and is reputed to be the first commercial traveler for an eastern firm in the West.

Jan 24: Discovery of gold on the estate of John Sutter made California and broke Sutter. From the day he settled in Nueva Helvetia, at the junction of the American and Sacramento rivers, Sutter prospered. Then gold was found by James W. Marshall, who was building a sawmill for Sutter. The workers on the estate left to look for gold. Every kind of adventurer squatted on Sutter's land. In four years he was ruined. For the rest of his life, Sutter petitioned the state and the federal government for aid. He died on June 18, 1880, at age 77, while the bill he sought was being argued in the House of Representatives. The boom provided a wealth of material for writers. Mark Twain, Joaquin Miller, Bret Harte, Ambrose Bierce, George Horatio Derby, Charles Warren Stoddard, and Edward Rowland Sill were all in the ranks of those who found inspiration in the volatile new atmosphere. There were few voices in the whole country to caution against the excesses of the gold rush. However, the Mormon Church in Salt Lake City, having heard reports of gold in California, cautioned its children to hoard up other riches: "The true use of gold is for paving streets. . . . When the Saints shall have preached the gospel . . . and built up cities enough, the Lord will open up the way for a supply of gold to the perfect satisfaction of his children. . . . Let them not be over-anxious, for the treasures of the earth are in the Lord's storehouses."

1849

I. Civil Rights
Exploration and Settlement
Government
Statistics
Wars

News of the discovery of gold in California in Jan. 1848 was slow in reaching the East. Word of it first appeared in the New York *Herald* on Aug. 19, but no

great excitement was created until Pres. James K.
Polk expressed enthusiasm about it in his message to
Congress on Dec. 5. The rush began by land across
the continent and by sea and land via the Isthmus of
Panama. The first shipload of prospectors arrived in
San Francisco via Cape Horn on Feb. 28. About
80,000 people made their way to California in 1849—
55,000 overland and 25,000 by sea. About 5000 who
started out overland never made it because Asiatic
cholera swept their ranks. By the end of 1849, gold
worth $10,000,000 had been mined.

Mar 3: The **U.S. Department of the Interior** was created by Congress as an administrative catchall for the
General Land Office, the Bureau of Indian Affairs, the
Pension Office, the Patent Office, and the Bureau of
the Census. Its prime purpose for many decades
seemed to be to locate resources in the West for exploitation by white settlers. Not until the end of the
century would the department regard the protection of natural resources as a part of its responsibility.

Mar 3: Minnesota Territory was established by Congress. Slavery within the territory was prohibited.

Sep 1: A **California convention** called by the territorial
governor, Gen. Bennett Riley, met in Monterey. The
convention created a state government without waiting for congressional action. On Oct. 20 the delegates
adopted a constitution. On Nov. 13 the constitution
was ratified by California voters, and a governor and
legislative representatives were chosen. Slavery was
prohibited.

II. Architecture
Arts and Music
Popular Entertainment
Publishing
Theater

Civil disobedience, which had been practiced by
many patriots before the Revolution and was to be
used as a means of protest again late in the twentieth

century, in 1849 found its most eloquent spokesman in Henry David Thoreau. A transcendentalist and observer of nature and of man, he opposed the Mexican War. In protest, Thoreau refused to pay his poll tax. He was jailed just overnight because, to his distress, a friend paid the tax for him. As a result of the experience, Thoreau wrote the essay "Civil Disobedience," in which he stated: "There will never be a really free and enlightened State until the State comes to recognize the individual as a higher and independent power, from which all its own power and authority are derived. . . ."

May 10: The **Astor Place riot,** a notorious theater riot, erupted outside the Astor Place Opera House in New York City, where the celebrated British actor William Charles Macready was performing. Angry crowds reacted against dress requirements for admission to the theater and against Macready's scornful public utterances on the vulgarity of American life. Macready's rival, the American actor Edwin Forrest, who had asserted the cause of the masses both in his stage roles and in his public statements, fueled the indignation of common citizens. On May 8 Macready's performance of *Macbeth* was stopped by Forrest's followers. Two days later, a mob led by E. Z. C. Judson, later to gain fame as Ned Buntline, used clubs, paving stones, and brickbats to shatter the windows of the theater during Macready's performance. Troops were summoned and when order could not be restored by their presence, they were ordered to fire, killing 22 and wounding 56.

III. Business and Industry
Education
Philosophy and Religion
Science

Spiritualism began to attract believers, who held that the human personality continues to exist after death and can communicate through a medium with the living. In 1848 two adolescent sisters of Wayne

County, N.Y., claimed they heard rappings on floors and walls and that these spelled out messages from the spirit world. Margaret Fox was the central figure in this new cult, along with her sister Katherine. Margaret later admitted it was all a fraud and that the sounds were made by cracking toe knuckles. Nevertheless, there were many believers. In the next decade séances became common and there were at least six spiritualist publications.

Elizabeth Blackwell became the first woman in the U.S. to receive a medical degree and the first female doctor of medicine of modern times. After some hospital experience in Paris and London, she and her sister in 1853 founded the New York Infirmary and College for Women, the first hospital run entirely by women.

IV. Fashion
Folkways
Holidays
Social Issues and Crime
Sports

Prize fighting was illegal but popular. Condemned for its brutality by many, the sport had many ardent followers. When Tom Hyer, the unofficial American champion, fought Yankee Sullivan this year, the participants and spectators were chased by militia and had to flee Peel Island, Md., the site of the match, to woods on the Western Shore. A few years later, when John C. Morrissey claimed the title vacated by Hyer, the site again had to be changed at the last minute. Bare fist boxing was brutal and there were few rules. In one bout that lasted three hours, one fighter, after being knocked down 81 times, dropped dead. A history of boxing in America was published this year. It was *The American Fistiana;* the book recorded the most important bouts of the previous four decades.

Jan: Amelia Bloomer, the temperance and woman's suffrage advocate, began publication of *Lily*. The first issue printed 200 copies, but by 1853 Bloomer was issuing 4000 copies twice monthly. The articles dealt with contemporary education, marriage laws, woman's suffrage, etc. Bloomer began to have a major influence on American society.

1850

I. Civil Rights
Exploration and Settlement
Government
Statistics
Wars

The territory acquired from Mexico in the Mexican War, particularly California, caused the reopening of the question of free or slave status for new states. After acrimonious debate, Congress passed five bills on the subject between Sept. 9 and Sept. 20. As signed by Pres. Millard Fillmore, they constituted what became known as the Compromise of 1850 and once more postponed a showdown on slavery. The compromise was the result of eight resolutions that had been introduced in the Senate on Jan. 29 by Henry Clay of Kentucky. The five final bills dealt with all the pressing questions, and for the most part reaction was favorable, but extremists in the North and South were displeased.

The seventh U.S. **Census** fixed the population of the 31 states of the Union at 23,191,876. The center of population was located 23 miles southeast of Parkersburg, W. Va.

The **number of immigrants** entering America in 1850 totaled 369,980. The figures reflected the Irish famine of the late 1840s, and social and political unrest in northwest Europe.

1850-1851: In **congressional elections** the Whigs lost one Senate seat, resulting in a Democratic majority of 35–24 with three seats going to minor parties. In the House the Democrats gained 28 seats for a 140–88 majority with five seats going to minor parties.

Mar 7: Daniel Webster supported Sen. Henry Clay's compromise in a famous speech to the Senate in which he espoused the provisions of the Fugitive Slave Bill. John Greenleaf Whittier had Webster in mind when he wrote in his poem "Ichabod":

> All else is gone; from those great eyes
> The soul has fled;
> When faith is lost, when honor dies
> The man is dead.

Apr 19: The **Clayton-Bulwer Treaty** was signed. The U.S. and Great Britain agreed to the neutrality of a canal to be built across Central America. Both governments were to act as joint protectors of the territory, and neither was to establish any military post on, or assume control over, any part of Central America.

May 25: New Mexico, impatient for statehood, formed its own state government. A convention set the boundaries of the state, banned slavery, and applied for statehood.

July 8: The **overland gold rush** to California through Fort Laramie, Wyo., involved 42,300 emigrants and 9720 wagons between Jan. 1 and July 8. Over 90% of the population of California was male. Nine years later men still outnumbered women six to one.

July 9: Pres. **Zachary Taylor died** of cholera at the age of 55. Vice Pres. Millard Fillmore was sworn in as the 13th president of the United States on July 10.

Sep 9: California was admitted to the Union as a free state, giving free states a majority in the Senate. This was one of the bargains of the Compromise of 1850 and a concession to the North. California was the 31st state admitted to the Union.

Sep 9: The **Texas and New Mexico Act** was passed by

Congress. The act established the Texas boundaries, authorized payment to Texas of $10,000,000 for relinquishing its claims to territories beyond the new state lines, and established the boundaries of New Mexico Territory. As a concession to the South, New Mexico would be a free or a slave state according to its constitution upon admission to the Union. This option was part of the Compromise of 1850.

Sep 9: The **Utah Act** established the territorial boundaries of Utah. It was to be a free or slave state according to the constitution it adopted on admission to the Union. Part of the Compromise of 1850, this option was a concession to the South.

Sep 18: The **Fugitive Slave Bill** was passed by Congress. Known as the second Fugitive Slave Law (a first, enacted on Feb. 1, 1793, was largely circumvented in the North), this legislation required return of escaped slaves to their owners. Fugitives were not permitted a jury trial and could not testify in their own behalf. The commissioners earned $10 if their decision favored the claimant but only $5 if it favored the fugitive. This law was part of the Compromise of 1850 and a concession to the South.

Sep 20: **Slave trade** was abolished in the District of Columbia. This was a concession to the North in the Compromise of 1850.

Oct 23-24: The **first national women's rights convention,** held in Worcester, Mass., was attended by delegates from nine states. The first women's convention in history had been held in Seneca Falls, N.Y., in 1848.

II. Architecture
Arts and Music
Popular Entertainment
Publishing
Theater

The extremes to which the public would go in its adulation of popular entertainers, especially when urged on by clever promotion, was nowhere better shown than in connection with the American tour of Jenny Lind, called the "Swedish Nightingale." Miss Lind was brought to the U.S. in 1850 by master showman and promoter Phineas T. Barnum. On her arrival 30,000 people surrounded her New York City hotel, hoping to see the coloratura soprano. Tickets for her Sept. 11 debut at Castle Garden Theater were auctioned at $225. Boston topped that with a $625 bid when she sang there. Miss Lind gave 95 concerts around the country from 1850 to 1852, for which she received $17,675. Barnum made a fortune.

The Scarlet Letter, a classic American novel by Nathaniel Hawthorne, was a best seller from the beginning. Four thousand copies were sold in the first ten days; the second printing immediately sold out. Its daring subject matter accounted in part for its immediate success.

Representative Men by Ralph Waldo Emerson was published. It was a collection of lectures he had given on Plato, Swedenborg, Montaigne, Shakespeare, Napoleon, Goethe and others. Emerson set forth his view of the roles played by great men. He believed that man was not the victim of his environment but had creative powers within him to change things and live his own life.

Washington Crossing the Delaware was painted in Düsseldorf, Germany, by Emanuel Leutze, an American historical and portrait painter residing abroad. Gen. Washington stands in a theatrical, unseamanlike pose in the boat; the Delaware R. is really the Rhine R. as seen from the artist's window. But in this and other U.S. historical subjects, such as *Westward the Course of Empire,* the gigantic mural on the wall of the west staircase of the House of Representatives, Leutze communicated the fortitude and courage of American national heroes and contributed significantly, if not realistically, to people's conceptions of American history.

Sep 27: The great American actor **Edwin Booth** made

his New York City debut at age 16 as Wilford in the play *The Iron Chest* at the National Theater. His acting debut had been at the Boston Museum on Sept. 10, 1849, when he played the role of Tressel in Colley Cibber's version of *Richard III*. His first major role also came at the National Theater, when he took over the role of Richard III in 1851 after his father, Junius Brutus Booth, became ill.

III. Business and Industry
Education
Philosophy and Religion
Science

The textile industry was the first U.S. manufacturing group to develop on a sizable scale. More than two-thirds of all cotton manufacturing was carried out in New England, where by 1850 there were 564 plants, capitalized at more than $58,000,000 and employing 61,893 operators. The South, by contrast, had only 166 plants, capitalized at $7,250,000 and employing 10,043 workers. The New England textile industry employed many female workers, most of them young girls.

A **cholera epidemic** swept through the Middle West after passing through the South the previous year. From New Orleans it fanned through the U.S. and was checked in successive advances only by cold weather.

The **house sparrow,** also known as the English sparrow, was imported from England by Nicholas Pike. The first flock of eight pairs died. In 1851 a new flock of sparrows was imported and released at Brooklyn, N.Y. They flourished and soon spread across the country.

A new **speed record for sailing ships,** 13 days from Boston Light to the Equator, was set by the *Stag Hound,* a clipper designed by Donald McKay, premier U.S. shipbuilder.

July 8: The **Mormon colony** on Beaver Island in Lake Michigan near the Straits of Mackinac crowned as its king James Jesse Strang, who founded the colony in 1847. In 1856 Strang was assassinated by disaffected followers. An expedition of mainlanders then broke up the colony, and some 2500 Mormons left Michigan.

IV. Fashion
Folkways
Holidays
Social Issues and Crime
Sports

Some advocates of women's rights attracted attention by means of odd dress. Amelia Bloomer, who edited *Lily*, a women's rights and temperance magazine, began wearing in public a skirt over full trousers, much like Turkish trousers. As a result, the fashion became known as the *bloomer costume*, although it had been designed in the mid-1840s by Elizabeth Smith Miller. With the pantaloon, called *bloomers*, Mrs. Bloomer wore an ordinary vest over her blouse. Because the outfit evoked derision, she abandoned it, but not before bloomers gathered higher on the leg were found suitable for women's gymnastics.

The memorable quote **"I would rather be right than be president"** was uttered by Henry Clay in the Senate during his impassioned plea for the compromises proposed by him to settle the dispute between slave and free factions. Bitter because of his failure to achieve the presidency, he threw off his famous remark when taunted by his colleagues.

A reflection of the rise of a new class, **the homeless,** was seen in the 18,456 persons sheltered in 8141 cellars in New York City. By 1856 tenements had been built to house some of these unfortunates.

The **federal policy toward Indians** at this time was summed up in the dictum that it was "cheaper to feed the Indians for a year than fight them for a day."

July 25: Gold in Oregon was discovered on the Rogue R., providing new prospecting territory for the forty-niners of California's gold rush.

1851

I. **Civil Rights**
   Exploration and Settlement
   Government
   Statistics
   Wars

The new, harsher Fugitive Slave Law of 1850 aroused immediate anger in the North. In turn, landowners and legislators in the South became upset because northern states refused to help enforce the act. The law provided for federal commissioners who could order warrants for arrest of fugitive slaves; it also provided heavy penalties for interfering with enforcement. Anyone aiding a fugitive slave could be fined and jailed. In reaction, a number of free states enacted "personal liberty laws," intended to make it difficult for a slave owner to repossess his property. The actual number of runaway slaves was small, estimated in 1850 at about 1000 out of 3,000,000 slaves. Most of the runaways were ultimately captured.

Feb 15: Shadrach, a **fugitive slave,** was rescued from forcible return to his master by a mob in Boston. Attempts to put the Fugitive Slave Act of 1850 into effect caused much bitterness in the North and increased abolitionist sentiment. Many states (Vermont, 1850; Connecticut, 1854; Rhode Island, 1854; Massachusetts, 1855; Michigan, 1855; Maine, 1855 and 1857; Kansas, 1858; and Wisconsin, 1858) passed personal liberty laws, in large part designed to circumvent the federal fugitive slave law. These state laws aroused much controversy and contributed greatly to the split between North and South that led to the Civil War. South Carolina later cited these laws as one of the grievances justifying its secession from the Union. Other outstanding rescues or attempted rescues included that of James Hamlet in New York City (1850), Thomas Simms in Boston (1851), "Jerry" M'Henry in Syracuse, N.Y. (1851), and Anthony Burns in Boston (1854).

Dec 24: A fire at the Library of Congress in Washington, D.C., destroyed two-thirds of its collection.

II. **Architecture**
   Arts and Music
   Popular Entertainment
   Publishing
   Theater

Americans in several fields were beginning to acquire reputations in Europe. In sculpture, the first was Hiram Powers, who had gone to Italy to study classical art in 1837. There in 1843 he produced his marble *Greek Slave* which, when exhibited in London in 1851 at the Crystal Palace, became the most celebrated statue of its time. The nude, a Greek maiden in chains, symbolized Greece's subjection to Turkey. The statue's nudity shocked many, but critics, including many clergymen, ultimately recognized the sculptor's moral purpose and the symbolism of the stark nudity. Several copies of the statue were made. Powers became wealthy and famous as a result of the busts he sculpted, but his fame did not last. Marble busts went out of fashion after his death.

The New York Daily Times was begun as a Whig paper under the editorship of Henry Jarvis Raymond. Its name was changed to *The New York Times* in 1857. During the Civil War it strongly supported Lincoln and his policies, while after the war it fought the Tweed Ring and Tammany in New York City. In 1896 it was purchased by Adolph S. Ochs. In 1935 control passed to Ochs's son-in-law, Arthur Hays Sulzberger.

The House of the Seven Gables by Nathaniel Hawthorne was published. The story centered on a curse laid on a house in Salem at the time of the witch trials (1692).

Moby-Dick, Herman Melville's powerful novel of the sea, was published and little understood. Ostensibly the story of a whaling captain's obsessive search for a white whale, it deals with man's conflict with evil in the universe. Not until 70 years later was the novel widely accepted as a masterpiece.

Francis Parkman began his multivolume account of the colonial French in America and their struggles with the British. The first volume was *The Conspiracy of Pontiac,* which ultimately proved to be the last of the series chronologically. Parkman combined a historian's temperament for painstaking scholarship with a love for the wilderness and respect for the Indians.

Stephen Foster composed "Old Folks at Home." Noting the prejudice against "Ethiopian songs" and wanting to preserve his name for more genteel compositions, Foster sold the first performance rights to Edwin P. Christy, the famous minstrel, and allowed Christy's name to appear on the published music as composer.

III. Business and Industry
Education
Philosophy and Religion
Science

The Young Men's Christian Association, founded in England in 1844, came to North America in 1851 with the organization of chapters in Boston, Mass., and Montreal, Canada. Other U.S. cities soon formed similar groups. The first convention of the North American association was held in Buffalo, N.Y., in 1854. In 1858 chapters for students were formed at the universities of Michigan and Virginia. The organization emphasized the improvement of the spiritual and moral well-being of young men. It also sponsored social and athletic activities.

Aug 12: A patent for a **practical sewing machine** was

granted to Isaac Merrit Singer, who quickly organized I. M. Singer & Company. The unique feature of Singer's machine was its continuous stitching action. Elias Howe, whose machine was then the most popular, initiated a royalty suit against Singer for producing a machine similar to Howe's. Singer lost and was forced to make a settlement of $15,000; his machine in the meantime had achieved a leading position. It was improved in the next decade by additional patented devices.

IV. Fashion
Folkways
Holidays
Social Issues and Crime
Sports

The first important U.S. victory in international sports came on Aug. 22, 1851, when the 170-ton schooner-rigged yacht *America* defeated 14 British vessels in a race around the Isle of Wight for the Hundred Guinea Cup. *America* was built for $30,000 by a syndicate headed by Commodore John C. Stevens, a wealthy Hoboken, N.J., financier and yachtsman who also served as captain. The trophy won became known as the *America's Cup* and has been in competition ever since. The cup was successfully defended by U.S. boats until 1984, when Australia became the first foreign country to win the event.

"**Go West, young man, go West**" originated as the title of an editorial by John B. L. Soule, editor of the Terre Haute *Express*. Horace Greeley, editor of the New York *Tribune* who had been deeply impressed with the West on his travels, reprinted the piece with full credit to Soule. Later, in a letter to a friend, Greeley repeated the advice, adding "and grow up with the country." The quote has since been attributed to Greeley because of his prominence in national affairs.

June 3: The **first baseball uniforms** were worn by the

New York Knickerbockers. The outfits consisted of straw hats, white shirts, and blue full-length trousers.

1852

I. Civil Rights
Exploration and Settlement
Government
Statistics
Wars

Disagreement over the Compromise of 1850 was not the only matter dividing the nation. The North was becoming more industrial, but the South remained tied to its slave-operated agricultural system. There were now 16 free and 15 slave states, causing the South to be outnumbered in the Senate as well as in the House, where the North had 144 seats to 90 for slave states. With improvement of transportation, the East and West were becoming more closely integrated by mutual economic interests. The West's interests were reflected particularly in the demand for laws to make it easier to acquire public land. Thus a prosperous and growing nation approached another presidential election with some disunity.

1852-1853: In **congressional elections** the Democrats gained three Senate seats for a 38-22 majority over the Whigs, with two seats going to minor parties. In the House they gained 19 seats for a 159–71 majority, with four seats going to minor parties.

June 1-6: The **Democratic National Convention nominated Franklin Pierce** of New Hampshire for the presidency and William R. King of Alabama for the vice presidency. The convention adopted a platform that favored the Compromise of 1850 as a solution to the slavery question.

June 16-21: The **Whig National Convention** nominated Gen. Winfield Scott of New Jersey for the presidency and William A. Graham of North Carolina for the vice presidency. The candidates were committed to strict enforcement of the Compromise of 1850.

Aug 11: The **Free-Soil National Convention** nominated John P. Hale of New Hampshire for the presidency and George W. Julian of Indiana for the vice presidency.

Nov 2: Franklin Pierce was elected president of the United States. William R. King was elected vice president. The electoral vote was Pierce, 254; Winfield Scott, Whig candidate, 42. The popular vote was Pierce, 1,601,474; Scott, 1,386,578; John P. Hale, Free-Soil candidate, 156,149.

II. Architecture
Arts and Music
Popular Entertainment
Publishing
Theater

The most important book of the 1850s, not for literary quality but for impact on the growing controversy over slavery, was *Uncle Tom's Cabin, or Life Among the Lowly* by Harriet Beecher Stowe. Her book appeared in 1852 and within a year 300,000 copies had been sold. For the first time blacks were treated as individuals, not stereotypes. The South denounced the book but in the North it was taken to be a true picture of the horrors of slavery. The novel may have hastened the final break between North and South. George L. Aiken, actor and playwright, dramatized *Uncle Tom's Cabin* and performed in it. It was first performed at Troy, N.Y., on Sept. 27, 1852, where it ran for 100 nights.

Stephen Foster composed "Massa's in de Cold Ground" and in 1853 "My Old Kentucky Home." In the latter, he dropped black dialect for standard English, thus ensuring widespread popularity for the song.

III. Business and Industry
Education
Philosophy and Religion
Science

The trend toward taller and taller buildings could only continue if two conditions were satisfied. Iron and steel to support such structures had to be readily available, and a practical way to get up and down had to be devised. Elisha Graves Otis, a Vermont-born inventor, solved the latter problem in 1852 when, while supervising construction of an industrial plant in Yonkers, N.Y., he developed a device to keep hoisting machinery from falling even if the lift chain or rope broke. From this start he developed a safe passenger elevator. The first of its kind was installed in E. V. Haughwout's store at 488 Broadway, New York City, on Mar. 23, 1857.

A **school attendance law** was enacted by Massachusetts. It required all children between the ages of 8 and 14 to attend school at least 12 weeks a year, 6 of them to be consecutive.

May 9: The **first U.S. Roman Catholic Church Council** was held at the Cathedral in Baltimore, Md.

Oct: **St. Ann's Church for deaf mutes** was founded in New York City by the Rev. Thomas Gallaudet. Its first service was held in the chapel at the University of the City of New York. In 1859 the church moved to a building on West 18th St.

IV. Fashion
Folkways
Holidays
Social Issues and Crime
Sports

About this time a Norwegian musician with a love for America and independence initiated a grandiose settlement scheme in western Pennsylvania. Ole Broneman Bull of Norway was a violinist who toured Europe and the U.S. giving concerts to raise money for his project. In 1852 he bought 125,000 acres,

which he called Oleana and which was to be a colony
for his countrymen, "consecrated to freedom, baptized in independence, and protected by the mighty
flag of the Union." The plan failed and Bull lost a
great deal of money.

Godey's Lady's Book began featuring paragraphs
with the heading "Employment of Women." The
items told of the most recent entries of women into
the world of business and industry. *Godey's* itself was
staffed largely by women in both editorial and press
rooms.

The trend toward **women teachers** in public
schools was reflected in the following figures. In Boston, 6000 of 8000 teachers were women; in Brooklyn,
103 of 120 teachers were women; and in Philadelphia, 699 of 781 teachers were women.

Jan 28: The famous sentence "**Eternal vigilance is the
price of Liberty**" was uttered by abolitionist Wendell
Phillips in an address before the Massachusetts Anti-
Slavery Society. Phillips' words are thought to have
been based on the statement "The condition upon
which God hath given liberty to man is eternal vigilance . . . ," made in a speech by the Irish politician
John Philpot Curran on July 10, 1790.

Apr 6: The word *telegram* was first used in the Albany
Evening Journal. It read in part: "A friend desires us
to give notice that he will ask leave . . . to introduce
a new word. . . . It is 'telegram,' instead of 'telegraphic
dispatch' or 'telegraphic communication.' " The British refused to accept this piece of Yankee slang until
1857, when the London *Times* used the word in a
heading over an official British dispatch.

Aug 3: The **first intercollegiate rowing race** was conducted by Harvard and Yale, whose crews rowed a
two-mile course on Lake Winnepesaukee, N.H. Harvard won by four lengths.

1853

I. Civil Rights
Exploration and Settlement
Government
Statistics
Wars

The U.S. became the first western nation to establish relations with Japan since the country was closed to foreigners in 1683. On July 8, 1853, Commodore Matthew Calbraith Perry sailed into Yedo (now Tokyo) Bay with a squadron of four vessels. For a time Japanese officials would have nothing to do with Perry, but on July 14 he was able to deliver the documents he carried from Pres. Millard Fillmore to two royal princes at the village of Kurihama. Perry then sailed away to give the Japanese time to consider the idea of external relations. He returned to Yedo the following March and on Mar. 31, 1854, signed a treaty that opened Japan to trade with the West.

Yellow fever took the lives of over 5000 persons in New Orleans, La., from 1853 to 1855. A few cases were reported in the spring, but epidemic proportions were not reached until mid-summer. Two hundred deaths were recorded in the week ending July 16. Vicksburg, Miss., lost one-sixth of its population in the epidemic.

The **Native American, or Know-Nothing, Party** was formed. Its adherents viewed with alarm the steadily growing number of immigrants. The party hoped to exclude anyone not native-born from holding federal, state, or municipal office, and urged the repeal of naturalization laws. "Know Nothing" became the party's unofficial name because its followers' typical reponse to questions regarding policy

was, "I don't know." The reply was not from igno-
rance but secrecy.

Mar 2: The **Territory of Washington** was formed after
separation from the Oregon Territory.

Dec 30: The **Gadsden Purchase,** negotiated by James
Gadsden, U.S. minister to Mexico, was signed. By its
terms the U.S. acquired 29,644 sq. mi. of territory,
comprising the southernmost portions of present-day
Arizona and New Mexico, for $15,000,000 (later re-
duced to $10,000,000). The purchase established the
final boundaries of the contiguous United States. The
treaty, amended with consent of the Mexican government, was ratified on June 30, 1854. The territory had
been sought for a route for the Southern Pacific Railroad.

II. Architecture
    Arts and Music
    Popular Entertainment
    Publishing
    Theater

The distinctive culture and humor of the old Southwest, along the Gulf of Mexico, were colorfully recorded by Joseph Glover Baldwin in *The Flush Times
of Alabama and Mississippi,* which was published this
year. The 26 sketches included a mixture of comic
anecdotes and biographies of notable lawyers and
judges of the 1830s and 1840s. The book was both
realistic and satirical and typified the humorous ex-
aggeration of the time as practiced by the region's
best orators, gamblers, and tellers of tall tales.

The **Crystal Palace** was built in New York City to
house the 1853 exhibition. Constructed of cast iron
and glass, it had the largest dome yet erected in the
U.S. It was hailed for integrating engineering and
decoration in a new national architectural style.

Feb: The women's suffrage magazine *Una,* published
by Paulina Wright Davis and edited by Caroline H.
Dall, issued its first number in Washington, D.C.

III. Business and Industry
Education
Philosophy and Religion
Science

The iron rails of the railroads were weaving a network of lines around the nation at an ever greater rate. In 1850 there were about 9000 miles of track, by 1860 more than 30,000. The Pennsylvania Railroad connected Philadelphia and Pittsburgh in 1852. The New York Central came into being in 1853, combining seven short lines between Albany and Buffalo, N.Y., into one. On Jan. 12, 1853, the Baltimore & Ohio Railroad began rail service to Wheeling, W. Va., from Baltimore. Rail service between New York and Chicago was available, although not in one continuous line. In 1856 the Illinois Central became the longest railroad in the world, with 700 miles of main line track. The Illinois Central was also the first railroad to which the federal government granted large tracts of public land as a subsidy; it was given 3,736,000 acres.

The **first terra cotta** in the U.S. was produced by James Renwick, professor of natural philosophy and experimental chemistry at Columbia University in New York City. Renwick, the father of the architect of the same name, proposed its use as paving material.

May: Gail Borden applied for a patent on his process for making evaporated milk in a vacuum. The Patent Office doubted its patentability until Borden reargued his application, after which the patent was issued, on Aug. 19, 1856. Production began in 1858. Originally conceived as a boon for immigrant and tenement-dwelling children who needed a source of safe, nutritious milk, evaporated milk skyrocketed in sales during the Civil War because of Army purchases.

IV. Fashion
   Folkways
   Holidays
   Social Issues and Crime
   Sports

Popular entertainment was taking new forms, and larger theaters were built to serve growing audiences. The Hippodrome, in New York City, which opened in 1853, could seat 4600 people. It offered chariot races as well as acrobats and clowns. Other entertainment included Swiss bell ringers and a steam calliope drawn by 40 horses.

The **Crystal Palace Exhibition of the Industry of All Nations** was held in New York City to demonstrate American inventions and industrial progress. Called a world's fair, it was inspired by the London Exhibition of 1851. The building that housed the exhibition was impressive enough to be referred to as Aladdin's palace.

Waitresses, now beginning to appear, were commented on by Amelia Bloomer, American feminist: "Stopping over night at the Delavan House in Albany, we were very agreeably surprised on entering the dining-room for supper to see about a dozen young women in attendance on the tables. This was something new. When we visited the house last winter the waiters were all men, as is usual in such places. Now not a man was to be seen in that capacity; but in place of their heavy tread, and awkward motions, was woman's light footfall and easy, graceful movements. In a conversation with the proprietor we learned that the change was made in May . . . entirely satisfactory . . . the only objectors being a few women . . . preferring black men."

The celebrated New York-Brooklyn **baseball rivalry** began when an all-New York team defeated an all-Brooklyn team in a best-of-three series, two games to one.

Oct 12: The **heavyweight boxing championship** was decided on a technicality. John C. Morrissey, claiming the title vacated by Tom Hyer, was losing to challenger Yankee Sullivan. But between rounds Sullivan left the ring to slug a few Morrissey supporters who had heckled him. He failed to get back into the ring to answer the bell for the next round, and the referee awarded the decision to Morrissey.

1854

I. **Civil Rights**
   Exploration and Settlement
   Government
   Statistics
   Wars

The signing of the Kansas-Nebraska Act on May 30 by Pres. Franklin Pierce brought civil war a step nearer. The bill, sponsored by Sen. Stephen A. Douglas, Democrat of Illinois, created two new territories and provided what Douglas called "popular sovereignty," also called "squatter sovereignty." This meant that those who settled in each territory would have the right to decide whether the territory, when admitted as a state, would be free or slave. In the North some people were infuriated because the law had the effect of repealing the Missouri Compromise of 1820, which said that there would never be slavery north of the southern boundary of Missouri, except for Missouri itself. Douglas was harmed politically by his sponsorship of the bill.

1854-1855: In **congressional elections** the fledgling Republican party gained 15 Senate seats but trailed the Democrats 40–15, with five seats held by minor parties. In the House the Republicans took a 108–83 majority, with 43 seats held by minor parties.

June 2: Fugitive slave Anthony Burns was the central figure in the most dramatic event of the year. Burns escaped by boat from Richmond, Va. On May 24 he had been arrested by federal officials in Boston on a trumped-up charge of theft. Abolition and women's suffrage groups were holding conventions in the city. When on June 2 Burns was taken from a jail to Long Wharf to begin his return trip to Richmond, the streets had to be guarded by thousands of troops and policemen. Buildings were draped in black, and church bells tolled. In a few months Burns was sold to a friendly master who in turn sold him to people in Boston interested in setting him free. It cost the U.S. government at least $100,000 to return this one fugitive slave to the South.

June 5: The **Canadian Reciprocity Treaty** opened the U.S. market to Canadian agricultural products, timber, and fish. In return American fishermen received new rights in Canadian waters and freedom of operation on the Great Lakes and the St. Lawrence R.

July 6: The **Republican Party was formed** in Jackson, Mich., and nominated the first Republican state ticket for the November elections. A preliminary meeting had been held at Ripon, Wis., on Feb. 28 by 50 disaffected Whigs, Free-Soilers, and northern Democrats, and the name "Republican" proposed. The Jackson meeting also attracted individuals from other splinter groups. The common bond was antislavery, more specifically anger over the Kansas-Nebraska Act.

II. Architecture
Arts and Music
Popular Entertainment
Publishing
Theater

Opera was thriving, as witnessed by a new and opulent opera house, the Academy of Music, which opened this year on 14th St. at Irving Place in New York City. It replaced the Astor Place Opera House, built in 1847. The new structure, which cost $335,000, opened on Oct. 2 with a performance of Vincenzo Bellini's *Norma*. The cast included two well-known artists of the day, Giulia Grisi and Giuseppe Mario, and was conducted by Luigi Arditi.

Walden, an American classic and the most famous work of Henry David Thoreau, was published. It was a series of 18 essays based on the two years Thoreau spent close to nature. The book stresses simplicity and holds that happiness is not to be had by pursuit of wealth. Descriptions of plants, birds, and animals are interspersed with reflections on life.

Novelist **Mary Jane Holmes** began her highly successful publishing career with *Tempest and Sunshine; or, Life in Kentucky.* By 1905 Mrs. Holmes had written 39 novels, many appearing originally in paperback, and had sold over 2,000,000 copies. In the decade or two after the Civil War, she was probably the most popular U.S. novelist. Her hallmark was highly sensitive heroines and noble heroes going through a series of stereotyped situations supported by a simplistic moral code.

The melodramatic ***Ten Nights in a Barroom and What I Saw There*** by Timothy S. Arthur was published. *Ten Nights* was second in sales to Harriet Beecher Stowe's *Uncle Tom's Cabin.* This favorite of the temperance forces was dramatized successfully by W. W. Pratt in 1858.

The **first fireproof building** in the U.S. was constructed for Harper & Brothers for its publishing headquarters in New York City. It was built with wrought-iron beams set in masonry walls.

III. Business and Industry
   Education
   Philosophy and Religion
   Science

The era of public libraries was beginning, and this year it received an important impetus with the opening of the Astor Library in New York City. The library was made possible by a bequest of $400,000 from John Jacob Astor, the wealthiest man in the U.S. at his death in 1848. The library was chartered in 1849 and opened its own building on Lafayette Place as a reference library in 1854. Astor had little formal education but maintained a lifelong interest in literature and science. Fitz-Greene Halleck and Washington Irving, two of America's leading authors, are said to have been instrumental in persuading Astor to make the bequest.

The **Boston Public Library** was opened to the public. The library had been founded two years earlier. The library is credited with having inaugurated the practice of having popular books kept in large enough supply to fill the demands of many readers while keeping a regular complement of books of more limited circulation. This policy permitted development of the libraries of manuscripts and rare books for which Boston Public Library is famous. The original building was replaced in 1895 with a new structure designed by Charles McKim. It is a masterpiece of the new Italian Renaissance style.

May 6: Transatlantic cable communication became possible when a company headed by Cyrus W. Field was granted a charter and a 50-year monopoly. Not until 1866 was a permanently successful cable laid.

IV. Fashion
   Folkways
   Holidays
   Social Issues and Crime
   Sports

Paris set the style in women's dress and the Empress Eugenie of France set the Paris style. This was the dawn of the era of the hoop skirt, which ballooned out from a woman's waist. Around 1870 the bustle, a horsehair pad or wire cage worn in back under a woman's skirt, became the fashion. With it went very long, elaborate dresses with puffed upper sleeves. For men, the long cutaway coat of the 1850s went out of fashion, but black suits and white shirts were still in style.

The trotting horse **Flora Temple** broke all records by running the mile at Kalamazoo, Mich., in 2:19½—the first time a horse had run a mile faster than 2:20. The news, flashed immediately throughout the nation by telegraph, made Flora Temple a national celebrity.

Growing interest in **baseball** in New York City was evidenced by the establishment of many clubs, including: the Eagle and the Empire of New York City and the Excelsior of Brooklyn. By 1855 Morrisania had the Union Club and Brooklyn had added the Atlantic and the Eckford.

Oct 31: In an article on **women postal workers** the *Nebraska Palladium* reported that "the number of females at present holding the office of Post Master is 128." An interesting aspect of this story was the report that women postmasters received the same pay as men. No other occupation could make that claim.

1855

I. **Civil Rights**
   Exploration and Settlement
   Government
   Statistics
   Wars

This period showed a great increase in immigration to America from Europe, both for economic and political reasons. The growth was reflected in the fact that this year the New York State Immigration Commission leased Castle Garden, at the tip of Manhattan Island, as a reception center. During the 1850s a total of 2,314,000 people arrived in the U.S. Almost all came from Germany, Ireland, England, Scotland, and Wales. Immigrants for the most part settled in the northeastern part of the country. The Irish tended to remain in the large cities, but many Germans moved west to farmland.

Feb 10: U.S. **citizenship laws** were amended to provide that all children born abroad of U.S. parents be granted U.S. citizenship.

Mar 30: Kansas's first territorial election chose legislators amid armed violence. Some 5000 so-called Border Ruffians invaded territory from western Missouri and forced the election of a proslavery legislature. The number of votes cast far exceeded the number of eligible voters. To prevent widespread bloodshed, Andrew H. Reeder, appointed territorial governor by Pres. Pierce, reluctantly allowed the fraudulent election to stand.

June 5: The **American Party** was chosen as the new name for the Native American Party, commonly called the Know-Nothing Party, during its national meeting at Philadelphia. Control had been won by southern and proslavery forces, resulting in the disaffection of northern members, most of whom turned to the Republicans. The party virtually ceased to exist after the 1856 presidential election.

Sep 5: Antislavery settlers in Kansas, at a convention held in Big Springs, repudiated the fraudulently elected territorial legislature. Arms were sent to the settlers from northern states and an army was formed, called the Free State forces. The abolitionist firebrand, John Brown, arrived in Kansas and became a leader of these forces.

Oct 23: The **Topeka Constitution** drawn up by Kansas Free State forces set up a governor and a legislature. Kansas now had two governments. The Topeka Constitution outlawed slavery.

II. Architecture
Arts and Music
Popular Entertainment
Publishing
Theater

American composers were still few in number. Two who became pioneer composers of opera in the U.S.

were William H. Fry and George F. Bristow. Fry wrote the first American opera, *Leonora*, in 1845, but it was not successful. Bristow's *Rip Van Winkle*, the second American opera, opened at Niblo's Garden in New York City on Sept. 27, 1855, and ran for four weeks. Richard Storrs, contemporary critic, announced, "A new American opera has succeeded in New York!" Fry and Bristow tried to encourage compositions by American composers.

Leaves of Grass by Walt Whitman, one of the most famous books of poetry of all time, was published at the author's expense. The first edition, containing only 12 poems, fared badly in the marketplace, but it did receive helpful praise from Ralph Waldo Emerson, ending with "I greet you at the beginning of a great career." A second edition, with 33 poems added, appeared in 1856; in 1860 a third, greatly enlarged and rearranged edition appeared. After the Civil War, revised and enlarged editions were published periodically; the final, ninth edition, under the author's direction, is dated 1892. In the 1940s a book club distributed 250,000 copies to its members. *Leaves of Grass* today is in many reprint series.

The Song of Hiawatha by Henry Wadsworth Longfellow was published. The poem was a broad collection of Indian legends tied together by a fictional character. Its publication marked the peak of Longfellow's fame. Using the meter of the Finnish epic *Kalevala*, Longfellow obtained musical effects by his repeated use of euphonious names for Indian persons and places. The poem epitomized the glorification of the American literary concept of the noble savage.

III. Business and Industry
Education
Philosophy and Religion
Science

Bridge building continued, and structures were getting longer and stronger. The most expert designer and builder of bridges was John Augustus Roebling.

Roebling came to the U.S. from his native Germany in 1831 and became a citizen in 1837. He was a pioneer in suspension bridge construction, completing the Allegheny Suspension Bridge at Pittsburgh in 1845 and the Niagara Suspension Bridge in 1855. In the latter bridge Roebling made the first full-scale use of a wire cable of his own design; the cable was made up of parallel wires that were wire-bound. Previous cables had consisted of twisted wire. Roebling first developed this wire cable, or wire rope, in 1841.

The **first lighthouse** on the Pacific coast was built on Point Loma, San Diego, Calif.

The **Panama Railroad,** owned and built by a U.S. company, was completed across the Isthmus of Panama.

IV. Fashion
Folkways
Holidays
Social Issues and Crime
Sports

Few blacks achieved any prominence or became well-known to the general public in the age of slavery. An exception was Frederick Douglass. Born a slave in Maryland, he escaped and made his way to Massachusetts in 1838. A speech delivered by Douglass at an antislavery meeting so impressed his hearers that the American Anti-Slavery Society engaged him as one of its lecturers. In 1847 Douglass founded an abolitionist newspaper, the *North Star.* During the Civil War he persuaded Pres. Abraham Lincoln to use blacks as soldiers. In 1889 he became U.S. ambassador to Haiti.

Mrs. **Sarah Josepha Hale** launched a campaign in the columns of *Godey's* against the use of the word "female" in reference to women in public life. Elimination of the term became one of the objectives of feminism in America.

The phrase *cotton is king* came into prominence. It was taken from the title of a book, *Cotton is King,*

or the Economical Relations of Slavery, by David
Christy, which was published this year. At this time
export of cotton amounted to one-half of all U.S. exports. Its value was more than $100,000,000 annu-
ally.

The practice of **selective law enforcement** was exemplified this year in instructions issued to New
York City police by Mayor Fernando Wood concerning prohibition. A statewide prohibition law had
gone into effect on July 4. Mayor Wood's instructions
read in part: "Whether liquors exhibited in your presence . . . are intoxicating liquors . . . you must judge
with great circumspection, and be careful to avoid
seizing any thus exempt. An error in this regard may
lay you liable to severe personal responsibility. . . .
Keeping liquor with intent to sell or give away, is not
an offense fully within the scope of the eye. . . . You
can not see the violation . . . for an intent can not be
seen. . . . These violations . . . do not . . . compel you
to arrest or seize without complaints." This situation
of selective law enforcement was disposed of by the
judiciary when it declared the New York State statute
unconstitutional in Mar. 1856. Twelve states and two
territories had prohibition by the end of 1855, but
drinking was an established American habit. Even
the cop on the beat liked his beer.

1856

I. **Civil Rights**
   Exploration and Settlement
   Government
   Statistics
   Wars

The presidential election campaign of 1856 saw two
new parties fielding candidates for the presidency.

One was the American Party, the Know-Nothings, which had reached its peak in 1854 and was disintegrating over the slavery issue. The other was the Republican Party, whose strength lay in the North and West and among antislavery forces. The main issue of the campaign was the fight between slavery and antislavery forces for control of Kansas Territory. Although the Democrats won the presidency, the combined popular vote for the American, Republican, and Whig candidates was more than that for the Democratic winner, James Buchanan.

1856-1857: In **congressional elections** the Democrats lost four Senate seats but kept a majority, 36–20, over the Republicans, with eight seats going to minor parties. In the House the Democrats took a 118–92 majority, with 26 seats going to minor parties.

Feb 22: The **Republican Party** held its first national meeting at Pittsburgh, Pa. Delegates met to plan a national presidential nominating convention to be held in June.

Feb 22: The **national convention of the American, or Know-Nothing, Party** met at Philadelphia and nominated former Pres. Millard Fillmore for president and Andrew J. Donelson of Tennessee for vice presi-

June 2: An **antislavery section of the Know-Nothing Party** met in New York City and nominated John C. Frémont of California for president and W. F. Johnston of Pennsylvania for vice president.

June 2-5: The **Democratic National Convention nominated James Buchanan** of Pennsylvania for president and John C. Breckinridge of Kentucky for vice president.

June 17-19: The **Republican National Convention nominated John C. Frémont** of California for president and William L. Dayton of New Jersey for vice president.

Aug 1: Bleeding Kansas, as the territory was known at this time, was without any settled government. Raids between the two factions continued, with an estimated 200 killed and $2,000,000 in property lost between Nov. 1855 and Dec. 1856. The House refused to seat either proslavery or Free State territorial delegates from Kansas.

Sep 17: The **Whig National Convention nominated** Millard Fillmore for the presidency and Andrew J. Donelson for the vice presidency. Fillmore and Donelson were also the candidates of the Know-Nothing Party.

Nov 4: James Buchanan was elected president of the United States. John C. Breckinridge was elected vice president. The electoral vote was Buchanan, 174; John C. Frémont, Republican, 114. The popular vote was Buchanan, 1,838,169; Frémont, 1,335,264; Millard Fillmore, Whig and American (Know-Nothing) Party candidate, 874,534. The election marked the end of the Whig Party as a national force.

II. Architecture
Arts and Music
Popular Entertainment
Publishing
Theater

Until this time American historians had mostly confined their writings to American and related British subjects. John Lothrop Motley went further afield and devoted his life's work to a study of the Netherlands. *The Rise of the Dutch Republic* appeared in 1856 in three volumes; it was followed by six more volumes in later years. Motley, writing with great enthusiasm for his subject, attempted to show how Protestantism in northern Europe had brought freedom there. Warmly partisan toward William of Orange, he created a dramatic narrative of the Dutch struggle against Spanish oppression. He drew analogies with the struggles of the U.S. and George Washington. The work sold over 30,000 copies in England and the U.S. in its first year.

"The Barefoot Boy" by John Greenleaf Whittier, one of America's most endearing poems, was included in his *The Panorama and Other Poems*, published this year. Turning here from his concerns about slavery, Whittier called up memories of his own boyhood and created a small masterpiece of local color.

Mar 1: George F. Bristow's *Second Symphony in D Minor* was performed by the New York Philharmonic Society. This was one of the few orchestral works by a native-born composer that it presented during the mid-nineteenth century.

Aug 18: A **copyright law** was passed by Congress, giving the author of a play "along with the sole right to print and publish the said composition, the sole right also to act, perform, or represent the same."

III. Business and Industry
Education
Philosophy and Religion
Science

Along with the growing railroad system, the telegraph was vital to the transportation and communication network that was uniting the nation from coast to coast. Ezra Cornell, a financier who had supported the experiments of Samuel F. B. Morse that led to the invention of the telegraph, set out in 1855 to organize a national telegraph system. Given the name Western Union Telegraph Company on Apr. 1, 1856, Cornell's company by 1866 became a national system controlling some 75,000 miles of telegraph lines. The telegraph was essential to the railroads because it was the only way a message could be sent ahead of trains to give operational orders.

The **first kindergarten** in the U.S. was opened in Watertown, Wis., under the guidance of Mrs. Carl Schurz, wife of the prominent German refugee and leading Republican figure in the Lincoln-Hayes administration. It was a German-language school. Mrs. Schurz was an ardent disciple of Friedrich Froebel, the progressive educator in Thuringia whose theories, including those on the kindergarten, had great influence on American education.

A patent for a **milk-condensing process** was

awarded to Gail Borden. Manufacture began in 1858. In 1851 Borden had won the Great Council Medal at the London Exposition for his development of a one-pound meat biscuit containing the nutritional qualities of five pounds of meat and ten ounces of flour. Borden was the first American food producer to win such an honor.

IV. Fashion
   Folkways
   Holidays
   Social Issues and Crime
   Sports

Gambling continued to be a favorite pastime of Americans. It was estimated that in the 1850s there were 2000 professional gamblers working the riverboats. Faro, monte, and chuck-a-luck were the favorite games. There was also three-card monte to help innocents lose their money even faster. The gamblers were easily recognized by their elegant, if gaudy, clothing, which featured a broadcloth coat and a ruffled white shirt.

By 1856 **baseball** was already considered a national pastime, as evidenced by the following passage from the sporting paper *Spirit of the Times:* "With the fall of the leaf and the diminution of the daylight, many of the out-of-door sports and pastimes come to a close for the season. The manly and exhilarating pastimes of Base Ball, Cricket, Foot Ball, and Racket are not playable. . . . We feel a degree of old Knickerbocker pride at the continued prevalence of Base Ball as the National game in the region of the Manhattanese."

1857

I. Civil Rights
Exploration and Settlement
Government
Statistics
Wars

A Supreme Court decision handed down on Mar. 6 in the case of *Dred Scott v. Sandford* was a setback for antislavery forces and further aggravated the growing ill feeling between North and South. Dred Scott was a slave whose owner had taken him from Missouri to Illinois, a free state, in 1834. Scott later returned to Missouri and in 1846 sued for his liberty on the grounds that his stay in free territory ended his slavery. The Court ruled, however, that Scott could not sue because slaves were not citizens. Going beyond the specific case, the Court also said that Congress had no power to prohibit slavery in territories and therefore the Missouri Compromise of 1820, already repealed by the Kansas-Nebraska Act, was un-

Jan 15: The **State Disunion Convention,** favoring peaceful separation of North and South, met at Worcester, Mass. The most fiery speech was delivered by William Lloyd Garrison, who declared, "No union with slaveholders."

May 1: A **literacy test** as a requirement for voting was adopted as an amendment to the Massachusetts state constitution.

Sep 11: The **Mountain Meadows Massacre** resulted in the death of 120 emigrants headed for California. They were killed in Utah by Indians incited by the Mormon fanatic John D. Lee. Lee's justification was that he was retaliating against Pres. Buchanan's order removing Brigham Young as governor of Utah.

Oct 5: Kansas elected a free-state legislature under Gov. Robert J. Walker. The elections were held under supervision, and thousands of fraudulent proslavery votes were rejected.

II. Architecture
   Arts and Music
   Popular Entertainment
   Publishing
   Theater

Books and articles attacking and defending slavery began to appear in increasing numbers. This year *Cannibals All! or, Slaves Without Masters* by George Fitzhugh, a lawyer and editor of the Richmond, Va., *Examiner,* challenged the idea that freedom was inherently better than slavery. Fitzhugh compared the northern wage system unfavorably with the slave system, arguing that factory workers were "slaves without masters" who had no guarantee of care in illness or old age. Another southerner, Hinton Rowan Helper of North Carolina, also published a book in 1857, *The Impending Crisis of the South,* which was at the same time antislavery and antiblack. He argued that slavery retarded the South and that white farmers who had no slaves suffered from competition with large plantations operated by slaves. Helper's book enraged the South. In 1860 the Republicans distributed 100,000 copies in a condensed version to aid Abraham Lincoln's presidential campaign.

Dec 8: *The Poor of New York* by Dion Boucicault, the Irish actor-playwright, opened in New York City during the panic of 1857, an event that was incorporated into the play. Boucicault wrote or adapted over 100 plays, among them *London Assurance,* produced in London Mar. 4, 1841, before he emigrated to the U.S.; *The Octoroon* (1859), dealing with the love of a white man for a black girl; and *Rip Van Winkle* (1865), in which the famous actor Joseph Jefferson played with so much success. Boucicault is credited with inaugurating the "road system." The revision of the copyright law that guaranteed a dramatist the sole right to "act, perform, or represent" his play was the result of his efforts.

III. Business and Industry
Education
Philosophy and Religion
Science

Awarding on June 23 of a patent for a process for the economical production of steel marked an important advance in a basic industry. The patent was awarded to William Kelly, whose process involved the oxidation of impurities in iron by blowing air through molten iron. He had first developed the process in 1851. Independently, Henry Bessemer had perfected the technique in England in 1856. Their rival claims were settled in 1866. The first Bessemer converter was built at Troy, N.Y., in 1864. Kelly's process was used in a converter at Wyandotte, Mich., the same year. Steel at once began to replace iron for railroad tracks, with 259,699 tons of steel rail produced in 1875.

Mar 3: A **U.S. subsidy of overseas cable** was voted by Congress, paying the company formed by Cyrus W. Field $70,000. The project was also supported by England and private resources on both sides of the Atlantic. The laying of cable from Ireland to Newfoundland began this year, but the cable broke some several hundred miles out from Valentia, Ireland. It was decided to use two ships, beginning from the midpoint between Newfoundland and Ireland and traveling in opposite directions. After three more failures, a copper wire 1950 miles long was laid between Trinity Bay and Valentia, the ships both arriving at their destinations on Aug. 5, 1858. Queen Victoria of England sent the first message on Aug. 16, 1858, to Pres. Buchanan. The feat was considered a glorious achievement until the cable broke two weeks later, perhaps from faulty insulation. After financial reverses and the interruption of the Civil War, Field succeeded in laying the cable in 1866, using the largest steamship of the time, *Great Eastern.*

Aug 24: A **financial panic** was precipitated by the failure of the New York City branch of the Ohio Life Insurance Company. Some 4932 businesses failed this year. By 1859 another 8000 had failed. The bankruptcies were primarily the result of overspeculation in railway securities and real estate.

IV. Fashion
   Folkways
   Holidays
   Social Issues and Crime
   Sports

One of the first large and well-planned city parks, and one that set an example, began to be laid out this year. It was Central Park in Manhattan, New York City, comprising 840 acres acquired in 1856. Frederick Law Olmsted and Calvert Vaux won a competition for designing it in 1857; Olmsted was appointed the park's chief architect in 1858. He and Vaux laid out a park that embodied the naturalistic and romantic ideas of the time. Olmsted spent most of his life designing parks and park systems in such cities as Brooklyn, Chicago, Buffalo, and Boston.

Charity balls were originated in New York City. The balls enabled society to dispense with its charitable obligations while displaying its wealth. The first annual charity ball was given at the Academy of Music.

The **New Orleans Mardi Gras** for the first time offered a pageant of decorative floats organized and paid for by societies called Krewes. The first society, Comus, began functioning this year as a patron and promoter of the festivities.

The **America's Cup,** won in England by the U.S. schooner-yacht *America,* was presented to the New

York Yacht Club by members who owned *America:* J.C. Stevens, Edwin A. Stevens, Hamilton Wilkes, J. Beekman Finley, and George L. Schuyler. The gift stipulated that the cup be used perpetually as a trophy in international challenge yacht races.

Oct 6: The **American Chess Association** was organized at the first American Chess Congress, held in New York City. There Paul C. Morphy, a 20-year-old chess wizard from New Orleans, La., won the American championship. Morphy toured Europe in 1858 and 1859, defeating all the masters who would meet him. Although he played only sporadically thereafter, he was recognized as the first American international chess master.

1858

I. Civil Rights
Exploration and Settlement
Government
Statistics
Wars

A landmark series of political debates took place this year between Aug. 21 and Oct. 15, when Sen. Stephen A. Douglas of Illinois and Abraham Lincoln, little known Republican of Illinois, held a series of seven debates in towns across Illinois, competing for a seat in the Senate. Their points of view showed clearly the growing gap between North and South. Lincoln opposed slavery. The nation, he said, would have to decide on the issue—either the whole country should accept slavery or eliminate it. Douglas did not defend slavery, but he did uphold the right of the people in a given territory to decide the issue for themselves. The Democratic majority in the Illinois legislature elected Douglas to the Senate seat, but Lincoln's efforts brought him into the national spotlight.

1858-1859: In **congressional elections** the Republican Party made a strong showing. In the Senate the Democrats took a majority of 38–26 over the Republicans, with two seats held by minor parties. In the House the Republicans took a 113–101 majority over the Democrats, with 23 seats going to minor parties. Abraham Lincoln, Republican candidate for senator from Illinois, was defeated by his Democratic rival Stephen A. Douglas.

Mar 23: The Senate voted to accept Kansas into the Union under the **Lecompton Constitution** after the constitution had been rejected by Kansas. The House, however, voted to resubmit the constitution to a popular vote.

May 11: Minnesota was admitted as a state, the 32nd to join the Union.

Aug 2: The **Lecompton Constitution** was submitted by the federal government to the people of Kansas for popular vote for the third time. It was rejected and the territory became nonslaveholding. Kansas did not enter the Union until 1861.

II. Architecture
   Arts and Music
   Popular Entertainment
   Publishing
   Theater

Changing critical standards in historiography were exemplified in the work of John Gorham Palfrey, a Unitarian clergyman of Boston and a former editor of the *North American Review*. He was the author of *History of New England,* which appeared in five volumes between 1858 and 1890. At the time the work was considered impartial and was praised for bringing colonial and English events together in its chronology. Later critics, however, considered the volumes biased in favor of New England, especially Massachusetts, and the clergy.

"The Courtship of Miles Standish" by Henry Wadsworth Longfellow, a verse account of a bit of Puritan history of the domestic kind, was published. Miles Standish, John Alden, and Priscilla became living traditions to millions through this work. In London 10,000 copies were sold on the day of its appearance. Longfellow's popularity among his contemporaries is revealed by the fact that over 300,000 of his books had been sold by 1857.

III. Business and Industry
Education
Philosophy and Religion
Science

Japan was further opened to American commerce in 1858, following Commodore Matthew C. Perry's original treaty of 1854. In 1855 the U.S. sent Townsend Harris, a New York merchant, to Japan as its first diplomatic representative. Harris came to exercise considerable influence with the Japanese government because of his sound advice. He signed agreements on June 18, 1857, and July 29, 1858, that opened more ports to U.S. commerce and gave Americans residence rights.

Philadelphia's first horsecar went into operation. As in New York City, where regular passenger runs began in 1852, the horsecar soon replaced the older omnibus. The horsecar effected a minor revolution in city planning, for the tracks it ran on were permanent and inflexible. Boston adopted a horsecar line in 1852, Chicago in 1859.

Aug 16: The **first cable message** was sent across the Atlantic Ocean from Queen Victoria of England to Pres. James Buchanan.

Oct 9: The stage inaugurating the **first overland mail service** connecting the West and East coasts reached St. Louis from San Francisco after a trip of 23 days 4 hrs. At St. Louis the mail was transferred to a train for the remainder of the journey to the East.

IV. **Fashion**
   Folkways
   Holidays
   Social Issues and Crime
   Sports

Another gold rush captured the nation's attention when gold was discovered in Colorado in the Pike's Peak area in 1857 and at Cherry Creek, Denver, in 1858. About 100,000 gold seekers headed west, but about half never made it to the gold regions. Within two years Denver was enough of a city to have a theater, circulating library, and debating club. The town of El Dorado, near present-day Colorado Springs, was founded by miners as Fountain Creek in 1859. The rallying cry of the fortune hunters in this period was "Pike's Peak or bust."

Birth control came to the fore with H. C. Wright's popular *The Unwelcomed Child; or the Crime of an Undesigned and Undesired Maternity.* It indicated a growing frankness about sexual matters in American society.

Apr 12: The **first U.S. billiard championship** was held at Fireman's Hall, Detroit, Mich. Michael J. Phelan defeated John Seereiter in a match lasting nine and a half hours. It was witnessed by a "genteel" audience that included a few ladies.

June 16: "**A house divided against itself cannot stand**" was included by Abraham Lincoln in his speech of acceptance of the Republican nomination for the U.S. Senate. "I believe," he went on, "this government cannot endure permanently half slave and half free."

July 20: The **first admission charge to a baseball game** (50 cents) was levied for the contest between Brooklyn and the New York All Stars at Fashion Race Course in Long Island. About 1500 spectators saw New York defeat Brooklyn 22–18.

1859

I. **Civil Rights**
   Exploration and Settlement
   Government
   Statistics
   Wars

A court case stemming from opposition to the Fugitive Slave Law of 1850 found a northern free state arguing for states' rights, usually the preserve of the South. In 1854 the Wisconsin Supreme Court freed Sherman M. Booth, an abolitionist editor who had been convicted in federal court of violating the Fugitive Slave Law, on the grounds that the law was unconstitutional. In *Abelman v. Booth* (Abelman was a U.S. marshall), the Supreme Court on Mar. 7, 1859, denied the right of a state to interfere in a federal case, and upheld the constitutionality of the law. The Wisconsin legislature then adopted a resolution defending state sovereignty.

The **Comstock Lode**, the richest known U.S. silver deposit, was discovered in western Nevada. It was the first major U.S. silver strike.

Feb 14: Oregon was admitted to the Union, the 33rd state.

July 5: The **Kansas constitutional convention** convened at Wyandotte, Kans. The chief issue was whether the state should be free or slave. On Oct. 4 an antislavery constitution was ratified by a vote of 10,421 to 5530.

Oct 16: The federal arsenal at **Harpers Ferry** (now in W. Va.) was seized by John Brown and 21 followers. Brown wanted to establish an abolitionist republic in the Appalachians and to fight slavery with fugitive slaves and abolitionist whites. On Dec. 2 he was hanged at Charlestown, Va., for murder, conspiracy, and treason against Virginia. In the South he was thought of as a murderer and traitor who deserved the gallows, but in the North his gibbet was described as "the cross of a martyr." In Concord, Mass., Henry David Thoreau wrote of Brown: "When a government puts forth its strength . . . to kill the liberators of the slave, what a merely brute . . . force it is seen to be." Lincoln was philosophical and brooded over the fates of historical zealots who had taken it upon themselves to end oppression. Longfellow sounded a prophetic note: "This will be a great day in our history, the date of a new revolution. . . . As I write, they are leading old John Brown to execution. . . . This is sowing the wind to reap the whirlwind, which will soon come."

II. Architecture
Arts and Music
Popular Entertainment
Publishing
Theater

Most of the opera singers heard in America were European-born and trained, and it was rare for an American-trained singer to reach the top ranks in Europe. The first to accomplish this was Adelina Patti, a coloratura soprano born of Italian parents in Madrid, Spain. She made her operatic debut in New York City on Nov. 24, 1859, in the title role of *Lucia di Lammermoor.* For years after that she sang in such cities as London, Paris, and Milan, returning to the U.S. in 1881. Patti was the most popular and highest paid singer of her time. It became a custom for audiences to demand that she sing "Home, Sweet Home" as one of her encores.

"Dixie," first known as "I Wish I Was in Dixie's Land," was composed by Dan Emmett as a "walk-around" for Bryant's Minstrels. The song was later claimed by both sides during the Civil War, but eventually became associated almost completely with the Confederacy. Emmett was a northerner from Ohio.

Sep 5: Probably the **first novel by a black** to appear in the U.S., *Our Nig; or Sketches from the Life of a Free Black* by Harriet E. Wilson, was issued in Boston. It had been privately printed for the author, about whom little is known, by the Boston printing firm of George C. Rand and Avery. Autobiographical in nature, the novel was intended by Mrs. Wilson to raise funds to care for her son, who died in 1860. Despite its significance, the novel remained virtually unrecognized until its rediscovery and republication in 1983.

III. Business and Industry
Education
Philosophy and Religion
Science

A turning point in the economic history of the U.S. came this year when on Aug. 27 the first producing oil well began to flow at the rate of 20 barrels a day. The well had been drilled to a depth of 60 feet by Edwin L. Drake, near Titusville, Pa. An oil rush, reminiscent of the California gold rush, began almost at once. Boom towns grew up overnight and within three years of Drake's discovery 128,000,000 gallons had been produced. Oil became an important export product and kerosene displaced whale oil and candles as a source of illumination.

The **first hotel passenger elevator** in the U.S. was installed in the Fifth Avenue Hotel, New York City. Many patrons continued to climb the stairs.

July: **Electric home lighting** was given its first successful demonstration by Prof. Moses G. Farmer in the parlor of his home at Salem, Mass. Current, supplied by a voltaic battery, was conducted to two lamps on a mantelpiece. Strips of platinum provided the illuminating medium. This device produced the best artificial light then known but was much more expensive than gaslight.

Sep 1: George M. Pullman's first sleeping car made its first run. It was a converted coach. In 1863 he built the *Pioneer*, the first modern sleeping coach with a folding upper berth and extensible seat cushions to form a lower berth. In 1868 he introduced a dining car, in 1875 a chair car.

IV. Fashion
Folkways
Holidays
Social Issues and Crime
Sports

Even though prizefighting was still bare-knuckled and brutal, it fascinated people of all classes. This was shown by the interest aroused when John C. Heenan sailed for England in 1859 to meet the British champion, Tom Sayers. Heenan had justly claimed the American heavyweight title on the retirement of John C. Morrissey. On Oct. 20, 1858, Morrissey had been awarded a decision over Heenan on a technicality. When Heenan and Sayers met on Apr. 17, 1860, they fought for 42 rounds in a bout that lasted 2 hrs. and 20 min. Heenan battered Sayers but the police broke up the illegal match. The crowd invaded the ring, and the bout was declared a draw. Even so, *The Spirit of the Times*, in an extra edition of 100,000 copies, hailed Heenan as the world champion.

June 30: Niagara Falls was crossed by a tightrope walker, Charles Blondin. In five minutes the sensational Frenchman, watched by 25,000 spectators, passed across a cable 1100 feet long and 160 feet above the seething water. In later performances Blondin made the same crossing blindfolded, pushing a wheelbarrow (July 4); carrying a man on his back (Aug. 19); and walking on stilts (Sept. 14, 1860). At age 72, in 1888, Blondin was still thrilling crowds in the U.S. and abroad with his high-wire skills.

July 1: In the **first intercollegiate baseball game** in history, Amherst defeated Williams, 66–32.

July 26: In the **first intercollegiate regatta,** Harvard defeated Yale and Brown at Lake Quinsigamond, Worcester, Mass. The race was in six-oared shells, at three miles. A similar regatta planned for the previous year was cancelled when the Yale stroke, George E. Dunham, drowned.

1860

I. Civil Rights
   Exploration and Settlement
   Government
   Statistics
   Wars

Even before the presidential election campaign of 1860 began, it was clear that slavery would be the only issue. The first result of this situation was a complete split in the Democratic Party between its northern and southern supporters. The Republican Party, drawing its strength from the North and West, was united in its antislavery stand and represented the largest part of the nation. There was also an attempt at a coalition of factions to hold the Union together at any cost. There were now 33 states, 18 of them free and 15 slave. This situation, combined with the split in the Democratic Party, made a Republican victory inevitable. Abraham Lincoln carried all the free states, except for a split in New Jersey. He won a clear majority in the electoral college but not in the popular vote.

The U.S. **Census** recorded a population of 31,443,321. The center of population was located 20 miles southeast of Chillicothe, Ohio. There were 448,070 free blacks and 3,953,760 slaves in the country.

1860-1861: In **congressional elections** the Republicans took control of both houses of Congress. As southern states seceded, the 37th Congress had the following representation: Senate, 31 Republicans, 10 Democrats, 8 other parties; House, 105 Republicans, 43 Democrats, 30 others.

Feb 27: Abraham Lincoln delivered his memorable address at Cooper Union, New York City. He set forth the issues on which the new Republican Party would appeal to voters and his no-compromise position on slavery. This projected Lincoln into the lead for the Republican presidential nomination.

Apr 23: The **national convention of the Democratic Party** met at Charleston, S.C. On Apr. 30 delegates from the South walked out over platform disputes. The remainder, led by Stephen A. Douglas, supported constitutional decisions and congressional noninterference on the issue of slavery in the territories. The convention adjourned on May 3 without making any nominations.

May 9: The national convention of the **Constitutional Union Party** nominated John Bell of Tennessee for the presidency and Edward Everett of Massachusetts for the vice presidency. The party was composed of remnants of the Whig and American parties.

May 16-18: The **Republican National Convention nominated Abraham Lincoln** of Illinois for the presidency and Hannibal Hamlin of Maine for the vice presidency.

June 18-23: Reconvening in Baltimore, Md., the **Democratic Party nominated Stephen A. Douglas** of Illinois for the presidency and Herschel V. Johnson of Georgia for the vice presidency.

June 28: The **southern Democrats nominated John C. Breckinridge** of Kentucky for the presidency and Joseph Lane of Oregon for the vice presidency. Their platform supported slavery in the territories.

Nov 6: Abraham Lincoln was elected president of the United States in a Republican victory over the divided Democrats. Hannibal Hamlin was elected vice president. The electoral vote was Lincoln, 180; John

C. Breckinridge, southern Democrat, 72; John Bell, Constitutional Union candidate, 39; Stephen A. Douglas, Democrat, 12. The popular vote was Lincoln, 1,866,252; Douglas, 1,375,157; Breckinridge, 849,781; Bell, 589,581.

Dec 20: South Carolina seceded from the Union, the first state to do so. Its action was taken as a consequence of Lincoln's election.

II. Architecture
Arts and Music
Popular Entertainment
Publishing
Theater

Poets of the period often devoted their talents to the controversy over slavery and the events of the Civil War. The leading voice of the South was Henry Timrod of South Carolina, who was to become known as the poet laureate of the Confederacy. Timrod's collection of *Poems* was published this year, but it was not until 1873 that his poetry dealing with the war appeared. Most notable was "Ode Sung at the Occasion of Decorating the Graves of the Confederate Dead," written in 1867, the year of his early death.

Dime novels made their first appearance under the aegis of the publisher Erastus Beadle. The first dime novel was *Malaeska; The Indian Wife of the White Hunter* by Mrs. Anna Sophia Stephens; it sold more than 300,000 copies in its first year. Another dime novel, *Seth Jones; or, the Captives of the Frontier* by Edward S. Ellis, also published this year, sold some 450,000 copies in less than a year. By 1865 Beadle's dime novel series had sold over 4,000,000 copies. The novels featured such larger-than-life characters as Deadwood Dick, Calamity Jane, and Kit Carson. Published in orange jackets, the books were read extensively by soldiers in camp. In 1870 a second series, Beadle's Pocket Novels, was begun. Literary fare in these novels consisted of tales of the West, Indians, hunters, pioneers, and the gunmen. In general, the morality of the books was unobjectionable if simplistic, for the villain and the hero were obvious from the opening pages, and evil was always punished.

"Old Black Joe," the last of Stephen Foster's "plantation songs," was published. Foster, suffering from alcoholism and financial problems, moved to New York City and began to write sentimental potboilers—as many as 46 songs in one year. He died in Bellevue Hospital, New York City, on Jan. 13, 1864.

The Conduct of Life by Ralph Waldo Emerson was published. For several years Emerson had lectured on the subject popularly and effectively. At the peak of his powers, he was now clearly an astute social commentator as well as moral philosopher. Among the book's topics were the discoveries of science, evolution, uses of wealth, importance of culture, faith, art, and a reevaluation of the position of the transcendentalists.

III. Business and Industry
Education
Philosophy and Religion
Science

Education of children at a very early age was a European innovation that now came to America. The first English-language kindergarten in the U.S. was opened in Boston this year by Elizabeth Palmer Peabody, a member of the New England intellectual elite. (A German-language kindergarten had been established in Watertown, Wis., in 1856.) Miss Peabody was interested in social reform and education and had been associated with A. Bronson Alcott and his experimental Temple School. In her kindergarten she followed the precepts of Friedrich Froebel, the German educator and founder of the kindergarten system. Miss Peabody was a member of the Transcendental Club, and her home was the setting of the notable conversation classes of Margaret Fuller, another of the transcendentalists.

A **U.S. Department of Education survey** showed a total of 321 high schools in the country; more than half were in Massachusetts, New York, and Ohio.

Feb 22: The **most significant strike of the period** began in Lynn, Mass. Shoemakers there struck for higher wages and union recognition. The strike, which followed the introduction of new machinery in the shoe industry, soon spread to include 25 towns and 20,000 shoemakers. The workers protested because youngsters were being brought in to work the new machines, cutting the salary of skilled men to $3.00 a week. The Mechanics' Association, formed in 1859 at Lynn, organized the strike. On Apr. 10 the manufacturers agreed to a 10% wage increase. Some 1000 workers went back to their jobs. The effort to win general union recognition was largely frustrated.

Apr 3: The first relay of the **Pony Express** mail service left St. Joseph, Mo., and arrived in Sacramento, Calif., on Apr. 13. The cost of mailing a letter was at first $5.00 a half-ounce, later reduced to $1.00. The Pony Express was discontinued in Oct. 1861, when the transcontinental telegraph began service.

May 10: The **Morrill Tariff Bill** was passed by the House of Representatives, opening the era of protectionism. The tariff became law in Mar. 1861. It became the regulator of imports and was superseded only by the McKinley Bill, passed by the 51st Congress in 1890.

June 23: The **Government Printing Office** was established by an act of Congress. Later the government bought an existing commercial press in Washington, D.C. Today, the Government Printing Office is the largest printing establishment in the world, with the plant valued at over $20,000,000.

IV. Fashion
   Folkways
   Holidays
   Social Issues and Crime
   Sports

The game of croquet was introduced to America from England. It was soon popular but did not reach the height of its popularity until after the Civil War. Croquet was the first outdoor athletic activity in

which women participated. Even more important, it
could be played by men and women together. Conse-
quently, it became as much a social as an athletic
activity and afforded fine opportunity for courting.
In the 1870s the vogue for croquet was so great that
sets with candle sockets for night playing were introduced.

Prices for shaves, haircuts, and curling were
raised at Tony Delight's in Chicago, one of the famous tonsorial enterprises in America. Shaves went
up from 5 cents to 6 cents, haircuts from 10 cents to
12 cents, and curling from 15 or 20 cents to 25 cents.
Shampoos were priced at 25 cents.

The term *seventh-inning stretch* became common at baseball games. It referred to the custom of
spectators standing up and stretching just before the
home team came to bat in the seventh inning. The
custom served two functions, one practical and one
superstitious. Spectators relieved cramped muscles
and brought good luck to their team as well, since the
number seven was seen as lucky.

The **popular attitude toward strikes** was reflected
in the reaction of the U.S. press this year to the Massachusetts shoemakers' strike, which was looked
upon as a virtual revolution. "Rebellion among the
workers in New England" and "Revolution at the
North" were among the warnings that greeted newspaper readers over their morning coffee. Some of the
newspapers were shocked by the part played by
women workers in the strike and bewailed the effects
of the feminist movement. Churches generally supported the strikers, while the New England manufacturers threatened the German and Irish immigrants,
who formed the bulk of the strikers, with legislative
retaliation that would take away their voting privileges.

1861

I. **Civil Rights**
Exploration and Settlement
Government
Statistics
Wars

The Civil War (1861–1865) began in the early morning hours of Apr. 12 when Confederate forces at Charleston, S.C., opened fire on the federal garrison at Fort Sumter in Charleston harbor. The action was the culmination of months of effort by Confederate officials to force federal troops out of Charleston harbor. They had been successful elsewhere in occupying federal arsenals and forts and in removing federal garrisons. Pres. Abraham Lincoln tried to deal firmly with South Carolina authorities without provoking violence, but the attempt failed. When the federal garrison at Fort Sumter surrendered on Apr. 13, the citizens of Charleston were filled with joy. Little did they realize that they had witnessed the beginning of four years of vicious warfare.

Jan 9: *Star of the West,* an unarmed federal supply ship, was fired on by the South Carolina state battery at Charleston harbor; the command to fire was given by Francis Wilkinson Pickens, governor of the state. The ship had been sent under orders from Pres. James Buchanan to supply and reinforce the federal garrison at Fort Sumter in Charleston harbor.

Jan 9: Mississippi became the second state to secede from the Union.

Jan 10: A **Florida convention** voted for secession from the Union. "United States" was changed to "Confederate States" in their constitution.

Jan 11: Alabama seceded from the Union.

Jan 19: Georgia seceded from the Union.

Jan 26: Louisiana seceded from the Union.

Jan 29: Kansas was admitted to the Union, the 34th state. It entered as a free state.

Feb 4: The **Confederate States of America was formed** at Montgomery, Ala. Jefferson Davis of Mississippi was elected president, Alexander H. Stephens of Georgia vice president. Both were chosen on Feb. 9.

Feb 9: The **Confederate Provisional Congress** asserted that all laws under the U.S. Constitution that were not inconsistent with the constitution of the Confederate states would be recognized.

Feb 13: The action that led to the awarding of the **first U.S. Medal of Honor** took place at Apache Pass, Ariz., where Col. Bernard John Dowling Irwin led his troops to victory over hostile Chiricahua Apache Indians. The medal was not given to Irwin until Jan. 24, 1894.

Feb 18: Jefferson Davis was inaugurated president of the Confederacy. The Confederate capital was established in Montgomery, Ala., where Davis lived at 626 Washington St., in a building known as the White House of the Confederacy. The capital was later moved to Richmond, Va.

Feb 23: Texas seceded from the Union, following a state convention's recommendation of Feb. 1. It was the seventh state to secede.

Mar 2: A congressional act establishing the **territories of Nevada and Dakota** was signed by Pres. James Buchanan. Nevada Territory was formed from Utah Territory, Dakota Territory from Nebraska Territory.

Mar 4: An official **Confederate flag,** "Stars and Bars," was adopted by a Confederate convention at Montgomery, Ala. The flag had seven stars and three stripes, and was raised over the Confederate capitol at Montgomery. Later, after the similarity between Union and Confederate flags created confusion at the Battle of Bull Run, the Confederate army adopted a battle flag consisting of a red field and the blue cross of St. Andrew, with 13 stars.

Mar 4: **Abraham Lincoln was inaugurated president** of the United States. A Republican, he was elected to two terms but was assassinated early in his second term. Hannibal Hamlin was inaugurated vice president.

Mar 11: The **Confederate constitution** was adopted unanimously by the Confederate congress in session at Montgomery, Ala. It declared the sovereignty of states and forbade passage of any law prohibiting slavery.

Apr 11: At **Fort Sumter,** surrender of the federal garrison was demanded by South Carolina authorities. Maj. Robert Anderson refused to surrender, but added that he would soon be forced to do so if supplies were not forthcoming.

Apr 12: The **Civil War began** at 4:30 A.M. when Confederate shore batteries under command of Gen. P. G. T. Beauregard opened fire on Fort Sumter. The federal garrison, out of supplies, surrendered on Apr. 13 and evacuated the fort the following day.

Apr 17: A **Virginia convention voted for secession** from the Union as a result of Lincoln's call for troops. The proposal was put before the people of Virginia on May 23 and passed. Virginia was the eighth state to secede.

Apr 19: A **blockade** of Confederate ports was ordered by Pres. Lincoln. The blockade would ultimately weaken the Confederacy by disrupting the importation of war supplies.

Apr 19-20: **Norfolk Navy Yard** was destroyed and evacuated by Union forces. Among the ships scuttled was the steam frigate *Merrimack,* which was burned to the waterline.

May 6: **Arkansas seceded** from the Union, the ninth state to join the Confederacy.

May 20: **North Carolina seceded** from the Union.

May 21: **Richmond,** Va., was made capital of the Confederate States of America. Virginia at this time was the most populous of the southern states.

June 8: **Tennessee seceded** from the Union.

July 21: At the first Battle of **Bull Run,** near Manassas, Va., Union forces under Gen. Irvin McDowell were defeated by the Confederates. McDowell delayed the attack for two days, allowing Confederate Gen. Beauregard to call on reinforcements from the Shenandoah Valley. Their arrival late in the day gave the Confederates a numerical advantage. It was in this battle that Confederate Gen. Thomas J. Jackson was nicknamed "Stonewall" for his firm stand at a crucial moment.

Sep 13: The **first naval engagement** of the Civil War took place at Pensacola, Fla. Lt. John Henry Russell sailed the frigate *Colorado* past shore batteries at night and, as day broke, with a force of 100 sailors and Marines, went for the southern privateer *Judah* in the shipyard. After hand-to-hand fighting, the contingent burned the vessel to the waterline and left with few losses. Pres. Lincoln thanked Russell personally, and the Navy Department honored him.

Nov 7: **Union forces captured Port Royal Island** on the South Carolina coast. A Navy fleet under Samuel F. Du Pont bombarded the protecting forts, Beauregard and Walker, which were then overrun by Army troops under Lt. Col. Thomas W. Sherman. The victory was important to the North, for it now had a base on the flank of the South. From this base its South Atlantic Blockading Squadron under Du Pont proceeded to capture or render inoperative nearly all the South's Atlantic ports below North Carolina.

II. Architecture
   Arts and Music
   Popular Entertainment
   Publishing
   Theater

East Lynne, a phenomenally successful novel and dramatization by Mrs. Henry Wood, an English author, was published in the U.S. this year. The tearjerker sold at least 1,000,000 copies, but its greatest success came as a stage play. The drama packed theaters for most of the rest of the century. *East Lynne*

later became a synonym for the crudest of melodramas.

Aug 15: Civil War events became theatrical material.
Charles Gayler's *Bull Run* was presented in New
York City less than a month after the battle itself.
Other plays dealing with the war were *Capture of Fort
Donelson* (1862) by Henry Seymour; *How to Avoid
Drafting* (1862), anonymous; *A Supper in Dixie* (1865)
by William C. Reynolds; *The Guerrillas* (1862) by
James D. McCabe, Jr.; and *Grant's Campaign* (1865)
by John Poole.

III. Business and Industry
Education
Philosophy and Religion
Science

An important step in the development of the nation's
communication system came on Oct. 24, 1861, when
Pres. Abraham Lincoln in Washington, D.C., received
the first transcontinental telegraph message, from
Sacramento, Calif. The lines of the Overland and the
Pacific telegraph companies had been linked at Fort
Bridger, Utah. A side effect of the completion of the
transcontinental line was the almost immediate demise of the far more romantic Pony Express, which
had begun operating in Apr. 1860 between St. Joseph,
Mo., and Sacramento.

Apr 20: Thaddeus Sobieski Coulincourt Lowe, inventor and balloonist, made a record balloon voyage
from Cincinnati, Ohio, to near the coast of South
Carolina—900 miles in 9 hrs.—to demonstrate the
value of balloons for observation by the military. He
was briefly held as a Union spy. On Oct. 1 Pres. Lincoln made him chief of the Army's aeronautic section.

Aug 5: Congress adopted an **income tax law** as a war
finance measure. Income was defined broadly as
"derived from any source whatever." The rates were
3% on incomes from $600 to $10,000 and 5% for
incomes above $10,000.

Oct 4: Construction of the *Monitor* **was** authorized by the U.S. Navy. This steam-powered, propeller-driven, armored, and rotary-turreted warship was designed and made by John Ericsson. It was launched at Greenpoint, L. I., on Jan. 30, 1862, less than 100 days after its keel was laid. Naval warfare was changed irrevocably by its design.

IV. Fashion
   Folkways
   Holidays
   Social Issues and Crime
   Sports

A change in American society's attitude toward light entertainment came in 1861 when Antonio "Tony" Pastor, a singer and dancer, opened his first theater at 444 Broadway in New York City. The variety theater had had a reputation for vulgarity, but Pastor's performers and acts were suitable for the whole family. He attracted women patrons by offering door prizes such as kitchenware and dress patterns. Pastor eventually became known as the father of American vaudeville. He introduced performers who were to become famous, such as Lillian Russell (born this year). His style of entertainment was soon copied in other cities.

Mar 4: In Abraham Lincoln's **first inaugural address** the new president began with a sentiment that has become an integral part of the literature and history of America: "This country, with its institutions, belongs to the people who inhabit it. Whenever they shall have grown weary of the existing government, they can exercise their constitutional right of amending it, or their revolutionary right to dismember or overthrow it." He concluded: "We are not enemies, but friends. We must not be enemies. . . . The mystic chords of memory . . . will yet swell the chorus of the Union, when again touched, as they surely will be, by the better angels of our nature."

1862

I. Civil Rights
   Exploration and Settlement
   Government
   Statistics
   Wars

An important milestone in settling the West was the
signing of the Homestead Act on May 20 by Pres.
Abraham Lincoln. This law gave 160 acres of public
land to any person who was head of a household and
21 years of age or older, provided that the person
settled on the land for five years and then paid a
nominal fee. If settlers wished to acquire title earlier,
they could do so after six months by paying $1.25 an
acre. The law was a boon to the approximately
2,000,000 people who ultimately found new homes
under it, but it was not the major contributor to the
overall settlement of the West. Far greater acreage
was available from other sources, particularly the
railroads, which received enormous grants of good
land as subsidies.

1862-1863: In **congressional elections,** the Republicans kept control of both houses of Congress with a
39–12 majority in the Senate and 103–80 majority in
the House.

Feb 8: **Union forces captured Roanoke Island,** N.C.
Gen. Henry A. Wise and his Confederate garrison of
2675 men were taken prisoner.

Mar 6-7: The Battle of **Pea Ridge,** Ark., was fought. A
Confederate army of 16,000 under Gen. Earl Van
Dorn attacked a Union army of 10,500 under Brig.
Gen. Samuel Ryan Curtis, whose last reserves pre-
vented a Union disaster on the second day. Among
the heavy losses on both sides were two Confederate

generals, Benjamin McCulloch and James McQueen McIntosh.

Mar 8: The **Confederate ironclad** *Virginia* destroyed two Union frigates at Hampton Roads, Va., sinking the *Cumberland* and setting the *Congress* on fire. The *Virginia* had been built from the raised hull of the Union ship *Merrimack*, which had been burned to the waterline when Union forces evacuated Norfolk Navy Yard in Apr. 1861.

Mar 9: In the **first battle between ironclad warships,** the Confederate ship *Virginia* and Union ironclad *Monitor* fought to a draw at Hampton Roads, Va., whereupon the *Virginia* retired, leaving the Union blockade intact. The crew of the *Monitor*, following naval regulations, had been using only half charges in its two 12-inch guns.

Apr 6-7: The Battle of **Shiloh** was fought near Pittsburg Landing, Tenn. The Union army of Tennessee was commanded by Gen. Ulysses S. Grant, the Confederate army of Mississippi by Gen. Albert S. Johnston. Over 100,000 men were engaged, the largest number yet in the Western Hemisphere. Johnston was close to a brilliant victory on the first day, but it cost him his life. Grant, with timely reinforcements on the second day, turned the tide against Gen. P. G. T. Beauregard. Losses were severe on both sides, sobering Washington and Richmond and the public perception of the struggle.

May 1: Capt. David G. Farragut and Union forces took **possession of New Orleans** after running past Forts Jackson and St. Philip on the Mississippi R. at night and then defeating a small Confederate flotilla. Farragut was promoted to rear admiral in July.

May 11: The Confederate ironclad *Virginia* was destroyed by its crew on the evacuation of Norfolk, Va.

June 1: Gen. **Robert E. Lee** was appointed commander of the Confederate Army of Northern Virginia.

July: The **first black troops** were organized by Maj. Gen. David Hunter in the Union's First Carolina Regiment. Many of the soldiers were former slaves.

July 1: The **Seven Days Campaign** ended with the indecisive Battle of Malvern Hill (Va.). Gen. Lee had

started the campaign with an attack on McClellan's
Union army at Mechanicsville, Va., on June 26. The
Confederates gradually pushed the timid McClellan
back to the safety of his base on the James River.
McClellan's Peninsular Campaign had failed and his
army was withdrawn. Casualties for the week stood
at Union, 15,849; Confederate, 20,141.

July 12: Congress authorized the **Medal of Honor** for
noncommissioned Army officers and privates who
exhibited supreme gallantry in action. This highest
U.S. military decoration had been authorized for
men of the Navy in 1861. In 1863 the award was
extended to include commissioned officers.

Aug 9: In the Battle of **Cedar Mountain,** Va., near the
Rappahannock R. northwest of Richmond, Confederate troops under Gen. Stonewall Jackson, planning
a move northward in advance of Gen. Lee's larger
forces, defeated two brigades of Union forces led by
Gen. John Pope and Gen. N.P. Banks. Badly outnumbered, the Union army suffered 2381 killed or
wounded; the Confederates, 1276.

Aug 29-30: At the second Battle of **Bull Run,** the maneuvers of Gen. Stonewall Jackson and his teamwork
with Gen. Lee were too much for the 45,000 Union
troops under Gen. John Pope, who broke and retreated to Washington, D.C. Union losses were 1724
killed, 8372 wounded, 5958 missing. Confederate
losses stood at 1481 killed, 7627 wounded, 89 missing.

Sep 15: The Union arsenal at **Harpers Ferry,** W. Va.,
was captured by Gen. Stonewall Jackson. A tremendous quantity of materiel was seized, and 12,500 men
were captured. Harpers Ferry was abandoned and
the captured troops set free by the Confederates on
Sept. 20 and reoccupied by the North on the 22nd.

Sep 17: At the Battle of **Antietam** Creek near Sharpsburg in western Maryland, Gen. Lee's first invasion
of the North was halted by Union troops under Gen.
McClellan. This was the bloodiest one-day battle of
the Civil War. Each side lost over 2000 killed and
9000 wounded.

Sep 22: A preliminary **Emancipation Proclamation**

was issued by Pres. Lincoln. It was announced that on Jan. 1, 1863, slaves within all areas still in rebellion would be declared free forever.

Dec 13: The Battle of **Fredericksburg,** Va., was a grave defeat for the North under Gen. Burnside. Gen. Lee's men killed or wounded 12,653 Union soldiers. Confederate casualties were 5300.

Dec 31: The Union ironclad *Monitor* sank in a gale off Cape Hatteras, N.C.

II. Architecture
   ## Arts and Music
   ## Popular Entertainment
   ## Publishing
   ## Theater

Typical of the style of humor favored by Americans of the period was that of Charles Farrar Browne, who wrote under the name of Artemus Ward. His writings began as newspaper columns in 1857, and in 1861 some of them were collected in *Artemus Ward, His Book.* Browne's column recounted the fictional adventures of Ward, a traveling carnival man. Ward's humor was based on naive sounding but shrewd comments on current events, with a great many misspellings that were considered amusing. Ward was an early influence on another writer, Samuel Langhorne Clemens, who began writing for the Virginia City, Nev., *Territorial Enterprise* this year. Clemens adopted the pseudonym Mark Twain in 1863.

An early romantic **western novel** set in the Rockies, *John Brent* by Theodore Winthrop, was published. The author, a Connecticut gentleman of leisure, had been killed in a Civil War skirmish in June 1861. That year saw the posthumous publication of Winthrop's novel *Cecil Dreeme,* about a young woman masquerading as a male artist in Washington Square, New York City. Another novel, *Edwin Brothertoft* (1862), and two travel books followed *John Brent.* Winthrop's popularity lasted for a generation.

III. Business and Industry
Education
Philosophy and Religion
Science

What eventually proved to be a cornerstone of higher education, especially in its practical aspects, was the Morrill Act, signed July 2 by Pres. Abraham Lincoln. The law took its name from Rep. Justin Smith Morrill, Republican of Vermont, who had first introduced the bill in 1857. The law granted to each loyal state 30,000 acres of land for each senator and representative serving in Congress. The schools to be established on the land were to emphasize agriculture, home economics, engineering, and mechanical arts. These land-grant colleges still exist in most states.

John D. Rockefeller, 23 years old, invested in an oil refining business $4000 he had accumulated through a partnership in a produce commission house, Clark & Rockefeller. Five years later he was the major owner of Rockefeller, Andrews, and Flagler, the progenitor of Standard Oil Company of Ohio, incorporated in 1870.

Aerial reconnaissance for Union forces was carried out by American balloonist Thaddeus Lowe, who photographed Confederate ground emplacements around Richmond, Va., at an altitude of 1000 ft. This was the earliest use of cameras to provide panoramic shots of military positions.

Congress established the **Department of Agriculture** "to acquire and diffuse useful information." In its first years its annual budget was about $50,000. Previously agriculture had been handled by the Patent Office, since many patents pertained to farm machinery.

Nov 4: The **Gatling gun,** designed by Richard Jordan Gatling, was given a patent. Its chief feature, six barrels revolving around a central axis, permitted high rates of fire. It was not employed by Union forces until the siege of Petersburg, Va., in 1864–1865.

IV. **Fashion**
    Folkways
    Holidays
    Social Issues and Crime
    Sports

Strong emotions aroused by the war were reflected in the use of such epithets as *Copperhead*. The term was applied to northern Democrats who opposed the war and the Republican administration. The Copperheads were particularly strong in Ohio, Indiana, and Illinois. The name came from the Copperheads' custom of cutting the head of the goddess of liberty from copper pennies to wear in lapels; it also referred to the venomous snake. Some Republicans used the term to condemn the entire Democratic party as disloyal to the Union. The term probably first appeared in print in the Cincinnati *Gazette* on July 30, 1862.

Dec 29: Walt Whitman wrote from Washington, D.C., to tell his mother about his brother George, whom he had visited in camp. He had a hard time locating his brother's outfit, and his pocket had been picked while he was changing trains in Philadelphia. But he found George safe and promoted to captain of the 51st New York Volunteers, at Falmont, Va., near Fredericksburg. George Whitman was sharing a tent with a Capt. Francis, and Walt lived with them: "There were five of us altogether, to eat, sleep, write, etc., in a space twelve feet square. George is about building a place, half hut and half tent, for himself. Every captain has a tent, in which he lives, transacts company business . . . has a cook (or a man of all work) and in the same tent mess and sleep his lieutenants, and perhaps the first sergeant. They have a kind of fireplace—and the cook's fire is outside on the open ground. . . ."

1863

I. Civil Rights
Exploration and Settlement
Government
Statistics
Wars

On Jan. 1, 1863, Pres. Abraham Lincoln issued his Emancipation Proclamation, which in spite of its title neither freed all the slaves nor satisfied the abolitionists. The proclamation applied only to slaves in territory under control of the Confederacy. It did not apply to areas occupied by Union forces or to the four slave states that had not seceded (Delaware, Kentucky, Maryland, and Missouri). In effect, it freed the slaves where Lincoln could not enforce the proclamation, and left slavery intact where the slaves could have been freed. Lincoln had no intention of driving the loyal slave states into the Confederate camp. The proclamation enraged many southerners, who saw it as an attempt to spark a slave insurrection.

Free delivery of mail in cities was initiated by Congress. Rural free delivery (RFD) did not begin until 1896.

Feb 24: The **Territory of Arizona** was formed from the Territory of New Mexico. Its first capital was established at Fort Whipple in 1864.

Mar 3: The **Territory of Idaho** was carved from four existing territories: Washington, Utah, Dakota, and Nebraska. It included the later states of Montana and Wyoming.

Mar 3: A **conscription act,** first in the nation's history, was passed by Congress. It called for registration of all male citizens between 20 and 45 years of age and aliens in the same age bracket who had declared their intention of becoming citizens. Conscripts could be exempted from military service by payment of $300 or by providing a substitute.

May 1-4: At the Battle of **Chancellorsville,** 50 miles southwest of Washington, D.C., Gen. Robert E. Lee won his greatest victory over huge Union forces under Gen. Joseph Hooker. In the North, 17,275 were killed or wounded; in the South, 12,821. Gen. Stonewall Jackson, one of the wounded, died a few days later.

June 20: West Virginia was admitted to the Union, the 35th state.

July 1-3: At the Battle of **Gettysburg,** Gen. Lee made a desperate bid to smash through Union forces and approach Washington, D.C., from the west. Gen. George G. Meade met him accidentally at Gettysburg, Pa. Lee's assaults on federal positions brought heavy losses to both sides. On July 3, when the famous charge of Gen. George E. Pickett's division failed, with one unit leaving 3393 out of 4800 men dead or wounded on the field, the battle was lost to the South. On July 4 both sides were exhausted. On July 5 Lee's army retreated across the Potomac R., never to return to northern territory. The South suffered 30,000 killed, wounded, or missing; the North, 23,000.

July 4: At the Battle of **Vicksburg** a Confederate army under Gen. John C. Pemberton surrendered to Gen. Ulysses S. Grant after a campaign that had begun on Mar. 29. The South lost 8000 killed and wounded; and more than 29,000 surrendered. Union casualties were 8910. This loss of manpower and control of the Mississippi R., atop the loss at Gettysburg, doomed the Confederacy.

July 13-16: Antidraft riots broke out in New York City, and nearly 1000 persons were killed or wounded before federal troops restored order.

Sep 19-20: At the Battle of **Chickamauga,** Tenn., Union forces under Gen. William S. Rosecrans were defeated by troops under Gen. Braxton Bragg. Both sides, evenly matched, saw over a quarter of their men killed or wounded. Union forces retreated to Chattanooga, Tenn.

Nov 23-25: At the Battle of **Chattanooga,** Tenn., Union reinforcements under Gen. Grant systematically captured Confederate positions around the city. The siege was broken and Confederate forces under Gen. Bragg fled to Dalton, Ga. Tennessee was no longer a battleground.

II. **Architecture**
   Arts and Music
   Popular Entertainment
   Publishing
   Theater

The Civil War continued to influence American literature. This year marked the appearance of a short novel that was destined to become a classic. *The Man Without a Country* by Edward Everett Hale, clergyman and author, first appeared anonymously in *Atlantic Monthly* in December. The story was inspired by a remark that had been made by Clement L. Vallandigham, leader of the northern antiwar Copperheads, in which he implied he did not care to live in a country that had Abraham Lincoln as president. In the story, Philip Nolan, charged with treason, declares that he never wants to hear of the U.S. again. He is sentenced to spend the rest of his life at sea, with all news of the U.S. withheld from him.

The first part of *Tales of a Wayside Inn,* stories in verse by Henry Wadsworth Longfellow, was published, demonstrating Longfellow's narrative skill. Using the convention of Chaucer and Boccaccio, he and six congenial acquaintances gather at an inn in Sudbury, Mass., and tell tales, including such favorites as "Paul Revere's Ride," "The Saga of King Olaf," "The Legend of Rabbi Ben Levi," and "The Birds of Killingworth."

Nov 19: The **Gettysburg Address** was delivered on the bloodstained battlefield at Gettysburg, Pa., by Pres. Abraham Lincoln, at ceremonies dedicating a national cemetery. The three brief paragraphs are marked by orderly thought, lucid expression, and a noble sense of the tragedy of the conflict.

III. Business and Industry
Education
Philosophy and Religion
Science

The Civil War increased the pace at which labor unions were organized. The war raised economic and social questions concerning free versus slave labor. At the same time, the increase in the cost of living caused by the war brought agitation for higher wages. As a result, at least ten national unions were organized between 1863 and 1866. Among them was the first of the railroad brotherhoods, the Brotherhood of Locomotive Engineers, formed this year as the Brotherhood of the Footboard. Conductors organized in 1868, trainmen in 1873, and firemen in 1883.

Butterick paper clothes patterns began when Ebenezer Butterick, a tailor and shirtmaker of Sterling, Mass., received a patent. The first patterns were cut from stiff paper and limited to children's wear, but were immediately successful. By 1864 Butterick had an office at 192 Broadway, New York City, and was making his patterns of tissue paper. In 1871 he sold 6,000,000 patterns.

Mar 3: The **National Academy of Sciences** was founded in Washington, D.C., as a private nonprofit organization to promote science and investigate scientific problems for the government. Today it has about 1250 members.

Apr 14: A **continuous-roll printing press** was patented by William Bullock, who put a press of this type into operation in his Pittsburgh, Pa., printing plant. He turned to manufacture of the press as soon as the Civil War ended. This was the first printing press capable of printing on both sides of a sheet.

IV. Fashion
Folkways
Holidays
Social Issues and Crime
Sports

A new sport became available to Americans this year with the introduction of roller skating by James L. Plimpton. Plimpton invented the four-wheel skate, which worked on rubber pads, thus permitting skaters to change direction by shifting their weight to one side or the other without lifting the wheels of the skate off the ground. Roller skating became fashionable in New York City and soon spread to other cities. In Newport, R.I., the Roller Skating Association leased the Atlantic House and turned its dining hall and plaza into a skating rink. In Chicago, the Casino could accommodate 3000 spectators and 1000 skaters. In San Francisco, a rink advertised 5000 pairs of skates available for rent.

The first attempt at **base-stealing** in baseball history was made by Eddie Cuthbert of Philadelphia, Pa., when his team, the Keystones, played against the Brooklyn Atlantics.

Oct 3: Thanksgiving Day was proclaimed a national holiday by Pres. Lincoln, to be observed on the last Thursday in November. In 1939 Pres. Franklin D. Roosevelt moved Thanksgiving Day one week back to stimulate Christmas shopping. In 1941 Congress adopted a joint resolution confirming the fourth Thursday, not the last Thursday, as Thanksgiving Day.

1864

I. **Civil Rights**
   Exploration and Settlement
   Government
   Statistics
   Wars

A presidential election while the Civil War was being fought posed special problems. In the North there was considerable dissatisfaction with the progress being made in defeating the Confederacy, so Pres. Abraham Lincoln did not think his chances of reelection were good. The Democrats were split between those who supported the war and those who wanted peace at almost any price. The Democratic nominee was Gen. George B. McClellan, commander of the Union Army, who had let several opportunities for victory slip away. The Democratic platform called for peace through reunification of the states but did not say how this was to be done. Fortunately for Lincoln and the Republicans, several important military victories were won in time to influence the outcome.

1864-1865: In **congressional elections** the Republicans increased their majorities to 42–10 in the Senate and 149–42 in the House.

Feb 7: A **Union expedition to Florida** to return the state to Union allegiance entered Jacksonville under command of Gen. Truman Seymour.

Feb 20: At the Battle of **Olustee,** Fla., near Jacksonville, Union forces under Gen. Seymour were badly defeated by Confederate troops under Gen. Joseph Finegan. The Union lost some 2000 killed or wounded. The effort to set up a loyal state government was severely hampered in what was the largest land engagement in Florida.

Apr 17: The **exchange of prisoners of war** was discontinued by Gen. Grant. He stated that the practice served to prolong the conflict.

May 5-6: The Battle of the **Wilderness** ended indecisively as the armies of Robert E. Lee and Ulysses S. Grant wrought mutual destruction near Chancellorsville, Va. Because of thick forest growth, most of the fighting was done at close hand. Despite heavy Union losses, Grant's progress southward was only briefly halted.

May 11: James Ewell Brown "Jeb" Stuart, Confederate general and cavalry leader, was mortally wounded at Yellow Tavern, Va., where an inadequate Confederate force was attempting to block Gen. Philip H. Sheridan. Sheridan, with Gen. Grant's approval, was making his first independent cavalry action.

May 12: The heaviest action of the Battle of **Spotsylvania** began at dawn, when Gen. Winfield Scott Hancock, with 20,000 men, attacked a Confederate salient. Creating a gap, Hancock's men captured some 4000 men and 20 guns.

May 26: The **Territory of Montana** was formed by Congress from the Territory of Idaho.

June 3: At the Battle of **Cold Harbor,** Gen. Lee won his last victory over Union forces, numbering 108,000 against his 59,000. On this day federal troops lost 7000 men against 1500 for the Confederate troops. In an eight-minute period more men fell in an assault on entrenched Confederate troops than in any other like period of time. Between May 7 and June 3, federal losses were 50,000 men, Confederate 32,000. The North could replace its losses fully, but the South could not.

June 7: The **Republican National Convention nominated Pres. Lincoln** for a second term. Andrew Johnson of Tennessee was nominated for the vice presidency.

June 15-18: At the Battle of **Petersburg,** Va., Union forces were unable to take the strategic city in the face of brilliant strategy by Gen. Lee. Gen. Grant began a siege that continued until Apr. 1865.

June 19: The Confederate cruiser *Alabama* was sunk by the U.S.S. *Kearsarge* off Cherbourg, France, while trying to escape into the Atlantic. Fifteen thousand Frenchmen watched the battle from shoreline cliffs. In two years of roaming the Atlantic, the *Alabama* had destroyed or captured 69 vessels.

Aug 5-23: At the Battle of **Mobile Bay,** Ala., David G. Farragut commanded a fleet of fourteen wooden ships and four ironclads. Running through a mine-field and past Confederate forts Gaines, Morgan, and Powell, Farragut's fleet defeated a Confederate flotilla, including the Confederate ironclad *Tennessee*, and took one of the South's last major ports. The city of Mobile was taken in 1865.

Aug 29: The **Democratic National Convention nominated Gen. George B. McClellan** for the presidency and George H. Pendleton of Ohio for the vice presidency. The party platform attacked Pres. Lincoln's prosecution of the war, calling his program a failure.

Sep 1: Atlanta, Ga., was evacuated by Confederate forces under Gen. John B. Hood. The next day the city was occupied by Union forces under Gen. William Tecumseh Sherman.

Oct 31: Nevada was admitted to the Union, the 36th state.

Nov 8: **Abraham Lincoln was reelected president** of the United States. Andrew Johnson of Tennessee was elected vice president. The electoral vote was Lincoln, 212; Gen. George B. McClellan, Democratic candidate, 21. The popular vote was Lincoln, 2,216,067; McClellan, 1,808,725.

Nov 16: Gen. **Sherman's march to the sea** with 62,000 men began. Leaving Atlanta, Ga., in flames and sweeping across a 60-mile front with little serious opposition, his army destroyed everything useful to the Confederates and ravaged the countryside. The South was cut in two. Gen. William J. Hardee and his remaining Confederate forces evacuated Savannah, Ga., on Dec. 21. Sherman occupied the city that day.

II. Architecture
Arts and Music
Popular Entertainment
Publishing
Theater

The Civil War created a large demand for statues of leading figures in the conflict. A sculptor who provided many such works was John Quincy Adams Ward. In 1861 Ward set up his studio in New York City. This year he completed what was perhaps his finest work, *Indian Hunter,* for New York City's Central Park. He completed this after a long trip among Indians in the West and Northwest. Ward later did other statues for Central Park and for several cities, including statues of Gen. William T. Sherman and Gen. George H. Thomas, as well as *Private of the Seventh Regiment.*

The Nasby Papers by Petroleum Vesuvius Nasby, pseudonym of the Ohio journalist David Ross Locke, was published. It was a collection of Locke's satiric "letters" to a newspaper by Nasby, an illiterate country preacher supposedly supporting the South but in effect caricaturing its positions. Pres. Abraham Lincoln enjoyed the Nasby letters, often reading them to his Cabinet and visitors.

III. Business and Industry
Education
Philosophy and Religion
Science

Efforts to educate the deaf, almost entirely the work of the Gallaudet family during the nineteenth century, were rewarded in 1864 when Congress authorized the granting of degrees by the new college division of the Columbia Institution for the Deaf, Dumb, and Blind, in Washington, D.C. The school was renamed Gallaudet College in 1894. Early in the century Thomas Hopkins Gallaudet had pioneered in the field. His eldest son, Thomas Gallaudet, was a clergy-

man who devoted almost all his time to missionary
work among the deaf; he founded St. Ann's Church
for Deaf-Mutes in New York City. The youngest son,
Edward Miner Gallaudet, had opened the Washington school about 1857. It remains the only liberal arts
college in the world for the deaf.

Feb 17: The **first successful submarine attack** was
made by the Confederate vessel *Hunley,* which sank
the federal sloop *Housatonic* while it was blockading
Charleston, S.C. In 1863 the Confederate submarine
David had damaged the federal ship *Ironsides.* Both
the *Hunley* and the *David* were lost in these engagements.

June 30: A new **Internal Revenue Act** was passed by
Congress. It increased taxes on many items, including tobacco, and introduced a second income tax.
The tax rate was 5% on incomes between $600 and
$10,000 and 10% on incomes over $10,000.

IV. Fashion
Folkways
Holidays
Social Issues and Crime
Sports

In the early days of baseball there was a rule against
paying players. However, by 1864 the rule had been
stretched or broken a number of times. At least as
early as 1860 the Brooklyn Excelsiors reputedly paid
Jim Creighton (under the table, of course), although
Albert J. "Al" Reach is often cited as the first professional baseball player. He accepted money in 1864 to
leave the Brooklyn Eckfords for the Philadelphia
Athletics. Reach later became a prominent manufacturer of sporting goods.

The motto **"In God We Trust"** appeared on a coin
for the first time, on the 1864 two-cent piece.

A **new political expression** was coined by Pres.
Lincoln in his campaign of 1864 when he observed,
" . . . it was not best to swap horses while crossing the
stream, and . . . I am not so poor a horse that they
might not make a botch of it in trying to swap."

The **first curve ball** by a baseball pitcher was thrown by William A. "Candy" Cummings of the Brooklyn Stars. He was pitching against the Brooklyn Atlantics. Skeptics thought it was an optical illusion.

May 11: "**I propose to fight it out on this line if it takes all summer**" was said by Gen. Ulysses S. Grant during the Spotsylvania campaign, reflecting the Union general's determination to take Richmond, Va., and win the war, despite the heavy losses he would suffer.

Aug 5: Adm. David G. Farragut exclaimed, "**Damn the torpedoes! Full speed ahead**" when the lead ship of his flotilla, the *Tecumseh*, struck a mine, then called a torpedo, and sank at the entrance to Mobile Bay. The federal fleet ran the minefield and the forts at the entrance and captured the small Confederate flotilla in the harbor.

1865

I. Civil Rights
   Exploration and Settlement
   Government
   Statistics
   Wars

The Civil War was scarcely over before Pres. Abraham Lincoln was assassinated, the first president to be killed. The assassin struck as Lincoln watched a comedy, *Our American Cousin*, at Ford's Theater in Washington, D.C., on the evening of Apr. 14. He died at 7:22 A.M. the next day. The assassin, John Wilkes Booth, an actor and Confederate sympathizer, escaped from Washington but broke his leg jumping from the president's box to the stage. He was cornered in a barn near Bowling Green, Va., on Apr. 26 and shot to death. Of the nine persons charged with the conspiracy, four were hanged and four were jailed. Dr. Samuel A. Mudd, the physician who, not recognizing Booth, set his broken leg, was sentenced to life imprisonment but was pardoned in 1869.

Jan 15: Fort Fisher, N.C., fell to Union forces under a joint sea and land assault. Some 2000 soldiers were captured, including Maj. Gen. William H.C. Whiting, mortally wounded. This engagement gave the federals control of Cape Fear R. Wilmington, the last Confederate port, was now closed.

Feb 17: Columbia, S.C., was set afire while being entered by federal troops under Gen. William Tecumseh Sherman. Bales of cotton were put to the torch, perhaps by Confederates to prevent their falling into federal hands. Strong winds scattered the burning cotton across most of the city.

Mar 2: Gen. Lee asked Gen. Grant for a conference to iron out differences between North and South. Pres. Lincoln rejected the proposal, demanding the surrender of the Confederates before such negotiations could take place.

Mar 3: The **Freedmen's Bureau was created by Congress** to help the destitute but free blacks of the South. In 1866 Congress greatly extended the bureau's power, over Pres. Andrew Johnson's veto. The first bureau commissioner was Union Gen. Oliver O. Howard, who later founded Howard University in Washington, D.C.

Mar 4: Pres. **Lincoln was inaugurated** for his second term. Sen. Andrew Johnson, Republican of Tennessee, succeeded Hannibal Hamlin as vice president.

Mar 25: At the Union siege of **Petersburg,** Va., Gen. Lee made a desperate attempt to break through the Union line at its weakest point, Ft. Stedman, east of the city. Despite initial success the Confederates were beaten back. Losses on both sides were heavy.

Apr 2: The **evacuation of Richmond** was urged by Gen. Lee, who informed Confederate Pres. Davis that he himself must withdraw from Petersburg, Va. Davis left the city that night with his cabinet, retreating to Danville. The now small Confederate army began evacuation of Petersburg.

Apr 3: Union forces occupied Petersburg, Va., one

day after the Confederate evacuation. Lee's forces moved south but were blocked by Union units.

Apr 9: At **Appomattox** Court House, Va., Gen. Lee surrendered to Gen. Grant. The Civil War was virtually ended.

Apr 14: Pres. **Lincoln was shot** by John Wilkes Booth at Ford's Theater in Washington, D.C. He died the following morning.

Apr 15: Vice Pres. **Andrew Johnson was sworn in** as 17th president of the United States. He completed Lincoln's term.

Apr 26: Gen. **Joseph E. Johnston surrendered** the Confederate Army of Tennessee to Gen. Sherman near Durham Station, N.C.

Apr 26: John Wilkes Booth was hunted down by military police in a barn near Fort Royal, Va. The barn was set afire, and Booth was mortally wounded, possibly by his own hand.

May 10: Jefferson Davis was captured at Irwinville, Ga., by a contingent of Gen. James H. Wilson's cavalry, led by Lt. Col. Benjamin Pritchard.

May 29: Pres. Johnson issued a **proclamation of amnesty,** specifying classes of persons who must make application for pardon. A second proclamation looked toward establishment of a loyal government in North Carolina, with the state to determine the voting rules.

Aug 14: Mississippi overturned its secession ordinance of 1861 at a state convention that also abolished slavery in the state.

Nov 9: North Carolina overturned its secession ordinance, prohibited slavery, and elected representatives to the U.S. Congress. The state was readmitted to the Union in 1868.

Dec 2: Adoption of the **Thirteenth Amendment,** prohibiting slavery, became a certainty when Alabama became the 27th state to ratify it, raising state ratifications to the necessary two-thirds. The declaration of ratification was issued on Dec. 18.

II. Architecture
   Arts and Music
   Popular Entertainment
   Publishing
   Theater

The end of the Civil War was marked by an outpouring of war-related writings: poetry commemorating the dead, accounts of wartime experiences, and reflections on its causes and consequences. One of the first and best of the war poems was James Russell Lowell's "Ode Recited at the Commemoration to the Living and Dead Soldiers of Harvard University," read on July 21, 1865. It was first privately printed and did not attract much attention until it appeared in the Sept. 1865 *Atlantic Monthly*. Lowell, who had lost three nephews in the war, portrayed Abraham Lincoln as the symbol of the courageous warrior. During the war Lowell had written two series of verses, *The Biglow Papers*, for the *Atlantic*. These were published in book form in 1867. They strongly supported the Union and criticized England for its unfriendly attitude toward the North.

The popular children's story ***Hans Brinker; or The Silver Skates*** by Mary Mapes Dodge, begun as a serial, quickly became a best seller.

Josh Billings, His Sayings by Henry Wheeler Shaw, rural apostle of horse sense, was published with the assistance of Charles Farrar Browne (Artemus Ward). Shaw's aphorisms, in the semiliterate vernacular, delighted the public and earned him the title of "Aesop and Ben Franklin condensed and abridged." Typical of his aphorisms is the following: "The muel iz haf hoss and haf Jackass, and then kums tu a full stop, natur diskovering her mistake."

Walt Whitman's ***Drum-Taps*** drew on the poet's experience as a nurse in Washington, D.C., during the Civil War. Later incorporated into Whitman's ever-expanding *Leaves of Grass*, this volume included such favorites as "Pioneers! O Pioneers!" and "Beat! Beat! Drums." A supplement published after Lincoln's death contained "O Captain! My Captain!" and "When Lilacs Last in the Dooryard Bloom'd."

Winslow Homer's *Prisoners from the Front* presented a series of paintings depicting the plight of men at the·front during the Civil War. Homer, now 25, had been engaged by *Harper's Weekly* as a special correspondent and artist.

Nov 18: Mark Twain (Samuel Langhorne Clemens) was catapulted to fame when his version of a California tall tale, "Jim Smiley and His Jumping Frog," was printed in the New York *Saturday Press.* It was quickly reprinted by major newspapers across the country. It is now known under the title "The Celebrated Jumping Frog of Calaveras County."

III. Business and Industry
Education
Philosophy and Religion
Science

Women were slowly being accepted in the professions and the sciences. Among them was Maria Mitchell, an astronomer. She discovered a comet in 1847. In 1865 she became the first woman professor of astronomy in the U.S., being appointed to a chair at Vassar College. Mitchell was noted especially for her studies of satellites, nebulas, and sunspots. She was the first woman to be elected to the American Academy of Arts and Sciences. Her reputation in the U.S. and abroad was a significant reflection of the rising reputation of Vassar.

Free delivery of mail was provided in all cities with populations of 50,000 or more.

Louis Agassiz began a 19-month expedition with his wife and six assistants to study the natural history of Brazil and add to his collection of specimens. Agassiz, who had become a naturalized American citizen, began his career at the University of Munich where, at 21, he published *The Fishes of Brazil* (1829), the most important work yet published in ichthyology. The study was based on a collection brought back to Germany by an expedition to Brazil in 1821. Agassiz always cherished the ambition to see the natural life of Brazil firsthand. The trip was financed primarily by Nathaniel Thayer of Boston, but other people, organizations, and government officials in the U.S. and Brazil also lent support. *A Journey to Brazil*, by Mrs. Agassiz, published in 1868, recounted the day-to-day experiences of the expedition.

IV. Fashion
Folkways
Holidays
Social Issues and Crime
Sports

Beards were fashionable at this time. Scarcely a picture exists of a Civil War general on either side who did not sport one. All presidents from Ulysses S. Grant (elected in 1868) to Chester A. Arthur had beards. Pres. Grover Cleveland (elected in 1884) broke the custom, although he had a large, drooping mustache. Men's clothing continued to be plain and conservative. Collars, cravats, and waistcoats were worn regardless of the weather, although some men were beginning to wear white linen or seersucker suits in summer.

Clara Barton was placed in charge of a government-sponsored search for missing soldiers of the Civil War. During the war, as a personal enterprise, she had obtained and distributed hospital supplies for Union troops. Her distribution agency often delivered supplies right at the front.

The popular **Stetson hat** had its origin this year when John Batterson Stetson opened a one-man hat factory in Philadelphia, Pa. Stetson, the son of a hatmaker, had previously attempted to establish himself in the business, but ill health had forced him to travel to Illinois, Missouri, and Colorado. During his travels he had noticed the style of hat favored by westerners and, after a slow start in Philadelphia, he began to design new hats based on the western styles. His business began to expand rapidly. By 1906 he employed 3500 workers and was selling 2,000,000 hats a year. The Stetson hat had a broad brim and its crown was tall enough to sport ten ornamental braids, known as galloons. It was the mispronunciation of the word *galloon* that gave the world the term *ten-gallon hat.*

Mar 4: Pres. **Lincoln's second inaugural address** brought tears to the eyes of many in the audience. It was a silent audience, befitting an occasion made even more solemn by Lincoln's words. The war was not over, but there was room for hope, if not certainty. Lincoln began by saying that the occasion did not call for an extended address, such as the one delivered at his first inaugural. The audience was as familiar as he with the progress of the war. Lincoln asked his listeners to relive with him the forebodings of four years before, when both sides were rushing toward war, though "neither party expected the magnitude or duration which it has already attained. Neither anticipated that the cause of the conflict might cease before the conflict itself should cease. Each looked for an easier triumph and a result less fundamental and astonishing. Both read the same Bible and pray to the same God. Each invokes His aid against the other. It may seem strange that any man should dare to ask a just God's assistance in wringing bread from the sweat of other men's faces; but let us judge not, that we be not judged." He expressed the common hope that the war would soon end, and bade his hearers to continue what they had begun: "With malice toward none, with charity for all, with firmness in the right, as God gives us to see the right, let us strive on to finish the work we are in, to bind up the nation's wounds, to care for him who shall have borne the battle, and for his widow and orphans; to do all which may achieve and cherish a just and lasting peace among ourselves and with all nations." The address was not followed by any demonstration, either public or personal, to indicate to Lincoln whether it had been effective. He felt himself that it was among the best he had ever delivered, and he expressed this sentiment in a letter to Thurlow Weed, thanking Weed for a few words of congratulation.

May 5: The **first railroad train robbery** took place at dawn at North Bend, Ohio, when an Ohio & Mississippi Railroad train was derailed by a gang. Male passengers were robbed and the express car looted.

Dec 24: The **Ku Klux Klan** had its beginning in the law office of Thomas M. Jones in Pulaski, Tenn. The name evolved from Greek *kyklos* (circle), suggested by John B. Kennedy. It was broken up into the more euphonious Ku Klux by James R. Crowe, who added Klan as a reflection of the predominantly Scotch-Irish population of the area.

1866

I. Civil Rights
Exploration and Settlement
Government
Statistics
Wars

Reconstruction, the process of dealing with the former Confederate states and the millions of freed black slaves, was to occupy the government and the nation for the next decade. Pres. Andrew Johnson proposed fairly lenient treatment of the secessionists but showed no interest in securing civil rights for blacks. Opposing him was a group of radical Republicans who wanted the South severely punished. The congressional election in the fall gave the radicals an overwhelming victory that paved the way for harsh treatment of the South.

A **cholera** epidemic decimated many U.S. cities. About 200 a day died in St. Louis, Mo., during the height of the epidemic.

1866-1867: In **congressional elections** the Republicans held a Senate majority of 42–11, the Democrats gaining one seat. In the House the Republican majority was 143–49.

Feb 19: The **New Freedmen's Bureau bill** was passed by Congress. The law authorized military trials for those accused of depriving newly freed blacks of their civil rights. Pres. Andrew Johnson vetoed the bill on the grounds that it violated the Fifth Amendment, and that the legislation affected 11 southern states not represented in Congress. The veto served to widen the rift between Congress and the president. Legislators retaliated by overriding the veto on July 16.

Apr 2: The **state of insurrection** was declared over by presidential proclamation in Georgia, South Carolina, Virginia, North Carolina, Tennessee, Alabama, Mississippi, Louisiana, Arkansas, and Florida. On Aug. 2 the president announced that the insurrection was at an end in Texas, and that civil authority existed in the U.S.

Apr 9: A **Civil Rights Act** was passed over Pres. Johnson's veto. It granted citizenship to all persons born in the U.S., except Indians. It declared that all citizens had the same civil rights and provided for the punishment of persons who prevented free exercise of these rights. The Fourteenth Amendment was proposed when the constitutionality of the first section of this act was questioned.

II. Architecture
    Arts and Music
    Popular Entertainment
    Publishing
    Theater

Southern writers of the war and postwar period tended to idealize both the recent and the colonial past, perhaps to compensate for loss of the struggle for secession. One such writer was John Esten Cooke, a Virginian who had served as a captain in the Confederate army. This year Cooke began a series of wartime romances with the publication of *Surry of Eagle's Nest.* The series continued with *Hilt to Hilt* (1869), *Mohun* (1869), and *Hammer and Rapier*

(1871). Cooke's writing showed sentimentality, but he achieved his aim: to entertain. Cooke also wrote *Life of Stonewall Jackson* (1863) and *Life of General Robert E. Lee* (1871).

Among the **books published** this year was *Snow-Bound,* the most famous poem by John Greenleaf Whittier. Drawing on his memories of youth and home life in rural New England, Whittier painted an inviting picture of a homestead buried in snow. The poem described the blazing hearth, the family members, the sparkling snowbanks, the schoolmaster, etc. Other books published this year included *Surry of Eagle's Nest* by John Esten Cooke, which harked back to the chivalry of antebellum Virginia and evoked vivid pictures of southern leaders and Civil War battles; and *Venetian Life* by William Dean Howells, who served as U.S. consul to Venice throughout the Civil War and described his impressions of the city, its life and literature.

III. Business and Industry
Education
Philosophy and Religion
Science

The steadily growing movement to promote animal welfare scored a major victory this year with the founding on Apr. 10 of the American Society for the Prevention of Cruelty to Animals. It was patterned after the Royal Society for the Prevention of Cruelty to Animals in England, which had been founded in 1824. The founder and first president of the ASPCA was the philanthropist Henry Bergh. Its purpose was to shelter homeless animals, help enforce game laws, and guide farmers in caring for livestock.

Apr. 1: Western Union, with capital of about $40,000,000, absorbed the U.S. Telegraph Company, with $6,000,000 worth of shares. This was on the tenth anniversary of the day that Western Union was named. The absorption of U.S. Telegraph made Western Union the first complete monopoly serving all parts of the country with uniform rates.

July 27: Final laying of the **Atlantic cable** between Great Britain and the U.S. was completed when the steamship *Great Eastern* reached the U.S. The final cable-laying voyage of the *Great Eastern* took two weeks, July 13 to July 27. The previous year the steamship had attempted to complete the laying of the cable, only to have it break in mid-ocean. Success came after 12 years of effort. Cyrus Field chartered his company on May 6, 1854, with Peter Cooper, Moses Taylor, Marshall Roberts, and Chandler White on the board of directors. Six hundred men worked on the first line, which had to be cut at sea because of a gale. Seven more efforts were needed before the cable was completed. A cable laid in 1858 was able to carry a message, but was probably badly insulated, and went out after three weeks of operation.

IV. Fashion
Folkways
Holidays
Social Issues and Crime
Sports

A lighter and more daring form of entertainment heralded the coming of what was to be known as burlesque. The first long-running musical show on Broadway, combining melodrama and ballet in a lavish production, was *The Black Crook*, which opened on Sept. 12 at Niblo's Garden and ran for 474 performances. Some considered it immoral because of its 50 lightly clad dancing girls. Even more daring was *British Blondes*, imported from England two years later. It played around the country for 20 years.

The expression **"Forty acres and a mule"** gained currency during the Reconstruction period. Many freed blacks had their hopes built up by the promise that Congress would divide southern estates and distribute acreage to each freed slave. The expression came to characterize vain expectations foisted on blacks by Reconstructionists.

1867

I. Civil Rights
   Exploration and Settlement
   Government
   Statistics
   Wars

Purchase of Alaska, 586,400 sq. mi. of almost un-known land in the far northwest of North America, added an unusual chapter to the story of the expansion of the U.S. On Mar. 30, 1867, Sec. of State William Henry Seward concluded negotiations with Russia whereby the U.S. agreed to pay $7,200,000, about two cents an acre, for the territory. The Senate ratified the purchase on Apr. 9, and ownership was transferred on Oct. 18. Alaska was known to be rich in furs and fish, but otherwise it seemed useless. It was many years before the natural riches of Alaska were appreciated and Americans began to settle it as a new frontier.

Jan 8: Suffrage was given to blacks in Washington, D.C., by a bill passed over Pres. Andrew Johnson's veto.

Mar 1: Nebraska was admitted as a state, the 37th to join the Union.

Mar 2: The **first Reconstruction Act** was passed by Congress over Pres. Johnson's veto. The bill imposed martial law on the southern states, which were split into five districts, and provided for the restoration of civil government as soon as the states were restored into the Union and passed the Fourteenth Amendment.

Mar 2: The **Tenure of Office Act** was passed. In substance, it denied power to the president to remove officials who had been appointed by and with the consent of the Senate. This act was ruled unconstitutional by the Court of Claims in 1926 in the case of *Myers v. U.S.*

Mar 23: The **second Reconstruction Act** was passed over Pres. Johnson's veto. It provided for the registration of all qualified voters, who were subsequently to decide on readmittance to the Union.

July 19: The **third Reconstruction Act** was passed over Pres. Johnson's veto. The bill was essentially a restatement of the two previous acts except for the added provision that the Fifteenth Amendment must be ratified before the southern states could be admitted to the Union.

II. Architecture
Arts and Music
Popular Entertainment
Publishing
Theater

In keeping with the spirit of the times were the novels of Horatio Alger, Jr. The mid-nineteenth century was an age when many proclaimed the virtues of the self-made man. Alger's books gave the formula for success. His first of the Ragged Dick series appeared in 1867. Like all those to come, it preached hard work and resistance to temptation as the road to wealth and renown. In most of the books, though, the young hero first gets a break by catching the eye of a well-to-do patron, perhaps by rescuing his pretty daughter from a runaway horse. Alger followed with the Luck and Pluck series (1869) and Tattered Tom tales (1871). These stories found a ready market in the steady wave of boys moving from farms or small towns to the cities to seek work. More than 20,000,000 copies of Alger's novels were sold.

Dec 2: Charles Dickens gave his first reading in a theater in New York City. This was his second visit to the U.S. Before the box office opened, people were standing in two lines, almost a mile long, waiting for tickets. Scalpers were asking $20 for a ticket. Thirty-one different editions of Dickens's collected works were published in 1867.

III. Business and Industry
Education
Philosophy and Religion
Science

The first organization of American farmers was founded in 1867 when Oliver H. Kelley, a Minnesota farmer and an employee of the Bureau of Agriculture in Washington, D.C., established the National Grange of the Patrons of Husbandry. The Grange movement had a slow start, but it greatly expanded as a result of the panic of 1873 and reached a membership peak of 858,000 in 1875. The Grange began as a social and educational organization but soon became involved in politics. Its main targets were the railroads and the owners of grain storage elevators who, the Grange claimed, charged exorbitant prices for their services. As a result of pressure from the Grange, some midwestern states passed laws to limit such rates.

The **eight-hour day,** a main goal of labor unions, was enacted in Illinois, New York, and Missouri, but it was not enforced.

A major **contribution to education** in the postwar South was made by George Peabody with a fund of $3,500,000. The Peabody fund hastened construction of town and city schools and provided for the training of teachers.

Cigarettes began to appear in America. Cigarette production had formerly been confined to Europe. Production in America did not provide a major source of revenue until the 1880s.

The **first elevated railroad** in America began operation in New York City. Built by the West Side Elevated Railroad Company, its single track ran from Battery Place through Greenwich St. and 9th Ave. to 30th St.

IV. Fashion
Folkways
Holidays
Social Issues and Crime
Sports

Life in the mining towns of the far West was boisterous and extravagant. The height of fun and games was achieved in Virginia City, Nev., site of the fabulous Comstock Lode, in the period from 1860 to 1880. The town had more than 100 saloons, five legitimate theaters, six variety houses, and other establishments such as dance halls. The single most popular performer was Adah Isaacs Menken, known for performing while clad only in a flimsy gown.

The phrase **Seward's folly** was coined to characterize the purchase of Alaska from Russia. The purchase was negotiated by Sec. of State William Henry Seward. Alaska was also ridiculed as *Seward's icebox*.

"Now is the time for all good men to come to the aid of the party," a slogan created by Charles Weller, a court reporter, was used to test the efficiency of the first practical typewriter, invented by his friend, Christopher Sholes.

June 19: The **first annual Belmont Stakes** was won by Ruthless, with a time of 3:05. The jockey was J. Gilpatrick. The race was held at Jerome Park, N.Y., from 1867 to 1889; at Morris Park, N.Y., from 1890 to 1905; and at Belmont Park, N.Y., from 1906 to the present. In the beginning the distance was $1\frac{5}{8}$ miles, but it has been changed from time to time. The Belmont Stakes is the oldest of the three classic American races.

1868

I. Civil Rights
   Exploration and Settlement
   Government
   Statistics
   Wars

For the first time in the nation's history a president was impeached. Pres. Andrew Johnson was accused by Congress of having violated the Tenure of Office Act of 1867, which forbade the president to discharge any federal officeholder appointed "by and with the consent of the Senate." Johnson tested the act by removing Sec. of War Edwin M. Stanton on Feb. 21. The impeachment was brought largely because the radical Republicans bitterly opposed Johnson's plans for Reconstruction. Johnson's firing of Stanton gave them the opportunity they had been seeking. On Feb. 24 the House of Representatives voted to impeach. The trial, conducted by the Senate, began on Mar. 13. On May 16 and again on May 26 the Senate voted on the charges brought against Pres. Johnson. Both times the vote was 35 for conviction and 19 for acquittal. Because a two-thirds vote was needed to convict, Johnson was judged not guilty. The radicals then dropped the matter.

Susan B. Anthony founded the suffragette newspaper *The Revolution*. It adopted the motto "The true Republic—men, their rights and nothing more; women, their rights and nothing less."

The **Ku Klux Klan** formulated its revised constitution, which declared that the organization was to be guided by chivalry, humanity, mercy, and patriotism. The southern states were to be its empire, with the grand wizard as supreme leader and its body of officers designated as "ghouls." In reality, the order was formed to intimidate blacks and carpetbaggers and to regain white supremacy in the South.

1868-1869: In **congressional elections** the Republicans kept majorities in both houses: 56–11 in the Senate and 149–63 in the House.

Mar 11: The **fourth Reconstruction Act** was passed. Under its provisions a majority of the votes actually cast would decide the adoption or rejection of a state constitution (the second Reconstruction Act required a majority of the registered voters). The measure was taken to counter the intimidation of black voters by the Ku Klux Klan and disenfranchised whites.

May 20-21: The **Republican National Convention** nominated Gen. Ulysses S. Grant for the presidency and Schuyler Colfax of Indiana for the vice presidency. At the same meeting, the convention adopted the name National Republican Party.

June 25: Congress passed a law providing an **eight-hour day** for laborers and workmen employed by the government. The concept of the eight-hour day was still something of a novelty, although ineffectual eight-hour laws had already been passed in a few states.

June 25: Congressional representation was granted to North Carolina, South Carolina, Louisiana, Georgia, Alabama, and Florida by an omnibus bill passed over Pres. Johnson's veto.

July 4-9: The **Democratic National Convention** nominated Horatio Seymour of New York for the presidency and Francis P. Blair, Jr., of Missouri for the vice presidency.

July 28: The **Fourteenth Amendment,** which granted citizenship to all those born or naturalized in the U.S., notably slaves freed by the Civil War, was adopted. It also validated debts incurred during the Civil War but denied federal or state responsibility for any debts incurred in aid of conspiracy or insurrection against the U.S.

Oct 21: A severe **earthquake** rocked San Francisco, Calif., causing about $3,000,000 in property damage.

Nov 3: Ulysses S. Grant was elected president of the United States, defeating Horatio Seymour. Schuyler

Colfax was elected vice president. Grant's popular majority was a scant 306,000 out of 5,715,000 votes, although his margin in the electoral college count was 214 to 80. The black vote, which totaled over 700,000, decided the election for Grant.

Dec 25: Unqualified **amnesty** was granted by presidential proclamation to all who participated in the "insurrection or rebellion" against the U.S.

II. Architecture
Arts and Music
Popular Entertainment
Publishing
Theater

The literary genre known as juvenile or children's literature received new vitality this year with publication of *Little Women* by Louisa May Alcott, daughter of A. Bronson Alcott. Up to this time, many of the books intended for children moralized to the extent that they did not entertain their readers. Miss Alcott's book, based on her own family experiences, was more realistic and less sentimental than most. The book became the most popular girls' story in American literature and has sold more than 2,000,000 copies. It earned its author about $200,000 by the time she died. Miss Alcott also wrote *Little Men* (1871), *Jo's Boys* (1886), and other books. Her writings brought financial security to her family, the head of which was well-intentioned but improvident. Miss Alcott greatly influenced the trend of juvenile literature by avoiding didacticism and by using characters drawn from life.

Hiram Powers completed his celebrated sculpture *Clytie*. Powers, who had settled in Florence, Italy, in 1837, was then enjoying great popularity, largely on the strength of such works as his statue of *Daniel Webster* (1859) in front of the Boston State House, as well as works in marble of other famous Americans, including John C. Calhoun, Andrew Jackson, and George Washington.

III. Business and Industry
Education
Philosophy and Religion
Science

As important as rail transportation had become, it still remained potentially dangerous for both passengers and freight. This year George Westinghouse solved a major problem with the invention of the air brake. This allowed equal and simultaneous braking, through one control, of each car in a train, and also provided for automatic braking if cars should accidentally uncouple or brake lines become disabled. Westinghouse's system was first put to use on a train this year. It made possible the safe braking of both long trains and high-speed trains, paving the way for a revolution in rail travel.

The **open-hearth process** in the American steel industry was introduced from England by Abram S. Hewitt in Trenton, N.J. The process expanded steel production by making more ore available through the extraction of sulfur and phosphorus.

Jan 16: A patent for a **refrigerator car** was granted to William Davis, a fish dealer in Detroit, Mich. Davis, wanting to increase his area of sales, had worked for many years to develop his "ice box on wheels." He used his new invention for the transportation of fish and fruit. He also designed the first railroad refrigerated car, which was built in 1869.

June 23: Two patents for the **typewriter** were granted to Christopher Sholes, Samuel Soulé, and Carlos Glidden. For five years afterward, Sholes worked to complete his machine but did not succeed. In 1871 he received an additional patent for improvements he had made to his original invention. Two years later he sold his rights to the Remington Arms Company for $12,000. Remington mechanics quickly converted Sholes's crude machine into a marketable product. The Remington Company had an improved model by 1873. Sholes carried on with ideas for improvements and took out another patent in 1875, but finally turned all of his work over to Remington,

which marketed the machine as the Remington typewriter.

IV. Fashion
Folkways
Holidays
Social Issues and Crime
Sports

Ice skating, which had begun a rise in popularity
around the 1850s, had become a major winter pastime. Steel skates had first been made in the 1850s.
They had straps and clamps to fasten them to shoes.
In the 1860s Jackson Haines, an American, invented
figure skating. By 1868 ice skating was so widespread
that a skating congress was held in Pittsburgh to set
regulations and encourage the sport. In a single winter some 200,000 skaters used the lakes in New York
City's Central Park. In Boston daily excursion trains
carried a thousand or more skaters to Jamaica Pond.
One reason for the sport's popularity was that both
sexes could participate, making skating a social as
well as athletic occasion.

The new sport of **velociped ing** (cycling) attained
great vogue in America three years after it had been
perfected in Paris. Schools for all ages and both sexes
were set up throughout the large cities. Newspapers
reported on the vogue. The fact that women could
participate added greatly to its rapid spread.

The **Benevolent Protective Order of Elks** was
formed in New York City.

May 30: Decoration Day was celebrated nationally for
the first time. The day was chosen by John A. Logan,
national commander of the Grand Army of the Republic, for decoration of Civil War graves. Previously, local communities had held decoration days at
various times.

Nov 11: The first indoor **amateur track and field meet**
was held by the New York Athletic Club. The club,
which had been organized Sept. 8, later held outdoor
meets, established rules for the conduct of meets, and

built the first cinder track. It continues to this day to promote track and field and other sports.

1869

I. Civil Rights
Exploration and Settlement
Government
Statistics
Wars

This year, Ulysses S. Grant was inaugurated 18th president of the United States. After a checkered career in and out of the Army, Grant began to rise in public esteem through his military exploits in the Civil War. Until 1862 it had seemed as though no Union commander was competent to win the war. By war's end Grant had become, after Abraham Lincoln, the leading figure in the Union war effort. Although Grant had had nothing to do with politics, the Republicans in 1868 were glad to nominate him, a certain winner, for the presidency. As it turned out, while Grant was honest and well-intentioned, he had almost none of the abilities required in a president and was fated to be the victim of dishonest friends and associates.

Arabella Mansfield was admitted to the Iowa bar as the **first woman lawyer** in the U.S. and the first woman lawyer in America since Mistress Margaret Brent, attorney for Cecilius Calvert, lord proprietor of Maryland in the 1640s.

Feb 6: The first caricature of **Uncle Sam** with chin whiskers appeared in *Harper's Weekly*. The figure had been used without whiskers by cartoonists for several years and had evolved from the Revolutionary caricature of Brother Jonathan. After 1869 Uncle

Sam became a stock device of political cartoonists.

Apr 10: The **Fifteenth Amendment** was ratified by Georgia, Mississippi, Texas, and Virginia, and these states were then readmitted into the Union. This amendment states that suffrage shall not be denied or abridged because of race, color, or previous condition of servitude.

May 15: The **National Woman Suffrage Association** was formed. Elizabeth Cady Stanton was chosen as first president and held the post until 1890. The other chief founder of the association was Susan B. Anthony.

Sep 1: The **Prohibition Party** was organized during the National Prohibition Convention in Chicago. The convention was called by the National Temperance Convention in Cleveland.

Dec 10: The **first women's suffrage** in the U.S. was granted by Wyoming Territory.

II. Architecture
   Arts and Music
   Popular Entertainment
   Publishing
   Theater

Musical performances were becoming widely available, although many of those providing music for American audiences were born abroad. One of the most able and energetic among them was Theodore Thomas, who came from Germany in 1845 and organized his own orchestra in 1862. Every year from 1869 to 1878 he toured the U.S. with the orchestra, introducing to Americans major works by Franz Liszt, Richard Wagner, Johannes Brahms, and others.

Among **books published** this year was *Innocents Abroad* by Mark Twain, a collection of articles written by Twain during a tour of Europe and the Near East. The extremely popular and humorous book poked fun at Old World institutions and distorted historical facts. Also published this year was *Oldtown Folks* by Harriet Beecher Stowe. The series of sketches, which demonstrated admirable use of local color, was based on Mrs. Stowe's memories of Litchfield, Conn., and those of her husband. Her description of New England life contributed to the later success of Sarah Orne Jewett and Mary Wilkins Freeman.

III. Business and Industry
Education
Philosophy and Religion
Science

Higher education was undergoing changes in the U.S., particularly at Harvard College in Cambridge, Mass., where Charles W. Eliot was inaugurated president on Mar. 10. Eliot was the first non-clergyman to hold the post and was an administrator rather than a teacher. He changed Harvard from a small undergraduate college into a modern university. Eliot introduced the elective system, organized graduate schools, insisted on written exams, and relaxed student discipline. He greatly influenced higher education throughout the country.

Henry J. Heinz and L. C. Noble established a food-packing company at Sharpsburg, Pa. Its first product was grated horseradish. Heinz eventually had widespread commercial success.

Jan 23: The **first state bureau of labor** in the U.S. was organized in Massachusetts.

May 10: The **first transcontinental railroad** in the U.S. was completed at Promontory Point, Utah, with the linkup of the Central Pacific Railroad from the west and the Union Pacific Railroad from the east.

Sep 24: Black Friday, a day of financial panic on Wall Street caused by the manipulation of Jay Gould and James Fisk, ruined thousands of gold speculators. In an attempt to corner the gold market, Gould and Fisk tried to keep Pres. Grant from selling government gold, and assured the public that they had been successful. However, Grant ordered the sale of $4,000,000 in gold, forcing the price down.

IV. **Fashion**
   Folkways
   Holidays
   Social Issues and Crime
   Sports

Although boxing would not become a major American sport until the 1880s, when John L. Sullivan popularized it, an important bare knuckle boxing match was fought this year between Tom Allen, an English boxer who had moved to the U.S., and Mike McCoole, an American who claimed the U.S. title. Allen challenged McCoole and the two squared off in St. Louis on June 15. McCoole won the fight on a ninth-round foul and claimed the American championship. The following year Allen lost a bid for the international bare knuckle championship. Allen and McCoole met again in 1873 for a bout near St. Louis. Allen beat McCoole, this time in seven rounds. McCoole quit the ring. Allen claimed the world championship but was whipped soundly in 1876 by the English fighter Joe Goss in a 27-round bout in Kentucky.

Mar 15: The **first professional baseball team** was the Cincinnati Red Stockings. The team announced regular payments to players and began a successful eight-month tour of the East and Middle West.

Nov 6: The **first intercollegiate football game** was played at New Brunswick, N.J. Rutgers beat Princeton 6–4 in a game more like soccer than football. There were 25 men on each team, and no running with the ball was allowed.

1870

I. Civil Rights
Exploration and Settlement
Government
Statistics
Wars

A short chapter in the history of American expansion ended this year in a personal defeat for Pres. Ulysses S. Grant. A group of land speculators interested Pres. Grant in a scheme to annex the Dominican Republic, which had gained independence from Spain in 1865. Ignoring the State Department and normal diplomatic procedure, Grant sent his private secretary, Orville E. Babcock, to negotiate a treaty of annexation. This treaty was submitted to the Senate on Jan. 10, and although Grant did his best to force its acceptance, the Senate rejected it on June 30.

The ninth U.S. **Census** recorded a population of 39,818,449. America's center of population was located 48 miles east by north of Cincinnati, Ohio.

1870-1871: In **congressional elections** the Democrats gained six seats in the Senate, but the Republicans still enjoyed a 52–17 majority, with five seats going to minor parties. In the House the Republicans lost 31 seats but still led 134–104, with five seats going to minor parties.

Jan 15: The first political cartoon to use the **donkey** as a symbol for the Democratic Party appeared in *Harper's Weekly.* The cartoon, by Thomas Nast, was called "A Live Jackass Kicking a Dead Lion."

Feb 25: The **first black in Congress,** Sen. Hiram R. Revels, Republican of Mississippi, took his seat. The first black member of the House was Joseph H.

Rainey, Republican of South Carolina, who also entered Congress this year.

Mar 30: The **Fifteenth Amendment was adopted.** It stipulated that no state shall deprive any citizen of the right to vote because of race, color, or previous condition of servitude.

June 22: Congress passed an act to create the **Department of Justice** under direction of the attorney general. The department today supervises all government police, the FBI, and the Bureau of Prisons.

Dec: The first **impeachment** of a state governor in the U.S. was conducted against Gov. William Woods Holden, the highly unpopular "scalawag" governor of North Carolina. He was replaced by Gov. Tod R. Caldwell.

II. Architecture
   Arts and Music
   Popular Entertainment
   Publishing
   Theater

John La Farge, a talented author and artist, was a pioneer in the art of stained glass. His celebrated work *Battle Window,* in Memorial Hall at Harvard University, was installed in 1870. In 1876 he did the mural decorations for Trinity Church in Boston. La Farge also executed stained glass windows for churches in Buffalo, N.Y., and Worcester, Mass., and for the chapel of Columbia University in New York City. What is referred to as American glass is an outgrowth of his experimentation.

Among the **books published** this year was *The Story of a Bad Boy,* a favorite boys' book by Thomas Bailey Aldrich. Semiautobiographical, the book provided a fresh account of boyhood, eschewing the moralizing that characterized most juvenile fiction. Other books published this year included the *Rubáiyát* of Omar Khayyám, translated by Edward Fitzgerald, and *The Luck of Roaring Camp and Other*

Sketches by Bret Harte, which catapulted the author to international fame.

Feb 14: Frontier drama burst on the stage with the popular *Kit the Arkansas Traveler* by Thomas Blades DeWalden. It was followed by *Horizon* (1871) by Augustin Daly, *Davy Crockett* (1872) by Frank Murdock, *The Gilded Age* (1874) by Mark Twain and Charles Dudley Warner, *The Two Men from Sandy Bar* (1876) by Bret Harte, and *The Danites in the Sierras* (1877) by Joaquin Miller.

III. Business and Industry
Education
Philosophy and Religion
Science

Formation of the Standard Oil Company this year marked the start of what was to become the biggest influence by far in the growing oil industry, and the first industrial combination to exercise a virtual monopoly. The moving spirit in the company was John D. Rockefeller, who had begun his career as a bookkeeper in Cleveland, Ohio, center of the oil refining industry at this time. Rockefeller and his partners, including his brother William, started with two refineries in Cleveland and a sales agency in New York City. From this modest beginning, Rockefeller set out to control not only the refining of oil but also its transportation from the oil fields and marketing of the finished product.

The **Great Atlantic and Pacific Tea Company** was organized "for the purpose of importing and distributing pure and reliable teas and coffees and subjecting the purchaser to but one profit from the foreign factor." The company grew into the largest single chain of grocery stores in the U.S. in terms of volume of business. The company's early advertising stressed that the chain could provide bargains by eliminating middlemen from grocery sales.

The **refrigerated railroad car** emerged in the 1870s as an important factor in the development of certain industries. Pioneer development of the refrigerated car is credited to Gustavus Franklin Swift, who in the 1870s began to ship dressed beef from Chicago to the East, the first time this was done successfully. He employed a railroad car in which fresh air was forced over ice and then circulated through the storage compartments. George Henry Hammond also pioneered at about this time in the use of refrigerated cars, shipping meat from Omaha, Nebr., and from Hammond, Ind.

The **growth of unions** in America was reflected in a total membership of 300,000.

Jan 2: Construction of the **Brooklyn Bridge** began. It was to span the East R. from Park Row, Manhattan, to Sands and Washington streets in Brooklyn.

Feb 9: The **U.S. Weather Bureau** was established by Congress. Originally part of the Signal Corps, it became part of the Department of Agriculture on July 1, 1891. On June 30, 1940, it was transferred to the Commerce Department.

IV. Fashion
Folkways
Holidays
Social Issues and Crime
Sports

The sporting year was marked by an important event in international yachting. For the first time since the U.S. won the America's Cup from England in 1851, a British yacht issued a challenge to win it back. Accordingly, on Aug. 8 in New York Bay, the *Cambria* sailed against 23 American boats of the New York Yacht Club. The winner was *Magic,* owned by Franklin Osgood. *Cambria* came in tenth. The bay was dotted with ships of all descriptions, and an estimated 100,000 people lined the shores to see the spectacle.

The craze for **roller skating** spread throughout the

U.S. as it did throughout the world. By 1863 four rollers had been added to "parlor skates" and a young skater, William H. Fuller, developed the art of figure skating, which he displayed on a tour around the world.

The **first boardwalk** in America was completed at Atlantic City, N.J.

Yale and Harvard met in a **crew race** on a circular course at Worcester, Mass. Yale came in first but was disqualified for having run into the Harvard team.

Aug 16: Fred Goldsmith demonstrated that the **curve ball** was not an optical illusion. Before a large crowd at the Capitoline Grounds, Brooklyn, N.Y., Goldsmith set up three poles in a straight line and hurled a ball that went to the right of the first pole, to the left of the second, and to the right of the third.

1871

I. Civil Rights
Exploration and Settlement
Government
Statistics
Wars

One of the great disasters in American history occurred between Oct. 8 and Oct. 11, when Chicago was burned nearly to the ground. According to legend, the fire began when a cow belonging to a Mrs. O'Leary kicked over a lantern. In fact, the fire started in the barn of a laborer named Patrick O'Leary, who lived on DeKoven Street on the West Side. Before the fire was out, about 17,500 buildings had been destroyed over an area of 2124 acres, with damage estimated at about $200,000,000. Some 250 people were killed and about 98,500 left homeless. It was a tribute to the spirit of the city and the times that rebuilding began at once and recovery took a surprisingly short time. Lost to fire was the original draft of Pres. Abraham Lincoln's Emancipation Proclamation, destroyed when the Chicago Historical Society building burned.

Feb 28: A **federal election law** was passed, providing for federal supervision of elections in any city having more than 20,000 inhabitants. The measure was taken primarily to protect black voters in the South.

Mar 3: The **Indian Appropriation Act** was passed. It made all Indians national wards and nullified all Indian treaties.

Mar 4: Pres. Ulysses S. Grant established the **first civil service commission,** headed by George William Curtis of New York City. The unwillingness of Congress to make additional appropriations rendered the commission ineffective.

May 8: The **Treaty of Washington** was signed between the U.S. and Great Britain at Washington, D.C. It provided for arbitration for the *Alabama* claims by an international tribunal to meet at Geneva. These claims were for damages to U.S. shipping during the Civil War by the raider *Alabama* and other Confederate vessels built or armed by the British. The treaty also renewed Canadian-American fishing arrangements in the North Atlantic.

II. Architecture
   Arts and Music
   Popular Entertainment
   Publishing
   Theater

America had never lacked for nature writers and in the later nineteenth century the best was John Burroughs, who followed in the footsteps of Ralph Waldo Emerson and Henry David Thoreau. His first work, *Wake-Robin*, was published this year. The book was poetic in manner, as was *Birds and Poets* (1877). *Wake-Robin* was an invitation to ornithology and imparted the author's enthusiasm for bird watching. Burroughs' later writings paid more attention to scientific observation, although in his final years he believed that the salvation of society depended more on teachers, prophets, poets, and mystics than on

Among **books published** this year was the best seller *The Hoosier Schoolmaster* by Edward Eggleston. A classic of regional literature, Eggleston's novel sold some 500,000 copies, a circulation never reached by Eggleston's *The Circuit Rider* (1874) or *Roxy* (1878), considered better novels. Also published this year were *Their Wedding Journey,* the first novel of William Dean Howells, a combination of travelogue and novel of manners tracing the honeymoon journey of the Marches (who appear in later novels) to Niagara, Montreal, and Quebec; and *Passage to India,* a collection of poems by Walt Whitman that reflected a broadening of the poet's scope and subject matter. In the 72 poems, Whitman's artistic powers embraced peoples of all lands.

Probably the **best-known painting** by an American, popularly known as *Whistler's Mother,* was exhibited by James McNeill Whistler at the Pennsylvania Academy of Fine Arts. It was entitled *Arrangement in Grey and Black.* Whistler remarked relative to the title that no one would have an interest in the identity of the sitter. Actually millions since have identified the canvas with their feelings for their own mothers.

III. Business and Industry
Education
Philosophy and Religion
Science

As communication and transportation improved, and as the U.S. came to be more concerned with events on other continents, an interest in religions other than Christianity was aroused. The outstanding scholar in this field was James Freeman Clarke, a Unitarian clergyman and liberal reformer. His *Ten Great Religions* (2 volumes, 1871–1883) was an important work in comparative religion. It went through 21 editions by 1886.

May 1: The **Legal Tender Act** was declared constitutional by a Supreme Court decision in the case of *Knox v. Lee.* Passed in 1862, when national credit was ebbing, the Legal Tender Act had authorized issuance of $450,000,000 in treasury notes, making them legal tender for all private debts and public dues except import duties and interest on public debt. A second act was passed in 1863. The Supreme Court, reduced to seven members, declared the Legal Tender Acts unconstitutional on Feb. 7, 1870, in the case of *Hepburn v. Griswold,* on the grounds that they exceeded any delegated or implied powers of Congress, violated the spirit of the Constitution, and deprived creditors of property without due process of law. Pres. Ulysses S. Grant made nominations to the empty Supreme Court posts on the same day the decision was handed down; four days later the Supreme Court voted to reargue the issues. The decision of May 1, 1871, found the power to issue legal tender implied in the power to coin money and wage war. It also declared that the Constitution forbade the states, but not Congress, from impairing contracts. Whether Pres. Grant actually packed the Court is still argued among historians.

IV. Fashion
Folkways
Holidays
Social Issues and Crime
Sports

An American type still popular in song, story, and movies is the cowboy of the western cattle country. He flourished from the late 1860s to the late 1880s, when cattle were driven long distances to market. The cowboy's heyday was brief; it was ended by the spread of railroad lines and by the fencing in of ranges and farms. The cowboy's life was not glamorous. It meant hard work, danger, and low pay. After a drive he would frequently spend all his pay in the saloons of such cow towns as Abilene, Kans.

Between 1867 and 1871 cowboys drove 1,460,000 cattle into Abilene, the first of the famous western railheads.

Mar 17: The **first professional baseball asssociation**, the National Association of Professional Baseball Players, was organized. It replaced the amateur National Association.

1872

I. Civil Rights
Exploration and Settlement
Government
Statistics
Wars

The presidential election campaign of 1872 was a strange one. As a result of the scandals in Pres. Ulysses S. Grant's administration, and because Grant sided with the radical Republicans in Reconstruction policies, many Republicans, liberals, and reformers split off to nominate their own candidate, Horace Greeley, editor of the New York *Tribune.* Greeley had been a leading figure in the antislavery movement and a key figure in the election of Abraham Lincoln. He was a champion of universal suffrage and other radical causes. He was also viewed by many as a champion of fads, a visionary. Even though the Democrats also nominated Greeley, Grant won the election handily. Greeley died less than a month after the election.

Susan B. Anthony tested the Fourteenth Amendment by leading a group of women to cast ballots in the presidential election. She was arrested, found guilty, and fined $100. She refused to pay the fine and never did. Her reward came 14 years after her death when in 1920 the Nineteenth Amendment, guaranteeing women's suffrage, was adopted.

1872-1873: In **congressional elections** the Republicans lost two Senate seats, for a 49–19 majority, with five seats held by minor parties. In the House, which had gained 50 seats since 1870, the Republicans made spectacular gains, leading 194–92, with 14 seats going to minor parties.

Feb 22: The **Prohibition Party** held its first national nominating convention in Columbus, Ohio. James Black of Pennsylvania was nominated for the presidency and the Rev. John Russell of Michigan for the vice presidency.

May 1: The first national convention of the **Liberal Republican Party nominated Horace Greeley** for the presidency and Gov. Benjamin Gratz Brown of Missouri for the vice presidency. The same slate was nominated by the Democratic convention on July 9.

June 5-6: The **Republican National Convention nominated Pres. Grant** for reelection. Sen. Henry Wilson of Massachusetts was nominated for the vice presidency. This was the first major party convention in which black delegates participated. Speeches were delivered from the rostrum by three black delegates, William E. Gray of Arkansas, B.B. Elliott of South Carolina, and John Roy Lynch of Mississippi.

July 9: The **Democratic National Convention nominated Horace Greeley,** editor of the New York *Tribune,* for the presidency and Gov. Benjamin Gratz Brown of Missouri for the vice presidency.

Nov 5: Ulysses S. Grant was reelected president of the United States, defeating Horace Greeley by an electoral vote of 286 to 66. Pres. Grant received a popular vote of 3,597,132 against 2,384,124 for Greeley.

II. Architecture
   Arts and Music
   Popular Entertainment
   Publishing
   Theater

Of the scores of magazines first published this year, two were especially notable. The first was *Publishers' Weekly*, originally issued with the title *The Publishers' and Stationers' Weekly Trade Circular*. Founded in New York City by Frederick Leypoldt, the first issue was dated Jan. 18, 1872. The second magazine of note was *Popular Science Monthly*, published by D. Appleton & Company and edited by Edward L. Youmans. Its first issue, which appeared in May 1872, carried the first part of *The Study of Sociology* by the British philosopher Herbert Spencer, and the first part of *Natural History of Man* by the French anthropologist Armand de Quatrefages. The magazine scored an immediate success, reflecting the growing American interest in science.

Among **books published** this year was *Roughing It* by Mark Twain, a "record of several years of variegated vagabondizing" in the West. A boisterous and exciting book, it described the rough-and-tumble life of the Nevada miners, stagecoach days on the Overland Trail, Western tall tales, hilarious optimism, and desperadoes and pioneers. Twain also included chapters on his stay in Hawaii. Other books published this year included *The Poet of the Breakfast Table* by Oliver Wendell Holmes; and *Barriers Burned Away* by Edward Payson Roe, a best-selling novel based on the Chicago fire of 1871.

III. Business and Industry
    Education
    Philosophy and Religion
    Science

A new era in retail merchandising began in 1872 with the establishment of Montgomery Ward & Company in Chicago. Its founder was Aaron Montgomery Ward, a clerk and traveling salesman who thought he could sell goods directly to people in rural areas by mail. He began with a one-sheet leaflet that offered bargains to Granges. Ward's business expanded and was copied by others.

The **Jehovah's Witnesses** was organized by Charles Taze Russell, a lay member of the Presbyterian Church. First called Russellites, International Bible Students, and Millennial Darwinists, Russell's fundamental followers officially became Jehovah's Witnesses in 1931. In 1939 the sect was incorporated in New York as the Watch Tower Bible and Tract Society.

The **Burbank potato** had its origin this year when Luther Burbank found an Early Rose potato plant that had produced a seed ball, a rare event for that type of potato. Burbank had bought a 17-acre plot in Lunenburg, Mass., in 1871 and had taken up market gardening as a livelihood. He collected the seeds and planted them the following year. Of the 23 seeds, only two produced plants worth investigating. In 1874 Burbank grew both varieties, then picked the more promising one. In Oct. 1875 Burbank sold this potato variety to James J.H. Gregory of Marblehead, Mass., for $150 and moved to California to continue his horticultural research. Gregory named the new variety the Burbank and made a fortune.

IV. Fashion
   Folkways
   Holidays
   Social Issues and Crime
   Sports

The nation was in its Gilded Age, and those who were reaping fortunes from enterprises honest or dishonest were eager to display their new wealth. Society in New York City came to be based almost entirely on wealth. A self-appointed leader of this glittering society was Ward McAllister, who had married a millionaire's daughter. In 1872 he chose a group of men from prominent New York families who were to lead society as "patriarchs." McAllister also groomed Mrs. William Astor to become the grande dame of New York high society.

Yellowstone National Park Reserve was established for the enjoyment of the public. It was designated the first Federal Forest Reserve by Congress in 1891. John Colter, a member of the Lewis and Clark expedition, is credited with reaching the region in 1806. His report on his adventures and the things he saw set the pattern for the fantastic stories about Yellowstone that were to circulate for years to come. The government finally sent exploratory parties to the area in 1859 and 1870. The reports on these expeditions were widely read and became the grounds for the act of Congress that established Yellowstone as a public park. Yellowstone is the oldest and biggest of the national parks. The area was originally marked off as 3348 sq. mi. In subsequent years, the boundaries of Yellowstone were substantially increased, and the Shoshone National Forest, a timber and land reserve, was added.

Nov 7: The brigantine *Mary Celeste,* commanded by Capt. Benjamin S. Briggs, sailed from New York harbor bound for Genoa, Italy, carrying some 1700 barrels of alcohol. On Dec. 4 the British brigantine *Dei Gratia* found the *Mary Celeste* between the Azores and Portugal, her sails slightly damaged, several feet of water in her hold, and completely abandoned. The cargo was intact, the ship was in good order, and there was plenty of food and water aboard, but the lifeboat was gone. The mystery of the disappearance of Capt. Briggs, his wife and daughter, and the eight crewmen aboard has never been solved, and the story of the *Mary Celeste*'s voyage has become a classic of sea lore.

1873

I. Civil Rights
Exploration and Settlement
Government
Statistics
Wars

After a period of unprecedented prosperity, fueled originally by the economic demands of the Civil War, the nation plunged into a depression. The panic of 1873 was triggered by the failure on Sept. 18 of the leading brokerage firm, Jay Cooke & Company, which had been financing construction of the Northern Pacific Railroad. The actual causes lay deeper: overspeculation in land and securities, issuance of too much paper money, and increasing inflation. Over 5000 businesses failed this year and another 5000 or so failed before recovery was complete about six years later.

Mar 3: An act prohibiting the **mailing of obscene literature** was passed by Congress. The bill was promoted by Anthony Comstock, secretary of the Society for the Suppression of Vice. Comstock, formerly a dry-goods store clerk, joined the YMCA and began to agitate for a New York vice society. He drew his inspiration from a London society that for 75 years had been engaged in ferreting out and bringing to trial moral offenders.

Oct 31: The U.S. steamer *Virginius* was captured by the Spanish gunboat *Tornado* while transporting supplies to Cuban revolutionary forces. Eight U.S. citizens from the steamer were subsequently executed in Cuba by Spanish authorities.

Nov 19: William Marcy "Boss" Tweed was convicted on 204 charges of fraud. He was sentenced to 12 years in prison and fined $12,550.

II. Architecture
Arts and Music
Popular Entertainment
Publishing
Theater

The founding of *St. Nicholas* magazine and the appointment of Mary Mapes Dodge as its editor marked 1873 as a notable year for children's literature. Mrs. Dodge edited the magazine and contributed to it until her death in 1905. In the process she had more influence on literature for young people than any other contemporary person or publication. Among the many contributors to *St. Nicholas* were Louisa May Alcott, Rudyard Kipling, Howard Pyle, Robert Louis Stevenson, Frank Stockton, and Mark Twain.

Among **books published** this year was the classic science fiction adventure story *Twenty Thousand Leagues Under the Sea* by Jules Verne, a French writer. Another Verne novel, *Around the World in Eighty Days*, topped the 1,000,000 mark in sales. Other books published this year included *Marjorie Daw* by Thomas Bailey Aldrich, a collection whose title story achieved both critical and popular success; *The Mystery of Metropolisville* by Edward Eggleston, a novel that included a preface by the author declaring that he considered the novel a proper vehicle for contributing to the history of civilization in America; and *Mrs. Skaggs's Husbands and Other Stories* by Bret Harte, which included some of the author's best writing of this period, notably the story "The Head of Sandy Bar."

III. Business and Industry
Education
Philosophy and Religion
Science

The first important railroad tunnel in the U.S., and the longest until 1927, was completed on Nov. 27. This was the Hoosac Tunnel, through the Hoosac Range in northwestern Massachusetts. Work on the tunnel had begun in 1851. The new explosive nitroglycerin had its first practical use in the U.S. in construction of the tunnel. So did the compressed air drill, which earlier had been used in the Mont Cenis Tunnel in the Swiss Alps, the only tunnel in the world longer than the Hoosac at that time. The Hoosac Tunnel was 4.75 miles long. It was traveled by trains of the Boston and Maine Railroad from New England to New York City. It was 20 feet high and 24 feet wide, and required 20,000,000 bricks for archwork support. It cost $20,000,000 to build and took the lives of nearly 200 workmen.

The **Union of American Hebrew Congregations,** the first national grouping of Jewish congregations, was organized. Two years later this group founded Hebrew Union College in Cincinnati, Ohio, the oldest rabbinical seminary in the U.S. A conference in Cleveland in 1855 had resulted in a breach between the eastern and the western rabbis; their division was not bridged until 1879. The Union of American Hebrew Congregations, therefore, consisted of congregations from the South and the West only.

Free mail delivery was provided in all cities with a population of at least 20,000.

May 1: The **first penny postcards** in the U.S. were issued.

IV. Fashion
   Folkways
   Holidays
   Social Issues and Crime
   Sports

By 1873 the American bison, also called the buffalo, was almost extinct, even though at the start of the nineteenth century estimates placed the North American bison population as high as 60,000,000. Bison were essential to the way of life of the Indians of the Great Plains, who depended on them for food, clothing, and shelter. The symbiotic relationship of the Indians and the bison threatened neither group.

However, with the coming of the railroad, professional buffalo hunters, and the settlement of the West, the situation changed. Bison were slaughtered far beyond any need for food or hides. Although in 1865 about 10,000,000 bison still roamed the plains, by 1890 only 1000 or so were left.

Memorial Day became a legal holiday in New York, the first state to recognize it. Rhode Island followed suit in 1874; Vermont in 1876; New Hampshire in 1877; and Wisconsin in 1879.

May 27: The first annual **Preakness Stakes** was won by Survivor, with a time of 2:43. The jockey was G. Barbee. The race was run at Pimlico, Md. The Preakness Stakes is one of the three classic races in American racing. It is grouped with the Kentucky Derby and the Belmont Stakes in importance. A horse that has won all three has earned the Triple Crown of American racing. The Preakness Stakes has been run over varying distances.

Aug 18: Mt. Whitney, the second highest mountain in the U.S., was scaled by an American team for the first time. The climbers were John Lucas, Charles D. Begole, and A. H. Johnson.

1874

I. **Civil Rights**
   Exploration and Settlement
   Government
   Statistics
   Wars

Growing out of the hardships caused by the panic of 1873, a convention in Indianapolis, Ind., formed the Greenback Party on Nov. 25, 1876. Its supporters were mostly farmers from the West and the South who wanted to inflate the currency so as to relieve themselves of the burden of debt they had incurred in times of high prices. Originally, the Greenback Party hoped to gain control of the Democratic Party, but it could not do so. It fielded its own candidates until 1884, when the party did so badly that it disbanded. In 1878, with the assistance of labor organizations, the Greenback-Labor Party elected 14 representatives to Congress. At the 1874 convention the party nominated Peter Cooper, New York industrialist and philanthropist, as its candidate for the presidency in 1876.

The **Woman's Christian Temperance Union,** called the WCTU, was established at Cleveland, Ohio. It stemmed from the women's crusade against liquor traffic in midwestern states. Mrs. Annie Wittenmyer was elected first president.

1874-1875: In **congressional elections** the Democrats picked up ten seats in the Senate but still lagged behind the Republicans 45–29, with two seats going to minor parties. In the House the Democrats took a 169–109 majority, with 14 seats going to minor parties.

June 20: Territorial government in the **District of Columbia** was abolished and replaced by a commission.

Nov 7: The first cartoon featuring an **elephant** to symbolize the Republican Party appeared in *Harper's Weekly*. Entitled "Third Term Panic," the cartoon by Thomas Nast showed Republican concern that Pres. Grant would be elected for a third term on the Democratic ticket.

II. Architecture
   Arts and Music
   Popular Entertainment
   Publishing
   Theater

The American theater prospered in the late nineteenth century and became completely professional, counting among its ranks numerous stars and a num-

ber of energetic and able producers. Among come-
diennes no one was better or more successful than
Ada Rehan, who first appeared on the stage in 1863
at the age of 13. She was for many years the leading
lady of Augustin Daly's company, popular both in
America and England. Her most famous part was
Katherine in *The Taming of the Shrew*.

Among **books published** this year was *The Gilded
Age* by Mark Twain and Charles Dudley Warner, a
novel that epitomized the corruption of post-Civil
War America. In the character of Colonel Sellers the
authors represented "the grandfather of all American
boosters . . . with his dreams of an immediate future
gilding a present of poverty-stricken, whiskey-
soaked, rough-and-tumble frontier." Other books
published this year included the first American edition of *Lorna Doone* by Richard Doddridge Black-
more; *The Circuit Rider,* a major novel by Edward
Eggleston, with a pioneer preacher as its main character whose pulpit was the saddle of his horse and
whose flock was the citizenry of communities without churches; *The Hanging of the Crane,* an ambitious
long poem by Henry Wadsworth Longfellow, not
generally classed among his best works; and *The Old
Regime in Canada* by Francis Parkman, a volume in
his cycle of histories about the struggles of the English and the French for dominion over North America.

III. Business and Industry
Education
Philosophy and Religion
Science

An invention that revolutionized life on the Great
Plains had its first practical use in 1874. The invention was barbed wire, the work of Joseph F. Glidden
of Illinois. Until 1874, considering the lack of timber
on the Great Plains, there had been no economical
way to fence the land. Cattle roamed where they

would. Now the range was fenced in. Cowboys had to become ranchers and farmers had to protect their crops from marauding cattle. At first there were battles between ranchers and farmers, but eventually barbed wire won. In 1874 only 10,000 lbs. of it were produced, but in 1880 the output was 80,500,000 lbs.

The **Chautauqua movement** was founded by Lewis Miller, an Ohio industrialist, and John H. Vincent, a Methodist clergyman, as an annual summer meeting for the training of Sunday school teachers. The movement derived its name from the site of its meetings on the shores of Lake Chautauqua, N.Y. The meetings gradually expanded their educational scope and the size of the student body.

IV. **Fashion**
    Folkways
    Holidays
    Social Issues and Crime
    Sports

A new sport, lawn tennis, appeared in the U.S. this year. Invented in England, the game came to the U.S. by way of Bermuda, where a New Yorker, Mary Ewing Outerbridge, was introduced to the game. She returned home with a net, balls, and rackets, and had the first lawn tennis court in the U.S. laid out on Staten Island. Another court soon was laid out in Nahant, Mass., and the game spread around the country. Tennis was such a genteel game that women could play despite their long skirts, since they were not expected to run about.

Rugby football was first introduced to an American campus in a match between Harvard and McGill University of Canada. Canadian rules for the game greatly interested sports-minded Americans and were instrumental in the development of modern football.

The **first public zoo** in the U.S., the Philadelphia Zoological Gardens of Philadelphia, Pa., was opened.

Aug 21: Henry Ward Beecher was sued for $100,000 by Theodore Tilton, accusing the famous preacher of committing adultery with Tilton's wife. The trial attracted national publicity and controversy, especially since the jury handed down a split decision, 9–3, in favor of Beecher. A special investigating committee made up of members of his congregation, the Plymouth Congregational Church, Brooklyn, N.Y., had previously exonerated Beecher after interviewing 36 people, including Tilton.

1875

I. Civil Rights
   Exploration and Settlement
   Government
   Statistics
   Wars

One of the worst scandals of the administration of Pres. Ulysses S. Grant surfaced this year with revelations involving what was called the Whiskey Ring. A group of distillers, chiefly in St. Louis, Mo., and corrupt Treasury Department officials had conspired to defraud the government of millions of dollars in taxes on liquor. Two hundred thirty-eight persons were indicted on May 10. Later in the year Grant's private secretary, Orville E. Babcock, was also indicted. Grant intervened to make sure Babcock was not convicted. Babcock retired shortly after his acquittal.

Jan 30: The **Hawaiian Reciprocity Treaty** was signed. It provided that no Hawaiian territory be turned over to any third power.

Mar 1: A **Civil Rights Act** was passed guaranteeing blacks equal rights in public places. The law also prohibited exclusion of blacks from jury duty.

Dec 4: William Marcy "Boss" Tweed escaped from prison at Ludlow St., New York City, and fled to Cuba.

II. Architecture
Arts and Music
Popular Entertainment
Publishing
Theater

The growing place of music in cultural life was indicated by the appointment in 1875 of John Knowles
Paine to a professorship of music at Harvard, the first
such post at any American university. Paine was a
composer and organist, but his importance in American music lay in his educational efforts. Many of his
pupils became notable composers.

A **masterpiece of realism** in the style of Jean Léon
Gérôme and Léon Joseph Florentin Bonnat was
Thomas Eakins' *Gross Clinic.* The objectivity with
which Eakins approached the subject corresponded
to the scientific objectivity of the doctor who is the
subject.

An **inspired sculpture** of Abraham Lincoln was the
famous *Emancipation* in Lincoln Park, Washington,
D.C., by Thomas Ball. A replica was set up in Boston
in 1877. Lincoln was shown with his hand lifted over
a kneeling slave.

III. Business and Industry
Education
Philosophy and Religion
Science

Dwight L. Moody, a new, forceful personality in
evangelical Christianity, began his life's work this
year with revival meetings in the East. Moody was to
play a major role in the religious life of the country
to the end of the nineteenth century. He preached a
simple biblical message, concentrating on the salvation of individual souls at a time when many clergymen were turning to social reform. Moody founded
the Northfield School for Girls (1879) and the Mt.
Hermon School for Boys (1881) in his native town of
Northfield, Mass., and the Moody Institute (1889) in
Chicago.

Luther Burbank set up a plant nursery in Santa

Rosa, Calif., in which he developed new strains of berries, fruits, vegetables, grains, and grasses.

Henry Bergh became the first president of the new **Society for the Prevention of Cruelty to Children.** In 1866 Bergh had incorporated the Society for the Prevention of Cruelty to Animals after a long and lonely crusade. The Society for the Prevention of Cruelty to Children was organized with the help of Elbridge T. Gerry, and quickly became the more prominent society, though Bergh remained more intimately asssociated with efforts to eliminate cruelty to animals.

The **Christian Science** movement received a powerful impetus with publication of *Science and Health* by Mary Baker Eddy.

Mar 15: The **first American cardinal,** Archbishop John McCloskey of New York City, was invested at St. Patrick's Cathedral.

IV. Fashion
   Folkways
   Holidays
   Social Issues and Crime
   Sports

The traveling circus was evolving into "the greatest show on earth," aided by that master of showmanship, Phineas T. Barnum, who had organized such a show in 1871. His tent covered the largest area of any in the world and he introduced the three-ring circus. In 1881 Barnum merged his circus with that of James A. Bailey to form an even bigger enterprise. Barnum's greatest single coup came in 1882 when he purchased Jumbo, the world's largest elephant, from the Royal Zoological Gardens of London.

Football uniforms were first worn at a match between Harvard and Tufts.

The **baseball glove** was introduced by Charles G. Waite, first baseman for a Boston team. The glove was unpadded.

May 17: The **first Kentucky Derby** was run at Churchill Downs, Ky. The winner was Aristides, with a time of 2:37¼. The jockey was Oliver Lewis.

1876

I. Civil Rights
Exploration and Settlement
Government
Statistics
Wars

For the first time since the Civil War, the Democratic Party was optimistic about its chances of winning a presidential election. The Grant administration was riddled with scandals, and the depression that had begun in 1873 had not completely disappeared. The Republicans were in disarray. Pres. Ulysses S. Grant would have liked a third term, but had strong opposition within the party. Rep. James G. Blaine, Republican of Maine, was favored by one faction but he too was touched by scandal. He lost the nomination but in July took a seat in the Senate. In the campaign the Democrats blamed the Republicans for the nation's ills, while the Republicans "waved the bloody shirt," still taking credit for having saved the Union during the Civil War. Neither party discussed the long-standing argument between so-called hard money businessmen and soft money proponents, mostly farmers.

1876-1877: In **congressional elections** the Republicans lost ground in the Senate but held a 39–36 majority, with one seat going to a minor party. In the House the Democrats held a 153–140 majority.

May 17: The **Prohibition Party** held its second national convention in Cleveland, Ohio. Green Clay Smith of Kentucky was nominated for president and Gideon T. Stewart of Ohio for vice president.

May 18: The **Greenback Party** held its first national convention at Indianapolis, Ind. The convention

named Peter Cooper of New York for president and
Samuel F. Perry of Ohio for vice president.

June 14-16: The **Republican National Convention
nominated Rutherford B. Hayes** of Ohio for president. His running mate was William A. Wheeler of
New York.

June 25: At the Battle of **Little Big Horn** in Montana,
Gen. George A. Custer and all of the 265 men of the
Seventh Cavalry were slaughtered by Sitting Bull's
Sioux Indians.

June 27-29: The **Democratic National Convention
nominated Samuel J. Tilden** of New York for president and Thomas A. Hendricks of Indiana for vice
president.

Aug 1: Colorado was admitted to the Union, the 38th
state.

Nov 7: The **presidential election** gave Samuel J.
Tilden, the Democratic candidate, a popular vote plu-
rality of 250,000, but Republicans refused to concede
on the grounds that returns from Florida, Louisiana,
South Carolina, and Oregon were in dispute. Hayes
needed the electoral votes of those states to win. On
Dec. 6 two different sets of electoral returns were
reported from the four states. The electoral vote ultimately was to be determined by a special 15-member
electoral commission.

Nov 23: William Marcy "Boss" Tweed, after his capture in Spain, was delivered to authorities in New
York City to serve his prison sentence.

II. Architecture
Arts and Music
Popular Entertainment
Publishing
Theater

An unusual book published this year was not intended for personal reading but to help organizations
of all kinds conduct their meetings with standard
rules. The book was *Pocket Manual of Rules of Order
for Deliberative Assemblies;* the author was Henry M.
Robert, an Army engineer. The small volume was at

once popular, as many groups recognized it as a means of ensuring order and fairness in business meetings. It was revised in 1915 and 1943 and has continued to be the standard work, known to millions as *Robert's Rules of Order*.

Among **books published** this year was *Clarel: A Poem and Pilgrimage in the Holy Land* by Herman Melville. Published in two volumes, the work was based on Melville's trip to the Holy Land in 1857. Its publication did nothing to enhance the reputation of the author, then working as a customs inspector in New York City. Other books published this year included *Helen's Babies* by John Habberton, a humorous novel that was enormously popular; *Roderick Hudson*, a novel by Henry James; *Among My Books: Second Series* by James Russell Lowell; *The One Fair Woman*, a novel by Joaquin Miller, the "poet of the Sierras"; *The Adventures of Tom Sawyer* by Mark Twain, an American classic that became his most popular book but was barred from libraries in Brooklyn, N.Y., Denver, Colo., and elsewhere as being unfit for young readers; and *My Winter on the Nile* by Charles Dudley Warner, a book of travel sketches based on the author's 1875 trip to Africa and the Middle East.

The gigantic **statue of *Daniel Webster*** now standing in Central Park, the work of Thomas Ball, was unveiled. Fourteen feet in height, the statue was cast in Munich. Popularity of the work brought Ball orders for statues of Josiah Quincy and Charles Sumner.

III. Business and Industry
Education
Philosophy and Religion
Science

Before the twentieth century most American scientists worked with practical objectives in mind. One of the few who devoted himself to what may be called pure research was Josiah Willard Gibbs, at Yale University. His work later had practical applications in industry. Gibbs's most important contribution was his theory of thermodynamics, the basis for modern physical chemistry and chemical engineering. His most important publication was "On the Equilibrium of Heterogeneous Substances," which appeared this year in *Transactions of the Connecticut Academy of Arts and Sciences*. The second half of this classic paper was published in 1878. Gibbs also contributed to statistical mechanics, vector analysis, crystallography, and electromagnetic theory.

The **first photograph of the solar spectrum** was taken by John William Draper, a physicist and astronomer at New York University. Draper was credited in 1840 with the first photograph of the moon.

A **mimeograph** device was invented by Thomas A. Edison in his laboratory at Menlo Park, N.J. The machine employed a stencil for making impressions. The impressions were inserted into a set frame and ink was applied. It was probably the first practical duplicating machine.

The **New York Society for Ethical Culture** was established by Dr. Felix Adler. In the same year Adler founded the first free kindergarten in New York City in connection with his Ethical Culture School.

Central Park was completed along the design of its planners, Frederick Law Olmsted and Calvert Vaux, as a growing part of New York City. It was to be expanded as the city expanded.

Mar 7: The first U.S. patent for the **telephone** was awarded to Alexander Graham Bell.

IV. **Fashion**
    Folkways
    Holidays
    Social Issues and Crime
    Sports

The nation celebrated its 100th birthday with a world's fair, the Centennial Exposition, held appropriately in Philadelphia, where the Declaration of Independence was written and proclaimed in 1776. The exposition covered 450 acres. Each state had its own building and 50 foreign nations sent exhibits. Between May and November, almost 10,000,000 people visited the fairgrounds. The most popular attraction proved to be Machinery Hall, with its vast displays of inventions heralding the latest technology.

Polo was brought to the U.S. by James Gordon Bennett, publisher of the New York *Herald*. The sport was launched at Dickel's Riding Academy, New York City.

In track, the **100-yard race** was run for the first time in ten seconds, by Horace H. Lee of Pennsylvania.

The **tenderloin section of New York City** (24th to 40th streets between 5th and 7th avenues) was so named by Police Captain A. S. Williams, who is reported to have said, on being transferred to the West 30th St. precinct: "I've been having chuck steak ever since I've been on the force, and now I'm going to have a bit of tenderloin." The expression was taken up by the press and soon was applied to the vice-laden sections of any city.

Jan 1: The **Philadelphia Mummers' parade** was organized in its present form in celebration of the American centennial. The parade was sponsored mainly by the Silver Crown New Year's Association. The Mummers' parade dates back to early colonial times. It combines the boisterous Swedish custom of celebrating the New Year with the English tradition of the Mummers' play, in which St. George slays the dragon. The city of Philadelphia did not officially recognize the parade until 1901, when 42 fraternal organizations received permits to stage a parade for which prizes would be awarded for costumes, music, and comic antics.

Apr 2: In the **first official National League baseball game,** Boston beat Philadelphia 6–5, with Jim O'Rourke getting the first hit.

May 23: The **first no-hitter** in National League history was pitched by Joe Borden of Boston. Borden lost his effectiveness soon after and ended the season as the club's groundskeeper.

June 6: The **Imperial Council of the Ancient Arabic Order of Nobles of the Mystic Shrine** for the U.S., a

Masonic order, was organized by Dr. Walter Fleming, assisted by Charles T. McClenachan.

Aug 11-12: The **America's Cup** was successfully defended by the yacht *Madeleine*, which won two straight races from the Canadian challenger *Countess of Dufferin*.

Nov: The **first cooking school** in the U.S., the New York Cooking School, was begun by Juliet Corson at St. Mark's Place in New York City. Corson was interested in teaching wives and daughters of workingmen how to buy and prepare good food. In Aug. 1877 she paid for the publication of 50,000 pamphlets entitled *Fifteen-Cent Dinners for Working-Men's Families*. She wrote other books and pamphlets on the subject in later years.

Nov 23: Rules for football were discussed at the invitation of Princeton, by delegates from Yale, Harvard, Rutgers, Columbia, and Princeton meeting at Massasoit House, Springfield, Mass. Princeton had recently adopted Harvard's rules, which in turn were chiefly based on the rules of the British Rugby Union, and these were adopted by all colleges represented at the meeting. The Intercollegiate Football Association grew out of the meeting.

1877

I. Civil Rights
Exploration and Settlement
Government
Statistics
Wars

The nation had never before faced a dispute over the results of a presidential election but it did this year. A candidate needed 185 electoral votes to win and Samuel J. Tilden, the Democratic candidate, clearly had 184. In dispute were the 19 electoral votes of three states still under carpetbag rule—Florida, Louisiana, and South Carolina—plus one vote in Oregon. In Congress both parties agreed on Jan. 29 to establish an electoral commission to decide the issue. The commission, with five members from each house of Congress and five members from the Supreme Court, was made up of eight Republicans and seven Democrats. All the commission's decisions were to fall along party lines. On Mar. 2 Congress accepted the commission's decision, which awarded all the disputed votes to the Republican candidate, Rutherford B. Hayes, who thus received 185 electoral votes to Tilden's 184. The Republicans were accused of offering southern Democrats economic favors for their region if they supported Hayes's claim. In any event, the new president showed a conciliatory attitude toward the South: the last federal troops were withdrawn and there was no further effort to protect the rights of blacks. Reconstruction was over.

Apr 24: Carpetbag rule ended in Louisiana, the last southern state to regain control of its internal government. Withdrawal of federal troops here and in South Carolina was a part of the bargain between Republicans and southern Democrats for quiet acceptance of the decision of the electoral commission.

June-Oct: Nez Percé Indians went to war with the U.S. in Idaho. The war ended when federal troops captured Chief Joseph and evacuated the Indians to a reservation.

June 15: The **first black was graduated** from the U.S. Military Academy at West Point, Henry O. Flipper.

II. Architecture
  Arts and Music
  Popular Entertainment
  Publishing
  Theater

Two actors destined to appear together many times and to be among the most popular and successful of their era made their debuts this year on opposite coasts. In Philadelphia, Otis Skinner appeared at the Museum Theater, and in San Francisco the Polish actress Helena Modjeska played the lead role in *Adrienne Lecouvreur*. The two would ultimately tour the U.S. together. Skinner became best known for his role in *Kismet* (1911). Madame Modjeska in 1883 played the role of Nora in *A Doll's House* in Louisville, Ky., the first American production of a play by Henrik Ibsen.

Among **books published** this year was *Deephaven* by Sarah Orne Jewett, one of America's finest novelists in the use of local color. The author's first major work, *Deephaven* contained sketches of a New England town that resembled her own South Berwick, Maine. Other books published this year included *Birds and Poets* by John Burroughs, marking the author as a worthy successor to Henry David Thoreau; *The American* by Henry James, continuing the author's exploration of contrasts and conflicts of American life in Europe; and *Poems* by Sidney Lanier, a volume which would be enlarged and reissued in 1884.

The **cakewalk** became a popular feature of minstrel shows following the success of a number called "Walking for Dat Cake" by the New York musical comedy team of Harrigan and Hart. The cakewalk now was an imitation of antebellum plantation cakewalks, set to syncopated tunes taken from black sources and later developed into ragtime.

May 1: The most popular **"cheap library,"** George Munro's *Seaside Library*, made its first appearance. Munro made a fortune publishing a novel a day, offering works by Charles Dickens, Sir Walter Scott, Charlotte and Emily Brontë, and many other foreign authors without paying any royalty.

III. Business and Industry
Education
Philosophy and Religion
Science

Strikes on a national scale, accompanied by violence, occurred this year for the first time in American history. The labor trouble began on July 17 when Balti-

more & Ohio Railroad workers struck. The line had
cut wages 10% even though it was paying large dividends to its stockholders. Violence broke out first in
Martinsburg, W. Va., where federal troops were used
to restore order. On July 20 nine strikers were killed
in Baltimore when state militia fired on a crowd. On
July 21 strikers in Pittsburgh rioted, destroying some
2000 freight cars. Police aided by cavalry troops attacked a gathering in Chicago on July 26, causing
more bloodshed. The strikes spread to other railroads and to many other industries. In the end, most
rail workers gained little or nothing, but coal miners
won a 10% wage increase. Although the strikes were
not especially successful, they did bring more unity
to labor and generally promoted the growth of labor
unions, which had suffered during the recent depression.

The detection of two **satellites of Mars** by Asaph
Hall made a major contribution to astronomy. This
discovery, made at the Naval Observatory in Washington, D.C., was ranked as the most significant since
the discovery of Neptune in 1846.

Dec 6: Thomas A. Edison completed his **phonograph.**
He filed for a patent for the device on Dec. 15. The
first full description of the phonograph appeared in
Scientific American (Dec. 22), at whose New York
offices Edison demonstrated its operation.

IV. Fashion
   Folkways
   Holidays
   Social Issues and Crime
   Sports

Flag Day was observed for the first time this year, on
June 14, to mark the centennial of the adoption of the
stars and stripes design by the Continental Congress.
It is not a legal holiday, but is observed by presidential proclamation. The question of who designed the
flag has never been resolved. Possibly it was Francis
Hopkinson, who was chairman of the Navy board of
the Congress, where the design originated.

The first annual **Westminster Kennel Club dog
show** was held at Gilmore's Garden in New York
City; it was sponsored by the Westminster Kennel
Club. Setters of English, Irish, and Gordon types,
pointers, spaniels, mastiffs, St. Bernards, terriers,
and poodles were well represented.

1878

I. Civil Rights
Exploration and Settlement
Government
Statistics
Wars

Epidemics struck the nation fairly often during this
period, when causes and cures were not known. Especially rampant this year was yellow fever, which
swept through the South. New Orleans was hardest
hit, and as people fled the disease there they spread
it elsewhere. Louisiana, Alabama, Mississippi, and
Tennessee were most affected, but the epidemic
reached as far north as Cincinnati, Ohio. There were
24,000 cases in New Orleans and 4000 fatalities. The
national toll was 14,000. Cigars and whiskey were
recommended by some as remedies. In Memphis,
Anna "Madame Annie" Cook, who operated the Mansion House brothel, discharged her prostitutes to provide hospital quarters. She died in September of yellow fever contracted while caring for patients. The
epidemic broke out again in 1879.

1878-1879: In **congressional elections** the Democrats
gained control of both houses of Congress for the first
time since 1858. The Democratic majorities were
42–33 in the Senate, with one seat going to a minor
party; 149–130 in the House, with 14 minor party
seats.

Jan 10: A **women's suffrage amendment** was introduced by Sen. Aaron A. Sargent of California in the exact words of its final form when adopted after World War I. Defeated in the Senate 16–34, the amendment would be reintroduced in each succeeding Congress.

Jan 14: The **Supreme Court** declared unconstitutional any state law requiring a railroad to provide equal accommodations for all passengers regardless of race or color.

June 11: The **District of Columbia** was given a new government by Congress. The three commissioners, two residents and one U.S. Army engineer, were empowered to recommend governing legislation to Congress. Residents would have no direct voice in either local or national government. The president made appointments to the commission on June 23.

II. **Architecture**
   Arts and Music
   Popular Entertainment
   Publishing
   Theater

This was a landmark year for newspaper publishing in the U.S., although it was not perceived as such at the time. On Dec. 9 Joseph Pulitzer, who had been involved in politics and publishing for a number of years, bought the St. Louis *Dispatch*, a bankrupt evening newspaper, for $2500. Pulitzer calculated that after the purchase he had enough operating capital to keep going for 17 weeks. Almost immediately he merged his paper with John A. Dillon's St. Louis *Post*, and within a year the new paper, the St. Louis *Post-Dispatch*, had doubled in circulation and was making money. From this point Pulitzer turned his interest away from politics and toward journalism. His influence would eventually change the newspaper business around the world.

Among **books published** this year was *The Leavenworth Case* by Anna Katharine Green, the first in a score or more of best-selling mystery novels. Other books published this year included *Roxy* by Edward Eggleston, a novel set in nineteenth-century Indiana;

The Europeans by Henry James, which reversed the usual plot in the author's novels by introducing European characters into an American setting; *Through the Dark Continent* by Henry M. Stanley, the explorer; and *History of American Literature, 1607–1765* by Moses Coit Tyler, a pioneering study of early American literature.

III. Business and Industry
Education
Philosophy and Religion
Science

Law had been a widely practiced profession in the U.S. from the start. It was taught as early as 1779 by George Wythe in Virginia, and in 1784 by Tapping Reeve in Connecticut. There was not, however, a national organization for the legal profession until Aug. 21, 1878, when the American Bar Association was formed at Saratoga, N.Y., at a meeting called by the Connecticut Bar Association. James O. Broadhead was chosen the first president.

Jan 1: The **Knights of Labor** was established as a national organization at its first general assembly. This was the first labor union to attempt to organize all workers into a single union. Its growth was rapid after the election in 1879 of Terence Vincent Powderly as its grand master workman.

Jan 28: The first commercial **telephone exchange** opened at New Haven, Conn. It provided eight lines and served 21 telephones.

Oct 15: The **first electric light company** was formed. It was the Edison Electric Light Company, located at 65 Fifth Ave., New York City.

IV. Fashion
Folkways
Holidays
Social Issues and Crime
Sports

The bicycle first attracted attention when exhibited at Philadelphia's Centennial Exposition in 1876. It was first manufactured in the U.S. in 1878. These bicycles had front wheels about five feet in diameter, but the rear wheels were no more than a third this size. Such a machine was difficult and dangerous to ride. Nevertheless, bicycling became a fad. It became a popular sport after the safety bike, basically like the modern bicycle, was introduced in 1887. By 1882 there were about 20,000 cyclists in the country; the League of American Wheelmen was formed in 1880. Cycling clubs held parades and competitive meets. Women could not ride the high-wheeled bikes but the tricycle

Oct 27: A celebrated **robbery** of $3,000,000 from the Manhattan Savings Institution in New York City was credited to a gang leader called George L. "Western" Leslie. Although two of his accomplices were convicted of the robbery, Leslie was not brought to trial because of lack of evidence. New York's chief of police attributed four-fifths of the bank holdups in the U.S. to Leslie, whose career was terminated by his murder in 1884.

1879

I. Civil Rights
Exploration and Settlement
Government
Statistics
Wars

Opposition to Chinese immigration, growing stronger in California in particular, came to a head with passage by Congress of a bill to restrict such immigration. Pres. Rutherford B. Hayes vetoed the bill on May 11 on the grounds that it violated the Burlingame Treaty of 1868, which established free immigration between the two countries. On May 7

California adopted a new constitution that forbade employment of Chinese laborers. Between 1850 and 1882 about 300,000 Chinese came to the U.S., almost all remaining on the Pacific coast. Chinese laborers had first been brought in large numbers in the 1860s to work on construction of the transcontinental railroad. The feeling against them at this time was economic rather than racial, since they worked for less than American workers.

Jan 1: Specie payment was resumed by the U.S. government for the first time since it was suspended in 1861. Lack of specie payment had kept the currency in an unsettled state, partly contributing to the panic of 1873. Its approaching resumption caused much apprehension that the government could not provide enough coin to meet the expected demand. Mints had been kept open after hours to produce additional coinage, and there was surprise when little currency was presented by the public for redemption. This showed the extent to which public confidence in government fiscal policies had been restored since the Civil War. Payment of specie has been maintained ever since.

Feb 15: Women attorneys won the right to argue cases before the U.S. Supreme Court by an act of Congress.

II. Architecture
   Arts and Music
   Popular Entertainment
   Publishing
   Theater

The history of one of the world's great entertainment palaces began this year when Madison Square Garden opened to the public in New York City. The first Garden was not elaborate, just a converted railroad structure at 26th St. In 1890 it was replaced by an elegant structure designed by the firm of McKim, Mead, and White; it featured a tower modeled after the Giralda in Seville, Spain. The second Garden was designed not for the average sports fan but for the wealthy and cultured citizens of New York and such events as the annual horse show of the Equestrian Society. This building was torn down and in 1925 replaced by a third Garden, on Eighth Ave. and 50th St. It was in turn replaced by the fourth and present Madison Square Garden, 31st to 33rd streets between Seventh and Eighth avenues.

Among **books published** this year was *Daisy Miller* by Henry James. It became the most popular of the author's early novels, perhaps because of an endearing young American heroine pitted against the complexities of Continental society. Other books published this year included *Old Creole Days* by George Washington Cable, the author's first collection of short stories, many of which first had appeared in *Scribner's Monthly; Progress and Poverty* by Henry George, a landmark work in economics concentrating on land and its value and advocating a "single tax" on land to replace all other forms of taxation; *A Lady of Aroostook* by William Dean Howells, the author's fourth novel; and *Rudder Grange* by Frank R. Stockton, a whimsically humorous novel that was so popular it inspired a sequel, *The Rudder Grangers Abroad* (1891).

III. Business and Industry
   Education
   Philosophy and Religion
   Science

A venture in retailing that began in 1879 set the stage for development of nationwide chains of stores in various merchandising fields. This year, Frank W. Woolworth, having had a five-cent store fail in Utica, N.Y., opened a five-and-ten-cent store in Lancaster, Pa. It was a success and by the 1890s Woolworth operated 28 stores. By 1911 the F. W. Woolworth Company owned over 1000 such outlets. Chain stores aroused the antagonism of local merchants, but the public approved, as their steadily increasing patronage showed.

The first public **electrical street lighting** system in the U.S. was installed in Cleveland, Ohio, by Charles

F. Brush. Wabash, Ind., was the first city to be completely lighted by electricity (Mar. 31, 1880). Brush used arc lights for illumination rather than incandescent lamps.

The **Church of Christ, Scientist** was organized by Mary Baker Eddy, founder of Christian Science. Mrs. Eddy, who resided in Lynn, Mass., was the author of *Science and Health with Key to the Scriptures*, published in 1875.

Oct 21: The first practical **incandescent electric lamp** was perfected by Thomas A. Edison in his laboratories at Menlo Park, N.J. He found that a carbonized filament of cotton would last for about 40 hrs.

IV. Fashion
    Folkways
    Holidays
    Social Issues and Crime
    Sports

Two popular forms of recreation during this period were fox hunting and coaching. Clubs of wealthy persons on Long Island, in the suburbs of Philadelphia, and in New England, Virginia, and Maryland took up fox hunting in the English style. One newspaper described the last hunt of the season at Newport, R.I., this way: "All Newport mustered at the meet, the road to Southwick's Grove being literally chock-full of vehicles of every sort, shape, size, and description." Coaching was also imported from England and such resorts as Tuxedo, N.Y., and Lenox, Mass., found roads jammed with expensive dog-carts, buckboards, landaus, and phaetons. In New York City there was an annual coaching parade during which such rigs as four-in-hands and tally-hos coursed down Fifth Ave. The elite of society rode atop these magnificent vehicles, the men in striped waistcoats and silk top hats, the ladies with parasols held over enormous picture hats.

The **National Archery Association** was founded at Crawfordsville, Ind., signalizing the beginning of modern archery in the U.S. The first target archery

tournament was held at Chicago this same year, with
Will Thompson the first champion.

1880

I. Civil Rights
   Exploration and Settlement
   Government
   Statistics
   Wars

The field for the presidential nominations of 1880
was wide open, Pres. Rutherford B. Hayes having
announced he would not seek a second term. For the
first time since the Civil War, the Republicans could
not claim they alone saved the Union: the Democratic
nominee, Gen. Winfield Scott Hancock, had fought in
both the Mexican and Civil wars. The tariff was the
only major issue and Hancock was inept at discussing it. The candidates for the most part stayed home,
and for the first time interested supporters came in
large numbers to visit them at their homes. James A.
Garfield especially received gifts and poems composed for the occasion, watching silently as supporters trampled his flowers and shrubs.

The U.S. **Census** recorded a population of
50,155,783. The center of population was located at
eight miles west by south of Cincinnati, Ohio (in
western Kentucky). New York became the first state
with a population above 5,000,000.

Mar 1: Excluding blacks from jury duty was held
unconstitutional by the Supreme Court. The decision
was based on section five of the Fourteenth Amendment. It advised jury commissioners that they were
forbidden to carry out their offices in such a way as
to discriminate on racial grounds in the selection of
jurors.

June 2-8: The **Republican National Convention nomi-**

nated **James A. Garfield** of Ohio for the presidency. Chester A. Arthur of New York was named as his running mate. During the convention's meetings Sen. Blanche Kelso Bruce of Mississippi was made temporary chairman of the convention, becoming the first black to preside over a major party convention.

June 22-24: The **Democratic National Convention nominated Winfield S. Hancock** of Pennsylvania for the presidency and William H. English of Indiana for the vice presidency.

Nov 2: James A. Garfield was elected president of the United States. Chester A. Arthur was elected vice president. The electoral vote was Garfield, 214; Winfield S. Hancock, Democratic candidate, 155. The popular vote was Garfield, 4,449,053; Hancock, 4,442,035; James B. Weaver, Greenback-Labor candidate, 308,578; Neal Dow, Prohibition candidate, 10,305. In congressional elections the Republicans fell into a 37–37 tie with the Democrats in the Senate, with one seat going to a minor party. In the House the Republicans took a 147–135 majority, with 11 seats going to minor parties.

Nov 17: The **Chinese Exclusion Treaty** was signed with China at Peking. It gave the U.S. the right to "regulate, limit, or suspend" but not to exclude completely the entry of Chinese nationals.

II. Architecture
   Arts and Music
   Popular Entertainment
   Publishing
   Theater

The riches accumulated by the new millionaires of the Gilded Age provided them with the opportunity to become art collectors. This was also the period when public art museums began to appear, led by the Metropolitan Museum of Art in New York City. Formed in 1870, it opened its doors ten years later on its present site in Central Park, facing Fifth Ave. It was destined to become the most comprehensive art museum in the U.S. and one of the great museums of the world. Its early sponsors were from families of wealth and social position who tended to look down on the new rich. However, the latter were not ignored for long; their financial support was vital to the growth of such institutions as the Metropolitan. The new rich, in turn, were eager to secure the favorable publicity that came through substantial gifts to the arts.

Among **books published** this year was *Ben-Hur* by Lew Wallace, a highly successful historical romance about early Christians in the Roman Empire. It has not been out of print since and has twice been made into Hollywood movie extravaganzas. Other books published this year included *Democracy* by Henry Adams, a novel set in Washington, D.C.; *Ultima Thule* by Henry Wadsworth Longfellow, the venerable poet's next to last collection; *Bricks Without Straw* by Albion W. Tourgee, a novel of life in postwar North Carolina; and *A Tramp Abroad* by Mark Twain, another delightful travel narrative, based on a walking tour of Germany, Switzerland, and Italy.

III. Business and Industry
Education
Philosophy and Religion
Science

The Salvation Army, one of the most energetic and successful evangelical and philanthropic organizations in the world, made its debut in the U.S. this year. The Salvation Army had been founded in England in 1865 by William Booth and his wife Catherine. In 1880 Commissioner George Railton and seven women members arrived in the U.S. to found a branch in Pennsylvania. In 1904 Evangeline Booth, daughter of the founder, took charge of the U.S. branch. From its early days the street bands of the Army have been familiar and popular. The organization has from the beginning treated its women workers the same as its men.

Illiteracy in America was estimated at 17% of the population, a decrease of 3% over the previous decade.

A **successful roll film** for cameras was patented by George Eastman of Rochester, N.Y. In 1885 he placed on the market his first commercial film, cut into strips and sealed in a box camera that was returned to the factory for removal and developing. The introduction of daylight loading film came in 1891, and the first pocket Kodak in 1895.

House paint was manufactured for the first time from standard formulas. The Sherwin-Williams Company of Cleveland, Ohio, began producing an all-purpose paint for wood from an unvarying formula. This production method was later applied to stains, varnish stains, varnishes, and enamels.

Jan 27: A patent for an **incandescent lamp** was received by Thomas A. Edison. The filament was made with a carbonized cotton thread. The first public demonstrations of the lamp had been held on Dec. 31, 1879, at Edison's laboratories at Menlo Park, N.J. The first commercial installation of these lamps was made in the steamship *Columbia* of the Oregon Railroad and Navigation Company.

IV. Fashion
Folkways
Holidays
Social Issues and Crime
Sports

Wrestling was more popular than boxing as an American combat sport, especially on the frontier and in mining towns, until well into the nineteenth century. Abraham Lincoln in his younger days had been a skilled wrestler. In 1880 the leading wrestler in the U.S. was William Muldoon, who won the heavyweight title this year. Muldoon wrestled in the U.S. and in England and toured America with John L. Sullivan, the boxing champion. Muldoon once had an eight-hour match with Clarence Whistler; the bout ended in a draw. Muldoon also organized the Police Athletic Association and invented the medicine ball.

The **world heavyweight bare knuckle boxing championship** was won by Paddy Ryan this year. Ryan beat the defender, Joe Goss of England, in an 87-round bout near Colliers Station, W. Va.

Orange Blossom, a pseudonym for Joseph M. Mulholland of Washington, Pa., became famous as the byline for implausible stories printed as serious news items. Mulholland's most spectacular hoax was his account of a flaming meteor that supposedly landed in western Pennsylvania, setting fire to a huge area. In later years his stories came to be printed as short works of the imagination, not to be taken literally.

1881

I. Civil Rights
Exploration and Settlement
Government
Statistics
Wars

For the third time in U.S. history, a vice president succeeded to the highest office after death of the incumbent. Chester A. Arthur of New York came to the presidency on the death of Pres. James A. Garfield. Arthur had a poor reputation, a result of his association with Sen. Roscoe Conkling of New York, who had made the most of the spoils system. Arthur was also considered too fond of high living. Nevertheless, his administration brought no scandal to the office and, to the surprise of many, supported badly needed civil service reform. Arthur also supported the rebuilding of the U.S. Navy, which had languished since the Civil War.

Jan 24: The **federal income tax law of 1862** was declared constitutional by the Supreme Court in the case of *Springer v. United States*. Counsel for Springer argued that the tax was a direct tax, forbidden by Article 1, sections 2 and 9 of the Constitution. The Supreme Court ruled that there were only two kinds of direct tax—real property tax and poll tax—and the income tax was neither of these.

July 2: Pres. **Garfield was shot** in a Washington, D.C., railroad station by Charles J. Guiteau, a disgruntled and perhaps insane office seeker. Garfield survived for 80 days after he was shot, being treated in Washington and Elberon, N.J., where the Garfield family was summering at the seashore. The doctors' reports provided no guidance on the president's ability to fulfill his duties. Vice Pres. Chester A. Arthur served as acting president. Garfield died Sept. 19, 1881, without ever leaving his bed. He was buried in Cleveland, Ohio. Guiteau was hanged in Washington on June 30, 1882.

Sep 20: **Chester A. Arthur was inaugurated president** of the United States, succeeding to the presidency on the death of Pres. Garfield. The 21st president and a Republican, he served three years and five months.

II. Architecture
Arts and Music
Popular Entertainment
Publishing
Theater

Literary magazines and their editors exercised great influence in this era. Among the best was Richard Watson Gilder, who this year became editor of *The Century Illustrated Monthly*, the successor to the celebrated literary journal *Scribner's Monthly*. He continued as editor until his death in 1909. In its first years *The Century* specialized in the memoirs of Civil War generals. The magazine published the works of such leading authors as William Dean Howells, Josh Billings, F. Marion Crawford, and Joel Chandler Harris. Gilder also wrote 16 volumes of poetry. His sister, Jeannette, assisted him at editing and wrote for newspapers what was probably the first American literary gossip column.

Among **books published** this year was *A Century of Dishonor* by Helen Hunt Jackson. Previously a writer of popular but minor fiction, poems, and prose sketches, and now living in the West, Mrs. Jackson provided an eye-opening account of the U.S. government's ruthless treatment of Indians. Among other books of this year were *Uncle Remus: His Songs and His Sayings* by Joel Chandler Harris, full of authentic black folklore in dialect; *Dr. Breen's Practice,* a novel about a society woman as a physician by William Dean Howells; and two novels by Henry James, *Portrait of a Lady,* the masterpiece of his early novels, and *Washington Square,* a story unusual for James about Americans in their home environment.

America's most talented woman painter, **Mary Cassatt,** an expatriate, for the third year in a row exhibited her work in Paris beside the works of other Impressionists. Cassatt, owing much to Edgar Degas and Gustave Courbet, abhorred conventional art and espoused naturalism. Her renderings of mothers and children in intimate scenes, her etchings and color prints soon won her an international reputation.

John Singer Sargent in his *Vernon Lee* and *Portrait of a Lady* foreshadowed the brilliant success of *Madame X* (1884) and the stream of portraits of the great and near great that followed. His work was marked by an air of aloof elegance, seemingly spontaneous poses, and technically brilliant use of light colors to reveal shapes.

III. Business and Industry
Education
Philosophy and Religion
Science

Founding of an American branch of the Red Cross on May 21, 1881, inspired by the establishment of the International Red Cross in Europe in 1863, was largely the work of one woman, Clara Barton. Miss Barton, a teacher, volunteered to nurse wounded

Union soldiers during the Civil War; in 1864 she was put in charge of all hospitals of the Union Army of the James. She became known to the soldiers as "the angel of the battlefield." At the request of Pres. Abraham Lincoln, she headed a search for missing Union soldiers after the war. The American National Red Cross received a federal charter in 1900 and is the only organization with such a charter. Miss Barton headed the Red Cross until 1904.

The **first central electric power plant** in the world was constructed on Pearl St., New York City, under the direction of Thomas Edison. Operations began with one generator. Edison had solved the problem of designing a system for the efficient distribution of power from a central generating system.

IV. Fashion
   Folkways
   Holidays
   Social Issues and Crime
   Sports

There were many organizations for Americans to join at this time. Some were patriotic, some religious, some social. Others, such as volunteer fire companies, combined civic service with sociability. Some carried extravagant names, such as the Ancient Arabic Order of Nobles of the Mystic Shrine, or Daughters of Isis. Some went in for gaudy uniforms and much ceremony and ritual. Patriotic groups were especially popular in the late nineteenth century. The Sons of the American Revolution, the Daughters of the American Revolution, and the Colonial Dames of America were all founded between 1875 and 1894. Largest of all was the Grand Army of the Republic, made up of veterans of the Union Army, which reached a peak membership of 400,000 in 1890.

The home of **William Kissam Vanderbilt**, at the corner of Fifth Ave. and 52nd St., was completed at a cost of $3,000,000. It marked the beginning of the great and often monumental edifices erected by

American millionaires in imitation of the chateaus and palaces of Europe.

Nov 9-10: The **America's Cup** was successfully defended by the yacht *Mischief*, which won two straight races from the Canadian challenger *Atlanta*.

1882

I. **Civil Rights**
  Exploration and Settlement
  Government
  Statistics
  Wars

The first federal law restricting immigration was passed by Congress on Aug. 3. It set a head tax of 50 cents on each immigrant and excluded convicts, the insane, and persons likely to become public charges. The law was the result of agitation by states controlling the main ports of entry. They had attempted to regulate immigration with state laws and to set a tax in order to support needy newcomers. The Supreme Court declared such laws unconstitutional in 1876 on the grounds that they attempted to regulate foreign commerce, a right reserved to Congress. In the decade from 1881 to 1890, over 5,000,000 immigrants arrived in the U.S.

Mar 16: The **Geneva Convention** of 1864 for the care of wounded war personnel, accepted by most European nations, was ratified by the U.S. Senate. Clara Barton, founder of the American branch of the Red Cross in 1881, did much to promote public sentiment in favor of ratification.

Mar 31: **A pension for widows of presidents** was voted by Congress. Mrs. Polk, Mrs. Tyler, and Mrs. Garfield were each voted $5000 a year. This initiated the custom of voting pensions to widows of presidents.

May 6: The first **Exclusion Act** barred further Chinese immigration for ten years. The act was regularly renewed by Congress and was still on the books in 1920.

Nov 7: In **congressional elections** the Democrats gained 50 seats in the House to take a 197–118 majority, with ten seats going to minor parties. In the Senate the Republicans gained one seat to take a 38–36 majority over the Democrats, with two seats going to minor parties.

II. Architecture
Arts and Music
Popular Entertainment
Publishing
Theater

English actors and actresses continued to be popular in the U.S., although in some cases not entirely for their abilities on stage. Such a figure was Lillie Langtry, who married into London society and became the first society woman to go on the stage. Having made her debut in London in Dec. 1881, she made her first visit to the U.S. this year. On Nov. 6 she appeared as Rosalind in Shakespeare's *As You Like It* at the Fifth Avenue Theatre in New York City. Although not a great actress, Langtry was welcomed wherever she appeared in the U.S., as much for her beauty and her scandalous reputation as for her acting.

Among **books published** this year was the realistic novel by William Dean Howells, *A Modern Instance*. In it Howells traced the history of a marriage that led to divorce and the disintegration of character. Other books published included *John Randolph* by Henry Adams, a biography that reflected the author's sustained interest in the Founding Fathers of the U.S.; *Mr. Isaacs,* the first of many romantic novels by Francis Marion Crawford, based on the adventures of a gem dealer the author had met in India; *L'Abbé Constantin,* by a French dramatist and novelist, Ludovic Halévy, which delighted American readers in translation with its likable village priest and his problems, including two American women who had acquired a home in his idyllic parish; *The Prince and the Pauper* by Mark Twain, set in the reign of England's King Edward VI; and *Anne* by Constance Fenimore Woolson, the first of her five novels dealing realistically with life in northern Michigan.

"The Lady or the Tiger?" by Frank R. Stockton was published in *Century Magazine.* Sensationally popular at the time, this short story has since appeared in nearly every American anthology of fiction.

III. Business and Industry
Education
Philosophy and Religion
Science

A development in 1882 in the way large businesses were organized had economic repercussions for many years. John D. Rockefeller of the Standard Oil Company sought a means of legally controlling under one management companies owned in several states. A lawyer, Samuel C. T. Dodd, hit on the idea of the trust. Stockholders set up a board of trustees to whom were turned over the stocks of about 40 companies. The stockholders received trust certificates, which gave the trustees, Rockefeller and his close associates, the right to operate the companies as they saw fit. The Standard Oil trust, organized on Jan. 2, 1882, was capitalized at $70,000,000. Rockefeller himself owned about a third of all the trust certificates. The trust idea was soon copied in such fields as sugar and tobacco processing. The result was monopolistic control of a number of industries, leading eventually to political action to restore competition.

Prof. **Granville Stanley Hall** of The Johns Hopkins University, Baltimore, Md., was appointed to a special lectureship in psychology and given $1000 to establish a psychological laboratory. William James at Harvard University had previously organized a laboratory for work in "psycho-physics," but Johns Hopkins soon took over leadership.

The nation's **first hydroelectric plant** was built at Appleton, Wis., where the first electric streetcar went into service in 1886.

Feb 2: The **Knights of Columbus,** the first fraternal benefit society of Catholic men, was founded in New Haven, Conn., by the Rev. Michael Joseph McGivney. The society was chartered on March 29, 1882.

IV. Fashion
   Folkways
   Holidays
   Social Issues and Crime
   Sports

Americans have a tendency to make folk heroes of outlaws; one of the first of these heroes was Jesse James. Born on Sept. 5, 1847, in Missouri, Jesse Woodson James fought for the Confederacy in Quantrill's Raiders. In 1866 he and his brother, Frank, became leaders of a Midwest gang that first held up banks, then turned to train robbery. A reward offered by the governor of Missouri tempted a member of the gang, Robert Ford, to shoot and kill Jesse on Apr. 3, 1882. After Jesse's death Frank James surrendered, was acquitted of the charges against him, and lived out his life on a Missouri farm. Much has been written about the James gang, including a song, "The Ballad of Jesse James."

Handball was an unknown sport in the U.S. until Phil Casey, one of Ireland's finest handball players, this year came to live in Brooklyn, N.Y. Casey soon built a court and opened a school. He introduced the sport in the U.S. with the help of fellow immigrants from the British Isles.

The phrase **"the public be damned"** was offered by William H. Vanderbilt in answer to a question by Clarence Dresser, a reporter for the Chicago *Daily News.* When asked whether Vanderbilt, owner of the New York Central Railroad, was running the railroad for the public or the stockholders, Vanderbilt tossed off his remark, which was to become a symbol of the arrogance of the railroad barons.

The **U.S. Intercollegiate Lacrosse Association** was founded. The original members were Harvard, Princeton, and Columbia; Yale and New York University were admitted in the following year.

Feb 7: The **world heavyweight bare knuckle boxing championship** was won by John L. Sullivan, who defeated Paddy Ryan in a nine-round bout in Mississippi City, Miss. This year Sullivan toured the country, giving boxing exhibitions under Marquis of Queensberry rules, and offering $500 to any person who could last four rounds with him. His efforts gave boxing new respectability and wider popularity.

June 24: The only major league **baseball umpire expelled for dishonesty**, Richard Higham left the National League.

Sep 25: The **first major league double header** was played between the Providence and Worcester teams.

1883

I. Civil Rights
Exploration and Settlement
Government
Statistics
Wars

Shocked by the suggestion that the assassination of Pres. James A. Garfield in 1881 by a disappointed office seeker was an indirect result of the spoils system, Congress on Jan. 16 passed the Pendleton Act, which was signed into law by Pres. Chester A. Arthur. The law established a three-man Civil Service Commission and specified rules for filling federal government positions by a merit system, including competitive examinations. At the start, only about 14,000 of

100,000 positions were covered by the act, but by 1900 about 106,000 of 250,000 were covered. The worst evils of political patronage were ended, but the question of whether the act improved the efficiency of government, as reformers declared it would, remained unanswered.

Oct 15: The **Civil Rights Act of 1875,** which forbade racial discrimination or separation in public accommodations, was vitiated by a narrow Supreme Court decision. The Court held that only state-imposed discrimination was forbidden, not that by individuals or corporations.

Nov 18: A system of **standard time** was adopted by the railroads of the U.S. and Canada to eliminate problems in printed schedules caused by the unsystematic setting of local times. In 1884, at an international conference in Washington, D.C., a worldwide system of standard time was adopted. The prime meridian was assigned to the meridian passing through the British Royal Observatory at Greenwich, England.

II. Architecture
Arts and Music
Popular Entertainment
Publishing
Theater

A marvel of design and engineering that captured the imagination of the public was officially opened on May 24. This was the Brooklyn Bridge, spanning the East R. between Brooklyn and New York City. John A. Roebling, a pioneer in suspension bridge design, planned the bridge. Shortly after work began in 1869, Roebling was injured when a barge crushed his foot against a pier. Tetanus set in and he died on July 22, 1869. His son, Washington A. Roebling, took over. In 1872 he too was felled, by nitrogen narcosis, or the bends, the result of too much time spent in the underground caissons built to sink the massive foundations of the bridge towers. From 1872 on, he directed construction from an apartment overlooking the bridge site. The bridge has a span of 1595 feet. The striking towers at either end are 272 feet high, with foundations 78 feet below water level. A great civic celebration, attended by Pres. Chester A. Arthur and Gov. Grover Cleveland, marked opening day.

Among **books published** this year was the semiautobiographical *Life on the Mississippi* by Mark Twain. Although soon recognized as a classic account of the difficult art of piloting steamboats on the Mississippi R., and written with the verve of Twain at his peak, the book was not a best seller until it was issued in a paperback edition in the 1940s. Other books published included *The Story of a Country Town* by Edgar Watson Howe, published privately after rejection by many commercial publishers. It was a frequently republished pioneering work of naturalistic fiction set in a midwestern community. *The Old Swimmin' Hole and 'Leven More Poems* by James Whitcomb Riley contained some of Riley's most famous verse depicting rustic life in Indiana. It was written in Hoosier dialect and reached a wide audience.

The **highest masonry building** in the U.S., the Monadnock Building, was erected in Chicago. All 16 stories rest entirely on masonry walls, which are five feet thick at the base.

III. Business and Industry
Education
Philosophy and Religion
Science

Two American scholars were the leading sociologists of the time, but differed completely on the meaning of the theory of evolution, which was much discussed by intellectuals. They were Lester Frank Ward and William Graham Sumner. Ward, whose *Dynamic Sociology* was published this year, believed that the human mind, when properly used, could take an active part in the process of human evolution. He did not believe that evolution is an inevitable and uncontrollable process. Ward further developed his ideas in *Psychic Factors in Civilization* (1893) and *Pure Sociology* (1903). Sumner, on the other hand, believed that the fittest survived and deserved to survive, and that the fittest were those who lived by hard work and individualism. His views were expressed in *What Social Classes Owe to Each Other* (1883).

Experiments leading to development of the **fountain pen** were begun by Lewis E. Waterman. The first to apply the principle of capillary action, Waterman obtained patents and produced a practical pen in 1884, thus founding the Ideal Pen Company in New York City. By 1887 his business had expanded vastly and a new L. E. Waterman Company was incorporated.

Mar 24: The **first telephone service** between New York and Chicago was initiated.

Sep 21: The first direct **telegraph service to Brazil** from the U.S. was established.

IV. **Fashion**
   Folkways
   Holidays
   Social Issues and Crime
   Sports

The far West fascinated Americans in the late nineteenth century, as it has continued to do ever since. A taste of that region was brought east and to Europe with some authenticity by William Frederick "Buffalo Bill" Cody. A Pony Express rider, buffalo hunter, and Army scout, he organized "Buffalo Bill's Wild West Show" in 1883. The show may have given its first performance at North Platte, Neb., on July 4. Buffalo Bill toured with the show for years, both in the U.S. and abroad. It was a smash hit in England. Queen Victoria enjoyed watching stage coaches being held up and Indian attacks repulsed, all to the accompaniment of heavy gunfire.

June 2: The **first baseball game played under electric lights** took place in Fort Wayne, Ind. Fort Wayne beat Quincy 19–11 in seven innings.

June 16: The **first Ladies' Day baseball game** was staged by the New York Giants. On Ladies' Day, both

escorted and unescorted ladies were admitted to the
park free.

Oct 22: The **first annual New York Horse Show**
opened at Gilmore's Gardens, New York City. It was
organized by the National Horse Show Association of
America. Represented were 165 exhibitors and 299
horses; many workhorses, including fire-engine
horses, police mounts, and draught horses, were
shown. The show was immediately popular and became an annual event. After 1913 the character of the
show altered; working breeds were no longer allowed, and entries were limited to show horses,
gaited horses, and the like.

1884

I. **Civil Rights**
Exploration and Settlement
Government
Statistics
Wars

The presidential election campaign of 1884 was
fought mainly with attacks on the reputations of the
rival candidates. The Republican candidate, James G.
Blaine, on the basis of letters he had written, was
accused of having profited from the Crédit Mobilier
scandal involving the building of the Union Pacific
Railroad. His opponents sang: "Blaine, Blaine, James
G. Blaine, the continental liar from the state of
Maine." The Democratic candidate, Grover Cleveland, was accused of having fathered an illegitimate
child, which in his forthright manner he admitted.
The turning point of the election was a remark made
on Oct. 9 by the Rev. Samuel D. Burchard in New
York, in the presence of Blaine, that the Democrats
were the party of "Rum, Romanism, and Rebellion."
Blaine did not disavow the remark, and the Irish-

American Roman Catholics of New York were outraged. Cleveland carried the state by 1149 votes and
thereby won the presidency.

The **National Equal Rights Party** was formed by
a group of suffragists who nominated Mrs. Belva A.
Lockwood of Washington, D.C., for president. Mrs.
Lockwood, a lawyer and the first woman admitted to
practice before the Supreme Court, was renominated
in 1888. She was the first woman candidate for the
presidency.

June 3-6: The **Republican National Convention** nominated James G. Blaine of Maine for the presidency on
the first ballot. Gen. John A. Logan of Illinois was
nominated for the vice presidency.

July 8-11: The **Democratic National Convention
nominated Gov. Grover Cleveland** of New York for
the presidency and Thomas A. Hendricks of Indiana
for the vice presidency.

July 23: The **Prohibition Party National Convention**
nominated John P. St. John of Kansas for the presidency and William Daniel of Maryland for the vice
presidency.

Aug 5: The cornerstone of the pedestal of the **Statue of
Liberty** was laid at Bedloe's Island (now Liberty Island) in New York harbor. The pedestal, which holds
the statue by the French sculptor Frédéric Auguste
Bartholdi, is 151 feet high.

Nov 4: Grover Cleveland was elected president of the
United States. Thomas A. Hendricks was elected vice
president. The electoral vote was Cleveland, 219;
James G. Blaine, Republican of Maine, 182. The popular vote was Cleveland, 4,911,017; Blaine, 4,848,334;
Benjamin F. Butler, Greenback Party candidate,
175,370; John P. St. John, Prohibition candidate,
150,369. In congressional elections the Republicans
gained five seats in the Senate to gain a 43–34 majority. In the House the Republicans gained 22 seats but
the Democrats held a 183–140 majority. Robert M. La
Follette, Republican of Wisconsin, was elected to his
first term in the House of Representatives.

II. Architecture
   Arts and Music
   Popular Entertainment
   Publishing
   Theater

Although newspaper chains had not yet come into existence, there was a market for news and feature material gathered by a news organization and made available for a fee to newspapers all over the country. The first such syndicate was founded on Nov. 8 by Samuel Sidney McClure, who had come to America from Ireland as a boy. In 1893 he founded *McClure's Magazine*, which became a great success under his editorship. The magazine was especially noted for the articles it published in the early twentieth century by such leading muckrakers as Ida Tarbell and Lincoln Steffens.

Among **books published** this year was *Huckleberry Finn* by Mark Twain. A world classic, this picaresque novel of Huck's adventures with his black friend Jim drew on the author's experiences on the Mississippi R. The river also served as a backdrop for a variety of rivermen, actors, and rascals, authentic vernacular speech, tall tales, and folklore. Also published this year were *A Roman Singer* and *To Leeward*, novels with an Italian setting by Francis Marion Crawford; *Excursions of an Evolutionist* and *The Destiny of Man in the Light of His Origin* by John Fiske, the best-known defender of Darwinism in the U.S.; the romantic novel *Ramona* by Helen Hunt Jackson, which reached millions of readers with its impassioned plea for justice for American Indians; *A Country Doctor*, another minor but solid novel by Sarah Orne Jewett; *In the Tennessee Mountains* by Mary Noailles Murfree, using the pseudonym Charles Egbert Craddock, the first collection of short stories with realistic settings and genuine Cumberland Mts. dialect; and *Montcalm and Wolfe*, the sixth and next-to-last of Francis Parkman's volumes in his mammoth history of French and English relations in North America.

John Singer Sargent, the brilliant American

painter living abroad, exhibited *Mme. Gautreau*, his portrait of a lady in a decolleté black dress. The painting caused a sensation. Critics accustomed to stodgy, rather unrealistic portraits charged Sargent with eroticism and provocativeness. Sargent withdrew the portrait to his studio, where as *Madame X* it remained until 1915. It was one of his masterpieces.

III. Business and Industry
Education
Philosophy and Religion
Science

The formation of national and local learned societies accelerated. At least 79 were organized in the 1870s and 121 in the 1880s. The American Historical Association, founded at Saratoga, N.Y., in 1884, was among the most important of these societies; it began publishing the *American Historical Review* in 1895. There were also more specialized groups, such as the American Society for Church History (1897) and the American Irish Historical Association (1897).

The **Linotype** automatic typesetting machine, which could form an entire line of type as one piece of metal, was patented by Ottmar Mergenthaler. Mergenthaler received patents for improvements in 1885. The first Linotype machines were put into operation by the New York *Tribune* on July 3, 1886. Mergenthaler's typesetter revolutionized the publishing industry.

IV. Fashion
Folkways
Holidays
Social Issues and Crime
Sports

One method of showing off newly acquired wealth in the Gilded Age was to build an elaborate and costly mansion. This went on chiefly in New York City, Chicago, and San Francisco, and at such summer resorts as Newport, R.I. At Fifth Ave. and 91st St. in New

York City, Andrew Carnegie, the steel magnate, erected a mansion with gold plumbing fixtures. In Chicago the Potter Palmers, society leaders, constructed a castlelike home with a tower 80 feet high. On Nob Hill in San Francisco, James C. Flood, whose wealth came from mining, built a 42-room house that was surrounded by a block-long bronze fence. It took the full-time services of a man to keep it polished.

The derisive term *mugwump* had wide currency during this election year. It was applied to those Republicans, reformist or liberal, who bolted the party to vote for the Democratic nominee, Grover Cleveland. The word derives from an Algonquian word meaning "big chief." Its first prominent use was by Charles Dana, editor of the New York *Sun,* with the implication that Republican bolters thought themselves above party affiliations. The term is now applied to bolters of any party.

The Knights of Labor, at their convention, designated that **Labor Day** be celebrated annually on the first Monday in September. Previously, the holiday had been celebrated sporadically. In 1887 several states established the first Monday in September as Labor Day; others followed suit shortly. Not until 1894 did Congress declare Labor Day a legal holiday for federal employees.

The **first black major league baseball player** was Moses Fleetwood Walker, who played for Toledo in the American Association.

June 5: Gen. **William Tecumseh Sherman,** a hero of the Civil War, declined the offer of the Republican presidential nomination with these words to the Republican convention: "I will not accept if nominated and will not serve if elected." Sherman was without political experience or inclination.

1885

I. Civil Rights
Exploration and Settlement
Government
Statistics
Wars

Under pressure from the Knights of Labor and other workers' groups, Congress on Feb. 26 passed the Contract Labor Law, or Foran Act, to further restrict immigration. The Knights had charged that American employers were signing up foreign workers with the promise of paying their passage to the U.S. and then were bringing them in for use as strikebreakers. Actually, most strikebreakers were hired from private labor agencies in large cities. The new law, virtually outlawing alien contract labor, did not, however, apply to skilled laborers needed by new industries or to certain other groups, such as actors and servants.

Feb 25: **Fencing of public lands** in the West was prohibited by an act of Congress. On Aug. 17 Pres. Grover Cleveland reinforced the act with orders to remove all illegal enclosures. Five years before, Carl Schurz, secretary of the treasury, had conducted an investigation into public land abuses. Since then, pressure mounted steadily to prevent railroad and cattle interests from exploiting the weak postwar management of western lands. By fencing in all water sources, special interests were concentrating great holdings. They reacted to the strictures of 1885 by forcing William A. J. Sparks, in 1887, from his presidential appointment as land commissioner. Agitation for reform persisted and eventually won out.

Mar 3: **Special delivery service** was inaugurated by the U.S. Post Office Dept.

II. Architecture
Arts and Music
Popular Entertainment
Publishing
Theater

Ragtime, the earliest form of jazz, began its rise to popularity with the arrival this year in St. Louis, Mo., of Scott Joplin. Joplin was born in Texarkana, Tex., in 1868, the son of a former slave. A self-taught musician, he was only 17 when he arrived in St. Louis. He began playing the piano in honky-tonks along Chestnut and Market streets. In ragtime the melody is syncopated on the piano with the right hand while the left keeps a regular beat in march style. In the late 1890s Joplin turned to composing. Among his best known works are "Maple Leaf Rag" and "The Entertainer," the latter supplying the background music for the 1973 movie *The Sting*. Joplin also composed a ragtime opera, *Treemonisha*.

Among **books published** this year, *The Rise of Silas Lapham* by William Dean Howells showed Howells at the peak of his form in depicting a self-made man and his family transplanted into Boston society. Also published were Ulysses S. Grant's unassuming *Personal Memoirs* in two volumes, a work that became a best seller and saved his heirs from penury; and the first major work by the Harvard philosopher and teacher Josiah Royce, *The Spirit of Modern Philosophy*.

The **Marshall Field Building,** designed by Henry Hobson Richardson, was completed, marking the beginning of a new era in commercial architecture. One of the Boston architect's masterpieces, it reflected Richardson's grasp of the realities of commercial problems and his talent for achieving, despite functional requirements, a logical, even exuberant, effect. His influence on Louis Sullivan and later Chicago architects is clear.

Feb 21: The **Washington Monument** was dedicated in the nation's capital, 37 years after the cornerstone was laid, four and a half years after construction began. Total cost was a bit less than $1,200,000. The monument is 555 feet 5 and one-eighth inches high. Ascent and descent can be made by elevator or by negotiating 898 steps. The monument was opened to the public on Oct. 9, 1888.

III. Business and Industry
   ## Education
   ## Philosophy and Religion
   ## Science

One of the most dreaded diseases of the time was tuberculosis, for which there was no specific remedy. Edward Livingston Trudeau, a New York physician, contracted the disease while taking care of his tubercular brother and went to live in the Adirondack Mts. in New York State. There, spending much time in the open air, he regained his health. He believed the cold dry air of the mountains and his way of life, which included much rest, were the cause of his cure. As a result, he opened the Adirondack Cottage Sanatorium in 1885 at Saranac Lake, N.Y. This first institution of its kind in the U.S. was initially a one-room cottage with simple furnishings and facilities. The sanatorium functioned until 1954, when it closed for lack of patients, modern methods of diagnosis and treatment having by then reduced deaths from tuberculosis in the U.S. by 95%.

Furnaces for **garbage disposal** began to be introduced in many cities, particularly in the landlocked Middle West, as a health measure. It had been discovered that swine fed with garbage from the cities contracted trichinosis, which could be transmitted to consumers of the infected meat.

IV. Fashion
   ## Folkways
   ## Holidays
   ## Social Issues and Crime
   ## Sports

A world's fair in the U.S., the New Orleans Exposition, attracted international attention when it opened on Jan. 24, 1885. It was the largest yet held in the U.S., being a third again larger than the Centennial Exposition in Philadelphia in 1876. Many nations, including England, France, China, Japan, Austria, and all the nations of South America, had exhibits. The U.S. was represented by exhibits from each department of the federal government and from the Smithsonian Institution, which had a display of "almost every survival of prehistoric times." Americans took special pride in what one observer termed "the unrivaled collection of American products and resources."

The **fashion in clothing** was described thus in *Harper's Bazaar:* " 'Moyen âge' is the term used to describe the new fashion in the spring of 1885. Scarfs, handkerchiefs, wide ribbons and fabrics are emblazoned to imitate medieval banners. Vieux rouge (old red) is showing two tones while the new blue is called vieille blouse usée, the color of workmen's shirts. Much beige and cream color and bright gold is being shown. Flowers and scarfs are replacing feathers on hats. Combinations of two materials with long drapery and plain lawn skirts are being used in both suits and dresses."

Sep 14-16: The **America's Cup** was successfully defended by the U.S. yacht *Puritan,* which won two straight races from the British challenger *Genesta.*

Dec 20: A **weightlifting feat** of incredible proportions was accomplished by William B. Curtis, who was reported to have lifted 3239 lbs. "with harness."

1886

I. **Civil Rights**
   Exploration and Settlement
   Government
   Statistics
   Wars

The nation was stirred by an incident on May 4 in Chicago's Haymarket Square. A labor rally there, which included speeches by anarchists, was breaking up when a large force of police arrived. A bomb exploded among them, killing seven officers and wounding about 60. The anarchists were blamed and the police arrested eight leaders of what came to be known as the Haymarket Riot. Their trial began on June 19. Although no evidence was ever presented to identify any of the accused as the bomb thrower, all eight were convicted on Aug. 20. Seven were sentenced to death, one to jail. Of the condemned, four were hanged on Nov. 11, one committed suicide in jail, and two had their sentences changed to life imprisonment. Seven years later, on June 26, 1893, Gov. John Peter Altgeld of Illinois pardoned the three still in jail. For this act he was denounced by some as little better than an anarchist himself.

Jan 19: A Presidential Succession Act was passed by Congress. It provided that in the event of removal, death, resignation, or inability of the president and vice president, the heads of the executive departments, in the order of the creation of their offices, would succeed to the presidency. A new order of succession was adopted in 1947, and it was superseded by the Twenty-fifth Amendment to the Constitution in 1967.

Sep 4: Geronimo, the inveterate Apache raider along the Mexican border, surrendered to Gen. Nelson A. Miles in Arizona. All the Chiricahua Apaches were then resettled in Florida as war prisoners. They were relocated to Fort Sill, Okla., in 1894.

Oct 28: The **Statue of Liberty** was unveiled and dedicated by Pres. Grover Cleveland in a ceremony on Bedloe's Island. The 225-ton, 152-ft. tall copper statue was presented to the U.S. by France in commemoration of 100 years of American independence.

Nov 2: In **congressional elections** the Republicans lost four seats in the Senate but held a 39–37 majority over the Democrats. In the House the Democrats lost 14 seats but held a 169–152 majority, with four seats going to minor parties.

II. Architecture
Arts and Music
Popular Entertainment
Publishing
Theater

Not surprisingly, the Civil War became a source of material for playwrights. The first important drama using this subject opened in Brooklyn, N.Y., on Feb. 22. It was *Held by the Enemy* by William Gillette, the actor and dramatist. Its plot concerned two soldiers in love with the same woman in an occupied southern city. In 1895 Gillette again used a Civil War setting, this time in a spy episode in *Secret Service*. Gillette's most popular play, however, was *Sherlock Holmes* (1899), in which Gillette was to act the title role until a few years before his death in 1937.

Among **books published** this year was an immensely popular story for children, *Little Lord Fauntleroy* by Frances Hodgson Burnett. The little gentleman-hero has long since lost any appeal for youngsters, but the illustrations by Reginald Bathurst Birch set a durable fashion for children's clothing, and 40 years later Mary Pickford played Fauntleroy in one of her box office successes. Also published were *The Midge* by Henry Cuyler Bunner, a graceful novelette by the poet-editor of *Puck; Indian Summer*, a romantic novel set in Florence, *Tuscan Cities*, a travel book, and *The Garroters*, a farcical play, all by William Dean Howells; *Princess Casamassima*, a novel by Henry James in which he uncovered the social ferment underlying the surface placidity of upper-class life in London; and *Hugh Wynne* by Silas Weir Mitchell, a noted Philadelphia physician and neurologist, partly a historical romance, partly a novel of psychology, first appearing as a serial in *Century Magazine*.

III. Business and Industry
Education
Philosophy and Religion
Science

A significant step in the growth of the labor movement was taken on Dec. 8 in Columbus, Ohio, when
the American Federation of Labor (AFL) was organized by about 25 labor groups representing 150,000
members. The new union grew out of the Federation
of Organized Trades and Labor Unions, formed in
1881. The first president of the AFL was Samuel Gompers, president of the Cigarmakers Union, who held
the office except for one year until his death in 1924.
The AFL was craft-oriented and favored skilled
labor. Under Gompers' leadership, it had nothing to
do with politics or socialistic programs, but put its
efforts into securing higher wages, shorter working
hours, and better working conditions. By 1890 the
AFL had 225,000 members; by 1900 its membership
was 550,000.

A cheap process for extracting **aluminum** from its
ore was invented by Charles Martin Hall. His electro-
lytic method caused the price of aluminum to drop
from $5.00 a lb. in 1888 to 18 cents in 1914.

The **Whiskey Trust** was formed on the model of
the Standard Oil Trust. It included 80 distilleries, of
which all but 12 were closed down; profits were distributed pro rata.

IV. Fashion
Folkways
Holidays
Social Issues and Crime
Sports

What a person will do to achieve instant notoriety
was demonstrated on July 23 when Steve Brodie, a
bookmaker, allegedly jumped off the Brooklyn
Bridge into the East R., a drop of about 140 feet.
Some said that a dummy was dropped while Brodie

hid under a pier, waiting to appear at the proper moment. In any event, Brodie opened a profitable saloon on the strength of the feat. Brodie later took to the stage and repeated his act by jumping from a "bridge" in the melodrama *Mad Money*, first performed at Niblo's Garden in New York City on Feb. 22, 1891.

The **first international polo match** was held between England and the U.S. at Newport, R.I.; it was a gala occasion. Both teams were colorfully dressed in satin and full-length leather boots. The grounds were lined with members of the social set of New England and New York. The visiting team, more practiced, swept the match 10–4 and 14–2.

Jan 1: The **first Tournament of Roses** was held in Pasadena, Calif., staged by the Valley Hunt Club, which had been founded by Charles Frederick Holder, a distinguished naturalist. Mr. Holder suggested that the members of the Valley Hunt Club decorate their carriages with the natural flowers of California on New Year's Day and that after a parade of these carriages a program of athletic events be devised to round out the day. Holder's floral motif has remained a feature of the tournament to this day.

Sep 9-11: The **America's Cup** was successfully defended by the U.S. yacht *Mayflower*, which won two straight races from the British challenger *Galatea*.

1887

I. Civil Rights
Exploration and Settlement
Government
Statistics
Wars

Growing agitation by farmers and others over the abuses of railroads in setting rates and in other matters resulted in the establishment of the first regulatory commission in U.S. history. This was the Interstate Commerce Commission, set up by the Interstate Commerce Act of 1887, which became law on Feb. 4. The law stated that interstate railroads must charge reasonable, not discriminatory, rates, and prohibited them from engaging in pooling operations. Drawbacks and rebates, both forms of rate reduction for preferred customers, were outlawed, and charging more for a short haul than a long haul was forbidden. In part, the law was an outgrowth of the Wabash case of 1886, in which the Supreme Court ruled that a state could not regulate an interstate railway that went through its territory. The railroads soon found ways to evade the act, and the Supreme Court reversed decisions of the commission.

Free delivery of mail was provided in all communities with a population of 10,000 or more.

Feb 3: The **Electoral Count Act** was created by Congress to avoid disputed national elections. It made each state responsible for its own electoral returns and forced Congress to accept the results except in the case of irregularity.

Mar 2: Pres. Grover Cleveland signed the **Hatch Act,** which called for establishment of an agricultural research and experiment station in each state with a land-grant college. The act also authorized annual appropriations to each state on the establishment of such a station.

II. Architecture
   Arts and Music
   Popular Entertainment
   Publishing
   Theater

The variety of American stage offerings in the late nineteenth century could be seen in a listing of plays that opened in New York City in 1887. Rapidly becoming a favorite was the young Edward Hugh Sothern, who played in a popular comedy, *The Highest Bidder*, which opened at the Lyceum Theater on May 3. *The Still Alarm*, which opened at the 14th Street Theater on Aug. 30, featured Harry Lacey playing a fireman. *A Hole in the Ground*, with William Mack, opened at the same theater on Sept. 12. David Belasco and Henry C. De Mille scored a resounding success with their first collaboration, *The Wife*, which opened at the Lyceum Theater on Nov. 1. That same night Ada Rehan, already popular, starred in *The Railroad of Love* at Daly's Theater, with Mrs. George H. Gilbert and John Drew in the cast. This year Rehan also gave her New York debut performance as Kate in Shakespeare's *The Taming of the Shrew*.

Augustus Saint-Gaudens completed his famous standing statue of Abraham Lincoln for Lincoln Park, Chicago. Lincoln, with slightly bowed head, stands before a chair from which he has seemingly just risen.

III. Business and Industry
Education
Philosophy and Religion
Science

Copying the lead of the Standard Oil trust in 1882, other industries rushed to establish trusts to secure monopolies and eliminate competition. In the decade beginning in 1887, 86 combinations of companies were made. Another 149 combinations were formed by 1900. This year saw formation of the Sugar Trust (American Sugar Refineries Company), the Whiskey Trust (Distillers' and Cattle Feeders' Trust), the Lead Trust, and the Cotton-Oil Trust, as well as monopolies in the wallpaper, shoelace, and oatmeal industries. When trusts were formed, some plants in the industry were closed to restrict supplies and raise prices, thus putting people out of work. In the case of the Sugar Trust, 11 out of 18 refineries were immediately shut down.

The interest of **Theodore Roosevelt** in the protection of big game and wildlife became manifest in his appeal for the formation of the Boone and Crockett Club, named for two of his heroes. Since 1883, Roosevelt had been buying Dakota ranchlands. He gave up these investments in 1887, but contact with the open spaces had stimulated his interest in nature. In 1888 he set down his western experiences in the book *Ranch Life and the Hunting Trail.*

IV. Fashion
Folkways
Holidays
Social Issues and Crime
Sports

Trade, manufacturing, transportation, and technology were greatly increasing the nation's wealth, yet there seemed to be a growing gap between the poorest and the richest Americans. For the poor, clothing tended to be drab and dark, as did furniture. Men went to work in overalls. Among women of all levels, clothing was mainly heavy and dark, except for the young and those in society who could spend freely. Gentlemen in society wore full dress suits to social affairs. The growing middle class enjoyed the good things of life to an increasing extent, living in comfortable homes. The average middle-class home was crowded with weighty furniture, thick draperies, and innumerable knickknacks.

The **first true golf club** in the U.S. was probably the Foxbury Golf Club, founded in Foxbury, Pa., as a result of John Mickle Fox's trip to Scotland, where he learned the game. The club is still in existence. There were golf clubs calling themselves such in Savannah, Ga., and Charleston, S.C., as far back as 1795 and 1796, but there is no record that their members ever played golf.

Mar 2: The **American Trotting Association** was organized at Detroit, Mich.

Sep 17-30: The **America's Cup** was successfully defended by the U.S. yacht *Volunteer*, which won two straight races from the British challenger *Thistle*.

1888

I. **Civil Rights**
   Exploration and Settlement
   Government
   Statistics
   Wars

The main issue in the presidential election campaign of 1888 was whether the tariff should be reduced; Democrats said yes, Republicans no. Pres. Grover Cleveland, the Democratic candidate, did not campaign, feeling it was beneath the dignity of the office of president. Benjamin Harrison, the Republican candidate, brought the front porch campaign to its peak. Republican groups were told when to visit Harrison's home, and the candidate was well prepared for each, including the Republican White Hat Club of Ohio. In all, he addressed about 300,000 people without leaving home. Late in the campaign, on Oct. 26, the British minister to the U.S. was tricked into writing a letter saying it would be best for England if Cleveland were reelected. Sensing there was still some latent dislike of the mother country, the Republicans turned this against Cleveland even though he had sent the hapless diplomat home.

The **secret ballot** was first used in the U.S. in local elections in Louisville, Ky. Adopted in Australia as early as 1858, the secret ballot came to be referred to in America as "kangaroo voting." Henry George, proponent of the single land tax, was among the earliest American public figures urging adoption of the secret ballot. In 1950 South Carolina became the last state to adopt the secret ballot.

Mar 12: A 36-hour **blizzard**, which struck the region

around New York City, cost 400 lives and destroyed millions of dollars of property. The city was virtually isolated from the world when the heavy snows halted transportation and disrupted communications. Messages to Boston had to be relayed via England.

June 5: The **Democratic National Convention nominated Pres. Grover Cleveland** for a second term. Allen G. Thurman of Ohio was nominated for the vice presidency.

June 25: The **Republican National Convention nominated Benjamin Harrison** of Indiana for the presidency and Levi P. Morton of New York for the vice presidency.

July 29: A **yellow fever epidemic** broke out in Jacksonville, Fla., and persisted until Dec. 7. Over 4500 cases were reported, and more than 400 persons died. Similar epidemics struck throughout the South during this period.

Nov 6: Benjamin Harrison was elected president of the United States. Levi P. Morton was elected vice president. The electoral vote was Harrison, 233; Pres. Grover Cleveland, the Democratic candidate, 168. The popular vote was Harrison, 5,444,337; Cleveland, 5,540,050; Clinton B. Fisk, Prohibition candidate, 250,125; Alson J. Streeter, Union Labor candidate, 146,897; Robert H. Cowdrey, United Labor candidate, 2808. In congressional elections the Republicans kept their 39–37 majority in the Senate and gained 14 seats in the House to take a 166–159 majority.

II. Architecture
   Arts and Music
   Popular Entertainment
   Publishing
   Theater

A new generation of musicians was emerging; they were to dominate American music until the time of World War I. These composers, whose works and writings reflected particularly the influence of Johannes Brahms, became known as the New England

Academicians or Boston Classicists. Among them was Arthur William Foote, the only important American composer of the period educated entirely in the U.S. His choral work *The Wreck of the Hesperus* was enthusiastically received in Boston this year. He composed an overture, *In the Mountains,* in 1887 and *Suite for Strings* in 1889.

Among **books published** this year was *Looking Backward, 2000–1887,* a Utopian fantasy by Edward Bellamy, a little-known journalist and novelist. Bellamy hit on the right medium for expressing his concern with social problems in an industrialized society. The book sold l,000,000 copies in a few years, and Bellamy clubs devoted to the nationalization of industry and redistribution of wealth sprang up everywhere. Also published this year were *The American Commonwealth,* a classic that ranks with Alexis de Tocqueville's *Democracy in America* as a sympathetic but penetrating analysis, by James Bryce, British historian, frequent visitor to the U.S., and later ambassador to the U.S. (1907–1913); *Acres of Diamonds* by Russell Conwell, an inspirational classic first delivered as a lecture in 1861 but polished through use on the Chautauqua circuit (over 6000 times); *The Critical Period of American History, 1783–1789* by John Fiske, who was now turning from evolution to history; *The History of the Inquisition in the Middle Ages* by Henry C. Lea, probably the best historical work to date by an American historian in a field other than U.S. history; *Political Essays,* the last published work of James Russell Lowell; and the first volumes in *The Library of American Literature,* edited by the poet, stockbroker, and critic Edmund Clarence Stedman.

May: "Casey at the Bat," by Ernest Thayer, was given its first public recitation by the popular actor DeWolf Hopper, at Wallack's Theater, New York City.

III. Business and Industry
Education
Philosophy and Religion
Science

Scientists and inventors were beginning to put electricity to practical use. Among the leaders in this field was Nikola Tesla, who was born in Austria-Hungary in 1857 and came to the U.S. in 1884. In 1888 he invented the alternating current motor, one of his most important contributions. Other inventions included an arc lighting system (1886), an alternating current transmission system (1888), and high-frequency current generators (1890). Tesla also worked on a system for transmitting power without wires. In his later years he was occupied with telephony and telegraphy.

George Eastman introduced the **Kodak,** a square box camera using roll film. Kodak camera No. 1 was at first marketed already loaded; the photographer mailed the Kodak to the factory, which returned prints and the reloaded camera. Photography became a practical hobby overnight, and sales skyrocketed.

June 13: A **Department of Labor** without Cabinet status was established by an act of Congress. In 1903 it was reduced to the status of a bureau in the Dept. of Commerce and Labor. On Mar. 4, 1913, Congress created a Department of Labor headed by a Cabinet member.

July 27: The **first electric automobile,** designed by Philip W. Pratt, was demonstrated in Boston. It was a tricycle driven by storage batteries, and was built by the Fred W. Kimball Company of Boston.

IV. Fashion
   Folkways
   Holidays
   Social Issues and Crime
   Sports

Although it was not the first golf club established in the U.S., St. Andrews Club in Yonkers, N.Y., founded this year, clearly marked the point at which the game became firmly rooted in the U.S. Clubs were soon set up in Boston, New York, and Philadelphia. By 1892 the game was moving westward, soon reaching the Pacific coast. In 1893 a course for women only was opened in Morristown, N.J., and by 1894 there were 100 courses in the country. At this time golf was a game for the well-to-do, and the players, who wore rather odd costumes, including scarlet coats, were often objects of ridicule.

The political slogan **"As Maine goes, so goes the nation"** was adopted by the Republican Party after the election of Benjamin Harrison. State elections in Maine for decades to come were held weeks before national elections, so they were used as gauges for predicting the results in the national balloting. Maine remained staunchly Republican until the era of Franklin D. Roosevelt.

Jan 21: The **Amateur Athletic Union** of the U.S. (AAU) was formed, winning control over amateur athletics from unscrupulous promoters. The AAU's ideal was to preserve "sport for sport's sake." It came to supervise and conduct programs and competitions in about 20 sports and to represent the U.S. in international amateur sports federations. Its influence has been reduced since World War II by the takeover of collegiate sports by the National Collegiate Athletic Association (NCAA) and by the increasing professionalization of many sports.

June 9: The 22nd annual **Belmont Stakes** was won by Sir Dixon, with a time of 2:40¼. The jockey was Jimmy McLaughlin, who picked up his sixth Belmont Stakes win. McLaughlin was the only jockey in Belmont history to twice win the race three times in a row (1882–1884, 1886–1888).

1889

I. Civil Rights
Exploration and Settlement
Government
Statistics
Wars

A controversy involving the U.S., Great Britain, and Germany over the Samoan Islands in the Pacific Ocean threatened to break out into armed conflict. In 1889 warships of the three nations converged in the region, reflecting the three powers' interest in the civil war being fought on the islands. A showdown among the naval vessels in the harbor of Apia was averted only when a fierce storm destroyed all the warships except one English vessel. On Apr. 29 a conference opened in Berlin and on June 14 the three nations agreed on a treaty that provided for a three-power protectorate to guarantee Samoan independence.

Feb 11: The **Department of Agriculture** was raised to Cabinet status by Congress. Pres. Grover Cleveland appointed Norman J. Colman as its first secretary. He served less than three weeks before being replaced by Jeremiah M. Rusk, appointed by incoming Pres. Benjamin Harrison.

Apr 22: At noon the great **Oklahoma land rush** began. The federal government, pressured by cattlemen, opened for settlement 1,900,000 acres in central Oklahoma bought from the Creek and Seminole tribes. Thousands of settlers raced in after a pistol shot signaled the opening. Many Oklahomans had already made illegal entry to stake claims to the best land. In fact, by 10 A.M. of the opening day, Guthrie, the designated central city for the new territory, had swelled with settlers seeking plots in the new territorial capital.

May 31: The disastrous **Johnstown flood** killed 2295 persons when the dam above Johnstown, Pa., broke after heavy rains had swelled the Conemaugh R. The flood destroyed four valley towns before drowning Johnstown in 30 feet of water. Every Johnstown survivor lost a relative or friend in this calamity.

Nov 2: **North and South Dakota** were admitted into the Union, the 39th and 40th states.

Nov 8: **Montana** was admitted into the Union, the 41st state.

Nov 11: **Washington** was admitted into the Union, the 42nd state.

II. Architecture
Arts and Music
Popular Entertainment
Publishing
Theater

A new approach to women's magazines was introduced this year by Edward W. Bok, who took over editorship of the *Ladies' Home Journal*. Hitherto such periodicals had offered only light entertainment and household hints. By publishing serious articles on civic affairs, waging crusades against social ills, and printing the writings of leading authors such as Mark Twain and Rudyard Kipling, Bok demonstrated that women's interests were wider than had been assumed. By the time Bok retired in 1919, the *Journal's* circulation had increased from 440,000 to 2,000,000.

Among **books published** this year was *A Connecticut Yankee in King Arthur's Court* by Mark Twain, in which the author further explored the ironies of human nature and existence by setting a Yankee industrialist in the not-so-romantic days of chivalry. Also published were the first two volumes of *The History of the United States* by Henry Adams, for many years the best account of the administration of Thomas Jefferson; *Sant'Ilario*, one of Francis Marion Crawford's better romantic novels of life in Italian society, part of his trilogy begun in *Saracinesca* and concluded in *Dr. Orsino* (1892); *A Little Book of Western Verse* by Eugene Field, which brought the Chicago columnist-poet a wider following; *Chita: A Memory of Last Island* by Lafcadio Hearn, the first novel by an atypical American author on an atypical theme, the destruction of an island and the hazards faced by a lost child; *Annie Kilburn* by William Dean Howells, a novel in which Howells took up the cause of labor; and the first two volumes of *The Winning of the West* by Theodore Roosevelt.

**III. Business and Industry
Education
Philosophy and Religion
Science**

Liberal thinkers within American Protestantism reacted to the problems caused by rapid industrializa-
tion with a movement that came to be known as the
Social Gospel, or Christian Socialism. These leaders
believed that Christian churches should do more
than strive for personal salvation. They worked to
abolish child labor, secure better working conditions
for women, and gain a living wage for all workers.
They believed that the growing concentration of
wealth was inimical to the teachings of Christ. The
early leader of the Social Gospel movement was the
Rev. Washington Gladden, who wrote *Burning Questions* (1890). Somewhat later, the Rev. Walter
Rauschenbusch became an important figure. Among
economists, Richard T. Ely took a forceful part.
Others active in the Society of Christian Socialists,
which held a meeting in Boston this year, were
Josiah Strong, David Jayne Hill, and E. Benjamin
Andrews.

Hull House, a settlement house that would become
famous, was established in a slum neighborhood in
Chicago by Jane Addams. Like other settlement
houses of this period, Hull House was patterned after
Toynbee Hall in London.

The **first movie film** was developed by Thomas A.
Edison on a base devised by George Eastman.

The **Singer Manufacturing Company** of Elizabeth-
port, N.J., produced and marketed the first electric
sewing machine known in the U.S.

**IV. Fashion
Folkways
Holidays
Social Issues and Crime
Sports**

As methods of transportation improved, there was a
temptation to see how far one could go in the shortest

time. Nellie Bly (Elizabeth Cochrane Seaman), a reporter for Joseph Pulitzer's New York *World,* set out on Nov. 14 to better the record of 80 days around the world set by Jules Verne's fictional hero Phileas Fogg. Using trains, boats, bullock carts, and her own energy, Nellie made it back to New York City on Jan. 25, 1890, with a time of 72 days, 6 hrs., 10 min., 58 sec. She was much acclaimed, especially by the *World.* She recounted her trip in *Nellie Bly's Book: Around the World in Seventy-Two Days* (1890). The year it was published, someone named George Train went around the world in 67 days, 12 hrs., 3 min., but no one paid him much attention. This was not Nellie Bly's first headline-grabbing exploit. Earlier she had had herself committed to a facility for the mentally ill on Blackwell's Island, New York City, and in 1887 recounted her adventures in *Ten Days in a Mad House.*

Walter Camp listed in *Collier's Weekly* the first **All-American football team,** selecting 11 college football players as best in the nation at their positions. The selection was made by Caspar Whitney, who chose the All-American teams through 1896. The selections appeared in articles in *Collier's* annually until Camp's death in 1925, when Grantland Rice took over the task. Today selections are made by various polls of sportswriters and coaches.

July 8: Bare knuckle boxing had its last and most memorable bout when John L. Sullivan knocked out Jake Kilrain in the 75th round for the U.S. heavyweight championship at Richburg, Miss. Sullivan then claimed the world's championship, for Kilrain had fought a draw with the champion of England, Jem Smith. After this bout boxing with gloves under Marquis of Queensberry rules was introduced.

1890

I. Civil Rights
Exploration and Settlement
Government
Statistics
Wars

Mounting pressure for federal restraint of monopolistic industrial trusts resulted in the passage on July 2 of the Sherman Antitrust Act, named for Sen. John Sherman, Republican of Ohio. The law stated: "Every contract, combination in the form of trust or otherwise, or conspiracy, in restraint of trade or commerce among the several States, or with foreign nations, is hereby declared illegal." In practice, the lack of definition of such words as trust weakened the law. Also, it was not clear whether the law applied to labor unions. The act did not accomplish as much as its advocates hoped because of the way federal courts interpreted it and because, for the first ten years at least, no vigorous attempt was made to enforce it.

The **Census** recorded a population of 62,947,714. The center of population was placed at 20 mi. east of Columbus, Ind.

Feb 10: Some 11,000,000 acres of **Sioux Indian territory,** ceded to the U.S. in 1889, were opened for general settlement.

Apr 14: The **Pan-American Union** was created by a resolution of the Pan-American conference held in Washington, D.C., between Oct. 2, 1889, and Apr. 21, 1890.

May 2: The **Oklahoma Territory,** the last territory in the contiguous United States, was created by an act of Congress. It was established by redefining Indian territory and creating an area for settlers within Indian lands.

July 3: Idaho was admitted to the Union, the 43rd state.

July 10: Wyoming was admitted to the Union, the 44th state. As a territory it had given women the vote in 1869. It was the first territory and the first state to do so.

Oct 1: The **Weather Bureau** was created in the Dept. of Agriculture by an act of Congress. Weather information had previously come from the Army Signal Corps.

Nov 4: In **congressional elections** the Republicans gained eight seats in the Senate to lead the Democrats 47–39, with two seats going to minor parties. In the House a Democratic landslide gave Democrats a 235–88 majority, with nine seats going to minor parties.

Dec 15: Sitting Bull, chief of the Sioux Indians, was killed in a skirmish with U.S. soldiers along the Grand R. in South Dakota.

II. Architecture
    Arts and Music
    Popular Entertainment
    Publishing
    Theater

Toward the end of the nineteenth century, light and comic operas became popular. The two leading composers were Victor Herbert and Reginald De Koven. The latter wrote 19 comic operas, of which the most popular by far was *Robin Hood,* first produced in Chicago this year on June 9. It contained his two most popular songs, "Brown October Ale" and "Oh, Promise Me." De Koven also wrote two grand operas, *Canterbury Pilgrims* (1917) and *Rip Van Winkle* (1920).

Among **books published** this year was *Poems,* a selection of poems among many by Emily Dickinson that were found after her death by her sister. It received mixed reviews because her poetry, often unrhymed and subtle, struck an unfamiliar note. Her place in U.S. poetry gradually became secure, and her popularity and reputation skyrocketed after World War II. Also published this year were *A Hazard* *of New Fortunes,* a long, complex novel by William Dean Howells, in which a cast of 15 major characters and many minor figures scramble for success in New York City; *The Influence of Sea Power upon History,* by Navy Capt. Alfred Thayer Mahan, a classic analysis of sea power; *Abraham Lincoln: A History* in ten volumes by John Nicolay and John M. Hay, wartime secretaries to the president which became a standard biography; and *Black Beauty,* by Anna Sewell, an English book for children issued in the U.S. under the aegis of the American Humane Society.

Louis H. Sullivan's Wainwright Building was erected in St. Louis. The Chicago architect has been called the father of modern architecture and the inventor of the skyscraper. The Wainwright Building was one of his best works. Also this year, Sullivan's Chicago Auditorium was completed. It was for many years the greatest structure of its type anywhere.

May 30: The cornerstone of the **Washington Memorial Arch,** in marble, was laid. The arch was originally built of wood. This masterpiece by architect Stanford White stands at the foot of Fifth Ave. in New York City.

III. Business and Industry
Education
Philosophy and Religion
Science

As the century neared its end, the U.S. developed a school of philosophy of its own—pragmatism. The term had been used in a magazine article as early as 1878 by Charles Sanders Peirce. Pragmatism taught that truth was to be found not in theoretical speculation, but in the practical outcome of ideas. It judged ideas and actions by their consequences, if any. This truly American philosophy was developed by William James, who became the most influential thinker of his time. He earned an international reputation and brought the concept of pragmatism to a wide audience. James's *Principles of Psychology,* published this year, became a classic. The book was thoroughly empirical and made a laboratory science of psychology.

The growth of **child labor** in the South was reflected in the fact that some 23,000 children were now employed in the factories of the 13 southern states. Adoption by industry of the traditional agricultural family system of employment was mainly responsible for the high number of children employed.

Illiteracy in America was estimated at 13.3% of the population, a decrease of 3.7% in a decade.

The establishment of **Sequoia and Yosemite national parks** by the federal government assisted the cause of conservation in the U.S. by protecting native species of animal and plant life from hunters and timber interests.

Formation of the **American Tobacco Company**, after a price war among cigarette companies, created a monopoly organized by James Buchanan Duke. Duke later created similar monopolies for plug tobacco and snuff. Ultimately he established the Duke Endowment, principally for the benefit of Trinity College in Durham, N.C., in 1924 renamed Duke University.

Pyramiding of wealth in the U.S. led to estimates that 1% of the people possessed more wealth than the rest of the people combined.

Jan 23: The **fastest railroad time** for an American train was claimed for the Atchison, Topeka & Santa Fe Railroad, which carried reporter Nellie Bly from La Junta, Colo., to Chicago at an average speed of 78.1 mph.

Oct 6: The sanctioning of **polygamy** was discontinued by the Mormon Church. Thereafter most cases in conflict with federal law concerned men who had married polygamously before 1890.

IV. **Fashion**
   Folkways
   Holidays
   Social Issues and Crime
   Sports

The existence of urban slums was well known by many, but it was not until the publication this year of *How the Other Half Lives* by Jacob A. Riis, a Danish-born New York City journalist, that the reality of the miserable lives led by thousands in the slums was brought home to the general public. The book triggered efforts to alleviate these conditions by improving labor conditions and instituting building codes. In his book Riis cited facts and figures and told of his experiences in the slums. Battling alone at first, Riis gained many supporters and found a powerful ally in Theodore Roosevelt. He also made enemies of landlords and politicians who were profiting from the slums.

Smoking by men at social functions became more acceptable during this decade, but the social taboo against women smoking in the company of men remained strong.

The **two-step** came into vogue. This lively dance step probably owed much to John Philip Sousa's fast "Washington Post March." In any case, the two-step replaced several older dances, such as the galop, quadrille, lancers, reel, polka, and Portland fancy.

Aug 6: The **first electrocution** took place at Auburn Prison, Auburn, N.Y. The executed prisoner was William Kemmler of Buffalo, who had been convicted of the hatchet murder of Matilde "Tillie" Ziegler, his common-law wife, on Mar. 28, 1889. The execution was botched. George Westinghouse, Jr., reported: "It has been a brutal affair. They could have done better with an axe."

Nov 29: The **first Army-Navy football game** was played at West Point, N.Y. The score was Navy 24, Army 0. The contest became an annual event between the two service academies (except for 1909, 1917–1918, and 1928–1929).

1891

I. **Civil Rights**
   Exploration and Settlement
   Government
   Statistics
   Wars

The tide of immigration continued to flow strongly. To help deal with it, the position of superintendent of immigration was created on Mar. 3. In this one year, 560,319 immigrants arrived at American ports, and during the 1890s the total was 3,687,000. Until the 1880s, most of the immigrants had come from western and northern Europe. However, in the 1880s such immigration decreased and the numbers arriving from southern and eastern Europe and the Middle East swelled greatly. These new immigrants were less equipped to fit into American life, and almost all had to start at the bottom of the economic ladder.

Mar 3: U.S. **Circuit Courts of Appeal** were created by an act of Congress. This relieved the Supreme Court of some of its appellate jurisdiction.

Mar 4: Congress passed the **International Copyright Act,** which gave British, French, Belgian, and Swiss authors copyright protection in the U.S. American publishers had previously pirated works by foreign authors, depriving them of their royalties and injuring American authors, whose books had to be priced higher than those of foreign authors because of the inclusion of royalties in the price. Copyright protection was later extended to include most other countries of the world.

May 19: The **People's, or Populist, Party** was launched in Cincinnati, Ohio. Farmers in the West and South were in desperate economic plight, and backers of the new party, thinking eastern bankers were hoarding gold, advocated free coinage of silver.

High railroad rates also were hurting farmers, so they advocated government ownership of railroads. Free silverites captured the Democratic Party in 1896, but lost the election by 600,000 votes.

Sep 22: Nine hundred thousand acres of **Indian land** in Oklahoma were opened for general settlement by a presidential proclamation. The land had been ceded to the U.S. by Sauk, Fox, and Potawatomi Indians.

II. Architecture
Arts and Music
Popular Entertainment
Publishing
Theater

One of the greatest careers of the American stage, extending over more than 40 years, came to an end on Apr. 4 at the Brooklyn, N.Y., Academy of Music when Edwin Booth appeared for the last time in *Hamlet.* Booth had always been popular and his restrained style of acting departed from the more emotional style of many others, but his career had been checkered, marked by bankruptcy and then by scandal when his brother, John Wilkes Booth, assassinated Pres. Abraham Lincoln. Among Booth's most notable achievements were the 100-night run of *Hamlet* in 1864 in New York City; the building of Booth's Theater in New York in 1869, where Booth presented the works of William Shakespeare; and the bequest of his New York home to the Players' Club, which he founded in 1888 and served as first president.

Among **books published** this year was *Tales of Soldiers and Civilians* by the San Francisco journalist Ambrose Bierce, a writer fascinated by the supernatural, the mysterious, the terrifying, and the intensely emotional. His *Tales,* based on his Civil War experiences, was later reissued under the title *In the Midst of Life.* It included the oft-anthologized "An Occurrence at Owl Creek Bridge" and "A Horseman in the Sky" and established his reputation in the East. Other

books published were *Poems, Second Edition,* by
Emily Dickinson; *The American Revolution* by the
skillful popularizer of U.S. history, John Fiske; *A New
England Nun and Other Stories* by Mary Wilkins
Freeman, offering expert portrayals of Massachusetts farm folk undergoing deformation of character
or spirit in an era that was leaving them behind;
Main-Traveled Roads, stark short stories and
sketches against a background of dreary midwestern
farm life, by Hamlin Garland; *Colonel Carter of Cartersville,* a novelette about a gentleman of the old
South down on his luck, which made Francis Hopkinson Smith a popular author; and a final collection
of poems and prose by the aging Walt Whitman,
Goodbye, My Fancy.

Nov 9: The **longest consecutive theatrical run** to date
was begun with the opening of *A Trip to Chinatown,*
a farce about San Francisco by Charles H. Hoyt. It
ran 650 performances, closing on Aug. 17, 1893, and
held the record until 1918. Hoyt had already satirized
spiritualism, the plumbing industry, railroad operations, and politics.

III. Business and Industry
Education
Philosophy and Religion
Science

As the nation grew, it became increasingly industrialized. Industrial and agricultural production was rising, and imports and exports rose steadily as well.
Agricultural products still represented the largest
part of exports, but in the 1890s they declined from
74.5% of the total to 61% by 1900. During the decade,
manufactured goods' share of exports rose from
17.87% to 31.65%. The value of imports increased
from $789,310,404 in 1890 to $849,941,184 in 1900.

Henry O. Havemeyer created the **American Sugar
Refining Company** under a New Jersey charter, after
having his Sugar Refineries Company in New York
broken up by the state's antitrust laws. Thus reorganized and without legal impediment, American Sugar

went on to control half the sugar consumed in the U.S. by the time of Havemeyer's death in 1907.

Aug 24: A **patent for a motion picture camera,** the first in its field in the U.S., was filed by Thomas A. Edison.

Oct 16: The **first correspondence school** in the U.S. was opened by Thomas Jefferson Foster, editor of the Shenandoah *Herald*. Now known as the International Correspondence School, Scranton, Pa., it was begun to teach mining methods to workers to increase safety in coal mines.

Dec 29: An early patent for **wireless telegraphy** was issued to Thomas Edison for a "means of transmitting signals electrically . . . without the use of wires." The patent was the result of experiments conducted in 1885. On Nov. 15, 1883, Edison had received a patent for his two-element vacuum lamp, the forerunner of the vacuum tube rectifier.

IV. Fashion
   Folkways
   Holidays
   Social Issues and Crime
   Sports

A unique event in sports history occurred this year when James Naismith, a physical education instructor at what is now Springfield College, Springfield, Mass., invented the game of basketball. No other sport is known to owe its origin to one person. Basketball is the only popular American game that does not have English origins. Naismith was seeking to create a game that could be played indoors in winter and allow fast action and competition but not be as rough as football, which was gaining a reputation for violence. The first basketball game employed a soccer ball and two peach baskets. The rules Naismith devised have not been changed basically in nearly 100 years.

Oct 18: The **first International six-day bicycle race** in the U.S. was run in Madison Square Garden, New York City. Riders used high-wheelers and worked alone, pumping until exhausted, then resting and starting again for 142 hours. The first winner was "Plugger Bill" Martin. The record under one-man rules was established in 1898 by Charlie Miller at Madison Square Garden, who rode 2093.4 miles. Most of his competitors ended up in hospitals, suffering from exhaustion.

1892

I. Civil Rights
Exploration and Settlement
Government
Statistics
Wars

As the 1892 presidential election approached, there was dissatisfaction among voters with both the Democratic and the Republican parties. Many thought the tariff rates too high, the farmers complained of low prices for their products, and there was a feeling that the government favored bankers and industrialists at the expense of the common man. The only party to show much concern about these issues, the People's Party, usually referred to as the Populists, was organized this year. The Populists campaigned vigorously for such proposals as public ownership of the railroads, an eight-hour day for labor, and a currency system controlled by the federal government, not the banks. In the election, the Populists became the first third party since 1860 to win electoral college votes, carrying Kansas, Colorado, Idaho, and Nevada.

Jan 1: Ellis Island in upper New York Bay became the receiving station for immigrants. On Nov. 12, 1954, it was closed after 62 years and the processing of 20 million immigrants. It is now part of the Statue of Liberty National Monument.

June 7-11: The **Republican National Convention**

nominated **Pres. Benjamin Harrison** for reelection and Whitelaw Reid of New York for the vice presidency.

June 21-23: The **Democratic National Convention nominated Grover Cleveland** of New York for the presidency and Adlai Ewing Stevenson of Illinois for the vice presidency.

Oct 15: The **Crow Indian reservation** in Montana was opened to settlers by presidential proclamation. The territory covered 1,800,000 acres.

Nov 8: Grover Cleveland was elected president of the United States. Adlai E. Stevenson was elected vice president. The electoral vote was Cleveland, 277; Pres. Benjamin Harrison, Republican incumbent, 145; James B. Weaver, Populist candidate, 22. The popular vote was Cleveland, 5,554,414; Harrison, 5,190,802; Weaver, 1,027,329; John Bidwell, Prohibition candidate, 271,058; Simon Wing, Socialist Labor candidate, 21,164. In congressional elections the Democrats gained five seats in the Senate for a 44–38 majority, with three seats going to minor parties. In the House the Democrats lost ground but kept a 218–127 majority, with 11 seats going to minor parties.

II. Architecture
Arts and Music
Popular Entertainment
Publishing
Theater

The cornerstone for what was intended to be the largest church in America, the Protestant Episcopal Cathedral of St. John the Divine, was laid on St. John's Day, Dec. 27. It was located on 11.5 acres of land in upper Manhattan, New York City. In a competition, the architectural firm of George Lewis Heins and Christopher Grant La Farge had won the award with plans for a structure in the Romanesque style. It was to be 601 ft. long, 146 ft. wide at the nave, and 320 ft. wide at the transept. Construction proceeded in fits and starts because of the great amount of money needed. In 1911 the trustees decided to change the partly built cathedral to the Gothic style, which would make it the largest Gothic cathedral in the world. Plans originally submitted by the architect Ralph Adams Cram were adopted. Today the cathedral is still incomplete, although work is once more in progress.

Among **books published** this year was the final edition of *Leaves of Grass* by Walt Whitman. Also published were *The West from a Car Window* by Richard Harding Davis, editor of *Harper's Weekly*, which collected reports on his extensive travels in the U.S.; *The Adventures of Sherlock Holmes*, the first collection of the short stories by Arthur Conan Doyle about literature's most famous detective; *The Quality of Mercy*, a novel by William Dean Howells in which he again probes the relationship between the economic order and the crimes of individuals; *Barrack-Room Ballads* by Rudyard Kipling, demonstrating the English poet's heroic view of his nation's imperialism; *The Old South* by Thomas Nelson Page, offering vivid if sentimental essays and sketches about plantation life; *Green Fields and Running Brooks*, another collection of Hoosier poems by James Whitcomb Riley; and *The History of David Grieve* by Mrs. Humphry Ward, a novel promoting the social application of Christianity.

Jack "Papa" Laine formed the Reliance Brass Band in New Orleans. A white musician, Laine was one of the first to imitate black styles of hot music. His later organization, Jack Laine's Ragtime Band, was probably the first white Dixieland jazz band.

"After the Ball Is Over," a perennial favorite song in the U.S., was composed by Charles K. Harris, one of the most successful songwriters of the 1890s and early 1900s. "After the Ball" became a tremendous hit during the Columbian Exposition of 1893 in Chicago.

The first home designed by **Frank Lloyd Wright,** it is widely believed, was Charnley House, built in Chicago. Wright made the plans while still working for the firm of Adler & Sullivan.

III. Business and Industry
   Education
   Philosophy and Religion
   Science

The growing conflict between capital and labor resulted this year in violent conflict in the Homestead Strike. On July 1, when a contract between the Amalgamated Association of Iron and Steel Workers and the Carnegie Steel Company expired, the company cut wages and refused to recognize the union. The workers struck on June 26. On July 6 the company brought in 300 Pinkerton guards to protect the Homestead plant, near Pittsburgh, Pa. A pitched battle resulted. The Pinkertons were turned away with three dead and many wounded; ten strikers were killed. The company hired strikebreakers and at its request the governor of Pennsylvania, Robert E. Pattison, sent in the state militia on July 12. The militia protected the strikebreakers hired by Carnegie. The strike ended on Nov. 20 with the workers admitting defeat. The union was destroyed and many of the men never got their jobs back.

The **fundamentalist-modernist controversy** was heated up by the heresy trial of Charles A. Briggs, professor of the Old Testament at Union Theological Seminary, New York City. Prof. Briggs, on his elevation to a distinguished chair at the seminary, delivered a paper taking a liberal approach on the authority of the Bible. Many orthodox Presbyterian ministers, sensing a threat in Briggs's modernist biblical views, persuaded the General Assembly of the Presbyterian Church, which held veto power over the seminary's appointments, to exercise its veto. The New York Presbytery then tried Briggs for heresy; he was acquitted. The prosecution appealed the decision to the assembly, which condemned Briggs and suspended him from the ministry. The case aroused partisan feelings among Presbyterian ministers across the country, and several defenders of Briggs were suspended, notably Prof. H. P. Smith of Lane Theological Seminary in Cincinnati, Ohio. At the end, the seminary broke off its Presbyterian relationship, became nondenominational, and kept its distinguished scholar.

The **First Church of Christ, Scientist** was founded in Boston, Mass., by Mary Baker Eddy and a small group of followers.

The **boll weevil,** a beetle of Mexican or Central American origin, was first seen in Texas; from there the pest spread widely, causing severe damage to U.S. cotton crops.

Nikola Tesla developed the first motor that could effectively utilize alternating current for power.

Sep: The **first successful gas-powered automobile** made in the U.S. was built by Charles and Frank Duryea, bicycle designers and toolmakers, at Chicopee, Mass. Afraid of ridicule if they tested the vehicle publicly, the builders tested it indoors. A more powerful model was given a successful trial run at Springfield, Mass., in 1893.

IV. Fashion
Folkways
Holidays
Social Issues and Crime
Sports

One of the most intriguing murder cases in U.S. history began on Aug. 4 when Andrew J. Borden and his second wife, Abby, were murdered with blows from an ax in their Fall River, Mass., home. Mr. Borden's 32-year-old unmarried daughter, Lisbeth A. Borden, was accused of the crime, although she denied it. Miss Borden did not testify at her trial. She was acquitted and the case was never solved, although it gave the world a still well-known jingle:

> Lizzie Borden took an ax,
> Gave her mother 40 whacks.
> When she saw what she had done,
> She gave her father 41.

Lizzie Borden spent the rest of her life as a virtual recluse and died in her Fall River home on June 1, 1927, at 68.

The phrase *the 400* with reference to society's elite achieved an almost instant place in American idiom after it was used by New York City's social arbiter, Ward McAllister. Asked to shorten a long list of persons to be invited to a ball in the Astor ballroom, which would hold only 400, McAllister commented that there were "only 400 persons in New York society." Social commentators and society gossips quickly gave the remark wide circulation. Those with social pretensions who were left off the list were outraged.

George W. G. Ferris designed the **Ferris wheel.** He built the first one in 1893 for the Columbia Exposition. Forty passengers could be carried 250 feet high in its 36 cars.

Sep 7: James J. Corbett won the **world heavyweight boxing championship** by knocking out John L. Sullivan in the 21st round. The bout, held at New Orleans, La., has been considered the first heavyweight title bout fought with gloves under Marquis of Queensberry rules, including three-minute rounds.

Oct 5: The notorious **Dalton gang** of robbers was virtually wiped out at Coffeyville, Kans., while attempting to rob a bank.

Oct 20-23: The **World's Columbian Exposition** was opened with magnificent dedication ceremonies at Chicago. Vice Pres. Levi Morton gave the opening address. John Philip Sousa, who resigned from the Marine Corps this year to organize his own band, conducted. The exhibition was the result of public demand for fitting commemoration of the discovery of America. On Apr. 25, 1890, Congress had passed an act that authorized an "exhibition of the arts, industries, manufactures, and products of the soil, mine and sea." Pres. Benjamin Harrison had recommended that a sum of "not less than $10 millions" be allotted to the fair. Total expenditures have been estimated as over $22,000,000. The fair was set out on an area of 644 acres, with the exposition itself covering 150 acres. There were 50 acres of concessions and 55 acres of state, transportation, electric, arts, and liberal arts buildings. It officially opened May 1, 1893.

1893

I. Civil Rights
Exploration and Settlement
Government
Statistics
Wars

A bitter political battle was fought over repeal of the Sherman Silver Purchase Act of 1890, which required that the U.S. treasury buy at market value 4,500,000 ounces of silver a month. When, by Apr. 15, 1893, the gold reserve in the treasury fell below the $100,000,000 level because silver had been overvalued in relation to gold, Pres. Grover Cleveland and others blamed the Sherman Act for creating too much money. Cleveland called a special session of Congress for Aug. 7, but it was Oct. 30 before both houses of Congress, after much debate, voted repeal. Cleveland was thus able to keep the U.S. on the gold standard, but he alienated members of the Democratic Party who wanted easy credit.

Jan 17: A **revolution in Hawaii** deposed Queen Lili-uokalani with at least the foreknowledge of the U.S. minister to Hawaii, John L. Stevens. A provisional government headed by Sanford B. Dole was protected by 300 U.S. Marines from the cruiser *Boston.* The provisional government requested the U.S. to annex the islands. The queen later protested her ouster to Pres. Grover Cleveland.

Apr 3: The **first U.S. ambassador to the Court of St. James** was named: Thomas Francis Bayard, secretary of state in Pres. Cleveland's first administration. Up to this time the highest U.S. diplomatic title had been minister.

July 17: Commissioner James H. Blount's **report on the Hawaiian revolution,** delivered to Sec. of State Walter Q. Gresham, accused Minister Stevens of active participation in all phases of the Hawaiian uprising. Stevens's supporters countercharged Blount with compiling a lopsided report based on a small sampling of Hawaiian opinion and of failing to question Stevens himself. Not until 1898 was Hawaii annexed as a territory.

Aug 24: A devastating **cyclone** ripped through Savannah, Ga., and Charleston, S.C., killing some 1000 persons and causing terrible damage.

Sep 16: The **Cherokee Strip,** between Kansas and Oklahoma, was opened for land rush settlement. More than 100,000 persons rushed into an area of 6,000,000 acres that had been purchased from the Cherokee Indians in 1891.

Sep 17: Yellow fever cases reached epidemic proportions in Brunswick, Ga.

Nov 7: Women's suffrage was adopted in Colorado.

II. Architecture
Arts and Music
Popular Entertainment
Publishing
Theater

American playwrights were relying more and more on domestic themes, characters, and settings for their plays, and were writing more realistic, if still melodramatic, plays. One such author, and also a leading actor, was James A. Herne, whose play *Shore Acres*, depicting life in New England, became a hit in 1893. The play deals with tensions in a family in a quietly realistic way. The play ran for 113 performances in Boston, beginning in Feb. 1893, and then became a success in New York City, opening on Dec. 25 at Daly's Theater.

Among **books published** this year was *Maggie: A Girl of the Streets*, by a 21-year-old newspaper reporter, Stephen Crane. Unable to find a publisher for a realistic novel about a prostitute, Crane published privately; no one paid attention to it until the success of his *Red Badge of Courage* in 1895. The significance of *Maggie* became clearer as grimly naturalistic portrayals of the seedy side of American life became increasingly the material of American writers. Also published this year were *Can Such Things Be?* by Ambrose Bierce, hair-raising tales of the supernatural; *The Cliff Dwellers*, a novel about the relationships of people working in a Chicago skyscraper, by Henry Blake Fuller; *Nights with Uncle Remus*, another of the popular collections of tales by Joel Chandler Harris; *The World of Chance* by William Dean Howells, expressing a stark view of life and society; *The Heavenly Twins* by Sarah Grand (pen name of Mrs. Frances Elizabeth M'Fall, an English women's rights activist), a best seller treating hitherto taboo subjects fictionally; and *The Strange Case of Dr. Jekyll and Mr. Hyde* by Robert Louis Stevenson, six years after its appearance in England.

The world premiere of **Antonín Dvořák's** *New World Symphony* was given in New York City. Dvořák, who had been in the U.S. only a year, produced the most American composition of the nineteenth century. Though no theme of the symphony is specifically drawn from folk music, many are close to the spirit of plantation songs and Indian melodies.

The first completely independent architectural commission of **Frank Lloyd Wright**, the Winslow residence in Chicago, was built this year.

Oct 23: *In Old Kentucky* by Charles T. Dazey opened in New York City, a melodrama so popular that it ran for 27 consecutive seasons either in New York City or on the road. The play makes use of fights, murder, horse racing, and conflict between mountaineers and plainsmen.

III. Business and Industry
Education
Philosophy and Religion
Science

A worldwide financial panic and economic depression began in the spring of 1893. Sensing weakness in the American economy, foreign investors began withdrawing their capital. Railroads began to go into bankruptcy, the steel industry declined, and the banking system was strained to the limit. On May 5 and June 27 stocks fell sharply on the New York Stock Exchange. On June 26 the value of the U.S. silver dollar had fallen from 67 cents to less than 60 cents in gold. A panic in New York City was averted on June 29 by a loan of $6,000,000 by clearinghouse banks. Pres. Cleveland directed the treasury to sell government bonds to New York City banks for gold; four issues of such bonds totaled $293,000,000. Nevertheless, by December about 600 banks had failed and by June 1894 no fewer than 194 railroads had gone bankrupt. Unemployment climbed, and by the winter of 1893–1894 there were about 2,500,000 persons out of work. Democrats blamed the high tariff and excess government spending by Republicans. Gold standard advocates blamed the depression on agitation for more and cheaper money. The populists blamed everything on the gold standard and a shortage of currency. The economy gradually improved, but it was 1897 before it could be said that good times had returned.

Frederick Jackson Turner made his famous contribution to American historiography with "The Significance of the Frontier in American History," an address delivered before the American Historical Association. Turner argued that the ever-expanding frontier of the U.S. provided the key to understanding the differences between Europeans and Americans.

A **zipper,** or slide fastener, was patented by Whitcomb L. Judson. It consisted of a series of hooks and eyes that fastened with a slider. An improved zipper with the meshed tooth type of slide familiar today was patented in 1913 by Gideon Sundbach.

Jan 4: Violators of the **Anti-polygamy Act** of 1882 were granted amnesty in a pronouncement by Pres. Grover Cleveland, with the stipulation that they observe the law henceforward. The pronouncement applied chiefly to elderly Mormons.

Dec 24: Henry Ford completed construction of his first successful gasoline engine. His first motor car was assembled in 1896. It made a successful run on June 4 powered by a two-cylinder, four-cycle gasoline motor.

IV. Fashion
Folkways
Holidays
Social Issues and Crime
Sports

The World's Columbian Exposition, on the shores of Lake Michigan in Chicago, was officially opened to the public on May 1 to mark the 400th anniversary of the discovery of America by Christopher Columbus. The exposition had been authorized by Congress in 1890 and formally dedicated on Oct. 12, 1892. The exposition's 150 buildings of Greek, Romanesque, and Renaissance styles of architecture became known as the White City; the buildings exhibited the talents of the foremost American architects and sculptors. Seven thousand workmen were employed in construction of the exposition. Popularly known as the Chicago World's Fair, the exposition covered 600 acres, brought exhibits from 72 countries, and by the time it closed on Oct. 30 attracted more than 27,000,000 visitors. The architecture and the landscaping had a powerful effect on the nation and was largely responsible for the so-called City Beautiful movement, which sought to make American cities more attractive and livable through the planning of buildings and parks.

The **rise of bicycling** as a means of transportation and recreation in the U.S. was indicated by the increase of bicycles in use from some 20,000 in 1882 to over 1,000,000 in 1893.

The first recorded **intercollegiate relay race** was run at Philadelphia between teams representing the University of Pennsylvania and Princeton University. In 1895 Penn initiated its Penn Relay Carnival with a series of mile relay races. Today the Penn Relay is considered the foremost annual track and field meet in the world. Relay races are an American contribution to an ancient sport.

June 14: Flag Day was first officially observed by the city of Philadelphia by order of the mayor, who ordered that the flag be displayed over every public building in the city. The mayor's order was pursuant to a resolution of the Colonial Dames of the State, whose president, Mrs. Elizabeth Duane Gillespie, was directly descended from Benjamin Franklin.

Oct 7-13: The **America's Cup** was successfully defended by the U.S. yacht *Vigilant*, which won three straight races from the British challenger *Valkyrie*.

1894

I. Civil Rights
Exploration and Settlement
Government
Statistics
Wars

A new form of protest over economic conditions appeared this year when Coxey's Army, a band of unemployed workers, began a march on Washington, D.C. Jacob S. Coxey was an Ohio businessman and social reformer who gathered together some hundred unemployed followers. Headed by a six-piece band, the group set out for the capital on Mar. 25 from Massilon, Ohio. Coxey expected to gather a large throng on the way to call attention to the plight of the unemployed and to demand government action, such as a large-scale road building program. The men were well received along the way but on Apr. 30, when they arrived in Washington, the army numbered only about 400 men. The next day Coxey and two others were arrested for trespassing on the Capitol lawn when they tried to present petitions to Congress. The army disbanded. Similar armies set out from other starting points, even from the West Coast, but of these, only 17 out of some 1200 persons reached Washington.

Jan 8: A **fire** at the site of the Chicago World's Columbian Exposition destroyed virtually all the buildings, with property damages estimated at $2,000,000.

Mar 17: A **Chinese Exclusion Treaty**, by which China agreed to exclusion of Chinese laborers from the U.S., was signed. The Senate ratified the treaty on Aug. 13.

June 21: The **Democratic Silver Convention** was held in Omaha, Neb.; 1000 delegates attended. William Jennings Bryan led the convention to the adoption of a free-coinage plank on a silver-to-gold ratio of 16 to 1.

Aug 8: The **Hawaiian Republic** was officially recognized by the U.S. government. On May 31 the U.S. had recognized that Hawaii should have its own government and that interference from any foreign power would be considered unfriendly to the U.S. On July 4 the Republic of Hawaii had been proclaimed and a progressive constitution adopted.

Aug 27: The **first graduated income tax law** was passed by a predominantly Democratic Congress after acrimonious debate. It was denounced by Sen. John Sherman (Ohio) as "socialism, communism, devilism." The law was declared unconstitutional in the next year by the Supreme Court. It was part of the Wilson-Gorman Tariff Act, which became law without the signature of Pres. Cleveland.

Nov 6: In **congressional elections** the Republicans regained control of both houses of Congress, taking a 43–39 majority in the Senate, with six seats going to minor parties, and taking a 244–105 majority in the House, with seven seats going to minor parties. William Jennings Bryan of Nebraska, defeated in his bid for a Senate seat, became editor in chief of the Omaha *World-Herald*. He became an enormously popular speaker on the national lecture circuit.

II. Architecture
Arts and Music
Popular Entertainment
Publishing
Theater

Few American women became professional painters at this time, but one who did so was Mary Cassatt, who spent most of her life in France. There she took part in the impressionist movement and became a friend of Edgar Degas and Edouard Manet. She was the only American invited by the impressionists to exhibit with them. Motherhood was one of her favorite subjects; she did several versions of *Mother and Child*. In 1893 she painted a mural, *Modern Women*, for the women's building at the Chicago World's Fair. In 1894 her painting *La Toilette* was exhibited in Paris.

Among **books published** this year was *Coin's Financial School* by William Hope Harvey, a free silver advocate. The book, on economics, was of little merit but sold 300,000 copies within a year. Also published this year were *A Kentucky Cardinal* by James Lane Allen, a novel about an amiable, nature-loving recluse in love with a girl of quite different interests; *Songs From Vagabondia* by Bliss Carman and Richard Hovey, the first of three refreshing poetic collaborations; *Glimpses of Japan* by Lafcadio Hearn, the best study to date of Japanese culture; *The Prisoner of Zenda* by Anthony Hope, a historical romance that became a classic; *A Traveler from Altruria* by William Dean Howells, a Utopian novel; *The Jungle Book* by Rudyard Kipling, a children's classic; *Wealth Against Commonwealth*, a study of the Standard Oil Company by Henry Demarest Lloyd, one of the first of the muckraking journalists; *Beautiful Joe* by Margaret Marshall Saunders, a dog story that eventually sold some 1,000,000 copies; and *The Tragedy of Pudd'nhead Wilson*, a generally underestimated novel by Mark Twain.

"The Sidewalks of New York" was written and composed by Charles Lawler, a buck-and-wing dancer in out-of-the-way music halls. The song was popular in the 1890s, but it became even more popular when Gov. Alfred E. Smith used it in his campaign for the Democratic presidential nomination in 1924.

III. Business and Industry
Education
Philosophy and Religion
Science

The Gilded Age might well have been called the Age of the Railroad. Railroad building and operation was the single largest economic enterprise by far. On the New York Stock Exchange in 1898, 60% of the stocks listed were those of railroads. The pace of track-laying was never surpassed: in 1880 the mileage was 93,261; in 1890, 167,191; in 1900, 198,964. By 1900 the railroads employed 1,018,000 persons and were valued at a little more than $10,000,000,000. One reason for the affluence of the lines was the generous way in which states and the federal government gave them public land as subsidies for building: nearly 50,000,000 acres from the states and about 130,000,000 acres from federal grants, most of it west of the Mississippi R.

The **American Federation of Labor** (AFL), under the leadership of Samuel Gompers, voted against adopting socialist reform programs. Gompers believed that U.S. labor should work with capitalism, not against it, and that the AFL's proper concerns were shorter hours, higher wages, and better working conditions. Gompers' victory set U.S. labor on a nonideological course quite different from that of labor in European countries.

Apr 20: A **strike by 136,000 coal miners** for higher wages began at Columbus, Ohio. This year, like the previous one, would be marked by widespread labor unrest.

May 11: The bitter **Pullman strike** began at the Pullman railroad car plant in south Chicago. The depression had induced the company to cut wages sharply without reducing the rents of the workers in company-owned housing. Considerable violence, pillaging, and burning of railroad cars ensued; mobs of nonworkers joined in.

June 26: A **general railway strike** followed the boycotting of the servicing of Pullman cars by the American Railway Union (ARU), an industrial union headed by Eugene V. Debs. Earlier this year Debs had led a successful strike against the Great Northern Railway. The ARU boycott tied up railroads across the nation.

Aug 3: The **Pullman strike** was declared over by the American Railway Union. Labor had been dealt a blow by being brought under the Sherman Antitrust Act and by the introduction of the court injunction as a weapon against it. The ARU specifically had been crushed. No further attempt to create an industrial union was made until the Depression of the 1930s. Only the AFL and the railroad brotherhoods survived. The AFL had 1,675,000 members by 1904.

Sep 4: A **garment workers' strike** was launched by some 12,000 tailors in New York City. They were protesting sweatshop conditions and the piecework system of payment.

IV. Fashion
   Folkways
   Holidays
   Social Issues and Crime
   Sports

Golf was becoming popular in the U.S. but was still largely pursued by the well-to-do at private country clubs. The United States Golf Association (USGA) was formed on Dec. 22 at a meeting of five golf clubs from Long Island, N.Y., Mount Hope, N.Y., Brookline, Mass., Newport, R.I., and Chicago. The association was to standardize rules, conduct national championship tournaments, and stimulate interest in the game. The USGA held its first amateur and open golf tournaments in 1895 at Newport. The new association did much to organize golf and establish consistent rules and guidelines, but it took another 20 years for golf to catch on with the American public.

The **highest batting average** for a season ever compiled by a major league baseball player was Hugh Duffy's .438. He was a member of the Boston Nationals.

June 16: The **squeeze play** was first employed in baseball by George Case and Dutch Carter, players on the
Yale team, in a game against Princeton. The squeeze
play is a batting maneuver in which, with a runner at
third base and with less than two out, the batter bunts
the ball slowly to the infield, enabling the runner on
third to come home safely. It was introduced in the
major leagues in 1904 by Clark Griffith, manager of
the New York Highlanders in the American League.
Two types of squeeze play are now in use. One is
called the delayed squeeze; in it the runner on third
base does not run until the ball has been bunted. The
other, more dramatic, type is called the suicide
squeeze, in which the runner on third base breaks
toward home plate as the pitcher begins his delivery.
June 28: Labor Day was made a legal holiday by a
congressional resolution.

1895

I. Civil Rights
Exploration and Settlement
Government
Statistics
Wars

A boundary dispute between Great Britain and Venezuela drew England and the U.S. to the verge of war
this year. The boundary between Venezuela and British Guiana had been in dispute for 80 years. Tension
grew when gold was discovered and Venezuelan
troops entered the disputed area. Great Britain
refused to submit the quarrel to arbitration, which
caused a belligerent reaction by Pres. Grover Cleveland's administration. Sec. of State Richard Olney,
on July 20, as much as told Great Britain that the U.S.
ruled the Western Hemisphere. This statement ir-
ritated Latin Americans and Canadians as well as the

British. On Nov. 26 the British prime minister, Robert A. T. Gascoyne-Cecil, Lord Salisbury, replied that the dispute did not concern the U.S., but the U.S. would not yield, citing the Monroe Doctrine. On Dec. 21 Pres. Cleveland asked Congress to establish a commission to settle the dispute and Congress did so. Great Britain, faced with pressing problems elsewhere in the world, wanted no more trouble and on Feb. 27, 1897, agreed to arbitration. On Oct. 3, 1899, a boundary was agreed on which largely upheld England's claim. In the aftermath, many Americans were appalled at how close to war the two English-speaking nations had come, especially since Great Britain was far stronger militarily than the U.S.

Feb 24: The **revolt of Cuba against Spain** broke out. On June 12 Pres. Cleveland called on U.S. citizens to avoid giving aid to the insurgents. A partial cause of the rebellion was the panic of 1893, which caused a severe depression in the Cuban sugar industry. Repressive measures taken by the Spanish aroused American sympathy, which was inflamed to a war pitch by the yellow journalism of William Randolph Hearst's New York *Journal* and Joseph Pulitzer's New York *World*.

Nov 5: Women's suffrage was provided for in the constitution of Utah. The constitution came into effect Jan. 4, 1896, the day Utah entered the Union. It was the second state to give women the vote.

II. Architecture
Arts and Music
Popular Entertainment
Publishing
Theater

The influence of William Morris, the English poet, craftsman, social reformer, and above all a devotee of the Middle Ages, was reflected in the career of the writer and editor Elbert Hubbard. Born in Illinois in 1856, Hubbard abandoned a career in business and turned to writing. This year he established the Roycroft Press at East Aurora, N.Y., and attempted with little success to imitate Morris's Kelmscott Press. He began publishing the monthly magazine *The Philistine*, noted for its inspirational writings and platitudes, contributed mainly by Hubbard. He started another magazine, *The Fra*, in 1908, the title coming from the sobriquet Hubbard had bestowed on himself. Hubbard was best remembered for the essay "A Message to Garcia" (1899), an enormously successful inspirational piece based on an incident in the Spanish-American War. It so appealed to employers that they distributed copies freely to their employees. By 1940 the total circulation of the article was estimated at 40,000,000.

Among **books published** this year was *The Red Badge of Courage*, a realistic Civil War novel by Stephen Crane. It was a remarkable performance: the author was 23 and without any war experience. The novel put American fiction on a firm path toward naturalism. Also published this year were *A House Boat on the Styx* by John Kendrick Bangs, a novel in a humorous vein drawing together various historical figures; *With the Procession* by Henry Blake Fuller, a novel of social strivings in Chicago; *Rose of Dutcher's Coolly*, a novel by Hamlin Garland about a girl's revolt against the bleak life on a Dakota farm; a second *Jungle Book* by Rudyard Kipling; *Amos Judd* by John Mitchell, founder of the original *Life* magazine, a novel about a young Indian rajah brought to the U.S. to save his life; and *The Jucklins* by Opie Read, a best-selling novel by the former editor of *The Arkansas Traveler*.

July 4: **"America the Beautiful"** by Katherine Lee Bates, a Wellesley College professor, was published in the *Congregationalist*, a church publication. The poem was revised in 1904 and put in final form in 1911.

III. Business and Industry
Education
Philosophy and Religion
Science

Advances in science and technology in the late nineteenth century included great progress in the field of astronomy, particularly in the construction of observatories. As early as 1874–1875, the Lick Observatory on Mt. Hamilton, Calif., was established through gifts from James Lick. The Lowell Observatory was founded in Flagstaff, Ariz., in 1894 by the astronomer Percival Lowell, who caught popular attention with his belief that intelligent life might exist on Mars. The Yerkes Observatory, on the shores of Lake Geneva, Wis., was founded in 1892 with money from Charles T. Yerkes, the financier and urban transportation system magnate. The Yerkes Observatory's 40-inch refracting telescope, then the largest of its type in the world, was completed in 1897.

June 11: The first U.S. patent for a **gasoline-driven automobile** by a U.S. inventor was issued to Charles E. Duryea. On June 26 of the previous year, the Patent Office had granted a patent for a motor car developed in Germany by Karl Benz.

IV. Fashion
    Folkways
    Holidays
    Social Issues and Crime
    Sports

The work of Charles Dana Gibson began to have a major influence on Americans' perceptions of themselves. Gibson's idealized depiction of the perfect American woman, who came to be known as the Gibson Girl, soon swept the country. She was slim, small-waisted, and had a pompadour hairstyle. She also had a cool, aloof beauty. The young man she was depicted with was created by Gibson somewhat in his own image. This ideal male was clean-shaven and had much to do with the disappearance of the hitherto popular mustache. He also had a strong jaw and broad shoulders, thus not needing padding in his jackets. Gibson's pair were frequently depicted in settings that made sharp and amusing comments on the social scene. Gibson's work appeared in many magazines and books, notably the works of Richard Harding Davis.

Women's skirts were shortened for bicycling wear. They were shortened an inch or two from the ankle, and the hems were weighted with lead.

Aug 31: The **first professional football game** was played in Latrobe, Pa., when Latrobe's team of profit-sharing players met the Jeannette, Pa., team. Latrobe hired a substitute quarterback, John Brallier, for $10 in expense money, making him the game's first professional player.

Sep 7-12: The **America's Cup** was successfully defended by the U.S. yacht *Defender,* which won three straight races from the British challenger *Valkyrie II.*

Oct 4: The **first U.S. Open golf tournament,** held at Newport Golf Club in Newport, R.I., under the auspices of the U.S. Golf Association, was won by Horace Rawlins. Rawlins, 19, had come from England earlier in the year to work at the Newport club.

Nov 28: The **first gasoline-powered automobile race** in the U.S., the Chicago to Evanston Thanksgiving Day Race, was won by the brothers Charles E. and J. Frank Duryea.

1896

I. **Civil Rights**
   Exploration and Settlement
   Government
   Statistics
   Wars

The presidential election of 1896 was decided after one of the hardest fought campaigns in U.S. history. The division between the Republicans and the Democrats was clear. Republicans were for hard money, a high tariff to protect American industry, and other conservative policies. The Democrats were now in the hands of the populists. The free coinage of silver was their primary campaign issue. This appealed to the farmers and miners of the South and West. The Republicans waged a front-porch campaign for William McKinley, spending about $7,000,000, mostly on mailings that reached 5,000,000 families a week. The Democrats, with only about $300,000 to spend, sent their candidate, William Jennings Bryan, on an 18,000-mile campaign trip, during which he made 600 speeches. But Bryan could not attract the votes of the urban workers, despite his personal attractiveness and oratorical power.

Jan 4: Utah was admitted into the Union, the 45th state.

May 18: The so-called **Jim Crow Car Law** of Louisiana was declared constitutional by the Supreme Court in *Plessy v. Ferguson,* which advanced the separate but equal doctrine. The court held that segregation was legal if equal facilities were offered to both races. The U.S. Supreme Court reversed this doctrine in civil rights decisions on May 17, 1954; May 31, 1955; and Nov. 7, 1955. Chief Justice Earl Warren said in the first of these decisions that the separate but equal doctrine had no place in the field of public education, and maintained that separate facilities were inherently unequal.

June 18: The **Republican National Convention nominated William McKinley** of Ohio for the presidency and Garret A. Hobart of New Jersey for the vice presidency.

July 11: The **Democratic National Convention nominated William Jennings Bryan** of Nebraska, a dark horse, for the presidency. Bryan's famous "cross of gold" speech united the silverite wing of the party and took the convention by storm. The platform advocated "free and unlimited coinage of both silver and gold at the present legal ratio of sixteen to one." Arthur Sewall of Maine was nominated for the vice presidency.

Oct 1: Rural free postal delivery was established.

Nov 3: William McKinley was elected president of the United States. Garret A. Hobart was elected vice president. The electoral vote was McKinley, 271: William Jennings Bryan, Democratic candidate, 176. The popular vote was McKinley, 7,104,779; Bryan, 6,502,925; John M. Palmer, National Democratic candidate, 133,148; Joshua Levering, Prohibition candidate, 132,007; Charles H. Matchett, Socialist Labor candidate, 38,274. In congressional elections the Republicans gained four seats in the Senate to lead 47–34, seven seats going to minor parties. In the House the Republicans lost 40 seats but still held a 204–113 majority, 40 seats going to minor parties.

II. Architecture
   Arts and Music
   Popular Entertainment
   Publishing
   Theater

A new form of American humor, art, and journalism came into being this year with the appearance of "The Yellow Kid," by Richard F. Outcault, in the New York *World*. It was soon to become the comic strip. A single-panel drawing, which appeared each week, showed the adventures of a boy in a long, yellow, sacklike garment; Outcault soon began to add words. This marked the first time a cartoon caption had appeared inside the frame of a picture. Circulation of the *World* boomed. In 1897 Rudolph Dirks introduced "The Katzenjammer Kids" and was the first to make use of a sequence of panels to tell a story. Another pioneer was Frederick Burr Opper with "Happy Hooligan" (1899). The first comic strip to appear six days a week made its appearance in 1907 in the San Francisco *Chronicle*. It was Harry C. "Bud" Fisher's "A. Mutt," a forerunner of "Mutt and Jeff."

Among **books published** this year was the immensely popular *Quo Vadis?* by the Polish novelist Henryk Sienkiewicz. This vivid, powerful tale of Roman life under Nero and of early Christians has been dramatized, filmed, and translated into all major languages. Also published were *Joan of Arc*, the last major work of Mark Twain, presenting a somewhat idealized Joan set against the malign

forces arrayed against her; *Poems, Third Series* by
Emily Dickinson, bringing to light more of the hundreds of her poems found by Lavinia Dickinson,
Emily's sister; *The Damnation of Theron Ware* by
Harold Frederic, a realistic novel about a hypocriti-
cal small-town Methodist minister; *The Country of
the Pointed Firs,* the masterpiece of the mistress of the
local-color novel, Sarah Orne Jewett; *The Seats of the
Mighty,* a historical novel by Sir Gilbert Parker about
the capture of Quebec; the first story about the fabulous fictional character Frank Merriwell, the creation of Gilbert Patten under the pseudonym Burt L.
Standish; *The Torrent and the Night Before,* poems by
Edwin Arlington Robinson, noteworthy only because
it was the first publication of this important American
poet; the fourth and final volume of *The Winning
of the West* by Theodore Roosevelt; *The Sense of
Beauty* by George Santayana, his first major philosophical work and a classic study of aesthetics; *In His
Steps* by Charles M. Sheldon, an all-time best seller
about a Kansas minister following the example of
Jesus, translated into 25 or more languages; and another religious classic, *The Story of the Other Wise
Man* by Henry Van Dyke, still in print.

Apr 23: The **first moving pictures** on a public screen
were shown at Koster and Bial's Music Hall in New
York City. The program included films of two blonde
girls performing the umbrella dance, a view of the
surf breaking on a beach, a comic boxing exhibition,
a bit of comic allegory entitled "The Monroe Doctrine," and a performance of the skirt dance. *The New
York Times* review the following day described the
exhibition as "all wonderfully real and singularly exhilarating."

III. Business and Industry
   ### Education
   ### Philosophy and Religion
   ### Science

Pulpit-thumping Christian evangelism was thriving
as the twentieth century neared. In these years the

most popular practitioner was William Ashley "Billy" Sunday. A professional baseball player from 1883 to 1900, Sunday had also worked for the YMCA in Chicago from 1891 until he turned evangelist in 1896. On Apr. 15, 1903, he was ordained a Presbyterian minister. Sunday was agile on the platform and colloquial in his speech. He preached the kind of Bible fundamentalism that many wanted to hear and promoted prohibition. It is said that by the time of his death in 1935 he had preached to more people than any other Christian.

Seven-eighths of the **wealth of the U.S.** was controlled by one-eighth of the people.

June 4: Assembly of the **first Ford automobile** was completed at 2 A.M. in a brick workshed in Detroit, Mich., by Henry Ford and his associates. The road test of the car was delayed an hour or so because genius had overlooked one detail: the car was wider than the shed door. The men had to use an ax to knock bricks out of the framework.

Aug 12: Gold was discovered on the Klondike R. about three miles from Dawson in the Yukon Territory of northwest Canada. This sparked the second great gold rush in U.S. history, the Klondike stampede of 1897–1898. News of the strike reached the U.S. in June of 1897, and within a month thousands were on their way by a variety of difficult routes. In 1898 there were about 25,000 people in the Klondike area. Total gold production there from 1885 to 1929 exceeded $175,000,000.

IV. Fashion
   ## Folkways
   ## Holidays
   ## Social Issues and Crime
   ## Sports

Newspapers, in search of greater circulation and more advertising, were becoming less political and more concerned with everyday interests of average people. They began to publish material to entertain as well as inform the reader. Among the innovations was the advice to the lovelorn column, which made its debut in 1896 in the New Orleans *Picayune*. Its author was Elizabeth Meriwether Gilmer, who used the pen name Dorothy Dix. Her column was later syndicated, and collections of her advice on various topics appeared in book form into the 1930s.

Apr 6: The **first modern Olympic Games** began in Athens, Greece. The games were dominated by a small team of Americans who arrived just as athletes for the first events were being called. The U.S. team, out of condition from the long ocean trip, with no time to limber up, won nine of the 12 events. James B. Connolly, who won the first event—the hop, step, and jump—was the first Olympic champion to be crowned in 15 centuries. Revival of the games was brought about by the efforts of a young French baron, Pierre de Coubertin of Paris. His plan to hold international contests every four years has been carried out for the most part.

July 7: The sentence **"You shall not crucify mankind upon a cross of gold"** marked William Jennings Bryan's stirring speech at the Democratic National Convention. The reference was to the insistence by the gold faction, which opposed free coinage of silver, on gold alone as the basis for U.S. currency.

July 18: The **U.S. Open golf tournament** was won by James Foulis.

1897

I. Civil Rights
Exploration and Settlement
Government
Statistics
Wars

The tariff continued to be a controversial issue, but after the presidential election of 1896 the Republican

Party was free to have its way. Pres. William McKinley called a special session of Congress, and on July 7 the lawmakers passed the Dingley Tariff Bill, named for its sponsor, Rep. Nelson Dingley, Republican of Maine. This law, which remained in effect until 1909, put tariffs at the highest level ever, raising them an average of 57%. It reimposed the duty on woolen goods and set the rate at 91%. The new tariff rates were much higher than was necessary because many American industries no longer needed protection against foreign goods.

Jan 12: The **National Monetary Conference** met at Indianapolis, Ind., and endorsed the existing gold standard. A commission appointed later in the year offered Congress a plan for the monetary system. With the free silver issue finally settled, the U.S. entered a decade of prosperity.

Mar 4: William McKinley was inaugurated president of the United States, the 25th. A Republican, he was elected to two terms but was assassinated before completing his second term.

II. Architecture
Arts and Music
Popular Entertainment
Publishing
Theater

Popular songs were being turned out by the hundreds. Many of them had a nostalgic air and expressed a yearning for rural life. Quite a few were humorous and, of course, many were about love. Among the most successful composers of the period was Paul Dresser, real name Dreiser, whose brother Theodore was to become one of America's greatest novelists. Dresser is remembered for "On the Banks of the Wabash, Far Away" (1897), on which his brother helped with the lyrics, and "My Gal Sal" (1905). Another popular songwriter of the day was Harry Von Tilzer, who is said to have composed more than 3000 songs, including "Wait Till the Sun Shines, Nelly" (1906).

Among **books published** this year was *Soldiers of*

Fortune by Richard Harding Davis, a novel that became a best seller. Davis was a newspaperman, war correspondent, and author. His work found a large audience from the early 1890s to his death in 1916; however, his novels and many stories did not stand the test of time and, except for a few, are largely forgotten. Other books published this year included *The Spoils of Poynton* and *What Maisie Knew* by Henry James; *Captains Courageous* by Rudyard Kipling, a novel of the sea that became a classic; *Hugh Wynne, Free Quaker* by S. Weir Mitchell, a novel of the American Revolution considered by some to be Mitchell's masterpiece; *The Children of the Night* by Edwin Arlington Robinson, the author's second collection of poems, which included "Richard Cory" and other well-known poems; and *The Literary History of the American Revolution* by Moses Coit Taylor.

III. Business and Industry
Education
Philosophy and Religion
Science

As the population of cities grew and their geographical boundaries expanded, transportation of large numbers of people became a serious problem. Elevated railroads had already been built, but they were noisy and dirty. Municipalities now turned to underground railways, or subways, as a solution. An experimental underground railway had been built in New York City more than 30 years before, yet New York City officials were still working out plans to finance subway construction. The first practical and successful subway line in the U.S. was the Tremont St. subway in Boston, which opened in 1897 and was completed the next year. It ran for only 1.8 miles and the cars were ordinary trolley cars. Later the Boston subway was extended to 22 miles.

July 2: A **coal miners' strike** shut down mines in Pennsylvania, Ohio, and West Virginia and put 75,000 men out of work. On Sept. 10 more than 20 miners were killed at Hazelton and Latimer, Pa., when deputy sheriffs opened fire on them. One day later the strike was settled. The miners won an eight-hour work day, semimonthly pay, abolition of company stores, and biennial conferences.

IV. Fashion
   Folkways
   Holidays
   Social Issues and Crime
   Sports

Conspicuous consumption in the Gilded Age exceeded anything ever seen before in the U.S. The most lavish party of all was that given in 1897 by the Bradley Martins of New York City. The ballroom of the Waldorf-Astoria Hotel was turned into a replica of the Palace of Versailles. Mrs. Martin attended dressed as Mary Queen of Scots, wearing a necklace that had once belonged to Marie Antoinette. The ball was held just as the nation was emerging from its worst depression ever, and thus produced a wave of criticism in the press. So much disapproval descended on the Martins that they fled to England and stayed there.

The **first Frontier Day** was conceived and celebrated by citizens of Cheyenne, Wyo., at the town's fair grounds. The celebration has since become a five-day Wild West Show, held annually at Frontier Park.

Mar 17: The **world heavyweight boxing championship** was won by Bob Fitzsimmons, who defeated James J. "Gentleman Jim" Corbett in a 14-round bout at Carson City, Nev. This was the first boxing match photographed by a motion picture camera.

Apr 19: The **first Boston Marathon** was won by John J. McDermott of New York City, with a time of 2 hrs., 55 min., 10 sec.

Sep 17: The **U.S. Open golf tournament** was won by Joe Lloyd of England.

1898

I. Civil Rights
   Exploration and Settlement
   Government
   Statistics
   Wars

Victory in the Spanish-American War made the U.S.
a nation with global interests. In one brief clash of
arms the U.S. acquired Guam, Puerto Rico, and the
Philippine Islands from Spain. In addition, Cuba was
granted independence, with Spain assuming its national debt. Many Americans were appalled by the
new U.S. foreign policy, which they equated with imperialism. Andrew Carnegie, the steel magnate and
philanthropist, offered to buy the Philippines for
$20,000,000 and give the country its freedom. Many
other Americans, however, talked of manifest destiny and the duty of the U.S. to spread its form of
civilization far and wide.

Feb 15: The U.S. **battleship** *Maine* exploded in
Havana harbor; two officers and 258 crew members
were killed. U.S. sympathies were already strongly
with Cuba in its revolt against Spanish tyranny, and
the *Maine* disaster made U.S. intervention inevitable.
The cause of the explosion and the people responsible
for it were never determined.

Apr 19: Congress adopted a **joint resolution on Cuba,**
which stated that the U.S. had no plans for Cuban
annexation, demanded Spain's withdrawal, and authorized the president to use military force. Spain
immediately severed diplomatic relations.

Apr 22: A **blockade of Cuban ports** was ordered by
Pres. McKinley. Rear Adm. William T. Sampson
sailed from Key West, Fla., with a sizable fleet.

Apr 22: The Spanish ship *Buena Ventura* was captured by the U.S. gunboat *Nashville,* the first prize of
the Spanish-American War.

Apr 24: The **Spanish-American War** officially began

when Spain declared war on the U.S. The following day Congress passed a declaration of war, effective Apr. 21.

May 1: At the Battle of **Manila Bay,** the six-ship Asiatic squadron of Commodore George Dewey decisively defeated a larger but outgunned and underprepared Spanish fleet. The U.S. flotilla emerged virtually unscathed, with only eight wounded. The Spanish fleet was destroyed, with heavy casualties. The action cleared the way for U.S. occupation of Manila in Au-

May 25: The **first troop expedition to Manila** set sail from San Francisco with some 2500 men.

June 11: About 600 **U.S. Marines landed at Guantánamo,** Cuba. They engaged Spanish forces the next day.

June 12-14: U.S. forces embarked from Key West, Fla. Some 17,000 troops under Gen. William R. Shafter sailed to undertake capture of Santiago de Cuba, the chief Spanish naval base in Cuba.

June 15: At **Guantánamo,** U.S. Marines repulsed a Spanish assault.

June 15: Annexation of Hawaii was approved in a joint resolution adopted by the House of Representatives, and by the Senate on June 17. It was signed by Pres. McKinley on July 7.

June 21: Guam, one of the Mariana Islands in the western Pacific, surrendered to Capt. Henry Glass on the U.S.S. *Charleston.* The Spanish commander on the island obviously had not heard of the outbreak of the war, for on the previous day when Capt. Glass fired on the island a message was sent to the *Charleston* with an apology for not having returned the salute— there was no ammunition on the island.

June 24: At the Battle of **Las Guasimas,** U.S. troops won the first major land battle of the war with Spain. The division of cavalry volunteers led by the aggressive Maj. Gen. Joseph Wheeler, with Col. Leonard Wood now a regimental commander and Col. Theodore Roosevelt leading the Rough Riders, performed well.

July 1-2: El Caney and San Juan Heights, Spanish

outposts to Santiago de Cuba, were stormed and taken over stubborn resistance by U.S. troops. There were heavy casualties on both sides. The Rough Riders participated in the attack.

July 3: The **Spanish fleet at Cuba,** under Adm. Pascual Cervera y Topete, was destroyed by U.S. ships in an attempt to break out of Santiago. The Spanish lost 323 dead, 151 wounded. The U.S. lost one man. The war was virtually over.

July 8: Isla Grande, in Subic Bay near Manila, was occupied by forces under Adm. George Dewey. The German gunboat *Irene,* which had attempted to hamper American operations, was forced to withdraw.

July 17: Santiago de Cuba was surrendered along with 24,000 Spanish troops by Gen. José Toral to U.S. Gen. William R. Shafter.

July 25: Puerto Rico was invaded by U.S. forces led by Maj. Gen. Nelson D. Miles. The landing was made at Guanica, on the southern coast. Resistance was minimal.

July 26: Spain sought peace terms through the French ambassador in Washington, D.C.

July 28: Ponce, Puerto Rico's second largest city, surrendered to Gen. Miles.

Aug 1: Casualties from disease were exceedingly high during the conflict in Cuba. At this time there were some 4200 sick U.S. personnel in Cuba, most suffering from yellow fever or typhoid. Fewer than 400 troops were killed in battle or died of wounds in Cuba. Fully 90% of U.S. casualties were caused by disease.

Aug 7: The **Rough Riders left Cuba,** along with other units, for Montauk Point, Long Island, to escape epidemics in Cuba.

Aug 9: At Coamo, Puerto Rico, U.S. forces under Brig. Gen. Oswald H. Ernst defeated a Spanish force.

Aug 12: Hostilities between Spain and the U.S. were halted by a protocol in which Spain agreed to give Cuba its independence and to cede Puerto Rico and Guam to the U.S. Spain agreed to negotiate the status of the Philippines in a postwar conference.

Nov 8: In **congressional elections** the Republicans continued to gain strength in the Senate and lose strength in the House, taking a 53–26 lead in the Senate, with eight seats going to minor parties, and holding a majority of 185–163 in the House, with nine seats held by minor parties. In New York State, Theodore Roosevelt was elected governor on the Republican ticket. The Republicans had chosen him partly because of his war service and partly to overcome the taint of corruption left by the previous administration.

Dec 10: The **treaty ending the Spanish-American War** was signed in Paris.

II. Architecture
Arts and Music
Popular Entertainment
Publishing
Theater

Sentimentality seemed to hold sway in the field of song, resulting in the composition of some musical pieces that were at least as popular for their words as for their music. An outstanding example, "The Rosary" by Ethelbert Nevin with lyrics by Robert Cameron Rogers, was published this year. It was the most popular song in the U.S. for a quarter of a century. Nevin was a pianist and composer who wrote other similar music, such as "Narcissus" (1891), and who set to music such poems as Eugene Field's "Little Boy Blue."

Among **books published** this year was *David Harum* by Edward Noyes Westcott, a Syracuse lawyer. The novel had been rejected by six publishers before being accepted by D. Appleton & Company. It was published shortly after Westcott's death from tuberculosis on Mar. 31. The story, centering on a shrewd, humorous, and lovable small-town banker, sold 400,000 copies by Feb. 1, 1901, and 1,000,000 in 35 years. It was dramatized in 1900 and twice made into a movie, the second time with Will Rogers in the title role. Other books published this year included

The Open Boat and Other Stories by Stephen Crane;
Mr. Dooley in Peace and War by Peter Finley Dunne;
The Turn of the Screw by Henry James, a masterpiece
of horror by a master of English prose; *Prisoners of
Hope* by Mary Johnston, a novel of colonial Virginia;
When Knighthood Was in Flower by Charles Major, a
historical romance that became a best seller; *The Adventures of Francois* by S. Weir Mitchell, a picaresque
novel of the French Revolution; and *Songs from the
Ghetto* by Morris Rosenfeld, an immigrant from Russian Poland, translation by Leo Wiener.

III. Business and Industry
Education
Philosophy and Religion
Science

As the end of the century neared, American industry
was becoming the most productive in the world. Steel
production had passed that of Great Britain in 1865;
by 1900 it was 10,000,000 tons a year, and the U.S.
was turning out more than Great Britain and Germany combined. Cotton textile mills were built in the
South as well as the North, and by 1900 the two regions were using 3,500,000 bales of cotton a year.
Meat packing was becoming an assembly line process, and large firms in the Midwest were leading the
way. The Niagara Falls power plant had ushered in
the era of hydroelectric power in 1894, and steam
turbines and electric motors were beginning to
change the face of American industry.

   Nome, Alaska, was founded as the result of a gold
strike on the Seward Peninsula, for which it was the
port. Nome was named for a misspelling of a nearby
cape on a map. The cape was referred to as "no
name."

June 1: The **Erdman Arbitration Act,** sponsored by
Rep. Jacob Erdman, Democrat of Pennsylvania, was
passed. It authorized governmental mediation between interstate carriers and their employees. It forbade interstate carriers to discriminate against or
blacklist union laborers. But on Jan. 27, 1908, the

Supreme Court held the provision against discrimination unconstitutional according to the Fifth Amendment. On July 15, 1914, Congress replaced the Erdman Act by the Newlands Act, which set up a mediation board.

IV. Fashion
   Folkways
   Holidays
   Social Issues and Crime
   Sports

A great deal of entertainment for the general public was being provided by amusement parks, usually located on the outskirts of cities and often built by traction companies to create traffic for their trolley car lines. Whole families could enjoy parks such as Palisades Amusement Park in New Jersey, just across the Hudson R. from New York City, which opened in 1897. Among the many attractions at these parks were roller coasters, merry-go-rounds, shoot the chutes, dance halls, bathing beaches, and, of course, food and drink.

The impassioned slogan **"Remember the Maine"** became the war cry of Americans urging war with Spain. The battleship *Maine* had been destroyed by an explosion while docked at Havana. The American public was led to believe that it had been blown up by agents of Spain. This feeling supported American resentment against Spanish oppression of Cuban nationalism.

June 18: The **U.S. Open golf tournament** was won by Fred Herd.

1899

I. Civil Rights
Exploration and Settlement
Government
Statistics
Wars

The first international discussion of the problems of armaments and warfare was held from May 18 to July 29 at The Hague, the Netherlands. Delegates from the U.S. and 25 other nations met at the invitation of Czar Nicholas II of Russia. The conference considered disarmament, limitations on methods of warfare, and establishment of a forum for arbitrating international disputes. Nothing was accomplished in disarmament and little in issues concerning warfare, except for conventions having to do with neutral shipping and the protection of noncombatants. The conference did establish the Permanent Court of International Arbitration, although arbitration was not compulsory and the U.S. specified reservations with regard to disputes that involved application of the Monroe Doctrine.

Feb 4: Philippine guerrillas under **Emilio Aguinaldo** fired on American forces at Manila, starting skirmishes lasting several days. Before the insurgents were driven out and scattered, 57 Americans were killed and 215 wounded. Some 500 Filipinos were killed, 1000 wounded, and 500 made prisoners. This was the beginning of a rebellion against U.S. rule that lasted until Mar. 23, 1901, when Aguinaldo was captured by Gen. Frederick Funston at Palawan, Luzon.

Feb 10: The **peace treaty** with Spain was signed by Pres. William McKinley. It had been ratified by Congress on Jan. 9. By its terms the U.S. acquired Puerto Rico and Guam, and Spain relinquished its claim to Cuba. The U.S. paid Spain $20,000,000 for specific Spanish holdings in the Philippines, but many interpreted the payment as purchase of the Philippines from Spain.

II. Architecture
Arts and Music
Popular Entertainment
Publishing
Theater

The last few years of the nineteenth century saw publication of a number of popular songs that were to endure. Among them were "A Bird in a Gilded Cage" (1899) by Harry Von Tilzer, "My Wild Irish Rose" (1899) by Chauncey Olcott, and "The Stars and Stripes Forever" (1897) by John Philip Sousa. The first named was not widely popular at first, but in later years it came to be identified closely with the 1890s. For every song that found a permanent place in U.S. musical history, there were many that did not make it to the new century, such as "Gold Will Buy Most Anything but a True Girl's Heart" (1898), and "She Was Happy Till She Met You" (1899), both by Monroe H. Rosenfeld.

Among **books published** this year was *The Theory of the Leisure Class* by Thorstein Veblen, professor of political economy at the University of Chicago. Though little read except among students of economics, this outspoken assault on the moneyed class made Veblen famous in his field. Also published this year were *Fables in Slang* by George Ade, who eventually found in the follies and foibles of his fellow Americans enough material for 12 books; *Richard Carvel* by Winston Churchill, a Revolutionary War romance, the first important novel by a writer capable of probing beneath historical events to underlying forces and ideals; *The School and Society* by John Dewey, a work that revolutionized American educational theory and practice; *Janice Meredith* by Paul Leicester Ford, a historical novel widely read, perhaps because the heroine and members of her family were involved in many of the major events of the Revolutionary War; *The Man with the Hoe and Other Poems* by Edwin Markham; *McTeague*, by Frank Nor-

ris, a novel about unromantic lower-class people in
San Francisco, written in a naturalistic manner; and
The Gentleman from Indiana by Booth Tarkington,
his first novel, about a crusading country editor.

Jan 15: "The Man with the Hoe," a poem by Edwin
Markham, a California schoolteacher, was published
in the San Francisco *Examiner.* The poem was a social protest; it pictured a farmer brutalized by forces
he could not control or understand. Within a week it
had been reprinted by newspapers across the country. Antitrust forces called it "the cry of the Zeitgeist
[cultural climate of the era]." It was the most popular
poem in the U.S. by far.

III. Business and Industry
   Education
   Philosophy and Religion
   Science

Propagation of the Christian faith was not left to the
clergy or the churches, especially among evangelical
Protestants. One group that came to play a unique
role in this endeavor was the Christian Commercial
Men's Association of America, formed by a group of
traveling salesmen meeting in Boscobel, Wis., on
July 1. The organization became better known as the
Gideons International, and best known for its chief
work, placing Bibles in hotel rooms. The first Gideon
Bible was placed in the Superior Hotel, Iron Mountain, Mont., in Nov. 1908.

Feb 14: Congress authorized **voting machines** for federal elections if desired by the individual states.

IV. Fashion
   Folkways
   Holidays
   Social Issues and Crime
   Sports

More attention was being paid to providing parks
and playgrounds in America's cities. By this time
Manhattan Island, the heart of New York City, had
1140 acres of parks, but most of it was accounted for

by Central Park; there was little parkland in crowded areas. An exception was Mulberry Park, opened in 1896, which consisted of only three acres but offered a little green space in one of the worst slum areas. Kansas City, Mo., in 1893 began planning a system of 16 miles of boulevards to connect 2000 acres of parkland. Boston began to organize a park system in the 1890s. By 1898 some 14 cities in the East had children's playgrounds, many of them in schoolyards.

June 9: The **world heavyweight boxing championship** was won by James J. Jeffries, who knocked out Bob Fitzsimmons in the 11th round of a bout at Coney Island, N.Y.

Sep 15: The **U.S. Open golf tournament** was won by Willie Smith.

Oct 16-20: The **America's Cup** was successfully defended by the U.S. yacht *Columbia,* which won three straight races from the British challenger *Shamrock I.*

1900

I. Civil Rights
   Exploration and Settlement
   Government
   Statistics
   Wars

Bitter antagonism against all foreigners in China broke into open warfare this year when a nationalist group, the Boxers, occupied Peking on June 20 and besieged members of the diplomatic corps, their families, and others in the British legation. The Boxers wanted to rid China of all foreigners. After a siege of nearly two months, troops from the U.S., Great Britain, France, Russia, Germany, and Japan reached Peking on Aug. 14 and put down the Boxer Rebellion. Under pressure from the U.S., the other powers agreed not to partition China further. On Sept. 7, 1901, China and eleven other nations signed the Boxer Protocol, by which China agreed to pay $333,000,000 in indemnity. The U.S. received $24,500,000, but in 1908 this amount was reduced and the money was used to educate Chinese students in the U.S.

The **Census** recorded a population of 75,994,575. The center of population was placed at six miles southeast of Columbus, Ind.

Mar 14: The currency act, which established a **gold standard** for all U.S. currency, was passed by Congress. The act was made possible by increased gold production in South Africa and the Klondike fields. It put an end to the free silver controversy, although William Jennings Bryan and other advocates of the free coinage of silver continued to agitate for ten years more.

Apr 30: An act establishing the **Territory of Hawaii** was passed by Congress. It went into effect on June 14. On that date Pres. McKinley appointed Sanford B. Dole the first governor of Hawaii. Dole had been born in Honolulu of American missionary parents.

June 19-21: The **Republican National Convention nominated Pres. McKinley** for reelection. Gov. Theodore Roosevelt of New York was nominated for the vice presidency, but he felt he was being sidetracked from the center of political activity. Roosevelt nonetheless conducted one of the most vigorous campaigns on record, visiting 24 states, traveling 21,000 miles, and delivering some 700 speeches. McKinley conducted a front-porch campaign, never stirring from his home.

June 21: **Amnesty** was granted to the Filipino insurgents by a proclamation issued by Gen. Arthur MacArthur, military governor of the Philippines.

July 5: The **Democratic National Convention nominated William Jennings Bryan** of Nebraska for the presidency and Adlai E. Stevenson of Illinois for the vice presidency.

Sep 8: A **hurricane** killed 6000 persons at Galveston, Tex. Winds up to 120 mph drove Gulf waters over land. Afterward looters were found with ringed fingers they had cut off the hands of the dead. Property damage amounted to $20,000,000.

Nov 6: William McKinley was reelected president of the United States. Gov. Theodore Roosevelt, Republican of New York, was elected vice president. The electoral vote was McKinley, 292; William Jennings Bryan of Nebraska, candidate on the Democratic and Populist tickets, 155. The popular vote was McKinley, 7,219,530; Bryan, 6,358,071; John G. Woolley of Illinois, Prohibition candidate, 209,166; Eugene V. Debs of Indiana, Social Democratic candidate, 94,768; and Wharton Barker of Pennsylvania, middle-of-the-road Populist, 50,232. In congressional elections both major parties gained Senate seats from the minor parties, the Republicans taking a 55–31 majority, with four seats held by minor parties. In the House the Republicans led 197–151, with nine seats held by minor parties.

II. Architecture
   Arts and Music
   Popular Entertainment
   Publishing
   Theater

The U.S. had produced painters of talent and accomplishment in the fields of portraiture, historical painting, and landscape studies. No American painter of standing, however, fell into quite the same class in this period as did Albert Pinkham Ryder. Mostly self-taught, Ryder many times used as his subject the sea or moonlight. His work evokes a feeling of loneliness and mysterious force of nature. Of some 160 paintings, perhaps his best known is *Toilers of the Sea* (1900), which includes a dark sail and a wan moon giving off an aura of ghostliness. Ryder also did paintings with such titles as *Death on a Pale Horse* and *Temple of the Mind*.

   Among **books published** this year was *Sister Carrie*, a first novel by Theodore Dreiser. An unflinchingly naturalistic novel, it examined in economic and moral terms the rise of a young woman from rural obscurity to success on the New York stage. Steeped in tragedy, the story was published only after Dreiser made extensive cuts. The book was issued, then recalled, by the publisher. The book's failure sent Dreiser into a deep depression. Reissued in 1912, the book was eventually recognized as an American classic. In 1981 it was republished with Dreiser's deleted text restored. Other books published this year included *Eben Holden, A Tale of the North Country* by Irving Bacheller, which sold 300,000 copies within six months; *The Wonderful Wizard of Oz* by L. Frank Baum; *Whilomville Stories* by Stephen Crane, a posthumous collection; *Literary Friends and Acquaintances* by William Dean Howells, a collection of the author's essays; *To Have and to Hold* by Mary Johnston, the author's best-known romance; *The Son of the Wolf* by Jack London, a first collection of stories; and *Alice of Old Vincennes* by Maurice Thompson, a historical novel set in Indiana in the late eighteenth century.

III. Business and Industry
Education
Philosophy and Religion
Science

The new century brought with it the automobile as a practical means of transportation. In 1900 there were only 8000 autos registered in the entire country and only about ten miles of paved roads for them to travel on. Only 4000 autos were produced in 1900, but ten years later 187,000 rolled out of the factories. The appearance of cars was changing, too. New autos looked less like horseless carriages and more like powered vehicles. The Automobile Club of America held its first meeting on Oct. 16, 1900; it sponsored the first automobile show, in Madison Square Garden, New York City, from Nov. 3–10. Nevertheless, the auto was viewed with displeasure by some. One editor wrote, "It is well named the devil-wagon." At the turn of the century there were still about 18,000,000 horses and mules providing transportation and power, and 10,000,000 bicycles for pleasure and work.

Rural free delivery served 185,000 customers. By 1924 this number would rise to 6,500,000.

A survey of **Protestant religious sects** in the U.S. at the end of the nineteenth century showed reformed and evangelical denominations in the vast majority: 6,000,000 Methodists; 5,000,000 Baptists; 1,500,000 Lutherans; 1,500,000 Presbyterians; 350,000 Mormons; and 80,000 Christian Scientists.

Illiteracy in the U.S. reached a new low of 10.7% of the population, a decline of 2.6% from 1890 and a decline of 9.3% from 1870.

The **International Ladies' Garment Workers Union** was established at a time when the average work week in the trade was 70 hours. Jacob A. Riis reported that women sewing at home for the clothing industry were earning 30 cents a day at best.

Telephone service in the U.S. had grown to 1,335,911 telephones in use.

Mar 5: The **Hall of Fame** was founded in New York City for the purpose of commemorating great Americans. It still exists today. New members are voted on every five years by a committee of 100 men and women from all the states. To be elected a nominee must have been dead at least 25 years, have been a citizen of the United States, and have the approval of three-fifths of the committee. Any citizen may make a nomination. A bust of a person elected is placed in the open air colonnade at the former campus in The Bronx of New York University.

IV. Fashion
   Folkways
   Holidays
   Social Issues and Crime
   Sports

The growth of tennis around the world received a tremendous impetus in 1900 when Dwight F. Davis, a player of championship caliber, offered a cup for international contests between male players of the

U.S. and Great Britain. The first five-match event was played in Boston, Mass. The U.S. won three matches, one match was not finished, and the last match was not played. The annual competition was soon opened to teams of other nations. Within a few years Australia and France presented teams that gave the U.S. and Britain strong competition.

Only 12,572 dozen pairs of **silk stockings** were sold in the U.S. this year, a ratio of one pair for every 2000 Americans. By comparison, 18,088,841 pairs were sold in 1921, one pair for every six persons.

Photography as a pastime received a tremendous boost when the Eastman Kodak Company introduced the Brownie Box Camera. The camera cost only $1.00 and a six-shot roll of film cost 10 to 15 cents, depending on the type of film the photographer chose. At these prices, virtually everyone who wanted to take pictures could afford to do so. The result was that photography made a grand leap out of the studio and into the real world. Brownie cameras were manufactured until the mid-1960s, when they were superseded by the equally popular Instamatic cameras.

Jan 29: The **American League** was formed in Chicago, Ill. The new baseball league demanded recognition as a major league, but was refused by the National League until 1903 when the National, American, and minor leagues joined forces and set up a ruling body known as the National Commission.

Apr 30: At 3:52 A.M. railroad engineer John Luther **"Casey" Jones** died at the throttle slowing down the *Cannon Ball* express train from Memphis, Tenn., to Canton, Miss., as it slammed into the rear of a stopped train. Although Jones was speeding to make up lost time, his final action saved his passengers' lives and he became a folk hero.

May 20-Oct 28: At the **Olympic Games** in Paris, France, the U.S. finished with 20 gold medals. France was first with 29 gold medals.

Oct 5: The **U.S. Open golf tournament** was won by Harry Vardon of England.

1901

I. Civil Rights
Exploration and Settlement
Government
Statistics
Wars

For the third time in the nation's history a president was assassinated. On Sept. 6 Pres. William McKinley visited the Pan-American Exposition in Buffalo, N.Y. While greeting visitors he was shot twice in the abdomen by a young anarchist, Leon Czolgosz, who was carrying a concealed pistol in a handkerchief. For a few days McKinley seemed to be recovering, but he took a turn for the worse and died on Sept. 14 at 2:15 A.M. McKinley, 58, was succeeded by Vice Pres. Theodore Roosevelt, who became the 26th president of the United States. Roosevelt took the presidential oath in the same house in Buffalo where the body of McKinley awaited transportation to Canton, Ohio, for burial. Roosevelt was not quite 43 years old and so was the youngest person to hold the office of president. Conservative Republicans, who had been happy with McKinley, were appalled. As governor of New York, Roosevelt had shown liberal tendencies. He had gained the vice presidential nomination in 1900 partly because Republican leaders sought to keep him in a harmless post.

The **Socialist Party** was organized by the merger of the Social Democratic Party under Eugene V. Debs with the reformist section of the Socialist Labor Party under Morris Hillquit.

Mar 4: Pres. **William McKinley was inaugurated** for his second term. Theodore Roosevelt was sworn in as vice president.

Apr 19: The **rebellion in the Philippines was ended** by proclamation. It had been the most unpopular war ever fought by the U.S., mainly because many Americans believed that the Philippines should have been given its independence.

Nov 18: The **Hay-Pauncefote Treaty** was signed, abrogating the Clayton-Bulwer Treaty of 1850. By its terms the British consented to U.S. control of an isthmian canal linking the Atlantic and Pacific oceans. The Senate ratified the treaty on Dec. 16.

II. Architecture
Arts and Music
Popular Entertainment
Publishing
Theater

For a number of years journalists had been documenting the corruption of the railroads and trusts. This year Frank Norris turned his skills as a novelist to a campaign against the excesses of big business. Concerned about the social and economic evils he saw, Norris planned a trilogy of novels, his *Epic of the Wheat*. The first volume, *The Octopus*, was published in 1901. It dealt with the struggle of farmers in the San Joaquin Valley of California against the power of the Southern Pacific Railroad. In *The Pit* (1903) Norris told the story of speculation on the Chicago wheat exchange and the damage it brought to individuals and society. Norris died on Oct. 25, 1902, at 32. *The Wolf*, which was to have concluded the trilogy, was never written. Norris viewed social and economic factors and nature itself as the determining elements in molding human lives.

Among **books published** this year were *D'ri and I* by Irving Bacheller, a novel set during the War of 1812; *Cardigan* by Robert W. Chambers, a novel of the American Revolution; *Graustark* by George Barr McCutcheon, a best-selling romance about a mythical Balkan kingdom; *Mrs. Wiggs of the Cabbage Patch* by Alice Hegan Rice; and *Springtime and Harvest* by Upton Sinclair, the author's first novel, which later was retitled *King Midas*.

III. Business and Industry
Education
Philosophy and Religion
Science

The extent to which the economy of the country had grown was made clear when the first billion-dollar corporation was formed this year. The United States Steel Corporation, formally organized on Mar. 3, was capitalized at $1,402,846,000. The actual value of the tangible property of the corporation was estimated at $682,000,000, indicating that a good deal of the capitalization was for good will. The enterprise netted the organizers, including the financier J. Pierpont Morgan, large sums. The corporation was formed primarily from the Carnegie Steel Company, but it brought in other mills as well. The new firm manufactured 60% of all iron and steel produced in the U.S. Andrew Carnegie received 5% bonds with a par value of $225,639,000 for his company and spent the next 20 years distributing his wealth in benefactions amounting to $350,000,000.

A report on **yellow fever** read by the Yellow Fever Commission to the Pan-American Medical Congress at Havana, Cuba, described experiments proving for the first time that the disease was transmitted by a mosquito *(Stegomyia calopus)*. Such a theory had been held for 20 years by Dr. Carlos Finlay of Havana, but he had been unable to offer proof and had been ridiculed by the medical profession. The Yellow Fever Commission, sent by the U.S. government to Cuba after the Spanish-American War, included Walter Reed, Aristides Agramonte, Jesse W. Lazear, and James Carroll. Doctors Lazear and Carroll both died from the effects of yellow fever contracted during the experiments.

Jan 10: The first great **oil strike in Texas** launched a fabulous era in the Southwest. The Spindletop claim near Beaumont, Tex., owned by Anthony F. Lucas, blew in on this date to open the door for the international petroleum industry.

IV. Fashion
    Folkways
    Holidays
    Social Issues and Crime
    Sports

Men who were to become legends of baseball were coming to the fore in the early years of the century. Among them was Connie Mack (Cornelius Alexander McGillicuddy), who began as a catcher for Washington (NL) in 1886, then played for Buffalo in the Players League in 1890 before joining Pittsburgh, where he ended his career as player-manager (1894–1896) with a .247 career batting average. In 1901 he was named manager of the Philadelphia Athletics (AL) and eventually became owner of the team. Under his long management the Athletics won nine league championships and five World Series. Mack was elected to the Baseball Hall of Fame in 1937. He did not fully retire until 1954, when the team was sold and moved to Kansas City, Mo.

June 15: The **U.S. Open golf tournament** was won by Willie Anderson.

Sep 2: "**Speak softly and carry a big stick**" was credited to Theodore Roosevelt a few weeks after becoming president. The saying, emphasizing the need for a strong foreign policy, caught the fancy of the entire nation and "the big stick" proved a favorite prop of political cartoonists.

Sep 28-Oct 4: The **America's Cup** was successfully defended by the U.S. yacht *Columbia,* which won three straight races from the British challenger *Shamrock II.*

1902

I. **Civil Rights**
   Exploration and Settlement
   Government
   Statistics
   Wars

Interest in conservation of natural resources was growing, and the nation found a strong advocate in Pres. Theodore Roosevelt. During his term of office Roosevelt added almost 150,000,000 acres of land to the government reserve. On July 17, 1902, Congress passed the Newlands Reclamation Act, named for its sponsor, Francis G. Newlands, Democratic congressman from Nevada. By its terms the government would build irrigation dams in 16 western states and use the proceeds from the sale of public lands for further projects. The law also set up the U.S. Bureau of Reclamation in the Department of the Interior.

Jan 24: A treaty with Denmark for the purchase of the **Virgin Islands** (Danish West Indies) was signed. The U.S. Senate approved the treaty, but the Danish Rigsdag rejected it. In 1917, after a Danish plebiscite (Dec. 14, 1916) favored the sale, the islands of St. Croix, St. Thomas, and St. John were finally purchased for $25,000,000.

May 20: Cuban independence was achieved, four years after the end of the Spanish-American War. The U.S. flag was lowered from government buildings in Cuba and replaced with the new Cuban flag.

June 28: The **Isthmian Canal Act** was passed by Congress. It authorized financing and building of a canal across the Isthmus of Panama, and also authorized an alternative route across Nicaragua in the event the president could not obtain a concession from the Panama Canal Company of France (which he eventually did for $40,000,000) and negotiate a proper treaty with Colombia. Treaty difficulties were ob-

viated by the successful rebellion and separation of
Panama from Colombia in Nov. 1903. The new republic immediately granted a ten-mile-wide strip of
land for the canal.

July 1: The **Philippine Government Act** was passed by
Congress. It declared the Philippine Islands an unorganized territory and all inhabitants territorial citizens. It authorized a commission, appointed by the
president, to govern the territory. On July 4 Pres.
Theodore Roosevelt issued an order establishing civil
government and granting amnesty to all political
prisoners.

Nov 4: In **congressional elections** both major parties
made gains in the Senate from minor party or vacant
seats, but the Republicans maintained their majority
over the Democrats, 57–33. In the House of Representatives the total number of seats rose from 357 to
386, and the Republicans kept their majority over the
Democrats, 208–178.

II. Architecture
   ## Arts and Music
   ## Popular Entertainment
   ## Publishing
   ## Theater

Plays dealing with strong characters, both virtuous
and otherwise, were successful at this time. Foremost
among American playwrights was Clyde Fitch, author of more than 30 popular plays. His play *The
Stubbornness of Geraldine,* a study of fidelity, opened
in New York City on Nov. 3, 1902. He also produced
this year *The Girl With the Green Eyes.* The play dealt
with the psychological aspects of jealousy; it was his
best work. *The Climbers* (1901) and *The City* (1909)
dealt seriously with New York City's financial and
political life. Fitch also wrote such popular farces as
Captain Jinks of the Horse Marines (1901).

Among **books published** this year was *The Virginian* by Owen Wister, a story of life in Wyoming that
became one of the most celebrated western novels of
all time. Wister dedicated the book to his friend Pres.

Theodore Roosevelt. *The Virginian* was reprinted 14 times in eight months, and in two years had sold some 300,000 copies. Other books published this year included *The Captain of the Gray-Horse Troop* by Hamlin Garland, a novel chronicling the exploitation of the Sioux by white men; *The Mississippi Bubble* by Emerson Hough, a historical novel; *The Wings of the Dove* by Henry James, a novel; *The Story of My Life*, the autobiography of Helen Keller; *A Daughter of the Snows* by Jack London, the author's first novel, and *The Cruise of the Dazzler*, for children, also by London; *Brewster's Millions* by George Barr McCutcheon, a novel that sold in the millions and was the basis for at least six motion pictures; *Dorothy Vernon of Haddon Hall*, a novel by Charles Major; and *The Blazed Trail* by Stewart Edward White, a novel.

III. Business and Industry
   Education
   Philosophy and Religion
   Science

As American business enterprises grew, debate increased as to whether large and powerful corporations were good for the nation. Experience so far indicated that industrial giants cared little for anything except profit and that only government regulation could restrain their actions. Into this argument came the International Harvester Company, incorporated in New Jersey on Aug. 12, 1902, with a capital of $120,000,000. The combination of interests represented by the concern produced 85% of all farm machinery in the U.S. However, Harvester conducted its business in such a moderate manner that there was little complaint. Both capitalists and consumers were beginning to recognize that, given the extent of the nation and its economy, bigness was here to stay.

Feb: Discovery of the **hookworm** was announced by Dr. Charles Wardell Stiles. He declared that the so-called poor whites in the South were neither lazy nor innately slovenly, but were suffering on a wide scale from the debilitating effects of the parasite. An antihookworm campaign began throughout the South, supported by the Rockefeller Foundation.

IV. Fashion
Folkways
Holidays
Social Issues and Crime
Sports

The early years of twentieth-century professional baseball saw the founding of the American League in 1900 out of the Western Association, the new league's first season in 1901, and the start of an annual championship series with the National League in 1903. This expansion created more heroes of the diamond. One of the most admired and successful managers of this period was John J. McGraw, nicknamed "Little Napoleon," who left as manager for Baltimore (AL) midway through the 1902 season to become manager of the New York Giants (NL). McGraw held that position for 31 years, during which the Giants won ten National League championships, four in succession, and three World Series. McGraw was elected to the Baseball Hall of Fame in 1937.

Jan 1: The **first Tournament of Roses Association football game,** and the first post-season football game, was held at Pasadena, Calif. Michigan defeated Stanford 49–0. The event came to be known as the Rose Bowl game in 1923.

Apr 19: The sixth **Boston Marathon** was won by Samuel A. Mellor of Yonkers, N.Y., with a time of 2 hrs., 43 min., 12 sec.

Oct 11: The **U.S. Open golf tournament** was won by Lawrence Auchterlonie.

1903

I. Civil Rights
   Exploration and Settlement
   Government
   Statistics
   Wars

By 1903 it became clear that legislation on the books could not keep railroads from engaging in business practices that gave certain shippers a decided advantage. As a result, on Feb. 19 the Elkins Act, named for Sen. Stephen B. Elkins, Republican of West Virginia, was passed by Congress. This law made it illegal for railroads to give rebates on their published freight rates. Finding that this did not solve the problem, Congress on June 29, 1906, passed the Hepburn Act, named for William P. Hepburn, Republican congressman from Ohio. That law empowered the Interstate Commerce Commission to regulate the rates charged by railroads, pipelines, and terminals.

Jan 22: The **Hay-Herrán Treaty,** granting a 99-year lease and U.S. sovereignty over a canal zone in Panama, was signed with Colombia. The U.S. Senate ratified it on Mar. 17, but on Aug. 12 the Colombian Senate rejected it.

Nov 3: A **revolt in Panama** against Colombian rule broke out one day after Pres. Roosevelt ordered U.S. naval forces to the area. The U.S. presence kept Colombian forces from halting the rebellion, which was engineered in part by officers of the Panama Canal Company and by Panamanian groups, all with the tacit approval of the Roosevelt administration. On Nov. 6 the U.S. recognized the Republic of Panama, three days after it had been proclaimed.

Nov 18: The **Hay-Bunau-Varilla Treaty** was negotiated. It gave the U.S. full control of a ten-mile-wide canal zone in Panama in return for $10,000,000 in gold plus a yearly payment of $250,000.

II. Architecture
  Arts and Music
  Popular Entertainment
  Publishing
  Theater

Realism was becoming an influence in adult American fiction, but it was not noticeable in children's literature. Sentimentalism and a happy ending were what sold, as witnessed by the popular books of Kate Douglas Wiggin. *The Birds' Christmas Carol* (1887) was the story of the life and death of an ethereal child. Wiggin's most successful book, *Rebecca of Sunnybrook Farm,* was published this year and sold more than 1,000,000 copies. This children's classic was about a girl's experiences on her widowed mother's farm. Another Wiggin classic was *Mother Carey's Chickens* (1911), about a warm-hearted widow who had a great many children.

Among **books published** this year was *The Ambassadors* by Henry James, a novel about Americans in Paris that showed the author at the peak of his literary powers. Other books published this year included *The Land of Little Rain* by Mary Austin, a collection of sketches; *The Bar Sinister* by Richard Harding Davis, a novel; *The Little Shepherd of Kingdom Come* by John Fox, Jr., a novel; *The Call of the Wild* by Jack London, a study of the forces of nature and civilization in the framework of a classic dog story, and *The People of the Abyss,* also by London, a study of the slums of London's East End; *Canterbury Pilgrims* by Percy MacKaye, a drama in blank verse that set Chaucer's characters in poetic adventures; *The Pit* by Frank Norris, the second volume of the author's *Epic of the Wheat* trilogy; and *The Testimony of the Suns* by George Sterling, a book of poetry.

The **first male motion picture star** made his debut in *The Great Train Robbery,* a landmark film considered the first motion picture with a plot. The actor, Max Aaronson, also used the names Max Anderson, G. M. Anderson, and Bronco Billy.

Mar: The vogue for what came to be called the **Nan-**

tucket limerick hit U.S. newspapers, inspiring many variations and sequels. The original went:

> There once was a man from Nantucket
> Who kept all his cash in a bucket;
> But his daughter, named Nan,
> Ran away with a man,
> And as for the bucket, Nantucket.

III. Business and Industry
Education
Philosophy and Religion
Science

A historic moment in technology and transportation arrived on Dec. 17, when Orville Wright made the first powered flight in a heavier-than-air machine. As early as 1898 Orville and Wilbur Wright, owners of a bicycle repair shop and factory in Dayton, Ohio, had been working on the problem of flight. Years of experimentation had led to their development of a working glider. Meanwhile, refinements of internal combustion engines gave them the power plant they needed to keep the glider aloft. On Dec. 17, 1903, on the beach at Kitty Hawk, N.C., Orville Wright flew the 750-lb. craft, which was powered by a 12-hp gasoline engine, for 12 seconds, traveling about 120 feet. Four flights were made that day, with Wilbur setting the record of 59 seconds in the air traveling 852 feet. The aviation age had arrived.

The **University of Puerto Rico** at Rio Pedras, P.R., was chartered. Its first classes had been held in 1900, when the institution was a normal school.

A **heavier-than-air flying machine,** built by Samuel P. Langley, was tested from a houseboat on the Potomac R. On takeoff, its wing hit a houseboat stanchion and the machine crashed. Langley was subjected to much public ridicule for his efforts. In 1914 the machine was reconditioned and flown. It was a 14-ft. model and flew without a pilot. There are those who maintain that Langley achieved powered flight before the Wright brothers.

Mar 21: In a **victory for organized labor,** the report of the Anthracite Coal Strike Commission, appointed by Pres. Roosevelt to investigate conditions in the mining industry, established that "no person shall be refused employment, or in any way discriminated against, on account of membership or non-membership in any labor organization."

July 4: The **first Pacific communications cable** was opened. Pres. Roosevelt sent a message around the world and back to him in 12 minutes.

IV. Fashion
Folkways
Holidays
Social Issues and Crime
Sports

This year was born an American sports institution, the World Series. For the first time, the champions of the National and American leagues met for a post-season playoff, which ran from Oct. 1 to Oct. 13; it was a best-of-nine series. The Pittsburgh Pirates, the National League champs, took three of the first four games from the Boston Red Sox, originally called the Red Stockings. On Oct. 7 the American League champs rebounded with an 11–2 romp over the Pirates, then won the next three games to take the series five games to three and prove to the world that the American League had arrived. Boston's win no doubt ruffled a few feathers in the National camp. In 1904, when Boston again took the American League pennant, John J. McGraw, manager of the champion New York Giants, already involved in a running feud with Ban Johnson, president of the American League, refused to allow a post-season playoff. The bitterness between the two leagues was only temporary. In 1905 the World Series resumed and has been played every year since.

June 27: The **U.S. Open golf tournament** was won by Willie Anderson.

Aug 8: The U.S. lost the **Davis Cup** international tennis challenge round to Great Britain, four matches to one.

Aug 22-Sep 2: The **America's Cup** was successfully defended by the U.S. yacht *Reliance*, which won three straight races from the British challenger *Shamrock III.*

1904

I. Civil Rights
   Exploration and Settlement
   Government
   Statistics
   Wars

By 1904 Pres. Theodore Roosevelt had achieved great popularity as well as control of the Republican Party. His nomination for a term in his own right was certain and his conservative Democratic opponent, Alton B. Parker, conducted a dull campaign. Roosevelt, although representing the conservative party in American politics, was the hero of the progressives. The progressives of this period inherited some of the goals of the populists of a few years earlier, but the populists represented chiefly southern and western farm interests. The progressives were urban-oriented, and concerned primarily with problems of industrial monopoly, corruption in government, assimilation of new immigrants, and the relief of poverty.

Jan 4: In a ruling on the **status of territorial citizens,** the Supreme Court ruled that citizens of Puerto Rico were not aliens and could not be refused admission to the continental limits of the U.S. However, they were not classified as U.S. citizens.

May 5: The **Socialist National Convention nominated Eugene V. Debs** of Indiana for the presidency and Benjamin Hanford of New York for the vice presidency.

June 21-23: The **Republican National Convention**

nominated **Pres. Roosevelt** for the presidency and
Charles W. Fairbanks of Indiana for the vice presidency.

July 6-9: The **Democratic National Convention nominated Alton B. Parker** of New York for the presidency and Henry G. Davis of West Virginia for the vice presidency.

Nov 8: Theodore Roosevelt was reelected president
of the United States. Charles W. Fairbanks was
elected vice president. The electoral vote was Roosevelt, 336; Alton B. Parker, Democratic candidate, 140.
The popular vote was Roosevelt, 7,628,834; Parker,
5,884,401; Eugene V. Debs, Socialist candidate,
402,460; Dr. Silas C. Swallow, Prohibition Party,
259,257; Thomas E. Watson, People's Party, 114,753.
The Republicans carried Missouri for the first time
since the Civil War in what was the biggest election
victory since 1872. They maintained a 57–33 majority
over the Democrats in the Senate and picked up 43
seats in the House for a 250–136 majority.

II. Architecture
   Arts and Music
   Popular Entertainment
   Publishing
   Theater

This was the era of the muckrakers, journalists and
authors who investigated and wrote about corruption in government and business. One of the leading
muckrakers was Lincoln Steffens, a magazine editor
who collected his articles on corruption in municipal
government in *The Shame of the Cities* (1904). Steffens held that such corruption stemmed from alliances between businessmen and politicians who
were able to enrich each other at the expense of the
taxpayer.

   Among **books published** this year was *The Golden
Bowl* by Henry James. Other books published this
year included *The Crossing* by Winston Churchill, a
novel set in Kentucky during the American Revolution; *The Deliverance* by Ellen Glasgow, a novel; *Cab-*

bages and Kings by O. Henry, the author's first collection of short stories; *The Sea Wolf* by Jack London, a study of human nature and the concept of the superman as embodied in the character of a brutal ship's captain; *Freckles* by Gene Stratton-Porter, a novel; and *The History of the Standard Oil Company* by Ida M. Tarbell, a muckraking classic.

The **American Academy of Arts and Letters** was founded by the National Institute of Arts and Letters. Membership was limited to 50, to be chosen from among the members of the institute.

III. Business and Industry
Education
Philosophy and Religion
Science

The first section of the New York City subway system, which was to become the largest in the country, was opened on Oct. 27, 1904. Work on the line had begun in 1900. It ran from the Brooklyn Bridge north to 145th St. and Broadway in Manhattan. Construction of this first part of the subway system was supervised by Alexander Ector Orr. Some of the present system runs on elevated tracks, but there are 134 miles of tunnels, some driven through rock. The first tunnel under the East R. was driven between 1903 and 1906 and put into service in 1908.

The **diesel engine** was shown for the first time in the U.S. at the St. Louis Exposition. The engine was based on the plans of the German inventor Rudolf Diesel.

Mar 14: The **Northern Securities Company** was ordered dissolved by the Supreme Court in a landmark case reflecting the federal government's relation to big business. Theodore Roosevelt's reputation as a trust-buster rested largely on the prosecution of this case and the angry comments he drew from J. P. Morgan, who controlled the railroad holding company.

Oct 19: The **American Tobacco Company** was formed by a merger of its two subsidiaries, the Consolidated

and the American & Continental tobacco companies.
Nov 2: Evangeline Booth was appointed commander
of the Salvation Army of the U.S.

IV. Fashion
Folkways
Holidays
Social Issues and Crime
Sports

As soon as automobiles were invented and manufactured, men began racing them against time and
against one another. Automobile racing as an organized sport began on Oct. 8, 1904, with the Vanderbilt
Cup race, sponsored by William K. Vanderbilt. Vanderbilt was an early auto fancier. It was said he had
garages that would hold 100 cars and that he hired 20
mechanics to service them. The race, on Long Island,
was as much a social as a sporting event, with about
25,000 spectators on hand. The winner was George
Heath, driving a 90-hp French Panhard. He defeated
17 other starters by completing ten laps around a
28.4-mi. course in 5 hrs., 26 min., 45 sec.

The **World Series** was called off this year by John
McGraw, manager of the New York Giants, the National League champions. Incensed by the abuse Ban
Johnson, president of the American League, had
heaped on him when he switched from the Baltimore
Americans in 1903, McGraw got even by refusing to
let the Giants meet Boston, the American League
leaders, for the post-season series. It took the persua-
sion of owners, managers, players and fans to
smooth the incident over. By that time it was too late
for the games to be played.

May 5: The **first perfect baseball game,** in which the
pitcher did not allow any opposing player to reach
first base, was pitched by Denton T. "Cy" Young of the
Boston Americans (AL), who led his team to a 3–0
victory over Philadelphia.

May 14: The first **Olympic Games** to be held in the U.S.
opened as part of the St. Louis Exposition in St.
Louis, Mo. The U.S. won 21 events and the unofficial

team championship in the third Olympiad of the
modern era.

July 9: The **U.S. Open golf tournament** was won by
Willie Anderson.

1905

I. Civil Rights
Exploration and Settlement
Government
Statistics
Wars

Pres. Theodore Roosevelt gained international prominence by arranging a peace conference between
Russia and Japan; the nations had been at war since
Feb. 10, 1904. Although Japan had fared better in the
military and naval engagements of the Russo-Japanese War, neither side was in a position to go on fighting much longer. In a note to the two powers on June
8, Roosevelt urged an end to hostilities and suggested
a conference. The peace conference met at Portsmouth, N.H., on Aug. 9, and the belligerents signed
the Treaty of Portsmouth on Sept. 5. The U.S. sought
to keep a balance of power in the Far East between
the two nations and also to preserve the Open Door
Policy in China. However, by the terms of the treaty,
Japan came out ahead and was on its way to becoming a world power. Japan's paramount interest in
Korea was recognized and it was given the South
Manchurian Railway and the Southern Liaotung Peninsula. Roosevelt was able to keep Japan from
securing more than half of Sakhalin Island. For his
efforts Roosevelt was awarded the Nobel Peace Prize
in 1906.

Jan 21: A **protocol with the Dominican Republic** was
signed, giving the U.S. complete charge of its customs
and international debt, with the purpose of satisfying
European creditors of Santo Domingo. The U.S. was

also to guarantee the territorial integrity of the republic. Though the U.S. Senate refused to ratify the protocol, Pres. Theodore Roosevelt made a temporary arrangement with the republic, incorporating the key elements of the protocol. The action was a reflection of the so-called Roosevelt Corollary to the Monroe Doctrine, which Roosevelt stated on Dec. 6, 1904. Roosevelt held that "in flagrant cases of wrongdoing or impotence" of nations in the Western Hemisphere, the U.S. might be obliged to undertake "the exercise of an international police power."

II. Architecture
Arts and Music
Popular Entertainment
Publishing
Theater

Higher education joined hands with theater this year when George Pierce Baker established his 47 Workshop at Harvard. He taught playwriting techniques and provided a laboratory for experimental stage productions. Among those whom Baker taught were Eugene O'Neill, Philip Barry, Sidney Howard, and S. N. Behrman. Baker taught at Harvard until 1925, when he went to Yale to continue his work there.

Among **books published** this year was *The House of Mirth* by Edith Wharton, a novel analyzing with great subtlety a group of wealthy, artificial, and oversophisticated people, and their tragic influence over the life of a young woman. Other books published this year included *Isidro* by Mary Austin, the author's first novel; *The Clansman* by Thomas Dixon, Jr., a novel about the Ku Klux Klan that was the basis for D. W. Griffith's landmark motion picture *The Birth of a Nation; The Game* by Jack London, a novel about prizefighting; *The House of a Thousand Candles* by Meredith Nicholson, a novel; and *Sandy* by Alice Hegan Rice, a novel.

III. Business and Industry
Education
Philosophy and Religion
Science

Life insurance had joined the ranks of big business, the three largest firms having combined assets of $1,250,000,000 by 1904. The major firms also had arrangements with certain banks by which the insurance company purchased large blocks of securities placed on the market by the banks. The funds for these lucrative transactions came from the thousands who paid insurance premiums. Reports of a scandal surfaced and an investigating commission was appointed by New York State in 1905. Headed by Charles Evans Hughes, it held 57 public hearings from Sept. 6 to Dec. 30 and uncovered numerous excesses. The probe disclosed, for example, that Charles Hazen Hyde, son of the founder of the Equitable Life Assurance Society, earned $100,000 a year, although still in his twenties. Hyde once charged to company expenses a $12,000 dinner for the French ambassador. The investigation resulted in reform legislation. It also brought Hughes into public life. He went on to become governor of New York, Republican candidate for president, and in 1930 chief justice of the U.S. Supreme Court.

The number of **automobiles** registered in the U.S. rose to 77,988, compared with 300 a decade earlier, but the automobile was still considered a useless toy by most people.

Feb 20: State compulsory vaccination laws were ruled constitutional by the U.S. Supreme Court in the case of *Jacobson v. Massachusetts.*

Apr 17: State laws limiting working hours were ruled unconstitutional by the U.S. Supreme Court.

July 7: The **Industrial Workers of the World** (IWW) was established in Chicago as a reaction against the more conservative American Federation of Labor. Its members came to be known as Wobblies.

IV. Fashion
   Folkways
   Holidays
   Social Issues and Crime
   Sports

Greyhounds had been chasing hares for several thousand years, but it was not until 1905 that an American developed the idea of racing the dogs around a circular track in pursuit of an artificial hare. Owen Patrick Smith of Hot Springs, S. Dak., decided to promote tourism through such races. There had been public opposition to the slaughter of live hares, so Smith substituted a stuffed rabbit skin attached to a motorcycle, thus launching the greyhound racing industry.

The **world heavyweight boxing championship** was won by Marvin Hart, who knocked out Jack Root in 12 rounds in the final bout of an elimination tourney. He filled the title vacated by James J. Jeffries' retirement this year.

Football rules were revised this season by the Rules Committee of Football as a result of Pres. Theodore Roosevelt's threat to abolish football after he had seen a newspaper picture of a badly mangled player. The changes included legalization of the forward pass and elimination of certain dangerous scrimmage plays.

At the **Wimbledon** tennis championships in England, May G. Sutton won the women's singles championship, becoming the first foreigner to win the women's singles and the first U.S. player to win any Wimbledon singles title.

Sep 22: The **U.S. Open golf tournament** was won by Willie Anderson.

Oct 9-14: The second annual **World Series** was won by the New York Giants (NL), defeating the Philadelphia Athletics (AL) four games to one.

1906

I. Civil Rights
   Exploration and Settlement
   Government
   Statistics
   Wars

The worst natural disaster in U.S. history occurred on the morning of Apr. 18, 1906, when a devastating earthquake struck San Francisco, Calif. Most of the damage came not from the shock but from the fire that followed. Flames swept the city for three days. By the time the fire was brought under control, 490 blocks had been leveled, 25,000 buildings had been destroyed, 225,000 people had been made homeless, and 452 had been killed. Damage was estimated to be at least $350,000,000. The nation rallied to the aid of the stricken city, whose residents began at once to rebuild. Banks offered to lend money and stores reordered stock.

The **first American Nobel Prize winner** was Pres. Theodore Roosevelt, who was awarded the Nobel Peace Prize this year for his role in mediating an end to the Russo-Japanese War (1904–1905).

June 30: The **Pure Food and Drug Act** was passed. It prohibited the sale of adulterated foods and drugs and demanded an honest statement of contents on labels. Dr. Harvey W. Wiley was mainly responsible for pointing up the necessity for this act. On the same day a Meat Inspection Act was passed by Congress. It was the result of the Reynolds and Neill report of June 4, which revealed shockingly unclean conditions in meat-packing plants. The Meat Inspection Act required sanitary conditions and federal inspection for all plants in interstate commerce.

Aug 23: A **request for U.S. intervention** in Cuba was issued by Tomás Estrada Palma, the first president of Cuba, to quell a revolt arising from election disputes.

Pres. Roosevelt held off but finally sent troops, who took over the Cuban government for 13 days in October.

Sep 22: Race riots in Atlanta, Ga., left 21 persons dead, including 18 blacks, and many more injured in one of the worst race riots in U.S. history. The city was placed under martial law.

Sep 29: The **Platt Amendment,** authorizing U.S. intervention in Cuba, was invoked and the U.S. assumed military control of the country. Sec. of War William Howard Taft was provisional governor.

Nov 6: In **congressional elections** the Republicans gained four Senate seats for a 61–31 majority. In the House the Republicans lost 28 seats but maintained a 222–164 majority.

II. Architecture
   Arts and Music
   Popular Entertainment
   Publishing
   Theater

The reading public's fascination with an American West more imaginary than real seemed insatiable. One man who did his best to feed this craving was Zane Grey, whose more than 60 books sold over 13,000,000 copies before he died in 1939. His first western novel, published in 1906, was *The Spirit of the Border.* His most popular novel was *Riders of the Purple Sage* (1912). Grey was quite authentic as to geography and topography, but his plots and characters were melodramatic and sometimes simplistic. Strong and brave heroes, nasty villains, and pretty, innocent heroines were his stock in trade. Many of his novels were made into movies.

Among **books published** this year was *The Jungle* by Upton Sinclair, a novel exposing the sordid aspects of the Chicago meat-packing industry, particularly the hardships imposed on its workers and the practice of selling questionable or tainted meat. The book came to the attention of Pres. Theodore Roosevelt, who summoned Sinclair for further information. Roosevelt then pushed for passage of the Pure Food and Drug Act of 1906. Other books published this year included *The Spoilers* by Rex Beach, a novel of Alaska based on actual events and the author's experiences in the territory; *Coniston* by Winston Churchill, a novel about boss rule in a state legislature; *The Awakening of Helena Ritchie* by Margaret Deland, a novel; *The Wheel of Life* by Ellen Glasgow, a novel; *The Four Million* by O. Henry, his second collection of stories; *White Fang* by Jack London, a sequel to *The Call of the Wild,* and *Before Adam,* a novel also by London; and *What Is Man?* by Mark Twain, a bitter essay in the form of a Platonic dialogue, published privately.

Ferdinand "Jelly Roll" Morton, the celebrated New Orleans ragtime piano player, wrote "The King Porter Stomp." Morton gave the St. Louis ragtime style of Scott Joplin a heavy beat. Among his many other ragtime compositions were "The Pearls," "Kansas City Stomps," "Chicago Breakdown," "Black Bottom Stomp," "Buddy Carter's Rag," and "The Perfect Rag."

III. Business and Industry
Education
Philosophy and Religion
Science

An event rare in U.S. religious history occurred this year when the Rev. Algernon Sidney Crapsey, rector of St. Andrew's Protestant Episcopal Church in Rochester, N.Y., was tried for heresy before an ecclesiastical court. His church was known for its social work, but it was charged that under the influence of the writings of Karl Marx and Ernest Renan, Crapsey had made heretical remarks about the divinity of Christ. The trial began on Apr. 18 at Batavia, N.Y., with detachments of lawyers, secular and clerical, representing both sides. The trial was fully reported by newspapers throughout the U.S. and England. Crapsey was convicted on Dec. 5 and expelled from the ministry.

Apr 7: Announcement was made of a successful **trans-atlantic wireless transmission** from a 40,000-watt transmitter at Manhattan Beach, New York City, to Lee De Forest at a receiving station in Ireland. This year De Forest invented the triode tube, the cornerstone for the development of modern wireless communication.

Dec 24: The first known **radio broadcast of voice and music** was made by Reginald A. Fessenden, a private radio experimenter, at Branch Rock, Mass. Fessenden had demonstrated his system at Branch Rock on Dec. 11. Also this year he established two-way wireless communication with Scotland.

IV. Fashion
   Folkways
   Holidays
   Social Issues and Crime
   Sports

The most talked about murder of the first decade of the twentieth century was the killing of Stanford White, the prominent architect. On the evening of June 25, 1906, White was at the roof garden of New York City's Madison Square Garden, which he had designed, when he was shot and killed by Harry K. Thaw. The wealthy playboy claimed that White had been having an affair with his wife, Evelyn Nesbit Thaw, a former chorus girl. Thaw's trial fascinated the country. After one hung jury, Thaw was found "not guilty because insane" in 1908. In 1913 Thaw escaped from the mental hospital where he was being held but was found in Canada and brought back. In 1915, at still another trial, he was declared sane and released.

Devil's Tower, Wyo., was designated the **first national monument** by Pres. Theodore Roosevelt. Devil's Tower, a natural rock formation 1000 ft. in diameter at its base and about 275 ft. in diameter at its top, is 865 ft. high.

Feb 23: The **world heavyweight boxing champion-**

ship was won by Tommy Burns, who defeated Marvin Hart in 20 rounds at Los Angeles, Calif. James J. Jeffries, who retired in 1905 because he could find no worthy adversary, refereed the fight.

Mar 17: The term *muckraker,* taken from a passage in John Bunyan's *Pilgrim's Progress,* was first used in its modern meaning by Pres. Theodore Roosevelt in an address to the Gridiron Club, Washington, D.C. Muckrakers were authors of "literature of exposure," who in the early 1900s helped stimulate reform by exposing unpleasant sides of American life. The best-known muckrakers included Lincoln Steffens, Ida M. Tarbell, Ray Stannard Baker, and David Graham Phillips. A prime example of the influence of muckraking literature can be seen in Upton Sinclair's *The Jungle,* which helped passage of the Meat Packing Act of 1906.

Apr 22-May 2: Olympic Games were held in Athens, Greece, but they were not accepted as official by the International Olympic Committee. The U.S. won 12 gold medals, behind France with 15.

June 29: The **U.S. Open golf tournament** was won by Alex Smith.

Oct 9-14: The third annual **World Series** was won by the Chicago White Sox (AL), who defeated the Chicago Cubs (NL) four games to two.

1907

I. Civil Rights
Exploration and Settlement
Government
Statistics
Wars

Pres. Theodore Roosevelt was especially interested in the preparedness and political value of the U.S. Navy.

Now that a powerful Navy existed, he proposed to show it to the world, partly to deter Japan from further adventurism in the Pacific. On Dec. 16, 1907, a squadron of 16 battleships, known as the Great White Fleet because of the ships' appearance, steamed out of Hampton Roads, Va., under Rear Adm. Robley D. Evans. Instead of causing alarm as some had feared, the fleet was enthusiastically received in many ports of call, including those in Japan, Australia, New Zealand, and Gibraltar. The fleet arrived back at Hampton Roads on Feb. 22, 1909, having convinced the world that the U.S. was a major naval power.

Feb 20: The **Immigration Act of 1907** was signed by Pres. Theodore Roosevelt. It included a provision empowering the president to restrict immigration by Japanese laborers.

Mar 14: Japanese laborers were excluded from immigrating to the continental U.S. by presidential order.

Mar 21: U.S. Marines landed in **Honduras** to protect life and property during a period of political disturbance.

Nov 16: Oklahoma was admitted to the Union, the 46th state.

II. Architecture
Arts and Music
Popular Entertainment
Publishing
Theater

The Broadway theater always offered a variety of productions, some dramatic, some humorous, and some appealing as much to the eye as to the ear or the mind. One of the most successful producers of visually lavish entertainment was Florenz Ziegfeld, who offered his first *Ziegfeld Follies* this year. Ziegfeld put on this annual revue for 24 years, featuring "the most beautiful girls in the world" together with comedians and singers. Among the stars he presented were Anna Held, Fanny Brice, Eddie Cantor, and W. C. Fields. Ziegfeld also staged such hits as *Rio Rita* and *Show Boat*.

Among **books published** this year was *Three Weeks,* a romantic novel by the English author Elinor Glyn that was suppressed in Boston because of its description of an illicit affair. It sold 50,000 copies in three weeks and eventually sold in the hundreds of thousands. Other books published this year included *The Trimmed Lamp* and *Heart of the West,* two more collections by O. Henry; *Songs of a Sourdough* by Robert W. Service, which included the celebrated ballad "The Shooting of Dan McGrew" and which was reissued as *The Spell of the Yukon; Christian Science* by Mark Twain; and *The Fruit of the Tree* by Edith Wharton, a novel.

The Education of Henry Adams, a masterpiece of autobiography by the noted historian and author, was privately printed and distributed to Adams's friends. Adams revealed that his education had not prepared him for modern living and expressed skepticism and loss of faith. The work was published posthumously in 1918 and was awarded the Nobel Prize for Biography in 1919.

The first public showing of a **color motion picture with sound** was held in Cleveland, Ohio. The Chromophone process was used in the film, which consisted of footage of grand opera, a bull-fight with naturalistic sound effects, and a political speech accompanied by derisive sounds.

The **Robey House,** one of Frank Lloyd Wright's earliest designs, was built in Chicago. The structure showed the broad low roofs and horizontal lines that were the hallmark of Wright's prairie houses.

III. Business and Industry
Education
Philosophy and Religion
Science

Once more overspeculation and a flawed and unregulated banking and credit structure caused a financial panic that turned into a brief depression. A large drop in the stock market on Mar. 13 presaged trouble. On Oct. 21 a run on the Knickerbocker Trust Company in New York City caused panic elsewhere. The bank was forced to close its doors. The government called on J. Pierpont Morgan, the nation's leading financier, for help. By the force of his personality, Morgan secured the cooperation of his fellow bankers, who combined their resources to import $100,000,000 in gold from Europe to restore confidence and end what came to be known as the panic of 1907. One result of the panic was passage of the Aldrich-Vreeland Act on May 30, 1908. It levied a tax of up to 10% on notes based on securities other than federal bonds. It also established a commission to investigate the currency and banking system.

The **Nobel Prize in Physics** was awarded to Prof. Albert Abraham Michelson, head of the Physics Department at the University of Chicago. Michelson was honored particularly for his studies of the speed of light, carried out with apparatus designed and built by himself.

Sep 12: The *Lusitania,* the largest steamship in the world, arrived in New York harbor on its maiden voyage. The liner set a new speed record of 5 days, 54 min. between Queenstown (now Cobh), Ireland, and New York.

IV. Fashion
Folkways
Holidays
Social Issues and Crime
Sports

One of the best-remembered infield combinations in the game of baseball is the trio of Joe Tinker, Johnny Evers, and Frank Chance, who played shortstop, second base, and first base, respectively, for the Chicago Cubs (NL). These three turned the double play into an art form. Chance had become manager of the Cubs in 1905. In 1907 the team finished first and went on to dominate the Detroit Tigers in the World Series. Evers and Tinker made six errors in the series, but the trio combined to steal eight bases and kept Detroit from scoring effectively. Franklin Pierce Adams later recalled them in a piece called "Baseball's Sad Lexicon":

Ruthlessly pricking our gonfalon bubble,
Making a Giant hit into a double,
Words that are weighty with nothing but trouble:
"Tinker to Evers to Chance."

At the **Wimbledon** tennis championships, May G. Sutton won the women's singles title.

May: An early **Mother's Day** observance was held in Grafton, W. Va., through the efforts of Miss Anna M. Jarvis, who arranged a special church service marking the second anniversary of her mother's death in 1905. She requested that those attending the service wear white carnations, which she supplied. The first formal observances of Mother's Day were held in Grafton and in Philadelphia, Pa., on May 10, 1908. The custom spread rapidly until, by 1911, every state in the Union was participating in Mother's Day exercises held on the second Sunday in May.

June 21: The **U.S. Open golf tournament** was won by Alex Ross.

Oct 8-12: The fourth annual **World Series** was won by the Chicago Cubs (NL), who swept the Detroit Tigers (AL) in four games after the first game ended in a tie.

Dec 2: The **world heavyweight boxing championship** was successfully defended by Tommy Burns, who knocked out Gunner Moir in ten rounds at London, England.

1908

I. Civil Rights
   Exploration and Settlement
   Government
   Statistics
   Wars

There was little doubt that Pres. Theodore Roosevelt, if he chose to run again in 1908, would be reelected. However, he had said in 1904 he would not seek a third term, although he had been elected in his own right only once. Instead he handpicked the Republican nominee, William Howard Taft, who had been a lawyer, judge, U.S. solicitor general (1890–1892), governor of the Philippines (1901–1904), and secretary of war (1904–1908). The campaign was a dull one, the Democratic candidate, William Jennings Bryan, having lost most of the glamor he showed when first nominated for the presidency 12 years before.

Feb 18: An agreement on the **restriction of Japanese immigration** was reached through a note sent to the American ambassador to Japan acknowledging Pres. Theodore Roosevelt's order of Mar. 14, 1907. The Japanese government agreed not to issue any more passports to Japanese laborers for immigration to the U.S.

May 10-17: The **Socialist Party National Convention** nominated Eugene V. Debs of Indiana for the presidency and Benjamin Hanford of New York for the vice presidency.

June 16-20: The **Republican National Convention nominated William Howard Taft** of Ohio for the presidency and James S. Sherman of New York for the vice presidency. When Chairman Henry Cabot Lodge spoke in praise of Pres. Theodore Roosevelt, who had chosen not to seek renomination, the delegates began a demonstration that lasted 45 minutes, breaking all previous records for both major parties.

July 7-10: The **Democratic National Convention nominated William J. Bryan** of Nebraska for the presidency and John W. Kern of Indiana for the vice presidency.

Nov 3: William Howard Taft was elected president of the United States. James S. Sherman was elected vice president. The electoral vote was Taft, 321; William Jennings Bryan, Democrat of Nebraska, 162. The popular vote was Taft, 7,679,006; Bryan, 6,409,106; Eugene V. Debs, Socialist candidate, 420,820; Eugene W. Chafin, Prohibition candidate, 252,683; Thomas L. Hisgen, Independence Party, 83,562; Thomas E. Watson, Populist, 28,131; August Gillhaus, Socialist Labor Party, 13,825. In congressional elections the Republicans held a 61–32 majority, the Democrats gaining one seat. In the House, which added five new seats, the Republicans lost three seats but maintained a majority, 219–172.

II. Architecture
Arts and Music
Popular Entertainment
Publishing
Theater

A new generation of American painters was arriving on the art scene. The work of these painters was realistic and showed concern with the contemporary world. In 1908 they became known as The Eight when they organized an exhibition of their work in February at the Macbeth Gallery in New York City. The eight artists were Arthur B. Davies, Maurice Prendergast, Ernest Lawson, Robert Henri, George Luks, William J. Glackens, John Sloan, and Everett Shinn. Henri was their leader. Their painting represented a turning away from the pretty but insipid pictures of the older, academic school of painting. Some of their works, depicting the seamier side of modern, urban life, won them the title of the Ash Can school from their detractors. Frank Jewett Mather of *The Nation* wrote that there "was more green, yellow and red sickness about their position than positive talent." Nevertheless, they brought to art a new vitality and proved that everyday scenes showing ordinary people could be worthwhile subjects for the painter, even when the subject was a city backyard, a crowded business street, or lonely city people at night.

Among **books published** this year was *The Trail of the Lonesome Pine* by John Fox, Jr., a novel set in the Cumberland Mts. of Kentucky. The author used his own experiences and knowledge of the region and its people in the novel, which became a best seller. Other books published this year included *The Barrier* by Rex Beach, a novel of adventure; *Mr. Crewe's Career* by Winston Churchill, a novel dealing with control of a state government by a railroad; *Friendship Village* by Zona Gale, stories of midwestern life; *The Iron Heel* by Jack London, a novel that predicted the rise of fascism; *The Circular Staircase* by Mary Roberts Rinehart, the mystery novel that launched her career; and *The Metropolis* by Upton Sinclair, a novel.

There were between 8000 and 10,000 **nickelodeons,** or movie theaters, in the U.S., drawing an estimated 200,000 customers a day. The first such theater had been launched in 1905 in Pittsburgh, Pa., by John P. Harris and Harry Davis.

Julia Ward Howe, author of the poem "The Battle Hymn of the Republic," became the first woman member of the American Academy of Arts and Letters. This year William Dean Howells was made president of the academy.

III. Business and Industry
Education
Philosophy and Religion
Science

The age of the skyscraper was dawning. In Chicago architects and engineers had pioneered in new technology and materials, especially the steel skeleton that made such structures possible. But it was in New York City that the first real skyscrapers were erected. The first New York City skyscraper was the Flatiron

Building, constructed between 1902 and 1904. Its
name came from the triangular plot on which it was
built, at the intersection of Fifth Ave. and Broadway.
Its 22 stories rose 180 ft. high. In 1908 the Singer
Building set a new record, its 47 stories rising to a
height of 612 ft. It held the title of the world's tallest
building for less than a year, however, being eclipsed
by the Metropolitan Life tower of 50 stories and 700
ft. The Woolworth Building, completed in 1913, set
still another record with its 55 stories and height of
760 ft. Although exceeded in height many times since,
this distinguished Gothic-ornamented tower remains
the proudest symbol of the age of early skyscrapers.

Feb 3: In an **antitrust decision** in the case of *Loewe v.
Lawlor*, the so-called Danbury hatters case, the Supreme Court ruled that the antitrust law applied to
labor combinations as well as to capital combinations and declared union boycotting illegal.

June 12: A new **transatlantic speed record** was set by
the liner *Lusitania*, which traveled from Queenstown
(now Cobh), Ireland, to New York, a trip of 2780
miles, in 4 days, 15 hrs.

Sep 17: Orville Wright crashed in his airplane at Fort
Myer, Va., when a propeller blade broke and the
plane fell 150 ft. to the ground, injuring Wright seriously and killing his passenger, Lt. Thomas W. Selfridge of the U.S. Signal Corps. Selfridge was the first
person killed in an airplane accident. Orville and Wilbur Wright, still using their original machine, though
with improvements, had made thousands of flights,
had remained in the air as long as 38 min., and had
flown distances up to 24 mi., but their work was still
unknown in the U.S. to all but a few hundred observers. This year Wilbur Wright went to Europe to make
tests for the French. Vast crowds watched his flights.
On Sept. 21 he set a new flight endurance record over
Le Mans, France—1 hr., 31 min., 25 sec. in a flight of
61 miles.

Oct 1: The celebrated **Model T Ford** was introduced.
It originally cost $850 but by 1926 the price, because
of efficient manufacturing, had dropped to $310 for

a machine that included a self-starter and other improvements.

IV. Fashion
Folkways
Holidays
Social Issues and Crime
Sports

The sporting event of the year turned out to be an around-the-world auto race, from New York City to Paris, France, by way of Alaska and Siberia. It was sponsored by *The New York Times* and *Le Matin*. The race began on Feb. 12, when six autos and their crews, French, German, Italian, and U.S., left New York City at 11 A.M. and traveled north toward Albany, N.Y. The cars drove west, across the U.S., Russia, and eastern Europe, experiencing breakdowns and encountering muddy roads, snow, ice, timber wolves, and gasoline shortages. The two lead cars were the huge German Protos driven by Lt. Hans Koeppen and the U.S. Thomas Flyer with George Schuster at the wheel. The German team was penalized 30 days for shipping their car by rail to Seattle, Wash., so, despite the fact the Germans arrived in Paris on July 26 and the Americans on July 30, the U.S. team was declared the winner. The only other entrant to finish, the Italian Zust, arrived two weeks later. When the U.S. team returned, New York City turned out in great numbers to greet them. Pres. Theodore Roosevelt received them at the White House on Aug. 20.

Apr 27-Oct 31: At the **Summer Olympics** in London, England, the U.S. won the unofficial team championship by taking 15 of 28 events, with 23 gold medals. The team was honored in New York City on Aug. 29 on its return from the games.

Aug 28: The **U.S. Open golf tournament** was won by Fred McLeod.

Sep 23: Perhaps the **greatest dispute in baseball** was a call made in what was supposed to be the decisive game, at the Polo Grounds, N.Y., of the Chicago Cubs-

New York Giants National League pennant race. In
the bottom of the ninth inning with two men out and
the score tied at 1–1, New York was at bat with two
men on. The batter hit safely to center field, scoring
the winning run. The Chicago players claimed, however, that when Fred Merkle, the man on first, saw
the winning run score, he started to walk toward the
clubhouse without advancing to second base, in-
validating the play. Johnny Evers, the Chicago second baseman, tried to get the ball and tag Merkle out,
but the fans streamed onto the field and bedlam
reigned. Days later Harry C. Pulliam, head of the
National Commission of Organized Baseball, decided
to call the game a tie. The teams were forced to play
a post-season playoff game, which the Cubs took 4–2.
Fans invented the terms "boner" and "bonehead" to
apply to Merkle's play.

Oct 10–14: The fifth annual **World Series** was won by
the Chicago Cubs (NL), who beat the Detroit Tigers
(AL) four games to one.

Dec 26: The **world heavyweight boxing championship** was won by Jack Johnson, who defeated
Tommy Burns in 14 rounds at Sydney, Australia.

1909

I. Civil Rights
Exploration and Settlement
Government
Statistics
Wars

The tariff remained a controversial issue. The new
president, William Howard Taft, had said he would
call a special session of Congress to lower rates.
When Congress finished with the matter, however,
the Payne-Aldrich Tariff Act, signed by Taft on Aug.
5, included some reductions but on the whole made

few changes. Sen. Nelson Aldrich, Republican of
Rhode Island, advocated a high tariff and led the fight
to keep rates high. In September, Taft defended the
bill in a speech at Winona, Minn., thus alienating
liberals and progressives who had thought he would
follow in the footsteps of their hero, Theodore Roosevelt.

The **National Association for the Advancement of
Colored People** was founded, principally by liberal
whites under the leadership of Oswald Garrison Vil-
lard, grandson of William Lloyd Garrison, to promote the rights and welfare of black Americans.

Apr 6: Robert Edwin Peary reached the North Pole.
With his servant Matt Henson, who was black, and
four Eskimos, Peary made a final dash from an advance base and reached latitude 90 degrees north for
the first time in recorded history.

July 12: A resolution for a **Sixteenth Amendment** to
the U.S. Constitution was passed by the Senate and
submitted to the states for ratification. The amendment authorized Congress to impose income taxes.

Sep 1: Dr. Frederick Cook, of Brooklyn, N.Y., claimed
to have reached the North Pole on Apr. 21, 1908,
beating Robert E. Peary in the feat by nearly a year.
The claim sparked a bitter debate, which continued
even after Congress and the scientific community at
large recognized Peary's claim.

II. Architecture
   Arts and Music
   Popular Entertainment
   Publishing
   Theater

The blues as a recognized musical form had been
around for some time, but 1909 was a landmark year
in the history of the blues. This year W. C. Handy, the
composer and bandleader, wrote "Mr. Crump" as a
campaign song for Edward H. Crump, the Democratic boss of Memphis, Tenn. In 1912 it was published as "Memphis Blues" and became a hit, the first
composition ever to be published as a blues song.

Among **books published** this year was *Martin Eden* by Jack London. It was an autobiographical novel about a strong and intelligent laborer and seaman who educates himself, strives for wealth and fame as a writer and, once he succeeds, finds life devoid of meaning and commits suicide on a voyage to the South Seas. Other books published this year included *The Silver Horde* by Rex Beach, a novel; *Roads of Destiny* and *Options*, two collections of stories by O. Henry; *54-40 or Fight!* by Emerson Hough, a historical novel about the conflict over the border between Canada and the Oregon Territory; *A Girl of the Limberlost* by Gene Stratton-Porter, a novel; *Three Lives* by Gertrude Stein, stories; and *A Certain Rich Man* by William Allen White, a novel.

The first notable **animated motion picture** shown in the U.S., *Gertie the Dinosaur*, utilized 10,000 drawings by Winsor McCay, a cartoonist for the New York *American*.

III. Business and Industry
   Education
   Philosophy and Religion
   Science

Although commercial production of celluloid, the first important synthetic plastic, had been achieved in 1872 by John W. Hyatt, it was in the early twentieth century that development of synthetics progressed significantly. In 1902 Arthur D. Little patented rayon (cellulose ester). In 1909 Leo H. Baekeland, Belgian-born inventor, announced his development of Bakelite, a synthetic thermosetting resin. It had many uses, and soon a large number of commercial products were being made in whole or in part of Bakelite. Because of its extremely high electrical resistance, it was used to make insulators and other components for the electrical, and later the radio, industry. Another feature of Bakelite was that it could be molded to any shape. It offered virtually limitless opportunities for manufacturers.

Henry Ford produced 19,051 **Model T Fords.** He

led the auto industry in production and sales by building only one model, the "universal" car, which "customers could have in any color as long as it was black."

July 27: Orville Wright made a new **flight duration record,** remaining in the air 1 hr., 1 min., 40 sec. and carrying a passenger in addition to Wright.

IV. Fashion
    Folkways
    Holidays
    Social Issues and Crime
    Sports

Former Pres. Theodore Roosevelt left for a hunting trip in Africa on Mar. 23, 1909, partly to let Pres. William Howard Taft have the limelight and partly because of his restless, energetic nature. Roosevelt received $50,000 from *Scribner's Magazine* for his account of the trip. When he returned in Feb. 1910 he brought back numerous animal trophies, which were given to the American Museum of Natural History in New York City. On June 18, 1910, he was off again on a trip to Europe. He reviewed troops with Kaiser Wilhelm of Germany and lectured at the Sorbonne in Paris and at Oxford University in England.

New standards of **fashion and beauty** were adopted as the automobile gained importance in American life. The suntanned, even red-faced Outdoor Girl replaced the soft, pale Gibson Girl when women took up automobile driving. "Automobile wrinkles" were soothed by application of freshly cut cucumbers. A new field was opened for fashion designers: special clothes for motoring, including a long veil to keep a lady's hat in place.

June 25: The **U.S. Open golf tournament** was won by George Sargent.

Oct 8-16: The sixth annual **World Series** was won by the Pittsburgh Pirates (NL), who defeated the Detroit Tigers (AL) four games to three.

1910

I. Civil Rights
Exploration and Settlement
Government
Statistics
Wars

The Mann-Elkins Act was passed by Congress on June 18. Named for Sen. Stephen B. Elkins, Republican of West Virginia, and Rep. James R. Mann, Republican of Illinois, the law increased the authority of the Interstate Commerce Commission in enforcing its rulings on rates. The new law also extended the ICC's jurisdiction to cover telegraph, telephone, and cable companies and authorized the commission to suspend railroad rate increases pending investigation and court decisions. A Commerce Court was set up to hear appeals of the commission's rulings.

The U.S. **Census** recorded a population of 91,972,266. The center of population was at Bloomington, Ind.

Prohibition had been adopted by the following states: Maine (1858), Kansas (1880), North Dakota (1889), Georgia (1907), Oklahoma (1907), Mississippi (1908), North Carolina (1908), Tennessee (1909).

The last five years had seen the worst period for **mine disasters** in U.S. history. From 1906 through 1910 there were 84 coal mine disasters that killed 2494 miners. Most of the accidents were explosions. The worst year was 1907 with a total of 919 fatalities; Dec. 1907 alone saw 702 fatalities.

Mar 26: An amendment to the **Immigration Act of 1907** was passed. It forbade entrance to the U.S. of criminals, paupers, anarchists, and persons carrying disease.

June 25: The **Mann Act,** popularly called the "white slave traffic act," was passed by Congress. The act

prohibited interstate or international transport of
women for "immoral purposes." It grew out of public
agitation over "white slavery," particularly the importation of European girls to work in American
brothels.

Nov 8: In **congressional elections** the Democrats took
control of Congress for the first time since 1894. In
the Senate the Republicans held a 51–41 majority, but
combination with insurgent Republicans opposed to
the policies of the Taft administration gave the Democrats control. In the House the Democrats took a
228–162 majority. The only minor party representative in the House was Victor L. Berger of Milwaukee,
Wis., the first Socialist ever sent to Congress. In state
elections, Franklin Delano Roosevelt was elected to
the New York legislature. Oregon adopted a presidential preferential primary, and Washington State
adopted woman suffrage.

II. Architecture
   Arts and Music
   Popular Entertainment
   Publishing
   Theater

Songs about unrequited love remained popular with
Americans. A songwriter who made a fortune from
such songs was Carrie Jacobs Bond, a self-taught
musician who wrote both the words and music for
some 175 songs. In 1910 she brought out one of her
most popular, "A Perfect Day." Other hits included
"Just a-Wearyin' for You" and "I Love You Truly"; the
latter has been sung at innumerable weddings since
its composition.

  Among **books published** this year was *The Spirit of
Romance* by Ezra Pound, the first book of essays by
the leading figure in the new imagist movement in
American poetry. Pound's subjects included the bar-
renness of American culture and the need for absolute criteria in evaluating art. Other books published
this year included *Molly Make-Believe* by Eleanor Abbott, a book for children; *The Rosary* by Florence

Barclay, a novel that sold some 500,000 copies in three years; *A Modern Chronicle* by Winston Churchill, a novel; *Whirligigs* and *Strictly Business*, collections of stories by O. Henry, who died this year; *My Mark Twain: Reminiscences and Criticisms* by William Dean Howells; *The Finer Grain* by Henry James, stories; *Burning Daylight* by Jack London, a novel, and *Lost Face*, also by London, a collection of stories including "To Build a Fire"; *The Town Down the River* by Edwin Arlington Robinson, a collection of poems including the classic "Miniver Cheevy"; and *The Bungalow Book* by Henry L. Wilson, which went through five editions and was immensely popular.

The first exhibition of the **Younger American Artists** took place with the opening of Alfred Stieglitz's "291." This show, at the Stieglitz Photo-Secession Gallery at 291 Fifth Ave. in New York City, offered works by Max Weber, John Marin, Abraham Walkowitz, William Zorach, Gaston Lachaise, Bernard Karfiol, Joseph Stella, and others.

III. Business and Industry
Education
Philosophy and Religion
Science

This year thousands of people became convinced that the end of the world was at hand. The cause of this prognosis was the passage of Halley's Comet, named for the English astronomer Edmund Halley, who had observed the comet's passage in 1682 and determined that it was the subject of similar observations made in 1531 and 1607. Enough people were frightened by stories of impending catastrophe that comet pills, supposed to protect from the comet's dire effects, went on sale. Miners refused to work on May 18, when the earth was due to pass through the fiery tail of the comet; they did not want to die underground. Many workers stayed home to spend their last day with their families. Farm families hid in cyclone cellars. Others took shelter in caves. In Milwaukee, Wis., two men were said to have committed suicide. Mark

Twain, who said he had come in with Halley's Comet and expected to go out with it, was not disappointed. He died on Apr. 21, at 74. Halley's Comet returned in 1985–1986, but did not make much of a show, since its path was much farther from the earth. In 1910, by contrast, the comet's tail could be seen across much of the night sky.

The **farm population** continued its steady decline. There were 32,077,000 farm inhabitants this year, 30,529,000 in 1930, and 25,058,000 in 1950.

Illiteracy in the U.S. reached a new low of 7.7% of the population, a decline of 3% from 1900 and 12.3% from 1870.

A **grade-school education** had been acquired by less than half the population over 25 years of age. Only about 4% of the population held college degrees.

Nov 14: The **first naval aircraft launching** from the deck of a U.S. warship was accomplished by Eugene Ely, who took off from the cruiser *Birmingham* at Hampton Roads, Va.

IV. Fashion
   Folkways
   Holidays
   Social Issues and Crime
   Sports

The most successful and popular organization for American boys was chartered on Feb. 6, 1910. It was the Boy Scouts of America. The incorporator was William D. Boyce, a Chicago publisher who took the idea from the English Boy Scout movement, founded in 1908 by Sir Robert Baden-Powell. Daniel Carter Beard, the illustrator and naturalist, had earlier founded the Sons of Daniel Boone, and Ernest Thompson Seton, author and artist, had organized the Woodcraft Indians. Both organizations had much the same purpose as the Boy Scouts.

This year's **national college football championship** was won by Harvard, with a record of eight wins, no losses, one tie.

Mar 16: A new **land speed record** of 133 mph was set by Barney Oldfield, who ran a timed mile in a Benz auto at Daytona Beach, Fla.

Mar 17: The **Camp Fire Girls** was organized by Dr. and Mrs. Luther Halsey Gulick, Mr. and Mrs. Ernest Thompson Seton, and others. It was incorporated in 1912. After 20 years there were more than 200,000 members in the U.S.

June 18: The **U.S. Open golf tournament** was won by Alex Smith.

June 19: Father's Day was celebrated for the first time in Spokane, Wash. Initiated by Mrs. John B. Dodd, it was backed by the Ministerial Association and the YMCA. Today it is celebrated on the third Sunday of June.

July 4: The **world heavyweight boxing championship** was successfully defended by Jack Johnson, who outclassed former champ Jim Jeffries in 15 rounds. After the match, Johnson's mother is reported to have said, "He said he'd *bring home the bacon,* and the honey boy has gone and done it." No earlier citation is known for this expression.

Oct 17-23: The seventh annual **World Series** was won by the Philadelphia Athletics (AL), who defeated the Chicago Cubs (NL) four games to one.

1911

I. Civil Rights
Exploration and Settlement
Government
Statistics
Wars

A tragic industrial disaster occurred on Mar. 25, 1911, when the Triangle Waist Company, a sweatshop in New York City, caught fire. About 850 employees were trapped in the building, which was full of inflammable materials used in making shirtwaists.

The fire began only minutes before the Saturday workday was to end and lasted but half an hour. The building was considered fireproof but had only one fire escape, and its exit doors were blocked. Some 146 persons were killed, most of them young women. The proprietors were tried but acquitted. However, the fire led to revision of the local building code and labor laws. The tragedy also added impetus to the organizational work of the International Ladies Garment Workers Union, which had been formed in 1900.

Jan 21: The **National Progressive Republican League** was formed in Washington, D.C., by Sen. Robert M. La Follette of Wisconsin. Sen. Jonathan Bourne of Oregon was elected president. The organization's chief aims were enactment of progressive legislation and promotion of popular government. It called for direct primaries, direct election of delegates to national conventions, and amendments to state constitutions providing for initiative, referendum, and recall.

Aug 22: **Arizona statehood** was vetoed by Pres. William Howard Taft on the grounds that its constitution permitted the recall of judges, which Taft considered a threat to the independence of the judiciary. After removing this provision, Arizona was admitted to the Union in 1912, after which it reinstated the provision.

II. Architecture
   Arts and Music
   Popular Entertainment
   Publishing
   Theater

The American appetite for fiction about the West, with rugged heroes and pure heroines, seemed insatiable. An author who catered to this appetite successfully was Harold Bell Wright, whose most popular novel, *The Winning of Barbara Worth,* was published this year; it eventually sold some 1,500,000 copies. Wright's stories were set in the Southwest. They were a careful mix of love story, adventure story, and moral instruction. Wright knew his craft and his readers. He turned out enormously popular novels for nearly 40 years. Other successful Wright books included *The Shepherd of the Hills* (1907), *The Calling of Dan Matthews* (1909), and *When a Man's a Man* (1916).

Among **books published** this year was the novel *Jennie Gerhardt* by Theodore Dreiser, which sold well enough to warrant republication in 1912 of Dreiser's first novel, *Sister Carrie* (1900). Other books published this year included *The Devil's Dictionary* by Ambrose Bierce, which originally appeared as *The Cynic's Word Book* (1906); *The Iron Woman* by Margaret Deland, a sequel to her novel *The Awakening of Barbara Richie* (1906); *Dawn O'Hara* by Edna Ferber, the author's first novel; *The Miller of Old Church* by Ellen Glasgow, a novel; *Sixes and Sevens* by O. Henry, a posthumous collection; *The Outcry* by Henry James, a novel; *South Sea Tales* by Jack London; and *Mother* by Kathleen Norris, the author's first novel, a best seller.

"Alexander's Ragtime Band" was composed by Irving Berlin. Although not strictly a ragtime tune, it was the first song to popularize ragtime outside the limited area of the Mississippi Delta.

III. Business and Industry
Education
Philosophy and Religion
Science

Before he left office, Pres. Theodore Roosevelt had ordered the Justice Department to act against the Standard Oil Company of New Jersey under the Sherman Antitrust Act of 1890, but it took more than four years for the case to reach the Supreme Court. Standard Oil controlled about 85% of the domestic oil industry at this time. On May 15, 1911, the Court ordered Standard Oil dissolved because it violated the antitrust law. In so doing, it added to the law by ruling that trusts were unlawful if they engaged in "unreasonable" restraint of trade.

Sep 17-Nov 5: The **first cross-country flight** was made by Calbraith P. Rodgers, who flew a Burgess-Wright biplane from Sheepshead Bay, N.Y., to Pasadena, Calif., in 82 hrs., 4 min. of flying time.

Nov 10: The Carnegie Corporation of New York was established by Andrew Carnegie with an initial endowment of $125,000,000. It was the first of the great foundations for scholarly and charitable endeavors. Other funds Carnegie established included the Carnegie Institute of Pittsburgh (1896), $24,000,000; the Carnegie Institute of Washington (1902), $22,000,000; the Carnegie Foundation for the Advancement of Teaching (1905), $15,000,000; and the Carnegie Endowment for International Peace (1910), $10,000,000.

IV. Fashion
   Folkways
   Holidays
   Social Issues and Crime
   Sports

Baseball continued to produce heroes for American sports fans. The best all-around player of the era was Tyrus Raymond "Ty" Cobb, who joined the Detroit Tigers in 1905 and played for 24 years in the American League. In his first year in the majors he batted .240. After that his batting average was never below .320. When he retired he held an incredible list of records, including a career batting average of .367, a record 2244 runs, 892 stolen bases, and 12 league batting championships. He was perhaps the most spectacular player the game has ever produced. In 1936 he became the first player elected to the Baseball Hall of Fame. His career total of 4191 hits stood as a record until 1985, when Pete Rose surpassed him.

May 30: The **first annual Indianapolis 500** auto race was won by Ray Harroun, completing the 500-mile course in 6 hrs., 42 min., 8 sec., with an average speed of 74.59 mph.

June 24: The **U.S. Open golf tournament** was won by John J. McDermott in a playoff round.

Oct 14-26: The eighth annual **World Series** was won by the Philadelphia Athletics (AL), who beat the New York Giants (NL) four games to two.

1912

I. Civil Rights
   Exploration and Settlement
   Government
   Statistics
   Wars

The 1912 presidential election began as a three-way race but soon became a contest between former Pres. Theodore Roosevelt, the Progressive Party candidate, and Woodrow Wilson, the Democrat. Pres. William Howard Taft, the Republican candidate, fell far behind. The mood of the country called for reform, and Roosevelt and Wilson differed only on the best way to achieve it. Roosevelt talked of the Square Deal and the New Nationalism; Wilson spoke of the New Freedom. Roosevelt would deal with industrial monopoly by regulating it; Wilson called for breaking up big business to restore competition. When Wilson won in November, he was only the second Democrat to be elected to the presidency since the Civil War.

Jan 6: New Mexico was admitted to the Union, the

Jan 22: U.S. troops began **occupation of Tientsin** for the protection of American interests in the Chinese Revolution, which had begun in Oct. 1911.

Feb 14: Arizona was admitted to the Union, the 48th state.

Apr 14-15: The British liner *Titanic* struck an iceberg off the coast of Newfoundland and sank on its maiden voyage, killing about 1500 persons, including many U.S. and British notables. An investigation showed that the ship had insufficient lifeboats and that safety procedures had not been followed. The company was blamed for poor equipment and for ordering the ship to speed through dangerous waters.

June 5: U.S. **Marines landed in Cuba** to protect American interests there.

June 18-22: The **Republican National Convention nominated Pres. William Howard Taft** for a second term, but only after bitter political maneuvering against the progressive elements favoring Theodore Roosevelt. James S. Sherman was renominated for the vice presidency. Taft forces won parliamentary control of the convention through the election of their candidate for convention chairman, Elihu Root, and through the seating of their delegates in disputed delegations. After Taft's nomination on June 22, Roosevelt announced the formation of the Progressive Party, under his own leadership.

June 25-July 2: The **Democratic National Convention nominated Woodrow Wilson** of New Jersey for the presidency and Thomas R. Marshall of Indiana for the vice presidency.

Aug 5: The **Progressive (Bull Moose) Party nominated Theodore Roosevelt** for the presidency and Hiram Johnson of California for the vice presidency. The party platform called for women's suffrage, direct primaries, and other progressive measures.

Oct 14: Theodore Roosevelt was shot from a distance of six feet by John Schrank of New York. The incident occurred in a Milwaukee, Wis., hotel during Roosevelt's campaign tour. The bullet struck a bulky manuscript and entered Roosevelt's chest. Despite the wound, Roosevelt insisted on delivering his speech before he was taken to a hospital.

Nov 5: Woodrow Wilson was elected president of the United States in a landslide Democratic victory. Thomas R. Marshall was elected vice president. The electoral vote was Wilson, 435; Theodore Roosevelt, Progressive Party, 88; William Howard Taft, Republican, 8. The popular vote was Wilson, 6,293,454; Roosevelt, 4,119,538; Taft, 3,484,980; Eugene V. Debs,

Socialist candidate, 900,672; Eugene W. Chafin, Prohibition candidate, 206,275. In congressional elections the Democrats took a 51–44 majority in the Senate, with one minor party seat, and a 291–127 majority in the House, with 17 seats going to minor parties.

II. Architecture
   Arts and Music
   Popular Entertainment
   Publishing
   Theater

The writing, or at least the publishing, of poetry in a modern style seemed to lag behind fiction. However, poetry received a decided stimulus in 1912 with the founding of *Poetry: A Magazine of Verse* in Chicago. The founder was Harriet Monroe, a poet. The magazine had a lasting influence on American poetry under her editorship, which continued until her death in 1936. *Poetry* published the work of such poets as Carl Sandburg, Amy Lowell, Ezra Pound, Hilda Doolittle, T. S. Eliot, Vachel Lindsay, and Hart Crane. Many new poets first came to public attention in its pages.

Among **books published** this year was *The Financier* by Theodore Dreiser, the first novel of a trilogy about Frank Cowperwood, a predatory businessman modeled after Charles T. Yerkes, the financier and transportation magnate. Dreiser continued the Cowperwood trilogy with *The Titan* (1914) and the posthumous volume *The Stoic* (1947). Other books published this year included *A Woman of Genius* by Mary Austin, a novel; *The Squirrel Cage* by Dorothy Canfield, a novel of domestic life; *Alexander's Bridge* by Willa Cather, the author's first novel; *Riders of the Purple Sage* by Zane Grey, the author's most popular novel; *The Autobiography of an Ex-Colored Man* by James Weldon Johnson, a novel; *Smoke Bellew* by Jack London, a novel; and the three-volume *Mark Twain, A Biography* by Albert Bigelow Paine.

III. Business and Industry
Education
Philosophy and Religion
Science

A strike of textile workers at Lawrence, Mass., in 1912 brought prominence in the East to the Industrial Workers of the World (IWW), a radical labor union that had hitherto been active chiefly in the West among miners, migratory farm workers, and lumbermen. The strike began on Jan. 12 over a reduction in wages. It lasted two months and there was considerable violence. The workers ultimately prevailed, and the strike established the IWW as a force to be reckoned with in the textile industry. The IWW's best-known leader was William D. "Big Bill" Haywood, an advocate of mass action, and violence if necessary, to achieve better conditions for workers.

May 1: A new **ship safety regulation** was issued by federal inspectors following the sinking of the *Titanic* in April. Steamships were ordered to carry enough lifeboats to hold all passengers.

June 19: A new **labor law** was passed by Congress. It extended the eight-hour working day to all workers under federal contract.

IV. Fashion
Folkways
Holidays
Social Issues and Crime
Sports

Americans had a new athletic hero to cheer in 1912, James Francis "Jim" Thorpe, perhaps the best all-around athlete in history. An American Indian, Thorpe attended Carlisle Indian School in Pennsylvania. There he participated in several sports and, under the tutelage of Glenn "Pop" Warner, led the small school to football triumphs over such powers as Harvard. At the Olympic Games in Stockholm in 1912, he won both the pentathlon and the decathlon, but his medals were taken from him the next year when it was discoverd that he had played semiprofessional baseball in 1909. On Jan. 18, 1983, 30 years after his death, his medals were restored to his daughter. In 1950 Thorpe had been voted by sportswriters "the greatest football player and male athlete of the first half of the twentieth century."

The spreading fad for **ragtime music** led at about this time to a series of so-called animal dances. The dances were execrated in press and pulpit. Among them were the fox trot, horse trot, crab step, kangaroo dip, camel walk, fish walk, chicken scratch, lame duck, snake, grizzly bear, turkey trot, and bunny hug.

May 5-July 22: At the **Olympic Games** in Stockholm, Sweden, the U.S. won 23 gold medals and took first place in the unofficial team championships.

Aug 2: The **U.S. Open golf tournament** was won by John J. McDermott.

Oct 8-16: The ninth annual **World Series** was won by the Boston Red Sox (AL), who beat the New York Giants (NL) four games to three in an eight-game series. The second game, played at Boston on Oct. 9, was a tie; it had been called in the 11th inning on account of darkness.

1913

I. Civil Rights
Exploration and Settlement
Government
Statistics
Wars

For many years tariff revenue had been the largest single source of government income. The adoption on Feb. 25, 1913, of the Sixteenth Amendment to the Constitution, permitting the levying of income tax on individuals and businesses without apportionment on the basis of the population of states, was soon to affect the importance of tariff revenues. The change did not come at once, however, for the first income tax law specified graduated rates of 1 to 6% of income.

Mar 1: The **Webb-Kenyon Interstate Liquor Act** was passed over Pres. Taft's veto. It stated that no liquor could be shipped into states where its sale was illegal. This was the first nationwide victory of the Anti-Saloon league.

Mar 21-26: What was called the **Dayton flood** raged in the Miami River Valley of Ohio, killing more than 400 people. Property damage was estimated at $100,000,000. An additional 200 or more persons were killed by floods along the Indiana R. and elsewhere in the West and South. In 1925 five dams were completed across the upper Miami R. and its tributaries at a cost of $32,000,000. These dams provided significantly increased protection against floods.

May 19: The **Webb Alien Land-Holding Bill** was signed by Gov. Hiram W. Johnson of California in the face of objections by Pres. Wilson and Japan. It excluded Japanese from ownership of land in California.

May 31: The **Seventeenth Amendment** to the U.S. Constitution went into effect. It provided for popular election of U.S. senators. Previously, senators had been chosen by their state legislatures. Thus, the amendment reduced the power and status of state governments and increased popular control of the federal legislature.

II. Architecture
   ## Arts and Music
   ## Popular Entertainment
   ## Publishing
   ## Theater

The single most important event to date in the American art world was held at the 69th Regiment Armory at Lexington Ave. and 26th St. in New York City, beginning Feb. 17. It was the International Exhibition of Modern Art, known to this day as the Armory Show. Organized originally to show works of younger U.S. artists, it came to include European artists as well. There were about 1600 paintings and sculptures in all. The show drew large crowds and horrified conservative critics. Ridicule was showered on Marcel Duchamp's cubist painting *Nude Descending a Staircase*, which one commentator called an "explosion in a shingle factory." In reviewing the show, Theodore Roosevelt was sympathetic but wrote that there was "apt to be a lunatic fringe among the votaries of any forward movement." The exhibition did much to change the direction of American painting.

Among **books published** this year was *O Pioneers!* by Willa Cather, the author's second novel and her first set in the Nebraska of her youth. The story dealt with Alexandra Bergsen, a second-generation Swedish-American who, through courage, diligence, and sacrifice, triumphed over the barren land. Other books published this year included *The Inside of the Cup* by Winston Churchill, a novel that became a best seller; *The Enjoyment of Poetry* by Max Eastman, which went through six editions by 1920; *Virginia* by Ellen Glasgow, a study of the life and values of a southern woman; *Rolling Stones* by O. Henry; *A Small Boy and Others* by Henry James, autobiographical writings; *General William Booth Enters into Heaven and Other Poems* by Vachel Lindsay; *The Valley of the Moon* by Jack London, a novel, and *John Barleycorn*, also by London, an autobiographical account of his struggles against alcohol; and *Pollyanna* by Eleanor Hodgman Porter, a juvenile novel that eventually sold more than 1,000,000 copies and inspired the term *Pollyanna*, meaning an irrepressibly optimistic person.

The **Woolworth Building**, tallest in the world, was built in New York City. It measured 792 feet and was considered a wonder by New Yorkers when it was first built.

III. Business and Industry
Education
Philosophy and Religion
Science

For many years the nation had needed a central banking system to bring stability to currency and credit markets. Bankers wanted a system they could control. Agrarian interests and others wanted a system controlled by the federal government that would provide easy credit. Pres. Woodrow Wilson pledged to reform the banking system and on Dec. 23, 1913, the Owen-Glass Act became law. It set up the Federal Reserve System. The act established a central Federal Reserve Board and a dozen regional banks. All national banks were required to join the system. State banks could do so if they wished. The system could issue currency and control credit by raising or lowering the discount rate it charged member banks. The general aim was to increase economic stability and make it impossible for speculators to upset the economy of the nation.

May 14: John D. Rockefeller donated $100,000,000 to the **Rockefeller Foundation,** chartered by the New York State legislature. His contribution was thought to be the largest single philanthropic act in history.

Summer: Henry Ford set up his **first automobile assembly line** for production of the inexpensive Model T. Ford introduced a revolutionary high wage for his workers of $5 a day. Between 1909 and 1924, the price of the Model T dropped from $950 to $290. Ford engineers had adapted the meat packers' conveyor belt system, and soon 1000 Fords a day were turned out.

Oct 10: The **waterway across the Isthmus of Panama** was completed when the Gamboa Dike was blown up. Pres. Woodrow Wilson set off the explosion by pressing an electric button at the White House.

IV. **Fashion**
   Folkways
   Holidays
   Social Issues and Crime
   Sports

This period is often looked back on as the golden age of professional baseball. The sport was truly national, with no competition as yet from professional football or basketball. Fans were as enthusiastic about their favorite teams. Millions of people attended National and American League games, and minor league teams were gaining in popularity as well. One of the top minor leagues was the United States League. In 1914 it was reorganized into the Federal League. It had good financial backing and started pulling top players from both the National and American leagues. Despite its claim to major league status, it lasted only through 1915.

July 25-28: The **Davis Cup** international tennis challenge round was won for the first time since 1902 by the U.S., beating the British team three matches to two.

Oct 7-11: The tenth annual **World Series** was won by the Philadelphia Athletics (AL), who beat the New York Giants (NL) four games to one.

Nov 1: The **first Army-Notre Dame football game** was a memorable one. The Notre Dame team was almost unknown in Eastern football circles, so its victory over Army, 35 to 13, stunned the losers. While legend tends to focus on the passing combination of Gus Dorais and Knute Rockne, the team from South Bend, Ind., was in fact bigger than Army and was favored to win. Its All-American fullback is said to have torn "the Army line to shreds." Notre Dame demonstrated that forward passes could be devastating.

1914

I. Civil Rights
Exploration and Settlement
Government
Statistics
Wars

In August the fragile peace that had prevailed in Europe was broken. European armies that had been preparing for the conflict for years mobilized, and guns began firing. The U.S. was completely unprepared for war, and Pres. Woodrow Wilson intended to keep the country out of the conflict. He viewed the U.S. as the nation that would bring the warring parties to the conference table and help fashion a lasting peace. The U.S. had only a small standing army, and much of it was tied down by the continuing dispute with Mexico. Its air arm was virtually nonexistent—a curious fact for the nation that had pioneered powered flight. Even the U.S. Navy was no match for either the British or German navies. Stories of German atrocities in Belgium hurt the Central Powers in U.S. public opinion, but the British blockade of Europe and subsequent seizure of neutral shipping hurt public perception of the Allies. Almost all Americans wanted the U.S. to stay out of the war.

Apr 9: In an incident at **Tampico,** Mexico, several U.S. Marines from the ship *Dolphin*, coming ashore for supplies, were arrested and detained for an hour and a half by Mexican authorities. Their release was followed by an apology from the Mexican commander at Tampico and an expression of regret by Pres. Victoriano Huerta, but the U.S. commander, Adm. Henry T. Mayo, demanded a special salute to the U.S. flag by the Mexican troops. On Apr. 11 Pres. Huerta refused the demanded salute and on Apr. 14 Pres. Wilson ordered the U.S. fleet to Tampico Bay.

Apr 16: A second **Coxey's Army** was organized at Massillon, Ohio, to march on Washington, D.C. Made up of unemployed workers, it was headed by Jacob S. Coxey, who had organized the first march in 1894.

Apr 21: At **Vera Cruz,** Mexico, U.S. forces seized the customhouse and Marines occupied the city. The detachment was sent to exact an apology from Pres. Huerta for the arrest of several U.S. Marines early this month. U.S. losses were 4 dead, 20 wounded.

Apr 22: Diplomatic relations with the U.S. were severed by Mexico.

Nov 3: In **congressional elections** the Democrats gained five Senate seats for a 56–40 majority. In the House they lost 61 seats but kept a 230–196 majority, with nine seats held by minor parties.

Nov 23: U.S. forces in **Vera Cruz,** Mexico, were withdrawn.

II. Architecture
   Arts and Music
   Popular Entertainment
   Publishing
   Theater

Most poets were content to write their poetry and see it published in magazines or books. One who was just as much interested in reciting his poetry in public as in writing it was Vachel Lindsay, who began his career by going on tours during which he exchanged his verses for food and lodging. It was not until publication this year of *The Congo and Other Poems* that he was recognized as a leading voice of the so-called new poetry movement. Lindsay's work is full of strong rhythms, sometimes pounding in their effect. He emphasized gestures and chant when he appeared in public, as he did regularly. *The Chinese Nightingale and Other Poems* (1917) probably saw his talent at its peak.

Among **books published** this year was *Tarzan of the Apes* by Edgar Rice Burroughs, an action-filled story of a man raised by apes in Africa. Burroughs' tale appealed to millions of readers and made the author famous and wealthy. Other books published this year included *North of Boston* by Robert Frost, a first collection of poems that included the classic "Mending Wall" and "The Death of the Hired Man"; *The Poet* by Meredith Nicholson, a biography in fictional form of Nicholson's fellow Hoosier writer James Whitcomb Riley; *Insurgent Mexico* by John Reed, who had been sent to cover the Mexican Revolution by *Metropolitan Magazine; Penrod* by Booth Tarkington, an enormously popular novel about the adventures of a 12-year-old midwestern youth that led to two sequels, *Penrod and Sam* (1916) and *Penrod Jashber* (1929); and *The Eyes of the World* by Harold Bell Wright, which became a best seller.

III. Business and Industry
   Education
   Philosophy and Religion
   Science

One of the greatest construction projects of all time, and one of strategic importance to the U.S. in terms of national defense and foreign commerce, was marked by completion and official opening of the Panama Canal on Aug. 15, 1914. To build the canal, about 240,000,000 cubic yards of earth were moved and $366,650,000 spent. The first passage through the whole length of the canal was made on Jan. 7, 1914, by a small boat, *Alexander la Valley.* On Aug. 15 the *Ancon,* carrying a full load of government officials, sailed from the Atlantic to the Pacific Ocean, a distance of just over 40 miles. In its first year of operation, 1108 ships passed through the canal.

The **death rate** in the Panama Canal Zone had dropped to six per 1000 against 14.1 per 1000 in the U.S. When work on the canal began in 1904, the area was dangerous to human health. The fight against yellow fever and malaria had been won by Gen. William Gorgas, whose campaign to eradicate mosquitoes had been pushed through in spite of official opposition.

The 1914 **Nobel Prize in Chemistry** was awarded to Theodore William Richards, the first American to receive the prize in that category. Richards was honored for his work in determining the exact atomic weights of a number of elements, in some cases correcting erroneous measurements. His investigation of the atomic weights of oxygen and hydrogen led ultimately to discovery of deuterium, commonly known as heavy hydrogen, a key component in atomic research.

Apr 10: Successful **heart surgery** on an animal was announced by Dr. Alexis Carrel. He said the operation was performed while he suspended blood circulation for several minutes.

May 18: The **Panama Canal** was opened to barge service.

IV. Fashion
   Folkways
   Holidays
   Social Issues and Crime
   Sports

American society's restless favorite son, former Pres. Theodore Roosevelt, set off on an exploring expedition in Brazil in Oct. 1913; he returned in May 1914. In the jungle he explored a 400-mile-long river that had been called Rio da Duvida [River of Doubt] and which was renamed Rio Roosevelt in his honor by the Brazilian government. Roosevelt wrote a book about his journey, *Through the Brazilian Wilderness* (1914).

America's favorite **dances** were changing. The colorful and elaborate cotillion, once the most fashionable dance of society, took second place about this time to the waltz and two-step.

May 7: A resolution establishing **Mother's Day,** to be celebrated on the second Sunday in May, was passed by Congress. On May 9 Pres. Wilson issued a proclamation calling on the public to display the U.S. flag on that day as an expression "of our love and reverence for the mothers of our country."

Aug 15: In the **Davis Cup** international tennis challenge round the U.S. was defeated by Australia three matches to two.

Oct 9-13: The 11th annual **World Series** was won by the Boston Braves (NL), who swept the Philadelphia Athletics (AL) in four straight games.

1915

I. Civil Rights
Exploration and Settlement
Government
Statistics
Wars

A major step in strengthening the country's coastal maritime services, with regard to lifesaving and prevention of smuggling, was taken on Jan. 28, 1915, when Congress established the U.S. Coast Guard. It combined the Revenue Cutter Service, which had been established in 1790, with the more recent Life Saving Service. The Coast Guard was placed under the authority of the Treasury Department, except in times of war. It absorbed the Lighthouse Service in 1939 and the Bureau of Marine Inspection and Navigation in 1942.

May 7: The British steamship *Lusitania,* queen of the Cunard fleet, was sunk without warning off Ireland by a German submarine. Of 1924 persons aboard, 1198 were drowned, including 63 infants. The number of Americans drowned was 114. American indignation over the sinking contributed to the U.S. entry into World War I against Germany in 1917.

July 29: U.S. Marines landed in Haiti one day after the assassination of Haitian president Vilbrun Guillaume Sam.

Aug 5: A **Latin-American conference** to debate ways to end the political disorder in Mexico opened in Washington, D.C. It was attended by representatives from Argentina, Brazil, Bolivia, Chile, Guatemala, Uruguay, and the U.S.

Sep 16: Haiti became a U.S. protectorate under the terms of a ten-year treaty. The Senate approved the treaty on Feb. 28, 1916.

II. Architecture
Arts and Music
Popular Entertainment
Publishing
Theater

Booker T. Washington, the most important black American of the late nineteenth and early twentieth centuries, died Nov. 14, 1915. Washington was born into slavery in 1856, the son of a mulatto mother and a white father. Securing an education by his own efforts, Washington, at age 25, was selected to organize what became Tuskegee Institute, a school he turned into a leading educational institution for blacks. Washington was a controversial figure after 1895 when he made a speech in which he said blacks should not attempt to achieve social and political equality until they had secured economic equality. This pleased many whites and resulted in financial support for Tuskegee, but other black leaders denounced his approach. Washington's autobiography, *Up From Slavery* (1901), is a classic.

Among **books published** this year was *Spoon River Anthology* by Edgar Lee Masters, a Chicago lawyer who had had a number of collections published but without much success. This collection of poems, written as epitaphs for people buried in a midwestern cemetery, made Masters a national literary figure. Other books published this year included *America's Coming-of-Age* by Van Wyck Brooks, nonfiction; *The Rivet in Grandfather's Neck* by James Branch Cabell, a novel; *The Song of the Lark,* a novel by Willa Cather; *Verse,* a posthumous collection by Adelaide Crapsey; *The Genius* by Theodore Dreiser, a novel; *Bib Ballads* by Ring Lardner, the author's first book, a minor collection of verse; *Dreams and Dust* by Don Marquis, poetry; *The Song of Hugh Glass* by John G. Neihardt, a long poem that was the first part of Neihardt's five-part *A Cycle of the West* (1949); and *The*

Harbor by Ernest Poole, a proletarian novel centering on New York harbor.

Margaret Sanger was arrested on obscenity
charges in connection with her book *Family Limitation,* a pioneer work on birth control. Taken to court
by the New York Society for the Suppression of Vice,
she was found guilty of circulating a work "contrary
not only to the law of the state, but to the law of God."
She was subsequently jailed.

Feb 8: *The Birth of a Nation,* D. W. Griffith's landmark motion picture, opened at Clune's Auditorium
in Los Angeles, Calif. The most spectacular film made
up to that time, it aroused bitter protests from liberals for its sympathetic treatment of the Ku Klux Klan
during Reconstruction. Black leaders objected to its
lurid racism. The film was based on the novel *The
Clansman* (1905) by Thomas Dixon.

III. Business and Industry
Education
Philosophy and Religion
Science

Although Thomas A. Edison had built his first phonograph in 1877, it was not until the early years of the
twentieth century that it became a practical machine.
In 1903 an American company issued recordings of
opera stars singing to piano accompaniment. About
ten years later, orchestral recordings were attempted
for the first time. The Victor Talking Machine Company brought out a phonograph in 1915 under the
name Victrola; the name soon was applied to all
phonographs. By 1919 Americans were spending
more on phonographs and recordings than on musical instruments, books and periodicals, or sporting
goods.

The **taxicab** made its appearance on the American
scene when automobile owners found that many people were willing to pay for a short ride. The price was
a nickel, or *jitney,* and the term soon was applied to
the cars themselves. Drivers were known as *hackers*
or *hackies* in the East, *cabbies* in the Midwest. Inter-
city bus lines sprang from regular jitney service.

Jan 25: The **first transcontinental telephone call** was made by the same men who had made the original telephone call in 1876. Alexander Graham Bell, speaking from New York City, said to Dr. Thomas A. Watson in San Francisco, "Mr. Watson, come here, I want you."

Dec 10: In a landmark for **Ford auto production,** the millionth Model T rolled off Ford's Detroit, Mich,, assembly line.

IV. Fashion
   Folkways
   Holidays
   Social Issues and Crime
   Sports

On Aug. 17 Leo M. Frank, 29, was lynched for the Apr. 26, 1913, murder of Mary Phagan, 14, at the National Pencil Company Factory in Atlanta, Ga. Frank had been superintendent of the factory and was charged with the murder after the girl's body was found there. In a sensational trial, Frank was convicted, largely on testimony by Jim Conley, the factory janitor. After futile appeals by Frank's attorneys, up to the Supreme Court, Gov. John M. Slayton commuted Frank's sentence to life imprisonment. An enraged mob took him from a jail in Marietta, Ga., and hanged him. Outside the South it was widely believed that Frank, a Jew, was a victim of hatred and bigotry. In 1982 Alonzo Mann, who had worked as Frank's office boy, revealed to the newspaper *The Tennessean* that on the day of the murder he had seen Jim Conley carrying the body of Mary Phagan to the factory basement, and that Conley had threatened him to keep quiet about the matter. In 1986 Frank's conviction was overturned, more than 70 years after his death.

   The quip "**What this country really needs is a good five-cent cigar**" originated with Indiana-born Thomas R. Marshall, vice president under Pres. Woodrow Wilson. During one of the tedious debates in the Senate he came out with the observation.

   Ty Cobb set a major league record for bases stolen

in one season, 96. The record stood until 1962 when Maury Wills stole 104 bases. In 1974 Lou Brock shattered the record again with 118 steals. During his career, Cobb set more records than any other player in the history of baseball.

A new **record for the mile run** was set in Cambridge, Mass., by Norman Taber, who completed the distance in 4:12.6, nearly two seconds under the old record.

Feb 23: An **easy divorce** bill, requiring only six months' residence, was signed into law in Nevada.

Apr 5: The **world heavyweight boxing championship** was won by Jess Willard, who defeated Jack Johnson in a 23-round bout in Havana, Cuba. It was not clear whether a blow by Willard or the blazing sun caused Johnson's descent to the canvas, described as a slow sinking.

June 18: The **U.S. Open golf tournament** was won by Jerome D. Travers.

Oct 8-13: The 12th annual **World Series** was won by the Boston Red Sox (AL), who beat the Philadelphia Phillies (NL) four games to one.

Oct 9: A new **auto speed record** of 102.6 mph was set by Gil Anderson, who won the celebrated Astor Cup at Sheepshead Bay, N.Y.

Dec 4: The **Peace Ship,** chartered by Henry Ford to carry a peace expedition to Europe, left the U.S. on a historic but futile mission. Ford's slogan "Out of the trenches and back to their homes by Christmas," became a rallying cry for the American pacifist movement. Ford's attempt to find a diplomatic end to the world conflict soon collapsed.

1916

I. Civil Rights
   Exploration and Settlement
   Government
   Statistics
   Wars

The presidential election campaign of 1916 was carried on in the shadow of World War I, then ravaging Europe and threatening to embroil the U.S. Pres. Woodrow Wilson, the Democratic candidate, made good use of the slogan "He kept us out of war," although he knew it was unlikely the country could remain neutral much longer. The Republican candidate, Charles Evans Hughes, might have won had he not snubbed Gov. Hiram Johnson of California when he visited that state. Johnson lost his enthusiasm for Hughes, and Hughes lost California.

Prohibition was voted in by Michigan, Montana, Nebraska, South Dakota, and Utah, making it law in 24 states. It now affected about 32,500,000 citizens.

Mar 9: The Mexican revolutionary and bandit **Francisco "Pancho" Villa** led a band of 1500 guerrillas across the border and attacked Columbus, N. Mex., killing 17 Americans. U.S. troops pursued the Mexicans, killing 50 on U.S. soil and 70 more in Mexico. Brig. Gen. John J. Pershing was ordered to Mexico to capture Villa.

June 3: The **National Defense Act** was passed. It increased the standing Army to 175,000 and the National Guard to 450,000.

June 7-10: The **Republican National Convention nominated Charles Evans Hughes** of New York for the presidency and Charles Warren Fairbanks of Indiana for the vice presidency.

June 14-16: The **Democratic National Convention renominated Pres. Wilson** for the presidency and

Vice Pres. Thomas R. Marshall for the vice presidency.

June 17: U.S. forces crossed into Mexico and an ultimatum was issued by the Mexican consul at Brownsville, Tex. It asserted that U.S. forces would be attacked unless withdrawn.

June 20: A note to Mexico by Sec. of State Robert Lansing asserted that troops would not be withdrawn from Mexico until order was restored on the border.

June 21: U.S. troops were attacked at Carrizal, Mexico. The Americans lost 17 killed or wounded; 38 Mexicans were killed, including the Mexican commander.

July 22: A bombing in San Francisco during a Preparedness Day parade killed 10 persons and wounded 40. In 1917 labor leader Tom Mooney was sentenced to hang and Warren K. Billings was sentenced to life imprisonment for the deed. Pres. Wilson commuted Mooney's sentence to life imprisonment in 1918, but because of confessions of perjured testimony at the trial the case was an international cause célèbre for many years. On Jan. 7, 1939, Mooney was pardoned by Gov. Culbert L. Olson of California. Billings was released later in the year.

Aug 4: A treaty for the purchase of the **Danish West Indies** (Virgin Islands) for $25,000,000 was signed by the U.S. and Denmark. It was ratified on Jan. 17, 1917.

Nov 7: Woodrow Wilson was reelected president of the United States. Thomas R. Marshall was reelected vice president. The election was so close that the outcome was uncertain for three days, when it became clear that Wilson had carried California, but by fewer than 4000 votes. The electoral vote was Wilson, 277; Charles Evans Hughes, Republican candidate, 254. The popular vote was Wilson, 9,128,837; Hughes, 8,536,380. In congressional elections the Democrats lost three seats in the Senate but maintained a 53–42 majority, with one seat going to a minor party. In the House the Democrats again narrowed their majority over the Republicans, 216–210, with six seats held by minor parties.

II. Architecture
   Arts and Music
   Popular Entertainment
   Publishing
   Theater

The nation's growing interest in the ballet was indicated by both the number of visiting foreign dancers and the development of American dance groups. Anna Pavlova, the Russian ballerina, had made her American debut in 1910. In 1916 Serge Diaghilev brought the Ballet Russe from Paris to New York City's Metropolitan Opera House for a January-to-May season. The noted Russian dancer Vaslav Nijinsky made his debut in New York on Apr. 12. Among American dancers, Ruth St. Denis and Ted Shawn were becoming well known.

Among **books published** this year was *Chicago Poems* by Carl Sandburg, a volume that heralded the arrival of a major new poetic voice and reflected the rise of the American Midwest as a force in American literature. Sandburg's book included the poems "Chicago" and "I Am the People, the Mob." Other books published this year included *The Certain Hour* by James Branch Cabell, short stories; *The Rising Tide* by Margaret Deland, a novel dealing with women's suffrage; *Life and Gabriella* by Ellen Glasgow, a novel; *A Heap o' Livin'* by Edgar Guest, verse; *The Man Against the Sky* by Edwin Arlington Robinson, poetry; *Seventeen* by Booth Tarkington, a novel; *The Mysterious Stranger*, a posthumous tale by Mark Twain; *Xingu and Other Stories* by Edith Wharton; and *When a Man's a Man* by Harold Bell Wright, a novel.

III. Business and Industry
    Education
    Philosophy and Religion
    Science

The automobile was seen everywhere, and the automobile industry was soon to become the largest single manufacturing section of the economy. In 1916 auto and truck production passed the 1,000,000 mark for the first time; the value of this production was nearly $1,000,000,000. The average price of a new car was just over $600, but Henry Ford's Model T, of which 577,036 were produced this year, was selling for only $360, down from the $850 price of just eight years earlier. It was estimated that there were about 3,500,000 cars on the nation's roads.

The theory of **progressive education** was formulated by John Dewey in his *Democracy and Education*. According to Dewey, intelligence should be seen as an instrument for changing one's environment and should be trained accordingly. He held that subject matter should be adjusted to the child, not child to the subject matter, and that there should be no distinction between cultural and vocational training.

The **submachine gun** was invented by Brig. Gen. John Taliaferro Thompson. The weapon came to be known as the Tommy gun.

Jan 24: The **federal income tax** was ruled constitutional by the U.S. Supreme Court in the case of *Brushaber v. Union Pacific Railroad Co.*

Jan 28: Louis D. Brandeis was appointed to the Supreme Court by Pres. Woodrow Wilson. The appointment was confirmed on June 1. Brandeis was the first Jew to become a justice of the Supreme Court.

Aug 25: The **National Park Service** was established as part of the Interior Department.

Sep 3: The **Adamson Eight-Hour Act** was signed by Pres. Wilson. The act made an eight-hour day standard for most railroad workers. The bill had been hurriedly passed by both houses of Congress to stave off a nationwide railroad strike called for Sept. 4. The strike was averted, but the president was severely critized and accused of wooing labor during an election year.

Oct 16: The **first birth control clinic** was opened by Margaret Sanger, Fania Mindell, and Ethel Burne at 46 Amboy St., Brooklyn, N.Y.

IV. **Fashion**
   Folkways
   Holidays
   Social Issues and Crime
   Sports

Among the baseball heroes of the early twentieth century was Grover Cleveland Alexander, a right-handed pitcher who between 1911 and 1930 played for the Philadelphia Phillies (NL), Chicago Cubs (NL), and St. Louis Cardinals (NL). In the 1916 season he set an unsurpassed record by pitching 15 shutouts for the Phillies. In all, Alexander recorded 90 shutouts during his career. He is exceeded in this respect only by Walter Johnson, who had 113 shutouts during his years with the Washington Senators (AL), from 1907 to 1927. Johnson also compiled a record 3503 strikeouts in his 27-year career.

Jan 1: In the second **Tournament of Roses Association football game** (the first had been played in 1902), and the first annual game, Washington State defeated Brown 14–0. This game marked the beginning of the annual football contest that in 1923 came to be called the Rose Bowl game.

June 15: Boy Scouts of America was incorporated by a bill signed by Pres. Woodrow Wilson.

June 30: The **U.S. Open golf tournament** was won by Charles Evans, Jr. The competition was suspended until 1919 because of U.S. entry into World War I in 1917.

Sep 30: The **longest baseball winning streak** on record was stopped at 26 games when the New York Giants (NL) were beaten 8–3 by the Boston Braves in the second game of a double header.

Oct 7-12: The 13th annual **World Series** was won by the Boston Red Sox (AL), defeating the Brooklyn Dodgers (NL) four games to one.

1917

I. **Civil Rights**
   Exploration and Settlement
   Government
   Statistics
   Wars

Pres. Woodrow Wilson had tried hard to keep the U.S. out of World War I, although his sympathies were with the Allied cause. Through the course of the war public opinion had shifted to the Allies' favor, but many still hoped to avoid U.S. involvement. By early 1917, however, it was clear that the U.S. would be unable to stay on the sidelines much longer. Wilson called a special session of Congress and on Apr. 2 delivered his war message. The Senate voted for war, 82–6, on Apr. 4 and the House followed on Apr. 6, 373–50. Wilson signed the war resolution the same day.

Jan 31: A note announcing the German renewal of **submarine warfare** against neutral and belligerent ships, effective Feb. 1, was delivered to the State Department by Count Johann-Heinrich von Bernstorff, the German ambassador.

Feb 3: Diplomatic relations with Germany were severed. On the same day the U.S. liner *Housatonic* was sunk by a German submarine after a one-hour warning.

Feb 24: The **Zimmermann note,** a coded message from German foreign minister Alfred Zimmermann to the German ambassador to Mexico, was given to Walter Hines Page, U.S. ambassador to Great Britain, by the British, who had decoded it. The note suggested that in the event of U.S. entry into the war against Germany, Germany would propose an alliance with Mexico. The contents of the note were made public on Mar. 1.

Mar 2: The **Jones Act** was passed, making Puerto Rico a U.S. territory and its inhabitants U.S. citizens.

Apr 2: The **first woman in the House of Representatives,** Rep. Jeannette Rankin, Republican of Montana, was seated.

Apr 24: The **Liberty Loan Act,** a war finance measure, authorized Sec. of the Treasury William G. McAdoo to issue for public subscription $2,000,000,000 worth of 3 1/2% convertible gold bonds.

May 18: The **Selective Service Act** was passed, authorizing federal conscription for the armed forces. The act required registration of all males from 21 to 30 years of age.

June 26: The **first U.S. troops in Europe** arrived at St.-Nazaire, France, under command of Maj. Gen. William L. Sibert.

Nov 3: The **first engagement** involving U.S. forces in Europe occurred near the Rhine-Marne Canal in France. German forces attacked American infantrymen training in front-line trenches. American losses: three dead, five wounded, twelve captured or missing.

Nov 6: Women's suffrage was made law in New York State by constitutional amendment.

Dec 18: The **Eighteenth Amendment** to the U.S. Constitution, outlawing manufacture, sale, or transportation of alcoholic liquors, was passed by Congress and submitted to the states for ratification. It was ratified on Jan. 29, 1919.

II. Architecture
Arts and Music
Popular Entertainment
Publishing
Theater

Middle West farm life in the last half of the nineteenth century was a subject that interested authors and readers. Hamlin Garland, who knew farm labor first-hand, had for a number of years been producing realistic books on the subject. In 1917 his autobiography, *A Son of the Middle Border,* was published. In

Main-Travelled Roads (1891) he fictionalized the hardships of farm life. Garland's influence on the development of realism helped prepare the way for a new wave of writers.

Among **books published** this year was *The Cream of the Jest* by James Branch Cabell, a novel about a jaded writer who escapes to a dream world called Storisende, has a number of adventures, and returns to the real world happier for the experience. Other books published this year included *The Innocents* and *The Job: An American Novel* by Sinclair Lewis, both novels; *Jerry of the Islands,* a posthumous novel by Jack London, who died in 1916; *Tendencies in Modern American Poetry* by Amy Lowell; *Parnassus on Wheels* by Christopher Morley, a novel; *Susan Lenox: Her Fall and Rise,* a posthumous novel by David Graham Phillips, considered his best work; *Merlin* by Edwin Arlington Robinson, the first volume of a poetic trilogy dealing with the Arthurian legends that concluded with *Lancelot* (1920) and *Tristram* (1927); and *King Coal* by Upton Sinclair, a novel about coal mining in Colorado.

June 4: The **first Pulitzer prizes** were awarded in the following categories: biography, *Julia Ward Howe* by Laura E. Richards and Maude H. Elliott assisted by Florence H. Hall; history, *With Americans of Past and Present Days* by Jean Jules Jusserand, the French ambassador to the U.S. The prizes also included awards in journalism.

III. Business and Industry
Education
Philosophy and Religion
Science

On Oct. 13 in New York City Mayor John P. Mitchell dedicated the Catskill Aqueduct at ceremonies in Central Park. The aqueduct, a remarkable work of engineering and construction, pointed up the need of cities for reliable sources of water. It had been under construction for 12 years and had cost $177,000,000. It was 92 miles long and at Storm King Mt. it passed under the Hudson R. at a depth of 1114 feet. Much of the aqueduct had to be cut through solid rock.

There were 4,842,139 **motor vehicles** registered in the U.S., 435,000 of them trucks. In all the other nations of the world it was estimated there were only 719,246 motor vehicles. This year alone, 1,795,840 passenger cars and 181,348 commercial vehicles were made in the U.S., and there were 25,500 garages and 13,500 repair shops to service them. The average price of a new car was $720.

Mar 19: An **eight-hour day** for railroad workers was accepted by railroad managers in cooperation with the defense program, thus removing the threat of a railroad tie-up. Labor also gained by keeping the same pay scale.

Sep 5: Federal **raids on IWW headquarters** in 24 cities were prompted by the labor organization's antiwar activities. Federal agents seized documents and books and made ten arrests, including William D. "Big Bill" Haywood, a leader of the organization.

IV. Fashion
   Folkways
   Holidays
   Social Issues and Crime
   Sports

Most professional baseball players of the era learned the game on sandlots or in school, but few played the game at college before entering the ranks of the pros. One of the game's top players during this period was Edward T. "Eddie" Collins, a Columbia College graduate of 1907. Beginning in 1906, Collins played for 25 years in the American League with the Philadelphia Athletics and the Chicago White Sox, becoming one of the best second basemen the game has known. His lifetime total of 3311 hits placed him eighth on the all-time list. Collins was four times the American League's base-stealing champion, in 1917 stealing 51 bases. In 1910 he stole 81 bases, his career high.

Apr 2: The memorable sentence **"The world must be made safe for democracy"** appeared in a speech by

Pres. Woodrow Wilson before Congress, requesting a declaration of war against Germany.

May 2: The **first double no-hit nine-inning baseball game** in the major leagues was played in Chicago. Jim Vaughn of the Chicago Cubs (NL) and Fred Toney of Cincinnati both pitched the full game without allowing a hit. The Reds scored in the tenth inning to win 1–0.

June 23: A **perfect baseball game,** no hits and no walks, was pitched by Ernie Shore of the Boston Red Sox (AL) in a 4–0 win over the Washington Senators.

Oct 6-15: The 14th annual **World Series** was won by the Chicago White Sox (AL), who defeated the New York Giants (NL) four games to two.

1918

I. Civil Rights
Exploration and Settlement
Government
Statistics
Wars

World War I ended on the 11th hour of the 11th day of November this year. At the designated moment, the entire western front opened up with gunfire as war-worn troops sought to fire the last shot. Then silence fell. In the U.S. and elsewhere enormous crowds poured into the streets for a noisy celebration. In New York City 150 tons of paper and ticker tape had to be cleaned off the streets after the festivities. Although the U.S. did not enter the war until nearly three years after the conflict began, the country had mobilized 4,743,829 men and women. Of these, 2,084,000 reached France. U.S. intervention was the deciding factor after years of heavy casualties brought England, France, and Germany to virtual exhaustion. U.S. casualties were 53,513 battle deaths; 63,195 other deaths, mostly from disease; 204,002 wounded. The cost was $21,850,000,000, not counting loans to allies.

Jan 8: Pres. Woodrow Wilson listed his **14 points** for a just and lasting peace in an address to Congress stating the "war aims and peace terms of the United States." It was translated and distributed to German soldiers and civilians throughout middle Europe by the Office of Public Information.

Apr 14: The **first American air ace** was Lt. Douglas Campbell, who shot down his fifth German aircraft.

May 16: The **Sedition Act** was passed. It provided heavy penalties for those who hindered the war effort by making false statements, obstructing enlistment, or speaking against production of war materials, the American form of government, the Constitution, the flag, etc. It was signed by Pres. Wilson on May 21.

June 4: At **Château-Thierry,** the U.S. Second Division halted German forces advancing toward Paris.

June 6-25: In the Battle of **Belleau Wood,** in France, the U.S. Second Division and Fourth Marine Brigade halted the Germans and recaptured the area after bitter fighting. American deaths: 285 officers and 7585 enlisted men.

July 15: In the Second Battle of the **Marne,** German forces attacked east and west of Reims but made no substantial gains. Some 85,000 U.S. troops fought in the battle.

July 18-Aug 6: The **Aisne-Marne offensive** was launched by more than 250,000 Americans in conjunction with French units to counter the German attack of July 15. The offensive forced the Germans out of the Soissons-Reims salient and gave the Allies the initiative.

Aug 8: At **Amiens** Allied forces began a prolonged offensive against the German salient at the Somme R.

Sep 12-13: At **St. Mihiel,** U.S. forces cut off and reduced the German salient, taking about 15,000 prisoners.

Sep 26-Nov 11: The Battle of the **Meuse-Argonne,** involving 1,200,000 U.S. troops, had as its objective the cutting of the German supply line, the Sedan-Mé-zières railroad. American forces cut the railway in early November. The armistice of Nov. 11 brought the American advance to a halt.

Nov 3: An **armistice with Austria-Hungary,** effective Nov. 4, was signed.

Nov 5: In **congressional elections** the Republicans gained control of both houses, taking a 49–47 lead in the Senate, and a House majority of 240–190, with three seats going to minor parties.

Nov 9: Kaiser Wilhelm II of Germany abdicated. Two days later the armistice went into effect and the war was ended.

Nov 21: The **Wartime Prohibition Act,** effective from June 30, 1919, until demobilization, was signed by Pres. Wilson. It banned manufacture or sale of liquor except for export.

II. Architecture
Arts and Music
Popular Entertainment
Publishing
Theater

Despite the many new plays being written and produced every year, interest in the works of great playwrights remained high. In fact, a number of actors and actresses spent all or most of their careers acting Shakespearean roles. A leading actor was Walter Hampden, an American who acted in England before making his New York City debut in 1907. In Shakespeare's plays he acted the roles of Caliban, Oberon, Romeo, Macbeth, Othello, Shylock, and Hamlet. His appearance as Hamlet in 1918 was hailed as the best American interpretation of the role since Edwin Booth. In 1925 Hampden took over the Colonial Theater in New York and renamed it for himself.

Among **books published** this year was *The Education of Henry Adams,* a posthumous volume, privately printed in 1907 that Adams had written to complement his *Mont-Saint-Michel and Chartres*

(1913). The work decried the multiplicity of modern society, symbolized by the electric dynamo, and the failure of modern education to prepare Adams for a happy and useful life. Other books published this year included *My Antonia* by Willa Cather, a masterly novel of prairie life; *Cornhuskers* by Carl Sandburg, a collection of poetry; and *The Magnificent Ambersons* by Booth Tarkington, a study of three generations of a family in Indianapolis from 1873 to 1916, years in which Indianapolis grew from a town to a city.

Aug 26: *Lightnin'* by Winchell Smith and Frank Bacon opened on Broadway at The Gaiety Theatre. It was destined to have one of the longest runs, 1291 performances, in U.S. stage history.

III. Business and Industry
Education
Philosophy and Religion
Science

The U.S. war effort required mobilization and control of the nation's economic life. The War Industries Board, established on July 28, 1917, was reorganized on Mar. 4, 1918, with Bernard Baruch, a financier, as its head. Food and fuel were rationed, taxes were increased, and millions of dollars worth of Liberty bonds were sold. The railroads were taken over by the government by a presidential proclamation on Dec. 26, 1917, an arrangement formalized by the Railroad Control Act of Mar. 21, 1918. Industries such as steel had already been stimulated by the war because of large purchases by the Allies. Between 1914 and 1917 the production of steel ingots and castings nearly doubled. During the 19 months the U.S. was at war, 875 seagoing vessels were built.

A **compulsory school attendance law** was passed in Mississippi, the last state to do so.

In 1918 there were 1,000,000 more **women employed** than in 1915. On Sept. 30 Pres. Woodrow Wilson told the Senate that women's suffrage was a "vitally necessary war measure." But the Senate lacked the strength to pass any legislation on the matter.

May 13: The **first airmail stamps** were issued by the Post Office Department, in denominations of 6 cents, 16 cents, and 24 cents.

May 15: The **first airmail service** was inaugurated with regular flights between New York City and Washington, D.C.

July 26: The **sugar ration** was reduced to two pounds a person a month by edict of the U.S. Food Board.

Oct: A devastating **influenza epidemic** reached its height. The disease had first appeared in early September in Boston, New York, and Philadelphia. By mid-October the death rate in these cities had risen over 700%. Doctors were baffled. The epidemic spread to 46 states and ultimately killed between 400,000 and 500,000 persons, far more than the number of Americans killed in the war. Many war plants shut down, telephone service was cut in half, and the draft was suspended in several cities. Panic spread rapidly. Newspapers were filled with outlandish theories of the epidemic's cause and long lists of the dead. The epidemic disappeared in 1919, but it left many afflicted with Bright's disease, cardiac diseases and tuberculosis.

IV. Fashion
Folkways
Holidays
Social Issues and Crime
Sports

The war prompted an innovation in time-keeping this year. On Mar. 31 Pres. Woodrow Wilson signed a law providing for Daylight Savings Time, by which clocks were to be set ahead one hour so that more daylight was available. Daylight savings was disliked by some, especially farmers, and the law was repealed in 1919. It was not reestablished nationwide until World War II.

Sep 5-11: The 15th annual **World Series** was won by the Boston Red Sox (AL), who beat the Chicago Cubs (NL) four games to two. Each player on the winning team received $1102.51, the all-time low payment to World Series winners.

1919

I. **Civil Rights**
   Exploration and Settlement
   Government
   Statistics
   Wars

With the war won, the Allies prepared to make the peace official. At the peace conference convened at Versailles, France, the American delegation was headed by Pres. Woodrow Wilson. His idealism contrasted with the attitudes of England and France, who wanted to punish Germany. When the Treaty of Versailles was signed on June 28, the war was officially ended. Germany was forced to admit guilt for the war and was stripped of Alsace-Lorraine, the Saar Basin, and its overseas colonies. Germany was also to pay reparations, later fixed at $56,000,000,000, and was required to disarm. Wilson got his wish to establish a League of Nations.

Jan 18: The **peace conference** opened in Paris. For Pres. Woodrow Wilson it was the beginning of a fight to preserve the principles of the 14 points on which he believed a lasting peace should be established. He failed to have many of his most important points included because of the demands of other victorious Allies.

Jan 29: The **Eighteenth Amendment** to the Constitution, prohibiting transportation and sale of alcoholic beverages, was ratified. It was the first amendment to have a time limit on ratification, seven years, and the only one that was subsequently repealed.

Feb 14: The draft of the **League of Nations covenant** was presented by Pres. Wilson to the Paris Peace Conference. Wilson embarked from Brest on Feb. 15 for the U.S. Later he returned to Europe, remaining at the peace conference until it ended on June 28 and returning to New York City on July 8.

July 10: The **Treaty of Versailles** and League of Nations covenant were sent by Pres. Wilson to the Senate for ratification. Wilson declared that acceptance of the treaty would ensure future peace.

Aug 31: The **Communist Labor Party** of America was founded at Chicago, Ill. The party adopted the platform of the Third International, including a badge featuring the hammer and sickle encircled by strands of wheat. The party motto was "Workers of the world unite!"

Sep 26: Pres. **Wilson suffered a stroke** while traveling to Wichita, Kans. His national tour was halted and he was taken back to Washington, D.C.

Oct 28: The **Volstead Act,** or National Prohibition Act, was passed by Congress over Pres. Wilson's veto of the previous day. The act defined as intoxicating liquor any beverage containing at least one-half of 1% alcohol and provided for enforcement of the provisions of the Eighteenth Amendment.

Nov 19: The **Treaty of Versailles** failed to achieve ratification in the Senate by a vote of 55–39.

II. Architecture
   Arts and Music
   Popular Entertainment
   Publishing
   Theater

A younger generation of composers was now presenting works that differed from the romantic style. Among them was Charles T. Griffes, whose *The White Peacock* (1915–1916), originally a piano piece, was presented in 1919 in a version orchestrated for ballet at the Rivoli Theater in New York City. It was received with considerable enthusiasm. Griffes composed a major work for orchestra, *The Pleasure Dome of Kubla Khan,* in 1920. That year he died at the age of 35.

Among **books published** this year was *Jurgen, A*

Comedy of Justice by James Branch Cabell, an excursion through the world of fantasy, allegory, and escape. A reworking of the story of Faust set in the mythical kingdom of Poictesme, the novel was suppressed because of the erotic adventures of its protagonist. The book became extremely popular and made Cabell's reputation. Other books published this year included *Winesburg, Ohio* by Sherwood Anderson, a series of connected stories hailed by critics and readers, and Anderson's most successful book; *Java Head* by Joseph Hergesheimer, a novel of East and West, and *Linda Condon*, also by Hergesheimer and also a novel; *On the Makaloa Mat* by Jack London, a posthumous collection of stories; *The American Language* by H. L. Mencken, the author's major scholarly work, which he subsequently augmented; and *Ten Days That Shook the World* by John Reed, a firsthand account of the Russian Revolution, later issued with an introduction by Lenin.

June 2: Pulitzer prizes were awarded for the following: fiction, *The Magnificent Ambersons* by Booth Tarkington; biography, *The Education of Henry Adams* by Henry Adams; poetry, *Old Road to Paradise* by Margaret Widdemer and *Cornhuskers* by Carl Sandburg.

III. Business and Industry
Education
Philosophy and Religion
Science

Charismatic religious leaders continued to attract followers in large numbers. The latest was Father Divine (George Baker), a black evangelist whose nonsectarian and interracial movement got its start in Harlem, in New York City, during this period. In 1919 his establishment at Sayville, L.I., attracted attention. Divine set up "heavens" for his "angels," mostly women, where he preached fundamentalist religion and stressed the value of economic and social equality and cooperation. Many of his followers believed he was God. During the years of the Great

Depression, Father Divine's heavens provided food and shelter for many people.

Sep 9: A **police strike in Boston** began when the policemen's union called its members off the job. Some 1117 out of 1544 patrolmen walked off their jobs. Many merchants locked up their shops, but looting occurred on a wide scale. New police were hired and the strike was put down. Gov. Calvin Coolidge told AFL president Samuel Gompers: "There is no right to strike against the public safety by anybody, anywhere, any time," a sentence that became well known.

IV. Fashion
Folkways
Holidays
Social Issues and Crime
Sports

Jack Dempsey, new and popular king of boxing, who was to set records in coming years, won the world heavyweight boxing championship on July 4. He scored a technical knockout against the defending champion, Jess Willard, after the third round of a bout at Toledo, Ohio. Dempsey fought four championship bouts and one non-title fight as champion, each of which grossed over $1,000,000, an enormous sum in those days. Dempsey was known as the Manassa Mauler (he was born in Manassa, Colo.) and earned more money than any previous boxer in history. In his fights he was ever on the attack, punching savagely. The crowds loved him for it.

May 10: The 45th annual **Kentucky Derby** was won by Sir Barton, ridden by Johnny Loftus, with a time of 2:09⅘. Sir Barton, ridden by Loftus, went on to win the Preakness and Belmont Stakes, thereby becoming the first horse to win racing's Triple Crown.

May 14: The 44th annual **Preakness Stakes** was won by Sir Barton, with a time of 1:53. The jockey was Johnny Loftus.

June 11: The **U.S. Open golf tournament** was won by Walter Hagen.

June 11: The 51st annual **Belmont Stakes** was won by Sir Barton, with a time of 2:17²/₅. The jockey was Johnny Loftus.

Sep 20: The **PGA golf tournament** was won by Jim Barnes.

Oct 1-9: The 16th annual **World Series** was won by the Cincinnati Reds (NL), who defeated the Chicago White Sox (AL) five games to three in a best-of-nine series, which the major leagues adopted from 1919 through 1921.

1920

I. Civil Rights
Exploration and Settlement
Government
Statistics
Wars

The presidential election of 1920 was in part a referendum on whether the U.S. should join the League of Nations. The Democratic nominee, James M. Cox, pledged to do his best to take America into the league. The Republican platform straddled the issue; candidate Warren G. Harding did not seem to feel strongly either way. Harding's election was an indicator that the American people wanted to forget the war. They rejected Woodrow Wilson's idealism and returned to everyday pursuits. This was the first presidential election in which women could vote, and they apparently voted the same way as the men—overwhelmingly Republican.

The U.S. **Census** recorded a population of 105,710,620. The center of population was placed at eight miles south-southeast of Spencer, Owen County, Ind. For the first time a decline was recorded in rural population to less than 50% of the total. The number of farm residents had dwindled to less than 30%.

Apr 15: In what came to be called the **Sacco and Vanzetti** case, Frank Parmenter and Alexander Berardelli, paymaster and guard for a shoe factory in South Braintree, Mass., were shot and killed. The payroll they were carrying was seized by the murderers. Three weeks later Nicola Sacco and Bartolomeo Vanzetti, workmen of Brockton, Mass., were arrested and charged with the crime.

May 8-14: The **Socialist Party National Convention** **nominated Eugene V. Debs** of Indiana for the presidency, for the fifth time, and Seymour Stedman of Ohio for the vice presidency. Debs was serving a ten-year prison sentence.

June 8-12: The **Republican National Convention** **nominated Warren G. Harding** of Ohio for the presidency and Gov. Calvin Coolidge of Massachusetts for the vice presidency. The nomination was decided on the tenth ballot.

June 28-July 5: The **Democratic National Convention** **nominated Gov. James M. Cox** of Ohio for the presidency and Franklin D. Roosevelt of New York for the vice presidency. Other chief candidates for the hotly contested presidential nomination had been A. Mitchell Palmer, attorney general in Pres. Woodrow Wilson's Cabinet, and former Sec. of the Treasury William G. McAdoo.

July 13-16: The **Farmer Labor Party National Convention** nominated Parley P. Christensen of Utah for the presidency and Max S. Hayes of Ohio for the vice presidency.

Nov 2: Warren G. Harding was elected president of the United States. Calvin Coolidge was elected vice president. The electoral vote was Harding, 404; James M. Cox, Democratic candidate, 127. The popular vote was Harding, 16,152,200; Cox, 9,147,353; Eugene V. Debs, Socialist candidate, 919,799; Aaron S. Watkins, Prohibition candidate, 189,408; W. W. Cox, Socialist Labor candidate, 31,175; Parley P. Christensen, Farmer Labor candidate, 26,541. The Republicans increased their majorities in both houses, leading 59–37 in the Senate and 301–131, with one minor party seat and two vacancies, in the House.

Nov 20: The **Nobel Peace Prize** was awarded to Pres. Woodrow Wilson in recognition of his efforts to promote world peace through the League of Nations.

II. Architecture
   Arts and Music
   Popular Entertainment
   Publishing
   Theater

What was to become a new industry and a new system of public entertainment and communication got its start on Nov. 2, 1920, when radio station KDKA in Pittsburgh, Pa., broadcast the results of the presidential election. There were few listeners, but for the first time radio broadcasting had become a service for the general public. By 1922 there were about 500 stations, but conditions were chaotic because all employed the same wavelength. Sec. of Commerce Herbert Hoover called a conference for Feb. 27, 1922; there, a system for allocating wavelengths was agreed on. In 1921 Americans were to spend about $10,000,000 on radio sets and parts.

Among **books published** this year was *Main Street* by Sinclair Lewis, a novel about life in a midwestern town that caused a sensation across the country and established Lewis as a leading literary figure. The novel, a bitter indictment of the drabness, hypocrisy, stupidity, and pride of the residents of Gopher Prairie, Minn., became an American classic. Other books published this year included *The Ordeal of Mark Twain* by Van Wyck Brooks, a controversial study of the great author; *This Side of Paradise* by F. Scott Fitzgerald, the author's first novel and a smashing success; *Miss Lulu Bett* by Zona Gale, a novel of rural life in the Middle West; *A Few Figs from Thistles,* a collection of poetry by Edna St. Vincent Millay; *The Great Impersonation* by E. Phillips Oppenheim, an adventure story that sold more than 1,000,000 copies; *Smoke and Steel* by Carl Sandburg, poetry; and *The Age of Innocence* by Edith Wharton, a novel of New York City society in the 1870s.

June 2: Pulitzer prizes were awarded for the following: biography, *The Life of John Marshall* by Albert J. Beveridge; history, *The War with Mexico* by Justin H. Smith; drama, *Beyond the Horizon* by Eugene O'Neill.

III. Business and Industry
Education
Philosophy and Religion
Science

A new era in transportation and communication was opened this year when the first New York to California mail plane left New York City on Sept. 7, arriving in San Francisco on Sept. 11. At first airmail service was difficult and risky. The planes were barely more than canvas and wood held together with wire, and instrumentation was virtually nonexistent. A plane's range was small, which meant the pilots had to hop from field to field to get across the country. Flying in bad weather was extremely dangerous. Nonetheless, many pilots who had learned to fly during World War I found the air service to their liking. Aircraft technology grew steadily through the 1920s and 1930s, and airmail service, like air transportation itself, became a fact of life.

Illiteracy in the U.S. reached a new low of 6% of the population, a decline of 1.7% from 1910 and a decline of 14% from 1870.

The average **life expectancy** in the U.S., as determined by the Bureau of Public Health, was 54.09 years; in 1901 it had been 49.24 years.

The **first measurement of a star** was accomplished by Albert A. Michelson, who calculated a stellar diameter with the aid of the interferometer he had invented in 1880. He demonstrated that the diameter of Alpha Orionis was 260,000,000 miles.

The **automobile** had become part of American life. By 1923 about 15,000,000 cars were registered. One out of every four families in the U.S. bought or sold an automobile each year. There were 1,000,000 fewer cars than telephones and only 7,000,000 fewer cars than dwelling places.

IV. Fashion
Folkways
Holidays
Social Issues and Crime
Sports

Whatever might happen in other sports, finance, or politics, American fans found it hard to believe scandal could ever touch baseball. Yet on Sept. 28, 1920, eight members of the Chicago White Sox (AL) were indicted on charges of having taken bribes to throw the World Series with the Cincinnati Reds the previous fall. Sportswriters soon referred to the team as the Black Sox, a name that stuck. On Aug. 2, 1921, after a few hours of deliberation, a jury acquitted the players. While spectators cheered, the jurors carried the players around on their shoulders. There was considerable doubt as to the justice of the verdict, and the players were banned from organized baseball.

The term *smoke-filled room* came into use to describe machine politics after the Republican National Convention in June. When the convention became hopelessly deadlocked over a presidential candidate, Ohio politican Harry M. Daugherty told the press: "The convention will be dead-locked, and after the other candidates have gone their limit, some twelve or fifteen men, worn out and bleary-eyed for lack of sleep, will sit down about two o'clock in the morning around a table in a smoke-filled room in some hotel and decide the nomination. When that time comes, Harding will be selected."

Apr 20-Sep 12: At the **Olympic Games** in Antwerp, Belgium, the U.S. won the unofficial team championship, winning nine gold medals. Finland was the second-place team.

July 3: At the **Wimbledon** tennis championships in England, William T. Tilden won the men's singles title.

July 9-16: The **Davis Cup** international tennis challenge round was won, for the first time since 1913, by the U.S., which swept Australia in five straight matches.

Aug 13: The **U.S. Open golf tournament** was won by Ted Ray of England.

Aug 21: The **PGA golf tournament** was won by J. Fowler Hutchison.

Oct 5-12: The 17th annual **World Series** was won by the Cleveland Indians (AL), who beat the Brooklyn Dodgers (NL) five games to two.

1921

I. Civil Rights
Exploration and Settlement
Government
Statistics
Wars

The 1920s witnessed several attempts to reduce armaments and lessen the danger of another war. The U.S. invited the major naval powers to the Washington Conference for Limitation of Armament, which opened in Washington, D.C., on Nov. 12, 1921. The U.S. proposed scrapping warships already built and limiting future construction. The conferees agreed on a 5–5-3 ratio for capital ships for the U.S., Great Britain, and Japan. In all, nine treaties were signed on Feb. 6, 1922, including one that restricted use of submarines in warfare and outlawed poison gas, and another in which the U.S., Great Britain, France, and Japan agreed to respect each other's rights over Pacific possessions. Eventually the work of this conference was destroyed by the events leading to World War II, but it did slow down the international arms race for a time.

Jan 13: A **report on urbanization** by the Census Bureau showed that 51% of Americans lived in cities and towns of more than 2500.

May 19: The **first generally restrictive immigration act** in the U.S. was signed by Pres. Harding. The act, effective June 3, initiated a quota system that restricted immigration in any given year to 3% of the number of each nationality reported in the Census of 1910. The total number of immigrants allowed to enter in any given year was set at 357,000.

June 10: The **Bureau of the Budget** and the office of Comptroller General of the U.S. were established by Congress as part of the Treasury Department. The first comptroller general was John Raymond McCarl, who took office on July 1.

July 2: The **state of war** between the U.S. and Germany was declared at an end by a joint resolution of Congress. The resolution also claimed all rights, reparations, or indemnities awarded to the U.S. under the Treaty of Versailles.

Aug: A reemergence in the South of the **Ku Klux Klan** was marked by lawlessness. Whippings, brandings, tarrings, and destruction of property were directed against blacks and whites, although no direct motive could be found for some of the violence.

Aug 25: A **peace treaty with Germany** was signed in Berlin. It stipulated that none of the provisions of the joint resolution of Congress of July 2, 1921, or of the Versailles Treaty would be vitiated by this treaty.

II. Architecture
Arts and Music
Popular Entertainment
Publishing
Theater

The 1920s saw the rise to national prominence of one of the great American humorists and political commentators, William Penn Adair "Will" Rogers, an authentic cowboy, with Indian ancestry, from Oklahoma. Rogers got his start on the stage as a rope twirler. Soon he was commenting wryly on public events. His perceptive remarks took him to fame in the movies and on the stage, especially in the *Ziegfeld Follies,* in which he first appeared in 1915. His newspaper column was syndicated nationally. The growth of radio as an entertainment medium in the late 1920s and early 1930s brought him an immense audience. Typical of his remarks were such gems as, "The U.S. has never lost a war or won a conference," "Everything is funny as long as it happens to somebody else," and "I tell you folks, all politics is applesauce."

Among **books published** this year, the runaway best seller was *The Sheik* by Edith W. Hull, the adventures of a beautiful girl carried off into the desert by an Arab chief. The novel inspired a motion picture of the same name, starring Rudolph Valentino, and a host of imitative books, including the parody *The Shriek* by Charles Somerville. Other books published this year included *The Brimming Cup* by Dorothy Canfield, a novel; *Three Soldiers* by John Dos Passos, a novel dealing with the aftermath of World War I; *A Daughter of the Middle Border* by Hamlin Garland, autobiography; *The Old Soak* by Don Marquis, the journalist and poet; *Collected Poems* by Edwin Arlington Robinson; *Alice Adams* by Booth Tarkington, a novel; and *Nets to Catch the Wind* by Elinor Wylie, poetry.

This year's **popular songs** included "Blue Moon," "If You Would Care for Me," "Look for the Silver Lining," "Kitten on the Keys," "I Never Knew," and "Down in Chinatown."

Oct 5: The **first radio coverage of the World Series** was carried by a wireless station set up at the Electrical Show at the 71st Regiment Armory in New York City, and by station WJZ in Newark, N.J. Both stations carried play-by-play bulletins. The first actual play-by-play coverage began in 1922.

Nov 11: The **Unknown Soldier** of World War I was buried at Arlington National Cemetery after lying in state at the Capitol rotunda in Washington, D.C.

III. Business and Industry
Education
Philosophy and Religion
Science

The war period had brought boom times to American industry and American workers. With the wartime demand for all kinds of goods ended, the nation experienced a depression by the middle of 1921. Fortunately, recovery began as early as the spring of 1922. In its initial stages, the depression brought wage reductions, such as a 22.5% pay cut imposed by the New York Central Railroad on 43,000 workers, and a 15% cut suffered by clothing workers. Sec. of Commerce Herbert Hoover called a national conference on unemployment. It opened on Sept. 21 and recommended a cut in prices instead of wages so that demand would be stimulated. It was also proposed that a program of public works be started to provide jobs.

    The **death rate** in the U.S. was 1163.9 per 100,000 population. In 1900 it had been 1755.

Apr 30: Ford Motor Company assets were reported to be $345,140,557. Henry Ford announced that a temporary crisis had ended. Six months previously, Ford had had 175,000 finished surplus automobiles. Ford then closed his plants and forced the surplus on unwilling dealers. An upsurge of buying saved the day.

June 25: Samuel Gompers was chosen president of the American Federation of Labor for the 40th time. He polled more than twice as many votes (25,022) as John L. Lewis (12,324), his opponent in the election.

July 21: The possibilities of **concentrated bombing** were shown by an Army test directed by Gen. William "Billy" Mitchell in which the former German battleship *Ostfriesland* was sunk by aircraft. The test was held off Hampton Roads, Va. Many believed that the demonstration vindicated Gen. Mitchell's belief in the superiority of air power over sea power.

IV. Fashion
Folkways
Holidays
Social Issues and Crime
Sports

The Volstead Act, the national prohibition law, was a year old on Jan. 16, but prohibition had not become the law of the land. In fact it fostered the rise of crime in the U.S. and thereby greatly changed America's social fabric. By 1921 bootleggers were doing a good business, although some of the liquor they supplied was of poor quality, even dangerous. Some people made their own, called bathtub gin or homebrew, but others depended on liquor smuggled over the Canadian border. Offshore lay ships loaded with alcoholic beverages, which small speedy boats brought ashore in darkness, defying the Coast Guard. Between 1920 and 1930 some 500,000 people were arrested for violating the Volstead Act.

June 29: At the **Wimbledon** tennis championships, Elizabeth Ryan won the women's singles title. William T. Tilden won the men's title on July 2.

July 2: The **world heavyweight boxing championship** was defended by Jack Dempsey, who knocked out Georges Carpentier in the fourth round. This was the first fight with a $1,000,000 gate.

July 22: The **U.S. Open golf tournament** was won by James M. Barnes.

Aug 3: In the **Black Sox scandal,** Judge Kenesaw Mountain Landis, the baseball commissioner, ruled that the Chicago White Sox players charged with throwing the 1919 World Series would not be allowed to play again despite their acquittal in 1920.

Sep 3: The **Davis Cup** international tennis challenge round was won by the U.S., defeating the Japanese team in five straight matches.

Sep 8: The **first Miss America** title was won by Margaret Gorman of Washington, D.C., at the end of a two-day pageant and festival at Atlantic City, N.J.

Sep 28: The **PGA golf tournament** was won by Gene Sarazen.

Oct 5-13: The 18th annual **World Series** was won by the New York Giants (NL), who beat the New York Yankees (AL) five games to three.

Nov 5: Armistice Day, Nov. 11, was proclaimed a legal holiday by Pres. Warren G. Harding.

1922

I. Civil Rights
   Exploration and Settlement
   Government
   Statistics
   Wars

A vexing problem of international relations in the postwar world was that of war debts. During World War I and after, U.S. loans to its allies and to newly formed nations totaled $10,350,479,074. Great Britain, France, and Italy were the largest borrowers. In turn, such countries as Great Britain and France were creditors of other nations. The European allies expected to pay their debts with the reparations assessed against Germany by the Treaty of Versailles. Britain had proposed canceling out debts but Pres. Woodrow Wilson had refused. On Feb. 9, 1922, Congress established a Foreign Debt Commission to settle the problem. In the final arrangement, debtor nations accepted obligations of about $11,500,000,000, payable to the U.S. over 62 years at an average interest rate of 2.135%. When Germany became unable to pay reparations, debts owed the U.S. were scaled down in 1925 and 1926.

Feb 27: The **Nineteenth Amendment** to the Constitution, providing for women's suffrage, was declared constitutional by a unanimous decision of the Supreme Court.

Apr 15: In the first formal action of the investigation that uncovered the **Teapot Dome** scandal, Sen. John

B. Kendrick of Wyoming introduced a resolution that called on Sec. of the Interior Albert B. Fall to explain why the Teapot Dome oil lands in Wyoming, which had been set aside by the Senate for use of the Navy, were being leased secretly to the Mammoth Oil Company, controlled by Harry F. Sinclair. Sen. Kendrick's information had come to him from one of his constituents, a small businessman in Wyoming.

Oct 3: The **first woman U.S. senator,** Mrs. W. H. Felton, 87, of Cartersville, Ga., was appointed by Gov. Thomas W. Hardwick of Georgia to the seat vacated by the death of Sen. Thomas E. Watson. Voters chose a successor to Felton in November.

Nov 7: In **congressional elections,** the Republicans suffered substantial losses but maintained majorities in both houses. In the Senate they led the Democrats 51–43, with two seats going to minor parties. In the House the Republicans lost 76 seats but still led 225–205, with five seats going to minor parties.

II. Architecture
    Arts and Music
    Popular Entertainment
    Publishing
    Theater

Jazz, a unique American contribution to music, hit a new peak of popularity and respectability in the 1920s. The period came to be known as the *jazz age.* One of the musicians who made jazz so popular was Louis "Satchmo" Armstrong, who in 1922 joined King Oliver's Creole Jazz Band in Chicago as a cornetist. The melodic development of jazz owed a great deal to Armstrong, and he made solo renditions an important part of band performances. Later Armstrong organized several big bands, appeared on Broadway, and made successful foreign tours.

Among **books published** this year was *The Enormous Room* by E. E. Cummings, the poet and artist. Cummings' only novel, it was based on the author's imprisonment by French authorities during World War I for some indiscreet remarks he made in letters home while serving on the front as an ambulance driver. Other books published this year included *One of Ours* by Willa Cather, a novel; *The Waste Land* by the expatriate poet T. S. Eliot, a remarkable poem echoing the disillusionment caused by war and modern life; *Tales of the Jazz Age* by F. Scott Fitzgerald, and *The Beautiful and Damned*, also by Fitzgerald, a novel; *The Covered Wagon* by Emerson Hough, a novel; *Babbitt* by Sinclair Lewis, a novel about a stereotypical midwestern businessman; *Vandemark's Folly* by Herbert Quick, a novel set in Iowa in the mid-nineteenth century, the first of a trilogy that included *The Hawkeye* (1923) and *The Invisible Woman* (1924); *Rootabaga Stories* by Carl Sandburg, a collection of stories for children; and *Merton of the Movies* by Harry Leon Wilson, a novel.

May 21: Pulitzer prizes were awarded for the following: fiction, *Alice Adams* by Booth Tarkington; biography, *A Daughter of the Middle Border* by Hamlin Garland; history, *The Founding of New England* by James Truslow Adams; poetry, *Collected Poems* by Edwin Arlington Robinson; drama, *Anna Christie* by Eugene O'Neill.

May 30: The **Lincoln Memorial** was dedicated in Washington, D.C.

III. Business and Industry
Education
Philosophy and Religion
Science

The year was marked by technical and commercial progress in radio broadcasting, an enterprise that was soon to foster a major industry and profoundly influence American society. On Aug. 28 the first commercial was broadcast over WEAF in New York City, which had begun operation on Aug. 16. The sponsor was the Queensborough Corporation, a real estate firm, that bought ten minutes of air time to extol Hawthorne Court, a group of apartment buildings in Jackson Heights, Queens. This year also saw one of the earliest long-distance relays; it used a telephone hookup to broadcast in New York a football game between the University of Chicago and Princeton University. On Oct. 4 the first radio play-by-play coverage of the World Series, reported directly from the Polo Grounds in New York City by Grantland Rice, was carried by radio station WJZ in Newark, N.J. Radio stations WGY in Schenectady, N.Y., and WBZ in Springfield, Mass., also carried World Series coverage.

The first successful use of the **Technicolor** film process was made by Herbert T. Kalmus. The process was not to become widely used for motion pictures until almost 20 years later.

Feb 21: The **aerial explosion** of the lighter-than-air ship *Roma,* after hitting high tension wires at Hampton Roads Army Airbase, Va., killed 34 of its 45-man crew. The airship had been purchased from the Italian government.

June 14: The **first president to be heard over radio** was Pres. Warren G. Harding, whose dedication of the Francis Scott Key Memorial in Baltimore was broadcast. The first official government message was not broadcast until Dec. 6, 1923.

Nov 15: Dr. **Alexis Carrel** of the Rockefeller Institute announced his discovery of leukocytes, or white corpuscles, agents in the blood that prevent the spread of infection.

IV. Fashion
    Folkways
    Holidays
    Social Issues and Crime
    Sports

The 1920s had more than their share of sensational murder cases, or perhaps it seemed that way because of the extravagant manner in which the press reported them. Typical was the Hall-Mills case, which began on Sept. 16 with the discovery, side by side under a crab apple tree in New Brunswick, N.J., of the bodies of the Rev. Edward Wheeler Hall and his choir leader, Mrs. Eleanor R. Mills. No one was indicted until four years later, when agitation by a New York City tabloid got the case reopened. The dead man's widow, two brothers, and a cousin were indicted for the murders. In the first 11 days of the trial, newsmen sent out some 5,000,000 words of copy. Billy Sunday, the evangelist, was also there to help report. In the end, all the defendants were acquitted and the case was never solved.

June 14: The **PGA golf tournament** was won by Charles Hoffner.

July 15: The **U.S. Open golf tournament** was won by Gene Sarazen.

Aug 31-Sep 5: The **Davis Cup** international tennis challenge round was won for the third straight year by the U.S., defeating Australia four matches to one.

Oct 4-8: The 19th annual **World Series** was won by the New York Giants (NL), who took four of five games from the New York Yankees (AL). The second game of the series (Oct. 5) had ended in a 3–3 tie after ten innings, when the game was called on account of darkness.

1923

I. Civil Rights
   Exploration and Settlement
   Government
   Statistics
   Wars

For the first time since Zachary Taylor's death in 1850, a president of the United States died in office of natural causes. Pres. Warren G. Harding was in poor health by early 1923. His reputation was in decline because friends he had appointed to federal office had proven corrupt or incompetent. Scandals were about to break all around him. To get away from the unpleasantness, Harding began a tour on June 20 of the West and Alaska. He took ill on the return journey and died in a San Francisco hotel on Aug. 2, at the age of 58. Harding died of an embolism while recovering from an attack of ptomaine poisoning and pneumonia, but there were rumors of foul play at the time. At 2:43 A.M. on Aug. 3, Vice Pres. Calvin Coolidge was sworn in as president by his father, a notary public, in the family home in Plymouth, Vt. Harding was buried at Marion, Ohio, on Aug. 10.

May 4: A bill repealing the **New York State Prohibition enforcement act** was passed by the state assembly. Despite Pres. Harding's warning that federal authorities would have to take over the enforcement of Prohibition in states that did not do the job themselves, Gov. Alfred E. Smith signed the repeal bill. This was thought by many to have been the beginning of the end of Prohibition.

Sep 15: Oklahoma was placed under martial law by Gov. John Calloway Walton because of terrorist activities of the Ku Klux Klan, which had become a powerful force in Midwest politics. This year several newspapers began exposing the Klan and its secret activities.

II. Architecture
Arts and Music
Popular Entertainment
Publishing
Theater

After jazz was brought north to Chicago by black musicians from New Orleans and other southern cities, white performers took up the style in greater numbers and became important contributors to it. Among them was Leon Bismarck "Bix" Beiderbecke, who was first influenced by recordings of the Original Dixieland Band. It did not take him long to win a reputation as a cornetist, and in 1923 he organized the Wolverine Orchestra in Chicago. Beiderbecke was also a pianist and a composer, one of his works being "In a Mist." A lonely, driven man, he died in 1931 at age 28.

Among **books published** this year was a slim volume entitled *Three Stories & Ten Poems* by Ernest

Hemingway, a young expatriate living in France, where the book was published. Two of the stories were republished in Hemingway's *In Our Time* (1925). Other books published this year included *A Lost Lady* by Willa Cather, a novel; *Tulips and Chimneys* by E. E. Cummings, the author's first volume of poetry; *Streets of Night* by John Dos Passos, a novel; *New Hampshire: A Poem with Notes and Grace Notes* by Robert Frost; *Collected Poems* by Vachel Lindsay; *Harmonium* by Wallace Stevens, poetry; and *Cane* by Jean Toomer, a collection of poetry, stories, and a play focusing on the black experience in the U.S.

May 13: Pulitzer prizes were awarded for the following: fiction, *One of Ours* by Willa Cather; biography, *The Life and Letters of Walter H. Page* by Burton J. Hendrick; history, *The Supreme Court in United States History* by Charles Warren; poetry, *The Ballad of the Harp-Weaver, A Few Figs from Thistles,* and *Eight Sonnets,* all by Edna St. Vincent Millay; drama, *Icebound* by Owen Davis.

III. Business and Industry
Education
Philosophy and Religion
Science

Inventors and scientists had been working for years at laying the technical groundwork for radio, talking pictures, and television. Lee De Forest, who came to be called "the father of radio" as early as 1906, had developed the triode vacuum tube, which made long-distance telephone and radio communications a possibility. On Mar. 13, 1923, in New York City, De Forest demonstrated a sound motion picture process called Phonofilm. The film he showed included a performance by an orchestra. De Forest held more than 300 patents, yet his career was not an easy one. Like many other inventors during this period, De Forest struggled to secure capital for research and was at times forced into court to protect his patent and licensing rights.

Auto production continued to climb. More autos were built this year than had been produced in the first 15 years of the twentieth century. About 15,000,000 passenger cars were in use in the U.S. New York, New Jersey, Pennsylvania, and Maryland combined had more autos than all the rest of the world outside the U.S.

The DuPont Corporation began the production of **cellophane** through the purchase of American rights to the Swiss patent of Jacques F. Brandenberger. Swiss factories had been producing cellophane, cellulose film, since 1912.

Jan: William Jennings Bryan stirred up controversy over evolution in addressing a group of ministers in St. Paul, Minn. The theory of evolution, he said, is a "program of infidelity masquerading under the name of science." The debate was taken up by newspapers, which gave the names *fundamentalist* and *modernist* to the two sides.

Oct 6: A new average **air speed record** of 243.76 mph was set by Lt. Al Williams, flying a Curtiss racer at the Pulitzer Trophy contest in St. Louis, Mo.

Nov 6: A patent for the **first electric shaver** was issued to Col. Jacob Schick. Schick received several additional patents and in 1931 established his own company, the Schick Dry Shaver Company, Inc., Stamford, Conn.

IV. Fashion
    Folkways
    Holidays
    Social Issues and Crime
    Sports

Thanks to the rugged personality and heroic achievements of Jack Dempsey as heavyweight boxing champion, the sport was more popular than ever and had attained a degree of respectability. On the night of Sept. 14, Dempsey met challenger Luis Angel Firpo, called the Wild Bull of the Pampas. The fight, held at the Polo Grounds in New York City, was one of the most exciting ever seen. Firpo was knocked out in the second round after 3 min., 57 sec. fighting time, but not before there had been 11 knockdowns, including one on a first-round punch by Firpo that knocked

Dempsey out of the ring. Sportswriters into whose
laps he fell shoved the champion back into the ring
in time to save him from losing his crown.

July 15: The **U.S. Open golf tournament** was won by
Robert T. "Bobby" Jones, an amateur who beat Robert Cruickshank by two strokes in a playoff round.

Aug 18: The **U.S. Lawn Tennis Association singles
championships** were won by Helen Wills in the
women's division and William T. Tilden in the men's
division (Sept. 15).

Aug 30-Sep 1: The **Davis Cup** international tennis challenge round was won for the fourth year in a row by
the U.S., defeating Australia four matches to one.

Sep 29: The **PGA golf tournament** was won by Gene
Sarazen, who beat Walter Hagen by one stroke.

Oct 10-15: The 20th annual **World Series** was won by
the New York Yankees (AL), defeating the New York
Giants (NL) four games to two.

1924

I. Civil Rights
Exploration and Settlement
Government
Statistics
Wars

Republican victory in the presidential election was
anticipated. The Democrats had torn themselves
apart in a struggle for the nomination. Gov. Alfred E.
Smith of New York represented the East and the big
cities, and William G. McAdoo of Tennessee, the
southern and western parts of the country. The eventual nominee was John W. Davis, an able man but
almost unknown to the voters. The Republicans, on
the other hand, could point with pride to Calvin Coolidge and a record of prosperity. The Democrats tried
to make much of the scandals of the Harding admin-

istration but failed to stir the electorate. In fact, despite a strong third party in the field, only about half of those eligible to vote did so.

June 12: The **Republican National Convention nominated Pres. Coolidge** for reelection and Charles G. Dawes of Illinois for the vice presidency.

June 19: The **Farmer-Labor Progressive Party National Convention** nominated Duncan MacDonald of Illinois for the presidency and William Bouck of Washington for the vice presidency. On July 10 the candidates stepped down and William Z. Foster and Benjamin Gitlow became the nominees.

June 30: In the **Teapot Dome** oil leasing scandal, a federal grand jury indicted Albert B. Fall, former secretary of the interior; Harry Sinclair, president of Mammoth Oil Company; Edward L. Doheny, president of Pan-American Oil and Transport Company; and Edward L. Doheny, Jr., on charges of bribery and conspiracy to defraud the United States. Sinclair was accused of bribing Fall to secure a lease for the Teapot Dome reserve in Wyoming. The Dohenys were charged with giving a $100,000 bribe to Fall in return for leases on the Elk Hills naval reserve in California.

July 4: The **Conference for Progressive Political Action nominated Sen. Robert M. La Follette,** Republican of Wisconsin, for the presidency and (July 18) Sen. Burton K. Wheeler of Montana for the vice presidency.

July 9: The **Democratic National Convention nominated John W. Davis** of West Virginia for the presidency on the 103rd ballot. Charles W. Bryan of Nebraska, brother of William Jennings Bryan, was nominated for the vice presidency.

July 10: The **Workers' Party National Convention** nominated William Z. Foster of Illinois for the presidency and Benjamin Gitlow of New York for the vice presidency.

Nov 4: Calvin Coolidge was reelected president of the United States. Charles G. Dawes was elected vice president. The electoral vote was Coolidge, 382; John W. Davis, Democratic candidate, 136; Robert M. La

Follette, Progressive candidate, 13. The popular vote
was Coolidge, 15,725,016; Davis, 8,385,503; La Follette, 4,822,856; Herman P. Faris, Prohibition candidate, 57,520; Frank T. Johns, Socialist Labor candidate, 36,429; and William Z. Foster, Farmer-Labor
Progressive and Workers' Party candidate, 36,386. In
congressional elections the Republicans picked up
five seats in the Senate for a 56–39 majority, with one
seat going to a minor party. In the House the Republicans picked up 22 seats for a 247–183 majority, with
four seats going to minor parties.

II. Architecture
Arts and Music
Popular Entertainment
Publishing
Theater

Light operas were a very popular form of theatrical
entertainment in the 1920s. They were upbeat and
romantic for the most part, and this went well with
the generally content American public. No composer
of such works was more popular than Rudolf Friml,
who was born in Prague in 1881 and settled in New
York City in 1906. Friml wrote the music for some 33
light operas, most of which now are long forgotten.
One of his most popular works was *Rose Marie,* with
libretto by Otto Harbach and Oscar Hammerstein II
and music by Friml and Herbert Stothart. It opened
at the Imperial Theatre in New York on Sept. 2 and
ran for 557 performances. *Rose Marie* contained two
of Friml's best remembered songs, "Indian Love Call"
and "Rose Marie." Two other well-known Friml oper-
ettas were *The Firefly* (1912) and *The Vagabond King*
(1925).

Among **books published** this year was *Billy Budd,
Foretopman* by Herman Melville, a work of beauty
and force that the author completed shortly before
his death in 1891. The manuscript was found in a tin
box among the Melville family possessions. The
novel's publication was an important event in the
growing movement to recognize Melville as a literary

giant. Other books published this year included *The Marble Faun* by William Faulkner, poetry; *Tamar and Other Poems* by Robinson Jeffers; *How to Write Short Stories* by Ring Lardner, a collection that brought him recognition as a perceptive and accomplished writer; and the *Autobiography* of Mark Twain.

May 11: Pulitzer prizes were awarded for the following: fiction, *The Able McLaughlins* by Margaret Wilson; biography, *From Immigrant to Inventor* by Michael I. Pupin; history, *The American Revolution—A Constitutional Interpretation* by Charles Howard McIlwain; poetry, *New Hampshire: A Poem with Notes and Grace Notes* by Robert Frost; drama, *Hell-Bent fer Heaven* by Hatcher Hughes.

III. Business and Industry
Education
Philosophy and Religion
Science

By early 1923 Germany, in default in reparations payments called for by the Treaty of Versailles, was undergoing extreme monetary inflation. It was clear that economic instability in Europe was a danger to U.S. economic growth. On Dec. 15, 1923, Pres. Calvin Coolidge had appointed Charles G. Dawes, a banker and government official, to head a commission to study the problem. On Apr. 9, 1924, the commission proposed what came to be known as the Dawes Plan, a program to reorganize German debt payments and stabilize its currency. The plan substantially reduced Germany's reparations, which had been set at the enormous sum of 132,000,000,000 marks. Payments would be graduated from 1,000,000,000 gold marks in the first year to 2,500,000,000 in the fifth. The plan was agreed to at an international conference that began in London on July 16, and that went into effect on Sept. 1. The economic crisis was alleviated for a time.

Ford auto prices hit their lowest point after a series of price cuts: $290 without a self-starter. The price for the Model T had been $950 back in 1909.

Jan 1: The number of **radios** in U.S. homes was over 2,500,000. In 1920 there had been no more than 5000 receivers in the U.S., most of them in the hands of experimenters and technicians.

June 2: The struggle against **child labor** took the form of a proposed amendment to the Constitution. But by 1950 only 26 of the necessary 36 states had ratified the amendment.

June 15: The **Ford Motor Company** announced manufacture of its 10,000,000th automobile. Ford had taken seven years to make the first million cars, but only 132 working days to make the tenth million.

IV. Fashion
   Folkways
   Holidays
   Social Issues and Crime
   Sports

Americans' general enthusiasm for sports made college football a natural for prime interest, professional football being in its infancy in the early 1920s. Among players of the time, the best known was Harold "Red" Grange of the University of Illinois, dubbed the Galloping Ghost of the Gridiron, who scored 31 touchdowns in his college career. The best-known team was Notre Dame, known as the Fighting Irish even though many of the team's players had no Irish connection. This year Notre Dame won all nine of its games and took the national college football championship. The team's success was due in large part to its coach, Knute Rockne, who did much to revolutionize the game by stressing the use of the forward pass and by drilling his players to near perfection.

Jan 25-Feb 4: The **first Winter Olympics** was held at Chamonix, France. The U.S. finished fourth in the unofficial team standings, behind Norway, Finland, and Great Britain, and won one gold medal.

May 4-July 27: At the **Summer Olympics** in Paris, France, the U.S. took first place in unofficial team standings for the eighth consecutive time and won 45 gold medals.

May 12: The **PGA golf tournament** was won by Walter Hagen.

June 6: The **U.S. Open golf tournament** was won by Cyril Walker, who beat Bobby Jones by three strokes.

July 21: **Nathan Leopold and Richard Loeb** were sentenced to life imprisonment for the kidnaping and murder of Bobby Franks in one of the strangest and most publicized crime cases of the twentieth century. The two well-educated young men had decided on a random killing, apparently to see what the experience would be like. Loeb was killed by a fellow inmate on Jan. 28, 1936, after 12 years in prison. Leopold was ultimately released on parole on Mar. 13, 1958. He died on Aug. 29, 1971, at age 66.

Aug 16: The **U.S. Lawn Tennis Association singles championships** were won by Helen Wills in the women's division and William T. Tilden in the men's division (Sept. 2).

Sep 11-13: The **Davis Cup** international tennis challenge round was won for the fourth year running by the U.S., defeating Australia in five straight matches.

Oct 4-10: The 21st annual **World Series** was won by the Washington Senators (AL), defeating the New York Giants (NL) four games to three.

1925

I. Civil Rights
Exploration and Settlement
Government
Statistics
Wars

The rapid development of aviation technology and the use of the airplane in World War I combat led to a controversy over the future of military air power. Gen. William "Billy" Mitchell, who had served during the war in the Army's air service, was convinced that air power would dominate future warfare. He set out to prove it and, in tests from 1921 to 1923, had land-based bombers attack and sink obsolete warships off the Virginia coast. In 1923 he predicted that bombers would make battleships useless, an opinion that was resented by Navy admirals. On Sept. 5 and 9, 1925, he charged government officials and military commanders with "incompetency, criminal negligence, and almost treasonable administration of national defense." As a result Mitchell was brought before a court-martial on Oct. 28, charged with "conduct prejudicial to good order and military discipline, insubordination, and utterances contemptuous of the War and Navy departments." On Dec. 17 he was found guilty and suspended without pay from rank, command, and duty for five years. Mitchell resigned from the service on Jan 29, 1926, and died in 1936.

Jan 5: The **first woman governor** in U.S. history, Mrs. William B. Ross, was inaugurated governor of Wyoming.

Aug 8: The **Ku Klux Klan** held a massive political demonstration in Washington, D.C. Some 40,000 white-robed klansmen and klanswomen marched down Pennsylvania Ave. in a massive parade that reflected the Klan's resurgence in strength during the 1920s. They did not wear their hoods, which were prohibited by a local ordinance against wearing masks. Many of the marchers were seen to raise their arms in a manner much like the fascist salute. It was probably the largest Klan parade on record, although there had been larger gatherings of Klan members.

II. Architecture
Arts and Music
Popular Entertainment
Publishing
Theater

The early 1920s saw first publication of several magazines that were unlike any published before. They were in keeping with the faster pace of life in the postwar world. *Reader's Digest*, with its condensed articles for quick reading, was founded in 1921. *Time*, a news magazine with a jazzy, know-it-all-style began publication in 1923. And on Feb. 21, 1925, a new type of magazine appeared with the founding of *The New Yorker*, edited by Harold Ross. It was said to be for the "caviar sophisticates" and "not for the old lady in Dubuque." It set new styles in fiction and humor, and featured cartoons that spoke for themselves or carried only one-line captions. Its reviews of books, plays, and films set high standards. The first issue was 32 pages and sold for 15 cents.

Among **books published** this year was *An American Tragedy* by Theodore Dreiser, a novel based on an actual murder in upstate New York in 1906. Dreiser explored the influence of money on human actions as well as the importance of heredity in this story. Other books published included *Manhattan Transfer* by John Dos Passos, a novel that presented in kaleidoscopic fashion a fictional cross-section of New York City; *The Great Gatsby* by F. Scott Fitzgerald, the classic novel of the Jazz Age; *Porgy* by Du Bose Heyward, a novel that was the basis for his successful 1927 play *Porgy and Bess*, written with his wife Dorothy, and George Gershwin's 1935 opera *Porgy and Bess*; *Roan Stallion, Tamar, and Other Poems* by Robinson Jeffers; *Arrowsmith* by Sinclair Lewis, a novel about an idealistic medical researcher and the forces at work in the world of scientific research; *The Song of the Indian Wars* by John G. Neihardt, the third installment of the poet's *Cycle of the West*; and *A Draft of XVI Cantos* by Ezra Pound, the first part of a continuing work remarkable for its scholarship, poetic versatility and, for most readers, its obscurity.

Apr 26: Pulitzer prizes were awarded for the following: fiction, *So Big* by Edna Ferber; biography, *Barrett Wendell and His Letters* by M. A. DeWolfe Howe; history, *A History of the American Frontier* by Frederic L. Paxson; poetry, *The Man Who Died Twice* by Edwin Arlington Robinson; drama, *They Knew What They Wanted* by Sidney Howard.

III. Business and Industry
   Education
   Philosophy and Religion
   Science

Labor unions did not benefit from the prosperity of the 1920s. In 1921 the American Federation of Labor had almost 4,000,000 members, but by 1929 it was down to 2,961,096. The recession of 1921–1922 hurt, and employers' associations offered strong opposition to organized labor. In addition, there were unfavorable court decisions, such as the 1923 Supreme Court ruling declaring unconstitutional a minimum wage law in the District of Columbia. The decision challenged the legality of similar laws in several states.

Of the many **automobile manufacturing companies** that were founded before 1905, only 15 were still in existence: Apperson (1901); Buick (1903); Cadillac (1902); Ford (1903); Franklin (1900); Haynes (1896); Locomobile (1899); Maxwell (1904); Olds (1897); Overland (1902); Packard (1902); Peerless (1900); Pierce-Arrow (1901); Stearns (1900); and Studebaker (1898). More than 1000 had failed.

A **National Spelling Bee** was initiated by the Louisville, Ky., *Courier Journal*. In 1939, the annual event came under sponsorship of the Scripps-Howard newspapers.

Jan 24: A **total solar eclipse** was seen in New York City for the first time in three centuries.

July 10-21: The celebrated **Scopes monkey trial** was held in Dayton, Tenn. John T. Scopes had been arrested on May 5 for teaching the theory of evolution to his students in violation of state law. Scopes was defended by Clarence Darrow and Dudley Field Malone. William Jennings Bryan was one of the prosecuting attorneys. Darrow questioned Bryan on his fundamentalist beliefs during the trial (July 20). The trial was thought to have been too severe a strain on Bryan, who died on July 26. Scopes was convicted and fined $100.

Sep 3: In an **airship disaster,** the U.S. Army dirigible

Shenandoah was wrecked in a storm near Ava, Ohio, killing 14 persons. In spite of this and similar disasters, advocates of lighter-than-air machines continued to espouse their craft.

Oct: The **Florida land boom** reached a peak about this time. Speculation in Florida properties was said to surpass any other business stampede in U.S. his-

Oct 16: Evolutionary theory was prohibited by the Texas State Text Book Board in any of its school textbooks.

IV. Fashion
    Folkways
    Holidays
    Social Issues and Crime
    Sports

The tempos of popular dances increased along with the pace of life in the Jazz Age. Sweeping the country in the early 1920s was the Charleston, an energetic dance that called for outward heel kicks and an up and down movement achieved by bending the knees to the syncopated rhythm of jazz. The dance had been performed in Charleston, S.C., as early as 1903, but its performance in the 1923 Broadway musical *Runnin' Wild* made the Charleston a hit elsewhere. The Charleston went well with short skirts and short hair. One writer claimed that in this period some 30,000,000 Americans danced frequently.

June 5: The **U.S. Open golf tournament** was won by Willie Macfarlane, who beat Robert T. "Bobby" Jones by one stroke in the second round of a playoff.

Aug 24: The **U.S. Lawn Tennis Association singles championships** were won by Helen Wills, for the third time running, in the women's division and William T. Tilden, for the sixth time in a row, in the men's division (Sept. 19).

Sep 12: The **Davis Cup** international tennis challenge round was won for the sixth straight time by the U.S., defeating France in five straight matches.

Sep 26: The **PGA golf tournament** was won by Walter Hagen.

Oct 7-15: The 22nd annual **World Series** was won by the Pittsburgh Pirates (NL), who beat the Washington Senators (AL) four games to three.

1926

I. Civil Rights
Exploration and Settlement
Government
Statistics
Wars

The question of whether the U.S. should join the Permanent Court of International Justice, which had been established in 1919 as part of the League of Nations, continued to be controversial. On Jan. 27, 1926, the Senate approved membership by a 76–17 vote, but it attached five reservations. Four were acceptable to the members of the World Court but one, relating to advisory opinions, was not. On Dec. 9, 1929, Pres. Herbert Hoover authorized the signing of a protocol of adherence that contained provisions agreed to by both the court and the U.S., but when this was submitted to the Senate, action on it was blocked. Pres. Franklin D. Roosevelt made another attempt, on Jan. 16, 1935, but the Senate rejected membership by a vote of 52–35.

May 10: U.S. **Marines landed in Nicaragua** following an uprising (May 2) led by Gen. Augusto César Sandino against Emiliano Chamorro, who had seized power in Oct. 1925. The force, under Rear Adm. Julian L. Latimer, was withdrawn on June 5.

Sep 18: A disastrous **hurricane** swept Florida and the Gulf states, killing 372 people and injuring more than 6000. Some 5000 homes were destroyed by the storm, leaving almost 18,000 families homeless. Property damage was estimated at more than $80,000,000.

Nov 2: In **congressional elections** the Democrats

made gains in both houses. In the Senate the Republicans led 49–46, with one seat going to a minor party. In the House the Republicans' majority was reduced to 237–195, with three seats going to minor parties.

Dec 10: The **Nobel Peace Prize** for 1925 was awarded jointly to Vice Pres. Charles G. Dawes, for his work on the Dawes Plan of 1924 for reconstruction of German finances, and to Sir Austen Chamberlain of England, for his years of work to promote peace in Europe.

II. Architecture
   Arts and Music
   Popular Entertainment
   Publishing
   Theater

About the turn of the century traditional music had begun to give way to a wave of highly original and experimental works by such composers as Charles Ives, Igor Stravinski, and Edgard Varèse. One of the exponents of a dissonant, neoclassic style was the composer Virgil Thomson. His *Sonata da chiesa* [Church Sonata] for E flat clarinet, C trumpet, viola, F horn, and trombone, completed this year, was in this vein. Its second movement incorporated a tango, which aroused considerable comment. Later Thomson changed his style. His works included several operas, the ballet *Filling Station* (1937), and music for the film *River* (1937). He also served as music critic of the New York *Herald Tribune* from 1940 to 1954.

Among **books published** this year was *Abraham Lincoln, The Prairie Years* by Carl Sandburg, the first two volumes of the poet's landmark six-volume biography of Lincoln. Other books published this year included *The Mauve Decade* by Thomas Beer, a study of American life in the 1890s; *The Story of Philosophy* by Will Durant; *Soldiers' Pay* by William Faulkner, the author's first novel; *The Sun Also Rises* by Ernest Hemingway, a novel of postwar disillusion that has become an American classic; *The Weary Blues* by

Langston Hughes, poetry; and *Topper* by Thorne Smith, a novel about a timid soul, Cosmo Topper, and two zany ghosts who befriend him.

Ferdinand "Jelly Roll" Morton began a series of recordings made with his Red Hot Peppers in Chicago. The records, some of the most important in the history of jazz, included "Black Bottom Stomp," "Smoke House Blues," "Original Jelly Roll Blues," and "Doctor Jazz." The band consisted of George Mitchell, Omer Simeon, Kid Ory, Johnny St. Cyr, John Lindsay, and Andrew Hilaire.

May 3: Pulitzer prizes were awarded for the following: fiction, *Arrowsmith* by Sinclair Lewis; biography, *The Life of Sir William Osler* by Harvey Cushing; history, *The History of the United States* by Edward Channing; poetry, *What's O'Clock* by Amy Lowell; drama, *Craig's Wife* by George Kelly.

May 5: Sinclair Lewis declined the Pulitzer Prize award for his novel *Arrowsmith*, declaring that prizes tend to make writers "safe, polite, obedient and sterile." Lewis urged all novelists to refuse such awards if they wished to remain free.

III. Business and Industry
Education
Philosophy and Religion
Science

Evangelists offering various approaches to salvation continued to attract followers. A leading figure in the movement was Aimee Semple McPherson, who had founded the International Church of the Foursquare Gospel and in 1923 had opened the Angelus Temple in Los Angeles, Calif. She was successful in attracting a following in California. Then, on May 18, 1926, she disappeared while at the beach. Her followers believed she had drowned. About a month later Sister Aimee, as she liked to be called, turned up in Mexico, claiming she had been kidnaped. Investigation revealed she had run off with a former operator of her radio station. The affair caused a sensation. McPherson was tried for fraud and acquitted, but her days of glory were coming to an end.

The **40-hour work week** was introduced by Henry Ford to boost the ailing automobile industry. American industrial leaders were shocked, but the proposition was warmly received by the AFL as a means of checking overproduction and limiting unemployment.

Feb 9: Teaching of the **theory of evolution** was prohibited in the public schools of Atlanta, Ga., by a decision handed down by the Board of Education.

Mar 7: The first successful **transatlantic radiotelephone conversation** was held between New York City and London at a demonstration by the American Telephone and Telegraph Company, The Radio Corporation of America, and the British General Post Office.

May 9: The **first successful flight over the North Pole** was made by Rear Adm. Richard E. Byrd and Floyd Bennett.

IV. Fashion
   Folkways
   Holidays
   Social Issues and Crime
   Sports

A new kind of heavyweight boxing champion was crowned in 1926. James Joseph "Gene" Tunney, born in New York City, reflected a more refined background than that of most professional fighters. A man of intellect as well as action, he liked the company of college professors. On Sept. 23 Tunney beat the champion, Jack Dempsey, on points in a ten-round bout in Philadelphia. The fight attracted a crowd of 118,736 and generated record receipts of $1,895,723. The next year, on Sept. 22, the two met in a rematch in Chicago and again Tunney won the decision. That fight was controversial because of a so-called long count in the seventh round, when Tunney was knocked down but the referee refused to start the count until Dempsey went to a neutral corner. The

rematch attracted an even larger crowd, about
145,000 people, and set another record for gate receipts, $2,658,660. Tunney, a better boxer but far less
colorful figure than the dethroned champion, retired
undefeated in 1928.

July 10: The **U.S. Open golf tournament** was won by
Robert T. "Bobby" Jones.

Aug 6: The **first woman to swim the English Channel**
was Gertrude Ederle of New York City, 19, who accomplished the feat in 14 hrs., 31 min.

Sep 11: The **Davis Cup** international tennis challenge
round was won for the seventh time in a row by the
U.S., defeating France four matches to one.

Sep 25: The **PGA golf tournament** was won by Walter
Hagen.

Oct 2-10: The 23rd annual **World Series** was won by
the St. Louis Cardinals (NL), who defeated the New
York Yankees (AL) four games to three.

1927

I. Civil Rights
Exploration and Settlement
Government
Statistics
Wars

On May 20, 1927, Charles A. Lindbergh, a 25-year-old
aviator, took off from Roosevelt Field, Long Island,
in the monoplane *Spirit of St. Louis,* and headed for
Paris, 3600 miles away. The world held its breath as
infrequent reports of his progress were heard. At last,
33½ hours after he took off, Lindbergh landed at
Orly, completing the first nonstop solo flight from
New York to Paris. He was welcomed by a crowd
estimated at 100,000. Lindbergh, tall, lanky, shy, and
soft spoken, was modest about his feat, but the world

considered him a hero. Pres. Calvin Coolidge sent a
Navy cruiser to bring him home. Lindbergh's ticker-
tape parade up Broadway in New York City was
watched by an estimated 4,000,000 people.

Aug 2: Pres. **Calvin Coolidge declined renomination,**
announcing "I do not choose to run for president in
1928." It had been generally assumed that he would
seek reelection.

Aug 23: Nicola Sacco and Bartolomeo Vanzetti were
executed in Massachusetts despite agitation in support of them. Many thought the two were innocent of
the 1920 killing of a factory guard and were being
railroaded for their radical beliefs.

Oct 10: The lease of the **Teapot Dome** oil reserve lands
in Wyoming to the Mammoth Oil Company by for-
mer interior secretary Albert B. Fall was ruled by the
Supreme Court to have been fraudulently negotiated
and therefore invalid.

Dec 17: In a **submarine disaster,** the entire crew of 40
of the U.S. submarine *S-4* died after the craft, attempting to surface off Provincetown, Mass., collided
with the Coast Guard destroyer *Paulding* and sank.
Divers said they heard tappings on the inside of the
submarine and pleas for food and water for three
days but were helpless to free the trapped men. On
Jan. 4 the first bodies were removed.

II. Architecture
    Arts and Music
    Popular Entertainment
    Publishing
    Theater

This year the monument at Mount Rushmore, S.D.,
was dedicated, a colossal 500-foot sculpture carved
on the side of the mountain by Gutzon Borglum. Visible for 60 miles were the busts of George Washington, Thomas Jefferson, Abraham Lincoln, and Theodore Roosevelt. Borglum died in 1941, and his work
was completed by his son, Lincoln. In 1916 Borglum
had begun a similar work on Stone Mt., Ga., as a

Confederate memorial, but he ended his association with the project in the mid-1920s because of disagreement with the sponsors.

Among **books published** this year was *The Bridge of San Luis Rey* by Thornton Wilder, a novel exploring the nature of destiny and divine providence in connection with the deaths of five persons in a bridge collapse. Other books published this year included *Blue Voyage* by Conrad Aiken, the author's first novel; *Death Comes for the Archbishop* by Willa Cather, a novel of the Southwest during the age of Spanish exploration and settlement; *Copper Sun* and *The Ballad of the Brown Girl*, both volumes by the poet Countee Cullen; *Elmer Gantry* by Sinclair Lewis, a novel; *archy and mehitabel* by Don Marquis, adventures in free verse of archy the cockroach and his friend mehitabel, a cat; *Giants in the Earth* by Ole Rölvaag, a novel of the Norwegian settlement of Dakota Territory in the nineteenth century; and *Oil!* by Upton Sinclair, a novel based in part on the Teapot Dome oil leasing scandal.

May 2: Pulitzer prizes were awarded for the following: fiction, *Early Autumn* by Louis Bromfield; biography, *Whitman* by Emory Holloway; history, *Pinckney's Treaty* by Samuel Flagg Bemis; poetry, *Fiddler's Farewell* by Leonora Speyer; drama, *In Abraham's Bosom* by Paul Green.

Oct 6: The **first talking motion picture** using the sound-on-film process was released. The film was *The Jazz Singer*, starring Al Jolson.

III. Business and Industry
Education
Philosophy and Religion
Science

This was a period of tremendous growth for the radio industry. As stations of all types proliferated and available output power climbed, it became clear that a supervisory body was needed. On Feb. 23, 1927, the

Radio Control Act was signed by Pres. Calvin Coolidge. It authorized establishment of a five-man Federal Radio Commission, each commissioner to supervise one of the five zones into which the country was divided. The commission was authorized to classify types of stations, assign frequency bands for each type, and issue rules and regulations to prevent interference between stations. It also was given power to rule on operating changes requested by radio stations. The Federal Radio Commission was temporary. Its authority reverted to the secretary of commerce after one year, after which the commission became an appellate body, ruling on appeals of decisions made by the secretary of commerce. Nonetheless, it brought some order to radio. In 1934 it was superseded by the Federal Communications Commission (FCC).

Jan 7: Commercial **transatlantic telephone service** was opened between New York City and London. Walter S. Gifford, president of the American Telephone and Telegraph Company, officially inaugurated the line by saying, "Hello, London."

Spring: The **15,000,000th Model T Ford** rolled off the assembly line. Shortly after this the Model T was discontinued and the Model A was introduced. Retooling took six months and cost $200,000,000, not counting losses attributable to nonproduction.

Apr 7: The first successful demonstration of **television** took place in New York City. Walter S. Gifford, president of the American Telephone and Telegraph Company, in New York City spoke with and saw Sec. of Commerce Herbert Hoover, who was in his office in Washington, D.C.

July 29: An electric respirator, later called the **iron lung,** was installed at Bellevue Hospital, New York City. Devised by two physicians, Philips Drinker and Louis A. Shaw of Harvard University, the new device was useful in overcoming many kinds of respiratory failure.

Nov 10: The **Nobel Prize in Physics** was awarded jointly to Arthur Holly Compton of the University of Chicago for his discovery of the Compton effect, ob-

served in collisions of x-rays and gamma rays and
their variation in wavelength; and to Charles Thomson Rees Wilson of Scotland for his development of
the vapor condensation method for tracking the
paths of electrically charged particles.

Nov 13: The **Holland Tunnel,** the first underwater
motor vehicle tunnel in the U.S., was opened to commercial traffic. The tunnel, linking Manhattan with
New Jersey, had two tubes, each large enough to accommodate two lanes of traffic.

IV. Fashion
Folkways
Holidays
Social Issues and Crime
Sports

In the 1920s baseball changed from a pitcher's game,
characterized by relatively few runs scored and even
fewer home runs, to a slugger's game. The leading
hitter was George Herman "Babe" Ruth, who had
begun his major league career in 1914 as a pitcher for
the Boston Red Sox (AL). Ruth joined the New York
Yankees (AL) in 1920 and hit 54 home runs that season, a new record. The next year his total was 59; in
1927 he knocked out a record 60, hitting the last one
on Sept. 30. The record-setting blow came on a pitch
by Tom Zachary, of the Washington Senators. Ruth's
record stood until 1961 when another Yankee, Roger
Maris, hit 61 home runs. (In Ruth's day the season
consisted of 154 games; in Maris's time, 162.) When
the Babe's career ended in 1935 he had hit 714 homers, a record surpassed only by Hank Aaron, of the
Milwaukee (and later Atlanta) Braves (NL), who
reached a total of 755 in 1976.

Walter Johnson, pitcher for the Washington Senators (AL), ended the last season of his 20-year career
by setting two major league career records. Johnson
had pitched a total of 113 shutouts and struck out
3503 batters.

June 16: The **U.S. Open golf tournament** was won by
Tommy Armour.

July 2: At the **Wimbledon** tennis championships,

Helen Wills won the women's singles title. Other titles won by U.S. players were men's doubles, Francis
T. Hunter and William T. Tilden (July 4); women's
doubles, Helen Wills and Elizabeth Ryan (July 5);
mixed doubles, Francis T. Hunter and Elizabeth
Ryan (July 5).

Aug 30: The **U.S. Lawn Tennis Association singles
championship** were won by Helen Wills in the
women's division and Rene Lacoste of France in the
men's division (Sept. 17).

Sep 10: The **Davis Cup** international tennis challenge
round was won by France, which defeated the defending U.S. team three matches to two. The U.S.
would not regain the cup until 1937.

Oct 5-8: The 24th annual **World Series** was won by the
New York Yankees (AL), who swept the Pittsburgh
Pirates (NL) in four straight games.

Nov 5: The **PGA golf tournament** was won by Walter
Hagen, for an unprecedented fourth time in a row.

1928

I. Civil Rights
Exploration and Settlement
Government
Statistics
Wars

The presidential election campaign of 1928 was
marked by a clash of personalities and positions. The
Republican candidate, Herbert Hoover, was known
as a manager who got things done. His Democratic
opponent, Gov. Alfred E. Smith of New York, was a
Catholic who favored repeal of the Eighteenth
Amendment. In addition, he was perceived as a big-
city politician, although he was a liberal reformer.
Radio played an important part in a campaign for the
first time, and Smith's harsh voice did not go over

well. The attack on his Catholicism was vicious, and the election brought out nearly two-thirds of the registered voters. For the first time since the Civil War, the Republicans carried some of the southern states.

Apr 13-18: The **Socialist Party National Convention** nominated **Norman Thomas** of New York for the presidency and James H. Maurer of Pennsylvania for the vice presidency.

June 12-15: The **Republican National Convention** nominated **Herbert Hoover** of California for the presidency and Charles Curtis of Kansas for the vice presidency.

June 26-29: The **Democratic National Convention** nominated **Gov. Alfred E. Smith** of New York for the presidency and Sen. Joseph T. Robinson of Arkansas for the vice presidency.

Aug 27: The **Kellogg-Briand Peace Pact** was subscribed to by 15 nations at Paris, France. The pact called for outlawing war and settling international controversies by arbitration. The pact was eventually signed by 62 nations.

Nov 6: Herbert Hoover was elected president of the United States in a landslide Republican victory. Charles Curtis was elected vice president. The electoral vote was Hoover, 444; Alfred E. Smith, Democratic candidate, 87. The popular vote was Hoover, 21, 392,190; Smith, 15,016,443; Norman Thomas, Socialist candidate, 267,835; William Z. Foster, Workers' Party candidate, 48,228; Verne L. Reynolds, Socialist Labor candidate, 21,181; William F. Varney, Prohibition candidate, 20,106; Frank E. Webb, Farmer Labor candidate, 6391. In congressional elections the Republicans increased their majorities in both houses, leading in the Senate 56–39, with one seat going to a minor party, and controlling the House 267–167, with one seat held by a minor party.

II. Architecture
   Arts and Music
   Popular Entertainment
   Publishing
   Theater

American poets have frequently used U.S. history as material for their works. The most prominent such writer in the 1920s was Stephen Vincent Benét, whose *John Brown's Body* was published this year. It was a long narrative poem about the abolitionist hero, evoking the period of strained North-South relations before the Civil War. Benét introduced an even larger project in poetic history with the publication of *Western Star* in 1943. It was the first part of an epic poem that was to trace the westward migration across the continent. *Western Star* depicted the settling of Jamestown and Plymouth colonies. Benét's death in 1943 put an end to the work.

Among **books published** this year was *Scarlet Sister Mary* by Julia Peterkin, a realistic and sympathetic chronicling of the life of a black woman on a South Carolina plantation. The novel was awarded the Pulitzer Prize in 1929 and was dramatized the following year. Other books published this year were *West-Running Brook* by Robert Frost, a collection of poetry; *The Man Who Knew Coolidge* by Sinclair Lewis, a novel; *Buck in the Snow,* a collection of poems by Edna St. Vincent Millay; *Good Morning, America* by Carl Sandburg, poetry; and *Boston* by Upton Sinclair, a novel.

Walt Disney introduced his most famous animated character, Mickey Mouse, in the cartoon *Plane Crazy,* the first cartoon released by Walt Disney Productions. It was followed by *Galloping Gaucho* and *Steamboat Willie,* the latter introducing sound to animated film.

May 7: Pulitzer prizes were awarded for the following: fiction, *The Bridge of San Luis Rey* by Thornton Wilder; biography, *The American Orchestra and Theodore Thomas* by Charles Edward Russell; history, *Main Currents in American Thought* by Vernon L. Parrington; poetry, *Tristram* by Edwin Arlington Robinson; drama, *Strange Interlude* by Eugene O'Neill.

May 11: The **first program of scheduled television broadcasts** was inaugurated by station WGY in Schenectady, N.Y.

III. Business and Industry
　　 Education
　　 Philosophy and Religion
　　 Science

Anthropology was advancing, now concerning itself to a greater degree with the implications of its findings for modern life. No one contributed more to this process than Franz Boas, who became Columbia University's first professor of anthropology in 1899 and held the post for 37 years. The most influential American anthropologist of his time, he taught and inspired generations of younger scientists. Boas was concerned with refuting the idea that race and culture could be correlated. He attacked the idea of a master race in works such as *Anthropology and Modern Life* (1928).

May 25: The **first woman to fly across the Atlantic,** Amelia Earhart, took off from Boston with two passengers in her airplane *Friendship.*

July 30: The **first color motion pictures** in the U.S. were exhibited by George Eastman at Rochester, N.Y. The scenes ran the gamut of colorful subjects, including goldfish, peacocks, scarlet-beaked doves, butterflies, flowers, Fifth Avenue fashion models, and pretty girls in pretty dresses. Maj. Gen. James Harbord, president of RCA, and E. F. A. Alexanderson, a pioneer in television, on the strength of the showing predicted the application of color to television.

IV. Fashion
　　 Folkways
　　 Holidays
　　 Social Issues and Crime
　　 Sports

No sport expanded more in the 1920s than golf. Some of this growth was related to the social status of the game rather than to its fun or healthful properties. Along with the growth of suburbia came a proliferation of golf courses and country clubs. This made the game expensive, adding club membership fees to the considerable cost of clubs, balls, and baggy plus-fours, but every rising young executive felt it was the thing to do. By the late 1920s there were more than 5000 courses, and golfers were spending about $200,000,000 a year on the sport.

Feb 11-19: At the second **Winter Olympics** in St. Moritz, Switzerland, the U.S. finished second in team standings and won two gold medals.

June 24: The **U.S. Open golf tournament** was won by Johnny Farrell, who beat Robert T. "Bobby" Jones by one stroke in a 36-hole playoff.

July 7: At the **Wimbledon** tennis championships, Helen Wills won the women's singles title for the second year in a row. The mixed doubles title was won by Elizabeth Ryan teamed with P. D. B. Spence of South Africa.

July 26: The **world heavyweight boxing championship** was successfully defended by Gene Tunney, who scored a 12th-round knockout over Tom Heeney in a bout in New Zealand. Shortly after, Tunney announced his retirement.

July 29-Aug 12: At the **Summer Olympics** in Amsterdam, Holland, the U.S. took first place in team standings and won 24 gold medals. U.S. athletes set 17 new Olympic records, 7 world records.

Aug 27: The **U.S. Lawn Tennis Association singles championships** were won by Helen Wills in the women's division and Henri Cochet of France in the men's division (Sept. 17).

Oct 4-9: The 25th annual **World Series** was won by the New York Yankees (AL), who swept the St. Louis Cardinals (NL) in four straight games.

Oct 6: The **PGA golf tournament** was won by Leo Diegel.

1929

I. Civil Rights
Exploration and Settlement
Government
Statistics
Wars

As the 1920s neared an end, many were convinced the prosperous times that had begun in 1922 would go on forever, but beneath the surface there were signs of trouble. Several aspects of the economy had begun to decline in 1927. The appearance of growth was, in fact, being produced by wild speculation in the stock market. On Sept. 3, 1929, stock prices reached their highest levels ever, but a slow decline began. On Oct. 24 an abrupt decline began. Leading bankers tried without success to stem the tide. On Oct. 29, Black Tuesday, a record 16,410,030 shares were traded as huge blocks of stock were dumped for whatever they would bring. By Dec. 1 stocks on the New York Stock Exchange had dropped in value by $26,000,000,000. The day after the crash, Pres. Herbert Hoover said, "The fundamental business of the country . . . is on a sound and prosperous basis." In actuality the Great Depression of the 1930s had begun.

Jan 15: The **Kellogg-Briand Peace Pact** was passed by the Senate 85–1, Sen. John J. Blaine of Wisconsin casting the only negative vote.

Sep: National **income statistics** showed that at about this time, some 60% of U.S. citizens had annual incomes of less than $2000, which was estimated as the bare minimum to supply a family with the basic necessities of life.

Oct 7: In the continuing **Teapot Dome** oil leasing scandal, the trial of former Secretary of the Interior Albert B. Fall began in the Supreme Court of the District of Columbia. He was accused of accepting a

$100,000 bribe from Edward L. Doheny in return for a lease on the Elk Hills, Calif., naval oil reserve. On Oct. 25 the court declared him guilty as charged. Fall was sentenced to one year in prison and fined $100,000.

II. Architecture
Arts and Music
Popular Entertainment
Publishing
Theater

American painters were taking up the abstract style. A painter who adapted the principles of abstract art to her own distinctive style was Georgia O'Keeffe, whose *Black Flowers and Blue Larkspur* was painted in 1929. Her depictions of flowers, of which she did many, used a close-up technique. O'Keeffe lived in New Mexico for many years, until her death in 1986. Her paintings, done in an almost bleak style, captured the vastness and forbidding beauty of the Southwest in brilliant representations of bleached bones, barren hills, and desert blossoms. Her later work was more abstract than that of her early years.

Among **books published** this year was *Sartoris* by William Faulkner, the author's first novel about the fictional Yoknapatawpha County and its people, including the Sartoris, Benbow, and Snopes families. Yoknapatawpha County was modeled after Lafayette County in Mississippi, Faulkner's home. Other books published this year included *Selected Poems* by Conrad Aiken; *Red Harvest* and *The Dain Curse* by Dashiell Hammett, both detective novels; *A Farewell to Arms* by Ernest Hemingway, a novel combining a love story with a realistic depiction of war; *Dear Judas and Other Poems* by Robinson Jeffers; *Laughing Boy* by Oliver La Farge, a novel depicting Navajo Indian life; *Round Up*, a collection of stories by Ring Lardner; *Dodsworth* by Sinclair Lewis, a novel chronicling the collapse of a midwestern auto manufacturer's marriage during a trip to Europe; *Cup of Gold* by John Steinbeck, the author's first novel; and *Look Homeward, Angel* by Thomas Wolfe, a novel

introducing Wolfe's celebrated alter ego, Eugene
Gant, a sensitive and gifted young man whose quest
for adventure closely mirrored the author's own.

May 12: Pulitzer prizes were awarded for the following: fiction, *Scarlet Sister Mary* by Julia Peterkin; biography, *Life and Letters of Walter H. Page* by Burton
J. Hendrick; history, *The Organization and Administration of the Union Army, 1861–1865* by Fred Albert
Shannon; poetry, *John Brown's Body* by Stephen Vincent Benét; drama, *Street Scene* by Elmer L. Rice.

May 16: The **first Academy Awards** were presented by
the Academy of Motion Picture Arts and Sciences.
Among the winners were best picture of 1927–28,
Wings; best actor, Emil Jannings; best actress, Janet
Gaynor.

**III. Business and Industry
    Education
    Philosophy and Religion
    Science**

Sociologists were beginning to apply accepted an-
thropological principles and methods to their examinations of contemporary communities. A pioneer
study in this field, *Middletown: A Study in American
Culture* by Robert S. and Helen M. Lynd, sociologists
of Columbia University, was published this year.
"Middletown" actually was the city of Muncie, Ind.
The Lynds' study covered such areas as education,
leisure, religion, government, and community affairs. A basic finding was that the people of Middletown learned and accepted "new ways of behaving
toward material things more rapidly than new habits
addressed to persons and non-material institutions."

Apr 15: The **Birth Control Clinical Research Center**
established in New York City by Margaret Sanger
was raided by New York police. They were acting on
a complaint by the Daughters of the American Revolution. Three nurses and two doctors were arrested
and thousands of records were confiscated. The case
caused an uproar as physicians and private citizens
indicated their support of the clinic. In May the case
was thrown out of court as an infringement of a physician's right to practice medicine.

Sep: The Standard Statistics index of **common stock prices** reached an average of 216. Its climb was as follows: 100 during 1926; 114 by June 1927; 148 by June 1928; 191 by June 1929. This increase represented the biggest bull market the U.S. had ever known.

Sep 24: The **first blind airplane flight,** in which the pilot used only instruments to guide the plane, was completed by Lt. James H. Doolittle at Mitchell Field, N.Y. Doolittle had received pilot training during World War I, then studied at the University of California and MIT. During this period, Doolittle was one of the leading figures in the development of flight. In 1930 he resigned from the Army Air Corps and went to work for Shell Oil Company as head of its aviation department.

Nov 29: The **first flight over the South Pole** was completed by Lt. Commander Richard E. Byrd. The flight, from a base at Little America over the Pole and back, with a stop at an advance fueling station, lasted 19 hours. The flight was made with a Ford trimotor airplane. Byrd had started from Little America on Nov. 28 with Bernt Balchen, pilot; Harold June, radio operator; and Capt. Ashley C. McKinley, photographer and aerial surveyor. The flight to the pole and back to Little America took about 18 hours. At one point, to gain enough altitude, Byrd jettisoned a month and a half's worth of food to lighten the plane.

IV. Fashion
   Folkways
   Holidays
   Social Issues and Crime
   Sports

Criminal gangs that battled to control the illegal liquor business were widespread in Chicago, where Al "Scarface" Capone was soon to emerge as the top gangster. Between 1920 and 1927, about 250 persons were murdered in gang warfare. The climax to this almost open warfare came on Feb. 14, 1929. Five members of one gang, some of them dressed as policemen, walked into a garage on Chicago's North

Side, where seven members of the rival George "Bugs" Moran gang were about to begin the day's illegal activities. They lined the seven up against a wall and mowed them down with submachine guns. The mass murder became known as the St. Valentine's Day Massacre and it was suspected that Capone was behind the killings.

The **world heavyweight boxing championship** was up for grabs this year. Max Schmeling of Germany became a contender after successful fights against Johnny Risko (Feb. 1) and Paulino Uzcudun (June 27). Jack Sharkey defeated William L. "Young" Stribling in a ten-round bout (Feb. 27). Schmeling and Sharkey met each other in a championship fight in 1930.

June 30: The **U.S. Open golf tournament** was won by Robert T. "Bobby" Jones, who beat Al Espinosa by 23 strokes in a playoff.

July 5: At the **Wimbledon** tennis championships in England, the women's singles title was won for the third straight year by Helen Wills. On July 6 the men's doubles was won by Wilmer Allison and John Van Ryn, and the mixed doubles was won by Helen Wills and Francis T. Hunter.

Aug 24: The **U.S. Lawn Tennis Association** singles **championships** were won by Helen Wills, for the sixth time, in the women's division and William T. Tilden, for the seventh time, in the men's division (Sept. 14).

Oct 8-14: The 26th annual **World Series** was won by the Philadelphia Athletics (AL), who beat the Chicago Cubs (NL) four games to one.

Dec 7: The **PGA golf tournament** was won for the second year in a row by Leo Diegel.

1930

I. Civil Rights
Exploration and Settlement
Government
Statistics
Wars

Early in 1930 Pres. Herbert Hoover called a special session of Congress to take up tariff revision, which he had promised in his presidential campaign the previous fall. Hoover primarily wanted to have tariff rates raised on agricultural products. By the time Congress finished its work, however, it sent Hoover the Smoot-Hawley Act, a bill that included some of the highest rates in history on manufactured products. In all, duties on 890 articles were raised to high levels. Hoover signed the act into law on June 17 despite the fact that on May 4 a petition signed by 1028 economists had been sent to Washington urging defeat of the proposed legislation. Within two years, 25 nations retaliated by raising duties on U.S. goods. The economic nationalism triggered by this legislation has been blamed for deepening the worldwide depression.

The U.S. **Census** recorded a population of 122,775,046. The center of population was located three miles northeast of Linton, Green County, Ind.

Mar 13: In the **Teapot Dome** oil leasing scandal, the trial of Edward L. Doheny, charged with bribing Albert B. Fall to obtain a lease for the Elk Hills naval oil reserve, began at the Supreme Court of the District of Columbia. Doheny was acquitted on Mar. 22.

May 26: In a decision affecting enforcement of **Prohibition,** the U.S. Supreme Court ruled that purchase of intoxicating liquor was not a violation of the Constitution.

Sep 9: Immigration of foreign laborers was virtually prohibited by an order issued by the State Department, a reflection of grave concern over U.S. unemployment.

Nov 4: In **congressional elections** the Republicans lost eight seats in the Senate for a nominal 48–47 majority, with one seat going to a minor party. In the House the Democrats took a 220–214 lead, with one seat going to a minor party.

II. **Architecture**
   Arts and Music
   Popular Entertainment
   Publishing
   Theater

This year was notable for a number of events that brought serious music to radio listeners. On Mar. 16, in the first opera broadcast directly from a stage in Europe (Dresden, Germany), station WEAF in New York City carried part of a performance of Beethoven's *Fidelio.* The program was relayed to New York via shortwave transmission. On Apr. 17 the National Broadcasting Company produced the premiere of Charles Sanford Skilton's one-act Indian opera, *The Sun Bride.* And on Oct. 5 the Columbia Broadcasting System began live Sunday broadcasts of the New York Philharmonic Symphony Orchestra. Arturo Toscanini was its conductor. Seven years later the NBC Symphony Orchestra was formed with Toscanini as conductor.

Among **books published** this year was *I'll Take My Stand: Humanism and America,* an anthology of the writings of a number of southern authors, including John Crowe Ransom, Allen Tate, and Robert Penn Warren. Other books published this year included *The Bridge,* Hart Crane's most memorable work; *The 42nd Parallel* by John Dos Passos, the first novel in the author's *U.S.A.* trilogy; *As I Lay Dying* by William Faulkner, a novel; *Cimarron* by Edna Ferber, a novel; *Collected Poems* by Robert Frost; *The Maltese Falcon* by Dashiell Hammett, the classic detective novel; and *Arundel* by Kenneth Roberts, a historical novel.

The painting ***American Gothic*** was completed by

Grant Wood. Wood had applied the techniques of Flemish and German primitives in the work, which he intended as a satire. The result came to be one of the best known American paintings.

May 12: Pulitzer prizes were awarded for the following: fiction, *Laughing Boy* by Oliver La Farge; biography, *The Raven* by Marquis James; history, *The War of Independence* by Claude H. Van Tyne; poetry, *Selected Poems* by Conrad Aiken; drama, *The Green Pastures* by Marc Connelly.

Nov 5: The **Nobel Prize in Literature** was awarded to Sinclair Lewis, particularly in recognition of his novel *Babbitt*. Lewis was the first American to win the prize in literature.

III. Business and Industry
Education
Philosophy and Religion
Science

The Institute for Advanced Study was chartered this year and opened its doors three years later in Princeton, N.J. Its establishment was made possible by gifts from Louis Bamberger and his sister, Mrs. Felix Fuld. The institute's first director was Abraham Flexner, a prominent educator; among its first members was Albert Einstein. The institute was formed as a center for graduate studies. It has no classes and does not confer degrees. As the institute developed, it became known particularly as a research center in mathematics and the natural sciences.

Illiteracy in America reached a new low of 4.3% of the population, a decline of 1.7% from 1920 and a decline of 15.7% from 1870.

According to an **automobile survey,** one of every 4.9 Americans owned an automobile.

Mar 13: Identification of the planet Pluto was made from a photograph taken on Jan. 21 at Lowell Observatory in Flagstaff, Ariz. The discovery boosted the prestige of mathematical astronomers, who had predicted existence of the planet.

Aug 11: The **American Lutheran Church** was formed at Toledo, Ohio, by the merger of the Lutheran Synod of Buffalo, the Evangelical Lutheran Synod of Iowa, and the Evangelical Lutheran Joint Synod of Ohio. On Oct. 31 the church, at an organizational convention, completed the merger of seven synods in the U.S. and Canada.

Oct 30: The **Nobel Prize in Physiology or Medicine** was awarded to Dr. Karl Landsteiner of the Rockefeller Institute for his discovery of human blood groups. Landsteiner was the first American citizen to win the prize for medicine.

Dec 11: The **Bank of the United States** in New York City, with 60 local branches and 400,000 depositors, closed. More than 1300 banks throughout the country had been closed down by the deepening economic crisis.

IV. Fashion
   Folkways
   Holidays
   Social Issues and Crime
   Sports

Golf's first nationally known figure and perhaps the best golfer who ever played, Robert Tyre "Bobby" Jones, Jr., announced his retirement on Nov. 17, after a year in which he set records never achieved by any other player. On Sept. 27 he became the only player ever to make the grand slam in golf by winning the 1930 U.S. Amateur golf tournament after winning the U.S. Open, the British Open, and the British Amateur tournaments. Jones had played serious golf for only eight years, spending much of his time studying law, literature, and engineering. But of the 27 major championship tournaments he entered, he won 13. In retirement he made instructional films and, with Clifford Roberts, founded the Augusta National Golf Club in Georgia and organized the Masters Tournament, one of the major U.S. golf tournaments.

Apr 19: The **Boston Marathon** was won for the seventh time by Clarence H. DeMar of Melrose, Mass., with a time of 2 hrs., 34 min., 48.2 sec.

May 9: The 55th annual **Preakness Stakes** was won by Gallant Fox, with a time of 2:00³/₅. The jockey was Earl Sande.

May 17: The 56th annual **Kentucky Derby** was won by Gallant Fox, with a time of 2:07³/₅. The jockey was Earl Sande, who scored his third Derby victory.

May 30: The 18th annual **Indianapolis 500** auto race was won by Billy Arnold, who completed the course in 4 hrs., 58 min., 39.72 sec., with an average speed of 100.44 mph.

June 7: The 62nd annual **Belmont Stakes** was won by Gallant Fox. The jockey was Earl Sande. This was the second time that a horse had won the Triple Crown. The winning time was 2:31³/₅.

June 12: The **world heavyweight boxing championship** was won by Max Schmeling of Germany. Schmeling was awarded the victory over Jack Sharkey, who fouled him in the fourth round of the bout in New York City.

July 4: At the **Wimbledon** tennis championships, the women's singles title was won by Helen Wills, now called Helen Wills Moody, her married name. Other titles taken by Americans were men's singles, William T. Tilden (July 5); women's doubles, Helen Wills Moody and Elizabeth Ryan (July 5); men's doubles, Wilmer Allison and John Van Ryn (July 7).

July 12: The **U.S. Open golf tournament** was won by Robert T. "Bobby" Jones.

Sep 13: The **PGA golf tournament** was won by Tommy Armour.

Sep 13-17: The **America's Cup** was successfully defended by the yacht *Enterprise,* which defeated the British challenger *Shamrock V* in four straight races.

Oct 1-8: The 27th annual **World Series** was won by the Philadelphia Athletics (AL), who defeated the St. Louis Cardinals (NL) four games to two.

1931

I. Civil Rights
  Exploration and Settlement
  Government
  Statistics
  Wars

Breakdown in enforcement of the Prohibition laws appeared to be affecting law enforcement in general. As a result, in May of 1929 Pres. Herbert Hoover had appointed a National Commission on Law Observance and Law Enforcement. He named George W. Wickersham, a former U.S. attorney general, as its head. The body came to be known as the Wickersham Commission. It issued its report on Jan. 19, 1931, noting that enforcement of antiliquor laws was hindered by the great profits to be earned in illegal traffic and by the apathy, even hostility, of the general public. The commission believed enforcement should be left to the federal government. It recommended revisions but not repeal of the Eighteenth Amendment. Pres. Hoover, in submitting the report to Congress on Jan. 20, said he also did not favor repeal. The report did not result in any effective action.

Sep: A **bank panic** spread across the nation. In September 305 banks closed; in October 522 shut down. Fear that the U.S. would go off the gold standard led to hoarding of the metal throughout the country.

Dec 10: The **Nobel Peace Prize** was awarded jointly to Nicholas Murray Butler, president of Columbia University, and to Jane Addams of Chicago. Butler had been the first major figure to support the Kellogg-Briand Peace Pact of 1928, and Addams had been the first international president of the Women's International League for Peace and Freedom. She was honorary president at the time of the award.

II. **Architecture**
   Arts and Music
   Popular Entertainment
   Publishing
   Theater

Widespread disillusionment with politics, prompted in large part by the seeming inability of the federal government to end the Depression, was reflected in this year's hit musical comedy, *Of Thee I Sing*, with music by George Gershwin, lyrics by Ira Gershwin, and book by George S. Kaufman and Morrie Ryskind. It was a sharp but good-natured satire on presidential politics. The show opened at the Music Box Theatre in New York City on Dec. 26 and ran for 441 performances. When the show won the Pulitzer Prize for drama the next year, it was the first musical ever to be so honored. The title song was a hit too. A sequel, *Let 'Em Eat Cake* (1933), was less successful, having only 90 Broadway performances.

Among **books published** this year was *The Good Earth* by Pearl S. Buck, the author's first novel. For two years this best seller was at the top of the sales list in bookstores. Other books published this year included *Shadows on the Rock* by Willa Cather, a beautifully written novel set in seventeenth-century Quebec; *ViVa* by E. E. Cummings, poetry; *Newspaper Days* by Theodore Dreiser, autobiography; *Sanctuary* by William Faulkner, a novel; *American Beauty* by Edna Ferber, a novel; *The Glass Key* by Dashiell Hammett; the *Autobiography* of Lincoln Steffens; *The Forge* by T. S. Stribling, the first novel of a trilogy dealing with the fictional Vaiden family of Alabama; *The Long Christmas Dinner* by Thornton Wilder, a collection of one-act plays; and *Axel's Castle* by Edmund Wilson, a collection of essays on symbolism and symbolist writers.

Mar 3: An act making **"The Star-Spangled Banner"** the national anthem was signed by Pres. Herbert Hoover. Francis Scott Key wrote the words in 1814 during the bombardment of Fort McHenry in the War of 1812.

May 4: Pulitzer prizes were awarded for the follow-

ing: fiction, *Years of Grace* by Margaret Ayers Barnes; biography, *Charles W. Eliot* by Henry James; history, *The Coming of the War: 1914* by Bernadotte E. Schmitt; poetry, *Collected Poems* by Robert Frost; drama, *Alison's House* by Susan Glaspell.

III. Business and Industry
Education
Philosophy and Religion
Science

Research in physics in the U.S. and Europe was leading to discoveries that in a few years would be applied in production of the atomic bomb. A leader in the U.S. was Harold C. Urey, a professor of physics at Columbia University. This year Urey announced that he and his associates had discovered an isotope of hydrogen with an atomic weight of two instead of one. This was heavy hydrogen, or deuterium. Molecules of water containing deuterium atoms instead of hydrogen atoms came to be known as heavy water. This was a key component in atomic fission experiments. Urey later served as director (1942–1945) of the Manhattan Project, which developed the world's first atomic bombs.

Jan 7: **Unemployment** was estimated at between 4,000,000 and 5,000,000 by Col. Arthur Woods, head of the President's Emergency Committee for Unemployment Relief.

May 1: The **Empire State Building,** the world's tallest building, was dedicated and opened to the public in New York City.

June 23: A **flight around the world** was begun by Wiley Post and Harold Gatty, who took off from Roosevelt Field, Long Island, N.Y., in their plane *Winnie May.* They landed back at Roosevelt Field 8 days, 15 hrs., 51 min. later.

Oct 5: The **first nonstop flight across the Pacific** Ocean was completed by Hugh Herndon and Clyde Pangborn, who flew from Sabishiro, Japan, to Wenatchee, Wash., a distance of 4860 mi., in 41 hrs., 13 min.

Oct 24: The **George Washington Bridge,** linking Manhattan with New Jersey across the Hudson R., was officially opened. Gov. Franklin D. Roosevelt of New York and Gov. Morgan F. Larson of New Jersey took part in the ceremonies. The Port Authority of New York had completed the bridge eight months ahead of schedule and under budget. The bridge, one of the most beautiful and best known in the world, was opened to traffic the next day.

IV. Fashion
   Folkways
   Holidays
   Social Issues and Crime
   Sports

The American gangster was a prominent personality in the 1920s and 1930s. Foremost was Alphonse "Al" Capone, also known as "Scarface." He ruled the Chicago underworld in the 1920s with unprecedented lawlessness and brutality. It was estimated that in 1927 alone he took in $105,000,000. Finally, in 1931, Capone was indicted for income tax evasion. He was convicted on Oct. 17 and sentenced to 11 years in prison. He was released in 1939, mortally ill from syphilis. In the East, Jack "Legs" Diamond attracted the most attention because of the unusual scrapes he got into and the number of times he was wounded, but not killed, by gunfire. On Dec. 18, 1931, he was shot to death in an Albany, N.Y., boardinghouse shortly after being acquitted of kidnaping.

July 3-4: At the **Wimbledon** tennis championships, the men's singles title was won by Sidney B. Wood, Jr., 20, the youngest winner in the history of the event. The men's doubles title was won by George Lott, Jr., and John Van Ryn, and the mixed doubles was won by George Lott, Jr., and Mrs. L. A. Harper.

July 6: The **U.S. Open golf tournament** was won by Billy Burke, who beat George Von Elm by one stroke after two 36-hole playoffs.

Aug 20: The **U.S. Lawn Tennis Association singles championships** were won by Mrs. Helen Wills

Moody in the women's division and H. Ellsworth Vines, Jr., in the men's division (Sept. 12).

Sep 19: The **PGA golf tournament** was won by Tom Creavy.

Oct 1-10: The 28th annual **World Series** was won by the St. Louis Cardinals (NL), who beat the Philadelphia Athletics (AL) four games to three.

1932

I. **Civil Rights**
   Exploration and Settlement
   Government
   Statistics
   Wars

It was a trying year for the nation. Pres. Herbert Hoover tried desperately to stem the Great Depression by granting generous credit to industry and ordering a stern check on government spending. Not only did he reduce his personal salary by 20%, but he also persuaded Vice Pres. Charles Curtis and nine members of the Cabinet to accept similar cuts. Public works programs were planned to alleviate staggering unemployment. Hoover's plans, however, were never realized, for the voters insisted on a change of administration, electing Franklin D. Roosevelt to the presidency in a Democratic landslide.

The number of **unemployed** in the U.S. reached 13,000,000. National wages were 60% less than in 1929, dividends 56.6% less. Total business loss during the year was placed at $5,000,000,000 to $6,000,000,000. Two and a half years after the Oct. 1929 stock market crash, U.S. industry as a whole was operating at less than half its maximum 1929 volume.

Jan 22: The **Reconstruction Finance Corporation** was

established with $2,000,000,000 at its disposal to lend to failing banks, farm mortgage associations, building and loan societies, railroads, and insurance companies.

Mar 1: In the **Lindbergh kidnaping**, one of the most highly publicized crimes of the twentieth century, Charles A. Lindbergh, Jr., an infant of 20 months, was kidnaped from his parents' home at Hopewell, N.J. The body of the child was found on May 12, after payment of a $50,000 ransom. Outraged public opinion made kidnaping a federal crime carrying the death penalty.

May 29: The so-called **Bonus Army**, a group of some 1000 former servicemen seeking cash payments for their veterans' bonus certificates, arrived in Washington, D.C. In June other groups of veterans arrived from every section of the country, swelling the army to about 17,000. Camped in the open or in unused buildings near the Capitol, they vowed to stay until Congress authorized immediate cash in full for their certificates. A bill authorizing payment passed the House on June 15, but was killed in the Senate on June 17. The government provided money for veterans to return to their homes, but about 2000 refused the offer and did not move. Finally, on July 28, federal troops under Gen. Douglas MacArthur drove them out.

June 14-16: The **Republican National Convention renominated Pres. Hoover** for the presidency on the first ballot. Charles Curtis was renominated for the vice presidency.

June 27-July 2: The **Democratic National Convention nominated Franklin D. Roosevelt** for the presidency, ending a deadlock produced by opposing factions supporting Roosevelt, John Nance Garner of Texas, and Alfred E. Smith of New York. The deadlock was broken and Roosevelt nominated on July 1, when Garner was persuaded to give his delegates to Roosevelt in return for the vice presidential nomination. Roosevelt broke precedent by flying to Chicago to accept the nomination. In his speech, he called for a "new deal for the American people."

Nov 8: Franklin D. Roosevelt was elected president of the United States in a Democratic landslide. John Nance Garner was elected vice president. Roosevelt carried all but seven states, with 472 electoral votes to 59 for Herbert Hoover. The popular vote was Roosevelt, 22,821,857; Hoover, 15,761,841; Norman Thomas, Socialist, 881,951; William Z. Foster, Communist, 102,785; Verne L. Reynolds, Socialist Labor, 33,276; William D. Upshaw, Prohibition, 81,869; Jacob S. Coxey, Farmer Labor, 7309. In congressional elections the Democrats gained 13 Senate seats for a 60–35 majority, with one seat held by a minor party. In the House the Democrats gained 90 seats for a 310–117 majority, with five seats going to minor parties.

II. Architecture
Arts and Music
Popular Entertainment
Publishing
Theater

This year 15,279 books were published or reprinted in the U.S. Of these, 1996 were novels. The novelists' main preoccupation this year seemed to be with the problems of the South. Despite the publication of several outstanding works, not much of literary value was offered to the public. In fact, a virtual paralysis had settled over the arts. Opera houses in Chicago and Philadelphia gave no performances. A number of new orchestral works were ventured, but none with serious claim to stature. Painters looking for inspiration found it in the formalized primitivism of the Mexican artist Diego Rivera and his compatriots. Architects, deprived of the opportunity to build, chose to quarrel over the so-called International school of design. The theater enjoyed only one real hit—Philip Barry's *The Animal Kingdom*.

Among **books published** this year was *Tobacco*

Road by Erskine Caldwell. This novel, dealing with the family of Jeeter Lester, a poor Georgia sharecropper, was the basis for an enormously successful dramatization in 1933 by Jack Kirkland; it has since become an American classic. Other books published this year included *Beyond Desire* by Sherwood Anderson, a novel set in the South; *1919* by John Dos Passos, the second novel in his trilogy *U.S.A.; Light in August* by William Faulkner; and *The Store* by T. S. Stribling, the second novel of a trilogy set in the South.

E. Y. "Yip" Harburg wrote one of the most popular songs of the year, "Brother, Can You Spare a Dime."

May 2: Pulitzer prizes were awarded for the following: fiction, *The Good Earth* by Pearl S. Buck; biography, *Theodore Roosevelt* by Henry F. Pringle; history, *My Experiences in the World War* by John J. Pershing; poetry, *The Flowering Stone* by George Dillon; drama, *Of Thee I Sing* by George S. Kaufman, Morrie Ryskind, and Ira Gershwin. This was the first time a musical received the drama award.

III. Business and Industry
   Education
   Philosophy and Religion
   Science

Poor demand for goods, uncertain manufacturing conditions, and a wobbly stock market combined to make this one of the most unfavorable business years in modern history. Labor, however, hailed its most important victory to date—passage of the Federal Anti-Injunction Law, or Norris-LaGuardia Act. The battle for the five-day work week was also being won, as Pres. Herbert Hoover made it standard for most government employees. With unemployment hovering at about 11,000,000, labor could make little headway in its demands for compulsory unemployment insurance. In science, progress was made in the study of cosmic rays; in the discovery of the neutron by

James Chadwick; in the enunciation of the uncertainty principle; and in laboratory production of gamma rays. In addition, an isotope of hydrogen was produced and vitamin C was isolated and identified. Automation was fast becoming a specialty of its own with the construction of large and versatile computing machines.

May 20: Amelia Earhart became the first woman to cross the Atlantic in a solo flight when she landed near Londonderry, Ireland, 2026½ miles from Harbor Grace, Newfoundland, her starting point. The flight took 13 hrs., 30 min.

Nov 10: The **Nobel Prize in Chemistry** was awarded to Irving Langmuir "for his discoveries and investigations in surface chemistry." Langmuir conducted his prize-winning research on surface actions of glass, water, and metals. His discoveries led to improvements in incandescent lighting, reduction of light glare from glass surfaces, and cloud seeding to induce rainfall.

IV. Fashion
   Folkways
   Holidays
   Social Issues and Crime
   Sports

The movement to repeal Prohibition received a boost when the redoubtable "dry" John D. Rockefeller spoke out for the repeal of the Volstead Act. Both presidential candidates asked for its erasure from the law books. With such powerful forces against it, Prohibition was doomed. In baseball Jimmy Foxx threatened to eclipse Babe Ruth's home run record of 60, falling short by two runs. Tennis had a dazzling new name—16-year-old Frankie Parker, who mowed down veteran opposition wherever he played. The greatest blot on the nation's conscience was its fantastic crime wave. The citizens of Chicago this year shelled out some $145,000,000 to racketeers.

Feb 4-13: At the 1932 **Winter Olympics** in Lake Placid, N.Y., the third such games in history and the first held in the U.S., the U.S. team won ten gold medals and the unofficial team championship.

June 21: The world **heavyweight boxing championship** was won by Jack Sharkey, who took a 15-round decision over Max Schmeling of Germany in New York City, thus returning the title to the U.S.

June 25: The **U.S. Open golf tournament** was won by Gene Sarazen.

July 1: At the **Wimbledon** tennis championships, Helen Wills Moody won the women's singles title. H. Ellsworth Vines, Jr., won the men's singles on July 2.

July 2: The term *New Deal* was introduced by Franklin D. Roosevelt in his speech accepting the Democratic nomination for the presidency. Before the assembled delegates in Chicago, Roosevelt said: "I pledge you, I pledge myself, to a new deal for the American people. Let us all here assembled constitute ourselves prophets of a new order of competence and courage. This is more than a political campaign; it is a call to arms."

July 30-Aug 14: At the 1932 **Summer Olympics** in Los Angeles, Calif., the U.S. won 16 gold medals and the unofficial team championship.

Aug 21: The **U.S. Lawn Tennis Association singles championships** were won by Helen Hull Jacobs in the women's division and H. Ellsworth Vines, Jr., in the men's division (Sept. 3).

Sep 4: The **PGA golf tournament** was won by Olin Dutra.

Sep 28-Oct 2: The 29th annual **World Series** was won by the New York Yankees (AL), who swept the Chicago Cubs (NL) in four games.

1933

I. Civil Rights
Exploration and Settlement
Government
Statistics
Wars

The change of administration deepened the economic crisis. The low point was reached by inauguration day, with the nation gripped by a bank panic. To meet the situation, the administration demanded and was given unprecedented powers. These led to wide changes in the monetary system and to creation of an array of federal agencies to regulate private industry and find jobs for millions on government-sponsored projects. While this program, known as the New Deal, restored some confidence, its more radical measures came under conservative attack. Its critics, however, failed to win popular support. In world affairs, America's Good Neighbor policy fostered an era of Pan-American political and economic cooperation. The gravity of domestic problems distracted attention from international affairs: the rise of Adolf Hitler in Germany, warfare in the Far East, and disintegration of the League of Nations.

Feb 6: The **Twentieth Amendment** to the U.S. Constitution was adopted. It abolished the so-called lame-duck session of Congress and changed the presidential inauguration date from Mar. 4 to Jan. 20. It also specified that the vice president-elect would succeed to the presidency if the president-elect died before inauguration.

Mar 1: Bank holidays were declared in six states, effectively preventing runs on bank assets by worried depositors. By Mar. 4 bank panics reached their greatest intensity. At 4:30 A.M. that day, Gov. Herbert H. Lehman of New York declared a state bank holiday; Gov. Henry Horner of Illinois immediately followed suit.

Mar 4: Franklin D. Roosevelt was inaugurated president of the United States. In his inaugural address, Pres. Roosevelt included the memorable sentence: "The only thing we have to fear is fear itself." The address outlined an aggressive policy to deal with the economic emergency.

Mar 4: Frances Perkins, the first woman to hold a Cabinet post, was appointed secretary of labor by Pres. Franklin D. Roosevelt.

Mar 12: The **first fireside chat,** a radio address to the entire nation, was delivered by Pres. Roosevelt on this Sunday evening. His subject was the reopening of the banks during the following week.

Mar 13: Banks began reopening across the country. Before the end of the month over 75% of all banks were operating again.

Mar 31: The **Civilian Conservation Corps** (CCC) was initiated by the Reforestation Unemployment Act to create jobs through a national reforestation program.

May 12: The **Agricultural Adjustment Act** (AAA) restricted production of certain crops, to be determined by farmers, and paid them bounties for uncultivated acreage. The bounties were to be paid from the revenue obtained from a processing tax. The Supreme Court ruled the AAA unconstitutional in 1936.

May 18: The **Tennessee Valley Act** was passed, establishing the Tennessee Valley Authority (TVA). Its purpose was to control Tennessee R. floods, institute a reforestation program on marginal lands in the Tennessee R. Valley, and provide rural electrification.

June 16: The **National Industrial Recovery Act** (NIRA) was created. It established the National Recovery Administration (NRA) and the Public Works Administration (PWA). Gen. Hugh Johnson was named administrator of the NRA, and Harold L. Ickes was named head of the PWA.

June 16: The **Banking Act of 1933** was passed by Congress, establishing the Federal Bank Deposit Insurance Corporation.

Nov 8: The **Civil Works Administration** was set up with an initial appropriation of $400,000,000. Its first director was Harry L. Hopkins. The plan was intended to provide work for about 4,000,000 unemployed and to put two-thirds of the families then receiving relief on a self-sustaining basis.

Dec 5: The **Twenty-first Amendment was adopted** when it was ratified by Utah, the 36th state to do so. Prohibition in the U.S. was thereby repealed.

II. Architecture
Arts and Music
Popular Entertainment
Publishing
Theater

Theater had a lackluster year despite offerings by established playwrights and stars. The most notable exception was Eugene O'Neill's *Ah, Wilderness!* Opera houses and symphonic societies curtailed their seasons. Painters and sculptors were helped by commissions from the Civil Works Administration. At one time, the government employed as many as 2500 artists and 1000 architects, most of whom worked at supplying murals for public buildings. The two most popular films of the year were *Little Women*, starring Katherine Hepburn, and *She Done Him Wrong*, featuring Mae West.

Among **books published** this year was *Anthony Adverse* by Hervey Allen, a long, sprawling novel set in the Napoleonic era. Despite criticism concerning Allen's historical accuracy, readers made the book a best-seller. Other books published this year included *Death in the Woods*, a collection of stories by Sherwood Anderson; *Winner Take Nothing* by Ernest Hemingway, also a collection of stories; *Give Your Heart to the Hawks, and Other Poems* by Robinson Jeffers; *Principles of Harmonic Analysis* by Walter Piston, one of the most influential textbooks on the methods of modern composition; *Rabble in Arms* by Kenneth Roberts, a historical novel; and *The Autobi-*

ography of Alice B. Toklas by Gertrude Stein, which sold surprisingly well.

A significant **obscenity ruling** was handed down in New York City concerning Erskine Caldwell's novel *God's Little Acre.* City Magistrate Benjamin Greenspan exonerated the book of the charge of obscenity made by the New York Society for the Prevention of Vice. The decision was based on three criteria: consideration of the book as a whole rather than a few isolated sections, the aptness of coarse language when spoken by coarse characters, and reactions of a cross-section of citizens on reading the work.

May 4: Pulitzer prizes were awarded for the following: fiction, *The Store* by T. S. Stribling; drama, *Both Your Houses* by Maxwell Anderson; history, *The Significance of Sections in American History* by Frederick J. Turner; biography, *Grover Cleveland* by Allan Nevins; poetry, *Conquistador* by Archibald MacLeish.

Dec 6: In a major ruling on **censorship,** the ban on *Ulysses* by James Joyce was lifted by Federal Judge John M. Woolsey, who wrote in part: "[It is] a sincere and honest book. . . . I do not detect anywhere the leer of a sensualist."

III. Business and Industry
Education
Philosophy and Religion
Science

Encouraged by sympathetic legislation, especially creation of the National Labor Relations Board (NLRB), organized labor became more militant in making its demands—particularly its right to organize. The American Federation of Labor boasted 4,000,000 members in 29,669 local bodies, and counted as allies the workers enrolled in the railroad brotherhoods. Scientists, meanwhile, confirmed the discovery in 1932 of the positron (positive electron). Television pioneers were jubilantly hailing a new communication medium and pointed with pride to a cathode-ray screen already on the market. American education presented a more somber picture. Two thousand rural schools failed to open in the fall. More than 1500 commercial schools and colleges were forced to suspend activities. Some 200,000 certified teachers were unemployed, and it was estimated that 2,280,000 children were not attending school.

Average **life expectancy** was 59 years, a gain of ten years since the turn of the century.

The first report of the **National Survey of School Finance,** authorized by Congress in 1931, was delivered. The report stated that one-third of America's schoolchildren were receiving an inadequate education.

Feb 25: The **first U.S. aircraft carrier** specifically designed for the purpose, the U.S.S. *Ranger,* was christened at Newport News, Va., by Mrs. Herbert Hoover. The U.S. had other carriers, but they were ships that had been converted for use as carriers.

Oct 20: The **Nobel Prize in Physiology or Medicine** was awarded to Thomas Hunt Morgan "for his discoveries concerning the function of the chromosome in the transmission of heredity." Morgan performed his most significant experiments as head of the California Institute of Technology in Pasadena, Calif.

IV. Fashion
Folkways
Holidays
Social Issues and Crime
Sports

The Depression damped most professional sporting activities. The exception was horseracing, which boomed as never before. State legislatures, recognizing the revenue produced by betting at tracks, compromised their moral positions by encouraging the sport. Maryland this year earned some $66,000,000 from racing revenues alone. League-leading baseball clubs played before packed parks, but the losing

teams could not fill their stands. College football contests enjoyed a 13% rise in attendance over the previous season—a popularity that extended to the professional game as well.

May 27-Nov 2: The **Century of Progress Exposition**
was held in Chicago, Ill., in honor of the centennial
of the founding of Chicago.

June 10: The **U.S. Open golf tournament** was won by
Johnny Goodman.

June 21: The **world heavyweight boxing championship** was won by the Italian giant, Primo Carnera,
who knocked out Jack Sharkey at Long Island City
Bowl.

July 6: In the **first all-star baseball game,** the American League defeated the National League by a score
of 4–2. The game was held at Comiskey Park in Chicago before 49,200 fans.

July 8: The **Wimbledon** women's singles championship was won by Mrs. Helen Wills Moody.

Aug 13: The **PGA golf tournament** was won by Gene
Sarazen.

Aug 26: The **U.S. Lawn Tennis Association singles
championships** were won by Helen Hull Jacobs in
the women's division and Frederick J. Perry of Great
Britain in the men's division (Sept. 10).

Oct 3-7: The 30th annual **World Series** was won by the
New York Giants (NL), defeating the Washington
Senators (AL) four games to one.

Dec 17: In the **first National Football League (NFL)
championship playoff,** the Chicago Bears defeated
the New York Giants 23–21 to become NFL champions of 1933. This year the NFL was divided into
Eastern and Western divisions, the leaders of the
divisions meeting in a playoff game to determine the
league winner. Previously the league championship
went to the team with the highest winning percentage.

1934

I. Civil Rights
   Exploration and Settlement
   Government
   Statistics
   Wars

Federal agencies continued to control many phases
of American life, but there was no controlling the
weather. Plagued by record cold snaps in February
and searing heat in July, farmers watched their crops
wither in the most destructive drought the Midwest
had ever seen. Rising agricultural prices afforded
temporary relief for them, but not for city dwellers.
Internal affairs were complicated by congressional
and local elections. Republican orators had only one
real issue—the dubious constitutionality of some of
the more radical New Deal provisions. According to
opponents of the New Deal, federal boondoggles had
reached outrageous proportions and were seriously
crippling the nation's financial resources, as witnessed by 33 new government agencies, 24,303 new
employees, and an increase in the national debt of
nearly 20%. Few voters responded, for conditions
were slowly improving; only 58 banks had failed in
1934—901 had been the annual average since 1921.

Mar 24: The **Tydings-McDuffie Act,** granting independence to the Philippines, was passed by Congress.
The Philippine legislature approved it on May 1.
Complete independence would not be proclaimed
until July 4, 1946.

June 6: The **Securities Exchange Act** was signed by
Pres. Roosevelt. It provided for creation of the Securities and Exchange Commission. It also provided for
licensing stock exchanges and declared certain speculative practices illegal.

June 28: The **Federal Farm Bankruptcy Act,** also
known as the Frazier-Lemke Act, was signed by Pres.

Roosevelt. It established a moratorium on farm mortgage foreclosures.

June 28: The **National Housing Act** was passed by Congress. It established the Federal Housing Administration to help home owners finance repairs and enlargements and to spur private building through federal mortgages.

July 22: John Dillinger, public enemy number one, was shot in Chicago, Ill., by FBI agents.

Nov 6: In **congressional elections** the Democrats gained nine Senate seats for a 69–25 majority, with two seats held by minor parties. In the House the Democrats gained nine seats for a 310–117 majority, with five seats going to minor parties.

II. Architecture
   Arts and Music
   Popular Entertainment
   Publishing
   Theater

Although the Depression was far from over, an up-beat mood in America was evidenced by a revitalization in publishing. Government-sponsored art projects encouraged the talented and were responsible for some 15,000 works of art being produced. Hollywood introduced to America a new child star, Shirley Temple.

Among **books published** this year was *Tender Is the Night* by F. Scott Fitzgerald, a novel exploring the lives of Dick Diver, a psychiatrist, and his schizophrenic wife Nicole. Now considered a masterpiece, the novel was published at a time when Fitzgerald's prestige as a writer was slipping and his own life was beginning to disintegrate. Other books published this year included *Doctor Martino and Other Stories* by William Faulkner; *The Thin Man* by Dashiell Hammett; and *Goodbye, Mr. Chips* by James Hilton.

May 7: Pulitzer prizes were awarded for the following: fiction, *Lamb in His Bosom* by Caroline Miller; biography, *John Hay* by Tyler Bennett; history, *The People's Choice* by Herbert Agar; poetry, *Collected*

Verse by Robert Hillyer; drama, *Men in White* by Sidney Kingsley.

III. Business and Industry
Education
Philosophy and Religion
Science

There was hope that the Depression was coming to an end. Unemployment had dropped by more than 4,000,000. Organized labor, which had claimed 58.3% of the national income in 1929, now earned 62.5%. Business failures dropped sharply. The purchasing power of industrial workers went up by 25%. The American Federation of Labor claimed 2,000,000 new members. The near-disastrous plight of the nation's schools was eased as capital outlay for education grew more generous. Scientists induced artificial radioactivity for the first time, extended the periodic table, tapped the sun's energy with two experimental solar motors, and predicted that man would soon harness atomic energy.

Jan 7: The Rev. Dr. William Ashley Sunday, better known as **Billy Sunday,** began an intensive two-week revival campaign in New York City at the Calvary Baptist Church. Dr. Sunday, 70, had not visited New York City for this purpose since 1917. At that time, he had evangelized for ten weeks in Washington Heights. People looked on Billy Sunday as the last of the old-fashioned revivalists.

May 23: What became known worldwide as **nylon** was first produced by Dr. Wallace H. Carothers, a research chemist in the Du Pont laboratories. Carothers succeeded in spinning a synthetic fiber that met exhaustive tests of durability. He called his invention polymer 66.

July 16: The **first general strike** in U.S. history took place in San Francisco, Calif., as an expression of support for the striking 12,000 members of the International Longshoremen's Association.

Oct 25: The **Nobel Prize in Physiology or Medicine** was awarded jointly to George R. Minot, William P.

Murphy, and George H. Whipple for their discovery of liver therapy to combat anemia. They were the fourth, fifth, and sixth Americans to receive the Nobel Prize in this field.

Nov 15: The **Nobel Prize in Chemistry** was awarded to Harold Clayton Urey for his discovery in Dec. 1931 of deuterium, or heavy hydrogen, an isotope of hydrogen. Deuterium and its oxide, commonly known as heavy water, were used in fission experiments to slow neutrons so they would split atomic nuclei on impact, a major advance in atomic physics.

IV. Fashion
   Folkways
   Holidays
   Social Issues and Crime
   Sports

Although Prohibition had been repealed nationally, the dry forces stubbornly refused to concede defeat, renewing their campaign on the local level. However, they were powerless to stop the revival of the huge liquor industry. Distillers this year produced 35,000,000 barrels of beer and 42,000,000 gallons of hard liquor. For the sports fan, the two most imposing figures in the country were Dizzy and Daffy Dean, brothers who rolled up 45 victories between them in pitching the St. Louis Cardinals into a world championship and the first million-dollar World Series gate.

June 9: The **U.S. Open golf tournament** was won by Olin Dutra, beating Gene Sarazen by one stroke.

June 14: The **world heavyweight boxing championship** was won by Max Baer, who scored a technical knockout over Primo Carnera in the 11th round of a fight held before a crowd of 48,495 in New York City.

July 29: The **PGA golf tournament** was won by Paul Runyan.

Aug 19: The **U.S. Lawn Tennis Association singles championships** were won by Helen Hull Jacobs in the women's division and Frederick J. Perry of Great Britain in the men's division (Sept. 12).

Sep 17-25: The **America's Cup** was successfully defended by the U.S. yacht *Rainbow*, which defeated the British challenger *Endeavour* four races to two.

Oct 3-9: The 31st annual **World Series** was won by the St. Louis Cardinals (NL), defeating the Detroit Tigers (AL) four games to three.

Dec 9: The **NFL championship** was won by the New York Giants, defeating the Chicago Bears 30–13.

1935

I. **Civil Rights**
   Exploration and Settlement
   Government
   Statistics
   Wars

The economic gains registered in 1934 seemed to produce a heady effect on the nation this year. Labor and capital squared off for a no-holds-barred brawl. The New Deal suffered a stunning setback when the Supreme Court declared the National Industrial Recovery Act unconstitutional. This provided anti-administration forces with effective ammunition to use against the New Deal, accusing it of being un-American, Bolshevistic, communistic, and socialistic. Rebellions minor and major destroyed Democratic unity in Congress and made it difficult for Pres. Franklin D. Roosevelt to maintain control of his own supporters. In short, the nation was feuding.

Jan 29: U.S. membership in the **World Court** was killed when the Senate refused by a vote of 52–36 to ratify participation in the court. The vote fell seven short of achieving the necessary two-thirds majority.

May 6: The **Works Progress Administration** (WPA) was instituted under the authority of the Emergency Relief Appropriation Act, which passed on Apr. 8.

May 11: The **Rural Electrification Administration** was established by executive order to build power lines and finance electricity production in areas not served by private distributors.

May 27: The **National Industrial Recovery Act was declared unconstitutional** by the Supreme Court. The decision invalidated the National Recovery Administration (NRA) and implied that any government attempt to legislate prices, wages, working conditions, etc., would be unconstitutional. This followed from the Court's strict interpretation of interstate commerce.

Aug 14: The **Social Security Act** was signed by Pres. Roosevelt. It established a Social Security Board to supervise payment of old-age benefits, such payments to be determined by the amount of money earned by recipients before their 65th birthdays.

Sep 8: Huey Long was assassinated. A powerful demagogue in Louisiana and national politics, he was shot to death in the corridor of the state capitol in Baton Rouge, La., by Dr. Carl Austin Weiss, Jr.

II. Architecture
   Arts and Music
   Popular Entertainment
   Publishing
   Theater

Conflicting social forces at work were reflected in the new, so-called proletarian novel, which found a receptive audience, and in the establishment of a left-wing book club. The trend even extended to the most conservative of all arts, the theater. Clifford Odets electrified audiences with his glorification of the little man. Imaginative artists discovered American primitivism through a surprising interest in African art. The Federal Music Project sponsored thousands of free concerts and employed some 18,000 musicians. Film makers produced a raft of epics, such as *Mutiny on the Bounty* and *A Tale of Two Cities*, as well as one of the finest films of all time, *The In-*

former. The death of Will Rogers in an airplane crash with Wiley Post on Aug. 16 near Point Barrow, Alaska, was widely mourned.

Among **books published** this year was *Of Time and the River* by Thomas Wolfe, the author's second novel about Eugene Gant. Here the young southerner comes in contact with the cosmopolitan world of New York City. Other books published this year included *Judgment Day* by James T. Farrell, the second novel of his trilogy about young Studs Lonigan; *The Last Puritan* by George Santayana, the philosopher's only novel; and *Tortilla Flat* by John Steinbeck, a novel lovingly recounting the lives of the *paisanos* of Monterey, Calif., and the first of Steinbeck's books to become a commercial success.

May 6: Pulitzer prizes were awarded for the following: fiction, *Now in November* by Josephine Winslow Johnson; drama, *The Old Maid* by Zoë Akins; history, *The Colonial Period of American History* by Charles McLean Andres; biography, *R. E. Lee* by Douglas S. Freeman; poetry, *Bright Ambush* by Audrey Wurdemann.

III. Business and Industry
Education
Philosophy and Religion
Science

Organized labor was furious over the Supreme Court's adverse decision on the NRA, and over management's attitude toward what labor considered to be workers' basic rights. However, labor found itself in the midst of a major civil war on the issue of craft unions vs. industrial unions. The chief opponents were John L. Lewis of the newly organized Committee for Industrial Organization and William Green, head of the American Federation of Labor. Crisis level was reached when Lewis resigned from the parent group and took his followers with him. Widespread unrest disturbed members of the Daughters of the American Revolution and the American Legion, who pressed state legislatures to pass laws requiring loyalty oaths for teachers. In all, 19 states put such measures on their books.

An epidemic of **infantile paralysis**, or poliomyelitis, sparked renewed interest in combatting the disease. The drive was led by Pres. Roosevelt, who had been stricken with the disease, also known as polio, in 1921.

June 10: **Alcoholics Anonymous** was organized in New York City.

Nov 9: The **Committee for Industrial Organization** was established by John L. Lewis from a dissenting faction within the American Federation of Labor. In 1938 its leaders were expelled from the older organization and reorganized their group as the Congress of Industrial Organizations.

IV. Fashion
   Folkways
   Holidays
   Social Issues and Crime
   Sports

Troubled times drew fresh blood into Prohibition ranks, and soon many counties were dry again. The highly charged emotional level of the people was reflected in an upsurge of lynchings in the South and intense interest in the trial of Bruno Richard Hauptmann, charged with the kidnaping and murder of the infant son of Charles and Anne Morrow Lindbergh.

May 4: The 61st annual **Kentucky Derby** was won by Omaha, with a time of 2:05. The jockey was Willis Saunders.

May 11: The 60th annual **Preakness Stakes** was won by Omaha, with a time of 1:58²/₅. The jockey was Willis Saunders.

May 24: The **first night baseball game** in the major leagues was played between the Cincinnati Reds (NL) and the Philadelphia Phillies (NL) before more than 20,000 fans at Crosley Field, Cincinnati, Ohio. The Reds beat the Phillies 2–1.

June 8: The 67th annual **Belmont Stakes** was won by Omaha, with a time of 2:30³/₅. The jockey was Willis

Saunders. This was the third time that a horse had won the Triple Crown.

June 8: The **U.S. Open golf tournament** was won by Sam Parks, Jr.

June 13: The **world heavyweight boxing championship** was won by James J. Braddock over Max Baer on points in 15 rounds.

July 6: At the **Wimbledon** tennis championships the women's singles title was won by Helen Wills Moody. This was her seventh victory.

Sep 11: The **U.S. Lawn Tennis Association singles championships** were won by Helen Hull Jacobs, for the fourth consecutive time, in the women's division and Wilmer L. Allison in the men's division (Sept. 12).

Oct 2-7: The 32nd annual **World Series** was won by the Detroit Tigers (AL), defeating the Chicago Cubs (NL) four games to two.

Oct 23: The **PGA golf tournament** was won by Johnny Revolta.

Dec 15: The **NFL championship** was won by the Detroit Lions, defeating the New York Giants 26–7.

1936

I. Civil Rights
Exploration and Settlement
Government
Statistics
Wars

Despite criticism of New Deal policies by its opponents, the administration received a vote of confidence in the national elections. Pres. Franklin D. Roosevelt carried all but two states, in the largest presidential vote cast to date. Democratic ranks closed and party leaders hailed the advent of good times. However, bad times continued for farmers as another scorching drought created a vast dust bowl and sent thousands westward in search of fertile land. Critics of the New Deal stressed the fact that since its election in 1932 the Roosevelt government had swelled the national debt by $12,000,000,000. Countering these statistics was the fact that at the same time the national income had risen by $30,000,000,000. In international affairs, Germany reoccupied the Rhineland, which had been taken from it after World War I; Italy annexed Ethiopia, which it had invaded the year before, thus crippling the League of Nations as an international peace-keeper; and civil war broke out in Spain.

Mar 2: The **Soil Conservation and Domestic Allotment Act** was signed by Pres. Roosevelt. It replaced the Agricultural Adjustment Act, which had been invalidated Jan. 6 by the U.S. Supreme Court. The new measure provided benefit payments to farmers who practiced soil conservation in a cooperative program to replace soil-depleting crops with soil-conserving crops.

June 9-12: The **Republican National Convention nominated Gov. Alfred M. Landon** of Kansas for the presidency and Col. Frank Knox of Illinois for the vice presidency. The Republicans were supported during their campaign by some conservative Democrats, among them Alfred E. Smith.

June 23-27: The **Democratic National Convention renominated Pres. Roosevelt** by acclamation for the presidency. It chose John Nance Garner for the vice presidency. In general the platform took its stand on the administration's record. The American Labor Party endorsed Roosevelt's candidacy.

Nov 3: Franklin D. Roosevelt was reelected president of the United States in a Democratic landslide that carried every state except Maine and Vermont. John Nance Garner was elected vice president. Congress became more than three-quarters Democratic in both houses. The electoral vote was Roosevelt, 523; Gov. Alfred M. Landon of Kansas, 8. The popular vote was Roosevelt, 27,751,612; Landon, 16,687,913; William

Lemke, Union Party, 891,858; Norman Thomas, Socialist, 187,342; Earl Browder, Communist, 80,181; Dr. D. Leigh Colvin, Prohibition candidate, 37,609; John W. Aiken, Socialist Labor Party, 12,729. The campaign was bitter. About 80% of the press opposed Roosevelt. In congressional elections the Democrats gained seven Senate seats, for a 76–16 majority, with four seats going to minor parties. In the House their majority was 331–89, with 13 seats going to minor parties.

II. Architecture
Arts and Music
Popular Entertainment
Publishing
Theater

The theater enjoyed one of the most distinguished seasons in years and was heartened by the founding of the Federal Theater Project under the Works Progress Administration (WPA). As the Depression eased, more concerts meant more new works performed and more musicians employed. Over 5000 artists in 44 states were employed by the Federal Art Project of the WPA. They painted between 600 and 700 murals for government buildings and a great number of works in oil and watercolor. The demand so far outstripped the supply that some artists were turning out a finished work each week. Movies enjoyed their most prosperous year since the Depression, even though four out of five films were called financial failures by their producers. The industry turned out some 500 feature films. Technicolor had been developed, but few ventured to use the innovation.

Among **books published** this year was *Gone With the Wind* by Margaret Mitchell, a blockbuster novel of Georgia in the Civil War that won a Pulitzer Prize in 1937 and was the basis for the classic 1939 motion picture. The novel sold 1,000,000 copies in six months. Other books published this year included *A Further Range* by Robert Frost, which included the poem "Two Tramps in Mud Time"; and *The Big*

Money by John Dos Passos, the third novel of his *U.S.A.* trilogy, which included *The 42nd Parallel* (1930) and *1919* (1932). The trilogy was collected in 1938.

May 4: Pulitzer prizes were awarded for the following: fiction, *Honey in the Horn* by Harold L. Davis; drama, *Idiot's Delight* by Robert E. Sherwood; history, *The Constitutional History of the U.S.* by Andrew C. McLaughlin; biography, *The Thought and Character of William James* by Ralph Barton Perry; poetry, *Strange Holiness* by Robert P. Tristram Coffin.

Nov 12: The **Nobel Prize for Literature** was awarded to Eugene O'Neill, the foremost American dramatist.

III. Business and Industry
Education
Philosophy and Religion
Science

The nation's commerce was much improved over the previous year. Farm prices were up, metals were up, and automobile production increased 20%. However, 8,000,000 still were unemployed. Labor warfare continued and unions discovered a new weapon in the sit-down strike. Education looked considerably brighter as fewer schools cried out for federal assistance. Teachers were granted slight increases in salaries; enrollment in lower grades dropped because of the falling birth rate; and 35,000 illiterates were taught to read and write by Civilian Conservation Corps instructors. Educators hailed widespread interest in adult classes.

The age of the **trailer** reached full swing. It was estimated that there were 160,000 trailers on the road. Observers on Jan. 1, 1937, counted an average of 25 trailers an hour crossing the state line into Florida. Some statisticians, like Roger Babson, predicted that soon half the population of the country would be living in trailers.

May 9: The first scheduled **transatlantic dirigible flight** was completed when the *Hindenburg* landed at Lakehurst, N.J. Built by the German Zeppelin Transport Company, the craft was 830 ft. long, 135 ft. in diameter, and propelled by four 1050 hp Daimler Benz Diesel engines. It had a range of 8000 mi.

Nov 12: The **Nobel Prize in Physics** was awarded jointly to Carl David Anderson of the California Institute of Technology for his discovery in 1932 of the positron, and to Victor Francis Hess of Austria for his discovery of cosmic radiation. The discoveries opened new areas of nuclear physics for scientists to explore. Anderson's research confirmed theories about the structure of matter.

IV. Fashion
Folkways
Holidays
Social Issues and Crime
Sports

More Americans attended athletic events this year than ever before. Football gate receipts were up 15% and there was a great increase in the popularity of basketball when it was included in the roster of Olympic Games for the first time.

Feb 5-16: At the **Winter Olympics** in Germany, the U.S. won two gold medals and placed fifth in the unofficial team scoring after Norway, Germany, Sweden, and Finland.

June 6: The **U.S. Open golf tournament** was won by Tony Manero, who shot a world's record 282 for a 72-hole title tournament.

July 4: At the **Wimbledon** tennis championships in England, the women's singles title was won by Helen Hull Jacobs.

Aug 5-16: At the **Summer Olympics** in Berlin, Germany, the U.S. won 20 gold medals and placed second in the unofficial team scoring behind Germany. The star of the games was the U.S. athlete Jesse Owens, who won four gold medals.

Sep 30-Oct 6: The 33rd annual **World Series** was won by the New York Yankees (AL), defeating the New York Giants (NL) four games to two.

Nov 22: The **PGA golf tournament** was won by Denny Shute.

Dec 13: The **NFL championship** was won by the Green Bay Packers, defeating the Boston Redskins 21 to 6.

1937

I. Civil Rights
Exploration and Settlement
Government
Statistics
Wars

The New Deal entered a period of transition in which its measures lost much of their emotional impact. As administration forces tried to press on, voices were increasingly raised against the program. Economic and political disputes rippled across the nation, aggravated to a degree by world events: civil war in Spain, German rearmament, and Japan's undeclared war on China. The worst of the Depression seemed over, but other dangers threatened.

Jan 20: Pres. **Franklin D. Roosevelt was inaugurated** for his second term. This was the first time the presidential inauguration was held on this date, as required by the Twentieth Amendment. Subsequent inauguration ceremonies have been held on this date, except in 1957 and 1985 when Jan. 20 fell on a Sunday and the ceremonies were conducted on Jan. 21.

Feb 5: In a move to alter composition of the **Supreme Court,** Pres. Franklin D. Roosevelt, after informing congressional leaders at a special Cabinet meeting in the morning, sent a message to Congress at noon recommending revision of statutes governing the federal judiciary. Although the recommendations were intended ostensibly to provide more efficient and younger judges in all federal courts, Roosevelt was charged with attempting to pack the Supreme Court, which in the past had invalidated important parts of the New Deal legislative program.

May 6: The dirigible ***Hindenburg*** was destroyed by fire as it approached its mooring mast at Lakehurst, N.J. It was thought that a spark caused while mooring set off the hydrogen contained within the giant airship. The *Hindenburg* burst into flames and fell to earth in a few horrifying seconds. The disaster marked the virtual end of lighter-than-air transport.

July 22: The **Supreme Court Bill**, by which Pres. Roosevelt sought to modify the federal judiciary, specifically the Supreme Court, was voted back into committee by Congress, effectively killing the bill. In the meantime, Justice Willis Van Devanter had resigned from the Supreme Court, allowing Pres. Roosevelt to appoint a liberal justice, Hugo L. Black, on Aug. 12 and swing the Court's balance in favor of the New Deal.

Sep 2: The **National Housing Act,** also called the Wagner-Steagall Act, was signed by Pres. Roosevelt. It created the U.S. Housing Authority for the purpose of administering loans to small communities and states for rural and urban construction.

Dec 12: The U.S. gunboat *Panay* was sunk in Chinese waters by Japanese air force planes, killing two and sparking a crisis in U.S.-Japanese relations. On Dec. 14 the U.S. demanded an apology and reparations. The Japanese complied immediately but continued to wage war in China.

II. Architecture
Arts and Music
Popular Entertainment
Publishing
Theater

Uncertainty in the nation's economic and political situation carried over to its creative life, resulting in a general sense of apathy. Federal support of the arts served merely to keep its practitioners alive and working. Architects debated the merits of functional design and drew much of their inspiration from builders abroad.

Among **books published** this year was *The Late George Apley* by John P. Marquand, a novel told in the form of a memoir recounting the stagnation of Boston's aristocracy. The story traced the history of several generations and showed the impact of new immigration on the old, settled society of Boston. Also published this year was the novelette *Of Mice and Men* by John Steinbeck that became a perennial favorite. It was the basis for a successful play and motion picture.

May 3: Pulitzer prizes were awarded for the following: fiction, *Gone With the Wind* by Margaret Mitchell; biography, *Hamilton Fish* by Allan Nevins; history, *The Flowering of New England* by Van Wyck Brooks; poetry, *A Further Range* by Robert Frost; drama, *You Can't Take It with You* by Moss Hart and George S. Kaufman.

III. Business and Industry
Education
Philosophy and Religion
Science

Labor placed the administration in the awkward position of having to choose sides between warring factions. However, despite internal difficulties, significant successes were won by unions in their effort to organize companies and industries that never before had recognized them. In medicine, the National Cancer Institute was founded, and Dr. E. C. Rosenow of the Mayo Clinic announced progress in the search for a serum against infantile paralysis, or polio. Experiments were based on the recent discovery that polio was caused by a transformed streptococcus.

In a wave of **industrial unrest** during the winter of 1936–1937, more than 500,000 workers quit their jobs. Many engaged in illegal sit-down strikes.

Mar 29: A minimum wage law for women was upheld by the U.S. Supreme Court in the decision of *West*

Coast Hotel v. Parrish. The judgment reversed two previous rulings.

Apr 12: The **National Labor Relations Act** of 1935 was upheld by the U.S. Supreme Court.

May 6: The **first coast-to-coast radio program** was conducted by Herbert Morrison, reporting the *Hindenburg* disaster.

May 12: In the **first worldwide radio broadcast** received in the U.S., listeners heard the coronation of King George VI of England.

May 27: The **Golden Gate Bridge** in San Francisco, Calif., was dedicated.

Aug: The first signs of a **new recession** became apparent in a selling wave on the stock markets. The retreat became sharper after Labor Day, and many stocks fell rapidly. On Oct. 19 the New York market was near demoralization, with total transactions of 7,290,000 shares—the largest since 1933.

Nov 11: The **Nobel Prize in Physics** was awarded jointly to Clinton Joseph Davisson of Bell Telephone Laboratories in New York City and Sir George Paget Thomson of Great Britain, for their independent "discovery of the interference phenomenon in crystals irradiated by electrons."

IV. Fashion
Folkways
Holidays
Social Issues and Crime
Sports

An event affecting the American people was the Spanish Civil War. While the U.S. government took no official position in the conflict, a considerable portion of the public offered highly emotional support to the Loyalist, antifascist side. American volunteers by the hundreds went to Spain, where they joined Loyalist armies.

May 8: The 63rd annual **Kentucky Derby** was won by War Admiral, with a time of 2:03 1/5. The jockey was Charles Kurtsinger.

May 15: The 62nd annual **Preakness Stakes** was won

by War Admiral, with a time of 1:58²/₅. The jockey
was Charles Kurtsinger.

May 30: The **PGA golf tournament** was won by Denny
Shute.

June 5: The 69th annual **Belmont Stakes** was won by
War Admiral, with a time of 2:28³/₅. The jockey was
Charles Kurtsinger. War Admiral thus became the
fourth horse to win the Triple Crown.

June 12: The **U.S. Open golf tournament** was won by
Ralph Guldahl.

June 22: The **world heavyweight boxing championship** was won by Joe Louis, who knocked out James
J. Braddock in the eighth round at Chicago.

July 2: At the **Wimbledon** tennis championship in England, the men's singles championship was won by J.
Donald Budge.

July 7: The fifth annual **baseball All-Star Game** was
won by the American League, which defeated the
National League 8–3 and picked up its fourth victory
in the event.

July 27: The **Davis Cup** tennis tournament was won
by the U.S., defeating Great Britain four matches to
one.

July 31-Aug 5: The **America's Cup** was successfully
defended by the yacht *Ranger,* which won four
straight races from the British challenger *Endeavour
II.*

Oct 6-10: The 34th annual **World Series** was won by
the New York Yankees (AL), defeating the New York
Giants (NL) four games to one.

Dec 12: The **NFL championship** was won by the Washington Redskins, defeating the Chicago Bears 28 to
21.

1938

I. **Civil Rights**
   Exploration and Settlement
   Government
   Statistics
   Wars

A return of economic adversity led to increased government spending. This eased the situation a little, but led to further disillusionment with the New Deal. Congressional elections saw a sudden increase in the number of Republican winners. However, the center of government activity and concern was swinging toward foreign affairs. German occupation and annexation (Apr. 10) of Austria, and the crisis in September sparked by German demands on Czechoslovakia, culminating in the Munich Pact (Sept. 29), showed the democratic nations to be paralyzed in the face of German aggression. For the first time, isolationism vs. limited intervention became an active national issue. There was widespread nervousness about the possibility of war, but few believed it likely.

Feb 16: The second **Agricultural Adjustment Act** was signed by Pres. Roosevelt. It maintained the soil conservation program; provided acreage allotments, parity payments, marketing quotas, and commodity loans to farmers; and authorized crop insurance corporations and the "ever-normal granary" proposals of Sec. of Agriculture Henry A. Wallace.

May 26: The **House Committee to Investigate Un-American Activities** (HUAC) was formed. It was also known as the Dies Committee after its chairman, Rep. Martin Dies, Democrat of Texas.

June 25: The **Wage and Hours Act** was signed by Pres. Roosevelt. It raised the minimum wage for workers engaged in interstate commerce from 25 cents to 40 cents an hour. Hours were limited to 44 per week in the first year of the law's enaction, dropping to 40 after the third year. Congress declared that it possessed the power in this act to ban interstate shipment of products made by unlawful exploitation of child labor.

July 17: Douglas G. **"Wrong-way" Corrigan,** unable to obtain a flight exit permit to Europe, took off from New York and landed in Dublin, Ireland, claiming he had headed for California. Despite his illegal action, he became a national celebrity for a time.

Sep 26: Pres. Roosevelt sent **private memorandums** to Britain, France, Germany, and Czechoslovakia. He recommended arbitration of the Sudetenland crisis, brought on by German demands in the Sudetenland, then part of Czechoslovakia. This set the stage for the Munich Pact (Sept. 29), which in effect surrendered the Sudetenland to Germany along with all Czechoslovakian fortresses on the frontier with Germany. British Prime Minister Neville Chamberlain, key figure in negotiations with Adolf Hitler, returned to England and announced he had secured "peace in our time."

Nov 8: In **congressional elections** the Democrats lost seven Senate seats but kept a 69–23 majority, with four seats going to minor parties. In the House Democrats lost 70 seats, for a 261–164 majority, with four seats going to minor parties.

II. Architecture
  Arts and Music
  Popular Entertainment
  Publishing
  Theater

It was an active year for performing and creative arts, although little of distinction was produced. Authors rediscovered the past and flooded the market with historical novels. The organization of two world fairs, scheduled for the following year at New York City and San Francisco, sent architects to their drawing boards and artists to their easels. Commissions were made subject to competition, so the level of work done was somewhat more imaginative than it had recently been. Movie attendance dropped some 40%. The top money maker of the year was Walt Disney's *Snow White and the Seven Dwarfs*, which made Disney famous around the world and became a film classic.

Among **books published** this year was *Our Town*, a play by Thornton Wilder that was also produced and awarded a Pulitzer Prize in 1938. A thoughtful fantasy set on a bare stage, the play examined the lives and relationships of the residents of a small New England village. A central character was the "stage manager," who served as narrator. Other books published this year included *The King Was in His Counting House* by James Branch Cabell, a novel; *The Unvanquished* by William Faulkner; the *Selected Poems* of John Gould Fletcher; *The Fifth Column* by Ernest Hemingway, a play dealing with the Spanish Civil War whose title came to mean a body of agents working secretly within a country to overthrow it; *The Selected Poetry of Robinson Jeffers*; *The Prodigal Parents* by Sinclair Lewis; *Land of the Free*, poetry by Archibald MacLeish; *Black Is My Truelove's Hair* by Elizabeth Madox Roberts, a novel; and *Uncle Tom's Children* by Richard Wright, a collection of stories that heralded Wright's arrival as a writer.

Estimates showed that the *Music Appreciation Hour*, a program conducted by Walter Damrosch over a national radio network, was heard by 7,000,000 schoolchildren each week.

May 2: Pulitzer prizes were awarded for the following: fiction, *The Late George Apley* by John P. Marquand; biography, *Pedlar's Progress* by Odell Shepard and *Andrew Jackson* by Marquis James; history, *The Road to Reunion, 1865–1900* by Paul Herman Buck; poetry, *Cold Morning Sky* by Marya Zaturenska; drama, *Our Town* by Thornton Wilder.

Oct 30: Orson Welles staged his radio play *War of the Worlds*, based on the novel by H. G. Wells. The program caused widespread panic when listeners took as true the realistically performed news reports of an invasion from Mars. The experience demonstrated the power of the new medium to influence large numbers of people.

Nov 10: The **Nobel Prize for Literature** was awarded to Pearl S. Buck, author of the novel *The Good Earth*.

III. Business and Industry
Education
Philosophy and Religion
Science

Because of government support, business conditions at year's end were healthier than at the start. Labor forces won two rousing victories—passage of the maximum hour and minimum wage bill and a long-sought measure that prohibited child labor in interstate industries. Isolated sit-down strikes still plagued industry, but public opinion seemed to swing against these tactics, so unions stopped them entirely. Technological advances were steady: James Slayter and John H. Thomas of Newark, Ohio, perfected methods to manufacture fiberglass. In addition, scientists made further advances in atomic physics.

Patents were issued for **nylon,** the pioneer synthetic fabric. Commercial production began immediately. Du Pont manufactured toothbrushes with nylon bristles, the first nylon product to reach the market.

Howard Hughes won the International Harmon Trophy for his flight around the world in the record time of three days, 19 hrs., 14 min.

Mar: The stock market **recession** reached its lowest point. Most of the leading stocks had fallen 50 points or more since the preceding August. The Federal Reserve Board's Adjusted Index of Industrial Production fell to 76.

May 27: The continuing **recession** prompted passage of the Revenue Bill of 1938 by Congress, on grounds that tax concessions were needed to stimulate business. The bill reduced taxes on corporations and was supported by Republican and Democratic opponents of the New Deal.

June 23: Civilian air transportation in the U.S. came under federal control with passage of the Civil Aeronautics Act, which established the Civil Aeronautics Authority as an independent agency of the federal government. The agency regulated the licensing of civil pilots, use of airways, introduction of new equipment, and rules of flight.

Nov: An early **radar** system, developed by the U.S. Army Signal Corps in 1936 and demonstrated before the secretary of war in 1937, was subjected to exhaustive tests by the Coast Artillery.

Nov 14-18: The **Congress of Industrial Organizations** (CIO) was established by the delegates to the annual convention of the Committee for Industrial Organization, held at Pittsburgh, Pa. John L. Lewis was unanimously elected president.

Dec 13: The number of Americans receiving **federal relief** had dropped to 2,122,960, compared with 3,184,000 the previous year, according to a report issued by the Works Progress Administration.

IV. Fashion
Folkways
Holidays
Social Issues and Crime
Sports

It was a good year for sports. The number of active golfers was up, winter sports showed phenomenal growth in popularity, and both football and baseball were thriving. In football some 1,100,000 fans flocked to see professional games in 1938. Major league baseball drew about 10,000,000 to the stadiums in a year when many longtime records were broken. The New York Yankees (AL) became the first team to win the World Series three times running (in 1939, the first to win the series four times in a row). Yankee star Lou Gehrig set eight new major league records, including most consecutive games (2122), most consecutive years with 150 or more games (12), and most home runs with bases filled (23).

The number of **automobile-related deaths** for the year was put at more than 32,000 by the National Safety Council. About one-third of the fatalities involved pedestrians. Almost 9000 deaths resulted from collisions between motor vehicles.

June 11: The **U.S. Open golf tournament** was won by Ralph Guldahl.

July 1: At the **Wimbledon** tennis championships in England, the men's singles title was won by J. Donald Budge. The next day Helen Wills Moody won the women's singles.

July 16: The **PGA golf tournament** was won by Paul Runyan.

Sep 5: In the **Davis Cup** international tennis matches, the U.S. defeated Australia three matches to two in the challenge round.

Oct 5-9: The 35th annual **World Series** was won by the New York Yankees (AL), defeating the Chicago Cubs (NL) in four straight games.

Nov 2: The projected **visit of the king and queen of England** to Canada and the U.S. prompted a letter from Pres. Roosevelt to King George VI. In the letter Roosevelt expressed his pleasure at the forthcoming visit, made suggestions for possible routes and schedules, and added some advice about what the American people would expect of their royal guests. He cautioned the king that the "essential democracy" of the royal couple would be the thing most likely to appeal to Americans. In particular, he urged the homely touch of a visit with the Roosevelts at Hyde Park, N.Y. He outlined stopovers in Washington, D.C., New York City, and Chicago, as well as at Hyde Park, but he did not think that it would be wise for the king and queen to drive through the "narrow, crowded" streets of New York City or Chicago.

Dec 11: The **NFL championship** was won by the New York Giants, defeating the Green Bay Packers 23 to 17.

1939

I. Civil Rights
   Exploration and Settlement
   Government
   Statistics
   Wars

Prosperity seemed just around the corner. Unfortunately, this was largely due to the tremendous volume of orders for military supplies that flooded the nation's factories. The administration could now concentrate for the first time on the problems engendered by approaching war in Europe. Germany completed the dismemberment of Czechoslovakia, and Adolf Hitler turned his attention to Poland. The signing in August of a nonaggression pact between Russia and Germany cleared the path to war between Germany and the other European powers. The principal question for the U.S. was how it would be able to stay out of the conflict.

June 8: King George VI and Queen Elizabeth of Great Britain arrived in Washington, D.C., on their visit to the U.S. (June 7–12). They were the first British sovereigns to visit the U.S.

Sep 1: Germany invaded Poland without declaration of war. On Aug. 24 Pres. Roosevelt had cabled Germany, Poland, and Italy, urging arbitration, conciliation, or negotiation to avoid war.

Sep 3: Great Britain and France declared war on Germany. On the same day Belgium declared its neutrality and Pres. Roosevelt, in a fireside chat, declared the U.S. to be neutral.

Sep 3: Thirty Americans died when the British passenger ship *Athenia* was sunk by a submarine. The following day, Sec. of State Cordell Hull advised U.S. citizens to travel to Europe only under "imperative necessity."

Oct 18: All **U.S. ports and waters were closed** to belligerent submarines by presidential order.

Nov 4: The **Neutrality Act of 1939** was passed by Congress. It repealed the prohibition of arms exports in the Neutrality Act of 1937 and authorized the "cash and carry" sale of arms to belligerent powers.

II. Architecture
Arts and Music
Popular Entertainment
Publishing
Theater

U.S. novelists were taking a long, fond look back on America's past. Historical novels had never been so plentiful. The theater mourned the passing of the Federal Theater Project but rejoiced in a sudden rebirth of interest in the legitimate stage. A shortage of New York City playhouses was felt for the first time in many years. Painters seemed to be exploring two areas: depiction of the regional American scene, which stressed people in relation to their land or locale; and the use of art as a vehicle for political statement or social satire. Film producers faced the bleak prospect of the loss of a lucrative European market. Nonetheless, this was the year of *Gone with the Wind,* one of the most expensive and most successful motion pictures of all time.

Among **books published** this year was *The Grapes of Wrath* by John Steinbeck, a powerful novel dealing with an Oklahoma farm family who lose their farm to the bank and are forced to travel to California to seek work as migrant laborers. Described as a proletarian novel, the book examined in moving detail the plight of the Okies, and by extension the plight of all people caught up in tragic circumstances not of their own making. The novel won a Pulitzer Prize in 1940 and was the basis for an outstanding motion picture. Also published this year were *Adventure of a Young Man* by John Dos Passos, the first novel of a trilogy entitled *District of Columbia; The Wild Palms* by William Faulkner, a novel; *Captain Horatio Hornblower* by C. S. Forester; *Collected Poems* by Robert

Frost; *Pale Horse, Pale Rider* by Katherine Anne Porter, stories; *Abraham Lincoln: The War Years* (four volumes) by Carl Sandburg; and *Collected Poems* by Mark Van Doren.

May 1: Pulitzer prizes were awarded for the following: fiction, *The Yearling* by Marjorie Kinnan Rawlings; biography, *Benjamin Franklin* by Carl Van Doren; history, *A History of American Magazines* by Frank Luther Mott; poetry, *Selected Poems* by John Gould Fletcher; drama, *Abe Lincoln in Illinois* by Robert E. Sherwood.

III. Business and Industry
   Education
   Philosophy and Religion
   Science

Business underwent a gradual decline from 1938 levels, followed by gradual recovery and then a spectacular upsurge in the fall, attributable to the outbreak of war in Europe. The biggest event of the year, however, received scant press attention. Scientists announced that they had succeeded in splitting uranium, thorium, and protactinium atoms by bombarding them with neutrons.

Discovery of the **Rh factor** in human blood by Dr. Philip Levine and Dr. Rufus Stetson of New York led to a clearer understanding of pregnancy and blood transfusion complications. The Rh factor is a component of red blood cells. Those with the factor are classified as Rh+, and those lacking it are Rh− Transfusion of one type of blood into a person with the other type can cause a serious immune reaction. In pregnancies, women with Rh− blood bearing Rh+ fetuses can develop an immune reaction to the baby's blood, leading to difficulties in subsequent pregnancies.

Frequency modulation, a new method of radio transmission and reception, was developed by Edwin H. Armstrong. Armstrong had devised the regenerative receiver during World War I. The latter type of radio became the standard for amplitude modulation, or AM, broadcast applications. However, AM broadcasting was susceptible to static, and in the 1930s and 1940s Armstrong worked to perfect FM transmission and reception, which was not affected by static emissions. He received virtually no support from public opinion, the radio industry, or the FCC. On Jan. 31, 1954, Armstrong, suffering from poor health, plagued by lawsuits, and lacking financial resources, committed suicide.

May 10: The **Methodist Church was reunited** after 109 years of division. The conflict within the church had been marked by two major crises. In 1830 the Methodist Protestant Church had separated from the Methodist Episcopal Church over the question of episcopal authority and had established a separate branch in which lay members were given a voice in church government. The Methodist Episcopal Church, South, had separated from the Methodist Episcopal Church in 1844, ostensibly over an administrative dispute, but probably over the slavery question. A Declaration of Union issued on this date unified some 8,000,000 American Methodists.

June 28: The first regular **transatlantic passenger air service** began when *Dixie Clipper*, a Pan American Airways airliner, left Port Washington, Long Island, with 22 passengers aboard. The flight reached Lisbon, Portugual, 23 hrs., 52 min. later.

Nov 9: The **Nobel Prize in Physics** was awarded to Ernest Orlando Lawrence of the University of California for his development of the cyclotron and for subsequent discoveries in the field of radioactivity, specifically the study of artificially radioactive elements. Lawrence's invention of the cyclotron provided nuclear scientists with an invaluable instrument with which to produce the subatomic particles required for study of nuclear reactions.

IV. **Fashion**
   Folkways
   Holidays
   Social Issues and Crime
   Sports

World fairs in New York City and San Francisco opened, and millions flocked to the expositions to glimpse wonders of the future. Observers noted the unreality of the enthusiasm, in face of the impending war in Europe. However, Americans paid little notice to the prophets of doom, instead lining up to take "death-defying" rides on the roller coaster and the parachute jump.

   The **latest fashions** were advertised in the Sears Roebuck catalog, which offered dresses "inspired by Schiapparelli." In the following year, Sears would announce that "the traditional lapse between the acceptance of new fashions . . . in metropolitan centers and on farms apparently no longer exists."

Mar 27: The **NCAA basketball championship** was won by the University of Oregon, which defeated Ohio State 46–33.

June 12: The **U.S. Open golf tournament** was won by Byron Nelson.

July 7-8: At the **Wimbledon** tennis championships in England, Robert L. Riggs won the men's singles title and Alice Marble won the women's singles. Riggs and Elwood T. Cooke took the men's doubles, Marble and Sarah Palfrey Fabyan the women's doubles.

July 17: The **PGA golf tournament** was won by Henry Picard.

Oct 4-8: The 36th annual **World Series** was won by the New York Yankees (AL), sweeping the Cincinnati Reds (NL) in four games.

Dec 10: The **NFL championship** was won by the Green Bay Packers, defeating the New York Giants 27 to 0.

1940

I. Civil Rights
Exploration and Settlement
Government
Statistics
Wars

With the outbreak of war in Europe in Sept. 1939, the key political question facing the U.S. became how to stay out of the conflict and still help the forces of democracy. Realizing that America was facing a crisis, Pres. Franklin D. Roosevelt decided to run for an unprecedented third term. His rival was a political newcomer, Wendell L. Willkie, whose plainspoken manner made him a powerful contender. Roosevelt won, largely because people felt it was better not to change administrations in dangerous times. This year Germany would invade Norway, overrun Denmark, Luxembourg, Belgium, and the Netherlands, and defeat France. In August Adolf Hitler launched the Battle of Britain, a brutal air assault intended to destroy the Royal Air Force and enable invasion of England.

The **U.S. population** was 131,669,275, according to Census Bureau figures. The center of population was two miles southeast by east of Carlisle, Sullivan County, Ind.

June 24-28: The **Republican National Convention nominated Wendell L. Willkie** of Indiana for the presidency and Charles L. McNary of Oregon for the vice presidency.

June 28: The **Alien Registration Act,** also known as the Smith Act, was passed by Congress. It was signed into law on the next day by Pres. Roosevelt. It required registration and fingerprinting of aliens and made it unlawful to belong to any organization advocating overthrow of the U.S. government. Subsequent registration showed approximately 5,000,000 aliens living in the U.S.

July 15-19: The **Democratic National Convention** nominated **Franklin D. Roosevelt** for the presidency on the first ballot. Henry A. Wallace of Iowa was nominated for the vice presidency.

Sep 3: The **U.S. gave 50 outdated destroyers** to Great Britain in exchange for 99-year leases on naval and air bases in Newfoundland and the West Indies.

Sep 16: The **Selective Service Act** was passed by Congress. The law, the first U.S. peacetime draft, provided for 900,000 selectees to be taken each year. All men between the ages of 20 and 36 were required to register. Length of military service was one year, but this was extended to 18 months in Aug. 1941.

Nov 5: Franklin D. Roosevelt was reelected president of the United States. Henry A. Wallace was elected vice president. The electoral vote was Roosevelt, 449, Wendell L. Willkie, Republican of Indiana, 82. The popular vote was Roosevelt, 27,244,160; Willkie, 22,305,198; Norman Thomas, Socialist candidate, 100,264; Roger W. Babson, Prohibition candidate, 57,812; Earl Browder, Communist, 48,579; John W. Aiken, Socialist Labor candidate, 14,861. In congressional elections the Democrats lost three Senate seats but kept a 66–28 majority, with two seats going to minor parties. In the House the Democrats gained seven seats for a 268–162 lead, with five seats going to minor parties.

II. Architecture
Arts and Music
Popular Entertainment
Publishing
Theater

Book production was up, with 11,328 titles published, and war novels led in popularity. The New York stage labored through an uninspired season, relying principally on foreign imports. On Broadway, the biggest musical hits of the season were *Du Barry Was a Lady* by Cole Porter and *Louisiana Purchase* by Irving Berlin. Musicologists noted a trend away from ultramodernism—the 12-tone system, for instance—which had intrigued composers. The art world showed the influence of European refugee painters, who were forced by war into American exile. Their work centered on the individual rather than on aesthetics. This tendency was seen in architecture as well, where outstanding work was done on buildings designed for shelter, care of the sick, social services, and recreation.

Among **books published** this year was *Native Son* by Richard Wright, a powerful novel considered by many to be Wright's masterpiece. It told the story of Bigger Thomas, a young black drawn into crime and ultimately to execution as a murderer. The novel was adapted for Broadway by Wright and Paul Green in 1941 and had a successful run. Other books published this year included *The Hamlet* by William Faulkner, the first novel of a trilogy about the Snopes family; *For Whom the Bell Tolls* by Ernest Hemingway, set in Spain during that country's civil war; and *You Can't Go Home Again* by Thomas Wolfe, who had died in 1938. Critics found this novel of Wolfe's quieter and better organized than his earlier works.

May 6: Pulitzer prizes were awarded for the following: fiction, *The Grapes of Wrath* by John Steinbeck; biography, *Woodrow Wilson, Life and Letters, Vols. VII and VIII* by Ray Stannard Baker; history, *Abraham Lincoln: The War Years* by Carl Sandburg; poetry, *Collected Poems* by Mark Van Doren; drama, *The Time of Your Life* by William Saroyan.

III. Business and Industry
Education
Philosophy and Religion
Science

Unemployment dropped dramatically because of the military conscription of many industrial workers as well as increased orders, resulting in increased hiring. Labor suffered setbacks in its right to organize and in efforts for better hours and wages. By and large, this was expected and accepted, as the labor force agreed that sacrifice was necessary to maintain America's pledge to support its allies. The next step toward development of the atomic bomb was taken when scientists determined that a chain reaction was possible and would soon become a reality.

The **first antibiotic** developed in the U.S., actinomycin, was produced by Dr. Selman Waksman of Rutgers University, a pioneer in antibiotics. However, it was found too poisonous for humans.

The average **life expectancy** was 64 years. This represented a major increase from 49 years in 1900.

Illiteracy in the U.S. reached a new low of 4.2% of the population, a decline of 0.1% from 1930, and a 15.8% drop from 1870.

Radios could be found in 30,000,000 homes, according to a survey.

Apr 20: An **electron microscope** was first publicly tested at the Radio Corporation of America laboratory in Camden, N.J. The instrument, about 10 ft. high and weighing 700 lbs., magnified by as much as 100,000 diameters. It had been developed by Dr. Ladislaus Marton and coworkers under the supervision of Dr. Vladimir Kasma Zworykin.

May 15: The first successful **helicopter flight** in the U.S. was completed by the VS-300, an experimental helicopter manufactured by the Vought-Sikorsky Corporation.

Oct 24: The **40-hour work week,** part of the Fair Labor Standards Act of 1938, went into effect.

Nov 7: A **suspension bridge collapse** over the Narrows at Tacoma, Wash., was caused by wind vibration. The bridge tumbled 190 feet into Puget Sound.

IV. Fashion
    Folkways
    Holidays
    Social Issues and Crime
    Sports

The coming of war to Europe threatened a complete halt in international sports competition. The 1940 Olympic Games were not held, and Olympic competition would not resume until 1948. Also suspended were the Davis Cup and Wimbledon tennis champi-

onships. Joe Louis did, however, defend the world
heavyweight boxing championship in two bouts
(Feb. 9 and June 20) against Arturo Godoy of Chile.
In baseball the New York Yankees ended up in third
place in the American League, losing a chance to
become the first team to win five consecutive World
Series.

Cornelius Warmerdam became the first person to
pole-vault 15 ft. Two years later he set a new record
when he vaulted 15 ft. 7¾ in. He retired from competition in 1943 after having vaulted 15 ft. or more 43
times.

Mar 30: The **NCAA basketball championship** was won
by Indiana University, defeating the University of
Kansas 60–42.

June 9: The **U.S. Open golf tournament** was won by W.
Lawson Little.

Sep 2: The **PGA golf tournament** was won by Byron
Nelson.

Oct 2-8: The 37th annual **World Series** was won by the
Cincinnati Reds (NL), defeating the Detroit Tigers
(AL) four games to three.

Dec 8: The **NFL championship** was won by the Chicago Bears, who defeated the Washington Redskins
by the incredible score of 73 to 0.

1941

I. Civil Rights
Exploration and Settlement
Government
Statistics
Wars

Two events overshadowed all others this year. On
June 22 Germany invaded the U.S.S.R. After several
weeks of spectacular German success it seemed that
Russia would fall before year's end. On December 7

Japanese forces launched a surprise attack on the U.S. base at Pearl Harbor, Hawaii. Almost instantly the American nation attained a unity it had not known since the dark days of 1933. No longer were Americans to debate the fact that the U.S. was a neutral power and yet had spent $13,000,000,000 on lend-lease appropriations—all of it for war materiel earmarked for use against Germany and Italy—and had created some 35 separate agencies and offices that in effect were war bureaus. The U.S. was in the war at last.

Jan 20: Pres. **Franklin D. Roosevelt was inaugurated** for an unprecedented third term. Henry A. Wallace was inaugurated vice president.

Feb 3: The **Federal Wage and Hour Law** was upheld unanimously by the U.S. Supreme Court. The law prohibited employment of children under 16 in mining and manufacturing and children under 18 in any dangerous occupation. The main provision of the law, however, was its regulation of minimum wages and maximum hours for industries engaged in interstate commerce.

Mar 11: The **Lend-Lease Bill** was signed by Pres. Franklin D. Roosevelt. It furnished a system by which the U.S. could lend goods and munitions to democratic countries in return for services and goods.

July 25: An **embargo** on shipments of scrap iron and gasoline to Japan was ordered by Pres. Roosevelt. The order also froze Japanese assets in the U.S.

Aug 9-12: The **Atlantic Charter** was formulated by Pres. Roosevelt and Prime Minister Winston Churchill at a secret meeting off Newfoundland. It contained eight articles of agreement and defined the aims of the two governments during and after the war.

Aug 18: A **Selective Service Act Extension** was signed by Pres. Roosevelt. It extended the period of military service to not more than 30 months in time of peace and removed the 900,000-man limit on selectees.

Oct 17: The U.S. destroyer *Kearny* was torpedoed and damaged by a German submarine off the coast of Iceland.

Oct 30: The U.S. destroyer *Reuben James* was torpedoed and sunk off the coast of Iceland by a German submarine during the night of Oct. 30–31. Some 100 lives were lost. It was the first American warship to be sunk in the war.

Dec 7: The **Japanese attacked Pearl Harbor,** Hawaii. The American battleships *Arizona, California, Oklahoma,* and *Utah* (an old target battleship) were sunk; the battleship *West Virginia* settled in shallow water and the *Nevada* ran aground. Damaged battleships were the *Pennsylvania, Maryland,* and *Tennessee.* Destroyers *Cassin, Downes,* and *Shaw,* and the minelayer *Oglala,* were sunk or badly damaged. In all, about 19 ships were sunk or damaged. About 3000 Americans lost their lives. The Japanese lost 28 planes and three midget submarines. Japanese forces also attacked Guam, Wake Island, the Philippines, and other strategic points in the Pacific at the same time Pearl Harbor was attacked.

Dec 8: A **declaration of war** against Japan was passed by Congress. The sole dissenting vote was cast by Rep. Jeannette Rankin, Republican of Montana. She had also cast the sole dissenting vote against entering World War I.

Dec 10: The **Japanese invaded** Luzon in the Philippines, where Gen. Douglas MacArthur commanded the defending U.S. and Philippine forces.

Dec 11: Germany and Italy declared war against the U.S., and Congress adopted a resolution recognizing a state of war.

Dec 22: Wake Island fell to the Japanese after a heroic 15-day stand by 400 U.S. Marines.

II. Architecture
Arts and Music
Popular Entertainment
Publishing
Theater

Of all the art forms, theater alone seemed concerned with the fact that the U.S. was at war. A number of propaganda plays were written by new as well as established writers. Unfortunately, many playwrights looked on the stage as a soapbox, and quality suffered. There were, however, the surprising flowering of a truly American painting style and a new musical awareness. New York City was no longer the sole arbiter of these arts; symphonic societies, ballet companies, opera houses, and museums mushroomed across the nation, sometimes presenting works of uncertain quality but always of unflagging enthusiasm despite wartime conditions.

Among **books published** this year was *Berlin Diary* by William L. Shirer, a study of Adolf Hitler and Nazi Germany that became a best seller. Other books published this year included *Random Harvest* by James Hilton; *H. M. Pulham, Esq.,* a novel by John P. Marquand; *The White Cliffs of Dover* by Alice Duer Miller, a book of verse celebrating the British people in wartime; and *My Friend Flicka* by Mary O'Hara, the story of a boy in Wyoming and his horse Flicka.

Mar 8: Sherwood Anderson, the writer, died at 64 of peritonitis in Cristobal, Canal Zone. He had achieved fame in 1919 with the publication of *Winesburg, Ohio,* a critically and popularly acclaimed collection of short stories.

May 5: Pulitzer prizes were awarded for the following: biography, *Jonathan Edwards* by Ola Elizabeth Winslow; history, *The Atlantic Migration, 1607–1860* by Marcus Lee Hansen; poetry, *Sunderland Capture* by Leonard Bacon; drama, *There Shall Be No Night* by Robert E. Sherwood.

III. Business and Industry
Education
Philosophy and Religion
Science

The nation's industry tooled up for full-scale war production. Realizing that wartime is usually a time of inflation, the government prepared to curb prices and limit consumption. Numerous bureaus were established to develop and direct America's vast economic potential. For the most part, the civilian population took controls in their stride, convinced that they were part of the price of winning the war. Anticipating a wage freeze, labor attempted to win boosts before it was too late. There were some 4000 strikes this year, twice as many as in 1940. Scientists turned their attention to increasing the U.S. arsenal of weapons. Federal educators prepared to meet the shortage of adequately trained personnel.

British pioneers in **penicillin** development, Sir Howard Florey and Dr. N. G. Heatley, flew to the U.S. to argue the necessity of large-scale production of the life-saving substance. American drug companies responded to their appeal, and penicillin in time became a household word.

Jan 3: A **shipbuilding program** of 200 merchant vessels was called for by the federal government.

Apr 11: The **Ford Motor Company** signed its first contract with a labor union. It settled a strike that began Apr. 2, when the CIO called out 85,000 workers at Ford's River Rouge plant. Ford closed the plant after rioting had injured 150.

Apr 11: The **Office of Price Administration and Civilian Supply** (OPACS, but better known as OPA) was established with limited powers to recommend price control measures. Its first head was Leon Henderson.

Apr 16: A **steel price freeze** at the levels of the first quarter of the year was announced by the OPA in its first official act. Industry cooperated.

Apr 17: A **cut in auto production** of 20% beginning Aug. 1 was agreed to by the auto industry.

May 1: **U.S. Defense Savings Bonds and Stamps** went on sale.

July 24: A **no-strike agreement** for the duration of the national emergency was signed by AFL building trade unions and the OPM.

Aug 3: A **gasoline curfew** was begun at midnight in 17 eastern states. The curfew closed filling stations from 7 P.M. to 7 A.M.

Dec 27: **Rubber rationing** was announced by the OPA. The measure decreased civilian consumption by 80%. Tire rationing was the first rationing regulation.

IV. **Fashion**
    Folkways
    Holidays
    Social Issues and Crime
    Sports

Remember Pearl Harbor became the war cry of the
man in the street, who used it more as a grim reminder than as an outburst of patriotism. Women's
fashions, reflecting the general restraint, kept to sub-
dued colors and inconspicuous lines. Prior to the
Pearl Harbor attack, the greatest fashion furor of the
year came when an embargo on Japanese silk was
announced. It caused a panic in the hosiery business
and sent thousands into shops to snatch up every
available silk stocking. In golf the top money winner
was Ben Hogan, with $18,358. In boxing, Joe Louis
defended the world heavyweight title five times.
When war came Louis entered the military, and title
competition was suspended. This year Americans
mourned the death of Lou Gehrig, longtime first
baseman for the New York Yankees (AL), who died
in New York on June 2 at age 37.

Jan 6: The term *Four Freedoms* was introduced by
Pres. Franklin D. Roosevelt in his annual speech
before Congress. These freedoms, which he en-
visaged as the cornerstone of a new world, were freedom of speech and expression, freedom of worship,
freedom from fear, and freedom from want.

Mar 29: The **NCAA basketball championship** was won
by Wisconsin, which defeated Washington State 39–
34.

May 3: The 67th annual **Kentucky Derby** was won by
Whirlaway, with a time of 2:01^{2}/5, a new Derby record. The jockey was Eddie Arcaro, who had won the
event in 1938.

May 10: The 66th annual **Preakness Stakes** was won
by Whirlaway, with a time of 1:58^{4}/5. The jockey was
Eddie Arcaro.

May 20: Pres. Roosevelt announced **Thanksgiving**
would be moved forward again, to the last Thursday

of November, after a two-year experiment during which the holiday was celebrated on the next-to-last Thursday in November. Roosevelt had originally moved the holiday to stimulate business activity.

June 7: The **U.S. Open golf tournament** was won by Craig Wood. This was the last time the U.S. Open would be played until 1946.

June 7: The 73rd annual **Belmont Stakes** was won by Whirlaway, with a time of 2:31. The jockey was Eddie Arcaro. Whirlaway thus became the fifth horse to win racing's Triple Crown.

July 13: The **PGA golf tournament** was won by Vic Ghezzi.

July 17: Yankee center fielder **Joe DiMaggio's hitting streak** was ended by pitchers Al Smith and Jim Bagby, Jr., of the Cleveland Indians. DiMaggio had hit safely in 56 consecutive games, from May 15 through July 16, a major league record.

Sep 23: A six-ton **monument marking a time capsule** from the New York World's Fair of 1939–1940 was unveiled in Flushing Meadow, Queens, N.Y., the site of the fair. The capsule contained artifacts and information about twentieth-century culture and was to be opened in the year 6939.

Oct 1-6: The 38th annual **World Series** was won by the New York Yankees (AL), defeating the Brooklyn Dodgers (NL) four games to one.

Dec 7: The wartime phrase *praise the Lord and pass the ammunition* was uttered by Howell M. Forgy, chaplain on the U.S. cruiser *New Orleans,* under attack at Pearl Harbor, Hawaii. While sweating sailors kept up a continuing antiaircraft barrage, he kept their spirits up with this phrase.

Dec 21: The **NFL championship** was won by the Chicago Bears, who defeated the New York Giants 37 to 9.

1942

I. Civil Rights
Exploration and Settlement
Government
Statistics
Wars

American military pride was subjected to rude shocks early this year as U.S. forces were forced from island after island in the Pacific. The chief defeat was the fall of the Bataan peninsula on Luzon in the Philippines, followed a month later by the fall of the island fortress of Corregidor in Manila Bay. Only days later, in early May, American fortunes changed when a U.S. fleet defeated the Japanese in the Battle of the Coral Sea, and again in June when U.S. torpedo bombers routed a second enemy naval task force in the Battle of Midway. At home, thousands of civilians over draft age flocked to Washington, D.C., to man the offices created to handle the mammoth war program.

Jan 2: In the Philippines, **Manila fell** to the Japanese, forcing U.S. and Philippine forces under Gen. Douglas MacArthur to withdraw to the Bataan peninsula.

Feb 10: The French liner *Normandie* burned and capsized at its pier in New York harbor. The world's fastest liner, it was being fitted out for service as a military transport when the fire broke out. The cause of the fire was never discovered, but sabotage was ruled out.

Feb 27-Mar 1: The **Battle of the Java Sea** was a major U.S. naval defeat. The Japanese inflicted heavy losses on the U.S. fleet commanded by Adm. Thomas C. Hart.

Mar 17: Gen. **MacArthur left Bataan** by presidential order when defense of the peninsula became hopeless. He withdrew to Australia and soon was named commander in chief of the Southwest Pacific Command.

Apr 9: Bataan fell to the Japanese after a heroic defense by a greatly outnumbered force. Gen. Jonathan M. Wainwright, with about 3500 soldiers and nurses, withdrew to Corregidor.

Apr 10: The **Bataan Death March** began at dawn. American and Philippine prisoners taken at Bataan were forced to march 85 miles in six days with but one meal of rice during the period. By the end of the march, which was punctuated with atrocities, more than 5200 Americans and many more Filipinos had lost their lives.

Apr 18: An **air raid on Tokyo** was conducted by carrier-launched bombers under command of Maj. Gen. James H. Doolittle. This was the first American offensive blow in the Pacific and did much to boost American morale. It also caused consternation in Japan.

May 4-8: In the **Battle of the Coral Sea**, U.S. naval air forces inflicted heavy losses on the Japanese fleet. This battle was the first ever fought in which neither fleet came within sight of the other. All the fighting was carried on by planes. The U.S. lost the carrier *Lexington*, the destroyer *Sims*, and a tanker. Seven Japanese warships, including one carrier, were sunk.

May 6: Corregidor fell to the Japanese. Gen. Wainwright surrendered the fortress to Japanese troops under Gen. Tomoyuki Yamashita.

June 4-6: In the **Battle of Midway** the U.S. gained an important victory over the Japanese. Americans repulsed an attempt to seize the island, sinking 17 Japanese ships, including four aircraft carriers. Japan lost 275 planes and 4800 men. The U.S. lost over 300 men and two ships.

June 28: The **first U.S. ground assault** on the Japanese in the South Pacific was executed when a contingent of commandos assaulted Salamaua, New Guinea, at night.

Aug 7: U.S. Marines landed on **Guadalcanal**, in the Solomon Islands, opening the first major U.S. amphibious operation in the Pacific. The struggle to force the Japanese off the island involved some of the bloodiest fighting of the war. The fighting continued until Feb. 1943.

Aug 18: Carlson's Raiders, a special guerrilla unit led by Lt. Col. Evans Fordyce Carlson, landed on Makin Island, at the northern end of the Gilbert Islands, with orders to destroy the radio station on the island. In 40 hours every Japanese member of a force of 350 was killed, 1000 gallons of gasoline were set aflame, and the island was rendered militarily useless.

Sep 15: The U.S. carrier *Wasp* was sunk off Guadalcanal.

Nov 3: In **congressional elections** the Democrats lost eight Senate seats but kept a majority of 58–37, with one seat held by a minor party. In the House they lost 50 seats but held a 218–208 majority, with four seats going to minor parties.

Nov 7: In **North Africa,** U.S. forces began landing with support of British naval and air units. Lt. Gen. Dwight Eisenhower commanded the 50 vessels and 400,000 troops employed in the operations.

Nov 12-15: In a **naval engagement off Guadalcanal,** the U.S. scored a major victory, inflicting heavy losses on a Japanese task force and preventing Japanese reinforcements from reaching the island.

II. Architecture
   Arts and Music
   Popular Entertainment
   Publishing
   Theater

Far from destroying the performing arts, World War II gave them an impetus they had not enjoyed for years. Producers scrambled for available playhouses, selling tickets at high prices and counting their profits. Entertainment-hungry civilians and servicemen were given escapist fare, in most cases unclad ladies of the chorus dancing to a loud pit orchestra. Hundreds of serious artists and musicians were absorbed into the armed forces. Architects responded to the demand for fast, prefabricated housing. This year Americans also mourned the loss of some artistic greats: John Barrymore, youngest member of the celebrated family of actors, May 29, at 60; Carole Lombard, actress and wife of Clark Gable, in a plane crash while returning home from a War Bond drive, Jan. 16, at 32; and Grant Wood, known best for *American Gothic* (1930), his portrait of a dour farm couple, Feb. 12, at 50.

Among **books published** this year was *The Moon Is Down* by John Steinbeck, a novel about the military occupation of a small town and the effect of that occupation on both conqueror and conquered. The book was published simultaneously with its dramatization on the New York City stage, an experiment that proved successful. Other books published this year included *The Just and the Unjust* by James Gould Cozzens, a novel about American lawyers; *The Robe* by Lloyd C. Douglas; *Go Down, Moses* by William Faulkner, a collection of stories that included Faulkner's novelette "The Bear"; and *See Here, Private Hargrove* by Marion Hargrove, an immensely popular chronicle of the soldier's life.

May 4: Pulitzer prizes were awarded for the following: fiction, *In This Our Life* by Ellen Glasgow; biography, *Crusader in Crinoline* by Forrest Wilson; history, *Reveille in Washington* by Margaret Leech; poetry, *The Dust Which Is God* by William Rose Benét.

III. Business and Industry
Education
Philosophy and Religion
Science

Anti-inflation measures, such as rent ceilings and wage and price freezes, were put into effect as the nation settled down to the grim business of war. The AFL and CIO voluntarily agreed not to strike for the duration of the war and to submit all labor disputes to a federal mediation board. The War Manpower Commission held virtually dictatorial power over all essential workers and was empowered, if the emergency warranted, to mobilize every adult in the country. Hard hit were colleges and universities, whose enrollments dropped off sharply. Adult education

classes, however, increased in number and helped
keep the schoolrooms at least partially filled.

Henry J. Kaiser, the industrialist, headed the Liberty Ship program, which incorporated techniques of
prefabrication and mass production to speed ship
production. By June of this year his four West Coast
shipyards had been assigned one-third of the U.S.
shipbuilding program. His yard in Vancouver built
and launched a 10,500-ton liberty ship in a record
four days.

Jan 30: The **Price Control Bill** was signed by Pres.
Franklin D. Roosevelt, officially giving the Office of
Price Administration the power to set all prices ex-
cept those for farm products.

Feb 9: War time became effective throughout the nation. Clocks were set ahead one hour, as in daylight
savings time, and were kept one hour ahead of standard time throughout the year.

Mar 17: A **no-strike agreement** was announced by
William Green of the AFL and Philip Murray of the
CIO.

Apr 28: Rents were stabilized by the OPA. The ruling
affected 86,000,000 people housed in 301 areas.

May 5: Sugar rationing began.

May 15: Gasoline rationing began in 17 eastern states.
The limit set was three gallons a week for nonessen-
tial driving. On July 22 a coupon system of rationing
was initiated.

June 13: The **Office of War Information** was established by Pres. Roosevelt to control dissemination of
official news and propaganda. Elmer Davis, the newspaperman and radio commentator, was named as
OWI head.

June 22: The **first V-mail** was sent overseas, from New
York City to London. V-mail involved the transfer of
letters written on prescribed forms to microfilm,
which was sent overseas. There the letters were
printed on photographic paper and delivered.

Oct 1: The first American **jet airplane,** the XP-59, was
tested at Muroc Army Base, Calif., by Robert Stanley,
chief pilot for Bell Aircraft Corporation.

Nov 29: Coffee rationing began.

Dec 1: Nationwide **gasoline rationing** went into effect.

Dec 2: The first sustained **nuclear reaction** was demonstrated in Chicago, Ill., before scientists at the University of Chicago, in a project known as the Argonne Project.

IV. Fashion
    Folkways
    Holidays
    Social Issues and Crime
    Sports

American society underwent enormous changes. Millions of young men went off to combat, women took up new posts in war industries and military support units, and rationing was introduced to control consumption and preserve resources for war production. In contrast to these changes, trends in fashion continued to emphasize simplicity and economy of design. Crime rates across the nation jumped; officials claimed that youths were having one last fling before entering the Army. In golf the top money winner again was Ben Hogan with $13,143.

Jan 9: The world **heavyweight boxing championship** was successfully defended, for the 20th time, by Joe Louis, who knocked out Buddy Baer in the first round.

Mar 28: The **NCAA basketball championship** was won by Stanford, which defeated Dartmouth 53–38.

May 31: The **PGA golf tournament** was won by Sam Snead.

Sep 30-Oct5: The 39th annual **World Series** was won by the St. Louis Cardinals (NL), defeating the New York Yankees (AL) four games to one.

Dec 13: The **NFL championship** was won by the Washington Redskins, who defeated the Chicago Bears 14 to 6.

Dec 21: Nevada divorces were ruled valid in all states by the U.S. Supreme Court.

1943

I. Civil Rights
   Exploration and Settlement
   Government
   Statistics
   Wars

An uncertain year dawned for U.S. military forces. The nation was engaged in a seesaw battle in North Africa and an agonizing struggle in the Pacific. U.S. forces advanced against the Japanese in New Guinea, the Solomons, and the Gilbert Islands, and new names were added to the American battle lexicon— Bougainville, Lae, Tarawa. In the European theater, American troops in North Africa swept across the Mediterranean to Sicily, then to the Italian mainland itself. To the north U.S. bombers wrought destruction in Europe and helped blast Nazi invasion ports in France.

A **polio epidemic** struck the U.S., killing 1151 and crippling thousands more.

Jan 14: The **Casablanca conference** opened in Morocco. It was attended by Pres. Franklin D. Roosevelt and other Allied officials. The Allies planned their military strategy for 1943 and agreed to demand unconditional surrender from the Axis nations.

Feb 20: At the **Kasserine Pass**, Tunisia, U.S. forces were driven back by Gen. Irwin Rommel's Afrika Korps using the 62-ton Mark VI tank. On Feb. 25 U.S. forces recaptured the pass.

Mar 2-4: In the **Battle of the Bismarck Sea**, a major U.S. victory in the Pacific, an entire Japanese convoy of 22 ships was sunk by American bombers. More than 50 Japanese planes were shot down.

May 7: Bizerte, Tunisia, was captured by American troops. The British took Tunis.

May 12: The **North African campaign** ended. Gen. Jurgen von Arnim, commander of Axis forces after

Rommel's recall to Europe, was captured in the Cape Bon peninsula along with other Axis officers.

May 30: Attu in the Aleutian Islands was retaken by U.S. forces after intense fighting.

July 10: Sicily was invaded by Allied forces, including Gen. George S. Patton's Seventh Army, British Field Marshal Bernard Law Montgomery's Eighth Army, and French and Canadian troops.

July 19: Rome was bombed by some 500 Allied planes. The highly strategic city, containing a network of railroads and freight yards, had been spared for four years by the Allies because of its religious significance.

Aug 11-24: The **Quebec conference** was held in Canada to work out the Pacific campaign. Some Chinese representatives were present during the conference. There was some difficulty in arriving at an accord with the Russians over future European operations and postwar problems. Pres. Roosevelt and British Prime Minister Winston Churchill met privately on Aug. 17.

Aug 15: Kiska in the Aleutians was retaken by American and Canadian units. When the troops landed, the Japanese were gone.

Aug 17: Sicily was conquered by Allied forces 37 days after it was invaded. The Axis powers had lost 167,000 men in the campaign, the Allies 25,000.

Aug 28: New Georgia in the Solomon Islands was secured by U.S. forces.

Sep 3: Invasion of Italy was commenced by Allied forces crossing the Strait of Messina.

Sep 8: Italy surrendered unconditionally to the Allied powers. German troops there fought on.

Sep 9: The **Allies landed at Salerno,** Italy. Upward of 700 American, British, Dutch, French, and Polish ships took part in the operation. The U.S. Fifth Army, under command of Gen. Mark Clark, participated in the landing.

Oct 13: Italy declared war on Germany. The new Italian government was headed by Pietro Badoglio. Mussolini, who had been placed under arrest, had been rescued (Sept. 12) by German commandos led by Col.

Otto Skorzeny. Mussolini formed a new fascist government in northern Italy.

Oct 19: The **Moscow conference** opened. Representatives of Great Britain, the U.S., the U.S.S.R., and the Chinese agreed to collaborate on surrender terms for the enemy. The powers recognized the need for an international organization to prevent future wars.

Nov 1: U.S. forces landed on **Bougainville** Island in the Solomons.

Nov 2: A U.S. **air raid on Rabaul,** New Britain, proved a major defeat for the Japanese. Gen. Douglas MacArthur, suspecting an attack would be launched from Rabaul on Empress Augusta Bay, off the west coast of Bougainville, had ordered the mission. Nearly every ship in Rabaul's harbor was hit or sunk, about 94,000 tons of shipping.

Nov 20: U.S. forces landed on **Tarawa and Makin** in the Gilbert Islands. On Nov. 22 landings were made on Abemama. Occupation of the Gilbert Islands was completed on Nov. 23.

Nov 22: At a **conference in Cairo,** Egypt, Pres. Roosevelt, Prime Minster Churchill, and Generalissimo Chiang Kai-shek planned military strategy against Japan and declared that Japan, when defeated, would be stripped of all Pacific territories seized since 1914.

Nov 28-Dec 1: At the **Teheran conference** in Iran, Pres. Roosevelt, Prime Minister Churchill, and Premier Joseph Stalin met to map strategy for the coming Allied invasion of western Europe.

Dec 17: A bill repealing the **Chinese Exclusion Acts** and setting an annual immigration quota of 105 Chinese was signed by Pres. Roosevelt. On the next day, in Chicago, Edward Bing Kan filed an application for citizenship. On Jan. 18, 1944, he became the first Chinese to be naturalized under the new law.

Dec 24: Gen. **Dwight D. Eisenhower** was named Supreme Commander of Allied forces for the invasion of Europe.

II. Architecture
Arts and Music
Popular Entertainment
Publishing
Theater

Roy Harris, Aaron Copland, and William Schuman all produced fresh, inventive works for the concert stage this year. Led by such painters as Thomas Hart Benton, American regionalism was rediscovered once again. Some artists painted with almost exotic lushness, others with defiant realism. Refugee artists, including Piet Mondrian, Marc Chagall, Fernand Léger, and Yves Tanguy, flourished in the U.S., producing such striking works as Chagall's *The Juggler* and Mondrian's *Broadway Boogie-Woogie*. In theater, Richard Rodgers and Oscar Hammerstein, II, elevated the musical comedy with their remarkable production of *Oklahoma!* The year was good for the motion picture industry as well. Top box office attractions were Betty Grable, Bob Hope, Abbott and Costello, Bing Crosby, and Gary Cooper. Notables who died included Lorenz Hart, the lyricist who collaborated with Richard Rodgers, Nov. 22, at 47; and Sergei Rachmaninoff, the Russian-born composer who had made his home in the U.S. after World War I, Mar. 28, at 70.

Among **books published** this year was *A Tree Grows in Brooklyn* by Betty Smith, a novel about a young girl and her family living in a Brooklyn slum. Also published this year were *The Human Comedy* by William Saroyan; *Thirty Seconds Over Tokyo* by Capt. Ted W. Lawson; *Here Is Your War* by Ernie Pyle; *God Is My Co-Pilot* by Col. Robert L. Scott, Jr.; *Guadalcanal Diary* by Richard Tregaskis; and *One World* by Wendell Willkie, an optimistic work that sold more than a million copies within two months of publication.

May 3: Pulitzer prizes were awarded for the following: fiction, *Dragon's Teeth* by Upton Sinclair; biography, *Admiral of the Ocean Sea* by Samuel Eliot Morison; history, *Paul Revere and the World He Lived In*

by Esther Forbes; poetry, *A Witness Tree* by Robert
Frost; drama, *The Skin of Our Teeth* by Thornton
Wilder. *Secular Cantata No. 2, A Free Song* by William Schuman won the first Pulitzer prize for a musical composition.

May 5: A **postal-zone numbering system** was inaugurated in 178 cities. Postmaster General Frank C.
Walker expected the use of numbers to speed up mail
deliveries.

III. Business and Industry
   Education
   Philosophy and Religion
   Science

The CIO and AFL generally kept to their no-strike
pledges, making this a quiet year on the labor front.
The United Mine Workers, however, stood in defiance of the War Labor Board, claiming that working
conditions and wages were unacceptable. A 48-hour
minimum work week was proclaimed by Pres.
Roosevelt for all essential war industries in labor-scarce areas. Colleges and universities were promised relief in a plan to send thousands of men to
school to be trained as officers for the Army and
Navy. In October the Swedish government announced that for the fourth year Nobel Prizes would
not be awarded. However, in 1944 retroactive prizes
were awarded for 1943. George Washington Carver,
the scientist and educator known best for his studies
on uses of the peanut, died on Jan. 5, at age 78.

Large-scale production of **penicillin** in the U.S. was
made possible by the discovery of a mold on a cantaloupe in a fruit market in Peoria, Ill. This mold was
found to yield ten times as much penicillin as the
original mold obtained by Sir Alexander Fleming of
England.

In **salvage drives** this year, 255,513 tons of tin
cans, 43,919 tons of fat, 6,000,000 tons of wastepaper,
and more than 26,000,000 tons of iron and steel scrap
were collected for use in essential industries.

Jan 18: The **American Medical Association** (AMA)

was found by the U.S. Supreme Court to have violated antitrust laws by preventing activities of cooperative health groups. The action had been initiated on Dec. 20, 1938.

Feb 7: Shoe rationing began, limiting civilians to three pairs a year.

Feb 9: **A minimum 48-hour work week** in war plants was ordered by Pres. Franklin D. Roosevelt.

Mar 1: Rationing of canned goods began.

Mar 29: Rationing of meat, fat, and cheese began.

Apr 17: Essential workers were frozen, that is, prohibited from leaving their jobs, by order of the War Manpower Commission. The order affected some 27,000,000 workers.

May 22: Radar detection devices, according to an article in *Collier's* magazine, were being used by Allied and Axis armed services. The U.S. War and Navy departments disputed the British claim to have discovered the principle of radar.

June 14: In a challenge of the **compulsory flag salute** brought by Jehovah's Witnesses, the Supreme Court ruled that under the Bill of Rights, schoolchildren could not be compelled to salute the flag if the ceremony conflicted with their religion.

June 20: Race riots hit Detroit, Mich. The influx of some 300,000 whites and blacks to war plants in the area contributed to the outbreak of violence. In two days, 35 people were killed, and more than 500, mostly blacks, were wounded. Police arrested 300 whites. Race riots also broke out this summer in Mobile (May 25), Los Angeles (June 4), Beaumont, Tex. (June 19), and Harlem, New York City (Aug. 1).

IV. Fashion
   Folkways
   Holidays
   Social Issues and Crime
   Sports

Conversation everywhere concerned war news; emergence of a new form of music called jive, a

danceable form of jazz; and a steady stream of baseball players drafted into the military. Their departure
made for a duller game, but the fans remained loyal.
This year Judge Kenesaw Mountain Landis, baseball's first commissioner, was elected to the Baseball
Hall of Fame. As in several years past, the standard
male garb of America's hepcats was the zoot suit. It
consisted of a long, one-button jacket for men, with
broad, padded shoulders and peaked lapels, high-
waisted trousers that ballooned at the knees and
gripped the ankles, a wide silk tie worn against a
colored or striped shirt, a knee-length key chain, and
a broad-brimmed hat. Jitterbug was the most popular
dance of the year, and variations on its basic routine,
called the Lindy hop, proliferated. In a nine-page article, *Life* magazine hailed the Lindy hop as "the true
national folk dance of America."

Women's fashions were emancipated from the
Paris tradition when American designers produced
clothing of fabrics available despite wartime shortages. Two silhouettes were featured: a slim, straight,
clinging line, caught at the waist by a belt; and a more
bulky figure created by wool box coats and suits.

A new **pitching record** for the twentieth century
was set by the New York Giants relief pitcher Ace
Adams, who pitched in 70 games, only one of them
a complete game for him.

Mar 30: The **NCAA basketball championship** was won
by the University of Wyoming, which defeated
Georgetown 56 to 43.

May 1: The 69th annual **Kentucky Derby** was won by
Count Fleet, with a time of 2:04. The jockey was
Johnny Longden.

May 8: The 68th annual **Preakness Stakes** was won by
Count Fleet, with a time of 1:57²/₅. The jockey was
Johnny Longden.

June 5: The 75th annual **Belmont Stakes** was won by
Count Fleet, with a time of 2:28¹/₅. The jockey was
Johnny Longden. Count Fleet thus became the sixth
horse to win racing's Triple Crown.

Oct 5-11: The 40th annual **World Series** was won by
the New York Yankees (AL), defeating the St. Louis
Cardinals (NL) four games to one.

Dec 26: The **NFL championship** was won by the Chicago Bears, who defeated the Washington Redskins 41 to 21.

1944

I. Civil Rights
   Exploration and Settlement
   Government
   Statistics
   Wars

In the European theater Russian forces made spectacular but costly progress against the Germans. In May Italy fell and on June 6 Allied forces landed in Normandy. In August American armored units began to move rapidly across France. By year's end Allied forces were poised on Germany's eastern and western borders, preparing for the final assault. Similar successes in the Pacific theater led many to hope for victory within the year despite repeated warnings by responsible leaders that the Axis war potential was still formidable. In mid-June the Germans introduced a new weapon, the V-1 pilotless bomb; they launched it against London and other British cities. In September they followed it with the V-2, a supersonic rocket causing great destruction.

Jan 22: Allied troops landed at **Anzio,** Italy, in a move to outflank the German defensive positions on the Gustav line across central Italy. British and American troops were unable to advance and the German line held.

Feb 2: Roi Island in the Marshall Islands was taken by the Fourth Marine Division and positions were secured on Namur and Kwajalein. For the first time Allied troops set foot on prewar Japanese territory.

Mar 6: Berlin was bombed by 800 U.S. Flying Fortresses. Some 2000 tons of bombs were dropped on the German capital.

Apr 22: Netherlands New Guinea was invaded by U.S. forces.

May 18: Cassino, the key point on the Germans' Gustav line in Italy, was evacuated after two months of bitter resistance.

June 4: Allied forces entered Rome on this day, Trinity Sunday. Out of respect for the religious holiday, the American Fifth and British Eighth armies did not occupy the city until the next morning.

June 6: The **Normandy invasion** began on this date, designated D-Day. Code named Operation Overlord, the invasion included landings on five beachheads in Normandy, France. The operation, under command of Gen. Dwight D. Eisenhower, involved more than 4000 ships, some 3000 planes, and Allied troops eventually numbering more than 4,000,000.

June 16: Bombing of Japan began with a raid on the island of Kyushu by U.S. Superfortresses.

June 26-28: The **Republican National Convention nominated Thomas E. Dewey,** governor of New York, for the presidency and Gov. John W. Bricker of Ohio for the vice presidency.

July 6: A circus tent fire at an afternoon performance in Hartford, Conn., destroyed the main tent of Ringling Brothers and Barnum & Bailey Circus. The blazing canvas fell on fleeing spectators. In the scramble 167 persons were killed and more than 175 were injured.

July 10: Saipan fell to U.S. forces after 25 days of hard fighting. Upward of 25,000 Japanese soldiers were killed. Some 2359 Americans died and more than 11,000 were wounded.

July 18: St. Lô, a key position in the German line in Normandy, fell to the U.S. First Army.

July 19-21: The **Democratic National Convention nominated Pres. Roosevelt** for his fourth term. Sen. Harry S Truman of Missouri was nominated for the vice presidency.

July 25: A breakout at St. Lô by the U.S. First Army

under Gen. Omar Bradley led to collapse of the German line in northwestern France.

Aug 8: Brittany fell to the rapid Allied advance south from Normandy. U.S. forces launched a powerful drive eastward toward Paris.

Aug 9: Guam fell to U.S. forces after 20 days of bloody fighting. The conquest cost the Americans 1214 dead and nearly 6000 wounded. Some 17,000 Japanese were killed and almost 500 prisoners were taken.

Aug 15: Southern France was invaded by the U.S. Seventh Army under Lt. Gen. Alexander M. Patch.

Aug 21: The **Dumbarton Oaks conference** opened at Washington, D.C. It was attended by delegates from the U.S., Great Britain, China, and the U.S.S.R. The conference agreed on "proposals for establishment of a general international organization," laying the groundwork for establishment of the United Nations.

Aug 25: Paris was liberated. The German commander Gen. Dietrich von Choltitz surrendered to French Gen. Jacques-Philippe Leclerc.

Sep 12: In the **first American engagement on German soil,** the U.S. First Army pushed five miles into west central Germany. For the first time the Allies fought where the local population was hostile.

Sep 17-27: An unsuccessful **airborne invasion of Holland,** code named Operation Market-Garden, was staged by combined British and American forces. Airborne units were dropped behind German lines to seize five bridges across the Rhine R., including the key bridge at Arnhem. The units met unexpected resistance and suffered heavy casualties. Relief forces were unable to link up with airborne troops, who were forced to evacuate.

Oct 20: Americans landed at **Leyte,** Philippine Islands, fulfilling Gen. Douglas MacArthur's promise to return. It was during the Leyte campaign that the kamikaze, or suicide plane, was first used.

Oct 23-26: In the **Battle of Leyte Gulf** the Japanese fleet, which had been unable to halt U.S. invasion of the Philippines, suffered heavy losses. It was the largest naval battle of the war.

Nov 7: Franklin D. Roosevelt was reelected president of the United States, the only person ever to win a fourth term. Harry S Truman was elected vice president. The electoral vote was Roosevelt, 432; Gov. Thomas E. Dewey, Republican, 99. The popular vote was Roosevelt, 25,602,504, Dewey 22,006,285. In congressional elections the Democrats lost two Senate seats but held a 56–38 majority. In the House they gained 24 seats for a 242–190 lead, with two seats held by minor parties.

Dec 15: The new rank **general of the Army** was conferred by Congress on Henry "Hap" Arnold, Dwight D. Eisenhower, Douglas MacArthur, and George C. Marshall. Popularly known as five-star generals, the new appointees wore insignia of rank consisting of five stars joined in a circle.

Dec 16: The **Battle of the Bulge,** last major German offensive of the war, began as German forces broke through Allied defenses in the Ardennes. Led by Gen. Karl von Runstedt, the drive was intended to seize Antwerp and split the Allies in the west. Bad weather hampered Allied air and supply operations. U.S. forces at Bastogne, a strategic point, were surrounded but did not surrender. American resistance stiffened after the massacre of American prisoners at Malmédy (Dec. 17). On Dec. 23 Allied air operations resumed when bad weather lifted. German armored columns halted for lack of fuel and were destroyed. By Dec. 27 a U.S. relief column reached Bastogne. By mid-January 1945 all ground taken in the offensive had been recaptured.

II. Architecture
Arts and Music
Popular Entertainment
Publishing
Theater

The arts enjoyed a boom year. Paper shortages forced publishers to experiment with soft-cover books, and the success of the experiment was overwhelming. Painters who had not been drafted profited when a plentiful supply of money created new buyers who could not shop in the European market. Broadway producers found eager audiences for practically everything they presented. The sellers' market did not improve the quality of the offerings. Architects were still learning a new trade—that of the efficiency builder, since the criterion for a contract was speed of construction. All their new ideas were confined to paper to await the end of the war. The movies enjoyed their greatest year in box office history, grossing close to $2,000,000,000 as the European market began to open in liberated areas. Such established stars as Bing Crosby and Gary Cooper took advantage of the tax laws by producing their own films. Top box office draws were Crosby, Cooper, Bob Hope, Betty Grable, and Spencer Tracy. The nation mourned the deaths of Charles Dana Gibson, the artist and illustrator who created the Gibson Girl, Dec. 23, at age 77; and Maj. Glenn Miller, director of the U.S. Air Force Band and, before the war, one of the most talented musicians and big band leaders. Miller was reported missing on a flight from Paris to London on Dec. 24.

Among **books published** this year was *Forever Amber* by Kathleen Winsor, a historical novel laced with sex. Set in England during the Restoration, the novel sold more than 1,000,000 copies in a year. Other books published this year included *Yankee from Olympus* by Catherine Drinker Bowen, a biography of Justice Oliver Wendell Holmes; *The World of Washington Irving* by Van Wyck Brooks; *A Bell for Adano,* a novel by John Hersey; *The Major Phase* by F. O. Matthiessen; *Brave Men* by Ernie Pyle; *Strange Fruit* by Lillian Smith, a novel whose central characters, a black woman and a white man, were torn between their love for each other and the strictures of southern society; and *Immortal Wife* by Irving Stone, a fictionalized biography of Jessie Frémont.

May 1: Pulitzer prizes were awarded for the following: fiction, *Journey in the Dark* by Martin Flavin; history, *The Growth of American Thought* by Merle Curti; biography, *The American Leonardo: The Life of Samuel F. B. Morse* by Carlton Mabee; poetry, *West-*

ern Star by Stephen Vincent Benét. A special award was given to *Oklahoma!* by Richard Rodgers and Oscar Hammerstein, II.

Oct 1: The **Declaration of Independence** and other historic documents sent away from Washington, D.C., for safekeeping in Dec. 1941 were put on display again at the Library of Congress.

Nov 11: An agreement on **record royalties** ended a two-year battle between recording companies and the American Federation of Musicians. Two major recording companies signed a contract agreeing to pay the union a fee on each record manufactured.

III. Business and Industry
   Education
   Philosophy and Religion
   Science

Industry had done such a remarkable job in producing war materiel that the government was able to relax many of its priority regulations. Manufacturers took advantage of the move by looking forward to a consumer economy. Labor controls remained in full effect, however, as did the many curbs against inflation. Despite these checks, living costs rose by nearly one-third, engendering unrest in union ranks. Institutions of higher education mourned the virtual end of the ASTP (Army Specialized Training Program). Some 110,000 of the 145,000 young men who had been enrolled in the nation's colleges were removed and sent to active service. Notables who died this year included Aimee Semple McPherson, the Canadian-born evangelist, fundamentalist preacher, and faith healer, Sept. 27, at age 54.

Penicillin, medical wonder of the year, was shown to be effective against wounds and a wide variety of infectious diseases. Further uses were also found for the sulfa drugs. In one of the more important medical feats of the war, the armed forces used the insecticide DDT to control and wipe out typhus, transmitted by body lice among troops and civilians.

In **salvage drives** this year, nearly 7,000,000 tons of wastepaper, 84,807 tons of fat, 18,500,000 tons of iron and steel scrap, 185,676 tons of tin cans, and 544,739 tons of rags were collected.

Apr 26: The **Montgomery Ward plant was seized** by the Army. Troops entered the Chicago plant after company chairman Sewell Avery refused to extend the firm's contract with the CIO as ordered by the WLB. Labor trouble continued, and on Dec. 28 troops again seized the plant and other company properties.

May 3: Meat rationing was ended, except for steak and choice cuts of beef, by order of the OPA.

May 8: The **first eye bank** was established by New York Hospital, New York City, in conjunction with 19 other New York hospitals. The eye bank was used to store human corneas, which could be used to restore sight in certain kinds of blindness.

May 20: The **Communist Party voted to disband** at a convention held in New York City. Its leaders formed a non-party group, the Communist Political Association.

Aug 14: Production of consumer goods such as vacuum cleaners, electric ranges, and cooking utensils was resumed under order of the WPB. The order was provisional and could be revoked depending on war needs.

Oct 26: The **Nobel Prize in Physiology or Medicine** was awarded to Joseph Erlanger of the Washington University Medical School in St. Louis and to Herbert Spencer Glasser of the Rockefeller Institute in New York for their research on the functions of single nerve fibers and their discovery that various types of nerve fibers conducted impulses at various speeds. At the same time the Nobel Prize in Physiology or Medicine for 1943 was awarded jointly to Edward A. Doisy of the St. Louis University School of Medicine and to Henrik Dam, the Danish biochemist. Dam was credited with discovering vitamin K, and Doisy with isolating vitamin K from alfalfa and determining its chemical nature.

Nov 10: The **Nobel Prize in Physics** was awarded to

I. I. Rabi of Columbia University for his studies of the magnetic properties of atomic nuclei. At the same time the Nobel Prize in physics for 1943 was awarded to Otto Stern of Carnegie Institute of Technology in Pittsburgh, Pa. A German-born physicist who came to America in 1933, Stern was honored for his contributions to the development of the molecular beam method for studying the magnetic attributes of atomic nuclei, and for his discovery of the magnetic movement of the proton.

IV. Fashion
Folkways
Holidays
Social Issues and Crime
Sports

Fashions swung toward bare midriffs, slim skirts, and large hats. Victories in both military theaters raised civilian morale and led to hopes the war would soon end. In boxing, a dispute over the lightweight championship arose in March when Bob Montgomery outpointed Beau Jack in 15 rounds at Madison Square Garden in New York City. Five days later his title, recognized by the New York State Athletic Commission, came into dispute when Juan Zurita defeated Sammy Angott in Hollywood and the National Boxing Association recognized Zurita as the lightweight champion. In golf the top money winner was Byron Nelson, with $37,967. Notables who died this year included Kenesaw Mountain Landis, commissioner of organized baseball for nearly 24 years, Nov. 25, at age 78.

Cartoonists **Bill Mauldin and George Baker** gave armed services newspapers their most popular features. In "Up Front with Mauldin," a pair of long-suffering GIs, Willie and Joe, endured combat stoically ("Just gimme th' aspirin. I already got a Purple Heart"). Baker created the "Sad Sack," an unlucky, confused, unkempt but well-meaning GI forever in trouble. In postwar years, Baker's "Sad Sack" became a regular feature of comic sections, and Mauldin took naturally to political cartooning.

Mar 28: The **NCAA basketball championship** was won by Utah, which defeated Dartmouth 42 to 40.

May 1: Ninety-year-old **Jacob S. Coxey,** standing on the steps of the Capitol in Washington, D.C., delivered the speech he was prevented from making 50 years before when he led Coxey's Army, a body of unemployed workers demanding a program of federal work projects.

Aug 20: The **PGA golf tournament** was won by Robert Hamilton, a relatively unknown pro from Indiana who beat Byron Nelson by one stroke in an upset victory.

Oct 4-9: The 41st **World Series** was won by the St. Louis Cardinals (NL), defeating the St. Louis Browns (AL) four games to two.

Dec 17: The **NFL championship** was won by the Green Bay Packers, who defeated the New York Giants 14 to 7.

1945

I. Civil Rights
Exploration and Settlement
Government
Statistics
Wars

It was a monumental year—the end of an era and the beginning of a new one. Germany and Japan were forced to accept unconditional surrender. Atomic bombs were dropped on two Japanese cities—a fact that changed the complexion of future wars and of the world in general. A new instrument of peace—the United Nations—was launched at San Francisco. The presidency of the United States changed hands as Franklin D. Roosevelt died in office. Another notable who died this year was Gen. George S. Patton, of injuries sustained in an auto accident on Dec. 9. Patton died in Heidelberg, Germany, Dec. 21, at age 60.

Jan 9: A **landing on Luzon** in the Philippines was made by the U.S. Sixth Army. In the operation, a task force of 850 ships sailed into Lingayen Gulf, 100 miles north of Manila.

Feb 4-11: The **Yalta conference,** a top-secret meeting in the Ukraine attended by Roosevelt, Winston Churchill, and Joseph Stalin, dealt with the postwar reorganization of Europe. Its communiqué, issued Feb. 12, called for a United Nations Conference on Apr. 25 to prepare a charter for a new peacekeeping organization.

Feb 7: Gen. **Douglas MacArthur returned to Manila** more than three years after he was forced out of the city by the Japanese.

Feb 23: On **Iwo Jima** the American flag was raised on Mt. Suribachi by Lt. Harold C. Shrier.

Mar 7: The **Remagen Bridge** over the Rhine R. was crossed by the U.S. First Army. Not since the days of Napoleon had an invading army crossed the Rhine.

Mar 16: Iwo Jima fell to the U.S. Marines after 36 days of bitter and bloody fighting. More than 4000 Marines were killed, 15,000 wounded. The Japanese lost more than 20,000 men.

Apr 1: Okinawa was invaded by U.S. forces.

Apr 12: Pres. **Franklin D. Roosevelt died** in Warm Springs, Ga., on the 83rd day of his fourth term; he was 63. He was succeeded by Harry S Truman.

Apr 24: The **United Nations conference** opened at San Francisco with delegates from 50 nations attending. The UN charter was signed June 26.

May 8: On this day, known as **V-E Day,** for victory in Europe, the instrument of unconditional surrender was ratified in Berlin, ending the European phase of World War II.

June 21: Japanese forces on **Okinawa** surrendered after two and a half months of deadly struggle. More than 100,000 Japanese soldiers were killed. American deaths ran to almost 13,000, with nearly 40,000 wounded.

July 5: The **Philippine Islands were declared liber-**

ated by Gen. Douglas MacArthur. In ten months of fighting since the first American landings at Leyte, more than 400,000 Japanese soldiers had been killed and upward of 12,000 Americans had lost their lives.

July 16: The **first atomic bomb** was detonated near Alamogordo, N. Mex., at 5:30 A.M.

July 28: In a bizarre **airplane crash,** a B-25 bomber flew into the Empire State Building in New York City. It became lodged between the 78th and 79th floors, killing 13 persons. The accident occurred on a foggy Saturday morning.

July 28: The **United Nations Charter** was ratified by the U.S. Senate by a vote of 89 to 2.

Aug 6: Hiroshima, Japan, was destroyed by the first atomic bomb to be used in war.

Aug 9: Nagasaki, Japan, was destroyed by the second atomic bomb to be used in war.

Aug 15: V-J Day, for victory over Japan, marked the end of the Pacific phase of World War II.

Sep 2: The formal **document of surrender** was signed aboard the U.S.S. *Missouri* in Tokyo Bay.

Nov 12: The **Nobel Peace Prize** was awarded to former secretary of state Cordell Hull for his contributions to the establishment of the United Nations. At the same time the 1944 prize was awarded to the International Red Cross. These were the first awards made since 1938.

II. Architecture
Arts and Music
Popular Entertainment
Publishing
Theater

Book publishing had a boom year, with the paperback trade continuing to create hundreds of thousands of book buyers. Hollywood, hungry for plots, was willing to pay as much as $250,000 for rights to a good story. With such prizes before them, writers tailored their techniques to fit the requirements of the screen. The result, by and large, was undistinguished. By war's end, the Hollywood Victory Com-

mittee had arranged for 55,619 personal appearances
of movie stars at bond rallies and military camps.
The motion picture industry kept up a high level of
production, even though the major companies were
under fire by government lawyers who charged them
with conspiring to form illegal trusts. Americans
mourned the passing of Robert Benchley, the humorist, Nov. 21, at age 56; and Ernie Pyle, the celebrated
war correspondent, who was killed on Iwo Jima on
Apr. 18, at age 44.

Among **books published** this year was *Black Boy*
by Richard Wright, the grim story of the author's
childhood. Other books published this year included
A Masque of Reason by Robert Frost; *Cass Timber-
lane* by Sinclair Lewis; *The Age of Jackson* by Arthur
M. Schlesinger, Jr., a fascinating account of the life
and times of Andrew Jackson; and *Captain from Cas-
tile* by Samuel Shellabarger, a historical novel.

May 7: Pulitzer prizes were awarded for the follow-
ing: fiction, *A Bell for Adano,* by John Hersey; history,
Unfinished Business by Stephen Bonsal; biography,
George Bancroft: Brahmin Rebel by Russel Blaine
Nye; poetry, *V-Letter and Other Poems* by Karl
Shapiro; drama, *Harvey* by Mary Coyle Chase; music,
Appalachian Spring by Aaron Copland.

III. Business and Industry
Education
Philosophy and Religion
Science

Aside from the war victory, the biggest news of the
year was the use of atomic energy. Scientists questioned the moral and ethical value of their contribution to victory in the war. At first, the public refused
to share the alarm of the physicists, believing that the
people who had created this new force would soon
tell the world how to control it. Unfortunately, this
did not come to pass.

Vitamin research in the U.S. continued with the
discovery of folic acid, a component of the large vita-

min B family and a necessary element for cell growth. Folic acid was found effective in the treatment of pernicious anemia, but later analyses revealed adverse affects on the nervous system.

Jan 15: A **nationwide dimout** was ordered to conserve diminishing fuel supplies.

Apr 30: **Sugar rations** were cut by 25% as reserves neared rock bottom.

May 8: The **nationwide dimout** was lifted.

July 1: The **New York State Commission Against Discrimination,** the first such agency in the U.S., was established. The commission was authorized to take steps to prevent "discrimination in employment because of race, creed, color, or national origin."

July 27: The **Communist Party** was reestablished by the Communist Political Association, which voted to disband itself.

Aug 14: All **manpower controls** were lifted by the War Manpower Commission.

Aug 18: Moving to **restore the civilian economy,** Pres. Truman ordered full restoration of civilian consumer production and collective bargaining, and a return of free markets.

Oct 30: **Shoe rationing** ended.

Nov 23: **Meat and butter rationing** ended.

Dec 20: **Tire rationing** ended.

IV. Fashion
Folkways
Holidays
Social Issues and Crime
Sports

It was a year of changes in sports. A new baseball commissioner was selected and both the Yankees and the Dodgers were sold to new owners. The annual baseball All-Star Game was canceled because of wartime transportation restrictions. In boxing a newcomer named Rocky Graziano scored five knockouts at Madison Square Garden. In golf the top money winner was Byron Nelson, with $63,335.66. American fashion designers stressed delicacy and pretti-

ness in their designs. Crime statistics recorded a star-
tling upward swing, which experts interpreted as
symptomatic of postwar uncertainty.

The phrase *Kilroy was here* appeared almost overnight throughout the world, at least wherever American GIs set foot. Kilroy represented a kind of abstract
conglomerate of all GIs. The phrase was scribbled by
U.S. Army gagsters on streets, billboards, latrines,
walls, and all other available surfaces.

Mar 29: The **NCAA basketball championship** was won
by Oklahoma A&M, which defeated DePaul 52–44.

Apr 24: Sen. **Albert B. "Happy" Chandler,** Democrat
of Kentucky, was named baseball commissioner,
filling the post vacated by the death of Kenesaw
Mountain Landis in 1944.

July 15: The **PGA golf tournament** was won by Byron
Nelson.

Oct 3-10: The 42nd annual **World Series** was won by
the Detroit Tigers (AL), defeating the Chicago Cubs
(NL) four games to three.

Dec 16: The **NFL championship** was won by the Cleveland Rams, who defeated the Washington Redskins
15 to 14.

1946

I. Civil Rights
   Exploration and Settlement
   Government
   Statistics
   Wars

Spiraling inflation, acute shortage of housing, and
bitter labor disputes were facing Americans. In addition there were rumblings of what came to be known
as the Cold War, and poverty-stricken Europe was
looking to the U.S. for aid. It quickly became appar-

ent that the U.S. would not be returning to a state of political isolation. Soviet expansionism became a new threat to world security, although some disagreed that Russia had territorial designs on the West. The administration took the view that complete isolation was a luxury Americans could not afford, primarily because of the existence of the atomic bomb, so the U.S. assumed the role of peacemaker in a world still in disorder.

July 1: Atomic bomb tests were held at Bikini Atoll in the Pacific. A Nagasaki-type bomb was dropped from 30,000 feet. It destroyed five ships, heavily damaged nine, and did varying amounts of damage to 45 others.

July 4: Philippine independence was proclaimed by Pres. Harry S Truman. He was keeping a promise made by the U.S. on acquiring the islands in 1898.

Aug 1: The McMahan Act, creating the **Atomic Energy Commission,** was signed by Pres. Truman. The commission was to be composed of a five-man control board without military representation but with military liaison. The act allowed the Army and Navy to manufacture atomic weapons and prohibited the distribution of fissionable materials or information on atomic energy.

Nov 5: In **congressional elections** the Republicans gained 13 Senate seats to take a 51–45 majority, and picked up 55 House seats for a 245–188 majority, with one seat held by a minor party.

Nov 14: The **Nobel Peace Prize** was awarded jointly to John Raleigh Mott and Emily Greene Balch. Mott, a Methodist layman and a leader in international church activities, headed the YMCA's relief activities for prisoners of war during World War I. Balch was a founder, in 1915, of the Women's International League for Peace and Freedom at The Hague, Netherlands.

Dec 14: The **UN accepted a gift** of $8,500,000 from John D. Rockefeller, Jr., for purchase of property along New York City's East R. for permanent UN headquarters.

II. **Architecture**
   Arts and Music
   Popular Entertainment
   Publishing
   Theater

Literary critics looked for a spate of fine books this year, calling up as their precedent the year immediately following World War I. Unfortunately, they were disappointed and had to be content with noting a new development in fictional technique—a modified stream of consciousness in which a highly sensitive story was told by a perceptive observer. Responding to high building costs, architects designed houses with small rooms and compensated by using more glass. U.S. painters exhibited in London and succeeded in shocking rather than boring viewers. Theatergoers were treated to one of the most extensive revival seasons in memory. The quality of motion pictures was up, as foreign producers made a strong bid for American markets, offering colorful spectacles and realistic dramas. Repeal of the federal excess profits tax and higher admission prices produced a record in box office receipts.

Among **books published** this year was *Memoirs of Hecate County* by Edmund Wilson, stories that caused a furor because of the author's treatment of sex. It raised a censorship issue reminiscent of the one inspired by James Branch Cabell's 1919 novel *Jurgen*. Lawsuits against Wilson and his publishers led eventually to withdrawal of the book for a time. Other books published this year included *Do I Wake or Sleep?* by Isobel Bolton, a novel written in the stream-of-consciousness style; *This Side of Innocence*, a novel by Taylor Caldwell; *Mr. Roberts* by Thomas Heggen; *B.F.'s Daughter* by John P. Marquand, a novel; *The Fields* by Conrad Richter, the second novel in a trilogy about a pioneer family that began with *The Trees* (1940); *The Hucksters* by Frederic Wakeman, a bitter novel about the advertising industry; *All the King's Men* by Robert Penn Warren, a novel about a southern political boss with parallels to the life of Huey Long; and *Delta Wedding*, a novel by Eudora Welty.

The first test of a new **Massachusetts obscene literature statute** was applied to Kathleen Winsor's 1945 best seller *Forever Amber*. The book was cleared in Suffolk County Superior Court and the decision upheld in the Massachusetts Supreme Court with the observation of Judge Frank J. Donahue that the book was more of a "soporific . . . than an aphrodisiac."

The **ranch style house** caught the architectural fancy of the public this year. Soon the countryside mushroomed with low-slung, one-story and split-level homes.

May 6: Pulitzer prizes were awarded for the following: biography, *Son of the Wilderness* by Linnie Marsh Wolfe; history, *The Age of Jackson* by Arthur M. Schlesinger, Jr.; drama, *State of the Union* by Russel Crouse and Howard Lindsay.

III. Business and Industry
Education
Philosophy and Religion
Science

It was a year of confusion and warfare between management and labor. Held down by years of wage controls, practically all the powerful labor unions struck for higher pay. Industry insisted that labor's demands were exorbitant, but could not afford walkouts at a time when consumer buying was at an unparalleled high. The country had a supply of ready money, saved from the days when nothing could be bought, and a new carefree desire to spend it. The changeover from war production to consumer goods took time, and tempers grew short when orders were not met immediately. The government, meanwhile, tried to convince people that the emergency was not yet over, that ruinous inflation still threatened, and that the shift to peacetime habits should be made cautiously.

Strikes this year involved some 4,600,000 workers, at a cost of 116,000,000 man-hours.

Feb 15: ENIAC, the electronic numerical integrator and computer, was dedicated at the Moore School of Electrical Engineering in Philadelphia, Pa. The first electronic digital computer, it had been developed by Dr. John W. Mauchly and J. Presper Eckert, Jr. It contained 18,000 vacuum tubes, occupied a 30 foot by 60 foot room, and weighed some 30 tons. The computer took 150,000 watts of power to run, had more than 500,000 soldered connections, and had taken 200,000 man-hours to build. Despite the fact that continual replacement of defective tubes was required to keep the machine running, ENIAC heralded a new age for science, engineering, industry, and mathematics.

July 7: Mother Frances Xavier Cabrini was canonized in ceremonies presided over by Pope Pius XII. She was the first American to be canonized. Mother Cabrini was the founder of the Missionary Sisters of the Sacred Heart of Jesus. Her principal shrine is at Mother Cabrini High School in New York City; her feast day is Dec. 22.

Oct 31: The **Nobel Prize in Physiology or Medicine** was awarded to Hermann Joseph Muller of Indiana University for his discovery of the production of mutations by x-ray irradiation. Muller obtained his first evidence of such mutations while at the University of Texas in 1926. His discoveries contributed greatly to genetics and radiology.

Nov 9: Wage and price controls were ended except for rent, sugar, and rice.

Nov 14: The **Nobel Prize in Physics** was awarded to Percy Williams Bridgman of Harvard University for his contributions to high-pressure physics. Bridgman developed an apparatus for production of very high pressures and made numerous discoveries in the study of high pressures.

Nov 14: The **Nobel Prize in Chemistry** was awarded jointly to James B. Sumner of Cornell University, for his work in the crystallization of enzymes, and to John Northrop and Wendell M. Stanley of the Rocke-

feller Institute, for their preparation of enzymes and
virus proteins in pure form. They were the fourth,
fifth, and sixth Americans to receive the Nobel Prize
in Chemistry.

IV. Fashion
   Folkways
   Holidays
   Social Issues and Crime
   Sports

Baseball stars returning from service improved the
game and afforded fans a breathtaking pennant race,
with a playoff necessary in the National League. In
golf the top money winner was Ben Hogan, with
$42,556.36. In keeping with peacetime optimism and
to retain leadership in the fashion world now that
styles again were coming from Paris, U.S. designers
showed lighthearted feminine collections. Chief topics of conversation included rising prices, the shortage of housing, the menace of Russian communism,
and the atomic bomb.

Mar 23: The **NCAA basketball championship** was won
by Oklahoma A&M, which defeated California 52 to
35.

May 4: The 72nd annual **Kentucky Derby** was won by
Assault, with a time of 2:06³⁄₅. The jockey was Warren Mehrtens.

May 11: The 71st annual **Preakness Stakes** was won
by Assault, with a time of 2:01²⁄₅. The jockey was
Warren Mehrtens.

June 1: The 78th annual **Belmont Stakes** was won by
Assault, with a time of 2:30⁴⁄₅. The jockey was Warren Mehrtens. Assault became the seventh horse to
win racing's Triple Crown.

June 16: The **U.S. Open golf tournament** was won by
Lloyd Mangrum, who defeated Byron Nelson and Vic
Ghezzi by one stroke.

July 6: At the **Wimbledon** tennis championships in
England, Pauline Betz won the women's singles title.
Louise Brough and Margaret Osborne won the

women's doubles, and Tom Brown and Jack Kramer won the men's doubles.

Aug 25: The **PGA golf tournament** was won by Ben Hogan.

Sep 8: The **U.S. Lawn Tennis Association singles championships** were won by Jack Kramer in the men's division and Pauline Betz in the women's division.

Oct 6-15: The 43rd annual **World Series** was won by the St. Louis Cardinals (NL), defeating the Boston Red Sox (AL) four games to three. On Oct. 3 the Cardinals had won the first National League playoff, beating the Brooklyn Dodgers in two games straight.

Dec 15: The **NFL championship** was won by the Chicago Bears, who defeated the New York Giants 24 to 14.

Dec 26: In the **Davis Cup** international tennis matches, the U.S. defeated Australia 5–0, regaining the trophy lost to Australia in 1939.

1947

I. Civil Rights
   Exploration and Settlement
   Government
   Statistics
   Wars

Economic equilibrium was the administration's chief concern. A restless population complained of constantly rising prices of food, clothing, rent, and other necessities of life. Manufacturers blamed rising costs on industry-wide wage boosts. Housing conditions everywhere became so tight that Pres. Harry S Truman called the shortage "the foremost of the many problems facing the nation." The most dramatic successes of the year were scored in foreign policy. The European Recovery program, or Marshall Plan, earned the gratitude of western European nations but the abuse of Iron Curtain countries. The intensity of the Cold War was stepped up as an executive order banned all members or sympathizers of the Communist Party from holding office in the executive branch of the U.S. government.

Apr 16-18: A **ship explosion** in Texas City, Tex., killed some 500 persons. The city itself was virtually annihilated by the blast. The nitrate-laden French freighter *Grandcamp* had caught fire early on the morning of Apr. 16. Fireman thought they had gotten the blaze under control until the ship exploded. Fire then swept the Monsanto Chemical Co. plant, and further explosions were set off in the ensuing conflagration. Also destroyed were a number of oil storage tanks. On Apr. 17 the freighter *High Flyer* exploded. The blasts and fires left the waterfront section of the city in complete devastation. Eyewitnesses said the scene was worse than anything they had seen in Europe during World War II.

May 22: The **Greek-Turkish Aid Bill** was signed by Pres. Truman. The bill authorized some $400,000,000 in aid to Greece and Turkey on their request. This authorization was subject to withdrawal on the disapproval of the interested countries, the U.N. Security Council or General Assembly, or the president if he deemed the aid to have been either improperly used or unnecessary. When Pres. Truman requested the legislation on Mar. 12 he said: "I believe that it must be the policy of the United States to support free peoples who are resisting attempted subjugation by armed minorities or by outside pressures." This political stance came to be known as the Truman Doctrine.

June 5: The **Marshall Plan** for reconstruction of Europe was proposed at Harvard University by Sec. of State George C. Marshall. He stated that careful study of European needs, on which U.S. aid should be based, was essential before progress could be made in the economic rehabilitation of Europe.

June 14: Peace treaties between the U.S. and Italy, Rumania, Bulgaria, and Hungary were ratified by the U.S. Senate and signed by Pres. Truman.

July 18: The **Presidential Succession Act** was signed by Pres. Truman. The act designated the Speaker of the House and then the president of the Senate pro tempore next in succession after the vice president.

Dec 27: A record-breaking **snowstorm** struck the Northeast, dumping a record 25.8 in. of snow on New York City and causing nearly 80 deaths in the North Atlantic states. Stalled trains stranded commuters. Marooned suburbanites crowded downtown hotels.

II. Architecture
Arts and Music
Popular Entertainment
Publishing
Theater

Two noticeable trends in American publishing were a reawakening interest in U.S. history and a turn toward philosophic introspection. The latter may have been prompted by increased concern with the fate of the human race now that it had discovered the power to destroy itself. Exhibitions of paintings featured non-objective and expressionistic works and leaned less on realism and surrealism. Composers took heart as orchestral societies encouraged production of new works. Despite a continuing boom on Broadway, producers found it difficult to find backers for their plays, with production costs twice what they had been five years earlier. Reluctant to risk so much on new scripts, producers resorted to revivals. Architects produced little that was new, since three-fourths of the building in the country was in the hands of large-scale developers. The biggest news in the movie industry was the investigation of alleged communist subversion. Senate committees claimed that ten screenwriters were communists or sympathizers and should not be allowed to work on films. A 20% federal amusement tax helped drive some customers away from movies to the new medium of television.

Among **books published** this year was *Under the Volcano*, a novel by the English-born writer Malcolm Lowry. The novel recounted the last day in the life of Geoffrey Firmin, an alcoholic British ex-consul in Mexico. The novel met with moderate success and critical acclaim, but eventually was recognized as a masterpiece. Other books published this year included *The Times of Melville and Whitman* by Van Wyck Brooks; *Butterfly* by James M. Cain, a novel; *Inside U.S.A.* by John Gunther; *The Big Sky* by A. B. Guthrie, a novel; *Gentleman's Agreement* by Laura Z. Hobson, a novel exploring anti-Semitism that became a best seller and was adapted for motion pictures; *Kingsblood Royal*, a novel by Sinclair Lewis; *Tales of the South Pacific* by James Michener; *The Harder They Fall*, a novel about boxing by Budd Schulberg; *I, the Jury* by Mickey Spillane; *The Wayward Bus* by John Steinbeck; and *Aurora Dawn* by Herman Wouk, the author's first novel.

Jan 28: A copy of the *Bay Psalm Book* was bought for $151,000 at an auction of the Parke-Bernet Galleries in New York City. This was the highest price paid to date for a book.

Apr 7: The first annual **Antoinette Perry, or Tony, Awards,** for outstanding contributions to the American theater during the 1946–1947 season, were presented. Among those honored were José Ferrer for his performance in *Cyrano de Bergerac;* Fredric March for *Years Ago;* Ingrid Bergman for *Joan of Lorraine;* Helen Hayes for *Happy Birthday;* and Patricia Neal for *Another Part of the Forest.* The awards were named after Antoinette Perry, who died in 1946. She served as director of the wartime board of the American Theater Wing.

May 5: Pulitzer prizes were awarded for the following: fiction, *All the King's Men* by Robert Penn Warren; biography, *The Autobiography of William Allen White;* history, *Scientists Against Time* by James Phinney Baxter, III; poetry, *Lord Weary's Castle* by Robert Lowell.

III. Business and Industry
Education
Philosophy and Religion
Science

Many of labor's hard-won gains were erased this year by passage of the widely debated Taft-Hartley Bill. While many citizens applauded the law's effective curb on alleged union excesses, labor leaders pledged an all-out effort to repeal the legislation, particularly the provision outlawing closed-shop contracts. Despite this setback, organized labor grew more powerful as a continuing business boom sent more and more workers into its ranks. American education was concerned with five major areas: improving the economic lot of teachers; meeting the challenge of increased enrollment; taking advantage of federal aid for schools while keeping schools free of government control; settling the growing controversy over the role of religion in education; and implementing a growing interest in international educational cooperation.

Enrollment of veterans in American colleges, spurred by the Servicemen's Readjustment Act of 1944, known as the G.I. Bill of Rights, reached its peak. Over 1,000,000 former servicemen were among some 2,500,000 students attending college classes.

Magazine circulation figures climbed. Thirty-eight magazines reported circulations of more than 1,000,000. In 1900 no U.S. magazine had a circulation of more than 500,000.

June 17: The **first globe-circling passenger airline** was inaugurated by Pan American Airways, Inc. A round-the-world fare was $1700. The new service began when the clipper *America,* a Lockheed Constellation, took off from La Guardia Airport en route to Gander, Newfoundland, the first stop on a 22,170-mile trip around the world. The plane was scheduled to return to New York on June 30.

June 23: The controversial **Taft-Hartley Act** was passed over Pres. Harry S Truman's veto. The act reduced or eliminated many labor union advantages provided for in the National Labor Relations Act of 1935, including the unconditional closed shop, the check-off system, which enabled unions to collect dues from all employed members; the unconditional right to strike at any time; and immunity from employer lawsuits over breaches of contract and strike damage. New obligations for labor unions included publication of financial statements and a mandatory affidavit of all union leaders attesting to nonmembership in the Communist Party.

Oct 14: The **first supersonic aircraft,** the Bell X-1 research airplane, was piloted faster than the speed of sound for the first time by Capt. Charles E. Yeager, USAF, during a test at Muroc Air Force Base, Calif.

Oct 23: The **Nobel Prize in Physiology or Medicine** was awarded jointly to Carl F. Cori and his wife Gerty T. Cori of Washington University in St. Louis for "the discovery of how glycogen is catalytically converted," and to Dr. Bernardo A. Houssay of Buenos Aires, Argentina, for his studies of the hormone produced by the pituitary gland. The Coris were the third husband and wife team to be awarded a Nobel Prize in the field of scientific research. Born in Czechoslovakia, they came to the U.S. in 1922.

IV. Fashion
Folkways
Holidays
Social Issues and Crime
Sports

Baseball took a historic step forward as Jackie Robinson signed with the Brooklyn Dodgers, of the National League, becoming the first black to play in the major leagues. Later in the year other black athletes played in the American League for the first time. In boxing, Joe Louis resumed his defense of the world heavyweight title, winning (Dec. 5) a split decision over "Jersey Joe" Walcott. In golf, the top money winner was Jimmy Demaret, $27,936.83. In women's fashion, the topic of conversation was the so-called New Look, inspired by the Paris designer Christian

Dior, who screened women's legs with a long skirt, pinched in their waists, and flattened their bosoms.

Mar 25: The **NCAA basketball championship** was won by Holy Cross, which defeated Oklahoma 58–47.

June 15: The **U.S. Open golf tournament** was won by Lew Worsham, who beat Sam Snead by one stroke on the last green in an 18-hole playoff.

June 24: The **PGA golf tournament** was won by Jim Ferrier.

July 4-5: At the **Wimbledon** tennis championships in England, Jack Kramer won the men's singles title and Margaret Osborne won the women's singles. Kramer teamed with Robert Falkenburg to win the men's doubles, Doris Hart and Patricia Canning Todd won the women's doubles, and Louise Brough teamed with John E. Bromwich of Australia to win the mixed doubles.

Sep 30-Oct 6: The 44th annual **World Series** was won by the New York Yankees (AL), defeating the Brooklyn Dodgers (NL) four games to three.

Dec 28: The **NFL championship** was won by the Chicago Cardinals, who defeated the Philadelphia Eagles 28 to 21.

Dec 30: In the **Davis Cup** international tennis challenge round, the U.S. defeated Australia four matches to one.

1948

I. Civil Rights
Exploration and Settlement
Government
Statistics
Wars

The administration and the lawmakers fought all year. Pres. Harry S Truman called the 80th Congress the "worst in our history." One of the chief areas of disagreement was over the supposed presence of communists in governmental positions. The House Committee on Un-American Activities wrote alarming reports, which the president largely ignored, calling one finding a "red herring." The president maintained that the FBI together with the Justice Department was more than equal to the task of cleaning house. Some 2,000,000 federal employees were investigated; as a direct result, 526 resigned and 98 were dismissed. In foreign affairs, the European Recovery Program continued with military aid to Greece, Turkey, and China. The most dramatic development of the year was the Soviet blockade of Berlin, which the U.S. broke by maintaining an airlift to resupply the beleaguered city.

Mar 30: The **Rent Control Bill**, which extended controls until Mar. 31, 1949, was signed by Pres. Truman. The bill also designated an Emergency Court of Appeals to decide on decontrols or increases recommended by local boards but rejected by the federal housing expediter.

Apr 3: The **Foreign Assistance Act** of 1948 was signed by Pres. Truman. The act provided $5,300,000,000 for a one-year European Recovery Program, known popularly as the Marshall Plan. The act also provided $275,000,000 for military aid to Greece and Turkey, $463,000,000 for economic and military aid to China, and $60,000,000 for a UN Fund for Children.

June 24: The **Selective Service Act** was signed by Pres. Truman. It provided for the registration of all men between 18 and 25 and the draft of enough men to constitute an Army of 837,000, a Navy and Marine Corps of 666,882, and an Air Force of 502,000.

June 25: The **Displaced Persons Bill** was signed by Pres. Truman. It admitted 205,000 European displaced persons, including 3000 nonquota orphans.

July 15: The **Democratic National Convention nominated Pres. Truman** for reelection, and Sen. Alben W. Barkley of Kentucky for the vice presidency.

July 17: The **States Rights Democrats** nominated Gov. Strom Thurmond of South Carolina for the presidency and Gov. Fielding L. Wright of Mississippi for the vice presidency. The political group, also known as the Dixiecrats, were members of the Democratic Party who had walked out of the national convention in opposition to the party's strong civil rights platform.

July 20: Twelve American **Communist Party leaders were indicted** and charged with advocating overthrow of the U.S. government.

Nov 2: Harry S Truman was reelected president of the United States in a major political upset. Alben W. Barkley was elected vice president. Political analysts and polls had predicted that Truman's Republican opponent, Gov. Thomas E. Dewey of New York, would win. The electoral vote was Truman 304, Dewey 189. The popular vote was Truman 24,104,836; Dewey 21,969,500; Strom Thurmond, States Rights Democrat, 1,169,312; Henry A. Wallace, Progressive, 1,157,172; Norman M. Thomas, Socialist, 132,138; and Claude A. Watson, Prohibition Party, 103,343. In congressional elections the Democrats gained nine Senate seats for a 54–42 majority. In the House they gained 75 seats for a 263–171 lead, with one seat going to a minor party.

Dec 15: Alger Hiss, a former State Department official, was indicted by a federal grand jury on two counts of perjury. Hiss, who had worked in the State Department in 1937 and 1938, denied giving official documents to Whittaker Chambers, a self-proclaimed courier for a communist spy group. He also denied ever meeting Chambers after Jan. 1, 1937.

II. Architecture
Arts and Music
Popular Entertainment
Publishing
Theater

World War II was one of the leading subjects of this year's books, and first novels dealing with the war by Norman Mailer and Irwin Shaw were among the

year's best. The newest communication medium,
television, was cursed in many quarters as the eventual destroyer of American reading, theater, and
movies. Actually, TV broadcasts of concerts and operas led to creation of music festivals and commissions for new composers, while movie studios suffered a 25% drop in employment, in part due to stiff
European competition.

Among **books published** this year was *Raintree
County* by Ross Lockridge, a first novel that achieved
both critical and popular success. It was to be the
author's only book. He died on March 6 at the age of
33, an apparent suicide. Other books published this
year included the best-selling religious novel *The Big
Fisherman* by Lloyd C. Douglas; *Crusade in Europe* by
Dwight D. Eisenhower; *The Naked and the Dead* by
Norman Mailer, the author's first novel and one of
the best fictional works about World War II; and *The
Young Lions* by Irwin Shaw, another first novel, also
about World War II and a critical and popular success.

The first **Supreme Court hearing on a state obscenity law** related to a specific book concerned Edmund Wilson's *Memoirs of Hecate County* and its suppression in New York State. The Court was
deadlocked on the question and thus upheld the
lower court conviction of the publisher.

May 3: Pulitzer prizes were awarded to the following:
fiction, *Tales of the South Pacific* by James Michener;
biography, *Forgotten First Citizen: John Bigelow* by
Margaret Clapp; history, *Across the Wide Missouri* by
Bernard De Voto; poetry, *Age of Anxiety* by W. H.
Auden; drama, *A Streetcar Named Desire* by Tennessee Williams.

Nov 4: The **Nobel Prize for Literature** was awarded to
T. S. Eliot. Born in St. Louis in 1888, Eliot moved to
England and in 1927 became a British subject.
Among his works of poetry were *The Waste Land*
(1922), and *Ash Wednesday* (1930).

III. Business and Industry
Education
Philosophy and Religion
Science

Bolstered by increased defense expenditures and a costly foreign-aid program, American industry enjoyed a peak year. Relations between labor and management were particularly mellow. General Motors granted an automatic cost-of-living increase to some 265,000 hourly workers. Strikes were fewer and less violent. However, education had a number of new problems to consider, including sharply rising enrollments; inadequate facilities; the failure of teachers to gain better economic status, mainly because rising prices offset salary increases; a shortage of teachers; a decline in enrollment of veterans at colleges and universities; and an ever-swelling tide of foreign students on exchange scholarships.

Conquest of **pernicious anemia** was completed with the discovery of vitamin B-12, the substance in liver extracts responsible for earlier cures. Vitamin B-12 was found to have phenomenal efficiency. A daily dosage equivalent to one hundredth of a grain of salt was sufficient to cure a victim of pernicious anemia, and the same quantity taken twice a week maintained the cured person in good health.

The **Polaroid Land Camera,** patented by Edwin H. Land in 1947, went on sale. The first camera to carry its own darkroom, it processed prints in one minute. It was an instant hit with professional photographers, who saw the value in obtaining instant prints of subjects. The Polaroid gave them greater flexibility in experimenting with lighting and settings for their subjects.

Mar 5: A new **U.S. rocketry record** was set by the Navy. A speed of 3000 mph and an altitude of 78 miles were achieved during tests at White Sands, N. Mex.

Mar 8: Religious education in public schools was declared a violation of the First Amendment by the U.S. Supreme Court.

June 3: The **world's largest reflector telescope** was
dedicated. It was the 200-inch Hale telescope at Palo-
mar Mountain Observatory, maintained by the California Institute of Technology.

Nov 20: A new **balloon altitude record** was claimed by
the U.S. Army Signal Corps. It was 140,000 feet (26 1/2
miles).

IV. Fashion
   Folkways
   Holidays
   Social Issues and Crime
   Sports

The major leagues provided baseball fans with the
first post-season playoff in the history of the American League when the Cleveland Indians ended the
year with the same won-and-lost record as the Boston
Red Sox. This year the Baseball Hall of Fame elected
two new members: Herbert J. Pennock, the pitcher,
and Harold "Pie" Traynor, longtime third baseman
for the Pittsburgh Pirates. Plaques honoring the two
were unveiled at Cooperstown, N.Y., in the 1949 annual ceremonies. In golf the top money winners were
Ben Hogan, $36,812, and Mildred "Babe" Didrikson
Zaharias, $3400. Meanwhile, the nation's crime rate
remained steady. Racketeers concentrated on large-
scale gambling operations, some of which had the
tacit approval of local authorities. In fashion, the so-
called New Look, in vogue last year, was rejected.
Women now wanted the more natural lines of the
body to show. Notables who died included George
Herman "Babe" Ruth, the Sultan of Swat, Aug. 16, at

Jan 30-Feb 8: At the **Winter Olympics** in St. Moritz,
Switzerland, the U.S. won three gold medals and finished third in unofficial team standings, behind Sweden and Switzerland.

Mar 13: The **NCAA basketball tournament** was won
by Kentucky, which defeated Indiana State 82 to 70.

May 1: The 74th annual **Kentucky Derby** was won by
Citation, with a time of 2:05 2/5. The jockey was Eddie
Arcaro.

May 15: The 73rd annual **Preakness Stakes** was won by Citation, with a time of 2:02³/₅. The jockey was Eddie Arcaro.

May 25: The **PGA golf tournament** was won by Ben Hogan.

June 12: The 80th annual **Belmont Stakes** was won by Citation, with a time of 2:28¹/₅. Citation thus became the eighth horse in history to win the Triple Crown of racing. The jockey was Eddie Arcaro, who chalked up his second Triple Crown victory.

June 12: The **U.S. Open golf tournament** was won by Ben Hogan, with a tournament record-breaking score of 276, five strokes lower than the previous tournament record.

June 25: The **world heavyweight boxing championship** was successfully defended by Joe Louis, who defeated "Jersey Joe" Walcott in an 11-round bout.

July 2: At the **Wimbledon** tennis championships in England, Robert Falkenburg won the men's singles title. The next day Louise Brough won the women's singles, then teamed with Margaret Osborne du Pont to win the women's doubles, and with John Bromwich of Australia to win the mixed doubles.

July 29-Aug 14: At the **Summer Olympics** in London, England, the U.S. won 33 gold medals and the unofficial team championship.

Sep 6: In the **Davis Cup** international tennis challenge round, the U.S. won its fifth straight match from Australia, sweeping the round 5–0 and retaining the trophy.

Oct 6-11: The 45th annual **World Series** was won by the Cleveland Indians (AL), defeating the Boston Braves (NL) four games to two. The Indians had won the American League pennant by beating the Boston Red Sox 8 to 3 in a single-game playoff, the first time a playoff was needed in the league.

Oct 24: The term *Cold War* to characterize East-West relations after World War II was given national prominence after a speech by Bernard M. Baruch before the Senate War Investigating Committee. "Although the war is over," said Baruch, "we are in the midst of a cold war which is getting warmer."

Dec 19: The **NFL championship** was won by the Phila-

delphia Eagles, who defeated the Chicago Cardinals
7 to 0.

1949

I. Civil Rights
   Exploration and Settlement
   Government
   Statistics
   Wars

In his message to Congress this year, Pres. Harry S
Truman presented a program of domestic legislation
that he called the Fair Deal. It included repeal of the
Taft-Hartley law, reenactment of the Wagner Act, a
law calling for a minimum wage of 75 cents an hour,
generous farm price supports, expansion of Social
Security, federal aid to local school systems, low-rent
public housing, slum clearance, and broad civil
rights proposals. In foreign affairs, the Senate ratified
the North Atlantic Treaty Alliance and pledged over
$1,250,000,000 to finance a military assistance pro-
gram. Worry over communists at home continued as
the U.S.S.R. disclosed that it too had atomic weapons,
and eleven Communist Party leaders in New York
City were found guilty of advocating overthrow of
the government.

Feb 7: The **Hoover Commission on Organization of
the Executive Branch of the Government** issued the
first part of its report, recommending streamlining of
the executive branch. On Feb. 17 the commission suggested that the Post Office Department be placed
beyond politics and run on a business basis. On Mar.
21 it suggested creation of a new Cabinet post, secretary of a department of national welfare and education. In its final report, on Apr. 1, the commission
characterized many government enterprises as corrupt and inefficient.

Apr 4: The **North Atlantic Treaty Organization** (NATO) was formed when the North Atlantic Treaty was signed in Washington, D.C., by representatives of Belgium, Canada, Denmark, France, Great Britain, Italy, Iceland, Luxembourg, The Netherlands, Norway, Portugal, and the U.S.

May 18: The first U.S. civilian **high commissioner of Germany** was appointed. He was John J. McCloy, president of the International Bank for Reconstruction and Development.

May 31: The perjury trial of **Alger Hiss** opened in New York City. Hiss had been indicted on Dec. 15, 1948, on two counts of perjury relating to his testimony to a federal grand jury on alleged espionage activities while a State Department official. Whittaker Chambers, a confessed courier for a communist spy ring, testified that Hiss had passed him official documents. Hiss denied giving Chambers any documents while at the State Department in 1937 and 1938, and denied seeing Chambers after Jan. 1, 1937. On July 8 the jury reported a deadlock and was dismissed. A new trial opened on Nov. 17.

June 29: The last **U.S. forces in Korea** were withdrawn. They had been occupying the southern portion of the peninsula since the end of World War II. Only a military mission remained.

Aug 31: The **Grand Army of the Republic,** veterans of the Civil War, held its 83rd and last encampment. It was attended by six of the 16 surviving veterans at Indianapolis, Ind.

Oct 14: Eleven American communist leaders were convicted of conspiring to advocate the overthrow of the government after a long, bitter trial marked by personal attacks on the presiding federal judge, Harold Medina. All were sentenced on Oct. 21 by Judge Medina to fines of $10,000. Ten were sentenced to five years imprisonment, one to three years. Originally, 12 leaders had been indicted but the case against William Z. Foster had been separated from the others because of Foster's ill health.

Oct 24: The permanent **UN headquarters** in New York City were dedicated.

II. Architecture
   Arts and Music
   Popular Entertainment
   Publishing
   Theater

The year in publishing was marked by an increasing popularity of books on religion, studies of world affairs, and books that discussed the plight of black Americans. Architects rejoiced in slightly decreased building costs, which enabled them to plan more luxury residences. The trend toward decentralization of cities afforded new opportunities to design factories, laboratories, and offices in rural areas. The League of New York Theaters instituted an investigation into the ills of the theater. Its findings recommended fairer policies toward the public in the matter of ticket distribution, pooling of production techniques, more careful advertising and promotion, and the training of theater staffs. The motion picture industry regained its momentum and enjoyed a healthy financial year.

Among **books published** this year was *The Man With the Golden Arm* by Nelson Algren, the powerful story of Frankie Machine, a Chicago poker dealer whose heroin addiction keeps him from escaping the slums and ultimately leads him to suicide. Other books published this year included *The Brave Bulls* by Tom Lea, the author's first novel; *The Waters of Siloe* by Thomas Merton, a history of the Trappist Order; *A Rage to Live* by John O'Hara, a novel; *The Greatest Story Ever Told* by Fulton Oursler; *A Guide to Confident Living* by Norman Vincent Peale; and *Peace of Soul* by Fulton J. Sheen.

Feb 19: The **first Bollingen Prize** for poetry was awarded to Ezra Pound for his 1948 collection The *Pisan Cantos.* The award sparked bitter controversy because Pound had been charged with treason for making pro-fascist broadcasts in Italy during World War II.

May 2: **Pulitzer prizes** were awarded for the following: fiction, *Guard of Honor* by James Gould Cozzens; biography, *Roosevelt and Hopkins* by Robert E. Sherwood; history, *The Disruption of American Democracy* by Roy Franklin Nichols; poetry, *Terror and Decorum* by Peter Viereck; drama, *Death of a Salesman* by Arthur Miller.

III. Business and Industry
Education
Philosophy and Religion
Science

A record national debt of $250,000,000,000 was offset by rising national income, estimated at $222,000,000,000. Agricultural productivity was at an all-time high. Economists noted a slight decline during the first half of the year, but pointed out that such a sag was inevitable after the inflation of 1948. Total salaries and wages reached new highs; the automotive industry sent some 6,000,000 cars and trucks off assembly lines—a new record. Unemployment increased by 1,500,000. Labor pressed for the fourth round of wage increases since the end of the war. The most significant development for labor was growing involvement in national politics. Candidates for elective office took great care to draw up platforms designed to attract the labor vote.

Feb 25: A **flight altitude record** was set when an American guided missile, the WAC-Corporal, was launched at White Sands, N. Mex., and reached an altitude of 250 miles. It was the highest altitude ever achieved by a manmade projectile.

Mar 2: The **first nonstop round-the-world flight** was completed by the U.S. Air Force Superfortress *Lucky Lady II*, which touched down at Carswell Air Force Base, Tex. The airplane had been refueled in the air four times.

Apr 20: The discovery of **cortisone** was announced. The hormone promised to bring relief to sufferers of rheumatoid arthritis, the most painful type of arthritis.

Oct 26: A **minimum wage bill** was signed by Pres. Truman, raising the minimum wage in certain industries engaged in interstate commerce from 40 cents to 75 cents an hour.

Nov 3: The **Nobel Prize for Chemistry** was awarded to William Francis Giauque for his work in chemical thermodynamics, specifically his studies of substances at very low temperatures. Giauque, born in Canada, was professor of chemistry at the University of Canada.

IV. Fashion
    Folkways
    Holidays
    Social Issues and Crime
    Sports

The two major league baseball leagues staged breathtaking shows for their fans as both pennants were clinched on the last day of the season. In golf the top money winners were Sam Snead, $31,593.83, and Mildred "Babe" Didrikson Zaharias, $4650. In boxing, Joe Louis officially retired in March. On June 22 Ezzard Charles defeated "Jersey Joe" Walcott in a 15-round decision and became the new world heavyweight champion. For a change, American men cheered Parisian fashion designers as they decreed daring decolletage for evening wear and bikini bathing suits for the beach.

Mar 26: The **NCAA basketball championship** was won by Kentucky, which defeated Oklahoma State 46 to 36.

May 31: The **PGA golf tournament** was won by Sam Snead.

June 11: The **U.S. Open golf tournament** was won by Cary Middlecoff.

July 1-2: At the **Wimbledon** tennis championships in England, Ted Schroeder won the men's singles title and Louise Brough won the women's singles. Louise Brough and Margaret Osborne du Pont won the women's doubles, and Frank Parker and Richard Gonzales won the men's doubles.

Aug 28: In the **Davis Cup** international tennis challenge round, the U.S. won the final two matches from

Australia to take the round 4 to 1 and retain the trophy.

Oct 5-9: The 46th annual **World Series** was won by the
New York Yankees (AL), defeating the Brooklyn
Dodgers (NL) four games to one.

Dec 18: The **NFL championship** was won by the Philadelphia Eagles, who defeated the Los Angeles Rams
14 to 0.

1950

I. Civil Rights
Exploration and Settlement
Government
Statistics
Wars

The nation was concerned with inflation, the threat
of communism, and a foreign policy that never
seemed to bring lasting peace. Profound pessimism
gripped the country when in June North Korean
troops crossed the 38th parallel and invaded South
Korea. The action was given over to the United Nations to handle; the organization sent an international police force with orders to end the hostilities.
Since no other nation could afford to enter the area
in force, the U.S. embarked on a costly, unpopular
war. Hatred of communist influences within the
country mounted as FBI director J. Edgar Hoover
announced that there were 55,000 party members
and 500,000 sympathizers active within the U.S. The
Senate appointed a special investigating committee
to probe charges of communist activity in the State
Department that had been leveled by Sen. Joseph
McCarthy, Republican of Wisconsin.

The U.S. **Census** reported a population of
150,697,361. The center of the population was placed

at eight miles north-northwest of Olney, Richland County, Ill.

Jan 21: Alger Hiss was convicted on two counts of perjury. The jury at this, his second trial on the perjury indictments, found Hiss guilty of lying to a federal grand jury. The jury was investigating allegations of espionage made by Whittaker Chambers, an avowed courier for a communist spy group. On Jan. 25 Hiss was sentenced to two concurrent five-year prison terms.

Jan 31: Development of the **hydrogen bomb** was authorized by Pres. Truman.

June 25: The **Korean War** (1950–1953) began when North Korean forces launched an invasion across the 38th parallel into South Korea. The UN ordered an immediate cease-fire and withdrawal of invading forces.

June 27: U.S. forces were ordered to Korea by Pres. Truman to help South Korea repel the North Korean invasion. The president received the approval of Congress for his action, and the UN Security Council adopted a U.S. resolution for armed intervention.

June 30: A **naval blockade** of the Korean coast and the use of U.S. ground forces were authorized by Pres. Truman.

July 1: The **first U.S. ground forces** landed in Korea.

July 8: Gen. **Douglas MacArthur** was named commander of UN forces in Korea.

Aug 4: The **U.S. Army** called up 62,000 enlisted reservists for 21 months of active duty.

Sep 8: Emergency powers over the entire national economy were granted to Pres. Truman under the Defense Production Act.

Sep 15: U.S. forces landed at **Inchon,** on the west coast of Korea just south of the 38th parallel, and began a drive inland. The operation was intended to relieve South Korean and UN forces hemmed in at Pusan on the southeastern end of the Korean peninsula, and to recapture Seoul, which had fallen to North Korean forces on June 28.

Sep 22: The **Nobel Peace Prize** was awarded to Dr. Ralph J. Bunche, director of the UN Trusteeship

Division, for his work as UN mediator between Israel and the Arab states from Sept. 1948 to Apr. 1949. Dr. Bunche was the first black to win the award.

Sep 26: Seoul, capital of South Korea, was recaptured by U.S. troops.

Sep 29: South Korean troops reached the 38th parallel.

Oct 7: U.S. forces invaded North Korea across the 38th parallel.

Nov 6: Chinese Communist troops were reported in action along with North Korean forces by Gen. Douglas MacArthur.

Nov 7: In congressional elections the Democrats lost five Senate seats but retained a 49–47 majority. In the House they lost 29 seats but kept a majority of 234–199, with one seat going to a minor party.

Nov 20: U.S. troops reached the Yalu R. on the Manchurian border.

Nov 29: U.S. forces retreated under heavy attack from Chinese Communist units.

Dec 16: A state of national emergency was declared by Pres. Truman. Charles E. Wilson was appointed director of defense mobilization.

II. Architecture
   Arts and Music
   Popular Entertainment
   Publishing
   Theater

The confusion and uncertainty of the times produced some curious results. The book *Dianetics* by L. Ron Hubbard, a science fiction writer, promulgated a new field of mental health. Architects expended their talents on shopping centers, supermarkets, motels, and outdoor movies, in response to a mass movement to suburbia. That chronic invalid, the theater, reported bad times. Production costs were so high that only smash hits could afford to pay their backers. Yet, with characteristic perversity, the Broadway stage produced some of its most interesting work in recent years. Particularly noteworthy was a renaissance of poetic drama, as witnessed by production of plays of T. S. Eliot, Christopher Fry, and Robinson Jeffers, all of which met with public acclaim.

Among **books published** this year was *World Enough and Time* by Robert Penn Warren, a novel based on an 1825 murder case known as the Kentucky tragedy. Other books published this year included *The Wall* by John Hersey, a story of the last days of the Warsaw ghetto under Nazi attack during World War II; *The Cardinal* by Henry Morton Robinson, the story of the rise of a Catholic priest; and *The Disenchanted* by Budd Schulberg, a biting novel of the struggle for success in Hollywood.

The **United Nations Secretariat,** designed by an international board of architects under the direction of Wallace K. Harrison, was built in New York City. It was a 39-story building with narrow end walls of white marble and wide elevations of green-tinted glass.

Mar 27: The **Bollingen Prize** for poetry was awarded to Wallace Stevens.

May 1: **Pulitzer prizes** were awarded for the following: fiction, *The Way West* by A. B. Guthrie; biography, *John Quincy Adams and the Foundations of American Foreign Policy* by Samuel Flagg Bemis; history, *Art and Life in America* by Oliver W. Larkin; poetry, *Annie Allen* by Gwendolyn Brooks; drama, *South Pacific* by Richard Rodgers, Oscar Hammerstein, II, and Joshua Logan.

Oct 11: A license to begin **color television broadcasting** was issued by the FCC to the Columbia Broadcasting System, effective Nov. 20. This touched off an industry-wide controversy. RCA charged that CBS's device was not the best. On Nov. 15 a temporary restraining order was issued by the Chicago Federal District Court.

Nov 10: The **Nobel Prize in Literature** for 1949 was awarded to William Faulkner at the 1950 awards ceremony in Oslo, Norway. The prize had not been awarded in 1949 because none of the candidates had won a majority of votes.

III. Business and Industry
Education
Philosophy and Religion
Science

A continuing upward trend in prices led organized labor to press for higher wages and improved working conditions. The Korean War cut the number of unemployed down to 1,900,000. The average weekly earning in industry was up to $60.53, an all-time high. Having pledged the defeat of Sen. Robert A. Taft of Ohio, labor entered into the state election campaign. But this, labor's first major attempt to function as a political force, ended in dismal failure when Taft was returned to office by an overwhelming majority. Growing financial difficulties faced colleges and universities. Public schools were beset by the charge that communists had filtered into school systems and by the issue of desegregation in classrooms. Religious leaders reported a rise in church membership. The Roman Catholic Church announced a 2% gain, Protestant churches a 2.9% gain.

The phenomenal popularity of **antihistamines** for the treatment of the common cold was reflected in sales amounting to $100,000,000 despite warnings by medical authorities.

Illiteracy in the U.S. reached a new low of 3.2% of the population, a decline of 1% from 1940 and 16.8% from 1870.

Jan 24: A **minimum wage** of 75 cents an hour went into effect under an amendment to the Fair Labor Standards Act. From 1950 to 1981 the federal minimum wage was increased 13 times, to $3.35 an hour. In 1967 the first minimum wage for farm workers, $1.00 an hour, went into effect.

Mar 13: The **largest corporate income** ever reported was announced by General Motors. Net earnings in 1949 were $656,434,232.

Mar 17: Discovery of a **new element, californium,** was
announced by the University of California, Berkeley.
This element, the heaviest yet known, was discovered
in experiments with the cyclotron, which also yielded
another element, berkelium. They were numbered 98
and 97 respectively.

Mar 23: Wages were up 130% from 1939 according to
a U.S. Labor Department report. However, buying
power increased only 35%.

May 25: The **longest vehicular tunnel** in the U.S., the
Brooklyn-Battery Tunnel in New York City, was
opened to traffic. Still the longest tunnel for automotive use, it has been surpassed in length by the 3.6-
mile Bay Area Rapid Transit (BART) tubes under San
Francisco Bay.

Oct 26: The **Nobel Prize in Physiology or Medicine**
was awarded jointly to Philip Showalter Hench of the
Mayo Clinic; Edward Calvin Kendall, head of the Department of Biochemistry, Mayo Foundation, University of Minnesota; and Tadeus Reichstein of the
University of Basel, Switzerland, for their research
into the nature of suprarenal cortex hormones and
the use of cortisone.

IV. Fashion
   Folkways
   Holidays
   Social Issues and Crime
   Sports

In boxing, Ezzard Charles successfully defended the
world heavyweight title against Freddie Beshore
(Aug. 15), Joe Louis (Sept. 27), and Nick Barone (Dec.
5). In golf the top money winners were Sam Snead,
$35,758.83, and Mildred "Babe" Didrikson Zaharias,
$14,800. In fashion, designers acted with more mod-
esty as the bikini bathing suit lost its popularity and
dresses became more wearable and natural. The biggest single fashion note was the reappearance of
stoles for use during the day as well as at night. The
younger set wore their hair short and dressed in dun-
garees and ballet shoes. This latter fad may have been

prompted by an outburst of activity in the dance world. American dance companies won over European audiences, and dancers from abroad toured the U.S., enjoying packed houses wherever they played.

Feb 8: Man o' War was named the greatest horse of the first half of the century by an Associated Press poll. Known as a horse that excelled as sprinter and distance runner, he ran as a two-year-old and a three-year-old, winning 20 out of 21 starts and breaking five track records.

Mar 28: The **NCAA basketball championship** was won by CCNY, defeating Bradley University 71 to 68.

Apr 8-23: The **first NBA (National Basketball Association) basketball championship** was won by the Minneapolis Lakers, who beat the Syracuse Nationals four games to two.

June 10: The **U.S. Open golf tournament** ended regular play with a three-way tie among Ben Hogan, Lloyd Mangrum, and George Fazio. On June 11 Hogan, in a spectacular comeback after an auto accident in 1949, won an 18-hole playoff round, beating Mangrum by four strokes and Fazio by six strokes.

June 27: The **PGA golf tournament** was won by Chandler Harper.

July 7: At the **Wimbledon** tennis championships in England, the men's singles title was won by V. Edward "Budge" Patty. The next day Louise Brough won the women's singles. Louise Brough and Margaret Osborne du Pont won the women's doubles and Brough teamed with Eric Strugess of South Africa to win the mixed doubles.

Sep 26: In the **Davis Cup** international tennis challenge round, the Australian team won its third straight match from the U.S., thereby ensuring victory. The Australians went on to win the round 4 to 1.

Oct 4-7: The 47th annual **World Series** was won by the New York Yankees (AL), defeating the Philadelphia Phillies (NL) in four straight games.

Dec 24: The **NFL championship** was won by the Cleveland Browns, who defeated the Los Angeles Rams 30 to 28.

1951

I. Civil Rights
Exploration and Settlement
Government
Statistics
Wars

The world hovered close to the brink of a third world war. Chinese Communist troops had unofficially entered the Korean campaign, operating from bases above the Yalu R. Gen. Douglas MacArthur advocated attacks on strategic positions within Chinese territory, a move that would be tantamount to declaring war on China, which had a military alliance with the U.S.S.R. American casualties had reached 100,000 and tempers at home were getting short. With this crisis before them, government leaders framed a foreign policy emphasizing preparation for war. A huge increase in taxes was asked, universal military training was urged, and a ring of bases around the U.S.S.R. was suggested. General war was averted when the administration stood with the UN on the decision not to attack Chinese bases.

Jan 1: Chinese Communist troops in Korea broke through the defense perimeter around Seoul and took Inchon and Kimpo airfield. Seoul was abandoned three days later.

Feb 26: The Twenty-second Amendment to the U.S. Constitution was adopted. It stipulated that no person may be elected to the presidency for more than two terms. A vice president succeeding to the presidency and serving more than half the term of his predecessor would be eligible for only one more term.

Mar 14: Seoul was recaptured by U.S. forces. This was the second time the South Korean capital was recaptured by UN forces. The reoccupation of Seoul marked a strategic and psychological victory over the

enemy forces, whose lines had been broken and who
were steadily being forced north, back over the 38th
parallel and into North Korea.

Mar 21: U.S. armed forces numbered 2,900,000 according to Defense Sec. George C. Marshall. This was
double the strength of U.S. armed forces at the outbreak of the Korean War (1950–1953).

Apr 4: SHAPE (Supreme Headquarters, Allied Powers
in Europe) was established in Paris. Gen. Dwight D.
Eisenhower assumed command.

Apr 11: Gen. **Douglas MacArthur was relieved** of all
commands by Pres. Harry S Truman. His posts as
supreme commander, Allied powers; commander in
chief, UN command; commander in chief, Far East;
and commanding general, U.S. Army, Far East were
all filled by Lt. Gen. Matthew Ridgway.

Apr 19: Gen. **Douglas MacArthur** addressed a joint
session of Congress, defending his Korean policies
and beliefs and declaring his military career to be at
its end. Recalling words of a ballad, "Old soldiers
never die, they just fade away," MacArthur stated: "I
now close my military career and just fade away, an
old soldier who tried to do his duty as God gave him
the light to see that duty."

June 23: A cease-fire in Korea was proposed by Jacob
Malik, Soviet delegate to the UN, who called for with-
drawal of troops from the 38th parallel. On June 30
Gen. Matthew Ridgway sent North Korea a proposal
to negotiate a cease-fire agreement. Kim Il Sung, the
North Korean commander, and Gen. Peng Teh-huai,
the Chinese commander, agreed the next day to meet
UN representatives to discuss cease-fire proposals.

July 10: The **first Korean truce talks** were held between UN and Korean representatives at Kaesong, on
the 38th parallel in North Korea.

July 11-25: The costliest **flood** to date in U.S. history
occurred when the Missouri R. and its tributaries
flooded more than 1,000,000 acres of farmland in
Kansas, Oklahoma, Missouri, and Illinois. Kansas
City suffered particularly severe damage on July 14.
Property loss was estimated at more than
$1,000,000,000.

Sep 8: A peace treaty with Japan was signed in San

Francisco by delegates of 48 nations. The U.S.S.R., Poland, and Czechoslovakia did not sign.

Oct 10: The **Mutual Security Act of 1951** was signed by Pres. Truman. It authorized $7,483,400,000 in U.S. foreign economic, military, and technical aid, and established a Mutual Security Agency. W. Averell Harriman was named head of the agency on the following day.

Oct 24: The **state of war with Germany** was declared officially ended by Pres. Truman.

II. Architecture
Arts and Music
Popular Entertainment
Publishing
Theater

Some 11,000 book titles were published this year. The phenomenal sale of paperback books led many publishers to launch a series of these editions. Architects were forced to concentrate on industrial and defense work, although some work was accomplished in the design of school buildings. Painters continued to work in abstractions, and American regionalism all but vanished from contemporary exhibitions. After a brief season of experimentation, the theater returned to the tried-and-true musical.

Among **books published** this year was *Requiem for a Nun* by William Faulkner, a novel written partly in the form of a play. The novel continued the story of Temple Drake, central character in Faulkner's 1931 novel *Sanctuary*. Other books published this year included *The Morning Watch* by James Agee, the author's first novel; *The Grass Harp* by Truman Capote, a novel; *The Sea Around Us* by Rachel Carson; *Mr. Lincoln's Army* by Bruce Catton; *Barbary Shore* by Norman Mailer, a novel; *Lie Down in Darkness,* a first novel by William Styron; and *The Caine Mutiny* by Herman Wouk, a novel.

Jan 22: The **Bollingen Prize** for poetry was awarded to John Crowe Ransom for his contributions to American poetry.

May 7: Pulitzer prizes were awarded for the follow-

ing: fiction, *The Town* by Conrad Richter; biography, *John C. Calhoun: American Portrait* by Margaret Louise Coit; history, *The Old Northwest, Pioneer Period 1815–1840, Volumes I-II* by R. Carlyle Buley; poetry, *Complete Poems* by Carl Sandburg.

III. Business and Industry
Education
Philosophy and Religion
Science

Employment of women in American industry reached its highest point in history, even higher than during World War II. Wages were up, but so were prices; total employment figures were robust. Alarmed over the growing inflation, the administration tried to institute a program of production controls. Two hundred thousand consumer items were placed under price controls, but attempts to freeze all prices and wages failed. Sen. Estes Kefauver of Tennessee, chairman of a Senate committee on organized crime in interstate commerce, opened hearings to television cameras. For weeks the nation watched as underworld figures testified—or refused to do so—before the committee. In education, universities and colleges saw a sharp drop in enrollment.

May 15: The **American Telephone and Telegraph Company** reported that it was the first corporation to have more than 1,000,000 stockholders.

June 14: UNIVAC, an electronic digital computer designed by Dr. John W. Mauchly and J. Presper Eckert, Jr., and the first such computer built for commercial purposes, was dedicated and demonstrated in Philadelphia, Pa. Mauchly and Eckert had developed ENIAC, the world's first electronic digital computer, in the 1940s, then set up their own company to develop computers for business and industry. They ran into financial difficulties, and their operation was ultimately taken over by Remington Rand.

June 25: The **first commercial color TV broadcast** was presented by the Columbia Broadcasting System, which had spent $5,000,000 over 11 years to develop the required new technology. The four-hour program was carried by stations in New York City, Baltimore, Boston, Philadelphia, and Washington, D.C. Unfortunately, no color TV sets were owned by the public. CBS itself had only 30 or 40 color receivers, and most of these were used for technical or monitoring purposes. It would be months before the first color sets would become available for purchase.

July 11: Released time for **religious studies** for schoolchildren in New York State was upheld by the New York State Court of Appeals. It was upheld again by the U.S. Supreme Court on Apr. 28, 1952.

Oct 18: The **Nobel Prize in Physiology or Medicine** was awarded to Dr. Max Theiler of the International Health Division of the Rockefeller Institute for development of vaccine 17-D to combat yellow fever.

Nov 10: The first transcontinental **direct dial telephone service** was inaugurated when Englewood, N.J., mayor M. Leslie Denning called Alameda, Calif., mayor Frank P. Osborn. The call marked the beginning of a test program involving some 10,000 customers of the New Jersey Bell system.

Nov 15: The **Nobel Prize in Chemistry** was awarded jointly to Dr. Edwin M. McMillan and Dr. Glenn T. Seaborg of the University of California for their research in transuranic elements. They were the eighth and ninth Americans to win the Nobel Prize in Chemistry.

Dec 20: The **first atomic-powered generator** began producing electricity at the U.S. Reactor Testing Station in Idaho.

IV. Fashion
Folkways
Holidays
Social Issues and Crime
Sports

The baseball season gave fans the ultimate home run thrill. The Brooklyn Dodgers and New York Giants battled their way to a tie for the National League pennant. Each team had won one of the playoff games. Brooklyn led in the third and deciding contest 4 to 1, going into the ninth inning. New York managed one run and then two men got on base. Finally, at the last moment, Bobby Thomson, the Giants' third baseman, slammed a home run off a pitch of Ralph Branca that decided the game and the season. In golf the top money winners were Lloyd Mangrum, $26,088.83, and Mildred "Babe" Didrikson Zaharias (for the fourth year in a row), $15,087.

Feb 3: The **largest purse** to date in horse racing, $144,323, was won by Great Circle in the Santa Anita Maturity at Santa Anita Park, Arcadia, Calif. The jockey was Willie Shoemaker.

Mar 27: The **NCAA basketball championship** was won by Kentucky, which defeated Kansas State 68 to 58.

Apr 7-21: The **NBA basketball championship** was won by the Rochester Royals, who beat the New York Knickerbockers 79 to 75.

June 16: The **U.S. Open golf tournament** was won for the second year in a row by Ben Hogan.

July 3: The **PGA golf tournament** was won by Sam Snead. It was his third PGA victory.

July 6-7: At the **Wimbledon** tennis championships in England, Dick Savitt won the men's singles title and Doris Hart won the women's singles. Hart and Shirley Fry won the women's singles.

July 14: The **first horse to win $1,000,000** was Citation, who brought his total earnings to $1,085,760 by winning the Hollywood Gold Cup at Inglewood, Calif. The bay horse had run out of the money only once in 45 starts during a four-year career.

July 18: The **world heavyweight boxing championship** was won by "Jersey Joe" Walcott, who knocked out Ezzard Charles in the seventh round at Pittsburgh, Pa. At 37 Walcott was the oldest person to gain the title.

Oct 4-10: The 48th annual **World Series** was won by the New York Yankees (AL), who defeated the New York Giants (NL) four games to two. The Giants had won the National League pennant by beating the Brooklyn Dodgers two games to one in a spectacular ninth inning recovery in the third game of the league playoff.

Dec 23: The **NFL championship** was won by the Los
Angeles Rams, who defeated the Cleveland Browns
24 to 17.

1952

I. Civil Rights
Exploration and Settlement
Government
Statistics
Wars

Early in the year British Prime Minister Winston
Churchill visited the U.S. to reestablish close ties between Great Britain and the U.S. and to formulate
unified policy on problems facing the West. The leading problem was the spreading danger of communist
domination. U.S. policy was to arm western Europe
and make it too costly for the U.S.S.R. to start a war.
Opponents of this U.S.-British alliance included former Pres. Herbert Hoover, who claimed the U.S. was
carrying Europe at disastrous expense. A far better
plan, he maintained, was to retire to the Western
Hemisphere and build a "bastion of liberty." Although 1952 was an election year, this issue was
never a serious part of the campaign since the two
major candidates, Adlai E. Stevenson and Dwight D.
Eisenhower, supported the NATO alliance. While
both Stevenson and Eisenhower enjoyed enormous
popularity, the Democrats suffered from charges of
corruption in the administration of Pres. Harry S
Truman. Eisenhower's eventual victory was interpreted by many as a rebuke to the Truman administration. In spite of truce negotiations in Korea, some
ground and air action continued; it intensified in October when truce talks were temporarily postponed.

Mar 8: Charges of **germ warfare** were formally lodged
against the U.S. by Chinese Foreign Minister Chou
En-lai. The charges, reported by Radio Peking, were

supported by the Soviet representative to the UN, Jacob A. Malik. An offer by the International Red Cross to investigate was rejected by Malik, and on Mar. 28 the UN ruled Malik's charges out of order.

Mar 20: The **Japanese Peace Treaty** was ratified by the U.S. Senate by a vote of 66 to 10.

June 25: The **McCarran-Walter Bill** to revise and limit immigration was vetoed by Pres. Truman as un-American and discriminatory. The following day the House of Representatives overrode the veto 278–113. The Senate took similar action on June 27 by a vote of 57–26. The law abolished racial restrictions on immigration and retained a quota system based on the national origins count of 1920.

July 11: The **Republican National Convention nominated Gen. Dwight D. Eisenhower** for the presidency. Sen. Richard M. Nixon of California was nominated for the vice presidency.

July 16: A **G.I. Bill of Rights** was signed by Pres. Truman. It offered Korean veterans with 90 days of service as of June 27, 1950, rights and benefits similar to those granted to veterans of World War II.

July 26: The **Democratic National Convention nominated Gov. Adlai E. Stevenson** of Illinois for the presidency and Sen. John J. Sparkman of Alabama for the vice presidency.

Oct 24: Gen. **Eisenhower vowed to go to Korea** to seek an early and honorable conclusion to the conflict there if elected to the presidency. Eisenhower spoke in Detroit, Mich., on the last stop of his whistle-stop campaign tour.

Nov 4: Dwight D. Eisenhower was elected president of the United States. Sen. Richard M. Nixon of California was elected vice president. The electoral vote was Eisenhower, 442, Gov. Adlai E. Stevenson, Democrat, 89. The popular vote was Eisenhower, 33,938,285; Stevenson, 27,312,217; Vincent Hallinan, Progressive, 140,138; Stuart Hamblen, Prohibition, 72,881; Darlington Hoopes, Socialist, 20,189. In congressional elections the Republicans gained one Senate seat for a 48–47 majority, with one seat going to a minor party. In the House they gained 22 seats, for a 221–211 majority, one seat going to a minor party.

Nov 29: President-elect **Eisenhower flew to Korea**, fulfilling his campaign promise, and inspected the UN forces there. On a three-day tour, he visited front-line positions. The tour was kept secret until he had returned from the zone of danger.

II. Architecture
Arts and Music
Popular Entertainment
Publishing
Theater

A building boom spurred architects to design with distinction, using new types of construction, notably employing prestressed concrete. The year saw much travel by musical organizations both in the U.S. and abroad. The Boston Symphony made its first European tour. George Gershwin's *Porgy and Bess* played to enthusiastic houses in Berlin, Vienna, and London. The most noticeable trend was a growing acceptance of so-called modern works. Igor Stravinsky, for instance, was slowly achieving full acceptance as a composer. In painting, a movement away from abstractionism toward representationalism was noted. This year's Broadway offerings were so lackluster that George Jean Nathan refused to issue his annual volume reviewing the season.

Among **books published** this year was *Invisible Man* by Ralph Ellison, a powerful novel about the struggle of a young black to find a sense of personal worth as a human being. The novel followed the young man as he moved from southern town to university to Harlem, from innocence to bitter pessimism. Other books published this year included *The Old Man and the Sea* by Ernest Hemingway, a short novel relating the symbolic tale of an old Caribbean fisherman struggling to catch a giant marlin; *Collected Poems 1917–1952* by Archibald MacLeish; and *East of Eden* by John Steinbeck, the author's longest novel, a panoramic story of a California family from the late nineteenth century through World War I.

Jan 11: The **Bollingen Prize** for poetry was awarded to Marianne Moore for her 1951 volume *Collected Poems.*

May 5: Pulitzer prizes were awarded for the following: fiction, *The Caine Mutiny* by Herman Wouk; biography, *Charles Evans Hughes* by Merlo J. Pusey; history, *The Uprooted* by Oscar Handlin; poetry, *Collected Poems* by Marianne Moore; drama, *The Shrike* by Joseph Kramm.

III. Business and Industry
Education
Philosophy and Religion
Science

Inflation was now a reality. Employment had reached a record high of 62,500,000. Prices continued to zoom. The U.S. Treasury recorded a deficit of $4,000,000,000. A major development on the labor front was the three-way struggle involving the steel industry, the Steelworkers of America (C.I.O.), and the U.S. president. When the union prepared to walk out for wage hikes, Pres. Truman seized the mills on the grounds that steel was vital to U.S. defense. Management retaliated by securing an injunction against the seizure; a federal district court then pronounced the president's action unconstitutional, a ruling upheld by the Supreme Court. This sent steelworkers out on what developed into a 54-day strike. Pres. Truman asked Congress for legislation permitting seizure of vital industries, but the Senate advised him to use the provisions of the Taft-Hartley law. Instead, he called both sides to the White House, where they settled the dispute in a conference.

Mar 2: Those considered **subversives could be barred from teaching** in public schools, according to a U.S. Supreme Court decision.

Apr 8: The nation's **steel mills were seized** by presidential order to prevent a shutdown by strikers. The next day three major steel companies instituted legal action in federal court, Washington, D.C., to contest the seizure. They were denied a temporary restraining order.

Apr 29: The **seizure of steel mills** was declared unconstitutional by U.S. District Judge David A. Pine. Steelworkers immediately went on strike.

May 2: The **steel strike was ended** by the steelworkers' union at presidential request.

June 2: Presidential **seizure of steel mills** was declared unconstitutional by the U.S. Supreme Court. Pres. Truman ordered the plants returned to their owners, and the steelworkers resumed their strike.

June 30: American stockholders numbered some 6,500,000. Of these, 76% earned less than $10,000 a year after taxes, according to a report made by the Brookings Institute.

July 7: A new **transatlantic speed record** for ships was set by the S.S. *United States* on its first round trip with an eastward crossing of 3 days, 10 hrs., 40 min. On July 14 it set a westward crossing record of 3 days, 12 hrs., 12 min.

July 24: The **steel strike was settled** when management and labor reached a compromise agreement at a White House conference called by Pres. Truman.

Oct 23: The **Nobel Prize in Physiology or Medicine** was awarded to Dr. Selman A. Waksman of Rutgers University for his discovery, with others, of streptomycin.

Nov 6: The **Nobel Prize in Physics** was awarded jointly to Dr. Edward Mills Purcell of Harvard University and to Dr. Felix Bloch of Stanford University for their work in the measurement of magnetic fields in atomic nuclei. They were the eighth and ninth Americans to receive the award in this field.

Nov 25: George Meany of New York was appointed president of the AFL to fill the unexpired term of William Green, who died on Nov. 21.

Dec 4: Walter P. Reuther, president of the United Auto Workers, was chosen to head the CIO.

IV. **Fashion**
   Folkways
   Holidays
   Social Issues and Crime
   Sports

This was a year of flying saucers, panty raids, and prison riots. Unidentified flying objects, frequently described as luminous disks or saucers, were reported flashing across night skies all over the nation. The Air Force even published photographs of the phenomena. There was widespread conjecture that these objects were manned by emissaries from outer space. While the nation watched the night skies, college boys across the country seemed intent on besieging sorority houses and girls' dormitories demanding as ransom articles of feminine underclothing, which were freely bestowed. Disturbances of a more serious nature plagued prison officials. Inmates pressing for more liberal treatment took guards as hostages while they bargained with prison authorities. These riots led to a review of state and federal prison systems.

Feb 15-25: At the **Winter Olympics** in Oslo, Norway, the U.S. won four gold medals and finished second in unofficial team standings .

Mar 26: The **NCAA basketball championship** was won by Kansas, which defeated St. John's 80 to 63.

Apr 12-15: The **NBA basketball championship** was won by the Minneapolis Lakers, who beat the New York Knickerbockers four games to three.

June 14: The **U.S. Open golf tournament** was won by Julius Boros, who beat Ed Oliver by four strokes and Ben Hogan, the defending champion, by five.

June 25: The **PGA golf tournament** was won by Jim Turnesa.

July 5: At the **Wimbledon** tennis championships in England, Maureen Connolly won the women's singles title. Doris Hart and Shirley Fry won the women's doubles.

July 19-Aug 3: At the **Summer Olympics** in Helsinki, Finland, the U.S. won 40 gold medals and finished first in the unofficial team standings.

Sep 23: The **world heavyweight boxing championship** was won by Rocky Marciano, who knocked out "Jersey Joe" Walcott in the 13th round of a bout in Philadelphia. It was Marciano's 43rd straight win as a professional boxer, with no losses.

Oct 1-7: The 49th annual **World Series** was won by the New York Yankees (AL), defeating the Brooklyn Dodgers (NL) four games to three.

Dec 28: The **NFL championship** was won by the Detroit Lions, who defeated the Cleveland Browns 17 to 7.

1953

I. Civil Rights
Exploration and Settlement
Government
Statistics
Wars

The nation watched with interest as a Republican administration took over the reins of government for the first time in 24 years. Pres. Dwight D. Eisenhower had uncertain control of Congress, the Republicans ruling there by the grace of conservative southern Democrats. The president made immediate attempts to improve his position with the legislative branch by announcing he favored a close presidential-congressional partnership. The new chief executive had four major areas of foreign policy to deal with: countering Russian expansion all over the globe; bolstering European allies by economic and military aid; fostering European unity; and forcing an equitable armistice in Korea. The most explosive internal problem was Sen. Joseph R. McCarthy, Republican of Wisconsin, charging Soviet espionage activities in the U.S. The administration's most outstanding success was a peace agreement in Korea. Pres. Eisenhower announced the agreement to a relieved country but warned, "We have won an armistice on a single battleground, not peace in the world."

In the **Korean War** (1950–1953), U.S. armed forces casualties totaled 137,051; of this number, 25,604 were killed; 103,492 were wounded; and 7955 were reported missing.

Jan 2: A report on the actions of Sen. **Joseph R. McCarthy** of Wisconsin issued by a Senate privileges and elections subcommittee stated that some of McCarthy's political activities had been "motivated by self-interest." McCarthy was known for his headline-grabbing charges of communist infiltration in various organizations.

Jan 21: Thirteen communist leaders were convicted by a federal jury in New York City of conspiring to advocate overthrow of the U.S. government.

Apr 1: The **Department of Health, Education and Welfare** (HEW) was created by joint congressional action. On Apr. 11 Mrs. Oveta Culp Hobby of Texas was sworn in as the department's first head.

Apr 24: Record **taxes** of $68,500,000,000 were collected in 1952 according to the U.S. Bureau of Internal Revenue.

Apr 25: A **record for filibustering** was set in the U.S. Senate by Sen. Wayne Morse, Independent of Oregon, who held the floor for 22 hrs., 26 min. opposing a bill that would return offshore oil reserves to the individual states. His marathon failed to sway the Senate, which passed the measure on May 5 by a vote of 56–35.

June 18: The worst **air accident** to date occurred near Tokyo, Japan, when a U.S. Air Force Globemaster crashed, killing 129 persons.

June 19: Julius and Ethel Rosenberg were executed at Sing Sing Prison in Ossining, N.Y. They were the first civilians to be executed in the U.S. for espionage. The couple had been convicted on Apr. 5, 1951, of passing secret information about the atom bomb to the U.S.S.R. Their deaths were the subject of protests around the world.

July 27: A **Korean armistice** was signed at Panmunjom by UN, North Korean, and Chinese delegates.

Aug 1: A broader **Social Security Act** was proposed by Pres. Eisenhower, who recommended provisions to include another 10,500,000 persons under the law. The proposed legislation was passed on Sept. 1, 1954.

Aug 7: The **Refugee Relief Act** of 1953 was signed by Pres. Eisenhower. It admitted 214,000 more refugees than permitted under existing immigration quotas.

II. Architecture
Arts and Music
Popular Entertainment
Publishing
Theater

There was a bountiful supply of good books this year, but few really distinguished ones. Of particular interest was the publication of a large number of books, mostly novels, by highly competent black writers. Architects looked forward to boom times with commercial construction up 43.2%. Important music festivals in the U.S. and abroad attracted many composers. American painting reverted to the abstract form, but it also discovered the primitivism of Grandma Moses, who received worldwide recognition. Despite Broadway's usual complaints of rising production costs and shortages of houses and scripts, the season showed a marked improvement. Filmgoers were treated to several innovations, including stereophonic sound; 3-D, intended to give the illusion of three dimensions; and several wide-screen processes. The most popular type of film was the science fiction thriller.

Among **books published** this year was *The Adventures of Augie March* by Saul Bellow, a novel offering a panoramic view of middle-class Chicago in the 1920s and 1930s. Other books published this year included *Go Tell It on the Mountain* by James Baldwin, the author's first novel; *Simple Takes a Wife* by Langston Hughes; *The Bridges at Toko-ri* by James Michener; *The Light in the Forest* by Conrad Richter; *Always The Young Strangers* by Carl Sandburg, an account of the poet's youth; *Battle Cry* by Leon Uris; and *The Outsider* by Richard Wright.

Jan 10: The **Bollingen Prize** for poetry was awarded jointly to Archibald MacLeish for his 1952 volume *Collected Poems, 1917–1952,* and to William Carlos Williams for his entire body of work.

May 4: Pulitzer prizes were awarded for the following: fiction, *The Old Man and the Sea* by Ernest Hemingway; biography, *Edmund Pendleton, 1721–1803* by David J. Mays; history, *The Era of Good Feeling* by George Dangerfield; poetry, *Collected Poems, 1917–1952* by Archibald MacLeish; drama, *Picnic* by William Inge.

III. Business and Industry
Education
Philosophy and Religion
Science

Americans numbered nearly 161,000,000. The country continued to enjoy unprecedented prosperity, even though the 1953 dollar was worth about 52 cents compared with its 1935–1939 equivalent. Greatly increased personal income more than made up the difference for much of the population. This year saw the end of wage and salary controls. Labor continued its fight for abolition of the Taft-Hartley law. A broad economic program was announced by the administration. It included revision of the tax laws—including modification or elimination of the excess profits tax to benefit corporations—and double taxation of dividends; shifting of the national debt to long-term bonds; and providing for a sliding scale interest rate based on demand. This last provision was designed as a check to inflationary borrowing.

The Ford Foundation established **The Fund for the Republic** and gave it $15,000,000 "to help fight restriction on freedom of thought, inquiry and expression."

Mar 30: Jet-propelled guided missiles were under production according to the U.S. Navy.

May 25: The **first atomic artillery shell** was fired at a military testing range in Nevada.

Oct 22: The **Nobel Prize for Physiology or Medicine** was awarded jointly to Dr. Fritz Albert Lipmann of Harvard University Medical School for his discovery of co-enzyme A and its function in metabolic processes; and to Dr. Hans Adolf Krebs of Sheffield University in England for his discovery of the citric acid cycle, known as the Krebs cycle.

Dec 16: A new **airplane speed record** was achieved by U.S. Air Force Major Charles E. Yeager, who flew a Bell X-1A rocket powered plane more than 1600 mph.

IV. Fashion
   Folkways
   Holidays
   Social Issues and Crime
   Sports

The year's biggest fashion news was a designers' invasion into the field of men's clothes. Bermuda shorts were promoted for the hot summer months. For the ladies, a mood of sleek elegance was decreed. Skirts were shorter, and so were hair styles. The Italian haircut became the vogue. It called for a carefully casual female crew cut that gave the wearer a gamin-like, windblown look. This year Rocky Marciano defended his world heavyweight title in bouts against "Jersey Joe" Walcott (May 15) and Roland LaStarza (Sept. 24). In golf the top money winners were Lew Worsham, $34,002, and Louise Suggs, $19,816. Fans mourned the death of one of the greatest athletes of all time, Jim Thorpe, Mar. 28, at age 64.

Mar 18: The **NCAA basketball championship** was won by Indiana, defeating Kansas 69–68.

Mar 18: The move of the **Boston Braves** baseball franchise to Milwaukee, Wis., was approved by the National League. This year Milwaukee led both leagues in attendance.

Apr 4-10: The **NBA basketball championship** was won by the Minneapolis Lakers, who defeated the New York Knickerbockers four games to one.

June 13: The **U.S. Open golf tournament** was won by Ben Hogan, who beat Sam Snead by six strokes to become the third person in history to win the tournament four times.

July 3: At the **Wimbledon** tennis championships in England, Victor Seixas won the men's singles title. The next day Maureen Connolly won the women's singles. Doris Hart and Shirley Fry won the women's doubles, and Hart and Seixas won the mixed doubles.

July 7: The **PGA golf tournament** was won by Walter Burkemo.

Sep 16: The shift of the **St. Louis Browns** baseball franchise to Baltimore, Md., was approved by the American League. The Browns would play the 1954 season as the Baltimore Orioles.

Sep 30-Oct 5: The 50th annual **World Series** was won by the New York Yankees (AL), defeating the Brooklyn Dodgers (NL) four games to two. This was the first time a team had won five consecutive World Series.

Dec 27: The **NFL championship** was won by the Detroit Lions, who defeated the Cleveland Browns 17 to 16.

1954

I. Civil Rights
Exploration and Settlement
Government
Statistics
Wars

Pres. Dwight D. Eisenhower declared that his foreign policy would be dedicated to regaining the initiative in the world fight against communism and to winning the confidence of U.S. allies. With regard to defense, the president advocated intensive research on atomic weapons and an integrated transcontinental transportation system for civil as well as military travel. It included development of the St. Lawrence

Seaway to open the central states to seagoing traffic via the Great Lakes. He advocated greater discretion in loyalty investigations, but promised decisive action in all cases of espionage or sabotage. He also revealed that some 2200 government employees had been dropped under the administration's new security system. Later in the year, the president asked Congress to enact legislation to enable the Atomic Energy Commission to share certain atomic secrets with U.S. allies and to pave the way for industrial development of the atom. The U.S. took part in the London conference (Sept. 28-Oct. 3) and the Paris conference (Oct. 20–23) in which it was agreed that U.S. and British forces would remain in Europe to help keep the peace. The West German Federal Republic (West Germany) was admitted to NATO on Oct. 23. But the major international event was the French defeat at Dien Bien Phu on May 7, causing withdrawal of French forces from Vietnam and the partition of the country into northern and southern states, with elections for reunification to be held in July 1956.

Mar 1: Five congressmen were shot on the floor of the House of Representatives by Puerto Rican nationalists. All recovered from their wounds.

Mar 8: A **mutual defense agreement** was signed by Japan and the U.S. It provided for gradual and partial rearming of Japan.

Mar 10: The **first atomic power plant** was planned for the Duquesne Power Co., Pittsburgh, Pa., by the Atomic Energy Commission. Pres. Eisenhower, using a special remote hookup, broke ground for it from Denver, Colo., on Sept. 6.

Apr 8: Construction of an **early warning radar net** stretching 3000 miles across the Canadian far north was announced by the U.S. and Canada.

Apr 23-June 17: The **Army-McCarthy hearings** were conducted by the Senate Permanent Subcommittee on Investigations. The hearings were held to investigate charges by its chairman, Sen. Joseph R. McCarthy, Republican of Wisconsin, that Sec. of the Army Robert T. Stevens and Army counsel John G.

Adams were hampering the committee's attempts to uncover communists in the military. Stevens and Adams countercharged that McCarthy and his staff had tried to get preferential treatment for one of its former staff members, Pvt. G. David Schine. The hearings, given broad television and newspaper coverage, did much to end the anticommunist witch hunt led by McCarthy.

May 17: Racial **segregation in public schools** was declared unconstitutional by the U.S. Supreme Court. The Court handed down a single ruling on four state cases, including *Brown v. Board of Education* of Topeka, Kans., and another involving the District of Columbia. The rulings outlawed the practice of "separate but equal" facilities in public school systems.

May 24: Communist Party membership was declared to be sufficient grounds for deportation of aliens in a U.S. Supreme Court decision that upheld the constitutionality of the Internal Security Act of 1950.

July 30: A **resolution of censure** against Sen. Joseph R. McCarthy for conduct unbecoming a senator was introduced in the Senate by Sen. Ralph E. Flanders, Republican of Vermont. A Senate select committee subsequently voted to censure McCarthy on two counts of the resolution.

Sep 1: Hurricane Carol struck Long Island, N.Y., and New England, killing 68. Property losses were estimated at $500,000,000.

Sep 3: The **Espionage and Sabotage Act** of 1954 was signed by Pres. Eisenhower. The death penalty was authorized for peacetime sabotage and the statute of limitations for these crimes was removed.

Sep 30: The **first atomic-powered submarine,** the U.S.S. *Nautilus,* was commissioned at Groton, Conn.

Oct 15: Hurricane Hazel, the most violent hurricane of the year, killed 99 persons in the U.S. and 249 in Canada. Combined U.S. and Canadian property losses were put at $100,000,000.

Nov 2: In **congressional elections** the Democrats gained one Senate seat for a 48–47 majority, with one seat going to a minor party. In the House they gained 21 seats, for a 232–203 majority.

Dec 2: Sen. **McCarthy was condemned** in a vote of a special session of the U.S. Senate for his conduct in Senate committees.

Dec 11: The **largest warship** ever built, the 59,650-ton aircraft carrier U.S.S. *Forestal*, was launched at Newport News, Va.

Dec 27: A new **land speed record** of 632 mph was announced by the Air Force. The speed was achieved by an experimental rocket-powered sled.

II. Architecture
Arts and Music
Popular Entertainment
Publishing
Theater

Books on the Cold War, U.S. foreign policy, government loyalty programs, subversion, and the A-bomb filled rental libraries and bookstore. Novelists favored an exploration of the psychopathic mentality, but said little new or surprising. A major development for poets was an ever-increasing list of awards and prizes open to them; they responded by writing more and better verse. The building boom of 1953 showed no signs of letup; in fact, July set a record with $3,135,000,000 in new construction. All areas of musical endeavor reported great demand. Established symphonic societies and popular musical festivals continued to give composers commissions. Four works by Igor Stravinsky were introduced this year: *Septet* for violin, cello, viola, clarinet, horn, bassoon, and piano; *Three Songs from William Shakespeare; In Memoriam: Dylan Thomas;* and *Four Russian Peasant Songs*. Filmgoers were treated to a rash of spectacular historical epics and westerns. Some 7448 movie houses had CinemaScope facilities.

Among **books published** this year was *A Fable* by William Faulkner, a retelling of the crucifixion and resurrection of Jesus set against the background of World War I. Other books published this year included *No Time for Sergeants* by Mac Hyman, a delightful tale of an innocent Georgia youth drafted into the Air Force; *The Bird's Nest* by Shirley Jackson, a novel about a girl with four personalities; *The Bad Seed* by William March, a novel depicting a young girl as the incarnation of evil; *Sweet Thursday* by John Steinbeck, a sequel to his novel *Cannery Row* (1945); *The Collected Poems of Wallace Stevens;* and *The Ponder Heart,* a novel by Eudora Welty.

Some 29,000,000 households had **television** sets. This represented about 60% of American households. Television had not been marketed seriously until about 1947.

Jan 10: The **Bollingen Prize** for poetry was awarded to W.H. Auden.

May 3: Pulitzer prizes were awarded for the following: biography, *The Spirit of St. Louis* by Charles A. Lindbergh; history, *A Stillness at Appomattox* by Bruce Catton; poetry, *The Waking: Poems 1933–1953* by Theodore Roethke; drama, *The Teahouse of the August Moon* by John Patrick.

Oct 28: The **Nobel Prize for Literature** was awarded to Ernest Hemingway "for his powerful style-forming mastery of the art of modern narration." Among Hemingway's works were *The Sun Also Rises* (1926), *A Farewell to Arms* (1929), and *For Whom the Bell Tolls* (1940).

III. Business and Industry
Education
Philosophy and Religion
Science

A business recession coupled with rising unemployment worried some Americans, but administration spokesmen told the nation that some fallback from unprecedented economic highs was desirable. The downward trend was reversed about the middle of the year. By September personal income had exceeded the August figure by $2,000,000,000. Unemployment, though, totaled 2,893,000, about twice the figure reported for 1953. The AFL and CIO agreed to merge, and AFL president George Meany predicted that the merger would take place in 1955. Huge crop surpluses resulted in stringent curbs by the Agriculture Department. Sec. of Agriculture Ezra Benson was given authority to barter surplus crops on the world market in exchange for strategic goods. Schools were suffering from overcrowding and, with the Supreme Court decision on May 14 outlawing segregation in public schools, there was confusion in the ranks of school administrators.

Feb 2: Detonation of the **first hydrogen bomb** was officially reported by Pres. Eisenhower. It had taken place at Eniwetok Atoll in the Pacific in 1952.

Feb 23: Antipolio inoculation of schoolchildren was begun in Pittsburgh, Pa., by Dr. Jonas E. Salk, developer of the serum.

Mar 24: A **hydrogen bomb** explosion in the Marshall Islands on Mar. 1 exceeded all estimates of its power, according to a statement made by Pres. Eisenhower.

May 13: The **St. Lawrence Seaway Bill,** authorizing construction of a joint U.S. and Canadian artificial waterway connecting the Great Lakes and the Atlantic Ocean, was signed by Pres. Eisenhower. On June 9 he named Sec. of Defense Charles E. Wilson director of the St. Lawrence Seaway Development Corporation.

Oct 13: The **first supersonic bomber,** the B-58, was ordered into production by the Air Force.

Oct 21: The **Nobel Prize for Physiology or Medicine** was awarded to John F. Enders of the Harvard School of Medicine, Thomas H. Weller of the Harvard School of Public Health, and Frederick C. Robins of Western Reserve Medical School for their work in the cultivation of the polio virus.

Nov 3: The **Nobel Prize in Chemistry** was awarded to Linus Pauling of the California Institute of Technology for his study of the forces holding together protein and other molecules.

Dec 31: New York Stock Exchange prices were the highest quoted since 1929. The volume of shares traded during 1954 (573,374,622) was the highest since 1933.

IV. Fashion
Folkways
Holidays
Social Issues and Crime
Sports

The continuing antics of Sen. Joseph R. McCarthy was a topic of conversation along with rising juvenile crime and delinquency. Families discussed discipline and examined outside influences. Lurid comic books and violence-spattered pulp magazines came under attack from parents' groups and, in some cases, legislators. Fashion designers introduced a softer silhouette that deemphasized the bust and showed a longer torso. In boxing, Rocky Marciano defended his world heavyweight title twice (June 17, Sept. 17) in bouts with Ezzard Charles. In golf, the top money winners were Bob Toski, $65,891.24, and Patty Berg, $16,011. Studies showed that the average American's favorite meal was fruit cup, vegetable soup, steak and potatoes, peas, rolls with butter, and pie à la mode. Some 90% of adult Americans drank three to four cups of coffee a day; 64% drank beer, wine, or liquor; and 45% smoked one pack of cigarettes a day. About 60% of the male population and 30% of the female population smoked.

Mar 20: The **NCAA basketball championship** was won by La Salle, defeating Bradley 92 to 76.

Mar 31-Apr 12: The **NBA basketball championship** was won by the Minneapolis Lakers, who defeated the Syracuse Nationals four games to one.

June 19: The **U.S. Open golf tournament** was won by Ed Furgol.

July 3: At the **Wimbledon** tennis championships in England, Maureen Connolly won the women's singles title, Louise Brough and Margaret Osborne du Pont the women's doubles, and Victor Seixas and Doris Hart the mixed doubles.

July 27: The **PGA golf tournament** was won by Chick Harbert.

Sep 29-Oct 2: The 51st annual **World Series** was won by the New York Giants (NL), defeating the Cleveland Indians (AL) in four straight games.

Nov 8: The shift of the **Philadelphia Athletics** baseball franchise to Kansas City, Mo., was approved by the American League.

Dec 26: The **NFL championship** was won by the Cleveland Browns, who defeated the Detroit Lions 56–10.

Dec 28: The **Davis Cup** international tennis challenge round was won by the U.S., which defeated Australia three matches to two.

1955

I. Civil Rights
Exploration and Settlement
Government
Statistics
Wars

The marked easing of the Cold War brought about by what was called the Geneva spirit was engendered by Pres. Dwight D. Eisenhower's proposal to the U.S.S.R. for exchange of military blueprints and mutual aerial inspection. Nations that had been suspicious of U.S. foreign policy began to trust the U.S. a little more. At home, Americans enjoyed a new prosperity. They remodeled their cities in an unprecedented building boom, bought more expensive cars, planned dream homes, and flocked to buy home appliances, especially color TV sets. The Far East, however, was still a sorely troubled area, particularly in Indochina following the French defeat at Dien Bien Phu in May 1954.

Jan 14: The U.S. **Senate investigation of communism** was approved for continuation in a Senate vote of 84–0.

Jan 19: The **first filmed presidential press conference** took place. Both TV and motion picture newsreel photographers covered the event.

Jan 28: Defense of **Formosa and the Pescadores Is-**

lands was pledged by the Senate by a vote of 85–3. On the following day the Chinese demanded that the U.N. order U.S. withdrawal from the entire Formosan area.

Feb 26: Some 4000 **atomic bombs** had been stockpiled by the U.S., and 1000 by the U.S.S.R., according to an unofficial estimate of Prof. Cecil F. Powell, the British scientist and winner of a Nobel Prize in Physics.

Mar 16: The **use of atomic weapons** in case of war was upheld in a statement made by Pres. Eisenhower.

July 18: The **Geneva conference**, attended by heads of state of the U.S., Great Britain, U.S.S.R., and France, opened at Geneva, Switzerland.

Aug 2: Funding for 45,000 new **public housing** units was approved by the House of Representatives, 187–168. The units were to be built by July 31, 1956.

Sep 8: A treaty establishing **SEATO,** the Southeast Asia Treaty Organization, was signed in Manila, the Philippines, by the U.S., Australia, France, Great Britain, New Zealand, Pakistan, the Phillipines, and Thailand. The mutual defense pact, the Southeast Asia Collective Defense Treaty, was ratified by the Senate on Feb. 1, 1955 and went into effect on Feb. 19. SEATO was formally ended on Feb. 20, 1976.

Nov 25: Racial segregation in interstate trains and buses was banned by the Interstate Commerce Commission.

II. Architecture
Arts and Music
Popular Entertainment
Publishing
Theater

A noteworthy trend in the year's publishing was the number of nonfiction books, especially those on child behavior. Architects hailed the continuing high level of construction, and church building reached its highest rate in history. New materials such as aluminum and plastics were being used in construction. The New York Philharmonic and Philadelphia orchestras embarked on extensive European tours. The Symphony of the Air headed east and played in Japanese concert halls. Highlights of the year in music included premieres of *Symphony No. Six* by Darius Milhaud (Boston, Oct. 7) and *Symphony No. Five* by Walter Piston (Boston, Nov. 25). A showing of contemporary American and European painters at the Museum of Modern Art, New York City, revealed that for the first time U.S. artists were surpassing their European peers in imaginative style and technique. The show featured Willem de Kooning, Jackson Pollock, Robert Motherwell, and Adolph Gottlieb.

Among **books published** this year was *Andersonville* by MacKinlay Kantor, a powerful Civil War novel about the notorious Confederate prison. Other books published this year included *The Day Lincoln Was Shot* by Jim Bishop; *A Good Man Is Hard to Find, and Other Stories* by Flannery O'Connor; *Band of Angels* by Robert Penn Warren, a novel set in the Civil War; *The Man in the Gray Flannel Suit* by Sloan Wilson; and *Marjorie Morningstar* by Herman Wouk, a novel.

Jan 9: The **Bollingen Prize** for poetry was awarded jointly to Louise Bogan for her *Collected Poems, 1922–1953* and Leonie Adams for her volume *Poems, A Selection,* both published in 1954.

May 2: Pulitzer prizes were awarded to the following: fiction, *A Fable* by William Faulkner; biography, *The Taft Story* by William S. White; history, *Great River, the Rio Grande in North American History* by Paul Horgan; poetry, *The Collected Poems of Wallace Stevens;* drama, *Cat on a Hot Tin Roof* by Tennessee Williams.

III. Business and Industry
Education
Philosophy and Religion
Science

The economy enjoyed a year of nearly full employment and peak production. Net business income was up 33% over the previous year. Labor stated new objectives, chief of which was attainment of a guaranteed annual wage. The organized labor force in the

U.S. totaled 15,000,000 after the AFL and the CIO merged to become the American Federation of Labor and Congress of Industrial Organizations (AFL-CIO). The major concern of labor leaders was the increasing use of automation in industrial plants. Walter P. Reuther, vice president of the newly merged labor group, predicted a second industrial revolution as a result of automation. Farm income was down $5\frac{1}{2}$% from 1954. Educators reported a shortage of 250,000 classrooms and 141,300 teachers.

Jan 8: **Thorazine and reserpine,** two new drugs, showed some success in the treatment of mental patients, according to the New York State Department of Mental Hygiene.

Feb 9: The **AFL-CIO merger** agreement was made public.

Apr 12: A successful **antipolio vaccine** was announced by Dr. Jonas E. Salk. Tests carried out in 44 states indicated its effectiveness against poliomyelitis.

May 23: The ordination of **women ministers** was approved by the General Assembly of the Presbyterian Church.

May 31: **Racial segregation** in U.S. public schools was banned by the U.S. Supreme Court.

Sep 12: A study of **foundations** by the American Foundations Information Service listed 7300 charitable, welfare, and research foundations in the U.S. Over 4000 had assets above $4,700,000.

Sep 26: The **New York Stock Exchange** recorded its heaviest single day dollar loss in history, $14,000,000,000. In all, 7,720,000 shares were traded, the highest volume since July 21, 1933. This sharp break in prices occurred two days after an announcement that Pres. Eisenhower had suffered a heart attack in Denver, Colo.

Oct 7: The aircraft carrier U.S.S. *Saratoga,* the world's most powerful warship, was launched at the Brooklyn (N.Y.) Navy Yard.

Oct 18: The **antiproton,** a new atomic subparticle, was discovered at the University of California.

Nov 2: The **Nobel Prize in Chemistry** was awarded to

Dr. Vincent du Vigneaud of Cornell University Medical College for his work on two hormones important in childbirth and in regulation of vital organs.

Nov 2: The **Nobel Prize in Physics** was awarded jointly to Dr. Willis E. Lamb of Stanford University and to Dr. Polykarp Kusch of Columbia University for their work on atomic measurements.

Dec 5: The **AFL and CIO formally merged.** The new organization, the American Federation of Labor and Congress of Industrial Organizations (AFL-CIO), was headed by George Meany, former president of the AFL.

Dec 27: Traffic fatalities over the Christmas weekend numbered 609, a new record.

IV. Fashion
Folkways
Holidays
Social Issues and Crime
Sports

Davy Crockett and rock 'n' roll highlighted the year 1955. Originally, the Davy Crockett fad was started by a Technicolor movie produced in Hollywood by Walt Disney. Publicity agents then parlayed the legend of the frontiersman who died at the Alamo into a national fad—millions of Davy Crockett coonskin hats were manufactured and distributed, and fur dealers in New York City enjoyed one of the most prosperous years ever. Equally contagious was the mania for rock 'n' roll music, which many attacked as immoral, allegedly because of its monotonous, primitive beat. It was a gala year in Flatbush. The faithful rejoiced as the Brooklyn Dodgers won their first baseball championship, doubly welcome since they beat the mighty New York Yankees. In boxing, Rocky Marciano successfully defended the world heavyweight title in bouts with Don Cockell of Great Britain (May 16) and Archie Moore (Sept. 21). In golf the top money winners were Julius Boros, $65,121, and Patty

Berg, $16,492. Fashion designers combined sophisticated sex appeal with fresh youthfulness, and favored a semifitted sheath of oriental design and color.

More than 1,000,000,000 **comic books** were sold annually, according to a report issued by the University of California, at an estimated cost of $100,000,000, four times the book budget of all U.S. public libraries combined. New York State passed a law banning the sale of lurid crime and horror comic books to persons under 18 years of age. Violations were punishable by a year in prison and/or a $500 fine.

Mar 19: The **NCAA basketball championship** was won by San Francisco, defeating La Salle 77 to 63.

Mar 21-Apr 10: The **NBA basketball championship** was won by the Syracuse Nationals, who beat the Fort Wayne Pistons four games to three.

June 19: The **U.S. Open golf tournament** was won by Jack Fleck, who beat Ben Hogan by three strokes in a playoff round.

July 1-2: At the **Wimbledon** tennis championships in England, Tony Trabert won the men's singles title and Louise Brough won the women's singles. Victor Seixas and Doris Hart won the mixed doubles.

July 26: The **PGA golf tournament** was won by Doug Ford.

Sep 28-Oct 4: The 52nd annual **World Series** was won by the Brooklyn Dodgers (NL), who defeated the New York Yankees (AL) four games to three.

Dec 26: The **NFL championship** was won by the Cleveland Browns, who defeated the Los Angeles Rams 38 to 14.

1956

I. **Civil Rights**
   Exploration and Settlement
   Government
   Statistics
   Wars

Tension with the U.S.S.R. still dominated the American scene. John Foster Dulles summed up the Cold War in his "brink of war" statement: "The ability to get to the verge without getting into the war is the necessary art." At home, there was bitter rivalry between the armed services, heightened in May by Army charges that the Air Force was not doing its job. Americans again found a conflict between the North and South. Southern states either ignored or rebelled against the Supreme Court ruling against segregation in the public schools. In Montgomery, Ala., blacks boycotted buses, and on November 13 the Supreme Court ruled that segregation on buses and streetcars was unconstitutional. Among those who died this year was Albert Woolson, the last surviving veteran of the Union Army, Aug. 2, at age 109.

Jan 9: In what was interpreted as a vote for **segregation,** Virginia amended a state prohibition against the use of public funds for private schools. The amendment helped support private education in a state where public schools had been shut down because of the 1954 Supreme Court ruling against segregation in public schools.

Feb 15: To enforce **school desegregation** in New Orleans, La., a federal court banned all Louisiana laws opposing the Supreme Court ruling against segregation in public schools.

Mar 27: The communist *Daily Worker* was seized by Internal Revenue Service agents for nonpayment of income taxes. The newspaper's New York, Chicago, and Detroit offices were returned on Apr. 3 after

Daily Worker officers posted $4500 against their tax bill.

Apr 8: Six Marine recruits drowned while on a disciplinary march at Parris Island, S.C. Platoon Sgt. Matthew C. McKeon was convicted on Aug. 3 of drinking on duty and negligent homicide. He was reduced in rank to private and served a three-month prison sentence.

June 30: In the worst **commercial air disaster** to date, 128 persons were killed when two airliners crashed into the Grand Canyon. The accident involved a Trans-World Airlines Super-Constellation and a United Air Lines DC-7, which were thought to have collided in midair.

Aug 13-17: The **Democratic National Convention nominated Adlai E. Stevenson** of Illinois for the presidency on the first ballot. Sen. Estes Kefauver of Tennessee was nominated for the vice presidency.

Aug 20-24: The **Republican National Convention nominated Pres. Dwight D. Eisenhower** for a second term. Vice Pres. Richard M. Nixon was renominated as Eisenhower's running mate.

Aug 24: The **first transcontinental helicopter flight** was completed by an Army H-21 helicopter, which flew nonstop from San Diego, Calif., to Washington, D.C., in 37 hrs. With a crew of five, it flew 2610 miles.

Nov 6: Dwight D. Eisenhower was reelected president of the United States in a landslide. Eisenhower was the first Republican president to win reelection since William McKinley in 1900. Although Eisenhower carried 41 states, the Democrats retained control of both houses of Congress. The electoral vote was Eisenhower, 457; Adlai E. Stevenson, Democrat of Illinois, 74. The popular vote was Eisenhower, 35,387,015; Stevenson, 25,875,408. In congressional elections the Democrats gained one Senate seat for a 49–47 majority. In the House they gained one seat for a 233–200 majority.

II. Architecture
Arts and Music
Popular Entertainment
Publishing
Theater

The year in publishing was marked by a growing market for books from abroad, perhaps a reflection of Americans' growing interest in world affairs. In architecture, the volume of construction, particularly of industrial and commercial buildings, continued to increase. The outspoken elder statesman of architecture, Frank Lloyd Wright, completed work on the Price Tower in Bartlesville, Okla., and began construction of the Guggenheim Museum in New York City. Contemporary American paintings by such artists as Jackson Pollock were characterized by a distinct abstractionism; in fact, abstractionism had become conventional. On Aug. 11 the art world mourned the death of Pollock, age 44, in an automobile accident.

Among **books published** this year was *The Last Hurrah* by Edwin O'Connor, a novel about an Irish-American politician in his final political campaign. Critics noted the similarities between the fictional politician Frank Skeffington and the Boston mayor, James M. Curley. The novel was a best seller. Other books published this year included *Seize the Day* by Saul Bellow, a collection including the title novella, a play, and several stories; *A Single Pebble* by John Hersey, a novel; *Peyton Place* by Grace Metalious, a racy novel about the residents of a New Hampshire town that became the best seller of the year; and *The Letters of Thomas Wolfe*, edited by Elizabeth Nowell, which revealed how close the author's novels were to his actual life.

Jan 8: The **Bollingen Prize** for poetry was awarded to Conrad Aiken for his 1955 volume *A Letter From Li Po, and Other Poems.*

May 7: Pulitzer prizes were awarded for the following: fiction, *Andersonville* by MacKinlay Kantor; biography, *Benjamin Henry Latrobe* by Talbot F. Hamlin; history, *The Age of Reform* by Richard

Hofstadter; poetry, *North and South—A Cold Spring* by Elizabeth Bishop; drama, *The Diary of Anne Frank* by Frances Goodrich and Albert Hackett.

III. Business and Industry
Education
Philosophy and Religion
Science

About 2,000,000 workers received pay increases during the first half of the year, while rising business investments and earnings were benefiting all of labor. The new federal hourly wage minimum of $1.00 an hour was expected to help approximately 2,000,000 workers. In addition, despite widespread drought and crop restrictions, American farmers produced a new all-time high in food and fiber output. Although there were no great discoveries in physics or astronomy during 1956, scientists were active in planning for the International Geophysical Year, to take place in 1957–1958.

Feb 6: Three days of **campus violence** at the University of Alabama were climaxed by the suspension of Autherine Lucy, the first black student to be enrolled there. On Mar. 1 she was permanently expelled for her accusations against the school in a legal suit handled by the National Association for the Advancement of Colored People.

Mar 20: A major **strike** at Westinghouse Electric Corporation, the longest walkout in more than 20 years, was settled after 156 days when the union accepted contract terms proposed by the company.

May 2: Racial **segregation in Methodist churches** was ordered abolished by the General Conference of the Methodist Church in Minneapolis, Minn.

June 11: In Chicago, reports on **polio** were presented to the American Medical Association by Dr. Jonas E. Salk and Surgeon Gen. Leonard A. Scheele. They stated that the crippling disease would be eliminated as a threat within three years through use of the Salk vaccine.

Aug 1: The **Salk antipolio vaccine** was put on the open market by manufacturers. It was sold through normal distribution channels.

Sep 24: The world's **first transatlantic telephone cable system** began operating. The twin cables, 2250 miles long, stretched from Clarenville, Newfoundland, to Oban, Scotland. The cable, which cost $42,000,000, had three times the capacity of radio telephone circuits between Europe and the U.S.

Oct 19: The **Nobel Prize in Physiology or Medicine** was awarded jointly to Dr. Dickinson W. Richardson and Dr. Andre F. Cournand of Columbia University, and to Dr. Werner Forssmann of West Germany, for their work in cardiology and their contributions to the treatment of heart disease.

Nov 1: The **Nobel Prize in Physics** was awarded jointly to William Shockley, Walter H. Brattain, and John Bardeen, all of Bell Telephone Laboratories, for their discovery of the transistor effect in semiconductors and the development of the transistor.

IV. Fashion
Folkways
Holidays
Social Issues and Crime
Sports

American society was being changed by political, social, and technological forces of great magnitude. One result of these pressures was a new spirit of youthful rebelliousness, as evidenced by the rise of a Tennessee rock-'n'-roll singer, Elvis Presley, who skyrocketed to fame despite objections from parents all over the U.S. A cult also grew up around the late James Dean, a promising young actor who had been killed in an automobile accident in 1955. Dean epitomized the American loner, daring to oppose a society that would not or could not understand him. In the more conventional world of boxing, Rocky Marciano retired as the undefeated world heavyweight champion. In golf, the year's top money winners were Ted Kroll, $72,835, and Marlene Bauer Hagge, $20,235.

Jan 20: Following an investigation of **tipping** conducted by the Internal Revenue Service, Hans Paul,
headwaiter at the Waldorf-Astoria Hotel in New York
City, was indicted on charges of not reporting tips
averaging $500,000 to $1,000,000 a year. Paul was
fined $7500 and sentenced to four months' imprison-
ment on Apr. 25.

Jan 26-Feb 5: At the **Winter Olympics** in Cortina d'Am-
pezzo, Italy, the U.S. won two gold medals. Hayes
Alan Jenkins and Tenley Albright took top honors in
singles figure skating competitions.

Mar 23: The **NCAA basketball championship** was won
by San Francisco, defeating Iowa 83 to 71.

Mar 31-Apr 7: The **NBA basketball championship** was
won by the Philadelphia Warriors, who defeated the
Fort Wayne Pistons four games to one.

Apr 19: Actress **Grace Kelly,** 26, was married in Monte
Carlo to Prince Rainier III of Monaco, 32, in one of
the most publicized marriages of the decade. Prince
Rainier was a member of the Grimaldi dynasty,
founded in 1017.

June 16: The **U.S. Open golf tournament** was won by
Cary Middlecoff, who beat Ben Hogan and Julius
Boros by one stroke.

July 7: At the **Wimbledon** tennis championships in
England, Shirley Fry won the women's singles title.
Althea Gibson teamed with Angela Buxton of Great
Britain to win the women's doubles, and Shirley Fry
and Victor Seixas won the mixed doubles.

July 16: The **Ringling Brothers and Barnum and Bailey Circus** performed its last show under canvas. Rising costs for a tented show had forced the move to
performances in permanent structures.

July 25: The **PGA golf tournament** was won by Jack
Burke.

Oct 3-10: The 53rd annual **World Series** was won by
the New York Yankees (AL), defeating the Brooklyn
Dodgers (NL) four games to three. On Oct. 8 Don
Larsen, the Yankee right-hander, pitched the first no-
hit, no-run game in World Series history, beating
Brooklyn 2 to 0.

Nov 22-Dec 8: At the **Summer Olympics** in Melbourne,

Australia, the U.S. won 32 gold medals and finished second in unofficial team standings, behind the U.S.S.R.

Nov 30: The **world heavyweight boxing championship** was won by Floyd Patterson, who knocked out Archie Moore in the fifth round in Chicago to win the title vacated by Rocky Marciano on Apr. 27. Patterson, 21, was the youngest fighter to win the championship.

Dec 30: The **NFL championship** was won by the New York Giants, who defeated the Chicago Bears 47 to 7.

1957

I. Civil Rights
Exploration and Settlement
Government
Statistics
Wars

On Oct. 4 the Soviet Union launched the first Earth satellite, Sputnik I. Americans were stunned by the Soviets' technological progress, and politicians, scientists, and educators called for a major U.S. initiative to regain superiority in missiles development and space technology. Thus 1957 was another year of world tension. Pres. Dwight D. Eisenhower presented the Eisenhower Doctrine; its aim was to resist communist aggression in the Middle East. Despite the race against the U.S.S.R. in outer space, the president continued to release uranium-235 for peaceful purposes; by the end of the year a total of 100,000 kilograms of U-235 had been made available for research and energy. The Air Force, which celebrated its golden anniversary (dating from the founding of the Army Air Corps—the Air Force was officially established in 1947), became the largest enterprise in the U.S.; its total assets for the year were over

$70,000,000,000. Notables who died included Sen. Joseph R. McCarthy, Republican of Wisconsin, whose widely publicized charges of communist subversion in government earned him Senate censure and condemnation, on May 2, at age 48.

Jan 5: The **Eisenhower Doctrine** was proposed by Pres. Eisenhower before a joint session of Congress. The plan offered protection to any Middle East nation seeking aid against communist aggression. Eisenhower requested authority to use U.S. forces to oppose communist or communist-backed attempts to overthrow any government in the region. He stated he would send such forces only under three conditions: first, only if requested by a Mideast nation under attack; second, only with hour-by-hour communication with Congress; third, only in accord with U.S. treaty obligations and the UN Charter.

Feb 8: The **European Atomic Energy Community** was pledged full U.S. support for establishment of an atomic energy industry in Europe within ten years.

Feb 9-12: The U.S. **Communist Party** held a convention in New York City during which its members adopted a new party constitution. One of the new rules in the constitution specified that party members could be expelled for subversion of the U.S. government. FBI chief J. Edgar Hoover stated that the new rules were merely an attempt by the party to gain acceptance by U.S. citizens.

Mar 30: The United States' second **atomic submarine,** the *Seawolf,* was commissioned. On May 16, *Skate,* the third atomic submarine and the first designed for assembly-line production, was launched at Groton, Conn.

July 16: A new **transcontinental speed record** (Long Beach, Calif., to Brooklyn, N.Y.) was set by Maj. John H. Glenn, Jr., USN, in a Navy F8U-1P jet. The time was 3 hrs., 23 min., 8.4 sec.

Aug 30: A new **filibuster record** was set by Sen. Strom Thurmond, Democrat of South Carolina, who held the floor arguing against civil rights legislation for 24 hrs., 27 min.

Sep 19: The **first underground atomic explosion** was set off at proving grounds near Las Vegas, Nev.

Sep 24: Racial violence in **Little Rock,** Ark., prompted Pres. Eisenhower to send a force of some 1000 U.S. Army paratroopers to enforce the desegregation of Central High School. The president said that violence had caused the removal of nine black students in the newly integrated school. The students entered the guarded school on Sept. 25.

Oct 8: Jack Soble, a confessed Soviet spy, was sentenced in New York to a seven-year imprisonment for espionage. Soble had pleaded guilty to obtaining national defense secrets with the knowledge that they would go to the U.S.S.R. His wife Myra Soble, and another member of the conspiracy, Jacob Albam, previously had been sentenced to seven years in jail, but their sentences were reduced to four and five years, respectively. Other charges against him were dropped, including one that carried the death penalty.

II. Architecture
Arts and Music
Popular Entertainment
Publishing
Theater

Architects continued to explore the use of new construction materials. A highlight of the year was the completion of the Seagram Building in New York City, the first such structure to be sheathed in bronze. Also in 1957 extraordinary prices were being paid for painting and sculpture. The Edward G. Robinson collection was sold for well over $3,000,000, and one painting in the Georges Lurcy collection, Renoir's *La Serre,* brought $200,000. Americans mourned the passing of Humphrey Bogart, actor, Jan. 14, at 57; James Francis "Jimmy" Dorsey, bandleader, June 12, at 53; Oliver Hardy, of the team of Laurel and Hardy, Aug. 7, at 55; Frederick Law Olmsted, landscape architect, Dec. 25, at 87; and Laura Ingalls Wilder, author of the popular "Little House" books, Feb. 10, at 90.

Among **books published** this year was *By Love Possessed* by James Gould Cozzens, the major novel of the year. Not all critics praised the book but it stayed on the top of the best-seller list. The novel depicted two days in the life of a middle-aged lawyer. Other books published this year included *A Death in the Family* by James Agee, the author's only full-length novel, dealing with a boy's reaction to his father's death; *The Wapshot Chronicle* by John Cheever, a novel; *The Town* by William Faulkner, part of the author's Yoknapatawpha County saga; *Simple Stakes a Claim* by Langston Hughes; and *On the Road* by Jack Kerouac, a semiautobiographical novel of the Beat generation in which the author explored the use of jazz, sex, and drugs by young people.

Jan 13: The **Bollingen Prize** for poetry was awarded to Allen Tate.

Feb 25: In a **censorship ruling**, the Supreme Court ruled unanimously against the conviction of a Detroit, Mich., bookseller for selling John Howard Griffin's book *The Devil Rides Outside*. The ruling voided the section of Michigan penal law banning the sale of books that might corrupt youth. Justice Felix Frankfurter said the law would reduce adults in Michigan to reading only what might be deemed fit for children.

May 6: Pulitzer prizes were awarded for the following: biography, *Profiles in Courage* by John F. Kennedy; history, *Russia Leaves the War* by George F. Kennan; poetry, *Things of This World* by Richard Wilbur; drama, *Long Day's Journey into Night* by Eugene O'Neill. A special award was made to Kenneth Roberts for his historical novels.

III. Business and Industry
Education
Philosophy and Religion
Science

In September wages for factory workers averaged $2.08 an hour, $82.99 a week. Employment remained high during most of the year, but in autumn began to decline. Farm production exceeded the crop yield record set in 1956, and farm prices continued the advance begun in 1956. In religion, leaders of various faiths played important parts in the fight to implement the Supreme Court's decision to bar racial segregation in public schools. Official bodies of several southern church groups requested peaceful compliance with the decision, and the Vatican approved the move by the archbishop of New Orleans to desegregate church schools. But at the end of the year, desegregation in the schools was still a major issue. Americans mourned the death of Adm. Richard E. Byrd on Mar. 11 at age 68. He had led five expeditions to Antarctica and was the first person to fly over the North and South Poles.

In a **survey** of 60,000 high school juniors and seniors, Dr. Ernest V. Hollis of the U.S. Office of Education discovered that 51% of students with an IQ of 133 or higher would not attend college because of the expense or because of a lack of goals.

Jan 21: The first **nationally televised videotaped TV broadcast** was carried by the National Broadcasting Co. The program was a recording of the presidential inauguration ceremonies in Washington, D.C. The first use of videotape in TV had occurred on Nov. 30, 1956, when taped broadcasts of *Douglas Edwards and the News* began running in the western U.S. The first national show to be videotaped was *Truth or Consequences,* beginning on Jan. 22, 1957.

May 2: Teamsters Union president **Dave Beck was indicted** by a federal grand jury in Seattle, Wash., on charges that he had evaded payment of $56,000 in income taxes in 1950. Further investigation revealed that Beck had used union funds for himself and his family.

June 13: The *Mayflower II* landed at Plymouth, Mass., 54 days after setting out from Plymouth, England, to duplicate the voyage of the Pilgrims.

July 1: The **International Geophysical Year** (July 1, 1957-Dec. 31, 1958) launched its first major scientific project, the firing of a rocket on San Nicolas Island, Calif., by the Naval Research Laboratory. The goal was to study the effects of the sun's radiation on communications. Scientists of 67 nations participated in

the International Geophysical Year, a coordinated
study of Earth, its atmosphere and oceans, and the
sun.

July 12: A link between **cigarette smoking and lung
cancer** had been established by scientific research,
Surgeon General Leroy E. Burney reported. Burney
stated that the studies showed a "direct relationship
between the incidence of lung cancer and the amount
smoked."

Aug 19-20: A new **balloon ascent record** was set when
Maj. David G. Simons, USAF, went up 101,486 feet
supported by a plastic balloon. The record also
marked man's longest stay on the edge of space.

Sep 18: **James R. Hoffa,** international vice president of
the Teamsters Union, was charged by the Ethical
Practices Committee of the AFL-CIO with fostering
criminals in the Teamsters Union. The AFL-CIO advised the union to expel Hoffa or leave the AFL-CIO.
On Dec. 6 the Teamsters Union was expelled.

Oct 16: The **first American objects launched into
space** were two aluminum pellets lofted by the U.S.
Air Force.

Oct 31: The **Nobel Prize in Physics** was awarded
jointly to Dr. Tsung Dao Lee of Columbia University
and Dr. Chen Ning Yang of the Institute for Advanced
Study at Princeton for their studies of the behavior of
subatomic particles.

Nov 1: The **world's longest suspension bridge,** the
Mackinac Straits Bridge between Michigan's upper
and lower peninsulas, was opened for traffic. The
bridge cost an estimated $100,000,000.

Dec 12: A new **jet speed record** was set by Maj. Adrian
E. Drew, USAF, in his F-101 Voodoo. Drew's speed,
over a course above the Mojave Desert, Calif., was
1207.6 mph.

IV. Fashion
Folkways
Holidays
Social Issues and Crime
Sports

The sack was the most discussed fashion since the

New Look. The sack's silhouette was an unfitted drape, and men were heard to comment: "It looks like a flour sack." The most highly praised man of the year in boxing was Carmen Basilio, who outpointed Sugar Ray Robinson in a savage fight for the middleweight championship. But by 1958 Robinson had defeated Basilio again. Floyd Patterson defended the world heavyweight title against Tommy "Hurricane" Jackson (July 29). In golf the top money winners were Dick Mayer $65,835, and Patty Berg, $16,272. Baseball was marked by the departure of the New York Giants for San Francisco and the Brooklyn Dodgers for Los Angeles, leaving the pennant-winning Yankees with sole dominion over New York baseball.

A new **baseball attendance record** for the National League was set by the Milwaukee Braves, who drew 2,215,404 fans to home games this year.

Mar 23: The **NCAA basketball championship** was won by North Carolina, which beat Kansas 54 to 53 in three overtime periods.

Mar 30-Apr 3: The **NBA basketball championship** was won by the Boston Celtics, defeating the St. Louis Hawks four games to three.

June 15: The **U.S. Open golf tournament** was won by Dick Mayer, who beat defending champion Cary Middlecoff by seven strokes in a playoff round.

July 6: At the **Wimbledon** tennis championships in England, Althea Gibson won the women's singles title. She then teamed with her opponent, Darlene Hard, to win the women's doubles. Gardnar Mulloy and V. Edward "Budge" Patty won the men's doubles. Hard teamed with Mervyn Rose of Australia to win the mixed doubles.

July 19: The **first U.S. runner to break the four-minute mile** was Don Bowden, who ran the mile in 3:58.7 at Stockton, Calif.

July 21: The **PGA golf tournament** was won by Lionel Hebert.

Oct 2-10: The 54th annual **World Series** was won by the Milwaukee Braves (NL), defeating the New York Yankees (AL) four games to three.

Oct 25: Umberto "Albert" Anastasia, an underworld figure, was slain by two gunmen as he sat in a barbershop. The gangster had been nicknamed "Lord High Executioner" of a crime syndicate known as Murder, Inc.

Dec 29: The **NFL championship** was won by the Detroit Lions, who defeated the Cleveland Browns 59 to 14.

1958

I. Civil Rights
Exploration and Settlement
Government
Statistics
Wars

The political scene was heated during the congressional election campaign by Republican charges that Democrats were guilty of radicalism. Former Pres. Harry S Truman countered with the claim that Pres. Dwight D. Eisenhower had surrendered in Korea. Informal polls showed that the Republicans were losing ground because of continued world tension, including that engendered by America's rush to beat the U.S.S.R. into space, but they continued the fight until election day. When the smoke cleared, the Democrats had scored the biggest gains in more than 20 years.

Mar 4: The verdict against Brig. Gen. **William "Billy" Mitchell,** the pioneer in military air power charged with bringing discredit to the Army more than 37 years earlier, was upheld by Sec. of the Air Force James H. Douglas. Douglas added that Mitchell's faith in air power had been vindicated.

Apr 18: Treason charges against **Ezra Pound,** accused

of making broadcasts for the fascists in Italy during World War II, were dropped in federal court in Washington, D.C. The poet had been confined at St. Elizabeths Hospital, a mental institution, since 1946. A key figure in securing Pound's release was his fellow poet Robert Frost. On July 1 Pound sailed with his wife for Italy.

May 1: Four antinuclear protesters were seized on their ship, *Golden Rule,* by the Coast Guard when they attempted to leave Honolulu for Eniwetok, the atomic testing area.

May 16: A new **world jet speed record** was set by Capt. Walter Irwin, USAF, who flew a single-jet F-104A Starfighter over Edwards Air Force Base, Calif., for an average speed of 1404.19 mph.

June 17: Sherman Adams, assistant to the president, denied before a House investigating committee that he had interceded with federal agencies on behalf of industrialist Bernard Goldfine. The president backed Adams on June 18, saying he was a man of integrity.

July 7: The **Alaska statehood bill** was signed by Pres. Eisenhower, making Alaska the 49th state on ratification by the voters of the territory in August. A formal declaration of statehood was planned for 1959.

Aug 5: The world's **first undersea crossing of the North Pole** was made by the U.S. atomic submarine *Nautilus.* The ship submerged near Point Barrow, Alaska, Aug. 1 and sailed under the 50-foot-thick ice cap for 96 hours before surfacing.

Sep 22: A new **underwater endurance record** was set by the atomic-powered submarine U.S.S. *Skate.* During a transpolar voyage it ran for 31 days under polar ice without surfacing.

Sep 22: Sherman Adams, assistant to the president, resigned under pressure from fellow Republicans who felt he was endangering GOP chances in the coming elections. In a nationwide radio-TV broadcast, Adams insisted he had done no wrong in accepting gifts from Boston industrialist Bernard Goldfine.

Oct 6: A new **underwater endurance record** was set by the atomic-powered submarine U.S.S. *Seawolf,* which surfaced after 60 days.

Nov 4: Congressional elections marked the greatest Democratic gains since the New Deal. The Democrats gained 13 Senate seats to take a 62–34 majority. In the House they won 47 new seats to take control 282–153. In state elections the Democrats made a net gain of five governorships to control 34 state houses against the Republicans' 14.

II. Architecture
Arts and Music
Popular Entertainment
Publishing
Theater

Book publishing had another year of growth in number of new titles and total number of books sold. At the beginning of 1958, some 45,592,000 households had television sets. TV was offering strong competition to the film industry, which produced fewer movies and showed a slight decline in attendance. Music experienced a few changes. Under the direction of a young, dynamic Leonard Bernstein, the New York Philharmonic Orchestra began to play more works by contemporary American composers. Painters were still fighting the battle of abstractionism versus representation, but abstractionism was the winner in most American exhibits. Among notables who died was Mike Todd, 49, the film producer, whose private plane crashed near Grants, N. Mex., Mar. 22.

Among **books published** this year was *Home From the Hill* by William Humphrey, a first novel that became a best seller. It told the story of a Texas family, concentrating on a boy who tried to emulate his father, a man obsessed with hunting and women. Other books published this year included *95 Poems* by E. E. Cummings; *The Ginger Man,* a novel by the expatriate American writer J. P. Donleavy; *The Affluent Society* by John Kenneth Galbraith; *J. B.* by Archibald MacLeish, a verse drama based on the biblical story of Job; and *Lolita* by Vladimir Nabokov, a novel about a middle-aged man and his love affair with a twelve-year-old girl. The book caused a sensation among readers and critics alike.

Jan 6: The **Bollingen Prize** for poetry was awarded to E.E. Cummings.

Jan 13: The Communist newspaper *Daily Worker* **suspended daily publication** because of declining revenue. Its final edition before becoming a weekly declared, "We'll Be Back."

Apr 11: Texas pianist **Van Cliburn,** 23, won the Tchaikovsky International Piano and Violin Festival held in Moscow. His playing of the *Third Piano Concerto* by Sergei Rachmaninoff filled the auditorium of the Tschaikovsky Conservatory with a frenzy of applause.

May 5: Pulitzer prizes were awarded for the following: fiction, *A Death in the Family* by James Agee; biography, *George Washington* by Douglas Southall Freeman; history, *Banks and Politics in America—from the Revolution to the Civil War* by Bray Hammond; poetry, *Promises: Poems 1954–1956* by Robert Penn Warren; drama, *Look Homeward, Angel* by Ketti Frings.

III. Business and Industry
Education
Philosophy and Religion
Science

A serious recession affected the entire country. In February the jobless represented 7.7% of the total labor force; by March the total number of unemployed had jumped to 5,198,000. After antirecession legislation, the situation began to improve by early fall. School desegregation was still a major issue. State authorities in Little Rock, Ark., closed the public schools and reopened them as private institutions that would not admit blacks. A new cry was heard for better educational standards as critics of American schools claimed that standards were lower than ever before.

The **Van Allen belt,** a zone of radiation around Earth about 600 miles in space, was detected by U.S.

satellites and named after James A. Van Allen, who led development of the satellite experiments. Radiation was shown to be 1000 times more intense than expected.

Jan 31: The **first U.S. Earth satellite,** Explorer I, was launched at 10:48 P.M. from Cape Canaveral, Fla. It was bullet-shaped, 80 in. long, 6 in. in diameter with the last stage attached, and weighed 30.8 lbs.

Mar 8: William Faulkner, the Nobel Prize-winning novelist, said at Princeton University that parents and educators were endangering U.S. education by not facing up to important realities and that schools were turning into "baby-sitting organizations."

Mar 17: Vanguard 1, a 3 1/4-lb. satellite, the second U.S. space vehicle, was launched after more than three months of highly publicized delays. The 6.4-in. aluminum sphere, the smallest satellite launched so far, went into a wider orbit than any other manmade satellite.

Apr 26: The **highest Vatican post held by an American** pro-prefect of the Vatican's Sacred Congregation for the Propagation of the Faith was given to Samuel Cardinal Stritch, archbishop of Chicago. On Apr. 28 a blood clot forced amputation of his right arm; on May 27 he died after a stroke.

Apr 28: Speaking on the **danger of nuclear fallout,** the Nobel-Prize-winning scientist Dr. Linus Pauling said that radioactive carbon-14 already left in the air by detonated atomic bombs would cause 5,000,000 genetically defective births and millions of cancer and leukemia cases in the next 300 generations.

June 27: A new **transatlantic speed record** from New York to London was set by Col. Harry Burrell, USAF, flying an Air Force KC-135. The new time was 5 hrs., 27 min., 42.8 sec., for an average of 630.2 mph.

Sep 30: The Supreme Court ruling against **racial segregation** in public schools was defied by Gov. Orval E. Faubus of Arkansas, who closed four high schools in Little Rock. On Sept. 17 the Little Rock Private School Corp. was chartered in a move to reopen the city's schools on a segregated basis as private but state-financed institutions.

Oct 11: In a **lunar exploration** mission, a Pioneer rocket was launched in an attempt to circle the moon. The mission failed on Oct. 12, but the vehicle obtained a record maximum altitude of 79,193 miles—30 times the altitude of any previous man-made object.

Oct 30: The **Nobel Prize in Physiology or Medicine** was awarded jointly to Joshua Lederberg of the University of Wisconsin for his studies of the genetic organization of bacteria; and to George W. Beadle of the California Institute of Technology and Edward L. Tatum of the Rockefeller Institute for their discovery that genes control specific chemical processes.

IV. Fashion
Folkways
Holidays
Social Issues and Crime
Sports

The year in international sports competition was highlighted by U.S. defense of the America's Cup and by American capture of the grand prize of tennis, the Davis Cup, which the U.S. had lost to Australia in 1955. Althea Gibson announced she would quit tennis for a year to launch a career as a popular singer. In boxing, middleweight champion Sugar Ray Robinson disproved the theory that former champions cannot make a comeback when he regained his crown for the fifth time, and heavyweight champion Floyd Patterson defended his title in a bout (Aug. 18) with Roy Harris. In golf the top money winners were Arnold Palmer, $42,407, and Beverly Hanson, $12,629.

Mar 22: The **NCAA basketball championship** was won by Kentucky, which defeated Seattle 84 to 72.

Mar 25: The **world middleweight boxing championship** was regained for an unprecedented fifth time by Sugar Ray Robinson, who outpointed Carmen Basilio in 15 rounds at Chicago.

Mar 29-Apr 12: The **NBA basketball championship** was won by the St. Louis Hawks, who defeated the Boston Celtics four games to two.

June 14: The **U.S. Open golf tournament** was won by Tommy Bolt.

June 28: A new **world swimming record** for the 100-meter butterfly was set by Nancy Ramey of Seattle, Wash., who won the event with a time of 1:09³/₅ during a meet in Los Angeles, Calif.

July 5: At the **Wimbledon** tennis championships in England, Althea Gibson won the women's singles title. She then teamed with Maria Bueno of Brazil to win the women's doubles.

July 20: The **PGA golf tournament** was won by Dow Finsterwald.

Aug 6: A new **world 400-meter hurdles record**, 49.2 sec., was set by Glenn Davis of Columbus, Ohio, during a meet in Budapest, Hungary.

Sep 20-27: The **America's Cup** was defended by the U.S. 12-meter sloop *Columbia,* which defeated the British challenger *Sceptre* in four straight races.

Oct 1-9: The 55th annual **World Series** was won by the New York Yankees (AL), defeating the Milwaukee Braves (NL) four games to three. Yogi Berra, the Yankees catcher, marked his tenth World Series, tying records set by Babe Ruth and Joe DiMaggio.

Dec 28: The **NFL championship** was won by the Baltimore Colts, who defeated the New York Giants 23 to 17.

Dec 31: The U.S. regained the **Davis Cup** when Alejandro "Alex" Olmedo defeated an Australian, Ashley Cooper, in singles competition for the third American match victory. The U.S. went on to win the international challenge round three matches to two.

1959

I. Civil Rights
Exploration and Settlement
Government
Statistics
Wars

The year was highlighted by a visit of Vice Pres. Richard M. Nixon to the U.S.S.R. in July and August, and by a visit of Soviet Premier Nikita S. Khrushchev to the U.S. in September. Nixon's well-publicized tour increased his chances of gaining the Republican presidential nomination in 1960. His major competitor was Gov. Nelson A. Rockfeller of New York. For the Democrats, however, no fewer than eight possible candidates were making their opening moves. Americans mourned the deaths of William J. "Wild Bill" Donovan, director of the Office of Strategic Services in World War II, Feb. 8, at 76; John Foster Dulles, secretary of state under Pres. Dwight D. Eisenhower, May 24, at 71; William F. "Bull" Halsey, Jr., one of the most colorful naval commanders in the Pacific during World War II, Aug. 16, at 76; and George C. Marshall, secretary of state under Pres. Harry S Truman and originator of the Marshall Plan for reconstruction of Europe after World War II, Oct. 16, at 78.

Jan 3: Alaska was proclaimed the 49th state by Pres. Eisenhower.

Mar 18: The **Hawaii statehood bill** was signed by Pres. Eisenhower. Statehood was conditional on a later vote for statehood by Hawaii's electorate.

Mar 30: Double jeopardy was upheld in two U.S. Supreme Court decisions stating that a person could be tried for the same offense in both federal and state courts.

Apr 7: Prohibition in Oklahoma was repealed after 51 years, leaving Mississippi the only dry state in the Union.

May 22: The **first black general** in U.S. history, Brig. Gen. Benjamin O. Davis, Jr., USAF, was promoted to the rank of major general.

June 8: Investigations of communist subversion conducted by Congress and by individual states were ruled constitutional by the U.S. Supreme Court in two 5–4 decisions.

July 7: An **omnibus housing bill** was vetoed by Pres. Eisenhower, who termed it excessive, defective, inflationary, and an obstacle to constructive progress toward better housing for Americans.

July 23: Vice Pres. **Richard M. Nixon arrived in Moscow,** beginning a two-week tour of the U.S.S.R. and Poland. The next day he held a highly publicized kitchen debate, a discussion with Soviet Premier Nikita S. Khrushchev while standing before a kitchen exhibit in the U.S. exhibition in Moscow. After the impromptu, so-called kitchen debate, Nixon formally opened the exhibition.

July 29: The **accidental death rate** for 1958 was declared by the National Safety Council to be the lowest since 1954, 52.5 persons in 100,000. Total deaths were 91,000, of which 37,000 were auto accident deaths, raising the all-time U.S. death toll in auto accidents to 1,265,000.

Aug 21: Hawaii was admitted to the Union as the 50th state, by a proclamation signed by Pres. Eisenhower. Hawaiians had voted by an overwhelming majority on June 27 for statehood in a special referendum. The president also issued the order for a new flag of 50 stars arranged in staggered rows: five 6-star rows and four 5-star rows, the flag to become official July 4, 1960.

Sep 7: In a move to ensure **voting rights** for blacks, the U.S. Civil Rights Commission requested Pres. Eisenhower to appoint federal registrars to supervise voting in areas where local officials had prevented blacks from voting.

Sep 15-27: Soviet Premier **Khrushchev visited the U.S.** Arriving at Andrews Air Force Base, where he was welcomed by Pres. Eisenhower, the premier stated he was visiting the U.S. with "open heart and good intentions." On Sept. 18 he addressed the UN, calling for total nuclear disarmament within four years, and on Sept. 25 he began a series of negotiations with Pres. Eisenhower at Camp David. On Khrushchev's departure for Moscow on Sept. 27, it was revealed that he and Pres. Eisenhower had reached understandings designed to relieve world tensions, including the withdrawal of a proposal Khrushchev had made in Nov. 1958 for major changes in the status of Berlin.

Nov 16: A **defense budget request** for 1961, totaling some $41,000,000,000, was presented by Pres. Eisenhower. It was also decided that there would be no immediate reduction in U.S. troops overseas.

Dec 7: Travel restrictions imposed by the federal government were upheld by the Supreme Court, which refused to consider lower court decisions banning American travel to China.

II. Architecture
   ### Arts and Music
   ### Popular Entertainment
   ### Publishing
   ### Theater

One of the year's cultural high points was the extensive foreign tour of Leonard Bernstein and the New York Philharmonic Orchestra. Commencing in Athens (Aug. 5) and concluding in London (Oct. 10), the tour included a series of 18 concerts in the U.S.S.R. The Soviet Union was the scene of another notable artistic event when *Welcome Home*, a painting by Jack Levine that had been sharply criticized by Pres. Eisenhower, proved popular with the Russians. Notables who died this year included Ethel Barrymore, the celebrated actress, June 18, at 79; Ernest Bloch, composer, July 15, at 78; Raymond Chandler, author, Mar. 26, at 70; Lou Costello, comedian, Mar. 3, at 50; Cecil B. DeMille, motion picture producer, Jan. 21, at 77; Edgar Guest, poet, Aug. 5, at 77; Billie Holiday, one of the greatest jazz vocalists of all time, July 17, at 44; and Frank Lloyd Wright, celebrated architect and pioneer of modern design, Apr. 9, at 89.

Among **books published** this year was *Advise and Consent* by Allen Drury, a novel dealing with a Senate confirmation hearing for a highly controversial nomination for secretary of state. Other books published this year included *Henderson the Rain King* by Saul Bellow, a novel; *Breakfast at Tiffany's* by Truman Capote, a short novel; *The Mansion* by William Faulkner, the author's last Snopes family novel; *The War Lover* by John Hersey, an antiwar novel; *History of the United States Naval Operations in World War II* by Samuel Eliot Morison; *Goodbye, Columbus* by Philip Roth, which included the title novella and five short stories; and *Poorhouse Fair* by John Updike, a collection of associated stories.

Jan 5: In a case involving **protection of journalists' sources,** Marie Torre of the New York *Herald Tribune* began a ten-day jail sentence for contempt of court for refusing to reveal a source used in one of her columns.

Jan 11: The **Bollingen Prize** for poetry was awarded to Theodore Roethke for his 1958 volume *Words for the Wind.*

May 4: Pulitzer prizes were awarded for the following: fiction, *The Travels of Jamie McPheeters* by Robert Lewis Taylor; history, *The Republican Era: 1869–1901* by Leonard D. White with Jean Schneider, who shared the prize with White's estate; biography, *Woodrow Wilson* by Arthur Walworth; poetry, *Selected Poems, 1928–1958* by Stanley Kunitz; drama, *J.B.* by Archibald MacLeish.

June 11: *Lady Chatterley's Lover,* by D. H. Lawrence, was banned from the mails by Postmaster General Arthur E. Summerfield, who said, "Any literary merit the book may have is far outweighed by the pornographic and smutty passages and words, so that the book, taken as a whole, is an obscene and filthy work."

June 15: An **equal time ruling** issued by the FCC earlier in the year was reaffirmed by the commission. It required radio and television stations to give equal time to opposing political candidates in debate and news broadcasts.

Sep 14: A bill lifting FCC **equal time** requirements for radio and television news broadcasts was signed by Pres. Eisenhower.

III. Business and Industry
Education
Philosophy and Religion
Science

After a two-week delay at the request of Pres. Dwight D. Eisenhower, the United Steelworkers of America began a nationwide walkout on July 15. Negotiations proceeded slowly. On the order of Pres. Eisenhower, an 80-day Taft-Hartley injunction was issued on Oct. 21 and, after a court fight ending in the Supreme Court, was executed on Nov. 7, halting the 116-day steel strike, the longest in U.S. history. The U.S. scored a spectacular success when it launched an Atlas missile designed to function as a satellite. This was the fifth and largest Earth satellite successfully launched by the U.S. Besides much information-collecting instrumentation, the missile contained a recording of Pres. Eisenhower's voice, which was automatically broadcast. The message was subsequently received and recorded by U.S. radio stations and distributed throughout the world.

Jan 19: Discriminatory school laws in Virginia, designed to prevent school integration by automatically closing schools receiving final federal court orders to integrate, were ruled invalid by the Virginia Supreme Court. On Feb. 2 schools in Arlington and Norfolk were desegregated with no serious disorders occurring.

Feb 17: Vanguard 2, a 21.5-lb. satellite designed to function as the first weather station in space, achieved orbit after being launched from Cape Canaveral, Fla., by the U.S. Navy.

Feb 28: Discoverer 1, the first satellite in the Discoverer military research satellite program, was launched successfully from Vandenberg Air Force Base, Calif.

Apr 5: The U.S. Naval Research Laboratory reported an increase in **atmospheric radioactivity** of 300% in the eastern United States following nuclear tests by the U.S.S.R. in Sept.-Oct. 1958.

Apr 9: The **first seven U.S. astronauts** were picked from the ranks of military test pilots by NASA. After a vigorous training and testing program, one would be selected to ride a Project Mercury space capsule into Earth orbit in 1961.

Apr 13: Discoverer 2, a military research satellite, was successfully launched from Vandenberg Air Force Base, Calif.

May 28: Two **monkeys were launched into space** by the U.S. Army from Cape Canaveral, Fla. They were recovered unhurt from the Caribbean area after a 300-mile-high space flight.

June 3: By **bouncing radio signals off the moon,** a message recorded by Pres. Eisenhower was transmitted from Westford, Mass., to Canadian Prime Minister John George Diefenbaker in Prince Albert, Saskatchewan.

June 15: It was announced by the New York Stock Exchange that **stock in public U.S. corporations** was owned by 12,490,000 persons as of early 1959.

June 18: The **Arkansas school law** used by Gov. Orval Faubus to close public schools in Little Rock and maintain de facto segregation was ruled unconstitutional by a three-judge federal court.

July 15: A nationwide **steel strike** was begun by the United Steelworkers against 28 steel companies after a breakdown of negotiations.

July 21: The **first U.S. nuclear merchant ship** was christened *Savannah* by Mrs. Dwight D. Eisenhower at Camden, N.J.

Aug 4: Teamster president **James R. Hoffa** and two of his chief aides were denounced for union abuses in a special U.S. Senate committee report.

Aug 7: Explorer 6, a 142-lb. satellite called the paddle wheel satellite because of its four vanes of solar cells, was placed in orbit from Cape Canaveral, Fla. It was the first satellite to be handled by NASA from initiation to orbit.

Aug 12: High schools in Little Rock, Ark., were reopened, integrating two previously all-white schools. About 200 to 250 segregationists demonstrated near Central High School, but policemen held them back with fire hoses and clubs.

Aug 13: Discoverer 5 was launched successfully into polar orbit from Vandenberg Air Force Base, Calif. This followed unsuccessful launchings of Discoverer 3 (June 3) and Discoverer 4 (June 25).

Aug 19: Discoverer 6 was launched into polar orbit from Vandenberg Air Force Base, Calif.

Sep 7: The National Council of Churches announced that **church membership** as of 1958 had increased to 109,557,741. This was a gain of 5% since 1957 and indicated that 64% of the population were church members.

Sep 11: A bill was passed by Congress authorizing **food stamps** in a program to distribute surplus food to impoverished Americans.

Sep 18: Vanguard 3, the 12th successful U.S. satellite, was launched from Cape Canaveral, Fla.

Sep 22: The **International Longshoremen's Association** was readmitted on two-year probation to the AFL-CIO. The ILA had been expelled from the labor organization because of corruption and crime, conditions that AFL-CIO president George Meany said were much improved.

Oct 1: In a **longshoremen's strike,** some 70,000 members of the International Longshoremen's Association walked off the job in Atlantic and Gulf Coast ports. Pres. Eisenhower invoked the Taft-Hartley Act on Oct. 6 by appointing a board of inquiry. An injunction on Oct. 8 halted the strike.

Oct 10: Initiation of the **first passenger service circling the globe** was announced by Pan American World Airways.

Oct 15: The **Nobel Prize in Physiology or Medicine** was awarded to Severo Ochoa of NYU College of Medicine and Arthur Kornberg of Stanford University Medical School for their joint work on the chemistry of heredity.

Oct 26: The **Nobel Prize in Physics** was awarded jointly to Emilio Segre and Owen Chamberlain of the University of California at Berkeley for their discovery of the antiproton.

Nov 7: Striking steelworkers were ordered back to work by the U.S. Supreme Court, which upheld a Taft-Hartley injunction against the strike.

Dec 30: The U.S.S. *George Washington,* the first nuclear submarine capable of carrying and launching missiles, was commissioned at Groton, Conn.

IV. Fashion
   Folkways
   Holidays
   Social Issues and Crime
   Sports

U.S. fans suffered a major blow when Floyd Patterson lost the world's heavyweight boxing title to Ingemar Johansson in the third round of a Yankee Stadium bout. Archie Moore retained the light heavyweight title by knocking out challenger Yvon Durelle of Canada, also in the third round. In baseball, the Los Angeles Dodgers, in their second season on the West Coast, gave California its first championship by winning the 1959 World Series. In golf, the top money winners were Art Wall, $53,142, and Betsy Rawls, $26,774.

Feb 14-15: A two-day **narcotics sweep** in New York City smashed a major heroin ring. Recovering an estimated 28.5 lbs. of heroin valued at $3,600,000, and $50,000 in cash, agents arrested 27 importers and distributors.

Mar 21: The **NCAA basketball championship** was won by California, defeating West Virginia 71 to 70.

Apr 4-9: The **NBA basketball championship** was won by the Boston Celtics, who defeated the Minneapolis Lakers in a four-game sweep.

May 20: Some 4978 **Japanese-Americans** who had renounced their U.S. citizenship during World War II and later applied for restitution were restored to citizenship by the Dept. of Justice.

May 25: A Louisiana ban on **boxing matches between blacks and whites** was declared unconstitutional by the U.S. Supreme Court.

June 13: The **U.S. Open golf tournament** was won by Billy Casper.

Aug 2: The **PGA golf tournament** was won by Bob Rosburg.

Aug 28-31: In the **Davis Cup** international tennis challenge round, Australia beat the defending U.S. team three matches to two.

Oct 18: The 56th annual **World Series** was won by the Los Angeles Dodgers (NL), defeating the Chicago White Sox four games to two. The Dodgers had won the National League pennant by sweeping two games from the Milwaukee Braves in a league playoff.

Nov 5: The newly formed **American Football League** announced that eight professional teams would begin play in 1965.

Nov 9: Consumers were warned against buying **cranberries** grown in Washington and Oregon. Arthur S. Flemming, secretary of Health, Education, and Welfare, announced that a weed killer causing cancer in rats had contaminated cranberries grown in Washington and Oregon during the 1958–1959 season.

Dec 19: The **last Civil War veteran,** Walter Williams, died in Houston, Tex., at the age of 117.

Dec 27: The **NFL championship** was won by the Baltimore Colts, defeating the New York Giants 31 to 16.

1960

I. Civil Rights
Exploration and Settlement
Government
Statistics
Wars

Relations with the U.S.S.R., which improved in 1959 after Vice Pres. Richard Nixon's trip to Moscow and Premier Nikita Khrushchev's tour of the U.S., deteriorated sharply after a U.S. U-2 reconnaissance plane was shot down inside the U.S.S.R. on May 1. The incident gave Khrushchev a propaganda advantage and led to cancellation of a planned Paris summit meeting. The U-2 incident and a later one concerning an American RB-47 airplane, together with U.S. involvement in Laos, the Congo, Germany, Cuba, and Japan, caused a sharp increase in the American public's concern with loss of national prestige. This concern may have played a decisive role in John F. Kennedy's successful bid for the presidency in the November elections after one of the most colorful campaigns and one of the closest votes in U.S. political history.

Jan 18: A controversial **mutual security treaty** was signed by the Japanese and U.S. governments. Among other pledges, the treaty stated that both the U.S. and Japan would "maintain and develop . . . their capacities to resist armed attacks."

Feb 23: Sen. Stuart Symington, Democrat of Missouri, declared in the Senate that the "American people are being misled" about the **missile gap** between the U.S. and the U.S.S.R. Pres. Eisenhower vehemently denied the charge.

Feb 24: The **U.S. population** had reached 179,245,000 by Jan. 1, 1960, according to a Census Bureau estimate.

Feb 29: A filibuster against **civil rights legislation** was begun by 18 southern senators.

Apr 8: A **civil rights bill** was passed by the Senate 71–18. Though it was the first civil rights legislation to survive a southern filibuster, Sen. Joseph S. Clark, Democrat of Pennsylvania, an advocate of civil rights, said his side had "suffered a crushing defeat," calling the bill "only a pale ghost of our hopes."

May 5: The **downing of a U.S. plane** over the U.S.S.R. on May 1 was announced by Premier Nikita S. Khrushchev, who called the captured pilot, Francis Gary Powers, a spy and vowed he would be put on trial. On May 7 the U.S. admitted that the unarmed U-2 plane had been on a spy mission.

May 9: The U.S. announced discontinuance of **U-2 flights** similar to the one intercepted by the U.S.S.R.

May 16: The **Paris summit conference** was canceled by Soviet Premier Khrushchev, who cited the U-2 incident as his reason. Khrushchev also canceled an invitation to Pres. Eisenhower to visit the U.S.S.R.

June 16: Pres. Eisenhower's **Japanese visit** was canceled in view of riots in Japan against the mutual security treaty between Japan and the U.S.

June 26: On return from his **Far East goodwill tour,** Pres. Eisenhower defended his foreign policies and proclaimed his tour a success despite cancellation of a visit to Japan.

July 4: The **50-star U.S. flag,** reflecting the admission of Hawaii to the Union in 1959, became official.

July 11: The U.S.S.R. announced that a **U.S. plane had been shot down** by a Soviet fighter on July 1. The U.S.S.R. alleged that the RB-47 reconnaissance bomber had been in Soviet air space over Arctic waters and accused the U.S. of continuing the espionage program revealed by the downing of a U-2 over Russia earlier in the year.

July 13: The **Democratic National Convention nominated Sen. Kennedy** of Massachusetts for the presidency. Kennedy was the second Roman Catholic in the party's history to be nominated for that office.

July 25: The **Republican National Convention nominated Vice Pres. Nixon** for the presidency. Nixon was virtually unchallenged for the nomination, although Sen. Barry Goldwater of Arizona received ten votes after his name had been put into nomination against his wishes.

Aug 19: Francis Gary Powers, pilot of the U-2 spy plane shot down in the U.S.S.R., was sentenced by the Soviets to ten years of "deprivation of freedom."

Sep 12: Sen. Kennedy stated that as president his **actions would be dictated solely by the public welfare** rather than by the Roman Catholic hierarchy, in a speech in Houston, Tex. Kennedy stated he would resign "if the time should ever come . . . when my office would require me to either violate my conscience or violate the national interest."

Sep 26: The first of a series of **television debates** between Vice Pres. Nixon and Sen. Kennedy took place in Chicago, Ill.

Oct 10-12: Former Pres. **Harry S Truman** was reported to be campaigning vigorously for Sen. Kennedy in the presidential campaign. It was reported that Truman said Vice Pres. Nixon "never told the truth in his life"; told a San Antonio audience that if it voted for Nixon, "You ought to go to hell"; and responded to a demand for an apology for his San Antonio remark by saying, "Tell 'em to go to hell."

Nov 8: John Fitzgerald Kennedy was elected president of the United States. Sen. Kennedy, Democrat of Massachusetts, was the second-youngest man ever to win the nation's highest office. Sen. Lyndon Baines Johnson, Democrat, was elected vice president. The electoral vote was Kennedy, 303; Nixon, 219; and Sen. Harry F. Byrd, 15. Kennedy won 49.7% and Nixon 49.6% of the popular vote, making the election one of the closest in U.S. history. In congressional elections the Democrats took a 65–35 majority in the Senate. In the House they lost 20 seats but kept a majority of 263–174.

Dec 16: The **worst air disaster** to date occurred when a United Air Lines DC-8 jet and a Trans-World Airlines Lockheed Super-Constellation collided in fog over New York harbor. The death toll was 132.

II. Architecture
Arts and Music
Popular Entertainment
Publishing
Theater

The opera year was highlighted by the performance in San Diego of *Die Frau ohne Schatten* by Richard Strauss, a gigantic musical drama replete with strange people and flying fish. The music season was tragically marked by the deaths of renowned musicians: Ernst von Dohnanyi, Feb. 9, at 82; Dimitri Mitropoulos, Nov. 2, at 64; Jussi Bjoerling, Sept. 9, at 49; and Leonard Warren, Mar. 4, at 48. The country also mourned the deaths of Franklin Pierce Adams, newspaper columnist, Mar. 23, at 78; H.L. Davis, winner of a Pulitzer Prize for his 1935 novel *Honey in the Horn*, Oct. 31, at 64; Oscar Hammerstein, II, lyricist and theatrical producer, Aug. 23, at 65; John P. Marquand, novelist and short story writer, July 16, at 66; and Richard Wright, who chronicled the black experience in America in *Native Son* (1940) and *Black Boy* (1945), Nov. 28, at 52.

Among **books published** this year was *To Kill a Mockingbird,* Harper Lee's first novel, which won a Pulitzer Prize in 1961. The novel, set in the South, concerned two children whose father, a lawyer, defended a black man charged with the rape of a white woman. Other books published this year included *Grant Moves South* by Bruce Catton, which dealt with the 1861–1863 campaign of Gen. U.S. Grant during the Civil War; *The Liberal House* by John Kenneth Galbraith, essays on the improvement of the U.S. economic situation; *The Child Buyer,* a novel by John Hersey; *Tristessa,* a novel by Jack Kerouac; *No High Ground* by Fletcher Knebel and Charles W. Bailey, an account of the development of the atomic bomb and the consequences of its use at Hiroshima; *Ourselves to Know,* a novel by John O'Hara; *Thrones* by Ezra Pound, the latest installment of his poetic work *Cantos; The Uncertain Trumpet* by Gen. Maxwell D. Taylor, which described U.S. military competence as dangerously diminished; *Apologies to the Iroquois* by

Edmund Wilson, which dealt with the history and social spirit of the Iroquois; and *Marilyn Monroe* by Maurice Zolotow, a biographical study.

Jan 10: The **Bollingen Prize** for poetry was awarded to Delmore Schwartz for his 1959 collection *Summer Knowledge.*

Jan 25: Payola, money illegally offered or accepted by disc jockeys for broadcasting phonograph records, would bring a $500 fine and one-year prison term in a law proposed by Donald H. McGannon, chairman of the National Association of Broadcasters' TV code review board. The proposal followed extensive investigations into payola practices in the broadcasting industry.

Feb 11: Jack Paar, protesting **NBC censorship** of one of his jokes the night before, walked off his late-night television show. Later, at a meeting with network officials, Paar agreed to return to the program Mar. 7.

Mar 25: *Lady Chatterley's Lover* by D.H. Lawrence was ruled not obscene, and therefore mailable, by the U.S. Circuit Court of Appeals in New York. Chief Judge Charles E. Clark, alluding to Postmaster General Arthur E. Summerfield, asked, "Should a mature and sophisticated reading public be kept in blinders because a government official thinks reading certain works of power and literary value is not good for him?"

Apr 29: In a **payola investigation,** Dick Clark, one of the nation's best paid and most influential disc jockeys, denied involvement in illegal payments. Clark stated before the Special House Subcommittee on Legislative Oversight, "I believe in my heart that I have never taken payola."

May 2: Pulitzer prizes were awarded for the following: fiction, *Advise and Consent* by Allen Drury; biography, *John Paul Jones* by Samuel Eliot Morison; history, *In the Days of McKinley* by Margaret Leech; poetry, *Heart's Needle* by W.D. Snodgrass; drama, *Fiorello!* by George Abbott, Jerome Weidman, Sheldon Harnick, and Jerry Bock.

May 19: In the **payola scandal,** Alan Freed, radio disc jockey, television personality, and originator of the term "rock 'n' roll," was arrested on charges of commercial bribery. Seven other persons accused of payola were also arrested.

Oct 17: Charles Van Doren, former star contestant on the TV quiz show *21,* and 13 others were arrested on charges of perjury. They had stated before a grand jury that the quiz shows involved in a recent scandal had not provided contestants with questions and answers before the shows were broadcast.

Nov 17: Anti-integration riots in New Orleans were the worst since initiation of school integration there. Almost 200 people were arrested.

III. Business and Industry
Education
Philosophy and Religion
Science

The U.S. demonstrated considerable technical progress by launching 17 space satellites and probes. The most spectacular of the objects sent into space were Tiros 1, which took 22,952 pictures of Earth's cloud cover; Discoverer 13, whose capsule was the first orbited object ever returned to Earth; and Discoverer 14, whose capsule was later retrieved in midair. Other aspects of national life, however, were showing less progress. A dangerous outflow of gold prompted the government to curtail spending abroad by military personnel, and there was a high rate of unemployment. The government continued its fight for southern school integration, but some public schools remained closed and were marred by mob violence and vandalism, such as that which erupted in November during attempts to integrate schools in New Orleans.

Jan 2: The age of the solar system was estimated by Dr. John H. Reynolds of the University of California (Berkeley) to be 4,950,000,000 years. His estimate was based on study of a meteorite found 41 years previously near Richardton, N.D.

Jan 4: The longest steel strike in the nation's history

was settled when the steel companies and the United Steel Workers agreed on a wage increase. The strike had begun on July 15, 1959.

Jan 7: A new **ocean diving record** was established when Lt. Donald Walsh, USN, and Jacques Piccard descended 24,000 ft. in the bathyscaphe *Trieste*. The world record dive was made in the Pacific Marianas Trench, 60 miles from Guam. The dive was surpassed on Jan. 23 when the *Trieste* made a dive of 35,800 ft. to the bottom of the Marianas Trench.

Jan 9: Some methods and instances of **birth control** were approved by the bishops and other leaders of the Protestant Episcopal Church. The approbation was limited to countries in which the population increase threatened the general welfare.

Mar 11: Pioneer 5, the third spacecraft to be orbited around the sun, was launched by the U.S. from Cape Canaveral. The other two were Pioneer 4 (U.S.) and Lunik 1 (U.S.S.R.).

Mar 22: Dr. J.R. Heller, director of the National Cancer Institute, reported that **cancer** of the stomach was declining and cancer of the lung increasing.

Apr 1: The **first weather satellite,** Tiros 1, was orbited by the U.S. It sent thousands of photographs of cloud cover back to Earth.

Apr 9: School integration had reached only 6% of southern schools, it was reported by *Southern School News,* in spite of the 1954 Supreme Court decision against segregation.

Apr 14: A **Polaris missile** was fired from under water off San Clemente Island, Calif., for the first time.

Apr 27: Sit-ins by blacks in the South were again endorsed by the National Council of the Protestant Episcopal Church.

Apr 28: Marital sex relations without procreative intentions were declared not to be sinful by leaders of the 100th General Assembly of the Southern Presbyterian Church.

May 10: The **first undersea voyage around the world** was completed by the nuclear submarine U.S.S. *Triton,* the largest known submarine.

May 12: Lockheed Aircraft announced that the **Electra**

crashes in Sept. 1959 and Mar. 1960 were caused by a structural deficiency. The cost of correcting the fault was estimated at $25,000,000.

May 15: Taxes reached 25% of earnings, according to a Tax Foundation report that lumped together federal, state, and local taxes.

May 20: The U.S. set a **world missile record** when an Atlas intercontinental ballistic missile flew 9000 miles, from Cape Canaveral, Fla., to beyond the tip of Africa.

May 24: Designed to act as an **early warning system** against surprise missile attacks, Midas 2, a 5000-lb. satellite, was launched from Cape Canaveral, Fla.

May 31: The Joint Commission on Mental Illness and Health reported that **mental illness** afflicted 25% of all Americans at one time or another in their lives to the extent that they required professional help.

June 6: For middle-aged men, **coronary death rates** "were found to be from 50% to 150% higher among heavy cigarette smokers" than among nonsmokers, according to the American Heart Association.

July 20: The first successful launching of **Polaris missiles** from a submerged craft was accomplished by the nuclear submarine U.S.S. *George Washington.* The missiles flew 1150 miles.

Aug 3: The first phone conversation in which **voices were bounced off the moon** was accomplished by U.S. scientists.

Aug 4: A **world air speed record** of 2196 mph was set by the X-15 experimental U.S. rocket plane. The plane was piloted by Joseph A. Walker, a civilian test pilot.

Aug 11: The **first payload recovered from orbit** was lifted from the Pacific Ocean by a U.S. helicopter. The capsule was placed in orbit by Discoverer 13 on Aug. 10.

Aug 19: A **spacecraft was snagged in midair** by the U.S. Air Force. The 300-lb. space capsule was ejected from Discoverer 14 at an altitude of 10,000 ft. and retrieved at 8500 ft.

Nov 3: The **Nobel Prize in Chemistry** was awarded to Prof. Willard Frank Libby of the University of California for discovering a method of radioactive carbon dating.

Nov 3: The **Nobel Prize in Physics** was awarded to Prof. Donald A. Glaser of the University of California for his development of the bubble chamber, a device that makes visible the paths of subatomic particles.

IV. Fashion
   Folkways
   Holidays
   Social Issues and Crime
   Sports

Floyd Patterson, using an eclectic boxing style, defeated Ingemar Johansson to become the first man in history to regain the heavyweight championship of the world. Another outstanding fighter, 40-year-old Sugar Ray Robinson, lost the world middleweight title to Paul Pender. Boxing was under fire, and a congressional investigation tried to determine the nature and extent of underworld influence in the sport. Congress also investigated the practice of payola in the recording and broadcasting industries.

Jan 2: The **U.S. chess championship** was successfully defended by Brooklyn's 16-year-old chess wonder, Bobby Fischer, in a tournament in New York City.

Jan 12: The **first 15,000-point NBA player,** Dolph Schayes of the Syracuse professional basketball team, reached a 15,013-point total for his career. Schayes was famed for his rebounding ability.

Jan 24: In a **Chicago police scandal,** Richard Morrison, an ex-convict awaiting trial for burglary, named eight Chicago policemen as confederates. In the ensuing investigation, 17 policemen were suspended on suspicion of robbery, bribery, and burglary.

Feb 18-28: At the **Winter Olympics** in Squaw Valley, Calif., the unofficial team championship was won by the U.S.S.R. Sweden was second and the U.S. was third.

Feb 23: Demolition of **Ebbets Field,** home park of the Brooklyn Dodgers (now the Los Angeles Dodgers), was begun. An apartment project was planned for the site.

Mar 7: In **racial violence,** Felton Turner, a black 27-year-old resident of Houston, Tex., was beaten with a tire iron and suspended upside down in an oak tree. The initials KKK were carved on his chest. Turner had been abducted by four masked youths, who said their actions were related to the sit-down strikes of Texas Southern University black students.

Mar 19: The **NCAA basketball championship** was won by Ohio State, which defeated California 75 to 55.

Mar 25: Wilt Chamberlain retired from professional basketball. Though he decried the rough tactics by opponents on the court, Chamberlain admitted that racial difficulties he encountered as a black had influenced his decision. Chamberlain relented later in the year and signed another pro basketball contract.

Mar 27–Apr 9: The **NBA basketball championship** was won by the Boston Celtics, who beat the St. Louis Hawks four games to three.

May 2: Caryl Chessman, convicted of kidnaping, rape, and robbery in Jan. 1948, was executed in the gas chamber at San Quentin Prison, Calif., after a 12-year battle for his life.

June 18: The **U.S. Open golf tournament** was won by Arnold Palmer, who beat Jack Nicklaus by two strokes.

June 20: The **world heavyweight boxing championship** was won by Floyd Patterson, who defeated Ingemar Johansson in a fifth-round knockout. Patterson thus became the first fighter in boxing history to regain the heavyweight championship.

July 24: The **PGA golf tournament** was won by Jay Hebert, beating Jim Ferrier by one stroke.

Aug 12: In a case of **racial discrimination,** a Troy, Mich., cemetery rejected the body of Winnebago Indian George V. Nash because he was not white. Nash, a World War I veteran, was buried in Pontiac, Mich., after his family refused to permit burial in Arlington National Cemetery.

Aug 25–Sep 11: At the **Summer Olympics** in Rome, Italy, the U.S. won 34 gold medals and took second place in team standings, behind the U.S.S.R.

Oct 3: In a **narcotics raid,** U.S. agents confiscated $3,500,000 worth of heroin (110 lbs.) and arrested four people, among them the Guatemalan ambassador to Belgium, Mauricio Rosal.

Oct 5-13: The 57th **World Series** was won by the Pittsburgh Pirates (NL), defeating the New York Yankees (AL) four games to three.

Oct 18: Casey Stengel, manager of the New York Yankee baseball team since 1949, was fired. Although the official announcement stated that Stengel had reached retirement age, he attributed dismissal to a controversy with the club owners.

Dec 26: The **NFL championship** was won by the Philadelphia Eagles, who defeated the Green Bay Packers 17 to 13.

1961

I. Civil Rights
  Exploration and Settlement
  Government
  Statistics
  Wars

John F. Kennedy was inaugurated president of the U.S. in a year that provided many explosive and dangerous situations. He was met with civil war in Laos and the Congo and continued Russian threats in Berlin. Rising tensions in Berlin culminated in the sealing off of East Berlin by East German and Soviet guards on Aug. 13, and the construction of a concrete and barbed wire barrier that came to be called the Berlin Wall. In September the Soviets resumed atmospheric nuclear testing. In the domestic arena, the president was confronted with several difficult problems. How to eliminate unemployment continued to be a major concern. Congress refused to provide substantial aid to U.S. education and passed an impotent civil rights bill. Notables who died included Whittaker Chambers, accuser of Alger Hiss, July 9, at 60; William Z. Foster, chairman of the American Communist Party from 1945 to 1957, Sept. 1, at 80; Learned Hand, distinguished jurist, Aug. 18, at 89; Sam Rayburn, longtime Speaker of the House, Nov. 16, at 79; Walter Bedell Smith, chief of staff to Gen. Eisenhower during World War II, Aug. 9, at 75; and Sumner Welles, diplomat, Sept. 24, at 68.

Jan 3: The **U.S. broke diplomatic relations with Cuba** after a series of mutually hostile actions, the last being Cuba's demand that the U.S. reduce its Havana embassy staff to 11 members.

Jan 20: John F. Kennedy was inaugurated president of the United States. A Democrat and the 35th president, Kennedy was assassinated on Nov. 22, 1963.

Mar 13: Elizabeth Gurley Flynn, 70, was named to succeed Eugene Dennis as national chairman of the U.S. Communist Party. She was the first woman to fill the office.

Apr 17: In what came to be called the **Bay of Pigs invasion,** some 1500 anti-Castro Cuban exiles landed at the Bay of Cochinos in Cuba. Organized by the U.S.-based National Revolutionary Council and trained by the CIA, the force enjoyed initial success but collapsed within a few days because of inadequate supplies, lack of air support, and overwhelming opposing forces. On Apr. 24 Pres. Kennedy stated he accepted full responsibility for failure of the invasion.

May 27: A bill establishing the **Alliance for Progress** was signed by Pres. Kennedy. The bill provided $600,000,000 in special aid to Latin America.

June 3-4: At the **Vienna summit meeting,** Pres. Kennedy and Premier Nikita S. Khrushchev discussed problems of mutual interest to the U.S. and the U.S.S.R., particularly nuclear disarmament and troubles in Laos and in Berlin.

July 24: A U.S. **passenger jet was hijacked.** An armed passenger forced the pilot of an Eastern Airlines Electra en route to Tampa from Miami to divert to Havana. Cuba later entrusted the plane to the UN Security Council to discourage what it alleged to be "imminent military aggression" by the U.S.

Aug 2: U.S. support for the Republic of China and its membership in the UN was reaffirmed in a joint communiqué issued following meetings between Pres. Kennedy and Premier Ch'en Ch'eng of the Republic of China. The statement reiterated U.S. opposition to UN membership for the People's Republic of China.

Sep 5: A hijacking bill making air piracy a crime punishable by death or imprisonment was signed by Pres. Kennedy.

Oct 6: Speaking on **civil defense,** Pres. Kennedy advised families to build or buy a shelter against atomic fallout. He said that the U.S. civil defense program should provide such protection for every American.

Nov 8: A plane crash killed 74 U.S. Army recruits flying in a chartered Imperial Airlines Constellation over an area near Richmond, Va. It was later revealed that the airline had been penalized twice for infractions of CAA regulations.

II. Architecture
Arts and Music
Popular Entertainment
Publishing
Theater

Tropic of Cancer by Henry Miller, originally published in France in 1934, became available in the U.S. after many years of prohibition on grounds of obscenity. Imported and reprinted by the same company that was responsible for U.S. publication of *Lady Chatterley's Lover, Tropic of Cancer* encountered considerably less legal difficulty than the D. H. Lawrence novel. The U.S. literary scene was saddened by the death of Ernest Hemingway; he was said to have shot himself while cleaning a shotgun. Joan Sutherland made an impressive U.S. debut at the Metropolitan Opera. She displayed a capacity for combining agility, color, subtlety, and volume of sound. Equally impressive was a New York City recital series by pianist Arthur Rubinstein, who enchanted U.S. music lovers. Playing ten Carnegie Hall recitals within 40 days, Rubinstein, at 72, announced joyfully that he had decided not to make the series his "final touch." Notables who died this year included Gary Cooper, actor, May 13, at 60; Hilda Doolittle, poet, Sept. 27, at 75; Dashiell Hammett, detective writer, Jan. 10, at 66; Moss Hart, playwright, Dec. 20, at 57; George S. Kaufman, playwright and producer, June 2, at 71; Chico Marx, Oct. 11, at 70; Grandma Moses, painter, Dec. 13, at 101; Eero Saarinen, architect, Sept. 1, at 51; and James Thurber, writer and cartoonist, Nov. 2, at 66.

Among **books published** this year was *Webster's Third New International Dictionary*. The massive new unabridged dictionary received a mixed response. Many linguists objected to its refusal to set standards of English and felt that too much valuable old material had been omitted. Other books published this year included *The Coming Fury* by Bruce Catton, the first volume of a trilogy to be called *Centennial History of the Civil War; Midcentury* by John Dos Passos, a novel; *Kaddish and Other Poems* by Allen Ginsberg; *Catch-22* by Joseph Heller, an antiwar novel that became a best seller; *Spirit Lake* by MacKinlay Kantor, a novel about frontier life in Iowa in the 1850s; *Franny and Zooey* by J. D. Salinger, stories; *Sinclair Lewis: an American Life* by Mark Schorer; *The Winter of Our Discontent* by John Steinbeck, a novel; and *The Agony and the Ecstasy* by Irving Stone, a novel based on the life of Michelangelo.

Jan 8: The **Bollingen Prize** for poetry was awarded to Yvor Winters for his 1960 volume of *Collected Poems*.

Jan 23: In a **film censorship** ruling, the U.S. Supreme Court upheld a Chicago, Ill., ordinance forbidding the showing of any motion picture without permission of the city censors.

May 1: Pulitzer prizes were awarded for the following: fiction, *To Kill a Mockingbird* by Harper Lee; biography, *Charles Sumner and the Coming of the Civil War* by David Donald; history, *Between War and Peace: The Potsdam Conference* by Herbert Feis; poetry, *Times Three: Selected Verse from Three Decades* by Phyllis McGinley; drama, *All the Way Home* by Tad Mosel.

May 9: Calling **television a "vast wasteland,"** Newton N. Minow, chairman of the FCC, in a vehement criticism of TV programming, said, "It is not enough to cater to the nation's whims—you must also serve the nation's needs."

Nov 15: A **record art price** of $2,300,000 was paid by the New York Metropolitan Museum of Art for Rembrandt's *Aristotle Contemplating the Bust of Homer*. The painting was formerly in the collection of the late Alfred W. Erickson and his wife.

III. Business and Industry
Education
Philosophy and Religion
Science

This was a year for adventure in space. Two Americans and two Russians invaded a frontier of the future. Though the U.S. was unable to equal the impressive Soviet feat of putting men into orbit, it succeeded in propelling two men to the threshold of space and then recovering them safely. The U.S. also launched an impressive series of Earth satellites and space probes, mostly designed to transmit data back to Earth. Progress of a different sort was made in civil rights in educational facilities. Court after court voided—but some upheld—various state laws designed to prevent school integration. Even though some civil rights battles were won, integration was slow and marked by sporadic violence, such as that encountered during the so-called freedom rides. Education as a whole became more of a national concern as it became increasingly evident that educational facilities were inadequate and growing more so and that the quality of instruction was poor in many parts of the country. Among the notables who died this year was Lee De Forest, whose invention of the audion tube in 1906 ushered in the age of radio, June 30, at 87.

Jan 28: Plans for establishing the **Peace Corps,** a project advocated by Pres. John F. Kennedy, were made public by the U.S. State Department.

Jan 31: In a **Project Mercury** suborbital test flight, the U.S. shot a 37½-lb. chimpanzee into space and recovered him successfully. The capsule containing the animal traveled 5000 mph to a height of 155 miles.

Feb 9: Earth is a "slightly irregular ellipsoid," according to photographic data received from Vanguard 1 and 2.

Feb 18: Discoverer 21 was launched into orbit by a Thor-Agena-B rocket. An unusual feature of the shot was a control mechanism that enabled the rocket engine to be restarted while in orbit.

Feb 22-23: Birth control as a means of family limitation was endorsed by the National Council of Churches at a meeting in Syracuse, N.Y.

Feb 23: The most costly **airline strike** in aviation history ended. The six-day strike had completely shut down Trans World, Eastern, Flying Tiger, American, and National airlines and had hampered operations of several others.

Apr 27: Explorer 11, a 95-lb. research satellite, was launched into orbit by a Juno 2 rocket. Carrying a "lensless telescope," the satellite was intended to determine the nature of interstellar matter.

May 4: A new **balloon altitude record** was set by two Navy scientists who acsended to 113,500 ft. aboard the balloon *Stratolab High No. 5.* One of the balloonists drowned after he fell from the sling of the helicopter that had picked him up.

May 5: A bill setting the federal **minimum wage** at $1.25 an hour and expanding coverage to include 3,624,000 workers not covered previously was signed by Pres. Kennedy.

May 5: The **first American in space** was Navy Commander Alan Bartlett Shepard, Jr., who made a successful suborbital flight aboard the Project Mercury capsule *Freedom Seven.*

June 16: Discoverer 25 was launched. Its capsule was

ejected and recovered on June 18. The satellite carried samples of various minerals to determine how they would be affected by space conditions.

June 29: Three satellites were launched simultaneously by a Thor-Able-Star rocket. These satellites, Transit 4-A, Greb 3, and Injun, constituted the first triple launching in history.

July 7: James R. Hoffa was reelected president of the International Brotherhood of Teamsters by an overwhelming vote. The election was held at the Teamsters' convention in Miami Beach, Fla.

July 21: The **second American in space** was Capt. Virgil I. "Gus" Grissom, USAF, who ascended to an altitude of 118 miles in a suborbital flight aboard the Project Mercury capsule *Liberty Bell Seven.*

Sep 8: In a report on **smoking and heart disease** in the *Journal of the American Medical Association,* it was held that there was statistical evidence connecting the two.

Oct 19: The **Nobel Prize for Physiology or Medicine** was awarded to Dr. Georg von Bekesy of Harvard University for his studies of the inner ear.

Nov 2: The **Nobel Prize for Chemistry** was awarded to Melvin Calvin of the University of California at Berkeley for determining the sequence of chemical reactions involved when a plant assimilates carbon dioxide.

Nov 2: The **Nobel Prize in Physics** was awarded jointly to Robert Hofstadter of Stanford University for his work on the atomic nucleus and to Rudolf L. Mössbauer of West Germany for developing a method of using radiation from excited nuclei to measure time.

IV. Fashion
Folkways
Holidays
Social Issues and Crime
Sports

In boxing Floyd Patterson again defeated Ingemar Johansson in a close but quick fight in Miami Beach,

Fla. Patterson withstood the power of the Swedish champion's savage right hand and scored a knockout, the second in a row for the American heavyweight. In golf, the top money winners were Gary Player, $64,540, and Mickey Wright, $22,236. In baseball, the National League announced that it would add two new franchises in 1962, the Houston Astros and the New York Mets. Americans mourned the death of Tyrus Raymond "Ty" Cobb, considered by many the greatest baseball player of all time, July 17, at 74.

Jan 2: The **AFL championship** for 1960 was won by the Houston Oilers, who defeated the Los Angeles Chargers 24 to 16.

Mar 13: The **world heavyweight boxing championship** was successfully defended by Floyd Patterson, who knocked out Ingemar Johansson in the sixth round in Miami Beach, Fla.

Mar 25: The **NCAA basketball championship** was won by Cincinnati, defeating the defending champions, Ohio State, 70 to 65.

Apr 2-11: The **NBA basketball championship** was won by the Boston Celtics, who defeated the St. Louis Hawks four games to one.

May 14: Two groups of **freedom riders,** people who traveled by private car and public transportation to sites in the South to protest racial segregation, were attacked by white citizens of Anniston and Birmingham, Ala., while on a journey from Washington, D.C., to New Orleans.

June 9: In a **college basketball bribery** scandal, four former players were indicted in New York City in connection with a point-shaving plot, in which players would deliberately control the score of a game as instructed by gamblers. Two gamblers, Aaron Wagman and Joseph Hacken, were named as co-conspirators. Both had been indicted earlier on related charges in the grand jury probe that began on Apr. 4. As the summer progressed, further revelations and indictments showed the practice of point-shaving to be widespread.

June 17: The **U.S. Open golf tournament** was won by Gene Littler.

July 8: At the **Wimbledon** tennis championships in England the women's doubles title was won by Karen Hantze and Billie Jean Moffitt.

July 30: The **PGA golf tournament** was won by Jerry Barber, who beat Don January by one stroke in a playoff round.

Oct 1: Yankee slugger **Roger Maris** hit his 61st homer, setting a new season record. He did it in a season of 162 games. Babe Ruth had hit 60 home runs in a 154-game season.

Oct 4-9: The 58th annual **World Series** was won by the New York Yankees (AL), beating the Cincinnati Reds (NL) four games to one.

Dec 4: The **world heavyweight boxing championship** was successfully defended by Floyd Patterson, who knocked out Tom McNeeley in the fourth round of a bout in Toronto, Canada.

Dec 24: The **AFL championship** was won by the Houston Oilers, who defeated the San Diego Chargers 10 to 3.

Dec 31: The **NFL championship** was won by the Green Bay Packers, who defeated the New York Giants 37 to 0.

1962

I. Civil Rights
   Exploration and Settlement
   Government
   Statistics
   Wars

In international affairs, Pres. John F. Kennedy appeared stronger and more sure. He visited Mexico and the Bahamas in an effort to strengthen alliances. Communist violation of a cease-fire in Laos in May led Kennedy to order U.S. troops into Thailand until guarantees of Laotian sovereignty could be secured. Chinese invasion of India in September prompted increased U.S. aid to India. The key event of the year came in October, when Pres. Kennedy, on national TV, revealed that Soviet nuclear missiles and jet bombers were located in Cuba and ordered a blockade of Cuba until the weapons were removed. The world appeared to stand on the brink of nuclear war until Premier Khrushchev agreed to withdraw the weapons. At home, the president was less successful. Congress continued to defeat or alter proposed legislation. The nation mourned the death of Eleanor Roosevelt, widow of Pres. Franklin D. Roosevelt and a key figure in the early years of the United Nations, Nov. 7, at 78.

Jan 15: **U.S. tanks were withdrawn** from the Berlin Wall in an effort to improve relations with the U.S.S.R. Two days later 12 Soviet tanks that had stationed near the wall since Oct. 1961 were removed.

Jan 29: The **nuclear test ban conference** of the U.S., U.S.S.R., and Great Britain in Geneva adjourned after 353 sessions in three years. The talks were deadlocked over a monitoring system for international control.

Feb 3: A **trade ban with Cuba,** effective Feb. 7 and including almost all products, was ordered by Pres. Kennedy.

Feb 8: Creation of the **Military Assistance Command** (MAC), a new U.S. military command in South Vietnam, was announced by the Defense Department.

Feb 10: U-2 pilot **Francis Gary Powers** was released in Berlin by Soviet authorities in exchange for Soviet spy Rudolf Abel. Frederic L. Pryor, an American student, was released by the Soviets at the same time.

Feb 26: **Segregation laws in transportation facilities,** both interstate and intrastate, were ruled unconstitutional by the U.S. Supreme Court. The Court ordered a federal court in Mississippi to act against state segregation laws in terminals.

Mar 19: The **Communist Party was sued** in New York by the Justice Department, which also sued four of its officials—Elizabeth Gurley Flynn, Gus Hall, Benjamin J. Davis, and Philip Bart—in an effort to collect $500,000 in income taxes and interest for 1951.

Apr 3: Full **racial integration in military reserve units,** exclusive of the National Guard, was ordered by the Defense Department.

Apr 8: Cuba announced that 1179 **Bay of Pigs prisoners** had been convicted of treason and sentenced to 30 years in prison. Officials offered to free all prisoners on payment of a $62,000,000 ransom. Six days later, 60 sick and wounded prisoners were returned to the U.S. on a promise to pay the ransom.

Apr 25: The **U.S. resumed nuclear testing** in the atmosphere after a three-year moratorium, with the explosion of a device near Christmas Island. The U.S.S.R. had broken the U.S.-Soviet moratorium the preceding September.

May 12: Some 1800 U.S. **Marines were sent to Thailand** with other naval, air, and land forces for defense against possible attack by communist forces from Laos. By May 29, more than 5000 U.S. military personnel were in Thailand.

June 16: Two U.S. **Army officers were killed** in an ambush by guerrillas north of Saigon, South Vietnam.

July 27: The last **Marines in Thailand** were withdrawn.

Aug 15: For the first time in history, the **national debt** exceeded $300,000,000,000.

Aug 27: At the **Geneva disarmament conference,** the U.S. and Great Britain proposed adoption of a total nuclear test ban open to international inspection. They also proposed an alternative plan that would reduce nuclear tests without international inspection. The U.S.S.R. rejected both proposals.

Aug 27: The **Twenty-fourth Amendment** to the Constitution, barring the poll tax as a requirement for voting in federal elections, was approved by Congress.

Oct 22: The **Cuban missile crisis** was the subject of a television address by Pres. Kennedy. He said that the U.S.S.R., contrary to its assurances, had been building missile and bomber bases in Cuba. Kennedy authorized a blockade of Cuba effective Oct. 24, to halt shipment of offensive weapons to Cuba. The day after Kennedy's address, the Council of the Organization of American States voted unanimously to authorize the use of armed force to prevent shipment of offensive weapons to Cuba.

Oct 25: Aerial photos of offensive missile bases in Cuba were displayed to the UN by Ambassador Adlai Stevenson. The next day the U.S. Navy boarded and searched a Soviet-chartered freighter en route to Havana.

Oct 27: Premier **Khrushchev offered to remove the Cuban missile bases** under UN supervision, demanding that the U.S. take corresponding action in Turkey. A U-2 reconnaissance plane was shot down over Cuba.

Oct 28: Withdrawal of Soviet missiles, under UN inspection, and a halt to construction of bases in Cuba, was agreed to by Premier Khrushchev. Pres. Kennedy agreed to lift the trade and weapons ban when the UN had acted, and pledged that the U.S. would not invade Cuba.

Oct 29: The U.S. **blockade of Cuba** was suspended for the duration of a trip by acting UN Secretary-General U Thant for a conference with Cuban Prime Minister Fidel Castro. No agreement was reached after UN inspection.

Nov 2: The **missile bases in Cuba were being dismantled,** Pres. Kennedy reported to the nation, adding that "progress is now being made toward restoration of peace in the Caribbean."

Nov 6: In **congressional elections** the Democrats gained two Senate seats for a 67–33 majority. In the House they lost five seats for a 258–177 majority.

Nov 7: Billie Sol Estes, a Texas financier whose business manipulations involving the Department of Agriculture had created a political scandal, was sentenced to eight years in prison after conviction on a charge of swindling a Texas farmer. He still faced numerous other state and federal indictments.

Nov 20: Lifting of the **naval blockade of Cuba** was

announced by Pres. Kennedy, following assurances by Premier Khrushchev that all Soviet jet bombers in Cuba would be removed within 30 days.

Nov 20: An **executive order prohibiting racial discrimination in housing** built or purchased with federal funds was signed by Pres. Kennedy.

Dec 23: The **Cuban government began releasing prisoners** captured in the Bay of Pigs invasion under an agreement with a U.S. committee of private citizens by which Cuba would get more than $50,000,000 in food and medical supplies.

II. Architecture
   Arts and Music
   Popular Entertainment
   Publishing
   Theater

In art, the interest of the general public and collectors focused on so-called pop art, the depiction and sometimes the actual display of the most banal objects of American life: canned foods, electric appliances, comic strips, and the like. An international art scandal broke when Canadian authorities questioned the authenticity of many of the paintings from Walter P. Chrysler's famous collection, then on tour in Canada. Formation of Citizens for Decent Literature kept the question of censorship in the news; two particular targets of this watchdog group were *The Carpetbaggers* by Harold Robbins and *The Tropic of Capricorn* by Henry Miller. In architecture, one of the year's most interesting structures was the 600-foot Space Needle, at the Century 21 Exposition in Seattle, Wash. Notables who died this year included Sylvia Beach, proprietor of the celebrated bookstore Shakespeare & Co. in Paris, about Oct. 5, at 75; William Beebe, naturalist, author, and explorer, June 4, at 84; E. E. Cummings, poet, Sept. 3, at 67; William Faulkner, winner of the 1949 Nobel Prize for Literature, July 6, at 64; Robinson Jeffers, poet, Jan 20, at 75; Franz Josef Kline, expressionist painter, May 13, at 51; Ernie Kovacs, television writer, performer, and producer, Jan. 13, at 42; Fritz Kreisler, violinist, Jan. 29, at 86; Marilyn Monroe, who died in her Los Angeles home of an apparent overdose of sleeping pills, Aug. 5, at 36; and Bruno Walter, conductor, Feb. 17, at 85.

Among **books published** this year was *Ship of Fools* by Katherine Anne Porter, a long-awaited novel 20 years in the writing. It was an account of a voyage from Mexico to Germany of a German ship in 1931, on the eve of Adolf Hitler's rise to power. Other books published this year included *Another Country* by James Baldwin, a novel; *Fail-Safe* by Eugene Burdick and Harvey Wheeler, a novel about the accidental launching of a nuclear strike against the U.S.S.R.; *Silent Spring* by Rachel Carson, a well-documented indictment of the indiscriminate use of pesticides and other chemicals; *In the Clearing*, a collection of poems by Robert Frost; *The Thin Red Line* by James Jones, a novel dealing with the invasion of Guadalcanal in World War II; *Seven Days in May* by Fletcher Knebel and Charles W. Bailey, II, a novel dealing with the military overthrow of the U.S. government; *Six Crises* by Richard M. Nixon; *A Simple Honorable Man* by Conrad Richter, a novel; and *Travels With Charley: In Search of America* by John Steinbeck.

WNYC-TV, the nation's first **municipally owned television station**, began operation in New York City. The city also received its first publicly supported educational television station, WNDT, this year.

Jan 7: The **Bollingen Prize** for poetry was awarded jointly to John Hall Wheelock for his 1961 volume *The Gardener*, and to Richard Eberhart for poetic excellence over a 30-year period.

May 7: Pulitzer prizes were awarded for the following: fiction, *The Edge of Sadness* by Edwin O'Connor; history, *The Triumphant Empire: Thunder-Clouds Gather in the West* by Lawrence Gibson; nonfiction, *The Making of the President, 1960* by Theodore H. White; poetry, *Poems* by Alan Dugan; drama, *How to Succeed in Business Without Really Trying* by Frank Loesser and Abe Burrows.

May 31-June 3: The **first International Jazz Festival,**

presented in Washington, D.C., by the President's Committee of the People-to-People Program, proved a disappointment. There was unanimous praise for the Duke Ellington orchestra and the old-style jazz of the Eureka Brass Band of New Orleans, but the classical-jazz hybrid composition called "Third Stream," by Ellington, Gunther Schuller, and André Hodeir, was received coolly.

Sep 23: Philharmonic Hall, the first building to be completed in New York City's **Lincoln Center for the Performing Arts,** opened with a gala concert. Live television coverage was supplied as Leonard Bernstein conducted the New York Philharmonic before an audience of dignitaries, musicians, and patrons of the arts. The hall's acoustics were to prove disappointing. For a long time afterward, engineers made adjustments in the ceiling baffles and other sound-enhancing devices.

Oct 23: A **postal error** involving a U.S. commemorative stamp issued on this date to honor the late secretary general of the UN, Dag Hammarskjold, was reported in early November by several stamp collectors, who had obtained stamps with one color printed incorrectly. Postmaster General J. Edward Day subsequently caused an uproar when he ordered 10,000,000 of the errors printed to prevent speculation in the rarities. A suit against Day by a New Jersey collector was withdrawn after the Post Office Department authenticated his 50-stamp pane as a "discovery" item.

Oct 25: The **Nobel Prize for Literature** was won by John Steinbeck, whose works included *Tortilla Flat* (1935), *Of Mice and Men* (1937), *The Grapes of Wrath* (1939), *The Moon Is Down* (1942), *Cannery Row* (1945), and *East of Eden* (1952). The award cited his "realistic and imaginative writing . . . distinguished by a . . . social perception." He was the sixth American, the seventh American-born, author to win a Nobel Prize for Literature.

III. Business and Industry
Education
Philosophy and Religion
Science

This year's space achievements included the launching of Telstar, a communications satellite, and the orbiting of three astronauts on perfect missions. Experimentation with nuclear submarines and with thermonuclear detonations added to U.S. technological development. In the South, segregation in university education was broken, but only after mob violence and several deaths. Official nondenominational prayers in public schools were ruled unconstitutional by the Supreme Court. Congress took no steps to provide funds for the improvement of educational facilities for the nation's youth. In industry, an effort by steel industry management to raise prices was stopped by Pres. John F. Kennedy. The AFL-CIO announced a drive to establish a national 35-hour work week.

Jan 12: A **railroad merger** of two of the nation's largest systems, the Pennsylvania and the New York Central railroads, was approved by the companies' boards of directors.

Jan 26: Ranger 3, a lunar probe designed to transmit close-up television pictures of the moon before landing scientific instruments on its surface, was launched from Cape Canaveral, Fla. Two days later, because of excessive velocity, it passed the moon and went into orbit around the sun.

Feb 14: Plans for an **underwater telephone cable** costing $84,000,000 and running between Hawaii and Japan, via Midway, Wake, and Guam islands, was announced by the American Telephone & Telegraph Company.

Feb 20: The **first American to orbit Earth,** Lt. Col. John Glenn, circled the globe three times aboard a Mercury capsule *Friendship 7* before splashdown. It was launched from Cape Canaveral, Fla.

Mar 1: In the **biggest antitrust case** in U.S. history, E. I. du Pont de Nemours & Company was ordered by a federal district court to divest itself of 63,000,000 shares of General Motors stock.

Mar 4: The Atomic Energy Commission announced that the **first atomic power plant in Antarctica** was in operation at McMurdo Sound.

Mar 8: A two-year **cultural agreement** was signed with the U.S.S.R. to expand cultural, scientific, technical, and educational exchanges.

Mar 16: Titan 2, the most powerful U.S. ICBM, on its maiden flight, covered more than 5000 miles from Cape Canaveral, Fla., to a spot near Ascension Island in the south Atlantic.

Mar 27: Segregation in all Roman Catholic schools in the New Orleans, La., diocese was ordered ended by Archbishop Joseph Francis Rummel.

Apr 19: Skybolt, the first U.S. airborne ballistic missile, was launched from a B-52 bomber at Cape Canaveral, Fla. Its second stage failed to fire and the missile fell short of its target.

Apr 26: The **first international satellite,** Ariel, bearing six British experiments and propelled aloft by a U.S. Delta rocket, was launched from Cape Canaveral, Fla. It was intended to study the ionosphere.

Apr 26: Ranger 4 crashed into the far side of the moon 64 hours after being launched from Cape Canaveral, Fla. Fifty-five hours into the flight, its radio system went dead.

May 6: In the **first submarine-launched nuclear detonation,** a Polaris missile armed with a nuclear warhead and launched from the nuclear submarine *Ethan Allen* was successfully exploded near Christmas Island. It was also the first U.S. test of a nuclear warhead carried by a long-range missile.

May 24: The **second American in orbit,** astronaut M. Scott Carpenter, circled Earth three times aboard the Mercury capsule *Aurora 7,* which was launched by an Atlas rocket from Cape Canaveral, Fla.

May 25: A nationwide campaign for a **35-hour work week** was announced by George Meany, president of the AFL-CIO.

May 28: In the **largest stock loss since Oct. 29, 1929,** shares on the New York exchange lost

$20,800,000,000 in value. The stock market quickly recovered.

June 25: A New York State law permitting recitation of an **official prayer** in public schools was ruled unconstitutional by the Supreme Court.

July 9: A **thermonuclear explosion** equivalent to 1,400,000 tons of TNT was set off by the U.S. 250 miles above Johnston Island in the Pacific. The blast caused a substantial radiation increase in the Van Allen belt, disrupting communications and satellite operations.

July 10: Telstar, the experimental communications satellite developed and owned by American Telephone & Telegraph and Bell Telephone Laboratories, was placed in orbit from Cape Canaveral, Fla. It later relayed live TV pictures from Andover, Maine, to France and Great Britain.

Aug 22: The *Savannah,* the world's first nuclear-powered ship, completed its maiden voyage from Yorktown, Va., to Savannah, Ga.

Aug 22: Pres. Kennedy announced that a **submarine rendezvous** beneath the North Pole had been effected by two U.S. nuclear submarines.

Aug 27: Mariner 2 was launched successfully from Cape Canaveral, Fla., on a projected 15-week trajectory toward the planet Venus.

Sep 20: The application by **James H. Meredith,** a black, for admission to the University of Mississippi was denied by Mississippi Gov. Ross R. Barnett in defiance of a federal court order.

Sep 28: Gov. **Ross R. Barnett** of Mississippi was found guilty of civil contempt by a U.S. court of appeals. He was ordered to cease interference with desegregation at the University of Mississippi or face arrest and a fine of $10,000 for each day of further interference.

Sep 30: James H. Meredith was escorted onto the University of Mississippi campus by U.S. marshals. Two men were killed in the ensuing mob violence, which was quelled with the aid of 3000 federal soldiers. The next day Meredith was enrolled and began to attend classes amid continuing disruption by protesters.

Oct 3: The **third American in orbit,** astronaut Walter

N. Schirra, completed five and three-quarter orbits aboard the Mercury capsule *Sigma 7* before splashing down near Midway Island in the Pacific within four miles of the recovery carrier U.S.S. *Kearsarge.*

Oct 18: The **Nobel Prize for Physiology or Medicine** was awarded jointly to Dr. James D. Watson of Harvard University, Dr. Maurice H. F. Wilkins of King's College in London, and Dr. Francis H. C. Crick of Cambridge, England, for their discovery of the molecular structure of deoxyribonucleic acid (DNA), the physical basis of heredity.

Dec 8: The **first black bishop** to serve a predominantly white diocese of the Protestant Episcopal Church in the U.S., the Right Rev. John Melville Burgess, was consecrated as suffragan bishop of Massachusetts.

Dec 13: Relay 1, an intercontinental communications satellite, was put in orbit. Two days later transmission was turned off for an indefinite period because of a power failure.

Dec 14: Mariner 2, on its 109th day of flight, transmitted information about Venus for 42 minutes.

Dec 21: Mississippi Gov. **Ross R. Barnett** and Lt. Gov. Paul B. Johnson were charged with criminal contempt of court in the U.S. Fifth Circuit Court of Appeals in New Orleans for their actions in September violating court orders for admission of James H. Meredith to the University of Mississippi.

IV. Fashion
Folkways
Holidays
Social Issues and Crime
Sports

In boxing Floyd Patterson lost his heavyweight crown to Sonny Liston in less than three minutes. In November 20-year-old Cassius Clay knocked out Archie Moore and moved closer to a title match against Liston. In baseball two new teams, the Houston Colt .45's and the New York Mets, joined the National League roster. The New York Yankees won their 20th World Series. In golf the leading money winners were Arnold Palmer, $81,448, and Mickey Wright, $21,641. A new dance craze, the twist, was born in a New York City nightclub, The Peppermint Lounge. In women's fashions wigs became popular, and boots became a fashion accessory. The romance between Elizabeth Taylor and Richard Burton on the set for the motion picture *Cleopatra* in Rome was in and out of the headlines all year. Notables who died in 1962 included Edward Britt "Ted" Husing, sports announcer, Aug. 10, at 50; Charles "Lucky" Luciano, gangster, Jan. 26, at 65; Clem McCarthy, sports announcer, June 4, at 79; and Benny "Kid" Paret, a welterweight fighter who died of injuries sustained in a bout with Emile Griffith, Apr. 3, at 24.

A **UPI survey** showed that in the 24 states with legalized betting at race tracks, 33,881,860 fans bet a total of $2,679,461,505. Attendance was up 1.28% over 1961, and betting was up 5.57%. Mrs. Richard C. du Pont's Kelso was named horse of the year for the third straight year. Kelso earned $254,585 to boost lifetime earnings of the horse to $1,011,940. Kelso became the fifth horse in racing history to top the $1,000,000 mark.

Jan: The use of **nudity in advertising** became a national controversy after Christina Paolozzi, a 22-year-old model, appeared in the nude in a full-page color ad in *Harper's Bazaar.* The photograph was the work of fashion photographer Richard Avedon.

Feb 2: The **first person to vault 16 feet** was a Marine Corps corporal, John Uelses, at the Millrose Games in Madison Square Garden in New York City. Using a springy fiberglass pole, he cleared 16 ft. 1/4 in. On the following night, in Boston, he raised the mark to 16 ft. 3/4 in.

Feb 10: Jim Beatty, the **first American to break the four-minute mile indoors,** was clocked at 3:58.9 in Los Angeles, a new indoor record. On June 8, also in Los Angeles, he set a new world record of 8:29.8 for two miles. Beatty won the James E. Sullivan Memorial Trophy as the outstanding amateur athlete of 1962.

Mar 2: The **first basketball player to score 100 points** in a game was Wilt Chamberlain, star of the Philadelphia Warriors, who made 36 goals and 28 foul shots in a game against the N.Y. Knicks.

Mar 24: The **NCAA basketball championship** was won by Cincinnati, which defeated Ohio State 71 to 59.

Apr 3: Eddie Arcaro, considered by many the greatest American jockey in modern turf history, retired from racing. During his 31-year career he had ridden 4779 winners and had brought home purses totaling $30,039,543.

Apr 7-18: The **NBA basketball championship** was won by the Boston Celtics, defeating the Los Angeles Lakers four games to three.

Apr 21: The **Century 21 Exposition,** the world's fair at Seattle, Wash., was opened by remote control from Palm Beach, Fla., by Pres. Kennedy, who activated the carillon in the 600-foot Space Needle tower.

June 17: The **U.S. Open golf tournament** was won by Jack Nicklaus, who beat Arnold Palmer by three strokes in a playoff.

July 7: At the **Wimbledon** tennis championships in England, Karen Hantze Susman won the women's singles title. Susman teamed with Billie Jean Moffitt to win the women's doubles, and Margaret Osborne du Pont teamed with Neale Fraser of Australia to win the mixed doubles.

July 22: The **PGA golf tournament** was won by Gary Player of South Africa, who became the first nonresident of the U.S. to win the championship.

Aug 14: In a **mail truck robbery** in Plymouth, Mass., thieves took a record cash haul of $1,551,277.

Sep 8: The **richest purse in thoroughbred racing history,** $357,250, was offered in the Arlington-Washington Futurity, a race for two-year-olds. The winner's share, $142,250, went to Candy Spots.

Sep 15-25: The **America's Cup** was successfully defended by the U.S. 12-meter yacht *Weatherly,* which defeated the Australian challenger *Gretel* four races to one. It was the closest competition in years and the first time since 1934 that the U.S. entry failed to sweep the first four races.

Sep 25: The **world heavyweight boxing championship**

was won by Sonny Liston, who knocked out the defending champion Floyd Patterson in two minutes and six seconds of the first round.

Sep 27: The **New York Mets,** a new National League baseball team, finished their first season, under former Yankee manager Casey Stengel. The Mets lost 120 of the 160 games they played. However, the fans loved them; nearly 1,000,000 came to the Polo Grounds to witness the heroic ineptitude of the players and the antics of their manager.

Oct 4-16: The 59th annual **World Series** was won by the New York Yankees (AL), defeating the San Francisco Giants (NL) four games to three. The Giants had won the National League pennant by beating the Los Angeles Dodgers two games to one in a league play-off.

Dec 23: The **AFL championship** was won by the Dallas Texans, who defeated the Houston Oilers 20 to 17. The game went to two extra quarters and was decided by a field goal by Tommy Brooker.

Dec 30: The **NFL championship** was won for the second year running by the Green Bay Packers, who defeated the N.Y. Giants 16 to 7.

1963

I. **Civil Rights**
   Exploration and Settlement
   Government
   Statistics
   Wars

The death of Pres. John F. Kennedy on Nov. 22 shocked the nation and the world. The 34th person elected president of the United States, Kennedy was the fourth to die by an assassin's bullet. The respect

he had evoked throughout the world was attested to
by the presence at his funeral of representatives of 92
nations, among them Charles de Gaulle of France,
Anastas I. Mikoyan of the U.S.S.R., and Prince Philip
of Great Britain. Although Kennedy did not live to
see the passage of his civil rights bill, his program of
medical care for the aged, or his tax-reduction bill,
Congress did approve his proposal for aid to the mentally retarded. This year also saw a $3,600,000,000
appropriation for foreign aid, a reduction of
$300,000,000 from the previous year. The signing of
a limited nuclear test-ban treaty in October was coun-
terbalanced by continuing conflict with Cuba and
with the U.S.S.R. The U.S. became more heavily involved in the war in Vietnam. On Nov. 1 the government of Pres. Ngo Dinh Diem of South Vietnam was
overthrown by South Vietnamese armed forces, and
Diem was assassinated. On Nov. 7 the U.S. recognized
the provisional government of Nguyen Ngoc Tho,
Diem's vice president. Notables who died this year
included W. E. B. Du Bois, a prominent black writer
and educator, Aug. 27, at age 95; and Medgar W.
Evers, civil rights leader, assassinated on June 12, at
age 37.

Jan 17: The largest **federal budget** to date, totaling
$98,800,000,000 with a projected deficit of
$11,900,000,000, was sent to Congress by Pres.
Kennedy.

Feb 8: Underground nuclear testing was resumed by
the U.S. A suspension of tests had been ordered on
Jan. 20 during the U.S.-U.S.S.R. test ban talks.

Feb 21: Medicare, a medical-hospital insurance plan
financed through Social Security, was submitted to
Congress by Pres. Kennedy.

Mar 13: Two **Soviet reconnaissance planes flew over
Alaska.** On Mar. 16 the U.S. protested what was
termed the "first clearly established incident of a Soviet overflight of the U.S."

Mar 18: The Supreme Court held that **free counsel for
all indigents** facing serious criminal charges must be
supplied by the states.

Apr 10: The nuclear-powered submarine *Thresher*

sank in the Atlantic with 129 men on board during a test dive. A Navy board of inquiry concluded that a system failure probably created progressive flooding and that the interference with electrical circuits caused loss of power.

June 12: Medgar Evers was assassinated by a sniper, who shot the civil rights leader in the back outside the Evers home in Jackson, Miss. The crime sparked numerous demonstrations, and Pres. Kennedy and many other leaders condemned the killing. After a funeral in Jackson, Evers was buried in Arlington National Cemetery.

June 23: Pres. Kennedy, beginning a **ten-day tour of Europe,** arrived in West Germany. On June 26, speaking to a crowd of more than 1,000,000 in West Berlin, Kennedy stated he was proud to say "Ich bin ein Berliner" [I am a Berliner].

July 8: Virtually all **financial transactions with Cuba were banned** by the U.S. in another move toward economic isolation of that country.

July 12: A modified form of **martial law** was declared in Cambridge, Md., after National Guard troops were sent into the city for the second time in a month to control racial violence.

July 25: A **limited nuclear test-ban treaty,** prohibiting testing in the atmosphere, in space, and under water, was initialed in Moscow by the U.S., Great Britain, and the U.S.S.R.

Aug 28: A **Freedom March** on Washington, D.C., brought an estimated 200,000 participants, who listened to speeches by ten civil rights leaders, among them Dr. Martin Luther King. Dr. King told the group, "I have a dream," describing a U.S. free of divisiveness, hatred, and injustice.

Aug 30: The **hot line** went into operation. It was an emergency communications link between Washington, D.C., and Moscow, intended to reduce the risk of accidental war.

Sep 15: A **church bombing** in Birmingham, Ala., left four young black girls dead. The attack on the 16th Street Baptist Church sparked further violence in the city, leaving two more dead and 19 injured.

Oct 7: Robert G. "Bobby" Baker resigned as secretary to the Senate majority after being charged with using his position for personal financial gain.

Oct 7: The **limited nuclear test-ban treaty was signed** by Pres. Kennedy. It went into effect Oct. 10.

Oct 10-12: A **U.S. military convoy to Berlin** was blocked by Soviet troops in a dispute over troop counting procedures. The U.S. lodged strong formal protests, and the convoy was allowed to proceed.

Oct 16: Two **U.S. military satellites** were secretly launched from Cape Canaveral, Fla., for the detection of any violation of the treaty banning nuclear tests in space.

Nov 4: A U.S. military convoy was blocked by Soviet troops at the western border of Berlin. The U.S. protested and after 41 hours the convoy was allowed to proceed.

Nov 12: Travel restrictions on diplomats were imposed by the State Department, which barred diplomats of Bulgaria, Czechoslovakia, Hungary, Poland, and Rumania from 355 U.S. counties, about 11% of the continental U.S., for "reasons of national security."

Nov 22: Pres. **John F. Kennedy was assassinated** while riding in a motorcade in Dallas, Tex. He was pronounced dead at 1 P.M. Gov. John B. Connally of Texas, accompanying Kennedy, was severely wounded. Vice Pres. Lyndon Baines Johnson was sworn in as the 36th president of the United States at 2:39 P.M. at Love Air Field in Dallas. That same afternoon, Lee Harvey Oswald, a suspect in the assassination, was captured by Dallas police.

Nov 24: Lee Harvey Oswald was shot and killed by a man named Jack Ruby while in the custody of Dallas police. The nation saw the murder on television. Ruby was apprehended immediately.

Nov 25: John F. Kennedy was buried at Arlington National Cemetery following a mass at St. Matthew's Roman Catholic Cathedral.

Nov 29: What came to be called the **Warren Commission** was established by Pres. Johnson. The special commission, headed by Chief Justice Earl Warren, was appointed to investigate the assassination of John F. Kennedy and related events.

II. Architecture
Arts and Music
Popular Entertainment
Publishing
Theater

The best plays on Broadway were revivals, such as Eugene O'Neill's *Strange Interlude;* British imports, such as John Osborne's *Luther;* and translations, such as Bertolt Brecht's *Mother Courage and Her Children.* New buildings at Harvard and Yale made most of the architectural news. Le Corbusier, the great Swiss-French master, designed the Visual Arts Center at Harvard, his first building in the U.S. At Yale two new college buildings, the first since the 1930s, were completed. Eero Saarinen and Associates were the designers. Also new at Yale were the Beinecke Rare Book and Manuscript Library and Paul Rudolph's Art and Architecture Building, a six-story structure that incorporated 36 different floor and ceiling levels. The Ford Foundation made history when it allocated $7,700,000 for development of ballet in the U.S. William Schuman, president of Lincoln Center for the Performing Arts in New York City, announced that $300,000 would be spent on improving acoustics in the center's Philharmonic Hall. Notables who died this year included Van Wyck Brooks, critic and biographer, May 2, at 77; Robert Frost, poet and four-time winner of the Pulitzer Prize, Jan. 29, at 88; Paul Hindemith, composer, Dec. 28, at 68; Oliver La Farge, author and anthropologist, Aug. 2, at 83; Elsa Maxwell, the celebrated New York City hostess, Nov. 1, at 80; Adolphe Menjou, actor, Oct. 29, at 73; Clifford Odets, playwright, Aug. 14, at 57; Zasu Pitts, film comedienne, June 7, at 63; Theodore Roethke, poet, Aug. 1, at 55; William Carlos Williams, poet and physician, Mar. 4, at 79; and Edgar Mantillon

"Monty" Woolley, the actor who gained fame in *The Man Who Came to Dinner,* May 6, at 74.

Among **books published** this year was *Terrible Swift Sword* by Bruce Catton, the second volume in Catton's trilogy *Centennial History of the Civil War.* The book covered the period from just after the first Battle of Bull Run in June 1861 through Lincoln's Emancipation Proclamation. Other books published this year included *Eichmann in Jerusalem: A Report on the Banality of Evil* by Hannah Arendt; *The Civil War: A Narrative, Fredericksburg to Meridian* by Shelby Foote, the second volume of a history of the war; *Idiots First* by Bernard Malamud, stories; *The Group* by Mary McCarthy, a novel; *The Sand Pebbles* by Richard McKenna, a novel; *The American Way of Death* by Jessica Mitford, a scathing study of American funeral customs; *The Two Ocean War* by Samuel Eliot Morison; *Raise High the Roof Beam, Carpenters* and *Seymour: An Introduction* by J. D. Salinger, two stories in one volume; and *Cat's Cradle* by Kurt Vonnegut, Jr., a novel.

The painting *Her Room* by **Andrew Wyeth** was bought by the William A. Farnsworth Library and Art Museum in Rockland, Maine, for $65,000. It was the highest price ever paid by a museum for the work of a living American artist.

The **Bollingen Prize** for poetry was awarded to Robert Frost, whose final volume, *In the Clearing,* was published in 1962.

Happenings, the name given to ultra avant-garde theatrical events, were performed in various places, except in theaters, in many cities. A series of abstract events generally of an absurd or comic nature, a happening combined mime, painting, music, and modern dance.

Jan 8-Mar 4: The *Mona Lisa* by Leonardo da Vinci was exhibited in New York City and Washington, D.C., on loan from the Louvre. Nearly 1,000,000 people waited on line to see the painting. Another Louvre masterpiece, James McNeill Whistler's *Portrait of My Mother,* was shown in Atlanta, Ga., in February as a memorial tribute to a group of Georgia art lovers killed in a plane crash near Paris in 1962.

Mar-June: The first large-scale exhibition of **pop art** was held at the Guggenheim Museum in New York City. The show moved on to other American cities later in the year, bemusing critics and public alike with its representational paintings of such prosaic subjects as soup cans and comic strips. Prominent in the three-year-old pop-art movement were Andy Warhol, Jasper Johns, Robert Rauschenberg, and Roy Lichtenstein.

May 6: Pulitzer prizes were awarded to the following: fiction, *The Reivers* by William Faulkner; biography, *Henry James, Vol. II: The Conquest of London, 1870–1881* and *Henry James, Vol. III: The Middle Years, 1881–1895* by Leon Edel; history, *Washington, Village and Capital, 1800–1878* by Constance McLaughlin Green; general nonfiction, *The Guns of August* by Barbara Tuchman; poetry, *Pictures from Brueghel* by William Carlos Williams. A furor was caused when it was announced that there would be no drama award. The advisory board for drama had recommended Edward Albee's *Who's Afraid of Virginia Woolf?* When their recommendation was not announced, both John Mason Brown and John Gassner resigned.

Oct 16: The **New York** *Mirror* ceased publication. Although the Hearst newspaper's circulation was the second largest among U.S. dailies, the paper fell victim to an economic squeeze, partly the result of the 114-day New York City newspaper strike (from Dec. 8, 1962 to Mar. 31, 1963), and partly the result of decreasing advertising income. The *Mirror's* assets were sold to the rival *Daily News.*

III. Business and Industry
   Education
   Philosophy and Religion
   Science

Progress toward civil rights was made when South Carolina and Alabama opened their colleges to blacks. The federal government appropriated nearly $2,000,000,000 for construction and improvement of U.S. college facilities and for student loans. The building and construction trades union of the AFL-CIO adopted a program to eliminate racial discrimination. In July demonstrations in New York City supporting increased hiring of minority workers at construction sites led to more than 700 arrests. During the year, the nation's unemployment rate rose. George Meany, president of the AFL-CIO, condemned automation as a "curse to society." A threatened national railroad strike resulted in a congressional act requiring arbitration, the first time arbitration was imposed in peacetime. Federal legislation required that women receive pay equal to that of men for similar work. The nation's farmers, in a referendum called for by the Food and Agriculture Act of 1962, overwhelmingly voted down a government program to decrease wheat production and to support the price of wheat. Traffic deaths reached an all-time high of 40,804.

Jan 3: Relay 1, a communications satellite launched Dec. 13, 1962, but silent since Dec. 15 owing to malfunction, was reactivated by radio signals from the ground. It began transmission between North and South America and Europe.

Jan 28: School desegregation in South Carolina, the last state to end segregation in its schools, was achieved when a student named Harvey B. Gantt was enrolled in Clemson College, Clemson, S.C.

Feb 14: Syncom 1, an experimental forerunner of a series of communications satellites, was launched from Cape Canaveral, Fla. Although a near synchronous orbit was achieved, radio contact with Earth was lost the same day.

Mar 17: Elizabeth Ann Seton was beatified by Pope John XXIII. She was the first native-born American to be so honored. She was declared a saint by Pope Paul VI in 1974 and canonized on Sept. 14, 1975.

Apr 5: J. Robert Oppenheimer, the U.S. physicist declared a security risk in 1954, was named winner of the Atomic Energy Commission's 1963 Fermi Award.

Apr 12: The Rev. **Martin Luther King, Jr., was arrested** in Birmingham, Ala., during a desegregation drive that had begun on Apr. 2.

Apr 18: Successful **human nerve transplants** were reported by Dr. James B. Campbell of the New York University Medical Center.

May 7: Telstar 2, the second communications satellite, was launched from Cape Canaveral, Fla. It began relaying color and black-and-white television signals between the U.S. and Europe.

May 9: A secret **military satellite** was launched by the Air Force from Point Arguello, Calif. It released some 400,000,000 tiny copper hairs into a polar orbit, providing a cloud of reflective material for relaying radio signals from coast to coast within the U.S.

May 15-16: The **fourth American in orbit,** Maj. L. Gordon Cooper, Jr., completed 22 orbits around Earth aboard the Mercury capsule *Faith 7,* in the final flight of Project Mercury.

June 4: A **Federal Reserve bill** changing the backing of $1.00 and $2.00 bills from silver to gold was signed by Pres. Kennedy.

June 8: A **drive against cigarette smoking** was opened by the American Heart Association, the first voluntary public agency to do so.

June 10: A bill requiring **equal pay for equal work,** regardless of sex, was signed by Pres. Kennedy.

June 11: The **University of Alabama was desegregated.** Gov. George C. Wallace, who had literally stood in the way of desegregation, stepped aside when confronted by federalized National Guard troops. Two black students were enrolled.

July 26: Syncom 2 was successfully launched and on Aug. 15 placed over Brazil in a geostationary Earth orbit. It transmitted telephone and Teletype messages between the U.S. and Nigeria.

Sep 7: Krebiozen, a so-called miracle drug, was declared by the Food and Drug Administration to be creatine, a common amino acid, and ineffective against tumors.

Sep 10: Public **school desegregation** in Huntsville, Ala.,

was effected after Pres. Kennedy federalized the Alabama National Guard, forcing Gov. Wallace to end
his attempt to block school integration.

Oct 10: The deferred 1962 **Nobel Peace Prize** was
awarded to Dr. Linus C. Pauling of the California
Institute of Technology. The award committee did
not specify Pauling's achievements, but his efforts to
secure a ban on nuclear testing were well known.

Nov 5: The **Nobel Prize in Physics** was awarded
jointly to Eugene P. Wigner of Princeton, Maria G.
Mayer of the University of California, and Hans Jen-
sen of the University of Heidelberg, Germany, for
their studies of atomic structure.

Dec 4: In a major change in the **Roman Catholic mass,**
the use of English in the U.S. in place of Latin for
parts of the mass and for the sacraments was approved by the Roman Catholic Ecumenical Council.

IV. Fashion
   Folkways
   Holidays
   Social Issues and Crime
   Sports

The sports world lost two of its most popular competitors in the retirements of baseball slugger Stan
Musial and basketball back-court artist Bob Cousy.
The strike zone in major-league baseball was enlarged at the beginning of the season. To compensate
for the bigger target, perhaps, National League umpires began applying the rule that a pitcher must wait
one second between windup and delivery. Rigorous
enforcement of the one-second rule evoked such outrage from fans and players that the Rules Committee
dropped it within a month. Golf's leading money winners were Arnold Palmer, $128,230, and Mickey
Wright, $31,269. Rogers Hornsby, the great slugger
whose .424 batting average for 1924 has never been
equaled, died on Jan. 5, at 66. Davey Moore, world
featherweight boxing champion, fell into a coma
shortly after losing his title on Mar. 21 in a bout with

Ultiminio "Sugar" Ramos. Moore died on Mar. 25, at age 29.

Mar 20: Hope Cooke, a recent graduate of Sarah Lawrence College, married Crown Prince Palden Thondup Namgyal of Sikkim in a Buddhist ceremony in Gangtok. On Dec. 2 the prince succeeded to the throne as maharajah on the death of his father, Sir Tashi Namgyal.

Mar 23: The **NCAA basketball championship** was won by Loyola, Ill., which defeated the University of Cincinnati 60 to 58.

Apr 24: The Boston Celtics' brilliant guard **Bob Cousy,** 34, retired from competition after leading the team to its fifth straight NBA championship. The Celtics had downed the Los Angeles Lakers four games to two (Apr. 14–24).

June 23: The **U.S. Open golf tournament** was won by Julius Boros, who beat Arnold Palmer and Jacky Cupit in a playoff.

July 6: At the **Wimbledon** tennis championships in England, Chuck McKinley won the men's singles championship.

July 21: The **PGA golf tournament** was won by Jack Nicklaus.

July 22: The **world heavyweight boxing championship** was successfully defended by Sonny Liston, who knocked out Floyd Patterson 2 min., 10 sec. into the first round.

Aug 5: Craig Breedlove set an unofficial **world auto speed record** of 407.45 mph on the Bonneville Salt Flats in Utah, driving a sleek three-ton, three-wheeled, jet-powered auto. The U.S. Auto Club established a new class for its records: "Jet-Powered Vehicles."

Aug 24: Don Schollander of Santa Clara, Calif., became the first person to break the two-minute mark for the 200-meter freestyle swim. At Osaka, Japan, he won the event with the time of 1:58.4.

Aug 24: John Pennel became the **first person to pole vault 17 feet,** reaching 17 ft. 3/4 in. at a meet in Miami, Fla.

Sep 27: Joseph M. Valachi, hoodlum turned informer,

identified the alleged chiefs of organized crime in the U.S. in televised testimony before the Senate Permanent Investigations Subcommittee.

Sep 29: Stan "The Man" Musial played his last game for the St. Louis Cardinals, retiring at 42 to take an executive position with the club. In his 22 years in baseball, all with the Cards, the great hitter set or tied 17 major league and 30 National League records.

Oct 2-6: The 60th annual **World Series** was won by the Los Angeles Dodgers (NL), who swept the New York Yankees (AL) in four games. Dodgers pitcher Sandy Koufax set a new series record by striking out 15 players in the opening game.

Dec 26-29: The U.S. regained the **Davis Cup,** which it had lost in 1959, by beating the Australian tennis team three matches to two.

Dec 31: The **NFL championship** was won by the Chicago Bears, who defeated the New York Giants 14 to 0.

1964

I. **Civil Rights**
   Exploration and Settlement
   Government
   Statistics
   Wars

Campaigning on the promise of achieving the Great Society, Pres. Lyndon Baines Johnson was elected to the presidency by a record-breaking vote. For the first time since 1920, the conservative wing had dominated the Republican campaign, alienating moderates and liberals. At the same time, the Democratic Party lost five southern states because of Pres. Johnson's success in putting through a civil rights bill in July. He was equally successful with the other primary legislative aim of his administration, the anti-poverty bill. His economy-in-government drive was

reflected in his first budget, which contained a
$1,100,000,000 cut in defense spending. Johnson
asked for $3,400,000,000 for foreign aid, the smallest
amount requested in 16 years. In domestic affairs, the
year was marked by racial violence in many U.S.
cities, including New York, Philadelphia, and St.
Augustine, Fla. In the summer a coalition of civil
rights groups mounted a voter registration and education drive in Mississippi; this sparked acts of violence. Foreign relations reflected continuing tension
with Cuba and in Berlin. Deterioration of the situation in Southeast Asia resulted in greater U.S. military and economic assistance to South Vietnam. In
the Congo, a number of American citizens were taken
hostage, along with many Europeans. Two Americans were killed after U.S. aircraft dropped Belgian
troops into the area, but most of the hostages were
freed. The U.S. and U.S.S.R. made efforts to reduce
threat of nuclear war by reducing stockpiles of materials for nuclear weapons. Steps were taken toward
international cooperation in developing peaceful
uses of atomic energy and sharing technological advances. Notables who died this year included Elizabeth Gurley Flynn, the American communist leader,
Sept. 5, at 74; Herbert Clark Hoover, 31st president of
the United States, Oct. 20, at 90; Douglas MacArthur,
Apr. 5, at 84; and Alvin C. York, whose bravery during World War I earned him some 50 medals, including the Medal of Honor, Sept. 2, at 76.

Jan 23: The **Twenty-fourth Amendment** to the U.S.
Constitution, abolishing the poll tax, was ratified by
South Dakota, the 38th state to do so. The amend-
ment was declared part of the Constitution on Feb. 4.

Mar 10: A **U.S. reconnaissance plane was shot down**
by Soviet air defense forces after it accidentally
crossed into East German airspace. It was the second
such incident in six weeks. Following U.S. protests,
the plane's three crewmen were released.

Mar 14: Jack Ruby was convicted by a Dallas, Tex.,
jury of the murder of Lee Harvey Oswald, the accused assassin of Pres. John F. Kennedy. Ruby was
sentenced to death.

Mar 27: A major **earthquake in Alaska,** centered in

Anchorage, killed 117 people and caused enormous damage. The next day Pres. Johnson declared Alaska a major disaster area.

May 18: In a ruling on **citizenship rights,** the Supreme Court declared unconstitutional a federal statute depriving naturalized citizens of U.S. citizenship if they return to the land of their birth for three years.

May 19: The State Department announced the **U.S. embassy in Moscow had been bugged.** A network of more than 40 microphones had been found embedded in the embassy's walls.

June 9: George Gessner was convicted of spying. The 28-year-old Army deserter and defector was found guilty of having passed U.S. nuclear secrets to the U.S.S.R. He was sentenced to life imprisonment, the first conviction under the 1946 Atomic Energy Act.

June 22: The provisions of the **Internal Security Act of 1950** denying U.S. passports to communists were ruled unconstitutional by the Supreme Court.

July 2: The **Civil Rights Act of 1964** was signed by Pres. Johnson in a televised ceremony a few hours after the House approved Senate amendments by a vote of 289 to 126.

July 8: The Senate Rules Committee reported that it had found **Robert G. "Bobby" Baker,** former secretary to the Democratic Senate majority, guilty of "many gross improprieties" while employed by the Senate; however, it did not accuse him of any specific violation of law.

July 15: The **Republican National Convention nominated Sen. Barry Goldwater** for the presidency. The next day Rep. William E. Miller of New York was nominated for the vice presidency.

July 18: A **race riot** broke out in Harlem, New York City, after an off-duty policeman shot a black youth who allegedly attacked him with a knife.

July 22: The section of the **Civil Rights Act of 1964** barring racial discrimination in public accommodations was upheld by a federal court in Atlanta, Ga. The court ordered a restaurant and motel in Atlanta to admit blacks.

July 24: An international **satellite communications**

agreement was initialed by representatives of 18 nations in Washington, D.C. The agreement specified international management and ownership of the global communications satellite system being developed in the U.S.

Aug 2: In what came to be called the **Gulf of Tonkin incident,** three North Vietnamese PT boats attacked the U.S. destroyer *Maddox* in the Gulf of Tonkin in international waters, but were fought off by fighter planes from the U.S. carrier *Ticonderoga.* Three days later U.S. planes bombed North Vietnamese installations and naval craft.

Aug 4: Three white **civil rights workers were found murdered** and buried in an earthen dam on a farm outside Philadelphia, Miss. The three, James Chaney, 21, of Meridian, Miss., and Andrew Goodman, 20, and Michael Schwerner, 24, both of New York City, had disappeared on June 21 after being held for six hours by Neshoba County police on charges of speeding. Their burned station wagon was found June 23, prompting Pres. Johnson to order an FBI search for the three men.

Aug 7: The **Gulf of Tonkin Resolution,** a joint resolution approving U.S. action in Southeast Asia, was passed by Congress. A resolution passed on Aug. 1 had granted authority to the president to use all necessary measures to repel armed attack and to help any SEATO nation asking assistance in defense of its freedom.

Aug 26: The **Democratic National Convention nominated Pres. Johnson** for the presidency. Sen. Hubert M. Humphrey of Minnesota was nominated for the vice presidency.

Aug 30: The **Economic Opportunity Act of 1964** was signed by Pres. Johnson. The bill authorized $947,500,000 for youth programs, community action antipoverty measures in rural areas, small business loans, and job training, including a Job Corps for youth.

Aug 31: The **most populous state** as of July 1, 1964, was California, the Census Bureau reported. New York dropped to second place.

Sep 3: A bill establishing a permanent **national wilderness** system comprising 9,200,000 acres was passed by Congress and signed by Pres. Johnson.

Sep 27: The **Warren Commission report** on the assassination of John F. Kennedy was released with the finding that there was no conspiracy, either domestic or international, in the assassination, and that Lee Harvey Oswald alone was responsible for it. The report found also that Jack Ruby, convicted murderer of Oswald, had had no prior contact with Oswald.

Nov 3: Lyndon Baines Johnson was elected president of the United States. Sen. Hubert Horatio Humphrey was elected vice president. The electoral vote was Johnson, 486; Sen. Barry M. Goldwater, Republican, 52. The popular vote was Johnson, 43,126,506; Goldwater, 27,176,799. In congressional elections the Democrats gained one Senate seat for a 68–32 majority, and 37 House seats for a 295–140 majority.

Dec 4: The **FBI arrested 21 Mississippians** on charges of conspiracy to violate the civil rights of the three civil rights workers found murdered on Aug. 4. On Dec. 10 the charges against 19 of the men were dropped in Meridian, Miss. Charges against the other two were dropped at the federal government's request.

Dec 5: The **Medal of Honor** was presented to Capt. Roger H. C. Donlon, U.S. Army, for heroism in South Vietnam. He was the first person to receive the medal since the Korean War.

II. Architecture
   Arts and Music
   Popular Entertainment
   Publishing
   Theater

Great interest was aroused by the purchase of the G. & C. Merriam Co. by Encyclopaedia Britannica, Inc. The Warren Commission's report on the assassination of Pres. John F. Kennedy was published by the U.S. Printing Office and by five commercial publishers. Bantam Books, with the help of *The New York*

Times, prepared a paperback edition that was available to the public 80 hours after the report was released. In the year that followed Kennedy's death, more than 50 books about him were published, some quick productions to catch the popular market, many moving tributes to the dead president. A new force in the theater world was The Repertory Theater of Lincoln Center, which had its first season in an off-Broadway theater while construction continued on its permanent home, the Vivian Beaumont Theater. The Robert Joffrey Ballet fell on hard times when the Harkness Foundation withdrew its subsidy and then took Joffrey's sets, scores, and ballets for the new Harkness Ballet. In November the Ford Foundation made a grant to keep the Joffrey Ballet going. Notables who died this year included Gracie Allen, the zany comedian, Aug. 27, at 58; Marc Blitzstein, composer, Jan. 22, at 58; Eddie Cantor, singer and comedian, Oct. 10, at 72; Rachel Carson, biologist and author, Apr. 14, at 56; Ben Hecht, playwright, Apr. 18, at 70; Alan Ladd, actor, Jan. 29, at 50; Peter Lorre, actor, Mar. 23, at 59; Arthur "Harpo" Marx, Sept. 28, at 70; Flannery O'Connor, the author, Aug. 3, at 39; and Cole Porter, songwriter, Oct. 15, at 71.

Among **books published** this year was the posthumous volume *A Moveable Feast* by Ernest Hemingway, a collection of sketches about Paris and its artistic colony during the years 1921–1926. Other books published this year included *The Rector of Justin* by Louis Auchincloss, a novel; *Herzog,* by Saul Bellow, the author's sixth novel; *Little Big Man* by Thomas Berger, a novel of the old West; *77 Dream Songs* by John Berryman, poems; *The Wapshot Scandal* by John Cheever, a novel; *Why We Can't Wait* by Rev. Martin Luther King, Jr., a forceful treatment of the civil rights movement; *Candy,* a sex farce by Terry Southern and Mason Hoffenberg; and *Julian* by Gore Vidal, a novel about the Roman emperor Julian the Apostate.

Feb 7: The **Beatles** arrived at Kennedy Airport in New York at the start of their first U.S. musical tour. After appearing on the *Ed Sullivan Show* on television, they gave their first concert on Feb. 12 at Carnegie Hall. Their second U.S. tour, a 33-day sweep beginning Aug. 19 in San Francisco, was a phenomenal success. Also successful were the group's album *Meet the Beatles,* which became an overnight best seller, and their movie *A Hard Day's Night,* which was released just before their second tour.

Apr 24: The **New York City Ballet,** under George Balanchine, opened its first season in its new house, the New York State Theater at Lincoln Center for the Performing Arts. A new ballet, *A Midsummer Night's Dream,* was performed in celebration of the 400th anniversary of William Shakespeare's birth. This was also the opening night of the new theater, which had been designed by Philip Johnson. In a modern interpretation of traditional theatrical elegance, the interior was red and gold and studded with giant faceted lamps that resembled jewels.

May 4: Pulitzer prizes were awarded for the following: biography, *John Keats* by Walter Jackson Bate; history, *Puritan Village: The Formation of a New England Town* by Sumner Chilton Powell; general nonfiction, *Anti-Intellectualism in American Life* by Richard Hofstadter; poetry, *At the End of the Open Road* by Louis Simpson.

Oct 1: An **equal time ruling** was issued by the FCC. It stated that any radio or television station carrying a presidential press conference in full must grant equal time to other presidential candidates.

III. Business and Industry
Education
Philosophy and Religion
Science

The first close-up pictures of the moon's surface were obtained by the U.S. At the same time, the U.S. successfully launched a spacecraft designed to fly by and photograph the surface of Mars. The first cooperative U.S.-U.S.S.R. space program—Echo 2, a communications satellite—was established. Also in this year, racial violence in both the North and South marked the nation's continuing efforts to assure equality in education for all. Harlem, Brooklyn, Rochester, northern New Jersey, Jacksonville, Fla., Chicago, and Philadelphia were scenes of violent rioting. Schools were boycotted in New York City, Cleveland, Cincinnati, Cambridge, Md., Boston, and Chicago to protest de facto segregation. Federal aid to universities was increased and extended. Notables who died this year included Leo Szilard, the atomic physicist who with Enrico Fermi produced the first nuclear chain reaction in 1942, May 30, at 66; and Norbert Wiener, the mathematician who was called the "father of automation," Mar. 18, at 69.

Jan 11: The **surgeon general's report on cigarette smoking** was released. A commission headed by U.S. Surgeon General Luther Terry found that the use of cigarettes "contributes substantially to mortality from certain specific diseases and to the overall death rate."

Jan 25: Echo 2, the first U.S.-U.S.S.R. cooperative space program, was launched from Vandenberg Air Force Base, Calif. It sent messages around the world by reflecting radio signals from one point on Earth to another.

Jan 29: A **new weight-into-orbit record** was set by the fifth Saturn rocket test in preparation for the manned Apollo program. A 20,000-lb. payload was boosted into orbit by the rocket from Cape Kennedy, Fla.

Mar 4: James R. Hoffa, president of the International Brotherhood of Teamsters, was found guilty of tampering with a federal jury in 1962 by a Chattanooga, Tenn., federal jury. He was sentenced to eight years in prison and fined $10,000.

Apr 8: An unmanned **Gemini spacecraft was successfully launched** into orbit from Cape Kennedy, Fla.

May 25: The **closing of schools to avoid desegregation** was ruled unconstitutional by the Supreme Court. The Court ruled that the schools of Prince Edward County, Va., which had been closed in 1959, must be reopened and desegregated.

June 14: An **agreement to end racial discrimination** in the steel industry was announced by the United

Steelworkers of American and 11 steel companies.

June 24: Health warnings on cigarette packages would be required starting in 1965, the Federal Trade Commission announced.

July 26: James R. Hoffa, president of the International Brotherhood of Teamsters, was convicted of fraud and conspiracy in the handling of his union's pension fund by a federal jury in Chicago. He was sentenced to five years in prison and fined $10,000.

July 31: The U.S. lunar probe **Ranger 7** crashed into the moon after sending back to Earth 4316 photographs of the lunar surface taken within a 1300-mile range.

Aug 14: Elementary school desegregation in Mississippi began without incident at previously white elementary schools in Biloxi, Miss. This marked the first desegregation of schools below the college level in that state.

Aug 19: Syncom 3, a communications satellite, was successfully launched from Cape Kennedy, Fla. In October it transmitted live broadcasts of the 1964 Olympic Games from Tokyo to California.

Aug 28: Nimbus 1, an advanced meteorological satellite, was launched from Vandenberg Air Force Base, Calif. Although it failed to achieve its intended circular orbit, it sent back exceptionally clear close-up pictures of Earth's nighttime cloud cover.

Oct 14: The **Nobel Peace Prize** was awarded to the Rev. Martin Luther King., Jr., civil rights leader of Atlanta, Ga. He donated the award, valued at $54,600, to the civil rights movement.

Oct 15: The **Nobel Prize for Physiology or Medicine** was awarded jointly to Dr. Conrad E. Block of Harvard University and Feodor Lynen, a German professor, for their work on the relationship between heart disease and cholesterol.

Oct 29: The **Nobel Prize in Physics** was awarded jointly to Charles H. Townes of the Massachusetts Institute of Technology and to Nikolai Basov and Aleksandr Prokhorov of the U.S.S.R. for their work in quantum electronics.

Nov 21: The **Verrazano-Narrows Bridge** between

Brooklyn and Staten Island, N.Y., was formally opened. At 6690 feet, it was the world's longest suspension bridge.

Nov 28: Mariner 4 was launched from Cape Kennedy, Fla., to transmit close-up TV pictures of Mars on its projected flyby within 8600 miles of that planet in July 1965.

IV. Fashion
   Folkways
   Holidays
   Social Issues and Crime
   Sports

At the New York World's Fair, the General Motors Futurama proved to be the most popular attraction. Ranking just behind GM in attendance was the Vatican Pavilion, its chief attraction being Michelangelo's *Pietà*. While this was the largest, most lavish, and in many ways the best fair of all time, attendance lagged behind fair president Robert Moses' predictions, and many exhibitors began to feel an economic pinch. Worst hit were the extravagant shows in the Lake Amusement Area that had been so popular at the 1939–1940 fair. Most of these shows closed before the end of the fair's first season. In baseball the St. Louis Cardinals beat the New York Yankees in the World Series; the following day Cardinal manager Johnny Keane resigned. Yankee manager Yogi Berra was moved to another position in the club, then quit to become player-coach of the New York Mets. Meanwhile, Keane was named manager of the Yankees. In boxing Cassius Clay gained the heavyweight title from Sonny Liston and enthralled many with his declarations of his own beauty, ability, and greatness. This year he also declared that he was a Black Muslim and changed his name to Muhammad Ali. In golf the top money winners were Jack Nicklaus, $113,284, and, for the fourth year in a row, Mickey Wright, $29,800.

Popular **rock 'n' roll dances** of the younger set had animal names: the Dog, the Monkey, the Chicken; but the favorites were the Watusi and the Frug. In these dances the partners gyrated, squirmed, jerked, and waved their arms—at a distance from one another, of course. The swinging set crowded into discothèques, where the music was supplied by records. The "in" places were Shepheard's and Trude Heller's in New York City and Whiskey à Go-Go in Los Angeles. Dancers were often abetted by scantily clad go-go girls, who performed in relays on raised platforms or in cages.

Jan 5: The 1963 **AFL championship** was won by the San Diego Chargers, who defeated the Boston Patriots 51 to 10.

Jan 29-Feb 9: At the **Winter Olympics** in Innsbruck, Austria, the U.S. finished eighth in the unofficial team standings, taking one gold, two silver, and three bronze medals.

Feb 25: The **world heavyweight boxing championship** was won by Muhammad Ali, in a bout at Miami Beach, when Sonny Liston could not answer the bell for the seventh round because of an injury to his left arm. Ali announced he would give Liston a rematch, but the World Boxing Association (WBA), claiming it had a rule forbidding return bouts, declared the heavyweight title vacant and made plans for an elimination tournament. When their contender Cleveland Williams was shot by Texas highway police, the WBA postponed its plans until 1965. The Ali-Liston bout, scheduled for Nov. 16 in Boston, was called off 70 hours before the bell, after Ali went to the hospital for a hernia operation.

Mar 21: The **NCAA basketball championship** was won by UCLA, which defeated Duke University 98 to 83. The victory climaxed a perfect season for UCLA, which won all 30 of its games, the first major team to have an undefeated season since 1957.

Apr 18-26: The **NBA basketball championship** was won, for the sixth time in a row, by the Boston Celtics, who defeated the San Francisco Warriors four games to one.

Apr 22: Opening-day ceremonies of the **New York World's Fair** of 1964–1965 were marred by threats of a massive traffic tie-up by members of the Congress of Racial Equality (CORE), who planned to have their cars run out of gas on all major arteries leading to the fair. The so-called stall-in, intended to dramatize CORE's demand for city action against racial discrimination, did not materialize, but it was probably a major factor along with bad weather in cutting attendance from an expected 250,000 to 92,646. Pres. Lyndon B. Johnson's dedication speech was interrupted by demonstrators' chants. When the fair closed its first season on Oct. 18, it was apparent that it was in dire financial straits. Low attendance was blamed on fear of racial violence, high prices, and characterization of the fair as a cultural desert.

May 31: In the **longest baseball game** to date, the San Francisco Giants beat the New York Mets 8–6 after 7 hrs., 23 min. of the second game of a double header. The end came in the 23rd inning, matching the fourth longest game in innings played.

June 20: The **U.S. Open golf tournament** was won by Ken Venturi, who beat Tommy Jacobs by two strokes.

June 21: A **perfect baseball game,** the first in a regular season since 1922, was pitched by Jim Bunning of the Philadelphia Phillies, who led his team to a 6–0 victory over the New York Mets at Shea Stadium in New York City.

July 19: The **PGA golf tournament** was won by Bobby Nichols, who beat both Arnold Palmer and Jack Nicklaus by three strokes.

Sep 12: In the **New Hampshire Sweepstakes,** the first legal sweepstakes in U.S. horse racing history, six persons won the first prize of $100,000 at Rockingham Park in Salem, N.H.

Sep 15-21: The **America's Cup,** yachting's oldest trophy, was successfully defended by the U.S racer *Constellation,* which easily outdistanced the British challenger *Sovereign* in four races off Newport, R.I.

Sep 25-28: For the first time in the history of **Davis Cup** tennis competition, the international challenge round was played on clay courts. The play took place in Cleveland, Ohio, where Roy Emerson and Fred Stolle led a strong Australian team to beat the U.S. defenders three matches to two.

Oct 7-15: The 61st annual **World Series** was won by the St. Louis Cardinals (NL), defeating the New York Yankees (AL) four games to three. Cardinal pitcher Bob Gibson struck out 31 batters in three games, a Series record. Mickey Mantle of the Yankees hit his 16th Series homer, breaking the record held by Babe Ruth.

Oct 10-24: At the **Summer Olympics** in Tokyo, Japan, the U.S. won the unofficial team championship with 36 gold medals.

Dec 26: The **AFL championship** was won by the Buffalo Bills, who defeated the San Diego Chargers 20 to 7.

Dec 27: The **NFL championship** was won by the Cleveland Browns, who swept the Baltimore Colts 27 to 0.

1965

I. Civil Rights
Exploration and Settlement
Government
Statistics
Wars

U.S. participation in the war in Vietnam was protested by many in demonstrations across the nation. Before year's end, U.S. losses in Vietnam since Jan. 1961 exceeded 1300 dead and 6100 wounded. The use of helicopters for medical evacuation helped keep the fatality rate below 2% of those wounded. Pres. Lyndon B. Johnson's administration obtained passage of most of its programs. Total appropriations were a record high for peacetime: $119,300,000,000, of which $46,900,000,000 went for defense. At the same time, Pres. Johnson's request for foreign aid was the smallest in the history of the program—$3,380,000,000, of which $3,200,000,000 was granted. The Medicare program was passed, as were antipoverty and voting rights bills and increased aid to education. Although turned down on his requests for repeal of Section 14-b of the Taft-Hartley Act, state right-to-work laws, and self-government for the District of Columbia, Pres. Johnson was given a $1,100,000,000 appropriation for development in Appalachia. In addition, excise taxes were cut, a new immigration law was passed to replace the 41-year-old national-origins quota system, and a new Cabinet-level Department of Housing and Urban Development was established. The nation's rate of population growth, 1.21%, was the slowest since 1945. Notables who died this year included Frances Perkins, secretary of labor from 1933 to 1945, May 14, at 83; Adlai E. Stevenson, unsuccessful Democratic candidate for the presidency in 1952 and 1956, July 14, at 65; and Henry A. Wallace, vice president of the United States from 1941 to 1945, Nov. 18 at 77.

Jan 28: Pres. Johnson asked Congress to propose **constitutional amendments** that would cover presidential disability; provide for filling a vice presidential vacancy; and reform the electoral college system so that voters could not be overridden by electors.

Feb 16: A **plot to dynamite the Statue of Liberty,** the Liberty Bell, and the Washington Monument was foiled. Four persons were arrested, including the self-styled leader of the Black Liberation Front and a woman member of a Quebec separatist party.

Feb 21: Malcolm X was assassinated by rival Black Muslims while addressing a gathering at the Audubon Ballroom in Washington Heights, New York City. Born Malcolm Little, the 39-year-old leader founded the extremist Black Nationalist movement after breaking with the Black Muslims in 1964. In recent months he had been moving toward a less violently anti-white stance. Two days after his death,

Black Muslim headquarters in San Francisco and New York City were burned.

Mar 8: Ruling on **conscientious objectors,** the Supreme Court held unanimously that a person holding a sincere belief in a Supreme Being, even though differing from the beliefs held by accepted religions, may be exempted from military combat training and service.

Mar 8-9: The **first U.S. combat forces in Vietnam,** more than 3500 Marines, landed in South Vietnam to guard the U.S. Air Force base at Danang. They joined 23,500 other Americans serving as advisers in South Vietnam.

Mar 11: The Rev. **James Reeb died** from a beating he received in Selma, Ala., on Mar. 9. A Unitarian minister from Boston, Reeb had been working in a civil rights drive. Three whites were subsequently indicted for the murder, but they were found not guilty on Dec. 10.

Mar 15: **Sweeping voting rights legislation** was requested by Pres. Johnson in a nationally televised address to a joint session of Congress. Later Johnson submitted a voting rights bill to Congress. One provision of the bill would empower the attorney general to assign federal registration examiners in the six states requiring literacy or other voter-qualification tests.

Mar 21: A five-day **civil rights march from Selma to Montgomery,** Ala., was begun by some 3200 marchers led by Dr. Martin Luther King, Jr. At the end of the march, some 25,000 demonstrators gathered in front of the state capitol in Montgomery.

Mar 25: **Viola Gregg Liuzzo,** a civil rights worker from Detroit, Mich., was shot and killed in Selma, Ala. On Dec. 3 Collie LeRoy Wilkins and two other Ku Klux Klansmen were convicted of conspiracy charges in the murder. They were sentenced to ten years' imprisonment.

June 7: An 1879 **Connecticut law banning the use of contraceptives** by anyone, including married couples, was ruled unconstitutional by the U.S. Supreme Court.

June 7: The 1962 conviction of **Billie Sol Estes** on swindling charges was overturned by the Supreme Court on the grounds that televising criminal trials was a violation of the due process clause of the Fourteenth Amendment, and that the presence of TV cameras might affect jurors, witnesses, and judges.

June 17: In the **first mass bombing raid** in the Vietnam War, Guam-based B-52s bombed a Vietcong concentration 30 miles north of Saigon. It was the first combat use of the heavy jet bombers since they were placed in operation in 1952.

June 30: In its final **report on the investigation of Robert G. "Bobby" Baker,** former secretary to the Senate Democratic majority, the Senate Rules Committee recommended that the Senate consider indicting Baker for violation of conflict-of-interest laws. It also recommended new Senate rules for control of outside business activities of Senate employees. Republican members of the committee termed the majority report a whitewash and filed a minority report criticizing the conduct of the investigation.

July 28: Pres. Johnson announced that **U.S. troop levels in South Vietnam** would be increased from 75,000 to 125,000, and the draft would be doubled from 17,000 to 35,000 a month.

Aug 11-16: Riots in Watts, a black section of Los Angeles, Calif., left 35 dead and hundreds injured. The riots, which caused about $200,000,000 in damage, were sparked when a white policeman stopped a black driver suspected of being drunk.

Aug 16: Total **U.S. casualties in Vietnam** since Jan. 1, 1961, were 561 killed, 3024 wounded, 44 missing in action, and 269 dead of noncombat causes.

Sep 24: Agreement in principle on a new **Panama Canal treaty,** to supersede the 1903 pact giving the U.S. sole control over the Panama Canal, was announced by Pres. Johnson. The new treaty would provide for joint administration of the canal.

Oct 4: Pope Paul VI visited New York City to address the UN General Assembly on world peace. During the visit he celebrated a papal mass in Yankee Stadium and attended the New York World's Fair.

Oct 15-16: Nationwide antiwar demonstrations were

held, followed by a series of rallies and petitions supporting U.S. policy. Several persons burned their draft cards publicly; one person was arrested three days later under a law effective Aug. 31 that made destruction of a draft card a crime.

Nov 9-10: A massive **Northeast power blackout** struck an 80,000-square-mile area comprising New York, most of New England, parts of New Jersey, Pennsylvania, and Ontario and Quebec, Canada. The blackout, lasting as long as 13 hours in some areas, was initiated by the malfunction of an automatic relay device at a generating plant near Niagara Falls.

Nov 20: **U.S. casualties** in Vietnam after a week-long battle in the Iadrang Valley were placed at 240 dead, 470 wounded, and six missing, exceeding the Korean War weekly average of 209 killed.

Nov 27: An **anti-Vietnam War demonstration in Washington, D.C.,** was conducted by some 15,000 to 25,000 protesters from 140 groups.

Dec 4: **Two airliners collided** in midair over Danbury, Conn. Four persons of the 112 passengers aboard the planes were killed.

II. Architecture
   Arts and Music
   Popular Entertainment
   Publishing
   Theater

The most sensational theatrical offering of the year was Peter Weiss's *The Persecution and Assassination of Marat as Performed by the Inmates of the Asylum of Charenton Under the Direction of the Marquis de Sade*, a production of the Royal Shakespeare Company directed by Peter Brook, which opened Dec. 27. The playwright's cynical view of the French Revolution was conveyed by actors manifesting a wide variety of psychoses. The Repertory Theater of Lincoln Center occupied its new home, the Vivian Beaumont Theater. The most significant development in art this year was the appearance of op (optical) art, abstract painting that commanded viewers' attention by the dazzling interaction of colors and/or optical illusion. The most important op art show, "The Responsive Eye," opened at the Museum of Modern Art in New York City; it was seen subsequently in St. Louis, Seattle, Pasadena, and Baltimore. Notables who died this year included Thornton W. Burgess, author of the Peter Rabbit stories, June 5, at 91; Nat "King" Cole, born Nathaniel Adams Coles, singer, Feb. 15, at 45; T.S. Eliot, the poet, Jan. 4, at 76; Lorraine Hansberry, playwright, Jan. 12, at 34; Judy Holliday, actress, June 7, at 42; Shirley Jackson, writer, Aug. 8, at 45; Stan Laurel, born Arthur Stanley Jefferson, comedian, Feb. 23, at 74; David O. Selznick, motion picture producer, June 22, at 63; and Edgard Varèse, the French-born composer regarded as the father of electronic music, Nov. 6, at 90.

Among **books published** this year were two biographies of John F. Kennedy that became the nonfiction standouts of 1965. *Kennedy* by Theodore Sorensen was an intimate account of Kennedy's career from 1953. *A Thousand Days* by Arthur M. Schlesinger, Jr., dealt with Kennedy's tenure as president. Other books published this year included *Going to Meet the Man* by James Baldwin, short stories; *Manchild in the Promised Land* by Claude Brown; *Never Call Retreat* by Bruce Catton, the third volume in the Civil War trilogy *Centennial History of the Civil War; Country Without Maps* by Jean Garrigue, a collection of poems; *Up the Down Staircase* by Bel Kaufman; *The Autobiography of Malcolm X; The Oxford History of the American People* by Samuel Eliot Morison; and *Everything That Rises Must Converge* by Flannery O'Connor, stories.

Jan 10: The **Bollingen Prize** for poetry was awarded to Horace Gregory for his 1964 volume *Collected Poems.* Beginning this year the cash award was increased to $5000 and the prize was to be awarded every other year.

May 3: **Pulitzer prizes** were awarded for the following: fiction, *The Keepers of the House* by Shirley Ann Grau; biography, *Henry Adams* by Ernest Samuels; history, *The Greenback Era* by Irwin Unger; poetry,

77 Dream Songs by John Berryman; drama, *The Subject Was Roses* by Frank D. Gilroy.

June 14: A **Festival of the Arts and Humanities** at the White House was attended by some 400 artists, who were welcomed by Pres. Johnson. The 13-hour event included exhibitions of paintings, sculpture, and photography; prose and poetry readings; music recitals; and a ballet. Robert Lowell, the poet, refused an invitation because of his distrust of U.S. foreign policy.

Sep 30: The Federal Aid to the Arts Act, establishing the **National Foundation on the Arts and the Humanities,** was signed by Pres. Johnson. The act appropriated $63,000,000 to finance the first three years of the program.

Oct 28: Eero Saarinen's steel **Gateway Arch** in St. Louis, Mo., the year's most awesome architectural project, was topped out. The 630-ft. parabolic arch commemorated the Louisiana Purchase and the city's role in westward expansion. It was part of the 40-block Jefferson National Expansion Memorial along the city's riverfront. The Spanish Pavilion from the New York World's Fair was to be reconstructed near the arch.

III. Business and Industry
Education
Philosophy and Religion
Science

The first U.S. walk in space and the successful rendezvous of two Gemini capsules 185 miles above Earth assisted NASA in its preparations for a manned trip to the moon. Photographs of the surface of Mars showed no trace of the famous canals and provided evidence that the planet had little atmosphere. Commercial communication using an Earth satellite was realized with the aid of Early Bird. The most spectacular comet since Comet Halley in 1910 was spotted by two Japanese amateur astronomers; it was named Comet Ikeya-Seki. The U.S. gross national product rose from $628,000,000,000 to $672,000,000,000, exceeding by $14,000,000,000 the predictions of the president's economic advisers. In December it was announced that the unemployment rate had fallen to 4.2%, an eight-year low. Notables who died this year included the religious leader Father Divine, real name believed to be George Baker, Sept. 10, at about 83; H. V. Kaltenborn, radio commentator, June 14, at 86; Edward R. Murrow, radio and television journalist, Apr. 27, at 57; and Paul Tillich, theologian, Oct. 22, at 79.

Feb 3: In a **cheating scandal** at the U.S. Air Force Academy, 105 cadets resigned for cheating on examinations. Four more resigned later, when the cadet wing honor board found they had had knowledge of the cheating but had not reported it.

Feb 16: Pegasus 1, a micrometeoroid detection station with 96-foot wings as sensors, was put into orbit.

Feb 17: Ranger 8, a moon probe, was successfully launched. It sent back 7137 photos of the moon's surface before crashing into the Sea of Tranquillity on Feb. 20.

Mar 21: Ranger 9 was launched. It transmitted 5814 photos of the moon's surface before crashing into Alphonsus crater on Mar. 24. It was the last moon probe of the Ranger series.

Mar 23: Gemini 3, the first manned Gemini flight, was successfully launched from Cape Kennedy, Fla. The craft, nicknamed "Molly Brown," was put through delicate maneuvers by its pilots, Maj. Virgil Grissom and Lt. Commander John Young, during its three-orbit flight. It was retrieved by the carrier *Intrepid* in the Atlantic Ocean.

Apr 6: Early Bird, the world's first commercial communications satellite, was launched and placed in orbit 22,300 miles above Earth. Owned by ComSat, Early Bird transmitted phone calls, TV, Teletype, and other communications.

Apr 16: The **Saturn S-1C rocket,** to be the first stage for the Apollo lunar flight and the largest U.S. booster ever produced, was successfully fired at Cape Kennedy, Fla.

May 24: A federal law authorizing **postal interception of communist propaganda** was declared unconstitutional by the Supreme Court. The law, empowering the postmaster general to hold foreign mail deemed to be communist propaganda and to make the addressee submit a written request for it, was ruled to violate the First Amendment.

June 3: Gemini 4, manned by Maj. James McDivitt and Maj. Edward White, was successfully launched from Cape Kennedy, Fla. During the four-day, 62-orbit mission White completed the first U.S. space walk; it lasted some 20 minutes while White, 135 miles above North America, was attached to the craft by a lifeline.

June 18: A **Titan 3C rocket** was launched into orbit with a total thrust of 2,400,000 lbs., the greatest thrust of any rocket ever to leave Earth's surface. The launching was the first to use large solid fuel rockets.

July 15: Mariner 4 began transmission of 21 pictures of the surface of Mars taken at a range of between 7000 and 10,500 miles. Continually transmitting data to Earth since its launch on Nov. 28, 1964, the craft flew within 5700 miles of Mars.

Aug 21: Gemini 5, piloted by Lt. Col. Gordon Cooper and Lt. Commander Charles Conrad, was launched on an eight-day, 120-orbit mission. The flight took as long as a round trip to the moon. There was some difficulty with a new fuel cell system.

Oct 12: The **Sealab 2** U.S. Navy research program, a series of 15-day stays 205 feet below the surface of the Pacific Ocean, was completed. The purpose was to study the effects on humans of living underwater and to conduct equipment tests.

Oct 21: The **Nobel Prize in Physics** was awarded jointly to Richard P. Feynman of the California Institute of Technology, Julian S. Schwinger of Harvard University, and Shinichero Tomonaga of Tokyo Education University in Japan for their work in quantum electrodynamics.

Oct 21: The **Nobel Prize in Chemistry** was awarded to Robert Burns Woodward of Harvard University for his work in synthesizing complex organic compounds.

Dec 4: Gemini 7, piloted by Lt. Col. Frank Borman and Commander James A. Lovell, Jr., was launched from Cape Kennedy on a 14-day, 206-orbit mission and rendezvous in space with Gemini 6.

Dec 15: Gemini 6, piloted by Capt. Walter Schirra and

Maj. Thomas Stafford, was launched. It made the first successful space rendezvous, with Gemini 7, some 185 miles above Earth. During its 14-orbit flight, it came within six feet of Gemini 7 and traveled in close formation with the sister ship.

IV. Fashion
   Folkways
   Holidays
   Social Issues and Crime
   Sports

In clothing and hairstyles, the trend was toward sexual ambiguity. Young men sprouted shoulder-length hair, and girls wore bangs and shingles, a style designed by London hairdresser Vidal Sassoon. The Mod look, also emanating from London, put the young of both sexes into tight, bell-bottom trousers. For dress-up, women wore skirts two inches above the knee and blouses ruffled at the throat and wrist. The Courrèges look was the high-fashion sensation. It featured a solid color A-line dress trimmed with contrasting bands, high white boots, and often a helmet-type hat. Art-inspired fashions included the Mondrian dresses of Yves St. Laurent and op art fabrics favored by Capucci. In sports Muhammad Ali defied World Boxing Association (WBA) rules against rematches and met Sonny Liston in a short and sweet, successful title defense. Nonetheless, the WBA stripped Ali of his title and declared the championship vacant. In golf the top money winners were Jack Nicklaus, $142,752, and Kathy Whitworth, $32,937. Deaths of this year included John Leonard "Pepper" Martin, of the St. Louis Cardinals, Mar. 5, at 61; Branch W. Rickey, baseball executive, Dec. 9, at 84; Helena Rubinstein, founder of a cosmetics empire, Apr. 1, at about 89; and Amos Alonzo Stagg, college football coach for more than 60 years, 41 of them at the University of Chicago, Mar. 17, at 102.

Mar 20: The **NCAA basketball championship** was won by UCLA, which defeated Michigan 91 to 80.

Apr 18-25: The **NBA basketball championship** was

won for the seventh straight year by the Boston Celtics, who defeated the Los Angeles Lakers four games to one.

May 25: The **world heavyweight boxing championship** was successfully defended by Muhammad Ali, who knocked out Sonny Liston about a minute into the first round of a rematch. Few fans saw the punch that floored Liston. Despite Ali's win, the World Boxing Association maintained that its heavyweight title belonged to Ernie Terrell, who had outpointed Eddie Machen on Mar. 5. Ali retained the National Boxing Association title.

June 21: The **U.S. Open golf tournament** was won by Gary Player of South Africa. He became the third man to win golf's four top pro titles; only Gene Sarazen and Ben Hogan had previously taken the U.S. and British Opens, the Masters, and the PGA.

Aug 15: The **PGA golf tournament** was won by Dave Marr.

Sep 9: A **perfect baseball game** was pitched by Sandy Koufax of the Los Angeles Dodgers (NL) against the Chicago Cubs. Koufax fanned 14 batters in the 1 to 0 victory. It was the fourth no-hit game of his career, a major league record, and only the eighth perfect game in baseball history.

Oct 6-14: The 62nd annual **World Series** was won by the Los Angeles Dodgers (NL), defeating the Minnesota Twins (AL) four games to three. In the seventh game, on Oct. 14, Sandy Koufax pitched his second World Series shutout, blanking the Twins 2 to 0.

Oct 17: The **New York World's Fair closed** after two years, drawing its largest crowd, 446,953, on the last day. The final days of the fair were marred by vandalism and looting by souvenir hunters. In its two-year run, the fair had the largest total attendance of any international exposition in history, 51,607,037, but not the predicted 70,000,000. Declared an "artistic, cultural, and educational success" by Robert Moses, president of the fair corporation, it was a financial disappointment; backers faced a return of 39 cents on the dollar of the $30,000,000 they had invested.

Nov 17: William D. Eckert was elected baseball com-

missioner. He succeeded Ford Frick, who retired
after having held the post since 1952.

Nov 22: **Muhammad Ali** stopped ex-champ Floyd Patterson in the 12th round of what had been billed as
a fight for the heavyweight championship. Although
the bout had been set up by Jim Deskin, new head of
the World Boxing Association, that organization afterward classified Ali as merely the top contender for
the crown the WBA had given to Ernie Terrell on
Mar. 5.

Dec 26: The **AFL football championship** was won by
the Buffalo Bills, who defeated the San Diego Chargers 23 to 0.

1966

I. Civil Rights
Exploration and Settlement
Government
Statistics
Wars

Steadily escalating participation in the Vietnamese
war resulted in 5008 U.S. troop deaths and 30,093
wounded in 1966, bringing total casualties since Jan.
1, 1961, to 6664 killed and 37,738 wounded. By the
end of the year, the U.S. had almost 400,000 troops in
Southeast Asia. Among the antiwar demonstrations
were the International Days of Protest (Mar. 25–27),
during which parades and rallies were held in seven
U.S. and seven foreign cities. The proposed budget
for fiscal 1967 set expenditures at $112,800,000,000,
with a predicted deficit of $1,800,000,000, the small-
est in seven years. Congress turned down the administration's proposed civil rights bill, largely because
of its open housing provisions, but it did pass measures giving the government a major role in determining automobile and highway safety standards, in

attacking urban decay, and in controlling air and water pollution. Notables who died this year included Christian A. Herter, secretary of state under Pres. Eisenhower from 1959 to 1961, Dec. 30, at 71; and Chester W. Nimitz, commander in chief of the U.S. Pacific fleet during World War II, Feb. 20, at 80.

Jan 17: Robert C. Weaver was unanimously confirmed as secretary of the newly created Department of Housing and Urban Development. He was the first black to hold a Cabinet position.

Jan 17: A military aircraft collision involving a U.S. B-52 bomber and a KC-135 jet tanker over Spain's Mediterranean coast killed seven of the 11 men aboard the planes. The B-52 was refueling. Four hydrogen bombs fell from the B-52, three on land. The fourth bomb was recovered from the Mediterranean Sea on Apr. 7.

Jan 29-31: The worst **blizzard** in 70 years struck an area stretching from North Carolina to New England, killing 165 people.

Jan 31: Pres. Johnson announced resumption of **bombing raids on North Vietnam.** They had been suspended on Dec. 24. The bombing had been halted in hope of furthering negotiations, but no move toward peace had been made by North Vietnam.

Feb 21: The first **air strike against North Vietnam** since the Jan. 31 resumption of bombing was made against a training center at the old French military base at Dien Bien Phu.

Feb 22: Operation White Wing, a month-long search and destroy mission by more than 20,000 U.S., South Vietnamese, and South Korean troops in Quang Ngai Province in South Vietnam, ended after enemy resistance collapsed. Communist troop deaths were reported at 1130.

Mar 2: U.S. troop strength in Vietnam was reported by Sec. of Defense Robert S. McNamara to have reached 215,000. Another 20,000 U.S. troops were said to be on the way.

Mar 10: A Green Beret camp was overrun by about 2000 North Vietnamese troops after a 72-hour siege. About 200 U.S. and South Vietnamese troops were

killed or captured at the Special Forces base in the
Ashau Valley.

Mar 25: Poll taxes were declared unconstitutional by
the Supreme Court on grounds that they represented
an economic barrier to voting.

Apr 12: B-52 strategic bombers were used for the first
time on targets in North Vietnam.

Apr 23: North Vietnamese aircraft for the first time
attacked U.S. aircraft flying over North Vietnam.

May 1: The **first intentional shelling of Cambodian
targets** occurred when U.S. artillery fired on forces
attacking U.S. troops operating along the Caibac R.

May 15: In an **antiwar demonstration in Washington,
D.C.,** more than 10,000 persons picketed the White
House. At a rally at the Washington Monument,
63,000 voters' pledges to vote only for antiwar candidates were displayed.

May 30: In the heaviest **air raids on North Vietnam** to
date, more than 300 U.S. planes bombed targets. On
May 31 an important North Vietnamese arsenal was
virtually destroyed by U.S. bombers.

June 3-13: A **major battle was fought in Kontum province,** in the Central Highlands of South Vietnam. No
figures on U.S. casualties were announced.

June 6: James Meredith was shot and wounded while
on a lone march from Memphis, Tenn., to Jackson,
Miss., to encourage black voter registration. On June
26 groups from across the country joined with Meredith to complete the march, which was highlighted
by a debate between Martin Luther King, Jr., the
leading advocate of nonviolence, and Stokely Carmichael and Floyd McKissick, militant advocates of political confrontation.

June 11: U.S. troop strength in Vietnam would be
increased by 18,000 within 45 days, Sec. of Defense
McNamara reported, bringing total troop strength to
285,000. U.S. dead since Jan. 1 were placed at 2100.

June 13: In the landmark case of ***Miranda v. Arizona,***
the U.S. Supreme Court ruled that the provision in
the Fifth Amendment to the Constitution against self-
incrimination applied to police interrogation of a

criminal suspect. Among other guidelines, the Court specified that suspects must be told they have the right to have a lawyer present while being questioned and that, if suspects choose to make a confession without a lawyer and are subsequently put on trial, the prosecution must prove that the defendants understood their rights when they confessed.

June 29: Hanoi and Haiphong were bombed for the first time in the Vietnam War. Oil storage and loading installations, highways, railroads, bridges, and ships were attacked. Approximately two-thirds of North Vietnam's oil supply was destroyed within a week.

July 30: The **demilitarized zone (DMZ)** separating North and South Vietnam was bombed by U.S. planes for the first time.

Aug 1: In what was called the **Texas tower massacre,** Charles J. Whitman, 25, barricaded himself in a tower at the University of Texas at Austin, Tex., and shot and killed 13 and wounded 31 before police killed him. Earlier he had killed his wife and mother.

Aug 6: Demonstrations against the Vietnam War were held across the country on the anniversary of the atomic bombing of Hiroshima in 1945. In Washington, D.C., pickets demonstrated in front of the White House and the church where Pres. Johnson's daughter Luci was being married. In New York City 5000 marched to Times Square. On Aug. 9, the anniversary of the atomic bombing of Nagasaki, 200 demonstrators attempted a sit-in at the New York office of the Dow Chemical Company, a manufacturer of napalm.

Sep 18-24: U.S. weekly casualties in the Vietnam War hit a record 970: 142 killed, 825 wounded, 3 missing. During the same period South Vietnamese losses were 98 killed, 280 wounded, 71 missing.

Sep 23: Aerial defoliation of areas immediately south of the Demilitarized Zone (DMZ) between North and South Vietnam had begun, the U.S. military command announced, to deprive infiltrating North Vietnamese of protective cover.

Oct 5: The **conviction of Jack Ruby** for the 1963 murder of Lee Harvey Oswald, alleged assassin of Pres.

John F. Kennedy, was reversed by the Texas Court of Appeals on the grounds of improperly submitted evidence.

Oct 13: The heaviest **air strike on North Vietnam** to date was made by 173 U.S. bombers. The next day 175 bombers renewed the raid. On Oct. 15 it was announced that 403 U.S. planes and three helicopters had been lost over North Vietnam since Feb. 7, 1965.

Oct 26: A **fire at sea** on the U.S. carrier *Oriskany*, in the Gulf of Tonkin, killed 43 men and injured 16.

Nov 8: In **congressional elections** the Republicans gained three Senate seats and 47 House seats, but the Democrats still held a 64–36 Senate majority and a 248–187 House majority. One of the new Republican senators was Edward W. Brooke of Massachusetts, the first black elected to the Senate since Reconstruction.

II. Architecture
Arts and Music
Popular Entertainment
Publishing
Theater

American theater this year offered a number of literate and entertaining productions. The strongest of these appeared to be the musicals, among them *Mame* and *Cabaret*. One of the year's highlights was the Broadway revival of Hal Holbrook's one-man show *Mark Twain Tonight!*. The New York City Opera moved into its new home in the Lincoln Center for the Performing Arts. The Metropolitan Opera announced in December that its two-year-old touring company, the Metropolitan Opera National Company, would be disbanded in 1967 for financial reasons. Among the year's top motion pictures were *Who's Afraid of Virginia Woolf?*; *Dr. Zhivago*; *Torn Curtain*, Alfred Hitchcock's 50th film; and *Thunderball*, the fourth of the James Bond films and a box office smash. By the time the fall television season began, nearly all network shows were being broadcast in color. Nearly half the 11,000,000 TV sets sold this year were color sets. In architecture, the use of steel and glass in conservatively designed structures continued to be the rule. The leader in this trend was Ludwig Mies van der Rohe. Notables who died in 1966 included Russel Crouse, playwright, Apr. 3, at 73; Walt Disney, pioneer in motion picture animation, Dec. 15, at 65; Hans Hofmann, abstract expressionist, Feb. 17, at 85; Buster Keaton, comedian, Feb. 1, at 69; Kathleen Norris, novelist, Jan. 18, at 85; Maxfield Parrish, painter, Mar. 30, at 95; Billy Rose, theatrical producer, Feb. 10, at 66; Mari Sandoz, novelist, Mar. 10, at about 65; Delmore Schwartz, poet, July 11, at 52; Deems Taylor, composer and music critic, July 3, at 80; Sophie Tucker, the Last of the Red Hot Mamas, Jan. 13, at about 79; and Ed Wynn, comedian and actor, June 19, at 79.

Among **books published** this year was *In Cold Blood* by Truman Capote. Described as nonfiction, the book employed fictional techniques to recreate the 1959 murder of a farm family in Holcomb, Kans. The book became a best seller. Other books published this year included *The Embezzler* by Louis Auchincloss, a novel; *Tai-Pan* by James Clavell, a novel about Japan in the mid-nineteenth century; *Papa Hemingway* by A.E. Hotchner, a biography; *Rush to Judgment* by Mark Lane, one of a spate of books criticizing the investigation of the Kennedy assassination; *The Fixer* by Bernard Malamud, a novel; *Valley of the Dolls* by Jacqueline Susann, a novel that critics hated but readers turned into a runaway best seller; and *Ariel* by Sylvia Plath, a collection of poems that further increased the posthumous recognition of the poet, a suicide in 1963.

Apr 16: At the end of the last performance of the **Metropolitan Opera** in its venerable house at Broadway and 39th St. in New York City, performers and audience joined hands and sang "Auld Lang Syne." The fabulous gold curtain later was cut into small patches and packaged with souvenir recordings of the occasion. A committee was formed to preserve the old house but failed to prevent its demolition.

May 2: Pulitzer prizes were awarded for the follow-

ing: fiction, *The Collected Stories of Katherine Anne Porter;* biography, *A Thousand Days* by Arthur M. Schlesinger, Jr.; history, *The Life of the Mind in America* by Perry Miller; general nonfiction, *Wandering Through Winter* by Edwin Way Teale; poetry, *Selected Poems* by Richard Eberhart.

III. Business and Industry
Education
Philosophy and Religion
Science

The movement for school integration showed signs of division, as did the entire civil rights movement. Pacifist followers of the Southern Christian Leadership Conference of Martin Luther King, Jr., differed with militants such as Stokely Carmichael of SNCC and Floyd McKissick of CORE. Carmichael and others used the term *black power* which, depending on the context of its use, meant anything from blacks taking control of their own political and economic destinies to the destruction of western capitalism. A corollary catch phrase, *white backlash*, came into use to describe the vocal and sometimes violent reaction to this emerging militancy and to continuing efforts by local and federal governments to end discrimination in education, housing, and jobs. Proposals to end de facto school segregation by redrawing district lines and busing children to and from black neighborhoods provoked bitter controversy At the same time, the Gemini space program came to a successful conclusion, and NASA began preparations for Apollo, a program to put U.S. astronauts on the moon. Notables who died this year included Gilbert H. Grosvenor, longtime president of the National Geographic Society, Feb. 4, at 90; and Sebastian Spering Kresge, founder of the S. S. Kresge store chain, Oct. 18, at 99.

Feb 9: The **New York Stock Exchange** reached the peak of a three-and-one-half-year bull market as the Dow Jones industrial average hit an all-time high of

995. A downturn in stock prices for most of the rest of the year set market analysts to worrying about a recession. A low of 744 was reached Oct. 7.

Mar 16: Gemini 8, manned by astronauts Neil Armstrong and David Scott, was launched and made the first successful space docking, closing on its target vehicle after a six-and-one-half-hour chase. A yaw thruster rocket on the Gemini malfunctioned, throwing the connected crafts into a frightening tumble and bringing the projected 71-hour flight to an end in less than 11 hours.

Apr 6: Cesar Chavez's **National Farm Workers Union,** which had started a strike against California grape growers Sept. 8, 1965, scored its first victory when it was recognized as the bargaining agent for farm workers of Schenley Industries, a major grower.

Apr 24: The **longest newspaper strike** in a major city began. Fearing loss of jobs as a result of a merger of three ailing New York City papers—the *World-Telegram and Sun,* the *Journal-American,* and the *Herald Tribune*—the Newspaper Guild struck the new World-Journal-Tribune Inc. The strike lasted until Sept. 11.

May 13: Federal funding for education was denied to 12 school districts in the deep South, the first such action against violators of the desegregation guidelines of the 1964 Civil Rights Act.

May 17: The **Gemini 9** launch was postponed because of the failure of an Atlas booster rocket to launch an Agena target vehicle into orbit.

June 2: Surveyor 1, launched May 30, made the first U.S. soft landing on the moon after a flight of 231,483 miles in 63 hrs., 36 min. It immediately began televising pictures of the moon's surface; by July 14, when its batteries went dead, it had sent more than 11,000 back to Earth. Shots of indentations made by the craft's legs showed that the surface was strong enough to support an astronaut.

June 3: Gemini 9, manned by astronauts Thomas Stafford and Eugene Cernan, was successfully launched and attempted to rendezvous with a target vehicle orbited several hours earlier. The astronauts found the target vehicle's nose shroud only partially detached, gaping open like the "jaws of an angry alligator" and making docking impossible. On the second day of the flight, Cernan spent a record 2 hrs., 5 min. in a space walk, but found his equipment so troublesome that he terminated his extravehicular activity early. Gemini 9 splashed down on June 6 after 70 hrs., 20 min. aloft.

July 1: The **Medicare** insurance program for the elderly was inaugurated. The new health plan, condemned by some as the first step toward socialized medicine, covered the cost of care in hospitals and, after Jan. 1, 1967, in nursing homes.

July 8: An **airline strike** that grounded the planes of all major airlines until Aug. 19 was called by the International Association of Machinists.

July 18: Gemini 10, manned by astronauts John Young and Michael Collins, was successfully launched and docked in space with an Agena target vehicle. Both astronauts suffered eye irritation when lithium hydroxide leaked from their life-support system. Gemini 10 splashed down on July 21 in full view of TV cameras after a 71-hour flight.

Aug 8: The **first successful artificial heart pump,** a left ventricle bypass, was installed in a patient at Methodist Hospital in Houston, Tex., by a team headed by heart surgeon Michael DeBakey. It was removed ten days later.

Aug 10: Lunar Orbiter 1, designed to photograph possible landing sites on the moon, was launched from Cape Kennedy. It went into lunar orbit on Aug. 14 and televised 215 pictures. On Oct. 29 it was crashed into the moon, lest its radio signals interfere with Lunar Orbiter 2, scheduled for launch on Nov. 6.

Aug 22: The **Consumer Price Index** hit a record high in July, making 1966 the most inflationary year since 1957.

Sep 12: Gemini 11, manned by astronauts Charles Conrad and Richard Gordon, was successfully launched and docked with an Agena target vehicle. On Sept. 14 the joined crafts achieved a record altitude of 851 miles. Gemini 11 landed Sept. 15, its descent controlled entirely by on-board instruments—a space first.

Sep 12: School violence broke out at two newly integrated public schools in Grenada, Miss. Police stood by as white mobs assaulted black children and their parents with ax handles, pipes, and chains, injuring 40.

Sep 22: Surveyor 2, launched two days earlier, crashed into the moon as attempts to correct its tumbling flight failed.

Oct 7: Stock prices hit the year's low, with the Dow Jones industrial average down to 744 from a February high of 995. It was the worst decline since the one-day crash of May 28, 1962.

Nov 6: Lunar Orbiter 2 was launched. On Nov. 17 it went into orbit, photographing possible landing sites along the lunar equator. NASA scientists said that photographs of domelike formations indicated that the moon formerly had volcanic activity.

Nov 11: Gemini 12, manned by astronauts James Lovell and Edwin Aldrin, was successfully launched and rendezvoused with an Agena target vehicle. This was the last mission of the Gemini program. On Nov. 12 the astronauts took pictures of a solar eclipse. Aldrin spent a total of five and a half hours in extravehicular activity, without the fatigue and equipment difficulties that had marked earlier Gemini flights. Gemini 12 landed safely on Nov. 15.

Nov 18: Abstinence from meat on Fridays would no longer be required of U.S. Roman Catholics, except during Lent. The change became effective Dec. 2.

Dec 10: The **Nobel Prize in Chemistry** was awarded to Robert S. Mulliken of the University of Chicago for his work on the chemical bond of atoms in a molecule.

Dec 10: The **Nobel Prize in Physiology or Medicine** was awarded jointly to Charles B. Huggins of the University of Chicago and Francis Peyton Rous, a member emeritus of the Rockefeller Institute, in recognition of their pioneer discoveries of the causes of specific types of cancer.

IV. **Fashion**
    Folkways
    Holidays
    Social Issues and Crime
    Sports

Southpaw Sandy Koufax made the Los Angeles Dodgers pay $130,000 for the use of his pitching arm for the season. He demonstrated its worth by winning 27 games and the National League pennant for his club, even though he had to take cortisone shots before each game for his arthritic arm. But the Baltimore Orioles swept the World Series in four straight games. After the season Koufax retired. The San Francisco Giants' Willie Mays hit 37 home runs for a career total of 542, second only to Babe Ruth's 714. Muhammad Ali consolidated his world heavyweight boxing championship by beating five contenders, the last being Cleveland Williams at the Houston Astrodome (Nov. 14) before 34,420 spectators, largest indoor crowd in boxing history. In golf the top money winners were Billy Casper, $121,944, and Kathy Whitworth, $33,517. In fashion the year's rage was the miniskirt, which put hemlines four or five— and occasionally a daring seven—inches above the knee. This year also saw a fad for paper throwaway clothes, especially inexpensive one-wearing dresses. The use of drugs became a national phenomenon, with the emphasis on LSD and other hallucinogens. The word *psychedelic,* first used to describe such drugs or their effects in the 1950s, came into popular use. The high priest of LSD was Timothy Leary, a psychologist fired from Harvard in 1963. Notables who died this year included James "Sunny Jim" Fitzsimmons, active in horse racing for 78 years, Mar. 11, at 91; Hedda Hopper, born Elda Furry, the Hollywood gossip columnist, Feb. 1, at 75; Tony Lema, golfer, July 24, at 32; Margaret Sanger, the pioneer in family planning, Sept. 6, at 82; and Abe Saperstein, founder of the Harlem Globetrotters, Mar. 15, at 63.

Jan 2: The 1965 **NFL championship** was won by the

Green Bay Packers, who defeated the Cleveland Browns 23 to 12.

Mar 5: A new indoor **pole vault record** of 17 ft., ¼ in. was set by Bob Seagren in Albuquerque, N. Mex.

Mar 12: Bobby Hull of the Chicago Black Hawks scored his 51st hockey goal of the season against the New York Rangers in Chicago. Hull thus became the first player to score more than 50 in a season; he later ran the total to 54.

Mar 12: Jockey **Johnny Longden,** 59, retired after 40 years of racing and after riding his 6,032nd winner—the most ever for a jockey—in the San Juan Capistrano Handicap at Santa Anita.

Mar 19: The **NCAA basketball championship** was won by Texas Western College, which defeated Kentucky 72 to 65.

Apr 17-28: The **NBA basketball championship** was won by the Boston Celtics, who beat the Los Angeles Lakers four games to three, thus enabling coach Red Auerbach to retire with his eighth successive championship. Auerbach was replaced by Bill Russell, Celtic center, the first black to coach a major U.S. sports team.

May 30: At the 50th annual **Indianapolis 500** auto race, nearly half of the 33 starters were involved in a first-lap crash, but only one driver was hurt. Graham Hill led the six finishers, completing the course in 3 hrs., 27 min., 52.53 sec., for an average speed of 144.317 mph.

June 8: A **merger** of the National and American football leagues, effective in 1970, was announced. The move provided for a common draft of college players in 1967, putting an end to costly competition between the leagues. It also set up a Super Bowl game between the league champions of the 1966–1967 season.

June 20: The **U.S. Open golf tournament** was won by Billy Casper, who beat Arnold Palmer in a playoff.

June 25: Buckpasser set a new world record of 1:32³/₅ for the mile in winning the Arlington Classic. He also became the first three-year-old to win more than $1,000,000. Kauai King, the Derby and Preakness winner this year, went lame in the race; his retirement from racing was announced three days later.

July 2: At the **Wimbledon** tennis championships in England, Billie Jean King beat Maria Bueno of Brazil to win the women's singles championship.

July 2-3: The **world decathlon record** of 8089 points, held by C.K. Yang, was bested twice at Salina, Kans., by Russ Hodge (8130) and Bill Toomey (8234).

July 9: Jack Nicklaus won the British Open, joining Gene Sarazen, Ben Hogan, and Gary Player as the only men to have won the four major golf championships of the world. (The other events are the PGA, Masters, and U.S. Open.)

July 17: A new **record for the mile run**, 3:51.3, was set by Jim Ryun, a 19-year-old college freshman, trimming 2.3 sec. from the world record.

July 23: A new outdoor **pole vault record** of 17 ft., 6¼ in. was set by John Pennel of Los Angeles, Calif.

July 24: The **PGA golf tournament** was won by Al Geiberger.

Oct 5-9: The 63rd annual **World Series** was won by the Baltimore Orioles (AL), who swept the Los Angeles Dodgers (NL) in four straight games, the last three being shutouts.

1967

I. Civil Rights
Exploration and Settlement
Government
Statistics
Wars

By mid-November this year, more than 17,000 Americans had died in Vietnam since 1961, 2000 more in the first ten months of 1967 than in the period 1961–1966. U.S. and UN efforts to achieve peace were entirely unsuccessful, with UN Secretary General U

Thant asserting that the impasse was caused by the U.S. bombing of North Vietnam. In South Vietnam, in the first election since the 1963 coup, Nguyen Van Thieu and Nguyen Cao Ky were elected president and vice president amid charges of election fraud. At home, Pres. Johnson got a $69,900,000,000 defense appropriation for the 1967–1968 fiscal year, the largest single appropriation ever passed by Congress. But he was unsuccessful in his request for an income tax surcharge that he said was needed to fight the war, to conduct the Great Society programs, and to fight inflation. Congress passed bills providing for increased Social Security benefits, aid to education, and anti-poverty funds. Administration legislation requests included the smallest appropriation for foreign aid in 20 years, a Civil Rights Act that would end discrimination in housing by 1969 and prevent discrimination in selecting juries, and revision of the Selective Service System through substitution of a lottery to select draftees. In what was called the long hot summer, the U.S. suffered the worst race riots in its history, with trouble in no fewer than 100 American cities. Notables who died this year included John Nance Garner, vice president of the United States from 1933 to 1941, Nov. 7, at 98; and Jack Ruby, convicted killer of Lee Harvey Oswald, alleged assassin of Pres. John F. Kennedy. Ruby died in Dallas, Tex., Jan. 3, at 55, while awaiting retrial after his conviction was overturned.

Jan 10: Lester Maddox, the Georgia restaurant owner who made headlines in 1964 by passing out ax handles to white customers to prevent desegregation of his eatery, was sworn in as governor of Georgia.

Jan 16: The **first black southern sheriff** since Reconstruction, former paratrooper Lucius Amerson, was sworn in at Tuskegee, Ala.

Jan 27: A 63-nation **space demilitarization treaty** was signed by the U.S. and the U.S.S.R. The treaty prohibited the orbiting of nuclear weapons and forbade territorial claims on celestial bodies. It became effective on Oct. 10.

Jan 29: Robert G. "Bobby" Baker, former secretary to

the Senate Democratic majority, was convicted of income tax evasion, theft, and conspiracy to defraud the government. He was sentenced Apr. 7 to from one to three years in prison.

Mar 1: Rep. **Adam Clayton Powell**, Democrat of New York, was denied his seat in the 90th Congress by a vote of 307 to 116. This was the third time the House had taken such action against a duly elected member. A committee investigating Powell's activities found that he had "wrongfully and willfully" misused approximately $46,000 of government money for private purposes and had "improperly maintained" his wife on his office payroll.

Apr 4: Military authorities announced that the **500th U.S. plane** had been shot down over North Vietnam since bombing began in 1964.

Apr 15: In an **antiwar demonstration** in New York City, some 100,000 to 400,000 persons marched from New York's Central Park to UN headquarters. A similar protest in San Francisco drew about 50,000.

Apr 20: The North Vietnamese port city of **Haiphong was bombed** by U.S. planes, which destroyed two power plants and struck at North Vietnamese Mig airfields for the first time.

Apr 21: Svetlana Alliluyeva, daughter of Joseph Stalin, the late premier of the U.S.S.R., arrived in New York City after receiving political asylum at the U.S. Embassy in New Delhi, India.

May 19: The **first U.S. air strike on central Hanoi,** North Vietnam's capital, was launched by U.S. planes.

June 1: U.S. casualties in Vietnam for the week of May 21–27 were reported as 313 killed and 2616 wounded, the greatest weekly casualty toll of the war.

June 8: The **U.S. communications ship** *Liberty* was attacked by Israeli torpedo boats and planes in international waters 15 miles north of the Sinai Peninsula; 34 seamen were killed and 75 were wounded. Israel apologized for the accidental attack.

June 12: State laws forbidding **interracial marriages** were ruled unconstitutional by the U.S. Supreme Court.

June 23 and 25: Ten hours of **U.S.-Soviet talks at Glassboro,** N.J., were held by Pres. Johnson and Premier Aleksei Kosygin. Kosygin had headed his nation's delegation to the UN during its attempt to have Israel branded the aggressor in the Six Day War (June 5–10) against Egypt, Syria, and Jordan.

June 30: The **General Agreement on Tariffs and Trade** (GATT), the result of four years of negotiations begun during the Kennedy administration, was signed in Geneva by the U.S. and 45 other nations.

July 2-7: U.S. Marines at **Con Thien,** just south of the DMZ in South Vietnam, suffered heavy casualties in fierce fighting with North Vietnamese units.

July 12-17: A **race riot in Newark,** N.J., left 26 dead and more than 1300 injured before police and National Guard troops restored order.

July 22: It was announced that **U.S. troop strength in Vietnam** was to be increased to 525,000 by the end of 1968.

July 23: **Puerto Rico voted to remain a commonwealth** of the U.S. Some 60.5% of the votes cast rejected statehood or full independence.

July 23: The **worst race riot** in U.S. history erupted in Detroit, Mich., killing 43 people and causing some $200,000,000 in damage in five days of violence.

July 25: A **riot in Cambridge,** Md., followed a speech by H. Rap Brown, chairman of SNCC. Brown was arrested by the FBI in Alexandria, Va., the next day. On Aug. 14 he was indicted in Cambridge for arson, inciting to riot, and disturbing the public peace.

July 29: An **aircraft carrier fire** aboard the U.S.S. *Forrestal* in the Gulf of Tonkin, caused by a punctured fuel tank, killed 134 people and injured 62.

Aug 21: The Defense Department announced that **two U.S. Navy jets had been shot down** over the People's Republic of China after straying off course from a bombing mission over North Vietnam.

Sep 1-Oct 4: A siege of the U.S. Marine base at **Con Thien,** just south of the DMZ in South Vietnam, raged for more than a month before U.S. firepower forced North Vietnamese gunners to withdraw from their artillery positions in the DMZ.

Sep 28: Walter Washington was sworn in as commis-

sioner of the District of Columbia, the first black to
head a major city government.

Oct 2: Thurgood Marshall was sworn in as the first
black Supreme Court justice in U.S. history.

Oct 20: Seven **Ku Klux Klan members were convicted**
of conspiracy in the 1964 murders of three civil rights
workers, James Chaney, Andrew Goodman, and Michael Schwerner, in Mississippi. The federal jury acquitted eight others and could reach no verdict on
three others.

Oct 21-22: An **antiwar march in Washington,** D.C.,
drew some 50,000 participants. At least 647 were arrested, most after a clash with police and troops at
the Pentagon.

Oct 26: Cancellation of draft deferments of college
students who violated draft laws or interfered with
recruiting was ordered by Lewis Hershey, director of
the Selective Service.

Oct 30-Nov 4: A North Vietnamese assault on **Loc
Ninh,** on the Cambodian border about 90 miles north
of Saigon, was broken after six days by U.S. artillery
and air strikes. The attack on the town and the U.S.
Special Forces camp there was unusually determined, possibly because the communists wanted a
victory to offset the Oct. 31 inauguration of Nguyen
Van Thieu as president of South Vietnam.

Nov 7: Carl B. Stokes, a Democrat, was elected the first
black mayor of Cleveland, Ohio, the eighth largest
city in the U.S.

Nov 20: The U.S. **population** reached 200,000,000, despite the lowest yearly birthrate in history, 17.8 per
1000.

Dec 5: More than 1000 **antiwar protesters** attempted
to close down a New York City induction center.
Among the 264 arrested were Dr. Benjamin Spock
and the poet Allen Ginsberg.

Dec 15: A **collapse of the Silver Bridge** on the Ohio R.
between Point Pleasant, W. Va., and Kanauga, Ohio,
killed 46 people. The collapse occurred during rush
hour.

Dec 20: U.S. troop strength in Vietnam reached
474,300.

II. Architecture
Arts and Music
Popular Entertainment
Publishing
Theater

The most important art news this year was the effort to save the cultural treasures damaged by a flood that struck Florence, Italy, on Nov. 4, 1966. U.S. art conservationists and concerned nonprofessionals volunteered their services, and many organizations helped raise money for salvage and restoration work. In theater, the 1966–1967 season was marked by scarcity of good new plays. Welcome visitors from abroad were the Old Vic, which began a 17-week tour of the U.S. in January; and the Jewish State Theater of Poland, which began a U.S. tour in October. In popular music a new element, Indian music, as popularized by the sitarist Ravi Shankar, appeared in the work of rock groups, notably the Beatles, whose new album *Sgt. Pepper's Lonely Hearts Club Band,* also showed signs of the growing influence of the drug culture. Notables who died this year included John Coltrane, jazz musician and composer, July 17, at 40; Nelson Eddy, singer and movie actor, Mar. 6, at 65; Mischa Elman, violinist, Apr. 5, at 76; Woodrow Wilson "Woody" Guthrie, folk singer, Oct. 3, at 55; Edward Hopper, realist painter, May 15, at 84; Langston Hughes, poet and writer, May 22, at 65; Bert Lahr, comedian and actor, Dec. 4, at 72; Henry R. Luce, founder of *Time* and *Life,* Feb. 28, at 68; Carson McCullers, writer, Sept. 29, at 50; Paul Muni, actor, Aug. 25, at 71; Dorothy Parker, writer, June 7, at 73; Claude Rains, actor, May 30, at 77; Basil Rathbone, actor, July 21, at 75; Carl Sandburg, poet, biographer, and folklorist, July 22, at 89; Alice B. Toklas, longtime companion of Gertrude Stein, Mar. 7, at 89; Spencer Tracy, actor, June 10, at 67; and Paul Whiteman, king of jazz, Dec. 29, at 77.

Among **books published** this year was *The Death of a President* by William Manchester, about the assassination of Pres. Kennedy. The Kennedy family

had sought to halt publication on the grounds that
they had not given final approval of the manuscript,
as had been agreed with the author. The book was
published after the Kennedys won the right to delete
from it some particularly sensitive material. Other
books published this year included *Tales of Manhattan* by Louis Auchincloss, short stories; *The Arrangement* by Elia Kazan, a novel; *Death at an Early Age*
by Jonathan Kozol, dealing with conditions in ghetto
schools; *Rosemary's Baby* by Ira Levin, a shocker that
was the basis for an enormously successful movie;
The Medium Is the Massage by Marshall McLuhan
and Quentin Fiore, a study of the impact of technology and communication on society; *Nicholas and
Alexandra* by Robert K. Massie, a biography of the
last czar and czarina of Russia; *The Complete Poems
of Marianne Moore*; *The Instrument* by John O'Hara,
a novel; *The Chosen* by Chaim Potok, a first novel that
became a best seller; *The Confessions of Nat Turner*
by William Styron, a novel based on an 1831 slave
revolt; and *Pulitzer* by W. A. Swanberg, a biography.

Feb 5: The **Bollingen Prize** for poetry was awarded to
Robert Penn Warren for his 1966 collection *Selected
Poems, New and Old, 1923–1966*.

Apr 26: A new **art auction record** was set by David
Mann, a New York City art dealer, who bought Pablo
Picasso's painting *Mother and Child* at Sotheby's in
London for $532,000, the highest price ever paid for
a work by a living artist.

May 1: Pulitzer prizes were awarded for the following: fiction, *The Fixer* by Bernard Malamud; biography, *Mr. Clemens and Mark Twain* by Justin Kaplan;
history, *Exploration and Empire* by William H.
Goetzmann; general nonfiction, *The Problem of Slavery in Western Culture* by David Brion Davis; poetry,
Live or Die by Anne Sexton; drama, *A Delicate Balance* by Edward Albee.

June 25: The **first global TV broadcast,** *Our World,*
originated live from 19 countries on five continents,
and was seen in 39 nations via satellite.

Nov 7: A law creating the **Corporation for Public**

Broadcasting, a nonprofit public corporation to aid noncommercial television, was signed by Pres. Johnson.

Dec 6: At a seminar on **art forgery** at New York City's Metropolitan Museum of Art, the museum revealed that one of its most prized pieces was a forgery. It was an elegant statue of a horse, estimated to be 2400 years old when it was acquired in 1923 and since then widely reproduced in casts and used as an illustration in many books on Greek art. A gamma-ray shadowgraph confirmed that the forgery had been cast by a technique developed in the fourteenth century but was probably no more than 50 years old.

III. Business and Industry
Education
Philosophy and Religion
Science

The space program suffered a setback when three astronauts were killed in a fire while taking their Apollo vehicle through tests at Cape Kennedy, Fla. Space exploration news was not all bad. The U.S. made three successful soft landings on the moon to obtain data about the lunar surface and possible landing sites for manned flights. Mariner 5 sent back information about the atmosphere of Venus, and the new Saturn 5 rocket, the world's largest launch vehicle, orbited Earth in a test to determine its use for eventual manned flights to the moon. The economy showed signs of vigor despite civil unrest in U.S. cities. School integration progressed, but campus violence continued, a reminder that change is rarely easy. Notables who died this year included Henry Kaiser, industrialist, Aug. 24, at 85; J. Robert Oppenheimer, nuclear physicist known as the father of the atomic bomb, Feb. 18, at 62; and Francis Cardinal Spellman, archbishop of New York, Dec. 2, at 78.

Jan 27: A **launch pad fire** during Apollo tests at Cape Kennedy, Fla., killed astronauts Virgil I. "Gus" Grissom, Edward H. White, II, and Roger B. Chaffee. An investigation concluded that a faulty electrical wire was the probable cause.

Feb 4: **Lunar Orbiter 3** was launched from Cape Kennedy, Fla., on its 92-hour mission to the moon. The spacecraft relayed pictures of possible landing sites for manned space vehicles.

Mar 7: James R. Hoffa, president of the International Brotherhood of Teamsters, began an eight-year prison sentence for jury tampering after the Supreme Court refused to review his 1964 conviction.

Apr 2: A report on **school desegregation** by the Southern Education Reporting Service stated that 16% of black students in 11 southern states were attending desegregated schools in 1967, an increase of 10% over 1966.

Apr 17: Surveyor 3 was successfully launched from Cape Kennedy, Fla. The second U.S. spacecraft to make a soft landing on the moon, it studied the lunar surface and sent back more than 6300 pictures.

May 11: Ceremonies marking installation of the **100,000,000th telephone** in the U.S. were attended by Pres. Johnson and representatives of the Bell System and the U.S. Independent Telephone Association. The U.S. had approximately half the telephones in the world.

May 29: A **California property law** giving owners "absolute discretion" in housing rental or sales was ruled unconstitutional by the U.S. Supreme Court on the grounds that it was discriminatory and violated the Fourteenth Amendment.

June 14: Mariner 5 was successfully launched toward Venus.

June 19: De facto **school segregation in Washington, D.C.,** was ordered ended by autumn by U.S. District Judge J. Skelly Wright.

July 17: Surveyor 4, launched from Cape Kennedy on July 14 and programed to land in Sinus Medii in the center of the near side of the moon, lost radio contact with Earth moments before it landed.

Sep 8: Surveyor 5 was launched from Cape Kennedy and made a soft landing on the moon 65 hours later.

By Sept. 24 it had transmitted a total of 18,006 pictures to Earth along with other important information.

Oct 18: The **Nobel Prize in Physiology or Medicine** was awarded jointly to Dr. Haldan Keffer Hartline of Rockefeller University, Dr. George Wald of Harvard University, and Dr. Ragnar Granit of Sweden for research on the eye and its transmission of sensory information to the brain.

Oct 18: The **Nobel Prize in Physics** was awarded to Dr. Hans Albrecht Bethe of Cornell University for his study of energy generation in stars.

Oct 19: Mariner 5 passed within 2480 miles of the planet Venus and sent back data indicating that the planet had no magnetic field and that its surface was unfit for human habitation.

Nov 7: Surveyor 6 was launched. On Nov. 9 it made a soft landing on the moon and began transmitting pictures and soil analysis data. On Nov. 17 it lifted off the moon's surface and landed a few feet away. Surveyor 6 then took pictures of its original landing site. It was the first spacecraft to lift off the moon.

Nov 9: The unmanned **Apollo 9** space vehicle completed an 8-hr., 37-min. test orbit of Earth. The capsule was recovered in the Pacific Ocean just ten miles from its target area. It had been launched from Cape Kennedy by the Saturn 5 rocket, the world's largest launch vehicle, designed for eventual manned flights to the moon. It was the first time Saturn 5 was used.

IV. Fashion
Folkways
Holidays
Social Issues and Crime
Sports

In baseball the Boston Red Sox outfielder Carl Yastrzemski led the American League in three batting categories. He finished the year with an average of .326, batted in 121 runs, and tied Harmon Killebrew in home runs, 44 for the season. The Kansas City Athletics moved to Oakland for the 1968 season, and the American League decided to expand to 12 teams in 1969 by creating a new Kansas City franchise and awarding a franchise to Seattle. The NFL granted a franchise to the New Orleans Saints, and split the league into two conferences and four divisions: Eastern Conference (Century and Capitol divisions) and Western Conference (Central and Coastal divisions). This year the AFL and NFL played the first Super Bowl game, the World Series of professional football. In boxing Muhammad Ali continued to support his claim to be the greatest of all time by successfully defending the world heavyweight crown against Ernie Terrell in a 15-round decision (Feb. 6) and Zora Folley in a seventh-round knockout (Mar. 22). When Ali refused to be drafted into the Army on religious grounds, the World Boxing Association again stripped him of his title. In golf the top money winners were Jack Nicklaus, $188,998, and Kathy Whitworth, $32,937. In fashion there was little new, but women began to wear maxis, which were ankle-length coats, over their miniskirts. A British model, named Twiggy caused a sensation with her closely cropped hair and tomboyish appeal. Notables who died this year included James E. "Jimmy" Foxx, a great hitter with a lifetime record of 534 home runs, July 21, at 59; John J. "Johnny" Keane, of the St. Louis Cardinals, Jan. 6, at 55; and Reese "Goose" Tatum, of the Harlem Globetrotters, Jan. 18, at 45.

Jan 15: The first annual **Super Bowl** was won by the Green Bay Packers (NFL), who defeated the Kansas City Chiefs (AFL) 35 to 10. The Packers had won the NFL championship Jan. 1 by beating the Dallas Cowboys 34 to 27. The same day the Chiefs won the AFL championship over the Buffalo Bills, 31 to 7.

Jan 18: Albert De Salvo, self-confessed **Boston strangler,** who allegedly murdered 13 women between June 1962 and Jan. 1964, was sentenced to life imprisonment for armed robbery, assault, and sex offenses. For lack of evidence, he was not tried for the murders.

Feb 2: Formation of the **American Basketball Association** (ABA), a second pro basketball league, with former NBA star George Mikan as commissioner, was announced. The new league, with 11 teams, failed to lure stars from the NBA.

Mar 25: The **NCAA basketball championship** was won for the third time in four years by undefeated UCLA, which beat Dayton 79 to 64. UCLA's center, sophomore Lew Alcindor, had an all-time high season field goal percentage of .667 in this, his first varsity year.

Apr 14-24: The **NBA basketball championship** was won by the Philadelphia 76ers, who defeated the San Francisco Warriors four games to two.

May 14: New York Yankee outfielder **Mickey Mantle** hit his 500th career home run at Yankee Stadium, becoming the sixth player to reach that mark.

June 18: The **U.S. Open golf tournament** was won by Jack Nicklaus with a score of 275, one stroke better than the record set by Ben Hogan in 1948.

June 20: Muhammad Ali was given a five-year sentence and fined $10,000 for refusing to be drafted into the Army. Boxing authorities had earlier stripped him of his world title, rejecting his claim to exemption as a minister of the Nation of Islam.

June 23: A new **world record for the mile** was set by Jim Ryun, who shaved two-tenths of a second from his old record with a run of 3:51.1 in the AAU championships at Bakersfield, Calif. At the same meet, Paul Wilson cleared 17 ft. 7¾ in., a new world record for the outdoor pole vault.

July 8: At the **Wimbledon** tennis championships in England, Billie Jean King swept the women's singles; the women's doubles, with Rosemary Casals; and the mixed doubles, with Owen Davidson of Australia.

July 14: Eddie Mathews of the Houston Astros became the seventh player to hit 500 home runs.

July 24: The **PGA golf tournament** was won by Don January in a playoff with Don Massengale.

Sep 12-18: The **America's Cup** was successfully defended by the U.S. yacht *Intrepid*, which swept the Australian challenger *Dame Pattie* in four straight races.

Oct 4-12: The 64th annual **World Series** was won by the St. Louis Cardinals (NL), who defeated the Boston Red Sox (AL) four games to three.

Dec 31: The **NFL championship** was won by the Green Bay Packers, who defeated the Dallas Cowboys 21 to 17 with a touchdown scored from the one-yard line by Bart Starr with 13 seconds remaining in the game.

Dec 31: The **AFL championship** was won by the Oakland Raiders, who routed the Houston Oilers 40 to 7.

1968

I. Civil Rights
Exploration and Settlement
Government
Statistics
Wars

Dissent and doubt regarding the war in Vietnam and the economy at home prompted several Democratic leaders to challenge Pres. Johnson in the run for the presidential nomination, and stimulated the third-party candidacy of George C. Wallace of Alabama. In March, in the wake of the enemy offensive in Vietnam that came to be known as the Tet offensive, Pres. Johnson announced he would not seek another term. Later, the country was shocked by the assassinations of Martin Luther King, Jr., and Sen. Robert F. Kennedy, and by violence surrounding the Democratic National Convention in Chicago. The Republican candidate, Richard M. Nixon, pledging to end the war in Vietnam and restore law and order in the U.S., narrowly won the presidency. Although inflation had become critical, Pres. Johnson's budget was a record $186,000,000,000, with the year's expenditure on Vietnam about $25,000,000,000. In August the U.S.S.R. and other Warsaw Pact forces invaded Czechoslovakia and ended that country's movement toward liberalism. Notables who died this year included Husband Edward Kimmel, commander of the U.S. Pacific Fleet at the time of the Japanese attack on

Pearl Harbor in 1941, May 14, at 86; Joseph Martin, Jr., Speaker of the House from 1946–1948 and 1952–1954, Mar. 6, at 83; Norman Thomas, head of the U.S. Socialist Party from 1926–1955, Dec. 19, at 84; and Lurleen Burns Wallace, who in 1966 succeeded her husband George C. Wallace as governor of Alabama, May 7, at 41.

Jan 5: Indictments for conspiracy to aid and abet draft evasion were handed down against Dr. Benjamin Spock, the eminent pediatrician, the Rev. William Sloane Coffin of Yale, and three other antiwar activists. On June 14 Spock, Coffin, and two others were convicted; the fifth defendant was acquitted.

Jan 17: In his **State of the Union** message, Pres. Johnson called for a 10% income tax surcharge to reduce the budget deficit estimated at $20,000,000,000 for fiscal 1968 and to curb inflation.

Jan 21: A nuclear-armed **B-52 bomber crashed** near Greenland. Some radiation was released from its four hydrogen bombs, which broke up in the crash.

Jan 23: The *Pueblo* incident began when the Navy intelligence ship U.S.S. *Pueblo* was seized off the coast of North Korea by North Korean patrol boats. It was claimed that the *Pueblo* had been caught within North Korean waters. Its crew of 83 were subjected to harsh treatment until their release on Dec. 23.

Jan 30-Feb 24: The **Tet offensive,** timed to coincide with the Vietnamese New Year, was a massive assault by enemy forces throughout South Vietnam. U.S. forces were surprised by the scope and size of the operation, whose key targets included Saigon, the Marine base at Khe Sanh, and the provincial capital Hue. Enemy forces suffered a devastating setback, but the offensive increased antiwar sentiment in the U.S.

Feb 1: Former Vice Pres. **Richard M. Nixon announced his candidacy** for the Republican presidential nomination.

Feb 8: Former Gov. of Alabama **George C. Wallace announced his candidacy** for president as a third-party candidate on a law-and-order platform.

Feb 14: In the *Pueblo* incident, talks intended to re-

solve the issue began at Panmunjom between the U.S.
and North Korea.

Feb 24: **Hue was recaptured** by U.S. forces in Vietnam.

Feb 29: The **Kerner Commission report** was released
by the President's National Advisory Committee on
Civil Disorders. The report condemned racism in the
U.S. and called for aid to black communities to avert
further racial polarization and violence.

Mar 12: Sen. **Eugene J. McCarthy** of Minnesota won
the majority of convention delegates selected in the
New Hampshire Democratic presidential primary.
Campaigning on an antiwar platform and aided by
student volunteers, McCarthy won 42% of the vote.
Although Pres. Johnson won 48% of the vote,
McCarthy won 20 of the 24 delegates.

Mar 13: It was announced that **nerve gas testing** by the
Army at Dugway Proving Grounds in Utah might
have caused the deaths of some 6400 sheep in the
area.

Mar 16: Sen. **Robert F. Kennedy announced his candidacy** for the Democratic presidential nomination.

Mar 28: **Violence in Memphis,** Tenn., erupted during
a march led by Dr. Martin Luther King in support of
a sanitation workers' strike. One black marcher was
killed. Dr. King urged calm as National Guard troops
were called to restore order. He promised to return
in April to attend another march.

Mar 31: Pres. **Johnson announced he would not seek
the presidency again.** Addressing the nation on television, the president also called for a partial halt to
the bombing of North Vietnam and the opening of
peace negotiations.

Apr 2: The **Wisconsin Democratic primary** was won
by Sen. McCarthy.

Apr 4: Dr. **Martin Luther King, Jr., was assassinated**
at age 39 by a sniper in Memphis, Tenn. The event
was followed by a week of rioting in urban black
ghettos. New York City remained calm but Washington, D.C., was seriously disrupted. King's funeral in
Atlanta, Ga., on Apr. 9 was attended by an estimated
75,000 people.

Apr 5: The **siege of Khe Sanh,** site of a U.S. Marine base in Vietnam, was lifted.

Apr 8: Operation Complete Victory, involving 100,000 allied troops in Vietnam, was begun. It aimed to drive enemy forces from the provinces around Saigon.

Apr 11: The **1968 Civil Rights Act** was signed by Pres. Johnson. Discrimination in housing was made illegal for almost all types of dwellings.

Apr 27: Vice Pres. **Hubert H. Humphrey announced his candidacy** for the Democratic presidential nomination.

Apr 30: New York's Gov. **Nelson A. Rockefeller announced his candidacy** for the Republican presidential nomination.

May 2: The **Poor People's March on Washington,** planned by Dr. Martin Luther King, Jr., before his death, got under way. It was led by the Rev. Ralph Abernathy. Later in the month some 3000 marchers camped on a muddy site, dubbed Resurrection City, near the Washington Monument.

May 3: Agreement to hold **peace talks in Paris** was reached between the U.S. and North Vietnam.

May 5: Another **major enemy offensive** was launched in South Vietnam against allied strongholds. Although Saigon came under attack from mortar and sniper fire, the assault was judged to be not as severe as the Tet offensive.

May 10: Peace talks opened in Paris with W. Averell Harriman representing the U.S. and Xan Thuy representing North Vietnam.

May 28: The **Oregon Democratic primary** was won by Sen. McCarthy.

May 29: The U.S. nuclear submarine *Scorpion* was reported missing off the Azores with 99 men aboard.

June 5: Sen. **Robert F. Kennedy was shot** in Los Angeles at 12:15 A.M., shortly after delivering a speech acknowledging his victory in the June 4 California Democratic primary. Sirhan B. Sirhan, a Jordanian, was seized for the shooting. Kennedy died June 6 and Sirhan was indicted for murder on June 7.

June 8: Ex-convict **James Earl Ray was arrested** in London for the murder of Martin Luther King, Jr., on Apr. 4.

June 10: Gen. **William C. Westmoreland** turned over command of U.S. forces in Vietnam to Gen. Creighton W. Abrams. Gen. Westmoreland had been appointed chief of staff by Pres. Johnson on Mar. 22 in a move interpreted as reflecting disappointment with the conduct of the war.

June 13: Chief Justice **Earl Warren submitted his resignation** to Pres. Johnson, effective on the approval of a successor.

June 23: The war in Vietnam became the **longest war in U.S. history.**

June 24: Resurrection City in Washington, D.C., was cleared by police, who arrested 124 people after expiration of their camping permit.

June 26: Associate Justice **Abe Fortas was nominated** by Pres. Johnson as chief justice of the Supreme Court.

July 1: The **nuclear nonproliferation treaty** was signed by the U.S., U.S.S.R., and 59 other nations, concluding four years of negotiations.

July 23: A **sniper attack** on police in Cleveland, Ohio, initiated four days of rioting, during which four civilians and three policemen were killed.

Aug 7: Rioting in Miami, Fla., broke out in the city's black section. Three people were killed and hundreds injured before National Guard troops could restore order.

Aug 8: The **Republican National Convention nominated Richard M. Nixon** for the presidency over Gov. Ronald Reagan of California and Gov. Nelson A. Rockefeller of New York. Gov. Spiro T. Agnew of Maryland was nominated for the vice presidency on Aug. 9 at the convention in Miami Beach, Fla.

Aug 10: Sen. **George McGovern of South Dakota announced his candidacy** for the Democratic presidential nomination.

Aug 28: John Gordon Mein, U.S. ambassador to Guatemala, was killed by terrorists.

Aug 29: In Chicago the **Democratic National Convention nominated Vice Pres. Hubert H. Humphrey** for the presidency. Sen. Edmund S. Muskie of Maine was named the vice presidential candidate. The convention, which began Aug. 26, was the most violent in U.S. history. Antiwar protestors clashed with police and national guardsmen. Hundreds of people, including bystanders and members of the press, were beaten by police, some in full view of television cameras.

Oct 2: Justice **Abe Fortas** asked to be withdrawn from consideration for confirmation as chief justice. The Senate had objected to his advisory services to the president while on the Court.

Oct 3: George Wallace named his running mate in his third-party bid for the presidency, former Air Force chief of staff Gen. Curtis E. LeMay.

Oct 31: Bombing of North Vietnam was ordered stopped by Pres. Johnson.

Nov 5: Richard M. Nixon was elected president of the United States, defeating his Democratic opponent Vice Pres. Hubert H. Humphrey in a close race. Spiro T. Agnew, Republican of Maryland, was elected vice president. The electoral vote was Nixon, 302; Humphrey, 191; George C. Wallace, third-party candidate, 45. One Nixon elector later cast his vote for Wallace. The popular vote was Nixon, 31,785,480; Humphrey, 31,275,166; Wallace, 9,906,473. The Republicans gained four seats in the House and five in the Senate, but the Democrats still held majorities of 58–42 in the Senate and 243–192 in the House. The Republicans gained five governorships in the election.

Dec 1: Condemning as a **police riot** the actions of Chicago police during the Democratic Convention in August, the National Commission on the Causes and Prevention of Violence warned against a national tendency toward violence.

II. Architecture
Arts and Music
Popular Entertainment
Publishing
Theater

This year several new theatrical companies opened,

notably the Negro Ensemble Company and Theatre
Atlanta. The motion picture industry adopted a new
voluntary film rating code to restrict viewing of inap-
propriate films by the young. The year in architecture
was marked by the opening in Chicago of the John
Hancock Building, a 100-story structure crisscrossed
with diagonal exterior braces and tapered for stability. Among the notables who died this year were Tal-
lulah Bankhead, stage and screen star, Dec. 12, at 65;
Edna Ferber, novelist, Feb. 23, at 78; Dorothy Gish,
actress, June 4, at 70; Harold Gray, creator of the
Little Orphan Annie comic strip, May 9, at 74; Fannie
Hurst, novelist, Feb. 23, at 78; Howard Lindsay, playwright, Feb. 11, at 78; Thomas Merton, Trappist
monk and writer, Dec. 10, at 53; Charles Münch, conductor of the Boston Symphony from 1949 to 1962,
Nov. 6, at 77; Edwin O'Connor, novelist, Mar. 23, at
49; Conrad Richter, novelist, Oct. 30, at 78; Ruth St.
Denis, choreographer of modern dance, July 21, at
about 90; Upton Sinclair, author, Nov. 25, at 90; John
Steinbeck, Nobel Prize-winning author, Dec. 20, at
66; and Walter Wanger, Hollywood producer, Nov.
18, at 74.

Among **books published** this year were two nonfiction works by Norman Mailer. His *The Armies of
the Night* was a personal account of the antiwar demonstrations in Washington, D.C., in Oct. 1967 that
culminated in a march on the Pentagon. *Miami and
the Siege of Chicago* was Mailer's equally personal
view of the 1968 political conventions. Other books
published this year included *Tell Me How Long the
Train's Been Gone* by James Baldwin, a novel; *Lost in
the Funhouse* by John Barth, a collection of stories;
A Brand New Life by James T. Farrell, a sequel to his
Studs Lonigan trilogy; *The Algiers Motel Incident* by
John Hersey, dealing with the murder of three blacks
by police during riots in Detroit; *A Small Town in
Germany* by John Le Carré, a master of the spy novel;
The Salzburg Connection by Helen MacInnes, an-
other master of the genre; *The Naked Ape* by Des-
mond Morris, a nonfiction study of human beings;
The First Circle and *Cancer Ward* by Alexander

Solzhenitsyn, the Russian writer's second and third novels; and *Couples* by John Updike, a novel.

Apr 6: San Antonio, Tex., celebrated its 200th anniversary with the **opening of HemisFair 68,** an attractive world's fair that featured many permanent buildings, including the 622-ft.-high Tower of the Americas, the largest construction of its type since the Eiffel Tower. One of the permanent buildings, the Theater for Performing Arts, opened with a performance of Verdi's *Don Carlo.*

May 8: Pulitzer prizes were awarded for the following: fiction, *The Confessions of Nat Turner* by William Styron; biography, *Memoirs 1925–1950* by George F. Kennan; history, *The Ideological Origins of the American Revolution* by Bernard Bailyn; general nonfiction, *Rousseau and Revolution* by Will and Ariel Durant; poetry, *The Hard Hours* by Anthony Hecht.

May 25: The **Gateway Arch** in St. Louis, Mo., designed by Eero Saarinen, was formally dedicated.

Oct 9: A record **art auction price** was paid at a Parke-Bernet auction in New York City by Norton Simon, the California industrialist. He bid $1,550,000 for Pierre Auguste Renoir's *Le Pont des Arts,* a record for an impressionist painting.

III. Business and Industry
Education
Philosophy and Religion
Science

The economy was seriously threatened by inflation, while unemployment remained low, averaging 3.6% of the labor force for the year. A record 9% increase brought the GNP to $860,000,000,000. In April and June William McChesney Martin, chairman of the Federal Reserve Board, warned that unless weaknesses in the economy were corrected, particularly inflation and the balance-of-payments deficit, the nation would face a serious crisis. Following passage of the income tax surcharge bill in June and exercise of fiscal restraints, interest rates dropped. By Decem-

ber, however, the prime rate had risen again, to a
record 6.75%. Labor made strong gains, but they
were offset in part by inflation and increased taxes.
In education, major strikes by teachers hit New York
City and Florida. On many campuses college students
demanded reforms, including separation of universities from government defense research projects,
greater student participation in college administration, increased enrollment of black and impoverished students, and introduction of black-studies programs. Students pressed their demands with calls for
strikes, in some cases met by police action. In medicine, new progress was made in organ transplants.
Dr. Denton Cooley of Texas, the most successful in
the field, performed 17 heart transplant operations.
This year Americans noted the deaths of Francis Cardinal Brennan of Philadelphia July 2, at 74; Chester
F. Carlson, inventor of xerography, Sept. 19, at 62;
Donald L. Hall, who designed the *Spirit of St. Louis*,
flown across the Atlantic by Charles A. Lindbergh in
1927, May 2, at 69; Helen A. Keller, who although
deaf, blind, and mute from childhood learned to
read, write, and speak and became a leader in the
drive for educational aid for the handicapped, June
1, at 87; Charles W. Mayo, the son and nephew of the
founders of the Mayo Clinic and a noted surgeon,
July 28, at 70; and Robert Reynolds "Bob" Jones,
founder of Bob Jones University, Jan. 16, at 84.

Jan 9: Surveyor 7 made a soft landing on the moon
and began sending back data, including photographs.
This was the last flight of the Surveyor series.

Jan 22: The unmanned **Apollo 5** spacecraft was successfully launched into Earth orbit. During the flight
its Lunar Excursion Module (LEM) was tested.

Feb 8: Four days of **student disorder in Orangeburg**,
S.C., culminated in the deaths of three black students
in a clash between police and students at South Carolina State College. The trouble began when students
from the college and nearby Claflin College protested
the barring of blacks from a local bowling alley.

Feb 19: The **first statewide teachers' strike** in U.S.

history began when more than half of Florida's public school teachers walked off the job. The strike lasted until Mar. 8.

Mar 17: A two-tiered **gold price system** was negotiated in Washington, D.C. by representatives of the U.S. and six European nation members of the London Gold Pool. All gold transactions between governments would be at the official price of $35 an ounce, but the private market would be allowed to fluctuate. This resolved a critical rush on gold that had threatened to disrupt the international economy.

Apr 4: **Apollo 6** was launched in an unmanned mission designed to test, for the second and last time, the Saturn 5 rocket prior to manned flight.

Apr 18: The **Bell Telephone System was struck,** for the first time in its history, by 178,000 members of the Communications Workers Union. The strike hardly affected telephone service, but the record-breaking settlement on May 5, amounting to an increase of 19.58% over three years, set a high standard for other unions to reach for in their wage negotiations.

Apr 23: A **sit-in at Columbia University** was begun by students protesting university plans to build a gymnasium on land used by the neighboring community. The sit-in, involving several university buildings, led to the closing of the university on Apr. 26. On the night of Apr. 30, the police cleared all buildings occupied by the students. In the police action, some 150 students and police were injured. The university did not resume normal operations until the opening of the fall semester.

June 13: A new **stock trading record** was set on the New York Stock Exchange, with 2,350,000 shares traded. The marked upsurge in business that had begun in April was attributed to general optimism that the war in Vietnam was coming to an end. The volume of paperwork became so great in this period that, starting on June 12, the exchange closed down trading on Wednesdays.

July 1: The **United Auto Workers formally separated from the AFL-CIO.** The split followed years of conflict during which UAW head Walter Reuther accused AFL-CIO head George Meany of blocking labor reforms and allowing the movement to stagnate. Three weeks later, the UAW joined with the Teamsters to form the Alliance for Labor Action.

July 4: Explorer 38, a giant radio astronomy satellite, was launched into Earth orbit. With its antennas extended, the satellite was 1500 feet in diameter.

July 15: The **first direct U.S.-U.S.S.R. commercial flights began** when a Soviet Aeroflot jet landed at Kennedy Airport in New York City. On the same day, a U.S. commercial jet took off for Moscow.

July 31: A statement on **birth control** was issued by the National Council of Catholic Bishops. It supported Pope Paul VI's encyclical of July 25, which reiterated condemnation of artificial methods of birth control. Nevertheless, some Catholic priests and laymen publicly disagreed with the pope's position.

Aug 8: In a **stock manipulation** case, financier Louis E. Wolfson and three associates were convicted of violating SEC regulations in connection with the liquidation of Merrit-Chapman & Scott Corp.

Oct 11: The **first manned Apollo mission,** Apollo 7, manned by Commander Walter M. Schirra, Jr., Donn F. Eisele, and Walter Cunningham, was successfully launched and began an 11-day Earth orbit during which the crew transmitted live television broadcasts from the spaceship. The men successfully performed a docking maneuver with the lunar module.

Oct 16: The **Nobel Prize in Physiology or Medicine** was awarded jointly to Dr. Robert W. Holley of the Salk Institute, Dr. H. Gobind Khorana of the University of Wisconsin, and Dr. Marshall W. Nirenberg of the National Institutes of Health for their studies of the genetic code.

Oct 30: The **Nobel Prize in Chemistry** was awarded to Lars Onsager of Yale University for his work in thermodynamic theory.

Oct 30: The **Nobel Prize in Physics** was awarded to Luis W. Alvarez of the University of California at Berkeley for his work in the field of subatomic particles, particularly his development of the bubble chamber.

Nov 6: A **student strike** was begun by dissident students at San Francisco State College. The students called for reforms, especially in the area of black-studies programs. This initiated almost four months of turmoil, during which the president of the school, S. I. Hayakawa, called in police to help end the strike.

Dec 4: A new **medical definition of death** was formulated by the American Medical Association in an effort to resolve controversy arising from organ-transplant operations. The AMA declared that a death had to be declared irreversible by two independent physicians before an organ could be removed from an apparently dead patient for transplanting. The term *brain death* was introduced by Dr. Henry K. Beecher of Harvard on Dec. 12 to denote irreversible death.

Dec 21-27: **Apollo 8,** manned by Commander Frank Borman, James Lovell, Jr., and William Anders, was launched from Cape Kennedy, Fla. It completed a pioneering five-day mission that included ten orbits of the moon (Dec. 24–25) and yielded spectacular photographs of Earth and the moon.

IV. Fashion
    Folkways
    Holidays
    Social Issues and Crime
    Sports

In fashion, hemlines remained high, and efforts to introduce the so-called midi length (hemline at mid-calf) were unsuccessful. Pantsuits for evening wear, with full flowing lines, gained wide acceptance. More and more men favored bold, extravagant fashions, and both men and women were wearing leather garments. For the first time the Gallup Poll reported that crime ranked number one among the issues that concerned the public. Another serious problem was the rising use of heroin by middle-class and upper-class youths along with an increase in drug abuse throughout American society. In sports, the National League added two new baseball franchises, San Diego and Montreal. Both the National and American leagues formed two divisions, Eastern and Western, with league championships to be determined by five-game playoffs beginning in 1969. In football, the NFL Players Association campaigned for better pensions. In golf there was a split between the PGA and the new American Professional Golfers, with both groups struggling for control of the ever more lucrative tournaments. A compromise agreement was reached on Dec. 13. The year's top golf money winners were Billy Casper, $121,944, and Kathy Whitworth, $48,380. In boxing, Jimmy Ellis became the World Boxing Association champion by outpointing Jerry Quarry in a bout on Apr. 27. New York State, Massachusetts, and Illinois recognized Joe Frazier, who had knocked out Buster Mathis in a title bout on Mar. 4. The new American Basketball Association concluded its first season with a $2,500,000 loss. This year tennis tournaments were opened to professionals as well as amateurs for the first time. Among the notables who died this year were Tommy Bridges, Detroit Tigers pitcher, Apr. 19, at 61; Samuel Earl "Wahoo Sam" Crawford, outfielder for the Detroit Tigers and Cincinnati Reds, June 15, at 88; Lawson Little, golfer, Feb. 1, at 57; Earl Sande, one of racing's most successful jockeys, Aug. 20, at 69; and Jess Willard, world heavyweight boxing champion from 1915 to 1919, Dec. 15, at 86.

Jan 14: Super Bowl II was won by the Green Bay Packers (NFL), who defeated the Oakland Raiders (AFL) 33–14 for their second Super Bowl victory. Shortly thereafter the Packers'coach, Vince Lombardi, retired to an executive post with the team. The Packers had won the NFL title on Dec. 31, 1967, by beating the Dallas Cowboys 21 to 17. The same day the Raiders had clinched the AFL title by beating the Houston Oilers 40 to 7.

Feb 6-18: At the 1968 **Winter Olympics** in Grenoble, France, the unofficial team championship was won by Norway. The U.S. won only one gold medal, the one taken by figure skater Peggy Fleming.

Mar 23: The **NCAA basketball championship** was won by UCLA, which defeated North Carolina 78–55. The day before, UCLA had beaten its archrival, the University of Houston, in the NCAA semifinals.

Apr 18-May 4: The **first ABA basketball championship** was won by the Pittsburgh Pipers, who beat the New Orleans Buccaneers four games to three.

Apr 21-May 2: The **NBA basketball championship** was won by the Boston Celtics, who defeated the Los Angeles Lakers four games to two.

May 4: The 94th annual **Kentucky Derby** was won by Dancer's Image, with a time of 2:02⅕. The jockey was Bob Ussery. Three days later Dancer's Image was disqualified when traces of a pain-killing drug were found in tests, and Forward Pass, ridden by Ismael Valenzuela, was declared the winner. This was the first recalled race in Derby history. Peter Fuller, owner of Dancer's Image, challenged the recall. Finally, on Dec. 23, the Kentucky Racing Commission ruled that Dancer's Image had won the race but not the purse.

May 8: A **perfect baseball game** was pitched by Jim "Catfish" Hunter of the Oakland Athletics, in leading his team to a 4 to 0 victory over the Minnesota Twins. This was the first American League perfect game since 1922.

June 16: The **U.S. Open golf tournament** was won by Lee Trevino, who beat Jack Nicklaus by four strokes and became the first person in the tournament's history to play all four rounds under par.

July 6: At the **Wimbledon** tennis championships in England, Billie Jean King won the women's singles title for the third straight year. King and Rosemary Casals won the women's doubles title for the second year running.

July 21: The **PGA golf tournament** was won by Julius Boros, who beat Arnold Palmer and Bob Charles by one stroke.

Aug 24: A new **horse racing record** for the mile was set by Dr. Fager, who ran the distance in 1:32⅕ at Arlington Park in Arlington, Ill. This year Dr. Fager was voted horse of the year and then was retired to stud.

Sep 9: The **first U.S. Open tennis championships** were won by Arthur Ashe in the men's singles division and by Virginia Wade of England (Sept. 8) in the women's singles division.

Oct 2-10: The 65th annual **World Series** was won for

the first time since 1945 by the Detroit Tigers (AL), who beat the St. Louis Cardinals (NL) four games to three.

Oct 12-27: At the **Summer Olympics** in Mexico City, the U.S. won 45 gold medals and took first place in the unofficial team standings. Despite the altitude, many records were broken, and spectacular performances were turned in by Bob Beamon, who broke the world broad jump record by 21 in. with a jump of 29 ft., 2½ in., and Dick Fosbury, who won the high jump at 7 ft., 4½ in., going over the bar backward. On Oct. 18 two U.S. track stars, Tommy Smith and John Carlos, were suspended from competition after giving the black power salute, a clenched fist raised high over the head, at an awards ceremony. Smith and Carlos had won the gold and bronze medals for the 200-meter dash.

Nov 17: In what became known as the **Heidi game,** a critical football game between the New York Jets and the Oakland Raiders televised on NBC, the network cut away the last minute of the game to broadcast a production of a children's program, *Heidi*. Oakland, behind at the time, scored twice in nine seconds to win 43 to 32.

Dec 26-28: In Australia, the **Davis Cup** international tennis round was won, for the first time since 1963, by the U.S., which beat Australia four matches to one.

1969

I. Civil Rights
Exploration and Settlement
Government
Statistics
Wars

Richard Milhous Nixon assumed the presidency, carrying the burden of the most unpopular war in U.S.

history. At the Paris peace talks little progress was made to end the Vietnam War. After Pres. Nixon made the first moves toward U.S. troop reductions in June, Sen. Charles Goodell, Republican of New York, demanded a complete pullout by the end of 1970. In October and November mammoth peace demonstrations were held in the nation's capital and other major cities. These rallies sparked prowar marches by what the president called "the great silent majority." As the year progressed, the new administration came under increasing criticism for allegedly pursuing a so-called southern strategy, a plan purportedly devised by Attorney General John Mitchell to frame policies and make appointments that would mollify the South and encourage Republican victories there in coming years. Congress voted a $5,000,000,000 cut in military spending, but failed by one vote to defeat construction of the Safeguard antiballistic missile system. This year skyjackers made off with 65 planes, a number that exceeded the total for all years since the first such seizure in 1952. Notables who died this year included Sen. Everett McKinley Dirksen, Senate Republican leader since 1959, Sept. 7, at 73; Allen W. Dulles, diplomat and director of the CIA from 1953 to 1961, Jan. 29, at 75; Joseph P. Kennedy, father of John F. and Robert Kennedy, Nov. 18, at 81; and Adm. Raymond A. Spruance, USN (ret.), who commanded the U.S. fleet at the Battle of Midway in 1942 during World War II, Dec. 13, at 83.

Jan-Mar: Torrential **rains,** the heaviest in 100 years, caused vast mud slides in southern California, killed more than 100, and destroyed nearly 10,000 homes. Damage exceeded $60,000,000. The worst storms hit on Jan. 18–26 and Feb. 23–26.

Jan 3: The House voted to seat Rep. **Adam Clayton Powell** of New York in the 91st Congress, but fined him $25,000 for improper use of government funds and stripped him of seniority.

Jan 16: At the **Paris peace talks,** U.S. and North Vietnamese delegates finally agreed on the shape of the table to be used when the South Vietnamese and the

National Liberation Front joined the negotiations. Four-party talks began Jan. 18.

Jan 20: **Richard M. Nixon was inaugurated president** of the United States. Spiro T. Agnew was inaugurated vice president. The inaugural ceremonies were marked by antiwar demonstrations.

Jan 20: At the **Paris peace talks,** Henry Cabot Lodge replaced W. Averell Harriman as chief U.S. negotiator.

Mar 4: Regular rail shipments of **nerve gas** were revealed by the Department of Defense, which reported it was spending $350,000,000 a year on chemical and biological weapons.

Mar 10: **James Earl Ray,** convicted assassin of Dr. Martin Luther King, Jr., was sentenced to 99 years in prison.

Apr 3: **U.S. combat deaths in Vietnam** since Jan. 1, 1961, reached 33,641, topping the 33,629 killed in the Korean War.

Apr 15: A **U.S. reconnaissance plane was shot down** by North Korean Mig jets over the Sea of Japan; 31 crewmen were lost.

Apr 23: **Sirhan Sirhan** was sentenced to death for the murder of Sen. Robert Kennedy.

Apr 24: In the **heaviest bombing raid** to date in the Vietnam War, U.S. B-52's dropped nearly 3000 tons of bombs on enemy positions near the Cambodian border northwest of Saigon.

May 14: An eight-point **Vietnam peace plan** was proposed by Pres. Nixon. It included pullout of most foreign troops within a year and elections supervised by an international body.

May 15: Supreme Court Justice **Abe Fortas** announced his resignation. He had been criticized for accepting a fee from the family foundation of Louis E. Wolfson, who was jailed for stock manipulation.

May 16: The $50,000,000 **nuclear submarine** *Guitarro* sank at dockside in San Francisco while undergoing final fitting. A House report later charged the Navy with "inexcusable carelessness."

May 20: U.S. and South Vietnamese troops captured

Hamburger Hill after ten days of bloody battle. Sen. Edward M. Kennedy of Massachusetts criticized such assaults as senseless. The hill was abandoned May 27 and later was reoccupied by North Vietnamese troops.

June 6: Court testimony revealed that the **FBI had tapped the phones of Martin Luther King, Jr.,** despite a 1965 order by Pres. Johnson to tap only for purposes of national security. The testimony was taken in a federal court in Houston, Tex.

June 23: Earl Warren retired as chief justice of the U.S. after swearing in Warren Burger as his successor.

July 11: The convictions of Dr. **Benjamin Spock** and three codefendants for conspiring to counsel draft evasion were overturned by a U.S. court of appeals.

July 18: Sen. **Edward M. Kennedy** was involved in an auto accident when the car he was driving crashed off a bridge into the waters off Chappaquiddick Island, Mass. Kennedy was unable to rescue his passenger, Mary Jo Kopechne, who drowned. He reported the accident to Edgartown, Mass., police on July 19. On July 25 he pleaded guilty to leaving the scene of an accident. That evening, in a television statement, he called his actions in delaying the report of the accident "indefensible." He asked his constituents to help him decide on whether to continue his political career. Supported by a favorable response, he resumed his Senate duties on July 31.

Sep 9: An **air collision** of a passenger jet and a light plane near Indianapolis, Ind., killed 83 people.

Sep 21: Operation Intercept, a U.S. drive to halt drug traffic from Mexico, brought border traffic to a virtual halt. Travel eased considerably on Oct. 10 after complaints by the Mexican government.

Sep 24: The trial of the **Chicago Eight** began. Eight radical leaders had been indicted on Mar. 20 on charges of conspiring to incite riots during the 1968 Democratic convention in Chicago. The eight—Rennie Davis, David Dellinger, John Froines, Tom Hayden, Abbie Hoffman, Jerry Rubin, Bobby Seale, and

Lee Weiner—claimed they were being tried for their political views. The trial was marked by numerous disruptions by the defendants, and on Oct. 29 Judge Julius J. Hoffman ordered Seale bound and gagged. On Nov. 5 Seale was sentenced to four years in prison on 16 counts of contempt, and his case was severed from that of the others, who then became known as the Chicago Seven. On Oct. 9–11 National Guard troops were called into Chicago to control demonstrators outside the courtroom.

Oct 15: The **first Vietnam Moratorium Day** was observed by millions with prayer vigils, candlelight processions, mass meetings, and black armbands. Pres. Nixon ignored it. Vice Pres. Agnew on Oct. 19 called protest leaders "an effete corps of impudent snobs."

Oct 28: Charges that an **illegal war in Laos** was being conducted without congressional knowledge or consent were leveled against the administration and the Pentagon by Sen. J. William Fulbright, chairman of the Senate Foreign Relations Committee.

Nov 3: Pres. Nixon said that **secret U.S. peace proposals had been rejected** by the North Vietnamese. Nixon asked the nation to support his plans to Vietnamize the war, that is, encourage Vietnam to pursue the war on its own, and withdraw U.S. troops.

Nov 11: Pro-America demonstrations in support of U.S. policy in Vietnam by U.S. citizens whom Pres. Nixon called "the great silent majority" marked this year's Veterans' Day observances.

Nov 14: The **second Vietnam Moratorium Day** began with a long, single-file "March Against Death" in Washington, D.C. On the next day 250,000 people marched there against the war. A San Francisco protest against U.S. participation in the war drew 100,000 demonstrators.

Nov 16: News reports charged a U.S. infantry unit with **massacre at My Lai 4,** a village in the Songmy district in South Vietnam, on Mar. 16, 1968. More than 450 villagers, including many women and babies, were said to have been slain. Pending an investigation, Lt. William L. Calley, Jr., in charge of the U.S. unit at that time, was kept on active duty beyond his official tour.

Nov 17: The first round of **Strategic Arms Limitation Talks** (SALT) between the U.S. and U.S.S.R. opened in Helsinki, Finland. The conference ended on Dec. 22 with an agreement to resume talks in Vienna on Apr. 16, 1970.

Nov 20: **Henry Cabot Lodge** resigned as chief U.S. negotiator at the Paris peace talks.

Nov 21: The nomination of **Clement Haynsworth** to the Supreme Court was rejected by the Senate after three months of consideration.

Nov 24: The **nuclear nonproliferation treaty** was signed by the U.S. and U.S.S.R., the 23rd and 24th signatories.

Dec 4: Fred Hampton, Illinois chairman of the Black Panther Party, was shot and killed along with another party member in a predawn police raid in Chicago. On the next day the Illinois ACLU demanded an investigation of the Panthers' charge that Hampton had been murdered in his bed.

Dec 8: An early morning police **raid on Black Panther headquarters** in Los Angeles led to a four-hour shootout before 11 party members surrendered.

Dec 15: U.S. troop strength in Vietnam would be cut to 434,000 by Apr. 12, Pres. Nixon announced. This would represent a total reduction of about 110,000 since he took office.

Dec 22: The most far-reaching **tax reform bill** in U.S. history was passed by Congress. Although it removed 9,000,000 of the very poor from federal tax rolls, it was criticized as a measure that aided the rich. The bill, signed by Pres. Nixon on Dec. 30, reduced the tax surcharge from 10% to 5% and extended it for six months, reduced the oil depletion allowance from 27.5% to 22%, closed numerous tax loopholes, and increased Social Security benefits by 15%.

II. Architecture
   Arts and Music
   Popular Entertainment
   Publishing
   Theater

Most of the year's theatrical excitement was generated on off-Broadway stages, where patrons saw an
unusual number of works by black playwrights, including Lorraine Hansberry, LeRoi Jones, and
Lonne Elder, III. *Ché,* a play about Guevara, the Latin
American revolutionist, opened in New York on Mar.
22; two days later its cast and production staff were
arrested on obscenity charges. *Oh! Calcutta!* by
Kenneth Tynan was panned by critics but soon became one of the season's hits. In December seven cast
members and the producer of its Los Angeles troupe
were arrested for indecent exposure and lewdness. A
strike by opera performers and musicians postponed
the opening of the Metropolitan Opera's season until
Dec. 29. In art, Pres. Lyndon B. Johnson presided
over the groundbreaking ceremonies for the Joseph
H. Hirshhorn Museum and Sculpture Garden in
Washington, D.C., in January. The museum was to
house the art collection Hirshhorn donated to the
U.S. in 1966. Also in January, the New York Museum
of Modern Art announced it had acquired the art
collection of Gertrude Stein, valued at more than
$6,000,000. In May Gov. Nelson A. Rockefeller of
New York announced he had donated his collection
of primitive art to the Metropolitan Museum of Art in
New York City. In September, the Metropolitan announced that its late chairman, Robert Lehman, who
had died on Aug. 9, had bequeathed his collection,
valued at more than $100,000,000, to the museum.
Other notables who died this year included Max Eastman, poet and author, Mar. 25, at 86; Judy Garland,
singer and actress, June 22, at 47; Walter Gropius,
founder of the Bauhaus school of design, July 5, at 86;
Jack Kerouac, Beat novelist, Oct. 21, at 47; Frank
Loesser, songwriter and composer, July 28, at 59;
Giovanni Martinelli, tenor for the Metropolitan
Opera for 33 years, Feb. 22, at 83; Ludwig Mies van

der Rohe, architect, Aug. 17, at 83; Drew Pearson, columnist, Sept. 1, at 71; Ben Shahn, painter, Mar. 14, at 70; and Gladys Swarthout, mezzo-soprano for the Metropolitan Opera from 1929 to 1945, July 7, at 64.

Among **books published** this year was *Naked Came the Stranger* by Penelope Ashe, a randy novel actually written in collaboration by 24 writers of the Long Island, N.Y., newspaper *Newsday*. Deliberately written as trash, it nonetheless made the best-seller list. Other books published this year included *Ernest Hemingway: A Life Story* by Carlos Baker; *Bullet Park* by John Cheever, a novel; *Henry James: The Treacherous Years 1895–1901* by Leon Edel, volume four in Edel's biography of James; *In This House of Brede* by Rumer Godden, a novel of life in an English convent; *An Unfinished Woman* by Lillian Hellman, autobiography; *Ada* by Vladimir Nabokov, a novel; *The Godfather* by Mario Puzo; *Portnoy's Complaint* by Philip Roth, a novel that became the year's publishing sensation; *Slaughterhouse-Five* by Kurt Vonnegut, Jr., a novel dealing with the Allied bombing of Dresden during World War II; and *The Making of the President 1968* by Theodore White.

Jan 5: The **Bollingen Prize** for poetry was awarded jointly to John Berryman for his 1968 collection *His Toy, His Dream, His Rest* and to Karl Shapiro for his 1968 volume of *Selected Poems*.

Feb 8: The last issue of the *Saturday Evening Post* was published. The magazine was first published on Aug. 4, 1821, but Cyrus H. K. Curtis, after acquiring it in 1898, claimed it had been "founded in 1728 by B. Franklin." In the 1970s the magazine was resurrected and issued nine times a year. The new publication lacked many of its predecessor's most attractive qualities.

Apr 7: Obscenity laws prohibiting the private possession of obscene materials were ruled unconstitutional by the U.S. Supreme Court. Justice Thurgood Marshall wrote: "Our whole constitutional heritage rebels at the thought of giving government the power to control men's minds."

May 5: Pulitzer prizes were awarded for the following: fiction, *House Made of Dawn* by N. Scott Momaday; general nonfiction, *So Human an Animal* by René Dubos and *The Armies of the Night* by Norman Mailer; biography, *The Man from New York: John Quinn and His Friends* by B. L. Reid; history, *Origins of the Fifth Amendment* by Leonard W. Levy; poetry, *Of Being Numerous* by George Oppen; drama, *The Great White Hope* by Howard Sackler.

III. Business and Industry
Education
Philosophy and Religion
Science

The U.S. economy continued to show danger signs. Inflation had not been adequately checked, and a recession threatened. The GNP rose to $932,300,000,000, about a 7.7% increase. Averaged over the year, the Consumer Price Index rose a sharp 7.2%. In an effort to fight inflation, the Federal Reserve Board acted to impose monetary restraint; by June 9 the prime lending rate had reached a record high of 8.5%. In science, the flights of Apollo 11 and Apollo 12 to the moon dwarfed all other achievements. These manned missions, exploring for the first time a heavenly body other than Earth, caused 1969 to be popularly called the year of the moon. The year in education was marked by increased unrest on college campuses as students watched the government's failure to bring the Vietnam War to an end or to address domestic problems. Notables who died this year included John L. Lewis, president of the United Mine Workers from 1920 to 1960, June 11, at 79; Willy Ley, science writer, June 24, at 62; and Bishop James A. Pike, the controversial Episcopal leader who was charged with heresy in 1966 and left the church in Apr. 1969. Pike died, probably on Sept. 3, after his car broke down in the desert in Israel. He was 56.

Jan 16: The first synthesized enzyme, ribonuclease, was announced by Merck Laboratories and Rockefeller University. It was produced by teams of scientists working independently at the two institutions.

Jan 20: The first optical identification of a **pulsar,** a dense neutron star, was announced by astronomers at the University of Arizona, who located such a body in the Crab Nebula.

Jan 29: The federal deadline for **school desegregation** was extended 60 days for five southern school districts before federal funds would be cut off. This reprieve was widely interpreted as a sign that the Nixon administration was not committed to enforcing integration.

Feb 14: The longest **dock strike** to date, a 57-day strike of Port of New York dock workers, which had begun on Dec. 20, 1968, was ended with agreement on a new three-year contract. But 43,000 other members of the International Longshoremen's Association continued to strike, closing ports along the Atlantic and Gulf coasts until Apr. 2.

Feb 25: Mariner 6 was successfully launched toward Mars. On July 30 it passed within 2120 miles of the Martian surface, sending back 74 photographs.

Mar 3: Apollo 9, manned by James A. McDivitt, Russell L. Schweickart, and David R. Scott, was successfully launched into Earth orbit on a ten-day mission to test the Lunar Excursion Module (LEM). Apollo 9 splashed down on Mar. 13.

Mar 27: Mariner 7 was successfully launched toward Mars. On Aug. 5 it passed over the planet's south pole and sent back 91 photographs.

Apr 4: The world's **first totally artificial heart**—made of Dacron and plastic—was implanted in a human by Dr. Denton A. Cooley in Houston, Tex. The patient died Apr. 8.

May 15: In Berkeley, Calif., the makeshift **People's Park** established by students and area residents on property owned by the University of California was attacked by police and National Guardsmen. Shotguns and tear gas were used. Five days later a National Guard helicopter dropped a stinging chemical powder on demonstrators, including faculty members.

May 18: Apollo 10, the first manned mission to the

moon, was successfully launched. Manned by Thomas P. Stafford, Eugene A. Cernan, and John W. Young, Apollo 10 went into lunar orbit. On May 22 the Lunar Excursion Module (LEM) descended to within ten miles of the moon's surface before returning to the Command Module. Apollo 10 returned to Earth and splashed down on May 26.

July 1: A federal **Truth-in-Lending Law** went into effect, requiring that charges for credit and loans be made clear to debtors.

July 3: It was announced that the Sept. 1969 **school desegregation deadline** would be enforced for all southern school districts except those with "bona fide educational and administrative problems." The next day, the National Education Association voted overwhelmingly to demand restoration of the deadline without modification.

July 16: Apollo 11, manned by Neil A. Armstrong, Edwin E. Aldrin, Jr., and Michael Collins, was successfully launched toward the moon. On July 20 Armstrong and Aldrin entered the Lunar Excursion Module *Eagle* and began the descent to a landing site near the Sea of Tranquillity. Touching down at 4:17 P.M. EDT, it became the first manned vehicle to land on the moon. Armstrong radioed "Houston, Tranquillity Base here. The *Eagle* has landed." About six and a half hours later, Armstrong became the first person to set foot on the moon, saying "That's one small step for [a] man, one giant leap for mankind." Aldrin joined Armstrong. The two spoke via telephone link to Pres. Nixon, set up experiments, and gathered samples of moon rocks during a two-hour moon walk. On July 21 *Eagle* lifted off and docked with the Command Module *Columbia*. Apollo 11 splashed down in the Pacific Ocean on July 24 at 12:50 P.M. EDT.

Aug 8: Pres. Nixon called for a guaranteed **minimum income** for families with children as part of a comprehensive reform of the welfare system.

Sep 14: The **first large vessel to navigate the Northwest Passage** was the SS *Manhattan*, an icebreaking tanker that sailed through the Prince of Wales Strait. The ship, the first commercial vessel to make the journey, had left Chester, Pa., on Aug. 24 and arrived at Point Barrow, Alaska, on Sept. 21. The project tested the feasibility of transporting crude oil by sea from northern Alaska. It cost the three sponsoring oil companies $40,000,000.

Oct 16: The **Nobel Prize for Physiology or Medicine** was awarded jointly to Dr. Max Delbruck of the California Institute of Technology, Dr. Alfred D. Hershey of the Carnegie Institute, Cold Spring Harbor, N.Y., and Dr. Salvador E. Luria of the Massachusetts Institute of Technology for their work on the genetic structure of viruses.

Oct 18: The use of **cyclamates,** artificial sweeteners, was banned by the Department of Health, Education, and Welfare. The ban was modified on Dec. 20 to permit use of specified amounts, except in soft drinks.

Oct 29: The Supreme Court ordered **immediate school desegregation** of the 33 Mississippi school districts for which the federal government had asked a delay. It was the first decision handed down by Chief Justice Warren Burger, who had been appointed by Pres. Nixon.

Oct 30: The **Nobel Prize in Physics** was awarded to Dr. Murray Gell-Mann of the California Institute of Technology for his contribution to the theory of elementary particles.

Nov 14: Apollo 12, manned by Charles Conrad, Jr., Richard F. Gordon, Jr., and Alan L. Bean, was launched on a lunar flight in rainy weather. Some 36.5 sec. after liftoff, it was hit by an electric charge, which briefly knocked out power in the spacecraft but not in the rocket. On Nov. 19 Conrad and Bean became the third and fourth humans to land on the moon when they brought down the *Intrepid,* their Lunar Excursion Module, on the plain of the Ocean of Storms. They made two moon walks, and the next day successfully blasted off to rejoin Gordon in the command ship, the *Yankee Clipper.* Apollo 12 splashed down on Nov. 24, only three miles from the carrier *Hornet.*

Nov 20: In the first step toward total **ban of DDT** by

1971, the U.S. Department of Agriculture ordered a halt to its use in residential areas.

Nov 22: Isolation of a single gene, the basic unit of heredity, was announced by scientists at Harvard University. Their feat promised to facilitate study of the mechanism of gene control.

Dec 2: The **Boeing 747,** which cost $21,400,000 to develop, made its first public flight, from Seattle, Wash., to New York City.

IV. Fashion
   Folkways
   Holidays
   Social Issues and Crime
   Sports

Major league baseball's 100th anniversary was a year of change and excitement. The National League added two teams, San Diego and Montreal, to its roster, and the American League added Kansas City and Seattle. Each league was split into divisions, and playoffs for league pennants were inaugurated. Players refused to report for spring training until owners increased their pension benefits. The outfields of six ball parks were shortened to make it easier to hit home runs and, in a further attempt to spark offensive play, the strike zone was narrowed and the pitcher's mound lowered. Mickey Mantle and Don Drysdale retired. The New York Mets astounded everyone with their first World Series victory. In soccer, the North American Soccer League continued to suffer organizational and financial growing pains. The league championship was won, on the basis of final team standings, by the Kansas City Spurs. In boxing, Joe Frazier twice defended his world heavyweight title, but Jimmy Ellis, recognized champion of the World Boxing Association, fought no championship bouts. In golf, the top money winners were Frank Beard, $175,223, and Carol Mann, $49,153. In fashion, bell-bottom pants were in vogue for women and men. Unisex fashions also became popular. People in the news who died this year included Vito

Genovese, considered the head of U.S. organized crime, Feb. 14, at 71; Walter Hagen, five-time PGA title winner, Oct. 5, at 76; Rocky Marciano, former world heavyweight boxing champion, in a plane crash on Aug. 31, at 46; and Tom Zachary, pitcher for the Washington Senators, Jan. 24, at 72.

Jan 12: **Super Bowl III** was won by the New York Jets (AFL), who defeated the Baltimore Colts (NFL) 16 to 7 to gain the first AFL victory. On Dec. 31, 1968, the Jets had won the AFL championship by beating the Oakland Raiders 27 to 23. The same day the Colts had won the NFL title from the Cleveland Browns, 34 to 0.

Feb 7: The **first woman jockey** to race at a U.S. pari-mutuel track was Diana Crump. At Hialeah, Fla., she rode her first mount to a tenth-place finish in a field of 12.

Feb 22: The **first winning woman jockey** at a U.S. thoroughbred track was Barbara Jo Rubin, with a victory at Charles Town, W. Va.

Mar 22: The **NCAA basketball championship** was won by UCLA, sparked by center Lew Alcindor, defeating Purdue 97 to 92. Alcindor became the first player to win the tourney's Most Valuable Player award three years in a row. Later, the Milwaukee Bucks were reported to have paid $1,200,000 for Alcindor's services during the next five years.

Apr 23-May 5: The **NBA basketball championship** was won by the Boston Celtics, who beat the Los Angeles Lakers four games to three. Following this, his tenth victory in 11 years, Celtics player-coach Bill Russell announced his retirement.

Apr 30-May 7: The **ABA basketball championship** was won by the Oakland Oaks, who beat the Indiana Pacers four games to one.

May 10: Plans for the 1970 **pro football merger** of the AFL and NFL were completed. The new National Football League was to have two conferences of 13 teams each. The old NFL was renamed the National Football Conference (NFC), and three of its teams (Baltimore, Cleveland, and Pittsburgh) were shifted to the new American Football Conference.

June 15: The **U.S. Open golf tournament** was won by

Orville Moody by a single stroke over Deane Beman, Al Geiberger, and Bob Rosburg.

June 21: A new **world pole vault record** was set by John Pennel, who cleared the bar at 17 ft., 10½ in. at a meet at Sacramento, Calif.

Aug 9: Sharon Tate and four others were found, apparently murder victims, at the Los Angeles home of the actress. In December, Charles Manson and several members of his nomadic hippie cult were indicted for the murders.

Aug 13: Bowie Kuhn, temporary commissioner of baseball since February, was formally appointed to that post with a seven-year contract.

Aug 15-18: At the **Woodstock Music and Art Fair,** a weekend folk-rock festival, inadequate planning and bad weather threatened for a time to make a disaster area of the site, Max Yasgur's farm near Bethel. The crowd was estimated at 300,000 to 400,000, and many more failed to reach the fair when traffic jams clogged all roads leading to the Catskill area. Helicopters were pressed into service to supply food, water, and medicine. Rains made a quagmire of the festival grounds. Drugs circulated freely, and a number of people were treated for bad drug reactions. Almost miraculously, there were only three deaths. The police adopted a hands-off posture, and the youths present enjoyed themselves in a general spirit of peace, coöperation, and enthusiasm. While many treated the affair as an idyll, others expressed alarm at the incontrovertible evidence of a mass drug culture.

Aug 17: The **PGA golf tournament** was won by Ray Floyd. The tournament was marred by the behavior of civil rights demonstrators, who harassed Gary Player of South Africa on Aug. 16.

Sep 7-8: The **U.S. Open tennis singles championships** were won by Margaret Smith Court of Australia (Sept. 7) in the women's division and Rod Laver of Australia (Sept. 8) in the men's division. With his victory, Laver completed the grand slam of tennis by winning the top four international championships—the Australian, French, Wimbledon, and U.S. singles titles. Laver had won the grand slam once before, in 1962.

Sep 19-21: The **Davis Cup** was successfully defended by the U.S., defeating Rumania in five straight matches.

Sep 22: San Francisco Giants outfielder **Willie Mays hit his 600th home run,** becoming the only player other than Babe Ruth to reach that mark.

Oct 11-16: The **World Series** was won by the New York Mets (NL), who won four straight games from the Baltimore Orioles (AL) after losing the opener to the Orioles. The Mets had beaten the Atlanta Braves in three straight games to take the National League pennant. The Orioles had swept three games from the Minnesota Twins for the American League pennant.

Oct 18: A new **football field goal record** was set by Chester Marcol of Hillsdale College in Michigan, who kicked a 62-yard field goal, the longest on record for either amateur or pro football.

Dec 11-12: A new **world record decathlon score** of 8417 points was set by Bill Toomey at the Southern Pacific AAU meet at UCLA.

1970

I. Civil Rights
Exploration and Settlement
Government
Statistics
Wars

One of the major problems confronting Pres. Richard M. Nixon and the nation was the faltering economy. Pres. Nixon countered rising inflation and joblessness with fiscal austerity, marked by severe cuts in U.S. aerospace programs. He also proposed a coordinated plan to improve the natural environment.

The president was disappointed in his second attempt to secure Senate approval of a so-called strict constructionist, and a southerner, to fill a vacant Supreme Court seat. Perhaps the most damaging event for the administration was the U.S. military invasion of Cambodia, which Pres. Nixon announced to the American people on Apr. 30. The incident sparked a nationwide shutdown of colleges and universities, violent demonstrations, and deaths on two college campuses. By late December U.S. troop strength in Vietnam had dropped to 340,000. By year's end, the total death toll of U.S. personnel had passed 44,000. Among notables who died this year were Brig. Gen. Benjamin O. Davis, Sr., the first black to attain the rank of general, Nov. 26, at 93; and Rep. L. Mendel Rivers, Democrat of South Carolina, chairman of the House Armed Services Committee, Dec. 28, at 65.

Jan 6: A **heroin-control agreement with France** was announced. It was aimed at halting the illegal production of the drug in France. The diplomatic agreement was part of an effort to halt heroin smuggling into the U.S.

Feb 14: Pres. Nixon, discussing **chemical warfare,** stated that the U.S. would not be the first to use lethal and incapacitating chemicals. He had previously renounced U.S. use of biological weapons.

Feb 26: The Army announced it would discontinue **surveillance of civilian demonstrations** and maintenance of files on civilians who might be involved in civil disturbances.

Mar 5: The **nuclear nonproliferation treaty,** ratified by the U.S., U.S.S.R., and 41 other nations, went into effect.

Apr 1: The 19th U.S. **Census** recorded a preliminary population count approaching 205,000,000.

Apr 8: The nomination of **G. Harrold Carswell** to the U.S. Supreme Court was rejected by the Senate after a prolonged debate. In 1969 the Senate had rejected the nomination of Clement F. Haynsworth, Jr., to the same vacant seat.

Apr 16: The second round of **Strategic Arms Limita-**

tion Talks (SALT) opened in Vienna, Austria. The talks recessed on Aug. 14, both sides agreeing to resume in Helsinki, Finland, on Nov. 2. The third round (Nov. 2-Dec. 8) ended on a less optimistic note than the Vienna round, but a fourth round was scheduled to begin in Vienna on Mar. 15, 1971.

Apr 29: A military **invasion of Cambodia,** called an *incursion* by the White House, was launched by some 50,000 U.S. and South Vietnamese troops. The operation, aimed at destroying Vietcong and North Vietnamese sanctuaries, was announced by Pres. Nixon in a televised address on Apr. 30.

May 4: At **Kent State University** in Kent, Ohio, four students were killed when National Guard troops fired at some 600 antiwar demonstrators, some of whom had been throwing rocks at the guardsmen and taunting them.

May 9: An **antiwar rally in Washington,** D.C., drew some 100,000 protesters to the nation's capital. Similar demonstrations were held in many parts of the country.

May 12: The nomination of Judge **Harry A. Blackmun** of Minnesota to the Supreme Court was approved by the Senate.

May 15: At **Jackson State College** in Jackson, Miss., two students were killed when city and state police opened fire on demonstrators.

June 15: The claim of **conscientious objector status** on moral grounds alone was found constitutional by the Supreme Court in the case of *Welsh v. United States.* Previously such status was granted only on the basis of long-standing religious belief and training.

July 4: Honor America Day was observed in Washington, D.C., as thousands gathered to show support for the administration's war policies.

Sep 22: A bill authorizing **congressional representation for the District of Columbia** through a nonvoting delegate to the House of Representatives was signed by Pres. Nixon. The district had not been represented in Congress since 1875.

Oct 13: Angela Davis, former faculty member at UCLA, black militant, and self-proclaimed communist, was seized in New York City in connection with an Aug. 7 courtroom shootout in San Raphael, Calif., in which a judge and three others were killed. She was wanted on kidnaping, murder, and conspiracy charges.

Oct 15: The **Organized Crime Control Act** was signed by Pres. Nixon, who pledged "total war against organized crime."

Oct 21: The **Nobel Peace Prize** was awarded to Dr. Norman E. Borlaug for his work on high-yield grains to help Third World nations boost food production and overcome the cycle of hunger and poverty.

Nov 2: Strategic Arms Limitation Talks (SALT) between the U.S. and U.S.S.R. were resumed at Helsinki, Finland.

Nov 3: In **congressional elections** the Democrats lost four seats in the Senate but maintained a majority of 54–44, with two seats going to independent and Conservative candidates. In the House the Democrats picked up 12 seats for a 255–180 majority.

Nov 12: The **court-martial of Lt. William L. Calley, Jr.,** a key figure in the massacre of some 102 South Vietnamese civilians at My Lai (Songmy), began at Fort Benning, Ga.

Nov 27: Testimony that an antiwar group called the **East Coast Conspiracy to Save Lives** was planning to kidnap a high government official and blow up the underground heating system for federal buildings in Washington, D.C., was given to a Senate subcommittee by FBI director J. Edgar Hoover. Hoover named Philip and Daniel Berrigan, both priests, as leaders in the plot. The government official was later identified as presidential adviser Henry Kissinger.

Dec 2: The **Environmental Protection Agency,** established in July by executive order, was activated. William D. Ruckelshaus was confirmed the same day as its director.

Dec 21: Reduction of the **voting age** in national elections to 18 years was ruled constitutional by the Supreme Court.

Dec 23: Plans for a speedy **phase-out of herbicide operations** in Indochina were announced by the Nixon administration.

II. Architecture
   Arts and Music
   Popular Entertainment
   Publishing
   Theater

The Broadway theater season was marked by the openings of a few outstanding serious plays, accompanied by an increased interest by both producers and theatergoers in comedies and musicals. The motion picture industry, suffering a financial pinch, reduced its offerings by 25%, but presented viewers with a number of excellent films, including *Catch-22, The Graduate, Patton,* and the rock documentaries *Woodstock,* which recounted the 1969 festival in upstate New York, and *Gimme Shelter,* about the ultimately disastrous 1969 U.S. tour of the Rolling Stones. This year the Metropolitan Museum of Art celebrated its centennial, and George Balanchine, director of the New York City Ballet, celebrated his 50th anniversary as a choreographer. The art world saw another year of record art prices. At the Parke-Bernet Galleries in New York City, Vincent van Gogh's *Le Cyprès et l'Arbe en Fleur* fetched $1,300,000, a record for a van Gogh work. On Nov. 27 Wildenstein Gallery of New York City paid $5,544,000, a record price for a single painting, for a Velázquez portrait. On May 12, 1971, the painting was acquired by the Metropolitan Museum of Art in New York City. On Dec. 10 Parke-Bernet sold Thomas Eakins' *Cowboys in the Badlands* for $210,000, a record for a U.S. painting. Notables who died this year included John Dos Passos, the novelist, Sept. 28, at 74; Erle Stanley Gardner, creator of Perry Mason, Mar. 11, at 80; Reuben Lucius "Rube" Goldberg, whose zany drawings of impossibly complex devices gave birth to the phrase *Rube Goldberg contraption,* Dec. 7, at 87; John Gunther, the author, May 29, at 68; James Marshall "Jimi" Hendrix, rock guitarist, Sept. 18, at 27; Richard Hofstadter, historian, Oct. 24, at 54; Janis Joplin, rock singer, Oct. 4, at 27; Gypsy Rose Lee, real

name Rose Louise Hovick, celebrated striptease artist and author, Apr. 26, at 56; John O'Hara, author,
Apr. 11, at 65; Erich Maria Remarque, German-born
novelist, Sept. 25, at 72; Mark Rothko, painter, Feb.
25, at 66; and George Szell, conductor of the Cleveland Orchestra from 1946, July 30, at 73.

Among **books published** this year was *Everything
You Always Wanted to Know About Sex* by Dr. David
Reuben, just one of a number of books about sex that
became best sellers, including *The Sensuous Woman*
by "J.," *Sexual Politics* by Kate Millett, a feminist
treatment of the battle of the sexes, and *Human Sexual Inadequacy* by the research team of Dr. William
H. Masters and Virginia Johnson. Other books published this year included *Mr. Sammler's Planet* by
Saul Bellow, a novel; *Ball Four* by Jim Bouton, which
took the baseball establishment to task; *Deliverance*
by James Dickey, the poet's first novel; *Islands in the
Stream,* a posthumous novel by Ernest Hemingway;
*You Might as Well Live: The Life and Times of Doro-
thy Parker* by John Keats; *The Art of His Life* by Jay
Martin, a biography of Nathanael West; *Culture and
Commitment* by Margaret Mead; *Zelda* by Nancy Mil-
ford, a biography of Zelda Fitzgerald; *The Greening
of America* by Charles A. Reich; *Hard Times, An Oral
History of the Great Depression* by Studs Terkel; *Bech:
A Book* by John Updike, a novel; and *QB VII* by Leon
Uris, a novel.

May 4: Pulitzer prizes were awarded for the following: fiction, *Collected Stories* by Jean Stafford; biography, *Huey Long* by T. Harry Williams; history, *Present at the Creation: My Years in the State Department*
by Dean G. Acheson; general nonfiction, *Gandhi's
Truth: On the Origins of Militant Non-violence* by Erik
H. Erikson; poetry, *Untitled Subjects* by Richard
Howard.

Oct 11: Natalia Makarova, the prima ballerina with
the Leningrad Kirov Ballet who defected from the
U.S.S.R. in September, joined the American Ballet
Theater.

Dec 23: The north tower of the **World Trade Center** in

New York City was topped out, making it the tallest building in the world. At 1350 ft., it was 100 ft. taller than the Empire State Building.

III. Business and Industry
Education
Philosophy and Religion
Science

The word *recession* crept back into the public vocabulary. The economic policies of Pres. Richard Nixon sought a controlled contraction in the economy, accompanied by reduced industrial output and temporarily higher unemployment to break the inflationary spiral that began some three years earlier. By year's end it was apparent that the brakes had been applied too strongly. On Dec. 4 it was announced that unemployment had risen to 5.8%. Officials began to move to reduce interest rates as a means of stimulating the economy. The space program suffered major cuts in the budget squeeze, and some of the best-known astronauts left the program to pursue other careers. NASA was hurt further by the near-disastrous Apollo 13 lunar mission in April. In education, the year was marked by explosive campus unrest. Pres. Nixon established a Commission on Campus Unrest, which reported that student disorders reflected student opposition to U.S. military activities, concern over racial injustice, and general dissatisfaction with American life. The commission urged Pres. Nixon to use his leadership to bring the nation together. Notables who died this year included Richard Cardinal Cushing of Boston, Nov. 2, at 75; Joseph Wood Krutch, naturalist and author, May 22, at 76; Walter Reuther, president of the United Auto Workers, who died with his wife and four others in a plane crash, May 9, at 62; John T. Scopes, Dayton, Tenn., central figure in the so-called Scopes monkey trial in 1925, Oct. 21, at 70; and Blanche Stuart Scott, a pioneer woman aviator, Jan. 12, at 84.

Jan 5: Joseph Yablonski, unsuccessful candidate for

president of the United Mine Workers, was found murdered in his home along with his wife and daughter.

Jan 14: A Feb. 1, 1970, **deadline for desegregation** of public schools in Alabama, Florida, Georgia, Louisiana, Mississippi, and Tennessee was issued by the Supreme Court, overruling the Sept. 1970 deadline set by a lower court.

Feb 4: An **ion propulsion engine** was launched into orbit aboard the satellite Sert 2 (for Space Electric Rocket Test). The engine was burned continuously for six months.

Feb 18: The **Chicago Seven** were acquitted of conspiracy charges in connection with riots during the 1968 Democratic convention in Chicago. Five were found guilty of crossing a state line with intent to incite a riot. On Feb. 20 they were sentenced to five-year prison terms.

Mar 16: The *New English Bible* was published in its entirety. Translated directly from ancient texts, it was the work of British scholars of the major Protestant churches, who were assisted by a panel of literary experts. It was the subject of debate because its language departed radically from the rich sonorities of the King James Bible.

Mar 18: The **first major postal workers' strike** in U.S. history began. On Mar. 23 Pres. Nixon ordered the National Guard to help alleviate mail delays. The strike ended on Mar. 25.

Apr 1: A **bill banning cigarette advertising** on radio and television, effective Jan. 1, 1971, was signed by Pres. Nixon.

Apr 11: Apollo 13 was successfully launched, carrying astronauts James A. Lovell, Jr., John L. Swigert, Jr., and Fred W. Haise, Jr., toward a lunar landing. The mission seemed to be going perfectly, but on Apr. 13 a tank of liquid oxygen exploded, damaging the spacecraft. The crippled spacecraft continued to the moon, circled it and returned to Earth on Apr. 17. Months later scientists reported that faulty design had caused the problem.

June 4: Use of the drug **L-dopa** for treatment of Parkinson's disease was approved by the Food and Drug Administration.

July 3: No **deaths from polio** were recorded in 1969, the National Communicable Disease Center reported. It was the first year without fatalities since record-keeping began in 1955.

Aug 11: The Rev. **Daniel J. Berrigan,** a Jesuit priest who was a fugitive for four months, was seized by FBI agents. Berrigan, his brother the Rev. Philip F. Berrigan, and seven others had been convicted of burning draft records at Catonsville, Md., in 1968. They were known collectively as the Catonsville Nine.

Sep 6: A **TWA airliner was hijacked** to Jordan by Palestinian terrorists. On Sept. 12 it was blown up along with two other western-owned airplanes.

Sep 30: The *New American Bible* was published in its entirety for the first time. It was the first Roman Catholic-sponsored translation in English created directly from original sources.

Oct 15: The **Nobel Prize in Physiology or Medicine** was awarded jointly to Dr. Julius Axelrod of the National Institute of Mental Health in Bethesda, Md., Sir Bernard Katz of Great Britain, and Ulf von Euler of Sweden for their study of the chemistry of nerves in controlling the vascular system.

Oct 16: The **Nobel Prize in Economics** was awarded to Paul A. Samuelson of MIT. It was the second such award, and the first won by an American.

Nov 18: Linus Pauling, the Nobel Prize-winning scientist, reported that high doses of vitamin C could ward off the common cold and the flu. Other scientists held that such doses given over a long period of time could be harmful.

Dec 31: The **National Air Quality Control Act** was signed by Pres. Nixon. It tightened air pollution standards and penalties and called for a 90% reduction in pollution from automobile exhausts by 1975.

IV. Fashion
Folkways
Holidays
Social Issues and Crime
Sports

The year in sports was marked by unrest. Curt Flood, of the St. Louis Cardinals, objected to being traded to the Philadelphia Phillies and brought an antitrust suit against organized baseball over the so-called reserve clause. The sports year was also marked by ever-increasing salaries for top athletes and record cash purses for major sports events. In golf, the top money winners were Lee Trevino, $157,037, and Kathy Whitworth, $30,235. In boxing, Joe Frazier was recognized as the world heavyweight champion, and Muhammad Ali, who had been stripped of the title in 1967, made a comeback with victories over Jerry Quarry (Oct. 26) and Oscar Bonavena (Dec. 7). In soccer the North American Soccer League (NASL) split into two divisions and added New York City and Toronto franchises for the 1971 season. In football, the American Football League added three franchises and became the American Conference of the National Football League. The old NFL roster was reorganized into the National Conference, each conference organized into three divisions. Winners of division playoffs in each conference would go to the Super Bowl. In fashion, many designers pushed the midi style, which dropped the hemline to mid-calf. Youth's influence in dress styles was reflected in such apparel as tie-dyed garments, granny dresses, and secondhand military attire. Americans mourned the passing of Charles "Sonny" Liston, 38, heavyweight boxing champion from 1962 to 1964, about Dec. 28; Vincent Thomas "Vince" Lombardi, celebrated coach of the Green Bay Packers, Sept. 3, at 57; and John J. "Johnny" Murphy, former pitcher for the New York Yankees, Jan. 14, at 61.

Jan 11: Super Bowl IV was won by the Kansas City Chiefs (AFL), who defeated the Minnesota Vikings (NFL) 23 to 7. On Jan. 4 the Chiefs had won the AFL championship by beating the Oakland Raiders 17 to 7. The same day the Vikings took the NFL title by beating the Cleveland Browns 27 to 7.

Feb 16: The **world heavyweight boxing champion-ship** was awarded to Joe Frazier, who knocked out Jimmy Ellis in the fifth round in New York City.

Mar 21: The **NCAA basketball championship** was won for the fourth straight time by UCLA, which defeated Jacksonville University 80 to 69.

Apr 24-May 8: The **NBA basketball championship** was won for the first time in 24 years by the New York Knickerbockers, who beat the Los Angeles Lak-ers four games to three.

May 15-25: The **ABA basketball championship** was won by the Indiana Pacers, who beat the Los Angeles Stars four games to two.

June 18-20: A new **world 440-yard hurdles record** of 48.8 sec. was set at the NCAA outdoor championships by Ralph Mann of Brigham Young University.

June 21: The **U.S. Open golf tournament** was won by Tony Jacklin of Great Britain, beating Dave Hill by five strokes to become the first Englishman to win the tournament in 50 years.

July 4: At the **Wimbledon** tennis championships, the women's doubles title was won by Billie Jean King and Rosemary Casals for the third time in four years. Casals teamed with Ilie Nastase of Rumania to win the mixed doubles title.

Aug 16: The **PGA golf tournament** was won by Dave Stockton, who topped Arnold Palmer and Bob Mur-phy by two strokes.

Aug 29-31: The **Davis Cup** international tennis chal-lenge round was won by the U.S., which swept West Germany in five straight matches.

Sep 2-13: The **U.S. Open tennis singles champion-ships** were won by Ken Rosewall of Australia in the men's division and Margaret Court of Australia in the women's division.

Sep 7: A new **world record for winning mounts** was set by Willie Shoemaker, who broke Johnny Long-den's record by winning his 6033rd race, at Del Mar, Calif.

Sep 12: Dr. **Timothy Leary,** the former educator who became a leading proponent of LSD use, escaped from prison near San Luis Obispo, Calif., and fled to Algeria.

Sep 15-28: The **America's Cup** was successfully defended by the U.S. yacht *Intrepid,* which beat the British challenger *Gretel II* four races to one. In the second race *Gretel II* was disqualified because it collided with *Intrepid* at the beginning of the race, the first such forfeit in the yachting classic's history.

Oct 2: Fourteen members of the **Wichita State University football team** were killed when their chartered plane crashed in the Rocky Mts.

Oct 10-15: The 67th **World Series** was won by the Baltimore Orioles (AL), defeating the Cincinnati Reds four games to one. On Oct. 5 the Orioles had clinched the American League pennant by sweeping the Minnesota Twins in three games; the Reds had taken the National League pennant by beating the Pittsburgh Pirates three straight.

Oct 23: A new **land speed record** of 622.407 mph was set by Gary Gabelich of Long Beach, Calif. He drove a rocket-powered car at the Bonneville Salt Flats in Utah.

Nov 8: A new **football field goal record** of 63 yards was set by Tom Dempsey of the New Orleans Saints in a two-point win over the Detroit Lions.

Nov 14: Forty-three players and coaches of the **Marshall University football team** died when their chartered plane crashed in Kenova, W. Va.

1971

I. **Civil Rights**
   Exploration and Settlement
   Government
   Statistics
   Wars

Pres. Richard Nixon announced in July that he would visit the People's Republic of China and the U.S.S.R. in 1972. The indication that the U.S. and China would move toward normalizing relations profoundly effected international relations. The U.S. continued to disengage from combat in Vietnam, and by December U.S. troop strength in South Vietnam had dropped to 184,000. Opposition to continued American involvement there made itself felt in Washington, D.C., in March, when a bomb planted by the radical Weather Underground exploded in the Capitol. In May thousands of people protesting the war were arrested by police when they attempted to shut down the government by blocking all traffic in the city. In other war-related events, Lt. William L. Calley, Jr. was convicted for his role in the My Lai massacre of 1968. His superiors were exonerated, prompting some to claim Calley was being used as a scapegoat. Pres. Nixon sought funds for the treatment and rehabilitation of Vietnam era veterans who suffered from drug addiction. As the 1972 presidential election approached, Pres. Nixon was faced with challenges for the Republican nomination from Rep. Paul N. McCloskey, Jr., of California, a liberal who sought more rapid deescalation of the war, and Rep. John M. Ashbrook of Ohio, a conservative campaigning to cut deficit spending and eliminate wage and price controls introduced in August. Eleven Democrats were registered for Democratic primaries. The Senate confirmed the nomination of Lewis F. Powell and William H. Rehnquist to the Supreme Court. Notables who died this year included Dean Acheson, former secretary of state, Oct. 12, at 78; Ralph Bunche, diplomat and winner of the 1950 Nobel Peace Prize, Oct. 11, at 67; Thomas E. Dewey, former governor of New York, Mar. 16, at 68; Adm. Thomas C. Hart, USN (ret.), commander in chief of the U.S. Pacific Fleet when Pearl Harbor was bombed, July 4, at 94; Audie Murphy, the most decorated U.S. soldier of World War II, May 28, at 46; Sen. Richard B. Russell, Democrat of Georgia, Jan. 21, at 73; Arthur B. Springarn, president of the NAACP from 1940–1965, Dec. 1, at 93; and Whitney M. Young, Jr., head of the National Urban League from 1961, Mar. 11, at 49.

Jan 12: The Rev. **Philip F. Berrigan** was indicted with five others for conspiring to kidnap presidential adviser Henry Kissinger and to bomb the heating systems of federal buildings in Washington, D.C. Berrigan was serving a sentence for burning draft cards.

Feb 9: An **earthquake** in southern California caused more than $500,000,000 in damage and killed 65 people, including 47 at a Veterans Administration hospital in Sylmar, near San Fernando.

Feb 11: A **treaty banning nuclear weapons from the seabed** beyond the standard 12-mile coastal limit was signed by the U.S. and 62 other nations at ceremonies in Washington, D.C., London, and Moscow. It was to become effective after ratification by 22 nations.

Feb 24: The Supreme Court ruled that **illegally obtained evidence,** generally inadmissible in a criminal trial, could be used to contradict a defendant's voluntary testimony. The decision marked a significant alteration of the Miranda ruling of 1966.

Mar 1: In Washington, D.C., the **Capitol was bombed** by the radical Weather Underground. The device, planted in a restroom in the Senate wing, caused some $300,000 in damage but no injuries.

Mar 8: Draft exemption for conscientious objectors, the Supreme Court ruled, must be based on opposition to all war, not just to the Vietnam War.

Mar 15: The fourth round of **Strategic Arms Limitation Talks** (SALT) between the U.S. and U.S.S.R.

began in Vienna, Austria. On May 28 the conference ended with an agreement to resume talks on July 8 in Helsinki, Finland.

Mar 29: Lt. **William L. Calley, Jr.,** was convicted of the premeditated murder of 22 people during the 1968 massacre of South Vietnamese civilians at My Lai. On Mar. 31 he was sentenced to life imprisonment. Exoneration on Sept. 22 of Calley's superior, Capt. Ernest L. Medina, coupled with the earlier dropping of charges against 11 superior officers, fueled the public outcry that Calley was being used as a scapegoat. On Apr. 1 Pres. Nixon ordered Calley released from the stockade and moved to his quarters at Fort Benning, Ga., pending the appeal process. Nixon announced that he would review Calley's case before sentence was carried out. On Aug. 20 Calley's sentence was reduced to 20 years' imprisonment.

May 3: In what was called the **Mayday antiwar protest** in Washington, D.C., the culmination of several weeks of antiwar activities in the nation's capital, thousands of demonstrators were arrested and confined when they tried to stop government activities by blocking traffic in the city. Most charges were dropped.

June 23: Claude E. Vealey confessed to the Dec. 1969 murders of dissident United Mine Workers leader **Joseph A. Yablonski** and his wife and daughter. In a Washington, Pa., court hearing, he stated he would testify against four others indicted for the murders, including Aubran W. Martin and Paul E. Gilly. On Nov. 12 Martin was convicted; he was sentenced to death the next day. Gilly was convicted on Mar. 1, 1972, and was sentenced to death the following day.

June 30: The **Twenty-sixth Amendment** to the U.S. Constitution, lowering the voting age for all elections to 18, went into effect when Ohio became the 38th state to ratify it.

July 8: The fifth round of the **Strategic Arms Limitation Talks** (SALT) convened in Helsinki, Finland. The talks recessed on Sept. 23 with unofficial reports that the U.S. and U.S.S.R. were approaching agreement on limitation of antiballistic missile (ABM) systems. The talks resumed in Vienna on Nov. 15. On Sept. 30 the two powers signed agreements on ways to reduce the risk of accidental nuclear war.

July 15: A projected **presidential visit to China** before May 1972 was announced by Pres. Nixon. He would be the first president to be received by a Chinese government.

Aug 2: Admission of the People's Republic of China to the UN would not be opposed by the U.S., it was announced. The U.S. also stated it would not agree to depriving Nationalist China of its representation. On Oct. 25 the UN General Assembly voted to admit the People's Republic of China and expel Nationalist China.

Sep 4: In the **worst single airplane crash** to date in the U.S., 111 people were killed when an Alaska Airlines Boeing 727 crashed into a mountain west of Juneau, Alaska.

Sep 9-13: A prison riot at Attica State Correctional Facility, Attica, N.Y., led to the deaths of 43 people. Nine prison guards held hostage and 28 prisoners were killed when some 1500 state police and other law enforcement officers staged an air and ground assault to end the uprising.

Sep 26: Japanese Emperor **Hirohito** was greeted by Pres. Nixon at Anchorage, Alaska, in the first foreign trip ever undertaken by a Japanese emperor. It was also the first meeting of a U.S. president and a Japanese monarch.

Dec 6: The nomination of **Lewis F. Powell, Jr.,** to the Supreme Court was approved by the Senate. Powell succeeded Justice Hugo L. Black, who resigned on Sept. 17 and died a week later.

Dec 10: The nomination of **William H. Rehnquist** to the Supreme Court was approved by the Senate. Rehnquist succeeded Justice John M. Harlan, who had resigned on Sept. 23.

Dec 26-30: Massive air bombardment of military installations in North Vietnam resumed. The heaviest attack since the Nov. 1968 bombing halt was conducted by U.S. Navy and Air Force planes.

II. Architecture
Arts and Music
Popular Entertainment
Publishing
Theater

The Broadway season offered few new shows, and museums reduced their hours of operation. The big publishing story of the year was the leak to *The New York Times* of a top secret Pentagon study of U.S. involvement in Vietnam. The series of excerpts that came to be known as the Pentagon Papers prompted heated debate over the newspaper's right to publish sensitive documents and the federal government's need to protect the documents. The motion picture industry continued to experience hard times as fewer pictures were produced by the major studios, even though more independent productions were filmed on location throughout the country. Film makers reported that sexually explicit films, which had been the rage for a time, were losing their box office appeal. Americans mourned the deaths of Duane Allman, rock guitarist, Oct. 29, at 24; Louis Daniel "Satchmo" Armstrong, the gravel-voiced jazz singer and trumpeter, July 6, at 71; Margaret Bourke-White, internationally renowned photographer, Aug. 27, at 67; Walter Van Tilburg Clark, author of *The Ox-Bow Incident* (1940), Nov. 10, at 62; Rockwell Kent, artist and illustrator, Mar. 13, at 88; Ted Lewis, real name Theodore L. Friedman, band leader and entertainer, Aug. 25, at 80; Harold Lloyd, comic genius of the silent film, Mar. 8, at 77; James Douglas "Jim" Morrison, rock singer, July 3, at 27; Ogden Nash, poet, known best for his humorous verse, May 19, at 68; Elmo Roper, pioneer pollster, Apr. 30, at 70; and Igor Stravinsky, the Russian-born composer, Apr. 6, at 88.

Among **books published** this year was *The Vantage Point* by former Pres. Lyndon Johnson. In these memoirs, Johnson recalled the events of his years in the White House and discussed many of the details that were revealed this year by *The New York Times* in the Pentagon Papers scandal. Other books published this year included *The Exorcist* by William

Peter Blatty, a shocker that was the basis for an enormously successful motion picture; *Bury My Heart at Wounded Knee* by Dee Brown, an account of the virtual destruction of American Indian society between 1860 and 1890; *The Book of Daniel* by E. L. Doctorow, a novel based on the Rosenberg spy case; *Eleanor and Franklin: The Story of Their Relationship Based on Eleanor Roosevelt's Private Papers* by Joseph P. Lash; *The Tenants* by Bernard Malamud, a novel; *Wonderland*, a novel by Joyce Carol Oates; *Honor Thy Father* by Gay Talese, a firsthand account of the life of an organized crime family; *The Other* by Thomas Tryon, a novel of the supernatural; *Rabbit Redux* by John Updike, a sequel to *Rabbit Run* (1960); *Meet Me in the Green Glen* by Robert Penn Warren, a novel; and *The Winds of War* by Herman Wouk, a massive novel of the early years of World War II.

Jan 10: The **Bollingen Prize** for poetry was awarded jointly to Richard Wilbur and to Mona Van Duyn for their contributions to American poetry.

May 3: Pulitzer prizes were awarded for the following: biography, *Robert Frost: The Years of Triumph, 1915–1938* by Lawrence R. Thompson; history, *Roosevelt, The Soldier of Freedom* by James McGregor Burns; general nonfiction, *The Rising Sun* by John Toland; poetry, *The Carriers of Ladders* by W.S. Merwin; drama, *The Effect of Gamma Rays on Man-in-the-Moon Marigolds* by Paul Zindel.

June 13: The first installment of what came to be known as the **Pentagon Papers,** excerpts from the Pentagon study *History of the U.S. Decision-making Process on Vietnam Policy,* was published in *The New York Times.* Publication of the documents was halted in federal court, but the decision was reversed on June 30 by the Supreme Court. On June 28 a former Defense Department official, Dr. Daniel Ellsberg, admitted that he had given the documents to the *Times.* He was subsequently indicted for theft and possession of secret documents.

July 21: *Fiddler on the Roof* became the longest-running Broadway musical, its 2845 performances surpassing the record set by *Hello, Dolly!*

III. Business and Industry
Education
Philosophy and Religion
Science

Projected GNP figures were off, unemployment was up to 6%, and inflation rose above 4% for the year. For the first time in the twentieth century imports exceeded exports. In August Pres. Richard M. Nixon announced a plan to control wages and prices, coupled with devaluation of the dollar to improve the U.S. balance of trade. In education, the National Science Foundation reported federal aid to colleges and universities was the lowest since 1966 and forecast an oversupply of scientists and engineers with Ph.D. degrees by 1980. The National Education Association reported that teacher demand was the lowest in 20 years. Despite serious cuts in NASA's budget, the U.S. completed two more manned lunar landings and launched Mariner 9 on its way to a Mars orbit. Late in the year Mariner sent back the first of many photographs of the surface of the planet. Back on Earth, underwater research produced a practical system for the recovery of manganese nodules from the ocean bottom, and at the California Institute of Technology, scientists reported they had successfully tested Albert Einstein's General Theory of Relativity. Notables who died this year included Philo T. Farnsworth, pioneer in the development of television, Mar. 11, at 64; Reinhold Niebuhr, Protestant theologian, June 1, at 78; James Cash Penney, founder of the J. C. Penney department store chain, Feb. 12, at 95; and David Sarnoff, a pioneer in television broadcasting, Dec. 12, at 80.

Jan 25: In its first decision on **sex discrimination in hiring** practices, the Supreme Court upheld the equal hiring provisions of the 1964 Civil Rights Act by ruling that businesses could not deny employment to women with preschool children unless they applied the same hiring criteria to men.

Jan 31: Apollo 14, manned by Alan B. Shepard, Jr., Edgar D. Mitchell, and Stuart A. Roosa, was successfully launched. After initial problems in docking the lunar and command modules, the mission proceeded to a successful lunar landing (Feb. 5–6). Apollo 14 returned to Earth on Feb. 9, bringing back more than 100 lbs. of rock for study.

Mar 2: William A. "Tony" Boyle, president of the United Mine Workers, was indicted on charges of conspiracy, embezzlement, and illegal campaign contributions.

Mar 29: Development of an apparently effective **serum hepatitis vaccine** for children was announced by the New York University Research Center.

Apr 14: Pres. Nixon announced the lifting of a **trade embargo** with the People's Republic of China, which had existed for more than 20 years.

Apr 20: The use of **school busing** to end racial segregation in public school systems was ruled constitutional by the Supreme Court.

May 1: Amtrak, also known as the National Railroad Passenger Corporation, began operation. It was to provide service by 182 trains to more than 300 cities.

May 8: Mariner 8 fell into the Atlantic Ocean after the launch vehicle's second-stage booster failed.

May 30: Mariner 9 was successfully launched from Cape Kennedy, Fla., toward a Mars orbit on Nov. 12. After achieving orbit, it began to send back spectacular pictures of the Martian surface as well as shots of the two moons of Mars.

June 28: State programs to underwrite **nonreligious instruction in parochial schools** were ruled unconstitutional by the Supreme Court.

July 1: The **U.S. Postal Service,** the semi-independent corporation organized to replace the Post Office Department, was officially inaugurated at the White House in Washington, D.C.

July 26: Apollo 14, manned by astronauts David R. Scott, James B. Irwin, and Alfred M. Worden, was successfully launched. Scott and Irwin were the fourth team to land on the moon (July 30-Aug. 2). They traveled 17.3 miles on the lunar surface using a four-wheeled lunar rover and collected what appeared to be a fragment of the moon's original crust.

Nicknamed Genesis rock, it was later found to be about 4,000,000,000 years old. Apollo 14 splashed down in the Pacific on Aug. 7.

Aug 2: A **federal bailout of Lockheed** Aircraft Corporation was authorized by Congress, which passed by a narrow margin a $250,000,000 loan guarantee for the aerospace giant's TriStar airbus program. The guarantee was officially approved by the administration on Sept. 9.

Sep 29: The **Orbiting Solar Observatory VII** was launched to study a solar flare through x-ray observations.

Oct 14: The **Nobel Prize in Physiology or Medicine** was awarded to Dr. Earl W. Sutherland of Vanderbilt University for his work with hormones.

Oct 15: The **Nobel Prize in Economics** was awarded to Simon Kuznets, formerly a professor at Harvard University, who pioneered the use of the gross national product as a means of measuring economic output.

IV. Fashion
  Folkways
  Holidays
  Social Issues and Crime
  Sports

Sports and politics found common ground this year when a team of U.S. table tennis players was invited to China in April for an impromptu tournament. They lost to the Chinese players but their presence in China, combined with the relaxation of U.S. foreign policy toward the People's Republic, led many to speak hopefully of an era of Ping-Pong diplomacy. This year Billie Jean King became the first woman athlete in history to win more than $100,000 in a year. In golf the top money winners were Jack Nicklaus, $244,490, and Kathy Whitworth, $41,182. Lee Trevino became the fourth U.S. golfer to win both the U.S. and British Open tournaments in the same year. In fashion, skirt lengths settled at just below the knee for daytime and just above the ankle for evening. Both blue denim and leather were popular, and short-shorts were jazzed up and renamed *hot pants*. A fad for 1940s styles reflected nostalgia for what some thought of as a simpler time. Among those who died this year were Robert T. "Bobby" Jones, great golfer, Dec. 18, at 69; Nathan Leopold, who was convicted with Richard Loeb for the "thrill murder" of Bobby Franks in 1924, Aug. 28, at 66; and Joseph Valachi, the crime figure who testified in Senate hearings in 1963 about the workings of Cosa Nostra, Apr. 3, at 66.

Jan 17: Super Bowl V was won in the last five seconds by the Baltimore Colts (AFC), who beat the Dallas Cowboys (NFC) 16–13 on a field goal by Jim O'Brien. On Jan. 3 the Colts had beaten the Oakland Raiders 27–17 to win the AFC championship and the Cowboys had topped the San Francisco 49ers 17–10 for the NFC championship.

Jan 25: Charles Manson was convicted, along with Susan Atkins, Leslie Van Houten, and Patricia Krenwinkel, of the 1969 murders of actress Sharon Tate and six others. On Apr. 19 they were sentenced to death. On Oct. 21 Charles Watson was also sentenced to death for the murders.

Feb 28: The **PGA golf tournament** was won by Jack Nicklaus, beating Billy Casper by three strokes.

Mar 8: The **world heavyweight boxing championship** was defended by Joe Frazier in a unanimous 15-round decision over Muhammad Ali. The fight, one of the richest sports events in history, grossed nearly $20,000,000, largely through receipts from closed-circuit television.

Mar 27: The **NCAA basketball championship** was won for the fifth straight year by UCLA, who beat Villanova 68 to 62.

Apr 8: The first legal **off-track betting** (OTB) system in the U.S. went into operation in New York City.

Apr 30: The **NBA basketball championship** was won by the Milwaukee Bucks in a four-game sweep over the Baltimore Bullets.

May 18: The **ABA basketball championship** was won by the Utah Stars, who beat the Kentucky Colonels four games to three.

June 21: The **U.S. Open golf tournament** was won by Lee Trevino, who beat Jack Nicklaus by two strokes in a playoff. On July 10 Trevino won the British Open, becoming the fourth U.S. player to win both championships in the same year.

June 28: Muhammad Ali won a four-year legal battle when the Supreme Court overturned his 1967 conviction for draft evasion.

July 3: At the **Wimbledon** tennis championships, the women's doubles title was won for the second year in a row by Billie Jean King and Rosemary Casals. King teamed with Owen Davidson of Australia to win the mixed doubles title.

Aug 21: George Jackson, 29, one of three black convicts known as the Soledad Brothers after being charged with the murder of a guard at Soledad prison in California, was killed while attempting to escape from San Quentin. Two convicts and three guards were also killed in the attempted mass breakout. Jackson's prison writings had been collected in *Soledad Brother* (1970).

Sep 5-15: The **U.S. Open tennis singles championships** were won by Stan Smith in the men's division and Billie Jean King in the women's division. It was the first time in 16 years both titles were won by U.S. players.

Sep 21: The **Washington Senators,** often fondly described by baseball fans as "first in war, first in peace, and last in the American League," would move to Texas for the 1972 season, it was announced. The team would be renamed the Texas Rangers.

Oct 8-11: The **Davis Cup** international tennis challenge round was won by the U.S., defeating Rumania three matches to two. This year it was decided to abolish the challenge round. Beginning in 1972, the defending team would be required to play through the entire competition.

Oct 9-17: The 68th annual **World Series** was won by the underdog Pittsburgh Pirates (NL), who beat the Baltimore Orioles (AL) four games to three. On Oct. 5 Baltimore had completed a three-game sweep over the Oakland Athletics to take the American League championship. On Oct. 6 the Pirates had clinched the National League pennant, beating the San Francisco Giants three games to one.

Oct 26: Bobby Fischer became the first U.S. chess player to make his way through the elimination matches for the world chess championship. Fischer defeated Tigran Petrosian of the U.S.S.R. in Buenos Aires, Argentina, thus qualifying for competition against Boris Spassky, the world champion, in 1972.

Oct 30: A new **college football rushing record** was set by Ed Marinaro of Cornell University, who scored a three-year career total of 4132 yards.

1972

I. Civil Rights
  Exploration and Settlement
  Government
  Statistics
  Wars

Pres. Richard M. Nixon enhanced his already substantial chances for reelection with trips to the People's Republic of China in February and to the U.S.S.R. in May. These successes were capped in October when two key strategic arms (SALT) agreements were signed. The Paris peace talks stalled when U.S. representatives walked out, claiming the North Vietnamese were not working for a settlement. On Mar. 30 North Vietnam moved into South Vietnam through the DMZ and from Cambodia. This was met by heavy air bombardment of North Vietnam. After initial losses, South Vietnamese forces began to turn back the North Vietnamese. On Apr. 27 the Paris talks resumed. Despite stepped-up air support for South Vietnamese military actions, U.S. disengagement continued. The last U.S. ground combat troops were withdrawn in August. On the eve of the presidential election, Henry Kissinger, security adviser to Pres. Nixon, reported that a Vietnam peace settlement was close. The Democratic Party proved unable to support its candidate, Sen. George S. McGovern of South Dakota, who had vowed to end the U.S. military presence in Vietnam within 90 days of his inauguration. McGovern also supported cuts in defense spending and proposed amnesty for those who had chosen prison or exile over military service in Vietnam. McGovern's charges of corruption in the Nixon administration, including the role of administration officials in the Watergate affair, failed to influence the electorate. Notables who died this year included J. Edgar Hoover, head of the FBI from 1924, May 2, at 77; and the Rev. Adam Clayton Powell, Jr., controversial Baptist minister and congressman from New York (1945–1970), Apr. 4, at 63.

Feb 4: The sixth round of the **Strategic Arms Limitation Talks** (SALT) in Vienna, Austria, begun on Nov. 15, 1971, ended with indications of progress. The seventh round opened in Helsinki, Finland, on Mar. 28 and led to the strategic arms agreements signed in Moscow on May 26.

Feb 21-28: A historic **presidential visit to China** was undertaken by Pres. Nixon. In the Shanghai Communiqué (Feb. 27), the two nations agreed to work to lessen the risk of war, to normalize relations, and to increase scientific and cultural ties. The Chinese held that Taiwan was part of China. The U.S. acknowledged that there was one China and stated that its policy was to withdraw U.S. military forces from Taiwan as tensions in the area decreased.

Mar 22: The **Twenty-seventh, or Equal Rights, Amendment** to the Constitution, prohibiting discrimination on the basis of sex, was passed by the Senate and sent to the states for ratification. Hawaii was the first to ratify. By the end of the year, 22 of the required 38 states had ratified it.

Mar 22: The **National Commission on Marijuana and Drug Abuse** urged an end to criminal penalties for the private possession and use of marijuana.

Apr 7: The **Federal Election Campaign Act** went into effect. The law set limits on advertising budgets and on candidates' financing of their own campaigns. It also required disclosure of contributors of more than $100.

Apr 10: A treaty banning **biological warfare** was signed by the U.S. and some 120 other nations.

May 8: The **mining of Haiphong harbor** and other major North Vietnamese ports was ordered by Pres. Nixon.

May 15: Alabama Gov. **George C. Wallace was shot** in Laurel, Md., by Arthur Bremer, 21, while campaigning in Maryland's Democratic presidential primary. Wallace was paralyzed from the waist down; three others were seriously injured.

May 22-30: The **first presidential visit to Moscow** in history was made by Pres. Nixon. U.S. and Soviet officials signed a number of agreements, including one for a joint space flight in 1975. On May 26 Pres. Nixon and secretary Leonid I. Brezhnev signed a treaty on antiballistic missile systems and an interim agreement on limitation of strategic missiles.

June 4: Angela Davis, the black militant, was acquitted in San Jose, Calif., of abetting a 1970 courtroom escape attempt that left four people dead.

June 17: In what became known as the **Watergate affair,** police arrested five men involved in a burglary of Democratic Party headquarters in the Watergate apartment complex in Washington, D.C. Among the five was James McCord, a former CIA agent then working for the Republican National Committee and the Committee to Reelect the President. Democratic Party Chairman Larry O'Brien, charging Pres. Nixon's campaign staff with "political espionage," filed a $1,000,000 civil suit on June 20.

June 19-23: Hurricane Agnes swept the East Coast, killing 127 and causing more than $1,000,000,000 in damage.

June 29: State death penalties were ruled unconstitutional by the Supreme Court, which held that they constituted cruel and unusual punishment.

July 10-14: The **Democratic National Convention nominated Sen. George S. McGovern** of South Dakota for president and Sen. Thomas F. Eagleton of Missouri for vice president. On July 25 Eagleton confirmed rumors that he had received psychiatric treatment three times from 1960 to 1966 for nervous exhaustion and fatigue. On July 31 Eagleton withdrew from the campaign. On Aug. 8, R. Sargent Shriver, former head of the Peace Corps, succeeded Eagleton on the ticket.

Aug 3: The **Strategic Arms Limitation Treaty** (SALT I) was passed by the U.S. Senate. The treaty limited the U.S. and U.S.S.R. to two antiballistic missile systems of 100 missiles each, one for defense of each nation's capital, one for defense of a portion of its ICBM system. A five-year interim agreement on limitation of strategic arms was approved by the House on Aug. 18 and by the Senate on Sept. 14. The two accords were signed in ceremonies at the White House on Oct. 3.

Aug 4: **Arthur Bremer** was convicted on nine counts in the May 15 shootings of Gov. George C. Wallace of Alabama and three others. He was sentenced to 63 years in prison.

Aug 12: The **last U.S. ground combat forces** in Vietnam were withdrawn.

Aug 21-23: The **Republican National Convention nominated Pres. Nixon** and Vice Pres. Spiro T. Agnew for reelection.

Aug 29: Pres. Nixon announced that a **White House investigation** of the Watergate break-in, conducted by White House counsel John Dean, revealed that administration officials were not involved in the burglary.

Sep 5: In what was known as the **trial of the Harrisburg Seven,** federal prosecutors moved to drop all conspiracy charges against the Rev. Philip F. Berrigan and six others accused of plotting to kidnap Henry Kissinger and blow up heating tunnels in Washington, D.C. The trial against the seven in Harrisburg, Pa., had ended in a hung jury.

Sep 15: In the **Watergate break-in** case, a federal grand jury indicted the five originally accused of burglary and former White House aides G. Gordon Liddy and E. Howard Hunt.

Oct 12-13: A **racial brawl on the carrier** *Kitty Hawk* off the coast of Vietnam left some 46 sailors injured. In November the carrier *Constellation* returned to port after more than 100 seamen protested what they termed racist actions by officers. On Nov. 10 Adm. Elmo R. Zumwalt, chief of naval operations, reprimanded some 90 naval officers and demanded an end to racist behavior in the Navy.

Nov 7: Richard M. Nixon was reelected president of the United States in the greatest Republican landslide in history. Spiro T. Agnew was reelected vice president. The electoral vote was Nixon, 521; Sen. George S. McGovern, Democrat, 17. The popular vote was Nixon, 45,767,218; McGovern 28,357,668. The Democrats picked up two Senate seats for a 57–43 majority. The Republicans gained 13 seats in the House, but the Democrats still led 255–179, with one seat going to an independent.

Nov 22: A 22-year-old **ban on travel to China** was lifted.

Dec 18: Full-scale bombing of North Vietnam was resumed after the Paris peace negotiations reached an impasse. The bombing was again halted on Dec. 30. Private talks were to resume on Jan. 8, 1973.

II. Architecture
   Arts and Music
   Popular Entertainment
   Publishing
   Theater

This year the publishing world was rocked by a hoax. The giant McGraw-Hill Company had paid Clifford Irving $750,000 for *The Autobiography of Howard Hughes,* supposedly based on some 100 talks with the reclusive billionaire. After telephone calls by a person claiming to be Hughes, the scheme began to unravel. Irving and his wife pleaded guilty to the hoax on Mar. 14, two weeks before the planned, but aborted, publication date of the book. In the art world, museum management came under fire for a practice called deaccessioning, the selling or trading of art works. Thomas Hoving of the Metropolitan Museum in New York City defended the practice as a way to improve collections. Critics charged the transactions put into private hands works that artists and donors had intended for public view. This year's theater season was noted for its numerous revivals, among them *A Funny Thing Happened on the Way to the Forum*. The music world also offered revivals, with a reemergence of '50s rock 'n' roll, ragtime music, and the big band sound of Benny Goodman and Duke Ellington. Many of Hollywood's film offerings were noted for their brutality, among them *The French Connection* and *The Godfather*. Notables who died this year included the poet John Berryman, a suicide, Jan. 7, at 57; Rudolf Friml, composer, Nov. 12, at 93; Ferde Grofé, composer of the *Grand Canyon Suite*, Apr. 3, at 80; Gabriel Heatter, the newscaster, Mar. 30, at 81; Mahalia Jackson, gospel singer, Jan. 27, at 60; José Limón, dancer, Dec. 2, at 64; Marianne Moore, poet, Feb. 5, at 84; Kenneth Patchen, poet, Jan. 1, at 60; Ezra Pound, poet, Nov. 1, at 87; Ted Shawn, dancer, Jan. 9, at 80; Helen Traubel, Wagnerian soprano, July 28, at 69; Edmund Wilson, author and critic, June 12, at 77; and Walter Winchell, columnist and broadcaster, Feb. 20, at 74.

Among **books published** this year was *August 1914* by Alexander Solzhenitsyn, a novel of the first weeks of World War I and culminating in the Russian defeat in the Battle of Tannenberg. Other books published included a slim volume by Richard Bach entitled *Jonathan Livingston Seagull*, a phenomenal best seller; *Delusions, Etc.*, poems by John Berryman; *The Late John Marquand* by Stephen Birmingham, a biography; *Captains and the Kings* by Taylor Caldwell, a novel; *The Best and the Brightest* by David Halberstam, an account of the Kennedy administration and the early years of American involvement in the Vietnam War; *The Boys of Summer* by Roger Kahn, a nostalgic look at the old Brooklyn Dodgers; *Eleanor and Franklin* by Joseph P. Lash, a study of the Roosevelts; *The Human Season: Selected Poems, 1926–1972* by Archibald MacLeish; and *The Optimist's Daughter* by Eudora Welty, a novel.

Jan 17: A report on TV violence by the surgeon general found little effect on children but found it harmful to people predisposed to aggressive behavior. Critics said the report was slanted in favor of the TV industry.

May 1: Pulitzer prizes were awarded for the following: fiction, *Angle of Repose* by Wallace Stegner; biography, *Eleanor and Franklin: The Story of Their Relationship* by Joseph P. Lash; history, *Neither Black nor White* by Carl N. Degler; general nonfiction, *Stilwell and the American Experience in China* by Barbara W. Tuchman; poetry, *Collected Poems* by James Wright.

June 29: In a landmark decision bearing on **freedom of the press,** the Supreme Court ruled that journalists have no right to withhold confidential information from grand juries. On Oct. 4 Peter Bridge of the Newark *News* became the first reporter to be jailed under this decision.

July 8-9: The largest **rock festival** since the 1969 Woodstock event drew some 200,000 rock music lovers to Pocono International Raceway at Long Pond, Pa.

Dec 29: *Life* magazine, a pioneer in photojournalism, suspended publication after 36 years of weekly publication.

III. Business and Industry
Education
Philosophy and Religion
Science

The inflationary spiral appeared to be coming under control. Unemployment was down, as was inflation, and economic growth was up. The economy's record was the best since 1967, and in November the Dow Jones average hit 1000 for the first time in history. The number of government employees had not risen and, for the first time in a decade, the number of agricultural workers had not dropped. Nevertheless, businessmen worried about the federal deficit, and many labor leaders withdrew from the Federal Pay Board, charging that wages were being more carefully monitored than prices. The big economic news was the $750,000,000 wheat sale to the U.S.S.R., prompting charges that grain dealers had known about the impending sale and had bought up grain at low prices, thus making big profits at farmers' expense. In medicine the leading topic was acupuncture, the Chinese practice of achieving anesthesia by inserting needles at specific points on the body. In transportation, the rise in airline hijackings sparked an international strike by pilots, which prompted U.S. officials to institute stricter airport screening procedures. Notables who died this year included Saul Alinsky, social activist, June 12, at 63; Lillian Gilbreth, a pioneer in time-motion studies, Jan. 2, at 93; Paul Goodman, writer and social critic, Aug. 2, at 60; Howard Johnson, founder of the restaurant chain bearing his name, June 20, at 75; Igor Sikorsky, developer of the helicopter, Oct. 26, at 83; Harlow Shapley, astronomer, Oct. 20, at 86; and Joseph F. Smith, Jr., president of the Church of Jesus Christ of Latter Day Saints, July 2, at 95.

Jan 11: A **stock-ordering scandal** rocked Wall Street when Abraham Treff, a college student, revealed he had violated a New York Stock Exchange "know your customer" rule by placing more than $200,000 in telephone orders through six member firms in Philadelphia without depositing any cash for the transactions.

Jan 14: Plans were announced for the **first breeder reactor,** a nuclear reactor that produces more fuel than it consumes. It was to be built in Tennessee by a consortium of government and private organizations.

Feb 5: In a move to prevent **airplane hijacking,** screening of passengers and their luggage became mandatory on all domestic and foreign flights by U.S. scheduled airlines.

Mar 1: The Supreme Court ruled that the **Federal Trade Commission** could extend its traditional authority in antitrust cases and bar unfair or deceptive marketing practices.

Mar 1: In the **Yablonski murder case,** Paul Gilly was convicted for the 1970 murders of United Mine Workers (UMW) dissident Joseph Yablonski, his wife, and his daughter. Gilly was sentenced to death the next day. On Apr. 11 Gilly's wife pleaded guilty and implicated several UMW leaders, including its president, William A. "Tony" Boyle. On May 2 Albert Pass, a union official, was arrested; on the following day, Tennessee local president Silous Huddleston confessed to his role in the killings. On Aug. 23 a federal grand jury indicted four union officials—Pass, Chester Philpot, William Prater, and Ernest Stults—and named three others as unindicted co-conspirators.

Mar 2: Pioneer 10 was successfully launched on a 22-month voyage that would take it past Jupiter.

Mar 27: In the wake of a huge **defense contract cost overrun,** Sen. William Proxmire, Democrat of Wisconsin, asked the Justice Department to investigate a report that the Air Force had overpaid $400,000,000 to Lockheed to build the C5-A cargo plane.

Apr 16: Apollo 16, manned by astronauts John W. Young, Charles M. Duke, and Thomas K. Mattingly, was successfully launched into orbit around the moon. On Apr. 20 Duke and Young descended to the moon's surface, remaining there until Apr. 23 to conduct tests and collect rock samples Apollo 16 splashed down on Apr. 27.

May 1: The 1969 election of **William A. "Tony" Boyle** as president of the United Mine Workers was declared void by a federal judge because union funds and facilities had been used in Boyle's campaign. On Dec. 19 Boyle resigned after Arnold Miller, a reform candidate, won a new election.

June 3: The **first woman rabbi in the U.S.,** Sally J. Priesand, 25, was ordained in Cincinnati, Ohio.

July 20: An agreement limiting **railroad featherbedding** settled the longstanding dispute over the use of firemen on railroads. A new contract allowed drastic reductions in the number of jobs, to be achieved by attrition.

July 23: ERTS-1, the first Earth Resources Technology Satellite, was successfully launched into Earth orbit. On July 25 it began sending photographic information about Earth's resources back to scientists on the ground.

Aug 21: Copernicus, an orbiting astronomical observatory designed to study the stars and the nature of the universe, was successfully launched into orbit.

Oct 12: The **Nobel Prize in Physiology or Medicine** was awarded jointly to Gerald M. Edelman of Rockefeller University and Rodney R. Porter of Great Britain for their studies of antibodies.

Oct 18: The **Water Pollution Control Act** was passed by Congress over Pres. Nixon's veto. It required industry to halt discharges by 1985, set industry-wide standards, and provided massive federal funding for building and improving sewage plants.

Oct 20: The **Nobel Prize in Physics** was awarded jointly to John Bardeen of the University of Illinois, Leon N. Cooper of Brown University, and John R. Schrieffer of the University of Pennsylvania for their development of the theory of superconductivity.

Oct 20: The **Nobel Prize in Chemistry** was awarded jointly to Christian B. Anfinsen of the National Institutes of Health, and Stanford Moore and William H. Stein of the Rockefeller Institute for their work in enzyme chemistry, particularly their studies of ribonuclease.

Oct 25: The **Nobel Prize in Economics** was awarded jointly to Kenneth J. Arrow of Harvard University and John R. Hicks of Great Britain.

Nov 13: An international convention to control **oceanic pollution** was signed by the U.S. and 90 other nations.

Nov 14: The **Dow Jones Index** of 30 industrial stocks closed above 1000 on the New York Stock Exchange for the first time in history.

Dec 7: Apollo 17, the sixth and last of the Apollo lunar landing missions, was successfully launched. It was crewed by Eugene Cernan, Ronald Evans, and Harrison Schmitt. During their lunar excursion (Dec. 11–14), Cernan and Schmitt found what they described as orange soil, which was taken to be a possible indication of volcanic activity, and collected some 249 lbs. of rock and soil samples. Apollo 17 splashed down in the Pacific Ocean on Dec. 19.

Dec 31: A near-total **ban on DDT use,** ordered by the Environmental Protection Agency, went into effect.

IV. Fashion
    Folkways
    Holidays
    Social Issues and Crime
    Sports

Professional sports were beset this year by organizational feuds. The new World Hockey Association attracted some of the NHL's best players with big contracts. After several months of conflict, the International Lawn Tennis Federation came to terms with Lamar Hunt's World Championship Tennis (WCT) group by dividing control over the scheduling of tournaments. Because the agreement was not approved until July, professionals under contract to the WCT were barred from playing in many major tournaments, including Wimbledon. In basketball, the American Basketball Association filed a $300,000,000 antitrust suit against the National Basketball Association, charging it with seeking to eliminate competition by encouraging ABA players to jump leagues. For the first time in history, major league baseball players struck, returning to play only after team owners agreed to an increase in players' pensions. Americans became interested in chess this year because of Bobby Fischer's antics in Reykjavik, Iceland. Fischer and the defending world chess champion, Boris Spassky of the U.S.S.R., argued for months about details leading up to the showdown. During play, Fischer made demands of match officials that kept him in the headlines for months. In golf the top money winners were Jack Nicklaus, $320,542, and Kathy Whitworth, $65,063. This year Americans

mourned the deaths of Charles Atlas, real name An-
gelo Siciliano, body builder, Dec. 24, at 79; Roberto
Clemente, star outfielder of the Pittsburgh Pirates,
who was killed in the crash of a cargo plane taking
relief supplies to earthquake victims in Managua,
Nicaragua, Dec. 31, at 38; Gilbert R. "Gil" Hodges,
former Brooklyn Dodgers star, Apr. 2, at 47; Norman
Norell, real name Norman Levinson, fashion designer, Oct. 25, at 72; Jackie Robinson, first black to
play in the major leagues, Oct. 24, at 53; Harold J.
"Pie" Traynor, in 1969 voted greatest third baseman
of all time, Mar. 16, at 72; and George Weiss, former
baseball executive, Aug. 13, at 78.

Jan 16: Super Bowl VI was won by the Dallas Cowboys
(NFC), who defeated the Miami Dolphins (AFC) 24 to
3. On Jan. 2 the Cowboys had stopped the San Francisco 49ers 14 to 3 for the NFC championship, and the
Dolphins had defeated the Baltimore Colts 21 to 0 for
the AFC title.

Feb 3-13: At the **Winter Olympics** at Sapporo, Japan,
U.S. athletes won three gold medals. The U.S.S.R. was
first, with eight gold medals, followed by East Germany, Switzerland, and the Netherlands, all with
four.

Mar 25: The **NCAA basketball championship** was won
by UCLA, defeating Florida State 81 to 76 and maintaining its 45-game winning streak.

Mar 27: In the trial of the two remaining **Soledad
Brothers,** John Cluchette and Fleeta Drumgo were
found innocent by a San Francisco jury of slaying a
prison guard at Soledad state prison in 1970. The
third convict charged, George Jackson, was killed
during a prison break attempt in Aug. 1971.

Apr 7: Reputed Mafia kingpin **Joseph "Crazy Joe"
Gallo,** 43, was murdered by four gunmen at his birthday party in a New York City restaurant.

Apr 28: In a settlement of the **1968 Kentucky Derby
controversy,** a Kentucky court of appeals awarded
the prize money to the second-place winner, Forward
Pass. The winner, Dancer's Image, was disqualified
from the money, but not the win, because the horse
had been given a pain-killing drug before the race.

May 7: The **NBA basketball championship** was won by the Los Angeles Lakers, who defeated the New York Knicks four games to one.

May 20: The **ABA basketball championship** was won by the Indiana Pacers, who beat the New York Nets four games to two.

June 18: The **U.S. Open golf tournament** was won for the third time by Jack Nicklaus, tying Bobby Jones's record of 13 major golf titles.

June 19: In a decision bearing on **baseball's reserve clause,** the Supreme Court ruled major league baseball exempt from antitrust statutes, thus ending Curt Flood's 1970 suit against organized baseball. The Court called the exemption an "anomaly" and called on Congress to correct the situation through legislation.

July 2: A new **world pole vault record** of 18 feet, 5¾ inches was set by Bob Seagren using a fiberglass pole in a meet at Eugene, Oreg.

July 7: The **first women FBI agents,** Susan Lynn Roley, a former U.S. Marine, and Joanne E. Pierce, a former nun, were sworn in.

July 7: At the **Wimbledon** tennis championships in England, Billie Jean King won the women's singles title. On July 9 Stan Smith won the men's singles title, completing the first U.S. singles sweep since 1955. King teamed with Betty Stove of the Netherlands to win the women's doubles, and Rosemary Casals teamed with Ilie Nastase of Rumania to take the mixed doubles title.

July 11-Sep 1: The **world chess championship** was won by Bobby Fischer, who triumphed over the defending champion, Boris Spassky of the U.S.S.R., in competition at Reykjavik, Iceland.

Aug 6: The **PGA golf tournament** was won by Gary Player.

Aug 26-Sep 11: At the **Summer Olympics** in Munich, West Germany, the U.S. won 33 gold medals to the Soviet Union's 50. Swimmer Mark Spitz set an Olympic record by winning seven gold medals. Frank Shorter was the first U.S. athlete in 64 years to win the gold medal for the marathon, and the U.S. basketball team lost for the first time since the game was introduced in 1936. On Sept. 5 Arab terrorists entered the Olympic village, killed two Israeli coaches and took nine Israeli athletes hostage. All nine were killed, along with a number of terrorists, in a shootout at a nearby airport. The Olympic Games were suspended for the first time in modern history. They were resumed on Sept. 6 after a memorial service for the dead athletes.

Sep 9-10: The **U.S. Open tennis singles championships** were won by Billie Jean King, for the third time, in the women's division and Ilie Nastase of Rumania in the men's division.

Oct 13-15: The **Davis Cup tennis championship** was successfully defended by the U.S., defeating Rumania three matches to two in Bucharest.

Oct 14-22: The **World Series** was won by the Oakland Athletics (AL), defeating the Cincinnati Reds (NL) four games to three. On Oct. 11 the Reds had won the National League pennant by beating the Pittsburgh Pirates three games to two. The next day the Athletics won the American League title over the Detroit Tigers, three games to two.

1973

I. Civil Rights
Exploration and Settlement
Government
Statistics
Wars

The landslide victory of Pres. Richard M. Nixon in Nov. 1972 was interpreted by some as a vote of confidence in the Nixon administration's policies. U.S. involvement in Vietnam seemed to be drawing to a close. As the year progressed, however, the story of the Watergate break-in was uncovered by journalists and by the Senate Select Committee on Presidential

Campaign Activities. Pres. Nixon's attempts to use executive privilege or national security as reasons to withhold evidence and limit testimony by administration aides caused further friction between the White House and investigators. The revelation that Pres. Nixon had had his official conversations recorded since 1971 set off a struggle for the tapes of conversations relating to Watergate. Key tapes became unavailable, and a portion of one was mysteriously erased. In August Vice Pres. Spiro T. Agnew revealed he was under investigation in connection with official corruption in Maryland that took place while he served as Baltimore County executive and governor of Maryland. By year's end the Nixon administration was in deep trouble. Nixon came under pressure to resign, and the House began an investigation to determine whether impeachment proceedings were in order. The year was marked also by the deaths of several national figures. Lyndon Baines Johnson, 36th president of the United States, whose efforts to realize the Great Society were overwhelmed by the tragedy of Vietnam, died on Jan. 22, at 64. Other notables who died this year included Earl Browder, head of the U.S. Communist Party from 1930 to 1945, June 27, at 82; Jeannette Rankin, who as Republican congresswoman from Montana (1917–1919 and 1941–1943) was the first woman elected to Congress and the only member to vote against U.S. entry into both world wars, May 18, at 92; and Winthrop Rockefeller, philanthropist, governor of Arkansas from 1967–1971, and grandson of John D. Rockefeller, Feb. 22, at 60.

Jan 22: A **Vietnam peace agreement** was signed in Paris by representatives of the U.S., North and South Vietnam, and the Vietcong. Its key provisions included a cease-fire throughout North and South Vietnam; withdrawal of U.S. forces and dismantling of U.S. installations within 60 days; release of North Vietnamese, Vietcong, and U.S. prisoners of war within 60 days; and reunification of the North and South through peaceful means. The South Vietnamese government was to remain until new elections were held. North Vietnamese forces in the South would remain in place, but could not be replaced or reinforced.

Jan 30: In the continuing **Watergate** scandal, James W. McCord and G. Gordon Liddy, former members of the Nixon reelection campaign, were convicted of breaking into and illegally wiretapping Democratic Party headquarters in 1972. Five others involved had earlier pleaded guilty.

Feb 28: Wounded Knee, S.D., was occupied by militant members of the American Indian Movement (AIM) to dramatize the group's demands for free elections of tribal leaders, investigation of the Bureau of Indian Affairs, and review of all U.S.-Indian treaties. The group surrendered on May 8 after officials promised to investigate the complaints.

Apr 11: In Mississippi, the **Mississippi R.** reached its highest flood level, 50.3 feet, in 30 years. By May 4 more than 35,000 in nine states had fled their homes, 11 had died, and damages had reached $500,000,000.

Apr 27: Acting FBI director **L. Patrick Gray resigned** following revelations he had destroyed records involving Watergate given him by White House counsel John Dean.

Apr 30: In a televised **address on Watergate,** Pres. Nixon announced he had accepted the resignations of his chief of staff H. R. Haldeman, domestic policy assistant John Ehrlichman, counsel John Dean, and Attorney Gen. Richard G. Kleindienst. He denied any involvement in the Watergate break-in or any subsequent cover-up.

May 14: In a major **equal rights decision,** the Supreme Court ruled that women in the armed forces were entitled to the same benefits for their spouses as those accorded male servicemen.

May 17: The **Senate Select Committee on Presidential Campaign Activities,** headed by Sen. Sam J. Ervin, Democrat of North Carolina, opened public hearings to explore the alleged cover-up of administration involvement in the Watergate affair.

May 25: Archibald Cox, a professor at Harvard Law

School, was sworn in as special Watergate prosecutor.

June 16-25: U.S.S.R. Party Sec. **Leonid I. Brezhnev** visited the U.S. He signed agreements to reduce the risk of accidental nuclear war, increase air travel, and promote scientific exchanges between the U.S. and U.S.S.R.

June 25-29: John Dean testified before the Senate committee investigating Watergate. He implicated himself, H. R. Haldeman, John Ehrlichman, Pres. Nixon, John Mitchell, and others in a cover-up. Dean testified that Nixon had discussed the use of executive privilege as a means of avoiding personal involvement in Watergate, and so-called hush money. Dean also produced what was described as a White House enemies list, naming scores of administration foes.

July 16: The existence of what were to be called the **Watergate tapes,** recordings of White House conversations, was revealed by former White House aide Alexander P. Butterfield. On July 23 special prosecutor Archibald Cox and the Senate committee subpoenaed the tapes. On July 26 Pres. Nixon refused to release them, appealing the case through the courts until Oct. 19, when he offered a summary of requested tapes in return for no further requests for tapes or papers. This was rejected by Cox.

Aug 6: Vice Pres. **Agnew** revealed he was being investigated by the Justice Department on charges of receiving kickbacks while serving as Baltimore County executive and governor of Maryland. He denied any wrongdoing on Aug. 8.

Sep 4: John Ehrlichman and G. Gordon Liddy were indicted along with two White House officials in connection with the burglary of the office of Daniel Ellsberg's psychiatrist in 1971. The action had been instigated by the so-called White House plumbers' unit, created to stop security leaks, following Ellsberg's release of Pentagon documents to the press.

Oct 10: Vice Pres. **Agnew resigned** and pleaded nolo contendere (no contest) to one charge of income tax evasion in return for the dropping of other charges.

Agnew was fined and given three years' probation.
He was only the second vice president to resign. John
C. Calhoun resigned in 1832 to take a Senate seat.

Oct 12: Rep. **Gerald R. Ford,** Republican of Michigan,
was nominated by Pres. Nixon for the vice presidency.

Oct 16: The **first black mayor of a major southern
city,** Maynard Jackson, was elected to office in Atlanta, Ga.

Oct 16: The **Nobel Peace Prize** was awarded jointly to
Sec. of State Henry A. Kissinger and to Le Duc Tho
of North Vietnam for their efforts in ending the Vietnam War. Tho declined the award.

Oct 20: In what came to be called the **Saturday night
massacre,** Attorney General Elliot Richardson resigned after refusing to fire special Watergate prosecutor Archibald Cox. Deputy Attorney General William Ruckelshaus was fired after refusing also.
Solicitor General Robert Bork then fired Cox, who
had earlier in the day announced he would not accept
White House summaries of the Watergate tapes.

Oct 23: Eight **impeachment resolutions** were introduced in the House, even as Pres. Nixon announced
he would turn over the subpoenaed Watergate tapes.

Nov 1: Leon A. Jaworski was appointed special Watergate prosecutor by Pres. Nixon, who pledged to seek
congressional approval before interfering with his
investigation.

Nov 7: The **War Powers Act,** requiring congressional
approval for commitment of U.S. forces in combat
abroad longer than 60 days, was passed by Congress
over Pres. Nixon's veto.

Nov 21: An **18½-minute gap** in a key Watergate tape
was revealed by the White House. The tapes requested were turned over to Judge John J. Sirica. On
Nov. 27 Rose Mary Woods, Pres. Nixon's personal
secretary, testified she had accidentally caused about
five minutes of the erasure. The remaining gap was
unexplained.

Dec 4: In the **Chicago Seven** conspiracy case, David
Dellinger, Abbie Hoffmann, Jerry Rubin, and their

attorney William Kunstler were convicted of contempt of court, but no sentence was imposed.
Dec 6: Gerald R. Ford was sworn in as vice president,
the first to take office under the terms of the Twenty-
fifth Amendment.

II. Architecture
   Arts and Music
   Popular Entertainment
   Publishing
   Theater

Broadway show revenues dropped to a ten-year low
during the 1972–1973 season. To avoid the financial
disaster accompanying a closing on opening night, a
number of producers made Broadway their last stop
on extensive national tours. *Lorelei*, starring Carol
Channing, was scheduled to arrive in New York City
in 1974 after a long 13-city tour. Joseph Papp, director of the New York Shakespeare Festival, took over
the Vivian Beaumont Theater in Lincoln Center. By
year's end he controlled productions on some ten
stages, a reflection of the importance of resident,
noncommercial theater. In motion pictures nostalgia
was popular with audiences, as evidenced by the success of such films as *American Graffiti*, about growing
up in the early 1960s, *Paper Moon*, *The Sting*, and
Dillinger. Nostalgia carried the day with television
audiences as well. The surprise hit was *The Waltons*,
a warm view of southern family life during the Great
Depression. A view of contemporary family life was
offered by a documentary called *An American Family*, about the Loud family of California. Notables
who died this year included Conrad Aiken, author
and poet, Aug. 17, at 84; W. H. Auden, one of the great
poets of the twentieth century, Sept. 28, at 66; S. N.
Behrman, playwright, Sept. 9, at 80; Pearl S. Buck,
Nobel Prize-winning novelist, Mar. 6, at 80; Lon
Chaney, Jr., actor, July 12, at 67; Eddie Condon, jazz

guitarist, Aug. 14, at 67; John Ford, director, Aug. 31, at 78; Betty Grable, 1940s pinup girl, July 2, at 56; William Inge, playwright, June 10, at 60; Gene Krupa, big band musician known for his drum solos, Oct. 16, at 64; Jacques Lipchitz, pioneer of cubist sculpture, May 26, at 81; Lauritz Melchior, leading Wagnerian tenor of the 1930s and 1940s, Mar. 18, at 80; Edward G. Robinson, actor, Jan. 26, at 79; Robert Ryan, actor, July 11, at 63; Edward Steichen, photographer, Mar. 25, at 93; and Max Yasgur, whose 600-acre Sullivan County, N.Y., farm had been the site of the 1969 Woodstock rock festival, Feb. 9, at 53.

Among **books published** this year was *Gravity's Rainbow* by Thomas Pynchon, a massive novel that explored the themes of sexuality, death, and warfare and their relationship to the development of twentieth-century history. Other books published this year included *Recovery* by John Berryman, an unfinished novel; *The Ascent of Man* by Jacob Bronowski, non-fiction; *The World of Apples* by John Cheever, stories; *Economics and the Public Purpose* by John Kenneth Galbraith; *The Taking of Pelham One Two Three* by John Godey, a novel about the hijacking of a New York City subway train; *Serpico* by Peter Maas, the true story of a policeman's struggle to overcome police corruption; *Marilyn* by Norman Mailer, another nonfiction novel; *Rembrandt's Hat* by Bernard Malamud, stories; *Do With Me What You Will* by Joyce Carol Oates, a novel; *The Implosion Conspiracy* by Louis Nizer, an account of the spy trial of Julius and Ethel Rosenberg; *The Great American Novel* by Philip Roth, a novel about a third baseball league, made up of misfits; *Breakfast of Champions* by Kurt Vonnegut, an example of the comic novel of despair; and *The Onion Field* by Joseph Wambaugh, a police novel based on fact.

Jan 7: The **Bollingen Prize** for poetry was awarded to James Merrill.

May 3: The 110-story **Sears Tower** in Chicago, Ill., was topped out at 1450 feet, making it the world's tallest building.

May 7: Pulitzer prizes were awarded for the following: fiction, *The Optimist's Daughter* by Eudora Welty; biography, *Luce and His Empire* by W. A. Swanberg; history, *People of Paradox: An Inquiry Concerning the Origin of American Civilization* by Michael Kammen; general nonfiction, *Fire in the Lake: The Vietnamese and the Americans in Vietnam* by Frances Fitzgerald and *Children of Crisis*, volumes two and three, by Robert Coles; drama, *That Championship Season* by Jason Miller.

May 11: In the **Pentagon Papers** trial of Daniel Ellsberg and Anthony Russo, Jr., charges of espionage, theft, and conspiracy in connection with release of sensitive Pentagon documents to the press were dismissed. Federal Judge William Byrne, Jr., cited "improper government conduct," including the burglary of the office of Ellsberg's psychiatrist.

May 26: In a major decision on **radio and TV advertising,** the Supreme Court ruled that stations were not obligated to sell equal air time for political or controversial issues.

June 21: In a series of decisions on **obscenity,** the Supreme Court ruled that juries could establish the prurient appeal of materials on the basis of prevailing attitudes in their own communities.

July 29: A **rock festival at Watkins Glen,** N.Y., drew some 600,000 fans to hear music by such groups as the Allman Brothers Band, the Grateful Dead, and The Band.

Sep 21: A new **record art price** for a painting by a U.S. artist, $2,000,000, was paid by the Australian National Gallery in Canberra for Jackson Pollock's *Blue Poles.*

III. Business and Industry
Education
Philosophy and Religion
Science

Record levels of retail sales, factory output, new car sales, employment, and personal incomes balanced against inflation of 8.5% and the second dollar devaluation in 14 months, added up to what a consumer columnist described as joyless prosperity. As food prices climbed, consumer groups organized a meat boycott. Toward the end of the year the situation was aggravated by an oil embargo imposed on the U.S. and other industrialized nations by members of the Organization of Arab Petroleum Exporting Countries (OAPEC). The oil shortage caused long lines at gas stations and shut down factories. The federal government organized an emergency gas rationing system, but it was not implemented. In education, the end of the military draft, skyrocketing tuition costs, and increasing competition among degree holders for jobs and for admittance to graduate and professional schools led students to question the value of a college education. Enrollment was up only 2%, but enrollment at less expensive public institutions was strong. Notables who died this year included Harvey S. Firestone, Jr., an industrialist, June 1, at 75; Harold B. Lee, president of the Church of Jesus Christ of Latter Day Saints, Dec. 26, at 74; Marjorie Post, a philanthropist whose wealth was estimated at some $200,000,000, Sept. 12, at 86; and Selman A. Waksman, winner of the 1952 Nobel Prize for Medicine for his discovery of streptomycin, Aug. 16, at 85.

Jan 18: In a **job discrimination** case, the American Telephone & Telegraph Company agreed to pay $15,000,000 to women and minority employees who had been treated unfairly, and to set up job-training programs and establish hiring quotas.

Jan 22: In a decision on **abortion,** the Supreme Court struck down state laws restricting abortions during the first six months of pregnancy.

Mar 22: The **National Commission on Marijuana and Drug Abuse** urged treatment for drug users and recognition that alcoholism is a drug problem.

Apr 2: Political intervention by big business was highlighted by the admission by International Telephone and Telegraph that it had offered funds to the CIA to oppose the election of Salvador Allende Gossens, a Marxist, to the presidency of Chile in 1970.

Allende was elected, but on Sept. 11, 1973, his government was overthrown by a military junta and he was killed.

Apr 5: Pioneer 11 was launched toward a December rendezvous with the planet Jupiter.

Apr 15: The signing of **contracts with California grape growers** by the International Brotherhood of Teamsters was announced. It prompted a strike by César Chávez's United Farm Workers Union, which charged the Teamsters with union busting by taking over contracts held by the UFW.

May 14: Skylab, the first U.S. space station, was launched into Earth orbit, but a launch mishap damaged one of its solar-power panels and jammed the other. On May 25, Skylab 2 carried astronauts Charles Conrad, Joseph Kerwin, and Paul Weitz to a rendezvous with the station. The crew deployed the stuck panel, made further repairs, and conducted scientific experiments before splashing down in the Pacific on June 22.

June 25: Several programs for **state aid to parochial schools** were declared unconstitutional by the Supreme Court.

June 29: Establishment of a **Federal Energy Office** to promote conservation and research into alternative sources of energy was announced by Pres. Nixon. It later assumed responsibility for mandatory fuel allocations and potential gasoline rationing.

June 30: The **largest merchant ship** built in the U.S., the 1094-foot, 230,000-ton supertanker *Brooklyn*, was christened at the Brooklyn, N.Y., Navy Yard.

July 28: Skylab 3 carried astronauts Alan Bean, Owen Garriott, and Jack Lousma to a rendezvous with the Skylab orbiting laboratory. They made repairs to the station and performed a number of experiments before returning to Earth on Sept. 25.

Sep 1: The nation's strongest **drug control law** went into effect in New York State. It imposed mandatory life sentences for those convicted of trafficking in hard drugs and for addicts who commit violent crimes.

Sep 6: Former United Mine Workers president **W. A.**

"Tony" Boyle was indicted on charges of ordering the 1969 murders of labor dissident Joseph Yablonski, his wife, and his daughter.

Oct 17: An **embargo on oil** shipped to the U.S. and other nations supporting Israel was instituted by 11 Middle Eastern oil-exporting states.

Oct 18: The **Nobel Prize in Economics** was awarded to Wassily Leontief of Harvard University.

Oct 23: The **Nobel Prize in Physics** was awarded jointly to Ivar Giaver of the General Electric Company in Schenectady, N.Y.; Leo Esaki, a Japanese citizen working for IBM in Yorktown Heights, N.Y.; and Brian D. Josephson of Great Britain for their theoretical work in the field of microelectronics.

Nov 3: **Mariner 10,** the first U.S. probe of the planet Mercury, was launched. It was to fly by Venus on its way to Mercury.

Nov 7: A **call for energy self-sufficiency** by 1980 was made by Pres. Nixon. He also asked for extension of Daylight Savings Time (passed Dec. 14) and reduction of the highway speed limit to 55 mph (passed Dec. 22); set heating oil allocations for homes, schools, and industries; reduced jet fuel allocations; and ordered lower temperatures in federal buildings. On Nov. 25 he called for a Sunday ban on gasoline sales. On Dec. 27 the Federal Energy Office outlined a standby gasoline rationing program.

Nov 13: Plans for a **trans-Alaska oil pipeline,** designed to supply 2,000,000 barrels of oil a day, were approved by Congress.

Dec 15: **Homosexuality** was not a mental illness, the American Psychiatric Association announced, overturning its 100-year-old position on the subject.

IV. Fashion
Folkways
Holidays
Social Issues and Crime
Sports

Salaries increased and attendance declined for football, basketball, and baseball, to the benefit of other sports, notably hockey, soccer, and tennis. In September the ban on local television coverage of football games was lifted for events sold out in advance, and many ticket-holders stayed home to watch the games. In baseball the American League adopted the designated hitter rule—which provided for a tenth player in the lineup to hit for the pitcher without forcing the pitcher to leave the game—in the hope of increasing scoring and boosting attendance. In hockey the NHL drew 9,299,028 fans for the 1972–1973 season, an increase of more than 1,000,000 over the previous year. In golf the top money winners were Jack Nicklaus, $308,362, and Kathy Whitworth, $82,864. As professional sports were changing and growing, so was the national passion for physical fitness. Some 60,000,000 Americans were involved in sports for exercise, including some 18,000,000 cyclists. Another carefully observed trend was the national crime rate. On Mar. 28 a preliminary report showed the 1972 crime rate was down 2%, but an FBI report released on Dec. 27 showed the rate for the first nine months of 1973 to be up 1%, and violent crime up 3%. Among those who died this year were Frank Costello, a leading underworld figure, Feb. 18, at 82; Walt Kelly, creator of the comic strip *Pogo*, Oct. 18, at 60; Edward V. "Eddie" Rickenbacker, World War I flying ace, July 23, at 82; and Murat B. "Chic" Young, creator of the comic strip *Blondie*, Mar. 14, at 72.

Jan 14: Super Bowl VII was won by the Miami Dolphins (AFC), defeating the Washington Redskins (NFC) 14 to 7. On Dec. 31, 1972, the Dolphins had defeated the Pittsburgh Steelers 21 to 17 for the AFC championship and the Redskins had beaten the Dallas Cowboys 26 to 3 for the NFC title.

Jan 22: The **world heavyweight boxing championship** was won by George Foreman, who defeated Joe Frazier in a second-round knockout. On Sept. 1 he defended the title with a one-round knockout of Joe Roman in Tokyo, Japan.

Feb 25: Juan Corona was sentenced to 25 consecutive life terms after being convicted for the 1971 murders of 25 migrant workers in California. In 1978 his conviction was overturned, on the grounds his lawyer did not defend him competently, and a new trial was ordered. He was convicted again on Sept. 23, 1982.

Mar 1: Robyn Smith became the first woman jockey to win a stakes race when she rode North Sea to victory in the Paumonok Handicap at Aqueduct Raceway.

Mar 1: The **birthrate** for the last six months of 1972 was reported at 1.98 children per couple, below the 2.1 rate for zero population growth.

Mar 26: The **NCAA basketball championship** was won for the seventh consecutive year by UCLA, defeating Memphis State 87 to 66.

Apr 28-May 12: The **ABA basketball championship** was won by the Indiana Pacers, who defeated the Kentucky Colonels four games to three.

May 5: The 99th annual **Kentucky Derby** was won by Secretariat, with a record time of 1:59^2/s. The jockey was Ron Turcotte.

May 10: The **NBA basketball championship** was won by the New York Knicks, who beat the Los Angeles Lakers four games to one.

May 19: The 98th annual **Preakness Stakes** was won by Secretariat, with a time of 1:55. The jockey was Ron Turcotte.

May 21: The **first athletic scholarship awarded to a woman** was given to Lynn Genesko, a swimmer from Woodbridge, N.J., by the University of Miami (Fla.).

May 27: A new **track record** for the 880-yd. run was set by Rick Wohlhuter, who ran the distance in 1:44.6 at the AAU meet in Los Angeles, Calif.

June 9: The 105th annual **Belmont Stakes** was won by Secretariat, with a time of 2:24, thus becoming the ninth horse to win racing's Triple Crown. The jockey was Ron Turcotte.

June 17: The **U.S. Open golf tournament** was won by Johnny Miller.

July 7-8: At the **Wimbledon** tennis championships in England, Billie Jean King won the women's singles title for the second straight year. King teamed with Rosemary Casals to win the women's doubles, and with Owen Davidson of Australia to win the mixed doubles. Jimmy Connors teamed with Ilie Nastase of Rumania to take the men's doubles. Many tennis professionals boycotted the championship because of the International Lawn Tennis Federation's suspension of Yugoslavian player Nikki Pilic for refusing to play on the Yugoslavian Davis Cup team.

Aug 12: The **PGA golf tournament** was won by Jack Nicklaus.

Aug 29-Sep 9: The **U.S. Open tennis singles championships** were won by John Newcombe of Australia in the men's division and Margaret Smith Court of Australia, for the fifth time, in the women's division.

Sep 20: In a nationally televised tennis mismatch billed as the **"Battle of the Sexes,"** Billie Jean King beat Bobby Riggs in three straight sets and went home $100,000 richer.

Oct 13-21: The **World Series** was won for the second year in a row by the Oakland Athletics (AL), defeating the New York Mets (NL) four games to three. The Mets had won the National League pennant on Oct. 10 by beating the Cincinnati Reds three games to two. The Athletics had won the American League title Oct. 11, beating the Baltimore Orioles three games to two.

Nov 30-Dec 2: The **Davis Cup** tennis championship was won in Cleveland, Ohio, by Australia, beating the U.S. in five straight matches.

Dec 1: Jack Nicklaus won the Disney World Open, becoming the first professional golfer to hit a career total of $2,000,000.

Dec 16: A new **NFL rushing record** was set by O.J. Simpson, running back for the Buffalo Bills, who broke Jim Brown's 1963 total of 1863 yds. Simpson later set a new pro record of 2003 yds.

1974

I. Civil Rights
Exploration and Settlement
Government
Statistics
Wars

The scandals revealed by the Watergate affair continued to cripple the Nixon presidency. The climax came when the Supreme Court ordered the White House to release transcriptions of recorded presidential conversations; the tapes indicated that Nixon had been involved in the cover-up of the Watergate burglary. The House Judiciary Committee, after several months of hearings, voted three articles of impeachment, and it seemed likely an impeachment trial would take place in the Senate. As Nixon's base of support disappeared, he made a tour of the Middle East (June 10–18) and traveled to the U.S.S.R. (June 25-July 3) to sign a limited accord on nuclear weapons testing. These trips were not enough to restore his popular support and in August, faced with impeachment, Nixon became the first U.S. president to resign. Meanwhile, Sec. of State Henry Kissinger followed a policy of shuttle diplomacy, flying from one capital to another in the Middle East. By year's end he had obtained agreement in principle by all parties to resume peace talks in Geneva. This success contrasted with disclosures that the FBI had carried out counterintelligence operations against civil rights groups in the U.S. and that the CIA had been involved in the destabilization or overthrow of foreign governments, particularly the elected Marxist government of Chile. Notables who died this year included Gen. Creighton W. Abrams, Army chief of staff, Sept. 4, at 59; former Sen. Wayne L. Morse of Oregon, July 22, at 73; Gen. Carl A. Spaats, the first chief of staff of the United States Air Force, in 1947, July 14, at 83; Lewis L.

Strauss, head of the Atomic Energy Commission from 1953–1958, Jan. 21, at 78; and Earl Warren, former chief justice of the Supreme Court, July 19, at 83.

Jan 15: In testimony on the **White House tapes,** an expert stated the 18½-minute gap in a critical tape had been caused by deliberate and repeated erasures.

Feb 6: An **impeachment inquiry** against Pres. Nixon by the House Judiciary Committee was approved by the House of Representatives.

Feb 28: The $6,400,000 **lawsuit against the Committee to Reelect the President** for its involvement in the Watergate break-in was settled. The Democratic National Committee accepted $775,000.

May 23: Following revelation of **cheating by Annapolis midshipmen,** some 900 were ordered by the U.S. Naval Academy to retake an examination .

July 24: In a decision on the **White House tapes,** the Supreme Court ordered that special prosecutor Leon Jaworski's subpoena of tapes and documents be honored by the White House. It ruled that presidential privilege did not apply to evidence required in prosecuting Watergate-related crimes. Pres. Nixon turned over the materials on July 30 and Aug. 5.

July 30: Three articles of impeachment were voted against Pres. Nixon by the House Judiciary Committee: for blocking the investigation of the Watergate affair, for abuse of presidential powers, and for hindering the impeachment process by not complying with the committee's subpoena for taped White House conversations.

Aug 5: Pres. **Nixon released tape transcripts** revealing he had impeded the Watergate investigation. One example of the evidence was an order to H. R. Haldeman on June 23, 1972, to tell the FBI: "Don't go any further in this case, period!"

Aug 8: Pres. **Nixon announced in a televised address that he would resign.** Nixon told an audience of some 100,000,000 he had made some wrong decisions but that he was resigning because he no longer had enough support in Congress.

Aug 9: Pres. **Nixon resigned.** Gerald R. Ford was sworn in as the 38th president of the United States.

Aug 20: Nelson A. Rockefeller, former governor of New York, was nominated for the vice presidency by Pres. Ford.

Sep 7: In a revelation of **CIA covert operations,** it was disclosed that in April CIA director William Colby had told a congressional committee that from 1970 to 1973 some $8,000,000 had been budgeted for operations against Chile's Marxist government.

Sep 8: Pres. **Nixon was pardoned** by Pres. Ford for any crimes he may have committed or may have participated in while in office. On Oct. 17 Ford defended this action before the House Judiciary Committee, saying he wanted to end the national divisions created by the Watergate affair.

Sep 16: Mary Louise Smith of Iowa became the first woman to head the Republican National Committee.

Sep 16: A limited **amnesty proclamation** was issued by Pres. Ford, offering clemency to thousands of Vietnam-era draft resisters and military deserters if they swore allegiance to the U.S. and performed up to two years of public service work.

Sep 16: Charges stemming from the 1973 **occupation of Wounded Knee,** S.D., against Russell Means and Dennis Banks, leaders of the American Indian Movement (AIM), were dismissed in federal court. The judge criticized the government's handling of witnesses and evidence.

Oct 10: Legislation providing for **public funding of presidential primaries and elections** was passed by Congress. It set limits on donations and outlays for congressional and presidential campaigns.

Nov 5: In **congressional elections** the Democrats gained a 61–37 majority in the Senate, with two seats held by independents. In the House the Democrats gained 43 seats, for a 291–144 majority. The Democrats also won four governorships, for a total of 36. Among the new Democratic governors was Ella Grasso of Connecticut, the first elected woman governor. In this election voters in the District of Columbia chose for the first time a mayor and a 14-member city council, posts previously filled by presidential appointment.

Nov 8: Charges against eight Ohio National Guardsmen stemming from the 1970 **Kent State** tragedy were dropped in federal court.

Nov 21: The **Freedom of Information Act,** providing expanded public access to government files, was passed by Congress over Pres. Ford's veto. The law provided that secrecy classification could be challenged in court and had to be justified by federal authorities.

Dec 10: Rep. **Wilbur D. Mills,** Democrat of Arkansas, resigned his chairmanship of the Ways and Means Committee. Several well-publicized incidents had linked him with Fanne Fox, a burlesque performer.

Dec 21: Allegations of illegal CIA activities were leveled by *The New York Times.* The newspaper reported that during the Nixon administration, the agency had maintained files on some 10,000 U.S. citizens and had engaged in illegal domestic operations against opponents of U.S. policy in Vietnam as well as other dissidents. On Dec. 26 CIA director William Colby acknowledged the truth of the allegations in a letter to Pres. Ford.

II. Architecture
   Arts and Music
   Popular Entertainment
   Publishing
   Theater

The year in theater was dominated again by British imports, notably works by Tom Stoppard and Alan Ayckbourn. In motion pictures nostalgia maintained its box office appeal. *That's Entertainment,* a pastiche of musicals from the 1930s to the 1950s, grossed $18,000,000, and *Chinatown* was reminiscent of the classic 1940s detective films. Disaster films such as *Towering Inferno* were also popular. In the art world, a study entitled *Museums USA* indicated the gravity of U.S. museums' financial woes. The report showed that 36% of the nation's museums had been forced to cut personnel and services since 1966, 37% had been forced to charge admission, and almost 57% of museum staffs were volunteers. Americans mourned the deaths this year of William A. "Bud" Abbott, straight man of the comedy team Abbott and Costello, Apr. 24, at 78; Jack Benny, the comedian, Dec. 26, at 80; Edward Kennedy "Duke" Ellington, the jazz composer and musician, May 24, at 75; Cassandra "Mama Cass" Elliot, the entertainer, July 29, at 33; Dorothy Fields, composer of such song hits as "I'm in the Mood for Love" and "The Way You Look Tonight," Mar. 28, at 68; Samuel Goldwyn, real name Goldfish, the Hollywood producer, Jan. 31, at 91; Adolph Gottlieb, the artist and pioneer in abstract expressionism, Mar. 4, at 71; Chester R. "Chet" Huntley, who was co-anchorman of NBC's nightly *Huntley-Brinkley Report* from 1956–1970, Mar. 20, at 62; Solomon I. "Sol" Hurok, the impresario, Mar. 5, at 85; Louis I. Kahn, the architect, Mar. 17, at 73; Walter Lippmann, the journalist, Dec. 14, at 85; John Crowe Ransom, the poet, July 3, at 86; Cornelius Ryan, known for his books about World War II, Nov. 23, at 54; Anne Sexton, the poet, Oct. 4, at 45; Edward V. "Ed" Sullivan, newspaper columnist and television host, Oct. 13, at 73; and Jacqueline Susann, the best-selling novelist, Sept. 21, at 53.

Among **books published** this year was *Something Happened* by Joseph Heller, the long-awaited second novel by the author of the 1961 classic *Catch-22*. In this new work Heller presented the perspective of a middle-aged man examining his life and finding it to be a mixture of stifled hopes, disillusionment, minor victories, and a sense of loss. Other books published this year included *Watership Down* by Richard Adams, an allegory of life, death, and continuity in the form of a touching animal story; *If Beale Street Could Talk* by James Baldwin, a novel; *Jaws* by Peter Benchley, a novel; *All the President's Men* by Carl Bernstein and Robert Woodward, a study of the people around Pres. Richard Nixon in the shadow of Watergate; *The Hawkline Monster* by Richard Brautigan, described as a Gothic western; *Fear of Flying* by Erica Jong, a novel; *The CIA and the Cult of Intelligence* by Victor Marchetti and John D. Marks, a study of the U.S. intelligence community; *Centennial* by James Michener, a novel examining the history of Colorado and Wyoming from prehistoric to recent times; *Plain Speaking, An Oral Biography of Harry S Truman* by Merle Miller; and *My Life as a Man* by Philip Roth, a novel.

Apr 1: In a decision on **censorship for national security,** a federal court ruled that *The CIA and the Cult of Intelligence* by Victor Marchetti and John D. Marks could be published with only 15 deletions made in the original text. The CIA had asked for 168 cuts.

May 7: Pulitzer prizes were awarded for the following: biography, *O'Neill, Son and Artist* by Louis Sheaffer; history, *The Americans: The Democratic Experience* by Daniel J. Boorstin; general nonfiction, *The Denial of Death* by Ernest Becker; poetry, *The Dolphin* by Robert Lowell.

Sep 27: A record price for an American painting was set with the sale of Willem de Kooning's *Woman V* to the Australian National Gallery for $850,000. The painting had been sold in 1953 for $30,000.

Nov 2: J. D. Salinger, ending a 21-year public silence, announced he was suing a publisher and several major bookstores for unauthorized publication and distribution of short stories he had written early in his career.

III. Business and Industry
   Education
   Philosophy and Religion
   Science

The economy slid into crisis. Inflation hit 10.3%, auto sales were off 20%, and housing starts were down 40%. Unemployment soared to 7.2% by December. Nevertheless, the economic depression feared by many did not occur. Foreign trade did not decline, and the international banking system withstood the impact of a dramatic rise in oil prices. In education, community control surfaced as a burning issue in the fall. In Kanawha County, W. Va., parents protested their schools' use of books reflecting contemporary sexual mores and dissident views about the U.S. In

Boston, the busing of students to achieve integration led to violence and to a confrontation between a citizens group and the federal judge who ordered integration of the city's schools. In science, there were questions regarding the safety of modern genetic research and warnings of possible environmental problems, such as depletion of the ozone layer in the atmosphere. In religion, even as membership in major church denominations declined, attendance at fundamentalist churches continued to climb. Notables who died this year included Vannevar Bush, who pioneered the development of electronic analog computers, June 28, at 84; Adelle Davis, the nutritionist, May 31, at 70; Haroldson Lafayette Hunt, one of the world's wealthiest men, Nov. 29, at 75; Charles A. Lindbergh, the pioneer aviator, Aug. 26, at 72; Alexander P. Seversky, an early advocate of strategic air power, Aug. 24, at 80; Stephen Gill Spottswood, bishop of the African Methodist Episcopal Zion Church and chairman of the NAACP from 1961, Dec. 1, at 77; Earl W. Sutherland, the Nobel Prize-winning pharmacologist, Mar. 9, at 58; and Arthur K. Watson, a key figure in the phenomenal growth of IBM in the 1950s and 1960s, July 26, at 55.

Mar 7: The Civil War ironclad *Monitor*, which had sunk in a gale in 1862, was reported found off Hatteras, N.C.

Mar 18: The **Arab oil embargo** against the U.S. was officially lifted following Sec. of State Henry Kissinger's efforts to mediate between Egypt and Israel.

Apr 8: A bill extending the **minimum wage** to some 8,000,000 additional workers, and gradually raising it to $2.30 an hour, was signed by Pres. Richard M. Nixon.

Apr 11: William A. "Tony" Boyle, former president of the United Mine Workers, was found guilty by a Media, Pa., jury of ordering the 1969 murders of Joseph Yablonski and Yablonski's wife and daughter.

Apr 30: Federal **wage and price controls were lifted.** A number of price increases by the steel and copper industries followed.

May 2: Legislation for a **Federal Energy Administration,** to be established by July 1975, was passed by

Congress. The new agency would be responsible for gas rationing, emergency planning, conservation measures, curbing exorbitant profits, and shaping foreign trade policies.

July 6: Heart disease, chief cause of death in the U.S., had declined 10% since 1963, according to a report by the National Center for Health Statistics.

July 29: The **first women Episcopal priests** were ordained by four bishops in Philadelphia, Pa. The ordination of the 11 women was ruled invalid by the House of Bishops on Aug. 15, but on Oct. 17 the same body approved in principle the ordination of women as priests.

Sep 2: The **Employee Retirement Income Security Act** was signed by Pres. Gerald R. Ford. It was to bring some 300,000 private pension plans under federal regulation by Jan. 1976, when uniform standards would become enforceable and a federal reinsurance program would go into effect to protect benefits if private plans should fail.

Sep 12: Opposition to **court-ordered school busing** in Boston turned into violence on opening day of classes. Subsequent violence prompted mobilization of the National Guard on Oct. 15.

Sep 29: Controversy over the accepted treatment **of breast cancer** was heightened by a report from the National Cancer Institute indicating that radical mastectomy, the prevailing treatment, was too drastic in many cases. The study pressed for surgery that was less deforming and that reduced the lingering pain, weakness, and other effects associated with radical mastectomy.

Oct 8: A program to control inflation, called **WIN (Whip Inflation Now),** was proposed by Pres. Ford. It called for voluntary energy conservation measures to help combat spiraling oil prices. Pres. Ford also asked for a 5% tax surcharge on corporate profits and on personal incomes of more than $15,000.

Oct 8: In the **biggest bank failure in U.S. history** to date, the Franklin National Bank, of New York, was declared insolvent. On Oct. 17 the Securities and Exchange Commission filed fraud charges against the bank's holding company and nine members of the firm.

Oct 10: The **Nobel Prize in Physiology or Medicine** was awarded jointly to Albert Claude, formerly of the Rockefeller Institute and currently director of the Institut Jules Bordet in Belgium, Emil Palade of Yale University Medical School, and Christian de Duve of Belgium, associated with the Rockefeller Institute and the University of Louvain, for their research into the inner workings of cells.

Oct 15: The **Nobel Prize in Chemistry** was awarded to Paul J. Flory of Stanford University for his research on macromolecules, which led to development of new plastics and other synthetic materials.

Nov 13: Blueprint for Project Independence, a plan to reduce U.S. reliance on oil imports, was released by the Federal Energy Administration. The study called for a federal tax of 15 cents a gallon on gasoline; a mandatory fuel standard of 20 miles a gallon for autos; tax credits for insulating homes and buildings; efficiency criteria for electrical appliances; and national standards for heating, cooling, and lighting.

Nov 15: The **retail price of sugar** soared to 65 cents a pound following the sixth major price increase by two leading U.S. refiners since Oct. 9. On Jan. 1 the price of a pound of sugar had been about 18 cents.

Nov 27: The **longest surviving heart transplant patient,** Louis B. Russell, Jr., died in Richmond, Va., at 49. He had received his new heart in 1968.

Dec 30: The **Boston School Committee was fined** by federal Judge W. Arthur Garrity, and its members were barred from participation in school integration matters unless they backed a new public school desegregation plan by Jan. 7, 1975.

Dec 31: A 41-year ban on **private possession of gold** was lifted. Early sales of bullion were light.

IV. Fashion
Folkways
Holidays
Social Issues and Crime
Sports

A Harris survey showed that tennis claimed 26% of 1974 sports audiences, compared with a 17.7% share in 1973. A Nielsen poll showed that 33,900,000 Americans played the game in 1974, a jump of 68% over the previous year. In golf the top money winners were Johnny Miller, $353,201, and JoAnne Carner, $87,094. In baseball Frank Robinson became the first black manager in major league baseball, Henry Aaron topped the home-run record set by Babe Ruth, and Lou Brock broke the record for stolen bases set by Maury Wills in 1962. Motorcycle stunt driving became a high-paying occupation this year as Robert Craig "Evel" Knievel managed (Sept. 8) to jump the Snake R. Canyon in Twin Falls, Idaho. The year's top fad was streaking, or running naked through a variety of settings. College students were especially fond of the new, short-lived sport. Among the notables who died this year were Jay Hanna "Dizzy" Dean, the baseball pitcher, July 17, at 63; Anne Klein, the fashion designer, Mar. 19, at 51; Peter Revson, a top U.S. race car driver, Mar. 22, at 35; Daniel R. Topping, New York Yankees baseball executive, May 18, at 61; and Amy Vanderbilt, writer on etiquette, Dec. 27, at 66.

Jan 13: Super Bowl VIII was won by the Miami Dolphins, defeating the Minnesota Vikings 24 to 7 for their second consecutive Super Bowl win. On Dec. 30, 1973, the Dolphins had defeated the Oakland Raiders 27 to 10 for the NFC championship, and the Vikings had defeated the Dallas Cowboys 27 to 10 for the AFC championship.

Feb 5: Patricia Hearst, daughter of publisher Randolph Hearst, was kidnaped from her Berkeley, Calif., apartment by members of a group calling itself the Symbionese Liberation Army. On Feb. 12 a ransom message from her abductors demanded $70 in food for every needy person in California. The Hearst family started a $2,000,000 food giveaway on Feb. 22.

Mar 24: The **NCAA basketball championship** was won by North Carolina State University, defeating Marquette University 76 to 64.

Apr 3: Patricia Hearst, in a tape to authorities sent by her abductors, declared she was joining the Symbionese Liberation Army of her own free will. On Apr. 15 a camera took a picture of her participating in the robbery of a San Francisco bank. On June 6 she was indicted by a federal grand jury for her role in the crime.

Apr 8: Henry "Hank" Aaron of the Atlanta Braves (NL) hit his 715th career home run in Atlanta against the Los Angeles Dodgers, breaking the record set decades earlier by the great Babe Ruth. Aaron finished the year with a career total of 733 homers.

Apr 28-May 12: The **NBA basketball championship** was won by the Boston Celtics, who took their 12th title win in 18 years by beating the Milwaukee Bucks four games to three.

Apr 30-May 10: The **ABA basketball championship** was won by the New York Nets, who beat the Utah Stars four games to one.

May 4: Expo '74 opened in Spokane, Wash. Its focus was environmental issues and solutions. The 100-acre site of the mini-world's fair was designed for future use as a park. Washington State's pavilion was intended to serve after Expo '74 as an opera house and convention center.

May 16: In a serial murder case known as the **Zebra killings,** four Black Muslims were indicted in San Francisco for the murder of three persons and attempted murder of six others. Twelve people, all of them white, had been killed, apparently at random, over a five-month period.

May 17: A shootout with the **Symbionese Liberation Army** in Los Angeles left six of eight known members of the terrorist group dead after police opened fire on their headquarters and the building caught fire. Among the dead were the group's leader, Donald D. DeFreeze, self-styled General Field Marshall Cinque. Patty Hearst and William and Emily Harris, wanted for bank robbery, were not in the building at the time of the attack.

June 12: Little League baseball announced that its teams would be open to girls.

June 16: The **U.S. Open golf tournament** was won by Hale Irwin, beating Forrest Fezler by two strokes.

July 5: At the **Wimbledon** tennis championships in England, Chris Evert won the women's singles title. On July 6 Jimmy Connors won the men's singles title. Peggy Michel teamed with Evonne Goolagong of Australia to win the women's doubles, and Billie Jean King teamed with Owen Davidson of Australia to win the mixed doubles.

Aug 11: The **PGA golf tournament** was won by Lee Trevino, beating Jack Nicklaus by one stroke.

Sep 9: The **U.S. Open tennis singles championships** were won by Jimmy Connors in the men's division and Billie Jean King in the women's division.

Sep 10: Lou Brock of the St. Louis Cardinals (NL) broke the major league record for stolen bases in a season, set by Maury Wills in 1962, when he stole base number 105 in a home game against the Philadelphia Phillies. Brock finished the year with a National League career record of 753 stolen bases.

Sep 10-17: The **America's Cup** was successfully defended by the U.S. yacht *Courageous,* which won four straight races from the Australian challenger *Southern Cross.*

Oct 3: Frank Robinson became the first black manager in major league baseball when he signed a $175,000-a-year contract as player-manager with the Cleveland Indians (AL).

Oct 12-17: The **World Series** was won for the third straight year by the Oakland Athletics (AL), who beat the Los Angeles Dodgers four games to one. On Oct. 9 the Athletics had won the American League pennant, beating the Baltimore Orioles three games to one. The same day the Dodgers took the National League pennant from the Pittsburgh Pirates, winning three games to one.

Oct 30: The **world heavyweight boxing championship** was regained by Muhammad Ali, who triumphed

over George Foreman with an eighth-round knockout in Kinshasa, Zaire.

1975

I. Civil Rights
Exploration and Settlement
Government
Statistics
Wars

The Vietnam War reached its conclusion this year. In
January the North Vietnamese stepped up military
actions in South Vietnam. In mid-March the South
Vietnamese army began a withdrawal from northern
South Vietnam that soon became a full-scale retreat.
On Apr. 30 the last U.S. citizens were airlifted out of
Saigon. On the same day, Gen. Duong Van Minh, who
had been installed as president two days earlier, surrendered to the Vietcong. In March the new government of Thailand announced it would seek complete
U.S. withdrawal from that country within a year,
conditions permitting. In mid-April Cambodia fell to
the Khmer Rouge. The agony of Vietnam would continue for the U.S. The war had divided the nation
politically and philosophically for more than a
decade, and its end prompted disillusionment and a
new spirit of isolationism. Thus, Congress and the
nation proved unwilling to commit itself against insurgents in Angola and Ethiopia. At home further
revelations in the Watergate scandal, investigations
of illegal FBI and CIA activities, and growing concern over the faltering national economy continued
to erode Americans' faith in their government and in
themselves. Notables who died this year included
Hannah Arendt, the political philosopher noted for

her writings on totalitarianism, Dec. 5, at 69; Gen. Anthony C. McAuliffe, acting commander of the 101st Airborne Division at Bastogne, Belgium, during the Battle of the Bulge in 1944, Aug. 11, at 77; and Raymond Moley, a member of Pres. Roosevelt's so-called Brain Trust, Feb. 18, at 88.

Jan 5: A **commission on CIA domestic activities** was appointed by Pres. Gerald R. Ford to investigate whether the agency had violated its charter by engaging in domestic intelligence operations. Headed by Vice Pres. Nelson A. Rockefeller, the commission reported on June 10 that the CIA had undertaken unlawful surveillance of some 300,000 persons or organizations and had supplied Pres. Nixon with information to use against political foes.

Jan 24: Fraunces Tavern was bombed in New York City, killing four persons and injuring 53. A terrorist group seeking Puerto Rican independence claimed responsibility.

Jan 27: A bipartisan **Senate investigation of FBI and CIA activities,** headed by Sen. Frank Church of Idaho, was begun. On Nov. 20 the committee released its report. It charged both agencies with illegal surveillance of U.S. citizens and the CIA with plotting to assassinate foreign leaders and maintaining a secret stockpile of poisons despite a presidential order to destroy the poisons.

Jan 31: Pres. Ford's **clemency program** for Vietnam-era military resisters was extended to Mar. 1.

Feb 21: For their parts in the **Watergate** cover-up, former White House aides H. R. Haldeman and John D. Ehrlichman, and former attorney general John Mitchell were each sentenced to 30 months' imprisonment.

Apr 4: A U.S. **C-5A transport plane crashed** shortly after takeoff from Saigon, South Vietnam. Some 200 of the refugees being airlifted to the U.S., most of them children, were killed.

May 12: The U.S. merchant ship *Mayaguez* was seized by Cambodian forces and its crew charged with spying within Cambodia's territorial waters. The crew of 39 was freed on May 14 in a U.S. military rescue operation. Fifteen U.S. soldiers died and 50 were wounded. The operation received virtually unanimous approval by U.S. citizens.

June 24: One hundred and thirteen people were killed when their **jet crashed while attempting to land** in a thunderstorm at Kennedy International Airport in New York City.

July 14: Allegations of **FBI burglaries and break-ins** were confirmed by agency director Clarence B. Kelley, who stated that such activities occurred in national-security cases. On July 16 the Washington *Post* revealed that some of the incidents involved ordinary criminal cases.

July 29: U.S. bases in Turkey were seized by the Turkish government after a U.S. embargo on military aid to Turkey. The embargo had been imposed because of a stalemate in negotiations between Turkey and Greece over Cyprus.

Aug 5: Alger Hiss was ordered reinstated to the Massachusetts bar 25 years after he lost his right to practice law because of a conviction for perjury before a grand jury investigating espionage against the U.S.

Aug 6: Literacy requirements for voting were abolished and a number of linguistic minorities were brought under the protection of the Voting Rights Act of 1965. The act itself was extended for seven years.

Sep 5: An **assassination attempt** against Pres. Ford in Sacramento, Calif., was ended when a Secret Service agent wrested a pistol from Lynette A. "Squeaky" Fromme, a follower of Charles Manson.

Sep 22: In a second **assassination attempt** against Pres. Ford, this time in San Francisco, Calif., the president was shot at by Sara Jane Moore, a police and FBI informer.

Sep 28: A bill authorizing **admission of women to the military academies** for the three major services by the fall of 1976 was passed by Congress.

Oct 22: Air Force Sgt. **Leonard Matlovich,** a much-decorated Vietnam veteran, was given a general discharge after publicly declaring his homosexuality. His intent was to challenge the ban against homosexuals in the military. His discharge was later upgraded to honorable.

Nov 3: In an **administration shakeup** that came to be known as the Halloween massacre, Sec. of State Henry Kissinger resigned his second post as head of the National Security Council, and Sec. of Defense James R. Schlesinger and CIA director William E. Colby were dismissed by Pres. Ford. The president subsequently nominated Donald Rumsfeld for secretary of defense and George Bush for CIA director.

Nov 12: William O. Douglas, 77, suffering from effects of a stroke incurred in 1974, announced his retirement from the Supreme Court after 36 years of service. During his tenure, longest of any Supreme Court justice in history, he earned a reputation as a civil libertarian.

Nov 18: Eldridge Cleaver, a former leader of the Black Panther Party, returned to the U.S. after seven years of exile to face criminal charges stemming from a shoot-out with Oakland, Calif., police.

Dec 4: A staff report of the Senate Committee investigating **illegal CIA activities** absolved the agency of direct participation in the 1973 military overthrow and subsequent murder of Chilean president Salvador Allende Gossens. The CIA was reported to have spent some $13,400,000 from 1963 on Chilean operations, mostly for anti-Allende activities.

Dec 19: U.S. covert aid to factions in Angola was cut by the Senate, despite warnings that U.S. security was at stake in the resolution of the civil war. The war had broken out after Portugal granted independence to Angola.

Dec 20: The last of some 130,000 **Indochinese refugees** resettling in the U.S. left the processing center at Fort Chaffee, Ark.

Dec 29: An **airport bombing** in the main passenger terminal at LaGuardia Airport in New York City killed 11 people and injured 70.

II. Architecture
   Arts and Music
   Popular Entertainment
   Publishing
   Theater

In New York City, hard times notwithstanding, Broadway revenues for the 1974–1975 season hit $57,400,000, almost 25% more than the preceding year. Inflation and recession, however, did take their toll on museums. As the value of endowments fell, museums attempted to reduce operating deficits. They fired employees, curtailed services, shortened schedules, and instituted or increased admission fees. By contrast, the motion picture industry enjoyed a second straight year of record revenues, some $2,000,000,000. Fewer films were made, but income from such blockbusters as *Jaws* and *The Godfather, Part II*, as well as such slick sex films as *Emmanuelle* and *The Story of O* helped boost the box office take. This year Americans mourned the passing of Julian E. "Cannonball" Adderley, the jazz musician, Aug. 8, at 46; Josephine Baker, the cabaret singer, Apr. 10, at 68; Thomas Hart Benton, the artist, Jan. 19, at 85; Walker Evans, the photographer known best for his stark portraits of Depression-era subjects, Apr. 10, at 71; Susan Hayward, the actress, Mar. 14, at 55; Vincent Lopez, the band leader and pianist, Sept. 20, at 80; Fredric March, the actor, Apr. 14, at 77; Ozzie Nelson, the radio and television performer, June 3, at 68; Rod Serling, the author and screenwriter, June 28, at 50; George Stevens, the film director, Mar. 8, at 70; Rex Stout, the creator of fictional detective Nero Wolfe, Oct. 27, at 88; Richard Tucker, the opera tenor, Jan. 8, at 60; Charles Weidman, the modern dancer and choreographer, July 15, at 73; Thornton Wilder, the author, Dec. 7, at 78; and P.G. Wodehouse, the English-born author and humorist, Feb. 14, at 93.

Among **books published** this year was *Ragtime* by E. L. Doctorow, a novel set in the U.S. at the turn of the century. The novel carefully intermingled its fictional characters with such real figures as Henry

Ford, Harry Houdini, and Stanford White. Other books published this year included *Humboldt's Gift* by Saul Bellow, a novel; *Thurber* by Burton Bernstein, a biography; *How the Good Guys Finally Won* by Jimmy Breslin, one of several books published this year dealing with the Watergate scandal and the Nixon administration; *Against Our Will: Men, Women and Rape* by Susan Brownmiller; *The Lonely Hunter: A Biography of Carson McCullers* by Virginia Spencer Carr; *Shogun, A Novel of Japan* by James Clavell; *Poems: Selected and New, 1950–1974* by Adrienne Rich; *Looking for Mr. Goodbar* by Judith Rossner, a novel that became one of the year's best sellers; *Passions,* stories by Isaac Bashevis Singer; *Breach of Faith* by Theodore H. White, a study of Richard M. Nixon and the Watergate scandal; *A Time to Die* by Tom Wicker, a study of the 1971 Attica prison riot; and *The Twenties,* a posthumous publication from the notebooks of Edmund Wilson.

Jan 7: The **Bollingen Prize** for poetry was awarded to A. R. Ammons for his work *Sphere: The Form of a Motion* (1974).

Apr 8: The principle of **family viewing time** was adopted by the directors of the National Association of Broadcasters, representing two-thirds of all television stations. For two hours in the early evening, stations were to avoid broadcasting shows with strong themes of violence or sex.

May 5: **Pulitzer prizes** were awarded for the following: fiction, *The Killer Angels* by Michael Shaara; biography, *The Power Broker: Robert Moses and the Fall of New York* by Robert Caro; history, *Thomas Jefferson and His Times* by Dumas Malone; general nonfiction, *Pilgrim at Tinker Creek* by Annie Dillard; poetry, *Turtle Island* by Gary Snyder; drama, *Seascape* by Edward Albee.

May 27: In a landmark case dealing with **government censorship,** the Supreme Court let stand a lower court ruling requiring former CIA agent Victor Marchetti to submit all writings about the CIA to the agency for prior approval. It was the first such ruling on record.

Aug 1: The **New Orleans Superdome,** the world's largest indoor sports and entertainment center, was dedicated. It cost $162,000,000 and seated 97,000 people.

Sep 25: The FCC lifted the **equal time ruling** that required radio and television stations to offer equal broadcast time for all political candidates.

III. Business and Industry
Education
Philosophy and Religion
Science

Soaring prices prompted many to turn to gardening and home canning to trim food expenses, which were at an eight-year high as a percentage of take-home pay. There were as many as 6,000,000 new gardeners, according to estimates by the Department of Agriculture. Recovery from the recession began in spring but was hampered by steep interest rates and record high savings levels. Pres. Ford secured a federal tax cut but was unsuccessful in trimming the federal deficit. The budget for 1976 included a deficit of about $52,000,000,000, about 11.5% more than in 1975. This year a Senate committee and the Securities and Exchange Commission investigated illegal payoffs by U.S. businesses overseas. In medicine the increasing number of malpractice suits and high court awards produced skyrocketing insurance premiums, and in some cases withdrawal of malpractice coverage. In a number of states physicians threatened job actions if legislative remedies were not taken. This year also saw publication of a landmark religious work, *The Torah—A Modern Commentary,* Reform Judaism's first comprehensive and authorized commentary on the first five books of the Old Testament. Notables who died this year included John R. Dunning, the physicist, Aug. 25, at 67; Euell Gibbons, the naturalist and author, Dec. 29, at 64; Elijah Muhammad, leader of the Nation of Islam for 41 years, Feb. 25, at 77; Charles H. Revson, the business executive, Aug. 24, at 69; and Henry P. Van Dusen, the Protestant theologian, Feb. 13, at 77.

Mar 11: The **proportion of blacks in predominantly white schools** was higher in the South than in the North, according to a report by the Commission on Civil Rights.

Mar 17-20: In the first major **doctors' strike** in U.S. history, some 2000 interns and resident physicians successfully struck New York City's 21 metropolitan hospitals. They achieved their goal of securing shorter work shifts.

Mar 28: Authorization for so-called **no-frills airline fares** was given for the first time, to National Airlines, by the Civil Aeronautics Board. The fares were for travelers willing to forego such amenities as free meals and drinks.

May: **Exxon Corporation** was listed as the nation's wealthiest company in the annual *Fortune* magazine listing of 500 top industrial firms. Exxon bumped General Motors, number one in the listing for 40 years. Of the top 20 corporations, ten were oil companies.

May 22: A bill providing broad **securities industry reforms** was passed by Congress. It abolished fixed brokerage fees and ordered the Securities and Exchange Commission to set up a national securities clearance system that would give investors up-to-date information on dealings across the country.

May 27: The number of **abortion-related deaths** had been drastically reduced by liberal abortion laws, a report by the National Academy of Sciences revealed. Compared with 320 deaths in 1961, when illegal abortions were common, there had been only 47 deaths in 1973, including 16 linked to illegal operations.

June 4: Discovery of the **oldest animal fossils** in the U.S., large marine worms dating back some 620,000,000 years, was reported by paleontologists in North Carolina.

June 26: **Forced confinement of mental patients** was barred by the Supreme Court, provided that the patients could care for themselves and did not endanger others.

June 30: The **discovery of a galaxy** approximately 8,000,000,000 light-years away from Earth, identified as Galaxy 3C123, was announced by astronomers at the University of California. The farthest known galaxy from Earth, 3C123 was estimated to be five to ten times larger than the Milky Way.

July 15: The **Apollo-Soyuz** joint space mission began with the launch of Soyuz 19 from the U.S.S.R. and the launch of Apollo, carrying astronauts Thomas P. Stafford, Donald K. Slayton, and Vance D. Brand, from Kennedy Space Center in Florida. On July 17 the craft docked with one another. During their 44-hour linkup, the crews performed a number of experiments. Soyuz returned to Earth on July 21, and Apollo splashed down on July 24.

July 31: Former Teamsters president **James R. Hoffa** was reported missing by his family. Hoffa, who had served a prison term for jury tampering and mail fraud, had been trying to regain leadership of the Teamsters. It was speculated that he had been murdered by organized crime figures.

July 31: The **cancer death rate** was placed at 176.3 persons per 100,000 by the National Center for Health Statistics. The rate was 105.9 in 1933 and

Sep 4: The first court-ordered **cross-district school busing** in a metropolitan area began in Louisville and adjacent Jefferson County in Kentucky. The National Guard was called in on Sept. 6 because of violence in two working-class suburbs.

Sep 11: Former United Mine Workers president **William A. "Tony" Boyle** was sentenced to three consecutive life terms in Media, Pa., for ordering the 1969 murders of union opponent Joseph Yablonski and Yablonski's wife and daughter.

Sep 14: Mother **Elizabeth Ann Bayley Seton** was canonized in Rome by Pope Paul VI. She was the first U.S.-born saint.

Oct 14: The **Nobel Prize in Economics** was awarded jointly to Tjalling C. Koopmans of Yale University and to Leonid Kantorovich of the U.S.S.R.

Oct 16: The **Nobel Prize in Physiology or Medicine**

was awarded jointly to David Baltimore of the Center for Cancer Research at MIT, Howard M. Temin of the University of Wisconsin, and Dr. Renato Dulbecco of Italy for their studies of tumor viruses and the effect of the viruses on genetic material.

Oct 17: The **Nobel Prize in Physics** was awarded jointly to James Rainwater of Columbia University and to Aage N. Bohr and Ben Mottelson of Copenhagen, Denmark, for their work on the asymmetry of the atomic nucleus.

Oct 20: In a decision on **corporal punishment,** the Supreme Court ruled that teachers could spank students if the students were told in advance of the behavior that would warrant such punishment.

Nov 10: The parents of **Karen Anne Quinlan,** a young woman who had been comatose in a hospital for seven months, lost a bid in New Jersey Superior Court to have the respirator believed to be keeping their daughter alive turned off. The court ruled that although her condition was irreversible, she was not dead according to legal or medical criteria. On Mar. 31, 1976, the New Jersey Supreme Court gave its approval for disconnecting the respirator. Quinlan proved able to breathe without assistance.

Dec 2: A federal law prohibiting the **mailing of firearms** that could be hidden on one's person was upheld by the Supreme Court.

Dec 6: Creation of the **first artificial animal** gene was reported by a team of four Harvard scientists.

Dec 9: South Boston High School was placed under federal court receivership by Judge W. Arthur Garrity after charging the Boston School Committee with failing to implement a court-ordered busing plan to desegregate the school.

Dec 11: Legislation for **voluntary conversion to the metric system** within ten years was passed by Congress.

IV. **Fashion**
   Folkways
   Holidays
   Social Issues and Crime
   Sports

Declining attendance and failure to secure a profitable television contract led to the demise of the World Football League. The American Basketball Association, reduced from eleven teams to eight by season's end, also faced collapse. Increasing violence in hockey led to the first criminal trial of a player for conduct during a game. New federal guidelines requiring equal access for women in school sports were criticized by officials as burdening schools with oppressive costs. Athletics for females traditionally had been neglected in sports budgets. For example, in 1974–1975 UCLA spent $180,000 of its $3,000,000 sports budget for women's athletics. At the University of Nebraska, women's athletics was allocated $45,000 of a $4,000,000 sports budget. In professional golf the top money winners were Jack Nicklaus, $323,149, and Sandra Palmer, $94,805. This year many Americans found recreation in discothèques, where they could dance to music they enjoyed and be treated to colorful lighting effects. Jewelry for men became popular this year. Among the most fashionable items were pendants, rings, bracelets, and neck chains with shark teeth, a fad sparked by the motion picture *Jaws*. Notables who died this year included Avery Brundage, president of the International Olympic Committee from 1952–1972, May 8, at 87; Ezzard Charles, world heavyweight boxing champion from 1949–1951, May 27, at 53; Leland Stanford "Larry" MacPhail, the baseball executive, Oct. 1, at 85; Perle Mesta, the Washington hostess with the mostest, Mar. 16, at 85; Joan Whitney Payson, owner of the New York Mets, Oct. 4, at 72; and Charles Dillon "Casey" Stengel, who managed the New York Yankees and later the New York Mets and mismanaged the English language to the endless delight of sports fans, Sept. 29, at 85.

Jan 12: Super Bowl IX was won by the Pittsburgh Steelers (AFC), who defeated the Minnesota Vikings (NFC) 16–6 for their first Super Bowl win. On Dec. 29, 1974, the Steelers had beaten the Oakland Raiders 24 to 13 for the AFC championship and the Vikings had defeated the Los Angeles Rams 14 to 10 for the NFC title.

Feb 1: Otis Francis Tabler, a computer scientist, became the first declared **homosexual to get security clearance** for work on a Defense Department con-

Mar 31: The **NCAA basketball championship** was won for the tenth time in 12 years by UCLA, defeating the University of Kentucky 92 to 85. On Mar. 29 UCLA coach John Wooden had announced he was retiring, after compiling a 620–147 career record.

Apr 3: Bobby Fischer was stripped of his world chess title after he failed to accept a match with U.S.S.R. challenger Anatoly Karpov. Karpov became champion by default.

May 13-22: The **ABA basketball championship** was won by the Kentucky Colonels, who defeated the Indiana Pacers four games to one.

May 18-25: The **NBA basketball championship** was won by the Golden State Warriors, who swept the Washington Bullets in four games.

June 3: It was reported that **Pelé**, the Brazilian soccer star (born Edson Arantes do Nascimento), would come out of retirement to play for the New York Cosmos. His three-year, $7,000,000 contract made him the highest-paid team athlete in the world.

June 23: The **U.S. Open golf tournament** was won by Lou Graham, who beat John Mahaffey in a playoff.

July 4-5: At the **Wimbledon** tennis championships in England, Billie Jean King won the women's singles title and Arthur Ashe became the first black to win the men's singles title. The men's doubles was won by Vitas Gerulaitis and Sandy Mayer. Ann Kiyomura teamed with Kazuko Sawamatsu of Japan to win the women's doubles, and Marty Riessen teamed with Margaret Court of Australia to win the mixed doubles.

Aug 10: Betty Ford, wife of Pres. Gerald R. Ford, created an uproar when she said during a television interview that she suspected all four of her children had tried marijauna, that she would not be surprised if her 18-year-old daughter Susan told her she was having an affair, and that the Supreme Court had made a "great, great decision" in legalizing abortion.

Aug 10: The **PGA golf tournament** was won by Jack Nicklaus, who beat Bruce Crampton and Tom Weiskopf by two strokes.

Sep 1: Tom Seaver, pitcher for the New York Mets (NL), set a new major league record of eight consecutive years with 200 strikeouts or more in a season.

Sep 6-7: The **U.S. Open tennis singles championships** were won by Chris Evert Lloyd in the women's division and Manuel Orantes of Spain in the men's division.

Sep 18: Patricia Hearst was captured in a San Francisco apartment, ending a 19-month FBI search for the kidnaped newspaper heiress who subsequently joined her abductors, the terrorist Symbionese Liberation Army. Hearst and William and Emily Harris were indicted by a Los Angeles jury on Oct. 2 on charges of assault, robbery, and kidnaping in connection with a 1974 shoplifting incident.

Oct 1: In what he called the **Thriller in Manila,** the Philippines, heavyweight champion Muhammad Ali defeated Joe Frazier in 14 rounds in his fourth title defense of the year.

Oct 11-22: The **World Series** was won for the first time in 35 years by the Cincinnati Reds (NL), who beat the Boston Red Sox (AL) four games to three. On Oct. 7 the Reds had beaten the Pittsburgh Pirates in three straight games for the National League pennant, and the Red Sox had swept the Oakland Athletics in three straight.

1976

I. **Civil Rights**
   Exploration and Settlement
   Government
   Statistics
   Wars

Former governor James Earl "Jimmy" Carter of
Georgia pulled off a clear-cut victory in the presidential election by sweeping the South and carrying four
of the most populous northern industrial states. Having served only one term as governor, Carter made
his neophyte status an asset by appealing to voters'
mistrust of politicians, particularly those in Washington, D.C. Voters appeared to believe he would keep
his promises. "I'll never tell you a lie," he pledged. In
Washington, Rep. Wayne Hays was forced to resign
in the wake of a sex scandal, and influential congressmen admitted to receiving illegal donations from
Gulf Oil Corporation, although they denied having
known the source of the donations. The Justice Department conducted a probe of a scheme by South
Korean lobbyists to secure support for the government of Park Chung Hee with lavish gifts and political contributions to congressmen. The scandal al-
most predictably became known as Koreagate.
Notables who died this year included Richard J.
Daley, longtime mayor and political boss of Chicago,
Dec. 20, at 74; James A. Farley, a leading political
figure during the first two terms of Pres. Franklin D.
Roosevelt, June 9, at 88; Sen. Philip A. Hart, Demo-
crat of Michigan (1958–1976), Dec. 26, at 64; and
Martha Mitchell, wife of former attorney general
John Mitchell, who herself made headlines during
Watergate by providing information of the scandal to
the press, May 31, at 56.

Jan 30: Ruling on the **Federal Election Campaign Act**
of 1974, the Supreme Court upheld the provisions for

government financing of presidential campaigns, disclosure of campaign contributions, and a ceiling on contributions. The court struck down limits on campaign expenditures except those placed on funds spent by candidates accepting federal subsidies. It declared unconstitutional the Federal Election Commission as set up, stating that its officers would have to be appointed by the executive branch, not the legislative.

Feb 10: U.S. officials confirmed that **microwave radiation** had been trained on the U.S. Embassy in Moscow. Soviet officials later contended that the emissions had been intended to incapacitate U.S. listening devices.

Feb 17: In a move to **restructure the U.S. intelligence community,** Pres. Gerald R. Ford announced creation of an independent board to oversee U.S. foreign intelligence operations. The next day he issued an executive order curtailing domestic surveillance of U.S. citizens and proscribing burglaries, illegal use of federal tax returns, and drug tests of unsuspecting subjects. Political assassination in foreign covert operations was also forbidden.

Apr 26 and 28: The heavily censored, two-part report of the **Senate Select Committee on Intelligence** was issued. It urged stricter guidelines for intelligence activities, closer congressional oversight, and more stringent safeguards against violation of civil liberties.

May 28: A **nuclear test pact** was signed by the U.S. and U.S.S.R. It limited underground tests to devices of no more than 150 kiloton yields and permitted examination of Soviet test sites by the U.S..

June 5: In Idaho, the **Teton R. Dam collapsed** as it was being filled for the first time, flooding an area of 300 sq. mi. Fourteen people were killed, and estimated damage was $1,000,000,000.

June 16: The **U.S. ambassador to Lebanon was assassinated.** Francis E. Meloy, Jr., and an aide were killed in Beirut by unidentified gunmen. Meloy and his aide were en route to a meeting with president-elect Elias Sarkis.

July 2: Death penalty laws in Georgia, Florida, and Texas were upheld by the Supreme Court, but those in North Carolina and Louisiana, which prescribed death sentences for specific crimes, were struck down.

July 14: The **Democratic National Convention nominated Jimmy Carter** for the presidency on the first ballot. The next day Sen. Walter F. Mondale of Minnesota was nominated for the vice presidency.

July 20: The last **U.S. forces in Thailand** were withdrawn at the Thai government's request.

July 27: Some 160 **Americans were evacuated from Beirut,** Lebanon, along with 148 other foreigners, by the U.S. Navy acting in conjunction with the Palestine Liberation Organization and the Lebanese Army.

Aug 18: Two U.S. soldiers were killed by North Korean troops, who attacked a work party setting out to prune a tree that blocked surveillance of the demilitarized zone between North and South Korea. The U.S. protested the slayings. On Aug. 21 North Korea called the incident regrettable but did not accept responsibility.

Aug 19: The **Republican National Convention nominated Pres. Ford** for reelection in a narrow victory over former governor Ronald Reagan of California. Sen. Robert J. Dole of Kansas was nominated for the vice presidency.

Sep 10-12: An **airplane was hijacked** at La Guardia Airport in New York City by five Croatian terrorists, who forced the crew of the TWA 727 to fly the airplane to Paris. There the Croatians surrendered on Sept. 12. On the day before, a bomb left in New York by the terrorists exploded, killing a police bomb expert and wounding three others. The five terrorists were returned to the U.S. to face charges of air piracy and murder.

Sep 27: In the **first presidential TV debate** between an incumbent and a challenger, Pres. Ford and Democratic candidate Jimmy Carter discussed domestic issues before a television audience estimated at 90,000,000. Two more debates were held on Oct. 6 and Oct. 22. A fourth debate was held between vice-

presidential candidates Walter Mondale and Robert
Dole (Oct. 15). It was the first televised debate between candidates for vice president.

Oct 20: In what came to be called **Koreagate,** the Justice Department reported that a major probe was
under way concerning the activities of a South Korean lobby, led by businessman Tongsun Park. The
purpose of the lobby was to influence congressmen
and other government officials through cash grants
and campaign contributions estimated at $500,000 to
$1,000,000 annually.

Nov 2: James Earl "Jimmy" Carter, Jr., **was elected
president** of the United States. Walter F. Mondale
was elected vice president. The electoral vote was
Carter, 297; Pres. Ford, 240. The popular vote was
Carter, 40,828,929; Ford, 39,148,940. In congressional elections the Democrats kept a 2–1 Senate majority, 61–38, with one seat going to an independent, and
a House majority of 292–143.

II. Architecture
Arts and Music
Popular Entertainment
Publishing
Theater

The year in theater was noteworthy for its excellent
revivals of *Porgy and Bess, My Fair Lady, Guys and
Dolls,* and *Fiddler on the Roof.* In film the year was
highlighted by such foreign works as Ingmar Bergman's version of Mozart's *The Magic Flute* and Lina
Wertmuller's *Seven Beauties.* But in Hollywood, the
biggest success came with *Rocky,* starring Sylvester
Stallone as a small-time boxer given an improbable
shot at the championship. The movie made Stallone
a star and led to several sequels. Television hits included the miniseries *Rich Man, Poor Man,* the lightweight series *Charlie's Angels,* featuring three eye-
catching private investigators, and the soap opera
spoof *Mary Hartman, Mary Hartman.* Notables who
died this year included Busby Berkeley, real name
William Berkeley Enos, the Hollywood choreogra-

pher, Mar. 14, at 80; Alexander Calder, the sculptor, Nov. 11, at 78; Lee J. Cobb, the actor, Feb. 11, at 64; Paul Gallico, the writer, July 15, at 78; Bobby Hackett, the jazz cornetist, June 7, at 61; Fritz Lang, the motion picture director, Aug. 2, at 85; Lotte Lehmann, the German-born soprano, Aug. 26, at 88; Johnny Mercer, writer of such songs as "Moon River" and "That Old Black Magic," June 25, at 66; Samuel Eliot Morison, the historian, May 15, at 89; Phil Ochs, songwriter and folk singer, Apr. 9, at 35; Walter Piston, the composer, Nov. 12, at 82; Lily Pons, the French-born Metropolitan Opera star for some 25 years, Feb. 13, at 71; Man Ray, the artist and leading exponent of Dada, Nov. 18, at 86; Paul Robeson, the singer and actor, Jan. 23, at 77; Rosalind Russell, the actress, Nov. 28, at 63; Mark Tobey, the abstract painter, Apr. 24, at 85; Dalton Trumbo, the novelist and screenwriter who was blacklisted in the late 1940s, Sept. 10, at 70; and Adolph Zukor, the motion picture executive who founded Paramount Pictures, June 10, at 103.

Among **books published** this year was *Roots* by Alex Haley, a fictionalized account of the author's discovery of his lineage in Africa. The book became a best seller and was the basis for an enormously popular television miniseries. Other books published this year included *The Black Family in Slavery and Freedom* by Herbert Gutman, which attacked the notion that blacks lacked strong family units in the past; *Scoundrel Time* by Lillian Hellman, memoirs; *World of Our Fathers* by Irving Howe, a study of the lives of Jews who emigrated from eastern Europe; *Lyndon Johnson and the American Dream* by Doris Kearns, a sympathetic portrait of the former president; *Agent in Place* by Helen MacInnes, a spy thriller; *The Russians* by Hedrick Smith, nonfiction; *Spandau* by Albert Speer, memoirs; *Adolf Hitler* by John Toland, biography; *Trinity* by Leon Uris, a novel; *Slapstick* by Kurt Vonnegut, a novel; and *The Final Days* by Robert Woodward and Carl Bernstein, an account of the end of the Nixon presidency.

Feb 11-18: The New York City weekly *The Village*

Voice published major portions of a secret House of Representatives report on intelligence agencies. CBS news reporter Daniel Schorr admitted on Feb. 12 that he had provided the *Voice* with a copy of the report. Schorr was suspended by CBS on Feb. 23, after the House ordered an inquiry to determine how he obtained the document. The inquiry proved unsuccessful and was halted on Sept. 22.

Apr 22: Barbara Walters became the first anchorwoman of a network television news program and the highest-paid journalist in history when she accepted a five-year, $5,000,000 contract with ABC.

May 3: Pulitzer prizes were awarded for the following: fiction, *Humboldt's Gift* by Saul Bellow; biography, *Edith Wharton: A Biography* by R. W. B. Lewis; history, *Lamy of Santa Fe* by Paul Horgan; general nonfiction, *Why Survive? Being Old in America* by Robert N. Butler; poetry, *Self-Portrait in a Convex Mirror* by John Ashbery; drama, *A Chorus Line* by Michael Bennett, Nicholas Dante, Marvin Hamlisch, James Kirkwood, and Edward Kleban.

May 18: What was billed as the **Concert of the Century** was presented at Carnegie Hall in New York City to benefit a $6,500,000 fund drive for the concert hall. Among the musical greats who participated were Leonard Bernstein, Yehudi Menuhin, Mstislav Rostropovich, Vladimir Horowitz, and Isaac Stern.

June 2: A journalist's car was bombed in Phoenix, Ariz. Don Bolles, an investigative reporter for the *Arizona Republic*, had been probing the role of leading politicians in land swindles. He died on June 13.

Sep 29: A new **record art price** for a painting by Rembrandt, $3,250,000, was set by the industrialist Armand Hammer, who announced acquisition of Rembrandt's *Juno.*

Sep 30: In the first major attempt at **copyright reform** since 1909, Congress approved legislation, effective Jan. 1, 1978, extending copyright protection for 50 years after the death of an author, artist, or composer. It also restricted reproduction of copyrighted material and set royalty rates for phonograph records played by broadcasters or used in jukeboxes.

Oct 6: The last privately owned painting by **Jackson**

Pollock, *Lavender Mist,* was reported to have been acquired by the National Gallery of Art in Washington, D.C., for $2,000,000. It had been bought in 1950 for about $1500.

Oct 21: The **Nobel Prize in Literature** was awarded to Saul Bellow "for the human understanding and subtle analysis of contemporary culture that are combined in his work."

III. Business and Industry
Education
Philosophy and Religion
Science

The state of the economy was probably a major contributor to Jimmy Carter's election to the presidency this year. Voters were wary of inflation, which fluctuated between 5% and 6%, and unemployment, which was about 8%. In this year, business ethics came under scrutiny following revelations of corporate payoffs to win sales abroad. Lockheed and Northrop were two major firms that were strongly criticized. Public indignation was also kindled by reports that a number of multinational corporations were cooperating with an Arab embargo on trade with Israel. Congress sought to discourage such behavior by eliminating tax incentives to participating firms. Census Bureau reports indicated that the number of Americans with high-school diplomas had doubled since 1950, but public concern about the quality of education was reflected in calls for greater emphasis on traditional educational skills. A number of states began to require high-school students to pass a comprehensive test before receiving diplomas. The year in science was highlighted by a clean sweep of Nobel Prizes by Americans. Notables who died this year included Jean Paul Getty, the billionaire oil tycoon, June 6, at 83; Howard R. Hughes, Jr., the reclusive billionaire, Apr. 5, at 72; Gerald L. K. Smith, the anti-Semitic, anti-Catholic founder of the so-called National Christian Crusade, Apr. 15, at 78; and Luther Allan Weigle, the biblical scholar who oversaw compilation of the Revised Standard Version of the Bible, Sept. 2, at 96.

Jan 12: The **first report on national health** issued by the Department of Health, Education, and Welfare indicated that Americans were generally healthy. Infant mortality rates had dropped from their 1950 level of 29.2 per 1000 births to 16.5. Heart disease among those 55 to 64 years of age had declined by almost 15% since 1970. The role of insurance companies in medical payments expanded. In 1950 they paid one-third of all health bills, but in 1975 they paid

Feb 12: Production of **Red Dye No. 2,** most frequently used in drugs, foods, and cosmetics, was banned by the Food and Drug Administration after studies indicated that the dye was carcinogenic.

Apr 1: Conrail, a federally funded corporation, took over operation of six bankrupt northeastern railroads. Federal subsidies were slated to end after five years.

Apr 21: Production of convertibles by the U.S. auto industry halted as General Motors rolled the last of its Cadillac Eldorado convertibles off the assembly line. The move was made in response to declining sales.

Apr 22: Widespread **cheating at West Point** was reported. By September, 700 cadets at the U.S. Military Academy were implicated in violations of the academy's honor code.

May 24: Concorde supersonic jet service between the U.S. and Europe was inaugurated when two Anglo-French Concorde jets arrived from Paris and London at Dulles International Airport, near Washington, D.C.

June 25: Discrimination by private nonsectarian schools was ruled unconstitutional by the Supreme Court.

July 9: The tranquilizer **Valium and alcohol** were the leading causes of drug-related ailments, according to a report of the National Institute on Drug Abuse. Valium, used by some 65,000,000 Americans, was the most often prescribed drug. The report stated that alcohol surpassed all other drugs in social costs.

July 18: Discovery of **Lyme arthritis,** a new, infectious strain of arthritis, was reported by researchers at Yale University's School of Medicine. Some 51 cases of the disease, apparently caused by an insect-borne virus, were recorded in and around Lyme, Conn.

July 20: **Viking 1,** launched on Aug. 20, 1975, landed on Mars. It was the first spacecraft to reach the planet. Data collected by Viking 1 and by **Viking 2,** launched on Sept. 9, 1975, and landed on Mars on Sept. 3, 1976, showed Mars to be a barren, rocky planet. Tests to detect the presence of life there were inconclusive.

July 27-Aug 31: What came to be called **Legionnaires' disease** claimed the lives of 29 people who had attended an American Legion convention in Philadelphia, Pa., on July 21–24. Another 151 were hospitalized for high fever and respiratory problems, symptoms of the disease.

Aug 28: **Synthesis of a bacterial gene** had been accomplished for the first time, scientists at the Massachusetts Institute of Technology reported. The gene functioned properly when implanted in a living cell.

Aug 30: **Medicaid waste** from fraud, abuse, and government bungling devoured some 25–50% of the $15,000,000,000 Medicaid budget, a Senate study reported. About half the $3,000,000,000 spent on physicians, dentists, pharmacies, and laboratories went for substandard or unnecessary care provided by Medicaid mills, privately owned clinics usually located in poor urban neighborhoods.

Sep 16: The **ordination of women** was approved by the 65th triennial General Convention of the Episcopal Church. By year's end, some of those who disapproved of the change were preparing to break with the church.

Sep 18: The Rev. **Sun Myung Moon,** head of the evangelical Unification Church, presided over a "God Bless America" rally in Washington, D.C., that drew some 50,000 persons. Moon, who advocated U.S. defense of South Korea, was denounced by established church leaders for perverting Christian doctrine. He was also under attack from parents who claimed brainwashing tactics had been used to recruit young people into the church. The converts, who solicited contributions in public places, were frequently referred to as *Moonies.*

Sep 28: The **Toxic Substances Control Act,** was passed by Congress. It prohibited the marketing of new chemical compounds before testing their impact on human health and the environment. The law also forbade production of polychlorinated biphenyls, or PCBs, after 1979. Studies of PCBs had shown they did not break down in the environment and were linked to cancer.

Sep 30: The first state **right-to-die law** was passed in California. It granted to adult patients the right to authorize a physician to shut off their life-support equipment when death was imminent. The law went into effect on Jan. 1, 1977.

Oct 14: The **Nobel Prize in Physiology or Medicine** was awarded jointly to Dr. Baruch S. Blumberg of the University of Pennsylvania Medical School and to Dr. D. Carleton Gajdusek of the National Institute for Neurological Diseases for their work on infectious diseases.

Oct 14: The **Nobel Prize in Economics** was awarded to Milton Friedman of the University of Chicago.

Oct 18: The **Nobel Prize in Chemistry** was awarded to William N. Lipscomb, Jr., of Harvard University for his studies of the structure and bonding of chemical compounds known as boranes.

Oct 18: The **Nobel Prize in Physics** was awarded jointly to Burton Richter of Stanford University and to Samuel C. C. Ting of MIT for their discovery of the psi, or J, particle.

Dec 15: A major **oil spill** began when the Liberian-registered tanker *Argo Merchant* ran aground near Nantucket Island, Mass., and its 7,700,000-gallon oil cargo leaked.

IV. Fashion
   Folkways
   Holidays
   Social Issues and Crime
   Sports

Professional athletes in baseball, basketball, and football gained greater freedom as team owners revised reserve and option clauses. The issue centered on the tying of players to clubs until retirement or disposal by the team. Owners' fears that so-called free agents would cripple sports proved groundless. Only 24 football players and 24 baseball players chose free-agent status. In basketball, free trading was slated to start in 1980. In boxing, Muhammad Ali defended his heavyweight title in three bouts and then announced his retirement. In golf the top money winners were Jack Nicklaus, $266,438, and Judy Rankin, $150,734. This year Americans found new sources of amusement in Citizen Band radios and in electronic games that hooked up to television sets. Among the year's deaths was that of Carlo Gambino, reportedly a leading figure in organized crime, Oct. 15, at 74.

Jan 9: A new amateur **pole vault record** of 18 ft. 1¼ in. was set by Dan Ripley at a National Invitational Indoor Track meet in College Park, Md.

Jan 18: Super Bowl X was won by the Pittsburgh Steelers (AFC), who defeated the Dallas Cowboys (NFC) 21 to 17 to pick up their second straight victory. On Jan. 4 the Steelers had beaten the Oakland Raiders 16–10 for the AFC championship and the Cowboys had beaten the Los Angeles Rams 37 to 7 for the NFC title.

Feb 4-15: At the **Winter Olympics** in Innsbruck, Austria, the U.S. won three gold medals and tied with West Germany for third place, behind the U.S.S.R. and East Germany. Dorothy Hamill, who won a gold medal on Feb. 13, emerged from the games as an Olympic star.

Mar 20: Patricia Hearst was convicted by a San Francisco jury of taking part in a 1974 bank robbery. She was sentenced to seven years in jail on Sept. 24 and released on bail pending appeal.

Mar 29: The **NCAA basketball championship** was won by Indiana, defeating Michigan 86 to 68.

May 1-13: The **ABA basketball championship** was won by the New York Nets, who defeated the Denver Nuggets four games to two to take their second championship in three years.

May 23-June 6: The **NBA basketball championship** was won for the 13th time by the Boston Celtics, defeating the Phoenix Suns four games to two.

June 17: In a **basketball merger,** the 18 teams of the NBA merged with four of the six remaining teams of the ABA.

June 20: The **U.S. Open golf tournament** was won in an upset by golf rookie Jerry Pate, who beat Tom Weiskopf and Al Geiberger by two strokes.

July 2-3: At the **Wimbledon** tennis championships in England, Chris Evert Lloyd won the women's singles title. Brian Gottfried teamed with Paul Ramirez of Mexico to win the men's doubles, and Evert Lloyd teamed with Martina Navratilova of Czechoslovakia to win the women's doubles.

July 4: A year of festivities celebrating the **bicentennial of U.S. independence** was capped at 2 P.M. by the ringing of bells nationwide. Among the special events this day were Operation Sail, a parade in New York harbor of more than 50 warships and 16 windjammers from many nations; convergence at Valley Forge, Pa., of six wagon trains that had trekked across the country; sealing of time capsules; and a 76-hour vigil (starting July 2) at the National Archives to honor the signing of the Declaration of Independence.

July 12: A change in the baseball **reserve clause** was agreed to by major league owners and players. The new rule allowed players to become free agents after five years.

July 17-Aug 1: At the **Summer Olympics** in Montreal, Canada, the U.S. won 34 gold medals and finished second in unofficial team standings behind the U.S.S.R. Among the stars of the games was decathlon champion Bruce Jenner.

Aug 16: The **PGA golf tournament** was won by Dave Stockton for the second time.

Aug 27: A new type of **sexual discrimination** in sports was highlighted when transsexual Renee Richards, formerly Richard Raskind, an eye surgeon, was barred from competing at the U.S. Open tennis championships at Forest Hills, N.Y., after refusing to submit to a chromosome qualification test.

Sep 11-12: The **U.S. Open tennis singles championships** were won by Chris Evert Lloyd in the women's division and Jimmy Connors in the men's division.

Oct 16-21: The **World Series** was won in a four-game sweep by the Cincinnati Reds (NL) over the New York Yankees (AL). On Oct. 12 the Reds had won the National League pennant over the Philadelphia Phillies in a three-game sweep, and the Yankees had taken the American League pennant from the Kansas City Royals three games to two.

Nov 4: In major league baseball's **first free-agent draft,** 24 players from 13 clubs participated. Reggie Jackson signed the most lucrative contract, calling for $2,900,000 over five years with the New York Yankees (AL).

1977

I. Civil Rights
Exploration and Settlement
Government
Statistics
Wars

In the first months of Pres. Jimmy Carter's administration, most Vietnam-era draft resisters were pardoned, the planned pullout of U.S. forces from South Korea was announced, and administration officials spoke out against human rights violations worldwide. Pres. Carter also established guidelines to prevent conflict of interest among officials, opened communication between the White House and ordinary citizens, ended U.S. opposition to the admission of Vietnam to the UN, and signed two treaties returning control of the Panama Canal to Panama. The new president suffered setbacks when Congress challenged the financial dealings of Bert Lance, director of the Office of Management and Budget, and opposed passage of Carter's energy conservation program. Vernon Jordan of the National Urban League charged the administration with not doing enough to reduce unemployment among blacks. Notables who died this year included Lewis B. Hershey, director of the Selective Service System from 1941 to 1973, May 20, at 83; Sen. John L. McClellan, chairman of the Senate Appropriations Committee, Nov. 27, at 81; and Francis Gary Powers, the pilot shot down over the U.S.S.R. in 1960, Aug. 1, at 48.

Jan 19: Tokyo Rose, real name Iva Toguri D'Aquino, was pardoned by Pres. Gerald R. Ford 27 years after her conviction for treason. She had made propaganda broadcasts from Japan during World War II in an attempt to demoralize U.S. troops.

Jan 21: A presidential pardon for most of the nation's Vietnam draft resisters was issued by Pres. Carter.

Jan 28-29: A blizzard paralyzed much of the East and Midwest, worsening a severe shortage of natural gas. Among the hardest hit cities was Buffalo, N.Y., which already had a cumulative snowfall of 160 inches.

Feb 28: A longstanding **land suit** against the state of Maine by the Passamaquoddy and Penobscot Indians prompted the federal government to warn that it would sue Maine if the state did not reach a settlement quickly.

Mar 2: A new **House ethics code** was adopted. It limited outside income for members of the House of Representatives, broadened financial disclosure requirements, and restricted gifts by lobbyists. The Senate adopted a similar code on Apr. 1.

Mar 9: U.S. ground forces in Korea would be withdrawn within five years, Pres. Carter announced.

Mar 18: U.S. **travel restrictions** to Cuba, Vietnam, North Korea, and Cambodia were lifted.

Apr 27: A **task force on illegal aliens** reported to Pres. Carter that 6,000,000 to 8,000,000 illegal aliens were living in the U.S. About 876,000 had been caught in 1976, compared with 89,000 in 1961.

Apr 28: In a major **espionage** case, a U.S. citizen named Christopher J. Boyce was convicted of supplying data on satellites and CIA codes to the U.S.S.R. in complicity with another American, Andrew Lee. On Sept. 12 Boyce was sentenced to 40 years in prison. Lee was convicted on May 14 and sentenced on July 18 to life imprisonment.

May 3: Normalization talks between the U.S. and Vietnam began in Paris. On the next day, the U.S. agreed to stop blocking Vietnam's request for admission to the UN.

May 4: Richard M. Nixon, in the first of five television interviews with David Frost, for which the former president was paid, acknowledged that he had "let the American people down" through his actions in the Watergate cover-up. In the May 19 interview, Nixon argued that sanctioning burglary and other illegal activities taken against dissidents is not illegal "when the president does it."

May 23: The end of the road in the **Watergate** scandal came for three former U.S. officials, John Ehrlichman, H. R. Haldeman, and John Mitchell, when the Supreme Court refused to hear their appeals. On June 22 Mitchell became the first former attorney general to begin serving a prison sentence.

June 6: Development of a **neutron bomb** by the U.S. was reported by the Washington *Post*. The weapon was designed to kill people but cause minimal destruction of property.

June 30: A halt in production of the **B-1 bomber** was announced by Pres. Carter.

July 13-14: A 25-hour **power failure** struck New York City and suburban Westchester County, leading to extensive looting and arson in the city. Some 3776 looters were arrested and 100 policemen injured. Property damage was estimated at $135,000,000.

July 19: Flooding struck the Johnstown, Pa., area, killing 76 people and causing some $200,000,000 in damage.

July 20: In the so-called **Koreagate** lobbying scandal, former Watergate prosecutor Leon Jaworski agreed to lead a House Ethics Committee probe into alleged congressional influence-buying by South Korean lobbyists. On Dec. 30 the Justice Department announced that South Korean businessman Tongsun Park had agreed to testify in return for immunity from prosecution.

Aug 4: Legislation creating the **Department of Energy,** the twelfth Cabinet-level department and the first new one since 1966, was signed by Pres. Carter. James R. Schlesinger was nominated and quickly confirmed as the first secretary of energy.

Aug 20: The **Republican Party** was reported by a Gallup poll to have the support of 20% of U.S. voters, the worst showing in 40 years.

Sep 7: Two **Panama Canal treaties,** transferring control of the canal to Panama by the year 2000, were signed by Pres. Carter and Panama's head of state, Brig. Gen. Omar Torrijos Herrera. The accords, capping 13 years of negotiations, were subject to ratification by each nation's legislature.

Sep 21: Bert Lance resigned as director of the Office of Management and Budget following severe criticism of his past financial practices as a banker in Georgia.

Nov 18-21: The first **National Women's Conference,** the largest feminist gathering since the Seneca Falls, N.Y., convention in 1848, drew 1442 delegates to Houston, Tex., to call for passage of the Equal Rights Amendment and elimination of institutional discrimination. Opponents of ERA and abortion held a so-called pro-family rally five miles away.

Dec 20: Legislation authorizing a **Social Security tax increase** was signed by Pres. Carter. The tax revision was expected to cost workers and employers $227,000,000,000 in the next ten years.

II. Architecture
   Arts and Music
   Popular Entertainment
   Publishing
   Theater

Even as the nation's interest in the arts boomed, the top 200 nonprofit performing arts groups were sinking under a $125,000,000 deficit incurred during the 1976–1977 season. The Metropolitan Opera in New York City confronted a $14,000,000 deficit; museums in New York, Chicago, and San Diego cut viewing hours to save costs. The American Shakespeare Festival in Stratford, Conn., failed to open for the season, and the City Center Joffrey Ballet in New York scrapped its spring season. In contrast, motion picture revenues were up to a record $2,300,000,000, largely because of such phenomenally successful films as *Star Wars* and *Close Encounters of the Third Kind*. Television's hit show of the year was the miniseries *Roots*, based on the book by Alex Haley. Americans mourned the passing this year of James M. Cain, the novelist, Oct. 27, at 85; Maria Callas, the opera singer, Sept. 16, at 53; Joan Crawford, the actress, May 10, at 69; Harry Lillis "Bing" Crosby, Oct. 14, at 73; Howard Hawks, the motion picture director, Dec. 26, at 81; James Jones, the novelist, May 9, at 55; Guy Lombardo, the band leader, Nov. 5, at 75; Robert Lowell, the poet, Sept. 12, at 60; Alfred Lunt, who performed with his wife Lynn Fontanne in numerous Broadway plays, Aug. 3, at 83; Julius Henry "Groucho" Marx, Aug. 19, at 86, and his brother, Milton "Gummo" Marx, Apr. 21, at 84; Samuel J. "Zero" Mostel, the actor, Sept. 8, at 62; Vladimir Nabokov, the writer, July 2, at 78; Elvis Presley, the king of rock 'n' roll, Aug. 16, at 42; and Ethel Waters, the blues singer and actress, Sept. 1, at 80.

Among **books published** this year was *A Rumor of War* by Philip Caputo. The book was hailed as one of the year's best of several works dealing with the Vietnam War. Other books published this year included

Falconer by John Cheever, a novel examining the soul of a convict; *Six Men* by Alistair Cooke, essays on six well-known figures of the twentieth century; *A Book of Common Prayer* by Joan Didion, a novel dealing with the inability of its middle-aged characters to find meaning in their lives; *The Immigrants* by Howard Fast, a novel; *The Age of Uncertainty* by John Kenneth Galbraith; *The Thorn Birds* by Colleen McCullough, a novel that became a runaway best seller; *Coming into the Country* by John McPhee, an excellent book about Alaska and Alaskans; and *Ring* by Jonathan Yardley, a biography of Ring Lardner.

Jan 11: The **Bollingen Prize** for poetry was awarded to David Ignatow.

Feb 8: Larry Flynt, publisher of the sexually explicit magazine *Hustler,* was convicted in Cincinnati of promoting obscenity and involvement in organized crime.

Apr 18: Pulitzer prizes were awarded for the following: biography, *A Prince of Our Disorder* by John E. Mack; history, *The Impending Crisis: 1841–1861* by David M. Potter; general nonfiction, *Beautiful Swimmers* by William W. Warner; poetry, *Divine Comedies* by James Merrill; drama, *The Shadow Box* by Michael Cristofer. A special award was given for *Roots,* written by Alex Haley.

June 30: The **Newport Jazz Festival,** citing prohibitive costs and acoustical problems, announced it was ending its six-year tenure in New York City and moving in 1978 to Saratoga Springs, N.Y.

Nov 13: The final installment of *Li'l Abner,* the comic strip created by Al Capp in 1934, marked Capp's retirement.

Nov 22: What was said to be a **record price for sculpture**—between $3,500,000 and $5,000,000—was reported to have been paid by the J. Paul Getty Museum in California for a fourth-century B.C. bronze.

III. Business and Industry
Education
Philosophy and Religion
Science

The U.S. faced a high trade deficit, primarily because of oil imports and the falling value of the dollar. Uncertainty about Pres. Carter's legislative program for tax reform and concern about new, inflationary social programs slowed investment by the private sector. The Dow Jones average declined more than 165 points during the year, and unemployment remained at 7% of the work force. The retail price of a pound of coffee hit $5.00, mainly because of a killing frost in Brazil in 1975. Many consumers struck back by switching to tea. Tea imports rose by nearly 30%, and tea prices rose as well. In transportation, the year was marked by sharp air fare reductions on domestic and transatlantic routes as airlines began offering no-frills flights. Transportation Sec. Brock Adams ruled that airbags or safety belts would be required automotive equipment beginning in 1984. In education, amendments to the Rehabilitation Act of 1973 required that handicapped children be included in regular school settings. Notables who died this year included Wernher von Braun, the German-born rocket pioneer, June 16, at 65; Loren C. Eiseley, the anthropologist and author, July 9, at 69; and John R. Powers, founder of the Powers modeling agency, July 19, at 80.

Jan 1: The **first woman Episcopal priest** in the U.S., Jacqueline Means, was ordained.

Jan 11: Henry Ford, II, resigned as trustee of the Ford Foundation, criticizing its staff for ingratitude for the capitalist wealth that made its work possible.

Jan 11: Discriminatory zoning laws, enabling suburbs to block racially integrated housing for low- and middle-income families, were upheld by the Supreme Court. The Court ruled that the refusal of a suburb to change zoning laws was not inherently unconstitutional.

Feb 23: The **Environmental Protection Agency** was

held by the Supreme Court to have the authority to establish industry-wide standards to control discharge of pollutants into waterways.

Mar 1: The U.S. extended its **fishing limits** to 200 miles offshore to protect depleted fisheries against the activities of foreign fishing fleets.

Mar 9: A ban on **saccharin** was proposed by the Food and Drug Administration after tests suggested that the artificial sweetener might be carcinogenic. Consumer resistance and intense lobbying led the FDA to allow saccharin to be sold as an over-the-counter drug. On Nov. 4 Congress postponed the ban for 18 months, pending new tests.

Apr 18: An all-out campaign for **energy conservation** was called for by Pres. Carter, who called the effort "the moral equivalent of war." On Apr. 20 he asked Congress for new legislation designed to discourage energy waste and encourage conservation measures.

Apr 30: Some 2000 **opponents of nuclear energy** occupied the construction site of a nuclear generating plant at Seabrook, N.H. By May 2 some 1414 protesters had been arrested for trespassing.

May 1: Controversy over **Laetrile,** a purported anti-cancer compound derived primarily from apricot pits, continued as the state of Indiana passed the first law legalizing its manufacture, sale, and use.

May 30: Viking 1 and 2 biological experiments on the planet Mars, which had proven inconclusive, were terminated by NASA scientists.

June 19: Bishop **John N. Neumann** of Philadelphia, known for his development of the parochial school system, was canonized by the Roman Catholic Church. He became the first American male to achieve sainthood.

June 20: Medicaid funding for elective abortions was ruled by the Supreme Court to be not obligatory under the Constitution or federal law.

June 27: Legal advertising of fees for specific, routine services was upheld by the Supreme Court in a decision with wide-ranging implications for a number of professions.

July 28: The 799-mile **trans-Alaska pipeline** went into full operation as the first oil from Alaska's Prudhoe Bay fields arrived at the loading port of Valdez at 11:02 P.M. (4:02 A.M. July 29, EST). Pumping operations had begun on June 20.

Aug 12: The **space shuttle** *Enterprise,* with astronauts C. Gordon Fullerton and Fred W. Haise, Jr., aboard, made its first free flight at Edwards Air Force Base after being lifted to 25,000 feet on the back of a Boeing 747.

Aug 23: The 77-pound aircraft *Gossamer Condor,* powered by its pilot, was flown by Bryan Allen over a one-mile, figure-eight course at Shafter, Calif. The craft won for its designer, Paul MacCready, the $86,000 Kremer prize for human-powered aircraft.

Sep 13: The **first U.S. diesel automobiles** were introduced by General Motors. The cars, Oldsmobile 88 and 98 models, were said to have 40% greater fuel efficiency than gasoline-powered cars.

Oct 11: The **Nobel Prize in Physics** was awarded jointly to John H. Van Vleck of Harvard University, Philip W. Anderson of Bell Laboratories and Princeton University, and Nevill F. Mott of Great Britain for their contributions to the field of solid state electronic circuitry.

Oct 13: The **Nobel Prize in Physiology or Medicine** was awarded jointly to Rosalyn S. Yalow of the Veterans Administration Hospital, Bronx, N.Y., Roger C. L. Guillemin of the Salk Institute, and Andrew V. Schally of Veterans Administration Hospital, New Orleans, La., and Tulane University for their independent studies of the production of peptide hormones in the brain and the relation of the hypothalamus in controlling the pituitary gland.

Oct 19: The **Concorde SST** made its first flight from France to Kennedy Airport in New York two days after the Supreme Court refused to stay a lower court ruling authorizing the flights. Concorde flights to Washington, D.C., had begun in May 1976.

Nov 1: A law raising the **minimum wage** from $2.30 to $3.35 an hour by 1981 was signed by Pres. Carter.

Dec 10: A nationwide **farmers' strike** was launched by the American Agriculture Movement, which held rallies in 30 state capitals in a drive to raise farmers' falling incomes.

IV. Fashion
Folkways
Holidays
Social Issues and Crime
Sports

With star player Pelé in action with an American professional team, soccer became the fastest growing team sport in the U.S. Growth of soccer (some 350,000 persons under 18 years of age were playing the game) was enhanced further by availability of inexpensive equipment, low injury rate, and accessibility for women players. The price of a professional soccer franchise had risen tenfold since 1971, when the going price was $10,000. Baseball attendance leaped 24% over 1976 levels, and basketball attendance edged the 10,000,000 mark. In horse racing 17-year-old Steve Cauthen drew wide attention for his remarkable achievements as a jockey. In boxing, Muhammad Ali decided not to retire and defended his heavyweight crown twice. In golf the top money winners were Tom Watson, $310,653, and Judy Rankin, $122,890. Also this year, skateboards became a new activity for vast numbers of youngsters. Notables who died this year included Robert Calvin "Cal" Hubbard, the baseball umpire, Oct. 17, at 77; Bernard "Toots" Shor, the celebrated New York City barkeeper, Jan. 23, at 73; and Philip K. Wrigley, owner of the Chicago Cubs baseball team, Apr. 12, at 82.

Jan 9: Super Bowl XI was won by the Oakland Raiders (AFC), who defeated the Minnesota Vikings (NFC) 32 to 14. On Dec. 26, 1976, the Raiders had beaten the Pittsburgh Steelers 24 to 7 for the NFC championship, and the Vikings had beaten the Los Angeles Rams 24 to 13 for the AFC title.

Jan 17: Convicted murderer **Gary Gilmore** was executed by a Utah firing squad, ending a ten-year halt on capital punishment in the U.S.

Mar 9-11: A **terrorist raid** was staged in Washington, D.C., by 12 Hanafi Muslim gunmen. The terrorists seized three buildings and demanded custody of five Black Muslims who had been imprisoned for the 1973 murder of seven Hanafis and of three more Black Muslims who had been imprisoned for the 1965 murder of Malcolm X. One person was killed during the raid, and 139 were held prisoner for 39 hours before the terrorists surrendered.

Mar 28: The **NCAA basketball championship** was won by Marquette University, defeating North Carolina 67 to 59.

May 7: The 103rd **Kentucky Derby** was won by Seattle Slew, with a time of 2:02^1/$_5$. The jockey was Jean Cruguet.

May 9: Patricia Hearst, serving a prison sentence for a 1974 robbery, was released on probation.

May 21: The 102nd **Preakness Stakes** was won by Seattle Slew, with a time of 1:54^2/$_5$. The jockey was Jean Cruguet.

May 22-June 5: The **NBA basketball championship** was won by the Portland Trail Blazers, who beat the Philadelphia 76ers four games to two after losing the first two games of the series.

May 26: One of the towers of the **World Trade Center was scaled** by George Willig, a toy designer, who climbed the south tower in three and a half hours. He was fined $1.10, one cent for each story of the building.

June 11: The 109th annual **Belmont Stakes** was won by Seattle Slew, finishing in 2:29^3/$_5$ to take the race and become the tenth horse to win racing's Triple Crown. The jockey was Jean Cruguet.

June 19: The **U.S. Open golf tournament** was won by Hubert Green, beating Lou Graham by one stroke.

June 29: Capital punishment for rape was ruled unconstitutional by the Supreme Court.

July 2: At the **Wimbledon** tennis championships in

England, the only U.S. player to win in finals play was Joanne Russell, who teamed with Helen Gourlay Cawley of Australia to win the women's doubles championship.

Aug 1: A return to **bell-bottom trousers,** white caps, and jumpers for sailors' uniforms was announced by the Navy after an experiment with coat-and-shirt uniforms.

Aug 10: The so-called **Son of Sam** serial murder case in New York City culminated in the arrest of David Berkowitz, 24, suspected of murdering six people and wounding seven more over a 13-month period.

Aug 14: The **PGA golf tournament** was won by Lanny Wadkins, who beat Gene Littler on the third hole of a sudden-death playoff.

Sep 10-11: The **U.S. Open tennis singles championships** were won by Chris Evert Lloyd, for the third straight time, in the women's division and Guillermo Vilas of Argentina in the men's division.

Sep 13-18: The **America's Cup** was successfully defended by the U.S. yacht *Courageous,* which beat the challenger *Australia* in four straight races.

Oct 1: The soccer superstar **Pelé** played his farewell game, playing the first half with the New York Cosmos and the second half with his former team, the Santos of Brazil.

Oct 11-18: The **World Series** was won by the New York Yankees (AL), defeating the Los Angeles Dodgers (NL) four games to two. On Oct. 8 the Dodgers had won the National League pennant over the Philadelphia Phillies, three games to one, and the following day the Yankees had clinched the American League pennant from the Kansas City Royals, three games to two.

Dec 10: Steve Cauthen became the first jockey to win more than $5,000,000 in purse money in one year. Cauthen ended 1977 with 488 wins.

1978

I. Civil Rights
   Exploration and Settlement
   Government
   Statistics
   Wars

Pres. Jimmy Carter returned on Jan. 6 from a nine-day, seven-nation tour of Europe, the Middle East, and India to a U.S. that was beset by grave domestic problems. The availability of energy was a major concern for the government and for business, and short supplies were reflected in rising inflation. To deal with inflation Carter announced (Apr. 11) that wage increases for federal employees would be held to 5.5% and asked (Oct. 24) for voluntary compliance on guidelines for wage and price increases. In the Koreagate lobbying scandal, Tongsun Park, a South Korean businessman, told the Justice Department he had given some $750,000 to members of Congress and political groups to influence legislation from 1970 to 1975. Americans mourned the passing of Gen. Lucius D. Clay, military governor of the U.S. zone in Berlin after World War II, Apr. 16, at 80; and Hubert Horatio Humphrey, former senator from Minnesota and vice president from 1965 to 1969 under Lyndon B. Johnson, Jan. 13, at 66.

Jan 6: A precedent-setting **Indian land claim suit** was lost by the Wampanoag Indians of Mashpee, Mass., who had gone to court to recover some 13,700 acres on Cape Cod. The jury decided the Indians did not legally constitute a tribe in 1870, when the land was supposedly taken from them, or in Aug. 1976, when they filed their lawsuit. The decision was expected to affect similar cases pending in the Northeast.

Jan 19: William H. Webster was appointed director of the FBI. A U.S. appeals court judge in St. Louis, Mo., Webster succeeded Clarence M. Kelley.

Feb 8: Pres. **Anwar el-Sadat** of Egypt began a six-day visit to the U.S. He conferred at length with Pres. Carter, urging the U.S. to exert pressure on Israel to negotiate a Middle East peace settlement.

Feb 22: Two days after a **train derailment** in Waverly, Tenn., two tank cars containing liquid propane exploded, killing 15 people and leveling two blocks of Waverly's business district.

Mar 16: A **Panama Canal treaty,** the first of two Canal treaties negotiated in 1977, was ratified by the Senate. The treaty guaranteed neutrality of the canal after Panama assumes control at the end of 1999.

Apr 6: A **retirement age bill,** giving most workers the option of retiring at age 70 rather than 65, was signed by Pres. Carter.

Apr 7: Production of the **neutron bomb** was deferred by Pres. Carter pending final decision on its construction and deployment.

Apr 18: The second **Panama Canal treaty** was ratified by the Senate. The treaty stated conditions for the operation and defense of the canal until 1999, when control of the canal passes to Panama. Ratification of both treaties was a triumph for Pres. Carter over strong opposition.

Apr 27: A **construction accident** at the site of a nuclear power plant at Willow Island, W. Va., killed 51 workers when a scaffolding collapsed inside a cooling tower. The workers, including 11 members of one family, fell 170 feet and were buried under tons of concrete.

May 11: The **first woman Marine Corps general,** Margaret A. Brewer, 47, was appointed.

June 6: Proposition 13, a California constitutional amendment that would reduce property taxes by 57%, was approved by 65% of the Californians who voted on the controversial proposal.

June 28: The concept of **racial quotas** came under fire when the Supreme Court ruled in the case of *Bakke v. the University of California* that the university had to admit Allan P. Bakke to its medical school. Bakke, who was white, claimed his civil rights had been violated when he was refused admission because of racial quotas designed to increase the number of minority students in the medical school.

Aug 7: The **Love Canal** area of Niagara Falls, N.Y., considered to be environmentally unfit for human habitation, was declared a disaster area by Pres. Carter. Evacuation of the area, which had been used as a toxic waste dump from 1947 to 1952, had begun on Aug. 4.

Sep 6-17: A **Middle East peace conference** at Camp David, Md., was attended by Pres. Carter, Pres. Anwar el-Sadat of Egypt, and Prime Minister Menachem Begin of Israel. On Sept. 17 Sadat and Begin signed an agreement at the White House to conclude a peace treaty between Egypt and Israel within three months.

Sep 25: A **midair collision** over San Diego, Calif., of a Southwest Airlines jet and a private plane killed all 137 people aboard the two craft and at least ten more on the ground.

Oct 6: The deadline for ratification of the **Equal Rights Amendment** was extended to June 30, 1982, by Congress. Since its passage in 1972, all but three of the required 38 states had ratified the measure. This was the first extension granted for ratification of a proposed constitutional amendment since 1917, when Congress set seven years as the limit for the process.

Oct 15: The **National Energy Act of 1978** was passed by Congress. The bill regulated natural gas prices, encouraged use of coal by utilities, set fuel efficiency standards, and provided tax credits for energy conservation. It was signed by Pres. Carter on Nov. 9.

Oct 30: In an **espionage case,** two Soviet citizens, former employees of the UN convicted for attempting to buy U.S. military secrets, were sentenced to 50 years in prison by a federal judge in Newark, N.J. The sentences were considered unusually severe.

Nov 7: In **congressional elections** the Republicans gained three Senate seats, but the Democrats still held a majority of 58–41, with one seat held by an independent. In the House the Republicans gained 12 seats, but the Democrats led 276–159.

Nov 18: A grisly **mass suicide in Guyana** was prefaced by the murder of Rep. Leo J. Ryan of California and four others visiting the People's Temple on a fact-finding mission to the country. When Jim Jones, leader of the religious sect, learned of the event he led the group in a mass suicide by poison. The final count was 911 dead, including more than 200 children. Most of Jones's followers, like Jones himself, were American citizens.

Nov 27: George Moscone and Harvey Milk, the mayor and city supervisor of San Francisco, respectively, were shot to death in City Hall by Dan White, a former supervisor.

Dec 15: The city of **Cleveland, Ohio, defaulted** on $15,500,000 in short-term notes, thus becoming the first major U.S. city to default on its obligations since the 1930s.

Dec 15: The **People's Republic of China** and the U.S. announced the two nations would initiate full diplomatic relations on Jan. 1, 1979. The U.S. was to sever diplomatic ties with the Republic of China (Taiwan).

II. Architecture
Arts and Music
Popular Entertainment
Publishing
Theater

The year in theater was disappointing despite a handful of above average plays. The year's biggest hit was the musical *Ain't Misbehavin'*. In May Mikhail Baryshnikov left the American Ballet and joined the New York City Ballet. Both companies had severe financial problems this year · but managed to stay afloat. Art auction prices continued to climb. George Caleb Bingham's *The Jolly Flatboatmen* brought $980,000, the highest price paid to date for an American painting. Notables who died this year included Faith Baldwin, a writer known for her romantic novels, Mar. 18, at 84; Edgar Bergen, ventriloquist, Sept. 30, at 75; Charles Boyer, actor, Aug. 26, at 79; Maybelle "Mother" Carter, grand old lady of the Grand

Ole Opry and matriarch of the musical Carter family, Oct. 23, at 69; Bruce Catton, author and historian known for his books on the Civil War, Aug. 28, at 78; James Gould Cozzens, Pulitzer Prize-winning novelist, Aug. 9, at 74; Charles Eames, designer known best for his molded plywood, form-fitting chairs, Aug. 21, at 71; Ruth Etting, Ziegfeld Follies girl and popular singer, Sept. 24, at 80; Phyllis McGinley, Pulitzer Prize-winning poet, Feb. 22, at 72; Jack Oakie, comedian, Jan. 23, at 74; Norman Rockwell, artist known best for his cover illustrations for the *Saturday Evening Post,* Nov. 9, at 84; Edward Durrell Stone, architect, Aug. 6, at 76; and Jack L. Warner, motion picture producer, Sept. 9, at 86.

Among **books published** this year was *The Stories of John Cheever,* a collection that won the Pulitzer Prize. Other books published this year included *The World According to Garp* by John Irving, a novel; *American Caesar* by William Manchester, a biography of Douglas MacArthur; *Chesapeake* by James Michener, a novel; *In Search of History: A Personal Adventure* by Theodore H. White; and *War and Remembrance,* a novel by Herman Wouk.

Apr 7: A **record book auction price** was set in New York City when The Stuttgart Museum bought a Gutenberg Bible for $2,000,000.

Apr 17: Pulitzer prizes were awarded for the following: fiction, *Elbow Room* by James A. McPherson; biography, *Samuel Johnson* by Walter Jackson Bate; history, *The Visible Hand* by Alfred D. Chandler, Jr.; poetry, *Collected Poems* by Howard Nemerov; general nonfiction, *The Dragons of Eden* by Carl Sagan; drama, *The Gin Game* by Donald L. Coburn.

July 7: The **censorship** controversy involving former CIA employees continued. On this date, Frank W. Snepp, III, who wrote an unauthorized book about the agency, was held by a federal judge to have violated his contract with the CIA. Snepp was ordered to hand over his earnings from the book to the federal government.

Oct 5: The **Nobel Prize for Literature** was awarded to Isaac Bashevis Singer, the Polish-born author who writes in Yiddish. He was cited for his "impassioned narrative art."

Oct 17: Congress voted the contralto **Marian Anderson** a special gold medal for her "unselfish devotion to the promotion of the arts" and her "untiring efforts on behalf of the Brotherhood of Man." In 1939 the black singer had been refused the use of Constitution Hall by the Daughters of the American Revolution. She subsequently performed before 75,000 at the Lincoln Memorial in Washington, D.C.

III. Business and Industry
Education
Philosophy and Religion
Science

The nation's economic woes continued. Inflation rose to 8%, productivity increased only 0.4%, the smallest rise since 1974, and the annual U.S. trade deficit reached $28,450,000. Pres. Jimmy Carter was not successful in pushing labor law reforms through Congress, nor was he able to get Congress to move toward a national health plan to be phased in during the 1980s. Health costs continued to rise, prompting the Department of Health, Education, and Welfare to ask hospitals to hold to a 9.7% increase in 1979. Congress voted a five-year, $50,000,000,000 extension of the Elementary and Secondary Education Act. This year the Mormon Church ended its 148-year ban on the ordination of black men. Notables who died this year included James Bryant Conant, longtime president of Harvard University, Feb. 11, at 84; John Donald MacArthur, billionaire insurance company tycoon, Jan. 6, at 80; Margaret Mead, anthropologist, Nov. 15, at 76; John D. Rockefeller, III, eldest of John D. Rockefeller's five grandsons and a noted philanthropist, Jan. 10, at 72; and Harry Winston, jeweler to the rich and famous, Dec. 28, at 82.

Jan 13: **Japan** agreed to some opening of its domestic market to U.S. products in order to reduce Japan's export trade surplus. Tariffs on some 300 items were

to be reduced, and quotas on 12 items, 11 of them
agricultural, were to be removed.

Mar 25: A 110-day **coal miners' strike,** longest in the
industry's history, ended when miners accepted a
new three-year contract and went back to work. The
strike had caused fears of power shortages and industrial layoffs, but stockpiling before the strike prevented them.

Apr 17: A new **stock trading record** was set by the New
York Stock Exchange, which saw 63,500,000 shares
change hands.

Apr 19: The **first black woman pilot** for a major U.S.
airline, Jill E. Brown, 27, from Baltimore, Md., began
working for Texas International Airlines.

May 5: Organized medicine was declared by Pres.
Carter to be the major obstacle to better health care.
Carter affirmed that doctors care about their patients,
but said the American Medical Association was concerned only with doctors' interests.

May 8: The **largest U.S. corporation,** according to *Fortune* magazine, was General Motors, with annual
sales of $54,000,000,000. Exxon Corporation was
rated second largest.

May 20: Pioneer Venus 1 was launched toward Venus.
On Dec. 4 it went into orbit around Venus and began
sending back data on the planet's atmosphere.

June 15: The $100,000,000 **Tellico Dam** project in Ten-
nessee was halted indefinitely when the Supreme
Court ruled that the snail darter, a rare species of
perch, was protected by the Endangered Species Act
of 1973 and that construction of the dam threatened
its extinction.

June 22: In studying photos of **Pluto,** James W. Christy
of the U.S. Naval Observatory discovered a hitherto
unknown small moon of Pluto in orbit around it,
only 12,000 miles from the planet.

Aug 8: Pioneer Venus 2 was successfully launched
toward a December rendezvous with Venus. On Dec.
9 it sent four probes to the planet's surface and began
relaying data about atmosphere and surface conditions of Venus.

Aug 11: The bacterium causing **legionnaires' disease** had been isolated, the Centers for Disease Control in Atlanta, Ga., announced. Previously it could only be studied in the tissue of a victim.

Oct 6: The **first woman university president** in the U.S., Hannah H. Gray, was inaugurated at the University of Chicago.

Oct 15: The **Humphrey-Hawkins full employment bill,** named for the late Hubert H. Humphrey of Minnesota and Rep. Augustus F. Hawkins, Democrat of California, was passed by Congress. A watered-down version of the original 1976 bill, it called for a national policy of reducing unemployment to 4% and inflation to 3% by 1983. It was signed by Pres. Carter on Oct. 27.

Oct 16: The **Nobel Prize in Economics** was awarded to Herbert A. Simon of Carnegie-Mellon University.

Oct 17: The **Nobel Prize in Physics** was awarded jointly to Arno A. Penzias and Robert W. Wilson of Bell Laboratories for their discovery of weak electromagnetic radiation existing throughout the universe, and to Per Kapitsa of the U.S.S.R. for his studies of liquid helium.

IV. Fashion
Folkways
Holidays
Social Issues and Crime
Sports

Professional sports prospered this year. Major league baseball drew a record 40,000,000 fans, and the Los Angeles Dodgers (NL) drew 3,347,776 customers to become the first team to break the 3,000,000 mark. In basketball, David Thompson of the Denver Nuggets negotiated an $800,000 contract for the year, highest to date for any professional athlete. Pro football increased its regular season from 14 to 16 games. In golf the top money winners were Tom Watson, $362,429, and Nancy Lopez, $153,097. The boom in jogging and physical fitness activities was good news for sportswear manufacturers, and even the fashion world began paying attention to Americans' interest in fitness and health. Americans also burned up the calories on the dance floors of discothèques, which became enormously popular in the wake of the hit film *Saturday Night Fever*. Notables who died this year included Ford C. Frick, former president of the National League (1934–1951), Apr. 8, at 83; Joseph V. McCarthy, who managed the New York Yankees to eight American League championships and seven World Series victories between 1931 and 1946, Jan. 13, at 90; and James Joseph "Gene" Tunney, undefeated heavyweight champion of the world from 1926 to 1928, Nov. 17, at 80.

Jan 9: In a major ruling on **coeducational sports,** a federal judge in Dayton, Ohio, ruled against preventing high-school girls from playing on the same sports teams as boys.

Jan 15: Super Bowl XII was won by the Dallas Cowboys (NFC), defeating the Denver Broncos (AFC) 27–10. On Jan. 1 the Cowboys had beaten the Minnesota Vikings 23 to 6 for the NFC championship and the Broncos had defeated the Oakland Raiders 20 to 17 to take the AFC title.

Feb 15: The **world heavyweight boxing championship** was won by Leon Spinks in a 15-round decision over Muhammad Ali at Las Vegas, Nev.

Mar 27: The **NCAA basketball championship** was won by the University of Kentucky, beating Duke University 94 to 88.

May 5: Pete Rose of the Cincinnati Reds (NL) made his 3000th base hit. He was the 13th player in baseball history to do so and, at 37, the youngest.

May 6: The 104th **Kentucky Derby** was won by Affirmed, with a time of 2:01 1/5. The jockey was Steve Cauthen.

May 20: The 103rd **Preakness Stakes** was won by Affirmed, with a time of 1:54 2/5. The jockey was Steve Cauthen.

May 21-June 7: The **NBA basketball championship** was won by the Washington Bullets, who beat the Seattle Supersonics four games to three.

May 26: The **first legal casino** in the U.S. outside Nevada was opened in Atlantic City, N.J., by Resorts International Hotel Casino.

June 9: The World Boxing Council **heavyweight boxing championship** was won by Larry Holmes, in a 15-round decision over Ken Norton.

June 10: The 110th **Belmont Stakes** was won by Affirmed, with a time of 2:26⁴/₅ to become the 11th horse to win racing's Triple Crown. The jockey, once again, was Steve Cauthen. As in the Kentucky Derby and Preakness, Alydar finished second. This was the first time there were Triple Crown winners in consecutive years, Seattle Slew having won in 1977.

June 18: The **U.S. Open golf tournament** was won by Andy North, beating J. C. Snead and Dave Stockton on the last hole after seeing a substantial lead vanish.

Aug 6: The **PGA golf tournament** was won by John Mahaffey, beating Tom Watson and Jerry Pate on the second hole of a sudden-death playoff.

Aug 11-17: The first successful **transatlantic balloon crossing** was made by Max Anderson, Ben Abruzzo, and Larry Newman, who flew from Presque Isle, Maine, to Paris, France, in 137 hrs., 18 min.

Sep 10: The **U.S. Open tennis singles championships** were won by Chris Evert in the women's division and Jimmy Connors in the men's division.

Sep 15: The World Boxing Association **heavyweight boxing championship** was won by Muhammad Ali, who beat Leon Spinks in 15 rounds to regain the title for an unprecedented third time.

Oct 10-17: The **World Series** was won by the New York Yankees (AL), defeating the Los Angeles Dodgers (NL) four games to two. On Oct. 7 the Yankees had won the American League pennant, beating the Kansas City Royals three games to one, and the Dodgers had taken the National League title, downing the Philadelphia Phillies three games to one.

Dec 8-10: The **Davis Cup** international tennis challenge round was won by the U.S., defeating Great Britain four matches to one.

1979

I. Civil Rights
   Exploration and Settlement
   Government
   Statistics
   Wars

The nation's attention was focused this year on
events in Iran, where in January a wave of revolutionary unrest toppled the regime of Shah Moham-
mad Reza Pahlavi and installed a fundamentalist Islamic dictatorship under the Ayatollah Ruhollah
Khomeini. In November Islamic revolutionaries
seized the U.S. embassy in Teheran, taking many hostages and demanding that the Shah, then in the U.S.
for medical reasons, be returned to Iran to stand trial
for alleged crimes. Pres. Jimmy Carter refused the
terrorists' demands and retaliated by banning the import of Iranian oil, freezing Iranian assets in the U.S.,
and threatening military action to free the hostages.
Thus began a diplomatic nightmare that came to be
known as the hostage crisis. Notables who died this
year included Nelson A. Rockefeller, four times governor of New York, and vice president of the United
States from 1974 to 1977, Jan. 26, at 70.

Jan 4: The legal battle over the **Kent State** University
shootings in Ohio in 1970 ended when an out-of-court
settlement was reached. The parents of the four students killed by National Guardsmen and the nine
wounded by the guardsmen were awarded a total of
$675,000.

Feb 8: Military ties with **Nicaragua** had been severed,
Pres. Carter announced, adding that economic aid to
the repressive regime of Anastasio Somoza DeBayle
would be reduced as well. The moves were intended
to force Somoza to negotiate with the revolutionary
Sandinista movement threatening to topple the Nicaraguan government.

Feb 14: The U.S. **ambassador to Afghanistan was kid-naped** in Kabul and then killed when Afghan govern-ment forces attempted to free him.

Mar 5: Alimony laws requiring payments by divorced husbands but not by divorced wives were ruled un-constitutional by the Supreme Court, which struck down an Alabama law as violating the Fourteenth Amendment.

Mar 26: An **Egyptian-Israeli peace treaty** ended the 30-year state of war between the two nations. The treaty was signed by Pres. Anwar el-Sadat of Egypt and Prime Minister Menachem Begin of Israel at the White House.

Apr 3: Jane Byrne was elected the first woman mayor of Chicago by the largest majority in that city since 1901.

Apr 27: A **prisoner exchange** with the U.S.S.R. was effected in New York City. The U.S. traded two Sovi-ets convicted in 1978 of spying for five Soviet dissi-dents, including Alexander Ginsburg, who had helped found a committee to monitor human rights violations in the U.S.S.R.

May 25: An **airline crash** of an American Airlines DC-10 jet shortly after takeoff in Chicago killed all 272 passengers and three people on the ground.

June 13: An **Indian land claim suit** was settled, grant-ing the Sioux nation $17,500,000 for an area of the Black Hills of South Dakota taken from them in 1877. Including interest, the award was estimated to ex-ceed $100,000,000. It was the largest award ever re-ceived by an Indian group.

June 18: The **SALT 2** strategic arms limitation treaty was signed in Vienna, Austria, by Pres. Carter and Pres. Leonid Brezhnev of the U.S.S.R.

July 2: Attendance at **criminal pretrial proceedings** is not a constitutional right of the public or the press, the Supreme Court ruled. The decision left open the possibility that public access to criminal trials could be limited as well.

July 19: In a major **Cabinet reorganization,** Pres. Carter dismissed four members, including the secretaries of the treasury and of energy; a fifth resigned. At a meeting of his Cabinet and staff, Carter had bluntly expressed his dissatisfaction, prompting the tendering of resignations by all his Cabinet members and by his senior White House staff.

July 25: Paul Volcker was appointed chairman of the Federal Reserve Board by Pres. Carter. He was confirmed on Aug. 2 and sworn in on Aug. 6.

Aug 15: Andrew Young resigned as U.S. ambassador to the UN following controversy over his unauthorized meeting with representatives of the Palestine Liberation Organization in July.

Sep 12-14: Hurricane Frederic struck the Gulf Coast, causing some $1,500,000,000 in damage with winds of up to 130 mph. Only eight people were killed, but some 500,000 were forced to evacuate.

Nov 3: A shootout in Greensboro, N.C., between Ku Klux Klan members and participants in an anti-Klan rally left five demonstrators dead and eight wounded. Fourteen Klansmen were arrested and 12 of them were charged with first-degree murder.

Nov 4: The U.S. embassy in Teheran was seized by Iranian revolutionaries, so-called students, who took some 90 hostages, including about 65 Americans. The revolutionaries released the non-U.S. hostages and 13 U.S. hostages, all women or blacks, but kept about 50. The revolutionaries demanded that the U.S. return the deposed Shah to Iran to stand trial. He was in the U.S. undergoing medical treatment. The U.S. refused to comply.

Nov 21: The U.S. embassy in Islamabad, Pakistan, was besieged for five hours before Pakistani soldiers restored order. One U.S. Marine was killed.

Dec 2: The U.S. embassy in Tripoli, Libya, was attacked by a mob. Two floors were damaged but the 21 people in the building escaped unharmed.

II. Architecture
Arts and Music
Popular Entertainment
Publishing
Theater

The Broadway theater prospered this year, with 119 productions generating $40,600,000 in profits, up 10% over the previous season. There were 46 off-Broadway shows. Among the year's hits were The *Elephant Man* and the musical *Sugar Babies*. On Dec. 8 the musical *Grease* gave its 3243rd performance and became the longest-running Broadway musical in history. The music industry faced hard times as oil price hikes translated into higher prices for records. Sales of recordings showed a decided drop after 25 years of steady growth. A new art auction price for an American work was set when *Icebergs*, a painting by Frederick Church that had hung unnoticed in England since 1863, sold for $2,500,000. Notables who died this year included Elizabeth Bishop, Pulitzer Prize-winning poet, Oct. 6, at 68; Al Capp, cartoonist, Nov. 11, at 70; James T. Farrell, author of the *Studs Lonigan* trilogy, Aug. 22, at 75; Arthur Fiedler, conductor of the Boston Pops Orchestra for 50 years, July 10, at 84; Emmett Kelly, clown, Mar. 28, at 80; Peggy Guggenheim, art collector and patron, Dec. 23, at 81; Roy Harris, composer, Oct. 1, at 81; S. J. Perelman, humorist, Oct. 17, at 75; Mary Pickford, first major star of silent movies, May 29, at 86; Richard Rodgers, composer, Dec. 30, at 77; Jean Stafford, writer, Mar. 26, at 63; and John Wayne, actor, June 11, at 72.

Among **books published** this year, the most talked-about work was Norman Mailer's nonfiction novel *The Executioner's Song*, a treatment of the life and death of Gary Gilmore, who was executed in 1977. The book became a best seller and won a Pulitzer Prize. Other books published this year included *A Streak of Luck* by Robert Conot, a biography of Thomas Edison; *Hanta Yo* by Ruth Beebe Hill, a historical novel that drew fire from some American Indians but became a best seller; *The Poems of Stanley Kunitz*, a collection of the poet's work over 50 years; *The Rise of Theodore Roosevelt* by Edmund Morris; *The Ghost Writer* by Philip Roth, fiction; *Sophie's Choice* by William Styron, a novel; and *Jailbird* by Kurt Vonnegut, a novel panned by critics but kept firmly on the best-seller lists by the public.

Jan 9: The **Bollingen Prize** for poetry was awarded to W. S. Merwin.

Feb 9: In the first major **art theft** from the Metropolitan Museum of Art in its 110-year history, thieves stole an ancient Greek marble head valued at $250,000.

Apr 16: Pulitzer prizes were awarded for the following: fiction, *The Stories of John Cheever;* biography, *Days of Sorrow and Pain* by Leonard Baker; history, *The Dred Scott Case* by Don E. Fehrenbacker; general nonfiction, *On Human Nature* by Edward O. Wilson; poetry, *Now and Then Poems* by Robert Penn Warren; drama, *Buried Child* by Sam Shepard.

Dec 3: A **rock concert disaster** claimed the lives of 11 youths who were trampled to death at Riverfront Coliseum in Cincinnati, Ohio. Fans were scrambling to get seats at a concert by The Who.

III. Business and Industry
Education
Philosophy and Religion
Science

The economic news continued bad: interest rates, inflation, and the foreign trade deficit all were higher. The Consumer Price Index was up 13.3%, the largest jump in 33 years. In December United States Steel announced it would close 13 plants, putting 13,000 steelworkers out of work and causing further unemployment in other industries. The Dow Jones Average of industrial stocks closed out the year at 838.4, up 4.2% over 1978. Trading was heavy, and a new record of shares traded was set: 8,155,915,314. Consumption of petroleum products declined 1.8%, the first drop since 1975. In education, costs were up and enrollment was down to 58,400,000, a full 3,000,000 fewer students than in 1975. Several events of religious significance highlighted the year. Reader's Digest announced it would publish a condensed version of the Bible, using the Revised Standard Version and reducing it by 40%. In September the Dalai Lama, religious leader of some 6,000,000 Tibetan Buddhists, came to the U.S. on a month-long visit. In October Pope John Paul II visited the U.S. Notables who died this year included Charles E. Coughlin, conservative, anti-Semitic "radio priest" of the 1930s, Oct. 27, at 88; Cyrus S. Eaton, Canadian-born multimillionaire, May 9, at 95; Conrad Hilton, founder of the Hilton hotel chain, Jan. 3, at 91; James Francis Cardinal McIntyre, Roman Catholic archbishop of Los Angeles, July 16, at 93; Samuel I. Newhouse, founder of the Newhouse publishing and broadcasting conglomerate, Aug. 29, at 84; Talcott Parsons, sociologist, May 8, at 76; A. Philip Randolph, labor and civil rights leader, May 16, at 90; Bishop Fulton J. Sheen, who reached millions through his radio and television broadcasts, Dec. 9, at 84; and Rexford Guy Tugwell, a leading figure in Franklin D. Roosevelt's so-called Brain Trust in the 1930s, July 21, at 88.

Jan 11: **Cigarette smoking** was labeled the "single most important environmental factor contributing to early death," in a report issued by U.S. Surgeon General Julius B. Richmond.

Feb 13: A report on **school desegregation** by the U.S. Civil Rights Commission stated that 46% of the nation's minority children were attending segregated schools 25 years after the Supreme Court declared segregation unconstitutional.

Mar 5: **Voyager 1,** launched in 1977, made its closest approach to Jupiter, coming within 172,000 miles of the planet's turbulent cloud cover.

Mar 28: A **nuclear near-disaster** occurred at Three Mile Island, near Harrisburg, Pa., when a power plant malfunctioned and its operators were unable to deal with the situation. The plant's containment building was flooded and a disaster of enormous magnitude was averted. However, two days later the governor of Pennsylvania advised pregnant women and preschool children living within five miles of the plant to leave the area.

May 5: The **largest U.S. corporation** in 1978, according to *Fortune* magazine's annual survey, was General Motors, with sales of more than $63,000,000,000.

June 27: The Supreme Court ruled that **black employees** could be promoted ahead of whites with greater work experience provided the move was part of an affirmative action program intended to offset racial discrimination.

July 11: Skylab, the 77-ton U.S. orbiting laboratory, reentered Earth's atmosphere and broke up, showering debris over the Indian Ocean and Australia. No one was hurt.

Sep 1: Pioneer 2, launched in 1973, flew past Saturn, discovering two new rings and an eleventh moon.

Oct 1-7: Pope John Paul II paid a six-day visit to the U.S., stopping at Boston, New York City, Philadelphia, Des Moines, Chicago, and Washington, D.C. On Oct. 6 he became the first pope to meet a U.S. president at the White House.

Oct 6: A **financial and stock panic** was sparked when the Federal Reserve Board announced—on a Saturday night—a raise in its discount rate from 11% to 12% and took stiff actions to tighten control of the money supply. In the next few days bond prices plunged, stock prices dropped in the heaviest trading since 1929, and banks raised their prime rates to 14.5%. By Oct. 11 the markets regained their balance and recovered most of their losses.

Oct 12: The **Nobel Prize in Physiology or Medicine** was awarded jointly to Allan M. Cormack of Tufts University and Geoffrey N. Hounsfield of Great Britain for their development of the CAT scan, an advanced type of x-ray equipment.

Oct 16: The **Nobel Prize in Chemistry** was awarded jointly to Herbert C. Brown of Purdue University and Georg Wittig of West Germany for their discoveries in the chemistry of boron and phosphorus.

Oct 16: The **Nobel Prize in Physics** was awarded jointly to Steven Weinberg and Sheldon L. Glashow of Harvard University, and to Abdus Salam of Pakistan for their contributions to the development of a unified field theory.

Oct 17: The **Nobel Prize in Economics** was awarded jointly to Theodore W. Schultz of the University of Chicago and Arthur Lewis of Princeton University for their work on the economic problems of developing nations.

Oct 17: A bill creating the **Department of Education,** the 13th Cabinet-level agency, was signed by Pres. Carter. On Oct. 30 the president appointed Shirley Hufstedler, a U.S. Court of Appeals judge in Louisiana, to head the new agency. The Department of Health, Education, and Welfare became the Department of Health and Human Services.

Dec 21: A bill authorizing a **federal bailout for Chrysler Corporation** by providing $1,500,000,000 in federal loan guarantees for the ailing automotive company was passed by Congress. It was signed by Pres. Carter on Jan. 7, 1980.

IV. Fashion
   Folkways
   Holidays
   Social Issues and Crime
   Sports

One incident reflecting the changes American society had undergone in the last several decades was the so-called palimony case involving the actor Lee Marvin and his former companion Michelle Triola Marvin. The couple had broken up in 1970, but Miss Marvin sued the actor for half of the $3,600,000 he had earned during their six-year relationship. In April a judge ruled against Michelle Marvin but awarded her $104,000 for purposes of rehabilitation. In sports, Muhammad Ali retired from boxing, leaving the World Boxing Association heavyweight crown up for grabs. John Tate won the heavyweight championship in October. In golf the top money winners were Tom Watson, $462,636, and Nancy Lopez, $215,987.

Jan 21: Super Bowl XIII was won by the Pittsburgh Steelers (AFC), defeating the Dallas Cowboys (NFC) 35 to 31. On Jan. 7 the Steelers had beaten the Houston Oilers 34 to 5 for the AFC championship and the Cowboys had defeated the Los Angeles Rams 28 to 0 for the NFC title.

Mar 26: The **NCAA basketball championship** was won by Michigan State, defeating Indiana State 75 to 64.

May 20-June 1: The **NBA basketball championship** was won by the Seattle Supersonics, who defeated the Washington Bullets four games to one after losing the opening game.

June 17: The **U.S. Open golf tournament** was won by Hale Irwin, repeating his 1974 victory.

Aug 6: The **PGA golf tournament** was won by David Graham of Australia, beating Ben Crenshaw on the third hole of a playoff.

Sep 9: The **U.S. Open tennis singles championships** were won by John McEnroe in the men's division and Tracy Austin, 16, in the women's division. Austin became the youngest player to win the women's singles title.

Oct 10-17: The **World Series** was won by the Pittsburgh Pirates (NL), defeating the Baltimore Orioles (AL) four games to three. On Oct. 5 the Pirates completed a three-game sweep of the Cincinnati Reds for the National League pennant. The following day the Orioles had taken the American League championship from the California Angels, three games to one.

Oct 21: The World Boxing Association **heavyweight boxing championship** was won in Pretoria, South Africa, by John Tate, who took a 15-round decision over Gerrie Coetzee.

1980

I. Civil Rights
Exploration and Settlement
Government
Statistics
Wars

It was a heartbreaking year for Pres. Jimmy Carter, whose administration seemed unable to achieve significant successes in domestic or foreign affairs. The national economy slumped under skyrocketing inflation and rising unemployment. The Carter administration was unable to bring the Iranian hostage crisis to a conclusion, and the Soviet invasion of Afghanistan in Dec. 1979 chilled U.S.-Soviet relations to the freezing point. Meanwhile, the Republican Party, solidly behind Ronald Reagan, expended great energy and vast resources in the presidential election campaign and swept their candidate into power in a Republican landslide. Another factor in U.S. politics was the 1980 Census, which reported a population of 226,504,825 and indicated a shift of 17 seats in the House of Representatives from the Northeast and Midwest to the South and West. This year Americans mourned the deaths of Helen Gahagan Douglas, former actress and Democratic congresswoman from 1944 to 1950 who lost her House seat to Richard M. Nixon in a bitterly fought campaign, June 28, at 79; and William O. Douglas, who had served on the Supreme Court for 36 years beginning in 1939, longer than any other justice in the Court's history, Jan. 19, at 81.

Jan 4: In a protest against the **Soviet invasion of Afghanistan** in December, Pres. Carter announced that the 17,000,000 metric tons of grain ordered by the U.S.S.R. would not be delivered. Carter also suspended the sale of high-technology equipment, postponed the opening of new consulates in the two countries, and curtailed Soviet fishing privileges in U.S. waters. Carter also entertained the idea of a U.S. boycott of the 1980 Summer Olympics in Moscow, a move he announced on Jan. 20.

Jan 23: In his **State of the Union** message, Pres. Carter said that Persian Gulf oil supply routes would be defended by force if necessary.

Jan 29: Six Americans escaped from Iran with the aid of Canadian embassy personnel, it was revealed. The U.S. citizens, who had posed as Canadians, had not been among those held in the U.S. embassy in Teheran.

Feb 2: Details of **Abscam,** an FBI sting operation to uncover official corruption, were released. Some 31 public officials were named as targets of the investigation, including Sen. Harrison Williams, Republican of New Jersey, and six members of the House of Representatives. In the operation an FBI agent posed as an Arab sheik and offered bribes for political favors.

Mar 15: An **Indian land claim suit** was settled when the Penobscot Indian tribe in Maine accepted an $81,500,000 settlement for land taken from it in violation of the Indian Non-Intercourse Act of 1790.

Mar 17: The **Refugee Act of 1980** was signed by Pres. Carter. It broadened the definition of the term *refugee* to include people from any part of the world, and increased the maximum annual number to be admitted to the U.S. from 290,000 to 320,000.

Apr 7: The U.S. broke **diplomatic relations with Iran** in the wake of the continuing hostage crisis. All exports to Iran were banned and Iranian diplomats in the U.S. were expelled.

Apr 11: Regulations prohibiting **sexual harassment of women** by their superiors in government or business were issued by the Equal Opportunity Commission.

Apr 24: A U.S. **hostage rescue mission** in Iran ended in disaster. During the operation, three of the eight helicopters of the airborne operation failed. At the staging area inside Iran, the mission was canceled, but during the withdrawal one of the remaining helicopters collided with one of six C-130 transports, killing eight and injuring five.

Apr 26: Sec. of State **Cyrus Vance resigned,** stating his opposition to the U.S. military rescue attempt in Iran. He was succeeded by Sen. Edmund Muskie, Democrat of Maine.

May 9: A **marine accident** killed at least 35 people when the freighter *Summit Venture* rammed the Sunshine Skyway Bridge over Tampa Bay, Fla., collapsing one of its twin highway spans. On Jan. 28 a Coast Guard cutter had struck an oil tanker near the bridge, killing 23 sailors.

May 17-19: Race riots in Miami, Fla., left at least 14 dead and more than 300 injured, and caused some $100,000,000 in damage. Nearly 1000 people were arrested in the violence, which erupted after an all-white jury acquitted four former Miami policemen charged with the fatal beating of a black man.

May 18: The eruption of **Mt. St. Helens** in southwestern Washington State blew the top of the mountain into the atmosphere, leveled some 120 sq. mi., and set off a series of fires, mudslides, and floods. About 400 people had been evacuated before the eruption, but a count in July showed 15 others dead and about 40 missing. The volcano had been dormant since 1857.

June 3: A total of 101,476 **Cuban refugees** had fled to the U.S. since mid-April with the tacit approval of Fidel Castro's government, it was reported. At first the refugees had been welcomed by the U.S., but by mid-May steps were taken to slow the tide and screen the refugees. It was feared Castro was using the exodus as a way to empty his prisons of criminals.

June 23-Aug 15: A summer-long **heat wave and drought** devastated crops and livestock and left 1272 people dead in 20 states. The mid-Mississippi R. Valley, the Southwest, and the South were hardest hit in the worst drought since the Dust Bowl days of the 1930s.

June 27: A law requiring **draft registration** by men 19 to 20 years of age was signed by Pres. Carter. Registration was to begin in July, but no actual draft was contemplated.

July 14-17: The **Republican National Convention nominated Ronald W. Reagan** for the presidency by a nearly unanimous vote. George Bush of Texas, former ambassador to the UN and former director of the CIA, was nominated for the vice presidency.

Aug 11-14: The **Democratic National Convention nominated Pres. Carter** and Vice Pres. Walter F. Mondale for reelection. Carter defeated Sen. Edward M. Kennedy of Massachusetts by a margin of nearly two to one.

Sep 19: A **fuel explosion** at a Titan 2 missile site near Damascus, Ark., killed one Air Force employee and injured 21. The blast left a crater 250-feet wide and forced the evacuation of 1400 people from the area for 12 hours.

Oct 2: In the **first House expulsion** since 1861, the House of Representatives expelled Michael Joseph Myers, Democrat of Pennsylvania. Myers had been convicted on Aug. 31 of bribery and conspiracy in connection with the Abscam investigation.

Nov 4: Ronald Reagan was elected president of the United States, carrying 44 states. The electoral vote was Reagan 489, Pres. Jimmy Carter 49. The popular vote was Reagan, 42,797,153; Carter, 34,434,100; John Anderson, independent candidate, 5,533,927. In congressional elections the Republicans picked up 12 Senate seats for a 53–46 majority, with one independent seat. In the House the Democrats lost 33 seats but kept a majority of 242–192, with one seat going to an independent.

    II. Architecture
        Arts and Music
        Popular Entertainment
        Publishing
        Theater

The Broadway theater season was marked by revivals of such former hits as *West Side Story, The Music*

Man, and *Brigadoon.* The American Ballet Theater celebrated its 40th anniversary this year, and Mikhail Baryshnikov became its director. Conflicts between the Metropolitan Opera Company and its orchestra led to cancellation of its 1980–1981 season. After a last-minute settlement on Dec. 10, the season was begun two months late. Plans for the long-awaited New York City Exposition and Convention Center were finally approved. The single structure would cover five blocks, have 500,000 sq. ft. of exhibition space, and be the largest structure of its kind. This year viewers crowded New York City's Museum of Modern Art to see more than 1000 works by Pablo Picasso. In May a Picasso painting brought $3,000,000 at auction. This sale soon was eclipsed by a $3,900,000 bid for a painting by Paul Cézanne, and $5,200,000 for a painting by Vincent Van Gogh. In music, digitally recorded LP records were widely marketed for the first time. In publishing, two of the nation's most respected magazines, *Harper's* and *Atlantic,* nearly failed but were saved at the last minute. Americans mourned the deaths this year of Gower Champion, choreographer, who died hours before his last show, *42nd Street,* opened, Aug. 25, at 61; Harold E. Clurman, director, drama critic, and author, Sept. 9, at 78; Jimmy Durante, entertainer, Jan. 29, at 86; Jane Froman, big band singer of the 1930s and 1940s, Apr. 23, at 72; José Iturbi, Spanish-born pianist, June 28, at 84; Andre Kostelanetz, conductor, Jan 13, at 78; Henry Miller, author of *Tropic of Cancer* and other controversial works, June 7, at 88; Katherine Anne Porter, Pulitzer Prize-winning author, Sept. 18, at 90; and Mae West, sex queen of the movies for 60 years, Nov. 22, at 87.

Among **books published** was *A Confederacy of Dunces* by John Kennedy Toole, who committed suicide after being unable to find a publisher for his work. Years later his mother found a publisher for his novel, which went on to win a Pulitzer Prize. Other books published this year included *Creek Mary's Blood* by Dee Brown, a novel; *Loon Lake* by E.

L. Doctorow, a novel; *Walt Whitman,* a biography by Justin Kaplan; *The White House Years* by Henry Kissinger, which focused on the Vietnam War and prompted much debate; *The Covenant,* another blockbuster by James Michener; and *The Second Coming* by Walker Percy, the author's fifth novel.

Mar 6: Marguerite Yourcenar became the first woman to be elected to the French Academy. A naturalized U.S. citizen, the author had resided in Maine for more than 30 years.

Apr 14: Pulitzer prizes were awarded for the following: fiction, *The Executioner's Song* by Norman Mailer; biography, *The Rise of Theodore Roosevelt* by Edmund Morris; history, *Been in the Storm So Long* by Leon F. Litwack; general nonfiction, *Gödel, Escher, Bach* by Douglas R. Hofstadter; poetry, *Selected Poems* by Donald R. Justice; drama, *Talley's Folly* by Lanford Wilson.

May 1: The first **American Book Awards,** formerly known as the National Book Awards, were presented for the following: fiction, *Sophie's Choice* by William Styron; general nonfiction, *The Right Stuff* by Tom Wolfe; biography, *The Rise of Theodore Roosevelt* by Edmund Morris; history, *The White House Years* by Henry Kissinger; poetry, *Ashes* by Philip Levine. The National Medal for Literature was presented to Eudora Welty.

May 29: A **world auction record** for a painting was set when J. M. W. Turner's *Juliet and Her Nurse* was sold in New York City for $6,400,000.

Oct 9: The **Nobel Prize in Literature** was awarded to Czeslaw Milosz, a self-exiled Pole living and teaching in California.

Nov 21: The so-called **Who Shot J.R.?** episode of the TV evening soap *Dallas* was seen by more U.S. viewers than any other television program in history. More than half the nation's audience watched to see who had tried to kill J.R. Ewing, a question unanswered at the end of the spring season.

Dec 8: John Lennon was shot and killed outside his apartment building in New York City. Mark David

Chapman, 25, a former mental patient, was held for the shooting.

III. Business and Industry
Education
Philosophy and Religion
Science

Inflation reached 12.4% by year's end, marking the second successive year of double-digit inflation. The Federal Reserve raised its discount rate to 13%, and unemployment hit an average of 7.1% for the year. Sales of U.S. automobiles were at a 19-year low, down 20% from 1979 levels, and the Ford Motor Co. reported a third-quarter loss of $595,000,000, the biggest ever for a U.S. corporation. This year the federal government took steps to deregulate the trucking industry and railroads. On July 1 Pres. Jimmy Carter signed a bill giving truckers more freedom to raise or lower rates without having to seek ICC permission. On Oct. 14 Pres. Carter signed a bill giving the railroads greater flexibility in setting rates. New federal assistance for railroads in financial trouble was also provided. A noteworthy development was the decline in computer prices. Sales of personal computers were up, although the expected production boom was hurt by short supply of integrated circuit chips. Notables who died this year included Jacqueline Cochran, first woman to fly faster than the speed of sound, Aug. 8, at 70; George Meany, president of the AFL-CIO from 1955 to 1979, Jan. 10, at 85; and Harland "Colonel" Sanders, founder of the Kentucky Fried Chicken food chain, Dec. 16, at 90.

Jan 16: The successful **synthesis of human interferon,** thought to be effective against viral diseases and possibly against some types of cancer, was announced by a group of scientists in Boston.

Feb 14: The 1500-lb. **Solar Maximum Observatory,** designed to study solar flares, was successfully launched into orbit.

Mar 13: In the **first criminal trial of a U.S. corporation** in a product defect case, the Ford Motor Company was found not guilty by a jury in Winimac, Ind., of reckless homicide. The case involved the 1978 deaths of three women killed in a Ford Pinto.

Apr 2: The **Crude Oil Windfall Profits Tax** bill was signed by Pres. Carter. It was expected to produce $227,000,000,000 in tax revenues from the nation's oil companies by 1990.

Apr 28: A report on **cancer death rates** issued by the American Cancer Society projected that 8,500,000 Americans would die from cancer in the 1980s, at least 2,000,000 more than had died in the 1970s.

May 5: The **largest U.S. corporation,** according to the annual report by *Fortune* magazine, was Exxon, with sales of $79,106,471,000 in 1979. Exxon moved from second to first place, dropping General Motors to number two.

June 16: In a landmark ruling on **genetic engineering,** the Supreme Court ruled that organisms created in the laboratory could be patented.

Sep 22: The risk of **toxic shock syndrome** led to recall of a tampon product manufactured by Procter and Gamble. Federal studies had linked use of the tampon with the deaths of 25 women.

Oct 10: The **Nobel Prize in Physiology or Medicine** was awarded jointly to Baruj Benacerraf of Harvard University, George Snell of the Jackson Laboratory in Maine, and Jean Dausset of France for their studies of antigens, protein-carbohydrate complexes found in the body.

Oct 14: The **Nobel Prize in Chemistry** was awarded jointly to Paul Berg of Stanford University for his studies of the manipulation of gene structures, and to Walter Gilbert of Harvard University and Frederick Sanger of England for their work on reading the fine details of the structure of DNA.

Oct 14: The **Nobel Prize in Physics** was awarded jointly to James Cronin of the University of Chicago and Val L. Fitch of Princeton University for their discoveries concerning the symmetry of subatomic particles.

Oct 15: The **Nobel Prize in Economics** was awarded

to Lawrence R. Klein of the Wharton School of the University of Pennsylvania for his development of models for forecasting economic trends.

Nov 12: Voyager 1, launched in Sept. 1977, flew within 77,000 miles of Saturn and found far more rings around the planet than had been previously identified, some with eccentric orbits. The spacecraft also found three new moons, making 15 known in all.

IV. Fashion
    Folkways
    Holidays
    Social Issues and Crime
    Sports

On Jan. 20 Pres. Carter announced U.S. withdrawal from the Summer Olympics, to be held in Moscow in July, in response to the Soviet invasion of Afghanistan in 1979. Some 50 nations followed suit, but many athletes who had trained for years for the games felt great bitterness at the move. In February Americans witnessed an athletic miracle as the U.S. Olympic hockey team defeated the favored Finnish and Russian hockey teams to take the gold medal and become national heroes. Another top story this year was Muhammad Ali's attempt to win the world heavyweight boxing title for an unprecedented fourth time. Ali had retired from boxing in 1979 after defeating Michael Spinks. On Oct. 2 he faced off against WBA champion Larry Holmes in Las Vegas, but his dream of victory was not to become reality. Nonetheless, the former champ earned $8,000,000 for his part in what many considered a terrible match. In golf, the year's top money winners were Tom Watson, $530,808, and Beth Daniel, $231,000. The year's fashion rage was the bulky coat, down-filled, quilted, and often reaching almost to the ground. Among those who died in 1980 were Alice Longworth Roosevelt, last surviving child of Theodore Roosevelt, Feb. 20, at 96; Richard "Rube" Marquard, one of baseball's all-time great pitchers, June 1, at 90; and Jesse Owens, track star who won four gold medals at the 1936 Olympics in Germany and shattered the Nazi myth of racial superiority, Mar. 30, at age 66.

Jan 20: Super Bowl XIV was won by the Pittsburgh Steelers (AFC), defeating the Los Angeles Rams (NFC) 31 to 19. On Jan. 6 the Steelers had beaten the Houston Oilers 27 to 13 for the AFC title and the Rams had defeated the Tampa Bay Buccaneers 9 to 0 for the NFC championship.

Feb 12-24: At the **Winter Olympics** in Lake Placid, N.Y., the U.S. won six gold medals and finished third behind the U.S.S.R. and East Germany. The U.S. hockey team scored a major upset over the U.S.S.R. team, which had been favored to win the gold medal. Eric Heiden swept the speed skating events, becoming the first athlete to win five gold medals in the Winter Olympics.

Mar 14: Twenty-two members of a **U.S. amateur boxing team died** when the Polish airliner they were traveling on crashed near Warsaw. The crash killed 87.

Mar 24: The **NCAA basketball championship** was won by the University of Louisville, beating UCLA 59 to 54.

Mar 31: The World Boxing Association **heavyweight boxing championship** was won by Mike "Hercules" Weaver, who knocked out John Tate in the 15th round at Knoxville, Tenn.

May 4-16: The **NBA basketball championship** was won by the Los Angeles Lakers, who defeated the Philadelphia 76ers four games to two.

May 12: The first nonstop **transcontinental balloon flight** was completed by Maxie Anderson and his son Kris, who flew 3100 miles from Fort Baker, Calif., to Matane, Quebec, on the Gaspé Peninsula, in four days aboard the balloon *Kitty Hawk*.

June 15: the **U.S. Open golf tournament** was won by Jack Nicklaus. It was his fourth U.S. Open win.

Aug 10: The **PGA golf tournament** was won for the fifth time by Jack Nicklaus.

Sep 6-7: The **U.S. Open tennis singles championships**

were won by John McEnroe in the men's division and
Chris Evert Lloyd in the women's division.

Sep 16-25: The **America's Cup** was successfully defended by the U.S. yacht *Freedom,* which beat the
challenger *Australia* four races to one.

Oct 14-21: The **World Series** was won by the Philadelphia Phillies (NL), defeating the Kansas City Royals
(AL) four games to two. On Oct. 10 the Royals completed a three-game sweep of the New York Yankees
to win the American League pennant. On Oct. 12 the
Phillies won the National League pennant, beating
the Houston Astros three games to two.

1981

I. Civil Rights
Exploration and Settlement
Government
Statistics
Wars

The UN Conference on the Law of the Sea, which had
worked for several years on the question of how to
apportion underseas resources, met in New York
City on Mar. 9 in what was expected to be its final
session. However, the fledgling administration of
Pres. Ronald Reagan, reversing the position of the
previous administration, objected to some of the
terms of the proposed treaty, and the U.S. did not sign
it. In domestic matters, the Bureau of the Census
estimated the nation's population as 230,500,000 at
year's end, an increase of 2,200,000 over 1980. Divorces in 1981 hit a record 1,210,000, the government
reported. Notables who died this year included Roger
Baldwin, a founder of the American Civil Liberties
Union, Aug. 26, at 97; Gen. Omar N. Bradley, called
the "GI's general" during World War II, Apr. 8, at 88;

Emanuel Celler, Democrat of New York, who served 50 years (1923–1973) in the House of Representatives, Jan. 15, at 92; David E. Lilienthal, former chairman of the Tennessee Valley Authority and first chairman of the Atomic Energy Commission, Jan. 15, at 81; Carl Vinson, Democrat of Georgia, who served 50 years (1914–1964) in the House of Representatives, June 1, at 97; and Roy Wilkins, leader of the NAACP from 1931 to 1977, Sept. 8, at 80.

Jan 20: Ronald Reagan was **inaugurated president** of the United States. A Republican, he was at 69 the oldest person ever to assume the presidency. George Bush was inaugurated vice president.

Jan 20: The Iranian **hostage crisis** ended when Iran released the 52 U.S. captives seized at the U.S. embassy in Teheran in Nov. 1979. The release was accomplished with the help of Algeria minutes after Ronald Reagan succeeded Jimmy Carter as president. On Jan. 21 Carter flew to Wiesbaden, West Germany, to greet the freed Americans.

Feb 18: In his first **State of the Union** message, Pres. Reagan called for cuts of $41,000,000,000 in the budget Pres. Carter had submitted. He also proposed a 10% income tax cut in each of the next three years, an increase of about $5,000,000,000 in defense spending, and more liberal depreciation rules for business.

Mar 30: Pres. **Reagan was shot** by John W. Hinckley, Jr., 25, outside a Washington, D.C., hotel. Reagan underwent two hours of surgery for a wound in his left lung. Presidential press secretary James Brady was shot in the head but survived. Also wounded were Secret Service agent Timothy J. McCarthy and Washington police officer Thomas K. Delahanty. Reagan returned to the White House on Apr. 11.

Apr 4: The **first Mexican-American mayor** of a major U.S. city, Henry Gabriel Cisneros, 33, was elected in San Antonio, Tex.

Apr 21: A major **Saudi arms sale** was announced. The U.S. agreed to sell $1,000,000,000 worth of military equipment to Saudi Arabia, including five AWACS electronic surveillance aircraft. Israel protested the sale.

Apr 24: The 15-month **embargo on grain** shipments to the U.S.S.R. would be lifted, Pres. Reagan announced, thus fulfilling a campaign pledge he had made.

June 8: In a ruling on **wage discrimination,** the Supreme Court ruled women could sue for equal pay even if the work they did was not identical with that of male employees.

June 25: The Supreme Court ruled that **draft registration** and, by extension, a military draft, could exclude women without violating the Constitution.

July 7: Sandra Day O'Connor, a judge of the Arizona Court of Appeals, was nominated by Pres. Reagan to become the first woman member of the Supreme Court. She was confirmed by the Senate on Sept. 21 and sworn in on Sept. 25.

July 17: A **hotel disaster** in Kansas City, Mo., in which two indoor aerial walkways collapsed, killed 111 people and injured 190. About 1500 persons were attending a tea dance when the steel and concrete structures plunged to the floor below.

Aug 4: Pres. Reagan's **income tax reduction plan** was passed by Congress with only a slight modification. The bill reduced income taxes by 5% (rather than the requested 10%) as of Oct. 1, 10% as of July 1, 1982, and 10% as of July 1, 1983.

Aug 10: Production of the **neutron bomb** as a warhead for missiles and artillery was authorized by Pres. Reagan. The decision reversed U.S. policy set by Pres. Carter in 1978. The weapons were to be kept in the U.S.

Aug 19: Two **Libyan jets were shot down** by U.S. Navy fighters about 60 miles from the Libyan coast after the Libyan fighters opened fire on the U.S. jets. Libya claimed control of all of the Gulf of Sidra, where the Navy was holding military exercises. The U.S. maintained that the gulf was an international body of water.

Dec 4: Covert **domestic intelligence operations** by the CIA and other agencies were authorized for the first time in an executive order issued by Pres. Reagan.

II. Architecture
Arts and Music
Popular Entertainment
Publishing
Theater

The worldwide recession weakened the art market, and a strong U.S. dollar discouraged foreign buyers. Nevertheless, in May a Picasso self-portrait sold in New York City for $5,300,000, a new auction record for a twentieth-century painting. The Joffrey Ballet celebrated its 25th anniversary in October. In the same month, theatergoers greeted the opening of a British import, *The Life and Adventures of Nicholas Nickleby*, which coincided with publication of new paperback editions of the Dickens novel. Tickets for the play cost $100. An advertisement for a $5 edition of the novel suggested buying the book and saving $95. Among the year's top motion pictures were *Superman II* and *Raiders of the Lost Ark*. In music, videocassettes became an important part of the marketing strategy for many rock groups, who found that airtime on MTV, a rock music channel carried by 252 cable television stations, translated into big sales in record stores. In architecture, increasing attention was being paid to preserving and restoring old buildings. A restoration of particular interest was that of the elaborate terra cotta facade of the Woolworth Building in New York City. Americans mourned the deaths of Nelson Algren, known best for his 1949 novel *The Man With the Golden Arm*, May 9, at 72; Samuel Barber, Pulitzer Prize-winning composer, Jan. 23, at 70; Hoagy Carmichael, popular composer, Dec. 27, at 82; Ariel and Will Durant, husband and wife authors of the 11-volume *The Story of Civilization*, she on Oct. 25, at 83, and he on Nov. 7, at 96; Howard Hanson, composer and director of the Eastman School of Music for 40 years, Feb. 26, at 84; Joseph H. Hirshhorn, millionaire art collector and founder in 1974 of the Hirshhorn Museum in Washington, D.C., Aug. 31, at 82; George Jessel, comedian, May 24, at 83; Anita Loos, novelist and playwright, Aug. 18, at 88; Rosa Ponselle, first U.S.-trained singer to star at the Metropolitan Opera, May 25, at 84; Robert Montgomery, actor, Sept. 27, at 77; William Saroyan, author and playwright, May 18, at 72; and Dewitt Wallace, founder in 1922 of *Reader's Digest*, Mar. 30, at 91.

Among **books published** this year was Dumas Malone's six-volume life of *Thomas Jefferson*, a work 40 years in the making. Its publication was greeted with unanimous acclaim. Other books published this year included *The Company of Women* by Mary Gordon, her second novel; *The Hotel New Hampshire* by John Irving, a novel that disappointed many who had praised his earlier novel *The World According to Garp; Tar Baby* by Toni Morrison, fiction; *The Collected Poems* of the late Sylvia Plath; and *Rabbit Is Rich* by John Updike, the author's third novel about Harry "Rabbit" Angstrom.

Jan 13: The **Bollingen Prize** for poetry was awarded jointly to May Swenson and Howard Nemerov.

Jan 14: **Broadcasting regulations** for radio stations were eased by the FCC, freeing stations to air as many commercials an hour as they pleased and removing any obligation to allocate time for news or public affairs programing.

Apr 13: **Pulitzer prizes** were awarded for the following: fiction, *A Confederacy of Dunces* by John Kennedy Toole; biography, *Peter the Great* by Robert K. Massie; history, *American Education: The National Experience, 1783–1876* by Lawrence A. Cremin; general nonfiction, *Fin-de-Siècle Vienna: Politics and Culture* by Carl E. Schorske; poetry, *The Morning of the Poem* by James Schuyler; drama, *Crimes of the Heart* by Beth Henley.

June 6: A nationwide competition to design a **Vietnam War Memorial** for Washington, D.C., was won by Maya Yang Lin, a 21-year-old Yale undergraduate in architecture. The winning design consisted of two long, low granite walls in the form of an open V, on which the names of all the U.S. war dead in the Vietnam War would be inscribed.

III. Business and Industry
Education
Philosophy and Religion
Science

The economy continued to falter in 1981. Inflation hit an annual rate of 14%. Unemployment hit 7.4% and continued to rise. The Census Bureau reported that average household income before taxes had declined 2.6%. Automobile production was at its lowest level in 20 years, with Detroit producing only 6,200,000 passenger cars. The cost of medical care climbed 12.5% and was the highest since records were begun in 1935. In January, Pres. Ronald Reagan lifted oil price controls. Crude oil and oil product prices shot up at once, but an oversupply of crude soon brought them back down. The U.S. imported 40% less oil than in the peak importing year of 1978. The ten major airlines reported a total operating loss of $577,000,000, more than double their losses in 1980. In July a potentially devastating pest, the Mediterranean fruit fly, was found in California. An area of 550 square miles was quarantined, and Gov. Jerry Brown ordered ground spraying and the stripping of fruit from trees. In September, threatened with a federal quarantine of the state's produce, Gov. Brown ordered aerial spraying in spite of protests from environmentalists. The last outbreak of fruit flies was reported in August. By October it appeared a disaster had been averted. Probably the year's brightest news concerned the introduction of a personal computer by IBM, a development that lent legitimacy to the growing personal computer industry and that was to turn it into a major economic force in a few short years. Among those who died this year were Donald W. Douglas, airplane designer, Feb. 2, at 88; John S. Knight, founder of the Knight newspaper empire, June 16, at 87; Lowell Thomas, broadcast pioneer, Aug. 30, at 89; and Harold C. Urey, winner of the Nobel Prize for his discovery of heavy hydrogen, Jan. 5, at 87.

Jan 7: A stock market run began when Joe Granville,

a popular market forecaster, advised investors to "sell everything." The Dow Jones average of industrial stocks fell 23.8 points, and trading on the New York Stock Exchange set a new daily record of 93,700,000 shares. By Jan. 19 the situation had stabilized and stocks had rebounded.

Jan 8: An increase in the risk of **coronary death** was linked to consumption of large amounts of cholesterol, according to a report in the *New England Journal of Medicine*. The report was based on a 20-year study of 1900 men.

Mar 5: Teaching evolution in public schools did not violate the rights of religious fundamentalists, a Superior Court judge ruled in a California case. He said, however, that dogmatic teaching about the origin of life was not to be permitted.

Apr 12-14: The **space shuttle** *Columbia,* with Robert L. Crippen and John W. Young aboard, was launched from Cape Canaveral, Fla., on its maiden flight. After a flight of 54 hrs., 20 min., 48 sec., including 36 orbits of Earth, *Columbia* touched down at Edwards Air Force Base, Calif., making the first wheels-down landing by any spacecraft.

May 4: The **largest U.S. corporation,** according to the annual survey by *Fortune* magazine, was Exxon, with sales in 1980 of $103,142,834,000. Mobil was second with $59,610,000,000. General Motors dropped to third place.

June 18: A vaccine produced by **genetic engineering** and effective against hoof and mouth disease was announced. The vaccine was believed to be the first product of gene splicing to provide protection against disease in animals or humans.

July 9: The **herpes simplex virus** had been successfully suppressed by an experimental drug, acyclovir, it was reported in the *New England Journal of Medicine*. Genital herpes, caused by the virus, was identified as the most rapidly spreading sexually transmitted disease in the U.S.

Aug 3: A nationwide **air traffic controllers' strike** was begun by the 13,000 members of the traffic controllers' union, PATCO. Pres. Reagan announced that the strikers had to return to work by Aug. 5 or face dismissal. Many stayed home and were fired. On Aug. 17 the Federal Aviation Administration began accepting applications for new air controllers. On Oct. 22 the federal Labor Relations Authority decertified PATCO, removing any possibility of a negotiated settlement with striking air controllers.

Aug 25: Voyager 2, launched in 1977, flew within 63,000 miles of Saturn. Data sent back by the spacecraft showed thousands of rings around the planet, many more than the several hundred previously believed to exist.

Oct 9: The **Nobel Prize in Physiology or Medicine** was awarded jointly to David H. Hubel and Tlosten N. Wiesel of Harvard University for their studies of the way the brain processes visual information; and to Roger W. Sperry of the California Institute of Technology for demonstrating the different functions of the right and left hemispheres of the brain.

Oct 13: The **Nobel Prize in Economics** was awarded to James Tobin of Yale University for his development of the portfolio selection theory of investment.

Oct 19: The **Nobel Prize in Chemistry** was awarded jointly to Ronald Hoffman of Cornell University and Kenichi Fukui of Japan for applying theories of quantum mechanics to predict the course of chemical reactions.

Oct 19: The **Nobel Prize in Physics** was awarded jointly to Nicolaas Bloembergen of Harvard University and Arthur Schawlow of Stanford University for their contribution to the development of laser spectroscopy.

Nov 14: The **space shuttle** *Columbia* completed its second mission, the second flight ever of a reusable spacecraft. The mission was cut short by the failure of a fuel cell.

Dec 8: The constitutionality of **religious services in campus buildings** by student organizations at public colleges and universities was upheld by the Supreme Court. Many considered this to be the most significant ruling on the issue of separation of church and state in years.

IV. **Fashion**
   Folkways
   Holidays
   Social Issues and Crime
   Sports

A trend toward dullness that had prevailed in fashion gave way to a new freshness, characterized by a simple, sexy look. A touch of opulence also became stylish, perhaps inspired by the dress of Nancy Reagan, wife of the president. This year a maintenance worker won $5,000,000 in the New York State Lottery, the largest lottery payoff to date. State lotteries in the U.S. were estimated to take in $3,600,000,000 annually. Crime continued to be a concern. The Burns Detective Agency estimated that white collar crime in 1981 would amount to between $1,200,000,000 and $1,800,000,000 and that only 15% of such crimes would be detected. Divorces in the U.S. totaled a record 1,200,000 this year, the government reported. In sports, the National Football League set a new attendance record of 13,392,000, an average of about 60,000 fans present at a game. In boxing Larry Holmes successfully defended his World Boxing Association heavyweight title in a three-round bout (June 12) against Leon Spinks. In pro golf the top money winners were Tom Kite, $375,699, and Beth Daniel, $206,977. Notables who died included John Kieran, sportswriter who became a star of the radio show *Information Please* in the 1930s and 1940s, Dec. 10, at 89; and Joe Louis, the "Brown Bomber," who held the heavyweight boxing title from 1937 to 1949, the longest reign ever, Apr. 12, at 66.

Jan 25: **Super Bowl XV** was won by the Oakland Raiders (AFC), defeating the Philadelphia Eagles (NFC) 27 to 10. On Jan. 11 the Raiders had beaten the San Diego Chargers 34 to 27 for the AFC championship and the Eagles had defeated the Dallas Cowboys 20 to 7 for the NFC title.

Mar 30: The **NCAA basketball championship** was won by North Carolina, which defeated Indiana 63 to 50.

May 5-14: The **NBA basketball championship** was

won by the Boston Celtics, who defeated the Houston Rockets four games to two.

May 24: The 65th **Indianapolis 500** auto race ended in controversy. A day after the race, Mario Andretti, who had finished second, was named winner over Bobby Unser because Unser had broken a rule during a slowdown period near the end of the race. On Oct. 8 the U.S. Auto Club (USAC) reversed the decision and gave the victory to Unser, but fined him $40,000 for his infraction. Unser had completed the race in 3 hrs., 35 min., 41.78 sec., with an average speed of 139.085 mph.

June 21: The **U.S. Open golf tournament** was won by David Graham of Australia, the fifth foreign player to win this title.

July 3-4: At the **Wimbledon** tennis championships in England, John McEnroe won the men's singles title and Chris Evert Lloyd won the women's singles. McEnroe teamed with Peter Fleming to win the men's doubles, and Pam Shriver teamed with Martina Navratilova to win the women's doubles.

Aug 9: The **PGA golf tournament** was won by Larry Nelson, beating Fuzzy Zoeller by three strokes.

Sep 9-13: The **U.S. Open Tennis singles championships** were won by John McEnroe in the men's division and Tracy Austin in the women's division.

Oct 20: What came to be called the **Brinks robbery**, a bungled armored-car holdup in Nanuet, N.Y., ended with two policemen and one guard dead and two guards wounded. Four persons were arrested, including three members of the terrorist Weather Underground group.

Oct 20-28: The **World Series** was won by the Los Angeles Dodgers (NL), defeating the New York Yankees (AL) four games to two. On Oct. 15 the Yankees had won the American League pennant over the Oakland Athletics in a three-game sweep. On Oct. 19 the Dodgers won the National League pennant, defeating the Montreal Expos three games to two.

Dec 11-13: The **Davis Cup** international tennis competition was won by the U.S., defeating Argentina three matches to one in Cincinnati, Ohio.

1982

I. Civil Rights
   Exploration and Settlement
   Government
   Statistics
   Wars

In January Pres. Ronald Reagan predicted that the recession, which had begun in 1981, would be short and followed by a strong recovery. His prediction proved overly optimistic, but at year's end there were encouraging signs in the economy. In foreign affairs the freeze in U.S.-Soviet relations continued as the U.S.S.R. stepped up its war in Afghanistan. The declaration of martial law in Poland on Dec. 13, 1981, viewed as a response to Soviet pressure, contributed to the broadening in June of a U.S. embargo on goods to the U.S.S.R. The Middle East again became a battleground as Israeli forces advanced into Lebanon in June in response to continued Palestinian attacks on Israel from Lebanon. Attempts by the U.S. to bring peace to the region were complex and generally fruitless, but the president decided to commit U.S. Marines as a peacekeeping force in Beirut, an action that provoked much controversy. Americans mourned the deaths this year of former Supreme Court Justice Abe Fortas, Apr. 5, at 71, and Bess Truman, widow of Pres. Harry S Truman, Oct. 18, at 97.

Jan 13: An Air Florida **jet crashed** into a bridge over the Potomac R. in Washington, D.C., shortly after taking off from National Airport, killing 78 people, including seven who were on the bridge.

Feb 6: Pres. Reagan's **proposed budget** for fiscal 1982 of $757,600,000,000 included a projected deficit of $91,500,000,000. Reagan called for deep cuts in domestic spending but asked for an 18% increase in the defense budget.

Mar 10: Economic sanctions against Libya were announced by the Reagan administration in response to Libya's involvement with international terrorist organizations. The sanctions included an embargo on Libyan oil shipments to the U.S. and a ban on export of high-technology products to Libya.

June 18: Exports to the U.S.S.R. of equipment to be used to build or operate the Siberian gas pipeline were banned. The ban also applied to the sale of such equipment produced by foreign subsidiaries or licensees of U.S. corporations. The move was protested four days later by the European Economic Community, but the ban was not lifted until Nov. 13.

June 21: John W. Hinckley, Jr., was found not guilty by reason of insanity in the Mar. 30, 1981, shooting of Pres. Reagan and three others. The verdict caused widespread shock and demands for revision of laws governing insanity pleas.

June 24: In a ruling on **presidential liability,** the Supreme Court ruled that a president could not be sued for damages for actions he took while in office. The decision was made in ruling on a suit brought against former president Richard M. Nixon by a government employee.

June 25: Alexander M. Haig, Jr., resigned as secretary of state following disagreements with Pres. Reagan and some of his advisers. George P. Shultz, a former Cabinet member and a businessman, was appointed to succeed Haig. Shultz was confirmed on July 15 and sworn in the next day.

June 30: The **Equal Rights Amendment** failed to achieve ratification despite an extension granted by Congress in 1978. At that time 35 of the required 38 states had ratified, but no others had done so in the intervening years.

July 9: A Pan American **jet crashed** after takeoff in New Orleans, La., killing 154 people. It was the second worst single-plane disaster in U.S. history.

Aug 20: About 800 **U.S. Marines landed in Beirut,** Lebanon, as part of a multinational force to oversee withdrawal of PLO fighters from the city. The Marines were withdrawn on Sept. 10, but they returned to Beirut on Sept. 29 following massacres of Palestinians in the Sabra and Shattila refugee camps by so-called Christian militiamen (Sept. 16–18) and a Lebanese request (Sept. 20) for assistance. On Sept. 30 one Marine was killed and three others wounded while attempting to defuse a bomb.

Sep 29-Oct 1: Cyanide placed in Tylenol capsules caused the deaths of seven persons in the Chicago area. By Oct. 6 a nationwide alert was sounded. Suspicious deaths in other parts of the country were reported but none appeared to be related to the Chicago murders. The makers of Tylenol, a pain reliever, recalled 264,000 bottles of the drug. The killer was never found.

Nov 2: In congressional elections the Republicans kept their 54–46 Senate majority, but the Democrats picked up 26 House seats for a 269–166 majority.

Nov 22: Construction of the **MX missile** was proposed by Pres. Reagan, who called for deployment of 100 of the multiple-warhead missiles in "dense pack mode," a relatively small area thought to be easier to defend against an enemy's first strike. The cost of the proposal was put at $26,000,000,000.

II. Architecture
Arts and Music
Popular Entertainment
Publishing
Theater

The Broadway season was relatively quiet. Biggest hits of the year were the musicals *Nine* and *Cats*. The cost of Broadway productions continued to climb. Cost of producing a musical approached $5,000,000. Opera companies and orchestras continued to have financial problems. The American Ballet Theater's season was shortened by a two-month lockout of its dancers in the fall. The dancers were finally given large salary increases. The Joffrey Ballet, in a move to gain a wider audience, decided to become a resident company in Los Angeles for part of the year while keeping its New York City season. This year movie theaters grossed $3,449,000,000, up 16% over 1981. The most successful film of the year was *E.T.: The Extraterrestrial*, which captured the hearts of millions. The recession was reflected in a softening of art auction prices, but a Henry Moore sculpture, *Reclining Figure*, brought $1,265,000. The 58-year-old *Saturday Review* suspended publication this year after losing $3,000,000 in the previous two years. Notables who died this year included Stringfellow Barr, educator known for his curriculum based on "100 Great Books," Feb. 2, at 85; Ingrid Bergman, actress, Aug. 29, at 67; John Cheever, writer, June 19, at 70; Frederick Dannay, who with his cousin Manfred B. Lee wrote the popular Ellery Queen mystery stories, Sept. 3, at 76; Babette Deutsch, poet, Nov. 13, at 87; Henry Fonda, actor, Aug. 12, at 77; John Gardner, novelist, Sept. 14, at 49; Melville Bell Grosvenor, president of the National Geographic Society, Apr. 22, at 80; Archibald MacLeish, poet, Apr. 20, at 89; Thelonius Monk, jazz pianist and composer, Feb. 17, at 64; Ayn Rand, novelist and champion of a controversial form of individualism, Mar. 6, at 77; Lee Strasberg, proponent of the method theory of acting, Feb. 17, at 80; King Vidor, pioneer film director, Nov. 1, at 87; and John Hay Whitney, millionaire horse breeder, Feb. 8, at 77.

Among **books published** this year were a number of volumes on the arms race and the threat of nuclear war. Perhaps the best was *The Fate of the Earth* by Jonathan Schell, which caused much discussion and gained a wide readership. Other books published this year included *The Dean's December* by Saul Bellow, a novel; *Oh, What a Paradise It Seems* by John Cheever, the author's last novel; *God's Grace* by Bernard Malamud, a novel; and *The Mosquito Coast* by Paul Theroux, the story of a modern, unsuccessful Swiss Family Robinson. This year the Library of America, embarking on a program to issue uniform, quality editions of works of major U.S. authors, issued volumes of the works of Nathaniel Hawthorne, Herman Melville, Harriet Beecher Stowe, and Mark Twain.

Mar 12: Pulitzer prizes were awarded for the following: fiction, *Rabbit Is Rich* by John Updike; biography, *Grant, A Biography* by William S. McFeeley; history, *Mary Chestnut's Civil War* by C. Vann Woodward; general nonfiction, *The Soul of a New Machine* by Tracy Kidder; poetry, *The Collected Poems* of Sylvia Plath; drama, *A Soldier's Play* by Charles Fuller.

July 10: A painting by **Samuel F. B. Morse**, *The Gallery of the Louvre*, brought $3,250,000 in a private sale, the most ever paid for an American work of art to date. The painting had been owned since 1884 by Syracuse University.

III. Business and Industry
Education
Philosophy and Religion
Science

The recession that began in the summer of 1981 had run its course by November of this year. In 1982 the rate of inflation dropped to 6% and the Consumer Price Index rose only 3.9% for the year, smallest increase since 1972. The gross national product fell 1.8%, largest decrease since 1946. Unemployment rose to 10.8% by December and averaged 9.7% for the year. Some 4,600,000 people were receiving unemployment compensation by October, the largest number since such payments began in the 1930s. More than 30 banks failed, and high interest rates crippled new housing starts. Yet there were signs that U.S. business was on the rebound. Boeing introduced a new jet, the 767, said to be 35% more fuel efficient than older aircraft. Kodak introduced the disc camera, its most important new product in nearly 20 years. The camera was about the size of a pack of cigarettes. In September IBM introduced its 3084 computer, almost twice as powerful as its predecessor and able to process instructions at the rate of 26,000,000 a second. The largest solar plant yet built, expected to produce 10,000 kilowatts of electricity, was completed in the Mojave Desert. The U.S. Institute of Medicine estimated that of the fatalities caused by the ten leading causes of death, fully 50% could be traced to their victims' styles of living, and that some 320,000 deaths a year were caused by smoking. The spread of genital herpes alarmed the nation. It was estimated that 20,000,000 Americans had the disease, and that 300,000 to 500,000 new cases were occurring every year. In education, there were 520,000 fewer students in all U.S. schools than in the previous school year. The College Board reported that black students on average scored 100 points lower on both verbal and math Scholastic Aptitude Tests than white students. Notables who died this year included William Bernbach, founder in 1939 of the Doyle Dane Bernbach advertising firm, Oct. 2, at 71; John Cardinal Cody, Roman Catholic archbishop of Chicago since 1965 and an outspoken advocate of integration, Apr. 25, at 74; and René Dubos, biologist, environmentalist, and author, Feb. 20, at 81.

Jan 5: An Arkansas law requiring the teaching of **creation science,** a theory of creation based on the Bible, in schools in which the theory of evolution was taught was struck down by a federal judge in Arkansas. The court ruled that the teaching of creation science violated the constitutional requirement of separation of church and state.

Jan 8: The **American Telephone and Telegraph Company** agreed to divest itself of its 22 Bell Telephone operating systems. The agreement ended an eight-year antitrust suit by the Justice Department that charged AT&T with monopolizing U.S. telephone service.

May 3: The **largest U.S. corporation,** according to the annual *Fortune* magazine survey, remained Exxon, with 1981 sales of $108,107,688,000. Mobil Oil was second.

May 13: Braniff International Corporation, operator of the nation's eighth-largest airline, filed for bankruptcy. Braniff was the first major U.S. airline to go bankrupt.

June 29: A major **Protestant church merger** brought together the United Presbyterian Church and the Presbyterian Church in the United States. The new church would have 3,000,000 members.

July 5: The **Penn Square Bank** in Oklahoma City, Okla., was closed by federal regulators. The bank had suffered heavy losses through loans to depressed energy-based businesses in the Southwest. Some of the bank's $2,000,000,000 in loans had been bought by other banks, causing tremors throughout the banking industry.

July 16: The Rev. **Sun Myung Moon,** leader of the controversial Unification Church, was sentenced to 18 months in prison and fined $25,000 after being convicted of tax fraud and conspiracy to obstruct justice.

Sep 8: Agreement on a Lutheran church **merger of three Lutheran denominations** was announced. The American Lutheran Church, the Association of Evangelist Lutheran Churches, and the Lutheran Church in America voted to form a single denomination, which would have 5,500,000 members.

Oct 15: A new **weekly stock trading record** was set by the New York Stock Exchange, 592,460,000 shares. On Oct. 7 the NYSE had reached a new one-day high of 147,070,000 shares.

Oct 18: The **Nobel Prize in Physics** was awarded to Kenneth G. Wilson of Cornell University for development of a mathematical system explaining changes in the behavior of matter at critical points of pressure and temperature.

Oct 20: The **Nobel Prize in Economics** was awarded to George Stigler of the University of Chicago for his study of government regulation and its effect on the economy.

Nov 11-16: The **first operational space shuttle flight** was completed by the shuttle *Columbia,* which successfully carried two satellites into orbit.

Dec 2: The first successful **artificial heart transplant** was completed at the University of Utah Medical Center. The recipient was Barney C. Clark, 61, who had been near death at the time of the operation.

IV. Fashion
   Folkways
   Holidays
   Social Issues and Crime
   Sports

This year the NCAA sponsored for the first time a major college basketball championship for women. The Association for Intercollegiate Athletics for Women (AIAW), which had been holding championship games since 1972, held its annual game this year, but it was clearly at the end of its existence and disgruntled at the NCAA takeover after years of lack of interest in women's competition. Major league baseball set an attendance record of 44,500,000. Tom Watson was the outstanding golfer of the year, winning both the British and U.S. Open championships. The top pro golf money winners were Craig Stadler, $446,462, and JoAnne Carner, $320,399. Fashions showed a tendency toward greater elegance. Women's winter styles included ponchos and knickers. Sports fans mourned the passing of Leroy "Satchel" Paige, one of the great pitchers of all time, June 8, at 75; and Walter W. "Red" Smith, Pulitzer Prize-winning sportswriter, Jan. 15, at 76.

Jan 24: Super Bowl XVI was won by the San Francisco 49ers (NFC), defeating the Cincinnati Bengals (AFC) 26 to 21. On Jan. 10 the 49ers had beaten the Dallas Cowboys 28 to 27 for the NFC title, and Cincinnati had beaten the San Diego Chargers 27 to 7 for the AFC championship.

Mar 29: The **NCAA men's basketball championship** was won by North Carolina, which defeated Georgetown 63 to 62.

May 27-June 8: The **NBA basketball championship** was won by the Los Angeles Lakers, who defeated the Philadelphia 76ers four games to two.

June 20: The **U.S. Open golf tournament** was won by Tom Watson, who beat Jack Nicklaus by two strokes.

July 3-4: At the **Wimbledon** tennis championships in England, Jimmy Connors won the men's singles title and Martina Navratilova won the women's singles. Navratilova teamed with Pam Shriver to win the

women's doubles, and Anne Smith teamed with
Kevin Curran of South Africa to win the mixed doubles.

Aug 8: The **PGA golf tournament** was won by Raymond Floyd, who posted a record opening round
score of 63.

Sep 11-12: The **U.S. Open tennis singles championships** were won by Jimmy Connors in the men's division and by Chris Evert Lloyd in the women's division.

Oct 12-20: The **World Series** was won by the St. Louis
Cardinals (NL), defeating the Milwaukee Brewers
four games to three. On Oct. 10 the Cardinals had
won the National League pennant over the Atlanta
Braves in three straight games. The same day the
Brewers won the American League pennant over the
California Angels, three games to two. The Brewers
became the first team to win a playoff after losing the
first two games.

Nov 26-28: The **Davis Cup** international tennis championship was won in Grenoble, France, by the U.S.,
defeating France four matches to one.

Dec 10: The **WBA heavyweight boxing championship**
was won by Michael Dokes, who knocked out Mike
Weaver in the first round of a bout at Las Vegas,
Nev.

Dec 12: The **largest cash robbery** in U.S. history occurred when thieves in New York City made off with
$9,800,000 from an armored truck company.

1983

I. Civil Rights
   Exploration and Settlement
   Government
   Statistics
   Wars

Pres. Ronald Reagan's administration faced a difficult year in foreign relations. In Lebanon the U.S. was unsuccessful in its attempt to secure withdrawal of Syrian and Israeli forces and to aid the Lebanese government in its struggle to assert authority over the many political and religious factions fighting in Beirut. Disaster struck the U.S. peacemaking effort in April when the U.S. embassy in Beirut was bombed. The crushing blow came in October when terrorists blew up U.S. Marine headquarters in Beirut. In Central America the U.S. sent military aid to the government of El Salvador in its long and bloody civil war. Pres. Reagan described the Salvadoran insurgents as terrorists. Meanwhile the U.S. sent aid to the anti-Sandinista, anticommunist "freedom fighters" in Nicaragua. Politicians and private citizens alike called for a consistent foreign policy for both the Middle East and Central America and voiced concern that U.S. policies would eventually involve the country in a war. In October U.S. forces were committed in an invasion of the island of Grenada, ostensibly to protect U.S. citizens there after a coup by Marxist radicals. In domestic affairs, the Census Bureau reported that the number of Americans living in poverty grew from 34,400,000 in 1982 to 35,300,000 in 1983, boosting the poverty rate to its highest level in 18 years. Even the weather was dismal in 1983. Heat, cold, and storms killed some 700 people, nearly twice the 1982 total, and caused an estimated $27,000,000,000 in damage. Among the notables who died this year were Benjamin V. Cohen, who wrote much of the precedent-setting legislation of the New Deal of the early 1930s, Aug. 15, at 88; Gen. Alfred M. Gruenther, a principal aide to Gen. Dwight D. Eisenhower in World War II and NATO commander from 1953 to 1956, May 30, at 84; and Sen. Henry M. "Scoop" Jackson, Democrat of Washington, who had served in Congress for nearly 43 years, Sept. 1, at 71.

Jan 15: Changes in the **Social Security system** were recommended by the National Commission on Social Security Reform. The changes, calculated to produce

$168,700,000,000 by 1989 and make the system solvent, included tax increases, a reduction in the growth rate of benefits, and an eventual raising of the retirement age. A bill incorporating these modifications was passed by Congress on Mar. 25 and signed by Pres. Reagan on Apr. 20.

Apr 11: A presidential panel reviewing the **MX missile** recommended that 100 of the ICBMs be installed in existing missile silos in Wyoming and Nebraska. The panel also recommended development of a smaller, single-warheaded missile, dubbed Midgetman.

Apr 12: The **first black mayor of Chicago,** Harold Washington, a Democratic congressman, was elected to office by a narrow margin.

Apr 18: The **U.S. embassy in Beirut,** Lebanon, was almost totally destroyed by a car-bomb explosion that killed 63 people, including 17 Americans. Pro-Iranian terrorists were blamed but the perpetrators were not found.

May 24: MX missile research and development funds, totaling $625,000,000, were authorized by Congress. Some Democrats supported Republicans on the measure after Pres. Reagan promised to be more flexible in arms control negotiations.

June 15: In a ruling on **legal abortions** involving five different cases, the Supreme Court curbed the power of state and local governments to limit access to such operations. The decision reaffirmed the 1973 ruling giving women unrestricted rights to abortions during the first three months of pregnancy.

June 23: The so-called **legislative veto,** by which Congress overruled actions of federal agencies, was ruled unconstitutional by the Supreme Court as an invasion of executive authority by the legislative branch.

June 28: A proposed **abortion amendment,** allowing legislation to curb or ban abortions, was rejected by the Senate. The vote was 50–49 in favor, but a two-thirds majority was required.

July 28: Soviet grain purchases were increased by at least 50% as a result of a new five-year agreement. The U.S.S.R. was to buy a minimum of 9,000,000 metric tons a year, up from 6,000,000, and could purchase as much as 12,000,000 tons.

Aug 27: A **march on Washington,** D.C., commemorating the famous 1963 civil rights march led by the Rev. Martin Luther King, Jr., brought some 250,000 persons to the nation's capital.

Sep 5: Sanctions against the U.S.S.R., in response to the Sept. 1 downing of a South Korean airliner by a Soviet fighter, were announced by Pres. Reagan. The largely token measures included suspension of negotiations for a U.S. consulate in Kiev. The airliner had been shot down after violating Soviet airspace, killing all 269 people aboard.

Sep 20: A resolution reaffirming the **War Powers Act of 1973,** the Multinational Force in Lebanon Resolution, was passed by Congress. The measure authorized U.S. Marines to remain in Lebanon for another 18 months as a peacekeeping force.

Oct 23: The **U.S. Marine headquarters in Beirut,** Lebanon, was destroyed when an explosive-laden truck evaded security measures and blew up outside the building. The driver of the truck was killed in the blast, which took the lives of 241 Marine and Navy personnel.

Oct 25: An **invasion of Grenada,** an island nation in the Caribbean, was launched by U.S. forces a week after a bloody coup by pro-Cuban Marxists. The guerrillas murdered Grenada's top leaders. By Nov. 2 the Department of Defense reported the end of hostilities. U.S. casualties were listed as 18 dead, 115 wounded. The action was taken to restore order and protect the 1100 U.S. citizens, mostly students, on the island.

Nov 11: The first U.S. **cruise missiles** arrived in Great Britain. In all, 572 of the intermediate-range missiles were to be deployed in Europe, including 160 in Great Britain.

Nov 23: The U.S.S.R. withdrew from **arms limitation talks** aimed at reducing the number of intermediate-range missiles in Europe. The action was in response to deployment of such weapons by the U.S.

Dec 4: Carrier-based **U.S. warplanes attacked Syrian positions** near Beirut, Lebanon, for the first time. Two planes were shot down. One pilot was killed and one captured. Syrian forces had fired on U.S. reconnaissance planes on the previous day, prompting the strike.

Dec 28: U.S. withdrawal from UNESCO, the United Nations Educational, Scientific, and Cultural Organization, as of Dec. 31, 1984, was announced. The reasons for the withdrawal included UNESCO's increasing political bias and financial mismanagement. The U.S. deferred withdrawing pending attempts to achieve improvements in UNESCO operations and management, but on Dec. 19, 1984, the decision to withdraw was reaffirmed.

II. Architecture
   Arts and Music
   Popular Entertainment
   Publishing
   Theater

Americans all over the country this year celebrated the 100th anniversaries of New York City's Metropolitan Opera and the Brooklyn Bridge. The celebrations at the Brooklyn Bridge on May 24, witnessed by an estimated 2,100,000 persons, were climaxed by a spectacular fireworks display staged by the master pyrotechnicians, the Grucci family. The year's major art exhibitions included *The Vatican Collections: The Papacy and Art*, which was seen in New York City, Chicago, and San Francisco; and a comprehensive exhibit of the works of Grant Wood, which was organized by the Minneapolis Institute of Art. A collection of 16 French impressionist works collected by Mr. and Mrs. H. O. Havemayer sold at auction for $16,800,000. Mark Rothko's *Black, Maroon, and White* sold for $1,815,000 and Willem de Kooning's *Two Women* fetched $1,200,000. Movie theaters had record attendance for the third consecutive year, with revenues of nearly $3,700,000,000. The two most popular films were *The Return of the Jedi*, the third completed film in George Lucas's projected nine-film *Star Wars* series; and *Never Say Never Again,* featuring Sean Connery as the super agent James Bond. Television offered two highly successful miniseries, *The Thorn Birds* and *The Winds of War,* both based on best-selling novels. The number of cable television subscribers reached 25,000,000. This year some 4,100,000 videocassette recorders were sold, auguring a strong new electronics market and promising a fundamental change in TV viewing habits. Sales of rock videos, records, and tapes were all up, but the craze for arcade video games came to a sudden halt in 1983. Rupert Murdoch, the Australian newspaper magnate, made headlines of his own by buying the Chicago *Sun-Times* for $90,000,000. Notables who died this year included George Balanchine, choreographer, Apr. 30, at 79; Eubie Blake, ragtime composer and pianist, Feb. 12, at 100; John Cowles, Sr., head of the Cowles publishing empire, Feb. 25, at 84; George Cukor, a leading film director for over 50 years, Jan. 24, at 83; Lynn Fontanne, who with her late husband Alfred Lunt starred in numerous Broadway plays, July 30, at 95; Ira Gershwin, celebrated lyricist, Aug. 17, at 86; Earl "Fatha" Hines, father of modern jazz piano, Apr. 22, at 77; Harry James, trumpeter and band leader, July 6, at 67; Raymond Massey, Canadian-born actor, July 29, at 86; José Luis Sert, architect, Mar. 15, at 80; Norma Shearer, actress, June 12, at 80; Gloria Swanson, film star, Apr. 4, at 84; and Tennessee Williams, playwright, Feb. 25, at 71.

Among **books published** this year was *Ironweed* by William Kennedy, a novel showing the seamier side of the author's hometown, Albany, N.Y. Kennedy had great difficulty securing publication for his book, but its release to enthusiastic reviews was accompanied by the reissue of two of Kennedy's earlier books, *Legs* (1975) and *Billy Phelan's Greatest Game* (1978). *Ironweed* went on to win the Pulitzer Prize. Other books published this year included *During the Reign of the Queen of Sheba* by Joan Chase, a novel; *Ancient Evenings* by Norman Mailer, a novel of ancient Egypt that received mixed reviews; *The Cannibal Galaxy* by

Cynthia Ozick, a novel; *In Search of Excellence* by Thomas J. Peters and Robert H. Waterman, Jr., a best-selling study of what the authors considered to be the best-run companies in the U.S.; and *The Anatomy Lesson* by Philip Roth, a novel.

Jan 21: The **Bollingen Prize** for poetry was awarded jointly to Anthony E. Hecht and John Hollander.

Mar 2: The **final episode of** *M*A*S*H*, a long-running series on U.S. medics in the Korean War, was seen by the largest television audience to date for a nonsports program, 125,000,000 viewers.

Apr 18: **Pulitzer prizes** were awarded for the following: fiction, *The Color Purple* by Alice Walker; biography, *Growing Up* by Russell Baker; history, *The Transformation of Virginia, 1740–1790* by Rhys L. Isaac; general nonfiction, *Is There No Place on Earth for Me?* by Susan Sheehan; poetry, *Selected Poems* by Galway Kinnell; drama, *'Night, Mother* by Marsha Norman.

III. Business and Industry
Education
Philosophy and Religion
Science

The economy showed strong signs of improvement this year. Consumer prices rose only 3.8%, slightly less than in 1982, and personal income was up 6.3%, slightly more than in 1982. Orders for manufactured goods rose 10.6%, the largest increase in four years. Automobile production increased 10.2%, and major appliance production was up 21.3%. The greatest increase of all was in new home construction, which jumped 60% over 1982. The country's top executives did spectacularly well. Forty-six captains of industry had cash compensation of more than $1,000,000, and the leader in total compensation took home $13,229,000. The New York Stock Exchange set a new record of 21,589,000,000 shares traded in 1982, and the Dow Jones industrial average closed the year at 1258.64, about 200 points ahead of the 1982 closing mark. The nation's airlines continued to have problems, however, and the foreign trade deficit hit a record for the year of $60,600,000,000. The worst drought since 1936 devastated the South and Midwest, wiping out crops and raising food prices. Elementary school enrollment was down for the eighth year in a row, but gifts to institutions of higher education were up 6.2% to a record $5,100,000,000. Hospital costs rose 10.7%. At the end of August the administration announced a new schedule of Medicare fees for hospital and medical costs in a move to slow the increase in medical bills. This year the number of persons killed in auto accidents dropped to 43,028, the lowest figure in 20 years, in part because of increased use of safety belts and a growing campaign against drunk driving. Notables who died this year included Terence Cardinal Cooke, Roman Catholic archbishop of New York and vicar of the U.S. armed forces, Oct. 6, at 62; R. Buckminster Fuller, architect and inventor of the geodesic dome, July 3, at 87; Herman Kahn, futurist and nuclear stragetist, July 7, at 71; and Humberto Cardinal Madeiros, Roman Catholic archbishop of Boston since 1973 and a noted conservative, Sept. 17, at 67.

Feb 2: Bishop **Joseph L. Bernardin,** archbishop of Chicago, was among 18 new cardinals invested by Pope John Paul II.

Mar 23: **Barney Clark,** 62, the first recipient of a permanent artificial heart, died 112 days after receiving the device.

Mar 30: The first **California condor chick** born in captivity was hatched at the San Diego Zoo. A second one was hatched on Apr. 5.

Apr 4-9: The **space shuttle** *Challenger,* the second U.S. space shuttle, made its maiden voyage into orbit with astronauts Paul Weitz, Donald Peterson, Karol Bobko, and Story Musgrave aboard.

Apr 13: The **largest U.S. corporation,** according to the annual survey by *Fortune* magazine, was Exxon, with sales of $97,172,523,000 in 1982. General Motors moved up from third to second place.

Apr 26: The **quality of American education** is so poor that it "threatens our very future as a nation and a people," a federal report announced. It decried what it called a "rising tide of mediocrity," which was reflected in high school test scores that were lower than those of 1957. It calculated that some 23,000,000 Americans were functionally illiterate.

May 3: The nuclear **arms race was condemned** in a pastoral letter issued by the Roman Catholic bishops of the U.S.

June 18-24: Sally K. Ride became the first U.S. woman astronaut in space as a member of the crew of the space shuttle *Challenger* in its second flight.

June 25: The **Washington Public Power Supply System** defaulted on debts of $2,250,000,000, becoming the largest governmental unit to fail in U.S. history. Of the five nuclear power plants it set out to build in Washington State, only one was ever completed.

Aug 9: The first direct evidence supporting the existence of **stellar systems** was reported by the Jet Propulsion Laboratory in Pasadena, Calif. An orbiting satellite had detected solid objects orbiting the star Vega. This was the first time that solid objects of any size had been identified in orbit around a star other than the sun.

Aug 30-Sep 5: The **first black astronaut in space,** Lt. Col. Guion S. Bluford, USAF, was part of the crew on space shuttle *Challenger*'s third mission. On Sept. 5 *Challenger* made the first nighttime shuttle landing.

Oct 10: The **Nobel Prize in Physiology or Medicine** was awarded to Barbara McClintock, a botanist at the Cold Spring Harbor Laboratory, Long Island, N.Y., for her studies of gene shifting on plant chromosomes and their effect on hereditary factors.

Oct 17: The **Nobel Prize in Economics** was awarded to Gerard Debreu, a French-born professor at the University of California, Berkeley, for his study of the way prices in a free-market economy work to balance consumer and producer forces.

Oct 19: The **Nobel Prize in Physics** was awarded jointly to Subrahmanyan Chandrasekhar of the University of Chicago for his work on the density of stars, and to William Fowler of the California Institute of Technology for his theory of the formation of the elements in the universe.

Dec 22: A joint **U.S.-Japanese auto venture** by General Motors and Toyota of Japan was approved by the Federal Trade Commission. The new plant, in Fremont, Calif., was expected to produce from 200,000 to 250,000 autos a year. Ford and Chrysler had both opposed the plan.

IV. Fashion
Folkways
Holidays
Social Issues and Crime
Sports

Baseball was the top spectator sport in 1983, drawing 78,051,343 fans and dropping horse racing, with 75,784,430 fans, to second place. In golf the year's top money winners were Hal Sutton, $426,668, and JoAnne Carner, $291,404. In fashion the key words were clean lines and classic shapes. Black was the favorite color, but winter brought a craze for brightly colored leg warmers. This year's top craze, however, was the Cabbage Patch doll, a soft cloth doll made by hand, so no two were exactly alike. The supply was nowhere near the demand, and by Christmas many a parent could not find one for sale at any price. Price was no object for some furniture buyers this year. A Rhode Island Chippendale dining table brought $687,000 at auction in 1983, a new record for American furniture. Notables who died this year included Paul "Bear" Bryant of the University of Alabama, the winningest football coach in history, Jan. 26, at 69; Jack Dempsey, world heavyweight boxing champion from 1919 to 1926, May 31, at 86; George Halas, longtime coach of the Chicago Bears, Oct. 31, at 88; and Meyer Lansky, reputed to have been for 40 years the top boss of organized crime, Jan. 15, at 80.

Jan 30: Super Bowl XVII was won by the Washington Redskins (NFC), defeating the Miami Dolphins (AFC) 27 to 17. On Jan. 22 the Redskins had beaten the Dallas Cowboys 31 to 17 for the NFC championship and the Dolphins had shut out the New York Jets 14 to 0 for the AFC title.

Apr 4: The **NCAA men's basketball championship** was won by North Carolina State, defeating the University of Houston 54 to 52.

May 22-31: The **NBA basketball championship** was won by the Philadelphia 76ers, who swept the Los Angeles Lakers in four straight games.

June 20: The **U.S. Open golf tournament** was won by Larry Nelson, who beat Tom Watson by one stroke.

July 2-3: At the **Wimbledon** tennis championships in England, John McEnroe won the men's singles title and Martina Navratilova won the women's singles. McEnroe teamed with Peter Fleming to win the men's doubles, and Navratilova teamed with Pam Shriver to win the women's doubles.

Aug 7: The **PGA golf tournament** was won by Hal Sutton, beating Jack Nicklaus by one stroke.

Sep 11: The **U.S. Open tennis singles championships** were won by Jimmy Connors in the men's division, and by Martina Navratilova in the women's division.

Sep 14-26: The **America's Cup** was lost by the U.S. for the first time in the yachting classic's 132-year history. The Australian challenger *Australia II* defeated the U.S. yacht *Liberty* four races to three.

Sep 23: The **World Boxing Association heavyweight boxing championship** was won by Gerrie Coatzee of South Africa, who knocked out Michael Dokes in ten rounds at Richfield, Ohio.

Oct 11-16: The **World Series** was won by the Baltimore Orioles (AL), defeating the Philadelphia Phillies (NL) four games to one. On Oct. 8 the Orioles won the American League pennant over the Chicago White Sox, three games to one, and the Phillies won the National League pennant from the Los Angeles Dodgers, three games to one.

Nov 2: A federal holiday honoring Dr. **Martin Luther King, Jr.,** the slain civil rights leader, was designated for observance on the third Monday of January in a bill signed by Pres. Reagan. King was the first person honored with a federal holiday since George Washington's birthday was so named.

1984

I. **Civil Rights**
   Exploration and Settlement
   Government
   Statistics
   Wars

The year's top domestic story was the presidential campaign, a race between former vice president Walter F. Mondale and Pres. Ronald Reagan, a highly popular incumbent and master of the media campaign. The Democrats tried unsuccessfully to challenge Reagan's ability to manage the government, even to comprehend the major issues of the day. The Republicans pointed to the booming national economy and assailed the Democrats for their free-spending ways and lack of political vision. In foreign affairs the U.S. and U.S.S.R. jockeyed for position in the debate over resuming nuclear arms limitation talks, so no progress was made. The U.S. appeared also to have lost the initiative in seeking peace in the Middle East. Congress and Pres. Reagan clashed on aid for El Salvador, where the established government was fighting insurgents, and on aid for the so-called *contras* in Nicaragua. There insurgents were fighting the established government, led by the Marxist-dominated Sandinistas. At home in midyear the Census Bureau estimated the U.S. population at 236,158,000. Almost all the population growth of the previous four years had been in the South and West. Two other items of current demographic information were also remarkable: Seven states had more than 1,000,000 residents aged 65 or older, and 454,136 people were in prison, almost double the total of ten years earlier. This year Los Angeles displaced Chicago as the nation's second largest city. Notables who died this year included George D. Aiken, Republican senator from Vermont from 1941 to 1975, Nov. 19, at 92; Ellsworth Bunker, a diplomat who served under six presidents, Sept. 30, at 90; Sen. Frank Church, Democrat of Ohio from 1957 to 1981, Apr. 7, at 59; Gen. Mark W. Clark, a top U.S. commander during World War II, Apr. 17, at 87; and Glen H. Taylor, former senator from Idaho who was Henry A. Wallace's vice presidential running mate on the Progressive ticket in 1948, Apr. 28, at 80.

Jan 10: Restoration of full **diplomatic relations with the Vatican** after a period of 117 years was announced in Washington, D.C. The move came at a time when the Vatican apparently was taking much interest in international affairs.

Feb 7: Withdrawal of U.S. Marines from Beirut, Lebanon was announced by Pres. Reagan. The troops were completely redeployed to Navy ships offshore by Feb. 29.

Mar 5: In a major decision on **separation of church and state,** the Supreme Court ruled that a city may make a Nativity scene part of an official Christmas display without violating the constitutional separation of government and organized religion.

Mar 20: A constitutional **school prayer amendment,** permitting organized spoken prayer in public schools, was rejected by the U.S. Senate. The 56–44 vote fell 11 short of the required two-thirds majority.

Apr 26-May 1: A presidential trip to China was made by Pres. Reagan. He was party to formal agreements on scientific and cultural exchanges, economic cooperation, and development of nuclear energy.

May 7: Establishment of an **Agent Orange victims' fund** of $180,000,000 was announced. The fund, provided by Dow Chemical Company and six other manufacturers of the herbicide, was intended to provide assistance for Vietnam veterans suffering from exposure to Agent Orange and for the families of victims.

May 22: In a decision on **job discrimination,** the Supreme Court ruled that law firms may not discriminate on the basis of sex, race, religion, or national origin in promoting associates to partnership. The decision affirmed that partnerships are covered by federal laws against discrimination, as are other forms of businesses.

June 6: On the **40th anniversary of D-Day**, Pres. Reagan joined with representatives from Great Britain, Canada, and other nations in ceremonies at Normandy, where Allied armies landed first in the invasion of France in 1944.

June 11: In a ruling on **admissibility of evidence**, the Supreme Court declared that illegally obtained evidence may be admitted at a trial provided it could be proved that the evidence would have been discovered inevitably by lawful means. On July 5 the Court ruled that some evidence obtained with defective search warrants could be used in a trial.

July 16-19: The **Democratic National Convention nominated Walter F. Mondale** of Minnesota for the presidency and Rep. Geraldine Ferraro of New York for the vice presidency.

July 17: To promote raising of the **legal drinking age** to 21, Pres. Reagan signed a bill giving states until Oct. 1, 1986, to do so or face a 5% cut in federal highway funds.

July 18: The **Deficit Reduction Act of 1984**, raising taxes by about $50,000,000,000 and cutting spending by $13,000,000,000 through 1987, was signed by Pres. Reagan.

Aug 20-23: The **Republican National Convention nominated Pres. Reagan** for reelection. George Bush was renominated for the vice presidency.

Sep 20: The **U.S. Embassy in Beirut was bombed.** A suicide car-bomb exploded outside the Embassy, killing at least 23, including two Americans.

Oct 3: The **first FBI agent charged with espionage,** Richard W. Miller, was arrested. He was accused of passing a classified document to two Soviet émigrés.

Oct 14: A bill introducing **major changes in U.S. criminal law** was signed by Pres. Reagan. The new law, permitting detention without bail for the first time in peacetime, was denounced by some as a threat to civil liberty.

Nov 2: In the first **execution of a woman** in 22 years, Margie Velma Barfield, 52, convicted of murder, was put to death in North Carolina.

Nov 6: Ronald Reagan was reelected president of the United States in the greatest Republican landslide in history. Reagan carried 49 states. Walter F. Mondale carried Minnesota and the District of Columbia. The electoral vote was Reagan, 525; Mondale 13. The popular vote was Reagan, 54,455,075; Mondale, 37,577,185. In congressional elections the Republicans gained two Senate seats for a 53–47 majority. In the House the Democrats lost 14 seats but kept a majority of 253–182.

Nov 26: The **World Court** declared it had jurisdiction in a case brought by Nicaragua to have the U.S. declared an aggressor nation. On May 10 the court had ruled unanimously that the U.S. should halt any attempts to blockade or mine Nicaraguan ports. The U.S. had stated it would not be bound by the decision of the World Court.

II. Architecture
   Arts and Music
   Popular Entertainment
   Publishing
   Theater

Although at year's end almost half of Broadway's 37 theaters were dark, prospects for the theater were promising. Gross receipts were up, and the 1983–1984 season had produced three sellout musicals, *La Cage aux Folles*, *Cats*, and *Sunday in the Park With George*. The American Academy of Dramatic Arts celebrated its centennial this year, and the Long Wharf Theater in New Haven, Conn., its 20th year anniversary. Major museum exhibits included the *Van Gogh at Arles* exhibit at the Metropolitan Museum in New York City, a complete sellout; an extensive James McNeill Whistler show at the Freer Gallery in Washington, D.C.; and a showing of works of traditional art of the Maori people of New Zealand at the Metropolitan Museum. In mid-May the Museum of Modern Art in New York City opened its new and greatly enlarged facilities. In the fall the Indianapolis Symphony Orchestra moved to a renovated movie palace, but orchestras in St. Louis, Pittsburgh, and Miami moved into new homes. Of the year's top films, *Indiana Jones and the Temple of Doom* earned $42,267,345 in its first six days of release, and went on to break virtually every box office record. The top recording artist of the year was Michael Jackson, whose album *Thriller* sold more than 20,000,000 copies worldwide in 1983 and 1984. Among those who died this year were Ansel Adams, photographer, Apr. 22, at 82; Brooks Atkinson, the drama critic, Jan. 13, at 89; William "Count" Basie, jazz pianist and band leader, Apr. 26, at 79; Richard Burton, the actor, Aug. 5, at 58; Truman Capote, the author, Aug. 25, at 59; Jackie Coogan, first major child star in U.S. film history, Mar. 1, at 69; Janet Gaynor, winner of the first Academy Award for best actress, Sept. 14, at 77; Lillian Hellman, the playwright, June 30, at 79; Alfred A. Knopf, founder of the publishing house bearing his name, Aug. 11, at 91; Mabel Mercer, a singer whose style greatly influenced popular music, Apr. 20, at 84; Ethel Merman, star of musical comedy, Feb. 15, at 76; Jan Peerce, tenor with the Metropolitan Opera for 27 years, Dec. 15, at 80; Lee Krasner Pollock, abstract expressionist painter, June 19, at 75; William Powell, the movie star, Mar. 5, at 91; Irwin Shaw, the author, May 16, at 71; Fred Waring, the band leader, July 29, at 84; Johnny Weissmuller, Olympic star and movie Tarzan, Jan. 20, at 79; and Meredith Willson, Broadway composer and lyricist, June 15, at 82.

Among **books published** this year was a reissue of George Orwell's 1949 classic novel of totalitarianism, *1984*. Critics noted that Orwell had intended the novel to be a warning of things that might occur, not a prediction of the inevitable. Readers put the book firmly on the best-seller lists. Other books published this year included *Him With His Foot in His Mouth and Other Stories* by Saul Bellow; *Lives of the Poets*

by E.L. Doctorow, six stories and a novella; *Iacocca*
by Lee Iacocca with William Novak, an autobiography of the man credited with returning Chrysler Corporation to prosperity from virtual bankruptcy; *The
Aquitaine Progression* by Robert Ludlum, a spy
thriller that topped the hardcover best-seller lists;
and *Walt Whitman*, a biography by Paul Zweig.

Mar 4: A Television Academy Hall of Fame was estab-
lished. Its first inductees were Lucille Ball, Milton
Berle, Paddy Chayefsky, Norman Lear, Edward R.
Murrow, William S. Paley, and David Sarnoff.

Apr 16: Pulitzer prizes were awarded for the following: fiction, *Ironweed* by William Kennedy; general
nonfiction, *Social Transformation of American Medicine* by Paul Starr; biography, *Booker T. Washington*
by Louis R. Harlan; poetry, *American Primitive* by
Mary Oliver; drama, *Glengarry Glen Ross* by David
Mamet.

May 9: A sculpture by **Alexander Calder,** a 24-foot-
high mobile entitled *Big Crinkly,* sold at auction in
New York City for $852,000, a new record for sculp-
ture by an American.

June 9: Donald Duck's 50th birthday was celebrated
at Disneyland in California. Donald's career began in
1934 with a bit part in the animated film *Wise Little
Men.*

Nov 1: A 1953 painting by **Willem de Kooning,** *Two
Women,* sold at auction for $1,980,000, the highest
auction price ever paid for a post-World War II art-
work.

III. Business and Industry
Education
Philosophy and Religion
Science

The year was excellent for businesses and consumers. The economy expanded 6.8%, its best performance since 1951. The rise in consumer prices was
only 4%, and personal income rose 6.8%. New housing starts hit 1,700,000, the highest number since
1979. Americans bought 14,100,000 cars and light

trucks, the largest volume since 1979. This helped put Detroit back on its feet, and the big three automobile makers earned $9,810,000,000, a new record. Not all the news was good, however. The foreign trade deficit hit a record $107,600,000,000, the Dow Jones average finished the year about 60 points below its opening price, and 79 banks failed, the largest number since 1938. Although employment was up, the unemployment rate stood at 7.1% in December, down only 0.3% from a year earlier. Organized labor's membership declined to 18.8% of wage and salary workers, compared with 23% in 1980. For the third year in a row, the value of farmland dropped, with the largest declines registered in Iowa and Nebraska. This was bad news for farmers, many of whom had borrowed heavily on their land and now were faced with bankruptcy. Medical costs continued to rise, contributing to the growth of prepaid medical plans and health maintenance organizations, known as HMOs. In November the Great American Smokeout saw more than 5,000,000 smokers kick the habit, according to the American Cancer Society; another 15,000,000 cut back their smoking. In education, this year's high-school graduates scored an average of four points higher on scholastic aptitude tests than the year before. Black students continued to improve their scores faster than white students but remained below the national averages. A study by the National Council of Churches showed members of the clergy to be among the lowest-paid professionals in the country, and women in the clergy to be the lowest paid. Among notables who died this year were the Rev. Martin Luther King, Sr., father of the slain civil rights leader, Nov. 11, at 84; John Rock, who helped develop the birth control pill, Dec. 4, at 94; and George G. Simpson, a world authority on vertebrate paleontology, Oct. 6, at 82.

Jan 13: A nuclear operating license was withheld from a nearly completed power plant in Illinois. It was the first time the Nuclear Regulatory Commission had refused to license a nuclear power facility that was close to completion.

Feb 3: In the first case of **surrogate conception,** the birth of a baby conceived in one woman's womb and brought to term by another woman was announced by a team of California physicians.

Feb 7: The **first human satellites** floated in space, two astronauts powered by jet packs and without lifelines connected to their spacecraft. The astronauts were Bruce McCandless and Robert Stewart, crew members on the fourth orbital flight (Feb. 3–11) of the space shuttle *Challenger*.

Feb 13: The **first heart and liver transplant** was performed on a six-year-old Texas girl, Stormie Jones.

Apr 11: The **largest U.S. corporation,** according to the annual survey by *Fortune* magazine, was Exxon, with 1983 sales of $88,561,134,000. General Motors was second.

Apr 23: Identification of a virus thought to **cause acquired immune deficiency syndrome** (AIDS) was announced by federal researchers. The disease, which destroys the body's natural immune system and is considered to be ultimately fatal, was estimated to have afflicted 4000 Americans to date.

May 9: Ordination of noncelibate homosexuals was prohibited by the General Conference of the United Methodist Church.

May 23: Kristine Holderied became the **first woman midshipman** to graduate at the top of her class at the U.S. Naval Academy at Annapolis, Md.

May 30: Scientists reported that an effective **chicken pox vaccine** had been developed. The disease claimed some 100 to 150 lives in the U.S. each year.

June 4: Successful **cloning of DNA** from an extinct animal was reported by scientists at the University of California. The gene fragments, cloned from an animal related to the zebra and the horse, were the first to be extracted from a vanished animal species.

June 12: In a decision supporting the **last hired, first fired** policy of many businesses, the Supreme Court ruled that courts could not overrule seniority programs to prevent layoffs of employees hired under affirmative action programs. Labor leaders applauded the decision, but civil rights groups and others condemned it.

June 14: A resolution opposing the **ordination of women** was passed by the Southern Baptist Convention. The resolution was nonbinding on local congregations and did not apply to women already ordained for the Baptist ministry.

June 21: In the **largest single stock transaction** in the history of the New York Stock Exchange, 10,000,000 shares of Superior Oil stock were sold for $423,800,000.

July 26: In the **largest federal loan guarantee** to a private enterprise, the U.S. government committed itself to $4,500,000,000 in loan guarantees to the Continental Illinois National Bank and Trust Company.

Aug 3: A new **daily volume record** of 236,600,000 shares was set by the New York Stock Exchange. It was the first time the volume exceeded 200,000,000 shares.

Aug 11: A bill protecting **student meetings** for religious or political purposes outside of normal school hours was signed by Pres. Reagan.

Aug 30-Sep 5: The **space shuttle** *Discovery,* the third of four U.S. space shuttles, made its maiden flight. Its crew of six included Judith Resnick, the second U.S. woman astronaut in space.

Oct 11: Dr. Kathryn D. Sullivan became the **first U.S. woman astronaut to walk in space.** She was one of seven crew members on the sixth flight of the space shuttle *Challenger* (Oct. 5–13). Also aboard in addition to the crew was the first Canadian astronaut, Marc Garneau.

Oct 16: A **baboon heart transplant to a human,** the first operation of its kind, was performed on a 15-day-old baby girl, identified only as Baby Fae, at Loma Linda University Medical Center in California. Baby Fae lived until Nov. 15.

Oct 17: The **Nobel Prize in Chemistry** was awarded to Dr. Bruce Merrifield of Rockefeller University for protein research offering promise of development of important new drugs.

Nov 11: In a pastoral letter on economic justice, a committee of Roman Catholic bishops called for sweeping economic changes to aid the poor, stating that the level of inequality between the wealthy and the poor was "morally unacceptable."

Nov 12: The **first space salvage operation** was performed during the second flight (Nov. 8–16) of the space shuttle *Discovery.* Astronauts Joseph Allen and Dale Gardner retrieved a nonfunctioning satellite and brought it into the shuttle's cargo bay. A second retrieval was accomplished on Nov. 14.

Nov 25: The **second artificial heart transplant** was performed at Humana Heart Institute International in Louisville, Ky. The recipient was William J. Schroeder, 52, of Jasper, Ind.

Nov 30: The basis for a **Protestant church merger** by nine major Protestant denominations was reached by the Consultation on Church Union, after 22 years of effort. The nine denominations were: African Methodist Episcopal Church; African Methodist Episcopal Zion Church; Christian Church (Disciples of Christ); Christian Methodist Episcopal Church; Episcopal Church; International Council of Community Churches; Presbyterian Church (U.S.A.); United Methodist Church; and United Church of Christ.

Dec 10: Discovery was announced of what was thought to be the **first planet detected outside the solar system.** U.S. astronomers had discovered a huge, gaseous object orbiting a star in the constellation Ophiuchus.

Dec 11-12: Discovery of **7000-year-old human skulls with brains virtually intact** was reported by archeologists in Florida. The skulls were found buried in peat at the bottom of a lake. They were described as the oldest skulls from which it had thus far been possible to extract and analyze DNA.

IV. Fashion
   Folkways
   Holidays
   Social Issues and Crime
   Sports

This year saw the centennial of the American Kennel Club, on Sept. 17. Another institution celebrating its centennial was the roller coaster, first put in operation at Coney Island, N.Y., on June 16, 1884. A different kind of celebration was held in Chicago, where a 28-year-old printer won $40,000,000 in the Illinois state lottery. It was the largest lottery win by one person in North America. The divorce rate dropped for the third year in a row, down to 4.9% of marriages. After three years of decline, traffic fatalities were up. Safety experts thought the increase was associated with the booming economy, which meant traffic was heavier than in recent years. Sales of home exercise equipment passed the $1,000,000,000 mark in 1984, and the growing U.S. mania for fitness and personal appearance also helped the cosmetics industry. It sold $10,000,000,000 worth of skin care products. The mania for Cabbage Patch dolls and their accessories continued. In fashion, the introduction of oversize men's clothing for women triggered a boom for used clothing stores, where women snapped up men's coats at bargain prices. In sports the NFL reported an increase in attendance at football games, but major league baseball showed a drop in attendance. A Gallup poll showed that swimming, bicycling, and fishing were the most popular activities of adult Americans. This year the memory of track star Jesse Owens, star of the 1936 Olympics in Berlin, was honored in West Berlin with the naming of an avenue after him. In professional golf, the year's top money winners were Tom Watson, $476,200, and Betsy King, $266,771. Americans mourned the deaths this year of Walter Alston, manager of the Los Angeles Dodgers for 23 years, Oct. 1, at 72; Joe Cronin, former star shortstop and later president of the American League, Sept. 7, at 77; Jim Fixx, whose books about running fueled the American passion for jogging, July 20, at 52; Waite Hoyt, former pitching great, Aug. 25, at 84; Oswald Jacoby, one of the great contract bridge players of all time, July 27, at 81; and Al Schacht, a player and coach who entertained fans at baseball games with pantomime antics that won him the title of Clown Prince of Baseball, July 14, at 91.

Jan 22: Super Bowl XVIII was won by the Los Angeles Raiders (AFC), defeating the Washington Redskins (NFC) 38 to 9. On Jan. 8 the Raiders had defeated the Seattle Seahawks 30 to 14 to win the AFC championship, and the Redskins had beaten the San Francisco 49ers 24 to 21 for the NFC title.

Mar 3: Peter V. Ueberroth, president of the Los Angeles Olympic Organizing Committee, was elected commissioner of baseball by the major league team owners.

Mar 9: The World Boxing Council **heavyweight boxing championship** was won by Tim Witherspoon, who outpointed Greg Page in a 12-round bout at Las Vegas, Nev.

Apr 2: The **NCAA men's basketball championship** was won by Georgetown, which defeated Houston 84 to 75.

May 8: The **U.S.S.R. withdrew from the 1984 Olympics.** The U.S.S.R. Olympic Committee said Soviet athletes could not compete because of "gross flouting" of Olympic ideals by the U.S. The move was seen in some quarters as revenge for the boycott of the 1980 games in Moscow by the U.S. and some other Western nations.

May 27-June 12: The **NBA basketball championship** was won by the Boston Celtics, who beat the Los Angeles Lakers four games to three.

June 18: The **U.S. Open golf tournament** was won by Fuzzy Zoeller in an 18-hole playoff with Greg Norman.

July 7-8: At the **Wimbledon** tennis championships in England, John McEnroe won the men's singles title and Martina Navratilova won the women's singles. McEnroe teamed with Peter Fleming to win the men's doubles, and Navratilova teamed with Pam Shriver to win the women's doubles.

July 18: A gunman killed 21 people in and near a McDonald's restaurant in San Ysidro, Calif. James Humberty, heavily armed, walked into the fast food store and began shooting, then continued killing people on the street before he was shot and killed by police officers.

July 28-Aug 12: At the **Summer Olympics** in Los Angeles, Calif., the U.S. won 83 gold medals and finished first in unofficial team standings. Carl Lewis won four gold medals in track and field events, and Mary Lou Retton won four in gymnastics. Joan Benoit won the first Olympic women's marathon.

Aug 19: The **PGA golf tournament** was won by Lee Trevino, who shot a 15 under par 273 to finish four strokes ahead of Gary Player and Lanny Wadkins.

Aug 31: The World Boxing Council **heavyweight boxing championship** was won by Pinklon Thomas, who outpointed Tim Witherspoon in a 12-round bout in Las Vegas, Nev.

Sep 8-9: The **U.S. Open tennis singles championships** were won by John McEnroe in the men's division and Martina Navratilova in the women's division.

Sep 14-18: The **first transatlantic solo balloon flight** was completed by Joe W. Kittinger, who flew 3535 miles from Caribou, Maine, to near Savona, Italy. He made the flight in the gondola of his ten-story-tall, helium-lifted craft named *Rosie O'Grady's Balloon of Peace.*

Oct 9-14: The **World Series** was won by the Detroit Tigers (AL), defeating the San Diego Padres (NL) four games to one. On Oct. 5 the Tigers had won the American League pennant over the Kansas City Royals in a three-game sweep, and on Oct. 7 the Padres had taken the National League pennant over the Chicago Cubs, three games to two.

Nov 9: The first world heavyweight boxing match under the auspices of the **International Boxing Federation** (IBF) was won by Larry Holmes, who knocked out James "Bonecrusher" Smith in the 12th round of a bout in Las Vegas, Nev. Holmes had vacated his WBC title when arrangements to fight Greg Page, the top contender, were not completed.

Dec 1: The WBA **heavyweight boxing championship** was won by Greg Page, who knocked out Gerrie Coetzee of South Africa in the eighth round of a bout in Sun City, Bophuthatswana.

Dec 16-18: The **Davis Cup** international tennis championship was won by Sweden, defeating the U.S. four matches to one at Göteborg, Sweden.

1985

I. Civil Rights
   Exploration and Settlement
   Government
   Statistics
   Wars

The nation was stunned by what appeared to be an epidemic of spying. Thirteen Americans were charged with espionage in the course of the year. Of those charged, most were past or present CIA or Navy personnel and one was an FBI agent. Most of those accused were said to have turned to spying not for reasons of ideology but for money. One of the accused had been supplying Israel, an ally, with information, much to the discomfiture of the U.S. and Israel. Late in November *The New York Times* reported that since 1968 U.S. citizens had been attacked by terrorists in 72 countries. In 1985 seventeen Americans were killed in terrorist attacks and 154 had been wounded. The government reported that 90 planned terrorist attacks had been foiled in a 12-month period. The Social Security system celebrated its 50th anniversary on Aug. 14, having paid $1,800,000,000 in benefits and carrying 36,700,000 people on its rolls. Americans mourned the passing of former Sen. Sam J. Ervin, Jr., Democrat of North Carolina, who headed the Senate Watergate investigation that led to Pres. Richard Nixon's resignation, Apr. 23, at 88; Patricia Roberts Harris, who served in two Cabinet posts under Pres. Jimmy Carter, Mar. 23, at 60; Henry Cabot Lodge, former Republican senator from Massachusetts and diplomat, Feb. 27, at 82;

former Sen. John J. Sparkman, Democrat of Alabama, who served 42 years in Congress, Nov. 16, at 85; Potter Stewart, who served on the Supreme Court from 1958 to 1981, Dec. 7, at 70; and Robert H. W. Welch, Jr., who in 1958 founded the John Birch Society and headed it until 1983, Jan. 6, at 85.

Jan 18: The **U.S withdrew from World Court proceedings** in a case brought against it by Nicaragua, stating that the court had overextended its jurisdiction. Nicaragua had charged the U.S. with conducting a secret war by aiding rebel *contra* forces and mining Nicaraguan harbors. On Oct. 7 the U.S. announced it no longer would comply automatically with World Court decisions because its procedures had been "abused for political ends."

Jan 20-21: A record **cold wave** hit much of the U.S., killing at least 40 people in 15 states. A record temperature of −27° F was reached in Chicago.

May 28: A plan for a **major tax revision** was unveiled by Pres. Reagan, who called for an income tax system that was "clear, simple, and fair for all." The new plan would reduce taxes for many Americans, but would increase corporate taxes. A bill along these lines passed the House in December, but no further action was taken on it in 1985.

June 14: A **TWA jetliner was hijacked in Athens,** Greece, by two Shiite Muslim terrorists, who forced the plane to Beirut, Lebanon, and demanded the release of 766 Shiites held in Israel. Some of the hostages were released, but 39 Americans were removed from the plane and kept hostage. Complicated negotiations led to their release on June 30, after Israel independently began to release the interned Shiites.

July 13: Pres. **Reagan underwent surgery** to remove a cancerous tumor from his colon. For eight hours Vice Pres. George Bush exercised the powers of the presidency.

Aug 2: An **airplane crash** of a Delta Airlines L-1011 at the Dallas-Fort Worth Airport killed 133 people. The plane crashed during an attempted landing in a violent thunderstorm.

Sep 1: The **wreck of the *Titanic***, the luxury liner that sank on its maiden voyage in 1912, was found by a U.S.-French exploratory team. The wreck was found about 500 miles south of Newfoundland, but its exact location was kept secret to discourage salvage attempts.

Sep 9: Sanctions against South Africa were announced by Pres. Reagan to protest that country's policy of apartheid. Sale of computers was banned, and imports of the Kruggerand were halted. The sanctions, which were relatively mild, were viewed as an effort to head off demands by Congress for sterner measures.

Sep 18: A **U.S. hostage in Lebanon,** the Rev. Benjamin Weir, was back in the U.S., Pres. Reagan announced. Weir had been held prisoner in Lebanon for 16 months. Six other Americans, kidnaped between Mar. 1984 and June 1985, were still in the hands of terrorists in Lebanon.

Sep 26-27: Hurricane Gloria struck off the coast of North Carolina, then moved north to the New York metropolitan region. The storm forced evacuation of some 280,000 coastal residents, but only three people were killed. Winds of up to 130 mph caused massive power line damage. Repairs on Long Island continued for more than a week after the storm.

Oct 7-10: The Italian liner ***Achille Lauro*** was hijacked in the Mediterranean by four members of the Palestinian Liberation Front (PLF). En route to Port Said, Egypt, the terrorists shot and killed a wheelchair-bound American, Leon Klinghoffer, 69, and dumped his body overboard. The hijackers surrendered in Egypt on Oct. 9. On the next day an Egyptian airliner flew them out of the country. The jet was intercepted by U.S. fighters and forced to land in Italy, where the four were arrested by Italian authorities. Also with them were Muhammad Abbas, head of the PLF, and another PLF representative, who had joined the others after the hijacking. Abbas was subsequently released and fled to Yugoslavia. The four original hijackers were convicted in Italy on Nov. 19 and imprisoned for possession of guns and explosives.

Oct 11: The **Nobel Peace Prize** was awarded to the International Physicians for the Prevention of Nuclear War, a Boston-based group founded by doctors from the U.S. and U.S.S.R. The cofounders were Dr. Bernard Lown of the Harvard School of Public Health and Dr. Yevgeny I. Chazov of the U.S.S.R.

Oct 27-Nov 7: Hurricane Juan struck the Gulf Coast, killing seven people and causing some $1,000,000,000 in damage in Louisiana. Downgraded to a tropical storm, Juan moved north, dumping heavy rains on West Virginia, Virginia, Maryland, and Pennsylvania, causing great damage and killing 42 more people.

Nov 4: A **Soviet defector changed his mind** and decided to return to the U.S.S.R. Vitaly Yurchenko, described as a senior KGB official, had defected in late July but on Nov. 2 escaped from CIA custody in Washington, D.C., and went to the Soviet Embassy there. He returned to the U.S.S.R. on Nov. 6.

Nov 20-21: A **summit meeting in Geneva,** Switzerland, was conducted by Pres. Reagan and Mikhail Gorbachev, Communist Party secretary of the U.S.S.R. The meeting was characterized as friendly. No major breakthroughs were reached, but both sides agreed to work toward strategic arms reductions and planned to hold another summit meeting in the U.S. in 1986.

Dec 11: The so-called **Gramm-Rudman bill** to eliminate the federal deficit by 1991 was passed by Congress. Pres. Reagan signed it the following day. The bill called on the president to impose automatic spending reductions if Congress did not meet each year's deficit ceiling. Social Security, interest on the national debt, and some programs for the poor were exempted from cuts.

Dec 12: An Arrow Airlines **charter jet crashed** in Gander, Newfoundland, killing all 248 U.S. Army soldiers aboard and the plane's crew of eight. The soldiers, members of the 101st Airborne Division, were on their way to Fort Campbell, Ky., after a tour of duty in the Sinai Peninsula. It was reported that the DC-8 had a history of mechanical problems.

Dec 27: A **terrorist attack at Rome airport** in Italy, and an almost simultaneous attack at the Vienna,

Austria, airport left 18 dead and 110 wounded, including five U.S. citizens.

II. Architecture
Arts and Music
Popular Entertainment
Publishing
Theater

On Broadway, fewer shows were staged than in any other year in the century. After two good seasons, attendance and ticket sales were down. Only musicals seemed to attract patrons. A surprise hit of the season was the musical *Tango Argentino,* which opened in October for a projected five-week run and made it big. The Dance Theater of Harlem celebrated its tenth anniversary this year, and the Metropolitan Opera Guild observed its 50th anniversary. The Boston Pops celebrated its centennial with a performance before a full house of 2000. Sales of compact discs and compact disc players far exceeded supply. Music lovers seemed to hover in record stores and buy up the discs as fast as they were unpacked. Manufacturers and audiophiles predicted that the CD would eventually replace the LP record. Books on cassettes were big sellers as well. Book lovers found they could enjoy literature while doing other things, even while driving to work. In art, Rembrandt Peale's portrait of his younger brother, *Rubens Peale With a Geranium,* sold for $4,070,000, the most ever paid at auction for an American painting. Museums across the country opened or planned new facilities. The Arthur M. Sackler Museum opened at Harvard in October. The Whitney Museum planned an addition, the design of which sparked instant controversy. The Metropolitan Museum proposed a new wing, the Dallas Art Museum opened one, and Ft. Lauderdale was finishing work on its first art museum. A landmark in book publishing was reached this year when Shel Silverstein's 1981 collection of poems and drawings, *A Light in the Attic,* made the best-seller list of *The New York Times* for the 112th week in a row, longer than any other book in the list's 59-year history. The movie industry suffered a 7% drop in ticket sales in 1985. Among the top films of the year were *Back to the Future, Rambo: First Blood Part II*, and *Rocky IV*. Videocassette recorder sales began to skyrocket, producing a new form of competition for movie houses. Notables who died this year included Yul Brynner, known for his almost nonstop acting role in *The King and I*, Oct. 10, at 65; Marc Chagall, the artist, Mar. 28, at 97; Stepin Fetchit, born Lincoln Theodore Perry, the first well-known black Hollywood actor, Nov. 19, at 83; Ruth Gordon, the stage and screen actress, Aug. 28, at 88; Rock Hudson, a movie actor who became the first major public figure known to have died of AIDS, Oct. 2, at 59; Eugene List, the concert pianist, Mar. 1, at 66; Helen MacInnes, master of the spy novel, Sept. 30, at 77; Robert Nathan, the author, May 25, at 91; Eugene Ormandy, musical director of the Philadelphia Orchestra for 44 years, Mar. 12, at 85; Roger Sessions, one of America's foremost composers, Mar. 16, at 88; Eric Sloane, the artist, Mar. 6, at 80; Orson Welles, director and actor, Oct. 10, at 70; E. B. White, author and longtime contributor to *The New Yorker* magazine, Oct. 1, at 86; and Efrem Zimbalist, internationally renowned violinist, Feb. 22, at 94.

Among **books published** this year was *Yeager* by Chuck Yeager with Leo Janos. The autobiography of the celebrated test pilot became a best seller. Other books published this year included *The Kingdom of the Wicked* by Anthony Burgess, a novel; *Chapterhouse: Dune* by Frank Herbert, the sixth novel in the author's science fiction epic; *The Cider House Rules* by John Irving, a novel; *Lake Wobegon Days* by Garrison Keillor, the witty host of the radio show *Prairie Home Companion; Skeleton Crew* by Stephen King, stories in the horror fiction genre; *Masters of Atlantis* by Charles Portis, a novel; *All Fall Down: America's Tragic Encounter with Iran* by Gary Sick; *Family Album* by Danielle Steel, a novel that became a best seller; *Dashiell Hammett* by Julian Symons, a biography of the celebrated mystery writer; *The Old Forest* *and Other Stories* by Peter Taylor; *Gods of War* by John Toland, the author's first novel; and *Galapagos* by Kurt Vonnegut, a novel.

Jan 15: The **Bollingen Prize** for poetry was awarded jointly to John Ashbery and Fred Chapell.

Apr 24: Pulitzer prizes were awarded for the following: fiction, *Foreign Affairs* by Alison Lurie; general nonfiction, *The Good War: An Oral History of World War II* by Studs Terkel; biography, *The Life and Times of Cotton Mather* by Kenneth Silverman; history, *Prophets of Regulation* by Thomas K. McCraw; poetry, *Yin* by Carolyn Kizer; drama, *Sunday in the Park With George* by Stephen Sondheim and James Lapine.

June 20: The **Metropolitan Opera** announced that it would abandon its national tour after 1986 because of rising costs and other considerations. The Met had gone on tour each year ever since its founding in 1883.

Nov 26: The rights to **Ronald Reagan's autobiography** were acquired by Random House for $3,000,000. The bid was believed to be the highest ever for a single book. The biography was to be written by Edmund Morris for completion early in 1991.

III. Business and Industry
Education
Philosophy and Religion
Science

The economy continued to expand, but at the low rate of 2.3%. The unemployment rate at the end of the year was 6.8%, lowest in nearly five years. Consumer prices rose only 3.8% and personal income rose 5.95%. Consumer spending rose by 6.6%. Americans bought a record 15,600,000 automobiles and light trucks. All this good news was balanced by some distressing statistics. The federal deficit hit a record $211,900,000,000 for the fiscal year ending Sept. 30, and the trade deficit for calendar 1985 climbed to a record $148,500,000,000. By mid-September the U.S. for the first time since World War I became a debtor nation, owing more to other countries than was owed to it. To alleviate this imbalance, the U.S., Great Britain, France, West Germany, and Japan agreed on Sept. 22 to take steps to lower the value of the dollar. On the next day the dollar fell in value by 4.29% against other major currencies. In business 1985 was the year of the corporate merger, with about $125,000,000,000 changing hands in buy-out transactions. There were 24 mergers involving $1,000,000,000 or more each. A government report released in October said that at least 6928 accidents involving toxic chemicals had occurred in the past five years, killing more than 135 people. The American Medical Association reported that nearly three times as many medical malpractice suits were being filed compared with ten years earlier. According to a congressional investigation, more than 500,000 persons had obtained false degrees or other credentials in fields ranging from architecture to medicine to zoology. Notables who died this year included Eugene Carson Blake, general secretary of the World Council of Churches from 1966 to 1972, July 31, at 78; Sarah G. Blanding, president of Vassar College from 1946 to 1964, the first woman to hold the position, Mar. 3, at 86; Stuart Chase, the economist and semanticist, Nov. 16, at 97; Archibald M. Crossley, a founder of modern public opinion polling, May 1, at 88; Gardner Cowles, Jr., head of the Cowles publishing and communications empire, July 8, at 82; Milton S. Eisenhower, diplomat, presidential adviser, and brother of Dwight D. Eisenhower, May 2, at 85; Spencer Kimball, president of the Mormon Church since 1973, Nov. 15, at 90; Simon Kuznets, Nobel Prize-winning economist, July 8, at 84; Charles F. Richter, for whom the Richter scale of earthquake measurement is named, Sept. 30, at 85; and Robert W. Woodruff, who turned the Coca-Cola Company into an international business giant, Mar. 7, at 95.

Jan 24-27: The first secret space shuttle flight was made by the shuttle *Discovery*. Even the launch time had been kept secret for the mission, which was devoted entirely to achieving military objectives.

Feb 17: A $120,000,000 libel suit against CBS was dropped by Gen. William C. Westmoreland, former commander of U.S. forces in Vietnam, after 18 weeks of court testimony. The case involved a 1982 CBS documentary that claimed Westmoreland had withheld important information on enemy troop strength.

Mar 4: A virtual **ban on leaded gasoline** was ordered by the Environmental Protection Agency, which required removal of 90% of the lead in automobile fuel by the end of the year. The agency contemplated ordering a total ban by 1988.

Mar 8: After having had **three heart implants** within 46 hours, Thomas Creighton, a 33-year-old Arizona man, died at the University Medical Center in Tucson, Ariz. Creighton had been given a human heart. When that failed he was given an untried artificial heart, then a second human heart.

Mar 18: The **largest U.S. corporation,** according to *The New York Times,* was Exxon, with 1984 sales of $97,276,000,000. General Motors was second.

Mar 18: The **American Broadcasting Company** was bought by Capital Cities Communications, Inc., for $3,500,000,000. It was the first time one of the three major networks had been sold.

Apr 8: The **Union Carbide Corporation was sued** by the government of India in connection with a plant disaster at Bhopal, India, on Dec. 3, 1984, that killed some 1700 persons and injured as many as 200,000.

Apr 24: Two new **U.S. Roman Catholic cardinals** were named by Pope John Paul II. They were Archbishop John J. O'Connor of New York and Archbishop Bernard F. Law of Boston.

May 12: The **first woman Conservative rabbi,** Amy Eilberg, 30, was ordained during graduation ceremonies at Jewish Theological Seminary in New York City.

May 21: In the **largest multiple birth** on record in the U.S., Patricia Frustaci gave birth to seven children, one stillborn, in California. Three died within a short time. The last of the three survivors did not leave the hospital until Oct. 4. On Dec. 3 the Frustacis filed a $3,200,000 malpractice suit against the physicians and the clinic that had given her fertility drugs.

June 4: In a decision on **school prayers** the Supreme Court struck down an Alabama law permitting one minute of prayer or meditation in public schools. The ruling suggested that other state laws might be found constitutional if they did not have as their sole purpose the fostering of religious activity.

July 1: In a decision on **separation of church and state,** the Supreme Court ruled that public school teachers could not enter parochial school classrooms to provide remedial or enrichment instruction. The ruling applied specifically to programs in New York City and Grand Rapids, Mich.

July 19: Christa McAuliffe, 36, a high-school teacher and mother of two from Concord, N.H., was selected from 11,000 applicants to become the first teacher to fly aboard a space shuttle.

Aug 23: The **TVA shut down its last nuclear plant,** the Sequoyah facility at Daisy, Tenn., because of doubts about the safety of nuclear power.

Oct 14: The **Nobel Prize in Physiology or Medicine** was awarded to Michael S. Brown and Joseph L. Goldstein of the University of Texas Health Center in Dallas for their discoveries in the field of cholesterol metabolism and contributions to the treatment of diseases linked to presence of the substance.

Oct 15: The **Nobel Prize in Economics** was awarded to Franco Modigliani of MIT for his work in analyzing the behavior of household savers and the functioning of financial markets.

Oct 16: The **Nobel Prize in Chemistry** was awarded jointly to Herbert A. Hauptman of the Medical Foundation of Buffalo, N.Y., and Jerome Karle of the Naval Research Laboratory, Washington, D.C., for developing techniques for determining the structures of molecules vital to life.

Dec 10: The **highest award for damages** in U.S. history was upheld by a Texas state judge. A jury had ordered Texaco, Inc., to pay $11,100,000,000 to the Pennzoil Company because it had interfered with an agreement for Pennzoil to acquire the Getty Oil Company in 1984. Texaco announced it would appeal the decision.

Dec 10: A complete **ban on tobacco advertising**, including smokeless tobacco products, was urged by the American Medical Association. On Dec. 19 the surgeon general of the U.S. said that cigarette smoking was a greater health threat to most Americans than hazards of the workplace.

Dec 16: A new **stock record** was set by the Dow Jones industrial average, which closed at 1553.10. It had gained 17.89 points in one day.

Dec 23: The **costliest farm bill** in history was signed by Pres. Reagan. Estimated to cost $169,000,000,000 over five years, it nonetheless reduced income and price supports to farmers for the first time since 1933.

IV. Fashion
   Folkways
   Holidays
   Social Issues and Crime
   Sports

The Coca-Cola Company shocked the public on Apr. 23 when it announced it was doing away with its 99-year-old recipe for the famous soft drink and offering a new formula. Faithful Coke drinkers responded so forcefully against the change that on July 10 Coca-Cola was forced to reintroduce the old Coke under a new name, Coca-Cola Classic. In fashion elegance continued to gain favor. Career women were beginning to wear more colorful suits, not just feminized copies of men's traditional wear. Meanwhile, the U.S. Army ruled that its male officers were not allowed to carry umbrellas. The national craze for Cabbage Patch dolls continued, and the classic Barbie doll was given a new French-designed wardrobe as well as a business suit with attaché case. In sports the North American Soccer League went out of business after heavy financial losses. Professional basketball and major league baseball, however, reported record attendance in 1985. This year the major league baseball playoffs were extended to best-of-seven series. Critics of the move said it would detract from the importance of the World Series. In golf the top money winners were Curtis Strange, $542,321, and Nancy Lopez, $416,472. Notables who died this year included James Beard, authority on cooking, Jan. 23, at 81; Rudi Gernreich, avant-garde fashion designer who introduced the topless bathing suit for women in the 1960s, Apr. 21, at 62; Burleigh Grimes, pitcher and member of the Baseball Hall of Fame, Dec. 6, at 92; John B. Kelly, Jr., president of the U.S. Olympic Committee, Mar. 2, at 57; Roger Maris, Yankee batting champ who broke Babe Ruth's home run record in 1961, Dec. 14, at 51; John Scarne, international authority on games and gambling, July 7, at 82; and Joseph "Smoky Joe" Wood, a pitcher who won 34 games for the Boston Red Sox in 1912, July 27, at 95.

Jan 20: Super Bowl XIX was won by the San Francisco 49ers (NFC), defeating the Miami Dolphins (AFC) 38 to 16. On Jan. 6 the 49ers had shut out the Chicago Bears 23 to 0 for the NFC championship, and the Dolphins had beaten the Pittsburgh Steelers 45 to 28 for the AFC title.

Mar 3: The **first jockey to win $100,000,000** in career purse money was Willie Shoemaker, who rode Lord at War to victory in the Santa Anita Handicap in Arcadia, Calif.

Apr 1: The **NCAA men's basketball championship** was won by Villanova, which beat Georgetown 66 to 64.

Apr 29: The **WBA heavyweight boxing championship** was won by Tony Tubbs in a 15-round decision over Greg Page at Buffalo, N.Y.

May 27-June 9: The **NBA basketball championship** was won by the Los Angeles Lakers, who defeated the Boston Celtics four games to two.

June 16: The **U.S. Open golf tournament** was won by Andy North, who came from behind to beat Tze-Chung Chen of Taiwan by one stroke.

July 6-7: At the **Wimbledon** tennis championships in England, Martina Navratilova won the women's singles title. Navratilova teamed with Paul McNamee of

Australia to win the mixed doubles, and Kathy Jordan teamed with Elizabeth Smylie of Australia to win the women's doubles.

July 11: **Nolan Ryan** of the Houston Astros (NL) became the first pitcher in major league history to strike out 4000 batters when he fanned Danny Heep of the New York Mets on three pitches in the sixth inning at Houston. The Astros won 4 to 3.

July 23: A new **record auction price for a thoroughbred** was set at Lexington, Ky., when a yearling son of Nijinsky II and My Charmer sold for $13,100,000.

Aug 11: The **PGA golf tournament** was won by Hubert Green, who beat defending champion Lee Trevino by two strokes.

Sep 7-8: The **U.S. Open tennis singles championships** were won by Ivan Lendl of Czechoslovakia in the men's division and Hana Mandlikova of Czechoslovakia in the women's division.

Sep 11: **Pete Rose** of the Cincinnati Reds (NL) set a new major league baseball record of 4192 career hits in a 2 to 0 win over the San Diego Padres at Cincinnati. The old record of 4191 hits was set by Ty Cobb in 1928.

Sep 21: The International Boxing Federation **heavyweight boxing championship** was won by Michael Spinks in a 15-round decision over Larry Holmes in Las Vegas, Nev.

Oct 5: Eddie Robinson of Grambling State University became the **"winningest" college football coach** in history when his team picked up its 324th win in his 44-year career. During that time Grambling State had lost 106 games and tied 15.

Oct 19-27: The **World Series** was won by the Kansas City Royals (AL), defeating the St. Louis Cardinals (NL) four games to three. On Oct. 16 the Royals had won the American League pennant against the Toronto Blue Jays four games to three, and the Cardinals had won the National League pennant against the Los Angeles Dodgers four games to two.

1986

I. **Civil Rights**
   Exploration and Settlement
   Government
   Statistics
   Wars

On New Year's Day Pres. Ronald Reagan appeared on television in the U.S.S.R., and Soviet leader Mikhail S. Gorbachev appeared on U.S. television. Both leaders expressed their hopes for world peace. Despite this apparent warming of U.S.-Soviet relations, the Reagan administration continued its tough policy toward the U.S.S.R. A statement of policy issued Mar. 14 committed the U.S. to "democratic revolution" around the world and implied a lessening of support for dictatorships based simply on the fact that they were anticommunist. On Jan. 28 Jonas Savimbi, leader of a rebel military group seeking to overthrow the Marxist government of Angola, was given a warm welcome in Washington. On Feb. 7 President-for-life Jean-Claude Duvalier of Haiti was forced to flee his country; he was flown to France aboard a U.S. jet. On Feb. 26 Pres. Ferdinand Marcos of the Philippines was forced out of office by a bloodless popular uprising. The Reagan administration had urged him to resign following his victory in a rigged election. On Mar. 12 the administration criticized the right-wing government of Chile for its abuses of human rights. In April a *New York Times*/CBS poll showed that 51% of Republicans, 74% of Democrats, and 59% of independents opposed a proposed $100,000,000 of aid to the Nicaraguan Contras. The Office of Management and Budget announced on Oct. 23 that the federal deficit for the year ended Sept. 30 reached $220,700,000,000, the fourth record figure in five years. Notables who died this year included Rep. Joseph P. Addabbo, Democrat of New York, a powerful figure in the shaping of defense policy, Apr. 10, at 61; Chester Bowles, senator, ambassador, and advertising executive, May 25, at 85; Sen. John P. East, Republican of North Carolina, June 29, at 55; James O. Eastland, Democratic senator from Mississippi for 36 years, Feb. 19, at 81; Charles A. Halleck, Republican of Indiana, who served 16 terms in the House of Representatives and was both minority and majority leader, Mar. 3, at 85; W. Averell Harriman, adviser to four presidents, July 26, at 94; Jacob J. Javits, Republican senator from New York from 1954 to 1981, Mar. 7, at 81; Philip C. Jessup, an authority in the field of international law who served on the International Court of Justice from 1960 to 1969, Jan. 31, at 89; and Adm. Hyman G. Rickover, the "father of the nuclear navy," July 8, at 86.

Jan 7: Economic sanctions against Libya were ordered by Pres. Reagan in retaliation for alleged Libyan involvement in terrorist attacks on Dec. 27, 1985, at the Rome and Vienna airports. Five U.S. citizens had been among the victims. All Libyan assets in the U.S. were frozen, and all U.S. citizens in Libya were ordered home.

Feb 19: A United Nations **treaty outlawing genocide** was ratified by the Senate. The treaty had been signed by the U.S. in 1948, but the Senate had never acted on it.

Mar 20: A controversial $100,000,000 **Contra aid bill** for Nicaraguan rebel forces was voted down by the House of Representatives, 222 to 210.

Mar 24: An armed clash with Libya occurred in the Gulf of Sidra after Libyan shore installations launched missiles at a U.S. fleet on maneuvers in the gulf. U.S. missiles damaged the Libyan missile site and destroyed two patrol boats advancing on the fleet.

Mar 25: Military aid to Honduras amounting to $20,000,000 was approved by Congress following reports of a Nicaraguan military incursion to destroy rebel Contra bases just inside the Honduran border.

Mar 25: A constitutional **amendment to require a balanced federal budget** was defeated in the Senate. The

66 to 34 vote in favor was one vote short of the two-thirds vote required for passage.

Apr 2: A **terrorist bombing** aboard a TWA jet flying from Rome, Italy, to Athens, Greece, killed four American passengers, including one infant. Nine other passengers were injured. An Arab terrorist group claimed responsibility.

Apr 5: A **terrorist bombing** in a West Berlin discothèque killed a U.S. soldier and a Turkish woman and wounded 155 other persons, including about 60 Americans. U.S. officials later stated they had firm evidence that Libya was involved in the crime.

Apr 14: A **U.S. air strike against Libya** was launched in retaliation for Libya's involvement in the West Berlin bombing of Apr. 5 and other terrorist acts. Sixteen U.S. F-111s flying from Great Britain were joined by U.S. carrier-based planes in attacks on five military bases and terrorist centers near Tripoli and Benghazi.

May 19: A new **gun control law,** weakening the 1968 federal gun control law, was signed by Pres. Reagan. Among other provisions, the new law allowed interstate retail sales of rifles. Police organizations had been among the groups that had lobbied against the bill.

May 27: Pres. Reagan announced that **U.S. strategic arms policy** would no longer be bound by the terms of the unratified SALT II arms agreement. At the same time, he announced that two Poseidon submarines would be dismantled to make room for a new Trident submarine and keep the U.S. in step with the treaty's provisions.

June 5: Ronald W. Pelton was convicted of espionage. The former National Security Agency employee had been charged with selling intelligence secrets to the U.S.S.R.

June 11: Constitutional protection for the **right to abortion** was narrowly reaffirmed by the Supreme Court. The decision voided a Pennsylvania law because some of its provisions were designed to deter women from having abortions and others would require doctors to risk the health of pregnant women.

June 17: Pres. Reagan announced that **Warren E. Burger** would retire as chief justice of the Supreme Court, effective July 10. The president named Associate Justice William H. Rehnquist as Burger's successor, and also named Antonin Scalia, of the U.S. Court of Appeals for the District of Columbia, to the Court. The changes were interpreted as a gain for conservative judicial philosophy.

June 18: A **midair collision** between a plane and a helicopter over the Grand Canyon killed all 25 persons aboard the two aircraft.

June 19: Richard W. Miller became the first FBI agent ever to be convicted of espionage. He was charged was passing information to the U.S.S.R.

June 19: Cyanide poisoning was declared the cause of death of two persons in the Seattle, Wash., area. Both had taken Extra-Strength Excedrin capsules containing the poison. Bristol-Meyers, the maker of Excedrin, announced the next day it was withdrawing all its nonprescription capsule drugs from sale.

June 27: U.S. actions against Nicaragua, including aid to antigovernment rebels, was ruled a violation of national law by the International Court of Justice. The U.S. was ordered to stop arming and training the insurgents and to pay Nicaragua for damages. U.S. officials had withdrawn from the case, stating the court had no jurisdiction.

June 30: The Supreme Court ruled that **homosexual relations,** even in private between consenting adults, are not protected by the Constitution. The decision upheld an 1816 Georgia law banning sodomy.

July 2: The use of **affirmative action** to remedy job discrimination was upheld by the Supreme Court, 6-3. The decision meant that it was legal to use numerical goals to increase minority representation among workers. The Reagan administration had opposed this interpretation of the law.

July 7: Part of the **Gramm-Rudman budget balancing act** of Dec. 1985 was found unconstitutional by the Supreme Court, 7–2. The court said the provision for automatic spending cuts violated the separation of powers within the federal government. The decision left standing a fall-back provision of the act requiring Congress to make budget cuts under certain conditions.

Aug 13: Congressional action on **Contra aid** supplied $100,000,000 to the Nicaraguan rebels. Pres. Reagan had requested the appropriation, which also added $300,000,000 for four neighboring Central America nations.

Aug 31: The **collision of two planes** near Los Angeles left all 67 persons aboard the two craft dead, and at least 15 others on the ground were believed killed also. One plane was an Aeromexico DC-9, the other a single-engine private plane. Ten houses were also demolished.

Oct 2: Pres. Reagan's **veto of a sanctions bill against South Africa** was overridden by Congress. The Senate vote was 78–21. On Sept. 29 the House had voted to override, 313–83. The law banned new investment by Americans in South Africa, prohibited the importation of such items as iron and steel, and cancelled landing rights in the U.S. for South African airlines.

Oct 9: The **Senate convicted federal judge Harry E. Clairborne** on three of four articles of impeachment, thus removing him from office. Clairborne had previously been convicted of tax evasion but had refused to resign his judgeship. It was the first impeachment trial in the Senate in 50 years.

Oct 11-12: No agreement on **arms control** was reached by Pres. Ronald Reagan and General Secretary Mikhail S. Gorbachev of the U.S.S.R. after two days of talks at a summit meeting in Reykjavik, Iceland. Reagan refused to accede to the Soviet insistence that the U.S. abandon its plan for a space-based missile defense system, popularly known as "Star Wars."

Oct 14: The **Nobel Peace Prize** was awarded to Elie Wiesel, author and human rights activist. He was cited as a "spiritual leader" against "violence, repression, and racism."

Oct. 22: A revised **federal income tax law** was signed by Pres. Ronald Reagan. The most complete revision of the tax code in more than 40 years, the new law lowered tax rates for almost everyone while eliminating many previous deductions and other tax preferences. The top rate for individuals was lowered from 50% to 38.5%. Most of the changes were to take place on Jan. 1, 1987. The total amount of taxes to be collected was expected to remain about the same.

Nov 2: One **American hostage,** David P. Jacobsen, director of the American Hospital in Beirut, Lebanon, held by kidnapers for 18 months, was freed. Another kidnap victim of Moslem terrorists, the Rev. Lawrence M. Jenco, had been released on July 26. However, on Apr. 17 another kidnap victim, Peter Kilburn, a librarian at the American University of Beirut, was found dead. The terrorists subsequently seized Frank Reed, an American educator, on Sept. 9; Joseph J. Cicippio, chief accountant at the American University, on Sept. 12; and Edward A. Tracy, an author, on Oct. 21.

Nov 3: What became known as the **Iran-Contra affair** began when a Lebanese magazine revealed that the U.S. had been secretly selling arms to Iran in the hope of securing the release of hostages held in Lebanon. American intelligence sources on Nov. 6 confirmed that the operation had taken place. On Nov. 12 Pres. Reagan admitted that he knew of the arms sale, but on Nov. 25 he said he had not been fully informed of all that went on. That same day it was revealed that some of the money received from the sale of arms to Iran had been secretly diverted to the Nicaraguan rebels, known as Contras. Also on Nov. 25 the two officials who were the major planners and overseers of the scheme left office: Vice Adm. John M. Poindexter, national security adviser, resigned, and his assistant, Marine Lt. Col. Oliver L. North, was dismissed. On Nov. 26 the president appointed a three-member panel, headed by former Sen. John G. Tower, to investigate the actions of the National Security Council staff. Meanwhile, Congress prepared to carry out its own investigation, and on Dec. 19 an independent counsel was named to head another inquiry into what was becoming a national scandal.

Nov 4: In the biennial **Congressional elections** the Democrats won control of the Senate, 53–47, with a

gain of eight seats. They retained control of the
House of Representatives, 253–182, a loss of five
seats.

Nov 6: Pres. Reagan signed into law an **immigration
act** that established new and drastically changed policies concerning aliens in the U.S. Employers were to
be prohibited from employing illegal aliens, but
many such persons would be given an opportunity to
secure legal status, by showing that they entered the
U.S. before Jan. 1, 1982, and had resided here continuously "in an illegal status."

Dec 31: At least **95 persons died in a fire** in a high-rise
hotel in San Juan, Puerto Rico. It was later determined that the fire was caused by a disgruntled employee who probably did not intend to do more than
shake up the management.

II. Architecture
Arts and Music
Popular Entertainment
Publishing
Theater

For the second year in a row, the Broadway theater
set a new record for fewest productions: 26, of which
only six were very successful. One of the latter was a
revival of an old-fashioned musical, *Me and My Girl.*
The movies continued to cater generally to teenagers
over other age groups with such films as *Ferris
Bueller's Day Off.* Major movies of the year included
Woody Allen's amusing *Hannah and Her Sisters; Top
Gun,* featuring the exploits of a fighter pilot; and *The
Color of Money,* with the ever-popular Paul Newman.
In art, the Brooklyn Museum presented *From Cour-
bet to Cezanne: A New 19th Century,* a show exhibit-
ing 130 works from the new Musée D'Orsay in Paris,
France. Brooklyn, N.Y., was also the site of the first
U.S. performance by the Central Ballet of China.
After the company's final appearance at the Brooklyn
Academy of Music on Mar. 16, the young dancers
from the People's Republic of China began a tour of
other U.S. cities. In publishing, the Louisville (Ky.)

Times and *Courier-Journal* newspapers, owned by the Bingham family for nearly 70 years, were acquired by the Gannett newspaper group on May 19 for $305,000,000. On May 28 the Baltimore *Sun* and *Evening Sun* papers were purchased by the Times Mirror Company of Los Angeles for some $450,000,000. In the newspaper world in general, the trend to abandon the publishing of evening papers continued, with 26 of them shifting to the morning field. In book publishing, the year was marked by the purchase on Sept. 28 of Doubleday & Co. by Bertelsmann AG, a large West German publisher, for $475,000,000. In November Bertelsmann sold the 95% interest Doubleday held in the Mets, New York's NL baseball team, to Nelson Doubleday, Jr., and Fred Wilpon for $95,000,000. Of magazines, one survey showed that the most popular among college students was *Cosmopolitan.* Notables who died this year included Harold Arlen, composer of such hit songs as "Over the Rainbow," Apr. 23, at 81; Desi Arnaz, prominent television actor, musician, and producer, Dec. 2, at 69; Cass Canfield, a leading book publisher for 40 years, Mar. 27, at 88; Lucia Chase, who helped found the American Ballet Theater in 1940, Jan. 9, at 88; John Ciardi, the poet and translator, Mar. 30, at 69; Broderick Crawford, the actor, Apr. 26, at 74; Benny Goodman, the "King of Swing," June 13, at 77; Cary Grant, suave leading man of the movies for 30 years, Nov. 29, at 82; Frank Herbert, the writer known best for his *Dune* series of science fiction novels, Feb. 11, at 65; L. Ron Hubbard, science fiction writer and founder of Scientology, Jan. 24, at 71; Joseph Kraft, the Washington columnist whose work appeared in some 200 newspapers, Jan. 10, at 61; Alan Jay Lerner, the lyricist and playwright known best for his collaboration with Frederick Loewe on *My Fair Lady* and other hits, June 14, at 67; Raymond Loewy, the father of "streamlining" and industrial design, July 14, at 92; Bernard Malamud, the Pulitzer Prize-winning novelist and short-story writer, Mar. 18, at 71; Una Merkel, one of the few silent film stars able to make the transition to sound films, Jan. 2, at 82; Gordon McRae, the movie actor and singer known best for his performance in *Oklahoma*, Jan. 24, at 64; Ray Milland, the actor, Mar. 10, at 81; Vincente Minnelli, producer of some of Hollywood's best musicals, July 25, at 76; Reuben Nakian, distinguished sculptor, Dec. 4, at 89; Georgia O'Keeffe, the artist, known for her desert paintings and exotic, colorful studies of flowers, Mar. 6, at 98; Otto Preminger, the movie director and producer, Apr. 23, at 80; Kate Smith, one of the most popular singers of the twentieth century, who made "God Bless America" an unofficial national anthem, June 17, at 79; Blanche Sweet, early film star who appeared in D. W. Griffith movies, Sept. 6, at 90; Rudy Vallee, an enormously popular singer and band leader in the 1920s and 1930s, July 3, at 84; Hal B. Wallis, producer of some 400 movies, including *The Maltese Falcon*, Oct. 5, at 88; Theodore H. White, the Pulitzer Prize-winning writer and acknowledged dean of political journalism, May 15, at 71; and Teddy Wilson, jazz pianist with a 50-year career, July 31, at 73.

Among **books published** this year was *The Garden of Eden*, a posthumous novel by Ernest Hemingway that received mixed reaction from critics. Another novel, *Gone With the Wind* by Margaret Mitchell, turned 50 on June 30 with publication of a facsimile edition of 50,000. The novel, which sold 25,000,000 copies in its first half century, hit the best-seller list once again. Among novels praised and popular were *Kate Vaiden* by Reynolds Price, *The Beet Queen* by Louise Erdrich, *A Summons to Memphis* by Peter Taylor, and *Roger's Version* by John Updike. Representative of an excellent array of nonfiction titles were *The Man Who Mistook His Wife for a Hat*, the recounting of a number of curious medical cases, by Dr. Oliver Sacks; *Ford: The Men and the Machine* by Robert Lacey; *Crabgrass Frontier: The Suburbanization of America*, winner of two prestigious history prizes, by Kenneth T. Jackson; *Tombee: Portrait of a Cotton Planter* by Theodore Rosengarten; and *The Triumph of Politics: Why the Reagan Revolution Failed* by David A. Stockman, former director of the Office of Management and Budget. None of these matched in sales Bill Cosby's *Fatherhood* or Tom Clancy's thriller *Red Storm Rising*.

Jan 11: A new **record book price** was set when William Morrow & Company and Avon Books bid $5,000,000 for North American hardbound and paperback rights to James Clavell's novel *Whirlwind*.

Feb 26: Robert Penn Warren became the first official poet laureate of the U.S. Daniel Boorstin, the Librarian of Congress, made the appointment.

Apr 17: Pulitzer prizes were awarded for the following: fiction, *Lonesome Dove* by Larry McMurtry; general nonfiction, *Move Your Shadow: South Africa, Black and White* by Joseph Lelyveld and *Common Ground: A Turbulent Decade in the Lives of Three American Families* by J. Anthony Lukas; biography, *Louise Bogan: A Portrait* by Elizabeth Frank; poetry, *The Flying Change* by Henry Taylor. No award was given for drama.

Apr 27: A **video pirate** interrupted the showing of a cable TV movie by Home Box Office by overriding the broadcast with a message saying he would not pay for his cable service. The FCC and commercial users of satellite transmissions expressed dismay that an unknown person could override the HBO signal.

Apr 29: Probably the worst **library fire** in U.S. history destroyed or damaged some 800,000 books at the Los Angeles Central Library. On May 5 officials reported that the fire, which caused $22,000,000 in damage, had been deliberately set.

May 6: A new record **auction price for a contemporary sculpture**, $1,300,000, was bid by a New York City art dealer for David Smith's 1963 welded-steel work *Voltri-Bolton XXIII*.

June 1: Television coverage of Senate proceedings was begun, in a test that was to continue until July 15. The House of Representatives had allowed such coverage since Mar. 19, 1979.

June 27: A **record auto auction price** of $6,500,000 was bid in Reno, Nev., by Jerry J. Moore, a Houston shopping center builder, for a 1931 Bugatti Royale. The French-built auto, one of seven built, had originally cost $42,000.

Aug 9: The popular artist **Andrew Wyeth** revealed for the first time 240 works of art secretly painted by him over 15 years. All but one of them were of a woman known only as Helga but later revealed to be a Wyeth neighbor. The collection was bought for an estimated $10,000,000 or more by a collector, Leonard E. B. Andrews.

Dec 15: America's most famous music auditorium, **Carnegie Hall** in New York City, reopened with a gala concert featuring many noted musicians. It had been closed for seven months for a $50,000,000 remodeling.

III. Business and Industry
Education
Philosophy and Religion
Science

The year's top story was the tragic loss of the NASA space shuttle *Challenger* and the deaths of all seven persons aboard. Investigations led to the conclusion that failure of a seal on one of the shuttle's solid-fuel booster rockets had caused the disaster. NASA records showed that agency officials had been warned of problems with the rocket joints. The disaster prompted fresh debate on the U.S. space program, particularly over use of the space shuttle as opposed to unmanned vehicles. For the most part it was a successful year for the national economy. Car and truck sales set a record of 16,000,000, with 28.2% of the vehicles imported. The price of oil fell as low as $12 a barrel in July, lowering the price of gasoline but damaging the domestic oil industry. By late December the price was back up to $16.90 as OPEC threatened to cut production. Hot weather and drought in some mid-Atlantic and southern states did great damage to crops and livestock, so that by the end of July losses were estimated at $2,000,000,000. At the year's end unemployment was down to 6.6%, the lowest figure in six years, while producer prices fell 2.5% for the year, the first decline since 1963. On the other hand the GNP grew only 2.5%, the worst showing in four years, but the CPI rose only 1.1%, the smallest increase since 1961. The foreign trade deficit, however, rose to $169,780,000,000, a record. The Labor Department reported that in February the number of women professionals in the U.S. topped for the first time the number of men holding professional jobs, by a margin of 29,000. A National Science Board report in March revealed that programs in college-level science, mathematics, and engineering had so declined as to constitute a "grave long-term threat" to the country. The Educational Testing Service of Princeton, N.J., announced it would spend $30,000,000 over 15 years to develop new tests that would focus less on absolute scores and concentrate more on what the test-taker knows and does not know. In June the federal government reported 21,915 cases of the disease AIDS in the U.S. and that 12,008 of these persons had already died. The sale of videocassette recorders continued to boom, with a total of 13,174,000 in 1986. Sales of compact discs reached $930,000,000, compared with $17,000,000 in 1983, while sales of LPs declined in the same period from $1,689,000,000 to $983,000,000. Notables who died this year included Herbert W. Armstrong, founder of the Worldwide Church of God, Jan. 15, at 93; Harrison Brown, pioneer in producing plutonium and later a foe of nuclear weapons, Dec. 8, at 69; Arthur F. Burns, Federal Reserve Board chairman and ambassador to West Germany, June 26, at 83; Edwin T. Dahlberg, former president of the National Council of Churches, Sept. 6, at 93; Edward Doisy, Sr., Nobel Prize winner who isolated vitamin K, Oct. 23, at 92; Dana McLean Greeley, president of the Unitarian Universalist Association, June 13, at 77; Fritz A. Lipman, joint Nobel Prize winner for the discovery of coenzyme, important in the body's metabolism, July 24, at 87; Robert S. Mulliken, Nobel Prize winner for his study of the chemistry of atoms, Oct. 31, at 90; James Rainwater, the Nobel Prize-winning physicist, May 31, at 68; Albert Szent-Györgyi, Nobel Prize winner for isolating vitamin C, Oct. 22, at 93; and Helen Taussig, the founder of pediatric cardiology, May 20, at 87.

Jan 12-18: The **space shuttle** *Columbia* completed its seventh orbital mission after liftoff had been postponed a record seven times. Its landing was postponed twice.

Jan 14: Local laws forbidding **backyard satellite dish antennas,** as distinct from other types of antennas, were banned by the FCC.

Jan 24: The spacecraft *Voyager 2* flew within 50,679 miles of the planet Uranus, discovering new moons and rings and obtaining the first evidence of a magnetic field around the planet.

Jan 28: The **space shuttle** *Challenger* exploded 74 seconds after liftoff at Cape Canaveral, Fla., killing all seven astronauts aboard, including Christa McAuliffe, 37, a Concord, N.H., schoolteacher, the first private citizen chosen for a space shuttle flight. On June 9 a presidential commission report identified failure of a seal on a solid-fuel booster rocket as the cause of the explosion and criticized NASA for a long history of managerial and engineering mistakes. On July 2 NASA announced it would modify the faulty booster rocket joints to eliminate the danger of further booster failures.

Mar 11: In a controversy over the **teaching of Roman Catholic doctrine,** the Rev. Charles E. Curran, a liberal theologian at the Catholic University of America in Washington, D.C., was ordered by the Vatican to retract his views on birth control and other sexual issues or lose the right to teach Roman Catholic doctrine. On Aug. 18 Father Curran's right to teach theology was revoked, and on Apr. 12, 1988, the trustees of Catholic University barred him from teaching in the theology department.

Mar 15: In a statement on the **treatment of terminal patients,** the American Medical Association said it was ethical for doctors to withhold "all means of life-prolonging medical treatment."

Apr 3: The **U.S. national debt** exceeded $2,000,000,000,000, having doubled in five years.

Apr 16: The first **surrogate birth of a test-tube baby,** a girl, was announced by spokesmen at Mount Sinai Hospital in Cleveland, Ohio.

Apr 17: Computers using the **megabit memory chip,** capable of storing more than 1,000,000 bits of electronic data, were being manufactured for the first time, IBM officials announced.

Apr 18: An Air Force **Titan rocket exploded** moments after launch. On May 4 a Delta rocket failed soon after launch and had to be destroyed. These failures, combined with the *Challenger* disaster, were seen as major setbacks for the U.S. space program.

Apr 22: The first **genetically altered virus** to be released into the environment was approved by the Department of Agriculture. It was to be used to fight a form of herpes affecting swine, which caused an annual $60,000,000 in damage.

Apr 28: The **largest U.S. corporation,** according to the annual *Fortune* magazine survey, was General Motors, with 1985 sales of $96,371,700,000. Exxon was second with sales of $86,673,000,000.

Apr 29: "Clear and unconditional" **opposition to use of nuclear weapons** was voted unanimously by the Council of Bishops of the United Methodist Church.

Apr 29: Settling a dispute over **AIDS virus research,** the Patent and Trademark Office designated the Pasteur Institute of Paris as the "senior party," rather than the U.S. National Institutes of Health, in the matter of which developed the first AIDS blood test. At stake were millions of dollars in royalties to be earned by the use of the test.

May 6: The **first American Indian to become a Roman Catholic bishop,** the Rev. Donald E. Pelotte, 41, was ordained in Gallup, N. Mex.

May 30: The first outdoor test of **genetically engineered plants** was begun when genetically altered tobacco was planted on a Wisconsin farm. The field test opened up the possibility of creating high-yield crops that would reduce farmers' dependence on toxic chemicals to control pests.

June 9: The **Dow Jones average** of industrial stocks marked a record one-day loss of 45.75 points.

June 12: The number of **deaths from AIDS** (acquired immune deficiency syndrome) would increase more than tenfold in five years, federal health officials predicted. By 1991 the disease would afflict some 270,000, causing 179,000 deaths, at a health cost of up to $16,000,000,000 annually.

June 19: The **third artificial heart recipient,** Murray P. Haydon, died at 59 in a Louisville, Ky., hospital. He had received the heart on Feb. 17, 1985.

July 2: **Affirmative action programs** to cure past discrimination in the work place were upheld by the Supreme Court, ruling in cases involving a New York City labor union and the Cleveland Fire Department.

Aug 2: **Leslie Alexander** became the first woman to take part in a service as a rabbi of a major Conservative Jewish congregation. Two days earlier she had been appointed assistant rabbi of Congregation Adat Ari El in Los Angeles. There were now reported to be 130 women rabbis in the U.S., mostly in Reform congregations.

Aug 6: The **longest-lived recipient of an artificial heart,** William J. Schroeder, died at age 54. He had suffered a series of strokes. Schroeder received the implant on Nov. 25, 1984, and lived 620 days. He was the second recipient and the last survivor of five persons to have had permanent artificial hearts implanted.

Aug 29: The **Evangelical Lutheran Church** in America was established by the merging of the Lutheran Church in America, the American Lutheran Church, and the Association of Evangelical Lutheran Churches. The new church, with 5,300,000 members, represented about two-thirds of all Lutherans in the U.S.

Sep 4: In an unusual action, **the Vatican** ordered an American archbishop to turn over to an auxiliary bishop authority in five areas involving such social issues as birth control and homosexuality. Archbishop Raymond Hunthausen of Seattle had previously been criticized for his liberal position on certain issues. The next day 140 Catholic leaders in the diocese protested in a letter to the Vatican. On May 27, 1987, full authority was restored to Archbishop Hunthausen.

Sep 11: On the **New York Stock Exchange** the Dow Jones average of industrial stocks fell 88.61 points, a record to this date, and closed at 1792.89. The volume of trading for the day was also a record at

237,600,000 shares. That record, however, lasted only until the next day, when 240,500,000 shares were traded.

Oct 13: The **Nobel Prize in Physiology or Medicine** was awarded to Rita Levi-Montalcini, holder of dual U.S. and Italian citizenship, of the Institute of Cell Biology in Rome and Stanley Cohen of Vanderbilt University. They were honored for their discovery of substances that influence cell growth.

Oct 15: The **Nobel Prize in Chemistry** was awarded to Dudley R. Herschback of Harvard University, Yuan T. Lee of the University of California, and John C. Polanyi of the University of Toronto for their discovery of a method of studying chain reactions molecule by molecule.

Oct 16: The **Nobel Prize in Economics** was awarded to James M. Buchanan of George Mason University for his studies in applying economic principles to political decision making.

Oct 20: Withdrawal from South Africa was announced by General Motors, the largest American company with business interests there. It said it was selling its operations. On Oct. 21 International Business Machines made a similar announcement, followed by Eastman Kodak on Nov. 19 and Citibank, formerly opposed to such action, on June 16, 1987.

Nov 3: Poverty in the U.S. was called a "social and moral scandal" in a pastoral letter adopted by America's Roman Catholic bishops. In preparation for over five years, the document said the government must do more to create jobs and help poor people. Less military spending, more economic planning, and an increase in the minimum wage were among the recommendations.

Dec 23: The **first nonstop flight around the world without refueling** was completed when the experimental airplane *Voyager* landed at Edwards Air Force Base, California, after a journey of 25,012 miles that took 9 days, 3 min., 44 sec. Made of plastic and stiffened paper, the fragile-looking plane carried five times its weight in fuel. The pilot was Richard G. Rutan and the copilot Jeana Yeager.

Dec 31: The production of alloys that provide **super-conductivity** at much higher temperatures than ever before was announced by Bell Laboratories and by University of Houston researchers. The Bell Labs material was reported to achieve full superconductivity at 36 K (0 on the Kelvin scale is equal to $-460°$, or absolute zero, on the Fahrenheit scale).

Dec 31: On the **New York Stock Exchange** the Dow Jones average of industrial stocks closed the year at 1895.95. On Dec. 2 it had reached a record high of 1955.57, and on Dec. 19 a record 244,700,000 shares were traded.

IV. Fashion
Folkways
Holidays
Social Issues and Crime
Sports

Drug use by professional athletes became an issue this year following 1985 courtroom revelations by baseball players concerning cocaine use in the major leagues. In February Michael Ray Richardson of the New York Nets basketball team was banned from playing in the NBA after his third drug violation, and John Lucas of the Houston Rockets was released after he failed a drug test. On June 19 Len Bias, a University of Maryland basketball star, died of cocaine poisoning, and on June 27 Don Rogers of the Cleveland Browns football team also died after using cocaine. In football, the major television networks announced they were dropping one-third of the 18 scheduled college bowl game broadcasts for lack of advertising support. A panel of medical experts said handball, squash, and swimming were the most effective sports in promoting fitness. This year marked the hundredth anniversary of the tuxedo, first worn by Griswold Lorillard to a ball in Tuxedo Park, N.Y., in the fall of 1886. A rise in tux sales and rentals this year was fueled, no doubt, by the growing popularity of weekend weddings, three-day affairs including dinners, brunches, barbecues, sports activities and,

of course, the wedding ceremony itself. The Statue of
Liberty also turned 100 this year. Its centennial celebration in New York City in July included a breathtaking parade of tall ships from around the world.
Texas celebrated the 150th anniversary of its independence from Mexico with 10,000 different events,
including the "World's Largest Rattlesnake
Roundup." The Oreo cookie marked its 75th anniversary this year. The ever-popular Popsicle underwent
a change, as the manufacturer announced the frozen
treat in future would sport only one stick. The company, which began manufacturing Popsicles more
than 50 years ago, reported annual sales of
100,000,000 dozen. Vanilla was reported to be the
nation's favorite flavor of ice cream. Bloomingdale's,
the trendy New York City department store, offered
eight rules on how to eat caviar properly (it should be
eaten with a fork, and never put lemon on it). The
Census Bureau reported there were 2,220,000 unwed
couples in the U.S., compared with 523,000 in 1970.
In fashion, dress design was more relaxed in comparison with the spare style of 1985. The lean silhouette
was in. Notables who died this year included James
H. "Jim" Crowley, last surviving member of the so-
called Four Horsemen of Notre Dame, the backfield
that made football history in the 1920s under coach
Knute Rockne, Jan. 15, at 83; Vincent Paul "Vince"
DiMaggio, oldest of the three DiMaggio brothers in
major league baseball, who played ten seasons in the
NL, Oct. 3, at 74; Henry "Hank" Greenberg, slugging
first baseman for the Detroit Tigers and member of
the Baseball Hall of Fame, Sept. 4, at 75; William
"Billy" Haughton, top harness racing driver, after a
racing accident, July 15, at 62; Robert L. "Bobby"
Layne, star quarterback of the Detroit Lions and
member of the Pro Football Hall of Fame, Dec. 1, at
59; Theodore H. "Ted" Lyons, pitcher for 21 years for
the Chicago White Sox and member of the Baseball
Hall of Fame, July 25, at 85; and William "Bill"
Veeck, the maverick baseball team owner known as
the "Barnum of Baseball," Jan. 1, at 71.

Jan 17: The **WBA heavyweight boxing championship**

was won by Tim Witherspoon in a 15-round decision over Tony Tubbs in Atlanta, Ga.

Jan 26: Super Bowl XX was won by the Chicago Bears (NFC), who defeated the New England Patriots (AFC) 46 to 10. The Bears had beaten the Los Angeles Rams 24 to 0 for the NFC title on Jan. 11. On the next day the Patriots had defeated the Miami Dolphins 31 to 14 for the AFC title.

Mar 22: The **WBC heavyweight boxing championship** was won by Trevor Berbick in a 12-round decision over Pinklon Thomas in Las Vegas, Nev.

Mar 31: The **NCAA men's basketball championship** was won by Louisville, defeating Duke 72 to 69.

Apr 2: The **three-point field goal** in men's basketball, made from a minimum distance of 16 ft., 9 in. from the basket, was adopted by the NCAA. The association also approved use of instant TV replays to check scoring and timing decisions.

Apr 11: A new **sailing record** for a solo nonstop circumnavigation of the globe was set by Dodge Morgan, 54, who arrived in St. George, Bermuda, aboard his 60-foot sloop *American Promise.* Morgan, the first American to complete such a voyage, had left Bermuda on Nov. 12, 1985, and had sailed 27,000 miles in 150 days. The previous record had been 292 days.

May 2: An **expedition to the North Pole** was completed by six U.S. and Canadian adventurers, the first expedition since 1909 to reach the pole assisted only by dogs. They made the 500-mile trek from Ward Hunt Island, Canada, in 56 days and returned from the pole by airplane.

May 3: The 112th **Kentucky Derby** was won by Ferdinand, with a time of 2:02⅘. The jockey was Willie Shoemaker, 54, who picked up his fourth Derby win and became the oldest jockey to win the annual racing classic.

May 25: In an event called **Hands Across America,** nearly 6,000,000 people linked hands in a chain that stretched 4150 miles from New York City to Long Beach, Calif., broken only along a few desert stretches. Sponsors hoped to raise $50,000,000 to aid the hungry and homeless in the U.S.

May 26-June 8: The **NBA basketball championship** was won by the Boston Celtics, beating the Houston Rockets four games to two for their 16th NBA title.

June 8: In the **longest nine-inning game** in American League baseball history, the Baltimore Orioles beat the New York Yankees 18 to 9 at Yankee Stadium in 4 hrs., 16 min.

June 15: The **U.S. Open golf tournament** was won by Raymond Floyd, 43, who beat Chip Beck and Lanny Wadkins by two strokes to become the oldest golfer to win the championship.

June 19: Len Bias, star forward for the U. of Maryland's basketball team, died of a heart attack, reported to have been brought on by using cocaine at a party celebrating his signing of a lucrative contract with the Boston Celtics.

June 21: Roger Clemens, Boston Red Sox (AL) ace pitcher, became the seventh pitcher in major league history to start a season with 13 straight wins, beating the Baltimore Orioles 7 to 2 at Boston. On Apr. 29 Clemens had struck out 20, a major league record, in a Boston win over the Seattle Mariners.

July 3-6: Liberty Weekend, a gala national celebration, capped a three-year, $70,000,000 restoration of the Statue of Liberty. On July 3 Pres. Reagan relighted the statue's torch, and new citizens were sworn in around the country. The next day a squadron of tall ships from around the world made its way up New York harbor. That evening saw the greatest fireworks display ever attempted, totaling some 40,000 pieces.

July 5-6: At the **Wimbledon** tennis championships in England, Martina Navratilova bested Hana Mandlikova of Czechoslovakia to win the women's singles title, her fifth consecutive and seventh career win in this event. Navratilova teamed with Pam Shriver to win the women's doubles. Ken Flach and Kathy Jordan won the mixed doubles.

July 27: Greg LeMond became the **first American to win the Tour de France,** the best-known bicycle racing event in the world. LeMond covered the 2500-

mile over-the-road route in 110 hrs., 35 min., 19 sec., beating his nearest competitor by 3 min., 10 sec. The race began on July 4.

Aug 11: The **PGA golf tournament** was won by Bob Tway, who sank a spectacular bunker shot on the final hole to edge out Greg Norman.

Aug 20: The third worst **mass murder** in U.S. history took place in Edmond, Okla. Patrick Henry Sherrill, described as always lonely and who had lost his post-office job for lack of competence, shot and killed 14 of his former coworkers, wounded 6 others, and then killed himself.

Sep 7: The **U.S. Open tennis singles championships** were won by Martina Navratilova over Helena Sukova of Czechoslovakia in the women's division and by Ivan Lendl of Czechoslovakia over his countryman, Miloslav Mecir, in the men's division.

Sept 23: Congress voted to make the rose the **official national flower** of the U.S. The subject had been debated off and on for about 100 years.

Oct 18-27: The **World Series** was won by the New York Mets (NL), who defeated the Boston Red Sox (AL) four games to three. New York lost the first two games at home, and the Sox lost the next two in Boston before winning game five to take a 3–2 advantage. The sixth game, played in New York, went to the Mets 6–5 in the tenth.

Nov 14: In one of the nation's **biggest financial scandals,** Ivan F. Boesky agreed to pay the government $100,000,000 as a penalty for illegal insider trading. The Securities and Exchange Commission announced that Boesky was barred for life from participating in the securities business, but he was allowed to liquidate stocks in order to pay off $1,400,000,000 of debt owed by his firm. On Apr. 23, 1987, he pleaded guilty to one charge of conspiracy to file false documents with the federal government; on Dec. 18 he was sentenced to three years in prison; and on Mar. 24, 1988, he began to serve his sentence.

Nov 22: The WBC **heavyweight boxing championship** was won by Mike Tyson, who knocked out Trevor

Berbick in the second round at Las Vegas, Nev. Tyson, 20 years old, became the youngest heavyweight champion in boxing history.

Dec 12: The WBA **heavyweight boxing championship** was won by James "Bonecrusher" Smith, who knocked out Tim Witherspoon in the first round of a bout in New York City.

1987

I. Civil Rights
Exploration and Settlement
Government
Statistics
Wars

The nation celebrated the 200th anniversary of its Constitution with two separate ceremonies in Philadelphia, where it was written in 1787. On May 25 delegates who had gathered from the 13 original states on May 22 held a ceremony on Independence Mall. On July 16, 200 members of Congress assembled in the Quaker City, ending their visit the next day with an observance of the signing of the document that featured the ringing of a replica of the Liberty Bell. In Washington the *Post* reported that in fiscal 1987 the U.S. gave $660,000,000 in military aid to the Afghans resisting the Soviet invasion. About the same time, in Waukee, Iowa, the plight of some farmers was dramatized when a bank foreclosed the mortgage on the home of Ann Zimmerman, who had been the state's first woman lieutenant governor. Back in Washington, it was revealed that for over 50 years the FBI had been busy keeping a number of America's leading authors under surveillance, including John Steinbeck, Gertrude Stein, Norman Mailer, and William F. Buckley, Jr. Also in Washington, in March, the "Grate American Sleep-Out" took place to publicize the distress of the homeless in the nation's capital. Taking part were actor Martin Sheen, Mayor Marion Barry, Jr., and Congressman Tony Coelho. The Hispanic population, the Census Bureau reported, had grown by 30% since 1980 and stood at 18,800,000. In the good old summertime a heat wave in the Midwest and East was blamed for nearly 100 deaths, with some areas suffering temperatures near or above 100° for 17 days. Notable people who died during the year included William J. Casey, director of the CIA and former chairman of the Securities and Exchange Commission, May 6, at 74; Ira C. Eaker, who was commander of U.S. air forces in Europe in World War II and helped establish the Air Force as a separate service, Aug. 6, at 91; Alfred M. Landon, Republican candidate for president in 1936, Oct. 12, at 100; Bayard Rustin, longtime civil rights leader, Aug. 24, at 77; and Maxwell D. Taylor, commander of airborne troops in World War II, Apr. 19, at 85.

Jan 4: The **crash of a 12-car Amtrak passenger train** with three Conrail freight engines near Chase, Md., killed 15 people and injured more than 175. It was the worst accident in Amtrak's history and occurred when the train and engines were mistakenly merged onto the same track.

Jan 22: An **East Coast blizzard** raged from Maine to Florida, causing at least 37 deaths. Parts of North Carolina received 20 inches of snow.

Jan 24: Three American members of the faculty of Beirut University College were **kidnaped by gunmen** in West Beirut, Lebanon. They were Allen Steen, Jesse Turner, and Robert Polhill. On June 17 another American, Charles Glass, a journalist, was kidnaped, but on Aug. 18 he either escaped or was allowed to escape. At this time five other Americans were being held captive by Moslem terrorists.

Feb 4: Pres. Ronald Reagan's veto of a **Clean Water Act** was overridden by Congress, the Senate acting today and the House having taken action the previous day. The law authorized the spending of

$20,000,000,000 through 1994 for sewer construction and the cleaning up of estuaries and toxic "hot spots" and for other purposes. Reagan said the bill was "loaded with waste and larded with pork."

Feb 19: Trade sanctions against Poland were lifted by Pres. Reagan after the Communist regime freed political prisoners. The action removed the ban on trade credits and restored Poland's "most favored nation" status for export-import purposes.

Feb 26: The **Tower Commission report** on the Iran-Contra affair was critical of Pres. Reagan for failing to understand or control the secret attempt to trade arms to Iran for the release of American hostages being held in Lebanon that ended with profits from the sale being improperly diverted to the Nicaraguan Contras. The commission, appointed by the president in Nov. 1986, said Reagan must take responsibility for the policy, which ended in "chaos" and caused the U.S. much embarrassment abroad. Blame was placed also on Donald T. Regan, the White House chief of staff, whom the president replaced with former Senator Howard H. Baker, Jr., on Feb. 27. In a television address on Mar. 4, the president said he took "full responsibility," but he did not admit that the plan for dealing with Iran was basically wrong.

Apr 27: Kurt Waldheim will not be allowed to enter the U.S., the Justice Dept. announced. The president of Austria and former secretary general of the United Nations was banned because he had "participated in activities amounting to persecution" of Jews and others while he was serving with the German army in the Balkans from 1942 to 1945. Waldheim was the first head of state ever put on a list of persons excluded from the U.S.

May 17: A missile attack on a U.S. frigate in the Persian Gulf killed 37 sailors and badly damaged the USS *Stark*. An Iraqi warplane fired two missiles by mistake and Iraq apologized for the attack. On July 22 U.S. warships began escorting Kuwaiti tankers re-registered under the American flag through the gulf to protect them from possible Iranian attacks. On Sept. 22 an American helicopter attacked and dam-

aged an Iranian minelayer, and on Oct. 19 U.S. naval
forces shelled two offshore installations in retaliation
for Iranian attacks on Persian Gulf shipping.

Aug 16: The **crash of a Northwest Airlines jet** on takeoff from the Detroit Metropolitan Airport killed 156
of the 157 persons on board. The only survivor was
a four-year-old girl, who was injured but recovered.
On May 10, 1988, a federal investigative report
blamed the crash on the failure of the two pilots to
follow required checklist procedures before takeoff.

Oct 1: A **severe earthquake** shook the Los Angeles
area, killing at least 8 people and injuring more than
100. It was the strongest quake in the region since
1971 and registered 6.1 on the Richter scale. Glass fell
from skyscraper windows and in Whittier 30 buildings collapsed.

Oct 23: The **Senate rejected the nomination of Robert
H. Bork** to the Supreme Court by a vote of 58–42.
Bork, a member of the federal Appeals Court in
Washington, had been nominated by Pres. Reagan to
fill the vacancy caused by the resignation of Justice
Lewis F. Powell, Jr., on July 1. Lobbying against Bork
by many liberal groups, who accused him of extreme
right-wing views on issues of civil rights and individ-
ual privacy, was intense. After two weeks of hearings
in September, the Senate Judiciary Committee on
Oct. 6 voted to recommend rejection of the nomination by a 9–5 tally. On Oct. 29 Reagan nominated
Douglas H. Ginsburg, also an Appeals Court judge.
Ginsburg withdrew on Nov. 7 after charges of a conflict of interest in the past and the admission that he
used marijuana while teaching at Harvard Law
School. The president then nominated Anthony
Kennedy, a federal judge in California, on Nov. 11.
Finally, on Feb. 3, 1988, the Senate unanimously con-
firmed Kennedy by a vote of 97–0.

Nov 15: Taking off in a snowstorm, a **Continental
Airlines jet crashed** at Denver's Stapleton Airport,
flipping over and breaking into three pieces. Of the 81
persons aboard, 28 were killed and more than 50
injured.

Nov 18: The **Congressional committees' report on the**

Iran-Contra affair blamed Pres. Reagan for failing in his constitutional duty and said he bore "the ultimate responsibility" for the wrongdoing of his aides. The committees' 690-page report also said "the rule of law was subverted" and that if the president did not know what his national security advisers were up to, he should have. The report provided the most complete accounting to date of what became of the nearly $48,000,000 that was raised by the sale of arms to Iran. The two committees had held joint hearings from May 5 to Aug. 15, during which they heard more than 250 hours of testimony from 28 witnesses. The chief witnesses were John M. Poindexter, national security adviser at the time of the affair, and his assistant, Lt. Col. Oliver L. North. The latter was briefly somewhat of a hero, with his gung-ho defense of his actions, which, in his view, had put his patriotic duty above the law.

Nov 20: Pres. Reagan and Congressional leaders agreed on **a plan to reduce the federal budget deficit** by $30,000,000,000 for the fiscal year that had begun on Oct. 1 and by $46,000,000,000 in the following year. On Dec. 22 Reagan signed budget bills totalling $603,900,000,000, a record that would presumably reduce the deficit by $3,400,000,000 more than previously agreed on.

Nov 21: **A federal prison riot** at Oakdale, La., by about 1000 Cuban refugees being held for possible deportation began with the seizure of 30 hostages. On Nov. 23 a similar group of 1392 detainees at the federal prison in Atlanta, Ga., also took action, seizing the prison and 75 hostages. The detainees were aroused by reports of a new agreement between the U.S. and Cuba whereby Cuba would take back more than 2000 "undesirables." After negotiations and without violence, the riot ended at Oakdale on Nov. 29 and at Atlanta on Dec. 4. The detainees were assured they would receive individual and full reviews of their status. By late Apr. 1988, 1153 of the detainees had been released, ten times more than in the previous five months.

Dec 8: The **first treaty that would reduce nuclear arse-**

nals was signed in Washington by Pres. Reagan and
General Secretary Mikhail S. Gorbachev of the
U.S.S.R. Under the terms of the treaty 2611 U.S. and
Soviet medium- and short-range missiles sited in
Europe would be destroyed. The pact provided for
on-site verification in both countries. The agreement
was seen as a first step toward agreement on the re-
duction of U.S. and Soviet long-range missiles.

Dec 16: Michael K. Deaver was found guilty on three
of five counts of perjury stemming from his lobbying
activities after he left the position of aide to Pres.
Reagan. He had been tried on charges of having lied
to a House subcommittee about efforts to arrange a
meeting between the president and a South Korean
trade representative and also of having lied to a federal grand jury. At the base of Deaver's troubles were
accusations that he violated the 1978 Ethics in Government Act, which regulates lobbying by former
government officials. White House deputy chief of
staff until May 1985, Deaver was the highest-ranking
Reagan administration official to be convicted of a
crime.

Dec 22: Aid to the **Nicaraguan Contras** of $14,000,000
for nonlethal use was approved by Pres. Reagan
when he signed a bill just passed by Congress as a
compromise with the executive branch.

II. Architecture
   Arts and Music
   Popular Entertainment
   Publishing
   Theater

Successful Broadway musicals were bigger, if not
better, than ever. *Les Misérables* (from England) had
advance ticket sales (some as high as $50) of
$11,000,000, and *Starlight Express,* a show whose
main features were its setting and gadgetry, cost
$8,000,000 to stage, a record. The only successful
drama was *Fences* by August Wilson. The movies provided a varied fare, including such comedies as *Three
Men and a Baby, Raising Arizona,* and *Moonstruck.*
Full Metal Jacket and *Good Morning, Vietnam* con-

cerned the war there. Also popular and worthy were *Broadcast News, The Last Emperor,* and *Empire of the Sun.* An unusual art exhibit opened in March in Leningrad, displaying 116 works by the three Wyeths—N.C., son Andrew, and grandson James. As another sign, perhaps, of more cordial relations between the U.S. and the U.S.S.R., a temporary exchange of masterpieces was arranged with the National Gallery of Art, sending an El Greco to the Hermitage in Leningrad, which in turn sent a Titian to Washington. Back home in Philadelphia, the Museum of Art staged the largest display of Chinese ceramic sculpture ever seen outside China, and in New York the Metropolitan Museum held the most important exhibit ever to come out of Israel, "Treasures of the Holy Land: Ancient Art from the Israel Museum." Both these exhibits were to go to Houston and Los Angeles. In North Adams, Mass., 28 vacant factory buildings were about to be taken over to house one of the largest collections of contemporary art, on loan from Count Giuseppe Pahza di Biumo. On the West Coast, Norton Simon, the industrialist, and the University of California at Los Angeles reached an agreement calling for the transfer of the large art collections owned by Simon to the school. The gift was said to be worth $750,000,000. At auction, artworks by Americans commanded higher prices than ever: a Georgia O'Keefe work selling for $1,900,000, a record for the artist; an Elie Nadelman sculpture going for $2,000,000; a Willem de Kooning painting bringing $3,600,000; and a George Caleb Bingham oil topping all with a reported price of $6,000,000 in a private sale. The American Ballet Theater sold $6,200,000 worth of tickets for its new production of *Sleeping Beauty,* but the dancers of the Dallas Ballet had to raise $500,000 or else disband. Publishing mergers continued to make news. In March media tycoon Rupert Murdoch, who owned newspapers and book publishing houses in Britain, Australia, and the U.S., acquired Harper & Row for $300,000,000. In June British publishing entrepreneur and corporate raider Robert Maxwell attempted to buy Harcourt Brace Jovanovich for $1,730,000,000, but HBJ fought back with a reorganization plan that saved the company from Maxwell but burdened it with an enormous debt. The circulation of daily newspapers dropped by a slight 0.4% and the number of papers from 1676 to 1657. In July it was estimated that 43,260,000 U.S. households, 49.5% of the total, had cable TV. This was an increase of about 2,000,000 in a year. Noteworthy persons who died included Fred Astaire, the popular dancer, June 22, at 88; the actress Mary Astor, Sept. 25, at 81; Bil Baird, master puppeteer, Mar. 18, at 82; James Baldwin, whose writings spurred the civil rights movement, Dec. 1, at 63; Michael Bennett, Broadway choreographer and winner of eight Tony Awards, July 2, at 44; Ray Bolger, actor best known as the Scarecrow in the movie *The Wizard of Oz*, Jan. 15, at 83; James Burnham, founding editor of the conservative *National Review*, July 28, at 82; Erskine Caldwell, author of novels about the South, such as *Tobacco Road*, Apr. 11, at 83; Jackie Gleason, comedian whose TV show of the 1950s, *The Honeymooners*, developed a cult following, June 24, at 71; Rita Hayworth, glamorous movie star, May 14, at 68; Jascha Heifetz, violin virtuoso, Dec. 10, at 86; Woody Herman, popular leader of big bands, Oct. 29, at 74; John Huston, noted movie director, Aug. 28, at 81; Danny Kaye, comedian, dancer, and singer, Mar. 3, at 74; Nora Kaye, ballerina who created a new, contemporary look among dancers, Feb. 28, at 67; Sammy Kaye, popular musician noted for the music of his "sweet bands," June 2, at 77; Mervyn LeRoy, who directed 75 films over 40 years, including *Little Caesar*, Sept. 13, at 86; Clare Boothe Luce, sharp-tongued playwright, ambassador, and politician, Oct. 9, at 84; Rouben Mamoulian, director of *Porgy and Bess* and *Oklahoma!* for the stage and of inventive films, Dec. 4, at 90; Pola Negri, exotic vamp of the movies of the 1920s and 1930s, Aug. 1, at 88; Geraldine Page, stage and screen actress, June 13, at 62; Andrés Segovia, who restored the guitar to top rank in classical music, June 2, at 94; Myron Stout, abstract artist of minimal black and white compositions, Aug. 2, at 79; Antony Tudor, who introduced psychological motivation in his choreography, Apr.

20, at 78 or 79; Andy Warhol, founder of Pop Art, Feb. 22, at 58; Glenway Wescott, novelist, acclaimed at age 26 for *The Grandmothers,* Feb. 22, at 85; and Marguerite Yourcenar, author, holder of dual French and U.S. citizenship, known particularly for *Memoirs of Hadrian,* an imaginary autobiography, and for being the first woman elected to the Académie Française, Dec. 17, at 84.

Among **books published** this year, most talked about novels were Toni Morrison's *Beloved,* the story of a woman escaped from slavery, and Tom Wolfe's *The Bonfire of the Vanities,* an account of a New York yuppie in big trouble. Other important novels were *The Counterlife,* the fourth in Philip Roth's Zuckerman series, and *Crossing to Safety,* Wallace Stegner's account of the friendship of two couples. The most popular suspense and thriller entries were *Patriot Games* by Tom Clancy and *Presumed Innocent* by Scott Turow. Among autobiographical works were *Man of the House* by former Speaker Thomas P. O'Neill, Jr., and *Trump: The Art of the Deal* by the successful New York real estate developer, Donald Trump. Two conservative critics of American education had their say in *The Closing of the American Mind* by Allan Bloom and *Cultural Literacy* by E. D. Hirsch, Jr.

Mar 30: Acquisition of the **Arturo Toscanini Archives** was announced by the New York Public Library. The large collection of scores, recordings, letters, and memorabilia of the late conductor, valued at $2,000,000, had been inaccessible since 1970 while negotiations went on.

Apr 6: The first American to win the **Ritz Paris Hemingway Award,** worth $50,000, was Peter Taylor for his novel *A Summons to Memphis.*

Apr 7: The **National Museum of Women in the Arts** opened in Washington, D.C., the first museum devoted entirely to women artists. It already held more than 500 examples of such art from the Renaissance to the 20th century. Some feminists felt it would segregate women's artistic work rather than promoting it.

Apr 16: Pulitzer prizes were awarded for the following: fiction, *A Summons to Memphis* by Peter Taylor; general nonfiction, *Arab and Jew: Wounded Spirits in a Promised Land* by David K. Shipler; biography, *Bearing the Cross: Martin Luther King, Jr., and the Southern Christian Leadership Conference* by David J. Garrow; history, *Voyagers to the West: A Passage in the Peopling of America on the Eve of the Revolution* by Bernard Bailyn; poetry, *Thomas and Beulah* by Rita Dove; drama, *Fences* by August Wilson.

Apr 17: Richard Wilbur was appointed the second **poet laureate** of the U.S. by the Librarian of Congress.

Sep 14: A new method of **measuring TV audiences** was introduced by the A. C. Nielsen Co., which for 20 years had relied on a system of diaries kept by a sampling of households. The new system featured "people meters," which registered opinion by viewers' pushing buttons. Early results of the new method made the TV networks unhappy, as it seemed to register fewer viewers than the diary system.

Sep 28: Two new museums opened in Washington, D.C., as part of the Smithsonian Institution. One was the National Museum of African Art, which had existed since 1964 but was now greatly expanded; the other was the all-new Arthur M. Sackler Museum for Asian and Near East Art. The museums, 96% underground, were on three levels and cost $73,000,000. They exhibited 6000 objects of African and 2500 of Asian art.

Oct 22: The **Nobel Prize for Literature** was awarded to Joseph Brodsky, Soviet-born exile, now a citizen of the U.S. A poet and essayist, in both English and Russian, Brodsky at 47 was the second youngest to win this award.

Nov 11: The **highest price ever paid for a painting**, $53,900,000, was bid at auction in New York for *Irises* by Vincent Van Gogh. The painting had been owned by John Whitney Payson, a member of a wealthy family. Some of the proceeds were to go to the Payson Foundation and to Westbrook College, Portland, Me. *Irises* was painted in 1889 soon after Van Gogh entered the asylum at Saint-Rémy, France.

III. Business and Industry
Education
Philosophy and Religion
Science

In spite of staging in October the greatest stock market crash in history, the national economy had a more or less successful year. Unemployment was down to 5.7%, the lowest since mid-1979, and the GNP rose 3.8%, increasing for the sixth consecutive year. On the other hand, the CPI was up 4.4%, the highest rate of inflation since 1981, and the trade deficit, at $171,220,000,000, set a record for the fifth year in a row, although the December deficit was the lowest in 11 months. The dollar weakened, ending the year at 121.05 to the Japanese yen, down 23% compared with the previous year end. Black-owned industrial and service businesses set a record, with $4,100,000,000 of sales. The TLC group, an investment concern, with $1,800,000,000 in sales, became the first such minority concern to pass the $1,000,000,000 mark. The recorded-music business prospered again. Unit sales of compact discs were up 93% to 102,000,000, with a value of $1,600,000,000. Sales of cassette tapes rose 19% to 410,000,000, worth about $2,900,000,000. However, sales of record albums and LPs declined 15% to 107,000,000, worth $793,000,000. *Forbes* magazine declared that Sam Moore Walton, 69, the founder of the Wal-Mart discount stores, was, for the third year in a row, the richest American, worth $8,500,000,000. But Albert J. Lowry, former supermarket butcher who had written widely on how to become a millionaire by dealing in real estate, filed for bankruptcy. During the year 30 states, compared with only five in 1983, appropriated money to fight the disease AIDS, and one estimate of what it would cost to battle AIDS nationwide in 1991 was $8,500,000,000. A report from the federal government said 40,000,000 Americans had blood cholesterol high enough to put them at risk of heart disease. The Mathematical Science Education Board found that, compared with 21 other countries, the achievement of American students was "lackluster." In 1987,

17% of college students were from minority groups, which comprise 21% of the U.S. population. Among notable persons who died were I. W. Abel, a founder of the United Steel Workers of America and its president from 1965 to 1977, Aug. 10, at 78; Walter H. Brattain, cowinner of the 1956 Nobel Prize in Physics for the invention of the transistor, Oct. 13, at 85; Henry Ford II, grandson of the founder of the giant automaking company, whose management brought the concern back from a sharp decline, Sept. 29, at 70; and Walter W. Heller, economic adviser to presidents Kennedy and Johnson, June 15, at 71.

Mar 19: The Rev. **Jim Bakker,** a successful TV evangelist, resigned his ministry, admitting that he had an extramarital sexual encounter with a church secretary seven years earlier. The founder of PTL (Praise the Lord, or People That Love) said he had paid what he called blackmail to the woman involved. His wife, Tammy, had also been active in the ministry and had her own line of cosmetics for sale. PTL operated a $172,000,000, 2300-acre theme park, Heritage USA, in Fort Mill, S.C., and in 1986 Bakker was paid $1,600,000 in salary and bonuses. On May 6 the Assemblies of God dismissed Bakker as a minister. On June 12 the new management of PTL filed for bankruptcy, noting $71,000,000 of debt, and on Feb. 1, 1988, sued Bakker for $52,800,000, charging mismanagement and unjustified compensation.

Mar 20: The **first drug to benefit AIDS patients** was approved by the federal government. The drug was azidothymidine, or AZT, and while it would not cure AIDS, tests showed it would let victims of the disease live longer. Because AZT could have severe side effects, its use was to be limited to selected categories of patients, totalling about 15,000. The drug was estimated to cost as much as $10,000 per patient per year. On Aug. 18 the Food and Drug Administration approved the trial use, for the first time in humans, of a possible AIDS vaccine. Similar tests were already being carried out in France. The test vaccine used a protein, CD4, that seemed to attract the AIDS virus, thus preventing it from entering nearby body cells.

Apr 4: Introduced by the nation's Roman Catholic

bishops, a **New Testament avoids the use of the word "man"** when the reference is to both men and women. A passage that read "Not on bread alone is man to live" had been changed to "One does not live by bread alone." Known as the Revised New Testament of the American Bible, it was now the authorized version for America's 50,000,000 Catholics.

Apr 16: The **patenting of new forms of animal life** created through gene splicing would be allowed, the federal government announced. The U.S. was the first country to take such a step. The policy allowed the patenting of animals with new traits created by recently devised reproductive technologies, including genetic engineering. Specifically banned was the patenting of new genetic characteristics in human beings.

Apr 27: The **largest U.S. corporation** in 1986, according to *Fortune* magazine, was General Motors, with sales of $102,813,700,000. Second was Exxon, whose sales were $69,888,000,000.

Apr 28: In the **third-largest U.S. takeover deal,** Standard Oil agreed to sell to British Petroleum for $7,800,000,000 the 45% of Standard not already owned by BP. The deal made BP the third-largest oil company in the world, behind Exxon and the Royal Dutch/Shell Group.

May 12: A **three-way heart and lung transplant,** believed to be a medical first, was performed in Baltimore, Md. A healthy heart was taken from a living person and transplanted to another. The heart donor then received the heart and lungs of an accident victim who had died in a nearby hospital. On May 14 a spokesman for a British hospital said similar operations had been performed there the last week in April and the first week in May.

June 2: A **new chairman of the Federal Reserve Board,** economist Alan Greenspan, was named by Pres. Ronald Reagan. He succeeded Paul A. Volcker, who had held the post for eight years and who was noted for the strong measures he had taken to quell the high inflation in the economy when he took office. In financial markets, where it had been expected Volcker would serve a third term, there was a sharp drop in bond prices. Greenspan, who had worked in both business and government, was known for his free-market sympathies and was not expected to change noticeably the policies Volcker had followed.

June 19: Teaching the **creationist theory** of human origin may not be required in public schools alongside the theory of evolution when the intent is to promote religious belief, according to the Supreme Court. Thus, by a 7–2 vote, the Court held unconstitutional a Louisiana law of 1984. The decision was seen as a serious blow to the efforts of fundamentalist Christians to mold public school curriculums to fit their beliefs.

June 30: By adopting the declaration **"Judaism has not been superseded by Christianity,"** The United Church of Christ became the first major U.S. Protestant denomination to so affirm the position of the Jewish religion. The declaration, adopted at the convention of the church in Cleveland, Ohio, also stated "God has not rejected the Jewish people."

Aug 25: On the New York Stock Exchange a **new record, 2722.42, was set by the Dow Jones industrial average.** The Dow had closed above the 2000 mark, at 2002.25, for the first time on Jan. 8. On Jan. 15 the exchange had set a new record for volume with 253,100,000 shares traded. On Sept. 22 the Dow Jones average scored its largest one-day gain, 75.23 points.

Sep 5-7: Infant **twins joined at the head** were separated in a lengthy and unusual operation at the Johns Hopkins University Hospital in Baltimore, Md. Metal plates were implanted over the skull holes caused by the operation. On Apr. 7, 1988, the hospital announced the twins would be discharged in a few days to return to West Germany, where they were born. They suffered some brain damage and might have vision problems but otherwise seemed likely to lead normal lives.

Oct 12: The **Nobel Prize in Medicine** was awarded to Susumu Tonegawa, a Japanese scientist working at the Massachusetts Institute of Technology. He had discovered how the human body marshals its immunological defenses against many different diseases it has never met before. Dr. Tonegawa was the first Japanese to win the Nobel Prize in this category.

Oct 14: The **Nobel Prize in Chemistry** was awarded jointly to Donald J. Cram of the University of California at Los Angeles, Charles J. Pedersen, formerly a research chemist with E. I. du Pont de Nemours & Co., and Jean-Marie Lehn, a French professor of chemistry. The three had carried out varied researches that included the creation of artificial molecules that mimic vital chemical reactions of life processes.

Oct 16: A baby only three hours old became the **youngest person to undergo a heart transplant.** The operation was performed at the Linda Loma (Calif.) Medical Center after the baby was delivered by Caesarean section. The donor of the heart was an infant who had been declared legally dead a few days earlier.

Oct 19: The **worst stock crash** in the history of the New York Stock Exchange occurred when the Dow Jones industrial average fell 508 points, closing at 1738.74, a decline of 22.6%, nearly double the decline in 1929 that ushered in the Great Depression. The volume of stocks traded, 604,330,000, was nearly twice the previous record of 338,500,000, set on Oct. 16. Computerized program trading, as well as various factors in the national and international economy, was blamed for the collapse of a market that had exhibited a case of the jitters in recent weeks. On Oct. 20 the Dow Jones rose 102.27 points and trading set another new record for volume with 608,120,000 shares traded. In spite of the gain, largely confined to blue chip issues, many more stocks fell than rose. The Dow gained another 186 points the following day but dropped 77.42 points on Oct. 22. The major markets set temporarily shorter hours in hopes of easing the tension, but on Oct. 26 there was another drop of 156.83 points. After a short period of relative quiet, the Dow fell 50.56 on Nov. 3, ending a five-day rally, and on Nov. 9 the average was down another 58.85 points, closing at 1900.20.

Oct 21: The **Nobel Prize in Economics** was awarded to Robert M. Solow of the Massachusetts Institute of Technology for his contributions to the theory of economic growth.

Nov 20: An agreement to reduce the **federal budget deficit** by $30,000,000,000 in the fiscal year that began on Oct. 1 was reached by Pres. Reagan and Congressional leaders after four weeks of complicated and sometimes rancorous negotiations, spurred by the stock market debacle of Oct. 19. Legislation would be required to make the agreement effective. Among steps to be taken were a reduction of $6,600,000,000 in domestic spending and a $5,000,000,000 cut in the defense budget.

Dec 2: A **free trade agreement** was signed by Pres. Reagan and Prime Minister Brian Mulroney of Canada. The pact, which included a mechanism for settling disputes, would eliminate tariffs and lower other trade barriers by the end of the century. All agricultural tariffs would be dropped within ten years. Approval by the legislative bodies of both countries was required before the agreement takes effect.

Dec 10: **Teaching about the use of condoms** in the battle against the disease AIDS was given qualified support by the Roman Catholic bishops of the U.S. in spite of the church's opposition to birth control. The bishops' position paper called on all Catholic schools to teach AIDS prevention.

Dec 11: To cover possible claims resulting from the use of the **Dalkon Shield birth control device,** a federal judge ordered the A. H. Robins Co., producer of the IUD, to establish a fund of $2,475,000,000 as part of its reorganization plan. The company had filed for bankruptcy in Aug. 1985 because of the thousands of claims against it by women who said they became infertile or suffered injuries as a result of using the shield. About 9500 women had already received compensation.

Dec 19: In the **largest cash settlement in U.S. corporate history,** Texaco agreed to pay Pennzoil $3,000,000,000 to settle a bitter lawsuit. In 1985 a Texas court had ordered Texaco to pay $10,100,000,000, plus interest, to Pennzoil for having illegally interfered with the latter's attempt to take over the Getty Oil Co. In its battle to overturn this decision, and in its very unfriendly negotiations to reach a less costly settlement with Pennzoil, Texaco filed for bankruptcy on Apr. 12, 1987. The agreed-upon settlement was paid to Pennzoil on Apr. 7, 1988. That same day Texaco ended 361 days in bankruptcy. On Apr. 15 Texaco, announcing it would sell at least $5,000,000,000 of its assets to recover its financial strength, said it would resume paying a quarterly dividend.

Dec 31: The **Dow Jones** average of industrial stocks closed the year at 1938.83. Although it was off 29% from its August peak, it was up 2.26% for the year in spite of the shattering crash of Oct. 19.

IV. Fashion
   Folkways
   Holidays
   Social Issues and Crime
   Sports

As in other years, Americans faced new problems, tried new or unusual things, set records, committed crimes. A commercial for condoms, a protection against the disease AIDS, first appeared on TV in a major market on Jan. 16, on KRON in San Francisco. Detroit and Indianapolis TV channels soon followed suit. In California an epidemic of random shooting at vehicles on its freeways resulted in four deaths, 16 injuries, and increased highway patrolling. Manufacturers, the Justice Department, and the Consumer Products Safety Commission agreed to a ban on the sale of three-wheeled all-terrain vehicles (ATVs), blamed for about 900 deaths since the early 1980s. Bob Barker, host for 20 years of the Miss Universe Pageant and an animal rights activist, refused to emcee this year's affair unless the contestants wore fake rather than real furs. In a case begun in California, where a wife can be entitled to half of an estate, the Supreme Court let stand a divorce settlement of $76,000,000 against Sheik Mohammed al-Fassi. In the suburbs the now adult baby boomers were interested in backyard gardening. Sales of lawn and garden materials and equipment reached $17,490,000,000, an increase of 47% since 1983. In fashion, for men of all ages there was good news, and for older women, bad: the miniskirt was back for the first time since the early 1970s. Many women refused to exhibit their thighs, and this time, more than before, the mini raised the question of appropriate wear at work for women aspiring to reach the executive suite. Noteworthy people who died included Wayne W. "Woody" Hayes, successful football coach at Ohio State, Mar. 12, at 74; Richard D. "Dick" Howser, baseball player and manager who led the Kansas City Royals to their only World Series victory, in 1985, June 18, at 51; Travis Jackson, shortstop for the New York Giants for 15 years and a member of the Baseball Hall of Fame, July 27, at 83; Thomas G. Lanphier, Jr., who in World War II shot down the plane carrying Adm. Isoroku Yamamoto, commander of the Japanese navy, Nov. 26, at 71; and William M. Masland, who in 1943 commanded the first round-the-world flight by a commercial aircraft, Feb. 20, at 79.

Jan 1-2: In **college football bowl games,** the results were Ohio State 28, Texas A&M 12 in the Cotton Bowl; Oklahoma 42, Arkansas 8 in the Orange Bowl; Arizona State 22, Michigan 15 in the Rose Bowl; and Nebraska 30, Louisiana State 15 in the Sugar Bowl. Both the AP and UPI polls chose Penn State as national champion for 1986 after Pennsylvania's Nittany Lions, in a battle of previously undefeated teams, triumphed over Miami (Fla.) 14–10 in the Fiesta Bowl on Jan. 2.

Jan 13: One of the **most successful prosecutions of organized crime figures** resulted in the conviction of eight key men, called "the board of directors." Seven of the Mafia leaders were given 100-year sentences in federal court. On Jan. 16 nine other racketeers were given shorter terms.

Jan 25: Super Bowl XXI was won by the New York Giants (NFC), defeating the Denver Broncos (AFC) 39–20. On Jan. 11, the Giants had won the NFC title by defeating the Washington Redskins 17–0 and Denver had won the AFC championship by defeating the Cleveland Browns 23–20 in overtime.

Jan 31-Feb 4: The **America's Cup** was regained by the

U.S. when the American challenger *Stars & Stripes*, skippered by Dennis Connor of San Diego, Calif., defeated the Australian yacht *Kookaburra III* in four straight races at Fremantle, Australia. Connor, the losing skipper in 1983, thus became the first American skipper to lose and regain the yachting trophy.

Feb 24: A **world record ice-fishing catch** was made by Omer J. Lebel of Van Buren, Me., when he caught a brook trout weighing 8 lbs., 4 oz.

Feb 25: The NCAA ruled that **Southern Methodist U.** could not field a football team this year because athletic officials had violated NCAA rules by paying about $61,000 to players. This, the stiffest penalty ever imposed on a football program, also provided that in 1988 SMU could play only seven games, all away from home and thus earning no revenue for SMU.

Feb 26: Michael Spinks was **stripped of his IBF heavyweight championship.** The action was taken because he failed to defend his title within nine months of winning the crown from Larry Holmes on Apr. 19, 1986, thus failing to live up to IBF rules.

Mar 7: The **combined WBA and WBC heavyweight boxing championship** was won by Mike Tyson, who defeated James "Bonecrusher" Smith by a unanimous decision in a 15-round bout at Las Vegas, Nev.

Mar 28: Setting a new **college basketball attendance record** before 64,959 fans, Indiana defeated the U. of Nevada, Las Vegas, 97–93 in the semifinals of the NCAA championship in the New Orleans Superdome.

Mar 29: The **NCAA women's basketball championship,** held in Austin, Tex., was won by Tennessee over Louisiana Tech 67–44.

Mar 30: The **NCAA men's basketball championship** was won by Indiana, defeating Syracuse 74–73. Hoosier guard Calvin Smith was voted the outstanding player among the final four teams.

Mar 31: After a grueling and precedent-setting legal battle, **custody of a baby born to a surrogate mother** was awarded to the father. Baby M, as the girl was known during the trial before a New Jersey judge, was born Mar. 27, 1986, the result of the artificial insemination of Mary Beth Whitehead by William Stern. Stern and his wife, Elizabeth, agreed to pay the mother $10,000 and she in turn would relinquish all rights to the child. Mrs. Whitehead, however, refused to give up the baby, and a suit brought by the Sterns to enforce the contract began on Jan. 5, 1987. Saying he was creating law, the judge in his decision upheld the legality of such a surrogate agreement and stripped the mother of all parental rights. On Feb. 3, 1988, however, the Supreme Court of New Jersey ruled unanimously that commercial surrogate motherhood contracts were illegal. It was the first ruling by a state's highest court in such a case and would probably influence courts and legislatures in other states. The Baby M dispute went back to a lower court, and on Apr. 6, 1988, the mother was granted broad rights to see the child, although the Sterns retained custody.

Apr 12: The **Masters golf tournament** was won by Larry Mize on the second hole of a three-way playoff, when he sank a 50-yard wedge shot to defeat Greg Norman and Seve Ballesteros.

Apr 18: An **unconscious sky diver was rescued** by another jumper. Debbie Williams was knocked out by colliding with another sky diver. Noticing her plight, Gregory Robertson dived to reach her and yanked open her ripcord when she was less than 3500 ft. from the ground. Williams was seriously injured, but Robertson resumed sky diving the same day.

May 2: The 113th **Kentucky Derby** was won by Alysheba, with a time of 2:03²/₅. The jockey was Chris McCarron.

May 3: The **richest prize in PGA tour history,** $225,000, was won by Paul Azinger when he captured the Panasonic Las Vegas golf tournament. In addition, Scott Hoch received a $118,299 Rolls-Royce for a hole-in-one at the 17th hole.

May 4: Women must be admitted to Rotary Clubs, hitherto all male, the Supreme Court ruled, 7–0. On

July 4 the Lions Club International voted to admit women and on July 7 Kiwanis International followed suit.

May 10-18: The **NHL Stanley Cup** championship was won by the Edmonton Oilers, who beat the Philadelphia Flyers four games to three.

May 14: An **1873 Colt revolver sold for $242,000,** a record, at auction. The single-action, .45-caliber weapon was the first six-shooter of the type known as the "Peacemaker" and the most famous gun ever produced in the U.S. The revolver was discovered in a New Hampshire farmhouse in 1925 and bought from the widow of an army major for $4.

May 16: The 112th **Preakness Stakes** was won by Alysheba, with a time of 1:55⁴/₅. The jockey was Chris McCarron.

May 24: A record **10,000th winning harness race** was won by Hervé Filion, a French-Canadian driver, at Yonkers Raceway, N.Y.

May 24: The 71st **Indianapolis 500 auto race** was won by Al Unser, completing the 500-mi. course in 3 hrs., 4 min., 59.147 sec. In winning this race for the fourth time, Unser became the oldest Indy winner, five days short of his 48th birthday.

June 2-14: The **NBA basketball championship** was won by the Los Angeles Lakers over the Boston Celtics four games to two.

June 4: The **longest winning streak in track history** ended when Edwin Moses lost a 400-m. hurdles race in Madrid to Danny Harris, another American. Moses had won 122 consecutive races, his last loss coming on Aug. 26, 1977, when he was beaten by Harald Schmid of West Germany. Moses holds the world record of 47.02 sec. for the 400-m. hurdle event.

June 6: The **119th Belmont Stakes** was won by Bet Twice by 14 lengths, with a time of 2:28²/₅. The jockey was Craig Perret. In addition, Bet Twice won $1,000,000 in the first Triple Crown participation bonus. Bet Twice finished second in both the Kentucky Derby and the Preakness Stakes. Alysheba had won those two races but finished fourth in the Belmont. On a 5-3-1 point basis, Bet Twice earned 11 points to Alysheba's 10. Had one horse won all three races, and thereby the Triple Crown, the bonus would have been $5,000,000.

June 15: In a bout promoted as deciding the **heavyweight championship,** Michael Spinks knocked out Gerry Cooney in the fifth round of a scheduled 15-round fight. The WBA and the WBC said they would not recognize the winner as champion, but several state boxing commissions said they would.

June 16: For the first time in a single meet, **three long jumpers cleared 28 ft.,** at the USA/Mobil Outdoor Track and Field Championships at San Jose, Calif. The winner, with a jump of 28 ft., 4½ in., was Carl Lewis. He thus extended his winning streak in track and field to 50 in six years. Lewis also won the 200-m. dash.

June 21: The **U.S. Open golf tournament** was won by Scott Simpson, who defeated Tom Watson by one stroke.

June 23: The **oldest living Olympic medalist in the U.S.** celebrated his 95th birthday by jogging along Fifth Ave. in New York City. He was Abel Kiviat, who won the silver medal in the 1500-m. race at the 1912 Olympics. He once held the records for 600 yards, 1000 yards, and the mile, all at the same time.

July 21: Lady's Secret became the **richest filly or mare in racing history** when she won a race at Monmouth Park, Oceanport, N.J. The victory brought total winnings to $3,015,764, surpassing the record set by All Along. Lady's Secret was sired by Secretariat, the Triple Crown winner in 1973.

July 22: Television sports fans favored pro football over baseball, the second most popular sport among watchers, according to a 1986 survey by Simmons Market Research. Pro football was watched frequently by 63,200,000 people, with baseball close behind at 62,700,000. The two leaders were followed by college football, 48,900,000; boxing, 37,200,000; and college basketball, 36,200,000.

July 29: The Dallas Cowboys became the first NFL

team to **test its personnel for AIDS.** The testing was described as voluntary and the results as confidential. All tests administered were reported to be negative.

Aug 1: Mary R. Stout, a former U.S. Army nurse, became the **first woman to head a national veterans' organization.** She was elected president of the Vietnam Veterans of America, which had 35,000 members, only about 300 of whom were women.

Aug 1: The unified **heavyweight boxing championship** was won by Mike Tyson, who earned a unanimous 12-round decision over Tony Tucker at Las Vegas, Nev. Tyson held the World Boxing Association and World Boxing Council titles, and Tucker was the champion of the International Boxing Federation. Tyson thus became the first undisputed titleholder since Feb. 1978, when Leon Spinks beat Muhammad Ali.

Aug 2: In the **fastest race in Indy car history,** Michael Andretti won the Marlboro 500 at Michigan International Speedway in Brooklyn, Mich., with an average speed of 171.490 mph. This bettered the mark of 170.722 mph set by Bobby Rahal when he won the Indianapolis 500 in 1986. One of the drivers who lost to Andretti was his father, Mario.

Aug 8-23: At the tenth **Pan-American Games,** in Indianapolis, Ind., the U.S. won 369 medals, including 168 gold medals. Cuba was second with 75 gold medals and 175 in all, and Canada was third with 30 and 162. For the U.S., track star Jackie Joyner-Kersee tied the world record for the long jump at 24 ft., 5.5 in., and Jeff Kubiak set a record for the games of 2 min., 17.62 sec. in the 200-m. breaststroke.

Aug 9: The **PGA championship** was won by Larry Nelson, who defeated Lanny Wadkins on the first hole of a sudden death playoff. The two had tied at 287 for the four rounds, only one under par, the highest winning score since the event became a stroke-play, 72-hole tournament in 1958.

Aug 16: The **tenth anniversary of the death of Elvis Presley,** rock-and-roll idol, was marked by the pilgrimage of 20,000 or so fans to his home, Graceland, in Memphis, Tenn. Carrying lighted candles, the singer's worshippers gathered at his grave, where a spotlight shone on a statue of Jesus Christ.

Aug 18: Donald Harvey, 35, was **found guilty of killing 24 people** since 1983 by a jury in Ohio. Of them 21 died, mostly by poison, in a Cincinnati hospital where he was an orderly. Harvey was sentenced to three consecutive life terms.

Aug 27: Edward W. Gillet, 36, **paddled a kayak alone from California to Hawaii,** arriving at Kahului after 63 days at sea. He left Monterey on June 25 expecting to make the 2200-mile crossing in 40 days. He ran out of food four days before landing and lost 25 pounds on the voyage.

Aug 29: Little League baseball celebrated the 40th anniversary of its world series. It claims 2,500,000 participants in 16,000 chartered programs. The world championship was won by Hua Lian, the Tai-wanese team, beating the Irvine, Calif., team 21-1 at Williamsport, Pa. Teams from the Far East had won 17 Little League championships in the last 21 years. It was Taiwan's seventh win in 11 years. Taiwanese teams had won 12 championships since 1969.

Sep 12: The women's division of the **U.S. Open tennis singles championship** was won by Martina Nav-ratilova over Steffi Graf of West Germany. It was Navratilova's fourth victory in this event in five years. After a 24-hour rain delay, Ivan Lendl on Sept. 14 defeated Mats Wilander of Sweden for the men's title.

Sep 29: A new **major league record for grand slam home runs** was set by Don Mattingly of the New York Yankees when he hit his sixth of the season. The op-posing pitcher was Bruce Hurst of the Boston Red Sox. In July, Mattingly had tied a major league record by hitting home runs in eight consecutive games.

Oct 9: A **world record price for a single postage stamp** was paid when a Japanese bank bought for $1,100,000 a stamp that had sold in Pittsburgh, Pa., in 1852 for two cents. The stamp was from a wedding invitation mailed to a Rev. and Mrs. McGill and is known as the Lady McGill. The previous highest price paid for a stamp was $935,000 in 1980.

Oct 17-25: The **World Series** was won by the Minnesota Twins (AL), who defeated the St. Louis Cardinals four games to three. In every game played, the home team won. Thus, with the Series opening in Minnesota, the Twins jumped out to a two-game lead. The next three games, played in St. Louis, were won by the Cardinals. On the teams' return to the Twins domed stadium, which provides a poor background against which to track high fly balls and with loyal hometown fans in full voice creating a din, the Cardinals folded in games six and seven. On Oct. 12, the Twins had won the American League pennant against the Detroit Tigers four games to one, and two days later the Cardinals won the National League pennant against the San Francisco Giants four games to three.

Nov 1: The **richest prize in tournament golf history**, $384,000, was won by Tom Watson at the $3,000,000 Nabisco Championship at San Antonio, Tex. The first place money brought Watson's total PGA tournament earnings to $4,701,629 in 17 years on the PGA tour. Although Curtis Strange finished last in this tournament, he won the title for highest golf earnings in 1987, a record $925,941.

Nov 5: A **27,000-mile solo voyage around the world** was completed by Tanis Aebi, 21, at Sandy Hook, N.J. She had sailed from New York on May 25, 1985, in a 26-foot sloop, *Varuna.* Her record as a solo sailor will not go into the record books, however, because she gave an acquaintance an 80-mile ride between two Pacific islands.

Nov 18: Paying the **highest price ever for such a car**, a Providence, R.I., business partnership paid $1,600,000 at auction for a 1963 Ferrari 250 GTO racing car. The vehicle, a red, two-seat hardtop made in Italy, of which only 32 exist, had been confiscated by the federal government from a murdered drug dealer's estate.

1988

I. **Civil Rights**
   Exploration and Settlement
   Government
   Statistics
   Wars

The nation entered another presidential election year with the certainty that it would be selecting a new tenant for the White House since Ronald Reagan would have served the maximum two terms allowed by the Constitution. More citizens than ever would be eligible to vote, the Census Bureau noting on Apr. 4 that as of July 1, 1987, there were 90,031,000 households. Within those households, the median age of Americans was increasing, exceeding 32 for the first time: 32.1 on July 1, 1987. Since there were so many baby boomers born in the early post-World War II years, they were now producing children in large numbers. The government reported in August that there were 3,829,000 births in 1987, the most in nearly a quarter of a century. Whether baby boomers or not, Americans were deserting their farms. About 240,000 left such rural places in 1987, bringing the nation's farm population to its lowest level since before the Civil War. Notables who died this year included Burnita S. Matthews, the first woman to serve as a federal district court judge, appointed in 1949, Apr. 25, at 93; Franklin D. Roosevelt, Jr., son of the late president, a U.S. representative, Aug. 17, at 74; J. Skelly Wright, federal judge who was a pioneer in the desegregation of schools and transportation in New Orleans, Aug. 6, at 77.

Jan 2: One of the **largest inland oil spills** ever, 20 miles up the Monongahela River from Pittsburgh, Pa., dumped 860,000 gallons into the stream when a 40-year-old tank of the Ashland Oil Co. collapsed. Flowing into the Ohio River, the spill caused extensive damage to water supplies and wildlife before dissipating.

Feb 5: Gen. **Manuel Antonio Noriega,** the most powerful figure in the government of Panama since he became commander of the armed forces on Aug. 12, 1983, was indicted by a federal grand jury in Miami, Fla., in connection with illegal drug dealings. It was charged that he had received more than $4,600,000 in payoffs for allowing large-scale drug dealers to use airstrips under his protection. The president of Panama, Eric Arturo Delvalle, on Feb. 25 tried to remove him from his post, but the general's armed forces drove the president from office. On Mar. 2 the U.S. government said it had asked New York banks not to distribute any government funds to Noriega. This and other economic measures caused great distress in Panama but did not dislodge Noriega. It was announced on Mar. 19 that the general had refused an American offer to leave the country with a promise of no attempt to extradite him. On May 25 the Reagan administration admitted it had failed to oust Noriega and said it would not carry on any further negotiations with him.

Feb 11: A federal jury convicted **Lyn Nofziger,** former White House political director, on three counts of illegal lobbying under the 1978 Ethics in Government Act. The law forbids lobbying a federal agency for a year after a person has left it. Nofziger was charged with violating this law on behalf of the Wedtech Corp., which sought defense contracts, and two other clients. On Apr. 8 he was sentenced to 90 days in jail and fined $30,000.

Feb 17: U.S. Marine Lt. Col. **William R. Higgins was kidnaped** in southern Lebanon, presumably by Palestinian terrorists. His abduction brought to nine the number of Americans missing in Lebanon. One of them, Terry A. Anderson, a journalist, had been held since March 16, 1985.

Feb 24: The **right to criticize public figures** was strongly endorsed by the Supreme Court, 8–0, when it overturned a $200,000 award to the Rev. Jerry Falwell, founder of the Moral Majority. The award had been made on the basis of an insulting parody in

Hustler magazine. The court said such free speech was to be protected even when it is "outrageous." Civil libertarians and press organizations hailed the decision.

Mar 16: In the **Iran-Contra affair** two key figures were indicted on charges of conspiracy to defraud the U.S. by illegally providing the Nicaraguan rebels with profits from the sale of American weapons to Iran. They were Vice Adm. John M. Poindexter and Marine Lt. Col. Oliver L. North. Indicted with them on 23 counts were two others involved in the scheme. The indictments came after a 14-month grand jury investigation conducted by independent prosecutor Lawrence E. Walsh. The indictments said that weapon sales to Iran totaled about $30,000,000 and that the U.S. government received $12,000,000. On June 8 the judge in the case ruled that the four defendants must be tried separately. The ruling permitted each defendant to use the testimony his codefendants gave to Congress. The ruling was seen as making it more difficult for the special prosecutor to obtain convictions. On June 9 Walsh announced he would bring North to trial first.

Mar 16: U.S. troops were ordered to Honduras on the basis of reports that 1500 or more Nicaraguan troops had made an incursion into Honduras to attack Contra bases there. The Nicaraguan government denied this. The American troops, four battalions of about 3200 men, were not involved in any fighting and were returned to the U.S. by Mar. 28.

Mar 22: The **Civil Rights Restoration Act** became law when both houses of Congress overrode a presidential veto. The new law stemmed from a Supreme Court decision of Feb. 28, 1984, known as the Grove City College case, in which the court held that if civil rights laws were violated in connection with a specific program receiving federal funds, other such programs at the same institution need not suffer. The new law said, in effect, that violations in connection with one program affected all parts of the institution receiving federal money.

Apr 1: Pres. Ronald Reagan signed legislation that provided $47,900,000 of **humanitarian aid for the Nicaraguan Contras.** The bill included $17,700,000 for children who were victims of the civil war. On Feb. 3, by a vote of 219–211, the House had rejected an administration proposal for $36,250,000 of aid that would have included money for military equipment.

Apr 4: The **governor of Arizona was convicted** of misconduct and removed from office by a vote of 21–9 in the state senate. It was the first impeachment trial of a governor in 60 years. Evan Mecham was found guilty of two charges of misconduct, one of which involved his lending $80,000 of state money to his auto dealership. He was also convicted of obstructing justice by trying to prevent an inquiry into charges that one of his aides had made a death threat against a grand jury witness. On June 16 a state jury found Mecham and his brother Willard not guilty of concealing a $350,000 campaign loan.

Apr 14: The **withdrawal of Soviet troops from Afghanistan,** which had invaded that country in Dec. 1979, was provided for in agreements signed by the U.S., the U.S.S.R., Afghanistan, and Pakistan. The U.S. and the Soviet Union agreed not to interfere in Afghan and Pakistani affairs, and Afghanistan and Pakistan would not interfere in each other's internal affairs. The troop withdrawal began on May 15.

Apr 18: The **U.S. Navy attacked Iranian forces** in the southern half of the Persian Gulf. The Americans destroyed two Iranian oil platforms and crippled or sank six armed Iranian ships. One American helicopter and its crew of two were lost. The U.S. said this strike was in retaliation for Iranian mining of gulf waters that resulted in damage to a Navy ship. On Apr. 29 the government announced that U.S. forces in the gulf would broaden their mission and protect all neutral ships attacked by Iran.

Apr 28: An **explosionlike rupture of the fuselage** of an Aloha Airlines Boeing 737 jet flying at 24,000 feet between Hilo and Honolulu, Hawaii, resulted in the death of a flight attendant, swept to her death, and injuries to 60 of the 94 other persons aboard. The plane made an emergency landing safely. Investigators said the cause of the disaster was apparently structural failure.

May 4: An **explosion in a chemical plant** near Henderson, Nev., injured about 200 people. The shock of the explosion was felt for 15 miles and hundreds of windows were shattered in nearby Las Vegas. The plant, which was leveled by four blasts, made fuel for the NASA space shuttles. On June 7 military and space agency officials said the loss of the plant would cause severe fuel shortage in 1989 that would remain a problem into the 1990s.

May 14: The **head-on, fiery crash** of a pickup truck and a bus carrying 67 people near Carrollton, Ky., took the lives of 27, mostly teenagers, returning from a church youth outing. The driver of the truck, who was traveling the wrong way on an interstate highway, was charged two days later with 27 counts of capital murder. Police said he was drunk at the time of the accident.

May 23: Maryland became the **first state to ban the sale of cheap pistols,** effective Jan. 1, 1990. The ban covered the manufacture and sale of pistols that were determined to be easily concealed, inaccurate, unsafe, or poorly made. Provision was made to ban plastic guns also.

May 24: Pres. **Ronald Reagan vetoed a trade bill** that Congress had been working on for three years. The House overrode the veto the same day, 308–113, but on June 8 the Senate failed to register a two-thirds vote to override, 61–37. The president objected particularly to a provision that would require businesses to give 60 days' notice of plant closings or large-scale layoffs. In general the bill was protectionist, intending to defend the nation's industries against what were considered by its supporters unfair trading practices of other countries.

May 27: By a vote of 95–3, the **Senate ratified the Intermediate-Range Nuclear Forces Treaty,** which called for the elimination of land-based medium-range and short-range missiles now installed in Europe by the U.S. and the Soviet Union. It was the first U.S.-Soviet arms accord approved by the Senate since 1972. The official documents were rushed to Moscow so that formal ratifications could be exchanged by Pres. Reagan and General Secretary Gorbachev at their forthcoming summit meeting.

May 29-June 1: Their **fourth summit meeting** was held in Moscow by Pres. Reagan and General Secretary Gorbachev. The meeting was notable chiefly for the extent to which Reagan pushed Gorbachev on the matter of human rights in the Soviet Union and the irritation publicly expressed in return by the Communist leader. Although some progress was made on a number of issues, there was no movement on arms reductions.

June 21: The **annual economic summit conference** of the Group of Seven—the leading industrial democracies Canada, France, Great Britain, Italy, Japan, the U.S., and West Germany—ended in Toronto, Can., with the heads of government expressing satisfaction with and confidence in the economic outlook. They called on the rapidly industrializing nations of Asia to do more for the world economy. The seven nations could not agree on how to reduce the enormous subsidies paid their farmers to help them export their products. The seven leaders agreed to set up a high-level task force to coordinate the fight against the illegal drug traffic.

June 29: The constitutionality of a federal law providing for **independent prosecutors** to investigate high-ranking government officials suspected of criminal activities was upheld by the Supreme Court, 7–1. The decision was a sharp rebuff for the Reagan administration, which had argued that the law was unconstitutional because it encroached on the executive power of the president. The law, enacted in 1978 as a result of the Watergate scandal, allowed the special prosecutors to be appointed by a three-judge federal appellate court.

July 3: An **Iranian passenger jet was shot down** by a U.S. Navy warship at the southern end of the Persian Gulf when it was mistaken for an Iranian F-14 fighter plane. A missile fired from the cruiser *Vincennes* resulted in the death of all 290 persons aboard the Airbus A300. The cruiser at the time was fighting off attacks by Iranian gunboats. There was confusion over what sort of signals, if any, were received from the passenger jet that led the commander of the *Vincennes*, Capt. Will C. Rogers 3d, to believe that his ship was about to be attacked. On Aug. 2 it was revealed that the report of an investigation by the military blamed crew error caused by psychological stress on men in combat for the first time.

July 5: Attorney General **Edwin Meese 3d,** under criticism for some time for alleged criminal or ethical wrongdoing, announced he would resign later in the summer. He asserted that the report of an independent prosecutor, who had been investigating the high official for 14 months, "vindicated" him because it recommended that no criminal charges be brought. The report, made public on July 18, said that Meese had willfully filed a false income tax return but had intended to pay. It also said there was insufficient evidence to seek indictments in two other matters. One concerned Meese's ties to the Wedtech Corp. of New York City, which had apparently tried to bribe its way into government defense contracts. The other involved an aborted plan to build a $1,000,000,000 oil pipeline in Iraq, the negotiations for which might have violated the Foreign Corrupt Practices Act.

July 18-21: The **Democratic National Convention** nominated Gov. Michael S. Dukakis of Massachusetts for president and Sen. Lloyd M. Bentsen, Jr., of Texas for vice president.

Aug 4: Rep. **Mario Biaggi** of New York City was convicted in federal court on 15 felony counts as the Wedtech racketeering trial ended. The case arose through the use of the Wedtech Corp. of the Bronx, New York City, as a source for extorted bribes paid to the defendants, who had lobbied in Washington on behalf of Wedtech, which was seeking contracts as, originally, a minority-owned business. Five other defendants were also convicted. On Aug. 5 Biaggi announced he would resign his House seat but would appeal his conviction.

Aug 10: Interned **Japanese-Americans** who were

forced into relocation camps during World War II would receive compensation for their ordeal, according to a bill signed by Pres. Reagan. The 120,000 surviving internees, about half the original number, and their beneficiaries would each receive $20,000 tax-free and an apology from the U.S. government.

Aug 15-18: The **Republican National Convention** nominated Vice Pres. George Bush of Texas for president and Sen. James Daniel Quayle of Indiana for vice president.

Aug 27: A settlement of Indian land claims, one of the largest in U.S. history, was confirmed by a vote of the tribe concerned, the Puyallup. The settlement gave the tribe $162 million in cash, land, and jobs, in return for surrendering further claims to land and buildings in Tacoma, Wash., valued at more than $750,000,000. Each adult member received $20,000 in cash at once; younger members would receive this sum when they reached 21.

Aug 31: So far this year 66,895 **forest fires** had burned 3.4 million acres in the U.S. It was the worst record since 1919 and approached the record of 1910, when more than 5 million acres were destroyed.

Sep 6: The **Hispanic population** of the U.S. had increased 34% since the 1980 census, the Census Bureau reported. There were now approximately 19.4 million people of Hispanic background, and they represented 8.1% of the total population. More than half of them lived in California and Texas.

Sep 14: The explosion of a **Soviet nuclear device** in Central Asia was witnessed for the first time by American officials. The U.S. government was in the process of deciding whether to agree to proposals that would allow each country to verify the other's underground tests.

Sep 22: Forest fires in Yellowstone National Park had by now burned half the park's 2.2 million acres in summer-long blazes. Controversy arose because park officials followed a policy of allowing naturally caused fires to burn themselves out.

Sep 30: Accidents in government-operated nuclear reactors at the Savannah River plant in South Carolina had been kept secret for as long as 31 years, Congressional committees reported. On Oct. 10 the Energy Dept. announced that it was shutting down the plutonium-processing plant near Boulder, Colo., because of safety problems. On Oct. 14 it was revealed that officials at a plant near Fernald, Ohio, knew for decades that it was releasing tons of radioactive uranium waste into the air. All the plants produced material for the nation's nuclear weapons.

Oct 3: Kidnapers released one hostage in Lebanon. He was Mithileshwar Singh, an Indian with resident alien status in the U.S. Nine Americans were still being held by terrorists.

Oct 13: A welfare reform bill was signed into law by Pres. Reagan. The most revolutionary change it made was to require single parents on welfare with children over three years old to get regular jobs. If they could not find work, they had to enroll in job training or educational courses. The law provided $3.34 billion for the first five years to carry out the law's provisions.

Oct 17: American military bases in the Philippines would continue to operate through Sept. 1991 by the terms of a modified agreement. The U.S. would provide the Philippines with $481 million a year in military and economic aid in 1990 and 1991. This was an increase over the current $180 million a year. The Subic Bay Naval Station and Clark Air Force Base were the two principal American installations.

Oct 18: Congress completed action on a bill to raise the **Veterans Administration** to Cabinet level. Pres. Reagan was expected to sign the measure. The Department of Veterans Affairs was to be officially established on Mar. 15, 1989. It would be the fifth addition to the Cabinet since 1953.

Nov 8: Vice President **George Bush,** the Republican candidate, was elected president of the United States, carrying 40 states. He defeated Governor Michael Dukakis of Massachusetts, the Democratic candidate. The electoral college vote was Bush 426, Dukakis 112. The popular vote was Bush 47,917,341, Dukakis 41,013,030.

II. Architecture
   Arts and Music
   Popular Entertainment
   Publishing
   Theater

In box office receipts, the 1987–1988 Broadway theater season was the best ever. Theaters took in $253 million, an increase of 21% over the previous year. Musicals—such as *The Phantom of the Opera, Les Misérables, Starlight Express,* and *Me and My Girl*—accounted for most of the ticket sales. Dramas like *Speed-the-Plow, Joe Turner's Come and Gone,* and *Walk in the Woods* were critical successes. The catastrophe of the season was the musical *Carrie,* on which work began seven years before and which closed after 16 previews and 5 regular performances with a loss of $7,000,000. The most talked about movie of the year received most of its attention before the public saw it. This was *The Last Temptation of Christ,* based on the novel by Nikos Kazantzakis and directed by Martin Scorsese. It was vociferously condemned by fundamentalist Protestants and some Roman Catholics, who had not yet viewed it, as being blasphemous and sacrilegious. Many viewers found it a well-meant but not overly successful cinematic effort to show how Christ might have been tempted to give up the role of messiah and live an ordinary family life. Hollywood was said to be making more movies to appeal to older audiences, but the year's production did not attest to that except perhaps for such different films as *Broadcast News,* a comedy, and *The Unbearable Lightness of Being,* a love story from the novel by Milan Kundera. On the other hand there was the popular *Who Framed Roger Rabbit,* which cleverly used both animated and live characters. Other box office successes included *Coming to America,* in which comedian Eddie Murphy played an African prince; *Crocodile Dundee II,* again starring Paul Hogan as a he-man from the outback; and *Bull Durham,* a baseball comedy with sex. In television there were both bright and dim spots. With the start of its reruns *The Cosby Show* sold $60,000,000 worth of commercials immediately. But there was a falling off of network viewing by children, costing millions in lost advertising revenue. The continued growth of cable television was also a factor in the loss of revenue, with 45 million American homes now subscribing. VCR and videocassettes also affected the home viewing market. Cassette sales continued to boom and were expected to reach nearly $7,000,000,000 in 1988, but there were so many videocassette stores selling and renting cassettes—25,000—that competition was driving profits down. A new recording by the group Run-D.M.C., *Tougher Than Leather*, was said to show that rap music was now in the mainstream of American culture. Rap began among young urban blacks, but now its rhymed chanting to a driving beat and its culture, known as hip-hop, were widely acceptable if not always respectable. The book publishing industry prospered, which perhaps accounted for the number of mergers, takeovers, and offers in the works. The big takeover news was the sale of the Crown Publishing Group to Random House on Aug. 15. No price was announced. One estimate projected the growth of book sales at an annual rate of 3.3% through 1992. Sales of children's books were increasing and might reach more than $800 million in 1988, double their sales of five years earlier. Export sales of American books were also expanding, to $739,000,000 in 1987, an increase in one year of 22%. Only in mass market paperbacks did the situation not seem rosy. Dollar sales were going up, but unit sales were down. Newspaper publishing was not as upbeat as book publishing. Although the number of households increased 41.4% from 1970 to 1987, weekday newspaper circulation rose only 1% and Sunday circulation 22.4%. Among notable persons who died were the poet Leonie Adams, June 27, at 88; Romare Bearden, collagist, Mar. 12, at 75; Barry Bingham, Sr., newspaper publisher, Aug. 15, at 82; Milton A. Caniff, comic strip artist, creator of *Terry and the Pirates,* Apr. 3, at 81; singer and actress Hazel Dawn, Aug. 28, at 98; Dennis Day, singer and comic with the Jack Benny radio show, June 22, at 71; Florence Eldridge, stage and movie star, Aug. 1, at 86; Gil

Evans, jazz composer and arranger, Mar. 20, at 75;
Robert A. Heinlein, science fiction writer, May 8, at
80; Robert Joffrey, founder and artistic director of
the ballet troupe bearing his name, Mar. 25, at 57;
Jim Jordan, star of the radio show *Fibber McGee and
Molly*, Apr. 1, at 91; Louis L'Amour, author of best-
selling westerns, June 10, at 80; composer Frederick
Loewe, Feb. 14, at 86; Joshua L. Logan, Broadway
director, July 12, at 79; James McCracken, dramatic
tenor, Apr. 30, at 61; Colleen Moore, who in the silent
movies was the personification of the 1920s flapper,
Jan. 25, at 87; Louise Nevelson, pioneering artist in
creating environmental sculpture, Apr. 17, at 88; Melvin James "Cy" Oliver, jazz composer and orchestra
leader, May 27, at 77; Irene Rich, star of silent movies, Apr. 22, at 96; Adela Rogers St. John, journalist,
author, and screenwriter, Aug. 10, at 94; Max Shul-
man, humorist and creator of the TV character Dobie
Gillis, Aug. 28, at 69.

Among **books published** this year were *A Brief History of Time* by Stephen W. Hawking and *Chaos:
Making a New Science* by James Gleick. Biographies
included *Freud: A Life for Our Times* by Peter Gay
and *Oscar Wilde* by Richard Ellmann. Historians offered *Battle Cry of Freedom* by James M. McPherson,
a vivid account of the Civil War, and *Reconstruction:
America's Unfinished Revolution* by Eric Foner. Fiction as usual offered a wide range of subject matter:
The Tenants of Time, about 19th-century Ireland, by
Thomas Flanagan; *Libra*, a recounting of the
Kennedy Assassination by Don DeLillo; *Quinn's
Book*, set in 19th-century Albany, N.Y., by William
Kennedy; and *The Mysteries of Pittsburgh*, a coming-
of-age first novel by Michael Chabon. There were,
too, the usual assortment of readable suspense and
mystery stories, such as *Freaky Deaky* by Elmore
Leonard and *The Cardinal of the Kremlin* by Tom
Clancy.

Mar 26: An exhibition of **art treasures from the Hermitage Museum** in Leningrad opened at the Metropolitan Museum in New York, consisting of 51 Dutch

and Flemish paintings from the 17th century, most of
which had never been seen in the U.S. The exhibit
was to go to the Art Institute of Chicago, which was
the joint organizer with the Metropolitan of the exhibit. In exchange, the two American museums arranged a display of 51 19th- and early-20th-century
French paintings that will be seen at the Hermitage
and later in Moscow.

Mar 31: Pulitzer prizes were awarded for the following: fiction, *Beloved* by Toni Morrison; general nonfiction, *The Making of the Atomic Bomb* by Richard
Rhodes; biography, *Look Homeward: A Life of
Thomas Wolfe* by David Herbert Donald; history, *The
Launching of Modern American Science, 1846–1876*
by Robert V. Bruce; poetry, *Partial Accounts: New
and Selected Poems* by William Meredith; drama,
Driving Miss Daisy by Alfred Uhry.

Apr 1: The **first nightly news anchorman** in American
broadcasting retired. He was Douglas Edwards, who
joined the CBS radio network in 1942 and held the
anchor position for 20 years.

Apr 8: Grolier, Inc., an American publisher of educational and reference materials, agreed to be taken
over by Hachette S. A., a French book and magazine
publisher, for about $450,000,000. On Apr. 13 Ha-
chette became the largest magazine publisher in the
world, with 74 publications in ten countries, by acquiring an American company, Diamandis Communications, Inc., for $712,000,000.

Apr 25: Publishing rights to a **sequel to *Gone With the
Wind*** by Margaret Mitchell, one of the most popular
novels of all time, were sold to Warner Books in an
auction for $4,940,000. The sequel, which was sched-
uled for publication in 1990, was to be written by
Alexandra Ripley, author of four novels. *Gone With
the Wind* was published in 1936 and had sold about
25,000,000 copies.

May 2: A **Jackson Pollock painting,** *Search* (1955),
was purchased at auction in New York for
$4,800,000, a record for the artist and for any post-
World War II work of art. The purchaser was a Tokyo

art dealer. On May 3, also at auction, Jasper Johns's *Diver* (1962), sold for $4,200,000, a record for the artist. The buyer was not identified.

May 3: Andy Warhol's collection of art and other objects sold for a total of $25,300,000 over a ten-day period of auctions. About 10,000 items were disposed of in the largest auction ever held by Sotheby's in New York. Warhol, who died in 1987, had an enormous collection of cookie jars, which brought $247,830. Other items included paintings, pottery, antiques, folk art, and American Indian art.

May 10: A record price for any work of sculpture was paid at auction in New York when *Little Dancer at 14 Years of Age* by Edgar Degas was sold for $10,120,000. An unidentified European was the purchaser. The bronze of Degas's 1881 wax sculpture is 37½ inches tall.

May 11: The **100th birthday of Irving Berlin,** America's most prolific and popular song writer, was celebrated with a gala concert at Carnegie Hall in New York City. Among the well-known performers paying tribute were Frank Sinatra, Willie Nelson, Ray Charles, Marilyn Horne, and Leonard Bernstein. Mr. Berlin could not attend but planned to watch the taped telecast.

May 18: Howard Nemerov, 68, was named the third **poet laureate** of the U.S., having been appointed by the Librarian of Congress.

June 7: Papers of Saul Bellow, consisting of notebooks, typescripts, and other materials relating to his novel *Mr. Sammler's Planet* (1969), were sold in New York City for $66,000, a record at auction for a work by a living author. It was the first manuscript the author, winner of the Nobel Prize for Literature in 1976, had sold. The items were bought as an anonymous gift to be presented to the Berg Collection of the New York Public Library.

June 15: A new edition of James Joyce's *Ulysses* published four years earlier became the center of a lively literary controversy. The edition, prepared by a team of German scholars, was claimed to correct some 5000 omissions, transpositions, and other errors in earlier editions. But John Kidd of the University of Virginia, in an 8000-word article in *The New York Review of Books*, said the edition had more flaws than its predecessors. Other scholars supported Kidd. As a result Random House, publisher of *Ulysses* in the U.S. since 1933, asked a textual scholar, G. Thomas Tanselle of Columbia University, to organize a committee to decide which edition it should publish.

Aug 7: The **sale of Triangle Publications**, Inc., publisher of *TV Guide*, the *Daily Racing Form*, and *Seventeen* magazine, to Rupert Murdoch, Australian publishing magnate with interests in the U.S., Great Britain, and Australia, was announced. At $3,000,000,000 the deal was the largest takeover ever in publishing.

Sep 17: The **Art Institute of Chicago** opened a large new gallery of 66,640 square feet. Limestone-sheathed, it was designed to blend with the original Beaux-Arts building of the Institute. The new building cost $23 million.

Sep 27: **Soviet and American curators** for the first time organized jointly a museum exhibition. It was entitled "Crossroads of Continents: Cultures of Siberia and Alaska" and opened for a six-month stay at the Smithsonian Institution, Washington, D.C. The exhibit contained nearly 600 objects showing the prehistoric life of peoples in those parts of the world.

Sep 29: **Union Station** in Washington, D.C., reopened after renovations that cost $160 million. The 81-year-old classical-style station was appropriate in its grandeur to a period when railroad travel was at its peak and when the U.S. capital was becoming an imperial city. It had been neglected and had gone to ruin since a failed attempt to renew it in 1976. It now had shops, restaurants, and theaters.

Oct 8: A very large collection of **Italian Renaissance manuscripts** and other documents had been acquired by Yale University. The material comprised the 500-year-old archives of the Spinelli banking family of Florence. The approximately 150,000 documents included business records as well as correspondence with a number of popes and such major figures as Lorenzo de' Medici.

III. Business and Industry
Education
Philosophy and Religion
Science

More than halfway through 1988, the national economy showed strong growth but also an increase in inflation. As a result, the Federal Reserve on Aug. 9 raised its discount rate a half point, to 6.5%. Banks in turn increased their prime rate to 10%, the highest since June 1985. In July the nation's factories, mines, and utilities operated at their highest level in eight years, aiding economic growth but also causing inflationary pressures. In June the unemployment rate, at 5.2%, was at its lowest since May 1974. It rose to 5.5% in August, but this in turn reduced fears of rising inflation. The most serious problem facing the economy was the Midwest and Southwest drought, with conditions not seen since the Dust Bowl years of the 1930s. In August the Department of Agriculture estimated that the grain harvest would be 31% lower than in 1987. Farmers were losing income and consumers could expect to pay higher prices for food. The government appropriated $3.9 billion for farm relief. In foreign trade, there was considerable improvement because the decrease in the value of the dollar stimulated exports of American goods. Imports, however, did not decrease as much as expected, so that the foreign trade deficit was not lowered very much. The environment was not in as good shape as the economy. In June a NASA scientist said global warming had begun, the earth having been warmer in the first five months of 1988 than in any comparable period in the past 130 years. The Environmental Protection Agency reported that clean air standards for ozone were violated in 1987 in more areas than before. The Fish and Wildlife Service revealed that the development of oil fields in northern Alaska had done far more environmental damage than the government originally predicted. For education, the report card showed mixed grades. At the college level the demand for admission was so great that some students near the top in high school were not being admitted anywhere. At the public school level, the children of the baby boomers were forcing the reopening of schools closed in the 1970s and early 1980s when the school population dropped. Young Americans who made it to college were revealed to be sadly lacking in geographical knowledge. In a survey of nine countries they ranked lowest. A bright spot was the growing interest young people were showing in the teaching profession. Education schools reported increases of up to 50% in applications. More racial unrest at predominantly white universities was noticeable and black students reported they were not welcome. Secretary of Education William J. Bennett stirred controversy when he said in April that the overall performance of American schools was "unacceptably low," an evaluation at once challenged by a number of educators. Charitable donations for religious, educational, and other purposes were a record $93.6 billion in 1987, but the rate of increase was the lowest in 12 years, which was blamed on the stock market collapse and the new income tax law. On July 27 the surgeon general of the U.S., in the most comprehensive report on nutrition and health ever issued by the government, said fat was a leading cause of disease and that its overconsumption was a major American health problem. In the business world, a boom in facsimile-transmission machines marked the year. Documents were being sent across the country in 20 seconds. American business was active in the Soviet Union. Pepsico, Inc., producer of Pepsi-Cola, claimed the honor of being the first American company to buy commercial time on Soviet TV, as of May 17. McDonald's in April prepared to open 20 stores in Moscow to sell the Big Mac—*Bolshoi Mak* in Russian. Notable persons who died in 1988 included Luis W. Alvarez, Nobel Prize-winning physicist, Sept. 1, at 77; John Cardinal Dearden, liberal Catholic prelate and archbishop of Detroit, Aug. 1, at 80; Richard F. Feynman, Nobel Prize-winning theoretical physicist, Feb. 15, at 69; Raymond W. Goldsmith, economist, July 12, at 83; James R. Killian, Jr., in 1957 the first presidential assistant for science and technology, and president of MIT, Jan. 29, at 83; Gardiner C. Means, economist, Feb. 15, at 91; Jackie Presser, president of the International Brotherhood of Teamsters, July 9, at 61; Isidor Isaac Rabi, pioneer atomic scientist and Nobel Prize winner Jan. 11, at 89; Sewall Wright, geneticist who established a mathematical basis for evolution, Mar. 3, at 98.

Jan 8: The **stock market plunge of Oct. 19, 1987,** was blamed on automatic trading programs of large money management firms, which generated huge sell orders, in a report of the Presidential Task Force on Market Mechanisms. The task force recommended that the Federal Reserve Board be made responsible for regulating trading. On Feb. 2 a staff report of the Securities and Exchange Commission said the crash was accelerated by trading in stock futures. It recommended that certain computerized trading in such futures be limited and that higher margins be required. The NYSE announced on Feb. 4 that it would curb the use of its electronic trading system when the Dow Jones average of industrial stocks rose or fell more than 50 points in a day.

Jan 13: The **oldest and most distant objects ever seen in the universe** were detected by astronomers, according to a report made before the American Astronomical Society. The objects appeared to be beyond any observed quasar and, being perhaps 17,000,000,000 years old, their radiations were coming from the creation of some of the universe's first galaxies.

Jan 28: The **risk of heart attack among men** could be sharply reduced by taking one aspirin tablet every other day, according to a report in *The New England Journal of Medicine*. The report was the result of a nationwide study carried on over a five-year period. On Jan. 30 a report involving 5000 British doctors found no strong evidence of this effect.

Jan 28: Controversy over a **nuclear power plant** caused the Public Service Co. of New Hampshire to file for bankruptcy. The Seabrook plant, 15 years in construction, was completed in July 1986 at a cost of $5,200,000,000 but had never been granted an operating license because of disputes over emergency evacuation plans. On May 27, in a similar dispute about emergency evacuation, the Long Island Lighting Co. agreed with New York State to abandon plans to operate its Shoreham nuclear plant, which over 20 years had cost $5,300,000,000 without ever being put to use.

Mar 14: A **treaty to protect the earth's ozone shield** was ratified by the Senate, 83–0, making the U.S. the first major user and producer of chlorofluorocarbons to approve an international agreement reached in Montreal in Sept. 1987. The agreement first froze and then called for a rollback of the use of such chemicals, which are believed to damage the ozone in the upper atmosphere. On Mar. 24 E. I. du Pont de Nemours & Co., the world's largest producer of chlorofluorocarbons, announced plans to phase out all production of such chemicals.

Mar 15: The **first black Catholic archbishop** in the U.S. was named by Pope John Paul II. Eugene Antonio Marino was installed on May 5 as head of the Archdiocese of Atlanta.

Apr 1: The **largest department store takeover** in the U.S. was completed when Federated Department Stores, Inc., accepted a bid of $6,600,000,000 from the Campeau Corp. of Canada. The deal was the fifth largest acquisition in U.S. history. Fifteen months earlier Campeau had purchased another American department store chain, Allied Stores Corp., for $3,600,000,000.

Apr 6: **Matthew Alexander Henson,** the black American who reached the North Pole with Robert E. Peary 79 years earlier on this date, was reburied in Arlington National Cemetery. Henson spent most of his life after 1909 in obscurity as a clerk in the Customs House in New York City, and when he died in 1955 at 88 he was buried in Woodlawn Cemetery, New York City.

Apr 8: Television evangelist the Rev. **Jimmy Swaggart was defrocked** as a minister of the Assemblies of God after he rejected punishment ordered by the church. He had been directed to stop preaching for a year after he publicly confessed "moral failure" on Feb. 21 following reports that he had committed lewd acts with a prostitute. He left his pulpit on Feb. 21 but on May 22 Swaggart appeared in the pulpit of his Family Worship Center in Baton Rouge, La., preaching without ministerial credentials.

Apr 11: Expansion of the **roles of women in the Roman Catholic Church** was recommended by a committee of Catholic bishops. Women's leadership roles would be expanded at almost all levels of the church except the priesthood. The report also condemned the "sin of sexism." Women should be encouraged to preach and to distribute communion, and the possibility of ordaining women as deacons should be studied.

Apr 12: The **world's first patent for a higher form of life,** a mouse, was issued to Harvard University. The patent for "transgenic nonhuman mammals" was in the names of two scientists, Dr. Philip Leder and Dr. Timothy A. Stewart, who injected a gene that causes cancer in many mammals into fertilized mouse eggs and so developed a new breed of genetically altered mice. The patented mouse was a more effective model for studying how genes contribute to the development of cancer.

Apr 13: Christian, Moslem, and Jewish **fundamentalism was rejected** by the Conservative movement of Judaism in the first statement of principles in its 143-year history. Conservative Judaism, the report said, should follow a moderate course, with loyalty to tradition but "without resigning from the 20th century." The report was the work of 35 scholars, rabbis, and laypeople.

Apr 22: A popular **antiacne drug caused severe birth defects,** according to the Food and Drug Administration. The drug, Accutane, was estimated to have caused defects in 900 to 1300 babies between 1982 and 1986. The drug's use may also have caused 700 to 1000 spontaneous abortions. Hoffmann-La Roche, maker of the drug, asserted that only 62 cases of birth defects were the result of taking Accutane. On Apr. 26 the FDA recommended that distribution of Accutane be greatly restricted.

Apr 23: A **ban on smoking** in passenger planes went into effect. The no-smoking rule applied to all flights of two hours or less, except for travel clubs, charter trips, and flights to foreign destinations. Northwest Airlines announced it would ban smoking on all domestic flights regardless of their duration.

Apr 25: The **largest U.S. corporation** in 1987, according to *Fortune* magazine, was General Motors, with sales of $101,781,900,000. Exxon was second, with sales of $76,416,000,000.

May 1: The Reagan administration announced an **increase in arms sales abroad.** Its aim was to sell $15,000,000,000 worth, which would be $3,000,000,000 more than it sold in the previous fiscal year. In that year another $2,000,000,000 worth was sold for export directly by manufacturers.

May 13: A **second genetic code** had been deciphered, according to a report in *Nature* by two scientists at MIT. This code directed one of several steps in the synthesis of proteins inside cells. Solution to the problem had been sought by molecular biologists for 20 years. It was a step in providing scientists a way to make proteins to order.

May 13: The **drug AZT** prolonged the lives of AIDS patients, according to the company that produced it. Of 144 patients who participated in the first human trials of azidothymidine (AZT), 84.5% were alive after one year. So far, however, experiments seeking a vaccine were discouraging. With nearly 35,000 Americans reported to have died of AIDS, Congress and Pres. Reagan approved a $1 billion program for education, treatment, and research.

May 16: Only slight changes in the **operations of stock markets** was recommended by the White House Working Group, the third federal government body to study the stock market crash of Oct. 19, 1987. The principal proposal was that trading be halted for one hour on all U.S. markets if any one of them fell or rose the equivalent of 250 points on the Dow Jones industrial average. Most experts were surprised that the group had so little to suggest and felt that the recommendations did not go far enough to prevent another crash.

May 26: A health advisory about AIDS, in the form of a pamphlet, was mailed by the federal government to every American with a mailing address. No such mailing had ever been made before. Written in language the 12-to-13-year level, the pamphlet was printed in an edition of 110 million copies in English and 4 million in Spanish.

May 29: Two **new American cardinals** of the Roman Catholic Church were among 25 prelates named to the high posts by Pope John Paul II. The Americans, who were officially installed on June 28, were James Aloysius Hickey of Washington and Edmund Casimir Szoka of Detroit. The appointments brought to ten the number of U.S. cardinals.

June 13: A cigarette manufacturer was found guilty for the first time in the cancer death of a longtime smoker. A federal jury in New Jersey awarded $400,000 damages to Antonio Cipollone, whose wife, Rose, died in 1984 and had smoked heavily for 40 years. However, the Liggett Group, found liable, and other tobacco companies were found not guilty of the charge that they had fraudulently misrepresented the risks of smoking and had conspired to misrepresent facts. The suit was the first of more than 300 since 1954 in which any tobacco company had lost a case.

June 14: The **Southern Baptist Convention** for the tenth consecutive year elected a conservative as its president. The victor was the Rev. Jerry Vines of Jacksonville, Fla., but he won by only 692 votes out of 31,274 cast by delegates. One of the most divisive issues was control of teaching at the denomination's seminaries. On June 16 the delegates voted to condemn homosexuality as "a manifestation of a depraved nature" and "a perversion of divine standards."

June 14: The **General Assembly of the Presbyterian Church** (U.S.A.) adopted a statement on Christian responsibilities in the nuclear age that declared nuclear war immoral. The statement said that under some circumstances noncooperation or disobedience to civil authority "has been deemed an appropriate Christian response." On June 25 the Roman Catholic bishops of the U.S. approved a report that questioned the morality of deploying a system of space-based defenses against missiles.

June 15: More than half of all **new mothers remained in the job market** for the first time in the nation's history, the Census Bureau reported. The figure reached 50.8% in 1987. Of new mothers with college degrees, 63% remained in the work force, compared with 38% of those with only a high school education. It was noted that women who had more education and more work experience before having children were better able to afford child care.

June 17: A federal law to **ban discrimination** against AIDS victims was recommended by a divided presidential commission appointed to consider all aspects of the spread of the disease. The Reagan administration did not at once accept this recommendation. In all, the commission's report contained almost 600 recommendations. One of them said "a top national priority" should be given to the problem of intravenous drug users.

June 20: Agreement was reached on a **new U.S.-Japanese trade pact** concerning the import of American beef and citrus products into Japan. Although under the arrangement U.S. exports will increase only about $1,000,000,000 a year, the dispute over these two items had been a symbolic one in America's effort to break down Japan's stiff barriers to trade. Under the terms of the agreement, Japan's import quotas on beef and fresh oranges will be abolished in three years and the quota on orange juice in four.

June 21: **No cavities** or other tooth decay were reported by half the nation's school children, according to a federal government survey. The increase to 49.9% of those with no decay, compared with 36.6% in a 1979–1980 survey, was attributed to the widespread use of fluoride and the high level of dental care. Officials said that if the situation continued to improve it would mean the end of dental disease as a major public health problem.

June 27: **Surrogate motherhood** was banned by a state for the first time when Gov. James J. Blanchard of Michigan signed a bill that outlawed commercial contracts for women to bear children for others.

Other state legislatures were considering similar measures.

July 1: A **catastrophic health care bill** was signed by Pres. Reagan. Effective Jan. 1, 1989, it provided the first major expansion of the Medicare program. Among its provisions were unlimited free hospital care after the recipient pays the first $564 annually; unlimited free physician care after the first $1400 annually; and an increase in payments for nursing-home care. Premiums were increased to pay the new costs.

July 3: A 19th-century **American woman was canonized** by Pope John Paul II at the Vatican. Sister Rose Philippine Duchesne, born in France in 1769 and who immigrated to the U.S. in 1818, was the fourth American to attain sainthood in the Roman Catholic Church. Sister Duchesne, who died in 1852, founded dozens of schools and a convent for young women as well as directing the American branch of her order, the Society of the Sacred Heart. Most of her work was done on the midwestern frontier, where she also nursed Indians and tried to spread Christianity among them. She opened in St. Charles, Mo., a free school that was the first such institution in the West.

July 11: The **General Convention of the Episcopal Church** closed in an atmosphere of compromise on several issues. On the subject of sexual morality, the delegates reaffirmed "the biblical and traditional teaching of chastity and fidelity," but also called for "an open dialogue" on human sexuality. Anticipating the likelihood of women becoming bishops, the convention provided for bishops to come in from outside a diocese where churches were at odds with their local bishop over women as clergy.

Aug 2: A bill requiring **notice of plant closings** became law without Pres. Reagan's signature. He opposed the bill but heeded Republican appeals that vetoing it would hurt the party's election chances in the fall. Under the bill's terms, a company with 100 or more full-time employees must give 60 days notice of plans to close a plant. The same notice must be given if 500, or a third, of a plant's workers are to be laid off.

Aug 17: The first joint American-Soviet **nuclear test**

verification experiment took place in Nevada. Teams of U.S. and Soviet scientists used different methods to determine the strength of a nuclear blast of an American device.

Aug 17: The **first hair growth drug** was approved for marketing by the Food and Drug Administration. It was a prescription drug called Rogaine and beneficial only under certain circumstances. A study of 1833 men found that 15% to 20% had cosmetically significant hair growth by using it.

Aug 23: A **foreign trade bill** with protectionist overtones was signed by Pres. Reagan. Covering a large number of areas, the new law was aimed particularly at what was alleged to be unfair trading practices of other nations. A most important provision allowed the president to negotiate international agreements to enlarge the markets for goods and services such as banking and insurance.

Sep 1: **Colon and rectal cancer,** in more than half such cases, could be traced to genetic predisposition, according to a new study. In the U.S. colon and rectal cancer cause more cancer deaths than any other form except lung cancer in men and breast cancer in women. The study showed that about a third of white Americans have this genetic disposition.

Sep 19: A **free trade agreement** with Canada was approved by the Senate, 83–9, completing U.S. action. The agreement would do away with almost all trade barriers and tariffs by 1999. The Canadian House of Commons had previously approved the agreement.

Sep 20: The **first Hispanic member** of the president's Cabinet took office as secretary of education. He was Lauro F. Cavazos, since 1980 president of Texas Tech University.

Sep 24: The **first woman to be elected a bishop** of the Episcopal Church was chosen to be suffragan bishop of the Diocese of Massachusetts. She was the Rev. Barbara C. Harris, a black who had been a priest for eight years.

Sep 28: A **bill to limit textile imports** was vetoed by Pres. Reagan. The bill would have limited the increase of textile imports to 1% per year and would have frozen at current levels the importation of footwear not made of rubber. On Oct. 4 the House of Representatives failed to override the veto by a vote of 272–152.

Sep 29-Oct 3: The **first U.S. manned space flight in 32 months** took place with five astronauts aboard the space shuttle *Discovery*. In the course of its journey the *Discovery* successfully launched a $100 million communications satellite. It was the first American manned flight in space since the *Challenger* blew up shortly after blastoff, on Jan. 28, 1986.

Oct 17: The **largest consumer products company in the world** would be formed by a proposed takeover of Kraft Inc. by Philip Morris Companies Inc. The latter offered $11.5 billion for Kraft. It would be the largest takeover in history after the $13.3 billion takeover of Gulf Oil Corp. by Chevron Corp. in 1984.

Oct 17: The **Nobel Prize in Physiology or Medicine** was awarded jointly to two Americans, Gertrude B. Elion and George H. Hitchings of the Burroughs Wellcome Co., and a Briton, James Black of London. The award was given for discoveries of "important principles for drug treatment." The winners developed drugs for treating such ailments as heart disease, gout, leukemia, and peptic ulcers.

Oct 19: The **Nobel Prize in Physics** was awarded to three Americans: Leon M. Lederman, of the Fermi National Accelerator Laboratory; Melvin Schwartz, of Digital Pathways Inc.; and Jack Steinberger, of the European Center for Nuclear Research. They received the award for their experiments in the early 1960s that produced the first laboratory-made beam of neutrinos. This work made possible detailed studies of radioactive decay involving the "weak" nuclear force.

IV. Fashion
   Folkways
   Holidays
   Social Issues and Crime
   Sports

Statistics reported in April for 1987 showed that baseball was still the national game. It attracted
88,200,000 spectators. Horse racing came in second
with attendance at 73,600,000, followed by football
with 50,000,000 fans. By opening day of the 1988
baseball season, the game had set a salary record:
major league owners were paying their players a
total of $300,511,924 for the season. The men who
officiated at professional sports did not do as well.
Major league umpires and NBA referees earned a
maximum of $100,000, while the NFL paid $1,800 per
regular game. "Tomboy" was an obsolete word, said
a Penn State professor in reporting that 82% of
today's young women participated in sports. The
100th anniversary of golf in the U.S. was observed on
June 20 at the St. Andrews Golf Club in Hastings-on-
Hudson, N.Y., near where the first match was played.
On the consumer front Americans had new, if not
better, products to rush out and buy. Among them
was a fake automobile telephone, of which 40,000
had been sold at $9.95; a vending machine that
cooked french fries while you wait; perfume and
other cosmetics for babies, under such names as Eau
de Senteur; a stopper to keep champagne corks on a
four-inch leash; chocolate that would not melt in hot
weather; and gourmet dog food for overweight
pooches. In a more practical way of life, a survey
found that teenagers were into cooking, and not just
with microwave ovens. One survey of 2200 young
people found that 80% said they had cooked a meal
for themselves in the previous week. On the crime
front, the Justice Department reported that there
were 581,609 inmates in state and federal prisons, an
increase of 6.7% in a year and more than double the
1970 prison population. Notable persons who died
included Alan Ameche, Baltimore Colts running
back, Aug. 8, at 55; Gregory "Pappy" Boyington, Marine ace of World War II who shot down 28 Japanese
planes and won the Medal of Honor, Jan. 11, at 75;
Glenn Cunningham, world-record holder for the
mile, Mar. 10, at 78; Robert Lee "Bobby" Dodd, famed
football coach at the Georgia Institute of Technology,

June 21, at 79; Ted Kluszewski, slugging first baseman, Mar. 29, at 63; Peter Press "Pete" Maravich,
college and professional basketball star whose 3667
points in his college career remained a record, Jan.
5, at 40; Arthur Joseph Rooney, Sr., a leading American sportsman and founder of the Pittsburgh Steelers
of the NFL, Aug. 25, at 87; Edd Roush, twice batting
champion of the National League, 1917 and 1919,
Mar. 21, at 94.

Jan 24: A year-long celebration of **Hawaii's 1000-year-
old native culture** ended with a party attended by
41,000 in Aloha Stadium in Honolulu, marking
Ho'olokah, or Hawaii Unity Day.

Feb 9: New York City's largest single **art theft** occurred
when 18 paintings and 10 drawings valued at
$6,000,000 were taken from the Colnaghi Ltd. gallery
on the Upper East Side. The most valuable items
taken were two paintings by Fra Angelico.

Feb 13-28: The **XVth Olympic Winter Games,** held in
Calgary, Can., saw the U.S. win only six medals: two
gold, one silver, and three bronze. The two American
gold medalists were Brian Boitano, men's figure skating champion, and Bonnie Blair, winner of the
women's 500-meter speed skating event. The Soviet
Union took the most medals, 29, including 11 gold.
East Germany was second with a total of 25.

Feb 27: A **new round-the-world speed record** was set
by a Gulfstream IV jet when it landed in Houston
after a flight of 36 hrs., 8 min. The former record had
been set as recently as Jan. 30 by a Boeing 747SP,
which made the flight in 36 hrs., 54 min., 15 sec.

Mar 15: The transfer of the **St. Louis Cardinals' NFL
franchise** to Phoenix was approved by the league.
The owners also voted to continue the use of the
instant replay by officials for another season.

Mar 31: The U.S. and Italy joined in a **drug case** that
brought charges against 233 suspected members of a
Sicilian Mafia drug ring. More than 100 suspects
were under arrest. The investigation had been under-
way for more than two years. Italian officials said it
showed that all three of Italy's major underworld
organizations were involved in the drug trade and

that New York's Mafia families had had more contact with them than previously thought.

Apr 4: The **NCAA men's basketball championship** was won by Kansas, which defeated Oklahoma 83 to 79.

Apr 20: The New York Yankees became the first team to hit more than 10,000 **home runs** in the major leagues when Jack Clark hit no. 10,001. It was his first home run of the season.

Apr 22: For the first time in its 37 years, the **Little 500,** a bicycle race held on the Indiana University campus in Bloomington, included an event for women's teams. Hitherto women had been restricted to a tricycle race and cheering the men. The Willkie Sprint team, representing a dormitory quadrangle, won this first women's event.

Apr 28: By **losing 21 consecutive games** at the start of the baseball season, the Baltimore Orioles set an American League record. They then won a game, but followed that with two more losses. The previous mark of 20 losses was set by Boston in 1906 and tied in 1916 and 1943 by Philadelphia.

May 2: The **most severe penalty** ever imposed on a major league baseball manager for an on-field incident was handed Pete Rose of the Cincinnati Reds by the president of the NL. Rose was suspended for 30 days for an incident in a game on Apr. 30 when he disputed a call by an umpire and pushed him. Aroused by comments of broadcasters of the game, fans threw a variety of things onto the field and forced one umpire to flee to safety.

May 3: The **largest cocaine seizure** in U.S. history was made by officials at Tarpon Springs, Fla., when they found 9200 pounds of the drug in hollowed-out lumber that had been shipped from Colombia. The cocaine was estimated to have a street value of more than $2,000,000,000. The largest previous cocaine seizure occurred in Fort Lauderdale, Fla., in Nov. 1987, when 8700 pounds were found.

May 4: Anthony "Fat Tony" Salerno, reputed to be the boss of the Genovese crime family, was convicted with eight other men of racketeering. The numerous crimes he was charged with included a multimillion-dollar scheme to rig bids in the construction industry. Those convicted faced up to 20 years in prison on the racketeering charge. Salerno was already serving a 100-year sentence for his conviction as a member of the Mafia's ruling "commission."

May 18: "Casey at the Bat," a poetic baseball classic and one of the most often recited poems in the English language, marked its 100th anniversary. On May 18, 1888, at Wallack's Theater in New York City, it was first recited by the popular actor William De Wolfe Hopper, who went on to repeat his performance about 10,000 times over the years. The saga of the mighty baseball hero who failed in the clutch was written by a 25-year-old Harvard graduate, Ernest L. Thayer. It was first published on June 3, 1888, in the San Francisco *Examiner* and Thayer was paid $5.

May 19: Carlos Lehder Rivas was convicted of smuggling tons of cocaine into the U.S. Lehder was the reputed leader of a violent Colombian drug ring and, with a codefendant, was found guilty of conspiring to bring 3.3 tons of cocaine into the U.S. between 1978 and 1980. Lehder could be sentenced to life plus 150 years in prison and fined up to $350,000.

June 7-21: The **NBA basketball championship** was won by the Los Angeles Lakers, defeating the Detroit Pistons four games to three. It was the first time since 1969 that a team had won the title two years in succession.

June 12: The **Tour of Italy bicycle race** was won by an American for the first time since the race was first held in 1909. The winner was Andy Hampsten, 26, who dropped out of the University of North Dakota to take up bicycling. He defeated 198 other cyclists and finished 1 min., 43 sec. ahead of his nearest challenger. The Tour of Italy is considered second only to the Tour de France in importance in professional bike racing.

June 20: A law to force the **admission of women to private clubs** was upheld unanimously by the Supreme Court. At issue was a New York City law requiring women to be admitted to large, private clubs that are said to play important roles in business and

professional life. In New York the University Club
had already voted to admit women. By the end of
August the Union League Club, the Century Association, and the Friars Club in New York agreed to
admit women. The Friars Club in California admitted its first female member in 1987. On June 18 the
exclusive Cosmos Club in Washington, D.C., unassail-
ably male for 110 years, voted by a large majority to
accept women. It too had been threatened with legal
action.

June 20: The **U.S. Open golf tournament** was won by
Curtis Strange, who defeated Nick Faldo by four
strokes in an 18-hole playoff.

June 25: "Axis Sally" died. Mildred E. Gillars (see Mildred Elizabeth Sisk) received her nickname during
World War II, when, although an American citizen,
she broadcast Nazi propaganda to U.S. troops fighting in Europe. Ms. Gillars was said to have been influenced by her lover, Max O. Koischwitz, a German
citizen and foreign-office official, who had at one time
taught at Hunter College in New York City. After the
war Ms. Gillars was arrested and tried for treason.
Convicted, she was sentenced to 10 to 30 years in
prison and fined $10,000. Ms. Gillars was released
after 12 years and later taught music in a convent
school in Columbus, Ohio, having earned a bache-
lor's degree in music in 1973.

June 27: The **heavyweight boxing championship** of
the world was retained by Mike Tyson when he
knocked out Michael Spinks in 1 min., 31 sec. of the
first round of a bout in Atlantic City, N.J. This was
Tyson's third defense of his title in 1988. On Jan. 22
he knocked out Larry Holmes, a former champion,
in the fourth round, and on Mar. 21 he knocked out
Tony Tubbs in the second round.

July 11: Unrestricted free agency for 280 members of
the NFL Players Association was denied by a federal
judge in Minneapolis. The players had sought an injunction that would free them to negotiate with any
team they chose because there was no collective bargaining agreement between the NFL owners and the
players at the time the players' contracts expired in
February. The decision meant players must sign with

their own teams or not at all. The players' association said it would continue to press an antitrust suit against the owners.

July 11: His **4000th career victory as a harness racing driver** was registered by John Campbell at the Meadowlands in New Jersey. He became the 15th driver in harness racing history to record that many wins. Campbell also led in career earnings, with $60 million in purses.

July 13: The **oldest U.S. veteran died.** He was Samuel Leroy Mendel, 104, of Galva, Ill. At 14 he attempted to enlist in the army to serve in the Spanish-American War of 1898 but was turned down. He served three years after 1901. His death left Nathan E. Cook, 102, of Tempe, Ariz., as the oldest U.S. veteran.

July 16: A new **world record for the women's heptathlon** was set by Jackie Joyner-Kersee, with a total of 7,215 points for the seven events. The record she broke was her own. Florence Griffith Joyner, Joyner-Kersee's sister-in-law, set a new world record of 10.49 sec. for the women's 100-meter dash. Both records were made at the Olympic trials in Indianapolis, Ind.

July 16: The **longest scoreless game** in professional baseball ended in the bottom of the 26th inning. The game was won by the San Antonio Missions over the Jackson Mets by 1–0 in a Texas League (Class AA) game in San Antonio. The game took 7 hrs., 23 min. to play.

July 31: The **last Playboy Club,** in Lansing, Mich., closed. The first opened in Chicago in 1960, and by 1972 a million men had joined 22 clubs. Daringly risqué for their time, the clubs featured as waitresses pretty girls barely stuffed into costumes that included bunny ears and tails.

Aug 8: The **first night baseball game at Wrigley Field,** Chicago, was played 53 years after the first major league night baseball game took place in Cincinnati, Ohio. Light for night games had never been installed until now. The game, however, was called after four innings because of heavy rain. For many years Wrigley Field was the only major league baseball park without lights.

Aug 9: The **largest trade in professional sports** occurred when the Edmonton Oilers of the NHL sent Wayne Gretzky, superstar of ice hockey, to the Los Angeles Kings for $15,000,000. The deal also sent two other Oiler players to the Kings, which in turn sent three of its skaters to Edmonton.

Aug 14: The **PGA golf tournament** was won by Jeff Sluman by three strokes. It was his first victory after six years on the pro tour.

Aug 20: **Jack Nicklaus** became the first professional golfer to win more than $5 million in tournament play. A small prize of $5275 in the International Golf Tournament at Castle Rock, Colo., brought his total to $5,002,825.

Aug 20: All **20 defendants were acquitted** in a racketeering trial that lasted 21 months, one of the longest trials in federal court history. Those acquitted constituted all the members of the Lucchese family, an alleged criminal organization of New Jersey. The jury apparently did not believe the government's witnesses, many of whom were convicted criminals. It was also thought that the jury felt the prosecution had needlessly prolonged the trial.

Aug 31: **Guilty of conspiring against free agents** was the finding of an arbitrator against the owners of the major league baseball clubs. These owners, the ruling said, violated baseball's collective bargaining agreement in relation to 79 players who became free agents at the end of the 1986 season. Almost none of the clubs attempted to sign such players from other clubs. Monetary damages if any were to be determined later. A similar finding was made in 1987 with regard to players who became free agents in 1985.

Sep 8: A **new commissioner of baseball,** A. Bartlett Giamatti, was named to take office on Apr. 1, 1989. He would succeed Peter Ueberroth. Giamatti, then president of the National League, was formerly president of Yale University and a professor there of Renaissance literature.

Sep 9: The **America's Cup** was retained by the U.S. when the *Stars & Stripes* defeated the *New Zealand* in two straight races. It was the most unorthodox contest for the cup in the 137-year history of the event. The *Stars & Stripes* was a 60-foot-long catamaran, and the *New Zealand* was a 132-foot-long monohull. A sharp dispute, which ended in court, resulted in this odd compromise as to how the races would be sailed.

Sep 16: The **14th perfect game** in major league baseball history was pitched by Tom Browning of the Cincinnati Reds. He defeated the Los Angeles Dodgers 1–0.

Sep 17-Oct 2: At the **Summer Olympics** in Seoul, South Korea, the U.S. finished third in medal winnings, taking 36 gold and 94 in all. The U.S.S.R. was first, with 55 and 132, East Germany second with 37 and 102. Among American winners were Matt Biondi, who won 7 medals, 5 of them gold, in swimming events; Greg Louganis, who became the first man to win the three-meter springboard event in consecutive Olympics; Jackie Joyner-Kersee, who won the heptathlon and the broad jump; and her sister-in-law Florence Griffith Joyner, who won the 100-meter and 200-meter dashes, setting a world record in the former.

Sep 23: **José Canseco** of the Oakland Athletics became the first major league baseball player ever to hit 40 home runs and steal 40 bases in one season.

Oct 4: A new major league baseball record of **67 innings of scoreless pitching** ended for Orel Hershiser of the Los Angeles Dodgers when the New York Mets scored on him in the ninth inning of the first game of the 1988 National League playoffs.

Oct 8: The **longest losing streak** in major college football came to an end when Columbia defeated Princeton, 16–13. The Lions had lost 44 games over five years before winning this one. The next week they lost again.

Oct 15: The **World Series** was won by the Los Angeles Dodgers (NL) who defeated the Oakland Athletics (AL) four games to one. On Oct. 12 the Dodgers had won the National League pennant over the New York Mets, four games to three. On Oct. 9 the Athletics took the American League pennant by defeating the Boston Red Sox, four games to none.

How to Use
the Index

Each index entry includes a date and section number. When a subject appears more than once in the book, the index supplies a date and section number for each instance.

When a text entry is dated by month and day, this information appears in the index. The citation

Adams, Leonie, 1955 Jan. 9, II

directs the reader to the time period 1955 and the entry dated January 9 in section II.

Introductory paragraphs, which appear at the beginning of each section for every time period, are identified in the index solely by year and section number. For example,

Acupuncture, 1972, III

means that information on acupuncture is to be found in the section III introductory paragraph of the time period 1972.

Undated text entries appear directly *after* the introductory paragraphs and are identified in the index by consecutive numbers in parentheses. Thus,

Actinomycin, 1940(1), III

directs the reader to the first undated entry *after* the introductory paragraph in section III of the time period 1940. Similarly, parenthetical numbers are used to identify multiple entries having the same date. The index entry

Adams, Sherman, 1958 Sept. 22(2), I

directs the reader to the time period 1958 and the second entry dated September 22 in section II.

The early time periods—from the beginning through 1799—are organized in multiple-year blocks. Therefore, for the index entry

Adultery: colonial divorce grounds, 1660(1), IV

the reader, realizing there is no discrete time period for the year 1660, turns to the time period 1660–1669, then locates the first entry dated 1660 in section IV.

Blacks (continued)
    first Roman Catholic archbishop
        (Atlanta, Ga.), 1988 Mar 15, III
    first senator since Reconstruction,
        1966 Nov. 8, I
    first southern city mayor (Atlanta,
        Ga.), 1973 Oct. 16(1), I
    first southern sheriff since Reconstruc-
        tion (Ala.), 1967 Jan. 16, I
    first Supreme Court justice, 1967 Oct.
        2, I
    first to head major city government,
        1967 Sept. 28, I
    first troops, 1862 July, I
    first U.S. general, 1959 May 22, I
    first U.S. Military Academy graduate,
        1877 June 15, I
    first woman pilot, 1978 Apr. 19, III
    intermarriage prohibitions (Mass.),
        1705, IV
    "Jim Crow" originated, 1828, IV
    juries, 1875 Mar. 1, I; 1880 Mar. 1, I
    Kerner Commission report, 1968 Feb.
        29, I
    literature, 1952(1), II; 1965(1), II
    mayors, 1967 Nov. 7, I
    Mormon ordination ban ended, 1978,
        III
    NAACP founded, 1909(1), I
    population, 1810(1), I; 1860(1), I
    portrayed on stage, 1823, II
    racism in Navy charged, 1972 Oct.
        12-13, I
    religion, 1816, III
    SAT scores, 1982, III
    sports, 1937 June 22, IV
    suffrage (Wash., D.C.), 1867 Jan. 8, I
    B. T. Washington on equality, 1915,
        II
    Wilson first novelist, 1859 Sept. 5, II
    woman bishop, 1988 Sept. 24, III
    writers, 1938(1), II; 1940(1), II; 1953,
        II
Blackwell, Elizabeth, 1849(1), III
Blaine, James G.:
    presidential candidacy, 1884, I; 1884
        June 3-6, I
Blaine, John J., 1929 Jan. 15, I
Blair, Bonnie, 1988 Feb 13-28, IV
Blair, Francis P., Jr., 1868 July 4-9, I
Blake, Eubie, 1983, II
Blake, Eugene Carson, 1985, III
Blanchard, Joshua, 1729, II
Blanchard, Thomas, 1820(2), III
Blanding, Sarah G., 1985, III
Blatty, William Peter, 1971(1), II
"Bleeding Kansas" (term), 1856 Aug.
    1, I

Blennerhassett, Harmon, 1806, I
Blitzstein, Marc, 1964, II
Blizzards see Snowstorms
Bloch, Ernest, 1959, II
Bloch, Felix, 1952 Nov. 6, III
Block, Conrad E., 1964 Oct. 15, III
Bloembergen, Nicolaas, 1981 Oct.
    19(2), III
Blondin, Charles, 1859 June 30, IV
Blood:
    anemia therapy, 1934 Oct. 25, III
    leukocytes discovered, 1922 Nov. 15,
        III
    Rh factor discovered, 1939(1), III
Bloody Marsh, Battle of (Ga.), 1742 9, I
Bloomer, Amelia, 1849 Jan., IV; 1850,
    IV; 1853(2), IV
Blount, James Henderson, 1893 July 17,
    I
Blue laws:
    Conn. travel, 1721 May, IV
    New Amsterdam, 1656(2), IV
    Va., 1618, IV
Bluford, Guion S., 1983 Aug. 30-Sept.
    5, III
Blumberg, Baruch S., 1976 Oct. 14(1),
    III
Bly, Nellie, 1889, IV; 1890 Jan. 23, III
Boas, Franz, 1928, III
Boating (see also America's Cup;
    Rowing):
    first intercollegiate regatta, 1859 July
        26, IV
    N.Y. Yacht Club founded, 1844 July
        29, IV
    popularity and social prestige, 1843,
        IV
    sailing circumnavigation record, 1986
        Apr. 11, IV
Bobko, Karol, 1983 Apr. 4-9, III
Bock, Jerry, 1960 May 2, II
Body of Liberties (Mass. code), 1641
    Dec., I
Boehm, John Philip, 1725, III
Boeing 747 airplane, 1969 Dec. 2, III
Boesky, Ivan, 1986 Nov. 14, IV
Bogan, Louise, 1955 Jan. 9, II; 1986
    Apr. 17, II
Bogardus, James, 1848, II
Bogart, Humphrey, 1957, II
Bohr, Aage N., 1975 Oct. 17, III
Boitano, Brian, 1988 Feb. 13-28, IV
Bok, Edward W., 1889, II
Bolles, Don, 1976 June 2, II
Bollingen Prize, 1949 Feb. 19, II; 1950
    Mar. 27, II; 1951 Jan. 22, II;
    1952 Jan. 11, II; 1953 Jan. 10, II;
    1954 Jan. 10, II; 1955 Jan. 9, II;

Cemeteries *(continued)*
  racial discrimination, 1960 Aug. 12, IV
Censorship *(see also* Freedom of information; Pornography):
  CIA controversy, 1978 July 7, II
  Citizens for Decent Literature, 1962, II
  Devil Rides Outside, The (Griffin), 1957 Feb. 25, II
  Lady Chatterley's Lover (Lawrence), 1959 June 11, II
  Memoirs of Hecate County (Wilson), 1946(1), II
  movie upheld (Chicago, Ill.), 1961 Jan. 23, II
  for national security decision, 1974 Apr. 1, II
  Supreme Ct. ruling on government, 1975 May 27, II
  textbook, 1925 Oct. 16, III
  Three Weeks (Glyn) (Boston, Mass.), 1907(1), II
  TV protested, 1960 Feb. 11, II
  Ulysses ban lifted, 1933 Dec. 6, II
Census *(see also* Population):
  first U.S., 1790 Mar. 1, I
Centennial of 1876 (Phila., Pa.), 1876, IV
Central America *see* Latin America
Central Intelligence Agency (CIA):
  absolved of direct role in Chile, 1975 Dec. 4, I
  alleged intervention in Chile, 1973 Apr. 2, III; 1974, I; 1974 Sept. 7, I
  Bush named director, 1975 Nov. 3, I
  censorship controversy, 1978 July 7, II
  Colby dismissed, 1975 Nov. 3, I
  commission on domestic activities named, 1975 Jan. 5, I
  covert domestic operations authorized, 1981 Dec. 4, I
  covert operations, 1974 Sept. 7, I
  illegal domestic operations, 1974 Dec. 21, I
  Marchetti-Marks book on, 1974(1), II; 1974 Apr. 1, II; 1975 May 27, II
  Senate investigation of, 1975 Jan. 27, I; 1975 Dec. 4, I
Central Park (N.Y.C.), 1857, IV; 1876(4), III
Century Illustrated Monthly, The (publication), 1881, II
Century 21 Exposition (Seattle, Wash.), 1962 Apr. 21, IV
Cernan, Eugene, 1966 June 3, III; 1969 May 18, III; 1972 Dec. 7, III

Cézanne, Paul, 1980, II
Chadwick, James, 1932, III
Chaffee, Roger B., 1967 Jan. 27, III
Chafin, Eugene W., 1908 Nov. 3, I; 1912 Nov. 5, I
Chagall, Marc, 1985, II
Challenger (space shuttle), 1983 Apr. 4-9, III; 1983 June 18-24, III; 1983 Aug. 30-Sept. 5, III; 1984 Feb. 7, III; 1984 Oct. 11, III; 1986 Jan. 28, III
Chamberlain, Austen (Sir), 1926 Dec. 10, I
Chamberlain, Wilt, 1960 Mar. 25, IV; 1962 Mar. 2, IV
Chamberland, Owen, 1959 Oct. 26, III
Chambers, Whittaker, 1948 Dec. 15, I; 1949 May 31, I; 1950 Jan. 21, I; 1961, I
Champion, Gower, 1980, II
Champlain, Samuel de, 1603, III
Chance, Frank, 1907, IV
Chancellorsville, Battle of (Va.), 1863 May 1-4, I
Chandler, Alfred D., Jr., 1978 Apr. 17, II
Chandler, Happy (Albert A.), 1945 Apr. 24, IV
Chandler, Raymond, 1959, II
Chandrasekhar, Subrahmanyan, 1983 Oct. 19, III
Chaney, James, 1964 Aug. 4, I; 1964 Dec. 4, I; 1967 Oct. 20, I
Chaney, Lon, Jr., 1973, II
Channing, William Ellery, 1819(2), III
Chapell, Fred, 1985 Jan. 15, II
Chapman, John (Johnny Appleseed), 1800, IV
Chapman, Mark David, 1980 Dec. 8, II
Chappaquiddick accident (Mass.), 1969 July 8, I
Charbonneau, Toussaint, 1805(1), IV
Charles, Ezzard, 1949, IV; 1950, IV; 1954, IV; 1975, IV
Charles II (King of Great Britain), 1661 Sept., III; 1681 Mar. 4, I; 1684 June 21, I
Charleston (S.C.):
  chief colonial cultural center, 1760-1764, II
  cyclone, 1893 Aug. 24, I
  epidemic, 1697, I
  founded, 1670 Apr., I
Charnley House (Chicago, Ill.), 1892(5), II
Charter Oak, 1687, I
Charters:
  colonial, 1606, I

China *(continued)*
U.S. support, 1961 Aug. 2, I
China, People's Republic of (Communist):
Nixon visit, 1971 July 15, I; 1972 Feb. 21-28,I
Nixon visit announced, 1971, I
Reagan's visit and U.S. cooperative agreements, 1984 Apr. 26-May 1, I
U.N. admission, 1971 Aug. 2, I
U.S. embargo lifted, 1971 Apr. 14, III
U.S. Ping-Pong team visit, 1971, IV
U.S. relations eased, 1971, IV
U.S. to enter full diplomatic relations, 1978 Dec. 15(2), I
U.S. travel ban lifted, 1972 Nov. 22, I
U.S. travel restrictions, 1959 Dec. 7, I
Chinese-Americans:
Calif. restrictions, 1879, I
limited immigration, 1880 Nov. 17, I
Chinese exclusion acts, 1882 May 6, I; 1894 Mar. 17, I; 1943 Dec. 17, I
Chinese Exclusion Treaty, 1880 Nov. 17, I
Chlorofluorocarbons, 1988 Mar. 14, III
Chocolate:
colonial popularity, 1710-1714, IV
first manufactured (Mass.), 1765, III
Cholera epidemics, 1850(1), III; 1866(1), I
Cholesterol, 1981 Jan. 8, III; 1985 Oct. 14, III
Chou En-lai:
U.S. germ warfare charges, 1952 Mar. 8, I
Christensen, Parley P., 1920 July 13-16, I; 1920 Nov. 2, I
Christian Observer (newspaper), 1813 Sept. 4, II
Christian Science:
church membership, 1900(2), III
Church of Christ, Scientist organized, 1879(2), III
First Church of Christ, Scientist founded (Boston, Mass.), 1892(3), III
Science and Health published, 1875(3), III
Christmas:
Mass. ban, 1660 May, IV
Nativity display upheld, 1984 Mar. 5, I
traffic fatalities, 1955 Dec. 27, III
Christy, James W., 1978 June 22, III
Chrysler, Walter P., 1962, II
Chrysler Corp.:

federal bailout, 1979 Dec. 21, III
Church, Frank, 1975 Jan. 27, I; 1984, I
Church, Frederick, 1979, II
Churches, National Council of, 1961 Feb. 22-23, III
Churchill, Winston:
Atlantic Charter, 1941 Aug. 9-12, I
Cairo conference, 1943 Nov. 22, I
Quebec conference, 1943 Aug. 11-24, I
Teheran conference, 1943 Nov. 28-Dec. 1, I
U.S. visit, 1952, I
Yalta conference, 1945 Feb. 4-11, I
Church of Christ, United, 1987 June 30, III
Church of England *see* Anglican Church
Church-state separation:
colonial, 1647 May 29-31, I
compulsory flag salute challenged, 1943 June 14, III
creationist theory teaching law unconstitutional (La.), 1987 June 19, III
creation science teaching law struck down (Ark.), 1982 Jan. 5, III
first guarantee (Quaker), 1677, III
Nativity display upheld, 1984 Mar. 5, I
public school teachers banned from parochial schools, 1985 July 1, III
religious services in public universities upheld, 1981 Dec. 8, III
school prayer banned (N.Y.S.), 1962 June 25, III
school prayer decision (Ariz.), 1985 June 4, III
school prayer reinstatement amendment rejected, 1984 Mar. 20, I
school prayer unconstitutional, 1962, III
Supreme Court religion in public schools decision, 1948 Mar. 8, III
CIA *see* Central Intelligence Agency
Cigars and cigarettes *see* Smoking; Tobacco
Cincinnati, Society of, 1783 May 13, IV
Cinema *see* Motion pictures
CIO *see* American Federation of Labor-Congress of Industrial Organizations; Committee for Industrial Organization
Circuses and entertainment *(see also* Burlesque; Freaks; Minstrel shows; Sports; Theater; Vaudeville; other specific types):

Drought: *(continued)*
  worst since Dust Bowl, 1980 June
    23-Aug. 15, I; 1983, III; 1988,
    III
Drug addiction *see* Narcotics
Drugs and drug products *(see also* Food
    and drug laws; Psychedelic
    drugs; Narcotics):
  antiacne linked to birth defects, 1988
    Apr. 22, III
  antihistamines, 1950(1), III
  AZT approved for AIDS, 1987 Mar.
    20, III
  AZT prolonged lives, 1988 May 13,
    III
  cyanide in Excedrin (Seattle, Wash.),
    1986 June 19(2), I
  cyanide in Tylenol capsules (Chicago,
    Ill.), 1982 Sept. 29-Oct. 1, I
  fertility malpractice suit, 1985 May
    21, III
  first antibiotic, 1940(1), III
  first hair growth, 1988 Aug. 17, III
  large-scale penicillin production,
    1941(1), III
Drumgo, Fleeta, 1972 Mar. 27, IV
Drury, Allen, 1959(1), II; 1960 May 2,
    II
Drysdale, Don, 1969, IV
Du Bois, W. E. B., 1963, I
Dubos, René, 1969 May 5, II; 1982, III
Duché, Andrew, 1741(2), III
Duchesne, Rose Philippine, 1988 July 3,
    III
Dueling:
  Decatur-Barron, 1807, I
  Hamilton-Burr, 1804 July 11, I
  Jackson-Dickinson, 1806, IV
Duffy, Hugh, 1894(.1), IV
Dugan, Alan, 1962 May 7, II
Dukakis, Michael, 1988 July 18-21, I;
    1988 Nov. 8, I
Duke, Charles M. 1972 Apr. 16, III
Duke, James Buchanan, 1890(4), III
Duke's laws (N.Y.S.), 1665 Feb. 28, I
Duke University (N.C.), 1890(4), III
Dulbecco, Renato, 1975 Oct. 16, III
Dulles, Allen W., 1969, I
Dulles, John Foster:
  "brink of war" statement, 1956, I
  died, 1959, I
Dumbarton Oaks conference (Wash.,
    D.C.) *(see* also United Nations),
    1944 Aug. 21, I
Dummer, William, 1720-1724, I
Dunlap, William, 1803 Feb. 4, II
Dunning, John R., 1975, III
Dunster, Henry (Rev.), 1636 Oct. 28, III

Duplicating machines:
  mimeograph invented, 1876(2), III
du Pont, Margaret Osborne, 1948 July 2,
    IV; 1949 July 1-2, IV; 1950
    July 7, IV; 1954 July 3, IV; 1962
    July 7, IV
Du Pont, Samuel F., 1861 Nov. 7, I
du Pont de Nemours, E. I., 1962 Mar.
    1, III; 1988 Mar. 14, III
Duquesne, Fort (Pa.), 1754 Apr. 17, I;
    1758 Nov. 25, I
Durant, Will, 1926(1), II
Durant, Will and Ariel, 1968 May 8, II;
    1981, II
Durante, Jimmy, 1980, II
Duryea, Charles E., 1895 June 11, III
Duryea, Charles E. and J. Frank, 1892
    Sept., III; 1895 Nov. 28, IV
Dutra, Olin, 1932 Sept. 4, IV; 1934
    June 9, IV
Duve, Christian de, 1974 Oct. 10, III
du Vigneaud, Vincent, 1955 Nov. 2(1),
    III
Dvořák, Antonín, 1893(2), II
Dwight, Timothy, 1822, II

Eagleton, Thomas F., 1972 July 10-14,
    I
Eaker, Ira C., 1987, I
Eakins, Thomas, 1875(1), II
Eames, Charles, 1978, II
Ear:
  inner, research, 1961 Oct. 19, III
Earhart, Amelia, 1928 May 25, III; 1932
    May 20, III
Early Bird (communications satellite),
    1965 Apr. 6, III
Earth:
  first American to orbit, 1962 Feb. 20,
    III
  "irregular ellipsoid," 1961 Feb. 9, III
Earthquakes:
  Alaska, 1964 Mar. 27, I
  Los Angeles (Calif.), 1987 Oct. 1, I
  San Francisco (Calif.), 1868 Oct. 21,
    I; 1906, I
  southern Calif., 1971 Feb. 9, I
  Winthrop study of, 1735-1739, III
East Coast Conspiracy to Save Lives,
    1970 Nov. 27, I; 1971 Jan. 2, I
Eastern Exchange Hotel (Boston, Mass.),
    1846(1), III
Eastman, George, 1880(2), III; 1888(1),
    III; 1889(4), III; 1928 July 30,
    III
Eastman, Max, 1969, II
Eastman Kodak Co., 1982, III
Eaton, Cyrus S., 1979, III

Indians *(continued)*
  smallpox epidemics, 1616, III
  Tecumseh's leadership, 1809, IV
  treaty with Pilgrims, 1621, I
  Wounded Knee (S.D.) occupation,
    1973 Feb. 28, I
  Wounded Knee (S.D.) occupation
    charges dismissed, 1974 Sept.
    16(3), I
Indian wars:
  Black Hawk, 1832 Apr. 6, I; 1832
    Aug. 27, I
  Creek, 1813, I; 1814 Mar. 29, I
  early, 1675-1676, I; 1675 June 24, I;
    1676 Feb. 10, I; 1676 Aug. 12, I
  first U.S. Medal of Honor, 1861 Feb.
    13, I
  Geronimo captured, 1886 Sept. 4, I
  Little Big Horn battle, 1876 June 25, I
  Nez Percé Indians, 1877 June-Oct., I
  Pequot, 1630-1639, I
  Pontiac's Rebellion, 1763 May 7, I
  Seminole, 1817 Nov. 20, 1; 1818, I;
    1835, I
  Tuscarora, 1711 Sept. 22, I; 1713
    Mar. 23, I
Indochina *see* Vietnam War; country
  names
Industrial Workers of the World
    (IWW):
  established, 1905 July 7, III
  federal raids on headquarters, 1917
    Sept. 5, III
  textile strike (Lawrence, Mass.), 1912,
    III
Industry *see* Business; Manufacturing
Infantile paralysis:
  epidemic, 1935(1), III; 1943(1), I
  first year of no deaths from, 1970 July
    3, III
  Salk vaccine, 1954 Feb. 23, III; 1955
    Apr. 12, III; 1956 June 11, III;
    1956 Aug. 1, III
  serum progress, 1937, III
  virus research, 1954 Oct. 21, III
Influenza:
  epidemic and deaths, 1918 Oct., III
  first serious epidemic, 1733, I
  vitamin C prevention, 1970 Nov. 18,
    III
Inge, William, 1953 May 4, II; 1973, II
Ingersoll, Charles, 1823(1), III
Insurance:
  life cos. scandal, 1905, III
Intelligence activities *see* Central Intelli-
    gence Agency; Espionage; Federal
    Bureau of Investigation; Wiretapping
Interferon, 1980 Jan. 16, III

Interior, Department of:
  created, 1849 Mar. 3(1), I
Intermediate-range ballistic missiles *see*
    Missiles Intermediate-Range Nu-
    clear Forces Treaty (INF), 1988
    May 27, I
Internal revenue *see* Taxation
  Internal Revenue Act, 1864 June
    30, III
Internal Security Act, 1954 May 24, I;
    1964 June 22, I
International Harvester Co., 1902, III
International Justice, Permanent Court of
    see World Court
International relations *see* Foreign relations
International Telephone and Telegraph
    Co. (ITT):
  Chilean political intervention, 1973
    Apt. 2, III
Interstate commerce:
  federal regulatory commission, 1887,
    I; 1910, I
  ICC's authority increased, 1910, I
  Wage and Hours Act, 1938 June 25, I
Interstate Commerce Act, 1887, I
Interstate Commerce Commission:
  increased jurisdiction, 1910, I
Intolerable Acts, 1774 Mar. 31, I; 1774
    June 22, I
Inventions *see* Patents; subject headings
Iowa:
  new territory formed, 1838 June 12, I
  statehood, 1846 Dec. 28, I
Iran:
  hostage crisis ended, 1981 Jan. 20(2),
    I
  hostage rescue mission aborted, 1980
    Apr. 24, I
  passenger jet downed by U.S., 1988
    July 3, I
  six Americans escaped, 1980 Jan. 29,
    I
  U.S. broke relations with, 1980 Apr.
    7, I
  U.S. hostage crisis, 1979, I; 1979
    Nov. 4, I
  U.S. Navy attacked forces in Persian
    Gulf, 1988 Apr. 18, I
Iran-Contra affair:
  Congressional report, 1987 Nov. 18, I
  key figures indicted, 1988 Mar. 16, I
  revealed, 1986 Nov. 3, I
  Tower report criticized Reagan, 1987
    Feb. 26, I
Iraq:
  missile attack on U.S., 1987 May 17,
    I
Ireland:

Tennis *(continued)*
  Richards barred from U.S. Open,
    1976 Aug. 27, IV
  tournaments open to pros, 1968, IV
  USLTA singles championships, 1923
    Aug. 18, IV; 1924 Aug. 16, IV;
    1925 Aug. 24, IV; 1927 Aug. 30,
    IV; 1928 Aug. 27, IV; 1929
    Aug. 24, IV; 1931 Aug. 20, IV;
    1932 Aug. 21, IV; 1933 Aug.
    26, IV; 1934 Aug. 19, IV; 1935
    Sept. 11, IV; 1946 Sept. 8, IV;
    1968 Sept. 9, IV; 1969 Sept. 7-8,
    IV
  U.S. Open, 1970 Sept 2-13, IV; 1971
    Sept. 5-15, IV; 1972 Sept.
    9-10, IV; 1973 Aug. 29-Sept. 9,
    IV; 1974 Sept. 9, IV; 1975 Sept.
    6-7, IV; 1976 Sept. 11-12, IV;
    1977 Sept. 10-11, IV; 1978
    Sept. 10, IV; 1979 Sept. 9, IV;
    1980 Sept. 6-7, IV; 1981 Sept.
    9-13, IV; 1982 Sept. 11-12, IV;
    1983 Sept. 11, IV; 1984 Sept.
    8-9, IV; 1985 Sept. 7-8, IV; 1986
    Sept. 7, IV; 1987 Sept. 12, IV
  Wimbledon, 1905(4), IV; 1907(1), IV;
    1920 July 3, IV; 1921 June 29,
    IV; 1927 July 2, IV; 1928 July 7,
    IV; 1929 July 5, IV; 1930 July
    4, IV; 1931 July 3-4, IV; 1932 July
    1, IV; 1933 July 8, IV; 1935
    July 6, IV; 1936 July 4, IV; 1937
    July 2, IV; 1938 July 1, IV;
    1939 July 7-8, IV; 1946 July 6, IV;
    1947 July 4-5, IV; 1948 July 2,
    IV; 1949 July 1-2, IV; 1950 July 7,
    IV; 1951 July 6-7, IV; 1952 July 5,
    IV; 1953 July 3, IV; 1954 July 3,
    IV; 1955 July 1-2, IV; 1956
    July 7, IV; 1957 July 6, IV; 1958
    July 5, IV; 1961 July 8, IV; 1962
    July 7, IV; 1963 July 6, IV; 1966
    July 2, IV; 1967 July 8, IV; 1968
    July 6, IV; 1970 July 4, IV; 1971
    July 3, IV; 1972 July 7(2), IV;
    1973 July 7-8, IV; 1974 July 5, IV;
    1975 July 4-5, IV; 1976 July 2-3,
    IV; 1977 July 2, IV; 1981 July 3-4,
    IV; 1982 July 3-4, IV; 1983 July
    2-3, IV; 1984 July 7-8, IV; 1985
    July 6-7, IV; 1986 July 5, IV
  Wimbledon boycotted, 1973 July 7-8,
    IV
  Wimbledon suspended, 1940, IV
  World Championship Tennis (WCT)
    tournament scheduling conflict,
    1972, IV
  youngest women's singles winner,
    1979 Sept. 9, IV
Tenure of Office Act, 1867 Mar. 2(2), I;
    1868, I
Terkel, Studs, 1970(1), II; 1985 Apr.
    24, II
Terra cotta, 1853(1), III
Terrell, Ernie, 1965 May 25, IV; 1965
    Nov. 22, IV
Terrorism *(see also* Bombs and bombing;
    Hijacking; Massacres):
  W. Berlin discothèque bombing,
    1986 Apr. 5, I
  Brinks robbery (Nanuet, N.Y.), 1981
    Oct. 20, IV
  Hanafi Muslim raid (Wash., D.C.),
    1977 Mar. 9-11, IV
  Lebanese, 1985 Sept. 18, I
  Olympic Games (W. Ger.), 1972 Aug.
    26-Sept. 11, IV
  Rome and Vienna airports, 1985 Dec.
    27, I; 1986 Jan. 7, I
  Shiite Muslim's hijacking (Athens),
    1985 June 14, I
  Statue of Liberty dynamite plot, 1965
    Feb. 16, I
  TWA jet bombing (Rome-Athens),
    1986 Apr. 2, I
  U.S. ambassador to Guatemala killed,
    1968 Aug. 28, I
  U.S. citizens victims abroad, 1985, I
  U.S. economic sanctions to protest
    Libyan, 1982 Mar. 10, I
  U.S. retaliation for Libyan, 1986 Apr.
    14, I
Terry, Luther, 1964 Jan. 11, III
Tesla, Nikola, 1888, III; 1892(5), III
Teton River Dam (Ida.), 1976 June 5, I
Texaco, Inc., 1985 Dec. 10(1), III; 1987
    Dec. 19, III
Texas *(see also* Mexican War):
  Alamo, 1836(2), IV
  Alamo captured, 1836 Mar. 6, I
  American settlements, 1823, I
  annexation and U.S. protection assur-
    ance, 1845 June 15, I
  Annexation Treaty voted down by
    Senate, 1844 June 8, I
  annexed by congressional joint resolu-
    tion, 1845, I
  capital punishment laws, 1976 July 2,
    I
  first American settlement, 1821 Dec.,
    I
  first European settlement, 1682(2), I
  Galveston hurricane, 1900 Sept. 8, I
  independence, 1836 Mar. 2, I; 1836
    Apr. 21, I; 1836 Oct. 22, I

Change the Course of History

Become one of history's most famous explorers as you relive the drama of Ferdinand Magellan's courageous expedition in **Galleons of Glory.**

On the 20th of September, 1519, Magellan's fleet of five galleons sailed from Spain searching for the *paso* – the legendary passageway to the riches of the Far East.

Take your place on the bridge and prepare for a challenging order. To succeed, you must overcome mutinous officers and crews, sabotage, disease, raging seas and unreliable maps.

Your fate – and the course of world history – will lie in your hands.

- Intuitive, menu driven interface.
- Three levels of increasing challenge.
- Colorful graphics (VGA Support).
- Based on the historical facts of Magellan's voyage.
- Supports Sound Blaster, AdLib, Tandy 3 voice.

Available for IBM PC/Tandy.

To buy: Visit your software dealer or, for credit card or mail orders, call **(800) 521-6263**, 8am – 5pm PT. For more information, write to: Brøderbund Software-Direct P.O. Box 12947 San Rafael, CA 94913-2947.